1928

• STANDARD & POOR'S 500 FUTURES TRADING BEGINS AT CME – April 21, 1982
• UNEMPLOYMENT HITS POSTWAR HIGH – December 1982

• TAX CUT EFFECTED – October 1, 1981
• GOVERNMENT NOTES TOP 16% – July 24, 1981

• PRIME RATE HITS 21% – December 19, 1980
• SPOT OIL PRICE EXCEEDS $40 – December 1980
• IRAN-IRAQ WAR – September 22, 1980

• HUNT BROTHERS SILVER CRISIS – March 28, 1980
• GOLD TOPS $850 – January 20, 1980

• IRAN TAKES HOSTAGES – November 4, 1979

• FED CUTS DISCOUNT RATE TO 3.5%
   – December 20, 1991

• USSR BECOMES COMMONWEALTH OF
   INDEPENDENT STATES –

• USSR COUP FAILS – August 1991

• VOLCKER HEAD OF FED. RES. – July 1979
• GOLD BOTTOMS AT $104 – August 23, 1976
• NIXON RESIGNS – August 9, 1974

• GULF WAR – January-February 1991

• CONTROLS ENDED – April 30, 1974
• ARAB OIL EMBARGO – October 22, 1973
• CBOE OPTIONS TRADING BEGINS – April 26, 1973
• VIETNAM AGREEMENT – January 27, 1973
• WAGE-PRICE FREEZE – August 15, 1971
• LIQUIDITY CRISIS – May 1970

• OIL PRICES TOP $40 A BBL. – October 1990
• IRAQ INVADES KUWAIT – August 1990
• RECESSION BEGINS – July 1990
• BERLIN WALL COMES DOWN – November 1989
• FRIDAY-THE 13TH MARKET PLUNGE – October 13, 1989
• RJR LBO (LARGEST YET) ANNOUNCED - October 1988

• JOHNSON ANNOUNCES WITHDRAWAL (FROM REELECTION CANDIDACY) – March 31, 1968
• POUND DEVALUED TO $2.40 – November 22, 1967
Y ASSASSINATED – November 22, 1963

CUT: PROPOSED – April 13, 1962, ADOPTED – February 26, 1964
EASE RESCINDED – April 13, 1962
ary 3, 1961
7, 1958

• BIGGEST ONE-DAY STOCK MARKET DECLINE – October 19, 1987
• GREENSPAN REPLACES VOLCKER AS CHAIRMAN OF FEDERAL RESERVE
   – August 1987
• IRAN ARMS AFFAIR – December 1986
• IVAN BOESKY SCANDAL - November 1986
• OIL PRICES FALL BELOW $7 A BBL. – July 1986
• INTEREST RATES REACH 8-YEAR LOW – April 1986
• G-5 DOLLAR-REDUCTION PACT – Septmeber 1985
• DOLLAR SETS HIGH AGAINST D MARK AND POUND – March 1985

• RUN ON CONTINENTAL ILLINOIS – May 1984
• PRIME RATE BOTTOMS AT 10 1/2% – February 1983

65 1966 1967 1968 1969 1970 1971 1972 1973 1974 1975 1976 1977 1978 1979 1980 1981 1982 1983 1984 1985 1986 1987 1988 1989 1990 199

575
550
525
500
475
450
425
400
375
350
325
300
275
250
225
200
175
150
125
100
75
50
25
0

65 1966 1967 1968 1969 1970 1971 1972 1973 1974 1975 1976 1977 1978 1979 1980 1981 1982 1983 1984 1985 1986 1987 1988 1989 1990 1991 1992 1993 1994 1995 1996 1997 1998 1999 2000

NSON   NIXON   FORD   CARTER   REAGAN   BUSH

VIETNAM WAR

MANAGEMENT OF INVESTMENTS

MANAGEMENT OF INVESTMENTS

Third Edition

JACK CLARK FRANCIS

McGraw-Hill, Inc.
New York St. Louis San Francisco Auckland Bogotá Caracas
Lisbon London Madrid Mexico Milan Montreal New Delhi
Paris San Juan Singapore Sydney Tokyo Toronto

MANAGEMENT OF INVESTMENTS

2 3 4 5 6 7 8 9 0 DOC DOC 9 0 9 8 7 6 5 4 3

ISBN 0-07-021818-8

This book was set in Stempel Garamond by Black Dot, Inc.
The editors were Kenneth A. MacLeod, Jeannine Ciliotta, and Sheila H. Gillams;
the text design was done by Robin Hoffmann;
the cover was designed by Armen Kojoyian;
cover illustration was done by Gary Eldridge;
the production supervisor was Kathryn Porzio.
New drawings were done by Hadell Studio.
R. R. Donnelley & Sons Company was printer and binder.

Library of Congress Cataloging-in-Publication Data

Francis, Jack Clark.
    Management of investments / Jack Clark Francis.—3rd ed.
        p.   cm.—(McGraw-Hill series in finance)
    Includes bibliographical references and indexes.
    ISBN 0-07-021818-8
    1. Investments.   I. Title.   II. Series.
HG4521.F688   1993
332.6'78—dc20   92-23156

ABOUT THE AUTHOR

Jack Clark Francis was born in Indianapolis, Indiana, received his Bachelor's and M.B.A. degrees from Indiana University, served as a Lieutenant in the U.S. Army for two years, and then earned his Ph.D. from the University of Washington in Seattle. He was a member of the finance faculty of the Wharton School of Finance, University of Pennsylvania for four years and served as a Federal Reserve Economist for two years. Dr. Francis has been a Professor of Economics and Finance at Bernard M. Baruch College in New York City since leaving the Federal Reserve.

Dr. Francis is a professor who likes to teach, and he likes to write the textbook for the courses he teaches. He has authored five editions of *Investments: Analysis and Management,* and two previous editions of *Management of Investments,* both books published by McGraw-Hill, Inc.; co-authored three editions of *Portfolio Analysis,* published by Prentice-Hall; co-edited *Readings in Investments,* published by McGraw-Hill; co-authored *Schaum's Investments Outline,* published by the Schaum's Division of McGraw-Hill; and co-edited *Interest Rate Risk Management,* published by Dow Jones–Irwin. Professor Francis has also had his research published in the *Journal of Finance, Journal of Financial and Quantitative Analysis, Financial Review, Financial Management, Journal of Economics and Business, Journal of Business Research, Quarterly Review of Economics and Business, Journal of Futures Markets, Journal of Monetary Economics, Journal of Portfolio Management, Review of Business,* and *Readings in Finance.* Dr. Francis is a noted speaker at various conferences dealing with finance, banking, business, economics, and computer technology, and he consults with various clients in these areas. He resides in Stamford, Connecticut.

Dedicated to
James Clark Francis

CONTENTS IN BRIEF

CONTENTS

PREFACE

The only thing that seems to remain constant in the area of investments and financial markets is the pace of change. New systems, new technology, new products make this field ever more sophisticated and ever more challenging for both teacher and student.

This third edition reflects both changes in the field and changes in the way it is taught: I have incorporated suggestions from users of the second edition, along with updating and refining material to take change into account. The fact that I teach the course myself, at Baruch College in New York City, not far from Wall Street, means that my students and/or members of their families often have Wall Street jobs and connections, so I learn from them as well. All this feedback has resulted in a thoroughly reorganized, streamlined, and rewritten third edition with fewer chapters but more material.

Special Features

- Comprehensive, up-to-date coverage of new financial products and strategies, such as the new combinations of options, new types of financial futures, asset-backed securities with different tranches, management buyouts, and indexed portfolios.

- In addition to a chapter entitled "International Investing," the third edition contains more on the international aspects of investing throughout the text. The chapter on investment performance evaluation, for example, contains material on global mutual funds and specialized country funds.

- Thorough analysis of the management risk factor and of agency theory: hostile takeovers, golden parachutes, poison pills, greenmail, and classified common stock are described and illustrated with actual cases.

- Broader incorporation of arbitrage concepts. Since the first edition, the text has focused on the various risk factors that make up *arbitrage pricing theory,* but this edition goes further. The law of one price, the basis for arbitrage, is discussed wherever appropriate, in addition to the chapter entitled "Arbitrage Pricing Theory."

- Use of the 1987 stock market crash throughout as a classic example of undiversifiable market risk: the crash is discussed in the chapters on law, stock valuation, technical analysis, options, futures, and international markets.

- Use of up-to-date real world mutual funds to illustrate concepts in a revised and expanded final chapter entitled "Investment Performance Evaluation."

- Definition, Computation, and Example boxes that present important material in easily accessible form.

- A new job opportunities appendix to Chapter 1 that provides guidelines to and information about career opportunities in investments.

- An end-of-book appendix that describes the kinds of data and software included in a supplement package that draws on a variety of resources to provide those who wish to work on computer with menu-driven programs containing Lotus 1-2-3 templates; Basic language programs to do computations similar to Lotus; and Business Week data for mutual fund analysis. None of the software is copy-protected.

- An end-of-book appendix that explains how to do investments analysis with hand-held calculators, written with the help of Professor Richard Taylor, that is applicable to more than the two calculators it specifically addresses—the Hewlett-Packard HP-12C and the Texas Instrument Student Business Analyst (model BA-35).

Organization of the Book

This edition has 28 chapters divided into 5 parts. It was written for front-to-back reading, but the various sections have been made as independent as possible so that readers and instructors can use the book as they need to.

Part 1, The Characteristics of Securities, focuses on risk and return, and on the various types of securities. Part 2, The Marketplace, describes the various markets and market indexes, the regulation of securities markets, and the application of current tax law to investing. The focus of Part 3, Financial Analysis, is on the basic tools the investor needs to analyze investments and make decisions: sources of information, financial statements, default and interest rate risk, bond selection, common stock analysis, and earnings analysis. Part 4 presents more risk factors and analysis techniques: technical analysis, efficient security prices, market risk, purchasing power risk, management risk, making buy-sell decisions. Part 5, Diversification, includes options, warrants, convertibles, futures, real assets, and portfolio analysis. The theory chapters have been grouped at the end in Part 5; they cover portfolio theory, the capital asset pricing model, and arbitrage pricing theory (APT), and they can be read and used at any point—or omitted altogether.

Teaching Aids

Several additional items can be of help for both students and instructors.

- The Schaum's Investments Outline Series (ISBN 0-07-021807-2, published by McGraw-Hill, and available in most school bookstores or by ordering directly from McGraw-Hill (1-800-338-3987 or 1-800-262-4729) or by writing McGraw-Hill, Inc., Schaum Division, Princeton Road, S-1, Hightstown, NJ 08520). This 288-page paperback, which I have co-authored with Professor Richard Taylor, is organized into 26 chapters and contains 396 solved problems with step-by-step solutions, 273 true-false questions and answers, and 260 multiple-choice questions and answers.

- An Instructor's Manual that includes several suggested course outlines plus step-by-step solutions to the text questions and problems, in addition to test bank questions. It also includes transparency masters containing full-page graphs and lecture notes/outlines.

- PC Software package containing data and programs for doing investments analysis on a PC (see Appendix A). Programs may also be uploaded to a mainframe computer; all programs are menu-driven and require no previous computer experience. The package includes Lotus 1-2-3 templates, Basic language programs that do the same computations as Lotus 1-2-3, and *Business Week* magazine data for mutual fund analysis.

- Investments casebooks for instructors who want to teach a case-oriented course: Keith V. Smith, *Case Problems and Readings: A Supplement for Investments and Portfolio Management* (McGraw-Hill, 1989, 351 pages); and Michael A. Berry and S. David Young, *Managing Investments: A Case Approach* (Dryden, 1990, 545 pages).

If you would like information and costs on any supplemental materials, please contact your local McGraw-Hill representative.

Acknowledgments

Many people have assisted me in preparing this third edition. Many of my colleagues at Baruch College helped in some way or another, but Professors Avner Wolf, Robert Ariel, Jae Won Lee, Giora Harpaz, Steve Katz, Harry Markowitz, Doug McCann, and Joel Rentzler made special contributions that were above and beyond the call of mere collegial duty.

Academics at other colleges also helped in numerous ways. Professors Frank J. Fabozzi at MIT, Cheng Few Lee at Rutgers University, Carl McGowan of the University of Michigan at Flint, Richard Taylor at Arkansas State University, Wi Saeng Kim of Rutgers University, Susan Jarzombek at Sacred Heart University, Raj Aggarwal at John Carroll University, K. C. John Wei at Indiana University, Professor Robert Greenleaf at Indiana University; Professor Jack Woods at Fairleigh Dickinson University; and Professor Joan C. Junkus at DePaul University, Chicago.

A number of gracious folks who are professional investment managers, financial analysts, traders, attorneys, accountants, and computer specialists also aided me. I am especially indebted to Peter A. Abken, Ph.D., Economist, Federal Reserve, Atlanta, Georgia; Joy Brown, MBA, Vice-President, Trans-Capital, Norwalk, Connecticut; Deborah Susan Francis, M.B.A., C.P.A., Seattle First National Bank; Duncan Goldie-Morrison, Senior Director, NatWest, London; Henry Green, Ph.D., Swiss Bank House, London; James L. Karl, Attorney, Marco Island, Florida; and Julian Walmsley, London. And from New York: Fischer Black, Partner, Goldman Sachs Asset Management; Richard Bookstaber, Ph.D., Vice President at Morgan-Stanley; Jane Brauer, Ph.D., Vice President, Citicorp; Seth Breidbart, Ph.D., Vice President, Morgan-Stanley; Russell Cornelius, Morgan-Stanley; Khosrow Dehnad, Ph.D., Vice President, Chase-Manhattan Bank; Emmanuel Derman, Ph.D., Vice President, Goldman, Sachs & Co.; Sam Eisenstadt, Senior Vice President, Value Line; Laurie Goodman, Ph.D., Vice President, Merrill Lynch; Robert Greenwald, Financial Consultant, Shearson Lehman Hutton; Mike Hogan, Ph.D., Vice President, Citicorp; Ira G. Kawaller, Vice President, Chicago Mercantile Exchange; Joseph A. Langsam, Ph.D., Vice President, Morgan-Stanley; Anlong Li, Ph.D., Shearson Lehman Hutton; Charlynn C. Maniatis, J.D., M.D.; Robert Mark, Ph.D., Managing Director, Chemical Bank; Richard Miller, Attorney, Katten Muchin & Zavis; Scott Newman, Attorney, Whitman & Ransom; Albert S. Pergam, Attorney, Cleary, Gottlieb, Steen, & Hamilton; Todd E. Petzel, Ph.D., Senior Vice President, Chicago Mercantile Exchange; Beth Pickens, L.L.B.; Shaiy Pilpel, Ph.D., Steinhardt Partners; Larry Pohlman, Ph.D., Blackstone Financial Management; Paul Potocki, Vice President, Shearson Lehman Hutton; R. S. Salomon, Jr., Salomon Brothers; David R. Smith, New York Life Insurance Company; Dee Ann Soder, Ph.D.; Leon Tatevosian, Morgan-Stanley; William Toy, Ph.D., Vice President, Goldman, Sachs & Co.; J. Gregg Whittaker, Ph.D., Director, County NatWest; Andrew F. Winning, Vice President, Merrill Lynch, Pierce, Fenner & Smith.

Although some of them have never met each other, numerous members of the huge McGraw-Hill family provided valuable aid in a gracious manner. It was a pleasure to work with Kenneth W. Lutz, Publisher, Trendline Services, who provided valuable artwork; Barbara Munder, Business Week Vice President and creator of the Mutual Fund Scoreboard; Ken MacLeod, my sponsoring editor; Jeannine Ciliotta and Lauren Shafer, my development editors; Sheila Gillams, a punctilious production editor; William O'Neal, a careful copyeditor; Judy Motto, a cheerful and conscientious software editor; John Aliano, Senior Editor in the Schaum's Division, and Terry Pace, an ancillary editor who adds value to each of my books.

McGraw-Hill and I would like to thank the following reviewers for their many helpful comments and suggestions: George Aragon, Boston College; M. E. Ellis, St. John's University; Joseph Finnerty, University of Illinois–Champaign; Christopher K. Ma, Texas Technical University; Abbas Mamoozadeh, Slippery Rock University; and Joseph Walker, University of Alabama.

All these people have made significant contributions to the third edition. However, I take full responsibility for whatever errors emerge.

Jack Clark Francis

MANAGEMENT

OF INVESTMENTS

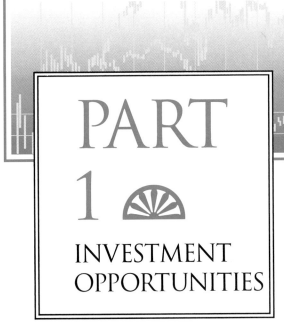

PART 1

INVESTMENT OPPORTUNITIES

SUCCESSFUL INVESTING requires clear-cut goals based on current information, as well as a thorough knowledge of the characteristics of the chosen investment vehicles. This is true whether you are an individual investor or the manager of a large institution's funds. Most investing, large or small, is done in securities, which are marketable financial instruments that give their owners the right to make specific claims on particular assets. But there are many kinds of securities, and new varieties are being developed every day. An investor needs to be familiar with them all in order to make sound decisions.

Chapters 1 through 3 focus on the variety of security investment opportunities and examine the characteristics of the major types of securities used as investment vehicles. Chapter 1 discusses the bottom line—risk and return, strategies and alternatives, and decision making. The focus is on analyzing investment objectives and matching goals with the available instruments and the various strategies that will lead to success. This means knowing how to calculate rate of return, assess risk, and weigh the risk-return relationship in order to make decisions that further investment goals. Chapter 2 focuses on debt securities—fixed-income securities, such as bonds, that pay contractually fixed periodic interest payments. It covers all the common forms of bonds, including various government securities. Chapter 3 focuses on investment opportunities that have ownership qualities, such as common and preferred stock, convertible securities, investment company shares, and new asset-backed securities.

All these chapters give the investor an overview of the major investment opportunities and their risk and return characteristics. They lay the foundation for the detailed analysis and evaluation of financial information and risk factors that is part of managing any investment program.

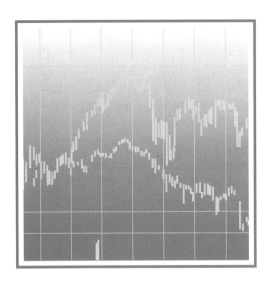

CHAPTER 1

INTRODUCTION

Investing involves making a current commitment of funds in order to obtain an uncertain future return. It is a risky business that demands information. This book will teach you how to become a better-informed investor of your personal funds, an entry-level security analyst, or a beginning investment manager or portfolio manager for yourself or for an employer.

3

When you finish this book you will know things about investing that most people never dreamed were possible—how to profit if an asset's price rises, how to profit if its price declines, and even how to profit if an asset's price doesn't change at all.

To process information effectively and select the best investments requires goals that are clear-cut and realistic. Therefore, let us begin our study of investing by focusing on what a good investment manager strives to achieve and the tools that investor needs to measure the two most important facts about any investment—its return and its risk.

1-1   The Investment Objective

The goal of investors and investment managers is to maximize their rate of return or, equivalently, the terminal value of their investments. As the following equation shows, maximization of rate of return and of ending wealth are equivalent objectives.

$$1 + \text{rate of return} = \frac{\text{terminal market value of investment}}{\text{beginning market value of investment}} \qquad (1\text{-}1)$$

If we view the beginning value of the invested funds as a fixed amount, any action that maximizes the rate of return will also maximize the ending value of the invested funds. Recasting Equation (1-1) shows that if $10,000 is initially invested and grows at a rate r of 10 percent for one period, it will grow to a terminal value of $11,000.

$$\text{Terminal wealth} = (1 + r)(\text{beginning wealth})$$

$$= (1 + 10\%)(\$10,000) = 1.1\,(\$10,000) \qquad (1\text{-}1a)$$

$$= \$11,000$$

Unfortunately, wealth maximization is neither simple nor straightforward. Its pursuit is frequently constrained by the investor's **risk aversion** (that is, dislike of risk), time limitations, lack of energy, lack of information, and even social opposition.

4

Some people claim that wealth maximization can be harmful to society. If we ignore criminal activities, that accusation is false. Law-abiding investment managers do not engage in fraud, theft, security price manipulation, insider trading, environmentally hazardous operations, unfair hiring practices, false advertising, or other harmful activities. Federal laws prohibiting these activities are backed by fines and prison sentences.

Law-abiding work to maximize the market value of investments is beneficial, to the investor and to the general population. Wealth maximizing investors seek out securities issued by efficient firms producing high-quality goods and services that many people want. Investors can encourage their firms to do research and development in search of product improvements and new technologies. These developments, in turn, can help the United States compete internationally and may also create new jobs and opportunities. Furthermore, to be profitable a corporation must provide goods and/or services in a courteous manner, make these products available at reasonable prices, and sell its products at locations and times that are convenient for consumers. Thus, actions that maximize rate of return also benefit the society at large.

Investing involves uncertainties that make risk-averse people reluctant to invest. The chance that an investment will yield a loss instead of a profit scares potential investors. Many are afraid to take the big risks necessary to earn big returns. Those who seek to maximize profits by assuming inappropriate financial risk can suffer a number of psychological and physical ailments. Realistically speaking, then, investing has two concurrent objectives—profit maximization and risk minimization.

In addition to risk aversion and time limitations, lack of information also constrains the accumulation of wealth. Many investors are amateurs: They "play the stock market" in their spare time and simply do not have the time or energy to investigate every potentially profitable opportunity. Many people either cannot or do not want to manage a number of different investments. And, of course, most people have only a limited amount of money to invest.

Investors can limit themselves to investments that involve modest risk. By doing this, they can usually limit the amount of time and effort they must devote to investment management. For example, a savings account in an FDIC-insured bank or short-term U.S. Treasury securities involve little risk and require only very modest management skills. Of course, bank accounts and Treasury securities do not yield high returns. Many intelligent investors recognize that there is a risk-return trade-off. Their desire to increase their wealth may be strong enough to motivate them to assume the higher levels of risk usually required to earn high returns.

Throughout this book we will assume that the investment objective is to obtain the greatest possible financial gain given a particular set of risk aversion, time, and skill constraints. We'll refine this assumption later in this chapter and in the chapters that follow.

1-2 The Investment Period

The period of time between the purchase and sale dates of an investment is called the investor's **investment horizon,** or **holding period.** If this holding period is very short, the position may not be a legitimate investment—it may be a gamble or a speculation. Let's see the difference.

Gambling A **gamble** is usually a very-short term investment in a game of chance.

Speculation Speculations typically last longer than gambles but not as long as investments. A **speculation** usually involves the purchase of a saleable asset in the hope of making a quick profit from a rapid increase in its price. Buying initial public issues of a common stock in the hope of selling it a few months later for a gain is a popular speculation that usually works.[1]

Investing There is no precise holding period to separate gambles from speculations and speculations from investments. The Internal Revenue Service (IRS) says that "long-term capital gains" are increases in the value of assets owned for more than 6 months. Using this reasoning, we might define an **investment** as a purchase with a holding period in excess of 6 months.

It is impossible to know how far ahead a planning horizon should extend. Investors cannot reasonably hope to see farther than about 1 decade ahead, and most investors cannot forecast even 2 years ahead. We will use 10 years as the maximum planning horizon. Figure 1-1 illustrates various holding periods within such a 10-year time span.

One important factor that is measured over the investment holding period is the rate of return. Let's see why.

1-3 The Rate of Return

We must define the rate of return in order to measure it. The **rate of return**, or **holding period return**, measures the speed with which the investor's wealth

---

[1] See Andrew J. Chalk and John W. Peavy, III, "Initial Public Offerings: Daily Returns, Offering Types and the Price Effect," *Financial Analysts Journal*, vol. 43, no. 5, 1987, pp. 65–69. This study shows that initial public offerings (IPOs) typically rise in price for 190 days after issue.

Box 1-1

7

Chapter 1
Introduction

DEFINITION: The Single-Period Rate Of Return, r

$$r = \frac{\text{total dollar income during some period}}{\text{purchase price (or dollars invested)}} \qquad (1\text{-}2)$$

increases (or decreases, if the investor suffers a loss). The rate of return is defined in Box 1-1.

Rate of return is simply the total income the investor receives during the holding period, stated as a percentage (or fraction) of the purchase price of the investment at the start of the holding period.

$$r = \frac{\text{ending wealth} - \text{beginning wealth}}{\text{beginning wealth}} \qquad (1\text{-}3)$$

Rates of return are usually stated at an annual rate to allow us to compare different returns. We'll look here at stock, home investment, and bond rates of return.

A Stock's Return

An investor can obtain two kinds of income from owning a share of stock: (1) income from price appreciation of the stock (or losses from price depreciation), which is sometimes called *capital gains* (or *losses*), and (2) income from cash dividend payments, which most corporations pay to common stockholders every year they can afford to do so. The sum of these two sources of income (or loss) equals the total change in invested wealth from the common stock investment during a given holding period. The rate of return formula is given below in a form appropriate for a common stock investment:

$$r = \frac{\text{price change} + \text{cash dividend (if any)}}{\text{purchase price}} \qquad (1\text{-}4)$$

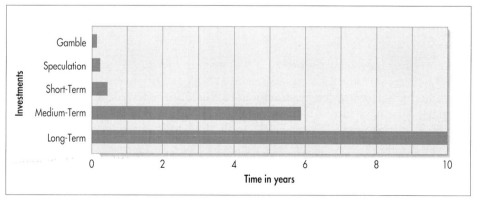

Figure 1-1 Different holding periods for gambling, speculating, and investing.

Box 1-2

COMPUTATION EXAMPLE: Rate of Return from GM stock

If a share of General Motors (GM) common stock is purchased for $44 on February 9 of one year and then sold on February 9 of the next year for $46, the investor's income from the price change over the 1-year holding period is $2. If the stock paid a cash dividend of $2.40 during the year, the investor's total income from the stock is $4.40 (or $2.00 + $2.40). The investor's rate of return for this 1-year investment in GM stock is 10 percent, as shown below:

$$r = \frac{\text{price change} + \text{cash dividend}}{\text{purchase price}} \tag{1-4}$$

$$= \frac{\$2.00 + \$2.40}{\$44.00} = \frac{\$4.40}{\$44.00} = \frac{1}{10} = .1 = 10\% \tag{1-4a}$$

The rate of return for a preferred stock investment is calculated the same way.

A Home Investment's Rate of Return

An investment in a house might yield two types of income: (1) rental income, which is the net income after all expenses have been deducted, and (2) price appreciation (or depreciation), known as *capital gains* (or *losses*).

Accountants follow a rule that price change is a source of *accounting income* only if the investment is sold and the price change is realized as cash. That is fine, but we are not studying accounting here. The fact that the price change could be realized and consumed if the investor wanted to do so makes it *economic income* that is too important for investors to ignore.

The sum of the two types of home income is given in relation to the cost of the investment in order to determine the home investor's rate of return:

$$r = \frac{\text{rental income} + \text{price change}}{\text{purchase price}} \tag{1-5}$$

Box 1-3

COMPUTATION EXAMPLE: The Rate of Return from Real Estate

An investor buys a house for $80,000. One year later the house has a value of $92,000; the investor has a capital gain of $12,000 (or 15 percent) for the year. If the house was rented for a net amount of $4000 (or 5 percent of the purchase price), then it yielded a total income of $12,000 + $4,000 = $16,000 or 20 percent, for the year. We can calculate the investor's rate of return as shown below:

$$r = \frac{\$4000 + \$12,000}{\$80,000} = \frac{\$16,000}{\$80,000} = \frac{2}{10} = .2 = 20\% \tag{1-5a}$$

Most bonds pay coupon interest instead of cash dividends or rental income and, thus, use the following rate-of-return formula:

$$r = \frac{\text{price change} + \text{coupon interest (if any)}}{\text{purchase price}} \tag{1-6}$$

To calculate a **net rate of return,** brokers' commissions, income taxes, and other transaction costs should be deducted from the income in the numerators of all one-period rate-of-return formulas.

1-4 Probabilities of Rates of Return

The rate of return is the most important outcome from any investment. However, it is impossible to know in advance precisely what rate of return a risky investment will yield. To assess the expected return and risk, a potential investor must assign a probability to each possible rate of return a security might yield.

What Are Probabilities?

A **probability** is a number that describes the likelihood of an event. Probabilities can vary from 0 to 1. The probabilities assigned to all possible outcomes for a given event must add up to exactly 1 (or, if stated as percentages, to 100 percent). If the outcomes under discussion are mutually exclusive, like rain and sunshine, probabilities must be assigned so that the probability of rain plus the probability of sunshine adds up to 1 (or 100 percent), indicating that there is 100 percent chance (or complete certainty) that one of the outcomes will occur.

Box 1-4

COMPUTATION EXAMPLE: A Bond's Rate of Return

Mary Smythe bought a U.S. Treasury bond with a $10,000 face value for a market price of $9000. One year later Ms. Smythe's bond was worth $9200. She therefore enjoyed a capital gain of $200 (or 2.22 percent) for that year. The bond also paid her coupon interest of $700 during the year. Mary's total income of $700 + $200 = $900 yields a 10 percent rate of return for the year, as shown below:

$$r = \frac{\$200 + \$700}{\$9000} = \frac{\$900}{\$9000} = \frac{1}{10} = .1 = 10\% \tag{1-6a}$$

If Mary had bought a zero coupon bond (paying no interest) and its price had behaved the same way, her total rate of return would have been 2.22 percent.

Box 1-5

FINANCIAL EXAMPLE: Maximizing Profits or Maximizing Return?

To see the fallacy of seeking an investment that has the largest dollar profits, consider Coke machines that hypothetically cost $1000 apiece and earn profits of $600 per machine in a typical year (a 60 percent rate of return). Compare investing in Coke machines with buying the whole Coca-Cola Corporation for $3 billion. Assume that the corporation normally earns a 20 percent rate of return. This rate of return for a $3 billion corporation equals profits of $600 million per year. Nevertheless, investing $3 billion in 3 million Coke machines that have a 60 percent per year rate of return is a better investment, because it would yield total profits of $1800 million per year. The key to allocating funds is to select investment alternatives with the highest rates of return.

Since it is possible that rain may occur while the sun is shining, rain and shine are not really mutually exclusive. In this case, the probability of rain plus the probability of sunshine is greater than one, $P(\text{rain}) + P(\text{shine}) > 1$. So we must subtract the common probabilities, denoted "$P(\text{rain and shine simultaneously})$," which are counted twice if the events are not mutually exclusive. Thus, for events that are not mutually exclusive we have

$$P(\text{rain}) + P(\text{shine}) - P(\text{rain and shine simultaneously}) = 1.0$$

Probabilities are sometimes called *relative frequencies* because they measure the relative frequency of some event. For instance, if it rains while the sun is out 10 percent of the time, then the probability, or relative frequency, of this event is

$$P(\text{rain and shine simultaneously}) = .10 = 10\%$$

Box 1-6

PRINCIPLES: The Laws of Probability

Probabilities are numbers that indicate the likelihood that an event will occur. Probabilities are governed by five rules.

1. A probability can never be a negative number.

2. A probability can never be larger than 1 (or 100 percent).

3. The probabilities attached to all the different possible outcomes must sum to exactly 1 (or 100 percent).

4. If an outcome is certain to occur, it has a probability of 1.0; no other outcome is possible.

5. Impossible outcomes are assigned a probability of 0.

Table 1-1
A Probability Distribution
for a Coin Toss

Outcome	Probability
Coin stands on edge	$P(\text{edge}) = 0 = 0$
Head	$P(\text{head}) = .5 = 50\%$
Tail	$P(\text{tail}) = .5 = 50\%$
Sum	$1.0 = 100\%$

Consider the tossing of a coin. Table 1-1 lists the possible outcomes and their respective probabilities. A *fair* coin toss has a fifty-fifty chance of coming up heads or tails—assuming that the coin cannot stand on its edge. Note that all the probabilities sum to 1, accounting for 100 percent of the possible outcomes.

Probability Distributions of Returns

An investor who wants to determine the riskiness and expected rate of return of a potential investment must come up with estimates of the probabilities of the possible rates of return. Analysis of an asset's risk and expected return focuses on the different plausible rates of return. Such considerations as whether a stock is a growth stock, whether the company's image is pleasing, or whether the firm's product is glamorous are relevant only to the extent that they affect the different rates of return and their associated probabilities.

This is an uncertain world. Investors cannot foretell exactly what rate of return an investment will yield. However, they can write down what they think the rate of return will probably be over the investment's holding period. A list of such probable rates of return is the probability distribution of rates of return. Broadly speaking, a **probability distribution** assigns (or distributes) a probability to every possible outcome of an uncertain situation. It can be expressed as a graph or a table. For example, Table 1-1 is a probability distribution. Figure 1-2 shows probability distributions of rates of return for American Telephone and Telegraph (AT&T), Borden, and Firestone common stock. Graphs of the probability distributions are on the left side of the figure. A table listing five possible rates of return for each asset is on the right side. The discrete rates of return in these lists represent a random sample of all the possible rates of return illustrated in the continuous graph. Interpreting the graphs requires additional explanation.

The horizontal axis of each graph in Figure 1-2 measures the single-period rates of return. The vertical axis gauges the probability that any given rate of return will occur. The five dots on each graph correspond to the five rates of return listed for each asset. The vertical line through the center of each graph indicates the expected rate of return, denoted $E(r)$.

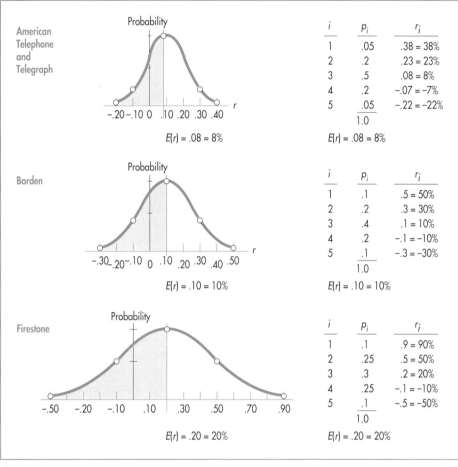

Figure 1-2 Probability distributions for three common stocks' rates of return.

Box 1-7

DEFINITION: The Expected Rate of Return, $E(r)$

The **expected rate of return** for any asset is the weighted average rate of return using the probability of each rate of return as the weight. It is denoted $E(r)$. An $E(r)$ is calculated by summing the products of the rates of return and their respective probabilities. Mathematically the expected rate of return is stated

$$E(r) = \sum_{t=1}^{T} (\text{probability}, P_t)(\text{return}, r_t) \tag{1-7}$$

$$= (P_1)(r_1) + (P_2)(r_2) + \cdots + (P_T)(r_T) \tag{1-7a}$$

The t subscripts in this formula are counters for each possible rate of return and its associated probability.

Box 1-8

13

Chapter 1
Introduction

> **COMPUTATION EXAMPLE:** Borden's Expected Return
>
> Calculation of the expected rate of return for the Borden probability distribution shown in Figure 1-2 is
>
> $$E(r) = (P_1)(r_1) + (P_2)(r_2) + (P_3)(r_3) + (P_4)(r_4) + (P_5)(r_5) \qquad (1\text{-}7a)$$
>
> $$= (.1)(.5) + (.2)(.3) + (.4)(.1) + (.2)(-.1) + (.1)(-.3)$$
>
> $$= .05 + .06 + .04 - .02 - .03 = .1 = 10\% \qquad (1\text{-}7b)$$

Expected Rate of Return and Risk

The width of a probability distribution of rates of return is a measure of **risk.** The word "risk" is synonymous with the phrase "variability of return" and the word "variance." The variance can be appraised visually. It is possible to look at Figure 1-2 and see which of the three probability distributions is the riskiest: Firestone, because its probability distribution is the widest. Borden is riskier than AT&T because the AT&T probability distribution is narrower. That is, AT&T has the least variability of return (or risk) of the three stocks in Figure 1-2.

1-5   Assessing Risk

To maximize the expected rate of return at some selected level of risk, we must define risk in such a way that it can be measured. Measuring an investment's risk is just as important as measuring its expected rate of return because minimizing risk and maximizing the rate of return are interrelated objectives in investment management.

   We will define an asset's **total risk** to be its *total variability of return.* An investment whose rate of return varies widely from period to period is riskier than one whose rate of return does not change much. One way to measure an asset's variability of return quantitatively is presented in Box 1-9.

Advantages of the Standard Deviation

There are different ways to measure variability of return. The range from the highest possible rate of return to the lowest is one measure, but the range is based on only two extreme values. Statisticians prefer to use as a measure of variability the standard deviation, which has the following three advantages:

1. Unlike the range, the σ considers *every* possible event. Furthermore, σ gives each event a weight equal to its probability.

2. The σ is well known among statisticians. As a result, some hand calculators and many computers are programmed to calculate it.

Box 1-9

DEFINITION: Quantitative Risk Statistics

The **variance** of an asset's rate of return equals the sum of the products of the squared deviation of each possible rate of return from the expected rate of return multiplied by the probability that the rate of return occurs.

$$\text{VAR}(r) = \sum_{i=1}^{T} P_i[r_i - E(r)]^2 \qquad (1\text{-}8)$$

$$= P_1[r_1 - E(r)]^2 + P_2[r_2 - E(r)]^2 + \cdots + P_T[r_T - E(r)]^2 \qquad (1\text{-}8a)$$

The **standard deviation,** denoted σ, of the rates of return is simply the square root of the variance of the rates of return:

$$\sigma = \sqrt{\text{VAR}(r)} \qquad (1\text{-}9)$$

The standard deviation and the variance are conceptually equivalent quantitative measures of total risk.

---

3. The σ is a measure of dispersion around the expected (or average) value. Thus, it corresponds nicely to the variability-of-return definition of risk, which says that risk is the degree to which actual returns vary from the expected return.

Calculating the Standard Deviation

Equations (1-8) and (1-9) in Box 1-9 can be used to calculate Borden's (or any other asset's) variance and standard deviation. The raw data for Borden are taken from Figure 1-2. Table 1-2 shows the calculations.

Calculations using the formulas from Box 1-9 show that the variance of AT&T is .018 and that of Firestone is .143. Taking the square roots gives a σ of .38 = 38 percent for Firestone, .22 = 22 percent for Borden, and .13 = 13 percent for AT&T.

Table 1-2
Calculation of Borden's Standard Deviation

$$(P_1)[r_1 - E(r)]^2 = .1[\ .5 - .1]^2 = .016$$
$$(P_2)[r_2 - E(r)]^2 = .2[\ .3 - .1]^2 = .008$$
$$(P_3)[r_3 - E(r)]^2 = .4[\ .1 - .1]^2 = \ \ \ 0$$
$$(P_4)[r_4 - E(r)]^2 = .2[-.1 - .1]^2 = .008$$
$$(P_5)[r_5 - E(r)]^2 = .1[-.3 - .1]^2 = \underline{.016}$$
$$\text{Total} = \text{VAR}(r) = .048 \qquad (1\text{-}8a)$$

$$\sigma = \sqrt{\text{VAR}(r)} = \sqrt{.048} = .219 = 21.9\% \qquad (1\text{-}9a)$$

Box 1-10   **15**

Chapter 1
Introduction

> **DEFINITION:** The Dominance Principle
>
> The **dominance principle:** Among all investments with a given expected rate of return, the one with the least risk is the most desirable. Among all assets with the same degree of risk, the one with the highest expected rate of return is the most desirable.

Thus Firestone is the riskiest of the three, and AT&T is the least risky. Note that taking the square roots of the variances does not alter their risk rankings.

The risk formulas in Box 1-9 can be used to calculate variability of return for an individual asset, such as a stock or a bond, or for a *portfolio* of diversified assets. Let us reconsider the assets listed in Figure 1-2 to see how this works.

1-6   Using Statistics to Make Investment Decisions

Visual inspection of Figure 1-2 shows that Firestone is the riskiest investment, Borden the next most risky, and AT&T the least risky. Figure 1-2 also shows that Firestone has the largest expected rate of return, Borden the next largest, and AT&T the smallest. These facts reveal an economic relationship that is no mere coincidence. Assets that involve the most risk tend to have the highest expected rates of return.

The Dominance Principle

A portfolio manager who examines the expected rate of return and risk statistics for many different bonds and stocks may select assets worthy of investment by using the dominance principle.

Table 1-3 lists five possible investments with risk and rate of return. Using the dominance principle reveals that the GM bond is "dominated" by AT&T stock because the telephone stock has a higher expected rate of return although both have the same risk. Figure 1-3 shows this graphically. Points that are higher on Figure 1-3 have higher expected rates of return; points farther to the right are riskier. The figure shows that the GM bond can be eliminated from consideration because it is a

Table 1-3
Risk and Expected Rate of Return for Five Assets

Security (symbol)	$E(r)$	Risk, σ
American Telephone & Telegraph (AT&T) common stock	8%	13.4%
Borden (BN) common stock	10	21.9
Firestone Tire and Rubber (FIR) common stock	20	37.8
General Motors (GM) common stock	10	18.0
General Motors (GM) bond	7	13.4

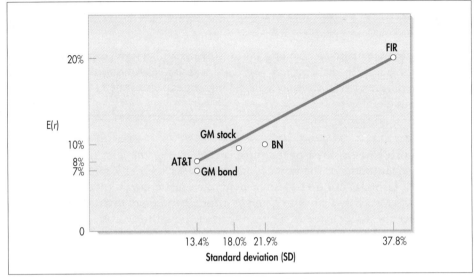

Figure 1-3   Expected rates of return and risk statistics for five assets.

dominated investment. General Motors (GM) stock dominates Borden's (BN) stock; their expected rates of return are the same, but GM's stock has less risk. So Borden is also dominated and can be ignored.

The dominance principle indicates that the GM bond and the Borden stock are inferior investments. The nondominated assets are the Firestone, General Motors, and AT&T stocks. The choices have been narrowed from five investments to three, but there is more to investments analysis.

Efficient Portfolios

Although GM's stock is a nondominated asset, a close examination of Figure 1-3 shows that its relative risk and return are not so appealing as those of AT&T and Firestone. To understand why, we need to consider the effect of the *combinations* of assets, or portfolios. A portfolio's expected rate of return is the weighted average of the expected rates of return of all the assets in that portfolio.

Suppose we constructed portfolios from AT&T and FIR. The different combinations of AT&T and FIR we might create are represented by the line from point AT&T to point FIR.[2] All of these points on the line between AT&T and FIR are *additional investment opportunities.*

The investment opportunities that can be created by forming diversified portfolios also create additional choices. It appears that the most dominant investment opportunities represented in Figure 1-3 are the portfolios lying along the

[2] The line representing portfolio possibilities in Figure 1-3 assumes that the individual assets' rates of return are perfectly positively correlated. The risk-reducing power of diversification is analyzed in Chapter 24, and the effects of lower correlations between the assets' rates of return will be considered in Chapters 24 and 25.

Box 1-11

17

Chapter 1
Introduction

> ### DEFINITION: Efficient Portfolios and the Efficient Frontier
>
> **Efficient portfolios** are the set of portfolios with the maximum expected rate of return at a given risk or, conversely, the set of portfolios with the minimum risk at a given level of expected rate of return. The set of all the efficient portfolios that can be created from a group of diversified investment possibilities is called the **efficient frontier.**

solid line from point AT&T to point FIR. These portfolio possibilities dominate any others between any other assets in the figure. Such dominant portfolios are called efficient portfolios, and the set of all possible efficient portfolios is the efficient frontier.

The efficient frontier in Figure 1-3 is represented by the line from AT&T to FIR. The efficient frontier dominates all other investment opportunities. Because diversification can reduce the risk of a portfolio that contains different assets, the efficient frontier will usually contain only portfolios. Individual assets cannot have their risk reduced by diversification. *The investment manager's job, therefore, is to select a diversified group of securities that will form a dominant portfolio on the efficient frontier.*

1-7   The Risk-Return Relationship

Investors require higher rates of return to invest in riskier assets because they dislike risk. These preferences result in a positive relationship between expected rate of return and risk called the **risk-return tradeoff.**

Empirical Evidence

Figures 1-4 and 1-5 illustrate what happened to investors who purchased different categories of assets over the past several decades.[3] Figure 1-4 contains probability distributions of rates of return and related summary statistics for six categories of securities and the inflation rate. Figure 1-5 traces how one dollar invested in each of these portfolios would have fared over time. The figures contain statistics documenting the positive risk-return tradeoff that forms the basis for many investment strategies.

Consider the positive tradeoff between expected rate of return and risk along the efficient frontier. As Figure 1-3 shows, the investment manager can maximize the return only by assuming more risk. Desirable investments can be found only along the efficient frontier, since all other investments are dominated. This means that diversification and risk management are as much a part of an investment manager's responsibility as seeking high returns.

---

[3] The geometric mean rate of return is explained in the appendix to this chapter. The standard deviation of returns was defined in Box 1-9.

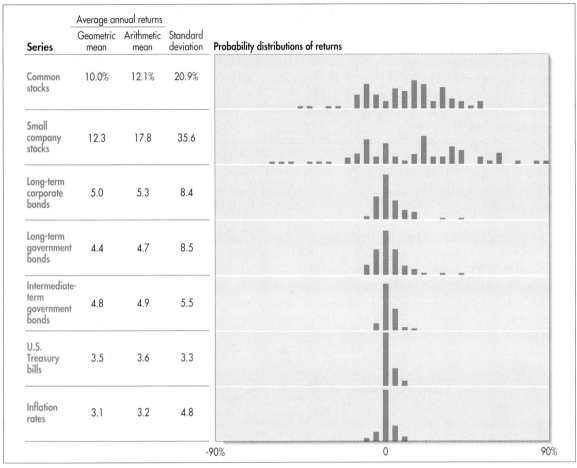

| Series | Average annual returns | | | Probability distributions of returns |
	Geometric mean	Arithmetic mean	Standard deviation	
Common stocks	10.0%	12.1%	20.9%	
Small company stocks	12.3	17.8	35.6	
Long-term corporate bonds	5.0	5.3	8.4	
Long-term government bonds	4.4	4.7	8.5	
Intermediate-term government bonds	4.8	4.9	5.5	
U.S. Treasury bills	3.5	3.6	3.3	
Inflation rates	3.1	3.2	4.8	

Figure 1-4 Average annual rate of return and risk statistics for different types of securities. (*Source: Stocks, Bonds, Bills, and Inflation: 1989 Yearbook,* Ibbotson Associates, 8 South Michigan Ave., Suite 707, Chicago, Ill. 60603.)

The Risk-Return Tradeoff: Three Examples

Not all high-risk assets will earn high rates of return, because some high-risk assets are bad investments. On average, however, high-risk assets should earn higher returns than low-risk assets. We can see the positive relationship between risk and return by comparing investment securities: consider T-bills, corporate bonds, and common stocks.

T-Bills Treasury bills are short-term bonds issued by the U.S. Treasury. There is virtually no chance that any U.S. Treasury bill will default, because the wealth of a mighty nation backs it. This minimal risk is the reason T-bills have such low returns, on average. Their small variability of return attracts risk-averse investors, even though the average returns are low.

Corporate Bonds   Corporate bonds represent investors' loans to corporations that must be paid back with interest. Unlike the U.S. Treasury, corporations can go bankrupt. So corporate bonds are riskier than Treasury bills and must therefore pay a higher average rate of return to attract investors. Bonds issued by a corporation typically yield lower average returns than common stock issued by the same corporation, however, for reasons that are explained next.

Common Stock   According to federal law, if a corporation goes bankrupt, all its assets must be auctioned off to pay its bills. The bankruptcy law states that certain classes of creditors must be completely paid off before other classes of creditors can receive anything. Essentially, all bills must be paid and all bondholders must be paid before the common stockholders of the bankrupt firm can be repaid. As a result, stockholders typically do not receive anything, because there is usually nothing left after all the bills are paid. Common stockholders' residual legal claim makes the investment more risky than bonds issued by the same corporation. This relatively high level of risk explains why a corporation's common stock tends to have the highest average rate of return of any security it issues.

Figure 1-5   Wealth indices for average investments in different types of securities, 1926–1988. (*Source: Stocks, Bonds, Bills, and Inflation: 1989 Yearbook*, Ibbotson Associates, 8 South Michigan Ave., Suite 707, Chicago, Ill. 60603.)

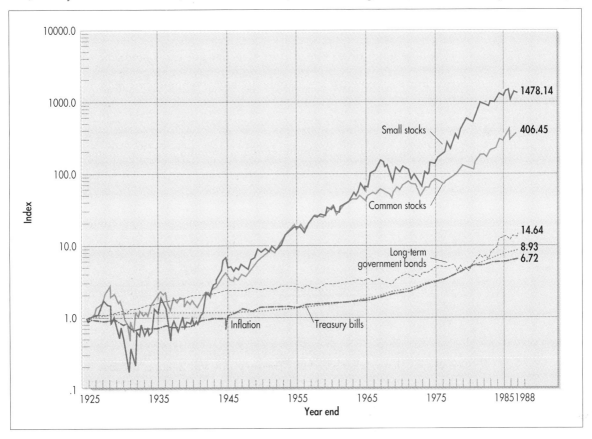

Box 1-12

DEFINITION: Securities

Securities are marketable financial instruments that give their owners the right to make specific claims on particular assets. An individual security provides evidence of either creditorship or ownership, depending on whether it is a bond or a stock. A share of **common stock** represents ownership; stock investors share in the business's profits. A **bond** is a loan that is paid off with interest; the investor lends money to the company that issued the bond. Bond investors get no share of the profits.

1-8 Investment Alternatives and Strategies

An investor can select from among many financial instruments and numerous investment strategies.

The Investments Menu

Table 1-4 lists the common types of securities and their general characteristics; it compares Treasury bonds and different securities that might be issued by the hypothetical XYZ Corporation.[4]

    The legal status of various securities, the income tax consequences of investment income, and the riskiness and average rates of return for each category of investments are examined in the early chapters of this book. Additional and more complicated

---

[4] Tax laws that exempt intercorporate cash dividend payments from income taxes under certain circumstances, the tax-free coupons on municipal bonds, the existence of certain tax-exempt investors, the existence of different classes of common stock issued by the same corporation, and other complications make Table 1-4 less than exhaustive. The table should be viewed as a framework for comparing securities. More comprehensive risk-return relationships are the topics of later chapters.

Table 1-4
**Ranking the Investment Characteristics
of Different Types of Securities**

Type of security	Risk	Average return	Investor control	Liquidity
XYZ Corporation's common stock	Most, 1	Most, 1	Most, 1	2
XYZ Corporation's preferred stock	2	2	2	3
XYZ Corporation's bond	3	3	3	Least, 4
U.S. Treasury bond	Least, 4	Least, 4	Least, 4	Most, 1

Note: The numbers represent ranking of the securities within a given heading, with 1 being the highest ranking.

investment alternatives, which include put and call options, commodity futures contracts, financial futures, and options on futures, are presented in later chapters. Table 1-5 gives a preview of what lies ahead.

Table 1-5
An Overview of Investment Alternatives

I. Financial assets
   A. Direct ownership (or equity) securities (Chapter 3)
      1. Common stock
      2. Preferred stock
      3. Asset-backed securities
        a. Mortgage-backed securities
        b. Lease-backed securities
        c. Receivables-backed securities
   B. Indirect ownership through investment company shares (Chapter 28)
      1. Closed-end investment companies
      2. Open-end investment companies, or mutual funds
   C. Monetary (or creditor) claims (Chapter 2)
      1. Nonmarketable
        a. U.S. savings bonds
        b. Savings accounts
        c. Time deposits and certificates of deposit
      2. Money market securities
        a. Repurchase agreements
        b. Banker's acceptances
      3. Bonds (or debt) securities
        a. Federal bonds
        b. Municipal bonds
        c. Corporate bonds
   D. Contingent claims (Chapters 21 and 22)
      1. Issuer-created
        a. Warrants
        b. Convertibles
        c. Rights
      2. Market-created
        a. Options
        b. Futures contracts
           (1) Traditional commodity futures
           (2) Financial futures
        c. Options on futures
II. Real (or nonfinancial) assets (Chapter 23)
   A. Real estate
   B. Gemstones
   C. Precious metals
   D. Collectibles
      1. Art
      2. Antiques
      3. Coins
      4. Stamps
   E. Other real assets (Chapter 23)

Table 1-6
Criteria for Selecting Investment Assets

Ownership or creditorship claims
Financial or real assets
Liquid (or marketable) versus illiquid assets
Taxable income or tax-exempt income
Direct or indirect investments
Long-term or short-term maturities
Convertible or nonconvertible securities
Callable or noncallable securities
Positive or zero cashflows (from interest or dividends)
Collateralized or uncollateralized claims
Underlying or derivative assets
Diversified or undiversified assets
Domestic or foreign investments
Investment risk factors:
   Default (or bankruptcy) risk (Chapter 10)
   Plus: Interest rate risk (Chapter 11)
   Plus: Bull-bear market risk (Chapter 17)
   Plus: Purchasing-power risk (Chapter 18)
   Plus: Political risk (Chapter 18)
   Plus: Management risk (Chapter 19)
   Plus: Foreign exchange risk (Chapter 27)
   Plus: Other risk factors
   Equals: Total risk

Table 1-7
Investment Strategies

Finding underpriced or overpriced assets
   (Chapters 10–20)
Speculating (Chapters 21–22)
Minimizing income tax (Chapter 7)
Taking long and short positions (Chapter 20)
Hedging (Chapters 20–22 and 24–26)
   Offsetting positions
   Options
   Futures
   Options on futures
Arbitraging (Chapters 20 and 26)
Diversifying (Chapters 24–26)
   Simple diversification
   Diversification across industries
   Markowitz diversification
International investing (Chapter 27)
Real asset investing (Chapter 23)
Immunizing (Chapter 12)
Mutual fund investing (Chapter 28)
Evaluating investment performance (Chapter 28)

Each of the investment alternatives listed in the table will be considered in the chapters that follow. The alternatives will be analyzed and categorized with respect to the investment characteristics listed in Table 1-6. Studying the financial characteristics of investment opportunities lets an investor see alternatives in terms of the risks they involve and the rates of return they can be expected to produce.

Investment Strategies

The last half of this book shows what investors and managers can do with the investment alternatives presented in the first half. Table 1-7 lists some of the investment strategies that will be presented.

Francis, Jack Clark, *Investments: Analysis and Management,* 5th ed. (New York: McGraw-Hill, 1991).
    Chapter 1 delves more deeply into the definition and sources of total risk. Algebra is used.

Markowitz, Harry, *Portfolio Selection* (New York: Wiley, 1959).
    Chapters 3 and 4 provide a well written yet rigorous exposition of finite probability by the Nobel laureate of portfolio theory. Algebra is used.

*Further
Reading*

Essay Questions

*Questions and
Problems*

1-1   Write out the formulas in words for the one-period rate of return for an investment in a corporate bond (*a*) before transactions costs and (*b*) after transactions costs. Assume the transactions costs include income taxes and broker's commissions.

1-2   What is implied when it is said that the probability of heads is six-tenths and the probability of tails is five-tenths when flipping a coin?

1-3   Compare and contrast the following phrases: (*a*) probability of occurrence in the future and (*b*) relative frequency in the past. Which one is more relevant in assessing an investment's expected rate of return?

1-4   Compare and contrast the following two investment goals: (*a*) maximizing the rate of return and (*b*) maximizing final wealth. Which is the better investment goal? *Hint:* Read the Appendix to this chapter about the geometric mean rate of return.

1-5   What is the risk-return tradeoff? Give a real-life example that illustrates this economic relationship.

1-6   A savings account earning a guaranteed 5 percent per annum in an FDIC-insured bank is a good example of a riskless asset. Construct the probability distribution of returns for this savings account. Calculate the variance of returns from the savings account.

1-7   Compare investing in U.S. Treasury bills with investing in the common stock issued by small corporations. (*a*) What are the advantages of the T-bill investment? (*b*) The disadvantages?

Problems

1-8   Calculate nine annual rates of return for Dynamics International Corporation's common stock from the stock price and cash dividend data below.

Year	Year's closing price*	Annual cash dividend	Annual rate of return, Eq. (1-4)
1	$ 60.00	$3.00	Insufficient data to calculate
2	69.00	3.00	($9.00 + $3.00)/$60 = .2 = 20.0%
3	100.50	3.00	
4	47.25	3.00	
5	39.525	3.00	
6	72.0975	3.00	
7	82.517	4.00	
8	70.2653	4.00	
9	80.31836	4.00	
10	92.382032	4.00	
11	134.573048	4.00	

* Stock prices are usually quoted in increments of one-eighth of $1 because the three-decimal-point quantity $.125 is the minimum price change allowed. Unrealistic stock prices that run to six-decimal-point accuracy were assumed here so that the annual rates of return would all work out to be exact multiples of 10 percentage points.

1-9   Calculate the average (or expected) rate of return, the variance of returns, and the standard deviation of returns from the 10 annual rates of return calculated for the Dynamics International Corporation's common stock in Problem 1-8.

1-10   Compare and contrast the following terms: (*a*) expected value, (*b*) weighted average using the probabilities for weights, (*c*) unweighted average, and (*d*) arithmetic mean. Calculate each of these quantities for the Firestone stock in Figure 1-2.

1-11   Reconsider the probability distributions in Figure 1-2. Show how to calculate the expected rate of return, variance, and standard deviation of Firestone's one-period rates of return.

1-12   The closing price of International Standard Corporation stock at the end of 19X0 was $40 per share. It is estimated that at the end of 19X1 there is a 10 percent probability that the price will have fallen to $32, a 20 percent probability that it will have remained the same, a 40 percent probability that it will have risen by 5 percent, a 15 percent probability that it will have increased 20 percent, a 10 percent probability that it will have increased 50 percent, and a 5 percent probability that it will have doubled. Calculate (*a*) the expected return, (*b*) the variance, and (*c*) the standard deviation for the period. (*d*) Do you think this probability distribution of returns forms a normal bell-shaped curve? Explain.

1-13   An investor has a choice of four stocks in which to invest. Their rates of return and their probabilities are given below.

Federal Systems Co.		Turtle Express, Inc.		Standard Pacific Co.		National Distributors, Inc.	
$E(r)$	P	$E(r)$	P	$E(r)$	P	$E(r)$	P
−30%	20%	−20%	15%	−20%	20%	−10%	10%
0	40	0	35	10	40	0	25
30	30	20	45	40	30	10	40
70	10	40	5	80	10	20	25

(*a*) Are all these stocks attractive investments? Why or why not?
(*b*) Of those that are attractive, how should the investor choose which to buy?

Multiple Choice Questions

1-14   What is the average or expected value of the number of dots that might turn up when you toss an ordinary six-sided die?

(*a*) 3.0
(*b*) 3.5
(*c*) 4.0
(*d*) 5.25
(*e*) 6.0

[handwritten:]
$e \ 167(1) + .167(2 B)$
$.167 + .334 + .501 + .668$
$+ .835 +$
1.002
$= 3.5$

1-15   Susan Ling is trying to decide which of the following common stocks to purchase.

Name of issuer	Expected return, $E(r)$	Standard deviation, σ
Able Corporation	7.0%	3.7%
Baker, Inc.	7.7	4.9
Charles & Company, Ltd.	15.0	15.0
Diamond Corporation	3.0	3.7 *dominate*
Energy Design, Inc.	7.7	12.0 *dominated*

[handwritten: D]

Which of the following statements is true?

(*a*) Able and Energy are dominated.
(*b*) Charles and Energy are dominated.
(*c*) Charles and Diamond are dominated.
(*d*) Energy and Diamond are dominated.
(*e*) Baker is dominated.

1-16   Calculate the expected rate of return $E(r)$ and the mode (or most likely) rate of return from the probability distribution of returns below for the Belfast Bearing Corporation's (BBC) common stock.

[handwritten: 20%   70%]

Five possibilities	Rate of return, r	Proba-bility, P
$i = 5$	−.5 = −50%	.1
$i = 4$	−.1 = −10%	.25
$i = 3$	.2 = 20%	.3
$i = 2$	.5 = 50%	.25
$i = 1$	.9 = 90%	.1
	Total	1.0

[handwritten:]
$$E(r) = .1(-.5) + .25(-.1) + .3(.2) + .25(.5) + .1(.9)$$
$$-.05 + -.025 + .06 + .125 + .09$$
$$= .195 \ .2$$
$$20\%$$

The expected rate of return $E(r)$ and mode return for BBC are which of the following?

(a) The $E(r)$ is 10 percent and the mode is 9 percent.
(b) The $E(r)$ is 20 percent and the mode is 20 percent.
(c) The $E(r)$ is 11 percent and the mode is 10 percent.
(d) The $E(r)$ is 20 percent and the mode is 19 percent.

1-17   Reconsider the probability distribution of returns for the Belfast Bearing Corporation (BBC) from the preceding question. Finish the calculations below to find the variance and the standard deviation of BBC's rates of return.

i	Rate of return, r	Proba-bility, P	Product $r \times P$	Deviation, $r - E(r)$	Deviation squared, $[r - E(r)]^2$	Product $P \times [r - E(r)]$
$i = 5$	$-.5 = -50\%$	.1	$-.05$	$-.7$	.49	.049
$i = 4$	$-.1 = -10\%$	.25	$-.025$	$-.3$	.09	.0225
$i = 3$	$.2 = 20\%$	.3	.06	0	0	0
$i = 2$	$.5 = 50\%$	.25				
$i = 1$	$.9 = 90\%$	.1				
		1.0				

Which of the following describes the variance and standard deviation?

(a) BBC's variance of returns is .143 and its standard deviation is .378.
(b) BBC's standard deviation of returns is 1.2 and its variance is 1.44.
(c) BBC's standard deviation of returns is .20 and its variance is .40.
(d) BBC's standard deviation of returns is 1.56 and its variance is 2.433.

1-18   Risk is best described by which one of the following statements?

(a) The phrase "total risk" is synonymous with the "total variability of return" from an asset.
(b) Bond quality ratings are essentially risk measures that measure the probability that an issue of bonds will default.
(c) Although U.S. Treasury bonds are free from default risk, they nevertheless contain management risk.
(d) Both (a) and (b) are true.
(e) All the above statements about risk are true.

1-19   Dominant assets have which one of the following characteristics?

(a) The highest rate of return
(b) The lowest risk
(c) The highest return in their risk class
(d) Both (a) and (b)
(e) (a), (b), and (c)

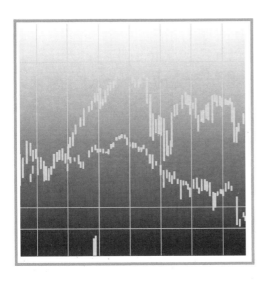

APPENDIX 1A

THE GEOMETRIC
MEAN RETURN

When dealing with several *successive* rates of return, we must distinguish between the *arithmetic average* rate of return and the *geometric average* return because only one of these average return measures is correct.

The Misleading Arithmetic Multiperiod Average Return

The **arithmetic average** of successive one-period rates of return over T time periods is defined in Equation (1A-1).

$$\bar{r} = \frac{1}{T} \sum_{t}^{T} r_t = \frac{1}{T} (r_1 + r_2 + r_3 + \cdots + r_T) \qquad (1A-1)$$

The r_t symbols represent the one-period rates of return defined in Equations (1-3) through (1-6), for the T successive time periods indicated by $t = 1, 2, 3, \ldots, T$.

Asset A's Arithmetic Average   If asset A is purchased at $40 at the end of time period 0 and its price rises to $60 at the end of the first time period, the asset earned a 50 percent gain, $r_1 = 50\%$. If the price of A then falls back to $40 at the end of the second period and the asset is sold at that price, a 33 percent drop was realized during the second period, $r_2 = -33.3\%$. The *arithmetic average* rate of return of 50 percent and -33.3 percent is 8.35 percent.

$$\text{Arithmetic average return from asset A} = \frac{50\% + (-33.3\%)}{2} = 8.35\%$$

Asset B's Arithmetic Average   Suppose asset B also has a purchase price of $40 at the end of time period 0, but asset B's price falls to $20 at the end of period 1; then it rises back to $40 at the end of period 2. The arithmetic average rate of return for asset B over the same two periods is the average of -50 percent and 100 percent, or 25 percent.

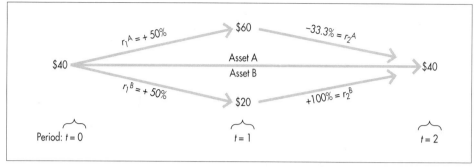

Figure 1A-1   The movements of assets A and B over two time periods.

$$\text{Arithmetic average return for asset B} = \frac{-50\% + 100\%}{2} = 25\%$$

The behavior of the prices of assets A and B over the two periods is illustrated in Figure 1A-1. In actuality, an asset purchased for $40 and sold for $40 two periods later returned neither 8.35 percent nor 25 percent: It earned zero return. The examples of assets A and B above demonstrate the fact that *the arithmetic average of successive one-period returns is not the true average rate of return over multiple time periods.*

Price Relatives and Link Relatives

The *geometric mean return* provides the correct answers. However, before examining the formula for the geometric mean return, we need to see that two new mathematical terms are equivalent.

Equating the **price relative,** p_t/p_{t-1}, to the **link relative,** $1 + r_t$, yields the following equation:

$$\frac{p_t}{p_{t-1}} = 1 + r_t \tag{1A-2}$$

For example, if a $40 investment grows to $60 in one time period, the price relative is $p_t/p_{t-1} = \$60/\$40$, the link relative is $1 + r_t = 1.5$, and the one-period rate of return is $r_t = 50$ percent, as shown below.

$$\frac{p_t}{p_{t-1}} = \frac{\$60}{\$40} = 1 + r_t = 1.5 \qquad \text{hence } r_t = 50\%$$

Price relatives and link relatives are used interchangeably in the geometric mean return formula.

Formulas for the Geometric Mean Return

The true rate of return over several successive time periods is called the **compounded rate of return** or **geometric mean return;** it is denoted GMR and defined in equation (1A-3).

$$(1 + \text{GMR})^T = \frac{p_1}{p_0} \frac{p_2}{p_1} \cdots \frac{p_T}{p_{T-1}} \tag{1A-3}$$

Using Equation (1A-2) allows us to rewrite Equation (1A-3) in an equivalent form of the GMR.

$$(1 + \text{GMR})^T = (1 + r_1)(1 + r_2) \cdots (1 + r_T) \tag{1A-4}$$

Asset A's GMR Calculations   The geometric mean return for asset A is calculated below and found to be zero.

$$(1.0 + \text{GMR})^2 = (\$60/\$40)(\$40/\$60) = (1.5)(.667) = 1.0$$

or $(1.0 + \text{GMR})^2 = (1.0 + .5)(1.0 - .333) = (1.5)(.667) = 1.0$

Therefore $1.0 + \text{GMR} = \sqrt{1.0} = 1.0$

and $\text{GMR} = 1.0 - 1.0 = 0$

Asset B's GMR Calculations   The geometric mean return for asset B is calculated below and found to be zero.

$$(1.0 + \text{GMR})^2 = (\$20/\$40)(\$40/20) = (.5)(2.0) = 1.0$$

or $(1.0 + \text{GMR})^2 = (1.0 - .5)(1.0 + 1.0) = (.5)(2.0) = 1.0$

Therefore $1.0 + \text{GMR} = \sqrt{1.0} = 1.0$

and $\text{GMR} = 1.0 - 1.0 = 0$

Only the geometric mean rate of return gives the true compounded rate of return over multiple time periods.

Maximizing the GMR as an Investment Objective

Equation (1A-3) simplifies to Equation (1A-5). Equation (1A-5) shows that maximizing the GMR from an investment is equivalent to trying to select assets that will have the maximum terminal price p_T.

$$(1 + \text{GMR})^T = \frac{p_T}{p_0} \tag{1A-5}$$

Thus, we see that wealth maximization is an investment objective equivalent to maximizing the GMR.[1]

[1] For more information about wealth maximization as an investment objective see H. A. Latane's classic paper, "Criteria for Choice among Risky Ventures," *The Journal of Political Economy,* April 1959, pp. 144–155. Also see Harry M. Markowitz, "Investment for the Long-Run: New Evidence for an Old Rule," *Journal of Finance,* vol. 31, December 1976, pp. 1273–1286.

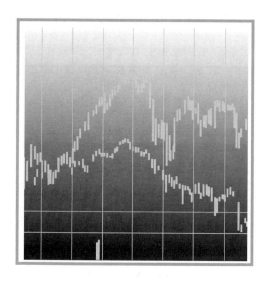

APPENDIX 1B

EMPLOYMENT
OPPORTUNITIES
IN INVESTMENTS

If you find yourself thinking of words like "exciting," "fun," and "glamorous" to describe the work of investment professionals, the following job descriptions and salary guidelines may interest you. About 200,000 people work in the securities industry, and if you include the whole financial services industry (commercial banking, investment banking, insurance companies, and so forth), there are millions of jobs in the field.

What You Can Do: Jobs

Registered Representative   Securities brokers are employed by brokerage houses to sell stocks, bonds, puts and calls, commodities, mutual funds, and other securities. Registered representatives also give clients investment advice and assist with portfolio management. Trainees must pass the Series 7 exam that is administered all over the United States periodically to demonstrate a knowledge of securities law and practices. It takes most beginners several years of "cold call selling" to build up a clientele, but then annual incomes in the $60,000 to $100,000 range can be expected from selling to individual (retail) investors. The average **retail brokers'** annual income was $79,169 in 1990.[1] **Institutional brokers** work with pension funds, banks, and mutual funds; they usually have MBAs and incomes that are about twice as high as those of retail brokers. Institutional brokers execute fewer, but larger, transactions than retail brokers; the institutional sales jobs are more difficult to obtain. Average annual income for institutional brokers was $166,335 in 1990.

Securities Analyst   Brokerage houses, pensions, trust departments of large banks, insurance companies, mutual funds, investment banks, charitable foundations, and other organizations that administer substantial pools of invested funds employ securities analysts to prepare written

[1] William Power, "Brokers Averaged Pay of $79,169 in 90, Survey Says," *Wall Street Journal,* June 24, 1991, p. C1. The salaries are from a survey of 35,000 brokers at 57 firms, less than half the brokers in the United States. The record year for salaries was 1986, when the average retail broker made $97,100 and the average institutional broker made $244,495.

investment recommendations and occasionally to talk to major clients. Annual salary plus bonus for a few widely acclaimed securities analysts exceeds $1 million per year. Over 400 of the top analysts are honored annually by being appointed to *Institutional Investors* magazine's All American Research Team and having their pictures in the October issue. It is estimated that these top analysts have annual incomes in excess of $500,000.

Those who are interested in becoming professional security analysts should consider getting an MBA and/or entering the chartered financial analyst (CFA) program. Many universities offer MBA programs. For more information about the CFA program, write to the Institute of Chartered Financial Analysts, P.O. Box 3668, Charlottesville, VA, 22903 (phone: 804-977-6600). Aspiring CFAs must pay annual fees, study security analysis at home, meet certain ethics requirements, pass three annual exams, and serve a financial apprenticeship.

Financial Planner   Financial planners usually work in sales or sales-related positions for life insurance companies, small financial consulting groups, brokerage firms, or on their own. They typically deal with affluent individuals who need security analysis, tax planning, investment management, or estate planning. Planners work with clients on a personal, one-to-one basis. Several schools that specialize in financial planning offer study programs to help people develop financial planning skills.[2] Some financial planners make more money from the commissions on the life insurance or securities they sell to clients than they do from consulting fees.

Where You Can Work: Employers

Registered representatives, securities analysts, and other investments professionals work for the kinds of employers listed below.

Investment Banks   The highest-paying investment banking jobs are usually found in New York City. Major New York investment banks hire analysts with bachelor's degrees to crunch numbers for $25,000 to $30,000 per year. These are 2-year apprentice jobs, and the apprentice is expected to obtain an MBA before advancing further. Typically, only top students from prestigious schools get investment banking jobs. Salaries for first-year associates with MBAs start at about $50,000, with another $25,000 in bonus. Investment bankers with 2 years of experience were paid a total compensation of from $100,000 to $195,000 in 1990—lower amounts than in previous years.[3] After a few more years, beginners work themselves into client contact, arbitrage, trading, and portfolio management positions where the sky is the limit for compensation. Base salary means little in these positions because bonuses can be several times larger than salary. In 1990 a 31-year-old Salomon Brothers managing director named Lawrence Hilbrand, an MBA from MIT, was paid an annual salary and bonus of $23 million as a high-tech bond trader.[4] This was, however, an unusually high amount.

[2] For more information, write to: (1) The International Board of Certified Financial Planners, Lincoln Avenue, Denver, Colorado, 80231-4993 (phone: 303-830-7543), (2) College for Financial Planning, 9725 East Hampden Avenue, Denver, Colorado, 80231-4993 (phone: 303-755-7101), or (3) the Investment Counselor's Association of America, 20 Exchange Place, New York, New York 10005 (phone: 212-344-0999).

[3] William Power and Michael Siconolfi, "Wall Street Bonuses for 1989 Are Even Smaller Than Expected," *Wall Street Journal*, February 5, 1990, p. C1. Also see "Wall Street Paychecks," *Wall Street Journal*, February 6, 1991, p. 1.

[4] "Sullied Solly: Hubris Led to Downfall," *Wall Street Journal*, August 19, 1991, p. A4.

On Wall Street, each year's pay is tied closely to the profit the individual generated for the firm that year. In contrast to Hilbrand, Salomon's chief executive officer (CEO), John H. Gutfreund (dismissed from the firm in 1991 for concealing improprieties in Salomon's Treasury bond trading), was paid only $3.5 million in 1989 and $2.3 million in 1990.[5] Salomon's Vice-Chairman, John Meriwether, was paid $10 million in 1990.[6] Morgan-Stanley and Goldman Sachs & Company typically pay much more than Salomon. All these firms reward those who earn millions for them with huge bonuses. You can become a millionaire at a young age on Wall Street, but the work is hard and life at the top can be short.

Mutual Funds   There are 2700 mutual funds in the United States, plus numerous foreign funds. These money management enterprises hire securities analysts, economists, portfolio managers, statisticians, computer programmers, and administrators. Fidelity Funds, which is headquartered in Boston, is the largest mutual fund company in the United States and operates over 80 different funds. Large mutual companies like Fidelity employ large professional staffs at salaries that are below Wall Street's, but the work is not as hard or as stressful.

Trust Departments at Commercial Banks   Large banks have trust departments to manage other people's money for fees of 1 to 2 percent of the market value of the managed assets per year for multimillion-dollar accounts. To do this, the banks need securities lawyers, securities analysts, economists, and portfolio managers. The manager of the trust department is usually a senior vice-president of the bank. Banking salaries vary with the size of the bank in the United States. Foreign bank executives are usually paid less than their American counterparts.

Commercial Bank Lending Departments   The presidents of most commercial banks start as financial analysts in the commercial lending department and work their way up through the lending officer ranks. There are about 15,000 banks in the United States, and those in medium- and large-sized cities typically employ several vice-president lending officers and assistant vice-president financial analysts. Again, salaries vary directly with the size of the bank. In addition, the largest banks in the United States perform some investment banking functions and offer positions comparable to those in investment banking firms.

Insurance Companies   Life insurance and casualty insurance companies employ securities analysts, economists, and portfolio managers to manage money entrusted to them by policyholders.[7] Insurance companies also provide money management services for large investors. The big insurance companies typically pay their executives a little less than the New York City commercial banks and a lot less than the largest investment banking firms. The tradeoff: Insurance companies are usually more stable, easier places to work.

---

[5] Michael Siconolfi, "These Days the Biggest Paychecks Don't Go to Chiefs," *Wall Street Journal,* March 26, 1991, p. C1.

[6] "The Big Squeeze: T-Note Market Is Jolted by Salomon's Admission," *Wall Street Journal,* August 12, 1991, p. A5.

[7] The Chartered Life Underwriter (CLU) is a program for life insurance salespersons and counselors. Training for the CLU designation is provided in the fundamentals of economics, finance, taxation, investments, and risk management by The American College, 270 Bryn Mawr Avenue, Bryn Mawr, Pennsylvania, 19010 (phone: 215-896-4500).

Investment Consulting Firms   Companies like Frank Russell and Company, headquartered in Tacoma, Washington (the world's largest pension fund consulting firm); BARRA, headquartered in Berkeley, California;[8] Roll and Ross Asset Management, headquartered in New Haven, Connecticut, and Los Angeles;[9] and other investment consulting firms manage billions of dollars in investments and employ highly educated professionals. Consulting firms employ people with degrees in finance, econometrics, computer science, and related fields.

[8] For details about BARRA's investment performance evaluation services, see H. Russell Fogler, "Common Stock Management in the 1990s," *Journal of Portfolio Management,* Winter 1990, pp. 26–35.

[9] Professors S. Ross of Yale University and Richard Roll of UCLA manage $7 billion of other people's money. For details, see Stephen E. Clark, "Practicing What They Teach," *Institutional Investor,* November 1991, pp. 92–99.

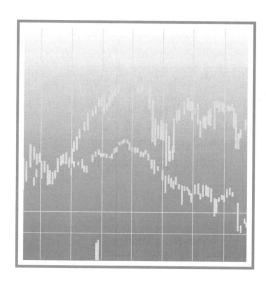

CHAPTER 2

DEBT
SECURITIES

Debt securities, which are the focus of this chapter, are sometimes called **fixed income securities** because they pay contractually fixed periodic interest payments that cannot vary during the life of the security. Zero coupon bonds pay annual incomes that are fixed at zero. In contrast, junk bonds usually promise investors the highest rates of interest.[1] Bonds are the most familiar kind of debt security. A bond is a component of a larger amount of debt. The big debt might arise, for example, because the General Motors Corporation or the U.S. Treasury Department wants to borrow, say, $10 million to buy some buildings. It is difficult to find a single lender who can make a $10 million loan. So, rather than seeking one $10 million loan, the potential purchaser of the buildings sells 100,000 bonds that each have a face value of $100. A $10 million **bond issue** results.

[1] Junk bonds are discussed in depth in Chapter 10.

Box 2-1   35

*Chapter 2
Debt Securities*

DEFINITION: Bonds

Bonds are negotiable promissory notes that can be issued by individuals, business firms, governments, or governmental agencies. These documents promise to repay their investors the principal amount plus a predetermined amount of interest. The principal and interest may be repaid as a single payoff or through a series of payments.

Stock (or equity) securities are the topic of Chapter 3. More sophisticated securities and real (nonfinancial) assets and their characteristics will be introduced in later chapters.

Let us begin our study of debt securities with the safest and simplest category, money market securities.

2-1   Nongovernment Money Market Securities

Money market securities are moneylike, highly marketable securities with short maturities and virtually no risk of default. The word **maturity** refers to the length of time an investor must wait to recover the investment in a debt security from the issuer (unless the bond is sold before it matures). All money market securities except U.S. Treasury bills mature within 270 days after issue, because a Securities and Exchange Commission regulation requires that all nongovernmental securities with longer maturities go through a costly legal registration process (described in Chapter 6). U.S. Treasury bills (T-bills) are money market securities that corporations and large investors sometimes buy from the Treasury, or from bond brokers, when they have cash to invest temporarily. T-bills, like all other money market securities, pay interest to investors by selling at a discount from their face (or maturity) value.

Here are some common nongovernment money market securities:

Negotiable Certificates of Deposit   A negotiable certificate of deposit, or **negotiable CD,** is a receipt from a federally insured commercial bank for a deposit of $100,000

Box 2-2

DEFINITION: Discount Pricing

A 90-day Treasury bill with a $100,000 face value might sell for $98,000 when it is initially issued by the Treasury Department. The $2000 difference between the T-bill's price and its face value is a **discount.** The buyer can either hold this bond for 90 days or sell it in the active T-bill market at any time before it matures. When the T-bill matures, whoever owns it can redeem it for its face value of $100,000. The $2000 discount is the interest income that is paid to the T-bill investor, or split among the series of investors who own the T-bill during its life.

---

or more. The bank issuing the CD is said to have "bought deposits" by offering CDs for sale with interest rates high enough to induce big depositors to buy them. One of the written legal provisions covering every CD is that the deposit cannot be withdrawn from the bank before a specific maturity date without some penalty; the typical penalty is a reduced rate of interest. Millions of dollars of negotiable CDs are traded daily between banks that have excess deposits and those that need deposits.

Most investors are probably familiar with the nonnegotiable CDs sold at neighborhood banks. Nonnegotiable CDs differ from negotiable CDs in several respects: (1) The interest rates on the nonnegotiable CDs are set by the issuing bank and are not negotiable. (2) The nonnegotiable CDs are not transferable securities that can be traded in the money markets. (3) The denominations of the nonnegotiable CDs are small—for example, as small as $100.

Banker's Acceptances   **Banker's acceptances** are money market securities that normally arise in foreign trade when an exporting seller is reluctant to grant credit to an unfamiliar foreign buyer (or importer). (For example, imagine that Boeing has an order for a jet plane from a new customer named Vietnam Airlines.) The buyer applies to a well-known international bank (say, the Bank of Tokyo) for a banker's acceptance to overcome the seller's fears that the debt might not be paid. The banker's acceptance is thus a written promise from the importer's bank to repay borrowed funds to the exporter's bank that assures the exporter of collecting. The buyer's bank is said to "accept" the banker's acceptance when it pays the exporter's bank in the United States.

If the importer's bank wants to recoup the money it has invested in the loan before the loan expires, it can sell the banker's acceptance to another bank. A banker's acceptance may be resold to new investors any number of times before the loan comes due and is repaid; there is an active market in banker's acceptances.

Any investor who buys a banker's acceptance can collect the loan on the date it is scheduled to be repaid. If the borrower defaults on the loan, the last investor holding the acceptance has legal recourse on (can collect from) the bank that accepted the banker's acceptance and thus originated the debt security. Banker's acceptances are practically default-free because a bank of international stature stands behind the instrument.

Commercial Paper   **Commercial paper** refers to short-term promissory notes issued by large, old, blue-chip corporations such as General Motors, Exxon, and IBM. The maturities vary from 5 to 270 days, and the denominations are $100,000 or more—usually more. These notes are not backed by any collateral; investors rely on the high credit rating of the issuing corporation.

It is customary for issuers of commercial paper to maintain open lines of credit (unused borrowing power at banks) sufficient to pay back all their outstanding commercial paper. Issuers operate this way because money can be borrowed more quickly and easily by issuing commercial paper than by applying for bank loans. The credit rating of most issuers is so high that the so-called prime (or highest-quality) commercial paper's interest rates are relatively low. The prime commercial paper rate approximates the yields on negotiable CDs and banker's acceptances. *Standard & Poor's Commercial Paper Rating Guide* provides default-risk analysis on commercial paper issued by hundreds of large corporations.

Repurchase Agreements **Repurchase agreements,** or repos, are instruments used by securities dealers to help finance part of their multimillion-dollar inventories of marketable securities for one or a few days. For instance, if a securities dealer (like Merrill Lynch, Pierce, Fenner & Smith) ends a day of trading with an increase of $30 million in its inventory of marketable securities, a repo may be sold (to Chase Manhattan Bank, for instance) to finance the $30 million inventory overnight. The securities dealer pays a repo broker a finder's fee (or broker's commission) to find an investor with $30 million in cash to invest overnight, while agreeing to repurchase the securities the next day at a slightly higher price. This slightly higher price represents the interest income for the overnight investor who purchased the repo. The investor is essentially making a short-term loan to the securities dealer using the securities dealer's inventory as collateral.

Repos that last longer than overnight, called *term repos,* can span 30 days or even longer. Term repos are marketable securities actively traded between the money market trading desks of large banks and brokerage houses.

Federal Funds Overnight loans between commercial banks are commonly called **federal funds.** Federal funds arise when some banks hold more reserves than the Federal Reserve requires. Federal funds, then, are simply excess reserves that banks lend to other banks with insufficient reserves. One bank borrows money from another and pays the federal funds interest rate to obtain the lending bank's excess reserves to hold as 1-day deposits. The borrowing bank needs these 1-day deposits to achieve the minimum legal reserve requirements.

The interest rate on these 1-day bank loans, called the **federal funds rate,** is followed closely by money market economists in finance and government policy-making agencies. This interest rate fluctuates quickly and in the United States is an indicator of the tightening or easing of credit. When the fed funds rate is high, credit may be tight and loans may be hard to obtain. Bankers obtain (or sell) federal funds every day simply by contacting other bankers by telephone to find the funds (or the buyers) they need.

Eurodollar Loans Sometimes called *petrodollar loans, Asian dollar loans,* or *hot money flows,* **Eurodollar loans** are large, short-term international loans denominated in dollars. These loans are usually arranged by banks with large international operations, such as Citibank in New York City or BankAmerica in San Francisco. Eurodollar loans tend to be made by businesses located in countries with low market interest rates. The **yield spread** between the two countries' interest rates is what motivates these loans across international boundaries. International bankers arrange Eurodollar loans for their banks' customers, and banks also frequently borrow or lend Eurodollars for their own account. An intermediary's fee of one-tenth of 1 percent or a yield spread of the same size is ample to motivate international bankers to arrange a multimillion-Eurodollar loan for a client or for their own account.

2-2 U.S. Government Securities

In 1990 the total debt of the federal government went over $3 trillion. Of that total, about $2.3 trillion was interest-bearing, publicly owned bond-type securities. Most of it was in the form of U.S. Treasury bonds, Treasury notes, Treasury bills, and savings bonds. All U.S. government securities are bonds of some sort, because governmental bodies cannot sell stock.

U.S. government securities are bonds of such high quality that investors around the world view them as being riskless or **default-free** securities. They are perceived to be very safe because the U.S. government has unlimited power to collect taxes or to print new money to pay its debts. Federal securities are divided between nonmarketable and marketable issues.

Nonmarketable Issues

About one-quarter of the U.S. public debt consists of **nonmarketable issues.** These issues cannot be traded in the securities market; they are not transferable or negotiable; they cannot be used as collateral for a loan; they can be purchased only from the U.S. Treasury; and they can be redeemed only by the U.S. Treasury. A major portion of these nonmarketable securities are U.S. savings bonds. Savings bonds do not have market-determined prices; redemption prices and yields are printed on the bond certificates.

EE savings bonds were introduced in 1982 to replace the old Series E bonds. The new bonds pay higher interest rates than their predecessors. E and EE savings bonds are zero coupon bonds available in denominations from $50 up to $10,000, with maturities as long as 10 years. EE savings bonds are sold at deep discounts from their face values to provide interest income for investors in the form of price appreciation. They are priced to yield at least 85 percent of the market yield on 5-year Treasury securities, if they are held to maturity. Furthermore, EE savings bonds guarantee a minimum yield of 6.0 percent if held to maturity, no matter how low other market interest rates may fall. If a savings bond is redeemed before its maturity date, the investor is penalized by receiving a low penalty rate of interest that starts at 4 percent after 1 year and graduates up to the 6 percent minimum after 5 years. Savings bonds are registered in the investor's name so that they can be replaced, at no charge, if they are lost. Federal income taxes on EE savings bonds can be deferred until the bonds are cashed in, and the interest is exempt from state and local income taxes.

Series HH savings bonds pay the same interest rates as EE bonds and have 10 years to maturity. These bonds are sold at their par (or face) value, rather than at a discount and pay fixed interest rates, which are printed on the bond. Many retired people use the interest income for living expenses. The semiannual coupons must be reported to the IRS and income taxes paid on them every year. The smallest denomination is $500.

Marketable Issues

Marketable issues make up about three-fourths of the federal debt. They include T-bills, T-notes, and T-bonds. Investors usually call a broker to purchase these securities from the supply of previous issues that are actively traded. Alternatively, the purchaser may subscribe for a part of a new issue through a Federal Reserve Bank. The holder of marketable government securities stands to gain not only from the interest paid on these bonds, but also from price appreciation if the selling price is higher than the purchase price. The market prices of these marketable issues are published daily in national newspapers such as *The New York Times* and *The Wall Street Journal.* Figure 2-1 shows a newspaper listing of Treasury security prices; it lists one day's prices for U.S. Treasury securities. Consider one particular issue, say, the 10¾ bonds of May 2003 (indicated by the arrow). The first (or farthest-left) column of Figure 2-1 contains the coupon rates of the different T-bond issues. The 10¾ issue of T-bonds pays a 10.75 percent coupon rate. Thus a $10,000 bond pays

TREASURY BONDS

Representative Over-the-Counter quotations based on transactions of $1 million or more.

Treasury bond, note and bill quotes are as of mid-afternoon. Colons in bid-and-asked quotes represent 32nds; 101:01 means 101 1/32. Net changes in 32nds. n-Treasury note. Treasury bill quotes in hundredths, quoted on terms of a rate of discount. Days to maturity calculated from settlement date. All yields are to maturity and based on the asked quote. For bonds callable prior to maturity, yields are computed to the earliest call date for issues quoted above par and to the maturity date for issues below par. *-When issued.

Source: Federal Reserve Bank of New York.

GOVT. BONDS & NOTES

Rate	Maturity Mo/Yr	Bid	Asked	Chg.	Ask Yld.
9¼	Apr 91n	100:01	100:03	....	-23.58
8⅛	May 91n	100:03	100:05	....	4.42
14½	May 91n	100:14	100:18	....	1.65
8¾	May 91n	100:08	100:10	....	5.00
7⅞	Jun 91n	100:10	100:12	....	5.52
8¼	Jun 91n	100:12	100:14	....	5.52
13¾	Jul 91n	101:21	101:23	....	5.37
7¾	Jul 91n	100:15	100:17	+ 1	5.55
7½	Aug 91n	100:14	100:16	....	5.71
8¾	Aug 91n	100:26	100:28	+ 1	5.67
14⅞	Aug 91n	102:20	102:24	− 2	5.35
8¼	Aug 91n	100:22	100:24	+ 1	5.90
8⅜	Sep 91n	100:31	101:01	+ 1	5.83
9⅛	Sep 91n	101:09	101:11	+ 1	5.81
12¼	Oct 91n	102:26	102:28	....	5.83
7⅝	Oct 91n	100:24	100:26	....	5.96
6½	Nov 91n	100:06	100:08	....	6.03
8½	Nov 91n	101:08	101:10	....	6.02
14¼	Nov 91n	104:09	104:13	− 1	5.91
7¾	Nov 91n	100:28	100:30	....	6.11
7⅝	Dec 91n	100:31	101:01	+ 2	6.04
8¼	Dec 91n	101:12	101:14	+ 2	6.04
11⅝	Jan 92n	103:24	103:26	+ 1	6.09
8⅛	Jan 92n	101:13	101:15	+ 2	6.11
6⅝	Feb 92n	100:07	100:09	+ 1	6.26
9⅛	Feb 92n	102:04	102:06	+ 1	6.28
14⅝	Feb 92n	106:29	107:01	....	5.52
8½	Feb 92n	101:24	101:26	+ 2	6.25
7⅞	Mar 92n	101:13	101:15	+ 3	6.21
8½	Mar 92n	101:29	101:31	+ 1	6.27
11¾	Apr 92n	105:00	105:02	+ 2	6.25
8⅞	Apr 92n	102:13	102:15	+ 1	6.30
6⅝	May 92n	100:08	100:10	+ 1	6.31
9	May 92n	102:18	102:20	+ 2	6.36
13¾	May 92n	107:10	107:12	+ 2	6.34
8½	May 92n	102:02	102:04	+ 1	6.45
8¼	Jun 92n	101:29	101:31	+ 2	6.48
8⅜	Jun 92n	102:01	102:03	+ 2	6.49
10⅜	Jul 92n	104:10	104:12	+ 2	6.57
8	Jul 92n	101:20	101:22	+ 1	6.58
4¼	Aug 87-92	95:27	96:27	....	6.83
7¼	Aug 92	100:25	100:29	+ 1	6.51
7⅞	Aug 92n	101:14	101:16	+ 2	6.65
8¼	Aug 92n	101:28	101:30	+ 2	6.67
8⅛	Aug 92n	101:27	101:29	+ 4	6.61
8⅛	Sep 92n	101:25	101:27	....	6.74
8¾	Sep 92n	102:25	102:27	+ 3	6.62
9¾	Oct 92n	104:01	104:03	....	6.76
7¾	Oct 92n	101:10	101:12	+ 2	6.77
7¾	Nov 92n	101:09	101:11	+ 2	6.82
8⅜	Nov 92n	102:07	102:09	+ 3	6.79
10½	Nov 92n	105:11	105:13	+ 3	6.76
7⅜	Nov 92n	100:25	100:27	+ 3	6.81
7¼	Dec 92n	100:18	100:20	+ 3	6.85
9⅛	Dec 92n	103:15	103:17	+ 3	6.86
8¾	Jan 93n	102:30	103:00	+ 4	6.87
7	Jan 93n	100:04	100:06	+ ?,	6.88
4	Feb 88-93	94:26	95:26	....	6.50
6¾	Feb 93	99:22	99:30	+ 1	6.79
7⅞	Feb 93	101:18	101:26	+ 2	6.79
8¼	Feb 93n	102:05	102:07	+ 1	6.92
8⅜	Feb 93n	102:12	102:14	+ 3	6.91
10⅞	Feb 93n	106:17	106:21	+ 3	6.88
6¾	Feb 93n	99:22	99:24	+ 2	6.90
7⅛	Mar 93n	100:11	100:13	+ 2	6.90
9⅝	Mar 93n	104:23	104:27	+ 2	6.89
7⅜	Apr 93n	100:24	100:28	+ 1	6.89
7	Apr 93n*	100:04	100:05	+ 4	6.92
7⅝	May 93n	101:05	101:09	+ 2	6.94
8⅝	May 93n	103:00	103:02	+ 2	6.99
10⅛	May 93n	105:24	105:28	+ 1	6.99
8⅛	Jun 93n	102:07	102:11	+ 3	6.94
7¼	Jul 93n	100:15	100:19	+ 1	6.96
7½	Aug 88-93	100:24	101:00	+ 3	7.02
8	Aug 93n	101:30	102:00	+ 2	7.04
8⅝	Aug 93	103:09	103:17	+ 2	6.94
8¾	Aug 93n	103:16	103:18	+ 2	7.05
11⅞	Aug 93n	109:31	110:01	+ 2	7.07
8¼	Sep 93n	102:16	102:18	+ 2	7.08

Rate	Maturity Mo/Yr	Bid	Asked	Chg.	Ask Yld.
8	Oct 96n	100:26	100:30	+ 1	7.79
7¼	Nov 96n	97:13	97:17	− 1	7.81
8	Jan 97n	100:19	100:23	− 2	7.84
8½	Apr 97n	102:26	102:30	....	7.87
8½	May 97n	102:24	102:28	− 1	7.89
8½	Jul 97n	102:22	102:24	− 2	7.93
8⅝	Aug 97n	103:10	103:14	− 2	7.92
8¾	Oct 97n	103:29	103:31	− 1	7.95
8⅞	Nov 97n	104:17	104:21	− 3	7.95
7⅞	Jan 98n	99:18	99:20	− 2	7.95
8⅛	Feb 98n	100:25	100:29	− 3	7.95
7⅞	Apr 98n	99:20	99:22	− 3	7.93
7	May 93-98	94:31	95:07	− 3	7.90
9	May 98n	105:08	105:12	− 4	7.99
9¼	Aug 98n	106:19	106:23	− 3	8.02
3½	Nov 98	94:02	95:02	+ 4	4.27
8⅞	Nov 98n	104:20	104:24	− 3	8.02
8⅞	Feb 99n	104:20	104:24	− 3	8.04
8½	May 94-99	102:00	102:08	− 5	7.66
9⅛	May 99n	106:02	106:06	− 3	8.06
8	Aug 99n	99:20	99:24	− 2	8.04
7⅞	Nov 99n	98:23	98:27	− 4	8.06
7⅞	Feb 95-00	98:18	98:22	− 4	8.09
8½	Feb 00n	102:13	102:17	− 6	8.09
8⅞	May 00n	104:24	104:28	− 4	8.10
8⅜	Aug 95-00	101:14	101:18	− 3	7.94
8¾	Aug 00n	104:01	104:03	− 4	8.11
8½	Nov 00n	102:15	102:17	− 4	8.11
7¾	Feb 01n	97:27	97:29	− 4	8.06
11¾	Feb 01	124:08	124:16	− 3	8.08
13⅛	May 01	133:29	134:05	− 4	8.09
8	Aug 96-01	99:18	99:26	− 4	8.03
13⅜	Aug 01	136:02	136:10	− 6	8.11
15¾	Nov 01	153:03	153:11	− 5	8.12
14¼	Feb 02	143:02	143:10	− 4	8.14
11⅝	Nov 02	125:07	125:15	− 4	8.17
10¾	Feb 03	118:26	119:02	− 4	8.20
10¾	May 03	118:30	119:06	− 6	8.21
11⅛	Aug 03	121:29	122:05	− 6	8.23
11⅞	Nov 03	127:29	128:05	− 6	8.23
12⅜	May 04	132:12	132:20	− 5	8.25
13¾	Aug 04	143:21	143:25	− 7	8.26
11⅝	Nov 04	126:21	126:25	− 5	8.30
8¼	May 00-05	100:11	100:15	− 8	8.18
12	May 05	130:07	130:11	+ 5	8.30
10¾	Aug 05	119:29	120:01	− 5	8.33
9⅜	Feb 06	109:18	109:22	− 5	8.23
7⅝	Feb 02-07	95:01	95:05	− 6	8.18
7⅞	Nov 02-07	97:02	97:06	− 7	8.19
8⅜	Aug 03-08	100:30	101:02	− 5	8.24
8¾	Nov 03-08	103:09	103:13	− 8	8.31
9⅛	May 04-09	106:07	106:11	− 5	8.32
10⅜	Nov 04-09	115:22	115:26	− 4	8.40
11¾	Feb 05-10	127:00	127:04	− 2	8.39
10	May 05-10	113:09	113:13	− 3	8.36
12¾	Nov 05-10	136:02	136:06	− 4	8.40
13⅞	May 06-11	146:08	146:12	− 2	8.39
14	Nov 06-11	148:05	148:09	− 1	8.39
10⅜	Nov 07-12	117:09	117:13	− 5	8.41
12	Aug 08-13	132:09	132:13	− 4	8.41
13¼	May 09-14	144:15	144:19	− 4	8.41
12½	Aug 09-14	137:25	137:29	− 4	8.41
11¾	Nov 09-14	131:06	131:10	− 4	8.39
11¼	Feb 15	129:21	129:25	− 2	8.35
10⅝	Aug 15	123:12	123:16	− 4	8.35
9⅞	Nov 15	115:25	115:29	− 4	8.34
9¼	Feb 16	109:12	109:16	− 5	8.34
7¼	May 16	88:26	88:30	− 6	8.31
7½	Nov 16	91:10	91:14	− 5	8.31
8¾	May 17	104:14	104:18	− 6	8.32
8⅞	Aug 17	105:24	105:28	− 5	8.32
9⅛	May 18	108:19	108:23	− 5	8.31
9	Nov 18	107:14	107:18	− 5	8.30
8⅞	Feb 19	106:02	106:06	− 5	8.30
8⅛	Aug 19	98:04	98:08	− 5	8.29
8½	Feb 20	102:11	102:15	− 5	8.27
8¾	May 20	105:11	105:15	− 6	8.25
8¾	Aug 20	105:11	105:13	− 6	8.26
7⅞	Feb 21	95:31	96:01	− 6	8.23

Figure 2-1 U.S. Treasury bond quotations from a daily newspaper.

coupon interest of $1075 each year, up to and including the year of its maturity. As indicated in the second column, this particular issue is scheduled to mature in May of 2003. Column 3 states that potential buyers for the 10¾s of 2003 are bidding 118:30 percent of face value for these bonds.

It is customary to quote Treasury bond prices in thirty-seconds of a point, because one thirty-second is the minimum allowable price change. One thirty-second equals .03125, or 3.125 percent of the bond's face value. As a result, the **bid price** of 118:30 means that the potential buyers' highest bid is 118³⁰⁄₃₂, or 118.9375 percent, of the bond's face value. If it is a $10,000-denomination bond, the bid price is $11,893.75. When a bond's market price exceeds its face value, as in this case, the bond is said to be selling at a **premium** over its face value.

Column 4 of Figure 2-1 shows an **asked price,** or **offer price,** of 119:06 for the 10¾s of 2003. This means that sellers require at least 119⁶⁄₃₂ percent of the bond's face value to induce them to sell. Column 5 indicates that the bond's market price dropped by ⁶⁄₃₂ from the closing price of the day before. This −6 means a price decline of ⁶⁄₃₂ points, or 1.875 percent of the face value. The last column in Figure 2-1 shows that the 10¾ bonds of 2003 offered investors a yield-to-maturity of 8.21 percent. Yields-to-maturity are discussed in Chapter 12.

The various types of marketable issues offered by the Treasury Department differ mainly in the length of time to maturity (see Figure 2-2).

Treasury Bills **Treasury bills,** which were introduced earlier in this chapter, mature in 13, 26, or 52 weeks from the date of issue.[2] The U.S. Treasury auctions millions of dollars worth of new bills every week to pay off maturing T-bills—a process called *rolling over the debt.* T-bills are sold in *book entry form,* and, thus, investors need not produce a physical security at maturity to claim their principal.

Treasury Notes **Treasury notes** differ from T-bills in two fundamental respects: (1) They are issued at par (or face) value, rather than at a discount, and (2) they make fixed periodic interest payments. The interest rates printed on the bonds are called

[2] T-bills are the only money market security to have maturities in excess of the 270-day maximum the SEC requires to avoid its registration process. This is because the U.S. Treasury need not register its securities with the SEC.

Figure 2-2 The various maturity ranges of marketable U.S. government securities.

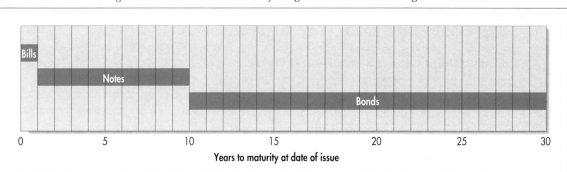

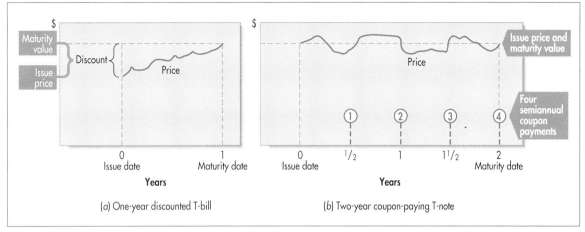

Figure 2-3   Price fluctuations of Treasury securities.

coupon rates. **Coupon bonds** promise scheduled coupon interest payments. The bond investor collects the interest income by tearing perforated coupons off the edge of the T-note and cashing them or depositing them at a bank. Each coupon is imprinted with its dollar value and the date it is to be paid. Figure 2-3 contrasts the way the prices fluctuate for a 2-year, coupon-paying T-note and a 1-year T-bill that is sold at a discount instead of paying coupon interest.

Notes mature within 1 to 10 years from the date of issue. After U.S. Treasury notes are issued, their market prices fluctuate continuously in response to changing credit market conditions.

Treasury Bonds   **Treasury bonds** are the smallest segment of the federal debt. Bonds differ from T-notes with respect to maturity—bonds mature and repay their face value within a period from 10 to 30 years from the date of issue. Some bond issues are **callable** (or **redeemable**) prior to maturity.

The T-bonds that pay a coupon rate of 13.25 percent and are usually listed in newspapers as the "13.25s of May 2009-14," for example, are callable as early as May of 2009. But this issue may not be called if the U.S. Treasury Department thinks it will be less costly to let it mature in May of 2014. The bonds may be called between 2009 and 2014 if, during that time, the Treasury thinks it can reduce its interest expense by calling in the bonds and issuing new bonds with a lower coupon rate to pay off the called issue.

Generally speaking, whatever interest expense bond issuers save by calling bond issues is income lost to the bond investors. As a result, investors dislike call provisions and will only buy callable issues if they pay slightly higher interest rates than similar issues that are noncallable.

Special Issues   Approximately 17 percent of government debt consists of special issues. These federal obligations cannot be purchased by the public; the Treasury sells them to government funds with cash to invest. The Government Employees' Retirement Fund, the Federal Old Age and Survivors Insurance Fund, and the National Service Life Insurance Fund buy these special issues.

41

Securities of Federal Agencies

The Federal Land Banks, the Federal Home Loan Banks, the Central Bank for Cooperatives, the Government National Mortgage Association (GNMA, also called *Ginnie Mae*), and the Federal Intermediate Credit Bank are all federal agencies that are allowed to issue their own debt obligations. **Federal agency bonds** are similar to other government bonds, but the federal government does not guarantee that the interest and principal will be paid. As a result, the yield on federal agency bonds is higher than that of federal government bonds. However, it would be poor political and economic policy for the government to allow any of its agencies to default, and the Treasury has on occasion provided funds to prevent financial embarrassment.

The Federal National Mortgage Association (FNMA, usually called Fannie Mae) and the Federal Home Mortgage Corporation (FHLMC, nicknamed Freddie Mac) started out as agencies of the U.S. government. Now (in theory, at least) they are independent mortgage finance businesses. Fannie Mae, Ginnie Mae, and Freddie Mac have helped issue billions of dollars of high quality mortgage-backed securities.

2-3   Corporate Bonds

Besides the federal government, corporations are the major issuer of bonds in the United States. Figure 2-4 shows daily corporate bond price quotations from a newspaper. Note that the American Telephone and Telegraph (AT&T) Corporation, for example, has many issues of bonds outstanding. To understand how to read the bond quotations in newspapers, consider the AT&T bond maturing in 2007 that pays 8⅝ (or 8.625) percent coupon interest rate (indicated by the arrow). This bond issue is referred to as "AT&T 8 5/8s07" in the first column of the listings. The bond has a face value of $1000, but this amount does not appear in the quotations. The coupon interest rate of 8.625 percent per year implies that every $1000 bond in this issue pays $86.25 per year of coupon interest. Column 2 gives an interest rate for this bond that is called the *current yield*. Column 3 tells how many of these $1000 bonds were traded that day—the *volume of trading*. The bond issue's highest and lowest trading prices for the day are reported in columns 4 and 5, respectively. Column 6 gives the last trading price reported for that day as 96⅛ percent of its face value, or $961.25 for a $1000-face-value bond. Dividing the bond's last price for the day into its annual coupon interest results in the **current yield** of 9.0 percent, which is shown in column 2. The last column shows that the price of the bond rose one quarter of a percentage point (or $25 for a $10,000 bond) from the previous day's closing price.

The major difference between corporate bonds and U.S. Treasury bonds is that Treasuries are perceived to be *default-free* because the federal government is considered to be bankruptcy-proof. Private companies are different.

Bankruptcy

Corporate executives face tough financial realities. Business executives are supposed to borrow money only to invest in ventures that will generate sufficient profits to pay off the debt. Since developing profitable undertakings in which to invest is not easy,

N.Y. Stock Exchange Bond Trading

MONDAY, SEPTEMBER 8

Bonds	Current Yield	Sales in $1,000	High	Low	Last	Net Chge.
A B C D						
AGS 7½11	cv	5	98½	98½	98½	+ ½
AMR 10¼06	10.3	41	100	99¾	100	...
ANR 8⅝93	8.9	1	97⅛	97⅛	97⅛	− 1¾
APL 10¾97	13.9	17	77¼	77⅛	77¼	...
ARX 9⅜05	cv	13	112	112	112	− ½
Advst 9s08	cv	37	108¼	107	107	− 1
AetnLf 8⅛07	8.7	20	94¾	92⅞	92⅞	− 2⅞
AlaBn 6.8s99t	6.8	5	100¼	100¼	100¼	+ ⅛
AlaP 9s2000	9.1	1	99	99	99	− ⅞
AlaP 8⅞s03	9.2	31	96¾	96⅛	96¾	+ ¼
AlaP 8¼s03	9.0	10	92	92	92	+ ¼
AlaP 9¾s04	9.6	11	101½	101⅜	101⅜	...
AlaP 10⅞05	10.4	5	105	105	105	− 2⅝
AlaP 8⅞06	9.2	4	96⅛	96⅛	96⅛	+ ⅝
AlaP 8¾07	9.3	15	93⅞	93⅞	93⅞	− ⅞
AlaP 8⅝87	8.6	10	100½	100½	100½	...
AlaP 9¼07	9.3	25	99½	99¼	99½	− ⅜
AlaP 9½08	9.5	5	100½	100½	100½	...
AlaP 9⅝08	9.6	1	100½	100½	100½	...
AlskH 16¼99	14.1	10	115¼	115¼	115¼	+ ⅜
AlskH 17¾91	14.5	5	122¾	122¾	122¾	+ 2⅛
AlskH 18⅜01	15.8	9	116⅜	115¾	116	+ ⅜
AlskH 15¼92	14.2	21	109	107¼	107¼	− 2½
AlskH 12⅞93	12.1	15	106½	106½	106½	+ ¼
Alco 8½10	cv	50	112	112	112	− 2
Alexn 5½96	cv	23	124	121	123⅛	+ 7⅛
Allgl 10.4s02	15.0	3	69½	69½	69½	+ ½
Allgl 9s89	10.8	5	83	83	83	...
AlldC 7⅞96	8.1	4	97¼	97¼	97¼	+ ⅞
AlldC zr87	...	35	94 11/16	94⅝	94 11/16	+ 9/32
AlldC zr96	...	2	46½	46½	46½	+ 2
AlldC zr2000	...	102	28⅝	28½	28½	− ⅜
AlldC d6s88	6.2	25	96¾	96½	96¾	...
AlldC d6s90	6.5	3	92⅞	92⅞	92⅞	...
AlldC zr99	...	10	30⅝	30⅝	30⅝	− 1⅜
AlldC zr05	...	15	18¼	18	18	...
AlldC zr09	...	90	12⅝	12⅛	12¼	− ⅝
AlldSt 8¾09	cv	104	216	213½	213½	− 3
AlsCha 16s91	14.6	57	110¼	109⅝	109⅝	− ⅝
Alcoa 6s92	6.7	1	89½	89½	89½	+ 1
Alcoa 9s95	8.9	4	101⅛	101⅛	101⅛	...
AluCa 9½95	9.5	5	100¼	100¼	100¼	...
AMAX 8½96	9.8	5	87	87	87	+ 2
AMAX 9⅜00	11.0	9	86	85⅛	85⅛	− 1⅛
AMAX 14¼90	13.1	27	108½	108½	108½	...
AFoP 4.8s87	4.8	12	99	99	99	− ¼
AAirl 4¼92	5.4	30	78½	78½	78½	− ⅛
ABrnd 4⅝90	5.1	1	90	90	90	...
ABrnd 9¾87	9.6	15	102	102	102	− ½
ACan 13¼93	11.5	18	116	115	115	− 1
ACeM 6¾91	cv	6	54½	54½	54½	− 3½
AmMed 9½01	cv	69	101	100½	101	− ¼
AmMed 8¼08	cv	17	92	92	92	...
AmMed 11s98	10.8	4	101⅞	101½	101⅞	+ ⅜
AmMot 6s88	cv	16	99	99	99	...
ATT 3⅞s90	4.2	15	92	92	92	+ ¾
ATT 3⅞90r	4.3	20	91⅜	91	91	...
ATT 8¾00	8.8	971	100	99⅜	99⅝	− ⅜
ATT 7s01	8.1	39	86⅝	86⅜	86⅜	− ½
ATT 7⅛s03	8.3	121	86¾	85¾	85¾	− 1¼
ATT 8.80s05	8.9	110	99	98½	98⅝	− ⅜
ATT 8⅝s07	9.0	263	96½	95⅝	96⅛	+ ¼
Amoco 9.2s04	9.1	8	101	101	101	− ⅞
Amoco 7s89t	7.0	25	100	100	100	...
Amoco 8⅜05	8.7	10	95⅞	95⅞	95⅞	− ¾
Amoco 7⅞07	8.7	75	91¾	91	91	− 1⅝
Amoco 14s91	12.6	5	111¼	111¼	111¼	− 1
Ancp 13⅞02f	cv	7	95¼	95¼	95¼	+ ¼
Apch 8.5s06	7.8	30	108½	108½	108½	+ 2
Aristr 9½89	9.4	4	101	99⅞	101	...
ArizP 7.45s02	8.8	4	85	85	85	− 1¾
ArkBst 7s11	6.1	11	114	114	114	...
ArmS 8.7s95	14.0	68	67	62	62	− 6
ArmS 9.2s00	15.3	180	67⅛	60	60	− 7⅞

	U.S. Gov't. Bonds	Other Dom. Bonds	Foreign Bonds	Total All Bonds
Today's Sales..........	$ ---	a$ 38,180,000	$ 170,000	$ 38,350,000
Friday's	---	a 35,659,000	337,000	35,996,000
Year to Date	1,064,000	a 7,347,834,000	21,938,000	7,370,836,000
1985	$ 870,000	a$6,273,540,000	$21,757,000	$6,296,189,000

a—Includes International Bank Bonds

BOND ISSUES TRADED

	Issues	Advances	Declines	New Highs	New Lows
Sept. 8.................	896	275	414	33	13
Sept.5	894	307	369	44	13
Sept. 4.................	901	400	301	62	7

Bonds	Current Yield	Sales in $1,000	High	Low	Last	Net Chge.
Citicp 8.45s07	9.2	5	92	92	92	− 1⅜
Citicp 8⅛07	9.2	30	90½	88⅛	88⅛	− 2⅜
Citicp 8.4s98t	8.4	36	100	100	100	...
Citicp 7.40s04t	7.4	48	99¾	99¾	99¾	− ½
Citicp 12s90	11.4	5	105⅛	105⅛	105⅛	− ½
Citicp 8s99	7.9	8	101	101	101	+ ¼
CitSv 13⅞11	12.3	5	112½	112½	112½	...
CitSvc zr87	...	36	91	90⅜	91	+ ¾
CitSvc zr88	...	30	83	82⅝	82⅝	− ⅛
CitSvc zr89	...	40	75⅞	75⅜	75⅞	...
ClkEq 7.85s91	8.4	8	94	94	94	− 1¼
ClkEq 8s87	8.0	30	100	100	100	− ¼
Claytn 7¾01	cv	51	101	100¼	100¼	− ¾
ClevEl 3⅞93	5.2	10	75	75	75	− ½
ClevEl 8¾05	9.7	20	91⅝	90	90	− 1⅞
ClevEl 9¼09	9.9	11	93	93	93	− 2
ClevEl 9.85s10	9.9	17	99¾	98	99¾	...
ClevEl 8⅜12	9.7	7	86	86	86	− ⅞
Coleco 11s89	cv	14	110	107	110	+ 4
Coleco 11⅛01	13.1	15	85	85	85	...
Coltln 10⅛95	10.8	201	94½	94	94	− ½
Coltln 11¼15	11.3	120	100	99⅝	99⅝	...
ColuG 9s94	9.0	5	100¼	100¼	100¼	...
ColuG 8¾95	8.8	5	100	100	100	+ ¾
ColuG 8⅜96	8.6	5	96⅞	96⅞	96⅞	− 1⅜
ColuG 7½97M	8.3	10	90½	90½	90½	+ 1
ColuG 7½97J	8.3	3	91⅜	90⅝	90⅝	− ½
ColuG 9⅝89	9.5	30	101⅜	101⅜	101⅜	+ ⅛
Cmdis 8s03	cv	30	100¾	99½	99½	− 1½
Cmdis 9.65s02	10.7	35	90	90	90	− 1
CmlCr 8¾91	9.2	10	95⅝	95⅝	95⅝	+ ¼
CmlCr 8¾88	8.8	36	99¾	99¾	99¾	+ ¼
CmlSo 4½91	cv	1	81⅛	81⅛	81⅛	− 1
CmwE 7⅝03J	8.8	25	86⅞	86⅝	86⅞	+ ¼
CmwE 8¾05	9.4	35	93⅛	93⅛	93⅛	...
CmwE 9⅜04	9.5	19	99	98⅝	98⅝	− ⅞
CmwE 8⅛07J	9.3	18	88	86¼	87	− 1¾
CmwE 8⅛07D	9.4	2	87¼	86¾	86¾	− 2¼
CmwE 8¼07	9.4	10	88½	88⅛	88⅛	− ⅝
CmwE 9⅛08	9.5	51	96½	95½	96½	+ 1
CmwE 14⅞87	14.3	18	104⅛	104 1/16	104 1/16	− 1 15/16
CmwE 14s91	13.0	24	108	107⅛	108	...
CmwE 16¼89	15.2	76	107	106½	107	+ ½
CmwE 17½88	14.7	47	118¾	118⅝	118¾	+ ⅜
CmwE 16s90	14.9	8	107⅛	107⅛	107⅛	...
CmwE 16¾11	14.5	40	115⅜	115⅜	115⅜	+ ⅜
CmwE 14¼92	13.0	35	110	110	110	− 1⅞
CmwE 15⅜12	13.0	10	118	118	118	− 1
CmwE 12⅛13	11.0	20	110½	110¼	110¼	...
Compq 9½05	cv	23	144½	144	144½	− 1½
Cmpvsn 8s09	cv	25	80⅛	79	79	− 3
ConEd 5s87	5.1	32	98⅛	98⅛	98⅛	...
ConEd 4s88	4.2	10	94¾	94¾	94¾	...
ConEd 4¾90r	5.3	5	90⅛	90⅛	90⅛	...
ConEd 5s90	5.5	5	90¾	90⅝	90⅝	− ⅜
ConEd 4¾91	5.5	2	86⅛	86⅛	86⅛	− 1⅝
ConEd 4⅝93	5.6	20	82½	82½	82½	+ ¼
ConEd 9⅜00	9.2	16	102¾	101	101½	− ½

Bonds	Current Yield	Sales in $1,000	High	Low	Last	Net Chge.
DuqL 8⅜07	9.7	6	87	86½	86½	− 1½
DuqL 10⅛09	10.1	5	100½	100½	100½	− ½
E F G H						
EasAir 5s92	cv	53	60	59½	60	+ 1
EasAir 11½99	cv	150	83½	83	83⅜	+ ⅜
EasAir 11¾05	cv	11	84½	84½	84½	− ½
EasAir 17½97	16.2	33	108	106	108	...
EasAir 17½98	16.0	1	109⅛	109⅛	109⅛	+ ⅛
EasAir 16⅛02	15.4	35	104¾	103⅞	104¾	+ ⅞
EKod 8⅝16	8.7	13	98⅞	98⅝	98⅝	− ⅛
ElPaso 15s00	13.6	15	110½	110½	110½	+ ¼
ElPaso 15¾92	14.2	5	111¼	111¼	111¼	− 1¼
Ens 10s01	cv	16	102¼	102	102¼	− ¼
EnvSys 6¾11	cv	25	101	101	101	− 1
EqutR 9s96	9.1	2	98½	98½	98½	− 4
EqutR 9½06	cv	16	180	180	180	+ 3
Equitc 10s04	cv	5	90	90	90	...
Estrl 12½95	12.4	7	100½	100½	100½	− ½
Exxon 6s97	7.0	45	85⅝	84¾	85⅝	− ⅛
Exxon 6½98	7.4	28	89	88⅜	88⅜	− ⅝
ExonFn 10½89	10.1	45	104⅛	104⅛	104⅛	− ⅜
ExxP 8⅞00	8.8	25	100½	100½	100½	− ¾
Feddr 5s96	cv	20	67	67	67	− ½
FdRty 8¾10	cv	7	132½	132½	132½	− 5½
FinCpA 6s88	6.8	7	88	88	88	+ ¾
FinCpA 11⅞98	12.6	41	94	94	94	...
FinCpA 6s10	10.5	1	57¼	57¼	57¼	− 1
FinCp d11½02	cv	1	103	103	103	− 1
FtSec 7s99t	7.0	4	99⅝	99⅝	99⅝	− ⅜
FtWis 8½96	8.7	6	98⅛	98⅛	98⅛	− ⅞
FishF 6½94	cv	5	86	85½	86	+ ½
FleetFn 9¼96	9.0	25	102½	102½	102½	+ ⅛
FleetFn 12½90	12.2	15	102⅜	102⅜	102⅜	− ⅝
FleetFn 8½10	cv	20	139½	139	139	− 2
FlaECs 5s01	7.6	1	66	66	66	− ½
Flwr 8¼05	cv	55	127½	126½	127½	+ 1
Ford 8⅛90	8.0	10	101½	101	101	− ½
Ford 9¼94	9.1	10	102	102	102	+ ¼
Ford 14¼90	13.4	26	106	105½	106	...
FrdC 8½91	8.5	2	100⅜	100⅜	100⅜	...
FrdC 7½91	7.5	15	100¼	100¼	100¼	− 1⅝
FrdC 7⅞93	7.9	15	100⅛	100⅛	100⅛	...
FrdC 9⅛01	9.1	1	100	100	100	...
FrdC 8⅜01	8.7	20	96	96	96	+ 2
FrdC 7⅞89	7.8	40	101½	100¼	101½	+ ½
FreptM 10½14	cv	78	105	104¾	105	...
Fruf 5½94	cv	11	151	150½	150½	− ½
Fuqua 9½98	9.9	6	96	96	96	...
GAF 11⅜95	10.9	7	104⅝	104⅝	104⅝	+ 1⅛
GATX 16⅜92	15.0	16	109	106	109	+ 3
GATX 11½96	11.5	410	100½	99¾	99¾	− ¾
Gelco 14⅝99	14.0	10	105½	104½	104½	− 1¾
GnATr 5¾99	cv	10	76	76	76	− ¾
GCinem 10s08	cv	20	210	210	210	...
GnDev 12⅝05	12.2	10	103½	103½	103½	− 1¼
GnEl 7½96	7.6	20	98½	98⅜	98⅜	− ½

Bonds	Current Yield	Sales in $1,000	High	Low	Last	Net Chge.
Grumn 9¼09	cv	10	106½	106½	106½	− ½
Gruntl 7½11	cv	70	95	95	95	...
GlfWn 6s88	6.2	6	97¾	96⅜	96⅜	− 1⅛
GlfWn 7s03A	8.9	27	79⅝	79	79	− ⅝
GlfWn 7s03B	8.8	45	79⅞	79½	79¾	− ¼
Hallb 16s88	15.9	3	100½	100½	100½	− ⅛
Harnis d12s04	12.0	10	100⅛	100⅛	100⅛	− ⅛
Hartfd 8½96	8.8	2	96⅞	96⅞	96⅞	...
Hawn 8.2s01	8.8	4	93	93	93	− ⅛
Hawn 7⅝02	8.5	6	89¼	89¼	89¼	+ ⅛
HltUSA 8¼03	cv	1	70¾	70¾	70¾	+ ¾
Heilm zr03	...	72	32¼	30⅝	30⅝	− 1⅞
Hellr 9½89	9.3	10	102	102	102	...
Hellr 8.1s87	8.1	10	100¼	100¼	100¼	...
Hercul 6½99	cv	6	164¾	164¾	164¾	...
Holidy 14⅛92	12.4	3	113¾	113¾	113¾	+ 5¾
HmeDp 8½09	cv	54	105½	104½	105	+ ⅛
HomFSD 6¾11	cv	189	100½	100½	100½	− ½
HoCp 8½08	cv	40	108¼	107¾	107¾	+ ¼
HoCp 9s98	cv	1	103⅝	103⅝	103⅝	− 1⅜
HugheT 9s08	12.9	319	72¾	69½	69⅞	− 1¾
HugheT 14¼88	14.1	30	102½	101	101	− ½
HugheT 9½06	cv	21	88⅝	88½	88⅝	− ⅜
Humn 8½09	cv	166	102½	102	102½	− ⅛
Hutton 12s05	11.4	10	105½	105½	105½	+ 1½
I J K L						
IllBel 8s04	8.7	10	92¼	92¼	92¼	− 1
IllBel 8¼16	9.0	33	93⅛	92	92	− 1⅞
IllPw 8⅝06	9.3	12	94⅛	93	93	− 1½
IndBel 8⅛11	8.7	5	93¼	93¼	93¼	...
IndBel 10s14	9.7	25	103⅛	103⅛	103⅛	− 1⅞
IndBel 8⅛17	8.9	10	90⅞	90⅞	90⅞	+ ½
Inexc 8½00	cv	32	78⅜	78¼	78⅜	+ ⅜
InldStl 11¼90	11.5	40	98	98	98	...
Insilco 9s10	cv	10	120¼	120¼	120¼	+ ¼
Intrfst 9¾99	11.7	20	83½	83¼	83¼	− ¾
Intrfst 7¾05	cv	40	70	70	70	+ ¾
Intrlk 8.8s96	9.0	7	98	98	98	...
IBM 9⅜04	9.1	132	102½	102¼	102½	+ ⅛
IBM 7⅞04	cv	421	120½	119	120¼	+ 1⅝
IPap 10⅞95	9.8	75	111	111	111	− 1
Intnr 10½08	...	75	117	115	115	− 3
JCP 9⅝06	9.6	3	99⅞	99⅞	99⅞	+ 1
vjJnM 7.8504f	...	7	101	100½	101	− 1⅜
vjJnM 9.7s85mf	...	89	106	105⅞	105⅞	+ 1/16
JonsLI 6¾94	33.8	2	20	20	20	+ ¾
vjJoneL 6¾94f	...	12	22	20⅛	22	...
vjJoneL 9⅞95f	...	17	45	44⅝	45	+ ⅜
vjJoneL 9¾96f	...	27	45	45	45	+ ⅜
K mart 6s99	cv	6	149¾	149¾	149¾	+ 1⅞
KaufB 12¼99	11.9	20	103½	103	103	− ½
KogerP 9¼03	cv	14	106	106	106	− 1
Krogr 14⅜91	13.3	1	108	108	108	− 1
Krogr 11s95	11.1	5	99	99	99	− 1¼
vjLTV 5s88f	...	35	27½	27	27¼	+ ¼
vjLTV 9¼97f	...	167	34¼	34¼	34¼	− ¼
vjLTV 11s07f	...	117	26⅜	25½	25½	− ⅜
vjLTV 13⅞02f	...	46	35¼	35	35	− ¼
vjLTV 14s04f	...	155	35¾	34⅞	35¾	+ ¾
vjLTV 11½97f	...	16	25¼	25	25	+ ¼
vjLTV 7⅞98f	...	4	23	23	23	+ 2
LaQuin 10s02	cv	23	104½	104	104½	...
LearS 10s04	9.9	1	101	101	101	− 1
Leget 6½06	cv	134	104½	104¼	104¼	...
Litton 11½95	10.5	5	109½	109½	109½	+ 1½
LomN 01s	...	115	30	28	28	− 3⅛
LomN 9s10	cv	41	130½	130	130	− 3
LomN 7s11	cv	25	99	99	99	− 2
LglsLt 13½13	12.8	27	105½	105	105½	...
LglsLt 17½89	15.5	11	114	113¼	113¼	− 1⅝
Lglsl	11.4	2	98½	98½	98½	− ⅜
LglsLt 11⅞15	12.0	100	99	99	99	...

Figure 2-4 Corporate bond quotations from a daily newspaper.

corporate bonds involve some risk of default. A bond issue is in **default** if any investor does not receive every penny of interest and if the bond's face value is not repaid as scheduled. A corporate bond issuer that defaults on its debt obligations will be sued. A bankruptcy court can reorganize the defaulted company or declare it bankrupt and liquidate the firm. To avoid this happening to their investment, bond investors study different bond issues to assess the default risk of each one.

Bond Indentures and Protective Provisions

A legally enforceable **indenture** contract backs every corporate bond issue and sets forth the relationship between the borrower (or issuer) and the lender (or investor). The indenture provisions that underlie bond issues can have a significant impact on the risk and return characteristics of the investment. In addition to analyzing the financial position of the issuing corporation, bond investors should study the indenture to learn about the issuer's legal obligations. Among other things, the issuer must give every potential bond buyer written answers to the following questions:

- What will the proceeds from the bond issue be spent for?
- What interest payments will investors receive?
- When will the bonds mature?
- What amount will be repaid?

Corporate bond issuers are required by federal law to promise in their indenture contracts to pay a trustee to act as a "watchdog" for the bond investors' interests. A **trustee,** usually some independent bank, is paid to see that the issuer keeps its promises and obeys the restrictions of the indenture contract. The trustee is a third party in every bond indenture contract; it is the trustee's job to make sure that the issuer lives up to whatever **protective provisions** are stipulated in the indenture.

The protective provisions written into a bond issue's indenture affect the bond's creditworthiness (or investment quality rating).[3] If, for example, an indenture says that the bonds are subordinated to another issue, this lowers the quality rating of the subordinated issue. This is because if hard times come to the firm, it can pay the holders of subordinated bonds only after it has paid off any senior, or prior-claim, bonds. Conversely, if an indenture gives a bond issue a mortgage claim on some of the firm's assets, that bond issue will tend to be rated higher than if it had no direct claim (if no specific assets had been pledged as collateral).

Types of Corporate Bonds

Sinking Fund Bonds **Sinking fund bonds** are issued by corporations that wish to repay a bond issue systematically by setting aside a certain amount for that purpose each year. The payment, usually a fixed annual dollar amount or a percentage of the debt, is made annually to the sinking fund agent, who is usually the trustee named in the indenture. This third person then uses the money to call the bonds at some **call premium** above their face value, or to purchase them on the open market if they are selling at a discount to their face value.[4]

---

[3] See Chapter 9 for techniques for measuring "creditworthiness." Default risk is explained in Chapter 10.

[4] For some insights see Andrew J. Kaloty, "On the Management of Sinking Funds," *Financial Management* (Summer), 1981, pp. 34–39.

Serial Bonds   **Serial bonds** are appropriate for firms that wish to divide their bond issues into a series, with the parts of the series maturing in consecutive years. Serial bonds are rarely callable before their maturity date; the issuer usually pays off each part of the series at its particular maturity date.

Secured Bonds   The most important protective provision for corporate bonds is **collateral,** or pledged assets. These are assets that have been pledged to help make payments to the investors if the issuer defaults.

If the indenture provides for a lien on a certain designated property, the bond is said to be **secured.** A **lien** is a legal right given to bondholders to sell the collateral to satisfy the unpaid interest or principal. Collateral is used to make bonds safer so that investors will pay a higher price for them. Collateral is seldom sold if the issuer defaults. It is more likely that the company will be reorganized and new securities issued to replace the defaulted bonds. But the existence of a lien on property has a very favorable influence on the treatment of the bondholders in a reorganization.

Mortgage Bonds   Bonds secured with a lien on real property or buildings are **mortgage bonds.** If all the assets of a firm are collateral under the terms of the indenture, it is called a blanket mortgage. Not all assets need be pledged; it may be that only some of the land or buildings of the company are mortgaged for the issue. There can be first, second, and subsequent mortgages, each with its respective subordinated claim to the assets of the firm in case of default. A first mortgage is the most secure because it has first claim on the assets. A mortgage bond may be open-end or closed-end, and it may contain an after-acquired property clause.

An *open-end mortgage* means that more bonds can be issued under the same mortgage contract. The creditors are usually protected by restrictions limiting such additional borrowing. Normally, an open-end mortgage will contain an *after-acquired property clause,* which provides that all property acquired after the first mortgage also be pledged as collateral. A *closed-end mortgage* allows no additional borrowing on the mortgage; this type of mortgage with an after-acquired property clause guarantees an increasing security base for the creditors.

Unsecured Bonds   Unsecured bonds are usually called **debentures,** and have no lien against any property. They may be seen as a claim on earnings, not on assets. This is not to say that debenture investors are not protected in case of default. These investors are classified as **general creditors** by law, since they have no collateral pledged. All assets that are not specifically pledged and any balance from pledged assets remaining after payment of secured debts are available to pay the legal claims of general creditors. To take this added riskiness into account, debenture indentures usually contain protective provisions. They may restrict any further issuing of debentures unless earnings over a certain number of years are 2 or 3 times what is needed to cover the original debentures' interest expense. Another common provision says that if any secured debt is issued, the debentures must be secured by an equal amount. Sometimes, unless working capital (that is, current assets minus current liabilities) is maintained at a high enough level to ensure that the bondholders will receive their coupon interest, the debtor is not allowed to pay any cash dividends on its common stock.

Subordinated debentures are simply debentures that are specifically made subordinate to other general creditors holding claims on assets. These other creditors are usually suppliers or financial institutions that have granted credit to the firm.

2-4 Municipal Bonds

Bonds issued by states, counties, parishes, cities, towns, townships, boroughs, villages, and special tax districts or municipal corporations are referred to as **municipal bonds** or, more commonly, just **munis.** They include the debt obligations of state and local commissions, agencies, and authorities, and those of state colleges.

Federal Tax Exemption

The Constitution of the United States provides for separation of state and federal governments. Federal taxation of municipalities has traditionally been interpreted as violating this separation. **Tax-exempt municipal bonds** grew out of this thinking. Tax-exempt munis are attractive investments to wealthy individuals and profitable partnerships that find themselves in high federal income tax brackets.

The federally tax-exempt coupon income from municipal bonds commands a premium in the market in the form of higher prices and lower interest rates. Consider a fully taxable (corporate or Treasury) bond that, except for the tax-exempt interest rate, is identical in all respects with a municipal bond that pays a 10 percent coupon rate. As Equation (2-1) illustrates, for an investor in the 33 percent federal income tax bracket, the 10 percent municipal yields the same after-tax return as a corporate or Treasury bond that pays 15 percent.

$$\begin{matrix} \text{Yield on} \\ \text{a fully} \\ \text{taxable issue} \end{matrix} = \frac{\text{municipal bond yield, 10\%}}{1.0 - \text{income tax rate, 33\%}} = 15\% \tag{2-1}$$

The federal income tax exemption that municipals enjoy also benefits the issuers; the exempt status makes the bonds easier to market. Only coupons are tax-exempt, however; federal income taxes must be paid on any capital gains that munis yield.

General-Obligation and Limited-Obligation Bonds

All municipal bonds, regardless of their exact contract provisions, fall into one of two major categories: general-obligation bonds or limited-obligation bonds.

General-Obligation Bonds   These bonds are sometimes referred to as **full faith and credit bonds** because of the unlimited nature of the pledge. **General-obligation bonds, or GO bonds,** originate from government units that have unlimited power to tax property to meet their obligations; they promise to pay without any limitations.

bonds.

Limited-Obligation Bonds Bonds originating from an issuer that is in some way restricted in raising revenues that can be used to pay debts are called **limited-obligation bonds.** The most significant form of limited-obligation bond is the **revenue bond;** this type of bond can be paid off only with the revenue from the specific assets for which it was issued. It is widely used to finance municipally owned utilities, such as waterworks, electric and gas utilities, sewage disposal systems, toll roads, toll bridges, public swimming pools, and dormitories at public colleges.

2-5   New Forms of Bonds

Bond underwriters continually develop new forms of bonds in hopes of making their products appealing to more investors. The put bonds, variable-rate bonds, and zeros that were issued by both governmental and corporate issuers for the first time in the United States during the 1980s are examples of new products.

Put Bonds and Variable-Rate Bonds

To induce bond investors to buy bonds that may plummet in price, issuers have developed put bonds and variable-rate bonds. A **put bond** allows the investor to "put" the bond back to the issuer at a predetermined price. That is, the issuer promises in the indenture to stand ready to buy the bond back at some fixed minimum price (for example, 95 percent of its face value). This promise establishes a "floor" beneath the bond's price. Municipalities originated put bonds during the 1980s, but corporate bond issuers quickly adopted the concept. Put bonds are sometimes called *option tender bonds* or *early redemption bonds.*

    Variable-rate bonds, or **floaters,** offer another risk-limiting provision. They promise a rate of interest that *fluctuates* as market conditions change. If market interest rates rise, the coupon interest rate on the variable-rate bond will also rise. The variable-rate provision protects the investor from being left with a bond that pays a fixed low rate of interest when market rates are rising. During the 1980s corporate bond issuers followed the municipalities and began to issue variable-rate bonds.

Zero Coupon Bonds

Zero coupon bonds are sold at a discount from their face value so that they provide interest income in the form of price appreciation (as with T-bills) instead of paying coupon interest (as with T-bonds). **Zeros,** as they are called, have original issue maturities that are measured in years. A zero coupon bond that will mature in 12 years with a face value of $10,000, for example, can be purchased for only $3971. This investment would yield a compound annual rate of return of 8 percent per year over the 12 years, if the zero is held to maturity.

    The default-free status of U.S. government securities makes them attractive, but some investors are not able to invest in them because their denominations are too large. The smallest Treasury bill denomination, for example, is $5,000. Several large security brokerages repackage these high denomination securities by purchasing multimillion-dollar blocks of Treasury bonds and reselling small shares in the pool of Treasury securities at a price slightly higher than their cost. The brokers profit by selling small shares in these large pools, and small investors get to buy Treasury bonds in denominations they can afford.

TIGRs and CATS Merrill Lynch, Pierce, Fenner & Smith has given the small-denomination shares in a big pool of Treasury obligations it creates the name Treasury investment growth receipts, or **TIGRs.** Salomon Brothers, another large brokerage, has created a similar product it calls certificates of accrual on Treasury securities, or **CATS.**

In order to create its first TIGRs in 1982, Merrill Lynch bought long-term Treasury bonds with a face value of $500 million and put them into a trust with a bank to act as custodian. Merrill *stripped* the coupons from the bond certificates and sold them separately. The **stripped bond,** called the *corpus,* is like a discounted Treasury security that has a long time until it matures. The stripped-off coupons were used to create a series of certificates that matured at 6-month intervals, just as the Treasury's semiannual coupon payments were made into the pool. TIGR investors buy certificates with whatever maturity they desire at a deep discount from their maturity value—the price gain is the investor's interest income. But the TIGR investor receives nothing until the selected maturity date arrives—which might be months, years, or decades in the future. The farther away the maturity date, the deeper the discount (and resulting price gain) for the investor.

Brokerage firms that originate securities like TIGRs or CATS usually promise their investors that they will maintain secondary markets where the certificates can be sold to other investors before they mature; this makes the certificates *liquid.* But under no circumstance can the Treasury securities held in the pool with a trustee be used as collateral by the investor, the custodian bank, or anyone else. The pool of T-bonds is held in trust until the last TIGR matures and the pool is liquidated to repay it.

One disadvantage of investing in zero coupon bonds like the TIGRs and CATS is that taxable investors must pay income taxes on the coupon interest each year, even though they do not receive any income. Zero coupon bonds cannot be used to delay income tax payments—only the income that is being taxed is postponed. Another disadvantage is the high commission rates (2 to 5 percent) investors must pay on zeros.

In 1985 the U.S. Treasury joined the stripping movement by creating its *separate trading of registered interest and principal securities,* or **STRIPS.** The investors do not get bond certificates, because STRIPS are **book entry securities;** evidence of ownership is maintained in computerized records at the Federal Reserve. Since STRIPS are direct obligations of the U.S. government, they are even safer than TIGRs and CATS. In recent years the market for STRIPS has surpassed the market for TIGRs and CATS.

In 1987 Salomon offered stripped municipal bonds, called **MCATS.** Each year brings the appearance of ingenious new securities.

LYONs   In 1985 Lehman Brothers and Merrill Lynch, Pierce, Fenner & Smith introduced another new form of corporate bond called the **liquidity yield option note**—or **LYON,** for short—that combined several new features into one package. The LYON is a unique combination of three features: (1) zero coupon bonds, (2) bonds that are convertible into common stock, and (3) put bonds.

The first issue of LYONs matures in 2001. When the first LYON was issued in 1985 a $1000-face-value bond could be purchased for $250. No coupon interest is paid on LYONs; the investor receives income in the form of price appreciation. The zero coupon feature of the bond frees investors from the *reinvestment rate risk* they might face if market interest rates were to fall in the future and they had to reinvest their coupons at lower rates of interest. However, income taxes must be paid on the accrued coupon interest income even though it is not received—a drawback common to all zero coupon bonds. Bond buyers who are afraid of price depreciation like the put-bond clause because it acts as a price support beneath the market price of the LYONs. Another attractive feature is the option to convert the bond into the issuer's common stock. Convertibility gives the LYON buyer a chance to participate in any large capital gains that the corporation's owners enjoy.

Some investors are not very impressed by the alternatives packaged into the LYON after they read the fine print in the indenture contract. It provides that the price at which a LYON could be put back to the issuer rises each year, so that investors would enjoy some price appreciation if they did put the bond back to its issuer. While this escalating price was a desirable feature, some analysts didn't think the escalating exercise price offered a high enough rate of return to make the option interesting. Furthermore, most potential LYON investors were disappointed to learn that the original conversion ratio of one LYON bond for 4.36 shares of common stock decreased every year, because it was tied to the escalating exercise price of the put option.[5]

YCANs   In the 1980s, the Morgan Stanley investment banking firm created a new kind of corporate bond called a **yield curve–adjusted note,** or **YCAN.** YCANs are **floating-rate bonds** because their coupon interest rate is reset to reflect current credit market interest rates every 6 months, instead of remaining fixed like most bonds' coupon rates. The first issue of YCANs was the Student Loan Marketing Association (Sallie Mae) notes in 1986. The floating coupon rate for this issue of 5-year notes was reset in accordance with the following formula:

YCAN floating coupon rate = 17.2% − LIBOR

The 17.2 percent in the formula is a constant number (which was changed for later issues of YCANs to reflect the current credit market conditions). What is interesting about the formula is that the London interbank offer rate (LIBOR), a fluctuating market interest rate that is widely quoted in international financial news, is *subtracted* from (instead of added to) the constant value of 17.2 percent. As a result of this subtraction, YCANs' coupon rate must rise and fall *inversely* with the LIBOR

[5] For more analysis of LYONs, see John J. McConnell and Eduardo S. Schwartz, "LYON Taming," *Journal of Finance,* July 1986, pp. 561–575.

and therefore with most other market interest rates. This *negative correlation* makes YCANs very desirable for risk-reducing purposes such as hedging and diversification, which will be explained in later chapters.

2-6   Some Conclusions

One of the first steps in decision making is to identify investment alternatives and their characteristics. Table 2-1 lists level of average return, degree of default risk, and amount of control investors have over management that characterize various categories of bond issues.

Table 2-1
The Income, Default Risk, and Control Characteristics
of Seven Different Types of Debt Securities

Type of bond	*Income or E(r) ranking*	*Ranking by risk of default*	*Investors' control over management*
U.S. Treasury securities	7 (lowest)	7 (zero)	None
Federal agency bonds	6	6 (near zero)	None
Money market securities	5*	5	None
Collateralized corporates			
Investment grade, AAA–BBB	4	4	Perhaps†
Junk bonds, grades BB–C	3	3	Perhaps†
Debentures			
Investment grade, AAA–BBB	2	2	Perhaps†
Junk bonds, grades BB–C	1 (highest)	1 (high)	Perhaps†
Municipal GO bonds‡			
Investment grade	§	Small ¶	None
Junk bonds, grades BB–C	§	Medium¶	None
Municipal revenue bonds‡			
Investment grade	§	Small¶	None
Junk bonds, grades BB–C	§	Medium¶	None

* The yields of money market securities fluctuate very rapidly over wide ranges; this makes return ranking dependent on the sample period.

† The indenture contracts of some debt issues grant the creditors limited voting privileges if the bonds go into default.

‡ The GO bonds of any given municipality typically involve less risk of default and therefore typically pay lower yields than the same issuer's revenue bonds.

§ The federal income tax exemption for the coupon income from municipal bonds militates toward their having low yields. However, municipal bond issues with low-quality ratings may be forced to pay high yields in spite of their tax-exempt status.

¶ It is usually not politically expedient to declare a municipality bankrupt and liquidate its assets. Furthermore, since municipal bonds cannot be downgraded to stock, a temporary default is about the worst that typically happens to municipals.

Most debt securities are small components of a large debt that the bond issuer incurs to finance a major purchase. Investors buy bonds because they come in convenient denominations, because they are marketable, because they yield cashflows from periodic interest payments, and because in most cases, they involve less risk than common stocks.

Debt securities are available with a wide array of different maturities and offer a spectrum of interest rates. Money market securities all have terms to maturity of less than 1 year. Treasury bills and commercial paper are short-term bonds issued by the U.S. government and corporations, respectively, in order to obtain short-term loans.

U.S. government bonds are issued by the U.S. Treasury Department. These bonds are generally considered to be safer from bankruptcy risk than any other bonds in the world. In contrast, corporate bonds offer higher rates of return than Treasury bonds in order to induce investors to buy these relatively riskier debt securities.

Municipal bonds are issued by cities, states, and other local governmental bodies to raise funds to pay for local projects. Interest income from municipal bonds has been declared free from federal income tax, and this tax exemption makes munis particularly attractive to investors in high income tax brackets.

There is a long list of investment alternatives that have been in existence for years. In addition, there is a growing list of new securities with acronyms like CATS, TIGRs, MCATs, STRIPS, and LYONs. There are junk bonds, put bonds, zeros, and other ingenious new debt securities that continuously emerge. Each new security provides a new investment opportunity to evaluate.

Fabozzi, F. J., S. G. Feldstein, I. M. Pollack, and F. G. Zarb, eds., *The Municipal Bond Handbook*, vols. 1 and 2. (Homewood, Ill.: Dow Jones–Irwin, 1983).
   Experts from every aspect of municipal bond investing each write chapters about their area of expertise. These chapters form a well-organized and comprehensive discussion of municipal bonds.

Fabozzi, F. J., and I. M. Pollack, eds., *The Handbook of Fixed Income Securities*, 2d ed. (Homewood, Ill.: Dow Jones–Irwin, 1987).
   A collection of nonmathematical chapters about every popular type of debt instrument. Each chapter is written by an expert in the area.

Standard & Poor's Corporation, *Standard and Poor's Rating Guide* (New York: McGraw-Hill, 1979).
   This book explains in detail how to evaluate the quality of various corporate and municipal bond issues.

Stigum, Marcia, *The Money Market: Myth, Reality and Practice*, 3d ed. (Homewood, Ill.: Dow Jones–Irwin, 1990).
   This volume provides a detailed and comprehensive discussion of all money market securities.

Weston, J. Fred, and Thomas Copeland, *Managerial Finance*, 8th ed. (New York: Dryden, 1986).
   Chapters 24, 25, 26, and 28 offer an easy-to-read explanation of the principal corporate securities.

Wood, John H., and Norma L. Wood, *Financial Markets* (New York: Harcourt Brace Jovanovich, 1985).

> *Chapter 6 contains an explanation of interest rate quotations and the yields on Treasury bills, notes, and bonds that includes a number of illustrations and numerical examples.*

Questions and Problems

Essay Questions

2-1   Compare mortgage bonds and debentures issued by the same corporation. Can one be a safer investment than the other even though they are issued by the same corporation? Why?

2-2   What are the differences between marketable and nonmarketable U.S. Treasury securities? Do these differences matter to bond investors?

2-3   What is a municipal bond? What characteristic of this type of security makes it unique?

2-4   What is a bond indenture? What does the trustee do? What is the single most important protective provision that bond investors may or may not be granted in the indenture?

2-5   What unique characteristics make money market securities different from other types of bonds and debt instruments?

2-6   What do TIGRs and U.S. savings bonds have in common? Explain.

2-7   Although bonds are commonly referred to as fixed income securities, not all bonds promise fixed interest payments. Name some so-called fixed income bonds that do not promise their investors constant periodic payments.

Problems

2-8   Find the price (and/or yield) quotations for U.S. Treasury securities in a newspaper. Ignore bonds issued by agencies of the U.S. government. Answer the following questions from your newspaper excerpt: (*a*) How many different Treasury security issues are outstanding? (*b*) What are the highest and lowest yields available on Treasury securities on that date? (*c*) What are the shortest and the longest terms until maturity for your sample of Treasury securities? (*d*) Do all the Treasury securities in your newspaper excerpt pay coupon interest? (*e*) Are the prices of any U.S. savings bonds quoted in the newspaper you checked?

2-9   On March 1, 199X, an investor paid $360 for a $1000-face-value zero coupon bond of Amalgamated Industries maturing in exactly 10 years. If the investor sells the bond a year later for $405, what was the investor's return on the bond during the 1-year holding period?

2-10   A 1-year Treasury bill is sold at a 5 percent discount from its maturity value. (*a*) What is the actual price an investor will pay for a $10,000 T-bill? (*b*) What is the actual return to the investor?

2-11   A $10,000 T-bill can currently be purchased for $9600. What rate of return (or percentage gain) will an investor earn from holding the T-bill until it matures in 65 days?

2-12   A 10-year zero coupon bond can be purchased for $285. What before-tax rate of return will an investor earn if he holds the bond to maturity?

2-13 John Q. Stone is considering the purchase of one of the following bonds: (*a*) a 7 percent annual coupon municipal bond and (*b*) a 12 percent annual coupon corporate bond. Mr. Stone is in the 33 percent tax bracket. If both bonds are selling at par, have similar maturities, and are equally risky, which bond should he purchase?

2-14 A bond of the XYZ Company sold for $980 on January 1, 199X; it was purchased for $910 on January 1 of the preceding year. If this bond paid $70 in interest during the year, what was its 1-year rate of return?

2-15 For the T-bill in Problem 2-11, annualize the rate of return to find the equivalent bond yield from the investment. *Note:* It is always assumed that there are only 360 days in the year when working with T-bills, so calculate both the 360-day return and the 365-day return, in case your boss asks for both.

2-16 An investor purchased a 90-day T-bill for $9600. Thirty days later, the investor sold the T-bill for $9700. What was the annualized rate of return on this investment? *Note:* It is always assumed that there are only 360 days in the year when working with T-bills, so calculate both the 360-day return and the 365-day return.

Matching Questions

2-17 Match the descriptions of bonds with the names of the U.S. Treasury securities listed below.

Time from issue until maturity	*Name of Treasury security*
1. 19 years, pays coupons	A. T-bond
2. 7 months, no coupons	B. T-bill
3. 6 years, pays coupons	C. T-note

2-18 Match the municipal bond names and phrases listed below with their definitions.

Names and phrases	*Definition*
1. Revenue bond D	A. A full faith and credit bond
2. Tax-exemption C	B. A town, school system, or toll bridge authority
3. Municipality B	C. Applies to coupons, but not price appreciation
4. General-obligation bond A	D. A limited-obligation bond

Multiple Choice Questions

2-19 Which of the following sequences best describes what happens to a financially troubled company?

(*a*) Bankruptcy is followed by default and reorganization.
(*b*) Default leads to reorganization by a court or maybe even a bankruptcy liquidation.
(*c*) The bankruptcy court reorganizes a company to avert default.
(*d*) Each of the above sometimes occurs.

B

2-20 Federal funds are best described by which of the following?

(*a*) Overnight loans between commercial banks.

(*b*) Bank reserves that are lent by banks with excess reserves to banks with insufficient reserves.

(*c*) Bank borrowings from the Federal Reserve that are obtained through the money markets.

(*d*) Both (*a*) and (*b*) are true.

2-21 Banker's acceptances (BAs) are best described by which one of the following statements?

(*a*) BAs are money market securities that are usually used in foreign trade when the seller is reluctant to grant credit to an unfamiliar foreign buyer.

(*b*) BAs are practically default-free because the borrower and the originating bank both stand behind the instrument.

(*c*) If the importer's bank wants to recoup the money it has invested in the loan before the loan expires, that bank can sell the BA to another investor.

(*d*) All the above are true.

2-22 Which of the following are zero coupon bonds?

(*a*) Series E and EE U.S. savings bonds.

(*b*) U.S. Treasury bills.

(*c*) Liquidity yield option notes.

(*d*) All the above are zeros.

2-23 The indenture governing an issue of corporate bonds might grant investors which of the following rights?

(*a*) The right to convert the bond into the issuer's common stock.

(*b*) The right to have the coupon interest rate reset periodically.

(*c*) The right to vote at all annual owners' meetings.

(*d*) Both (*a*) and (*b*) are true.

(*e*) All of the above are true.

2-24 How is the income from a zero coupon bond taxed by the federal government?

(*a*) Coupons and price appreciation are taxed in the year when the income is received.

(*b*) Income taxes must be paid on coupon income each year, even though the coupons are not paid.

(*c*) Price appreciation income is taxed in the year when the income is realized, but not necessarily when it is received.

(*d*) Both (*b*) and (*c*) are true.

(*e*) Both (*a*) and (*c*) are true.

2-25 Which one of the following statements best describes corporate bonds?

(*a*) Bond investors are creditors of the corporation.

(*b*) A bond is an engraved certificate evidencing corporate borrowing.

(*c*) All corporate bonds make coupon interest payments once per annum.

(*d*) Both (*a*) and (*b*) are true.

(*e*) None of the above is true.

2-26 An indenture may contain protective clauses dealing with which of the following topics?

(*a*) Collateral.
(*b*) A sinking fund.
(*c*) Subordination clauses.
(*d*) All the above are true.
(*e*) None of the above are true.

2-27 Zero coupon corporate bonds are correctly described by which of the following?

(*a*) They were first issued in 1881.
(*b*) The investor must pay income taxes on the coupons even though no cash is received.
(*c*) They may be purchased at deep discounts from their face values.
(*d*) Both (*b*) and (*c*) are true.
(*e*) All the above are true.

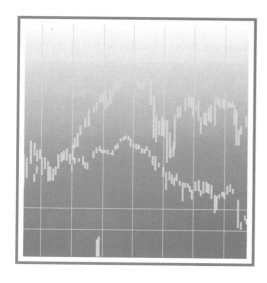

CHAPTER 3

EQUITY AND ASSET-BACKED SECURITIES

In the Dartmouth College case of 1819, Chief Justice Marshall of the U.S. Supreme Court formulated the following definition of a corporation:

> A corporation is an artificial being, invisible, intangible, and existing only in the contemplation of the law. Being a mere creature of the law, it possesses only those properties which the charter of its creation confers upon it either expressly or as incidental to its very existence. . . .

Box 3-1   57

> **DEFINITION: Stock**
>
> **Stock** is a security that evidences an ownership or equity claim on a share of income and the assets of a corporation. Stockholders have residual claims that are junior (or subordinate) to the claims of all the firm's debtors. Not all shares of stock in a corporation are necessarily equal; some corporations issue different classes of stock. The rights and privileges of each class are specified in the corporate charter.

The founders of a corporation obtain a corporate charter from the state, have ownership (or equity) shares printed, and sell the shares to as many different people as they wish in order to raise the capital to start the new business.

Many people prefer to invest in a corporation's stock rather than investing in a sole proprietorship of their own because investing in stock offers several advantages over more direct forms of business ownership. (1) A well-managed corporation can have a perpetual life. (2) Stock ownership can be transferred more easily than the ownership interest in an unincorporated business. (3) Stockholders enjoy **limited liability.** If the corporation goes bankrupt, the stockholders are not liable for its debts. (4) Shares of stock are available in convenient amounts (that is, odd lots and small denominations) that small investors can afford.

This chapter focuses on equity securities and securities that possess equity or ownership characteristics. *Common stock* is the purest equity security. *Preferred stock* is a hybrid that contains elements of ownership. *Convertible securities* can be converted into stock, and so have equity potential. *Investment company* shares are ownership securities. In addition, there are various new *asset-backed securities.* Let us begin with the most junior equity security.

3-1   Common Stock

Common stock is the first security a corporation issues and, in the event of bankruptcy, the last to be retired.[1] The chance that a common stockholder will get anything after a bankruptcy is minimal. But common stock's potential for dividend payments and price appreciation is unlimited. In contrast, bonds and preferred stock are contracts with fixed interest or dividend payments. An investor's risk is higher with common stock than with any other category of security. As a result, investors ordinarily refuse to invest in common stock unless it promises rates of return above those offered by debt securities.

When investors buy common stock, they can obtain certificates as proof of ownership. Stock certificates state the number of shares purchased, their par value (if

---

[1] *Master limited partnerships* are an alternative to the corporate form of business organization. Those who invest in a master limited partnership can enjoy many of the benefits of common stock investment without suffering the burden of double taxation (see Chapter 7). For more information see J. M. Collins and R. P. Bey, "The Master Limited Partnership: An Alternative to the Corporation," *Financial Management,* vol. 15, no. 4 (Winter), 1986, pp. 5–14.

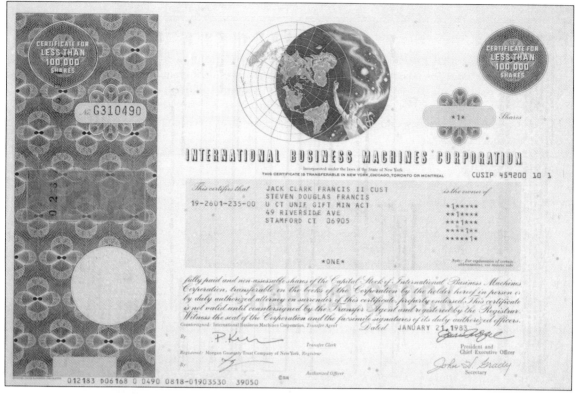

Figure 3-1 Common stock certificate. (Courtesy of IBM.)

any), and usually the name of the transfer agent. Figure 3-1 shows a common stock certificate. When stock is purchased, the new owner and the number of shares bought are noted in the stock record book of the **transfer agent.** The **registrar** checks to verify that the transfer agent made no errors. The functions of the transfer agent and the registrar are usually carried out by the appropriate departments in large city banks.

Voting Rights

Since they are the owners of the corporation, common stockholders have a voice in management through their voting rights. They elect the board of directors and vote on major issues. Most stockholders do not vote themselves; they sign and return **proxies** mailed to them by the company, which allow a named person, usually a member of corporate management, to vote the shares of the proxy signer at the stockholders' meeting. Proxies allow management, which seldom owns a majority of the shares, to control a majority of the votes and implement its decisions.

Many corporate charters provide for **cumulative voting.** This permits stockholders to have as many votes as they have shares of stock times the number of directors being elected. The stock owner may cast all these cumulative votes for one director or divide them among several. Stockholders with a significant minority of shares can thus gain representation on the board of directors.

Table 3-1
Comparison of 1990 Par, Book, and Market Values
for Shares of Randomly Selected Corporations

Corporation	Par per share	Cash dividend, $/share	No. of common shares (000)	Book value per share, $	Range of market price, $
AT&T	$1.00	$1.32	1,092,143	$12.90	$ 46–29
COMPAQ Computer	0.01	0	86,089	21.59	67–35
Ford Motor Co.	1.00	3.00	462,713	49.12	50–25
General Motors	1.66	3.00	601,200	45.17	50–33
GTE Corporation	0.05	1.52	664,000	12.90	36–29
General Electric	0.63	1.92	887,552	24.43	75–50
IBM	4.73	6.47	572,647	74.79	123–94
Microsoft	0.001	0	119,412	8.08	78–25

The **preemptive right** (not always provided) gives existing stockholders the right of first refusal on any new issue of stock so they can maintain their previous fraction of the total outstanding shares. If exercised, the preemptive right prevents dilution of ownership control when additional stock is issued.

Par Value and Book Value

Par value is the face value of a share of stock. It was introduced to guarantee that the corporation would receive a fair price for the interest in the firm represented by a share. However, the concept was undermined during the early 1900s when dishonest dealers sold stock for less than its par value; this is called "watering the stock" because the new shares being sold for below-par prices diluted the older stockholder's value, earnings, and cash dividends per share. In 1912 New York acknowledged the inadequacy of the par value mechanism by becoming the first state to allow stock to be issued with no par value. No-par stock can be issued at any price because it has no par value to dictate a minimum value. No-par stock's peak of popularity was reached in the 1920s; corporations today have largely given it up in favor of low-par shares. Most companies now set a par value for their stock at a level below the price the shares will command on the market; $1 per share is common. So the par value of a stock tells us nothing about the value of the share.

A common stock's **book value** per share is defined in terms of the balance sheet.

Box 3-2

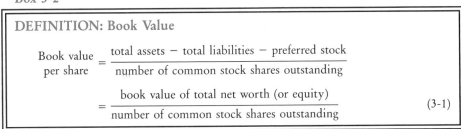

DEFINITION: Book Value

$$\text{Book value per share} = \frac{\text{total assets} - \text{total liabilities} - \text{preferred stock}}{\text{number of common stock shares outstanding}}$$

$$= \frac{\text{book value of total net worth (or equity)}}{\text{number of common stock shares outstanding}} \qquad (3\text{-}1)$$

NEW YORK STOCK EXCHANGE COMPOSITE TRANSACTIONS

Quotations as of 4:30 p.m. Eastern Time
Monday, April 22,

	52 Weeks Hi	52 Weeks Lo	Stock	Sym	Div	Yld %	PE	Vol 100s	Hi	Lo	Close	Net Chg
			-A-A-A-									
	24¼	9⅛	AAR	AIR	.48	3.3	14	636	14¾	14¼	14½	− ⅛
	11½	8¾	ACM Gvt Fd	ACG	1.26	11.1	...	1140	11⅜	11¼	11⅜	...
n	9⅜	7¾	ACM OppFd	AOF	1.26e	13.8	...	146	9¼	9⅛	9⅛	...
x	11	8⅝	ACM SecFd	GSF	1.26	11.6	...	x1135	11	10⅞	10⅞	+ ⅛
	9	7¼	ACM SpctmFd	SI	1.01	11.4	...	416	9	8⅞	8⅞	− ⅛
n	8¼	6½	ACM MgdIncFd	AMF	1.01	12.6	...	633	8⅛	8	8	...
	12⅝	10	ACM MgdMultFd	MMF	1.50	12.0	...	261	12⅝	12½	12½	− ⅛
	28¼	17	AL Labs A	BMD	.24	.9	22	103	27¼	26⅝	27⅛	+ ⅜
	2⅞	1	AM Int	AM		...	...	393	1⅝	1½	1½	...
	13½	4⅝	AM Int pf		2.00	18.6	...	95	10¾	10⅝	10¾	+ ⅛
	10⅜	8⅝	AMEV Sec	AMV	1.05a	10.4	...	48	10¼	10	10⅛	+ ⅛
	70¼	39¾	AMR	AMR		...	...	4666	62½	60⅝	62	− ¾
	24⅝	22¼	ANR pf		2.12	8.9	...	5	23¾	23¾	23¾	...
	44¼	29¾	ARCO Chm	RCM	2.50	5.9	15	138	42½	42¼	42½	− ¼
	3⅝	1¼	ARX	ARX		...	...	94	2½	2⅜	2⅜	...
	56¼	38¼	ASA	ASA	3.00	6.6	...	749	45½	44⅝	45½	+ ¾
▲	**4⅜**	**1⅞**	**ATT Cap yen wt**			...	...	**5825**	**4⅝**	**4⅜**	**4½**	**+ ¼**
	54	33⅜	AbbotLab	ABT	1.00	2.0	22	6051	51⅜	50⅝	51⅛	− ⅛
	14	9⅞	Abitibi g	ABY	.50	3.7	...	5	13⅜	13⅜	13⅜	− ⅛
	9⅛	4¾	AcmeElec	ACE		...	2	32	5	4¾	5	+ ⅛
	9⅝	4½	AcmeCleve	AMT	.40	6.2	19	110	6½	6¼	6½	+ ¼
s	40	22	Acuson	ACN		...	26	1876	34¼	33¼	34⅛	+ ¼
	17⅜	14⅛	AdamsExp	ADX	1.72e	10.1	...	125	17⅛	17	17	− ⅛
	14½	7	AdobeRes	ADB		...	...	26	7⅞	7¾	7¾	− ¼
	21¼	18⅞	AdobeRes pf		2.40	12.2	...	8	19⅝	19⅝	19⅝	+ ⅛
	19⅞	16	AdobeRes pf		1.84	10.9	...	41	16⅞	16⅝	16⅞	− ¼
	14¼	**3⅝**	**AdvMicro**	**AMD**		...	...	**22577**	**13 7/16**	**12⅜**	**12½**	**−1**
	35⅜	**13**	**AdvMicro pf**		**3.00**	**9.2**	...	**180**	**33½**	**32¼**	**32½**	**−1¾**
	5¼	1⅝	Advest	ADV		...	...	140	4⅝	4¼	4⅜	− ⅛
x	54⅜	29	AetnaLife	AET	2.76	5.8	9	x1835	48	47	47½	...
	10⅞	6¼	AffilPub	AFP	.24	2.7	35	1399	9	8⅝	8¾	...
	22½	10⅝	Ahmanson	AHM	.88	5.4	11	4563	17¼	16⅜	16⅜	− ⅝
	5⅞	2	Aileen	AEE		...	9	335	5½	5¼	5⅜	− ⅛
	70⅜	42⅞	AirProduct	APD	1.44	2.2	15	935	67	65⅜	65⅜	−1⅝
s	27	13½	AirbornFrght	ABF	.30	1.5	12	1674	21	20	20½	− ½
	20	**11¼**	**Airgas**	**ARG**		...	**17**	**321**	**15⅛**	**14⅜**	**14½**	**−1**
	19⅛	10	Airlease	FLY	1.60	12.9	6	44	12½	12¼	12⅜	...
	25½	21	AlaPwr pf		2.05e	8.5	...	96	24⅛	23¾	24⅛	...
	10¼	9	AlaPwr pf		.87	8.7	...	2	10	10	10	+ ⅛
	100¼	90	AlaPwr pf		9.00	9.0	...	z130	100¼	100	100¼	+ ¼
	25⅜	**13⅞**	**AlaskaAir**	**ALK**	**.20**	**.9**	**138**	**925**	**23⅝**	**21¾**	**22**	**−1⅝**
	18	8	AlbanyInt	AIN	.35	2.6	68	772	13⅞	13½	13½	− ⅜
	34¼	19⅛	AlbertoCl	ACV	.22	.8	22	81	29⅛	28⅝	29⅛	+ ⅜
	24⅞	15⅛	AlbertoCl A	ACVA	.22	1.0	17	520	23	22⅞	23	− ½
s	51⅜	27½	Albertsons	ABS	.56	1.2	28	1555	48⅞	48	48¼	− ¼
	24½	16⅝	Alcan	AL	1.12	5.2	14	2858	21⅝	21¼	21⅜	− ⅜
	37⅞	27⅝	AlcoStd	ASN	.88	2.9	12	689	30¼	29¾	29⅞	+ ⅛
	28	16⅛	Alex&Alex	AAL	1.00	3.7	20	337	27	26⅜	26⅞	+ ⅝
	51⅜	19¾	Alexanders	ALX		...	...	30	26⅛	26	26	− ¼
	101¾	73	AlleghanyCp	Y	1.86t	1.9	9	15	100¼	99	99	−1⅝
s	34¼	18⅛	AllegLud	ALS	.88	3.4	13	50	26⅜	26⅛	26¼	− ⅜
	40⅛	34	AllegPwr	AYP	3.16	8.2	11	280	38¾	38⅝	38¾	− ⅛
	20	9¾	AllenGp	ALN		...	8	63	13⅜	13¼	13¼	− ¼
	21¾	14¼	AllenGp pf		1.75	9.1	...	10	19¼	19	19¼	+ ¼
	25½	12½	Allergan	AGN	.32	1.3	20	493	23⅞	23⅝	23¾	− ¼
	24⅛	11½	AllncCapMgt	AC	1.76e	7.9	19	422	22½	21¾	22¼	− ½
n	**17**	**8⅝**	**AllncGlblEnv**	**AEF**	**.34e**	**3.1**	...	**1579**	**11¾**	**11**	**11⅛**	**− ⅝**
n	24½	8⅝	AlliantTech	ATK		...	8	137	21¼	21	21⅛	− ⅛
	23¾	15¾	AlldIrishBk pf		2.97	13.1	...	140	22¾	22⅜	22⅝	− ⅛
n	22	17½	AlldIrishBk	AIB	2.97e	16.1	...	12	18½	18¼	18½	− ¼
	9⅛	3	AlliedPdts	ADP		...	5	10	3⅝	3½	3½	− ⅛
	37⅞	24⅞	AlliedSgnl	ALD	1.80	6.1	9	1105	29⅝	29¼	29½	− ¼
	56	48¼	BaltimrGE pfB		4.50	8.2	...	z20	55	55	55	−1
	39⅛	19	BancOne	ONE	1.16	3.0	14	2005	38¼	37½	38¼	+ ½
	13/16	**⅛**	**BancTexas**	**BTX**		...	...	**220**	**9/16**	**15/32**	**15/32**	**− 1/32**
	36¾	23⅜	BancoBilV	BBV	1.59e	5.5	8	3	28¾	28¾	28¾	− ¾
	25½	19¼	BancoCentrl	BCM	1.05e	4.8	7	6	22	22	22	− ¼
	55⅞	37½	BancoSantdr	STD	2.16e	4.2	9	2	51⅜	51⅜	51⅜	−1½
	100½	66	Bandag	BDG	1.10	1.1	18	74	97⅞	96¾	97	−1
	15⅝	3	BankBost	BKB	.40	4.7	...	5075	8¾	8¼	8½	...
	31	11¼	BankBost pfA		3.56e	13.1	...	53	27½	26¾	27¼	+ ⅝
	30⅛	10¾	BankBost pfB		3.44e	13.2	...	92	26½	25¾	26	+ ⅛
	52	16	BankBost pfC		6.32	13.5	...	z1820	46¾	46½	46¾	− ¼
	39¼	13¼	BankNY	BK	1.52	5.7	17	1522	26¾	26¼	26½	− ⅜
	39½	17½	BankAmer	BAC	1.20	3.2	9	8015	38¾	37⅞	37⅞	− ⅜
	40	30½	BankAmer pf		3.42e	8.8	...	44	39¼	38⅞	38⅞	− ¼
	67⅝	55¼	BankAmer pf		6.00	9.0	...	11	67	66¾	66⅞	+ ⅛
▲			BankAmer pf			...	...	951	25⅞	25⅛	25⅜	...
	51⅜	28½	BankTrst	BT	2.54	5.2	6	3055	49½	47½	49	+ ½
n	14⅛	6¾	BannerAero	BAR		...	...	141	10¾	10⅜	10⅜	− ⅛
	25⅜	21	Barclays pr		2.78	11.2	...	54	25⅛	24¾	24¾	− ¼
	25⅜	20⅝	Barclays prB		2.72	10.9	...	68	25	24¾	24⅞	...
	25½	21	Barclays pfC		1.90e	7.5	...	92	25⅜	25	25⅜	+ ⅜
	25¾	24¾	Barclays pf			...	...	449	25½	25¼	25¼	− ¼
s	36	22	Barclays	BCS	2.15i	6.8	17	88	31⅞	31	31¾	− ½
	28¼	13	Bard CR	BCR	.44	1.6	32	3279	27¼	26	27⅛	− ⅛
	32¾	23⅞	BarnesGp	B	1.40	4.6	12	55	30½	30¼	30¼	− ⅜
	37¾	14⅛	BarnettBks	BBI	1.32	4.9	16	1155	27½	26⅜	26⅞	− ½
	60½	52¼	BarnettBks pf			...	...	42	59½	58½	58⅞	− ⅜
n	9	4¾	BaroidCp	BRC	.20	2.9	25	546	6⅞	6¾	6⅞	...
n	21⅜	14½	Bass	BAS	.82e	5.0	8	7	16½	16¼	16⅜	− ⅜
	14¼	5½	BattleMtn	BMG	.10	1.3	37	3668	7⅞	7⅜	7¾	+ ¼
	84¾	54¾	BauschLomb	BOL	1.44	1.8	18	559	83¼	82¼	82¼	− ⅞
	37⅛	20½	BaxterInt	BAX	.74	2.1	19	6530	36½	34⅞	35⅜	− ½
▲	43⅜	35	BaxterInt pfA		3.59e	8.3	...	105	43½	43	43½	+ ⅜
	21⅝	18	BayStGas	BGC	1.28	6.3	12	44	20⅜	20⅛	20¼	− ⅛
	16⅝	7½	BearStearns	BSC	.60b	3.8	12	1711	15⅞	15½	15⅝	− ⅜
	24¼	13⅜	BearingsInc	BER	.64	3.0	51	26	22⅛	21⅝	21⅝	...
	13¾	6¼	Beazer	BZR	.77e	6.2	7	1811	12⅝	12¼	12⅜	− ½
	19½	11⅞	BeckmanInstr	BEC	.28e	1.5	15	283	19⅜	18¾	18¾	− ½
	81½	58	BectonDksn	BDX	1.16	1.5	16	1212	78⅛	76	76	−2
	30¼	16½	BeldenHem	BHY	.64	3.4	21	6	18⅞	18⅞	18⅞	...
	56¼	39½	BellAtlantic	BEL	2.52	5.2	14	3010	48⅞	48⅜	48⅞	+ ¼
	18¾	9⅜	BellIndus	BI	.40	3.7	8	127	11⅛	10¾	10⅞	− ⅛
	57⅝	49	BellSouth	BLS	2.76	5.2	16	3237	52⅞	51¾	52⅝	+1
	38¼	26⅛	Belo AH A	BLC	.52	1.7	23	88	30½	30⅜	30½	...
	41¼	25⅝	Bemis	BMS	.84	2.4	18	483	35¼	34½	34⅞	− ½
	60⅜	34⅜	Beneficial	BNL	2.40	4.1	12	514	59¾	58	58	−1¾
	18⅛	12½	Benetton	BNG	.97e	7.3	...	56	13½	13¼	13¼	− ⅝
	1⅞	¾	Benguet	BE		...	16	180	1¼	1⅛	1¼	...
	8275	5500	BerkHathwy	BRK		...	23	z120	8075	8025	8025	+15
	23¼	12½	Berlitz	BTZ	.50	3.1	29	117	16⅛	15¾	16⅛	− ¼
	19	13	BerryPete	BRY	.60	4.2	17	109	14⅛	13⅞	14⅛	+ ⅜
	12⅝	**4½**	**BestBuy**	**BBY**		...	**18**	**524**	**10¾**	**9⅞**	**9⅞**	**−1**
	18¾	10⅝	BethSteel	BS	.40	2.8	16	2972	14⅜	14	14¼	− ¼
	49	37⅛	BethSteel pf		5.00	10.8	...	41	46½	46	46½	+ ¼
	25⅛	19¼	BethSteel pfB		2.50	10.5	...	77	24	23¾	23¾	− ¼
	12⅜	3⅞	BeverlyEnt	BEV		...	58	8200	11	10⅜	11	...
	18½	10⅜	BiocraftLabs	BCL	.10e	.6	...	289	18⅛	17½	17⅝	− ⅜
	21	10½	BirmghamStl	BIR	.50	3.4	15	48	15⅜	14⅞	14⅞	− ½
	17⅞	8	BlackDeck	BDK	.40	3.0	16	1108	13⅞	13½	13½	− ¼
	36½	25½	BlackHills	BKH	1.76	5.1	14	107	35½	34⅝	34¾	− ⅞
n	10½	9¼	BlackstnAdv	BAT	.98	9.6	...	273	10⅜	10¼	10¼	− ⅛
	9½	7⅝	BlackstnIncTr	BKT	1.05	11.1	...	1148	9½	9⅜	9½	+ ⅛
n	10¼	9⅞	BlackstnStrat	BGT	.98	9.7	...	715	10¼	10	10⅛	...
	10½	9	BlackstnTgt	BTT	.95	9.2	...	1131	10⅜	10¼	10⅜	...
	55¾	34¼	BlockHR	HRB	1.56	3.0	24	416	52⅛	51¼	51¾	+ ¼
s	15¼	8⅜	BlockbstrE	BV		...	27	20184	12	11½	11¾	− ¼
	7⅝	5⅛	BluChipValFd	BLU	.74e	10.2	...	434	7⅜	7¼	7¼	− ⅛
	25¼	11½	BrushWell	BW	.72	4.2	16	108	17⅜	17⅛	17⅛	− ½
	27⅝	22⅞	BuckeyePtr	BPL	2.60	10.1	9	129	26⅜	25⅝	25¾	− ¾
	16⅜	12	BunkerHill	BHL	1.64a	11.2	...	17	15	14⅝	14⅝	− ½
	14⅜	10⅛	BurgerKgInv	BKP	1.64	12.5	11	61	13⅜	13⅛	13⅛	− ¼
	16⅛	**8½**	**BurlgtnCoat**	**BCF**		...	**12**	**99**	**11¾**	**11¼**	**11¼**	**− ¾**
	39¼	22¼	BurlgtnNthn	BNI	1.20	3.9	11	1904	31¼	30¼	30¾	+ ½
	9⅜	8	BurlgtnNthn pf		.55	6.6	...	5	8⅜	8⅜	8⅜	− ⅛
	50⅛	32⅞	BurlgtnRes	BR	.70	1.8	26	760	38⅝	38¼	38¼	− ¼
	17¼	10½	BurnhmPacif	BPP	1.36	8.8	53	26	15⅜	15⅛	15⅜	+ ¼
	9¾	⅞	BusinssId	BLI		...	...	971	1⅞	1¾	1⅞	...
			-C-C-C-									
	28⅛	14¾	C&S Sovran	CVN	1.56	7.8	20	1848	20	19½	19⅞	+ ¼
	50⅞	30¾	CBI Ind	CBH	.60	1.3	20	299	48¼	47⅞	48	− ⅛
	206¼	150¼	CBS	CBS	1.00	.6	207	638	161½	160¼	161½	− ⅜
	3	**11/16**	**CCX**	**CCX**		...	...	**2**	**¾**	**¾**	**¾**	**− 1/16**
	13⅛	5⅝	CDI	CDI		...	15	58	8⅞	8¾	8⅞	− ⅛
	5¾	**13/16**	**CF IncoPtnr**	**CFI**	**.16**	**6.7**	...	**51**	**2⅜**	**2⅜**	**2⅜**	**+ ⅛**
	56¾	33¼	CIGNA	CI	3.04	5.5	13	1667	55⅞	55	55¼	− ¾
x	7⅝	3⅝	CIGNA High	HIS	.90	14.7	...	x688	6⅛	5⅞	6⅛	+ ⅛
	24½	19½	CIPSCO	CIP	1.84	7.7	12	250	24	23¾	23⅞	− ⅜
	38¾	12¾	CML	CML		...	14	338	37⅜	36¾	36⅞	−1
	33	24⅞	CMS Engy	CMS	.48	1.7	12	2860	28½	27¾	28⅜	− ¼
	6⅞	**1¾**	**CMS Enhanc**	**CME**		...	**26**	**91**	**4**	**3⅝**	**3⅝**	**− ¼**
	92½	49½	CNA Fnl	CNA		...	15	443	85⅞	85	85⅜	+ ⅝
	11⅝	8½	CNA IncShrs	CNN	1.16a	11.0	...	120	10⅝	10½	10½	+ ⅛
	88⅝	66¾	CPCInt	CPC	2.20	2.6	17	1536	85½	84½	84½	−2½
	34¾	23¾	CPI Cp	CPY	.56	1.7	15	150	33	32⅞	33	− ⅛
	9	6¼	CRIIMI	CMM	1.08	12.7	9	267	8⅝	8½	8½	− ⅛
	13⅛	11⅛	CRI Liq	CFR	2.03e	16.9	...	43	12	11⅞	12	− ⅛
	18¾	9⅝	CRSS	CRX	.12	.8	14	1131	14⅝	14	14¼	− ½
	41½	26	CSX	CSX	1.40	3.4	10	3710	41½	40¾	41	...
	22¼	16	CTS	CTS	.75	3.5	15	41	21½	21⅜	21½	+ ⅛
s	23⅞	10¼	CUC Int	CU		...	43	794	22⅝	21½	22⅛	−1
	7¾	**2½**	**CV REIT**	**CVI**		...	...	**41**	**4¾**	**4⅜**	**4⅜**	**− ¼**
	31⅜	21⅝	CablWirels	CWP	.80e	2.9	18	485	27¾	27⅛	27¼	− ¾
	44	13⅛	CabltrnSys	CS		...	30	813	41¾	39	40½	−1⅛
	35⅞	23	Cabot Cp	CBT	1.04b	3.0	13	1623	35⅜	34⅞	35	− ½
	18½	13⅜	CabotO&G	COG	.16	.9	26	475	17	16⅞	16⅞	− ⅛
	34⅝	13¼	CadenceDsgn	CDN		...	22	2141	27¾	26½	26¾	−1⅜
	23⅜	10⅛	CaesarWld	CAW		...	14	1037	21⅝	20⅞	20⅞	− ⅞
	21¾	2⅛	CalFed	CAL	.12	1.7	...	1217	7¾	7¼	7¼	− ⅜
	3	2¼	CalifREIT	CT	.40e	14.5	...	34	2¾	2¾	2¾	...
	14⅞	5¼	CallahnMng	CMN		...	...	69	7⅝	7½	7⅝	− ⅛
	36⅜	17¾	CalMat	CZM	.64a	2.6	23	85	25⅛	25	25	− ¼
	1¼	**¼**	**Calton Inc**	**CN**		...	...	**209**	**13/16**	**¾**	**¾**	**− 1/16**
	1	¼	CampblRes g	CCH		...	...	270	5/16	9/32	5/16	...
	87⅛	43¾	CampblSoup	CPB	1.16	1.4	178	1637	84	82⅞	83½	− ⅞
	20	14⅞	CdnPac g	CP	.92	5.4	4	377	17¼	17	17⅛	...
	3⅝	⅝	Canal Cap pf		.43t	34.4	...	5	1¼	1¼	1¼	...
	633	380	CapCities	CCB	.20	.0	18	190	468	455	461¼	−7¾
	52½	26¼	CapHldg	CPH	1.20	2.4	15	638	52¼	51	51	−1⅛
	19⅝	11¾	CapstdMtg	CMO	2.40	12.6	8	66	19⅛	18¾	19	...
	16¼	10½	CapstdMtg pf		1.60	10.0	...	40	16	16	16	+ ⅛
	3¾	**¾**	**Careercom**	**CCM**		...	...	**114**	**15/16**	**13/16**	**⅞**	**− 1/16**
	38⅜	26⅝	Carlisle	CSL	1.24	3.6	13	72	35	34⅝	34⅝	− ⅜
	13⅞	**5⅛**	**CarolcoPic**	**CRC**		...	**14**	**386**	**7⅜**	**7**	**7**	**− ⅜**
	21	10¼	CarolFrght	CAO	.60	3.5	...	65	17⅝	17⅜	17⅜	− ¼
	49	38	CarolPwr	CPL	3.04	6.4	15	400	47¾	47¼	47⅜	+ ⅛
	57	36½	CarpTech	CRS	2.40	4.8	13	213	51⅞	49½	50	−2
	6¾	**1⅛**	**vjCarterHaw**	**CHH**		...	**33**	**754**	**2**	**1⅞**	**2**	**+ ⅛**
▲	67½	44⅞	CarterWal	CAR	.92	1.4	19	253	67⅝	65¾	65¾	−1⅛
	20⅛	15⅛	CascadeNG	CGC	1.36	6.9	10	20	19⅞	19⅝	19⅝	− ⅛
s	20½	8⅝	CashAmInv	PWN	.08	.6	20	39	14½	14⅜	14½	+ ⅛
	38⅝	26¼	CastlCook	CKE	.20e	.6	18	1005	36¼	35⅝	35¾	− ¾
n	15	8½	CatellusDev	CDX		...	33	275	12¾	12⅝	12¾	...
	68½	38⅛	Caterpillar	CAT	1.20	2.4	40	2909	49⅞	48⅝	49	− ½

Figure 3-2 Stock price quotations: (*a*) New York Stock Exchange.

Book value gives some indication of the amount of net assets per common share, but it has little effect on stock prices. Stock often sells for prices below book value. Book and market values may be equal on the day the stock in a new corporation is issued, but after that, it appears that only coincidence will ever make them equal. Table 3-1 shows how book value and par value compare with the actual market price of the stock for a few corporations.

NASDAQ BID & ASKED QUOTATIONS

Stock & Div		Sales 100s	Bid	Asked	Net Chg.
-A-A-A-					
A&A Fd g		91	3 1/8	3 3/8	...
ACSEn		40	2	2 1/4	-1/8
ACTV		10	2 1/2	2 3/4	...
ACTV wt		10	1 1/4	1 1/2	...
AFN s		254	2 3/8	2 9/16	-1/8
ANB		3	29	30	...
APA		2	4 1/2	5	...
ASA In s		53	1 1/16	1 3/16	...
ATC		134	5 3/4	6 1/4	-1/4
ATC Inc		85	2 5/8	2 7/8	-1/8
Accuhlt		20	6 5/8	7	...
Accuh wt		63	2 3/4	2 7/8	-1/16
Acqua		38	5 15/32	6 3/16	...
Acqua wt		19	2 31/32	3 11/32	+1/32
ActnPr		20	3 5/8	4 1/4	+1/8
ActnSt pf		62	2 3/4	3 1/4	...
AdvMed		20	2 3/16	2 1/4	...
AdNMR		757	4 1/2	4 5/8	...
A NMR wt		113	5 3/8	5 5/8	-1/8
AdvPho		105	8	8 3/8	...
AdvLfe		14	1 5/16	1 9/16	...
Advatex		8	1 1/8	1 1/4	-1/16
AerSyE		5	4	4 3/8	...
Aeroson		143	2	2 1/8	...
AgBag		294	3 5/8	3 7/8	...
AirSen		114	7/8	1 1/16	...
AirCure		120	6 1/4	6 3/8	+1/8
AirCur wt		105	2	2 1/8	...
AirInt		3585	1 5/8	1 23/32	+1/8
Airsh wt		50	1 1/4	1 3/8	...
Ajay un		16	10	10 3/4	-1/2
Alden	.12e	5	4 3/8	4 3/4	...
AldCap		1251	3 1/2	4	...
Alpha1		600	6 3/4	7 1/8	-3/8
Alph1 wt		315	2 5/8	3	-3/8
Alpnet		100	1	1 1/8	...
AltaEn s		209	1 3/16	1 3/8	...
AAcft		646	9/16	19/32	...
AmBiogn		81	5 1/2	5 19/32	...
AmBio wt		28	4 5/8	4 13/16	...
AmBio un		15	29	31	-1/4
AmBdy		115	5	5 1/2	-1/4
ABsCpt		481	12 1/2	12 3/4	-1/2
ACty pf	1.50	2	16 1/2	18	...
AClam s		91	3 1/2	3 3/4	...
ACGold		97	1 11/16	1 13/16	...
AmCred		20	7/8	1 1/4	-1/8
AmDrg		673	1 5/16	1 3/8	+1/32
AmFB		20	2 1/4	2 3/4	...
AShd rt		12	11/16	13/16	...
AIM 84	.80e	67	4 1/2	5	-1/8
AIM 85	1.44e	97	12 1/4	13	...
AMobl s		17	4 7/8	5 1/2	...
ANtPt		8	3 15/16	3 31/32	...
ARecr	.16	70	5 1/2	6	...
ASLFL		120	3/16	9/32	...
Amrhst		31	3 1/8	3 3/8	...
Amtech		20	1 1/4	1 1/2	...
AnlySur		56	1 9/16	1 3/4	...
Angecn		561	8 1/8	8 3/8	-1/4
Apco	.82e	1307	14 3/4	16 1/2	+1/2
Aphton		90	8 1/8	8 1/4	-1/8
ApogRb		52	1 5/16	1 7/16	...
ApogeTc		45	5 1/4	6	+1
ApdMicr		64	4 3/8	4 5/8	...
Aquant		104	1 9/16	1 11/16	-1/16
ArchPt		13	2 9/16	2 11/16	...
ArchCm		125	8 5/8	8 7/8	-1/8
Arcus		10	3 1/4	3 1/2	...
ArdenIn		9	2 1/4	2 1/2	...
ArizInst		15	3	3 1/8	...
Arhyth		40	3 3/4	4 1/4	...
Asar wt91		7	9 1/2	11	-1
ASEA	1.69e	317	91 1/4	92	-3/4
Atratc s		134	2 1/8	2 1/4	...
AtrixL		400	9 3/8	9 7/8	-3/4
Ault		32	2 1/8	2 3/8	-1/8
AuraSy		3814	7	7 1/4	-1/4
Aurora		46	1 13/16	2 1/16	-1/8
AutProt		390	1 1/2	1 9/16	+3/32
AutPr un		47	5 3/4	5 15/16	+1/16

Stock & Div		Sales 100s	Bid	Asked	Net Chg.
EnvDi s		431	1 7/8	2 1/16	+1/16
EnvSvc s		21	5 5/8	5 3/4	...
Esrc un		10	2 1/4	3	...
EvnsFS		30	5	5 3/4	...
EverMd		113	8	8 1/4	...
Evgrn s		151	4	4 1/4	+1/8
ExecTl		305	4 7/8	5 1/8	-3/8
ExpFb s		18	4	4 1/4	-1/8
ExpCsh		68	7 1/4	7 3/4	...
-F-F-F-					
FNB Cp	.28b	133	11 1/2	13	...
FahnVin		10	3 3/4	4 1/4	...
FallFn	.78e	19	15	16	...
FastCm		55	1 7/8	2 1/8	-1/16
FidlMd		777	1 1/2	1 9/16	-1/8
FinNw h		1179	5/8	3/4	...
Fingmx		276	1 7/8	2	...
FBkPhl		7	9 1/2	11	...
FtCarIn	.50	5	27	29	...
FComrB	.60	11	28 1/2	33 1/2	...
FtFdTn		2	5 1/2	7	...
FFncrp		10	3 3/4	4 3/4	...
FtTeam		154	10 7/8	11 3/8	-1/4
FUtdSv	.30e	5	7 1/2	8 1/4	...
Fisons	.64e	179	32 1/2	32 5/8	-1 1/4
Flexwat		4	7/8	31/32	...
FlghtIn		160	2 1/8	2 3/8	-1/8
Fonar		1096	1 3/4	1 13/16	+1/16
ForeInd		40	1 5/16	1 7/16	...
FndrBk		2	3 1/2	4 1/2	...
FountP		403	1 11/16	1 3/4	...
FtnPh un		53	10 1/4	11	...
Frnchtx	.03e	159	6 1/8	6 5/8	-3/8
FrntAd	.04a	6	3 1/8	3 7/8	...
FutCm s		1413	4 7/8	5	+1/4
-G-G-G-					
GB Fds		229	3 1/4	3 3/8	...
GTEC 5pf	1.00	25	11 1/2	12 1/4	...
GTS		41	2 1/4	2 3/4	-1/8
Gambro	.33e	13	27	28 1/4	-1/2
GamaIn		70	3 1/2	3 11/16	...
Gaml wt		50	1 1/4	1 1/2	...
Gaml un		20	5	5 1/4	...
GemEng		260	4 3/32	4 3/16	+1/32
GnCom		100	2 3/4	2 15/16	-1/8
GnKinet		109	8 1/2	8 3/4	...
GnNtr pf		56	1/4	5/16	...
GnPrcl		11	7	7 3/8	...
Gentnr		9	1 1/4	1 7/16	...
GeoTek		225	1 1/16	1 1/4	...
GldStd		75	1 3/16	1 1/4	...
Goldex		10	3/4	1	...
GoodTm		4	1 1/2	1 5/8	...
GoodT un		25	1 5/8	1 7/8	...
GtAMg	.84e	1	32	35	...
GtLk pf		4	80	87	...
GrnDan		2	2 5/8	3 1/4	...
-H-H-H-					
Haladr s		50	1/4	1/2	-1/4
HalwIn		15	2 1/2	2 3/4	...
Harmny		1	1 1/2	2 1/4	...
Hrrier s		90	2 3/4	2 7/8	...
HausCh		101	7 1/8	7 1/4	...
HlthClb		80	3 1/2	3 11/16	...
HltCl un		16	4 13/32	4 21/32	...
Hlthtek		100	1/4	1/2	...
HemaC		355	2 1/4	2 1/2	-1/8
Highldr		1	1 11/16	1 7/8	...
-I-I-I-					
ICC Tc s		77	4 1/4	4 3/8	...
I-Flw un		23	2 13/16	3	-1/16
IPS		53	9 1/2	9 7/8	...
IPS wt		2	4 3/4	5 1/4	...
Identix		333	4 13/16	4 15/16	...
ImgFl un		1	13 1/2	14 3/4	-1
ImgMgt		1465	1 3/16	1 5/16	-1/32
Imatr 91wt		186	1 7/16	1 9/16	-1/16
Imex		135	1 3/8	1 1/2	...
ImpTc un		60	3 3/8	3 5/8	...
Imreg		325	2 1/8	2 1/4	-1/8
InHome		1476	3 3/8	3 7/16	-1/16
IHme un		9	5	5 1/4	-1/8
Inamed		272	3	3 1/8	-1/8

Stock & Div		Sales 100s	Bid	Asked	Net Chg.
ParkAut		139	1 3/8	1 3/4	+1/8
Parlux		46	2 1/8	2 3/8	...
Perfdta		5	1 3/8	1 3/4	...
PerDia		173	1 11/32	1 19/32	-3/32
PhnxA s		177	2 13/16	2 7/8	...
PhnxLa		3604	5 1/16	5 3/32	-11/32
PhL wt95		425	2 3/8	2 7/16	-1/4
PhxNet		10	2 1/2	2 7/8	...
Photcm		359	1 5/16	1 19/32	...
PhotScl		382	7 1/8	7 3/8	-1/8
PiedMn		131	1 5/16	1 1/2	...
Pikevle	1.08	2	24	25	...
PinBG s	.80	z2	24	26	...
PitStop		25	1 5/16	1 7/16	...
PlasmT		274	11/16	13/16	-1/16
Polymrx		67	2 1/4	2 1/2	...
Ponder		140	5 3/4	6 1/8	...
PwSpec		33	2 3/8	2 5/8	...
PrabRbt		1	1 1/4	1 1/2	...
PrmCell		130	1 3/4	2	...
PrmEgy		10	1 1/2	1 5/8	...
PrvB pf	.32	1	1 7/8	2 1/16	...
PrfBcp		3	5 1/4	6 3/4	...
PrfCr un		19	8	9 1/4	...
Pictvs un		35	1 5/8	2	...
Protch		30	2	2 1/4	...
PrvAm		290	3 7/8	4 1/4	...
PsycCp		92	2 3/4	2 7/8	-1/16
PubcC s		3	7 1/4	8	...
PurTc un		45	5 3/4	6 3/8	...
Purflw		12	7 3/4	8 1/4	...
Qdrax		1173	1 3/32	1 1/8	+1/16
Questch		7	2 1/4	2 3/4	...
-R-R-R-					
RCM		804	4 5/16	4 3/8	-3/16
RF&P	1.20	119	30 1/2	32 1/4	-2
RTI		64	23/32	7/8	+1/32
RamHO		74	14	14 3/4	-1/2
Ramtrn		89	4 3/8	4 9/16	-3/16
RndAcc		350	2 7/8	2 15/16	...
RndA un		20	6 3/4	7 1/8	-1/8
ReaGld		60	5/8	13/16	-1/8
RegalC		10	1 1/8	1 1/4	...
RegBnc	.07e	38	10 1/4	12 1/4	...
Regenx		202	2 1/4	2 3/8	-1/8
Rntrak		335	8 1/8	8 1/2	-5/8
RschFt		324	3 3/4	4	-1/8
Ringer		73	7 1/2	7 7/8	-1/4
Roadmst		1485	1 1/16	1 1/8	-1/8
RkMCh		2	4 3/4	5	...
RoylnOp		5	1 3/4	2 1/4	...
Rubicn		14	1 3/8	1 5/8	-1/8
-S-S-S-					
SGI Int		290	2 7/16	2 9/16	-1/8
SI Hand		6	5	5 3/4	...
SK Tch		350	2 1/4	2 7/16	+3/16
SOI Ind		68	1 1/4	1 5/8	...
SSMC pf	2.85	154	30 1/2	31 1/2	+1/2
STOR		4	1 1/8	1 3/4	...
S2 Golf		98	1 1/2	1 11/16	+3/16
SageAnl		534	2 1/4	2 1/2	...
SIM wt s		2068	12 5/8	13	-1 1/4
Sandata		3	1 7/32	1 5/16	+3/32
Sasol	.19e	1	3 5/8	4	...
SchrHl		10	11	13 1/2	...
SchdM s		265	2 15/16	3	...
ShdM pf		12	2 7/8	3 1/8	...
Secom s		6	6	6 1/2	...
Selvac		20	7/16	9/16	...
Senetek		285	1 1/8	1 1/4	...
SenrSv		780	1 3/4	1 7/8	-1/16
ShrdTc		76	3 5/8	4	...
Smtl wtA		45	8 1/4	8 5/8	-1/4
Smtl wtB		28	3 3/4	4	-1/8
Softkey		245	3 1/8	3 5/16	...
SftwrDv		259	2 7/8	3 1/8	+1/2
SolvEx		285	1 11/16	1 3/4	...
SoPcPt		360	23/32	25/32	-1/16
SouldCp h		5655	2 9/32	2 11/32	-1/16
SprtSu		308	1 1/4	1 1/2	...
SprtTch		291	3 3/8	3 5/8	...
StarSr s		296	3 7/16	3 5/8	-5/16
StakeTc		35	1 11/16	1 15/16	-1/8

(*b*) NASDAQ. Supplemental list of over-the-counter stocks.

Stock Price Quotations

On any business day, stock prices at the close of trading on the previous day are listed in leading newspapers. Figure 3-2 shows listings for two different exchanges: (*a*) the New York Stock Exchange and (*b*) the over-the-counter stocks. The two left-hand columns of Figure 3-2*a* show the highest and lowest prices for each NYSE stock during the past year. The name of the issuing corporation and an abbreviated form are in the third and fourth columns. The lowercase letters refer to footnotes that provide details (for example, "pf" indicates an issue of preferred stock). The most recent cash dividend per share (if any) is in column 5. Columns 6 and 7 contain each stock's cash dividend yield and price-earnings ratio. The volume of shares traded (in hundreds) during the last trading day is in column 8. Columns 9, 10, and 11 contain the high, low, and closing prices, respectively, from the most recent day of trading. The change in the closing price between the last two trading days is in the right-hand column.

Figure 3-2*b* contains the prices of over-the-counter (OTC) stocks obtained from the National Association of Security Dealers Automated Quotations (NASDAQ). [The NASD creates what is called the *over-the-counter (OTC) market;* see Chapter 4.] The two columns at the left side of Figure 3-2*b* list the abbreviated name of the issuing corporation and the latest cash dividend per share (if any). Column 3 tells how many hundreds of shares traded during the previous trading day. The bid (or highest offer to buy) and asked (or lowest offer to sell) prices for each stock are in columns 4 and 5, respectively. The right-hand column shows how much the price of each stock changed from the most recent trading day's closing price.[2]

Classified Common Stock

A minority of corporations issue more than one category of common stock. Multiple-category stock is called **classified common stock.** Traditionally, stock referred to as *class A* is nonvoting, dividend-paying stock that is issued to the public. Class B stock is voting stock held by management, which therefore has control of the firm. Class B pays no dividends, but the owners enjoy the residual price appreciation benefits of a growing company.

Cash Dividend Payments

Fast-growing corporations tend to pay little or no cash dividends to their stockholders in order to retain as much capital as possible to finance the firm's growth and expansion. A few firms (Teledyne, Tosco, Data General, Penn Central, and Memorex) even have a corporate policy against paying cash dividends. In contrast, many established firms pay out a large portion of their earnings in dividends. Most public utilities, for example, take pride in their regular, substantial cash dividend payments.

It used to be widely believed that the market price of a corporation's shares tended to rise when the firm maintained stable cash dividend payments; that idea is

---

[2] Prices from the NASD's Supplemental List (of inactively traded stocks) are shown in Figure 3-2*b* because it reveals both bid and asked prices. Prices from NASD's National Market System (the more actively traded stocks) are not shown because bid and asked prices are not published, although both are used in trading. The NYSE, AMEX, and NASD do not publicize the fact that every stock has two prices and a bid–asked spread comes out of every share traded to pay for the market-making operations. See Chapters 4 and 18.

less common today. Now more companies determine dividend policy on the basis of financing needs. Cash dividends are important to some investors, but not to others. The **cash dividend clientele** can buy stocks that consistently pay large dividends; the **price appreciation clientele** can look for stocks that retain earnings to finance expansion. If a corporation makes a drastic change in its dividend policy, the market price of its shares typically immediately reflects whatever "the market" sees as the **information content** implicit in the change. In order to avoid causing price changes that may be disconcerting to investors, most corporations endeavor to make only small, infrequent, upward adjustments in their cash dividends.

Stock Splits and Stock Dividends

When a company divides its shares, it is said to have had a **stock split.** If a corporation had 2 million shares outstanding and split them 2 for 1, it would then have 4 million shares outstanding. A stock split causes certain accounting changes. The firm must correspondingly reduce the par value of the common stock, but it does not change its capital stock and retained earnings accounts (see Chapter 9). If the corporation's shares had a par of $1 before the split, then the 2-for-1 split would give a par of 50 cents. Corporations often split their stock to reduce the stock's market value per share. The split divides the market price per share in proportion to the split. For example, a $100 per share stock will sell at $50 after a 2-for-1 split.

Stock dividends are dividends paid in shares of the issuing corporation's stock instead of cash. When a stock dividend is paid, the accountant must increase the stock account and decrease the retained earnings account within the net worth section of the balance sheet. Except for these accounting entries, stock dividends and stock splits are identical. Just as a $200 per share stock will sell at $100 after a 2-for-1 stock split, a $200 per share stock will sell at $100 after a 100 percent stock dividend. For this reason, the NYSE has adopted a rule calling all distributions of stock under 25 percent (that is, one share for every four held) *stock dividends* and distributions over 25 percent *stock splits,* even if the corporation calls its action something different.

In a 100 percent stock dividend or a 2-for-1 stock split, there will be twice as many shares outstanding but *the total market value of the firm is not changed by changes in the unit of account.* Contrary to popular belief, stock splits and stock dividends do not affect the total value of the firm or the shareholder's returns. The effect of stock dividends and splits is analyzed further in Chapter 16.

3-2   Preferred Stock

Preferred stock is a hybrid security with elements of both debt and equity. Although it is technically a form of equity investment, it has many of the characteristics of debt, such as fixed income and call provisions. Its one-period rate of return is calculated as for a common stock return [see Equation (1-4)].

Most preferred stock has a par value. However, as with common stock, preferred with a par value has no real advantage over preferred that has no par value. Preferred stockholders have legal priority (or seniority) over common stockholders with respect to earnings and also, in the event of liquidation, with respect to assets. But preferred stockholders are in a more risky (subordinate, or junior) position compared with the corporate bondholders. As compensation for the risk they bear, preferred stockholders generally receive a higher rate of return than bondholders in the same corporation. Unlike common stock, preferred is limited (except for participating preferred, which is discussed below) in the amount of dividends it can receive. If the firm prospers, the preferred receives only the stipulated dividend; all the residual earnings go to the firm's common stockholders.[3]

Voting Rights

While preferred stock may put its owner in a riskier position than bonds do in the case of liquidation, in terms of control over management, the preferred stockholder is usually in a better position. Bondholders have virtually no voice in management, but some preferred stockholders get voting rights.

Before 1930, preferred stockholders had few voting rights. The theory was that so long as holders of this class of stock received their dividends, they should have no voice in the company. Currently, however, the trend is to give preferred shares more voting rights. Moreover, nonvoting preferred may become voting stock if preferred dividend payments are missed for a stated length of time or in special circumstances, such as authorization of a new bond or stock issue, or a merger. Since such events may affect dividends, granting of voting privileges is consistent with the idea that so long as dividends are paid, preferred stockholders should have no voice in management.

Cash Dividend Payments

Dividends are the most significant feature of preferred stock, since preferred stockholders gain more from dividends than from capital appreciation. The dividend paid is usually a stipulated percentage of par value or, for a stock with no par, a stated dollar amount per year.

Most preferred issues outstanding today have a **cumulative cash dividend** clause: The preferred stockholder is entitled to a dividend whether or not the firm earns it. If the corporation omits a preferred dividend payment or any part of it, the omitted dividend must be made up later before any dividend can be paid to the common stockholders.

Not all preferred stock is cumulative. **Noncumulative preferred stock** entitles the stockholder to the stock's promised rate of cash dividends only if the issuing corporation earns enough to pay them. To protect investors in noncumulative

---

[3] For detailed studies of preferred stock see J. S. Bildersee, "Some Aspects of the Performance of Preferred Stock," *Journal of Finance,* December 1973, pp. 1187–1201; D. B. Smith, "A Framework for Analyzing Non-convertible Preferred Stock," *Journal of Financial Research* (Summer), 1983, pp. 127–139; D. Emanuel, "A Theoretical Model for Valuing Preferred Stock," *Journal of Finance,* September 1983, pp. 1133–1155; and E. H. Sorensen and C. A. Hawkins, "On the Pricing of Preferred," *Journal of Financial and Quantitative Analysis,* November 1981, pp. 515–528.

preferred from being exploited by common stockholders who want to keep all the corporation's earnings for common stock dividends, some state laws say that a corporation cannot legally pay dividends on its common stock if it has missed a preferred dividend during that dividend period.

Call Feature

Because of the various cash dividend guarantees and other inducements needed to make a preferred stock issue attractive, issuing companies want to be in a position to call in their preferreds when financially feasible. A **redemption clause** gives the company the right to call in the issue. As with a bond redemption, a preferred stock redemption is allowed after public announcement of such action. A **call premium** must be paid above the par value of the stock and its regular dividend. Call premiums usually equal 1 year's cash dividend if the preferred is called in the first year after issue, and they decline slightly each year after that.

Call features are usually disadvantageous to investors but advantageous for the firm, since they allow a corporation to end the high fixed costs of preferred cash dividends. For investors, the call price acts like a ceiling that limits upward movement of the market price of the callable security.

Participating Preferred Stock

Participating preferred stock is an uncommon issue in which the stockholder is entitled to a stated rate of dividends plus a share of any cash dividends paid to common stock that are in excess of the participating preferred dividends. Financially troubled firms typically use such a provision to help sell preferred stock. Because preferred stock is basically a fixed-income investment like a bond, but has few, if any, of the legal guarantees inherent in a bond, the preferred issuer may add protective clauses to an issue to make the stock safer and more saleable.

Adjustable-Rate Preferred Stock

Issues of preferred stock with adjustable, rather than fixed, cash dividend payments were marketed in the United States for the first time in 1982. The dividend rates on these innovative issues were tied to the market interest rates on Treasury bonds and were adjustable quarterly. Most allowed their cash dividend rates to fall to no less than 7.5 percent or rise to no more than 15.5 percent. Federal income tax law in the United States allows corporate investors that hold a preferred stock investment 46 days or more to be exempt from federal income tax on 70 percent of the cash dividends received. This intercorporate tax exemption explains why some corporations invest in preferred stock.[4]

---

[4] Sophisticated investment strategies using adjustable-rate preferred stock have been analyzed by Bernard J. Winger, Carl R. Chen, John D. Martin, J. William Petty, and Steven C. Hayden, "Adjustable Rate Preferred Stock," *Financial Management,* vol. 15, no. 1 (Spring), 1986, pp. 48–57.

Money Market Preferred Stock (MMPS)

Money market preferred stock (MMPS) is like an adjustable-rate preferred that is periodically reissued with a new cash dividend rate. The MMPS has a brief life—some issues have lives of only 7 weeks.[5] MMPS shares are typically offered in large denominations, such as $100,000, because they are targeted at large corporate investors. Issues are sold via a **Dutch auction** at which potential buyers bid for the stock by offering to accept a certain rate of cash dividends for the short life of the MMPS. The entire issue is sold at the lowest dividend rate bid that allows all the bids submitted to be filled.

3-3   Convertible Securities

A **convertible security** can be converted by its owner into another security that has different rights and privileges. Most convertible securities are preferred stocks or bonds that can be converted into common stock. Once converted into stock, they cannot be changed back. If the convertible security is a bond, it provides the investor with a fixed interest payment; if it is preferred stock, it provides a stipulated dividend. Since convertible investors get the option to convert the instrument into common stock, this allows them to participate in any stock price appreciation. A convertible bond (or preferred stock) may be viewed as equivalent to a nonconvertible bond (or preferred stock) with an **embedded call option.** Chapter 21 shows how to value call options.[6] Convertibles allow their investors to earn the guaranteed fixed return until they are assured of a capital gain, then convert to get the common stock's price appreciation.

Many convertibles specify the period during which the issue may be converted. The convertible may stipulate that conversion cannot take place until 2 or 3 years after the date of issue. This stipulation allows the corporation to use money obtained from an issue of convertibles for investments that will show up in higher common stock prices later. A limited issue will also place a time limit, typically 10 to 15 years, during which the conversion can take place. Convertible preferred stocks usually allow unlimited time; an unlimited bond is eligible for conversion for the entire time it is outstanding.

An Overhanging Issue

Most convertible securities are callable. The purpose of the call provision is not to redeem the convertible securities, but to force conversion of the issue when the conversion value of the security is well above the call price. Investors will convert to

---

[5] For an empirical analysis of so-called dividend-stripping (or cash-dividend-capture) investment strategies see Theoharry Grammatikos, "Dividend Stripping, Risk Exposure, and the Effect of the 1984 Tax Reform Act on the Ex-Dividend Day Behavior," *Journal of Business,* vol. 62, no. 2, April 1989, pp. 157–173.

[6] Valuing the option portion of a convertible has been investigated by M. H. Brennan and E. S. Schwartz, "Convertible Bonds: Valuation and Optimal Strategies for Call and Conversion," *Journal of Finance,* December 1977, pp. 1699–1715. Also see J. E. Ingersoll, Jr., "A Contingent Claims Valuation of Convertible Securities," *Journal of Finance,* May 1977, pp. 463–478.

common stock, if that is profitable, rather than have their convertible securities called away from them at a lower price.[7]

Ordinarily a company will plan for an issue to be converted within a certain period of time. A growth company, for example, may expect conversion as soon as 18 months after issue. When a company is unable to force the conversion of an issue because the market price of the common stock has not risen to a point that will induce investors to convert, the issue is said to be an **overhanging issue.** Failure for conversion to occur might indicate that the company has failed to perform as expected. An overhanging issue can cause serious problems, since the company may find it difficult to gain market acceptance for additional issues when it has a convertible issue overhanging.

The Conversion Ratio

The **conversion ratio** is the ratio of exchange between the common stock and the convertible security. For example, a $1000 convertible bond with a conversion ratio of 10 may be convertible into 10 shares of common stock. The *par conversion price* is simply the bond's $1000 face value divided by the conversion ratio ($1000/10 = $100 per share conversion price). In this case the ratio may be stated as 10 shares of stock for each bond.

The conversion price need not be constant over time; it may change with the length of time outstanding or with the proportion of the issue converted. A bond issue might have a par conversion price of $100 per share for the first 5 years, $105 per share for the next 5 years, $110 for the third 5 years, and so on. Under a provision stipulating an increasing price with the number of outstanding securities that have been redeemed, a bond might have a conversion price of $100 per share for the first 25 percent of the shares converted, $105 for the second 25 percent, $110 for the third, and $115 per share for the final 25 percent converted. Such provisions give the issuer some ability to induce investors to convert, thus enabling the issuer to avoid an overhanging issue.

Effects of Convertible Financing

Common stock investors fear having the value of their holdings and their control of the corporation diluted by a conversion. The increased number of outstanding common shares after the conversion dilutes the corporation's earnings per share (EPS) because total income is divided by a larger number of outstanding shares. Likewise, the preexisting common stock investors' control of their corporation is diluted because the shares they own will represent a smaller proportion of the outstanding stock after a conversion. As a result, when a convertible issue is announced, the market price of the issuer's common stock usually declines.

---

[7] Changes in the issuer's unit of account caused by stock splits and/or stock dividends affect the terms of conversion. If the issuer splits its stock or declares a stock dividend, the conversion value of the convertible instrument is lowered appropriately. For example, if the conversion price of a bond were $100 per share and the conversion ratio were 10 shares of common stock per bond, a 2-for-1 stock split would change the conversion ratio from 10 to 20 (as the number of shares doubled) and the conversion price from $100 to $50 (as the market price of the common stock was halved).

To maintain the current stockholders' position, the convertible security can be covered by a provision for preemptive rights under which the convertibles must be offered to the existing stockholders before they can be sold to the general public (see Box 3-3).

Box 3-3

FINANCIAL EXAMPLE: How Good Is Blough?

A few years ago the Blough Corporation issued $1 million of convertible debenture bonds that had a 7 percent coupon rate and a conversion ratio that allows the issue to be converted into 40,000 new shares of common stock at any time. Assume that Blough already has 80,000 shares of common stock outstanding, is in a 50 percent income tax bracket, and has no other outstanding debt. If the corporation has taxable earnings of $400,000 per year, its earnings per share will be $2.06 before the debentures are converted, as shown below. This level of earnings supports a stock price of $22.66 per share so long as Blough's price-earnings ratio stays at 11 times earnings.

Earnings before interest and taxes (EBIT)	$400,000
Less: Interest on 7% debentures	− 70,000
Profit before taxes	$330,000
Less: 50% income taxes	− 165,000
After-tax profit	$165,000
Number of shares outstanding	80,000
Earnings per share (EPS)	$2.06
Price-earnings ratio (P/E)	11 times
Market price per share of common stock	$22.66

Whether or not you should invest in Blough's common stock with the issue of convertible debentures overhanging depends on the stock price after conversion. Using Blough's earnings per share after the debentures are converted and the price-earnings ratio of 11 times to estimate the new price per share of common stock suggests the following forecast.

Earnings before interest and taxes (EBIT)	$400,000
Less: Interest on 7% debentures	0
Profit before taxes	$400,000
Less: 50% income taxes	$200,000
After-tax profit	$200,000
Number of shares outstanding	120,000
Earnings per share (EPS)	$1.67
Price-earnings ratio	11 times
Market price per share of common stock	$18.33

These results indicate that the conversion will dilute Blough's earnings per share so much that the common stock will be a bad buy as it falls from ($2.06 × 11=) $22.66 per share before the conversion to ($1.67 × 11=) $18.33 after the conversion.

Investment companies take in money from people who want to have it managed for them by professional money managers. They typically charge a management fee of about 1 percent of the value of the assets managed per year; it is deducted from each client's account. The investment managers commingle the funds from different investors and buy a diversified list of securities. The securities are selected to achieve some investment objective, which the law requires the company to publish before shares in it can be sold.

Mutual Funds

Mutual funds, a synonym for **open-end investment companies,** are the most popular kind of investment company. The law allows mutual funds to keep selling more shares so long as they can continue to find more investors—the company is open-ended. These investment companies pursue many different objectives and offer investors many different kinds of investment opportunities:

- *Growth funds* try to maximize investors' capital gains through aggressive common stock investing.

- *Balanced funds* seek to conserve the owners' principal by investing only in high-grade bonds and high-quality preferred stock.

- *Tax-exempt funds* generate tax–exempt interest income by investing in municipal bonds.

- *High-yield funds* seek high levels of coupon interest income by investing in a diversified portfolio of junk bonds.

- *Index funds* are designed to achieve the same rate of return as some selected stock or bond market index by investing in about (or exactly) the same securities in the same proportions (more or less) as the chosen index.

Closed-End Funds

Closed-end investment companies are similar to open-end companies in some ways, but different in others. Both sell shares for cash, commingle investors' funds, and seek investments that conform to some stated investment objective. Some closed-end funds pursue the same investment objectives as mutual funds, but many seek riskier goals. One big difference between open-end and closed-end investment companies is that the law forbids closed-end funds from selling more shares after their initial public offering is completed. Another difference is that the law requires mutual funds to sell and redeem shares at their net asset value per share. In contrast, the shares in closed-end investment companies can be bought and sold only in a secondary market, where their prices are determined by supply and demand (and usually deviate from their net asset value per share). Investment companies are examined in more detail in Chapter 28.

3-5 Asset-Backed Securities

Asset-backed securities are marketable debt securities collateralized by financial assets like mortgages, accounts receivable, leases, and installment loan contracts. These debt securities are, in some respects, like the equity shares in a closed-end investment company. They are created by a process called *securitization,* which is cheaper than traditional lending techniques that need financial intermediaries.

The Development of Asset-Backed Securities

The major asset-backed securities, in chronological order by date of inception, are described in the following list. The mortgage-backed securities listed in items (2) through (4) are the largest category of asset-backed securities. They have evolved into several forms that are blueprints for other asset-backed securities discussed later in the chapter. The maturities of mortgage-backed securities range from 15 to 30 years. At the other end of the spectrum, the maturities of auto-loan-backed bonds never exceed 5 years. The pools of asset-backed securities in items (2) through (5) were insured against default losses by U.S. government agencies. The profitability of these government-subsidized financing plans set the stage for the private securitization programs in items (6) through (14).

1. Repurchase agreements (repos), the oldest asset-backed security, are money market securities that date back to the 1950s. Repos were discussed in Chapter 2.

2. **Mortgage pass-through securities (MPTS)** are bonds that are backed by a pool of mortgages insured against default losses. **Mortgages** are loans to finance the purchase of real estate that have the real estate which is being purchased pledged as collateral. MPTS were first sold in 1970 by the Government National Mortgage Association (GNMA), nicknamed *Ginnie Mae.* As their name implies, MPTS immediately pass through all cash flows from the mortgages to those who invest in the pool. Most borrowers buy and sell their real estate and pay off the mortgages before they mature. As a result, MPTS investors face the uncertainties of mortgage prepayments. Even mortgage defaults result in prepayments, because the mortgages in the pool are insured against default and are prepaid by the insurer when a default occurs.

Box 3-4

DEFINITION: Securitization

Securitization is a process in which financial intermediaries like commercial banks and other lenders are eliminated and marketable debt securities are sold directly to investors. An investment bank forms a pool of financial assets and sells debt securities to external investors to finance the pool. The primary goal of securitization is liquidity. Most asset-backed securities issues are liquid because the investment banking firm that securitizes the assets agrees to maintain an active secondary market in them.

3. **Mortgage-backed bonds (MBBs)** are debt securities issued to finance a pool of mortgages. MBBs modify the uncertain mortgage payments flowing into the pool and transform them into cashflows to investors that are like fixed coupons. The MBB issuer must overcollateralize the pool to enhance its credit rating and make the MBBs easier to sell. By doing this, the MBB issuer takes a residual (or equitylike) risk position in the pool that requires an unattractive entry on the issuer's balance sheet.

4. **Collateralized mortgage obligations (CMOs)** are securities issued by the Federal Home Loan Mortgage Corporation (FHLMC), called *Freddie Mac.* They are multiclass debt securities used to finance a pool of insured mortgages. Issuers are allowed to repackage the uncertain mortgage payments flowing into the pool and use them to service several different **tranches** of debt securities. If two tranches are used, say, a fast-pay tranch and a slow-pay tranch, the slow-pay tranch would presumably be the class of securities with the higher risk. The disadvantages of CMOs are that the issuer must market the pool's residual (which is like an equity investment in the pool), and must show the pool's assets and liabilities on its balance sheet.

5. Student loans were combined into pools created by the Student Loan Marketing Association (SLMA), called *Sallie Mae,* in 1973. Student loans are personal loans, so Sallie Mae securities are not mortgage-backed assets.

6. **Trade-credit-receivable-backed bonds** were first issued by the AMAX Corporation in 1982.

7. **Equipment-leasing-backed bonds** were first issued by the Comdisco Corporation in 1984.

8. **Certificates of automobile receivable securities (CARS)** were first issued by Salomon Brothers, the investment banking firm, in 1985.

9. Loans issued by the Small Business Administration were pooled, and debt securities were issued by the First National Bank of Wisconsin in 1985.

10. **Collateralized lease equipment obligations (CLEOs)**, securities designed to finance a pool of computer leases, were issued by First Boston in 1985. This was the first use of leases in asset-backed financing.

11. **Certificates amortizing revolving debts (CARDs)** are shares in a pool of credit card receivables first issued by Salomon Brothers in 1986.

12. Subtitle H of the Tax Reform Act of 1986 created an instrument called the **real estate mortgage conduit investment (REMIC)**. A REMIC is a separate legal entity into which mortgage originators can sell mortgage assets, and thus simplify their balance sheet. In addition, REMICs can use the cash flows from their mortgages to service multiple classes of debt securities (like the CMO tranches).

13. **Shared appreciation mortgages (SAMs)** are arrangements in which a real estate buyer who is seeking a mortgage at a lower interest rate gives a cooperating lender an **equity kicker** in the form of a share of the appreciation when the property is sold.

14. **Policy-holder loan bonds (PHL bonds)** were underwritten by Morgan Stanley in 1988 to securitize a pool of loans from Prudential Life Insurance Company's whole life insurance policyholders who had borrowed against the cash value of their policies.

The Costs and Benefits of Securitizing

Financial-asset-backed securitization became a multibillion-dollar business during the 1980s, increasing faster than any other type of financing. Securitization is a trend that will reshape the investment banking and commercial banking industries in the years ahead.

The costs involved in securitizing financial assets include the administrative costs (such as investment bankers' fees), the cost of providing information to the public and credit rating agencies, and the cost of providing the insurance and/or guarantees needed to enhance the credit ratings of the underlying financial assets. Some form of credit enhancement is needed to raise the quality rating of the pool of financial assets high enough to make it marketable to investors.

Because securitization usually involves the creation of debt securities, the default risk traditionally borne by equity investors must be assumed by some other entity. **Credit enhancement** techniques provide for this. First, the assets to be financed are placed in trust with some third party (such as a bank). The next challenge is to obtain AAA, or at least AA, quality ratings for the collateral from rating agencies. If the proper credit enhancement arrangements are not made, fear of default risk will keep investors from buying asset-backed securities. There are several ways to obtain credit enhancement for securitized assets:

1. If the seller of the financial assets has a bond rating of AAA, and that seller will grant the investors financial recourse in case the assets default, the rating agencies will usually give the asset-backed securities the same AAA rating that they give the corporation that stands behind them.

    For example, a AAA-grade commercial bank could finance its inventory of home mortgages by selling CMOs. However, the bank would have to show the mortgages as both an asset and a liability on its balance sheet, since the CMO investors have recourse to the bank in case the mortgage pool defaults.

2. Credit enhancement can be obtained through a letter of credit from a bank or insurance company that has a high-quality rating. If the financial assets that might default are guaranteed by a company with a AAA rating, the rating agencies will usually assign the guarantor's AAA grade rating to the insured securities.

3. Credit enhancement can be obtained through a surety bond purchased from a AAA-rated bank or insurance company. The pool of financial assets that might default gains a AAA rating because the insurance indemnifies investors against potential losses.

4. The seller of the financial assets can **overcollateralize** the pool by posting collateral that has a value exceeding the value of the assets in the pool. Overcollateralization at 125 percent of the value of the financial assets in the pool

is customary, so that even if 25 percent of the collateral assets default, there is still enough left to fully collateralize the assets in the pool. The disadvantage to the issuer is that the excess is, in effect, like an equity investment in the pool that the issuer must hold until the pool is liquidated.

5. Insurance can be purchased from an insurance company (or another AAA-rated third party) on a pool of financial assets that involve some default risk. The insured collateral can usually obtain AAA ratings if the insurer has a AAA-grade rating.

6. Creating a pool of assets that are highly diversified by geographical area, by debtor, by collateral, or in other ways is a venerable method of reducing risk. Securities issued against a low-risk pool can obtain higher credit ratings than the individual assets that make up the pool.

The benefits obtained from securitization vary with the form of the issue. Typical benefits are:

1. The seller of the financial assets can avoid the risks (namely, the interest rate risk and default risk) associated with carrying the assets in inventory.

2. Prepayment risks borne by the seller of the financial assets may be transferred to the investors.

3. Diversification opportunities are increased for both the seller of the financial assets and those who invest in them.

4. Lower-cost financing for inventories of financial assets may be available.

5. Funds flow more efficiently from investors to borrowers.

6. The seller of the financial assets gains liquidity. Stated differently, assets that may not be liquid individually (such as mortgages) are repackaged and turned into liquid asset–backed securities.[8]

3-6 Other Investments

The menu of investment opportunities is extensive, exotic, and tantalizing. Additional investments will be examined in the chapters that follow. It may be helpful, however, to introduce put and call options, futures contracts, options on futures contracts, American Depository Receipts, real estate, silver, gold, and some other investment assets here.

Put and Call Options   Options are financial instruments that give their owners the right but not the obligation to buy or sell a particular security at a fixed price within a predetermined time period. There are two basic types of options: put options and call options (options are the topic of Chapter 21).

---

[8] See Christine A. Pavel, *Securitization* (Chicago: Probus, 1989). In addition, the entire fall 1988 issue of the *Journal of Applied Corporate Finance*, vol. 1, no. 5 is devoted to securitization.

Futures Contracts   A **futures contract** is a legal agreement between a potential buyer and a potential seller of a commodity. The futures contract stipulates that the seller will deliver a specified quantity of a particular commodity to a designated location for the buyer of the futures contract to accept at a prearranged price at some specific time in the future. For example, bank A agrees to deliver one $100,000 Treasury bond for $94,562 to bank B in Chicago during December of next year, and bank B agrees to accept the T-bond and pay cash on delivery. Such a futures contract would be called a *December contract for a T-bond.* Commodity futures contracts are negotiable financial instruments that can be bought and sold for a profit or loss.

The volume of agricultural commodity futures contracts traded has been exceeded in recent years by the volume of financial futures contracts, which did not exist 20 years ago. Today they are popularly called **financial futures.** Financial futures are like the traditional commodity futures contracts in many ways, but at the same time are significantly different. Financial futures treat Treasury bonds, stock market indexes, and esoteric financial quantities as the underlying commodity. In many cases financial futures call for a cash settlement based on some market-determined outcome instead of the delivery of a commodity or security. (Futures contracts are examined in Chapter 22.)

American Depository Receipts   **American depository receipts (ADRs)** are certificates used by international investors. They represent shares of a foreign common stock and can be purchased instead of the stock itself by those who want to make dollar investments in a foreign stock that is not dollar-denominated. ADRs are legal claims on the equity shares in the foreign corporation. Foreign shares are purchased by an American investment bank or brokerage firm and held in trust at a commercial bank. The trustee bank issues the ADRs to acknowledge that it holds the underlying shares. For a small fee, the trustee bank collects cash dividends in the foreign currency, converts them to U.S. dollars, makes dollar-denominated dividend payments to investors who paid dollars for the ADRs, and performs the necessary bookkeeping. (International investing is the topic of Chapter 27.)

Real Assets   Real estate, diamonds, gold, silver, art objects, and collectibles are real physical goods that tend to appreciate in value with the general rate of price inflation. During any given time period, some real asset investments perform better than some categories of securities. Furthermore, during special periods specific real assets have enjoyed some spectacular price rises. Chapter 23 analyzes the investment characteristics of real assets.

Summary

Common stockholders have the right to receive certificates to evidence share ownership, the right to receive dividends, the right to vote at stockholders' meetings, and, in many states, the preemptive right to maintain a proportionate share in the corporation's assets, earnings, and voting control. In return for these advantages, common shareholders are forced to accept (1) only a residual claim on the corporation's earnings after all other bills have been paid and (2) the last claim on the assets if the corporation goes bankrupt. If the corporation prospers, however, these residual rights can be lucrative privileges.

Unlike common stockholders, preferred stockholders participate in the corporation's earnings only to a limited extent. Preferred stock promises a fixed rate of cash dividends that has a prior claim on corporate earnings over common stock dividends. If the preferred issue is cumulative, any missed cash dividend payments will be collected eventually, unless the issuer goes bankrupt. Some issues of preferred stock allow their owners to vote at stockholders' meetings if the preferred dividends are in arrears (that is, not fully paid). High-grade preferred stock thus offers good security and a stable income if the issuing corporation flourishes.

Convertible preferred stocks combine all the features of ordinary preferred with the added benefit of being convertible into common stock if the common appreciates. Convertible preferred thus offers both safety features not found in common stock and the opportunity to participate in the price appreciation of the common stock.

Asset-backed securities include bonds backed by mortgages, credit cards, and other financial assets. Asset-backed bonds are shares in a pool of diversified assets that pass through the asset buyers' installment loan repayments to those who bought the bonds that financed the pool.

Mutual fund shares, put and call options, futures contracts, international investments, and real assets are other types of investments we explore in later chapters.

*Further
Reading*

Cottle, Sidney, R. F. Murray, and F. E. Block, *Security Analysis*, 5th ed. (New York: McGraw-Hill, 1988).
This nonmathematical book about fundamental analysis explores many facets of common stocks, preferred stocks, and bonds.

Fabozzi, Frank J., *The Handbook of Mortgage-Backed Securities*, 2d ed., and *Mortgage-Backed Securities* (Chicago: Probus, 1987).
These nonmathematical books explore investing in mortgage-backed securities. Tables and graphs of empirical data are analyzed. The book presumes the reader knows the definition of the word "mortgage" and understands "present values."

Schall, Lawrence D., and Charles W. Haley, *Financial Management*, 6th ed. (New York: McGraw-Hill, 1991).
Chapters 11 and 22 provide an easy-to-read and informative discussion of common stock, long-term debt, preferred stock, convertible securities, and warrants.

Wiesenberger Services, Inc., *Investment Companies* (New York, published annually).
This large reference book explains investment companies, summarizes the relevant laws, and gives raw financial data for many open-end and closed-end funds.

Essay Questions

Questions and Problems

3-1   Define (*a*) a corporation and (*b*) common stock.

3-2   Do you expect the market price of a corporation's common stock to fluctuate the same way as the price of its preferred stock? Explain.

3-3   What are the advantages of investing in the common stock rather than the bonds of a corporation? What are the relative disadvantages of common stock investing?

3-4 "Stock dividends and stock splits have no effect on the value of a company." True, false, or uncertain? Discuss.

3-5 Is preferred stock more like a common stock or a bond? Explain.

3-6 The U.S. concept of shareholder democracy holds that one share gets one vote. Recently there has been a renewed interest in *classified common stock*. (*a*) Do you think that the two concepts are mutually exclusive? (*b*) Which is better for the average U.S. citizen? Explain.

Problems

3-7 The convertible bond of the GGG Corporation has a conversion ratio of 20. If the common stock of the GGG corporation is currently selling for $40 per share, what is the conversion value of the bond?

3-8 The *conversion premium* is the amount by which the market price of a convertible security exceeds its conversion value. If the convertible bond of the GGG Corporation in Problem 3-7 has a current market price of $950, what is its conversion premium?

3-9 Ms. J. J. Evans recently sold 200 shares of BGO Company stock for $40 per share. (*a*) If she purchased the stock 1 year ago for $30 per share and during the year received a $2 dividend per share, what return did she earn before taxes? (*b*) Assume Ms. Evans is in a 33 percent tax bracket. What return did she earn on an after-tax basis? (*c*) If Ms. Evans's broker charged a $150 commission to buy the 200 shares and another $150 to sell them, for a total buy-sell commission of $300, what was her one-period return after taxes and total commissions?

3-10 The Frame Corporation fell on hard times and suspended payment of the cash dividends on both its 5 percent cumulative preferred stock and its common stock last year. This year the corporation earned an after-tax income of $200,000, and Frame's president is anxious to resume paying cash dividends on the common stock in order to placate a group of stockholders who are angry because their dividend was suspended last year and the price of Frame's stock is depressed. Many common stockholders are threatening to come to the annual stockholders' meeting and vote to replace the president unless he does something to increase the price of Frame's stock. Will the president be able to resume the common stock cash dividend this year? Assume that there are 20,000 shares of preferred with a face value of $100 per share and 100,000 common shares outstanding.

3-11 The Gorman Manufacturing Corporation was founded with an initial offering of 100,000 shares of common stock that had a par value of $1 per share. These shares were sold for a price of $10 per share. (*a*) What did the net worth section of Gorman's balance sheet look like after this initial offering?
   Gorman had after-tax earnings of $100,000 during its first year of operations. Half these first-year earnings were paid out as cash dividends, and the other half were retained in the firm. (*b*) What did Gorman's balance sheet look like after its first year of manufacturing was complete? *Hint:* Consult an introductory accounting textbook.

3-12 On May 1, 19X1, Eagle Tire Company sells a new issue of 8 percent convertible bonds, convertible into Eagle's common stock at a price of $25 per share. Eagle's common stock is then selling for $20 a share and pays a $0.60 per share cash dividend. (*a*) What is the conversion premium at the time the convertible is issued? (*b*) If the price of the common rises to $30 over the next year, who would receive a higher return, an investor in the common or an investor in the convertible? Assume that interest rates do not change during the year. (c) Repeat part (b) if the common rises to $21. (d) Repeat part (b) if the price of the common falls to $18.

3-13   National Gas and Electric Company has two issues of preferred stock outstanding, an 8 percent cumulative issue and a 13 percent noncumulative issue, in addition to common stock. In 19X0, both convertible issues paid their normal dividend, and an $0.80 per share dividend was paid on the common stock (which sold for $40). In 19X1, because of an increase in fuel prices, National was forced to omit the dividend on all three issues. Earnings rebounded in 19X2, and the company resumed paying dividends on all three issues, raising the dividend on the common to $1 per share. (a) How much would an investor holding $1000 of each issue receive over the three 1-year periods? (b) Does the performance of these issues over this period necessarily reflect their relative performance under all economic conditions? Why or why not?

3-14   Sally Stein is an investment officer at a life insurance company that is in the 25 percent marginal corporate income tax bracket. Which of the following two securities will provide the company's portfolio with the higher yield-to-maturity if neither defaults? (a) A new issue of AAA-grade (that is, a high grade that entails virtually no chance of default) corporate bonds selling at par with a coupon rate of 10 percent. (b) An issue of AAA-grade preferred stock with an 8 percent cash dividend rate. Hint: Consider the tax rate on intercorporate cash dividends in Section 7-4.

3-15   The common stock of the Biddle Corporation had the following end-of-year prices and dividend record for three consecutive years.

Year	Ending price	Dividend
t + 1	$50	$2.00
t + 2	30	1.00
t + 3	45	1.50

(a) Calculate the rate of return for Biddle for years 2 and 3. (b) Recalculate the rate of return for Biddle for the same years if a 2-for-1 stock split took place anytime during year t.

Multiple Choice Questions

3-16   Common stockholders have the right to vote on which of the following?

(a) Dissolution or consolidation of the corporation
(b) Selection of the board of directors
(c) Amendments to the corporate charter or bylaws
(d) Both (a) and (c)
(e) All the above

3-17   Preferred stockholders receive priority over common stockholders in which of the following ways?

(a) Cash dividends cannot be paid to common stockholders unless the preferred stockholders receive their stated cash dividend.
(b) In the event of bankruptcy and liquidation, the preferred shareholders are paid before the common stockholders.
(c) Preferred shareholders (not common stockholders) get to elect the chairman of the corporation's board of directors.
(d) Both (a) and (b).
(e) All the above.

3-18 What are the primary reasons that convertible securities are desirable investments?

(a) They provide fixed cash income from either coupon interest or cash dividends.
(b) They provide an opportunity to benefit from upward movement in the price of the issuer's common stock.
(c) Their fixed income before conversion provides a "floor" or "price support" below which the convertible's price in unlikely to drop.
(d) Both (a) and (b) are true.
(e) All the above are true.

3-19 The consequences of converting bonds or preferred stock to common stock are best described by which of the following statements?

(a) Converting an issue to common stock reduces the corporation's risks of going bankrupt because the corporation rids itself of the fixed cost of the coupon interest or cumulative cash dividends on the convertibles.
(b) Converting an issue to common stock may anger those longtime shareholders that hate to experience any decrease in their proportion of voting control in the corporation.
(c) Converting an issue to common stock tends to decrease the earnings per share because the corporation must divide its earnings among the larger number of outstanding shares that exist after the conversion.
(d) Both (b) and (c) are true.
(e) All the above are true.

3-20 Mr. Farley owns 52 percent of the outstanding shares of the Farley Corporation and is chairman of the board. If the Farley Corporation expands by selling a new stock issue that doubles the number of shares outstanding, Mr. Farley's share of ownership and control of the new larger corporation will be what percent if he exercises his preemptive right to the maximum extent permitted?

(a) 13 percent   (c) 52 percent
(b) 26 percent   (d) 100 percent

3-21 Calculate the quarterly rate of return for IBM's common stock for the second quarter of 1979 from the data below. Your assignment is complicated by the 4-for-1 stock split IBM's board of directors declared in June 1979. *Hint:* Remember that every investor owned four times as many shares after the split as before the split.

Year/qtr.	End-of-quarter price	Unadjusted per share cash dividend	Change in unit of account	Adjusted for change Ending price	Adjusted for change Per share cash dividend	Adjusted for change Quarterly return
1979/4Q	$ 64.375	$0.86		$64.375	$0.86	−11.99%
1979/3Q	74.125	0.86		74.125	0.86	2.15
1979/2Q	73.375	3.44	4-for-1	73.375	0.86	?
1979/1Q	315.50	3.44		78.875	0.86	6.54
1978/4Q	298.50	2.88		74.625	0.72	8.56
1978/3Q	277.625	2.88		69.406	0.72	9.04

Which one of the following is correct for IBM's 1979/2Q rate of return?

(a) −76.51 percent   (c) −6.38 percent
(b) −75.65 percent   (d) −5.88 percent

3-22 Merrill Brothers investment banking firm purchased $400 million worth of U.S. Treasury bonds at their initial public offering, stripped the coupons off the bonds, repackaged the cashflows from the pool of bonds for sale as zero coupon bonds, and sold the corpus portion of those bonds for $250 million. How much do you think Merrill will get for the stripped coupons? *Hint:* You might consult F. J. Fabozzi and T. D. Fabozzi, *Bond Markets, Analysis and Strategies* (Englewood Cliffs, N.J.: Prentice-Hall, 1989), chap. 5.

    (*a*) Less than $150 million.
    (*b*) Exactly $150 million.
    (*c*) More than $150 million.
    (*d*) Each of the above is equally likely.

3-23 The General American Corporation's (GAC's) common stock was selling at $80 and its book value was $44 per share when the corporation declared a 100 percent stock dividend. What was GAC's common stock and book value per share immediately after the 100 percent stock dividend?

    (*a*) $60 and $33
    (*b*) $50 and $28
    (*c*) $40 and $22
    (*d*) $30 and $18

PART 2
THE MARKETPLACE

IN THE UNITED STATES and most other countries of the world, securities are bought and sold through mechanisms known as markets, which are run by traders and usually regulated by government. Investors not only go to the market to buy and sell; they also check its movements—the amount of trading and the changes in prices from day to day—to see how their investments are doing and whether it is a good time to adjust their portfolios. The four chapters of this part focus on the market system for securities; later chapters cover the specialized markets for options, futures contracts, and other more complex financial instruments.

Chapter 4 describes the primary and secondary securities markets and how they operate, and the kinds of traders who work in these markets and what they do; it also gives an overview of the emerging global markets. Chapter 5 describes the major market indexes and averages and how they are constructed; it also compares and contrasts the various measures and their uses in making investment decisions.

Chapters 6 and 7 focus on government regulation both of markets and trading (through laws and regulatory agencies) and of individuals (through tax laws and policies). Chapter 6 focuses on the regulation of the markets and on the history of federal securities regulation from the onset of the Great Depression and the Great Crash of 1929 until the present. Chapter 7 describes the federal tax system as it affects investing for both individuals and corporations.

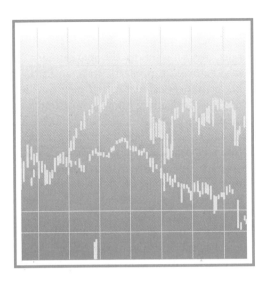

CHAPTER 4

SECURITIES MARKETS

Securities markets are a fast-moving, glamorous, complex, multibillion-dollar business. New York City, London, and Tokyo are the biggest securities markets in the world. Telecommunications link these and other markets so that the whole world now operates as one international securities market. At any hour of the day or night, securities are being traded somewhere in the world.

This chapter initially focuses on the functions, operations, and trading arrangements of securities markets in the United States. Then the discussion is broadened with a look at how securities markets around the world operate. We begin by exploring how securities issues originate in primary markets.

83

4-1 Primary Markets

Billions of dollars worth of new issues are brought to the market each year. A **primary issue** occurs when the issuer gets the cash proceeds from an **initial public offering (IPO)** of stocks or bonds. The agent responsible for finding buyers for IPOs is called an *investment banker.* This name is misleading because investment bankers do not invest their own funds, and they are not at all like commercial banks.

The largest brokerage firms in the United States underwrite new issues, act as brokers, and provide a wide range of financial services. Merrill Lynch, Pierce, Fenner & Smith, for example, has large brokerage operations in the markets for federal government securities, securities issued by agencies of the federal government, municipal bonds, corporate bonds, preferred stocks, common stocks, commodity futures contracts, and put and call options. Merrill Lynch employs 12,300 brokers, but only a few hundred of its highest-paid people do the investment banking.

In contrast, firms like Salomon Brothers and Goldman Sachs, which each employ less than 2000 brokers, are primarily investment banking firms. Salomon Brothers and Goldman Sachs limit their retail brokerage activities to clients with at least a $1 million initial balance. (Merrill Lynch will open an account if the client has as little as $5000.)

Functions of the Investment Banker

Advice Initially, the investment banker serves a potential security issuer in an advisory capacity. The underwriter helps the issuing firm analyze its financing needs and suggests different ways to raise funds. The underwriter may also function as an adviser in mergers, acquisitions, and refinancing operations.

If the issuer and the investment banker agree to proceed with an IPO, further investigations must be conducted by accountants, engineers, and attorneys. Once these experts give their assessments, the investment banking firm draws up a tentative underwriting agreement between the potential issuer and the investment banking house specifying all terms of the issue except the market price for the new security.

The investment banking firm that first reaches an agreement with the issuer is called the **originator** or **managing underwriter.** The originator coordinates two temporary groups in an effort to "float the issue" or, what amounts to the same thing, keep the issue's price from "sinking." Members of the first group, the **underwriting syndicate,** pool their money and share the underwriting risk;

Box 4-1

DEFINITION: Investment Banker

Investment bankers purchase new securities from the issuers and sell these securities to the investing public as quickly as possible. Investment bankers are also called **underwriters** because they insure the issuer against loss from the sale of new securities. Investment bankers help create new issues; they advise IPO clients, handle administrative tasks, underwrite the issue, and distribute the securities.

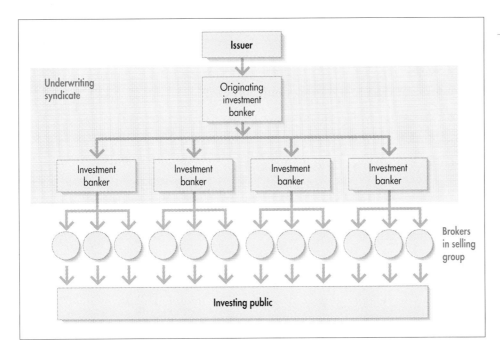

Figure 4-1   Flowchart for a primary offering made through a syndicate of investment bankers.

syndicates range from 5 to 200 investment banking houses, depending on the total dollar value of the issue. The second group, the **selling group,** is made up of brokerage firms that have agreed to sell the primary offering to investors. Figure 4-1 illustrates the relationship between the originator, the underwriting syndicate, and the selling group.

Administration   The investment banker shares with the issuer the responsibility of conforming with the securities laws. This involves preparing the registration statement and prospectus, or applying for an exemption. The Securities and Exchange Commission (SEC) requires that most primary issues be accompanied by a **registration statement,** which must disclose information that will allow potential investors to assess the quality of the new issue. The information that must be published in registration statements is set by law (see Principles Box 4-2). After filing the registration statement with the SEC, there is usually only a brief waiting period until the new issue may be offered for sale. But the SEC may delay approval by requesting additional information, and in these cases the waiting period may last for weeks.

The **prospectus** is a detailed summary of facts about the issuer and is part of the registration statement. Once SEC approval is obtained and the price has been set, the prospectus is reproduced and made available to potential investors. According to SEC requirements, all investors must have a prospectus before they can invest, and every prospectus must disclose all the facts a potential investor needs to evaluate the new securities. SEC approval of the registration statement and the prospectus is not an endorsement of the offering. SEC approval means only that the legally required information has been disclosed.

Box 4-2

PRINCIPLES: The Information Required in an SEC Registration Statement

1. Copy of the issuer's articles of incorporation

2. Purpose for which the proceeds of the issue will be spent

3. Offering price to the public

4. Offering price for special groups, if any

5. Fees promised to developers and/or promoters

6. Underwriter's fees

7. Net proceeds to the issuer

8. Information on the issuer's products, history, and location

9. Copies of any indentures affecting the new issue

10. Names and remuneration of officers in the issuing firm

11. Details about any unusual contracts, such as a managerial profit-sharing plan

12. Detailed statement of capitalization

13. Detailed balance sheet

14. Detailed income and expenses statements for 3 preceding years

15. Names and addresses of the issuer's officers and directors and of the underwriters

16. Names and addresses of any investors owning more than 10 percent of any class of stock

17. Copy of the underwriting agreement

18. Copies of legal opinions on matters related to the issue

19. Details about any pending litigation

Not all issues must be registered with the SEC. Issues from governmental bodies and (if they apply for it) issues from companies regulated by governmental agencies are exempt from registration. Other issues that are likely to be exempt include intrastate offerings, issues that are offered to only a few investors, and issues of less than $1.5 million (the most frequently exempted group). Exemption does not make the issuer and underwriters immune from legal action in case of fraud; it merely simplifies the administrative work.[1]

[1] Shelf registration, an expeditious procedure for registering primary offerings, is discussed in Chapter 6.

Underwriting **Underwriting** refers to the guarantee by the investment banker that the issuer of the new securities will receive a certain amount of cash for them. The brief period between the time the investment banking houses purchase an IPO from the issuer and the time they subsequently sell it to the public is *very risky.* Because of unforeseen changes in market conditions, the underwriters may not be able to sell the entire issue, or they may have to sell it at less than the price they paid for it.

Perhaps the most difficult decision in any IPO is setting the price. The right price is not too low; this would be unnecessarily costly to the issuer. The right price is not too high either; this might cause losses for the underwriters. When the price is right, when the market conditions are good, and when the issuer and the underwriters are reputable, the IPO will "go out the window"—it will be sold in 1 or a few days. When one or more of these conditions is lacking, it may become a **sticky issue;** it may take a week, a month, or even longer to sell, and result in multimillion-dollar losses for the underwriters.

Distribution Investment bankers distribute securities to investors in several ways. As we have seen, they may buy the issue and then sell the securities; this is called an *underwriting.* Or they may simply act as an intermediary in bringing together issuer and investors.

If the investment banker finds one buyer for an entire issue and arranges for a direct sale from the issuer to this large investor, a **private placement** occurs. The investment banker is compensated for bringing buyer and seller together, for helping

Box 4-3

FINANCIAL EXAMPLE: Junk Bond IPOs

Initial issues of high-yield bonds are often used to finance new companies, small companies whose names are not well known, leveraged buyouts (LBOs), and very risky investments. Investment bankers have difficulty finding buyers for these IPOs. Mike Milken, a senior vice president at Drexel Burnham Lambert, was widely recognized as the investment banker who created the $175 billion junk bond market and financed Drexel's incredible development during the 1980s. Unfortunately, Milken's successes did not extend into the 1990s. In 1990 he was given a 10-year jail sentence for securities fraud. As soon as Milken was sentenced the multibillion-dollar Drexel went bankrupt, and the junk bond market collapsed.

During his heyday Milken invested Drexel millions in IPOs of high-yield bonds that other investment bankers turned down. When Milken overpriced an issue or when bad news about an issuer emerged before the syndicate could sell all of a risky IPO to investors, the investment bankers were left holding the bag. When Milken was not able to find buyers for junk bond issues that he originated, Drexel Burnham Lambert suffered millions of dollars of losses and inadvertently became the major investor in these issues. A few of Milken's IPOs were so sticky it took months to sell them, and even then they were sold at much less than Drexel paid for the issue. However, Milken was right more than he was wrong: He earned billions of dollars for Drexel.

Table 4-1
Debt Placement Costs Are Less for Private Placements Than for Public Offerings

Issue size $ millions	Private Placements			Public Issues		
	Underwriting expenses, %	Other expenses, %	Total, %	Underwriting expenses, %	Other expenses, %	Total, %
Under 0.50	1.7%	1.1%	2.8%	7.3%	2.9%	10.2%
0.50 to 0.99	1.4	0.9	2.3	5.5	3.2	8.7
1.00 to 2.99	0.9	0.5	1.4	3.5	2.1	5.6
3.00 to 4.99	0.6	0.4	1.0	1.4	1.3	2.7
5.00 to 9.99	0.6	0.3	0.9	0.9	1.0	1.9
10.00 to 24.99	0.3	0.3	0.6	1.0	0.7	1.7
25.00 and above	0.2	0.2	0.4	0.7	0.4	1.1

Source: A. B. Cohan, *Yields on Corporate Debt Directly Placed,* (Washington, D.C.: National Bureau of Economic Research, 1967), p. 127.

to determine a fair price, and for executing the transaction. Table 4-1 shows that bond issuers, especially small issuers, get their bond issues sold more cheaply by using direct placement rather than public offerings.[2] In some IPOs, the investment banker may agree to distribute new shares on a **best-efforts basis,** while assuming no financial responsibility if all the securities cannot be sold. The banker's charges for best-efforts offerings are typically more than for a direct placement but less than for a fully underwritten public offering.[3] Best-efforts offerings are not common.

Figure 4-2 illustrates the decision alternatives issuer and investment banker must work through as they plan a primary issue.

Pricing   After an underwriting, the investment bankers sometimes must stabilize the price of an IPO during the distribution period to prevent it from drifting downward. The underwriting syndicate's manager supports the price by placing orders to buy the newly issued security at a specified price in a secondary market where the new securities are trading. Although this price support might seem like price-fixing, which is illegal, the SEC approves of it so long as full, prior disclosure of intent to stabilize is made. Price stabilizing is defended on the grounds that if it were not allowed, the syndicate's risk would be greater and the underwriting cost to the issuer would increase. Price-pegging may continue for as long as 30 days after the IPO.

If an IPO has been badly priced, the price stabilization operation will not work. In the most extreme case, the managing underwriter would start buying back every share that had been sold in an effort to keep the price up, and all the underwriters in the syndicate would experience severe losses.

[2] For more information about private placements and public issues see Burton Zwick, "Yields on Privately Placed Corporate Bonds," *Journal of Finance,* March 1980, pp. 23–29. Also see "Two Cheers for 144A", on pp. 117–119, and "The Wiring of 144A", on pp. 219–220, both in the July 1990 issue of *Institutional Investor.*

[3] For more details about best-efforts offerings see Jay R. Ritter, "The Costs of Going Public," *Journal of Financial Economics,* December 1987, pp. 269–282.

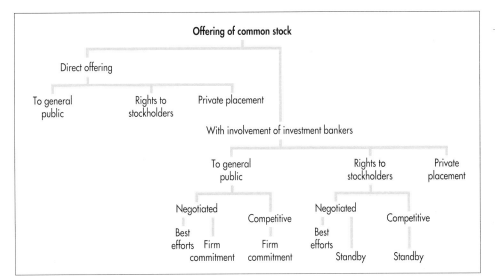

Figure 4-2 The decision alternatives for a primary issue. (*Source:* Adapted from Sanjai Bhagat, "Wealth Effects of Preemptive Rights Removal," *Journal of Financial Economics,* November 1983, p. 290.)

Flotation Costs

To keep down underwriting costs, some issuers solicit bids from competing investment banking firms. The underwriter that offers to pay the highest net cash proceeds for the IPO gets the deal. The law requires that public utility holding companies seek competitive bids for IPOs. Research to determine the advantage of seeking competitive bids versus negotiating with only one investment banker suggests that the issuer gets about the same price for the issue either way.

Investment bankers profit by selling IPOs at prices above what they paid for them. The difference between the buying and selling prices is called the **spread.** A normal spread for a bond issue, for example, is four percentage points. The spread is stated as a percent of the bond issue's face value. The four-percentage-point spread in a bond issue is typically divided as follows:

1. The managing underwriter keeps half of one point for originating and managing the syndicate.

2. The entire underwriting group earns about 1½ percentage points.

3. The members of the selling group earn the remaining two percentage points.

If the managing underwriter sells to the ultimate buyers, that underwriter receives the full four-percentage-point spread, since no other parties are involved.

On a multimillion-dollar issue, the 4 percent spread adds up to a lot of cash. Issuing firms turn many investment bankers into millionaires. Table 4-2 shows the results of surveys of investment banker charges. It is considerably more expensive to issue common stock than to issue the same amount of fixed income securities. A large

CASE

Selecting a Broker

In selecting a firm to be your broker, you might want to choose from among the largest. The accompanying table gives 1990 rankings by total capital. Brokerage houses could be ranked on their ability to make profits. Profit is related to the amount of capital the firm can control, because this is what allows the firm to underwrite bigger deals. Statistics show that the big profits are in underwriting, not in brokering, even though number of offices or number of brokers can be helpful factors. And total capital is more important than equity capital because borrowed capital is equal to equity when a large underwriting must be financed.

Firms like Salomon Brothers and Goldman Sachs (19 and 20 offices, respectively) make much higher profits than firms with many more retail offices, like Edward D. Jones & Co., which in 1990 had 1523 offices. This is because although Salomon and Goldman Sachs do fewer deals, they do much bigger and much more profitable investment banking deals. On the other hand, these firms also require clients to open accounts with large minimum balances, such as $1 million.

So how you make your decision depends on a number of factors: how well the firm is doing, how much money you have to invest, how much time you have to spend monitoring your investments, and the kinds of services you need.

Rank	Name of firm	Total capital, $ millions	Equity capital, $ millions	Long-term debt, $ millions	"Excess" net capital, $ millions
1	Merrill Lynch & Co.	$10,048.4	$3,151.3	$6,897.1	$1,052.8
2	Shearson Lehman Hutton	8,966.0	2,200.0	6,766.0	1,140.0
3	Salomon Brothers Holding Co.	5,757.0	3,906.0	1,851.0	878.7
4	Goldman Sachs & Co.	4,018.0	2,145.0	1,873.0	684.0
5	Morgan Stanley & Co.	2,648.0	2,021.0	627.0	382.7
6	Prudential-Bache Securities	1,840.4	959.5	880.9	275.1
7	First Boston Corp.	1,783.0	1,056.0	727.0	508.0
8	Paine Webber Group	1,523.1	1,001.2	521.9	386.6
9	Bear, Stearns & Co.	1,444.0	1,060.0	384.0	277.0
10	Dean Witter Reynolds	1,429.0	940.0	489.0	604.0
11	Smith Barney, Harris Upham	927.0	758.0	169.0	184.0
12	Donaldson, Lufkin & Jenrette	900.0	289.0	611.0	189.0
13	Kidder, Peabody & Co.	728.0	391.0	337.0	161.0
14	Shelby Cullom Davis & Co.	550.7	550.7	—	397.1
15	BT Securities Corp.	479.0	479.0	—	380.0
16	J. P. Morgan Securities	469.0	469.0	—	264.0
17	Nomura Securities International	376.0	226.0	150.0	153.0
18	Charles Schwab & Co.	344.0	279.0	65.0	77.0
19	A. G. Edwards & Sons	304.0	304.0	—	135.0
20	UBS Securities	293.0	118.0	175.0	185.5

Source: Institutional Investor, "Ranking America's Biggest Brokers," April 1990, p. 91.

part of the investment banking costs is fixed and does not vary with the size of the issue. As a result, considerable economies of scale exist in investment banking. One way of reducing costs is through *preemptive rights offerings,* the subject of the next section.

Table 4-2

Average Underwriting and Administrative Costs as a Percentage of IPO Proceeds

Size of issue, $ millions	Bonds			Preferred stock			Common stock		
	Underwriting commissions	Administrative expenses	Total costs	Underwriting commissions	Administrative expenses	Total costs	Underwriting commissions	Administrative expenses	Total costs
Under 1.0	9.8%	4.0%	13.8%	11.1%*	5.3%*	16.4%*	12.7%	9.1%	21.8%
1.0–1.99	8.0	2.9	10.9	9.5*	3.9*	13.4*	10.9	5.8	16.7
2.0–4.99	4.1	2.0	6.1	5.7*	2.9*	8.6*	8.5	3.9	12.4
5.0–9.99	2.4	.9	3.3	2.1	0.7	2.8	6.4	2.9	9.3
10.0–19.99	1.3	.8	2.1	1.5	.5	2.0	5.1	1.0	6.1
20.0–49.99	1.0	.5	1.5	1.4	.4	1.8	4.2	.5	4.7
50 and over	.9	.3	1.2	1.3	.2	1.5	3.2	.2	3.4

* Lack of information necessitated considerable interpolation to estimate the preferred stock small-issues costs.

Sources: See R. Hillstrom and R. King, eds., "1960–69: A Decade of Corporate and International Finance," Investment Dealers Digest, New York, p. 18. Also see R. Beatty and J. Ritter, "Investment Banking, Reputation, and the Underpricing of Initial Public Offerings," Journal of Financial Economics, vol. 15, March 1986, pp. 213–232; A. J. Chalk, and J. W. Peavy III, "Initial Public Offerings: Daily Returns, Offering Types, and the Price Effect," Financial Analysts Journal, vol. 43, no. 5, 1987, pp. 65–69; R. Rock, "Why New Issues Are Underpriced," Journal of Financial Economics, vol. 15, January–February 1986, pp. 187–212.

An IPO of stock with voting rights can be underwritten and sold to the investing public, or it can be sold to the company's existing investors through a **preemptive rights offering.** Most issues of common stock in countries outside the United States are sold by preemptive rights offerings to reduce the underwriting costs, and to eliminate the possibility that an IPO to the general public will be priced so low that it transfers wealth from the existing shareholders to the new investors. For reasons that investigators have not yet discerned, these **privileged subscriptions,** as they are also called, are not much used in the United States. Table 4-3 contrasts the costs of underwritten and nonunderwritten issues of common stock with and without rights.

Registering a rights offering with the SEC is the same as registering a nonrights issue. However, as Figure 4-2 shows, the issuer must decide how to distribute the shares. In the United States, it is common to grant shareholders one warrant for each share of stock. The terms of the **warrants** granted in each offering differ. For example, an issue of warrants might entitle its holders to use 10 warrants to buy 1 share of the new stock at a favorable exercise price anytime within 25 days. Thus, a stockholder with 10 shares is entitled to purchase 1 new share at the advantageous *exercise price.* (Each such warrant is like a call option on one-tenth of a new share that has a specified exercise price and expires in 25 days.) The warrants may be exercised, sold, or thrown away.

Many of the warrants granted in rights offerings are sold in an active market that lasts until the warrants expire. The warrants will be worthless if the price of the optioned stock is below the exercise price of the warrant. However, it is simple for the issuer to increase the probability that its warrants become profitable to exercise. If the issuer sets the exercise price substantially (for instance, 20 percent) *below* the

Table 4-3
Common Stock Issue Costs Stated as a Percentage
of the Proceeds for Rights and Nonrights Issues

	General Underwritten cash offers			Underwritten rights issues			Nonunderwritten rights issues
	Underwriters'	*Other*	*Total*	*Underwriters'*	*Other*	*Total*	*Total*
Under 0.50	—	—	—	—	—	—	9.0
0.50 to 0.99	7.0	6.8	13.7	3.4	4.8	8.2	4.6
1.00 to 1.99	10.4	4.9	15.3	6.4	4.2	10.5	4.9
2.00 to 4.99	6.6	2.9	9.5	5.2	2.9	8.1	2.9
5.00 to 9.99	5.5	1.5	7.0	3.9	2.2	6.1	1.4
10.00 to 19.99	4.8	0.7	5.6	4.1	1.2	5.4	0.7
20.00 to 49.99	4.3	0.4	4.7	3.8	0.9	4.7	0.5
50.00 to 99.99	4.0	0.2	4.2	4.0	0.7	4.7	0.2
100.00 to 500.00	3.8	0.1	4.0	3.5	0.5	4.0	0.1
Average	5.0	1.2	6.2	4.3	1.7	6.1	2.5

Source: C. W. Smith, "Alternative Methods for Raising Capital: Rights versus Underwritten Offering," *Journal of Financial Economics,* vol. 5, December 1977, pp. 273–307, table 1, p. 277.

market price of the new stock, the warrant is likely to remain profitable (unless the stock price falls more than 20 percent). Issuers want to guarantee that their warrants will be exercised because, if that happens, they get the proceeds from the rights issue needed to expand. To eliminate the possibility that warrants go unexercised, an investment banker can be retained on a standby basis. A **standby underwriting agreement** is a contract in which the issuer pays an investment banker to be ready to support the price of its stock at a level above the exercise price of the warrant. Stated differently, in case the price of the stock falls, the investment banker is paid an insurancelike fee to buy any unsubscribed rights and, if necessary, exercise their warrants.

4-2 Secondary Markets

When investment bankers underwrite IPOs in the *primary market,* the issuers receive the cash proceeds from the sale. The securities continue to trade between investors in a **secondary market,** but the issuers no longer receive any cash proceeds.

Investors usually initiate securities purchases in the secondary markets by calling a securities brokerage firm. After an account has been opened, a broker relays the client's order to a dealer that makes a market in the securities the investor wants.

Securities markets perform a variety of functions:

- Markets *maintain active trading* so investors can buy or sell securities immediately at a price that varies little from transaction to transaction. A continuous market increases the marketability (or liquidity) of the assets traded there.
- Markets *facilitate the* **price-discovery process.** Price is determined by the transactions that flow from investors' demand and supply preferences. Security markets usually make their transactions prices public, and that information helps investors make better decisions.
- Markets indirectly *stimulate new financing.* If it is easy for investors to trade securities in a liquid secondary market, they will be more willing to invest in IPOs.
- To some extent, all securities markets in the United States are **self-regulating organizations.** The markets monitor the integrity of members, employees, listed

Dealers invest own $$
Brokers dont

Box 4-4

> **DEFINITION: Dealers, Market Makers, and Brokers**
>
> A **dealer** is an individual or a firm that puts its own capital at risk by investing in a security in order to carry an inventory and make a market in that security. Dealers that provide other parties with immediate supply and/or demand by trading the security they inventory at posted prices are called **market makers.** **Brokers** are commission salespeople who need not invest their own funds in the securities they sell. Most brokers are employed by dealers.

firms, and clients. Continuous internal audits help guard against unfair trading practices. Market makers willingly pay the costs of the performance reviews and expel dishonest members because they realize that survival depends on a good reputation. (The SEC oversees all securities trading and supplements these self-regulating activities.)

Organized Exchanges in the United States

Our discussion of secondary markets begins with the organized stock exchanges. The New York Stock Exchange (NYSE) is the largest and most widely known, but there is another large organized exchange in New York, the American Stock Exchange (AMEX), plus several regional exchanges. Table 4-4 shows that the NYSE handles about half the volume of shares traded in the U.S. secondary markets. The AMEX follows its next-door neighbor with 3.6 percent of total share volume. The other organized exchanges listed in Table 4-4 (the Midwest, Pacific, Philadelphia, Boston, and Cincinnati Exchanges) are called the **regional exchanges.** Their volume makes up the balance of the trading in exchange-listed stocks. These smaller exchanges provide a valuable market-making service for local businesses and for the issuers of municipal bonds.

Approximately 90 percent of the trading volume on the regional exchanges is in stocks that have **dual listings:** many of the NYSE-listed stocks that trade in high volume can also be bought and sold at one or more of the regional exchanges and/or in the over-the-counter (OTC) market. The regional exchanges thus provide

Table 4-4
Volume of Equity Trading on NYSE, AMEX, Regional
Exchanges, and OTC Markets in the United States, 1989

	Number of shares		*Dollar volume*	
	Millions of shares	*Percent of total*	*Billions of dollars*	*Percent of total*
NYSE	41,699	48.0%	$1,543	67.0%
NASDAQ OTC trading	33,530	38.6	431	18.8
American Stock Exchange	3,125	3.6	44	1.9
OTC's third market	1,794	2.1	66	2.9
Regional stock exchanges:*				
Midwest				
Pacific				
Philadelphia				
Boston				
Cincinnati				
Regionals subtotal	6,733	7.7	217	9.4
Total	86,881	100.0	$2,301	100.0

* For histories of these exchanges see chapter 10 of *The Stock Market*, 5th ed., by R. J. Tewles and E. S. Bradley (New York: Wiley, 1987).

Source: NASDAQ Fact Book 1990, p. 8, an annual of the National Association of Security Dealers.

market-making competition for the NYSE that helps keep brokerage commissions low.

All firms whose stock is traded on an organized exchange must have filed an application for listing. Principles Box 4-5 compares and contrasts the listing requirements on the NYSE, the AMEX, and the over-the-counter market. The

Box 4-5

PRINCIPLES: Listing Requirements

NYSE Listing Requirements

1. Earnings before taxes of at least $2.5 million in the most recent year

2. Earnings before taxes of at least $2 million during the 2 preceding years

3. Net tangible assets of at least $18 million

4. Total market value of common stock of at least $18 million

5. At least 1.1 million publicly held shares outstanding

6. More than 2000 investors holding at least 100 shares each

Summary of listings: The NYSE lists almost 1700 of the largest and best-known corporations.

AMEX Listing Requirements

1. Earnings before taxes of at least $750,000 in the most recent year

2. Net tangible assets of at least $4 million

3. At least 500,000 publicly held shares outstanding

Summary of listings: The AMEX lists almost 900 smaller and younger corporations. (In addition to being a stock market, in recent years the AMEX has become a large put and call option exchange.)

NASD Listing Requirements

1. NASDAQ's National Market System
   a. Net tangible assets of at least $2 million
   b. At least 100,000 publicly held shares outstanding
   c. At least 300 owners of round-lot or larger positions
   d. At least two competing market makers

2. NASD's Supplemental List (or the pink sheets)—lists stocks that are not traded actively enough to be listed in the NASDAQ system.

Summary of listings: About 31,000 of the smallest and youngest corporations are traded over the counter, through the NASD. About 2700 of these are traded actively enough to be listed in the NASDAQ system. Many computer and financial service corporations are NASD stocks.

NYSE has the most stringent listing requirements of all the exchanges. Listing requirements tend to screen out stocks that will not generate enough trading volume for the exchange members to earn significant transactions fees.

Once a company has met the requirements for listing, it must meet certain additional requirements established by the exchange and the SEC. For example, the listed firm must publish quarterly earnings reports, fully disclose financial information annually, and obtain SEC approval of proxy forms before they can be sent to stockholders.

Given the strict requirements, why would corporations seek listings on organized exchanges rather than be traded OTC? One possibility is that a firm may benefit from the publicity. Being listed on an organized exchange and having its trading data reported daily in the newspapers and on television may enhance the prestige of the firm. However, research casts doubts on claims that NYSE- and AMEX-listed securities sell at higher prices or are less risky than OTC stocks.[4]

Organization of the NYSE

The NYSE is the major stock exchange in the United States. Its organization, however, is not superior to that of the OTC or any other securities market. In fact, each market has unique organizational strengths and weaknesses.

The NYSE is a *corporation* led by a board of directors elected by the members of the exchange. The board represents both member firms and the public; it is the chief policy-making body of the exchange. Some of the functions of this powerful body are:

- Approval or rejection of applications of new members
- Acceptance or rejection of budget proposals
- Discipline of members through fines, suspension, or expulsion
- Acceptance or rejection of proposals for new listings
- Submission of requests for changes to the SEC
- Assignment of securities to posts on the trading floor
- Administration of the affairs of the exchange

The main trading floor of the NYSE is about the size of a football field. Bonds and the less actively traded stocks are bought and sold in an annex. Around the edges of both rooms are telephone booths, used primarily to transmit orders and transaction confirmations between the brokers' offices and the exchange floor. On the floor are about 400 (this number varies) assigned **trading posts.** Every one of the 1670 corporations listed on the NYSE (the number changes constantly) is assigned to

---

[4] See Arvind Bhandari, Theoharry Grammatikos, Anil Makhija, and George Papaioannou, "Risk and Return on Newly Listed Stocks: The Post-listing Experience," *Journal of Financial Research,* vol. 12, no. 2 (summer), 1989, pp. 93–102.

be traded at one of these trading posts. Some listed corporations have common stock, preferred stock, bonds, and/or warrants to be traded. About 2200 different securities of various kinds are traded on the NYSE.

NYSE Members

There are 1366 members of the NYSE; this number has remained constant since 1953. Memberships are frequently referred to as *seats,* although trading is conducted without the benefit of chairs. Figure 4-3 is a photograph of the NYSE trading floor. All NYSE members are brokers and/or dealers. In most years there are about 40 sales of exchange memberships, as old members die or retire. Empty seats are auctioned off to a list of bidders that the NYSE has approved for membership. In 1977 a seat sold for as low as $35,000, but by 1987 it had reached a high of $1,150,000. In the early 1990s seat prices dropped below $500,000. The value of the seats varies directly with the amount of income purchasers think they can earn. Commission income in one form or another is a primary determinant of seat price (and the behavior of the NYSE, its members, and the entire securities industry). In addition to the 1366 owned memberships, in recent years another 78 memberships have been rented from the NYSE for about $100,000 per year.

NYSE members can perform one of several specialized functions.

Commission Brokers   Several hundred of the seats on the NYSE are owned by **commission brokers,** agents on the exchange floor who buy and sell securities for clients of brokerage houses. They act like employees of a brokerage house. Commis-

Figure 4-3   Trading on the floor of the New York Stock Exchange.

sion brokers communicate via telephone with brokerages; they receive transactions from the brokerages that employ their services and they send back confirmation messages. They may also act as dealers and seek profits by trading for their own account.

Floor Brokers   Floor brokers are sometimes called **two-dollar brokers** because, for a commission that was $2 per order years ago, they execute orders for commission brokers who have more orders than they can handle. Floor brokers are free-lance members of the exchange. Floor brokers help prevent backlogs of orders, and they allow many firms to operate with fewer exchange memberships than would be needed without their services.

Floor Traders   Floor traders, sometimes called **registered traders,** differ from floor brokers because they trade primarily for their own accounts. Floor traders are speculators who search the exchange floor for profitable buying and selling opportunities. They trade free of commission, since they own their own seats and deal for their own account. As a result, floor traders sometimes buy and sell the same stock on the same day, an activity called **day trading,** in order to profit from small price moves.

When trading accelerates, floor traders sometimes act as floor brokers and may even assist the specialists. However, NYSE rules forbid floor traders from acting as both agent (or broker) and principal (or dealer) for the same stock in the same day. In recent years the number of floor traders has declined sharply.

Specialists   About 400 seats on the NYSE are owned by people called **specialists.** They are assigned to posts on the trading floor, where they "make a market" in one or more stocks assigned to them by the NYSE. These market makers act as both a *broker* and a *dealer* in the stocks assigned to them. As a broker, specialists execute orders for other brokers for a commission. As a dealer, the specialists buy and sell shares of their assigned stock for their own accounts; they put their own capital at risk as they trade.

To become a specialist requires experience, ability as a dealer, a seat on the exchange, selection by the board of directors, and a minimum amount of capital. All specialists are required to have adequate capital to own a position of at least 4000 shares of the stock in which they specialize. Most specialists join others to form **specialist firms.** These help them obtain operating capital and achieve economies of scale in processing paperwork. As a result, most specialists on the floor of the NYSE are members of one of approximately 90 specialist firms.

Specialists make more money, on average, than any other category of NYSE member. However, *specialists must accept the obligation to maintain a fair and orderly market for their assigned stocks*—or they run the risk of losing their position. To keep the market in a stock fair and orderly when there are more buy orders than sell orders, specialists must raise the market price of the security they control or sell shares out of inventory to meet the excess demand. When there are more sell orders than buy orders, specialists must lower the price of the stock or buy shares for their own account in order to equalize supply and demand. Within the limits set by shifts in supply and demand and their desire to earn enough profit to survive, each specialist is continually resetting the market prices for his or her assigned securities.

BID: $42 and ?/8			ASKED: $42 and ?/8	
0/8	4 Wentz 9 Mirandi 3 Dalton		0/8	
1/8	1 Sullivan 4 Jacoby		1/8	
1/4	3 McGovern		1/4	
3/8	2 Gabelli		3/8	
1/2			1/2	
5/8			5/8	3 Dart
3/4			3/4	2 Wu 4 Zachs 2 Theodakis
7/8			7/8	5 Emerson 9 Moran 4 Fallon

Figure 4-4   Computer printout from a specialist's book for a stock with a bid of $42⅜ and $42⅝ asked.

There is a conflict of interest because specialists act as a principal trading for their own self-interest while simultaneously acting as an agent in their role as a monopolistic market maker for other traders. The NYSE denies that this conflict of interest is a problem and points out that, in order to create a level playing field, many specialists let the crowd standing around their post see their specialist books.

NYSE specialists keep a separate **specialist's book,** or **limit order book,** for each stock in which they make a market. These books are administrative diaries used to record unexecuted buy and sell orders that come in from customers. Figure 4-4 shows the pages from a specialist's book that list 1 day's orders for one stock. The information in the book includes the names of the customers, the quantity they want to buy or sell, and the limit on the price at which they want the specialist to execute their transaction. The list of potential trades in the book outlines the supply and demand pressures that determine the price of the security. A monopoly on this valuable information helps specialists set an equilibrium trading price and also earn trading profits for themselves.

The Impact of May Day

The efficiency of the NYSE was improved by competition from other market makers and by a law that took effect on May 1, 1975, a day Wall Streeters call **May Day.** Before May Day, all NYSE member firms charged a substantial brokerage commission on every trade. The NYSE enforced this *fixed minimum commission schedule* because its members thought it would maximize profits. As a result, before May Day the NYSE was a system of monopolistic market makers, since the NYSE specialists never competed with each other by offering to lower their commissions. The NYSE was also a price-fixing cartel, because its commission rates were not negotiable.

The Securities and Exchange Commission decreed that the NYSE must replace its fixed commissions with negotiated commissions on May 1, 1975. The lower commission rates offered by competing market makers from outside also pressed the NYSE to cut its transactions costs. These pressures forced rapid improvements in operational efficiency. The commission rate NYSE brokerages charged for their services dropped approximately 25 percent soon after May Day.

In hindsight it is clear that the high fixed minimum commissions had restricted the exchange's volume of shares traded and lowered the members' profits. After May Day, with lower negotiated commissions, trading volume and member profits soared to new highs year after year.

Liquidity in Secondary Markets

Perfectly liquid assets are perfectly marketable; they suffer no price decrease if they are sold hastily. Cash and demand deposits at a bank are examples of perfectly liquid assets. Real estate is not a liquid asset because sellers typically must grant large price discounts in order to sell it quickly. In addition, real estate brokerage commission rates of 5 to 7 percent must commonly be paid.

Most securities have more "moneyness" than real estate but are not perfectly liquid assets like cash. Investors pay a slightly higher price, called a **liquidity premium,** for assets that are more liquid.[5]

Illiquid assets are assets that cannot be sold quickly unless the seller incurs significant execution (or transaction) costs. **Execution costs** are the costs of transacting; they include:

- Price concessions the seller must grant to the buyer to accomplish a quick sale.

- The bid–asked spread. (Figures 2-1 and 3-2*b* show examples of some bid–asked spreads.) The size of the bid–asked spread varies inversely with the liquidity of a security.

[5] For more detail see Y. Amihud and H. Mendelson, "Liquidity and Asset Prices: Financial Management Implications," *Financial Management,* vol. 17, no. 1 (Spring), 1988, pp. 5–15.

Box 4-6

DEFINITION: Liquidity

In the absence of new information that might affect the supply of or the demand for an asset, **liquidity** is the ability to buy or sell the asset quickly without causing any significant change in its price. Liquidity increases directly with the ease and speed with which something can be converted into cash, or can be bought. Liquidity varies inversely with the costs incurred when buying or selling. The liquidity of a market or the liquidity of an asset usually increases as the volume of trading in it increases.

Box 4-7

101

Chapter 4
Securities
Markets

Four Examples of the Bid Page from a Market Maker's Limit Order Book

Bid price	Examples of possible shares ordered at each bid price			
$50	100	100	500	500
49⅞	200	200	500	500
49¾	0	300	0	700
49⅝	0	300	0	900
49½	0	300	0	1500
Condition of the market	Thin and shallow	Thin and deep	Broad and shallow	Broad and deep

Source: Adapted from Kenneth Garbade, *Securities Markets* (New York: McGraw-Hill, 1982), table 20-1, p. 421.

• The amount of work that is required to find a buyer or seller.

• Brokers' commissions and transfer taxes.

Dealers, market makers, and brokers work together to create markets that are liquid because their work is easier and their cost of doing business is less in liquid markets. Three qualities that **liquid markets** possess are depth, breadth, and resiliency.

• A market has **depth** if buy and sell orders exist (or can be easily uncovered) both above and below the price at which the security is trading. A market that lacks depth is called a **shallow market.**

• A market has **breadth** if buy and sell orders exist in *volume.* Markets that lack the volume of orders needed to provide liquidity are called **thin markets.**

• A market has **resiliency** if new orders pour in immediately in response to price changes caused by temporary order imbalances. A speedy price discovery process is essential for a resilient market.

Breadth, depth, or the lack thereof are illustrated for the bid page of a market maker's limit order book (for instance, a specialist's book) in Example Box 4-7, which illustrates four different sets of bid orders for a security that has $50 as the highest bid price.

The OTC Markets

The phrase "over-the-counter market" originated in the days when securities were bought and sold over the counters in the offices of securities dealers. Today, OTC trades occur in brokers' offices, dealers' offices, homes, cars, trains, and planes and over the phone in all 50 states and in foreign countries. The OTC market is more a way of doing business than a place. The OTC market competes with investment bankers and the organized exchanges because OTC dealers can operate as both a primary and a secondary market.

The geographically decentralized broker-dealer members of the National Association of Securities Dealers (NASD) who trade OTC securities are linked by an international network of telephone lines and computer systems (see also Chapter 6). OTC prices are arrived at through negotiations that take place over these communication lines. This communications system allows investors to select among competing market makers instead of being forced to trade through one monopolistic market maker (such as a NYSE specialist). Although competing market makers will probably all sell any given stock at about the same price, they may offer to execute transactions faster and/or for smaller commission charges.

Securities Traded OTC   Securities traded over the counter range from risk-free U.S. government bonds to the most speculative common stocks. Historically, the OTC markets have been more important as bond markets than as stock markets. Currently, virtually all U.S. government, corporate, and municipal obligations are traded OTC, although U.S. government bonds and many corporation bonds are also traded at organized exchanges. The organized exchanges prefer to trade the stocks of the corporations they list instead of their bonds, because the common stock commission rates are higher.

The OTC stock market is not quite so large as the OTC bond market. Over 31,000 different common stock issues are traded OTC, but many of these issues generate virtually no trading activity because they are shares in small, local corporations that are closely held by the founders' families. Many preferred stock issues are traded OTC, and some of the same securities listed on the NYSE are also being traded OTC in the "third market" (which is discussed below).

OTC Broker-Dealers   Some of the OTC broker-dealers registered with the SEC are organized as sole proprietorships, some as partnerships, and many as corporations. Many have memberships at more than one stock exchange. Some are wholesalers (who buy from and sell to other dealers), some are retailers (selling mostly to the public), and some perform both functions. Dealers who buy and sell a particular security regularly are said to *make a market* in that security (somewhat like the specialists on the NYSE). Broker-dealer firms can be categorized according to their specialties:

- An *OTC house* specializes in OTC issues and rarely belongs to an exchange.

- An *investment banking house* that specializes in IPOs may diversify by acting as dealer in both listed and OTC securities.

- A *commercial bank* or a *trust company* may also be an OTC dealer or broker that deals in U.S. government, state, and local obligations. It might also trade local stocks, and even NYSE-listed stocks.

- A *stock exchange member house* may have a separate department specifically formed to carry on trading in OTC markets.

- Some *bond houses* deal almost exclusively in municipal issues or federal government bond issues that are traded OTC.

The NASDAQ   Bid and asked prices are determined primarily by approximately 500 OTC market-making firms via competitive negotiations. A computerized communications network called NASDAQ connects 50,000 computer terminals operated by these 500 OTC market makers. "NASDAQ" (pronounced "NAZ-dak") is an acronym for National Association of Security Dealers Automated Quotations. NASDAQ provides instantaneous bid and ask prices for about 5000 securities in response to pressing a few keys on a computer terminal.

When an NASD broker or dealer makes an inquiry, the NASDAQ computer and telecommunications system flashes prices on the screen of any terminal linked to NASDAQ's central computer. This allows registered representatives to obtain bid–ask quotations of all OTC market makers in the security they wish to trade. The OTC broker then contacts the dealer offering the best price plus commission total cost and executes a trade. The advantage to investors using this system is the assurance that, although they are usually getting about the same security price from the competing market makers, they can select the trade with the lowest commission cost.

NASDAQ is designed to handle up to 20,000 stocks, but currently lists only about 5000 (still considerably more than the 1700 listed on the NYSE). Not all OTC stocks are listed in NASDAQ, because some are not traded actively enough to be included in the system. Many economists hope that NASDAQ's excess capacity may eventually be put to use by including stocks listed on the exchanges.

The thousands of stock prices quoted in NASDAQ are not all published in daily financial newspapers. To be included in NASDAQ's widely publicized **national daily list,** a stock must have at least three market makers, a minimum of 1500 stockholders throughout the country, and command what NASDAQ calls "significant investor interest." For OTC stocks not included in the national daily list, a more comprehensive quotation service is provided by the National Quotation Bureau (NQB), whose subscribers are primarily security dealers. The NQB quotes prices of over 8000 securities on its daily **pink sheets** using information derived chiefly from OTC dealer firms. The pink sheets are widely disseminated to the investing public.

The Third and Fourth Markets

The **third market** is an OTC market in NYSE-listed stocks. The OTC dealers that make up the third market provide minimal services for their clients—only execution of buy-sell orders and record keeping. These dealers pass on the cost savings they achieve by providing minimal client services in the form of lower commissions.

Direct investor-to-investor trades occur in what is called the **fourth market**—a communications network between block traders. A **block** is a single transaction that involves 10,000 or more shares. Fourth-market participants bypass the normal dealer system. Figure 4-5 illustrates the relationship between the organized exchanges, the OTC market, the third market, and the fourth market.

The fourth-market organizer collects only a small commission or an annual retainer for helping to arrange block transactions. The costs of trading blocks are very

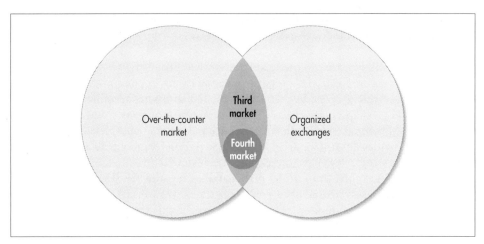

Figure 4-5 Venn diagram of the organized exchanges, the OTC market, and the third and fourth markets.

small (a fraction of 1 percent) relative to the dollar value of the transaction. Traders operating in the fourth market may also obtain a better price through direct negotiation, more rapid executions, and anonymity. Anonymity can be valuable when the General Motors pension fund is buying a block of Ford stock, for instance.

There are several privately owned fourth-market organizations, and each one

Box 4-8

EXAMPLE: Instinet

Instinet* is a fourth-market firm that uses a computer network to connect geographically dispersed terminals. An Instinet subscriber who wants to buy or sell begins by entering the name of the stock, its bid or asked price, respectively, and the desired number of shares into Instinet's computer network, along with a private identification number. This entry is an offer to buy or sell that prints out on the computer terminals of other subscribers around the world. Another subscriber who wants to trade may contact the first subscriber and negotiate via the computer. If the two parties agree on the price and size of a trade, Instinet's computer prints out confirmation slips for both subscribers. The deal is completed without the services of a market maker, who would extract a bid–asked spread and/or charge a commission. The buyers and sellers never even learn each others' identities; this anonymity is valued by some fourth-market clients.

* Instinet is a registered trademark of the Institutional Networks Corporation, 122 E. 42 St., Suite 1001, New York, NY 10168. Instinet is a subsidiary of Reuters, a large international financial news and quotation service. (Telerate, owned by Dow Jones, is the largest of several competitors that Reuters faces in its drive to automate the world's security markets.)

operates somewhat differently. Most use telephones to communicate with institutional customers; others, like Instinet, use computers.

The Block Positioners

A special type of broker called a **block positioner** has developed to line up the multiple buyers needed to purchase a block of securities. Block positioners routinely process multimillion-dollar block transactions and rarely cause the market price of the issue to change significantly. Most block positioners are employees of brokerage firms that own seats on the NYSE. These large firms have both the capital to carry a block in inventory and the connections to distribute it. Block positioners also operate in the third and fourth markets. Some people say that the block positioners operate in the **upstairs market,** meaning an office that trades NYSE-listed stocks but is on floors located above the NYSE-trading floor.

The commission rates charged by block positioners are small; one-fourth of 1 percent is not unusual. In contrast, because economies of scale are not possible in small transactions, odd-lot traders typically incur commission rates of 2 to 6 percent. The low commission rates offered by the block positioners are another source of competitive pressure that helps reduce brokerage commissions.

Discount Brokers

Discount brokerages attract clients by offering lower commissions than the full-service houses. Merrill Lynch, Shearson Lehman Hutton, and Prudential-Bache are examples of **full-service brokerages.** These firms typically require their brokers to be college graduates. They provide free investment research advice for their clients, free safekeeping of the clients' securities, monthly statements, year-end tax summaries, air-conditioned offices that clients may visit, and other customer services that are paid for by their high commission rates. Clients of full-line brokerage firms pay brokerage commission rates (stated as a percent of the market value of the total transaction) approximately equal to those illustrated in Figure 4-6. Essentially, the larger the transaction, the lower the commission rate.

Figure 4-6 Typical common stock commission rates for a full-service brokerage house.

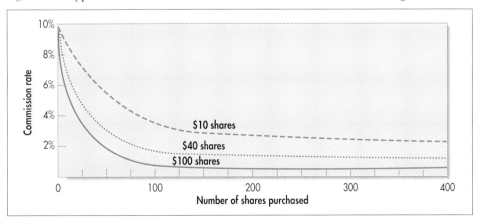

Discount firms do not provide many services and amenities for their clients—they just do the trades and paperwork every brokerage must do. However, their clients pay commission rates only a fraction of those charged by the full-service brokerages. Charles Schwab & Company, Rose & Company, Olde Discount Corporation, and Quick & Reilly are large discount brokerage firms. Trading through a discount brokerage is a good way for investors to reduce transactions costs.

Bond Markets

Municipal bonds are traded OTC. Corporate and Treasury bonds are traded in two secondary markets—the OTC market and organized exchanges. Some exchange members make markets in T-bonds and the bonds of listed corporations. But, most trading in Treasury and corporate bonds takes place in the OTC market.

Issues of corporate and municipal bonds that are placed privately and bond issues that are not rated by agencies like Standard & Poors or Moody's are not marketable. If a bond issue has a quality rating and a dealer quotes bid-asked prices for it, the bond is marketable. But some marketable bond issues are more liquid than others. Active traders want to know how liquid the market is for a bond before they buy.

The marketability of any security is simply determined by measuring the size of the issue's bid-asked (or bid-offer) spread from its quoted prices. If bond dealers quote a spread equal to or less than one-half of 1 percent of the bond's price, the issue is highly marketable (for example, all Treasury issues; see Figure 2-1). In contrast, a bid-asked spread of more than 2 percent indicates low marketability. The primary determinants of the size of the bid-asked spread are the number of dealers competing to make a market in the issue and the volume of trading activity in the issue. Active trading by a number of dealers makes a competitive market in which the bid-asked spreads are small and liquidity is high.

4-3   Making a Trade

In order to manage their portfolios, investors must give their securities brokers orders to execute transactions. There are a number of arrangements from which investors can choose.

Types of Buy and Sell Orders

- *Market orders:* The fastest, most common, easiest, and most surely executed kind of order is a **market order.** A customer instructs the broker to buy or sell specified securities at the best possible price as soon as the order reaches the trading floor of the exchange. Market orders are usually executed immediately. If a market order is sent to a NYSE specialist when the stock exchange is closed, the order is recorded in the appropriate specialist's book to be executed as soon as the market opens (see Figure 4-4).

- *Limit orders:* Both types of limit orders set price limits. A **limit buy order** stipulates the maximum price the investor is willing to pay for some quantity of a

Box 4-9

107

Chapter 4
Securities
Markets

> **FINANCIAL EXAMPLE: Ms. Morgan Guards Her Profits**
>
> Mary Morgan bought stock in the Bellemore Corporation for $50 per share. Its current market price is $75. As a result, Mary's position in the stock has an *unrealized paper profit* of $25 per share. Ms. Morgan fears a drop in the stock's market price might erase her gains, so she calls her broker and gives him a stop order to sell at a market price of $70 per share. This stop order will, in effect, become a market order if Bellemore's price falls to $70. The $70 liquidating price is not guaranteed, however. The stock might be down to $69 or $68 or even lower by the time the market maker can execute Mary's stop order. However, her profits are pretty well protected.

given security. A **limit sell order** specifies the minimum price at which the investor is willing to sell some quantity of a security. If the limit price is not available when a trading order reaches the floor, that order is recorded in the market maker's limit order book and held for execution if and when the limit condition is attained. If an expiration time is affixed to the order, it may expire before it is executed.

- *Stop orders:* **Stop orders,** often called **stop-loss orders,** are designed to protect a customer's existing profit or to limit potential losses. Stop-loss orders instruct a broker to sell certain securities if the price goes down to whatever level the investor specifies.

  The danger of using stop-loss orders is that the investor runs the risk of being **whipsawed**—selling a security with long-run price appreciation that happens to be in a temporary downturn. Stop orders are executed in order of priority, as are all limit orders; i.e., the first stop order received at a given price is the first order executed at that price. The NYSE specialist, e.g., must keep a record of stop orders. An accumulation of stop orders at a certain price can cause a sharp break in the market price of the issue. In such an event, the exchange may suspend the stop orders just when the traders most need the protection.

- *Stop-limit orders:* These orders specify both the stop price and the limit price at which the customer is willing to buy or sell. The customer must be willing to run the risk that the security will not reach the limit price, resulting in no trade. If the trade cannot be executed by the broker when the order reaches the trading floor, the broker will turn the order over to the market maker, who will execute it if the limit price or better is reached.

  A stop-limit order to buy is the reverse of a stop-limit order to sell. As soon as the stock's price reaches the stop level, the order to buy is executed at the limit level or better—that is, below the limit price, if possible. Unfortunately, prices may change so quickly in a fast-moving market that even a well-placed stop-limit order will be passed over without being exercised.

- *Day orders:* Orders to buy and sell can have time limits. A **day order** remains in effect only for the day it is brought to the exchange floor. The vast majority of

Box 4-10

FINANCIAL EXAMPLE: Mr. Morgan's Stop-Limit Order

Tom Morgan owns 2000 shares of a stock that is currently selling at $40, but he fears the price may drop. Tom therefore gives his broker the following order: "Sell 2000 shares at $39 stop, $38 limit." If the price of the stock falls to $39, the broker will immediately try to execute the stop portion of the stop-limit order. If the stop order cannot be executed at $39, it may be executed at the $38 limit price or better. But the stock will not be sold at a price below $38.

---

orders are day orders. At the end of the day it was submitted, a day order is automatically extinguished.

- *Good-till-canceled (GTC) orders:* As its name suggests, a **GTC order** remains in effect indefinitely. It is also called an **open order.** Customers may prefer a GTC order instead of a day order when they are willing to wait until the price reaches some limit they set. GTC orders must be confirmed periodically to remain in effect.

Margin Trading

A new client opening an account at a securities brokerage must choose between a cash account and a margin account. Investors applying for a **cash account** need furnish only their name, address, and social security number, because they must pay cash for any securities they buy. **Margin account** investors are applying to the brokerage for permission to buy securities on credit and, so, must furnish more information. Investors who open a margin account are required by the NYSE to make a minimum initial deposit of $2000, but some brokerages require much larger balances. A minimum initial deposit of $2000 is enough for Merrill Lynch, but Salomon Brothers and Goldman Sachs require $1 million.

Margin trading includes both margin buying and margin short selling. However, only a small portion of total trading on the margin is short selling. (Short selling is discussed in detail in Chapter 20.)

Margin Requirements   When investors buy securities on margin, they buy some shares with cash and borrow from their brokerage to pay for additional shares, using the paid shares as collateral. Investors must pay interest on the amount borrowed. The shares paid for with the investors' money are like the equity (or down payment) on an installment purchase agreement. The Federal Reserve's Board of Governors controls the amount that may be borrowed. If the Federal Reserve Board stipulates a 55 percent margin requirement, for instance, the investor must pay cash for at least 55 percent of the value of the securities purchased. The Federal Reserve's margin requirements have varied from a low of 25 percent in the 1930s to a high of 100 percent in the 1940s. The margin requirement was 55 percent at the time this book was written, but it may be changed at any time.

When discussing margin trading, it is helpful to remember that, when opening a new account, the following terms all mean the same thing:

Margin = initial cash investment = initial equity in a margin account

The amount of money the brokerage firm lends the investor is called the **debit balance** in a margin account. Equation (4-1) measures the percentage margin in an investor's account.

$$\text{Margin percentage} = \frac{\text{AMV} - \text{TD}}{\text{AMV}} = \frac{E}{\text{AMV}} \qquad (4\text{-}1)$$

where AMV = aggregate market value of all securities in the account

TD = total debt, or account's debit

E = equity, or net worth

Box 4-11

EXAMPLE: Trading on 55 Percent Margin

Assume the margin requirement is 55 percent. An investor named Jan Timms, with $5500 of initial cash to invest, purchases a $100 per share stock that pays no cash dividends. Jan sells the stock 1 year after buying it. What kind of an account should Jan open?

Ms. Timms could open a cash account and use the entire $5500 of beginning equity to pay cash for 55 shares. Her $5500 would be fully invested, and she could not buy more shares until she added more cash or sold some securities. Effectively, all cash accounts have 100 percent margin requirements. Ms. Timms could also open a margin account. With a margin account, she could also use her $5500 to purchase 55 shares at $100 each. She could then use these 55 shares as collateral and obtain a loan as large as $4500 from her brokerage firm, and then have as much as $5500 margin + $4500 loan, or $10,000, invested in the stock. Ms. Timms will have borrowed the maximum the 55 percent *initial margin* requirement allows. Consider her positions if the $100 per share stock (*a*) doubles in price to $200 or (*b*) drops by half to $50.

The Good News

If the price of the shares doubles, Ms. Timms will have a nice gain. If she had opened a *cash account,* she will be able to sell for a gain of $100 per share on 55 shares, or $5500, before interest, commissions, and taxes. A *margin account* would have allowed Jan to have up to $10,000 invested in 100 shares. After the price doubled, her profit would be $100 per share times 100 shares, or $10,000, before interest, commissions, and taxes, and the balance in her margin account would be as shown below.

Assets	Liabilities and net worth
Market value . . . $20,000	Debit balance (the loan) . . . $ 4,500
	Equity (Jan's net worth) . . . 15,500
	Total market value $20,000

Note that the investor's debt never changes; Jan's debit remains at $4500. The $10,000 gross gain brings her margin up from an opening value of 55 percent to the higher level of ($15,500 equity ÷ $20,000 total value = .775, or) 77.5 percent. The $10,000 gross gain attained with margin far exceeds the $5500 gross profit that Jan would have earned if she had opened a cash account.

Jan's One-Period Margined Return

When an investor buys on margin, the one-period rate of return, net of interest and commission expenses, is as defined in Equation (4-2).

$$r_t = \frac{p_{t+1} - p_t + d_t - i(1 - m)p_t - C}{mp_t} \qquad (4\text{-}2)$$

where r_t = one-period rate of return per share

p_{t+1} = price per share at end of period

p_t = initial price per share

d_t = dividend per share for the period

i = interest rate

m = margin percent

C = commissions per share

For Jan Timms, the margin percentage m = 55 percent = .55 in Equation (4-2). The denominator, mp_t = (.55)($100) = $55, is the dollar amount of her initial equity investment per share. Jan borrowed $(1 - m)p_t$ = (1 − .55)($100) = $45 per share at an interest rate of i = 10 percent = .10, so the dollar amount of the interest expense is $i(1 - m)p_t$ = ($45)(.10) = $4.50 per share for a 1-year loan. This is deducted from the numerator to obtain the net income return on equity. Assume total broker's commissions C for buying and selling were 30¢ per share and that there were no dividends d_t. Jan's net rate of return on equity is r = 173.1 percent, as shown below:

$$= \frac{\$200 - \$100 + 0 - (10\%)(1.0 - .55)(\$100) - 30¢}{(.55)(\$100)}$$

$$= \frac{\$100 - \$4.50 - 30¢}{\$55} = 1.731 = 173.1\% \text{ net return}$$

(4-3)

Jan Timms' margined gain of $10,000 minus interest and commission expenses equals a 173.1 percent net return on an initial investment of $5500. Favorable financial leverage magnified the 100 percent gain in the stock's price to a 173.1 percent rate of return after all expenses are deducted.

What if the shares decreased in price from $100 to $50 per share? In this case, if Jan Timms had spent $5500 cash to buy 55 shares in a *cash account,* her gross loss would have been $50 per share times 55 shares, or $2750. If she had opened a *margin account* with her $5500 cash, the story would be different. Jan could have used her $5500 cash as margin to obtain a $4500 loan from her brokerage and used the total of $10,000 to buy 100 shares. If the market value of the shares then drops from $100 to $50, Jan loses $50 per share times 100 shares for a $5000 total loss. By buying stock on 55 percent margin, Jan's losses nearly doubled. Her margined account's final position is summarized below:

Assets	*Liabilities and net worth*	
Market value . . . $5,000	Debit balance (the loan) . . . $ 4,500	
	Equity (Jan's net worth). . .	500
	Total market value	$5,000

The gross loss was $5000, plus the interest expense of $450 on a $4500 debit balance. On an initial $5500 margin investment, a total loss of $5,000 + $450 = $5,450 is 99 percent ($5450 loss/$5500 margin = .99) of Jan's equity. Adverse financial leverage magnified the 50 percent price drop into a 99 percent decline in equity. Furthermore, since the margin in her account is now down to only 10 percent ($500 margin/$5000 total value), Jan is below the 55 percent margin requirement. She can expect to receive a "margin call" soon.

A Margin Call   If a margined stock decreases in value sufficiently, the investor will receive a **margin call** from the broker, who will inform the client that it is necessary to put up more margin money. If the investor cannot come up with the additional cash within a day or two, the broker must liquidate enough of the investor's securities to bring the equity in the account up to the legally required minimum. Liquidating the margined client's shares is easy because margin customers must keep their securities deposited at the brokerage house as collateral for their loan. If anything is left in the margin account after the margin call, forced sale, and loan repayment, the investor will receive that remaining balance. You might ask, by how much must a stock decrease in value before there is a margin call?

The New York Stock Exchange has a **maintenance margin requirement,** which stipulates that a margin call must occur when the equity in the account is less than 25 percent of the market value of the account. For Jan Timms, this means a margin call would be required when the market value of her $10,000 margined purchase of common stock falls below $6000. Stated differently, a maintenance margin requirement of 25 percent means the client's loan cannot exceed 75 percent (or $4,500/$6,000) of the account's aggregate market value. The Federal Reserve Board's Regulation T specifies only the initial margin requirement; it has no maintenance requirement. Most brokerage firms set maintenance margin requirements that are between the 25 percent required by the NYSE and the Federal Reserve's initial margin requirement.

Buying on margin allows investors to magnify their gross profits by the reciprocal of the margin requirement (that is, 2 times if the margin requirement is ½, 3 times if it is ⅓, and so forth). The major risk is that it causes magnified losses of the same reciprocal if stock prices decline. There is the added disadvantage of the fixed interest payments. In sum, margin trading increases both potential profits and potential losses.

4-4 Secondary Markets: Global Comparisons

Trading practices in the United States accommodate our economic system and business practices. There are other systems that work equally well. Here we'll look at different market-making procedures around the world and at the advantages and limitations of various types of organization. Table 4-5 summarizes some characteristics of stock markets around the world.

Call, Continuous, and Mixed Markets

In a **call market,** trading orders that come in from clients over a period of time are accumulated into batches and then executed simultaneously. Call markets are used where the volume of trading is not large—in Austria and Norway, for instance. Simultaneous execution is done by crossing all buy and sell orders for the called financial instrument at one price. If that single price is outside the limits stipulated in some orders, those trades are not executed at that call. Unfilled orders may be resubmitted at the next call. It is common to have trading calls once or twice each trading day, and at the same time each day. Each financial instrument traded in the market is called sequentially until the batches of trades for all financial instruments have been cleared.

The stock exchanges in Canada, Britain, and the United States have enough volume to support **continuous markets;** trades are executed anytime during the trading day. It is more convenient for investors to trade in continuous markets because transactions are executed faster and more surely.

Markets that lack the volume to sustain a continuous market but have too much activity to be limited to a call market have developed a compromise. The stock exchanges in Sweden, Switzerland, Denmark, and France have **mixed markets** in which one group of stocks is traded continuously for, say, 10 minutes, and then a different group of stocks is traded continuously for the next 10 minutes. This pattern continues throughout the day until all groups of stocks have been actively traded.

Geographically Fragmented versus Centralized Markets

The NYSE and AMEX are **geographically consolidated markets** that bring together trades from all over the world to be executed on the floors of those exchanges. NASDAQ is a **geographically fragmented market** because the competing market makers operate in 50 different states and several foreign countries. NASDAQ's fragmentation does not diminish its ability to make liquid markets, however. The bid and asked quotes from market makers are brought together in the NASDAQ computer to create one electronically centralized market. Various econo-

Table 4-5
Institutional Arrangements in Stock Markets around the World

Country	Type of auction	Official specialists	Forward trading on exchange	Automated quotations	Program trading	Options/futures trading	Price limits	Transaction tax (round-trip)	Margin requirements	Trading off exchange
Australia	Continuous	No	No	Yes	No	Yes	None	.6%	None	Infrequent
Austria	Call	Yes	No	No	No	No	5%	.3%	100%	Frequent
Belgium	Mixed	No	Yes	No	No	No[a]	10%/None[b]	.375%/.195%	100%/25%[b]	Occasional
Canada	Continuous	Yes	No	Yes	Yes	Yes	None[c]	0	50%[d]	Prohibited
Denmark	Mixed	No	No	No	No	No	None	1%	None	Frequent
France	Mixed	Yes	Yes	Yes	Yes	Yes	4%/7%[e]	.3%	100/20%[f]	Prohibited
Germany	Continuous	Yes	No	No	No	Options	None	.5%	None	Frequent
Hong Kong	Continuous	No	No	Yes	No	Futures	None[g]	.6%+	None	Infrequent
Ireland	Continuous	No	No	Yes	No	No	None	1%	100%	Frequent
Italy	Mixed	No	Yes	No	No	No	10–20%[b]	.3%	100%	Frequent
Japan	Continuous	Yes	No	Yes	Yes	No[i]	−10%	.55%	70%[j]	Prohibited
Malaysia	Continuous	No	No	Yes	No	No	None	.03%	None	Occasional
Mexico	Continuous	No	Yes	No	No	No	10%[k]	0	None	Occasional
Netherlands	Continuous	Yes	No	No	No	Options	Variable[l]	2.4%[m]	None	Prohibited
New Zealand	Continuous	No	No	No	No	Futures	None	0	None	Occasional
Norway	Call	No	No	No	No	No	None	1%	100%	Frequent
Singapore	Continuous	No	No	Yes	No	No[n]	None	.5%	71%	Occasional
South Africa	Continuous	No	No	Yes	No	Options	None	1.5%	100%	Prohibited
Spain	Mixed[o]	No	No	No	No	No	10%[p]	.11%	50%[p]	Frequent
Sweden	Mixed	No	No	Yes	No	Yes	None	2%	40%	Frequent
Switzerland	Mixed	No	Yes	Yes	No	Yes	5%[q]	.9%	None	Infrequent
United Kingdom	Continuous	No	No	Yes	Yes	Yes	None	.5%	None	Occasional
United States	Continuous	Yes	No	Yes	Yes	Yes	None	0	Yes	Occasional

[a] Calls only on five stocks.
[b] Cash/forward.
[c] None on stocks; 3–5% on index futures.
[d] 10% (5%) for uncovered (covered) futures.
[e] Cash/forward; but not always enforced.
[f] Cash/forward; 40% if forward collateral is stock rather than cash.
[g] "Four spread rule": offers not permitted more than four ticks from current bids and asks.
[h] Hitting limit suspends auction, then tried a second time at end of day.
[i] Futures on the Nikkei Index are traded in Singapore.
[j] Decreased to 50% on October 21, 1987, "to encourage buyers."

[k] Trading suspended for successive periods, 15 and then 30 minutes; effective limit: 30–40%.
[l] Authorities have discretion; in October, 2% limits every 15 minutes used frequently.
[m] For nondealer transactions only.
[n] Only for Nikkei Index (Japan).
[o] Groups of stocks are traded continuously for 10 minutes each.
[p] Limits raised to 20% and margin to 50% on October 27, 1987.
[q] Hitting limit causes 15-minute trading suspension. Limits raised to 10–15% in October 1987.

Source: Richard Roll, "The International Crash of October 1987," Financial Analysts Journal, September–October 1988, table 3, p. 29.

mies can be achieved by using a geographically fragmented but electronically centralized market that are not available to exchanges with costly trading floor operations, like the NYSE and the AMEX.

Daily Price Change Limitations

Most stock exchanges in the world, and all stock exchanges in the United States, allow the prices of the traded securities to fluctuate freely. Exchanges in Italy, Spain, Switzerland, Austria, France, and some other countries, however, impose daily price change limitations. If changes in the price of any stock reach that exchange's maximum daily limit, trading is stopped—usually for the rest of that day. These maximum daily limitations range from 4 percent to as much as 20 percent.

Price fluctuation limitations have been used for decades in commodity exchanges in the United States and around the world to control destabilizing price swings. Recently, the NYSE has adopted certain daily price change limitations to prevent another international stock market crash like that of October 1987. These **circuit breakers** call for trading to stop for 1 hour if the Dow Jones Industrial Average (DJIA) drops 250 points during 1 day, to allow the market to consolidate and stabilize, and for 2 hours if the DJIA drops 400 points. Similar circuit breaking procedures have been implemented by the Chicago Mercantile Exchange on its S&P 500 Stocks Index futures contract, because it was felt that trading in this futures contract could destabilize prices of the 500 stocks that are included in the index.

Margin Requirements

In the United States, Federal Reserve regulations mandate a complex array of margin requirements, ranging from tiny down payments for investments in Treasury securities to initial margins of over 50 percent for purchases of common stocks. Security markets in many other countries, including Britain, Australia, and Switzerland, are not subject to margin requirements. At the other extreme, margin requirements are 100 percent in Ireland, Italy, and Austria.

Margin requirements are supposed to restrain speculative excesses financed with borrowed money, but in the United States their administration has been questionable. Although market conditions change continuously, the Federal Reserve does not adjust margin requirements very often. The initial margin requirement for common stocks remained at 50 percent from 1975 until 1992, for instance. In 1985, the U.S. Treasury and the Federal Reserve both asked Congress to transfer responsibility for setting margin requirements from the Federal Reserve to the securities exchanges. Congress has not yet responded to that request.

Crowds, CLOBs, or Specialists?

Members of a commodity exchange in the United States who wish to trade a particular commodity go to a designated floor space, called a **trading ring,** where the commodity exchange requires all trading in that commodity be conducted.[6] Once in

---

[6] Commodity futures contracts and commodity exchanges are the topic of Chapter 22.

the trading ring, traders indicate their desire to buy or sell by public outcry and/or hand signals. Other traders in the same pit, or ring, consummate trades, and clerks immediately communicate the price and quantity of every transaction around the world via telecommunications. Some knowledgeable financial economists have asserted that a *crowd* of traders with similar interests which meets at a designated place provides a better way to make a market than having a monopolistic market maker like a NYSE specialist standing ready to transact at an assigned post. Another way of making markets is to use what is called a CLOB.

CLOB stands for **consolidated limit order book.** A CLOB should contain all limit orders from all exchanges in publicly accessible form so that all traders from all markets can freely transact trades through it. The CLOB can be maintained by administrative assistants (called the *saitori* at the Japanese market, for example), by telecommunications links to a central computer (like NASDAQ), or by some other device. The primary advantages of a CLOB are that all orders would be fully exposed to the market so that none get sidetracked and executed at less than the most advantageous price; the **rules of trading priority** are never violated. These rules state that the highest bidder should always get the trade, and if there is a tie for the highest bid, then the first party to submit the best bid gets the trade.

4-5 Some Conclusions

Today a wide array of market-making procedures are being employed successfully around the world. Some of these markets differ substantially from the NYSE. In addition, competing markets are growing within the United States. Many of these markets, both foreign and domestic, are expanding by taking trading volume away from the NYSE and the AMEX. Furthermore, Congress has ordered changes to make U.S. security markets more competitive (see Chapter 6). All these trends make it clear that there will be changes on Wall Street. Table 4-5 can be viewed as a menu of alternative scenarios suggesting what might lie ahead for secondary markets in the United States.

Summary

Primary securities markets are made by investment bankers who help originate new issues of stocks and bonds. Investment bankers advise clients, handle administrative tasks, underwrite the issue, help make pricing decisions, and distribute the securities. The issuing company receives the proceeds of the sale, less flotation costs. One way of reducing these costs is the preemptive rights offering.

After the distribution is complete and the company has received the proceeds, the securities continue to trade in secondary markets; the issuer receives no benefit from these sales. Secondary markets in the United States perform a number of functions, including maintaining an orderly market, facilitating the price-discovery process, stimulating new financing, and maintaining fair trading practices.

Secondary markets include organized exchanges like AMEX and the NYSE, as well as the electronic OTC market. Firms that work the secondary market range from the more expensive full-service brokerages to discount brokerages that supply basic services. The NYSE is a corporation that regulates its broker or dealer members, who perform a variety of specialized functions: commission broker, floor broker, floor trader, or specialist.

On May 1, 1975, the SEC abolished the fixed minimum commissions that had been the hallmark of organized exchanges like the NYSE; investors have benefited from negotiated commission rates ever since. Dealers, market makers, and brokers work together to create markets that are liquid, markets where assets can be bought and sold quickly without causing any significant change in price.

The OTC market, which is a network of geographically decentralized broker-dealers who trade securities via telephone and computer, competes with organized exchanges. The securities traded OTC range from risk-free government bonds to the most speculative common stocks. A computerized communications network called *NASDAQ* connects the computer terminals operated by OTC market makers and allows for instantaneous worldwide trading. The third market is an OTC market in NYSE-listed stocks; the fourth market is a communications network for investor-to-investor block trades.

In making a trade, investors can choose from a variety of buy and sell orders: market orders, limit orders (buy and sell), stop orders, stop-limit orders, day orders, and good-till-canceled orders. Investors who open accounts at brokerage firms can deal in cash, or buy securities on credit (trade on margin). Margin trading is regulated by law.

The market systems used in the United States are not the only systems; there are call, continuous, and mixed markets; geographically fragmented and centralized markets; markets with limitations on daily price fluctuations; and markets with very different margin requirements. Many of these other markets, both domestic and foreign, are expanding by taking trading volume from the NYSE and the AMEX, and Congress has now ordered changes to make U.S. securities markets more competitive.

**Further
Reading**

Bloch, Ernest, *Inside Investment Banking,* 2d ed. (Homewood, Ill.: Dow Jones–Irwin, 1989).
  This nonmathematical book provides rich detail about investment banking.

Loll, Leo M., and Julian G. Buckley, *The Over-the-Counter Securities Market* (Englewood Cliffs, N.J.: Prentice-Hall, 1981).
  Chapters 8 through 11 describe various securities markets in significant detail. This book is studied by many people who are preparing to take the NASD exam (or Series 7 Exam) to be a registered representative (that is, a securities broker).

National Association Of Securities Dealers, *The NASDAQ Handbook* (Chicago: Probus, 1989).
  This book describes the OTC market and the NASDAQ system and provides a wealth of descriptive statistics.

Schwartz, Robert A., *Equity Markets* (New York: Harper & Row, 1988).
  This book provides a detailed economic analysis of the markets where stocks are traded. Some mathematical statistics are used.

Stigum, Marcia, *The Money Market,* 3d ed. (Homewood, Ill.: Dow Jones–Irwin, 1990).
  This book describes money market securities and explains in easy-to-read, nonmathematical detail how money markets work.

Tewles, Richard J., and Edward S. Bradley, *The Stock Market* (New York: Wiley, 1982).
  This book goes into detail explaining the institutions and practices that make up securities markets in the United States. No mathematics is used.

4-1   Compare and contrast the way that stock prices are determined (*a*) in the OTC market and (*b*) on organized exchanges like the NYSE. (*c*) Do you think that OTC stocks traded through NASDAQ would bring higher prices if they were listed instead on the NYSE?

4-2   "Price pegging assures the investment banking syndicate that no losses will be incurred." Is the preceding statement true, false, or uncertain? Explain.

4-3   (*a*) Do you see any conflict of interest between a stockbroker's roles as a sales representative working to maximize commission income and an investment adviser who is trying to give clients advice to maximize their wealth? (*b*) Does *agency theory* gives us any clues about this situation? *Hint:* See Chapter 19.

4-4   Assume you are a specialist on the floor of an organized exchange like the NYSE or AMEX and that you are operating within the typical specialists' environment. More specifically, assume that (*a*) your exchange's rules for its specialists permit you to trade only to help stabilize the market or to liquidate inventories or short positions accumulated in stabilization operations, (*b*) you cannot accurately anticipate either long- or short-run price trends, and (*c*) you will occasionally encounter very large bids or offers from institutional investors that you must stand ready to execute. In this situation, what would you do to earn the maximum trading profits for yourself in your role as a specialist?

4-5   Who are the people called *floor brokers* within an organized exchange like the NYSE and what do they do?

4-6   What are the advantages and disadvantages of trading on margin instead of paying cash for your trades?

4-7   Some financial economists are critical of the market-making function performed by the specialists on the NYSE and AMEX. These critics have suggested that the United States could attain a better resource allocation if these specialists were replaced by a better market-making system. (*a*) What prompts these criticisms? (*b*) What better market-making system might be devised?

4-8   How do you suppose the market price of Xerox stock would behave if buy orders were allowed to reach the Xerox specialist on the floor of the NYSE only on Tuesdays and Thursdays, and sell orders reached that specialist only on Mondays, Wednesdays, and Fridays? Explain your idea.

4-9   What is the advantage of buying stocks by giving your broker a market order rather than a limit order? What are the disadvantages of this approach?

4-10   During the 1970s the NYSE tried unsuccessfully to get the SEC to outlaw the third market by claiming that it "fragmented" the stock market in the United States. Comment on the NYSE's charge of "market fragmentation."

Problems

4-11   If the initial margin requirement is 60 percent and an investor purchases 500 shares of a $40 per share stock, what is the minimum initial margin that is required for this transaction?

4-12 Reconsider Problem 4-11. If the initial margin requirement were 75 percent, what minimum margin would be required?

4-13 If the margin requirement is 65 percent and an investor intends to purchase 100 shares of $50 per share stock, what is the minimum down payment? Show your calculations.

4-14 Assume an investor purchased a $100 stock on 55 percent margin and then its price rose to $150 in one year and the stock was sold. The interest rate the brokerage firm charged for the loan to make the margined investment was 10 percent. No cash dividends were received while the investor held the stock. What was the investor's one-period rate of return on this transaction, net of all costs? Show your calculations.

4-15 John Jones recently opened a margin account with the Enrichment Services Investment Company (ESIC). ESIC currently has a 65 percent initial margin requirement and a 35 percent maintenance margin. Mr. Jones initially purchased 300 shares of YXZ stock at $50 per share. By how much must the price of YXZ stock decline before a margin call occurs?

4-16 If the price of YXZ from Problem 4-15 falls to $15, how much must Mr. Jones deposit in his brokerage account to maintain the minimum margin requirement?

4-17 If the price of YXZ stock of Problem 4-15 rises to $75 per share, what will Mr. Jones's one-period return be if he purchased the stock on margin? Ignore commission cost, but assume an interest rate of 12 percent and no cash dividends received.

4-18 What would the 1-year return of Mr. Jones be if he did not purchase the stock in Problem 4-17 on margin? Ignore commission cost.

4-19 Consider the four hypothetical numerical examples from a NYSE specialist's book that are listed below. The numbers in the body of the table refer to the number of shares available at each bid price. The highest bid price is $68 per share.

Bid price	Case 1	Case 2	Case 3	Case 4
$68	100	100	600	500
67	100	100	600	600
66	0	200	0	700
65	0	300	0	1000
64	0	300	0	1400

Describe the four cases above in terms of the breadth and depth of each market situation (or the lack of these qualities, called *thinness* and *shallowness*).

4-20 The following formula is used to calculate the percent of margin left in an account based on the current market value of the securities:

$$\text{Current margin} = \frac{\text{current market value of securities} - \text{amount borrowed}}{\text{current market value of securities}}$$

Brokers use the phrase "buying power" to refer to the amount of additional stock that can be purchased with the equity in an existing account. Compute the buying power in the following four accounts if the margin requirements are (*a*) 50 percent; (*b*) 75 percent.

Name of account	Market value of investments	Equity	Margin requirement	
			50%	75%
Robert Able	$ 0	$ 8,000	$16,000	
Thomas Baker	8,000	4,000		
Samuel Jones	20,000	16,000		
Joseph Smith	30,000	10,000		

(c) Why do stock brokers calculate their clients' buying power and lend them money to buy more securities?

4-21 When an investor pays 100 percent cash (or 100 percent margin), the one-period rate of return on the cash account is defined below as r_c.

$$r_c = \frac{\text{price change + cash dividend}}{\text{purchase price}}$$

In contrast, when an investor buys on margin, the rate of return on the margin account is defined below as r_m.

$$r_m = \frac{\text{price change + cash dividend − interest expense}}{\text{investor's down payment (or margin)}}$$

Assuming the margin requirements are 55 percent, calculate the rates of return for both a cash and a margin transaction in which one share of a stock is purchased for $60 when (a) the price doubles to $120 and (b) when the stock's price falls 50 percent to $30. A total of four different rates of return should be calculated. Ignore interest expense, commissions, taxes, and other transaction costs in your calculations.

Matching Questions

4-22 Match the following words and phrases with the definitions listed below.

	Definition
1. Block	A. A booklet of financial facts about the issuer that the SEC legally requires primary issuers to give to prospective investors.
2. Best-efforts offering	B. The market for new issues that investment bankers make.
3. Fourth market	C. An investment banker accepts the responsibility to sell an issue, but not to underwrite the risks of the distribution.
4. Underwriting	D. 10,000 or more shares.
5. Primary market	E. A communications network through which blocks of securities are traded at negotiated prices and low commissions.
6. Prospectus	F. When a dealer buys new securities into inventory and assumes the risks associated with distributing them.

4-23   What are specialists who make markets in a stock at the organized exchanges called?

    (*a*) Brokers.
    (*b*) Dealers.
    (*c*) Market makers in the secondary market.
    (*d*) All the above are true.
    (*e*) Agents of the exchange who control market prices.

4-24   Why do the organized exchanges usually stipulate in their listing requirements that the issuing corporation have some minimum number of shareholders (several hundred to several thousand)?

    (*a*) To prevent manipulation of the stock's price by a handful of people who own most of the stock.
    (*b*) To help ensure that a market for trading the stock exists that is sufficiently large to generate trading fees and commissions to support that stock's market maker.
    (*c*) To make it hard for "corporate raiders" and merger specialists to take over the corporation by enlisting the aid of only a few of the largest stockholders in the corporation.
    (*d*) Both (*a*) and (*c*) are true.
    (*e*) Because stockholders usually become customers for the corporation's products; therefore, if the corporation has numerous stockholders, they will help support its sales at a high and profitable level.

4-25   If the margin requirement is 65 percent and you intend to make an initial purchase of 100 shares of $50 per share stock, what is the minimum cash payment you would be required to make?

    (*a*) $3250   (*d*) $5500
    (*b*) $4100   (*e*) $6500
    (*c*) $4400

4-26   The OTC market is best described by which of the following statements?

    (*a*) It is a market where different prices may be posted by different market makers for the same security instead of having only one price determined by a specialist.
    (*b*) It is a market where unlisted securities are traded.
    (*c*) In order to survive in the OTC market, it is essential to be a member of a trade association called the NASD.
    (*d*) All the above are true.
    (*e*) It is a market where proprietors and partners sell their small companies.

4-27   If an investor pays 50 percent margin for a stock purchased at $80 per share, collects $6 cash dividends, sells the stock at $90, pays interest expense of $4, and incurs commission costs and income taxes of $4 per share, what is the investor's one-period rate of return?

    (*a*) 10 percent   (*d*) 40 percent
    (*b*) 20 percent   (*e*) 50 percent
    (*c*) 30 percent

4-28   Full-service brokerage firms feel pressure to reduce their commission rates from which of the following?

(a) The third market
(b) The fourth market
(c) Discount brokers

(d) Block positioners
(e) All the above

4-29   Block positioners are best described by which one of the following statements?

(a) Sometimes they act as brokers, and sometimes they act as dealers.
(b) They do not trade through the organized exchanges.
(c) Both (a) and (b) are true.
(d) They transact business only in the primary market.
(e) They act only as dealers.

C

4-30   Margin money is defined by which of the following?

(a) The minimum amount of credit that may be borrowed against the margined securities
(b) The maximum amount of credit that may be borrowed against the margined securities
(c) The maximum amount of investor's cash down payment that is required by the margin laws
(d) The minimum amount of investor's cash down payment that is required by the margin laws
(e) Both (a) and (c)

D

4-31   The regional stock exchanges are best described by which one of the following statements?

(a) The regional exchanges have been faster to automate their operations with computers and telecommunications than the NYSE.
(b) Sometimes the same stocks listed at the NYSE can be purchased at a better price plus commission total cost through one of the regional exchanges.
(c) Relative to the NYSE the regional exchanges tend to be slow in the implementation of modern market-making technology.
(d) Both (a) and (b) are true.
(e) None of the above are true.

D

1 stock costs 40

$$\frac{40 + 6 + 10 - 4 - 4}{80} \quad .2$$

$$\frac{90 - 80 + 6 - 4(1 - .5) - 4}{.5(80)} = \frac{10}{40}$$

$$(t =$$

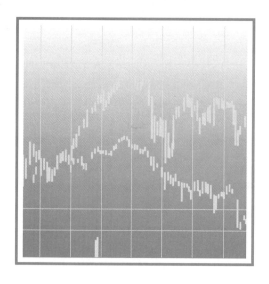

CHAPTER 5

MEASURES OF MARKET PRICE MOVEMENTS

Investors who are too busy to look up the current prices of their assets often ask, "How's the market doing?" One way to answer this question quickly and easily is to consult a security market indicator. The Dow Jones Industrial Average (DJIA) is probably the best-known indicator, the one we hear about on radio during the day and see on the televised business news. The DJIA is quoted and discussed in the business sections of most newspapers, and if it is up or down by very much, it can be front-page news. The Dow Jones Industrial Average is probably the only market indicator most people could name.

But the DJIA is by no means the only indicator available: hundreds of security market averages and indexes are tabulated every day. They include indicators for each different stock market and for various categories within each stock market, bond market indicators for different categories of bonds, commodity indexes for various categories of commodities and for each commodity exchange, and foreign exchange indexes. There are many different market indicators because stock prices may be

Box 5-1

123

Chapter 5
Measures of
Market Price
Movements

DEFINITION: Bull and Bear Markets

A **bull market** is a period of time during which there are usually more buyers than sellers. As a result, the prices of most assets traded in the market are rising. Bull markets may last for as long as several years. For most investors, bull markets are a better time to buy than to sell. In contrast, there is more selling than buying during a **bear market.** As a result, the prices of most assets are falling. Bear markets are usually much shorter than bull markets. Some investors endeavor to buy at the beginning of a bull market, which is delineated by a **trough** in the appropriate market indicator, and sell before the **peak,** which marks the start of a new bear market.

[handwritten: bull prices ↑]

rising, for instance, while bond prices are declining. Each index or average aims to give an indication of the level of prices for some group of market assets.

A well-constructed index uses a significant sample of the population being surveyed, and this sample is selected so that it provides a representative indication of the population of interest. A good index also employs a logical weighting system. For example, an equally weighted securities index indicates how the average investor should do picking stocks randomly. An equally weighted indicator thus serves as a good standard of comparison against which to judge the performance of someone who claimed to be an investment expert. Market indicators have other uses too—some will be explained in this chapter and some in later chapters.

When the consensus view of a particular market or a particular asset is optimistic, a *bull market* is said to be occurring in that market or for that asset. Bullish times are punctuated by periods of prevailing pessimism called *bear markets.* Thousands of investors study market indicators in an effort to delineate bull and bear markets so they will know whether it is a good time to buy or sell.

5-1 Well-Known Indexes and Averages

The DJIA is an average, not an index. A **security market average** can be a weighted or an unweighted average price for a group of securities. Like the averages, stock market indexes also track the average price for a sample of securities. But index calculations are usually more complex.

A **market index** is a series of pure numbers that is devoid of units of measure such as dollars, inches, or pounds. Financial indexes are typically ratios of underlying dollar values; they are used for making comparisons between different index numbers. Index numbers are constructed with a fixed base date and base value. The base date is usually selected to give a meaningful time perspective to the index; the base value is usually set at 100, 10, or 1.

Security market indexes and averages are tabulated and published each day, all over the world, by different organizations for different reasons. Some of the more popular stock market averages and indexes are listed below:

The Dow Jones Industrial Average (DJIA)

The Dow Jones Transportation Average

The Dow Jones Utility Average

Moody's Industrial Average

Moody's Railroad Stock Average

Moody's Utility Stock Average

Standard & Poor's Indexes for 90 different industries

Standard & Poor's 400 Industrial Stocks Index

Standard & Poor's 20 Transportation Stocks Index

Standard & Poor's 40 Utility Stocks Index

Standard & Poor's Financial Stocks Index

Standard & Poor's 500 Stocks Composite Index (S&P 500)

New York Times Index

Value Line Average

Wilshire 5000 Equity Index

New York Stock Exchange Index

Center for Research on Security Prices (CRSP) Index

NASDAQ National Market System Index

American Stock Exchange (ASE) Index

Barron's 50 Stock Average

Nikkei Stock Market Index (from Tokyo)

TSE 300 Composite Index (from Toronto Stock Exchange)

FT-SE, or "Footsie," the Financial Times–Stock Exchange Index (from London)

Europe, Australia, and Far East (EAFE) Index

This list is suggestive, but not exhaustive, for there are even more bond market indexes than there are stock market indicators. One listing shows approximately 400 different bond indexes for corporate bonds, U.S. government bonds, U.S. government-agencies, corporate bonds, municipal bonds, Yankee bonds, Eurodollar bonds, foreign bonds, zero coupon bonds, and high-yield bonds. Salomon Brothers has 45, Standard & Poor's has 15, Shearson Lehman has 36, Moody's has 19, and Merrill Lynch has 95 bond indexes. Dozens of commodity price indexes covering various categories of physical commodities and commodity futures contracts are published. There are also cost-of-living and cost-of-doing-business indexes. The U.S. Department of Commerce disseminates dozens of price indexes monthly. Trade associations, businesses, universities, and foreign countries also publish price indexes and indexes of business activity.

Every index that is compiled is important. Some are incredibly important. For example, all Americans are affected by the consumer price index (CPI), released monthly by the U.S. Department of Commerce. The monthly social security checks received by millions of retirees are indexed to the CPI, the wages of millions of labor union members contain cost-of-living adjustments (called *COLAs*) based on the CPI, and thousands of alimony and child support payments are indexed to the CPI. Furthermore, professional money managers are alert to the monthly CPI announcements, because inflation affects prices (as explained in Chapter 18).

The economic statistics business is a large industry. The U.S. Department of Commerce, the Federal Reserve, Standard & Poor's, Moody's, the economic research departments of large banks, and other organizations employ thousands of people. Since the statistics they calculate affect many people every day, it is important to learn how these statistics are determined and how they should be interpreted.

5-2   Constructing an Indicator: Basic Principles

Market indicators are handy price summaries that have many uses. First, investors can get a quick indication of how market movements affected the market value of their portfolio. Second, market indicators can be used for historical analysis. By analyzing market indexes and other economic indicators, an analyst may detect relationships between different indexes and sectors of the economy. Third, some economic relationships can be used to make predictions. If an index is a dependable *leading index,* for instance, it may be useful for forecasting. Fourth, some people believe that by charting an index over time, it is possible to detect repetitive patterns that may be used to make forecasts. This approach to security analysis is called **technical analysis,** and it is the topic of Chapter 15.

Finally, securities market indexes can form the basis for investment strategies. For instance, a group of mutual funds called **index funds** became popular during the 1980s. The *investment objective of index funds is to invest in the same stocks used to compute some stock market index in order to earn the same return as that market index.* The Standard & Poor's 500 Stocks Composite Index is popular with the stock market indexers.

If it is well constructed, a market index will give a representative and unbiased indication of the prices of the entire population under consideration. A poorly constructed index may be misleading because it is based on a tiny or an unrepresentative sample of the population. In selecting a market index with which to work, or in designing a new index, the following factors should be considered.[1]

1. *Sample size:* The **sample size** should be a significant fraction of the total group being studied, because larger samples usually provide more reliable indications of the direction in which the population is headed.

---

[1] Almost all averages and indexes use arithmetic average computations. A less popular alternative exists, however. Value Line publishes both an arithmetic mean and a geometric mean index of stock prices. (See Appendix 1A about geometric means.) The Kansas City Board of Trade had a futures contract that was originally based on Value Line's geometric mean. Because of complaints about the complicated formula, the contract based on the geometric mean was replaced in February 1988 by a new contract based on Value Line's arithmetic mean. Value Line publishes both the geometric mean index and the arithmetic mean.

2. *Representativeness:* The sample should contain heterogeneous elements so that it can be **representative** of all sections of the population that is being sampled. A sample of securities, for example, should not contain just large firms (unless the index was designed to report only the price behavior of large firms).

3. *Weighting:* The various elements in the sample should be assigned **weights** that correspond to actual investment opportunities. A security might be **market value–weighted** so that its weight would be proportional to the fraction of total market value represented by each firm's outstanding shares. **Equal weights** could be used to represent the probability of selecting any given security randomly. Indexes constructed with value weights or equal weights represent the results of a "no skill" investment strategy and make useful standards of comparison.

4. *Convenient units:* An index should be stated in **units** that are easy to understand and that facilitate answering relevant questions.

5. *Availability:* An index should be easily accessible to many people at a low cost.

In the next section we use these principles to evaluate some real-world stock market indicators.

5-3 Contrasting the DJIA and S&P 500

Since many investors use market indicators to help them make investment decisions, you should know how to evaluate averages and indexes. This section compares and contrasts two famous stock market indicators, the highly publicized DJIA and the Standard & Poor's 500 Stocks Composite Index (S&P 500), on five criteria.

Sample Size   The S&P 500 Index contains 500 common stocks, almost 30 percent of the NYSE-listed stocks. The DJIA is an average of 30 securities and samples less than 2 percent of the NYSE-listed stocks.

The main advantage of a small sample size used to be that it was cheap and easy to tabulate, but with the advent of computerized data bases and sophisticated programs, the advantages of small sample size have disappeared. A small sample is more likely to be affected by **sampling errors**. Suppose, for example, that an ornithologist who went out to study crows observed only one crow, which happened to be an albino.

Representativeness   The 30 blue-chip stocks that make up the DJIA are listed in Table 5-1. Note that the DJIA is made up entirely of large, old, blue-chip, NYSE-listed firms. No small firms, no new firms, and no stocks listed in other markets are used. The S&P 500 includes stocks of large and small, new and old, profitable and unprofitable, NYSE-listed and AMEX-listed companies, and of manufacturing and service corporations. The only disadvantage of using a representative sample is the cost of constructing and maintaining it, costs that are now much less because so much of the work has been computerized.

Table 5-1
The 30 Stocks of the Dow Jones Average (and Their Ticker Symbols)

Allied Signal (ALD)	International Paper (IP)
Aluminum Company of America (AA)	McDonald's (MCD)
American Express (AXP)	Merck (MRK)
American Telephone & Telegraph (T)	Minnesota Mining & Manufacturing (MMM)
Bethlehem Steel (BS)	Navistar (NAV)
Boeing (BA)	Philip Morris (MO)
Chevron (CHV)	Primerica (PA)
Coca-Cola (KO)	Procter & Gamble (PG)
Du Pont (DD)	Sears (S)
Eastman Kodak (EK)	Texaco (TX)
Exxon (XON)	Union Carbide (UK)
General Electric (GE)	USX Corp. (X)
General Motors (GM)	United Technology (UTX)
Goodyear Tire (GT)	Westinghouse (WX)
International Business Machine (IBM)	Woolworth (FW)

Weighting   The S&P 500 weights each security in proportion to the aggregate market value of all its outstanding shares of stock. Market value weights correspond to the investment opportunities each issue of stock provides in the market. The DJIA's weighting system is not so intuitive.

In 1928, when the DJIA was expanded to include 30 stocks, the 30 market prices were simply summed and divided by 30 to obtain the DJIA, as shown below.

$$\text{DJIA}_t = \frac{\sum_{i=1}^{30} p_{i,t}}{\text{divisor}_t} \qquad \begin{array}{l} \text{divisor} = 30 \text{ in } 1928 \\ \text{divisor} = .505 \text{ in } 1990 \end{array} \qquad (5\text{-}1)$$

The symbol $p_{i,t}$ denotes the price of stock i at time period t.

Over the years some of the 30 securities underwent stock splits and stock dividends, and as a result the weights had to be changed. Computation Box 5-2 demonstrates how the weights in an average calculated like the DJIA are changed by stock dividends and splits.[2] The adjustments for stock splits and stock dividends started off allright with the original 30 stocks in 1928, but by the 1990s the divisor of

---

[2] The Dow Jones Industrial Average is explained on p. 5 of the June 28, 1979, *Wall Street Journal* article entitled "Revised Dow Jones Industrials to Add IBM and Merck, Delete Chrysler and Esmark." Dow Jones also gives away a free booklet entitled *The Dow Jones Averages: A Non-Professional's Guide.* Write to Educational Service Bureau, Dow Jones & Company, P.O. Box 300, Princeton, NJ 08540. Half-price student subscriptions to *The Wall Street Journal* can also be obtained through the same address. Also see H. L. Butler, Jr., and R. F. DeMong, "The Changing Dow-Jones Industrial Average," *Financial Analysts Journal*, July-August 1986, pp. 59–62.

Box 5-2

COMPUTATION: How the Divisor for a Three-Stock Average,
Calculated Similarly to the DJIA, Changes When One Stock Is Split

Stock	*Prices just before stock X is split 2 for 1*	*Prices just after stock X is split 2 for 1*
X	$40	$20
Y	30	30
Z	20	20
Total	$90 ÷ 3 = 30	$70 ÷ divisor = 30
Divisor	3	2.333

---

less than 1 resulted in average values that lack intuitive appeal. Box 5-3 illustrates another problem with a price-weighting system: the average fluctuates differently if different stocks experience the same 10 percent increase in price.

Convenient Units   The DJIA ranged between 500 and 3000 points from 1980 to 1990. The Dow Jones Company has explained that each of these points equals about a 7-cent change in the market value of an "average share of stock." Unlike the DJIA, the S&P 500 is an index. It is calculated from a 1941–1943 base value of 10, using the formula

$$\text{S\&P 500} = \frac{\displaystyle\sum_{i=1}^{500} p_{i,t}\, n_{i,t}}{\displaystyle\sum_{i=1}^{500} p_{i,B}\, n_{i,B}} \times 10 \tag{5-2}$$

$$= \frac{p_{1,t}\, n_{1,t} + p_{2,t}\, n_{2,t} + \cdots + p_{500,t}\, n_{500,t}}{p_{1,B}\, n_{1,B} + p_{2,t}\, n_{2,t} + \cdots + p_{500,B}\, n_{500,B}} \times 10$$

where $p_{i,t}$ and $n_{i,t}$ represent the market price per share and number of shares outstanding at time period t for the ith stock issue, $p_{i,B}$ and $n_{i,B}$ stand for the same values during the 1941–1943 base period, and the index is calculated over $i = 1, 2, \ldots, 500$ issues. Note that in the base year (when the subscripts t and B in the formula are equal), the S&P 500 Index equals $1 \times 10 = 10$.

Availability   The S&P 500 Index is widely distributed to those who subscribe to the appropriate Standard & Poor's Corporation publications. The DJIA is published daily by the Dow Jones Company through the two financial newspapers it owns—*The Wall Street Journal* and *Barron's*. Fortunately, business libraries generally have current copies of both the Dow Jones newspapers and the Standard & Poor's publications.

Box 5-3

129

Chapter 5
Measures of
Market Price
Movements

COMPUTATION: How a Price-Weighted Average Reacts to 10% Changes in the Prices of Stocks X and Z

Stocks	Price at time t	If X increases 10%	If Z increases 10%
X	$40	$44	$40
Y	30	30	30
Z	20	20	22
Total	$90	$94	$92
Divisor	3	3	3
Average	30	31.3	30.6
Percent change in three-stock average		4.4%	2.0%

5-4 Revising the Two Indicators: A Historical Perspective

The three main problems that cause an existing index to need revision are (1) adjusting for stock splits, (2) changing the number of stocks in the sample, and (3) making substitutions to replace stocks that disappear (because companies go bankrupt or are swallowed up in a merger, for example). These problems and the effects they have on the DJIA and the S&P 500 are considered next.

Stock Splits

The way that stock splits are reflected in the divisor of an average like the DJIA was explained in Box 5-2. As a result of this weighting procedure, the relative importance of stocks that split is decreased in the computation of the DJIA, and the importance of stocks that have not split increases. There is no economic or statistical logic behind these shifts in the DJIA weights.[3]

The S&P 500 Index is a value-weighted index that handles stock splits logically. It is constructed from presplit and postsplit market prices that nullify the effects of stock dividends or splits. In the S&P 500 Index Equation (5-2), the market price per share of each stock p is multiplied by the number of shares outstanding n. As a result, the S&P 500 Index is unaffected by stock splits. For example, if a stock undergoes a 2-for-1 split, there are twice as many shares outstanding after the split (that is, $2n$ split shares) and the price of each stock is halved (to $p/2$ dollars per split share). The aggregate value of the corporation's outstanding stock is unchanged.

---

[3] See Harold Bierman, Jr., "The Dow Jones Industrials. Do You Get What You See?" *Journal of Portfolio Management,* vol. 15 (Fall), 1988, pp. 58–60.

Box 5-4

COMPUTATION: A Value-Weighted Index with a Base Value of 10 Is Unchanged after Stock X Splits 2 for 1

Just before stock X splits 2 for 1

Stock	Price	Number of shares outstanding	Corporation's aggregate market value
X	$40	1,000,000	$ 40,000,000
Y	30	9,000,000	270,000,000
Z	20	2,000,000	40,000,000
			$350,000,000*

Just after stock X splits 2 for 1

Stock	Price	Number of shares outstanding	Corporation's aggregate market value
X	$20	2,000,000	$ 40,000,000
Y	30	9,000,000	270,000,000
Z	20	2,000,000	40,000,000
			$350,000,000†

* Base value—corresponds to index value of 10.

† Market value after split.

$$\text{Index value just after split} = \frac{\text{after-split value}}{\text{base value}} \times \text{initial index value}$$

$$= \frac{\$350,000,000}{\$350,000,000} \times 10 = 1 \times 10 = 10 \qquad \text{unchanged}$$

$$\begin{array}{c}\text{Total market value} \\ \text{before the split}\end{array} = \begin{array}{c}\text{total market value} \\ \text{after the split}\end{array}$$

$$n \times p = 2n \times \frac{p}{2}$$

Box 5-4 shows that a three-stock, value-weighted index is unaffected by a 2-for-1 split in one of its stocks.

Sample Size

When the DJIA was first constructed in 1884, it contained 12 stocks. The sample size was increased to 20 stocks in 1916, and the present size of 30 was adopted in 1928.

The S&P Composite Stocks Index was first computed in 1923 with a sample of 233 stocks. The sample was gradually increased to 500 stocks by 1957. The total market value of the stocks that form the S&P 500 is equal to approximately 75 percent of the total value of all NYSE stocks. An index based on such a large sample size is not prone to sampling errors.

Substitutions

131

*Chapter 5
Measures of
Market Price
Movements*

Substitutions can be a recurrent and troublesome problem for any price-weighted average or for an index computed from a small sample. Over the decades there have been many substitutions in the DJIA. One of the more interesting involved IBM stock. IBM was *added* to the DJIA in 1932 and then *deleted* in 1939 in order to make room for American Telephone and Telegraph (AT&T). But AT&T is a utility stock. The DJIA is an average of *industrial* stocks; utility stocks should be in the Dow Jones Utility Average. It is not clear why Dow Jones included AT&T in the DJIA. Another perplexing change is the addition of IBM in 1979, after it had been added in 1932 and dropped since 1939.

In the S&P 500 substitutions are of only minor importance because of the small weight given to each individual stock. Stocks are added or deleted only when they are listed or delisted from an exchange or disappear because of mergers or acquisitions.

5-5   Making Comparisons

All the stock market indicators in the United States are highly positively correlated.[4] Table 5-2 shows that the American Stock Exchange, which has the lowest correlations with the other U.S. stock markets, still has a robust .675 for even its lowest correlation coefficient. The other U.S. stock market indicators are even more highly correlated.

---

[4] Correlation coefficients are defined in the appendix to this chapter.

Table 5-2
Correlation Coefficients between Different U.S. Stock Market Indicators
(Monthly Returns from 1975–1988)

	DJIA	S&P 400	S&P 500	NYSE	AMEX	OTCIND	OTCCOMP	CRSPEQ	CRSPV
DJIA	1.0								
S&P 400	.958	1.0							
S&P 500	.953	.977	1.0						
NYSE	.889	.909	.911	1.0					
AMEX	.675	.738	.736	.736	1.0				
OTCIND	.735	.770	.753	.737	.762	1.0			
OTCCOMP	.768	.782	.785	.784	.782	.881	1.0		
CRSPEQ	.937	.944	.945	.940	.844	.743	.801	1.0	
CRSPVW	.944	.949	.959	.956	.853	.765	.813	.922	1.0

Note: DJIA = Dow Jones Industrial Average; S&P 400 = Standard & Poor's 400 Industrial Stocks Index; S&P 500 = Standard & Poor's 500 Stocks Composite Index; NYSE = New York Stock Exchange Index; AMEX = American Stock Exchange Average; OTCIND = Over-the-Counter Index; OTCCOMP = OTC Composite Stocks Average; CRSPEQ = CRSP Equally Weighted Stocks Index; CRSPVW = CRSP Value-Weighted Stocks Index.

Table 5-3
S&P 500 Average Common Stock Rates of Return, 1926–1988

To the end of	1926	1927	1928	1929	1930	1931	1932	1933	1934	1935	1936	1937	1938	1939	1940	1941	1942	1943	1944	1945	1946
1926	11.6																				
1927	23.9	37.5																			
1928	30.1	40.5	43.6																		
1929	19.2	21.8	14.7	-8.4																	
1930	8.7	8.0	-0.4	-17.1	-24.9																
1931	-2.5	-5.1	-13.5	-27.0	-34.8	-43.3															
1932	-3.3	-5.6	-12.5	-22.7	-26.9	-27.9	-8.2														
1933	2.5	1.2	-3.8	-11.2	-11.9	-7.1	18.9	54.0													
1934	2.0	0.9	-3.5	-9.7	-9.9	-5.7	11.7	23.2	-1.4												
1935	5.9	5.2	1.8	-3.1	-2.2	3.1	19.8	30.9	20.6	47.7											
1936	8.1	7.8	4.9	0.9	2.3	7.7	22.5	31.6	24.9	40.6	33.9										
1937	3.7	3.0	0.0	-3.9	-3.3	0.2	10.2	14.3	6.1	8.7	-6.7	-35.0									
1938	5.5	5.1	2.5	-0.9	-0.0	3.6	13.0	16.9	10.7	13.9	4.5	-7.7	31.1								
1939	5.1	4.6	2.3	-0.8	-0.1	3.2	11.2	14.3	8.7	10.9	3.2	-5.3	14.3	-0.4							
1940	4.0	3.5	1.3	-1.6	-1.0	1.8	8.6	11.0	5.9	7.2	0.5	-6.5	5.6	-5.2	-9.8						
1941	3.0	2.4	0.3	-2.4	-1.9	0.5	6.4	8.2	3.5	4.3	-1.6	-7.5	1.0	-7.4	-10.7	-11.6					
1942	3.9	3.5	1.5	-1.0	-0.4	2.0	7.6	9.3	5.3	6.1	1.2	-3.4	4.6	-1.1	-1.4	3.1	20.3				
1943	5.0	4.7	2.9	0.6	1.3	3.7	9.0	10.8	7.2	8.2	4.0	0.4	7.9	3.8	4.8	10.2	23.1	25.9			
1944	5.8	5.5	3.8	1.7	2.5	4.8	9.8	11.5	8.3	9.3	5.7	2.6	9.5	6.3	7.7	12.5	22.0	22.8	19.8		
1945	7.1	6.9	5.4	3.5	4.3	6.6	11.5	13.2	10.4	11.5	8.4	5.9	12.6	10.1	12.0	17.0	25.4	27.2	27.8	36.4	
1946	6.4	6.1	4.7	2.8	3.5	5.6	10.1	11.6	8.8	9.7	6.8	4.4	10.1	7.7	8.9	12.4	17.9	17.3	14.5	12.0	-8.1
1947	6.3	6.1	4.7	3.0	3.7	5.6	9.8	11.2	8.6	9.4	6.7	4.5	9.6	7.5	8.5	11.4	15.8	14.9	12.3	9.9	-1.4
1948	6.3	6.1	4.7	3.1	3.8	5.6	9.6	10.8	8.4	9.1	6.6	4.6	9.2	7.3	8.1	10.6	14.2	13.2	10.9	8.8	0.8
1949	6.8	6.6	5.3	3.8	4.5	6.3	10.1	11.2	9.0	9.7	7.4	5.6	10.0	8.3	9.2	11.5	14.8	14.0	12.2	10.7	5.1
1950	7.7	7.5	6.4	4.9	5.6	7.4	11.1	12.3	10.2	11.0	8.9	7.3	11.5	10.0	11.0	13.4	16.6	16.1	14.8	13.9	9.9
1951	8.3	8.1	7.1	5.7	6.4	8.2	11.7	12.9	11.0	11.7	9.8	8.4	12.4	11.1	12.1	14.3	17.3	16.9	15.9	15.3	12.1
1952	8.6	8.5	7.5	6.2	6.9	8.6	12.0	13.2	11.3	12.1	10.3	9.0	12.8	11.6	12.5	14.6	17.4	17.1	16.1	15.7	13.0
1953	8.3	8.1	7.2	5.9	6.5	8.2	11.4	12.4	10.7	11.4	9.6	8.3	11.9	10.7	11.5	13.4	15.7	15.3	14.3	13.7	11.2
1954	9.6	9.5	8.6	7.4	8.1	9.7	12.9	14.0	12.4	13.1	11.6	10.4	13.9	12.9	13.9	15.8	18.2	18.0	17.4	17.1	15.1
1955	10.2	10.2	9.3	8.2	8.9	10.5	13.7	14.7	13.2	13.9	12.5	11.4	14.8	13.9	14.9	16.8	19.1	19.0	18.5	18.4	16.7
1956	10.1	10.1	9.2	8.2	8.8	10.4	13.4	14.4	12.9	13.6	12.2	11.2	14.4	13.5	14.4	16.1	18.2	18.1	17.5	17.3	15.7
1957	9.4	9.3	8.5	7.4	8.1	9.5	12.3	13.2	11.8	12.4	11.0	10.0	13.0	12.1	12.8	14.3	16.2	15.9	15.2	14.9	13.2
1958	10.3	10.2	9.5	8.5	9.1	10.6	13.3	14.3	12.9	13.6	12.3	11.4	14.3	13.5	14.3	15.8	17.6	17.5	16.9	16.7	15.3
1959	10.3	10.3	9.5	8.6	9.2	10.6	13.3	14.2	12.9	13.5	12.3	11.4	14.2	13.4	14.1	15.6	17.3	17.1	16.6	16.4	15.1
1960	10.0	10.0	9.3	8.3	8.9	10.3	12.8	13.7	12.4	13.0	11.8	10.9	13.5	12.8	13.5	14.8	16.4	16.1	15.6	15.3	14.0
1961	10.5	10.4	9.7	8.8	9.4	10.8	13.3	14.1	12.9	13.4	12.3	11.5	14.1	13.4	14.0	15.3	16.9	16.7	16.2	16.0	14.8
1962	9.9	9.9	9.2	8.3	8.8	10.1	12.5	13.2	12.1	12.6	11.4	10.7	13.0	12.3	12.9	14.1	15.5	15.3	14.7	14.4	13.3
1963	10.2	10.2	9.5	8.7	9.2	10.5	12.8	13.5	12.4	12.9	11.8	11.1	13.4	12.7	13.3	14.5	15.8	15.6	15.1	14.9	13.8
1964	10.4	10.4	9.7	8.9	9.4	10.6	12.9	13.6	12.5	13.0	12.0	11.3	13.5	12.9	13.5	14.5	15.8	15.6	15.2	14.9	13.9
1965	10.4	10.4	9.8	9.0	9.5	10.7	12.9	13.6	12.5	13.0	12.0	11.3	13.5	12.9	13.4	14.5	15.7	15.5	15.0	14.8	13.8
1966	9.9	9.8	9.2	8.4	8.9	10.1	12.2	12.8	11.8	12.2	11.2	10.5	12.6	12.0	12.4	13.4	14.5	14.3	13.8	13.6	12.6
1967	10.2	10.2	9.6	8.8	9.3	10.4	12.5	13.1	12.1	12.5	11.6	10.9	12.9	12.4	12.8	13.8	14.9	14.7	14.2	14.0	13.1
1968	10.2	10.2	9.6	8.9	9.3	10.4	12.4	13.1	12.1	12.5	11.6	10.9	12.9	12.3	12.8	13.7	14.7	14.5	14.1	13.9	13.0
1969	9.8	9.7	9.1	8.4	8.9	9.9	11.8	12.4	11.4	11.8	10.9	10.3	12.1	11.6	12.0	12.8	13.8	13.6	13.1	12.9	12.0
1970	9.6	9.6	9.0	8.3	8.7	9.7	11.6	12.2	11.2	11.6	10.7	10.1	11.9	11.3	11.7	12.5	13.5	13.2	12.8	12.5	11.7
1971	9.7	9.7	9.1	8.4	8.9	9.9	11.7	12.2	11.3	11.7	10.8	10.2	11.9	11.4	11.8	12.6	13.5	13.3	12.8	12.6	11.8
1972	9.9	9.9	9.3	8.7	9.1	10.1	11.9	12.4	11.5	11.9	11.0	10.5	12.1	11.6	12.0	12.8	13.7	13.5	13.0	12.8	12.0
1973	9.3	9.3	8.7	8.1	8.5	9.4	11.1	11.7	10.8	11.1	10.3	9.7	11.3	10.8	11.1	11.8	12.7	12.4	12.0	11.7	10.9
1974	8.5	8.4	7.8	7.2	7.5	8.4	10.1	10.6	9.7	10.0	9.1	8.5	10.1	9.5	9.8	10.5	11.2	10.9	10.5	10.2	9.4
1975	9.0	8.9	8.4	7.7	8.1	9.0	10.6	11.1	10.2	10.6	9.8	9.2	10.7	10.2	10.5	11.1	11.9	11.6	11.2	11.0	10.2
1976	9.2	9.2	8.7	8.0	8.4	9.3	10.9	11.4	10.5	10.9	10.1	9.5	11.0	10.5	10.8	11.5	12.2	12.0	11.6	11.3	10.6
1977	8.9	8.8	8.3	7.7	8.1	8.9	10.5	10.9	10.1	10.4	9.6	9.1	10.5	10.0	10.3	10.9	11.6	11.4	11.0	10.7	10.0
1978	8.9	8.8	8.3	7.7	8.0	8.9	10.4	10.8	10.0	10.3	9.6	9.0	10.4	9.9	10.2	10.8	11.5	11.3	10.9	10.6	9.9
1979	9.0	9.0	8.5	7.9	8.2	9.1	10.6	11.0	10.2	10.5	9.8	9.2	10.6	10.1	10.4	11.0	11.7	11.4	11.1	10.8	10.2
1980	9.4	9.4	8.9	8.3	8.7	9.5	11.0	11.4	10.6	10.9	10.2	9.7	11.1	10.6	10.9	11.5	12.2	11.9	11.6	11.4	10.7
1981	9.1	9.1	8.6	8.1	8.4	9.2	10.6	11.0	10.3	10.6	9.9	9.4	10.7	10.2	10.5	11.1	11.7	11.5	11.1	10.9	10.3
1982	9.3	9.3	8.8	8.3	8.6	9.4	10.8	11.2	10.5	10.8	10.1	9.6	10.9	10.5	10.8	11.3	11.9	11.7	11.4	11.2	10.6
1983	9.6	9.5	9.1	8.5	8.9	9.6	11.0	11.5	10.7	11.0	10.3	9.9	11.1	10.7	11.0	11.5	12.2	12.0	11.6	11.4	10.9
1984	9.5	9.5	9.0	8.5	8.8	9.6	10.9	11.3	10.6	10.9	10.3	9.8	11.0	10.6	10.9	11.4	12.0	11.8	11.5	11.3	10.7
1985	9.8	9.8	9.4	8.9	9.2	9.9	11.3	11.7	11.0	11.3	10.7	10.2	11.4	11.1	11.3	11.8	12.4	12.3	12.0	11.8	11.2
1986	10.0	9.9	9.5	9.0	9.4	10.1	11.4	11.8	11.2	11.4	10.8	10.4	11.6	11.2	11.5	12.0	12.6	12.4	12.1	11.9	11.4
1987	9.9	9.9	9.5	9.0	9.3	10.0	11.3	11.7	11.0	11.3	10.7	10.3	11.5	11.1	11.3	11.8	12.4	12.2	11.9	11.8	11.2
1988	10.0	10.0	9.6	9.1	9.4	10.1	11.4	11.8	11.1	11.4	10.8	10.4	11.6	11.2	11.4	11.9	12.5	12.3	12.1	11.9	11.4

Source: R. G. Ibbotson and Rex A. Sinquefield, *Stocks, Bonds, Bills and Inflation (SBBI): 1982 Edition*, updated in *SBBI 1989 Yearbook*, Ibbotson Associates Inc., 8 South Michigan Ave., exhibit C-1, pp. 200–201.

To the end of	1947	1948	1949	1950	1951	1952	1953	1954	1955	1956	1957	1958	1959	1960	1961	1962	1963	1964	1965	1966	1967
1947	5.7																				
1948	5.6	5.5																			
1949	9.8	11.9	18.8																		
1950	14.9	18.2	25.1	31.7																	
1951	16.7	19.6	24.7	27.8	24.0																
1952	17.0	19.4	23.1	24.6	21.2	18.4															
1953	14.2	15.7	17.9	17.6	13.3	8.3	−1.0														
1954	18.4	20.4	23.0	23.9	22.0	21.4	22.9	52.6													
1955	19.8	21.7	24.2	25.2	23.9	23.9	25.7	41.7	31.6												
1956	18.4	19.9	21.9	22.3	20.8	20.2	20.6	28.9	18.4	6.6											
1957	15.4	16.4	17.7	17.6	15.7	14.4	13.6	17.5	7.7	−2.5	−10.8										
1958	17.5	18.7	20.1	20.2	18.8	18.1	18.1	22.3	15.7	10.9	13.1	43.4									
1959	17.1	18.1	19.3	19.4	18.1	17.3	17.2	20.5	15.0	11.1	12.7	26.7	12.0								
1960	15.8	16.6	17.6	17.5	16.2	15.3	14.9	17.4	12.4	8.9	9.5	17.3	6.1	0.5							
1961	16.5	17.3	18.3	18.3	17.1	16.4	16.2	18.6	14.4	11.7	12.8	19.6	12.6	12.9	26.9						
1962	14.8	15.4	16.1	15.9	14.7	13.9	13.4	15.2	11.2	8.5	8.9	13.3	6.8	5.2	7.6	−8.7					
1963	15.2	15.8	16.6	16.4	15.3	14.6	14.3	15.9	12.4	10.2	10.8	14.8	9.9	9.3	12.5	5.9	22.8				
1964	15.3	15.9	16.6	16.4	15.4	14.7	14.4	16.0	12.8	10.7	11.5	15.1	10.9	10.7	13.5	9.3	19.6	16.5			
1965	15.1	15.7	16.3	16.2	15.2	14.6	14.3	15.7	12.8	11.1	11.6	14.7	11.1	11.0	13.2	10.1	17.2	14.4	12.5		
1966	13.7	14.2	14.7	14.4	13.4	12.7	12.4	13.4	10.7	9.0	9.2	11.7	8.2	7.7	9.0	5.7	9.7	5.6	0.6	−10.1	
1967	14.2	14.6	15.1	14.9	14.0	13.4	13.1	14.2	11.6	10.1	10.5	12.8	9.9	9.6	11.0	8.6	12.4	9.9	7.8	5.6	24.0
1968	14.0	14.5	14.9	14.7	13.8	13.3	13.0	14.0	11.6	10.2	10.5	12.7	10.0	9.8	11.0	8.9	12.2	10.2	8.6	7.4	17.3
1969	13.0	13.3	13.7	13.4	12.5	11.9	11.6	12.4	10.1	8.7	8.9	10.7	8.2	7.8	8.7	6.6	9.0	6.8	5.0	3.2	8.0
1970	12.6	12.9	13.2	13.0	12.1	11.5	11.1	11.9	9.7	8.4	8.6	10.2	7.8	7.5	8.2	6.3	8.3	6.4	4.8	3.3	7.0
1971	12.6	12.9	13.3	13.0	12.2	11.6	11.3	12.0	10.0	8.8	8.9	10.5	8.3	8.0	8.7	7.1	9.0	7.4	6.1	5.1	8.4
1972	12.9	13.2	13.5	13.3	12.5	12.0	11.7	12.4	10.5	9.4	9.5	11.0	9.0	8.8	9.5	8.1	9.9	8.6	7.6	7.0	10.1
1973	11.7	11.9	12.2	11.9	11.2	10.6	10.3	10.8	9.0	7.9	7.9	9.2	7.3	6.9	7.5	6.0	7.4	6.0	4.9	4.0	6.2
1974	10.1	10.2	10.4	10.1	9.3	8.7	8.2	8.7	6.9	5.7	5.7	6.7	4.8	4.3	4.6	3.0	4.1	2.5	1.2	0.1	1.4
1975	10.9	11.1	11.3	11.0	10.3	9.7	9.4	9.9	8.2	7.1	7.1	8.2	6.4	6.1	6.5	5.2	6.3	5.1	4.1	3.3	4.9
1976	11.3	11.5	11.7	11.5	10.8	10.3	9.9	10.4	8.8	7.8	7.9	9.0	7.3	7.1	7.5	6.3	7.5	6.4	5.6	5.0	6.6
1977	10.7	10.8	11.0	10.7	10.0	9.5	9.2	9.6	8.1	7.1	7.1	8.1	6.5	6.2	6.6	5.4	6.4	5.4	4.6	3.9	5.3
1978	10.5	10.7	10.9	10.6	9.9	9.4	9.1	9.5	8.0	7.1	7.1	8.0	6.5	6.2	6.6	5.5	6.5	5.4	4.7	4.1	5.4
1979	10.8	10.9	11.1	10.8	10.2	9.7	9.4	9.8	8.4	7.5	7.6	8.5	7.1	6.8	7.2	6.2	7.1	6.2	5.6	5.1	6.3
1980	11.3	11.5	11.7	11.5	10.9	10.4	10.2	10.6	9.2	8.4	8.5	9.4	8.1	7.9	8.3	7.4	8.4	7.6	7.1	6.7	8.0
1981	10.8	11.0	11.2	10.9	10.3	9.9	9.6	10.0	8.7	7.9	7.9	8.8	7.5	7.3	7.6	6.8	7.6	6.9	6.3	5.9	7.1
1982	11.1	11.3	11.5	11.2	10.7	10.2	10.0	10.4	9.1	8.4	8.4	9.3	8.1	7.9	8.2	7.4	8.3	7.6	7.1	6.8	8.0
1983	11.4	11.6	11.8	11.6	11.0	10.6	10.4	10.8	9.6	8.8	8.9	9.8	8.6	8.5	8.8	8.1	8.9	8.3	7.9	7.6	8.8
1984	11.3	11.4	11.6	11.4	10.9	10.5	10.2	10.6	9.4	8.7	8.8	9.6	8.5	8.4	8.7	8.0	8.8	8.2	7.8	7.5	8.6
1985	11.8	11.9	12.1	11.9	11.4	11.1	10.8	11.2	10.1	9.5	9.6	10.4	9.3	9.2	9.6	8.9	9.7	9.2	8.8	8.7	9.7
1986	11.9	12.1	12.3	12.1	11.6	11.3	11.1	11.4	10.4	9.7	9.8	10.6	9.6	9.5	9.9	9.3	10.1	9.6	9.3	9.1	10.2
1987	11.8	11.9	12.1	11.9	11.4	11.1	10.9	11.3	10.2	9.6	9.7	10.4	9.5	9.4	9.7	9.1	9.9	9.4	9.1	8.9	9.9
1988	11.9	12.0	12.2	12.0	11.6	11.2	11.1	11.4	10.4	9.8	9.9	10.6	9.7	9.6	10.0	9.4	10.1	9.7	9.4	9.3	10.2

To the end of	1968	1969	1970	1971	1972	1973	1974	1975	1976	1977	1978	1979	1980	1981	1982	1983	1984	1985	1986	1987	1988
1968	11.1																				
1969	0.8	−8.5																			
1970	1.9	−2.4	4.0																		
1971	4.8	2.8	9.0	14.3																	
1972	7.5	6.7	12.3	16.6	19.0																
1973	3.5	2.0	4.8	5.1	0.8	−14.7															
1974	−1.5	−3.4	−2.4	−3.9	−9.3	−20.8	−26.5														
1975	2.7	1.6	3.3	3.2	0.6	−4.9	0.4	37.2													
1976	4.9	4.1	6.0	6.4	4.9	1.6	7.7	30.4	23.8												
1977	3.6	2.8	4.3	4.3	2.8	−0.2	3.8	16.4	7.2	−7.2											
1978	3.9	3.2	4.5	4.6	3.3	0.9	4.3	13.9	7.0	−0.5	6.6										
1979	5.0	4.5	5.9	6.1	5.4	3.2	6.6	14.8	9.7	5.4	12.3	18.4									
1980	6.9	6.5	8.0	8.4	7.8	6.5	9.9	17.5	13.9	11.6	18.7	25.2	32.4								
1981	6.0	5.6	6.9	7.2	6.5	5.2	7.9	14.0	10.6	8.1	12.3	14.3	12.2	−4.9							
1982	7.0	6.7	7.9	8.3	7.7	6.7	9.4	14.9	12.1	10.2	14.0	16.0	15.2	7.4	21.4						
1983	7.9	7.7	8.9	9.3	8.9	8.0	10.6	15.7	13.3	11.9	15.4	17.3	17.0	12.3	22.0	22.5					
1984	7.8	7.6	8.7	9.1	8.7	7.9	10.2	14.8	12.5	11.2	14.1	15.4	14.8	10.7	16.5	14.1	6.3				
1985	9.0	8.9	10.1	10.5	10.2	9.6	11.9	16.2	14.3	13.3	16.2	17.6	17.5	14.7	20.2	19.8	18.5	32.2			
1986	9.5	9.4	10.6	11.0	10.8	10.2	12.4	16.4	14.7	13.8	16.4	17.7	17.6	15.3	19.9	19.5	18.5	25.1	18.5		
1987	9.3	9.2	10.3	10.6	10.4	9.9	11.9	15.5	13.9	13.0	15.3	16.3	16.0	13.8	17.3	16.5	15.0	18.1	11.7	5.2	
1988	9.6	9.5	10.6	11.0	10.8	10.3	12.2	15.6	14.1	13.3	15.4	16.3	16.1	14.2	17.2	16.5	15.4	17.8	13.3	10.9	16.8

In spite of the various statistical techniques that are needed to construct a market index, it is easy to construct one for the United States because to a large extent the prices of all common stocks are simultaneously affected by the same basic economic forces. As a result, the various stock market indicators all move together through alternating bull and bear markets, and a poorly constructed average like the DJIA is highly positively correlated with the more scientific S&P 500 index.

Some markets are not so homogeneous as the U.S. stock markets. The commodity markets, for instance, are driven by unrelated and sometimes even opposing forces that determine the prices of the goods traded there. So it is more difficult to construct commodity indexes for the United States than it is to construct stock market indexes. The result is that we can compare some market measures easily, but not others.

The Naive Buy-and-Hold Strategy

One typical question market indexes are used to answer is, "What kind of return can I earn if I invest in a certain type of asset?" Table 5-3 provides some answers for common stock investors. It displays the annual rates of return from the Standard & Poor's 500 Stocks Composite Index for every year and every combination of consecutive years from 1926 to 1988. These returns show what investors who reinvested all cash dividends and paid no income taxes or brokerage commissions would have earned if they did not suffer either bad or good luck. The returns in Table 5-3 are referred to as the *returns from a naive buy-and-hold strategy.* These common stock returns were converted to the price indexes illustrated in Figure 5-1. (Tables 5-2 and 5-5 contain other statistics that describe the results of different naive buy-and-hold strategies.)

The Standard & Poor's 500 Stocks Composite Index (S&P 500) represents a naive buy-and-hold portfolio constructed with a value-weighting system. Its market value weights correspond to the investment opportunities that each issue of stock in the market provides an unskilled stock picker.

The **equally weighted index** is another example of a naive buy-and-hold portfolio. Box 5-6 shows that an equally weighted index can be constructed by computing an unweighted average of the one-period of rates of return from different assets.

Box 5-5

DEFINITION: Naive Buy-and-Hold Strategy

Naive buy-and-hold strategy is an umbrella term for different nonaggressive and uninformed approaches to the management of investments. A portfolio selected by a blindfolded investor who chose assets by throwing an unaimed dart at the stock exchange listing page in a newspaper and then held this portfolio regardless of whatever new information became available is a naive buy-and-hold portfolio. Such portfolios are used as standards of comparison against which other investment strategies may be compared.

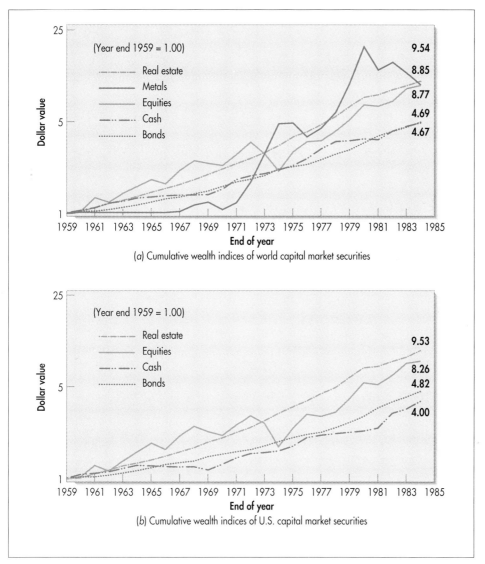

Figure 5-1 Illustrations of average wealth cumulations from $1 invested in different categories of assets from the United States and the whole world, 1960–1984. (*Source:* Roger G. Ibbotson, Laurence Siegel, and Kathryn S. Love, "World Wealth: Market Values and Returns," *Journal of Portfolio Management*, Fall 1985, figs. 5 and 6, p. 10.)

Contrasts among Different Market Measures

The correlations between the stock market indicators in Table 5-2 are all high and positive. In contrast, the correlations between the heterogeneous markets shown in Table 5-4 are lower, for several reasons. Many of the items are real, physical goods that are good inflation hedges (such as grains, meats, gold and silver, and real estate). In

Table 5-4
World Capital Market Security Returns Correlation Matrix

	NYSE	AMEX	OTC	U.S. total equities	Europe equities	Asia equities	Other equities	Foreign total equities	World equities	U.S. Treasury notes	U.S. Treasury bonds	U.S. agencies	U.S. total government bonds
NYSE	1.000												
AMEX	0.851	1.000											
OTC	0.900	0.897	1.000										
U.S. equities	0.997	0.883	0.929	1.000									
Europe equities	0.618	0.689	0.651	0.640	1.000								
Asia equities	0.237	0.123	0.244	0.237	0.391	1.000							
Other equities	0.792	0.848	0.766	0.807	0.731	0.320	1.000						
Foreign equities	0.656	0.657	0.666	0.672	0.908	0.695	0.765	1.000					
World total equities	0.955	0.879	0.914	0.964	0.787	0.409	0.853	0.841	1.000				
U.S. Treasury notes	0.105	-0.102	-0.117	0.068	-0.159	-0.108	-0.252	-0.192	-0.037	1.000			
U.S. Treasury bonds	0.091	-0.153	-0.094	0.056	-0.130	-0.005	-0.266	-0.165	-0.041	0.904	1.000		
U.S. agencies	0.007	-0.201	-0.187	-0.030	-0.280	-0.178	-0.342	-0.327	-0.156	0.962	0.904	1.000	
U.S. total government bonds	0.033	-0.183	-0.189	-0.006	-0.201	-0.067	-0.296	-0.226	-0.105	0.972	0.950	0.964	1.000
U.S. intermediate-term corporate bonds	0.361	0.078	0.132	0.322	0.099	0.045	-0.028	0.072	0.242	0.900	0.865	0.848	0.887
U.S. long-term corporate bonds	0.341	0.058	0.110	0.302	0.095	0.022	-0.033	0.052	0.219	0.858	0.912	0.808	0.859
U.S. total corporate bonds	0.361	0.083	0.132	0.323	0.117	0.033	-0.019	0.075	0.243	0.865	0.902	0.809	0.863
U.S. total bonds	0.206	-0.047	-0.031	0.166	-0.045	-0.007	-0.160	-0.074	0.075	0.954	0.956	0.915	0.967
Foreign domestic corporate bonds	0.044	0.025	0.107	0.050	0.315	0.269	-0.028	0.314	0.156	0.035	0.172	-0.008	0.085
Foreign domestic government bonds	0.010	0.078	0.097	0.024	0.345	0.084	0.058	0.255	0.115	0.061	0.190	0.044	0.117
Foreign crossborder bonds	0.270	0.116	0.172	0.255	0.253	0.154	0.017	0.215	0.249	0.560	0.716	0.552	0.607
Foreign total bonds	0.042	0.067	0.112	0.052	0.343	0.153	0.028	0.281	0.144	0.097	0.239	0.072	0.153
World total bonds	0.136	0.035	0.069	0.124	0.248	0.122	-0.041	0.194	0.155	0.511	0.619	0.473	0.561
U.S. business real estate	0.159	0.227	0.138	0.164	0.268	0.218	0.243	0.332	0.233	0.262	0.036	0.179	0.206
U.S. residential real estate	0.123	0.213	0.090	0.125	0.207	-0.080	0.356	0.141	0.133	0.068	-0.039	0.095	0.066
U.S. farm real estate	-0.164	-0.093	-0.223	-0.171	-0.097	-0.003	-0.063	-0.065	-0.139	-0.315	-0.256	-0.273	-0.267
U.S. real estate total	0.054	0.166	0.006	0.054	0.156	-0.033	0.288	0.129	0.083	-0.051	-0.138	-0.024	-0.040
U.S. Treasury bills	-0.055	-0.063	-0.160	-0.070	-0.169	-0.157	-0.101	-0.153	-0.114	0.395	0.111	0.328	0.325
U.S. commercial paper	-0.112	-0.130	-0.210	-0.127	-0.211	-0.176	-0.150	-0.199	-0.174	0.394	0.115	0.348	0.330
U.S. total cash	-0.064	-0.080	-0.170	-0.079	-0.178	-0.159	-0.112	-0.162	-0.125	0.400	0.119	0.340	0.332
Foreign total cash	-0.393	-0.355	-0.289	-0.386	-0.127	0.009	-0.270	-0.107	-0.311	-0.203	-0.183	-0.154	-0.143
World total cash	-0.225	-0.240	-0.284	-0.238	-0.212	-0.115	-0.225	-0.180	-0.242	0.270	0.032	0.237	0.236
Gold	-0.094	-0.024	-0.067	-0.088	0.032	0.046	0.140	0.044	-0.058	-0.277	-0.252	-0.178	-0.206
Silver	-0.093	0.374	0.142	0.116	0.052	-0.181	0.410	-0.020	0.070	-0.131	-0.140	-0.064	-0.109
World total metals	-0.093	-0.011	-0.064	-0.086	0.032	0.036	0.152	0.039	-0.058	-0.279	-0.253	-0.177	-0.207
U.S. market wealth portfolio	0.915	0.837	0.831	0.917	0.605	0.209	0.754	0.626	0.886	0.214	0.162	0.139	0.152
Foreign market wealth portfolio	0.493	0.498	0.544	0.510	0.823	0.602	0.556	0.865	0.678	-0.086	0.021	-0.201	-0.083
World market wealth port. (excl. metals)	0.853	0.799	0.814	0.861	0.782	0.406	0.765	0.815	0.914	0.109	0.119	0.007	0.066
World market wealth port. (incl. metals)	0.747	0.723	0.727	0.757	0.706	0.351	0.753	0.732	0.805	-0.010	0.016	-0.059	-0.023

	U.S. intermediate corporate bonds	U.S. long-term corporate bonds	U.S. total corporate bonds	U.S. total bonds	Foreign corporate bonds	Foreign government bonds	Cross-border bonds	Foreign total bonds	World total bonds	Business real estate	Residential structures	Farm real estate	Total U.S. real estate
U.S. intermediate-term corporate bonds	1.000												
U.S. long-term corporate bonds	0.941	1.000											
U.S. total corporate bonds	0.960	0.996	1.000										
U.S. total bonds	0.956	0.956	0.962	1.000									
Foreign domestic corporate bonds	0.211	0.263	0.264	0.180	1.000								
Foreign domestic government bonds	0.203	0.269	0.266	0.192	0.890	1.000							
Foreign cross-border bonds	0.741	0.814	0.807	0.721	0.626	0.628	1.000						
Foreign total bonds	0.260	0.326	0.323	0.242	0.950	0.985	0.689	1.000					
World total bonds	0.635	0.693	0.692	0.646	0.829	0.860	0.866	0.895	1.000				
U.S. business real estate	0.335	0.107	0.152	0.192	0.165	0.249	0.203	0.228	0.256	1.000			
U.S. residential real estate	0.085	-0.039	-0.030	0.017	0.091	0.293	0.108	0.225	0.191	0.493	1.000		
U.S. farm real estate	-0.252	-0.255	-0.273	-0.274	0.176	0.103	0.049	0.125	-0.013	0.016	0.214	1.000	
U.S. real estate total	-0.004	-0.129	-0.123	-0.082	0.164	0.303	0.123	0.256	0.172	0.518	0.916	0.570	1.000
U.S. Treasury bills	0.336	0.094	0.135	0.244	-0.269	-0.224	-0.060	-0.240	-0.091	0.685	0.428	-0.053	0.389
U.S. commercial paper	0.313	0.070	0.108	0.230	-0.289	-0.232	-0.078	-0.254	-0.108	0.655	0.462	-0.040	0.415
U.S. total cash	0.339	0.096	0.136	0.247	-0.265	-0.217	-0.054	-0.234	-0.085	0.681	0.447	-0.046	0.405
Foreign total cash	-0.191	-0.225	-0.225	-0.192	0.616	0.617	0.101	0.608	0.393	0.231	0.317	0.306	0.399
World total cash	0.222	-0.005	0.029	0.141	0.048	0.080	0.007	0.065	0.106	0.705	0.528	0.096	0.529
Gold	-0.235	-0.316	-0.323	-0.280	0.001	0.107	-0.046	0.062	-0.079	0.219	0.586	0.517	0.684
Silver	-0.150	-0.177	-0.187	-0.153	-0.286	-0.054	-0.076	-0.136	-0.177	0.188	0.532	0.351	0.580
World total metals	-0.239	-0.318	-0.326	-0.282	-0.011	0.104	-0.047	0.056	-0.085	0.220	0.596	0.526	0.696
U.S. market wealth portfolio	0.446	0.367	0.393	0.284	0.153	0.171	0.395	0.191	0.288	0.394	0.422	-0.019	0.371
Foreign market wealth portfolio	0.192	0.221	0.236	0.080	0.723	0.687	0.517	0.718	0.603	0.329	0.174	-0.008	0.177
World market wealth port. (excl. metals)	0.390	0.354	0.377	0.231	0.431	0.428	0.504	0.455	0.471	0.407	0.365	-0.014	0.332
World market wealth port. (incl. metals)	0.238	0.193	0.207	0.093	0.380	0.426	0.404	0.429	0.389	0.390	0.552	0.133	0.531

	U.S. Treasury bills	U.S. commercial paper	U.S. total cash	Foreign total cash	World total cash	Gold	Silver	World total metals	U.S. market wealth portfolio	Foreign market wealth portfolio	World market (excl. metals)	World market (incl. metals)
U.S. Treasury bills	1.000											
U.S. commercial paper	0.990	1.000										
U.S. total cash	0.999	0.995	1.000									
Foreign total cash	-0.008	0.033	0.010	1.000								
World total cash	0.881	0.895	0.891	0.460	1.000							
Gold	0.179	0.256	0.210	0.419	0.366	1.000						
Silver	0.125	0.127	0.123	-0.203	-0.014	0.438	1.000					
World total metals	0.177	0.253	0.207	0.401	0.355	0.999	0.477	1.000				
U.S. market wealth portfolio	0.133	0.088	0.130	-0.233	0.013	0.104	0.291	0.111	1.000			
Foreign market wealth portfolio	-0.254	-0.298	-0.258	0.218	-0.122	0.025	-0.110	0.018	0.533	1.000		
World market wealth port. (excl. metals)	-0.033	-0.083	-0.037	-0.059	-0.053	0.075	0.142	0.077	0.925	0.812	1.000	
World market wealth port. (incl. metals)	-0.014	-0.027	-0.004	0.105	0.046	0.427	0.283	0.427	0.873	0.727	0.924	1.000

Source: Roger G. Ibbotson, Laurence Siegel, and Kathryn S. Love, "World Wealth: Market Values and Returns," *Journal of Portfolio Management* (Fall), 1985, table 5, pp. 19–20.

Box 5-6

COMPUTATION: The One-Period Return for an Equally Weighted Three-Stock Average

Stocks	Price at time t	Price at time t + 1	One-period rate of return	Weights	Return times weight
X	$40	$44	+10%	.333	+3.33%
Y	30	30	0	.333	0
Z	20	18	−10	.333	−3.33%
Totals:				1.0	0

Weighted average return = 0

contrast, bonds are *monetary* assets that are denominated in fixed dollar amounts that cannot change with inflation. Bonds are bad inflation hedges. Furthermore, bond prices do not rise with the rising profits that characterize periods of economic boom. The prices of common stocks typically do appreciate considerably whenever profits are increasing. Different economic forces drive commodity, bond, and common stock prices in different directions. These examples suggest why the correlations among the different types of markets shown in Table 5-4 differ.

The correlations among different common stock market indicators shown in Table 5-2 are all high and positive because they all represent domestic U.S. stock market indexes; the same factors simultaneously tend to affect the prices of all the underlying common stocks. Economic recessions in the United States, for example, usually bring lower levels of corporate profits and reduced cash dividends that lead to selling off of common stock investments and lower prices for almost all domestic stocks. Such "chain reactions" tend to move all common stock prices together *systematically.*

Table 5-5 contains summary statistics calculated from the different investment indexes. The geometric mean rate of return,[5] the arithmetic average rate of return, and the standard deviations of the year-to-year rates of return for each different index are given in Table 5-5. The geometric mean and the arithmetic mean are two similar but slightly different ways of calculating the average rate of return. The standard deviation is a statistic that measures the variability of returns the investment experienced—it is a *risk measure.* Risky investments have larger standard deviations than safe investments.

By comparing the average return and risk statistics in Table 5-5 and the correlation coefficients in Table 5-4, an investor can gain insights into the different investment possibilities, which otherwise would take years of experience to accumulate.

---

[5] The geometric mean rate of return is defined in Appendix 1A.

Table 5-5
Risk and Average Return Statistics for
Different Categories of Investments, 1960–1984*

Asset category	Geometric mean return†	Arithmetic mean return	Standard deviation of returns
Common stocks			
United States			
NYSE	8.71%	9.99%	16.30%
AMEX	7.28	9.95	23.49
OTC	11.47	13.88	22.42
U.S. total	8.81	10.20	16.89
Foreign			
Europe	7.83	8.94	15.58
Asia	15.14	18.42	30.74
Other	8.14	10.21	20.88
Foreign total	9.84	11.02	16.07
Common stock total	9.08	10.21	15.28
Bonds			
U.S. corporate			
Intermediate-term	6.37	6.80	7.15
Long-term	5.03	5.58	11.26
U.S. corporate total‡	5.35	5.75	9.63
U.S. government			
Treasury notes	6.32	6.44	5.27
Treasury bonds	4.70	5.11	9.70
U.S. agencies	6.88	7.04	6.15
U.S. government total	5.91	6.10	6.43
U.S. total	5.70	5.93	7.16
Foreign			
Corporate domestic	8.35	8.58	7.26
Government domestic	5.79	6.04	7.41
Cross-border	7.51	7.66	5.76
Foreign total	6.80	7.01	6.88
Bonds total	6.36	6.50	5.56
Cash equivalents			
United States			
Treasury bills	6.25	6.29	3.10
Commercial paper	7.03	7.08	3.20
U.S. cash equivalents total	6.49	6.54	3.22
Foreign	6.00	6.23	7.10
Cash total	6.38	6.42	2.92

* See Table 5-4 for the correlation coefficients among these assets' rates of return.

† See Appendix 1A about the geometric mean return.

‡ Including preferred stock.

Table 5-5 *(continued)*

Asset category	Geometric mean return†	Arithmetic mean return	Standard deviation of returns
Real estate§			
Business	8.49	8.57	4.16
Residential	8.86	8.93	3.77
Farm	11.86	12.13	7.88
Real estate total	9.44	9.49	3.45
Metals			
Gold	9.08	12.62	29.87
Silver	9.14	20.51	75.34
Metals total	9.11	12.63	29.69
U.S. total wealth portfolio	8.63	8.74	5.06
Foreign total wealth	7.76	8.09	8.48
World wealth portfolio			
Excluding metals	8.34	8.47	5.24
Including metals	8.39	8.54	5.80
U.S. inflation rate	5.24	5.30	3.60

§ U.S. only.

Source: Roger G. Ibbotson, Laurence Siegel, and Kathryn S. Love, "World Wealth: Market Values and Returns," *Journal of Portfolio Management* (Fall), 1985, table 4, p. 17.

Summary

Security market indicators fall into two major categories—averages and indexes. Market indexes (like the S&P 500) are usually more scientific measures than market averages (like the DJIA) for several reasons: (1) the indexes have been constructed with explicit consideration given to the logic of the weighting system, (2) the indexes have been developed with base years to facilitate comparisons, and (3) the index is usually in more convenient units of measurement (such as percent changes) than an average of dollar prices, which becomes distorted over the years by differing rates of price gains.

After a good average or index is selected, it must be properly maintained. Securities market indexes must be adjusted for stock dividends and splits so that these changes in the unit of account do not distort the index. Additions and substitutions in the list of assets being sampled should be made judiciously.

Averages and indexes are constructed for many reasons. Some security market indicators are designed to represent a naive buy-and-hold strategy. These can be used as standards of comparison for evaluating the skills of professional investment managers. Hundreds of other security market indicators have been created to track the prices of selected market assets. Economic indicators are used to measure things like the level of business activity in various sectors and the rates of inflation for meaningful categories of goods. They are all tools for the investor to use in making wise buy and sell decisions.

Fabozzi, Frank J., and Gregory M. Kipnis, eds., *The Handbook of Stock Index Futures and Options* (Homewood, Ill.: Dow Jones–Irwin, 1989).

> Chapter 7, entitled Stock Market Indicators, explains details about stock market index construction.

Ibbotson Associates, *Stocks, Bonds, Bills and Inflation: 1989 Yearbook* (Chicago: Capital Market Research Center, 1989).

> This annual book presents an easy-to-read explanation of how different security market and economic indicators are constructed, with the aid of a little freshman college algebra. Graphs and tables of the summary statistics lend themselves to comparisons that will be insightful to astute investors. Annual data from 1926 to 1989 are presented.

Ibbotson, R. G., R. C. Carr, and A. W. Robinson, "International Equity and Bond Returns," *Financial Analysts Journal*, July-August 1982, p. 66.

> Empirical data about international investments in common stocks and bonds are compiled and analyzed to provide a helpful selection of international indexes. No mathematics is used in this easy-to-read article.

Ibbotson, Roger G., Laurence Siegel, and Kathryn S. Love, "World Wealth: Market Values And Returns," *Journal of Portfolio Management* (Fall), 1985.

> This easy-to-read article suggests how worldwide diversified investments in both real and monetary assets performed over the 1960 to 1984 sample period.

Teweles, Richard J., and Edward S. Bradley, *The Stock Market*, 5th ed. (New York: Wiley, 1987).

> Chapter 18 is an easy-to-read, nonmathematical discussion of stock market averages and indexes. The chapter ends by explaining how the Dow theory (about charting stock prices in hopes of finding revealing patterns) uses stock market averages.

Essay Questions

5-1   What is the difference between (*a*) a stock market average and (*b*) a stock market index?

5-2   Compare and contrast the following two weighting systems that are frequently used in the construction of stock market indexes: (*a*) equal weights; (*b*) market value weighting. Define each of them. For what purposes are these different weighting systems appropriate?

5-3   What is a naive buy-and-hold strategy? Have any stock market indicators been constructed to correspond to such an investment strategy? Would a serious investor ever follow a naive buy-and-hold strategy? If so, explain why.

5-4   Consider the two following stock market indicators: (*a*) Standard & Poor's 500 Stocks Composite Index (S&P 500) and (*b*) the Dow Jones Industrial Average (DJIA). Which of these market indicators is better? Why?

5-5   If you were searching for a stock market index to track a portfolio of small new growth stocks, would you be better off using a value-weighted or an equally weighted index? Explain why.

5-6   Consider briefly the 30 individual stocks that make up the Dow Jones Industrial Average (DJIA). *Hint:* See Table 5-1. Can you think of a new name that would be more appropriate for the DJIA? If so, explain.

5-7 The Laspeyres (L) and the Paasche (P) price index formulas are well known in economics. These two indexes are formulated below as security market indicators.

$$L = \frac{\sum_i p_{i2}\, w_{i1}}{\sum_i p_{i1}\, w_{i1}} \qquad P = \frac{\sum_i p_{i2}\, w_{i2}}{\sum_i p_{i1}\, w_{i2}}$$

The subscripts refer to time periods $t = 1$ and $t = 2$ when the securities' prices (denoted p) and the securities' weights (represented by w) in the two specific indexes were established. You can think of $t = 1$ as representing some historical base date for the index and $t = 2$ as representing some later date that is of interest. Which of these two indexes would be more appropriate for a stock market index? Explain why. *Hint:* What do the two different weighting systems imply? (No outside research is needed here, but it is permitted if you are having trouble with the question.)

Problems

5-8 Consider forming a stock price index from the three common stocks listed below. These three stocks were selected to expedite the computations because they (*a*) issued no additional shares and (*b*) had no stock dividends or splits. Cash dividend payments are ignored in the computation of this price index.

Stock	Base period market price, July 1, 1960	More-recent-period market price, July 1, 1991	Percentage price change	Total shares outstanding on both dates
Mite	$20	$70	+250%	10,000
Middie	40	60	+ 50	50,000
Maxum	60	80	+ 33	100,000

(*a*) If the new three-stock index is value-weighted, what will its value be on July 1, 1991? (*b*) If the new three-stock index is price-weighted, what will its value be on July 1, 1991? (*c*) If the new three-stock index is equally weighted, what will its value be on July 1, 1991? (*d*) Compare and contrast the value-weighted, the price-weighted, and equally weighted index numbers you obtained from the same three stocks and explain why they differ.

5-9 Consider the effect of a 10 percent change in the price of one stock on the computation of the following hypothetical three-stock portfolio.

Stock	Price at time period $t = 0$	Price at time period $t = 1$ Low-price change	Price at time period $t = 1$ High-price change
Ace	$ 80	$ 80	$ 88*
Black	50	50	50
Case	20	22†	20
Total	$150	$152	$158
Divisor	3	3	3
Average	50	50.66	52.66
Percent change in the average		1.3%	5.3%

* $80 (1.1) = $88.
† $20 (1.1) = $22.

To what do you attribute the fact that the average rose 1.3 percent when the price of Case's stock rose 10 percent, but the same average rose 5.3 percent when the price of Ace went up 10 percent? What implications do your findings have for the DJIA?

5-10   The Gurlz Cloz Corporation's (GCC) stock has had the following returns the past 10 years: 20%, −5%, 35%, 5%, 10%, −10%, 25%, 2%, 15%, and 18%. Calculate Gurlz Cloz stock's (a) average return, (b) standard deviation of returns, and (c) geometric mean return over the 10-year period. (See Appendix 1A for the formula for the geometric mean return.)

5-11   (a) Calculate the standard deviation of IBM's stock returns with the following data:

Year/quarter	IBM's quarterly return
1984/Q3	18.53%
1984/Q4	−.02
1985/Q1	4.04
1985/Q2	−1.69
1985/Q3	.99
1985/Q4	26.42

(b) Calculate IBM's geometric mean return.

Multiple Choice Questions

5-12   What considerations are relevant when either constructing a new market indicator or selecting an existing one?

   (a) The size of the sample used to compute the index
   (b) The representativeness of the securities in the sample   *E*
   (c) Whether the index is stated in units of measurement that are convenient
   (d) Whether or not the weighting system used is rational
   (e) All the above

5-13   The weights used in constructing a value-weighted stock market index are best described by which of the following statements?

   (a) The same (or equal) weights are assigned to every security in the index.
   (b) The weight assigned to each stock is proportional to its price per share.   *C*
   (c) The share price of every stock in the index is multiplied times the number of shares outstanding to determine the weight of that issue based on its total value stated as a proportion of the aggregate market value of all the stocks in the index.
   (d) The weight assigned to each stock in the index is proportional to the number of shares that that issue has outstanding, stated as a proportion of the aggregate number of shares outstanding for all issues that make up the index.
   (e) Both (a) and (d) are true.

5-14   Standard & Poor's 500 Stocks Composite Index is best characterized by which one of the following statements?

   (a) It is constructed from a large sample size.
   (b) It employs a representative sample of stocks.   *E*
   (c) It suggests the results from using a naive buy-and-hold strategy to invest.
   (d) Both (a) and (b) are true.
   (e) All the above are true.

5-15 Summary statistics like the ones shown in Figure 5-1 and Tables 5-3 and 5-5 are best described by which of the following statements?

(a) If the statistics are calculated over a long sample period that includes several complete business cycles, they may be representative of the market's long-run equilibrium tendencies.

(b) If the statistics are calculated over sample periods so short that they do not include at least one complete business cycle, they are unique summary statistics that will probably be unrepresentative of any long-run equilibrium relationships.

(c) Geometric mean rates of return will be larger than arithmetic mean returns calculated on the identical sample.

(d) Both (a) and (b) are true.

(e) All the above are true.

5-16 A weighted or unweighted mean stock price is called which one of the following?

(a) An index (d) A base number
(b) An average (e) None of the above
(c) A parameter

5-17 Stock price indexes can provide which of the following kinds of information?

(a) The prices of individual securities
(b) Aggregate corporate profits
(c) Historical price levels
(d) An indication of future prices
(e) All the above

5-18 The Dow Jones Industrial Average is best described by which one of the following statements?

(a) It has a tiny sample size.
(b) It is constructed from an unrepresentative sample of only blue-chip stocks.
(c) It is measured in inconvenient units.
(d) It is calculated with an arbitrary and confusing weighting system.
(e) All the above are true.

5-19 Maintaining and continually updating a stock price index is made difficult by which of the following problems?

(a) Stock splits and stock dividends.
(b) Substitutions for troublesome stocks.
(c) Necessity of using a significant sample size.
(d) All the above.
(e) The computational costs can rise to unbearably high levels if the index is to be computed frequently (for example, several times each trading day) and/or the sample size is large.

5-20 All stock market indexes for the different stock markets in the United States are most accurately characterized by which of the following statements about the degree to which they covary together?

(a) They are perfectly positively correlated.
(b) They are highly positively correlated.
(c) They are uncorrelated.
(d) They are negatively correlated.
(e) It is impossible to generalize—some are highly positively correlated and some are negatively correlated.

APPENDIX 5A

CORRELATION

The correlation coefficient is represented by the lowercase Greek letter rho, ρ. Correlation coefficients are index numbers that are never larger than positive one and never smaller than negative one. Symbolically, $+1.0 \geq \rho \geq -1.0$. The **correlation** measures the direction and strength of the relationship between two variables.

Correlation Examples and Illustrations

If two variables (such as the annual sales of left shoes and the annual sales of right shoes) rise and fall together in unison, these variables are said to be **perfectly positively correlated.** The correlation equals its upper limit of positive unity in this case. Figure 5A-1*a* is a scatter diagram of two highly positively correlated variables called x and y. The variables x and y might represent the annual sales of right and left shoes. Each dot in Figure 5A-1*a* might represent 1 year's sales of each type of shoe for a given year, for instance.

If two variables move perfectly *inversely,* they are said to be **perfectly negatively correlated.** In this case the correlation between the variables equals the lowest possible value of -1.0. A correlation of $\rho = -1.0$ indicates a perfect inverse (or negative) relationship. For example, the miles per hour that a car averages between two points is perfectly inversely correlated with the travel time for the trip. If two variables are perfectly negatively correlated, all the data points would fit precisely on a negatively sloped line in a two-dimensional graph.

If two variables *tend* to move inversely, but this negative relationship is not perfectly inverse, then the correlation is a negative number between 0 and -1. The monthly average temperature readings outside a home and that home's monthly heating bills over several months are an example of two variables that are **negatively correlated,** but not perfectly inversely correlated. Figure 5A-1*b* shows how two variables that are negatively correlated might covary. The horizontal axis measures the outdoor temperature; the vertical axis measures the home's monthly heating bill.

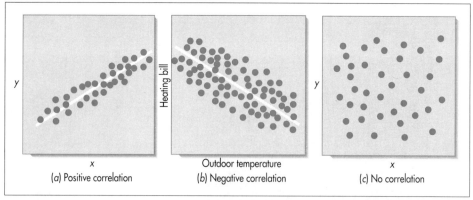

Figure 5A-1 Scatter diagrams showing different correlations.

If the movements of two variables are independent, they are said to be **uncorrelated.** In this case the correlation coefficient equals zero. For example, the correlation between each month's left shoe sales across the United States and your home's monthly heating bill should be zero because these two variables are totally unrelated. Figure 5A-1c is a scatter diagram for two variables, denoted x and y, that have zero correlation.

Measuring the Correlation Statistically

Equation (5A-1) defines the correlation between two variables x and y.

$$\rho = \frac{\text{covariance between } x \text{ and } y}{(\text{standard deviation of } x)(\text{standard deviation of } y)} \tag{5A-1}$$

The standard deviation was defined in Box 1-9 and calculated in Table 1-2. The covariance is a statistic that measures how two variables covary. The covariance is defined in Equation (5A-2).

$$\text{Cov}(x,y) = \frac{1}{T} \sum_{t=1}^{T} [x_t - E(x)][y_t - E(y)] \tag{5A-2}$$

where t is a counter that counts the pairs of x_t and y_t variables used in the computation, T denotes the total number of observations, and $E(x)$ and $E(y)$ represent the expected values of the x and y variables. The arithmetic averages of x and y can be used instead of their expected values since $E(x) = \bar{x}$ and $E(y) = \bar{y}$.

Covariance calculations may be found in Tables 25-2 and 25-3. The standard deviations and the covariance are used to compute correlation coefficients in these boxes.

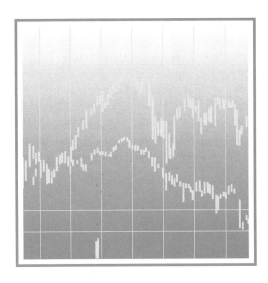

CHAPTER 6

REGULATING
SECURITIES
MARKETS

Savers go to securities markets in search of good investments. Corporations go to securities markets to finance expansion. The exchange that results transfers billions of dollars annually into productive enterprises. This exchange is a vital part of the capitalist system; the U. S. federal government has passed laws to promote the safety and stability of these markets.

Legal procedures and safeguards ensure that U.S. capital markets are fair places where hardworking investors can find rewarding investments. Laws forbid fraud and price manipulation, and federal agencies uphold these laws. Professional associations such as the National Association of Securities Dealers, the Municipal Securities Rule Making Board, and the Association for Investment Management and Research require members to observe strict codes of ethics.

The laws and procedures that govern securities markets in the United States were established as the need for them became clear. Before examining the regulatory system, let's look at the abuses that brought about the federal laws. We begin with the wrongdoing state laws were unable to remedy or control.

6-1 Illegal Trading Practices

Securities regulations enacted by state legislatures are commonly called **blue sky laws.** Kansas passed the first one in 1911; in 1917, Supreme Court Justice McKenna explained blue sky laws by saying: "The name that is given to the law indicates the evil at which it is aimed; that is, to use the language of a cited case, 'speculative schemes which have no more basis than so many feet of blue sky.'"[1] But whether state laws were well or poorly written, when a state threatened to prosecute, the criminals simply fled to the next state. Clearly, federal laws were needed

Some of the illegal practices current federal laws prohibit are listed and described below.

- **Churning:** Transaction activity that is disproportionate in amount and frequency to the size and nature of a client's account in order to generate commission income for a broker. The practice is called *churning* because it involves turning the client's account over again and again to generate sales commissions.

- **Cornering of the market:** The purchase by some individual of all the securities or all of a commodity available for sale. This person then owns the total supply and controls the price, and will typically try to liquidate the position at a high price for a gain.

---

[1] Justice McKenna in *Hall v. Geiger-Jones Company*, 242 U.S. 539, 550, in 1917.

Box 6-1

> DEFINITION: Fraud
>
> **Fraud** is defined as deliberate deception performed in order to obtain unfair or illegal gain. In securities markets, insider trading, wash sales, matched orders, price manipulation schemes, cornering the market, misrepresentation of yourself or someone else, misrepresentation or concealment of any relevant investment-related facts, and churning are examples of fraudulent activities.

Bertha Hecht—A Churning Victim

Bertha, a poor young immigrant when she arrived in the United States, worked most of her life as a $125 per month housekeeper for a Mr. Hecht. Later in life her fortunes improved; Bertha became Mrs. Hecht. In 1939, before her marriage, Bertha opened a brokerage account with $2000 of her hard-earned money with a securities broker named Asa Wilder. From 1939 to 1955 Bertha's account grew from $2000 to $65,000 as a result of additional deposits, dividend income, and capital gains. During those 16 years the account showed a total of 32 sales and 41 purchases; it was traded infrequently. And over those years Asa Wilder and Bertha became friends, even though Wilder had moved to a different brokerage firm.

In 1955 Mr. Hecht died and left his 62-year-old widow an estate with a net value of $502,532. After Hecht's death, Bertha and Asa Wilder started a close business and social relationship. She transferred $42,000 of her personal account and the proceeds from Mr. Hecht's estate to Hooker and Fay, where Wilder was then employed. In 1957, when Wilder left Hooker and Fay to become a broker at Harris, Upham and Company, the Hecht account of $533,161 was transferred to Wilder's new firm. Bertha Hecht dealt with Asa Wilder through Harris, Upham and saw him socially for several years after her husband died. Then, in 1964, Mrs. Hecht's tax accountant advised the perky 71-year-old widow that her account at Harris, Upham was down to $251,161.

Bertha Hecht brought suit against Asa Wilder and Harris, Upham for recovery of $1,109,000. This suit claimed damages for three reasons: (1) The Hecht account had been converted from a blue-chip investment account to an inappropriately low-grade, speculative account by Wilder. (2) Wilder traded excessively in the account for the purpose of generating commissions. (3) Wilder had defrauded Bertha Hecht by trading between the accounts in such a manner that he profited from her losses in two different securities transactions.

The court found that, if it were still intact, Mrs. Hecht's original Harris, Upham account would have had a value of $1,026,775. Dividend and bond interest would have amounted to $194,135 instead of the $124,237 earned under Wilder's guidance. The court

also learned that during the 6 years and 10 months that Wilder handled Hecht's account at Harris, Upham he entertained his client socially. During this time Mrs. Hecht had paid $91,000 in commissions and markups on securities, $98,000 in commissions on commodity trades, and $13,000 in interest on loans advanced to her margin account. These charges covered 1300 transactions in 200 different corporate stocks and 9000 commodity transactions—very active trading.

In assessing the role of Wilder's employer in allowing Mrs. Hecht's account to be depleted, the court pointed out that although the Hecht account amounted to only one-tenth of 1 percent of the total of all accounts in the firm's San Francisco office, it had supplied, in commissions and interest, at least 4.7 percent of the office's total income. Furthermore, the charges against the Hecht account, stated as a percent of the value of the account, were about 50 times the average. If the brokerage firm had monitored its accounts properly, these statistics would have alerted management to what Asa Wilder was doing and the abuse could have been stopped.

In defending his actions Wilder claimed that, as he was paid on salary rather than straight commission, he had no incentive to churn the account. The court pointed out, however, that Wilder had received bonuses and pay increases which corresponded chronologically with the periods when he was depleting the Hecht account most actively. Furthermore, 3 months after Wilder lost the Hecht account, his salary was reduced from $1250 to $850 per month. Thus, it appeared that his income was related to the brokerage's income from the Hecht account.

The court concluded that Mrs. Hecht had not monitored her account and therefore could not rightfully assert that it was wrongfully or unwillingly converted to a speculative account. On the issue of excessive trading (or churning), the court ruled that Mrs. Hecht should receive $143,000 in damages, which equaled the full amount of commissions she had paid to Harris, Upham and Co. On the issue of the two fraudulent self-dealing securities transactions perpetrated by Wilder on Hecht, the court granted Hecht $232,000 in damages.

In 1862 Commodore Cornelius Vanderbilt obtained a spectacular market corner. He started buying stock in the Harlem Railroad in New York City for $8 per share and continued buying until the price was up to $100 per share and he had control of the railroad. He then invested more money in the railroad to extend its lines into Manhattan. Daniel Drew, a ruthless price manipulator, also purchased shares in the railroad as the price rose. Drew, who wanted more profit, conspired to sell his shares to drive the price down and simultaneously took a short position* in the stock to profit from the price decline. The unscrupulous Drew then influenced Boss Tweed and other crooked New York City politicians to repeal the railroad's legal franchise to operate in New York City. Once it was unable to operate legally, the railroad was worthless. Then Drew sold all his holdings and also sold short 137,000 shares he did not own, with the expectation that the price would fall rapidly. The price fell to $72. Vanderbilt then used his great wealth to purchase every available share and raised the price of his shares to $179. Drew took a loss on his short sale of 137,000 shares. There were only 27,000 shares of stock outstanding. Drew was forced to settle with the buyers of the 137,000 shares that he had contracted to deliver at prices well below $100, while Vanderbilt held the price at $179. Since Vanderbilt had cornered the market, Drew's losses became Vanderbilt's gains.

* *Short sellers* are speculators who contract to sell an asset they do not own. Short selling is examined in more detail in Chapter 20.

• **Due diligence violation:** Failure of a dealer, managing director, or partner to learn every essential fact about every underwriting that falls within his or her area of responsibility, and/or failure to ensure that all these relevant facts are made available to investors.

• **Illegal pool:** An association of two or more people with the objective of manipulating prices and profiting therefrom. When this objective is attained, the pool is dissolved. Pool members may provide capital or inside information; some may manage the pool's operations. During the early 1890s there were two kinds

The Sinclair Consolidated Oil option pool of 1929 was spectacularly profitable. While Sinclair stock was selling in the $28 to $32 range, a contract was obtained from the company granting the pool an option to buy 1,130,000 shares at $30 per share. The pool then purchased 634,000 shares in the open market to bid up prices. Next, the pool exercised its options to buy at $30, and then liquidated its holdings while the stock was selling in the $40 range. The pool also sold 200,000 shares short as the price fell. The pool's total profit was approximately $12.5 million from the following sources: $10 million from optioned shares purchased at $30 per share, $500,000 from shares purchased in the market, and $2 million from the short sales.

of pools that have since been made illegal: a **trading pool** purchased the target securities in the open market, and an *option pool* acquired all or most of its securities at advantageous prices under *option contracts* (see Chapter 21).

- **Illegal solicitation:** Failure of a broker or dealer who is trying to convince someone to invest to give the potential client a prospectus that reveals all the relevant facts.

- **Inadequate disclosure:** Failure to deliver an SEC-approved prospectus before or during the time that a trade is solicited. Failure to register with the SEC before the securities are sold is another form of inadequate disclosure (unless the issue is explicitly exempted from the registration process).

- **Insider trading:** Securities transactions based on material nonpublic information obtained in breach of a fiduciary trust. Inside information may be procured by **insiders** such as corporate directors, owners of 10 percent or more of the equity shares, and executives who have access to material, nonpublic information about their corporation. In addition, federal regulators and common law cases have determined that auditors, consultants, financial analysts, bank lenders, and printers can be **temporary insiders** because they are exposed to material, nonpublic information. These temporary insiders (even part-time secretaries) are guilty of a breach of fiduciary trust if they profit from information to which they had temporary access. Insider trading is defined by case law instead of legislated law, and so the definition continues to evolve.

- **Matched orders:** Illusory transactions in which two individuals act in concert to get misleading transaction information onto the ticker tape (called *painting the tape*). The conspirators create a record of a trade and give the impression that delivery was made, without any true change in ownership. As with a wash sale, the record is needed to deceive others into believing that a market price has changed, or that someone else has purchased the securities.

- **Pyramiding of debt:** Speculative purchase of securities with small cash margins (of, say, 3 percent of the purchase price) with the rest borrowed (in this example, 97 percent of the cost). If the securities rise in price, aggressive lenders will treat these unrealized paper profits as new equity. These lenders then advance the borrower even more money, based on the speculator's "additional margin" or "paper profits." Such pyramiding of debt on top of unrealized paper profits is disastrous when prices decline significantly. Price declines equal to the down payment (3 percent, in this case) may bankrupt imprudent speculators. When lenders then try to sell the securities held as collateral, they may find that their declining market value is not enough to cover the debt. To avoid further losses, lenders may hurriedly dump the shares on the market, accelerating the price decline and further aggravating the financial problem.

- **Unauthorized exchange:** A securities exchange that operates without obtaining written SEC approval, or exemption.

- **Unauthorized trading:** Trades executed for a client's account that are not authorized verbally and/or in writing by the client before the transaction occurs. (Today, NYSE and NASD rules require written client authorization, but during the early 1900s such authorizations were not required. A client could be bankrupted by an unscrupulous broker.)

- **Unqualified salesperson:** Any broker or dealer who solicits trades without first passing the appropriate examination and/or without being registered with the National Association of Securities Dealers (NASD).

- **Unregistered securities:** Securities that are traded on a registered exchange without having been properly registered with the SEC. Or any securities issued by a corporation that has more than a few shareholders, is significant in size, and sells the securities across a state line without having its registration statement approved by the SEC in advance of the offering.

- **Unsuitability:** Inappropriateness of a sale to a client because the amount or kind of investment does not match the person's wealth, health, age, risk-taking abilities, and/or other circumstances.

- **Wash sale:** A deceptive transaction in which a seller of securities repurchases the securities (possibly even the same certificates) almost immediately. The purpose of a wash sale is to create a record of a sale, which is needed to establish the appearance of a loss for income tax purposes or to deceive someone into believing that a market transaction occurred.

6-2   The Straws That Broke the Camel's Back

The securities frauds and abuses outlined above were not illegal in the United States during the early 1900s; in fact, they still are not illegal in many foreign countries.[2] It took the painful lessons of the 1930s to motivate the U.S. Congress to pass laws against them.

The Depression

The Depression was a period of swift, severe economic decline that lasted for a good part of the 1930s. The demand for goods and services sank as pessimism prevailed. Consumer spending plummeted. Millions were unemployed and thousands were homeless, left to survive on handouts. As demand for goods continued to drop, prices fell. Between 1929 and 1931 the price of a dozen eggs dropped from 30 to 18 cents, and corn sank from 80 to 32 cents per bushel. The unemployment rate reached a peak of 24.9 percent in 1933. Thousands of businesses went bankrupt because of lack of sales. Borrowers fell behind on their repayments. Lacking liquid assets, many commercial banks defaulted when depositors tried to withdraw their money. A banking panic caused even some of the most soundly managed banks to become insolvent. Between 1930 and 1932 over 5000 commercial banks went bankrupt; many families lost their life savings.

---

[2] International investing is the topic of Chapter 27.

The Great Crash

153

Chapter 6
Regulating
Securities
Markets

The Depression was preceded by a stock market crash that began in September 1929. As with all business downturns, the smart investors foresaw the economic downturn, predicted decreases in corporate sales and earnings, and liquidated their investments several months before business activity began to drop off. The **Great Crash** thus preceded the Depression by a few months, because it was *anticipation of the Depression that caused the stock market's crash.*[3]

The Great Crash was spectacular. The Dow Jones Industrial Average (DJIA) closed at a peak of 381 on September 3, 1929. On October 2 the DJIA fell 49 points, and it dropped another 43 points the next day. By October 23 the DJIA had slipped to 306—a decline of nearly 20 percent in less than 2 months—and it continued to drop. The worst market collapse in American history had begun. The decline continued for over 3 years. On July 8, 1932, the DJIA closed at 41—less than 11 percent of its peak in 1929. Stated differently, 89 percent of the market price of the average investment was wiped out.

The Demand for Reform

The massive unemployment, widespread losses, thousands of bankruptcies, deprivation, and anguish caused by the Great Crash and the Depression brought public demand for reform. Securities markets, which were partly to blame for the creation of the economic bubble that burst in 1929, were dealt with swiftly. Congress passed the Securities Act of 1933 and the Securities Exchange Act of 1934. The purpose of these laws was to promote the public welfare. The legislators who passed the securities laws believed they would foster fair dealing, promote saving and investing, and thereby tend to maximize per capita national income. These and other regulations passed at about the same time forbade wash sales, cornering the market, pools, dissemination of fraudulent information, and the use of inside information. Such laws have diminished the frequency of price manipulation schemes and other destabilizing forms of speculation and have increased the stability of U.S. securities markets.

6-3   Federal Securities Regulation, 1933–1939

The federal laws passed in the 1930s are presented in chronological order to show how legislative thinking about securities laws evolved from the fraud schemes of the early 1900s and the economic disasters of the early 1930s.

The Glass-Steagall Act of 1933

In 1933 the United States was mired in the Depression. In Congress, Representative Henry Bascom Steagall and Senator Carter Glass pushed through a law to decentralize financial power that applied primarily to the commercial banking industry. It

---

[3] Because the Great Crash started before the Depression, some people have erroneously claimed that the Great Crash caused the Depression. This view is economically naive.

also affected the investments industry. The Banking Act of 1933, usually called the Glass-Steagall Act (GSA, hereafter), prohibits commercial banks from doing investment banking and vice versa. It also established the Federal Deposit Insurance Corporation (FDIC) to insure bank deposits and gave the banking industry a huge subsidy by forbidding commercial banks from paying interest on demand deposits.[4]

The part of the law that affects the investments industry is the section forbidding commercial banks to underwrite primary issues of corporate stock and bonds. To give just one example, this section of the act split the venerable House of Morgan into what are today known as the Morgan-Guaranty Bank (America's fourth-largest, most prestigious, and very profitable bank) and the equally prestigious Morgan-Stanley investment banking firm. Today the Glass-Steagall Act's mandated separation of commercial and investment banking is widely considered to be against the nation's better interests. This part of the law was weakened in the 1980s when the Federal Reserve allowed commercial banks to acquire brokerage houses that handled secondary trades (but not primary corporate issues).

The Securities Act of 1933

The Securities Act of 1933 (SA, hereafter), also known as the *truth in securities law*, requires full disclosure of all relevant information about new issues of corporate securities. The SA mandates that almost all new securities issues by large corporations be registered with a branch of the federal government that had not yet been established when the act was passed. It also requires that every security issue's registration statements contain financial statements audited by an independent accountant and other information relevant for potential investors.

Registration of IPOs The main objective of the 1933 SA is to provide potential investors in initial public offerings (IPOs) with the facts they need to make informed investment decisions. The act specifies that the issuing firm and the investment banker must register the issue, unless an applicable exemption applies. **Registration** means filing audited financial statements, information about the underwriting agreement, and other data about the firm with the federal government. See Principles Box 4-2 for a list of the information that must be disclosed.

After a firm "registers" with the federal government, it must usually wait a few weeks before issuing the securities. During the waiting period, a federal government agency called the *Securities and Exchange Commission (SEC)* investigates to ensure that all the required information has been disclosed. The **prospectus** contains most of the information in the registration statement and is prepared for public distribution. Every investor who buys the new securities must be provided with one. If the prospectus is distributed before the end of the waiting period, it must have a note in red ink on its cover stating that it has not yet received SEC approval for issuance as a final prospectus—such a prospectus is called a **red herring.** SEC approval, when it is

---

[4] The prohibition on paying interest on demand deposits was largely voided in the 1970s by the development of negotiable order of withdrawal (NOW) accounts, which are not covered by the GSA.

granted, does not imply that the securities are a good investment. It merely indicates that the legally required information has been properly disclosed and is available for investors to analyze if they wish.

In the 1980s the SEC modified the registration process to reduce the red tape. **Rule 415** allows large corporations to file **shelf registration** statements with the SEC that give details about the firm's long-term financing plans. Thereafter, the corporation can quickly float new issues of stocks or bonds without filing a separate registration statement for each individual issue.

Exemptions   The following types of securities offerings are exempted from the full registration requirements of the Securities Act of 1933:

- *Small issues:* Issues offered by firms issuing less than $1,500,000 of new securities per year.

- *Secondary trading:* Trades between private individuals in which the original issuer receives no money. (Secondary trades are regulated by the Securities Exchange Act of 1934.)

- *Private offerings:* Stock issues offered to small groups of private investors who are experienced or informed enough not to require disclosure statements for their own protection. Such purchasers sign a letter saying they are buying the shares for investment purposes and not for resale to the public. As a result, these issues are sometimes called **letter stocks.** Investors must keep the shares for at least 2 years.

- *Government securities:* Securities issued by the U.S. federal government and some municipal securities were exempted from the SEC registration procedure by later regulations. (Nevertheless, most issues of municipals are registered and have prospectuses, because many states' laws require it.)

Antifraud Provisions   In addition to requirements for full disclosure, the SA of 1933 contains antifraud provisions. It provides remedies against securities salespeople or others who disseminate untrue or misleading information about securities. Courts finding fraudulent statements being made about securities can issue injunctions to stop the actions and require other civil law remedies, such as reimbursement for damages.

The SA of 1933 limited the techniques that can be used to sell securities. It provided the basis for a later legal ruling that all public securities dealers imply, by offering their services to the public, that they will deal fairly. This ruling in turn provides a basis for prosecuting salespeople who give misleading advice or perpetrate frauds.[5]

---

[5] For an empirical economic study which suggests that securities laws are not so effective as some people might think, see Carol J. Simon, "The Effects of the 1933 Securities Act on Investor Information and the Performance of New Issues," *American Economic Review,* June 1989, pp. 295–318.

The Securities Exchange Act of 1934

The limitations of the 1933 Securities Act were quickly recognized. One of its main shortcomings was that no federal agency existed to enforce it. As a result, Congress enacted the Securities Exchange Act (SEA) of 1934, which established the Securities and Exchange Commission (SEC) and extended the Securities Act of 1933 requirement of full disclosure to also include the secondary markets. The specific provisions of the Securities Exchange Act of 1934 included these:

Establishment of the SEC   The Securities Exchange Act of 1934 created the SEC and charged it with the responsibility for regulating securities markets. The SEC is located in Washington, D.C., and is headed by five commissioners appointed by the president with the consent of the Congress.

The SEC has offices in New York City, Boston, Atlanta, Miami, Chicago, Detroit, Houston, Fort Worth, Los Angeles, San Francisco, Seattle, and Philadelphia; it is heavily staffed with lawyers. Investors can write to the SEC about allegations of fraud and wrongdoing, and the SEC lawyers will consider taking action to rectify the alleged wrongdoing. The SEC also initiates investigations of its own.

The SEC may take action to require conformity with the securities laws. The commission is granted the right to:

- Suspend trading in particular stocks, bonds, put and call options, and other securities

- Suspend the registration of a securities exchange

- Expel officers or members of an exchange who operate illegally

- Suggest changes in an exchange's rules and bylaws and require their implementation

- Collect financial statements and records

- Conduct investigations and hearings as needed to enforce the law

- Obtain injunctions requiring the cessation of activities violating the securities laws

- Obtain writs requiring violators to comply with the law

Disclosure Requirements for Secondary Securities   The main difference between the SA of 1933 and the SEA is that the SEA extends disclosure requirements to secondary markets. To ensure full disclosure of information about securities traded in secondary markets, the 1934 act requires that annual reports and other periodic reports be filed for public inspection at the SEC offices before listing securities for trading on an organized exchange. The **Securities Acts Amendments of 1964** extended these registration requirements to securities traded OTC and established other requirements.

Registration of Organized Exchanges   The SEA of 1934 grants the SEC considerable authority over organized exchanges. It requires that all exchanges register with the

Box 6-2

157

Chapter 6
Regulating
Securities
Markets

> PRINCIPLES: Registration Requirements
>
> Companies must provide the SEC with the following reports about their operations:
>
> 1. The audited annual **10-K Report,** which contains four parts: Part I, description of operations; Part II, financial statements; Part III, information about executive personnel; and Part IV, additional financial details about assets.
>
> 2. The quarterly **10-Q Report,** which may or may not be audited. It contains condensed quarterly financial statements.
>
> 3. The event-oriented **8-K Report,** which is required within 15 days after a merger, acquisition, resignation of a director, change in certifying account-ant, or other event.
>
> 4. The event-oriented **13-D Report,** which is required within 10 days after any entity acquires 5 percent or more of any class of any corporation's stock, and whenever such positions are increased or decreased.

SEC, comply with the law, adopt rules for disciplining members who do not conduct their business in a legal and ethical manner, and furnish the SEC with copies of their rules and bylaws. Within these guidelines the exchanges are free to regulate themselves. However, the SEC can intervene in the operations of an exchange and alter penalties, expel members, or even close the exchange. In fact, the SEC has rarely intervened. It has been hypothesized that the mere prospect of federal regulators intervening motivates the exchanges to work to avoid any embarrassing investigations.

Credit Regulation When Congress wrote the 1934 law, it wanted to prohibit pyramiding debt. Since the Federal Reserve Board is charged with controlling the money supply and credit conditions, Congress gave it the authority to set margin requirements for credit purchases of securities.[6] The Fed then wrote Federal Reserve Regulations T and U to cover **initial margin requirements.** The Securities Exchange Act of 1934 also limited securities dealers' total indebtedness to 20 times their owners' equity capital.

As we saw in Chapter 4, the initial margin is the percentage of the purchase price that investors must pay with their own funds (like a minimum down payment).

---

[6] The Board of Governors of the Federal Reserve also controls banks' reserve requirements and Federal Reserve open-market operations, and it sets the discount rate at which banks may borrow from the Federal Reserve system. The Treasury and the Federal Reserve publicly suggested in 1984 that the securities exchanges be allowed to take over setting the margin requirements for themselves. Congress has not yet responded to this suggestion.

Regulations T and U allow the Board of Governors of the Federal Reserve to set the margin requirements for loans made to securities buyers. In recent years the initial margin requirement has varied between 50 and 60 percent for common stocks. (See Chapter 4 about how to calculate margin requirements.)

Proxy Solicitation   The SEA of 1934 requires the SEC to establish rules governing solicitations by registered issuers of stock to obtain their shareholders' voting rights on matters to come before the shareholders' meeting. These borrowed shareholders' voting rights are called **proxies** (see Chapter 3). The SEC requires that all proxy solicitations contain some information about the issues to be voted upon, a proxy card for the shareholder to express approval or disapproval of each issue, and a complete list of candidates if the solicitation is for the election of directors.

Exemptions   Securities of federal, state, and local governments, securities that are not traded across state lines, and any other securities the SEC wishes to specify are exempt from registering with the SEC. Certain organized exchanges may also be exempted from registering if the SEC chooses. As a matter of practice, certain small local exchanges have been exempted (the exchanges in Honolulu and in Wheeling, West Virginia). Many of the provisions of the SEA do not apply to exempted securities and exchanges.

Insider Activities   Section 16(a) of the SEA requires that those most likely to possess material, nonpublic information (every officer, director, and owner of more than 10 percent of a listed corporation's shares) must file a statement, called an *insider report,* of their holdings of that firm's securities in every month in which a change in those holdings occurs. In 1991 this rule was extended to include transactions involving options and other derivative financial instruments that apply to the employing firm's securities. These insider reports are public information—some newspapers publish them.

Recent common law cases have established policies that extend the prohibition against insider trading beyond those explicitly mentioned in the 1934 act. The current view is that both part-time and full-time employees of a corporation at all levels have a *fiduciary responsibility* to the shareholders of the corporation. Stated differently, practically anyone who has access to material, nonpublic information about the firm can be considered an insider. Insiders are forbidden by the Securities Exchange Act of 1934 to earn gains by trading in the firm's securities if they have held the securities less than 6 months.

Section 16(b) of the SEA requires that insiders' profits from investments held for less than 6 months be returned to the issuing corporation. Section 16(c) forbids insiders to make short sales in the firm's shares. Section 32, as amended in 1975, provides for penalties in the form of fines and/or up to 10 years' imprisonment.

Outlawing Price Manipulation   The SEA of 1934 forbids price manipulation practices such as wash sales, pools, circulation of manipulative information, and false and misleading statements about securities.

Box 6-3

159

Chapter 6
Regulating
Securities
Markets

FINANCE: Insider Trading Is Just Fine

In keeping with the philosophy that the "government that governs least governs best," some informed thinkers have argued that insider trading should be legal here, as it is in many foreign countries. They argue that if insiders were permitted to act on the valuable information they sometimes possess, their trading would help align each security's market price more closely with its true underlying (but unobservable) value. It is desirable to have prices equal to values in a free-market economy because market prices are the signals used to allocate the nation's resources. The buyer who bids the highest price gets the resource. To the extent that prices differ from values, resources will tend to be allocated to uses that are not optimal for the nation's welfare.

For the detailed arguments in support of insider trading as a way to increase market efficiency, see Harold Demsetz, "Corporate Control, Insider Trading and Rates of Return," *American Economic Review*, vol. 76, no. 2, May 1986, pp. 313–316, and Henry Manne, "In Defense of Insider Trading," *Harvard Business Review*, November-December 1966. See also George Benston, "Required Disclosure and the Stock Market: An Evaluation of the Securities Exchange Act of 1934," *American Economic Review*, March 1973, pp. 132–155. Try to read Henry G. Manne et al., *Wall Street in Transition: The Emerging System and Its Impact on the Economy* (New York: New York University Press, 1974). Also see George J. Stigler, "Public Regulation of the Securities Markets," *Journal of Business*, vol. 37, no. 2, April 1964, pp. 117–142.

On the other side, for a rigorous explanation of how insider trading is harmful to society, see Norman S. Douglas, "Insider Trading: The Case Against the 'Victimless Crime' Hypothesis," *The Financial Review*, vol. 33, no. 2, May 1988, pp. 127–142.

The Public Utility Holding Company Act of 1935

In 1928 investigators for the Federal Trade Commission (FTC) discovered a system of huge utility empires that were organized to profit the owners of the utility holding companies rather than serve the public. The result was the Public Utility Holding Company Act of 1935. Section 11(a) of this act gave the SEC the responsibility and the authority to "determine the extent to which the corporate structure . . . may be simplified, unnecessary complexities thereby eliminated, voting power fairly and equitably distributed . . . and the properties and business thereof confined to those necessary and appropriate to the operations of an integrated public utility system." The act also gave the SEC the power to regulate the terms and form of securities issued by utility companies, to regulate the accounting systems they use, to approve all acquisitions and dispositions of assets and securities, and to regulate intercompany transactions such as the payment of cash dividends and the making of loans. There have been no major problems with this industry since the law was enacted.

The Maloney Act of 1938

The Maloney Act of 1938 is an extension of the Securities Exchange Act of 1934, adopted at the request of over-the-counter securities dealers to provide for their self-regulation. The act stipulates that one or more associations of OTC brokers and dealers may apply for registration with the SEC, that these groups may regulate themselves within the guidelines laid down by the SEC, and that the groups may grant discounts on securities traded among their members. OTC dealers who are not members of an association deal with association members by paying full retail prices for any securities they purchase. The price concessions provide a strong incentive for all OTC dealers to belong to an association.

Only one association of OTC dealers registered with the SEC under the provisions of the Maloney Act—the **National Association of Securities Dealers (NASD).** Today NASD's more than 7000 member firms operate over 20,000 branch offices and employ approximately 500,000 registered representatives who sell securities in the OTC market. The Association has a test individuals must pass to join; a set of rules forbidding fraud, manipulation, and excessive profit taking; a uniform-

Box 6-4

PRINCIPLES: Dealing with Bankruptcy

As amended in 1978, the Federal Bankruptcy Act of 1938:

- Requires that a court-appointed **trustee** oversee the affairs of the firm against which bankruptcy charges have been filed.

- Provides for **liquidation** of hopelessly troubled firms (Chapter 10). The court-appointed trustee typically holds a public bankruptcy auction, sells all assets, and uses the proceeds to pay all the firm's debts in accordance with the legal priority of claims.

- Provides for **reorganization** of seriously troubled firms that might be able to survive (Chapter 10). For example, the bankruptcy judge might downgrade all securities in a reorganization. All common stock is declared null, void, and worthless, and all preferred stock is downgraded to common stock. Uncollateralized bonds are downgraded to preferred stock. The reduced fixed interest costs may then allow the firm to survive.

- Provides for **arrangements** to govern troubled firms that show promise of being able to survive (Chapter 10). A typical arrangement is that the court protects the troubled firm from bankruptcy or other legal proceedings while the firm's managers try to convince its lenders to accept repayments of, say, 50 cents per dollar of debt, in order to avoid a bankruptcy that would yield even less.

- Provides for **repayment plans** to govern moderately troubled firms that should be able to survive (Chapter 10). The bankruptcy court may order all the creditors to grant the firm payment extensions of 6 months, for example.

practices code standardizing and expediting such routine transactions as payments and deliveries; and a procedure for disciplining members who engage in illegal or unethical conduct.

Penalties involving suspensions and fines may be levied by the NASD. Expulsion is the most severe, since nonmembers cannot obtain the purchase discounts they need to stay in business. All decisions may be appealed to NASD's board of governors, the SEC, or the courts. The SEC has direct power over the NASD. It must be given copies of all rules adopted by the NASD (or any other association of OTC dealers that may be formed). It may suspend or revoke an association's registration for failure to follow SEC guidelines. And the SEC may review and alter the verdict in any judicial proceedings.

The Federal Bankruptcy Act of 1938, as Amended in 1978

Corporations that are teetering on the precipice of bankruptcy can be enticing investments: Their shares can be purchased at low prices, and if they turn themselves around and regain prosperity, share prices will skyrocket. Before entering into such *special situations,* however, investors should know how to evaluate both the upside and the downside possibilities. The Federal Bankruptcy Act explains the downside risks.

Bankruptcy law is the foundation on which default risk (see Chapter 10) is defined; anticipated actions by bankruptcy courts can have dramatic effects on the prices of securities issued by distressed firms. Interestingly, the prices of firms that are affected by the bankruptcy laws do not react directly to court declarations of bankruptcy, reorganization, or other financial trauma. Because analysts forecast these events, securities prices typically change in *anticipation* of court actions months before they occur.

The Trust Indenture Act of 1939

The Trust Indenture Act of 1939 requires that an **indenture,** or contract setting forth the promises the issuing company makes to its investors, accompany every corporate bond issue. The act was intended to protect absentee bond investors from the results of unwise or unscrupulous acts by the managers of the firm that they knew nothing of. One protective provision common in indentures stipulates that the issuing corporation can pay no dividends on common stock if the coupon interest payments on its bonds are past-due; this helps ensure that the bond investors will receive their interest income. Some indentures stipulate that certain assets (such as a specific building) serve as collateral for a bond issue; the collateral belongs to the bond investors until they are all fully paid off. The Trust Indenture Act of 1939 requires that a trustee (usually a bank) be appointed to make certain that the indenture's provisions are not violated. If a protective provision is violated, the trustee is empowered to sue the issuing corporation on behalf of the bond investors. For example, the trustee can urge management to make all coupon payments on time and to keep a building that serves as collateral in good repair. If the issuer is unable to fulfill these conditions, the trustee can force the issuer into bankruptcy and see that the bond investors are treated fairly. For instance, the trustee would see that the bond investors received either the title or the sale proceeds from any collateral that might have been promised in the indenture.

6-4   Securities Regulation, 1940–1990

The laws enacted in the 1930s established the foundation of U.S. securities law. More recent laws are narrower in scope, but they are also important. Some expand on the earlier regulations or are amendments to them. This section summarizes these more recent provisions.

The Investment Company Act of 1940

The **Investment Company Act of 1940** is the main piece of legislation governing the management of investment companies. As explained in Chapter 3, an investment company takes in money from various investors, commingles the funds, and invests the money in a diversified portfolio of securities that it manages for a fee. There are two types of investment company fund—the popular open-end type (or mutual fund) and the less common closed-end fund.

The Investment Company Act of 1940 requires that investment companies avoid fraudulent practices, fully disclose their financial statements, give prospectuses to potential investors, publicly disseminate statements outlining their investment goals (for example, growth, income, or safety), not change their published goals without the consent of the shareholders, obtain stockholders' approval of contracts for the portfolio's management, limit the issuance of debt, not employ people convicted of securities frauds as officers, have some outsiders on their board of directors, follow uniform accounting procedures, and operate the fund for the benefit of shareholders rather than for the benefit of its managers.

The Investment Advisors Act of 1940

The **Investment Advisors Act** requires that investment advisers register with the SEC and disclose certain information about their background. Advisers are forbidden to assign their investment advisory contracts to another adviser without the client's consent, to enter into profit-sharing agreements with their clients, and to use selected testimonials in their advertising. It is, however, not the intent of the act to deny the right to sell investment advice to an applicant (even if that person is incompetent). As with all securities laws, the law expects that the investor will evaluate the information the law provides and then make an informed judgment.

The Real Estate Investment Trust Act of 1960

Real Estate Investment Trusts are usually called **REITs;** they are like mutual funds that invest in real estate. The 1960 act grants REITs exemption from federal income taxes if they obtain at least 75 percent of their income from rent and mortgages, have at least 75 percent of their assets invested in real estate, and pay out at least 90 percent of each year's income to shareholders. The 1960 act also requires REITs to have at least 100 different investors—which are also called *shareholders* or *certificate holders*. The five largest shareholders are not allowed to control more than 50 percent of the shares in any REIT. These rules are similar to the requirements governing mutual funds; their purpose is to ensure that REITs are not used for income tax evasion and that they invest primarily in real estate.

The Securities Investor Protection Corporation Act of 1970

The Securities Investor Protection Corporation, or **SIPC** (pronounced "SIP-ic"), was established to protect the clients of brokerage firms that go bankrupt. The act requires that all registered securities brokers and dealers and all firms that are members of national securities exchanges join SIPC and pay dues equal to approximately 1 percent of the firm's gross income.

SIPC dues are placed in a fund that is used to repay clients of a bankrupt brokerage firm if the firm loses the client's securities and/or does not have the capital to repay client losses arising from the brokerage's failure. SIPC was formed to free investors from worry by providing insurance in case their brokerage firm fails.

The Employment Retirement Income Security Act of 1974

The rapid growth of pension funds from 1940 on led Congress to pass the Employee Retirement Income Security Act of 1974, called **ERISA.** ERISA requires employers that promise pension benefits to set aside the funds needed to pay for these pension liabilities, requires employers to give employees *vested rights* in their pension fund after several years of service, and establishes the *Pension Benefit Guarantee Corporation* to insure pensioners against loss if the employer underfunds the pension plan. Pension funds are of particular interest to investment managers today, because they are the largest pools of investment money in the United States.

Among ERISA's provisions is a novel application of the "prudent man rule" of law. ERISA refers to the *overall investment portfolio* rather than to each individual asset in the portfolio (which is how the *prudent man rule* is usually applied). It appears that junk bonds or options or other investments that might ordinarily be judged to be imprudent when viewed individually are acceptable pension assets so long as they are appropriate within the pension portfolio's overall investment strategy. The act also resolved certain inherent conflicts of interest—for example, a pension fund cannot invest in the employer's securities. This provision helps ensure that the pensioners will not be bankrupt if their former employer is.

The Commodity Futures Trading Commission Act of 1974

Commodity futures contracts are marketable financial instruments that have a long legislative history. Starting in 1884, a new bill about trading futures contracts was introduced in Congress almost every year. Most sought to ban trading in futures contracts. In the early days of large financial markets, many people believed that trading in futures contracts destabilized market prices and/or was just another form of gambling. Today people are aware that speculators help make markets more liquid and tend to diminish price fluctuations.[7]

The Commodity Exchange Authority (CEA) Act of 1936 established the CEA to regulate trading in domestic agricultural commodities. It granted approval for new futures contracts to be publicly traded, policed the registration of the commodity futures commission merchants, investigated charges of cheating and fraud in commodity trading, and prevented price manipulation in U.S. commodities. Commodity futures trading started growing rapidly in the 1960s, and the tiny CEA was inadequate. The Commodity Futures Trading Commission Act of 1974 passed all the CEA's regulatory authority to a new, larger independent regulatory agency it established, the **Commodity Futures Trading Commission,** or **CFTC.**

The CFTC is an independent federal regulatory agency overseen by five commissioners appointed by the president of the United States. It has a staff of economists and other regulatory officials who study the commodity markets to discern what rules and regulations about commodity futures trading will best promote the public welfare. The CFTC Act of 1974 also gave the agency authority to sue any person or organization that violated the CFTC Act, to take charge of a commodity market in an "emergency" situation and take whatever actions it deemed necessary to restore an orderly market, and to issue "cease and desist" orders backed by criminal or civil sanctions and fines.

One of the most sweeping changes brought about by the CFTC Act was to grant the CFTC authority over commodities from all over the world when they are traded in the United States. This gives the CFTC power over all silver and gold futures contracts in the United States, for example, even though the precious metals and the competing contracts on them may come from foreign countries.

The Securities Reform Act of 1975

The **Securities Reform Act of 1975** established the **Municipal Securities Rule Making Board,** or **MSRB.** The MSRB is a self-regulating body for the municipal bond market; it has 15 board members and is overseen by the SEC. The MSRB requires that all municipal bond dealers and brokers register with the SEC, disclose their involvement in any new issues of muni bonds they might sell, pass the NASD's securities brokers exam, keep records of all transactions, accept whatever disciplinary action the MSRB might hand down in case of fraud or deception, and participate in an industrywide system for clearing muni bond trades.

The Securities Acts Amendments of 1975

The Securities Acts Amendments (SAA) directed the SEC to oversee the development of a vaguely defined national securities market. Other provisions of this amendment amended the Securities Exchange Act of 1934 by requiring the SEC to

---

[7] See William L. Silber, "Marketmaker Behavior in an Auction Market: An Analysis of Scalpers in Futures Markets," *Journal of Finance*, vol. 39, no. 4, September 1984, pp. 937–953. Also see Robert Forsythe, Thomas R. Palfrey, Charles R. Plott, "Futures Markets and Informational Efficiency: A Laboratory Examination," *Journal of Finance*, vol. 39, no. 4, September 1984, pp. 954–981.

nullify exchange rules that are anticompetitive; prohibit the use of fixed commission rate schedules; clarify the jurisdiction of the courts and the process of judicial review in securities law; call for fair competition among brokers, dealers, and securities market makers; call for wide public availability of information on securities transactions; and require provision of opportunities for investors' orders to be executed without the participation of a dealer (such as an NYSE specialist).[8]

Rule 144A

In 1990 the SEC passed its **Rule 144A,** which allows professional investors with over $100 million of securities holdings to trade securities that have not gone through the slow and costly SEC registration procedure. Professional investors have always been allowed to trade holdings of nonregistered securities in foreign markets; one of the purposes of Rule 144A is to make U.S. securities markets more competitive with the foreign markets. Rule 144A does not permit issues of securities from publicly traded corporations to be traded without being registered, however.

The Arbitration Rulings

During the 1980s securities brokerage firms endeavored to reduce their legal expenses by asking clients to sign an agreement stating that any misunderstandings between the client and the broker would be submitted to **binding arbitration** rather than being adjudicated in the courts. The U.S. Supreme Court declared such agreements legal in 1989. The ruling provided a sound way to control runaway legal expenses, but many of the arbitrators used during the 1980s were securities brokers. To provide a fairer procedure, the brokerage firms agreed in 1991 to let an independent body called the *American Arbitration Association* handle arbitrations.

In capitalist systems, the securities markets are vital to the success of the economy, which is why governments intervene to ensure their safety and stability. In the United States, a complex array of laws and regulations have developed in response to various unforeseen and catastrophic events. The most far-reaching event in this century was the Great Crash of 1929 and the Depression that followed. They inspired legislation that became the backbone of federal securities law: the Securities Act of 1933 and the Securities Exchange Act of 1934, which established the federal Securities and Exchange Commission (the SEC). Legislation has continued to flow from Congress ever since: laws aimed at regulating public utility companies, OTC markets, bankruptcies, bond issue indentures, investment companies and advisers, real estate investing, pension management, commodity futures trading, municipal bond trading, and competition among markets.

    All these statutes—and the active regulation provided by the federal agencies charged with overseeing the operations of securities markets—provide the United States with what is widely regarded as the best securities laws in the world, and the best-regulated markets.

Summary

---

[8] Chapter 4 describes some of the new securities market developments that are emerging under this legislation.

Further Reading

Hammer, Richard M., Gilbert Simonetti, Jr., and Charles T. Crawford, eds., *Investment Regulation around the World,* (Somerset, N.J.: Ronald Press, 1983).
> *A collection of readings about the investment regulations in foreign countries.*

Loll, L. M., and G. Buckley, *The Over-the-Counter Securities Markets,* 4th ed. (Englewood Cliffs, N.J.: Prentice-Hall, 1981).
> *This is an easy-to-read book about securities markets, securities trading, and securities law. The book is widely used by people studying to pass the NASD exam to become securities brokers.*

Lowenstein, Louis, *What's Wrong with Wall Street?* (Reading, Mass.: Addison-Wesley, 1988).
> *Professor Lowenstein is a professor of law and finance, and as such, he offers some ingenious suggestions to make securities markets in the United States more efficient and less prone to speculative excesses.*

Schwartz, Robert A., *Equity Markets* (New York: Harper & Row, 1988).
> *Chapter 5 of this financial economics book discusses securities law.*

Securities and Exchange Commission, Securities Act of 1933, Release No. 4725; Securities Exchange Act of 1939, Release No. 7425.
> *The SEC provides these and numerous other releases to document and explain its legal activity in the securities industry.*

Tewles, Richard J., and Edward S. Bradley, *The Stock Market,* 5th ed. (New York: Wiley, 1987).
> *Chapters 16 and 17 provide some good legal discussion for investors who are not lawyers.*

Questions and Problems

Essay Questions

6-1 Is it legal to trade securities on the basis of a so-called hot tip from someone who has access to inside information about the issuing company?

6-2 Compare and contrast the Securities Act of 1933 and the SEA of 1934 with respect to the registration of securities issues. What federal agency does each act specify to do the required registration? Which act provides for the registration of IPOs? Of previously issued securities that are traded in secondary markets?

6-3 What is a prospectus? What is the purpose of a prospectus? To whom should prospectuses be provided, and at what time should the prospectus be provided? When the SEC releases a prospectus for public dissemination, what is the implication of this release?

6-4 What is the SEC? How did it develop? What functions does it perform?

6-5 How is credit that is used to purchase securities regulated?

6-6 What is the NASD? How did it develop? What are its functions? What powers does it have to enforce the law?

6-7 What is an indenture? Who is an indenture contract supposed to protect? What precautions discourage violation of an indenture?

6-8 What harm can come to a national economy if some investors occasionally corner a market or operate pools?

Matching Questions

167

*Chapter 6
Regulating
Securities
Markets*

6-9 Match the following 12 brief descriptions of securities laws with the title of the appropriate law.

Act	Description of securities laws
1. Glass-Steagall Act	A. The contracts governing bond issues must clearly specify the rights of bond owners. Trustees must not allow anything to impair their willingness or legal right to sue the issuer.
2. Securities Act of 1933	B. Mutual funds and closed-end investment companies were brought under federal control.
3. Securities Exchange Act of 1934	C. Sellers of investment advice are required to register with the SEC.
4. Public Utility Holding Company Act	D. The federal insurance program to reimburse clients for losses resulting from bankrupt brokerage firms was established.
5. Maloney Act	E. Pension fund management was brought under federal control.
6. Trust Indenture Act	F. This law established a federal agency to oversee futures markets.
7. Investment Company Act	G. The SEC was directed to establish a new national market system (NMS) with negotiated commission rates.
8. Investment Advisors Act	H. This forbids commercial banks from engaging in investment banking.
9. Securities Investor Protection Corporation (SIPC)	I. Firms issuing securities must register new issues with federal authorities. Registration information is made available to the public in the form of a prospectus.
10. Employee Retirement Income Security Act (ERISA)	J. The SEC was set up to regulate the securities industry. All securities exchanges must register with the SEC. The SEC must regulate proxy voting. Regulations of earlier laws were extended to cover secondary sales.
11. Commodity Futures Trading Act	K. This empowers the SEC to oversee the finances, accounting, organization, and activities of public utilities to ensure the public welfare is served.
12. Securities Acts Amendments	L. Associations of qualified over-the-counter brokers and dealers can register with the SEC and regulate themselves within SEC guidelines.

6-10 Match the terms in the left column with the corresponding descriptions in the right column.

1. Churning	A. A phony transaction carried out to create the illusion that a significant transaction occurred.
2. Cornering the market	B. The Dow Jones Industrial Average fell drastically from a high reached in 1929.
3. The Depression	C. The common practice of brokers to get their clients to generate commissions by fruitless securities trading.
4. Insider	D. An executive, owner of shares, or internal or external employee having access to nonpublic information that may affect the firm's securities prices.
5. Pool	E. Buy almost all the supply of a good that is available.
6. Wash sale	F. Several years in the early 1930s when unemployment was high and bankruptcies were rampant.
7. The Great Crash	G. An association of people formed to profit from manipulating securities prices.

Multiple Choice Questions

6-11 Which of the following does the Commodity Futures Trading Commission regulate?

C

(*a*) Securities markets
(*b*) Trading in options
(*c*) Trading of futures
(*d*) All the above

6-12 The NASD is best described by which of the following?

C

(*a*) A trade association of securities dealers.
(*b*) The organization that oversees and regulates the over-the-counter market.
(*c*) Both the above are true.
(*d*) Non-Active Securities Dealers (NASD) are limited partners who have no voice in the management of the firm.

6-13 Investors are insured against loss if their brokerage firm goes bankrupt by which one of the following bodies?

A

(*a*) SIPC
(*b*) FDIC
(*c*) SEC
(*d*) Federal Reserve

6-14 The Securities Exchange Act of 1934 forbids insiders to do which of the following activities?

D

(*a*) Pass inside information to other investors
(*b*) Sell short in their company's stock
(*c*) Take profits from price appreciation on their firm's stock if they have owned it for less than 6 months
(*d*) All the above

6-15   Which of the following categories of people are insiders?

(a) Members of the board of directors
(b) Investment bankers, external accountants conducting a periodic audit, and consultants
(c) The president and vice presidents of competing firms
(d) All the above
(e) Both (a) and (b)

E

6-16   Which of the following statements describes a wash sale?

(a) There is no sale at all.
(b) Transactions performed merely to establish the record of a sale.
(c) It may be done to establish a tax loss.
(d) All the above are true.
(e) None of the above is true.

D

6-17   Insider activities are required to be reported under which of the following laws?

(a) The Securities Act of 1933
(b) Securities Exchange Act of 1934
(c) Maloney Act of 1936
(d) Trust Indenture Act of 1939

B

6-18   The National Association of Securities Dealers registered with the SEC under the provision of which one of the following laws?

(a) Securities Act of 1933
(b) Securities Exchange Act of 1934
(c) Maloney Act of 1936
(d) Trust Indenture Act of 1939

C

6-19   The Securities Acts Amendments legislation is best described by which one of the following statements?

(a) It is a law passed in 1975.
(b) It requires the SEC to establish a national market system (NMS).
(c) The law is vague and leaves much discretion to the SEC about how it is to be implemented.
(d) (a), (b), and (c) are true.
(e) Brokerage commission rates should be determined by the market makers.

D

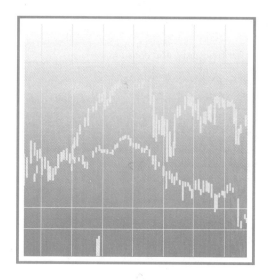

CHAPTER 7

FEDERAL
TAXES

Since 1913, when the first federal law requiring U.S. citizens to pay income taxes went into effect, two tax trends can be discerned. The first is that federal tax laws constantly change. A substantial change has occurred about every 2.5 years since 1976, for example. Second, taxes have been increased a great number of times, but rarely reduced. More recently, taxpayers have had some good news. A law passed in 1986 requires that federal tax brackets be widened every year into the foreseeable future, which effectively *reduces most people's tax rate*. This reduction is indexed to the inflation rate.

The 1986 Tax Reform Act tied certain parts of the federal tax structure to the rate of inflation to stop bracket creep. **Bracket creep** occurs as incomes inflate with the general price level. The higher incomes then push people into progressively higher income tax brackets. Indexing the progressive income tax rate structure to the rate of inflation means that income can increase as much as the inflation rate every year and the taxpayer will not have to pay a higher percentage of income in taxes.

Since the tax brackets change automatically every year, depending on the inflation rate during the past year, it is impossible to prepare tax rate tables that apply to future years. So while this chapter will give you a good grounding in the basics of the tax system, you must consult the tax tables that are published annually to prepare your tax return for the Internal Revenue Service (IRS).

The 1986 Tax Reform Act lowered both individual and corporate income tax rates, which reduced the incentives for trying to avoid taxes. Understanding the tax structure is nevertheless a worthwhile endeavor. Most people find that their tax payments still rival housing payments as their single largest expense. So *legally minimizing* taxes is important. Furthermore, there are substantial penalties for noncompliance with the tax law, and ignorance of the law is not a legally acceptable defense. This chapter will present an overview of the federal tax structure, plus some legal and ethical ways to minimize, defer, and occasionally even avoid taxation.

This chapter presents only a thumbnail sketch of the federal tax laws. Many details are omitted, and state taxes are ignored completely. Therefore, do not think that this chapter can be used to train tax experts. There are college-level tax-accounting courses available for would-be tax experts.

186
66
―――
252

7-1 Federal Personal Income Taxes

The federal income tax system is more than assigning a flat tax rate to some individual's income. Taxpayers are eligible for a number of deductions and exemptions, and payment schedules vary depending on marital status and household status. Income derived from investments may be taxed differently than income from salary or wages. And taxpayers may benefit from various retirement savings plans.

In this section, we look at the various components of the federal income tax structure, beginning with the steps needed to derive "taxable income" from "gross income."

How to Determine Taxable Income

Gross income is the starting point for computing someone's taxable income. The gross income figure equals *all income,* with certain exclusions specified in the Internal Revenue Code. Specific tax-exempt items include, to name a few, interest on most municipal bonds, gifts, a portion of social security benefits, and most life insurance proceeds. Unless the Internal Revenue Code specifically excludes a source of income from taxation, *all income is subject to taxation.*

Adjusted gross income is gross income after adjustments are subtracted. Some IRA contributions, Keogh contributions, alimony payments, and penalties on early withdrawal of savings are examples of **adjustments** that can be deducted. Adjustments are valuable; they benefit both taxpayers who itemize deductions and those who use the IRS's standard deduction.

The **taxable income** computation begins with adjusted gross income. Adjusted gross income is reduced by exemptions and the greater of either the standard, nonitemized deduction or the itemized deductions. Box 7-1 illustrates the computation of an individual taxpayer's taxable income. The remaining portion of this section describes in more detail the meaning of some of these terms, including "standard deductions," "itemized deductions," and "exemptions."

The Standard Deduction   Approximately 80 percent of taxpayers claim the standard, nonitemized deduction rather than itemize their deductions. The **standard deduction** is a flat amount used when itemized deductions are presumably too little. The

Box 7-1

COMPUTATION: The Procedure for Deriving Taxable Income

Gross income: Includes wages, salaries, net rents, etc., but excludes such things as interest on most municipal bonds, gifts, some social security benefits, and most life insurance proceeds

Less: Alimony payments, some IRA contributions, Keogh contributions, and other *adjustments*

Equals: Adjusted gross income (AGI)

Less: The greater of the *standard deduction* or itemized personal deductions. The latter includes such items as:

1. Medical expenses in excess of 7.5% of adjusted gross income
2. State and local taxes, except sales taxes
3. Charitable contributions (with certain limitations)
4. Some but not all interest payments
5. Casualty losses in excess of $100 per loss and 10% of adjusted gross income
6. Various miscellaneous deductions in excess of 2% of adjusted gross income*

Less: $2150 (in 1991) for each allowable exemption (the amount is adjusted for inflation annually)

Equals: Taxable income

---

* The total of deductions for charity, taxes, noninvestment interest and miscellaneous items are reduced for all taxpayers with adjusted gross incomes (AGI) over $100,000. To figure the reduction in deductions, subtract $100,000 from AGI and multiply the remainder by 3 percent. This adjustment effectively adds almost 1 percent to an individual's marginal tax rate.

standard deduction that is allowed depends on the taxpayer's filing (that is, family) status and is increased to adjust for inflation each year.

	Standard deductions		
Filing status	*1989*	*1991*	*1992, 1993, . . .*
Married, filing jointly	$5200	$5700	Increasing
Head of household	4550	5000	inflation-
Single	3100	3400	adjusted
Married, filing separately	2600	2850	amounts

In addition, the standard deduction is increased by $650 for each elderly (65 or over) or blind person who is married (or $1300 for a married person who is both blind and elderly). An additional standard deduction of $850 is allowed for an unmarried person who is elderly or blind ($1700 if both). Both the basic standard deduction and the additional allowances are subject to inflation adjustments every year. The tax benefits for being elderly and/or blind apply to taxpayers using the standard deduction, but not to those who itemize.

Itemized Deductions If itemized deductions exceed the standard deduction, it is always to the taxpayer's advantage to itemize. Allowable itemized deductions are explained below:

Medical expenses: Medical expenses unreimbursed by insurance are deductible to the extent that they exceed 7.5 percent of the taxpayer's adjusted gross income. For example, a taxpayer with $100,000 of adjusted gross income will have a medical expense deduction limited to unreimbursed medical payments in excess of $7500. Few individuals qualify for this deduction.

State and local sales taxes: State and local income taxes, real estate taxes, and personal property taxes qualify as itemized deductions. (The 1986 Tax Reform Act excluded state and local sales taxes from itemized deductions.)

Charitable contributions: Charitable contributions are, generally speaking, fully deductible for itemizing taxpayers only. Such taxpayers are limited to a deduction of no more than 50 percent of adjusted gross income for cash contributions to qualifying charities. Any excess deductions can be carried forward to the next 5 tax years, however. Donations of appreciated property are subject to stricter limitations.

Interest expense: Before 1986, almost all personal interest expense was allowed as tax-deductible, including interest on credit card and auto loans. The 1986 Tax Reform Act phased out consumer interest deductions, but added one loophole. Interest on up to $100,000 of *home equity loans* is fully deductible, regardless of the purpose for which the funds are used. Therefore, mortgage loans and home equity loans may be obtained to pay off other consumer loans in order to turn nondeductible interest into deductible interest. The wisdom of mortgaging one's home to pay for consumer purchases is dubious, but the tax law encourages it.

The individual taxpayer is allowed to deduct some other types of interest expenses. These include:

- Interest paid on business loans.

- Interest expense on loans incurred to finance investments, to the extent of investment income; any excess can be carried forward to future years when "unused" or "leftover" investment income may exist.

- Mortgage interest (with some restrictions).

- Interest from passive activity (involving no material participation by the investor), to the extent allowed by the passive activity rules (which are explained below).

Possibly the only rule that has remained constant regarding interest deductions over the past few decades is the nondeductibility of interest on loans used to finance tax-exempt income, such as municipal bonds. This rule makes sense; the costs of generating tax-exempt income should not be granted a tax deduction.

Miscellaneous deductions: Miscellaneous deductions include personal expenses incurred to generate business or investment income, and/or to preserve or protect income-producing assets. These expenses are deductible to the extent that they exceed 2 percent of adjusted gross income. Examples of miscellaneous deductions include 80 percent of business meals and entertainment, 100 percent of other unreimbursed employee expenses, tax-preparation fees, union dues, dues for professional organizations, subscription fees for business and investment-related periodicals, and safety-deposit box rentals. Certain moving expenses are also miscellaneous itemized deductions but are not subject to the 2 percent limitation. To illustrate: a taxpayer who has adjusted gross income of $20,000 and total qualifying miscellaneous deductions (not including moving expenses) of $1000 would be allowed an itemized miscellaneous deduction of $600, since only those items in excess of $400 (that is, 2% of $20,000) are deductible.

Casualty losses: A **casualty loss** may arise from fire, storm, shipwreck, or other events emanating from sudden, unexpected, or unusual causes. Casualty losses are deductible only to the extent that they cumulatively exceed 10 percent of adjusted gross income and $100 per loss. The amount of the loss is reduced by insurance awards in arriving at the proper deduction.

Exemptions **Exemptions** represent additional reductions of taxable income for qualifying individuals. Each taxpayer is allowed a personal exemption. Each taxpayer is also allowed an exemption for a spouse (if filing a joint return), as well as for each

---

CASE

The Case of the Dead Horse

A businessman named James Silver owned a very expensive pet horse, Lightning, that had a voracious appetite.

Lightning accidentally ate some rodent poison and died. The IRS allowed James a casualty deduction for the horse.

qualifying dependent. In the case of divorced parents, the custodial parent claims the dependent child exemption unless a legal agreement in effect before 1985 gives the noncustodial parent the exemption or unless the custodial parent signs IRS Form 8332 giving the noncustodial parent the exemption. Each exemption claimed has a value; it is $2150 for each exemption in 1991, and the amount increases each year with the rate of inflation. For high-income taxpayers, however, the benefit of exemptions is phased out. Exemptions are reduced by 2 percent for every $2500 by which adjusted gross income exceeds $100,000 for singles and $150,000 for married couples. This effectively adds half of 1 percent to an individual's top marginal tax bracket per exemption.

Calculating Tax Liability

The 1991 tax rate structure is shown in Table 7-1.

Marginal tax rate is the phrase used to describe the rate at which a taxpayer pays tax on his or her last dollar of income (or the rate at which the taxpayer saves on his or her last dollar of deductions). The marginal rate is the appropriate rate to consider for investment decisions. The **average tax rate,** the amount of tax divided by taxable income, has limited usefulness for decision-making purposes. The taxpayer is more interested in how decisions will affect tax liability at the margin—that is, the last dollars earned or last dollars saved from deductions. For example, if Ms. Taxpayer, whose taxable income is otherwise $50,000, is about to receive a year-end bonus of $5000, she should know she will pay Uncle Sam 31 percent on that $5000. Ms. Taxpayer's tax calculations are shown in Box 7-2; it shows that her marginal tax rate is (28% + 3%), or 31 percent. Her average tax rate is 23.5 percent (that is, $12,925 of tax/$55,000 of taxable income).

The Changing Federal Income Tax Laws   Major tax acts in recent years include:

- Tax Reform Act of 1976
- Revenue Act of 1978
- Economic Recovery Tax Act of 1981 (ERTA)
- Tax Equity and Fiscal Responsibility Act of 1982 (TEFRA)
- Tax Reform Act of 1984
- Tax Reform Act of 1986
- The Revenue Reconciliation Act of 1990

Table 7-1
1991 Tax Rates on a Person's Taxable Income

Tax rates	Joint returns	Single individuals
15% on incomes of:	$0–$34,000	$0–$20,350
28% on incomes of:	$34,001–$82,150	$20,351–$49,300
31% on incomes of:	Above $82,150	Above $49,300

COMPUTATION: Ms. Taxpayer's Marginal Tax Rate

A single person with a taxable income of $55,000 would calculate the 1991 tax as follows:

15% of first $20,350	$ 3,052.50
28% of ($49,300 − $20,350)	8,106.00
31% of ($55,000 − $49,300)	1,767.00
Total tax	$12,925.50

Therefore, this person is paying tax at a *marginal rate* of 31 percent.

The 1986 tax law was the most dramatic change of all—but most financial and political commentators expect continuing tax changes. By the time you read this text, the rate structure reported here may well have been changed by new legislation.

One of the messages Congress sent the public in 1986 was that the tax structure's primary objective is to raise revenue, not to encourage particular behaviors. Many proinvestment portions of the Internal Revenue Code were repealed or watered down. Investment credit was repealed, the capital gains exclusion was repealed, tax-sheltered investments were shut down, real estate investment lost many of its tax benefits, and individual retirement account benefits were lost to many taxpayers.

How long the pendulum will swing in the direction of revenue raising is anyone's guess. The only certainty is that taxes have changed so rapidly and become so complex that the average person's ability to comply with the law is questionable. The U.S. Treasury Department is years behind in drafting the IRS Regulations used to interpret the volumes of new tax laws. A stabilization of tax law is in order before the weight of change makes voluntary compliance a dream rather than an accepted standard.

Special Taxes on Investors

Speculators and investors face special taxes. Here are some tax considerations they should bear in mind.

Capital Gains and Losses   Capital gains and losses arise out of the sale or disposition of capital assets, which include such things as securities and real estate. The exchange of these capital assets can result in a long-term capital gain or loss or a short-term capital gain or loss, depending on the length of the holding period. According to IRS codes, if a capital asset has been held for more than 1 year, it is classified as a long-term asset. If a capital asset is held 1 year or less, it is called *short-term* and gains are taxed as ordinary income. The 1990 tax act reinstated a slight preferential tax treatment for long-term capital gains. As of January 1991, long-term capital gains are subject to a maximum tax rate of 28 percent. Thus, people in the 31 percent tax

Box 7-3

177

Chapter 7
Federal
Taxes

COMPUTATION: Ms. Gaynor's Long-Term Gain

Ms. Gaynor is a single taxpayer who earned $60,000 of taxable income in 1991. Her income included a $10,000 long-term capital gain. Thus, Ms. Gaynor's ordinary (or non-capital gains) income was $50,000 in 1991, which exceeds the $49,300 of ordinary taxable income that would be taxed at a rate of 28 percent or below. Ms. Gaynor's 1991 income taxes cannot exceed $14,175.50. If her $60,000 income came exclusively from salary or wages, her tax would rise to $14,475.50.

1. $60,000 income including $10,000 capital gains:

15% of first $20,350	$ 3,052.50
28% of ($49,300 − $20,350)	8,106.00
31% of ($50,000 − $49,300)	217.00
28% of the $10,000 net capital gain	2,800.00
Total taxes due	$14,175.50

2. $60,000 income without capital gains:

15% of first $20,350	$ 3,052.50
28% of ($49,300 − $20,350)	8,106.00
31% of ($60,000 − $49,300)	3,317.00
Total taxes due	$14,475.50

---

bracket benefit by the 3 percent differential (31 percent − 28 percent), as can be seen in Box 7-3. Between 1987 and 1991 there was no difference between the taxation of ordinary income and long-term capital gains income.

Capital losses can be used to offset ordinary income. A maximum of $3000 per year of *net* capital losses (that is, total capital losses in excess of total capital gains) can be used to reduce taxable ordinary income. Capital losses in excess of the $3000 may be carried forward to future years, until the taxpayer dies.

The historic intent of a preferential capital gain tax rate was to foster and reward risk-taking investors. Theoretically, because some people are willing to risk money developing products and processes, the U.S. economy should be stronger and a better competitor in the world markets. Congress seemed to believe this theory. The capital gains tax rate was significantly preferential until 1986, when it was repealed. But beginning in 1991, a token preferential capital gains rate reappeared. The taxation of capital gains has become a political football, with one side saying it is designed to benefit the rich and the opposing side saying it will stimulate the economy and thereby help everyone.

Wash Sales　A **wash sale** is the nearly simultaneous purchase and sale (or vice versa) of the same security. As explained in Chapter 6, it is illegal to use wash sales to create the illusion that a transaction occurred in order to perpetrate a fraud. The law also prohibits the use of wash sales to evade income taxes. The IRS prohibits deduction of loss on sale or exchange of securities if substantially identical securities are acquired within 30 days before or after the sale or exchange. The wash sale rules apply whether the taxpayer voluntarily sells the stock in order to register a loss for income tax purposes, is forced to sell, or sells in order to prevent a greater loss. These provisions also apply when the taxpayer enters into a futures contract or option to acquire substantially similar stock or securities. Note, however, that the wash sale rules apply only to loss transactions, not transactions involving gains. And the loss is not gone forever; recognition of a loss is merely postponed until the replacement security is sold at a loss.

Home Ownership   Two provisions of the tax law affecting capital gains are helpful to homeowners: (1) the one-time exclusion of up to $125,000 of gain on the sale of a principal residence by a taxpayer who is 55 or older and (2) the nonrecognition rule for gains on the sale of a principal residence, when the proceeds from the old home are reinvested in a new residence within 2 years of sale and when the purchase price of the new residence equals or exceeds the selling price of the old residence. These two provisions, in addition to the mortgage interest deduction and real estate tax deduction, continue to make home ownership a tax-favored investment.

Commodity Futures Contracts and Hedges   **Commodity futures contracts** are considered capital assets and are subject to a unique rule of taxation.[1] Any gain or loss is treated as if (1) 40 percent of the gain or loss is a short-term gain or loss and (2) 60 percent of the gain or loss is a long-term gain or loss.

Hedges are risk-reducing strategies in which the hedger buys and sells the same asset at the same time in order to attain a position that is equivalent to having no position at all. Hedging is analyzed in Chapter 20. Nonspeculative hedges are not considered capital assets, and, therefore, any income or loss is treated as ordinary gains or losses. When futures contracts are entered into *solely as hedges against speculative risks* due to commodity price fluctuations inherent in a taxpayer's business (such as a farmer's agricultural commodities, or a silverware manufacturer's inventory of silver bullion), such operations are recognized for income tax purposes as a legitimate form of business insurance—a nonspeculative hedge. The costs are deductible as ordinary and necessary business expenses, and any profits are considered ordinary income. Speculative hedges are taxed as capital assets.[2]

---

[1] The commodity futures contracts must be *marked to the market* (as most U.S. contracts are) to determine the settlement prices and margin requirements, or else the contracts' gains or losses are all treated as ordinary income and taxed at the higher ordinary income rate.

[2] The line drawn between a hedging transaction involving futures contracts and a speculative commodity futures contract can become very fine. In order for a hedge not to be classed as a speculative capital asset, there must be (1) a risk of loss by unfavorable changes in the price of something expected to be used or marketed in one's normal business, (2) a possibility of shifting such risk to someone else through the purchase or sale of futures contracts, and (3) an intention and attempt to so shift the risk. When losses are incurred, it is to the investor's advantage to have a nonspeculative hedge to enjoy the unrestricted benefit of ordinary losses. When a hedged position incurs gains, the investor is better off obtaining the favorable capital gains treatment. To avoid retroactive changes in one's intent, the Internal Revenue Code requires the hedger to clearly identify, before the close of the day on which the transaction was entered into, which transactions are for hedging purposes.

Put and Call Options   Put and call options were introduced in Chapter 3; they are capital assets and are afforded capital gains and loss treatment. If they are held for periods of less than 1 year (which is the usual case), they receive short-term capital gain or loss treatment when they are traded or allowed to expire. When an option is exercised, however, its premium (or purchase price) is added to the sales proceeds of the underlying security and thus receives the same short-term gain or loss treatment as the underlying asset. Puts and calls are explored in more detail in Chapter 21.

Tax-Exempt Municipal Bonds

Municipal bonds are issued by municipalities such as states, counties, townships, cities, and school districts to finance local public projects (see Chapter 2 for more details). The Internal Revenue Code specifies that *the interest income from most municipal bonds is exempt from federal income taxes.*[3] The exemption comes from a traditional separation in this country between federal and local governments. This tax exemption makes it easier for small, unheard-of municipalities to sell their bonds and thus obtain financing for projects to improve their community.

Municipal bonds pay lower rates of interest than practically all taxable bonds. On an after-tax basis, however, municipal bonds pay competitive yields. See Box 7-4. Most municipalities need the tax exemption to help attract investors—it is like a federal subsidy.

[3] When a municipality issues industrial development bonds to finance business development, the income may be *alternative minimum taxable income* (AMTI) and may be subject to the AMTI tax (instead of ordinary income tax). Since the AMTI is very complicated and affects very few people, it is not discussed further in this introductory tax chapter.

Box 7-4

COMPUTATION: The After-Tax Yield on a Municipal Bond

Consider an investor in the 28 percent income tax bracket who is trying to decide between a municipal bond and a corporate bond of equivalent riskiness, both of which pay a 10 percent rate of interest. On an after-tax basis, the municipal bond will pay 10 percent interest, whereas the corporate bond will pay only 7.2 percent.

$$\begin{array}{ccc}
\text{Pretax} & & \text{aftertax}\\
\text{interest} \times & \left(1.0 - \begin{array}{c}\text{investor's}\\\text{income}\\\text{tax rate}\end{array}\right) = & \text{interest}\\
\text{rate} & & \text{rate}
\end{array}$$

$$.1 \times (1.0 - .28) = .072 = 7.2\%$$

This formula shows that 28 percent of the corporate bond's interest income goes for taxes, leaving 72 percent for the investor. Since 72 percent of the 10 percent interest rate equals a 7.2 percent after-tax return, the investor will earn 2.8 percentage points more with the municipal bond.

Table 7-2
After-Tax Returns for Investors
in Three Tax Brackets

Before-tax return, %			
15% *tax bracket*	*28%* *tax bracket*	*31%* *tax bracket*	*After-tax return*
5.29%	6.25%	6.52%	4.50%
5.88	6.94	7.25	5.00
6.47	7.64	7.97	5.50
7.06	8.33	8.70	6.00
7.65	9.03	9.42	6.50
8.24	9.72	10.14	7.00
8.82	10.42	10.87	7.50
9.41	11.11	11.59	8.00

The higher an investor's income tax bracket, the more incentive there is for that investor to seek tax-exempt bond interest. Table 7-2 illustrates the after-tax rates of return for investors in three income tax brackets. For instance, an investor in the 31 percent tax bracket earning a before-tax rate of return of 12 percent gets an after-tax return of 8.28 percent. This 8.28 percent after-tax return is computed by multiplying the 12 percent before-tax return by 69 percent (1.0 minus the 31 percent tax rate).

Although the highest marginal tax rate shown on the tax tables is 31 percent, the effective marginal tax rate can be higher as a result of two changes made in the 1990 Revenue Reconciliation Act: (1) The phaseout of the personal exemptions for single taxpayers with incomes in excess of $100,000 and married taxpayers with incomes in excess of $150,000 equates to a one-half of 1 percent increase in the effective marginal tax rate *per exemption.* A family of six whose tax table marginal tax rate is 31 percent would have an effective marginal tax rate of 34 percent during the exemption phaseout. (2) Taxpayers with incomes in excess of $100,000 are subject to a 3 percent reduction for most of their itemized deductions up to a maximum 80 percent reduction. This itemized deduction phaseout equates to nearly a 1 percent increase in the effective marginal tax rate.

Rental Real Estate

The IRS has defined **passive activities** as those that do not involve material participation by the investor. Real estate investing, for example, has been classified as a passive activity. Losses from passive activities can be used only to offset other passive income (but not ordinary salary income or income from a portfolio of investments).[4] Even investors who actively participate in the management of rental

---

[4] The 1986 Tax Act eliminated virtually all traditional passive investments designed to generate tax losses in excess of income in order to reduce total tax liability. These traditional tax shelters generally involved oil and gas exploration, equipment leasing, and real estate.

real estate cannot offset excess real estate losses with ordinary income or portfolio income. There is one small exception: When an individual or a married couple actively participates in rental real estate activities, up to $25,000 of losses from all such activities may be used in each year to offset ordinary and portfolio income.

7-2 Tax-Sheltered Retirement Plans

Tax shelters for individuals' contributions to their own retirement funds are provided because the federal government does not want elderly people to become wards of the state. Further, such **tax-sheltered retirement plans** encourage long-term investing, which benefits the economy. These are essentially savings plans, with two tax incentives. First, any part of current income put in these retirement plans may be deducted from gross income to reduce the taxable income. Second, the interest income, cash dividends, and any capital gains are not taxable until the taxpayer retires and actually receives the funds. This tax deferment is advantageous because most people will be in a lower income tax bracket after they retire. To discourage people from using retirement plans as savings pools to evade (or at least delay) income taxes, a penalty of 10 percent is levied on most withdrawals made before the saver reaches the age of 59.5. In addition, the entire amount of the early withdrawal becomes immediately subject to ordinary income taxes. Therefore, tax-sheltered retirement plans are not useful as tax shelters for short-run savings.

Congress has allowed the tax-sheltered retirement plans to remain fairly well intact. While the law is constantly changing and evolving, and is extraordinarily complex, it may nevertheless be fair to say that qualified retirement plans may be the last remaining significant tax shelter for the average American taxpayer. The benefits of these plans are fairly simple; Box 7-5 shows how they work.

Box 7-5

COMPUTATION: Saving for Retirement Cuts Income Taxes

A person who has $20,700 taxable income and is subject to a marginal tax rate of 28 percent places $1500 in a tax-sheltered retirement plan.

	Without retirement plan	*With retirement plan*
Taxable income	$20,700	$20,700
Contribution to retirement plan	0	1,500
Taxable income	$20,700	$19,200
Tax rate	× .28	× .28
Income tax	$5,796	$5,376

Thus, this prudent planner saves $420 in income taxes ($5,796 − $5,376).

There are many types of tax-sheltered retirement plans—pension plans, profit-sharing plans, 401K plans, IRAs, SEPs, and Keogh plans, to name a few. Pension and profit-sharing plans typically are employer-paid benefits, and most large corporations provide one or more such plans. Let's look at some of the more common plans.

Pension and Profit-Sharing Plans

The provisions of employer-provided pension and profit-sharing plans vary with each corporation. Each plan must stay within certain parameters defined by the Pension Reform Act of 1974, also known as the *Employment Retirement Income Security Act (ERISA),* introduced in Chapter 6. Vesting is one of many issues for which ERISA provides guidelines. **Vesting** occurs when an employee obtains a legally enforceable claim on pension benefits, such that the benefits cannot be taken away even if that person resigns or is dismissed. There are many different vesting plans, but in general complete vesting must occur after an employee has been with a firm from 3 to 7 years. Each corporation's written pension plan must meet official government approval before adoption.

401K Plans

A plan gaining popularity in recent years is the **401K plan** (named for Section 401 of the Internal Revenue Code, which created it). This plan differs from corporate pension plans in that it provides for employee contributions in addition to employer contributions. Both employee and employer contributions, as well as earnings from previous contributions, are excluded from the employee's taxable income until the person begins making withdrawals as a retiree.

Plans differ from company to company, and Congress changes the guidelines frequently. The maximum employee contribution is the lesser of some stipulated percentage of wages (as provided for in the plan) or $7979, adjusted annually for inflation. Such tax-sheltered retirement plans have become increasingly popular in recent years, as they provide employees with retirement income and a tax shelter on current income.

Keogh Plans

Keogh plans are sometimes referred to as *H.R. 10 plans* or *self-employed retirement plans.* In the past the rules governing Keogh plans were much more restrictive than those for corporate profit-sharing plans. Recent legislation, however, has established parity between corporate plans and Keogh plans. One effect of this new parity is that a major reason for incorporating a business (the more favorable corporate retirement plan benefits) has been eliminated.

Self-employed taxpayers can deduct up to 25 percent of their annual net income from their business and put it into a tax-deferred Keogh plan. There is a $30,000 annual maximum allowable deduction. People who are employed and also operate a business can benefit from Keogh plans as well. These people are limited to a 15 percent maximum annual deduction from the income they receive from their employer. Keogh plan investing can be used to supplement the 15 percent maximum on the pension plan provided by an employer.

All taxpayers are allowed to contribute the lesser of $2000 per year or their total earned income to an individual retirement account, or IRA, (or $2250 for spousal IRAs). But, not all taxpayers are allowed to deduct their IRA contributions from their gross income in order to arrive at their taxable income. Only those people who are not active participants in employer-maintained retirement plans *and* who have adjusted gross incomes of not greater than $40,000 ($25,000 for single individuals) are allowed to fully deduct their IRA contributions. For those who are active participants in an employer-maintained retirement plan with adjusted gross incomes over $40,000 ($25,000 for single individuals), the deductible portion of the IRA contribution is reduced on the basis of adjusted gross income. Zero deduction is allowed for people with adjusted gross income of $50,000 or more ($35,000 or more for single individuals), before reductions for tax-deductible IRA contributions. These rules are summarized in Table 7-3. For married taxpayers, the phaseout and loss of deductions applies when either spouse is covered by an employer-provided retirement plan. That is, when one spouse is covered by an employer-provided retirement plan, *neither* spouse is allowed to have an IRA deduction—one of several marriage penalties built into the federal tax system.

Those people *not* qualifying for an IRA income tax deduction for their contributions must meet IRS bookkeeping requirements. These requirements are designed to keep track of earnings from IRA contributions, and to determine which portion of eventual IRA payments is taxable. Form 8606 must be filed with the person's annual income tax return; failure to file subjects the taxpayer to a $50 penalty. Since the nondeductible IRA contribution achieves tax deferral only on the investment income earned by the IRA, some taxpayers have decided that the additional bookkeeping costs are greater than the tax benefit and have chosen other investment options.

An IRA participant may make contributions every year or only occasionally. People who establish IRAs must select investment vehicles for their retirement contributions. Popular vehicles include common stocks, bonds, and savings accounts. Since 1987 taxpayers may also hold gold and silver coins issued by the United States.

Simplified Employment Pensions

Simplified employment pensions (SEPs) are emerging as the primary retirement plan for small businesses and professional practices. Although Keogh plans are still widely used for small businesses, SEPs offer several advantages:

Table 7-3
IRA Deductions for Joint Filers

Gross income	With a corporate retirement plan	Without a corporate retirement plan
Zero to $40,000	Full IRA deduction	Full IRA deduction
$40,000 to $50,000	Partial deduction	Full deduction
$50,000 and up	No deduction	Full deduction

- They are less expensive and are easier to implement.

- No government filings are required, and there are no annual disclosure requirements other than reporting SEP contributions on an employee's W-2 Form.

- A SEP plan can be established at any time up to the date an employer files its tax return, whereas a Keogh plan must be in place prior to year-end.

- A SEP can contain a "mini-401K" salary-reduction feature (sometimes given the acronym SAR/SEP) permitting employers to make elective deferrals of up to $7979 (in 1990, and adjusted annually for inflation); most important, employers do not have to contribute.

SEPs use IRAs rather than trusts to collect and administer retirement funds. Thus, the IRA rules apply rather than the qualified-plan rules of pension, profit-sharing, 401K, and Keogh plans. SEPs and SAR/SEPs provide greater flexibility at a fraction of the cost and complexity associated with comparable 401K and profit-sharing plans.

Tax planning should not be discontinued after a taxpayer reaches retirement age. Estate taxes must be paid on the value of a deceased person's assets. Furthermore, gift taxes, which are imposed to stop people who are near death from giving away wealth to avoid taxes, must also be considered.

7-3   Estate Taxes and Gift Taxes

Estate taxes are the most steeply progressive of all federal taxes. After a $600,000 exemption per person, the rates range from 37 percent on taxable estates valued at over $600,000 to 55 percent on taxable estates over $3 million. Note that the lowest estate tax rate is higher than the highest individual income tax rate. Further, in most cases, the estate tax represents a double tax. Throughout their lifetimes, individuals pay tax on the income they earn. The after-tax income that is saved builds up the saver's estate. But when the saver dies, that accumulated after-tax income is taxed again. High and progressive estate tax rates make estate planning for the affluent a prudent course. We will first discuss estate taxes and then consider tax-exempt gifts as a legal way to reduce estate taxes.

Estate Taxes

The estate tax is levied on the deceased's *taxable estate*. The *gross estate* comprises all the assets owned by the decedent, valued as of date of death. Date-of-death values are easily derived for assets such as cash, publicly traded stocks and bonds, life insurance proceeds, certificates of deposit, and other monetary assets. But valuation can be difficult for a closely held business, real estate, jewelry, art, and other real (or physical) assets. These assets may require costly appraisals by experts, and they are always subject to close IRS scrutiny on audit. The total of all assets owned at the date of death values make up the **gross estate.** The estate tax is levied on the **taxable estate** which is determined by subtracting from the gross estate certain deductions, expenses, and gifts, as shown in Box 7-6.

Box 7-6

185

*Chapter 7
Federal
Taxes*

DEFINITION: The Taxable Estate

Gross estate

Less:
    Unlimited marital deduction
    Unlimited charitable deductions
    Funeral expenses
    Estate administrative expenses
    Debts of the decedent

Equals: Taxable estate

Gift Taxes

To maximize the portion of an estate that heirs may inherit, some people make gifts to eliminate the appreciated value of the donated assets from their taxable estates. But not all gifts are tax-free. Anytime one person gives money to another without receiving goods or services of equal value in return, the IRS considers this transfer of wealth to be subject to tax. The estate and gift taxes are both also known as **unified transfer taxes.** They are subject to the same tax rates, as shown in Table 7-4.

Table 7-4
Unified Federal Estate and Gift Tax Rates*

Over (1)	But not over	Tax on (1)	Tax rate on excess over (1)
$ 0	$ 10,000	$ 0	18%
10,000	20,000	1,800	20
20,000	40,000	3,800	22
40,000	60,000	8,200	24
60,000	80,000	13,000	26
80,000	100,000	18,200	28
100,000	150,000	23,800	30
150,000	250,000	38,800	32
250,000	500,000	70,800	34
500,000	750,000	155,800	37
750,000	1,000,000	248,300	39
1,000,000	1,250,000	345,800	41
1,250,000	1,500,000	448,300	43
1,500,000	2,000,000	555,800	45
2,000,000	2,500,000	780,800	49
2,500,000	3,000,000	1,025,800	53
3,000,000		1,290,800	55

* Lifetime transfers (gifts) and transfers at death are added together for the purpose of determining the applicable rate for transfers at death.

Note: Since the first $600,000 from an estate is tax-exempt, the relevant estate tax rates are 37 percent through 55 percent, which are shaded.

COMPUTATION: Mr. John White's Estate Taxes

John White, a widower, dies with a taxable estate of $800,000. Four years before his death John gave his son and his daughter gifts of $100,000 apiece. The net estate tax of the late Mr. White is calculated below:

John White's taxable estate	$800,000
Two $100,000 gifts*	+200,000
Two annual gift tax exclusions	− 20,000
Adjusted taxable estate	$980,000
Estate tax from Table 7-4	
[$248,300 + .39($980,000 − $750,000)]	$338,000
Tax reduction due to $600,000 exemption	
[$155,800 + .37($600,000 − $500,000)]	−192,800
Net estate tax	$145,200

* After his death, if Mr. White's accountant forgot to report his gifts, the IRS could pick them up with its computerized records of his children's tax reports, canceled checks, bank records, or other parts of the "paper trail" left by the transactions. Remember, jail sentences are typical penalties for failure to report income and gifts and pay the taxes due.

However, there is a generous tax credit applicable to the unified transfer tax, and there are also some exemptions.

Up to $10,000 per year may be gifted to as many people as a taxpayer desires without incurring any tax. Unlimited amounts may be given to one's spouse tax-free. When the gift giver dies, the deceased person's *total taxable gifts* must be added back to the estate, and the unified estate and gift-tax schedule shown in Table 7-4 is applicable to this aggregate amount.

Table 7-4 applies to the total amount of taxable gifts given before the donor dies, plus the taxable estate of the donor. The first $600,000 of transfers are exempt from the unified estate and gift tax. This $600,000 exemption is equivalent to a tax credit of $192,800 subtracted from the estate and gift unified tax. The $192,800 credit is in addition to the $10,000 annual exclusions and the unlimited marital deductions. Box 7-7 provides a hypothetical example of how a person's estate tax would be calculated.

7-4   Federal Corporate Income Taxes

Unlike people, corporations may live forever. If a corporation's life does end (for instance, in bankruptcy), it incurs no gift or estate taxes. However, corporations must pay taxes on income annually, just as individuals do.

Corporations are legal entities that exist to allow the ownership of a firm to be subdivided into shares that are readily transferable. Unlike a proprietorship or a partnership, both of which are considered to be extensions of their owners, corporations are treated by the law as separate entities. As a result, income earned by corporations is taxed twice. First, profitable corporations pay corporate income taxes of about one-third of every dollar of earnings. Second, the people who own the corporation's shares pay federal income taxes on whatever cash dividends and capital gains their shares yield. Some economists believe that this **double taxation** not only seems wrong, it also weakens the incentive to make investments that would strengthen the economy. The double taxation of corporate earnings cannot be avoided by accumulating profits year after year within the corporation instead of paying the after-tax profits out as cash dividends. Two federal penalty-like taxes prevent such tax evasion schemes—the accumulated earnings tax, and the personal holding company tax.

Corporate Tax Structure

The corporate income tax structure is simple. A corporation must pay federal income tax according to the progressive tax rates in Table 7-5. There is no preferential treatment of capital gains. Consider a corporation that earns $80,000 of taxable income. This corporation would pay a total federal income tax of $15,450, as indicated in Box 7-8. As Table 7-5 shows, corporations' *marginal tax rates* on income vary from 15 percent to 34 percent. Box 7-8 shows that the *average tax rate* for a corporation with $80,000 of taxable income is 19.3 percent (that is, the total tax of $15,450 is 19.3 percent of the total income of $80,000). The average corporate tax rate starts at the minimum marginal tax rate of 15 percent for incomes of $50,000 or less and rises toward a maximum marginal tax rate of 34 percent.

Table 7-5
Federal Corporate Income Tax Rates

Taxable income	Tax rate
Not over $50,000	15%
Over $50,000 but not over $75,000	25
Over $75,000	34

Note: The benefit of the lower and progressive 15 and 25 percent corporate income tax brackets begins to be phased out when a corporation's taxable income reaches $100,000. This phaseout occurs via a *5 percent surcharge.* The benefit of graduated rates is fully phased out for corporations with more than $335,000 of taxable income. Stated differently, the corporate marginal income tax rate is effectively 39 percent for incomes between $100,000 and $335,000.

COMPUTATION: Federal Income Tax on a Corporation's Annual
Income of $80,000

Marginal tax rate	Times	Portion of total income	Equals	Portion of total tax
15%	×	$50,000	=	$ 7,500
25	×	25,000*	=	6,250
34	×	5,000†	=	1,700
Total		$80,000		$15,450‡

* The amount between the first $50,000 and $75,000.

† The amount over the first $75,000.

‡ The corporation's *average tax rate* is 19.3 percent because the total tax of $15,450 is 19.3 percent of the total income of $80,000.

Intercorporate Cash Dividends

When a parent corporation owns a subsidiary corporation and receives cash dividend income from it, **triple taxation** occurs—(1) the subsidiary corporation pays income taxes, (2) the parent corporation pays taxes on cash dividend income from the subsidiary, and (3) the parent's shareholders are taxed on cash dividends they receive. In order to reduce this triple taxation, corporations are allowed to receive certain income free from tax. They are permitted to keep 70 percent of the cash dividend income paid to them from subsidiary corporations free from federal income taxes.[5] Thus, if a corporation in the 34 percent income tax bracket receives cash dividends from another corporation in which it owns shares, the effective tax rate on the intercorporate cash dividends is 10.2 percent (which is 34 percent of the 30 percent that is taxable).

Interest Expense

Corporations are allowed to deduct interest expense they pay on borrowed funds from their gross income to arrive at their taxable income. As a result, borrowing reduces the tax bill. The deductibility of interest encourages borrowing money rather than waiting until enough cash has been saved to pay for the purchase. Such borrowing accelerates spending and has the positive effect of stimulating the economy by creating more sales of goods and, thus, more jobs. A negative effect is a

[5] If the parent corporation owns more than 80 percent of a subsidiary corporation, then the parent's intercorporate cash dividend income from that corporation is 100 percent exempt from federal income taxes. For example, the General Motors Corporation need not pay income taxes on any cash dividends from its Chevrolet division if Chevy is a subsidiary that is more than 80 percent owned by GM.

proliferation of borrowing—by both corporations and households. Consumers borrow to finance consumption, corporations borrow to finance expansion and LBOs, and as a result, the United States entered the 1990s with huge amounts of debt that will cripple its progress.

Corporate Income Statements

The two main determinants of a corporation's income taxes are, first, the corporate income tax structure and, second, the accounting methods used to derive a corporation's taxable income. Box 7-9 outlines the essentials of accountants' income statements. Despite the seeming simplicity, many questions arise concerning definitions and measurements of the items that determine income.

Generally accepted accounting procedures (GAAP) are followed by virtually all practicing accountants in the United States, but nevertheless, more than one procedure may be acceptable for reporting a business transaction. The American Institute of Certified Public Accountants (AICPA), the IRS, and the SEC hand down opinions on which practices are acceptable and which are unacceptable. Often these opinions eliminate the extreme or the completely ambiguous alternatives while still allowing several accounting choices. The result is a narrowing of practices but not the

Box 7-9

DEFINITION: The Format for Corporate Income Statements

Sales revenue

Less: Cost of goods sold

Equals: Gross operating margin

Less: Selling and administrative expenses and depreciation

Equals: Net operating income (earnings before interest and taxes)

Less: Interest expense

Equals: Income before taxes

Less: Taxes

Equals: Net income

Less: Dividends on preferred stock

Equals: Net income for common equity

Less: Dividends to common equity

Equals: Retained earnings

---

creation of uniform accounting. Thus, the same economic event can often be legitimately reported in several different ways. This affects the corporation's taxable income.

People unfamiliar with the complexity of accounting procedures often assume that corporate income is a clearly defined quantity; the financial statements published in annual reports do not seem open to dispute. The following quotation from a widely used intermediate accounting textbook gives a truer picture.

> The measurement of periodic income of a business enterprise is perhaps the foremost objective of the accounting process. The word *estimate* is appropriate because income is one of the most elusive concepts in the business world. The art of accounting probably never will progress to the point where "income" can be defined to everyone's satisfaction.[6]

The point is that accounting procedures can have as much impact on the taxes a corporation pays as the tax laws themselves. Chapter 14 goes into more detail about what to do if a company has "cooked its books."

7-5 Tax-Exempt Investors

To prevent double taxation and to encourage charitable giving, the IRS allows certain conduit-type investment organizations to operate either partially or totally free from federal income taxes. Some of these income tax exemptions are granted to the biggest investment organizations in the world. These large investors do not need to consider tax strategies such as investing in tax-exempt municipal bonds.

Investment Companies

Investment companies (which include mutual funds and closed-end funds) can choose to be classified as **regulated investment companies,** which qualifies them for income tax exemption. To be considered a regulated investment company the funds must invest in a diversified portfolio of securities and pay out all capital gains, cash dividends, and interest income in the same year the income was realized. The purpose of these two stipulations is to stop investment companies from being used as holding companies for accumulating assets and thus building corporate empires, or as tax-avoidance devices that accumulate tax-free income for investors. The income paid out by regulated investment companies becomes a taxable part of the shareholder's total income when it is received by the shareholder. This realized income may be automatically reinvested in the same investment company immediately, if the individual desires; however, income taxes must be paid even though the income was reinvested.

---

[6] A. N. Mosich and E. John Larsen, *Intermediate Accounting*, 5th ed. (New York: McGraw-Hill, 1982), p. 85.

Trusts

A **trust** is a contractual agreement under which a party called the **trustee** (usually the trust department of a bank) holds and manages assets that are put into the trust by a second party, the **benefactor.** The trust is established for the benefit of a third party who is the trust's **beneficiary.** Benefactors place monies into trusts to obtain asset management, asset protection, tax management, estate planning, and to support a beneficiary. Charities and incapacitated family members are common examples of beneficiaries. The contract between the benefactor and the trust manager that governs how the trust assets should be managed is called a **fiduciary agreement.** If a trust distributes all its income to the trust's beneficiary, the beneficiary must pay income taxes on that income (unless the beneficiary is also tax-exempt—for example, a university). But, the trust pays no income taxes if all income is distributed. If income is accumulated in the trust, however, it is taxable. Morgan-Guaranty Bank in New York City, for instance, has a large trust department, which manages over $100 billion of trust assets.

Pension Plans

Monies accumulated in employee pensions and profit-sharing plans earn tax-free income. These funds are taxable income to the retired employees when they receive them.

Pension funds are the largest investors in the United States; they constitute an investment pool of income tax–free money that exceeds $1 trillion, in aggregate. Exxon, IBM, the State of California, and General Motors, for example, each hold billions of dollars in segregated pension funds to pay their employees' retirement incomes. In some corporations, pension fund managers control more assets than any other executive.

Charities and Foundations

Nonprofit charities, religious groups, and educational foundations are allowed to invest their endowments and earn income that is free from income taxes if certain minimum annual donationlike payments are made to beneficiaries. There are different tax regulations for different types of charities and foundations. However, a minimum of 5 percent of the assets or all earned income, whichever is larger, must be given to the beneficiaries every year. If a foundation makes this annual donation, it need pay only an excise tax of 1 to 2 percent on its income.

7-6   Some Conclusions

Both private individuals and corporate entities are required by law to pay income taxes. As of this writing, individual federal income tax rates are mildly progressive, from 15 to 31 percent; corporate rates range from 15 to 34 percent. Highly progressive gift and estate taxes encourage careful estate planning.

One of the many objectives of the 1986 Tax Reform Act was to restore a perception of fairness to the federal income tax. Too many wealthy people had been paying very little in taxes via perfectly legal means. And too many taxpayers knew of people who did not declare income and thus evaded taxes.[7] For these reasons the 1986 Tax Reform Act was a tax bill with teeth. Gone are tax shelters as we once knew them; gone is the low preferential tax rate on long-term capital gains; perhaps most important, gone is much of the driving incentive to cheat on taxes. The top tax rates have tumbled from 1981's high of 70 percent to 1991's high of 31 percent. Perhaps these lower rates are the best tax shelter ever contrived. But perhaps they also represent too much of a good thing. Many analysts believe that federal budget deficits will continue to force legislators to raise tax rates; the first step in this trend occurred in 1990.

Summary

Because of the federal tax structure in the United States, investors and investment managers need to anticipate the tax consequences of their money management decisions. Both individuals and corporations pay taxes on income, though at different rates and with different deductions and exemptions. Although the general structure of the federal income tax has remained the same since its inception in 1913—ours is a progressive system—the tax laws have changed constantly and substantially (about every 2.5 years since 1976), and although there have been cases of tax reduction, for the most part the rates have been increased many, many times.

Tax payments for most individuals rival housing payments as their single largest expense; for corporations, the tax structure encourages borrowing rather than saving, because of the interest deduction. So tax policies have a significant impact on our financial lives.

As individuals, we need to know how our taxable income is derived from our gross income, and how to decide to take the standard deduction or to itemize; we need to know about exemptions, marginal tax rates, and the structure of the special taxes on investors (capital gains and losses, wash sales, home ownership, the tax rules for futures contracts and hedges, put and call options, tax-exempt municipal bonds, and real estate investing). For the future, we must make investment decisions about tax-sheltered retirement plans, and about estate and gift taxes.

Corporations have their own tax rates, deductions, and exemptions. Special rules apply to tax-exempt investors—which are today some of the biggest investment organizations in the world: investment companies, trusts, pension plans, and charities and foundations.

Further Reading

Kess, Sidney, and Bertil Weslin, *Estate Planning Guide* (Chicago: Commerce Clearing House, 1990).
   This is a comprehensive analysis of estate planning for most types of situations.

[7] Peter M. Gutmann, "The Subterranean Economy," *Financial Analysts Journal,* November-December 1977; P. M. Gutmann, "Are the Unemployed, Unemployed?" *Financial Analysts Journal,* September-October 1978; P. M. Gutmann, "The Subterranean Economy Five Years Later," *Across the Board,* vol. 20, no. 2, February 1983, the Conference Board magazine.

Prentice-Hall, *Federal Tax Course* (Englewood Cliffs, N.J.: Prentice-Hall, annual).
 A comprehensive text, revised annually, that explains with numerous examples the tax law.

U.S. Treasury Dept., Internal Revenue Service, *A Guide to Federal Estate and Gift Taxation,* Pub. 448 (Washington, D.C.: U.S. Government Printing Office, annual).
 This is a concise summary of federal estate and gift taxes. Examples are sparse; legal terms are plentiful. There is no math.

U.S. Treasury Department, Internal Revenue Service, *Tax Guide for Small Business,* Pub. 334, (Washington D.C.: U.S. Government Printing Office, annual).
 This explains the tax laws that apply to businesses, including sole proprietorships, partnerships, and corporations. There is no math.

U.S. Treasury Department, Internal Revenue Service, *Your Federal Income Tax,* Pub. 17 (Washington D.C.: U.S. Government Printing Office, annual).
 This explains many specific problems and gives examples. There is no math.

Essay Questions

7-1   Name three allowable deductions from adjusted gross income that can be used in arriving at a person's taxable income; do the same for a corporation's taxable income.

7-2   How is the corporate federal income tax rate structured?

7-3   (*a*) What are the major benefits of investing in an IRA? (*b*) What are the disadvantages of investing in an IRA?

7-4   A wealthy singer named Randy Trump lost his $400 camera while in Nashville. Will Randy's lost camera qualify as a casualty loss for tax purposes? If so, how much can he write off?

7-5   What is the difference between marginal and average tax rates?

7-6   Do you believe that the income tax system in the United States should be (*a*) graduated upward (made more progressive) or (*b*) graduated downward (made more regressive)? Explain your choice. *Hint:* It would probably be a good idea to get a *welfare economics* textbook and read about progressive and regressive taxes.

7-7   The Gamma Fund is a large common stock mutual fund with thousands of shareholders. Its holdings are diversified across hundreds of stocks. Last year Gamma paid out its total income from cash dividends of $4 million and, in addition, the $6 million it earned from capital gains to its stockholders. How much federal income tax did Gamma owe on the $10 million it earned?

7-8   Anthony Cava bought a common stock for $20 per share on January 22, 1988, and it appreciated to a price of $50 on December 27, 1991. Correctly anticipating a temporary downturn, Anthony sold the stock for $50 on December 27, 1991, and repurchased it on January 15, 1992, for $40. The stock resumed its price climb, and Anthony finally liquidated it at a price of $60 per share on November 19, 1992. What were Anthony's total capital gains from the stock over the entire 1988 through 1992 period that he owned it?

7-9   (*a*) Define *capital assets*. (*b*) Should the following four assets be called *capital assets:* General Motors' inventory of automobile engines; GM's inventory of finished cars; Widow Jones's inventory of stocks and bonds; the inventory of securities owned by Merrill Lynch, Pierce, Fenner & Smith?

Problems

7-10   Assume the adjusted gross income (not including capital gains and losses) of Mr. and Mrs. Taylor, filing a joint return, is $20,000 in 1991. During that tax year the Taylors also had $5000 in long-term capital gains and $6000 in long-term capital losses. Calculate the Taylors' tax due, assuming no other deductions or inflation adjustment in 1991.

7-11   Jack Lind has a marginal tax rate of 33 percent and must choose between a tax-free municipal bond paying 6 percent and an equally risky taxable security paying 8 percent. Which security should he choose? Explain why.

7-12   After being happily married for many years, Mary Jones died in 1987. Her husband, John, passed away in 1988. The value of their estate was $1.8 million at the time of Mary's death and $2 million when John died. In 1983 John and Mary had given $500,000 to their only child. Given these facts, determine Mary's taxable estate and estate tax due. What is John's taxable estate and estate tax due?

7-13   The one-period rate of return from an investment in common stock is calculated with the following formula:

$$\text{One-period rate of return} = \frac{\text{price change} + \text{cash dividend, if any}}{\text{purchase price}}$$

If an investor purchases a stock at $50 per share, sells it at $58 per share, collects $2 per share cash dividend, and is tax-exempt, the rate of return that is calculated with the formula is 20 percent.

$$\frac{(\$58 - \$50) + \$2}{\$50} = \frac{\$8 + \$2}{\$50} = \frac{\$10}{\$50} = .2 = 20 \text{ percent return}$$

(*a*) Calculate the after-tax one-period rate of return from this common stock investment if a tax rate of tr = 28 percent is charged on both capital gains (that is, changes in the stock's price) and cash dividends. Show the formula you use (with all parts labeled) and your calculations. (*b*) How is the after-tax one-period rate of return calculated if the tax rate on capital gains, denoted tg, is half the tax rate on ordinary income and the tax rate on ordinary income and cash dividends is ot = 28 percent? Show the formula you use and your calculations.

7-14   Rose Dimaggio bought $6000 worth of Cleveland municipal bonds, held them for 4 months and collected semiannual coupons in the amount of $300, and then sold the bonds for $6400. If Rose is in the 25 percent federal income tax bracket, how much tax will she owe on this transaction?

7-15   The Sontab Corporation's total taxable income was $60,000 in 1991. Sontab paid federal corporate income taxes of $7500 on the first $50,000 of its income and $2500 on the last

$10,000, for a total tax bill of $10,000. What were Sontab's average and marginal corporate income tax rates?

7-16 Fred Chambers has a written commitment from his bank stating that it will lend him $50,000 at x percent interest for 20 years. Fred is considering borrowing this money and using it all to buy a 20-year, coupon-paying U.S. Treasury bond that pays x percent interest. Fred thinks he can make money on this transaction because he thinks the interest expense will be tax-deductible. Should Fred borrow the money to buy the bond?

Multiple Choice Questions

7-17 Zoe Cava bought 100 shares of the Mystical Magic Corporation's stock for $20 per share on February 9 and sold them on June 20 for $40 per share. If Zoe is in the 28 percent income tax bracket, how much will her taxes be?

    (*a*) $460
    (*b*) $560
    (*c*) $660
    (*d*) $760

B   2000 × .28

7-18 The Whale Corporation earned $10 million of taxable income from its operations and is in the 34% income tax bracket. In addition, Guppie Inc., Whale's totally owned subsidiary, paid cash dividends of $100,000 to Whale. How much federal income tax will Whale have to pay?

    (*a*) $3,300,000
    (*b*) $3,400,000
    (*c*) $3,405,100
    (*d*) $3,434,000

B

7-19 All of the following might describe a person who sells a stock with no intention of ever delivering it, but which one is illegal?

    (*a*) The person might be selling short to form a hedge.   C
    (*b*) The person might be postponing a profit until the next year.
    (*c*) The person might be converting a short-term gain into a long-term gain.
    (*d*) The person might be selling short in order to profit from an expected price decline.

7-20 All of the following are regressive taxes except:

    (*a*) Sales tax
    (*b*) Gasoline tax
    (*c*) Inheritance tax   C
    (*d*) Food tax

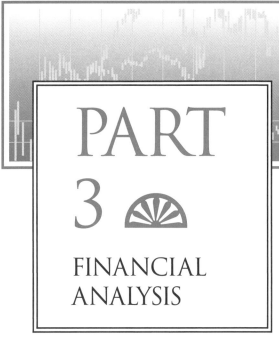

PART 3

FINANCIAL ANALYSIS

FINANCIAL ANALYSIS is a vital part of investing successfully: the investor or investments manager must be able to interpret the various performance indicators in order to make sound investment decisions. The seven chapters of this part focus on the various kinds of financial analysis, from how to read corporate financial statements to analyzing such major risk factors as default risk and interest rate risk, to bond selection and common stock and earnings analysis.

Chapter 8, on sources of investment information, sets the stage by presenting information sources on world affairs, national economies, industries, and industrial firms. Chapter 9 reviews the principal financial statements that are used to report the progress of every firm, and presents the various ratios that can be calculated in order to assess a firm's financial health.

Chapter 10 focuses on default or bankruptcy risk, the risk that results from changes in the financial strength of an investment. Chapter 11 describes and analyzes interest rate risk, the risk that arises because fluctuations in market interest rates cause the prices of bonds and other securities to vary. Chapter 12 describes the bond selection process, including how to calculate yields and interpret bond price movements. Chapter 13 does the same for common stock, and includes a number of the computations that help illuminate a firm's likelihood of success in the future. Chapter 14 continues the analysis of the firm by focusing on earnings.

CHAPTER 8

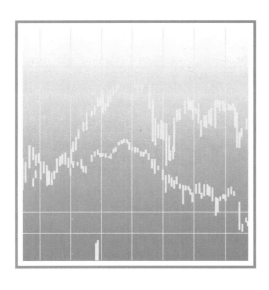

INVESTMENT
INFORMATION
SOURCES

Investment analysis usually begins with an inquiry into world affairs. Wars, epidemics, earthquakes, and international trade all affect nations' economies and their securities markets. Financial analysts typically develop a picture of world conditions and then an estimate of the impact of these conditions on the nation in which they are considering investing. At the next stage, the analysis can focus on specific industries. Labor negotiations, changes in legislation, sales of the industry's product, and competition within the industry are considered. After all this background investigation has been completed, the financial analyst can focus on particular firms.

This chapter presents and discusses information sources about world affairs, national economies, industries, and individual firms—in that order. Computer facilities that may be helpful are discussed later in the chapter.

8-1 National and International Newspapers

Investor's Business Daily, The Wall Street Journal, and *The New York Times* are daily U.S. newspapers that publish financial information. They carry current reports on political and economic conditions around the world, as well as the financial news. The *Economist* and the *Financial Times* are London financial newspapers of particular interest to international investors. The London papers are expensive to obtain in the United States, but libraries carry them.

- *Investor's Business Daily:* Some say that **Investor's Business Daily** (*IBD*) is the best investments newspaper in the United States. It carries the most extensive listing of security prices and other financial data of any daily newspaper. The previous day's trading results are reported daily, along with detailed financial analyses of individual securities. Five days a week *IBD* carries in-depth economic and financial news that is useful to investors. The *IBD* is narrowly focused; it does not contain society, fashion, or cultural material unless the event affects investment values.[1]

- *The Wall Street Journal:* **The Wall Street Journal** (*WSJ*), published 5 days a week, is written for a national business audience.[2] The *WSJ* reports world, national, and financial news as well as current events in various industries and firms. The *Journal* also reports the opinions of economists and various financial personnel about the course of future events. In addition, the paper contains articles on art and leisure interests, human interest stories, and stories on topics unrelated to investments.

- *The New York Times:* **The New York Times** (*NYT*) is published 7 days a week and is noted for its objective coverage of a wide range of topics. Each day the *NYT* contains a large business and financial section that reports financial news,

---

[1] Annual subscriptions costing $149 can be obtained from *Investor's Business Daily,* 1941 Armacost Ave., Los Angeles, Ca. 90025. Student subscriptions are available at half price.

[2] Subscriptions to the *WSJ* cost $139 per year for second-class postage delivery to your door. Instructors interested in using the *WSJ* in class may contact Educational Service Bureau, Dow Jones & Co., P.O. Box 300, Princeton, N.J. 08540, for information about student subscription programs at discounted prices and various free teaching materials.

market data from various markets, and stories about individual firms and industries. In addition, the daily and Sunday *NYT* has extensive coverage of art, leisure interests, local news, and other topics.

8-2   National Affairs

Price movements of most securities are partially attributable to bullish (upward) and bearish (downward) trends in the price levels of an entire securities market. Thus, if the level of market indexes can be forecast, much information about future securities prices will be provided. Forecasting the level and direction of the national economy can be useful in predicting the trend of security price movements. Newsletters published by large banks, U.S. government periodicals, and investment analysis companies are helpful sources of information about how national affairs affect financial conditions.

Bank Newsletters

Various banks publish newsletters on economic conditions. These newsletters usually focus on the general economic outlook, but they also often refer to expected effects of economic changes on the financial markets.

The large commercial banks listed below publish economic periodicals that are available free:

Chase Manhattan Bank (New York)

Bank of New York (New York)

Citibank (New York)

Chemical Bank (New York)

Harris Trust and Savings Bank (Chicago)

Continental Bank (Chicago)

Bank of America (California)

Morgan Guaranty Trust Company (New York)

The *Federal Reserve Bulletin* is a monthly summary of economic data published by the Federal Reserve Board.[3] The bulletin is a handy source of raw economic data on many topics. The St. Louis Federal Reserve Bank also publishes weekly and monthly economic newsletters which it sends to subscribers and which contain some of the best monetary economic analyses available to the public.[4]

---

[3] Annual subscriptions cost $25.00 and may be obtained by writing to Publication Services, Board of Governors of the Federal Reserve System, Washington, D.C. 20551.

[4] For low-cost subscriptions, write to Research Department, Federal Reserve Bank of St. Louis, P.O. Box 442, St. Louis, Mo. 63166.

U.S. Government Publications

Most government publications are oriented toward the national economy and the effects of its cycles and other fluctuations on various industries. Summaries of macroeconomic data may be obtained from U.S. government sources. The U.S. Department of Commerce publishes the monthly **Survey of Current Business** (*SCB*) for example. The front section of the *SCB* contains comments about and studies of business conditions. The second section contains attractive graphic displays of voluminous economic data and tables of raw statistical data covering prices, wages, production, business activity, and many other factors. Weekly statistical updates are also available. Figures 17-3 and 17-5 provide samples of graphs from the *SCB*.[5]

The President's Council of Economic Advisors publishes the monthly *Economic Indicators,* which is a compendium of time series and graphs, and the *Annual Economic Review.* Figure 8-1 shows a page from *Economic Indicators*.[6]

The Federal Trade Commission and the SEC publish the *Quarterly Financial Report for Manufacturing Corporations,* which contains aggregate balance sheet and income statement information for manufacturing corporations. The categories "profits per dollar sales" and "annual rate of profit on stockholder's equity at end of period" are shown by industry and by asset size. This information can be quite helpful when comparing different industries.[7]

Commercial Publications

Some business organizations that are of public interest publish information about their activities. In addition, financial information corporations like Standard & Poor's publish survey data and related facts.

NYSE Fact Book: The NYSE publishes an annual pamphlet (cost is $10) that contains extensive current and historical data about the exchange, NYSE activities, and comparisons with competing markets.

AMEX Fact Book: This annual booklet is analogous to the *NYSE Fact Book* but contains data about the American Stock Exchange—activities, members, and administration.

NASDAQ Fact Book: The *NASDAQ Fact Book* is an annual booklet comparable to the *NYSE Fact Book* and the *AMEX Fact Book*. It provides facts and figures about the over-the-counter securities market.

Barron's: Barron's is a weekly newspaper published by the Dow Jones Company that contains articles about investing, extensive securities price data, and extensive statistics summarizing the week's activities in financial markets.

---

[5] *SCB* may be obtained from the Superintendent of Documents, U.S. Government Printing Office, Washington, DC 20402. Subscriptions to the *SCB* are $29 per year.

[6] Subscriptions to *Economic Indicators* are $14.00 per year. Write to the Superintendent of Documents. See fn. 5 for the address.

[7] Subscriptions are $22.00; write to the Superintendent of Documents. See fn. 5 for the address.

CORPORATE PROFITS

In the second quarter of 1991, according to current estimates, corporate profits before tax fell $2.3 billion (annual rate) and profits after tax fell $5.8 billion.

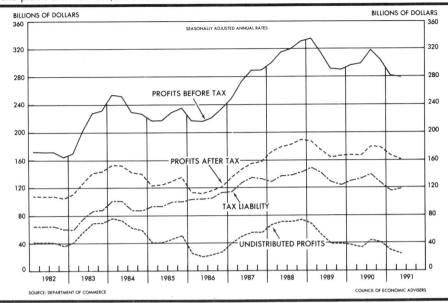

SOURCE: DEPARTMENT OF COMMERCE

COUNCIL OF ECONOMIC ADVISERS

[Billions of dollars; quarterly data at seasonally adjusted annual rates]

Period	Profits (before tax) with inventory valuation adjustment [1]						Profits before tax	Tax liability	Profits after tax			Inventory valuation adjustment
	Total [2]	Domestic industries							Total	Dividends	Undistributed profits	
		Total	Financial	Nonfinancial								
				Total [3]	Manufacturing	Wholesale and retail trade						
1980	194.0	159.6	21.0	138.6	77.1	21.6	237.1	84.8	152.3	54.7	97.6	−43.1
1981	202.3	173.8	16.5	157.3	88.5	32.5	226.5	81.1	145.4	63.6	81.8	−24.2
1982	159.2	131.2	11.8	119.4	58.0	34.6	169.6	63.1	106.5	66.9	39.6	−10.4
1983	196.7	166.6	18.1	148.5	70.1	38.9	207.6	77.2	130.4	71.5	58.9	−10.9
1984	234.2	203.3	13.0	190.3	88.8	51.2	240.0	93.9	146.1	79.0	67.0	−5.8
1985	222.6	191.4	22.8	168.6	79.7	44.1	224.3	96.4	127.8	83.3	44.6	−1.7
1986	228.3	195.2	32.0	163.2	59.5	44.1	221.6	106.3	115.3	91.3	24.0	6.7
1987	255.9	218.4	20.7	197.8	86.7	37.9	275.3	126.9	148.4	98.2	50.2	−19.4
1988	289.8	246.5	22.4	224.1	106.5	37.1	316.7	136.2	180.5	110.0	70.5	−27.0
1989	286.1	235.2	15.4	219.8	96.1	38.7	307.7	135.1	172.6	123.5	49.1	−21.7
1990	293.3	236.4	18.7	217.7	88.8	41.5	304.7	132.1	172.5	133.9	38.7	−11.4
1982: IV	150.7	121.6	18.7	102.9	46.8	33.6	164.1	59.8	104.3	68.5	35.8	−13.4
1983: IV	223.4	190.7	15.5	175.2	88.6	43.1	231.5	88.1	143.4	73.9	69.5	−8.1
1984: IV	224.6	193.9	13.6	180.3	79.8	51.8	226.1	87.0	139.2	80.8	58.4	−1.6
1985: IV	228.4	193.6	26.0	167.6	83.8	38.5	235.0	99.8	135.2	84.0	51.2	−6.6
1986: IV	226.1	193.4	28.6	164.8	64.8	41.0	234.1	113.1	121.0	93.6	27.4	−8.0
1987: IV	268.6	226.2	19.8	206.4	98.2	37.8	289.7	132.1	157.6	102.2	55.4	−21.1
1988: IV	308.7	261.9	24.1	237.8	112.6	42.3	331.1	142.1	189.1	115.3	73.8	−22.5
1989: IV	275.3	218.4	6.9	211.5	83.7	41.9	289.8	123.5	166.3	127.7	38.6	−14.5
1990: I	285.5	232.6	16.1	216.5	90.1	39.2	296.9	129.9	167.1	130.3	36.8	−11.4
II	298.8	249.9	18.2	231.7	100.8	44.4	299.3	133.1	166.1	133.0	33.2	−.5
III	298.7	241.1	21.7	219.3	91.2	39.5	318.5	139.1	179.4	135.1	44.3	−19.8
IV	290.3	222.3	18.8	203.4	73.1	42.8	304.1	126.5	177.6	137.2	40.4	−13.8
1991: I	289.7	221.4	22.5	198.9	67.1	46.2	281.5	115.1	166.4	137.5	29.0	8.1
II	284.1	226.3	23.2	203.0	72.0	47.6	279.2	118.6	160.6	136.4	24.2	4.9
III P									137.9			−3.2

[1] See p. 4 for profits with inventory valuation and capital consumption adjustments.
[2] Includes rest of the world, not shown separately.

[3] Includes industries not shown separately.

Source: Department of Commerce, Bureau of Economic Analysis.

Figure 8-1 Corporate profits and related economic indicators vary over the business cycle, from *Economic Indicators*. (*Source: Economic Indicators,* December 1991, p. 8, U.S. Department of Commerce, U.S. Government Printing Office, Washington, D.C.)

203

S&P Trade and Security Statistics: Standard & Poor's *S&P Trade and Security Statistics* is an annual book of numerical data that, for an additional fee, can be supplemented with weekly updates. The book contains historical data on 90 Standard & Poor's stock price indexes monthly from 1926 to the present: cash dividends, earnings, dividend yields, and price-earnings ratios. Bond price and yield data are available for different types of bond indexes (such as industrials, utilities, transportation, and financial corporations) for various quality ratings (AAA, AA, A, BBB), and for municipal and federal government bonds. *S&P Trade and Security Statistics* also contains decades of statistics covering other business and financial topics. See Figure 8-2, for example.

The Dow Jones Investor's Handbook: The Dow Jones Investor's Handbook contains data on the Dow Jones Industrial Average (DJIA) from 1939 to the present. Values of the DJIA, the cash dividends, and the earnings per share are reported. In addition, data on other Dow Jones averages and activity in the NYSE and AMEX are provided.

8-3   Investment Information Services

Syntheses of financial and other information about industries and individual firms are published by investment information services. These firms offer subscriptions to daily, weekly, and monthly publications. The cost of a subscription is deductible from an investor's income, according to federal income tax regulations. Many public libraries carry the publications of one or more of these services, which readers may consult free of charge. The leading services are Standard & Poor's Corporation (owned by McGraw-Hill), Moody's Investor Services, Inc. (owned by Dun & Bradstreet), and the Value Line Investment Survey (owned by Arnold Bernhard & Co.).

The Standard & Poor's Corporation

Standard & Poor's publications may be purchased by calling or writing Standard & Poor's Corporation, 25 Broadway, New York, N.Y. 10004.

S&P Corporation Records   Much of Standard & Poor's information is based on facts from thick, bound reference volumes entitled *S&P Corporation Records,* which give complete investment data on hundreds of companies over a period of years. The *S&P Corporation Records* is arranged alphabetically by the corporations' names. Frequent bulletins keep the semiannual *S&P Corporation Records* up to date.

The massive *S&P Corporation Records* discusses the affairs of each company listed, under the following topic headings: Capitalization and Long-term Debt; Corporate Background, with such subheadings as Sales Backlogs, Subsidiaries, Affiliates, Principal Properties, Capital Expenditures, Employees, Officers, Directors, and Executive Offices; Bond Descriptions, with such subheadings as Trustee, Purpose of Issue, Sinking Fund, Redemptions, Security, Dividend Restrictions, and Price Range; Stock Data, with such subheadings as Voting Power, Capital Changes, Capital Stock Offered through Rights, Stock Issued under Convertibles, Capital Stock Sold, Stockholders, Transfer Agent, Listings, and Dividends; and Earnings and

EARNINGS, DIVIDENDS AND PRICE-EARNINGS RATIOS—QUARTERLY

Quarterly	Earnings Per Share—Adjusted To Index: Actual Quarterly Ind.	Rails	Utils.	Comp.	4 Qtr. Total Ind.	Rails **	Utils.	Comp.	Dividends Per Share—12-Mos. Moving Total Adjusted to Index: Ind.	Rails	Utils.	Comp.	Price Earnings Ratio: Ind.	Rails **	Utils.	Comp.	Yield: Ind.	Rails	Utils.	Comp.	†Stock Price Indexes 1941-43 = 10: Ind.	Rails	Utils.	Comp.
1979																								
1	3.79	1.94	2.08	3.51	14.26	8.06	6.92	13.30	5.49	2.68	4.40	5.20	7.95	5.56	7.31	7.64	4.84	5.98	8.70	5.12	113.38	44.79	50.58	101.59
2	4.23	2.89	1.54	3.86	15.07	8.71	7.05	13.98	5.64	2.72	4.48	5.34	7.57	6.06	7.21	7.36	4.94	5.15	8.82	5.19	114.14	52.79	50.81	102.91
3	4.02	1.93	1.88	3.70	15.92	9.00	7.16	14.63	5.83	2.78	4.57	5.51	7.67	6.22	7.12	7.47	4.78	4.97	8.96	5.04	122.09	55.96	50.98	109.32
4	4.17	2.89	1.66	3.79	16.21	9.65	7.16	14.86	5.98	2.85	4.66	5.65	7.47	5.85	7.02	7.26	4.94	5.04	9.28	5.23	121.02	56.50	50.24	107.94
1980																								
1	4.40	2.43	1.91	3.94	16.82	10.14	6.99	15.29	6.15	2.94	4.74	5.80	6.86	5.97	6.46	6.68	5.33	4.85	10.50	5.68	115.31	60.56	45.15	102.09
2	3.84	2.36	1.51	3.51	16.43	9.61	6.96	14.94	6.31	3.03	4.82	5.94	7.81	6.92	7.56	7.65	4.92	4.56	9.16	5.20	128.34	66.48	52.63	114.24
3	3.62	2.68	2.03	3.40	16.03	10.36	7.11	14.64	6.46	3.12	4.89	6.07	8.91	7.99	7.01	8.57	4.52	3.77	9.81	4.84	142.82	82.80	49.87	125.46
4	4.27	3.18	2.08	3.97	16.13	10.65	7.53	14.82	6.55	3.23	4.96	6.16	9.58	10.05	6.96	9.16	4.24	3.02	9.46	4.54	154.45	107.00	52.45	135.76
1981																								
1	4.01	2.82	2.23	3.70	15.74	11.04	7.85	14.58	6.67	3.26	5.04	6.28	9.80	9.78	6.51	9.33	4.33	3.02	9.86	4.62	154.19	107.92	51.13	136.00
2	4.41	2.07	1.78	3.94	16.31	10.75	8.12	15.01	6.77	3.36	5.12	6.39	9.01	8.66	6.42	8.71	4.59	3.61	9.81	4.87	147.58	93.06	52.20	131.21
3	3.85	3.01	2.26	3.66	16.54	11.08	8.35	15.27	6.90	3.47	5.22	6.52	7.93	6.98	6.20	7.71	5.31	4.48	10.37	5.61	130.04	77.39	50.36	116.18
4	4.43	3.40	2.05	4.06	16.70	11.30	8.32	15.36	7.00	3.58	5.34	6.63	8.34	7.86	6.53	8.12	5.11	4.03	10.08	5.41	137.12	88.87	52.98	122.55

Quarter	Earnings Per Share—Adjusted to Price Index (Quarterly) 400 Ind.	20 Trans.	40 Utils.	40 Finan.	500 Comp.	Dividend Per Share—Adjusted to Price Index (4 Qtr. Total) 400 Ind.	20 Trans.	40 Utils.	40 Finan.	500 Comp.
1982										
1	3.30	0.02	2.57	0.51	3.15	7.09	0.80	5.44	0.81	6.72
2	3.60	0.47	1.83	0.44	3.30	7.18	0.82	5.55	0.81	6.81
3	3.05	0.44	2.44	0.60	3.05	7.19	0.83	5.65	0.82	6.85
4	3.26	0.33	1.94	0.65	3.14	7.16	0.83	5.72	0.84	6.87
1983										
1	2.98	0.15	2.38	0.59	2.93	7.19	4.23	5.81	0.86	6.91
2	3.69	2.85	1.92	0.58	3.47	7.20	4.23	5.90	0.88	6.94
3	3.90	3.92	2.82	0.49	3.76	7.27	4.18	5.96	0.89	7.00
4	4.16	4.43	2.32	0.46	3.87	7.37	4.13	6.05	0.90	7.09
1984										
1	4.38	3.09	2.75	0.47	4.16	7.37	4.18	6.17	0.90	7.18
2	5.03	4.57	2.43	0.10	4.41	7.41	4.19	6.27	0.91	7.31
3	4.29	4.59	2.73	0.43	4.12	7.36	4.29	6.38	0.92	7.38
4	4.28	3.09	2.40	0.35	3.95	7.43	4.39	6.47	0.92	7.53
1985										
1	4.03	2.20	2.76	0.49	3.91	7.57	4.50	6.52	0.92	7.66
2	3.74	3.95	2.38	0.42	3.63	7.62	4.60	6.60	0.92	7.74
3	3.51	4.33	3.01	0.59	3.74	7.71	4.67	6.67	0.92	7.84
4	3.96	2.17	1.41	0.16	3.33	7.74	4.74	6.73	0.92	7.90
1986										
1	3.80	0.98	2.71	0.68	3.82	7.86	4.76	6.80	0.92	8.02
2	4.20	d3.47	2.67	0.47	3.82	7.95	4.80	6.86	0.92	8.10
3	3.59	3.99	3.09	0.68	3.88	8.10	4.82	6.95	0.91	8.23
4	2.82	d0.04	1.90	0.78	2.96	8.14	4.88	7.03	0.90	8.28
1987										
1	4.53	1.54	2.75	0.78	4.44	8.17	4.93	7.13	0.91	8.34
2	5.25	4.13	2.38	d2.06	3.14	8.39	4.96	7.22	0.91	8.52
3	5.45	3.61	3.26	0.81	5.32	8.53	5.01	7.31	0.93	8.66
4	5.06	3.71	2.23	0.53	4.60	8.68	4.99	7.38	0.96	8.81
1988										
1	6.31	2.39	2.72	0.49	5.53	8.82	5.01	7.44	0.98	8.95
2	6.94	4.37	2.40	0.83	6.22	9.14	5.04	7.49	1.02	9.23
3	6.62	8.11	3.35	0.82	6.38	9.47	5.11	7.54	1.03	9.46
4	6.16	6.15	1.58	0.94	5.63	9.75	5.33	7.62	1.04	9.73
1989										
1	7.52	3.40	2.83	0.83	6.74	10.11	5.44	7.48	1.04	9.98
2	7.02	7.49	2.48	0.90	6.48	10.46	5.51	7.56	1.08	10.30
3	6.27	5.24	2.83	d0.35	4.85	10.82	5.81	7.69	1.09	10.67
4	5.53	0.95	2.26	0.45	4.83	11.21	5.99	7.89	1.14	11.05

Quarter	Price/Earnings Ratios 400 Ind.	20 Trans.	40 Utils.	40 Finan.	500 Comp.	Earnings Per Share—Adjusted to Price Index (4 Qtr. Total) 400 Ind.	20 Trans.	40 Utils.	40 Finan.	500 Comp.
1982										
1	7.77	11.03	6.05	6.33	7.56	15.99	1.63	8.66	2.24	14.81
2	8.06	10.45	5.98	5.78	7.74	15.18	1.68	8.71	2.16	14.17
3	9.34	13.57	6.30	6.46	8.87	14.38	1.45	8.89	2.17	13.56
4	11.92	19.19	6.88	7.53	11.12	13.21	1.26	8.78	2.20	12.64
1983										
1	13.32	21.03	7.14	8.31	12.32	12.89	6.46	8.59	2.28	12.42
2	14.63	22.24	7.29	8.19	13.35	12.98	6.92	8.68	2.42	12.59
3	13.60	17.89	7.41	8.00	12.52	13.83	8.60	9.06	2.31	13.30
4	12.64	13.99	7.01	8.55	11.76	14.73	11.35	9.44	2.12	14.03
1984										
1	11.20	9.83	6.58	8.72	10.43	16.09	14.29	9.81	2.00	15.26
2	10.02	7.82	6.10	9.92	9.46	17.43	16.01	10.32	1.52	16.20
3	10.52	8.41	6.97	12.03	10.03	17.82	16.68	10.23	1.46	16.56
4	10.38	9.38	7.36	13.93	10.05	17.94	15.34	10.31	1.35	16.64
1985										
1	11.44	10.71	7.79	15.04	11.02	17.63	14.45	10.32	1.37	16.39
2	12.97	12.49	8.54	13.79	12.29	16.34	13.83	10.27	1.69	15.61
3	13.09	12.17	7.28	11.11	11.96	15.56	13.57	10.90	1.85	15.23
4	15.39	14.92	9.75	15.49	14.46	15.24	12.65	9.56	1.66	14.61
1986										
1	17.56	18.97	11.07	16.77	16.45	15.01	11.43	9.51	1.85	14.52
2	18.09	50.55	11.39	15.66	17.05	15.47	4.01	9.80	1.90	14.71
3	16.47	52.18	11.04	13.47	15.58	15.55	3.67	9.88	1.99	14.85
4	18.73	135.12	10.83	10.31	16.72	14.41	1.46	10.37	2.61	14.48
1987										
1	22.16	111.02	11.11	10.99	19.32	15.14	2.02	10.41	2.71	15.10
2	21.80	26.23	11.17	184.1	21.06	16.19	9.62	10.12	0.16	14.42
3	20.82	28.87	11.36	103.2	20.29	18.05	9.24	10.29	0.29	15.86
4	14.09	14.64	9.62	N.M.	14.12	20.29	12.99	10.62	0.04	17.50
1988										
1	13.61	15.23	9.84	N.M.	13.93	22.07	13.84	10.59	−0.25	18.59
2	13.29	15.47	10.43	9.37	12.62	23.76	14.08	10.61	2.66	21.67
3	12.50	11.70	10.45	9.72	11.96	24.93	18.58	10.70	2.67	22.73
4	12.35	10.85	11.21	7.95	11.69	26.02	21.02	10.05	3.08	23.76
1989										
1	12.46	11.06	11.57	8.14	11.81	27.24	22.03	10.16	3.42	24.96
2	13.30	10.46	12.92	8.64	12.61	27.32	25.15	10.24	3.49	25.22
3	14.73	14.03	14.65	14.74	14.71	26.97	22.28	9.72	2.32	23.69
4	15.31	16.30	15.00	17.10	15.43	26.34	17.08	10.42	1.83	22.90

Quarter	Yield—End of Qtr. (Annual $) 400 Ind.	20 Trans.	40 Utils.	40 Finan.	500 Comp.	Stock Price Indexes (End of Period) 400 Ind.	20 Trans.	40 Utils.	40 Finan.	500 Comp.
1982										
1	5.71	4.45	10.37	5.72	6.00	124.23	17.98	52.47	14.17	111.96
2	5.87	4.67	10.66	6.49	6.21	122.42	17.56	52.05	12.49	109.61
3	5.35	4.22	10.09	5.85	5.69	134.45	19.68	55.99	14.01	120.42
4	4.56	3.43	9.46	5.07	4.88	157.62	24.18	60.45	16.58	140.64
1983										
1	4.19	3.11	9.48	4.54	4.52	171.65	135.85	61.30	18.94	152.96
2	3.79	2.75	9.32	4.44	4.13	189.96	153.87	63.32	19.82	168.11
3	3.88	2.72	8.88	4.82	4.22	187.38	153.82	67.11	18.47	166.07
4	3.96	2.60	9.14	5.96	4.30	186.24	158.81	66.17	18.13	164.93
1984										
1	4.09	2.98	9.55	5.16	4.51	180.14	140.40	64.58	17.43	159.18
2	4.24	3.34	9.96	6.03	4.77	174.73	125.25	62.94	15.08	153.18
3	3.93	3.06	8.95	5.24	4.44	187.41	140.20	71.27	17.56	166.10
4	3.99	3.05	8.53	4.89	4.50	186.36	143.91	75.89	18.80	167.24
1985										
1	3.75	2.91	8.11	4.47	4.24	201.67	154.80	80.36	20.60	180.66
2	3.60	2.66	7.53	3.95	4.03	211.92	172.74	87.66	23.30	191.85
3	3.79	2.83	8.41	4.48	4.31	203.67	165.17	79.34	20.55	182.08
4	3.30	2.51	7.22	3.58	3.74	234.56	188.72	93.17	25.72	211.28
1986										
1	2.98	2.20	6.46	2.97	3.36	263.51	216.83	105.27	31.02	238.90
2	2.84	2.37	6.16	3.06	3.23	279.78	202.70	111.67	29.75	250.84
3	3.16	2.52	6.37	3.40	3.56	256.06	191.50	109.09	26.80	231.32
4	3.02	2.47	6.26	3.34	3.42	269.93	197.27	112.29	26.92	242.17
1987										
1	2.44	2.20	6.17	3.05	2.86	335.53	224.27	115.63	29.79	291.70
2	2.38	1.97	6.39	3.09	2.80	352.98	252.35	113.07	29.46	304.00
3	2.27	1.88	6.24	3.11	2.69	375.85	266.79	117.11	29.92	321.83
4	3.04	2.62	7.23	4.44	3.57	285.85	190.17	102.12	21.63	247.06
1988										
1	2.94	2.38	7.14	4.39	3.46	300.39	210.80	104.21	22.32	258.89
2	2.89	2.31	6.77	4.09	3.37	315.73	217.79	110.66	24.92	273.50
3	3.04	2.35	6.74	3.96	3.48	311.67	217.37	111.86	25.96	271.91
4	3.03	2.34	6.76	4.25	3.50	321.26	228.17	112.64	24.49	277.72
1989										
1	2.98	2.23	6.36	3.74	3.38	339.42	244.20	117.60	27.83	294.87
2	2.88	2.09	5.72	3.58	3.24	363.48	363.05	132.27	30.17	317.98
3	2.72	1.86	5.40	3.19	3.06	397.95	312.53	142.35	34.19	349.15
4	2.78	2.15	5.04	3.64	3.13	403.49	278.48	156.34	31.30	353.40

PRICE-EARNINGS RATIOS shown above are obtained by dividing the stock price index, as of the end of the period, by the 4 Qtr. Total of Earnings through the corresponding quarter.

Date for the period 1926–1934 are based on annual earnings of all companies. During the period 1935 through the third quarter of 1950, earnings data are based only on those companies, reporting quarterly earnings. During this period the coverage was changing, gradually changing from meager coverage to close to full coverage at the end of the period. Beginning with the fourth quarter of 1950 estimates of quarterly earnings for the missing companies have been used, thereby maintaining uniform coverage. †Rails Discontinued.

% End of period. **Rail earnings have been revised beginning 1967 to reflect consolidated earnings, if reported. Prior to 1967, earnings are on "company only" basis. P-preliminary.

EARNINGS, DIVIDENDS and BOOK VALUES are calculated in the same manner that the Stock Price Indexes are calculated (see Description of Method used in Computation pages 2 and 3). The only difference in the formula is the substitution of earnings, dividends or book values in place of prices (P1) in the numerator.

Figure 8-2 Quarterly stock market statistics from *Standard & Poors Trade and Security Statistics.* (Source: *Standard & Poors Trade and Security Statistics,* 1990, Standard & Poor's Corporation, 25 Broadway, New York, N.Y. 10004, p. 118.)

Finances, with such subheadings as Auditors, Consolidated Earnings Statements, Adjusted Earnings, Quarterly Sales, Property Account Analysis, Maintenance and Repairs, Consolidated Income Statement, and Consolidated Balance Sheet.

The Outlook Standard & Poor's weekly publication entitled *The Outlook* surveys market conditions and recommends common stocks to investors. It also contains special articles, reports on individual firms, discussions of stocks now in favor, a report on overall business conditions, a market forecast and recommendations, and sometimes a "stock for action." A special annual issue of *The Outlook* is published with a forecast for the coming year; the forecast is divided into such categories as best low-priced stocks, candidates for dividend increases, rapid-growth stocks for long-term profits, and stocks for action in the year ahead. Market indexes are also tabulated and published in *The Outlook* each week (see Figure 8-3).

Figure 8-3 Over 90 different stock market indexes from *The Outlook*, December 11, 1991, p. 16. (*Source:* Standard & Poors, 25 Broadway, New York, N.Y. 10004.)

†MONTHLY STOCK PRICE INDEXES

	NOV. MONTH END	% CHANGE FROM PREV. MONTH	†NOV. AVG.	DEC. 4	1991 RANGE HIGH	1991 RANGE LOW
500 Composite	375.22	- 4.4	385.92	380.07	397.41	311.49
Industrials	442.42	- 4.4	454.97	447.83	472.01	364.90
Transportation	295.88	- 9.2	315.86	314.44	329.05	226.22
Utilities	145.22	- 1.5	146.66	146.15	149.85	133.52
Financial	29.77	- 7.0	31.22	30.31	32.54	21.97
MidCap 400	131.34	- 3.6	134.62	134.00	139.07	95.11
Capital Goods	282.58	- 6.9	294.10	283.10	320.69	252.81
Consumer goods	558.96	- 2.1	568.32	572.67	585.59	419.86
Energy Composite	348.90	- 8.4	366.32	347.32	389.62	337.21
High Tech Composite	183.35	- 4.9	189.06	181.45	213.89	167.09
High Grade	276.59	- 3.8	283.07	281.66	290.94	222.79
Low Priced	677.59	+ 4.2	686.34	680.54	702.33	398.56
INDUSTRIALS						
Aerospace/Defense	388.69	- 5.6	402.69	377.94	419.31	333.23
Aluminum	241.55	- 9.0	254.20	240.47	297.51	237.05
Automobile	107.22	- 11.5	112.87	105.30	153.19	105.30
Excl. General Motors	59.49	- 10.2	61.99	59.54	87.13	59.40
Auto Parts: After Mkt.	37.21	- 4.4	38.52	37.95	40.05	22.96
Heavy Duty Trucks & Parts	57.51	- 3.7	59.30	58.51	65.69	48.15
Beverages: Alcoholic	361.30	- 1.6	365.14	376.81	376.81	275.09
Soft Drinks	1111.47	+ 4.1	1084.49	1144.86	1144.86	764.78
Broadcast Media	3905.60	- 9.5	4178.53	3895.73	4845.15	3895.73
Building Materials	185.35	- 12.2	200.26	187.55	241.40	158.14
Chemicals	170.36	- 7.8	178.19	172.20	191.60	136.71
Chemicals: Diversified	47.04	- 10.1	49.67	48.82	54.52	38.67
Chemicals: Specialty	196.47	- 5.0	204.57	202.75	214.55	154.57
Coal	427.21	- 4.3	437.71	443.43	480.08	403.46
Commercial Services	271.13	- 7.1	276.86	270.26	329.12	252.04
Communication—Equip./Mfrs.	70.16	+ 3.5	71.08	70.68	73.92	43.97
Computer Software & Serv.	75.87	- 5.6	78.21	78.39	83.88	55.84
Computer Systems	154.06	- 5.9	159.59	150.08	217.61	150.08
Excl. I.B.M.	332.57	- 5.9	340.30	324.91	433.51	313.66
Conglomerates	49.68	- 6.8	51.28	49.70	57.29	46.12
Containers: Metal & Glass	319.95	- 6.3	336.28	328.78	355.24	223.82
Paper	1171.93	- 10.4	1270.66	1197.86	1345.07	746.62
Cosmetics	219.07	+ 2.5	222.16	225.63	229.08	160.13
Electrical Equipment	923.90	- 6.0	957.59	915.30	1100.45	793.14
Electronics: Defense	179.07	+ 0.8	180.83	182.24	201.10	137.86
Electronics: Instrumentation	80.93	- 4.3	82.82	81.01	94.39	53.99
Electronics: Semiconductors	62.79	- 2.7	64.27	63.10	79.94	56.63
Engineering & Construction	151.94	- 14.0	160.31	154.19	215.90	138.23
Entertainment	1215.44	- 9.8	1266.01	1230.33	1438.48	1144.49
Foods	763.74	+ 2.3	767.19	785.97	790.38	567.41
Food Wholesalers	356.84	- 3.7	366.91	367.45	407.45	296.17
* Gaming Cos.	46.94	- 5.0	49.16	50.36	55.04	32.35
Gold Mining	167.13	+ 1.0	161.06	165.14	196.19	149.65
Hardware & Tools	17.86	- 7.1	18.51	18.09	20.55	13.77
Homebuilding	55.61	+ 3.2	57.11	57.36	59.96	38.63
‡ Health Care: Composite	225.67	- 3.1	230.01	232.96	236.20	160.14
Diversified	389.97	- 3.9	399.66	402.96	411.70	283.91
Miscellaneous	190.93	+ 2.2	190.26	198.85	198.85	129.61
Drugs	1495.92	- 1.5	1512.98	1539.64	1540.98	1003.56
Hospital Management	65.20	- 18.0	70.50	67.69	116.63	65.20
Medical Prod. & Sup.	241.69	- 2.7	245.69	251.21	254.84	161.14
Hotel-Motel	126.72	- 9.8	134.68	128.09	162.14	97.59
Household Furnish. & Appliances	377.05	- 7.2	401.86	387.75	432.48	284.74
Household Products	774.89	- 0.7	784.06	792.24	813.25	716.34
Housewares	620.81	- 3.0	637.53	646.27	654.56	375.46
Insurance Brokers	253.07	- 3.7	256.97	259.79	307.38	250.05
Leisure Time	122.32	- 10.3	131.94	118.86	145.87	95.34
Machine Tools	49.38	- 13.5	50.79	50.11	78.85	48.20
Machinery: Diversified	241.21	- 11.6	256.68	238.45	284.44	217.19
Manufactured Housing	160.61	- 5.5	169.77	165.81	181.14	116.93
Manufacturing: Div. Industrials	252.05	- 6.0	259.51	253.13	296.99	219.47
Metals: Miscellaneous	211.23	- 10.8	226.33	209.54	247.79	190.98
Miscellaneous	115.44	- 3.8	118.37	116.73	122.73	96.42
Office Equipment & Supplies	211.83	- 5.5	218.01	215.42	224.23	148.98
Oil & Gas Drilling	39.44	- 14.1	43.26	38.38	64.97	38.38
Oil: Composite	673.33	- 7.9	705.00	669.00	748.10	647.45
Domestic Integrated	583.77	- 13.5	633.56	574.20	707.55	574.20
Int'l Integrated	340.25	- 6.2	352.82	338.95	367.89	314.82
Oil Well Equip. & Service	1676.13	- 13.8	1812.46	1700.67	2144.24	1675.15
Paper & Forest Products	709.80	- 10.7	748.33	709.30	818.65	607.02
Pollution Control	296.95	- 1.9	296.24	306.66	363.38	283.11
Publishing	1364.34	- 6.0	1402.12	1377.61	1604.65	1219.85
Publishing: Newspapers	92.31	- 6.0	95.33	94.00	112.11	91.12
Restaurants	199.21	- 3.0	203.99	201.46	210.38	156.70
Retail: Composite	517.11	- 0.1	523.47	530.65	567.28	359.14
Department Stores	1087.49	- 2.2	1116.35	1118.12	1328.02	828.59
Drug Stores	138.71	- 4.9	143.73	140.71	158.20	116.95
Food Chains	390.56	- 9.3	412.35	392.39	559.12	390.56
Gen. Merchandise Chains	41.42	+ 1.7	41.70	42.62	44.72	26.62
Specialty	707.19	- 0.8	712.56	723.46	772.74	498.59
Specialty-Apparel	366.31	+ 6.1	362.58	380.38	380.38	200.16
Shoes	544.63	+ 1.8	556.74	545.28	595.16	303.74
Steel	44.05	- 6.9	46.80	44.44	50.03	38.60
Telecommunication: Long Dist.	219.34	- 4.6	224.18	220.70	242.06	175.96
Textiles: Apparel Mfrs.	228.56	- 6.9	237.98	241.43	260.29	167.48
Tobacco	1208.18	- 3.6	1231.69	1218.61	1315.48	886.84
Toys	49.08	+ 2.9	48.27	48.71	49.60	23.80
UTILITIES						
Electric Companies	73.42	+ 2.2	72.58	73.53	73.63	61.24
Natural Gas	346.56	- 5.1	361.26	346.26	409.58	341.36
Telephone	257.13	- 4.1	264.13	260.29	279.15	247.03
TRANSPORTATION						
Airlines	253.94	- 6.4	259.98	259.40	315.02	230.60
Railroads	272.50	- 10.3	293.12	294.89	309.37	189.29
Truckers	272.63	- 8.0	290.21	281.78	317.00	227.15
Transportation Miscellaneous	11.84	- 8.5	12.50	12.32	14.26	10.60
FINANCIAL						
Bank Composite	151.17	- 9.9	161.67	155.21	172.15	100.44
Money Center Banks	90.65	- 9.6	96.41	91.97	102.28	66.44
Major Regional Banks	119.06	- 6.5	125.65	122.17	131.98	73.02
Other Major Banks	112.13	- 21.9	127.98	118.47	149.56	79.86
Life Insurance	983.46	- 1.5	1008.22	983.09	1043.75	744.77
Multi-Line Insurance	50.62	- 2.5	51.16	50.94	57.95	40.95
Property-Casualty Insurance	372.14	- 2.6	376.83	376.16	415.57	326.78
Savings & Loan Holding Cos.	47.64	- 12.2	50.84	49.97	66.03	37.24
Personal Loans	208.49	- 12.2	224.40	212.91	270.52	147.56
Financial Miscellaneous	34.40	- 6.1	35.68	34.83	39.09	24.27
Brokerage Firms	90.82	- 6.3	98.36	94.57	108.41	42.31
Real Estate Investment Trusts	1.77	- 0.6	1.76	1.69	2.18	1.60

*NOT INCLUDED IN COMPOSITE INDEXES. †FIGURES FOR 500 COMPOSITE, INDUSTRIALS, TRANSPORTATION, UTILITIES AND FINANCIAL BASED ON DAILY INDEXES. ALL OTHERS BASED ON WEEKLY INDEXES. ‡GROUP ESTABLISHED IN JANUARY 1987.

S&P publishes the monthly, pocket-sized *Stock Guide, Bond Guide,* and *Chart Guide.* Each is a concise summary of investment information about various issues. Figure 8-4 shows two adjacent pages of the *Stock Guide.* The *Stock Guide* contains lists under the categories Stock for Potential Appreciation, Recommended Stocks Primarily for Appreciation, Candidates for Dividend Increases, Candidates for Stock Splits, and 25 of the Best Low-Priced Stocks. The back pages of the *Stock Guide* contain data about the hundreds of publicly available mutual funds. Figure 8-5 shows a page from S&P's *Bond Guide.* The *Chart Guide* contains graphs of stock prices and other technical analysis (see Chapter 15) information for hundreds of corporations.

Moody's Investor Services

Moody's publications may be obtained by calling or writing Moody's Investor Services, Inc., 99 Church St., New York, N.Y. 10007.

Moody's Manuals Comprehensive investment information and the financial history of hundreds of companies are published in *Moody's Manuals.* These *Manuals* are specialized: there are different books for industrial, transportation, utility, bank and financial, and government securities. Twice weekly, Moody's publishes a report to keep its manuals current. *Moody's Manuals* are similar to the *S&P Corporation Records.*

The voluminous *Moody's Industrial Manuals* contain fundamental financial information about hundreds of firms. For each firm, information is presented under the following headings and subheadings: Capital Structure, with subheadings on long-term debt and capital stock history, subsidiaries, business and products, and principal plants and properties; Management, with subheadings on officers, directors, general counsel, auditors, stockholders, employees, general office address, and unfilled orders; Income Accounts, with subheadings on comparative income account, supplementary profit and loss data, comparative balance sheets, property account, and description of reserves; Financial and Operating Data, with subheadings on statistical records, data adjusted for stock splits and stock dividends, financial and operating ratios and analysis of operations; Long-term Debt, with subheadings on authorized debt, call dates, sinking fund, security sales and leasebacks, dividend restrictions, rights on default indenture modification, term loans, notes payable, revolving credit agreement, and other notes; and Capital Stock, with subheadings on authorized stock, dividend restrictions, voting rights, preemptive rights, transfer agent, registrar, stock subscription rights, and debenture subscription rights.

Moody's Handbook of Common Stocks Quarterly issues of *Moody's Handbook of Common Stocks* give a brief summary of about 1000 firms. Figure 8-6 shows a sample page. The market price of each firm is charted and compared with the industry's price trend. Financial background, current developments, and future prospects are reported, along with the financial statistics for several years. S&P's counterpart to *Moody's Handbook* is the *Stock Market Encyclopedia,* which also covers about 1000 stocks. Moody's *Stock Survey* is a weekly publication that is like *The Outlook* from Standard and Poor's.

¶ S&P 500 # MidCap 400 • Options Index	Ticker Symbol	Name of Issue (Call Price of Pfd. Stocks)	Market	Com. Rank. & Pfd. Rating	Par Val.	Inst. Hold Cos	Inst. Hold Shs. (000)	Principal Business	Price Range 1971-89 High	1971-89 Low	1990 High	1990 Low	1991 High	1991 Low	Nov. Sales in 100s	November, 1991 Last Sale Or Bid High	Low	Last	%Div Yield	P-E Ratio
1	INSMA	**Insituform Mid-Amer'A'**	OTC	B	1¢	38	2303	Sewer,pipeln,conduit repair	9½	3¼	7¼	4⅝	16¾	5¾	5325	15⅝	13½	15B	0.9	21
2	INSUA	**Insituform North Amer'A'**	OTC	B−	1¢	29	1470	Mkts sewer/PL repair process	25½	1⅛	8⅝	2 7/16	18⅛	3¼	34099	18⅛	14¼	17⅝B	...	10
3	IRC	**Inspiration Resources**	[1]NY,B,M,Mo,P	C	No	39	13157	Base mtls,agribus,lsg,coal	33⅞	3¾	7	2⅝	4⅝	2½	41629	4½	3¼	3⅞	...	d
4	III	**Insteel Industries**	AS	B	No	29	1572	Mfrs welded wire fabric	11	3½	10⅜	4¾	9¼	6¼	1238	9¼	7⅜	8⅛	3.0	25
5	ISN	**Instron Corp**	AS,B,M	B+	1	27	1880	Material testing equip	18⅜	7/16	11⅛	7½	14⅞	7¼	2845	11	9⅛	9¾	1.2	14
6	ISY	**Instrument Systems**	AS,B,M,Ph	B−	25¢	28	5628	Home furnish'gs,electr equip	123¾	⅞	2⅜	1¼	6⅜	1⅜	35377	6⅜	4¼	4⅜	...	9
7	Pr I	**2nd[51]Pfd'I'Cv(10)vtg**	AS	NR	25¢	1	139	specialty plastic films	24	1	2⅞	1⅞	6⅜	2⅜	903	6⅜	4⅞	4⅞	5.1	..
8	INMRY	**Instrumentarium 'B' ADR[54]**	OTC	NR	No	2	697	Mfr,dstr hosp'l eqp/supplies	16⅞	3¼	14⅛	6	8¾	4¾	....	4¾	4¾	4¾B	4.4	d
9	INTE	**Intech Inc[55]**	OTC	C	No	3	61	Mfr assembled elec circuits	4½	1	1⅜	5/16	11/16	5/16	55	11/16	⅝	⅝B	...	d
10	ITG	**Integra-A Hotel/Rest't**	NY,B,M	NR	10¢	12	1838	Indep oper:Holiday/Days Inn	875	¼	11/16	1/16	⅜	1/32	3530	⅛	1/32	1/16B	...	d
11	ITGR	**Integra Fin'l Corp**	OTC	NR	1	50	9504	Commercial banking, Penna	30¾	23¼	25¾	15¼	29½	13	3889	29½	26¾	26¾B	4.8	26
12	ICST	**Integrated Circuit Sys**	OTC	NR	No	4	155	Design, mfr integrated circuits	....	....	....	....	9¼	6½	6239	8¾	8	8B	...	13
13	IDTI	**Integrated Device Tech**	OTC	B−	0.001	57	13338	Mfrs integrated circuits	16¼	4⅜	8	3¼	9¾	3⅛	29505	5	3⅝	3¾B	...	d
14	IHSI	**Integrated Health Svcs**	OTC	NR	0.001	46	3630	Oper geriatric medl facilities	....	....	....	....	20¼	13¾	10925	20¼	17	17¾B	...	..
15	INTS	**Integrated Systems Inc**	OTC	NR	No	25	2923	Dvlp CAE/CASE software prod	....	....	15	7⅜	17¼	9¾	8041	16¼	10	10¼B	...	d
16	IWSI	**Integrated Waste Svcs**	OTC	NR	1¢	16	861	Non-hazardous waste mgmt	....	....	9⅜	4⅝	12¾	5¼	16634	10½	8⅜	9B	...	22
17	IDCC	**INTEK Diversified**	OTC	B	1¢	2	22	Mfr indust'l plastic prod	4⅛	½	1¾	¼	⅞	¼	200	7/16	⅜	7/16B	...	d
¶18•[2]	INTC	**Intel Corp**	OTC	B−	.001	714	143466	Semiconductor memory circts	41⅞	5/16	52	28	59¼	37¾	343775	44¼	39¾	41B	...	10
19	ICL	**Intellicall Inc**	NY	NR	1¢	39	1710	Mfr/mkt pay telephones	18½	3¼	17¼	7¼	13½	4⅜	9561	7⅜	4⅜	6	...	12
#20•[3]	INEL	**Intelligent Electronics**	OTC	NR	1¢	115	9352	Franchise:computer stores	17⅝	2½	23¾	9⅝	37½	17½	66645	24¾	19¾	24¼B	...	11
21	INP	**Intelligent Sys Master Unit**	AS,P	C	5¢	2	1	Personal computer enhanc'mt	32¾	1⅞	2½	⅞	1⅞	1	1435	1¼	1	1	...	d
22	IT	**Intelogic Trace**	NY,B,P,Ph	NR	1¢	12	4556	Computer maintenance svcs	18⅛	2	2⅝	½	1¼	½	6518	1	⅝	⅞	...	d
23	IPR	**Inter-City Products**	AS	NR	No	8	776	Mfr heat/cooling equip,pipe	....	....	8	2¼	5½	2⅜	543	5½	4½	4¾	...	d
24	Pr	**8% cm Cv Cl C Pref(25)**	AS	NR	No	2	150		....	....	22½	14⅝	18	14¼	8	18	17	17¾B	11.3	..
25	IITCF	**INTERA Info Tech'A'**	OTC	NR	No	25	1384	Gather spec site engin'g data	....	....	20¾	8¾	17	8¾	1352	12⅜	9	9¼B	...	14
26	ICB	**Intercapital Inc Sec**	NY,M	NR	1	13	11	Closed-end inv:fixed income	25⅞	13⅞	22⅜	16¾	21¼	16¾	1290	21	20¼	20⅝	9.6	..
27	IMB	**Intercapital Ins Muni Bd Fd**	NY	NR	1¢	1	.3	Closed-end muni bond fund	....	....	....	....	16	14½	1359	15⅞	15¼	15⅝	⊙6.7	..
28	IQT	**Intercapital Qual Muni Inv**	NY	NR	1¢	..	...	Closed-end muni bond fund	....	....	....	....	15¾	14¾	1874	15⅜	14¾	14⅞	6.9	..
29	ISB	**Interchange Finl Svcs**	AS	A−	No	2	3	Commercial banking,New Jersey	21¾	1⅞	12	5⅝	12	6½	58	12	10⅝	10⅝	6.6	12
30	ITCM	**INTERCIM Corp**	OTC	NR	1¢	3	660	Computer integrated mfg	8⅝	⅞	2¾	½	¾	½	559	⅝	⅝	⅝B	...	63
31	ISS	**INTERCO Inc**	NY,B,M,Ph,P	D	No	27	920	Mfr/retailer,consumer prod	73⅝	3/16	13/16	1/16	9/16	1/16	11316	¼	¼	¼	...	d
32	IFSIA	**Interface Inc'A'**	OTC	A	10¢	75	12128	Mfrs free lying carpet tile	19⅜	3¼	19¾	6¾	14¼	7⅞	10397	9¾	8⅜	8¾B	2.7	14
33	INTF	**Interface Systems**	OTC	B+	10¢	16	371	Mfrs IBM compatible printers	11	⅝	7	2½	5¾	2⅝	1102	4¾	3⅛	3⅝B	...	24
¶34•[4]	INGR	**Intergraph Corp**	OTC	B+	10¢	194	28488	Computer graphics systems	40½	3⅞	23½	10½	31½	13	49458	20½	16½	17¼B	...	10
35	IGHC	**Intergroup Healthcare**	OTC	NR	.001	13	1309	Managed hlth care svc, Arizona	....	....	....	....	17½	11	4273	17½	15½	16B	...	15
¶36	IK	**Interlake Corp**	NY,B,M,P	NR	1	83	3024	Diversified ind'l mfg co	61¾	6½	14⅜	3⅛	5⅝	2¾	3597	5⅝	4⅛	5⅛	...	d
37	LEAF	**Interleaf Inc**	OTC	NR	1¢	36	4869	Computer aids for publishing	24⅛	5⅜	8	2½	10½	3	31902	10½	8⅛	8⅝B	...	43
38	INMA	**Intermagnetics Gen'l**	OTC	B−	10¢	24	1832	Mfr superconductive mtls	22¾	3	7¼	4⅜	13⅞	5¼	19240	11⅜	8½	8⅞B	...	18
39	IMI	**Intermark Inc**	AS	C	1	29	2302	Broadly diversified holding co	15	⅛	10¾	1½	3½	7/16	5262	¾	7/16	11/16	...	d
40	INMT	**Intermet Corp**	OTC	B	10¢	42	5125	Iron foundry-auto indus	19	4¾	9⅝	3⅝	9	4½	7545	8¼	6½	6¾B	1.8	d
41	IMET	**Intermetrics Inc**	OTC	B−	1¢	10	698	Computer software prod & svc	20¾	2¼	5⅛	2⅜	6¾	2⅝	260	4¾	4¼	4¼B	4.7	7
42	IASG	**Intl Airline Support Grp**	OTC	NR	.001	[illegible]	[illegible]	Sell used&new aircraft parts			3¾	[illegible]	5¾	[illegible]	[illegible]	6¼	[illegible]	5¾B	...	12
43	IAL	**Intl Aluminum**	NY,B,M,P	A−	1	31	1650	Mfr & sale aluminum prod	30¾	1	27¼	18⅞	30	20⅝	808	24½	20⅝	20¾	4.8	24
¶44•[5]	IBM	**Intl Bus. Machines**	[6]NY,B,C,M,P,Ph,Mo	A	1¼	1245	281205	Lgst mfr business machines	175⅞	37⅝	123⅛	94½	139¾	92	291235	101⅜	92⅜	92½	5.2	27
45	BZU	**IBM,Americus(Unit)**	AS,M	NR	No	4	74	Unit Trust for IBM	166	97¾	123	99	131¼	95	153	99⅜	95	90B	5.3	..
46	BZS	**Score**	AS,M	NR	No	7	2505	capital appreciation	58	7⅜	9⅞	15/16	4½	⅜	4404	⅝	⅜	7/16	...	..

Uniform Footnote Explanations-See Page 1. Other: [1]Ph,To [2]ASE,CBOE,P:Cycle 1. [3]ASE,CBOE,P:Cycle 3. [4]ASE:Cycle 1. [5]CBOE:Cycle 1. [6]To [51]$0.25 cash or $0.25 shr common. [52]Paid $0.25 in com stk (0.08 shr). [53]Paid $0.25 in com stk (0.16 shr). [54]Exch ADR represents¼'B' shr. [55]Invest grp plan acq, $0.875. [56]Stk dstr of Showbiz Pizza Time. [57]®$0.44,'91. [58]®$1.00,'89. [59]△$30.15,'90. [60]©$0.0243,'91. [61]Special cash & debs dstr,'88. [62]Liabs Subj to compromise. [63]®$1.24,'90. [64]Special divd. [65]®$0.39,'91.

Index	Splits ◆ Cash Divs. Ea. Yr. Since	Dividends Latest Payment Period $	Date	Ex. Div.	Total $ So Far 1991	Ind. Rate	Paid 1990	Financial Position Mil-$ Cash& Equiv.	Curr. Assets	Curr. Liab.	Balance Sheet Date	Capitalization Lg Trm Debt Mil-$	Shs. 000 Pfd.	Com.	Earnings $ Per Shr. Years End	1987	1988	1989	1990	1991	Last 12 Mos.	Interim Earnings Period	$ per Shr. 1990	1991	Index
1	1988	S0.07	1-10-92	12-6	0.10	0.14	0.08	5.31	18.0	5.33	6-30-91	0.37	...	±8030	Sp	*±0.21	±0.15	±0.28	±0.45	P±0.70	0.70				1
2	....	None Since Public			...	Nil	....	28.0	41.0	7.68	9-30-91	5.92	...	±7870	Dc	d0.10	0.52	0.46	0.22	....	1.75	9 Mo Sep	0.17	*1.70	2
3	1989	0.03	11-14-90	11-2	...	Nil	0.12	19.5	525	340	6-30-91	p111	...	±p68885	Dc	*0.15	0.63	0.38	d1.64	....	d4.06	9 Mo Sep	0.10	△d2.32	3
4◆	1986	Q0.06	1-2-92	12-5	0.229	0.24	0.208	0.03	59.7	31.5	6-30-91	32.8	...	5249	Sp	*0.68	△1.59	1.30	□0.67	P△0.32	0.32				4
5	1973	Q0.03	1-3-92	12-9	0.12	0.12	0.12	3.95	60.5	26.6	9-28-91	11.9	...	6269	Dc	0.54	0.40	0.53	0.58	....	0.68	9 Mo Sep	0.29	0.39	5
6	....	©Wrrt	7-1-69	5-23	...	Nil	....	12.8	197	76.7	6-30-91	112	1707	28364	Sp	*□0.01	*d0.05	d0.54	*△0.32	P*△0.51	0.51				6
7	....	[52]....	6-28-91	6-10	[52]...	0.25	[53]....	Cv into 1 common				....	1844	...	Sp	b1.10	b0.74	b0.04	n/a	....	....				7
8◆	1984	0.21	5-17-91	4-26	0.21	0.21	0.266	56.4	268	130	12-31-90	105	...	±6650	Dc	1.02	2.16	1.60	d0.66	....	d0.66				8
9◆	....	5%Stk	9-5-89	7-28	...	Nil	....	0.34	5.53	2.65	9-13-91	....	...	3268	Mr	d0.09	d0.01	d0.09	d0.39	....	d0.08	24 Wk Sep	d0.27	0.04	9
10◆	....	h[56]....	12-30-88	1-3	...	Nil	....	0.15	5.93	38.1	9-27-91	27.2	115880	10529	Dc	*0.34	d0.57	□d1.30	d2.85	....	d1.35	9 Mo Sep	d1.68	d0.18	10
11	1989	Q0.32	12-1-91	11-8	1.22	1.28	1.20	Book Value $21.05			12-31-90	p143	...	p24233	Dc	p2.49	2.62	1.42	1.06	....	1.05	9 Mo Sep	2.13	2.12	11
12	....	None Since Public			...	Nil	....	7.58	12.3	2.62	6-30-91	0.19	...	4563	Je	0.11	0.08	0.05	0.11	[57]0.50	0.62	3 Mo Sep	d0.01	0.11	12
13◆	....	None Since Public			...	Nil	....	24.4	119	54.7	6-30-91	54.4	...	26148	Mr	0.46	0.70	0.66	0.05	....	d0.70	6 Mo Sep	0.02	d0.73	13
14	....	None Since Public			...	Nil	....	29.5	60.6	18.8	6-30-91	47.4	...	8266	Dc	...	...	...	....	....	....	9 Mo Sep	0.15	0.55	14
15	....	None Since Public			...	Nil	....	21.2	27.0	4.44	8-31-91	....	...	9075	Fb	0.15	0.21	0.29	0.47	....	d0.95	6 Mo Aug	0.17	d1.25	15
16	....	None Since Public			...	Nil	....	7.57	19.2	8.53	6-30-91	8.39	...	7843	Dc	d0.04	0.08	0.22	0.37	....	0.41	9 Mo Sep	0.27	0.31	16
17	....	None Paid			...	Nil	....	0.35	3.05	1.19	6-30-91	0.17	...	2816	Dc	0.11	0.25	0.26	d0.06	....	d0.10	9 Mo Sep	d0.08	d0.12	17
18◆	....	None Paid			...	Nil	....	1918	3348	1213	6-29-91	353	...	202649	Dc	*0.98	2.51	2.07	3.20	E3.95	3.81	9 Mo Sep	2.40	3.01	18
19	....	None Since Public			...	Nil	....	0.70	107	30.9	6-30-91	49.3	...	6717	Dc	0.31	0.53	0.79	1.10	....	0.51	9 Mo Sep	0.79	0.20	19
20◆	....	None Since Public			...	Nil	....	65.7	342	310	7-31-91	29.9	...	18036	Oc	0.35	0.59	[58]1.02	2.09	E2.20	2.40	9 Mo Jul	1.41	1.72	20
21	....	0.10	9-19-89	8-25	...	Nil	....	3.26	19.2	9.51	9-30-91	....	...	6691	Dc	1.03	1.57	d0.45	d1.43	....	d1.15	9 Mo Sep	d0.55	d0.27	21
22	....	None Since Public			...	Nil	....	10.2	41.2	52.9	7-27-91	73.2	...	11911	Jl	□0.58	△0.19	0.01	△d2.15	△d1.59	d1.50	3 Mo Oct	△d0.23	△d0.14	22
23	....	None Since Public			...	Nil	....	9.90	435	368	j6-30-91	110	2440	7227	Dc	...	p1.19	p1.21	△[59]d1.25	....	jd2.70	6 Mo Jun	△0.71	d0.74	23
24	1990	gQ0.50	10-1-91	9-10	g2.00	2.00	0.451	Cv into 2.866 ord shrs				....	1528	...	Dc	...	...	...	....	....	....				24
25	....	None Since Public			...	Nil	....	0.14	30.7	19.9	6-30-91	7.79	...	5449	Sp	d1.46	0.61	0.33	1.01	....	0.68	9 Mo Jun	0.74	0.41	25
26	1973	0.16½	11-1-91	10-11	0.19	1.98	2.10	Net Asset Val $18.02			11-22-91	....	...	11949	Sp	§18.79	§19.28	§18.83	§16.97	....	....				26
27	1991	[60]0.111	12-20-91	12-2	[60]0.714	1.05	....	Net Asset Val $14.48			11-22-91	....	★1	★4607	Dc	...	...	...	....	....	....				27
28	1991	0.08½	12-20-91	12-2	0.08½	1.02	....	Net Asset Val $13.90			11-22-91	....	★3	★17007	Dc	...	...	...	....	....	....				28
29◆	1981	Q0.17½	1-21-92	12-16	0.70	0.70	0.70	Book Value $8.14			6-30-91	0.48	100	1727	Dc	1.34	1.44	1.54	0.99	....	0.91	9 Mo Sep	0.91	0.83	29
30	....	None Since Public			...	Nil	....	0.35	3.82	2.27	6-30-91	0.05	...	15088	Je	d0.35	d0.10	d0.04	d0.23	0.02	0.01	3 Mo Sep	0.01	Nil	30
31◆	....	[61]....			...	Nil	....	File bankruptcy Chapt 11				[62]2142	3332	38729	Fb	®3.50	®1.53	d1.22	d7.03	....	d4.57	6 Mo Aug	d3.21	d0.75	31
32◆	1977	Q0.06	11-22-91	11-4	0.24	0.24	0.24	9.23	245	99.4	6-30-91	242	...	±17232	Dc	±0.87	±1.18	±1.43	±[63]1.37	....	0.65	9 Mo Sep	±1.04	±0.32	32
33◆	....	None Since Public			...	Nil	....	0.86	17.9	3.59	6-30-91	2.44	...	4206	Sp	0.54	△0.66	0.67	0.44	....	0.15	9 Mo Jun	0.40	0.11	33
34	....	None Since Public			...	Nil	....	125	668	195	6-30-91	17.9	...	48106	Dc	1.23	1.55	1.48	1.28	E1.70	1.52	9 Mo Sep	0.88	1.12	34
35	....	None Since Public			...	Nil	....	38.2	58.0	47.6	6-30-91	16.0	...	★9750	Dc	...	...	...	p0.51	....	1.08	9 Mo Sep	p0.45	p1.02	35
36◆	....	[64]45.00	9-28-89	9-29	...	Nil	....	12.5	228	176	9-29-91	434	...	10491	Dc	4.69	3.75	0.09	d2.07	Ed1.25	d1.21	9 Mo Sep	d1.72	d0.86	36
37	....	None Since Public			...	Nil	....	15.9	38.9	21.4	6-30-91	1.62	2143	12140	Mr	*0.47	0.07	d1.37	d0.11	....	0.20	6 Mo Sep	d0.24	0.07	37
38◆	....	3%Stk	9-16-91	8-30	3%Stk	Stk	....	2.13	31.3	6.92	8-25-91	9.60	...	6882	My	d0.60	0.13	0.25	0.13	[65]0.40	0.49	3 Mo Aug	0.06	0.15	38
39◆	1978	0.03	7-2-90	6-12	...	Nil	0.09	13.8	114	93.9	9-30-91	286	2709	15018	Mr	□1.55	0.01	△d1.90	d4.77	....	d4.69	6 Mo Sep	d1.52	△d1.44	39
40	1985	Q0.03	11-21-91	11-1	0.14	0.12	0.20	15.1	88.0	52.8	6-30-91	39.3	...	20895	Dc	1.00	0.76	0.68	d0.49	....	d0.25	9 Mo Sep	0.06	0.30	40
41	1990	A0.20	5-23-91	4-24	0.20	0.20	†1.00	7.20	22.7	10.7	8-31-91	0.26	...	3691	Fb	*0.40	0.79	0.43	0.59	....	0.61	6 Mo Aug	0.28	0.30	41
42	....	None Since Public			...	Nil	....	0.01	11.8	9.19	8-31-91	0.18	...	3825	My	...	0.02	0.19	0.20	0.37	0.48	3 Mo Aug	0.09	0.20	42
43	1966	Q0.25	1-10-92	12-16	1.00	1.00	1.00	15.0	79.7	18.0	6-30-91	2.79	...	4205	Je	1.58	3.06	2.91	3.52	1.46	0.86	3 Mo Sep	0.74	0.14	43
44	1916	Q1.21	12-10-91	11-4	4.84	4.84	4.84	4700	35516	22285	6-30-91	11991	...	572138	Dc	8.72	△9.27	6.47	10.51	E3.45	5.73	9 Mo Sep	6.21	□1.43	44
45	1987	Q1.198	12-19-91	11-4	4.79	4.79	4.79	Net Asset Val $113.00			12-31-90	....	...	7783	Dc	§115.50	§121.88	§94.12	§113.00	....	....	Expires 6-30-92			45
46	....	None Since Public			...	Nil	....	....	....	....	....	....	...	...	Dc	...	...	...	....	....	....				46

◆Stock Splits & Divs By Line Reference Index [4]3-for-2,'89:10%,'87,'88,'90,'91. [8]6-for-5,'88. [9]Adj for 5%,'89. [10]No adj for dstr of Showbiz Pizza Time,'88. [13]3-for-2,'87. [18]3-for-2,'87. [20]2-for-1,'90. [29]3-for-2,'87. [31]No adj for spl dstr,'88. [32]2-for-1,'87. [33]10%,'87. [36]No adj for spl $45 dstr,'89. [38]Adj for 3%,'91. [39]10%,'89.

Figure 8-4 Information on common and preferred stocks from Standard & Poors *Stock Guide*, November 1991 (shown opposite page). (*Source:* Standard & Poors, 25 Broadway, New York, N.Y. 10004.)

In addition to its weekly *Bond Outlook,* Moody's publishes the *Bond Survey.* Both publications include some similar data about the corporate and municipal bond markets, attractive convertibles and new issues, changes in bond ratings, bonds called for payment, and similar terms.

Value Line Investment Survey

Value Line's publications may be purchased by calling or writing The Value Line Investment Survey, 711 Third Ave., New York, N.Y. 10017. The **Value Line Investment Survey** differs somewhat from the Moody's and S&P publications. Value Line reports on 1700 stocks in 60 industries, covering each stock in detail once

Figure 8-5 A sample page of information from Standard & Poor's *Bond Guide,* November 1991. (*Source:* Standard & Poors, 25 Broadway, New York, N.Y. 10004.)

Corporate Bonds

AME-AME 27

Title-Industry Code & Co. Finances (In Italics) / Exchange — Individual Issue Statistics	*Ind* / Interest Dates	*Fixed Charge Coverage 1988* / S&P Debt Rating	*1989* / Date of Last Rating Change	*1990* / Prior Rating	Eligible	*Year End* / Bond Form	*Million $ Cash & Equiv.* / Redemption Provisions: Regular Price	*Curr. Assets* / Regular (Begins) Thru	*Curr. Liab.* / Sinking Fund Price	*Balance Sheet Date* / Sinking Fund (Begins) Thru	*L. Term Debt (Mil $)* / Refund/Other Restriction Price	Refund/Other Restriction (Begins) Thru	*Capital-ization (Mil $)* / Outst'g (Mil $)	*Total Debt % Capital* / Underwriting Firm	Underwriting Year	Price Range 1991 High	Price Range 1991 Low	Mo. End Price Sale(s) or Bid	Curr. Yield	Yield to Mat.
***American Greetings** (Cont.)*																				
Nts 8⅛s '96	jJ15	**A**	11/89	A−	X	R	100	(7-15-93)	....	....	....	....	100	K2	'86	103¼	97¼	103¼	7.87	7.28
Amer Hospital Supply	***43***	***Mgr into Baxter Travenol,see***																		
• SF Deb 7⅞s 2007	fA15	**A−**	7/91	BBB+	X	R	103.333	8-14-92	100	....	....	....	16.7	M3	'77	92¼	70	89⅜	8.81	9.16
Amer Medical Int'l[1]	***31***	***1.69***	***1.29***	***[2]0.92***		***Au***	***42.00***	***244.0***	***565.0***	***5-31-91***	***★2186***		***2278***	***86.7***						
SF Deb 11¼s 2015	Jd	**B+**	7/91	B	Y	R	107.884	5-31-92	100	(6-1-96)	®105.632	5-31-92	38.8	G2	'85	98½	58	96½	11.66	11.69
Sr Nts[3] 11s 2000	aO15	**B+**			Y	R	103.14	(10-15-96)	....	....	....	....	100	F2	'91	100¾	99¼	100	11.00	11.00
Nts 14⅜s '92	fA15	**B+**	7/91	B	Y	R	NC	....	....	....	....	....	62.6	G2	'82	103¼	84⅝	99⅞	14.39	14.47
Nts 9¾s '93	Fa	**B+**	7/91	B	Y	R	100	....	....	....	....	....	79.1	G2	'86	99¾	78½	97¼	10.03	12.31
Nts 13⅛s '94	fA15	**B+**	7/91	B	Y	R	100	(8-15-93)	....	....	....	....	50.0	G2	'84	103¼	74	103	12.74	11.78
Nts 11⅜s '95	Fa	**B+**	7/91	B	Y	R	NC	....	....	....	....	....	84.7	G2	'85	101½	67⅞	98½	11.55	11.94
Nts 10¼s '95	Jd	**B+**	7/91	B	Y	R	100	(6-1-92)	....	....	....	....	56.2	G2	'85	98¾	63	91⅞	11.16	13.22
Sub SF Deb[4] 11s '98	aO	**B−**	7/91	CCC+	Y	R	100	....	100	....	....	....	3.80	F2	'78	90⅝	56½	90⅝	12.14	13.11
Sub SF Deb[4] 11¾s '99	Jd	**B−**	7/91	CCC+	Y	R	100	....	100	....	....	....	8.00	F2	'79	93⅛	58⅜	93⅛	12.62	13.22
Sr Sub Nts[5] 13½s 2001	fA15	**B−**			Y	R	103.86	(8-15-96)	....	....	....	....	210	F2	'91	107⅝	100	106	12.74	12.41
Amer President Cos Ltd[6]	***63***	***3.93***	***1.40***	***1.33***		***Dc***	***27.10***	***388.0***	***323.0***	***6-28-91***	***463.0***		***967.0***	***48.8***						
Nts 11s '96	Jj15	**BBB**	3/91	BBB+	X	R	100	(1-15-93)	....	....	....	....	94.5	S1	'86	108⅜	100⅛	103½	10.63	9.94
Amer President Lines[7]	***70***	***Gtd by U.S. Gov't agency***																		
Bonds 7⅝s '96	Mn	**AAA**			X	R	101.05	4-30-92	100	....	Z100	....	5.81	L4	'71	100¾	95	100¾	7.57	7.42
American Shared Hosp Svcs	***43***	***1.50***	***0.64***	***0.53***		***Dc***	***1.44***	***15.20***	***18.90***	***6-30-91***	***46.90***		***66.90***	***89.4***						
◆Sr Sub[8]Nts[9] 16½s '96	aO15	**NR**	10/91	C		R	100	....	100	(10-15-95)	....	....	23.8	D9	'88	63½	55	57	....	Flat
American Standard[10]	***13f***	***[11]0.67***	***0.97***	***0.86***		***Dc***	***25.20***	***1186***	***903.0***	***6-30-91***	***1966***		***2218***	***100.0***						
SF Deb 9¼s 2016	jD	**B+**	6/88	A+	Y	R	106.938	11-30-92	100	(12-1-97)	®104.625	11-30-96	150	F2	'86	83½	56¾	79	11.71	11.89
Sr Sub Deb 12⅞s 2000	Jd31	**B−**			Y	R	104.83	(6-30-93)	100	(6-30-98)	....	....	550	F2	'88	102	62	98½	13.07	13.17
Sub Disc[12]Deb 14¼s 2003	Jd30	**B−**			Y	R	105	6-29-94	100	(6-30-01)	....	....	[13]546	F2	'88	84	22	79¾	....	Flat
American Tel & Tel[14]	***67b***	***5.61***	***6.02***	***6.11***		***Dc***	***1273***	***23089***	***18903***	***9-30-91***	***8816***		***29809***	***47.1***						
Deb 4¾s '92	mN	**AA**	8/84	AAA	X	CR	100	....	....	....	....	....	250	M6	'60	99½	94⅜	98⅞	4.80	6.02
Deb 4⅝s '94	Fa	**AA**	8/84	AAA	X	CR	100	....	....	....	....	....	300	F2	'62	97⅛	90½	96⅝	4.79	6.31
• Deb 5⅝s '95	fA	**AA**	8/84	AAA	X	R	100	....	....	....	....	....	250	M6	'66	97⅞	88	s97	5.80	6.55
Deb 4⅜s '96	aO	**AA**	8/84	AAA	X	CR	100	....	....	....	....	....	250	F2	'62	89½	82¼	89½	4.89	6.97
• Deb 5½s '97	Jj	**AA**	8/84	AAA	X	R	100	....	....	....	....	....	250	F2	'67	95	84¼	92	5.98	7.41
Deb 4¾s '98	Jd	**AA**	8/84	AAA	X	CR	100.34	5-31-92	....	....	....	....	250	M6	'61	86⅝	79½	86⅝	5.48	7.38
Deb 4⅜s '99	Mn	**AA**	8/84	AAA	X	CR	100.56	4-30-92	....	....	....	....	250	M6	'63	82⅜	74⅛	80¾	5.42	7.84
• Deb 6s 2000	fA	**AA**	8/84	AAA	X	R	100.91	7-31-92	....	....	....	....	250	H1	'67	90	80	s89¾	6.69	7.64
• Deb[15] 8¾s 2000	Mn15	**AA**	8/84	AAA	X	R	101.40	5-14-92	....	....	....	....	713	M6	'70	104	99½	s103¼	8.47	8.21
• Deb 7s 2001	Fa15	**AA**	8/84	AAA	X	R	101.25	2-14-92	....	....	....	....	500	B9	'71	94¾	85⅞	s94⅜	7.42	7.87
• Deb 5⅛s 2001	Ao	**AA**	8/84	AAA	X	R	100.85	3-31-92	....	....	....	....	250	F2	'66	83	73⅝	s82¼	6.23	7.84
• Deb 7⅛s 2003	jD	**AA**	8/84	AAA	X	R	101.85	11-30-92	....	....	....	....	350	M6	'72	94⅜	84⅜	s93⅝	7.61	7.96
• Deb 8.80s 2005	Mn15	**AA**	8/84	AAA	X	R	103.05	5-14-92	....	....	....	....	500	M6	'74	103⅜	97⅛	s102¾	8.56	8.45
• Deb 8⅝s 2007	Fa	**AA**	8/84	AAA	X	R	103.51	1-31-92	....	....	....	....	300	S1	'75	102½	95½	s102½	8.41	8.33
• Deb 8⅝s 2026	Ao	**AA**			X	R	106.21	3-31-92	....	....	....	....	300	S1	'86	100	90⅜	s99¾	8.65	8.65
American TV & Commun'ns	***12a***	***3.88***	***3.43***	***3.79***		***Dc***	***0.74***			***6-30-91***	***776.0***		***1377***	***56.4***						
Deb 9¾s 2016	jD	**BB**	10/89	A−	Y	R	107.33	11-30-92	100	(12-1-97)	®104.87	11-30-96	150	S1	'86	97	74⅛	97	10.05	10.08
Nts 8⅜s '93	jD	**CALL**	11/91	BB		R			Called 12-1-91 at 100				150	S1	'86	100	95	99⅝	8.41	Call

Uniform Footnote Explanations-See Page 1. Other: [1] Subsid of Amer Medical Hldgs. [2] 10 Mo Aug'90. [3] (HRO)At 101 for a Chge in Ctrl. [4] Was Lifemark Corp. [5] (HRO)On Chge in Ctrl at 101. [6] See Amer President Lines. [7] Subsid of Amer Pres Cos. [8] Int incr fr 14% on 10-15-89. [9] Int of 4-15-91 pd 5-15-91. [10] Subsid of ASI Holding. [11] 8 Mo Dec'88. [12] Int accrues at 14.25% fr 6-30-93. [13] Incl disc. [14] See Western Elec,Pac Tel&Tel. [15] Issued in $100 denomin.

INTERNATIONAL BUSINESS MACHINES CORPORATION

LISTED	SYM.	LTPS♦	STPS♦	IND. DIV.	REC. PRICE	RANGE (52-WKS.)	YLD.
NYSE	IBM	71.4	83.5	$4.84*	101	140 - 96	4.8%

HIGH GRADE. WEAK DOMESTIC DEMAND WILL PRESSURE RESULTS DESPITE STRONG OPERATING MARGINS.

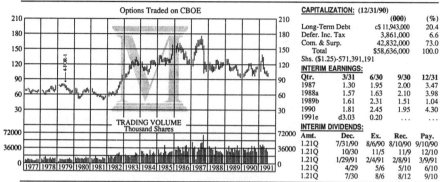

CAPITALIZATION: (12/31/90)

	(000)	(%)
Long-Term Debt	c$ 11,943,000	20.4
Defer. Inc. Tax	3,861,000	6.6
Com. & Surp.	42,832,000	73.0
Total	$58,636,000	100.0

Shs. ($1.25)-571,391,191

INTERIM EARNINGS:

Qtr.	3/31	6/30	9/30	12/31
1987	1.30	1.95	2.00	3.47
1988a	1.57	1.63	2.10	3.98
1989b	1.61	2.31	1.51	1.04
1990	1.81	2.45	1.95	4.30
1991e	d3.03	0.20	...	...

INTERIM DIVIDENDS:

Amt.	Dec.	Ex.	Rec.	Pay.
1.21Q	7/31/90	8/6/90	8/10/90	9/10/90
1.21Q	10/30	11/5	11/9	12/10
1.21Q	1/29/91	2/4/91	2/8/91	3/9/91
1.21Q	4/29	5/6	5/10	6/10
1.21Q	7/30	8/6	8/12	9/10

BACKGROUND:

IBM is the largest manufacturer of information processing equipment and systems. IBM applies advanced information technology to solve the problems in business, government, science, space, defense, education, medicine and other areas. IBM offers customers solutions that incorporate information processing systems, software, communication systems and other products and services to address specific needs. While most products are sold or leased through IBM worldwide marketing organization, IBM utilizes external distribution channels through IBM Business Partners. In 1990, revenues were derived: sales, 64%; support, 16%; software, 14% and rentals & financing, 6%.

RECENT DEVELOPMENTS:

IBM announced a strategic alliance with Apple Computer to develop a new operating system that makes computing more user-friendly. For the quarter ended 6/30/91, net income plunged 92% to $114 million compared with $1.41 billion a year ago. Revenues fell 11% to $14.73 billion.

Poor results were attributed to the drop in sales of computer equipment, unfavorable foreign currency exchange rates and higher charges related to severance packages. However, demand for workstations and midrange mainframes improved and sales from support services rose 16%.

PROSPECTS:

Intense discount pricing within the computer industry accompanied by lower demand from both domestic and European markets clouds the near-term outlook. Meanwhile, long-term prospects are brightened by IBM's new comprehensive product offerings which include the System/390 ES 9000 line of mainframes, entry level models of the AS/400 minicomputers, two high-end models of the PS/2 computer and the PS/1 home computer. In addition, IBM's alliance with Apple to design an operating system centered around an object oriented software bode well for long-term growth. Brisk demand, competitively-priced workstations and the laptop computer will boost sales.

STATISTICS:

YEAR	GROSS REVS. ($mill.)	OPER. PROFIT MARGIN %	RET. ON EQUITY %	NET INCOME ($mill.)	WORK CAP. ($mill.)	SENIOR CAPITAL ($mill.)	SHARES (000)	EARN. PER SH.$	DIV. PER SH.$	DIV. PAY. %	PRICE RANGE	P/E RATIO	AVG. YIELD %
81	29,070	20.7	18.2	3,308	2,983	2,669	592,294	5.63	3.44	61	71½ - 48⅜	10.7	6.0
82	34,364	23.4	22.1	4,409	4,805	2,851	602,406	7.39	3.44	47	98 - 55⅝	10.4	4.5
83	40,180	23.9	23.6	5,485	7,763	2,674	610,725	9.04	3.71	41	134¼ - 92¼	12.5	3.3
84	45,937	24.5	24.8	6,582	10,735	3,269	612,686	10.77	4.10	38	128½ - 99	10.6	3.6
85	50,056	22.4	20.5	6,555	14,637	3,955	615,418	10.67	4.40	41	158½ - 117⅜	12.9	3.2
86	51,250	15.3	13.9	4,789	15,006	4,169	605,923	7.81	4.40	56	161⅞ - 119¼	18.0	3.1
87	54,217	14.3	13.7	5,258	17,643	3,858	597,052	8.72	4.40	50	175⅞ - 102	15.9	3.2
88	59,681	14.7	13.9	a5,491	17,956	8,518	589,741	a9.27	4.40	47	129½ - 104½	12.6	3.8
89	62,710	11.0	9.8	b3,758	14,175	10,825	574,700	b6.47	4.73	73	130⅞ - 93⅜	17.3	4.2
90	69,018	16.0	14.1	6,020	13,644	11,943	571,391	10.51	4.84	46	123⅛ - 94½	10.4	4.4

♦Long-Term Price Score — Short-Term Price Score; See page 4a. STATISTICS ARE AS ORIGINALLY REPORTED. a-Excludes $315 million ($0.53 per share) credit for an accounting change. b-Includes $2.4 billion ($4.16 a share) charge for restructuring. c-Includes debentures convertible into common stock. e-Includes a net charge of $2.3 billion ($3.96 a sh.) related to changes in accounting for post-retirement benefits.

INCORPORATED:
June 16, 1911 — NY

PRINCIPAL OFFICE:
Old Orchard Road
Armonk, NY 10504
Tel.: (914) 765-7777

ANNUAL MEETING:
Last Mon. in April

NUMBER OF STOCKHOLDERS:
789,046

TRANSFER AGENT(S):
First Chicago Trust Co. of N.Y.
New York, NY

REGISTRAR(S):
First Chicago Trust Company of N.Y.
New York, NY

INSTITUTIONAL HOLDINGS:
No. of Institutions: 1,441
Shares Held: 302,584,660

OFFICERS:
Chairman & C.E.O.
J. F. Akers
Presidnet
J. D. Kuehler
S.V.P. & C.F.O.
F. A. Metz, Jr.
Treasurer
R. Ripp
Secretary
J. E. Hickey

Figure 8-6 Page discussing IBM from *Moody's Handbook of Common Stocks,* November 1991. (*Source:* Moody's, 99 Church Street, New York, N.Y. 10007.)

every quarter. Figure 8-7 shows one of Value Line's quarterly reports for a firm. Supplements are issued to Value Line subscribers each week to keep the financial reports up to date. About 85 stocks are usually included in the three- or four-page supplements. Once per quarter Value Line issues industry reports like the one shown in Figure 8-8 for every industry it researches.

A unique feature of Value Line's service is its investment scoring system. Value Line rates every stock from 1 to 5 with respect to four factors: quality, performance in the next 12 months, appreciation potential in 3 to 5 years, and income from dividends.

A second distinctive feature of Value Line is the quality of its investment advice. In studies to determine the profitability of the investment advice given by various brokerages and investment advisers, Value Line ranks as one of the better sources. On average, studies have suggested that Value Line's recommendations yield a portfolio that earns a few percentage points more return per year than could be earned by picking a diversified portfolio randomly. Such favorable studies have never been published for other investment advisory services by unbiased outside researchers.[8]

8-4   Brokerage Houses

Brokerage offices usually carry one or more of the leading investment surveys, and the brokers are happy to provide these at no charge for customers' use. In addition, the largest brokerage houses maintain research departments that generate information for their customers. The largest securities brokerages listed in the case on page 90 have their own internal research departments. Such a research department provides publications, usually in the form of market newsletters or reviews, free upon request. The analyses cover industries and individual companies. Upon request, some research departments will also analyze portfolios and make specific recommendations tailored to a customer's investment goals. A brokerage that is too small to maintain a research staff may provide free research published by a company like Standard & Poor's and/or Moody's.

Although the large retail brokerages strive to maintain a reputation for fair dealing, their salespeople's advice should not be followed blindly. Every time a securities broker makes an investment recommendation, *the investor should remember that the broker will make a commission whether or not the customer profits from the trade.* A wise investor never relies on investment advice from a broker or one brokerage house's investment newsletter.

---

[8] See Fisher Black, "Yes, Virginia, There Is Hope: Tests of the Value Line Ranking System," *Financial Analysts Journal*, September-October 1973. Also see L. D. Brown and M. S. Rozoff, "The Superiority of Analyst Forecasts as a Measure of Expectations: Evidence from Earnings," *Journal of Finance*, vol. 33, no. 1, March 1978, pp. 1–16. For a study that employed Value Line's approach for selecting stocks see S. Basu, "The Investment Performance of Common Stocks in Relation to Their Price-Earning Ratios," *Journal of Finance*, vol. 32, no. 3, June 1977, pp. 663–682. Also see T. E. Copeland and D. Mayers, "The Value Line Enigma (1965–1978): A Case Study of Performance Evaluation Issues," *Journal of Financial Economics*, November 1982, pp. 289–321.

| | | High: | 8.5 | 26.4 | 23.5 | 29.8 | 53.8 | 103.0 | | Target Price Range 1994 1995 1996 |
| | | Low: | 3.5 | 7.9 | 15.1 | 15.3 | 28.0 | 48.7 | | |

TIMELINESS 1 Highest
(Relative Price Perform-
ance Next 12 Mos.)

SAFETY 3 Average
(Scale: 1 Highest to 5 Lowest)

BETA 1.40 (1.00 = Market)

1994-96 PROJECTIONS
	Price	Gain	Ann'l Total Return
High	135	(+30%)	7%
Low	90	(−10%)	−3%

Insider Decisions
	J	F	M	A	M	J	J	A	S
to Buy	0	0	0	0	0	0	0	0	0
Options	0	4	0	0	0	7	1	4	6
to Sell	1	3	4	1	3	12	11	11	11

Institutional Decisions
	1Q'91	2Q'91	3Q'91
to Buy	110	106	140
to Sell	97	110	77
Hld's(000)	52176	49583	55245

Percent shares traded: 30.0 / 20.0 / 10.0

Options: ASE, PACE

Microsoft was founded in 1975 as a partnership between William Gates and Paul Allen. Mr. Allen temporarily ended his ties with the company in April of 1985. He now owns 16.2% of Microsoft's stock and serves as a member of the Board of Directors.

Microsoft was incorporated in 1981, and an initial public offering was held in March of 1986 at a price of $5.25 a share.

CAPITAL STRUCTURE as of 9/30/91

Total Debt $19.3 mill.   **Due in 5 Yrs** $19.3 mill.

LT Debt Nil

Leases, Uncapitalized $14.9 mill.

Pension Liability None - No defined benefit pension plan.

Pfd Stock None

Common Stock 176,197,000 shs. (100% of Cap'l) as of 10/31/91

CURRENT POSITION
($MILL.)	1990	1991	9/30/91
Cash Assets	449.2	686.3	858.9
Receivables	181.0	243.3	237.7
Inventory (FIFO)	55.6	47.1	58.4
Other	34.1	51.8	46.2
Current Assets	719.9	1028.5	1201.2
Accts Payable	51.0	85.9	103.6
Debt Due	6.5	19.5	19.3
Other	129.3	188.0	191.7
Current Liab.	186.8	293.4	314.6

ANNUAL RATES
of change (per sh)	Past 10 Yrs.	Past 5 Yrs.	Est'd '89-'91 to '94-'96
Sales	--	48.0%	28.5%
"Cash Flow"	--	52.0%	28.0%
Earnings	--	56.0%	29.0%
Dividends	--	--	Nil
Book Value	--	60.0%	38.5%

QUARTERLY SALES ($ mill.) A
Fiscal Year Ends	Sep.30	Dec.31	Mar.31	Jun.30	Full Fiscal Year
1988	102.6	155.9	161.8	170.5	590.8
1989	176.4	209.9	197.0	220.2	803.5
1990	235.2	300.4	310.9	336.9	1183.4
1991	369.4	460.5	486.9	526.6	1843.4
1992	580.5	650	675	694.5	2600

EARNINGS PER SHARE A B
Fiscal Year Ends	Sep.30	Dec.31	Mar.31	Jun.30	Full Fiscal Year
1988	.13	.21	.22	.18	.74
1989	.22	.28	.24	.27	1.01
1990	.29	.42	.41	.44	1.56
1991	.47	.61	.65	.74	2.47
1992	.75	.87	.90	.98	3.50

QUARTERLY DIVIDENDS PAID
Calendar	Mar.31	Jun.30	Sep.30	Dec.31	Full Year
1987					
1988		NO CASH DIVIDENDS			
1989		BEING PAID			
1990					
1991					

1981	1982	1983	1984	1985	1986	1987	1988	1989	1990	1991	1992	© VALUE LINE PUB., INC.	94-96
--	.20	.39	.76	1.09	1.29	2.19	3.67	4.91	6.94	10.58	14.45	Sales per sh A	26.25
--	--	--	--	.21	.29	.54	.87	1.19	1.91	3.09	4.15	"Cash Flow" per sh	7.15
--	.03	.05	.12	.17	.26	.47	.74	1.01	1.56	2.47	3.50	Earnings per sh B	6.00
--	--	--	--	--	--	--	--	--	--	--	Nil	Div'ds Decl'd per sh	Nil
--	--	--	--	.05	.09	.37	.44	.55	.93	1.52	.95	Cap'l Spending per sh	1.20
--	.07	.11	.24	.42	.91	1.51	2.33	3.43	5.39	7.75	11.90	Book Value per sh	28.00
--	123.88	128.21	127.56	129.20	153.12	158.14	160.99	163.76	170.55	174.23	180.00	Common Shs Outst'g C	190.50
--	--	--	--	--	--	19.5	19.8	25.2	17.8	19.9	22.6	Avg Ann'l P/E Ratio	19.0
--	--	--	--	--	--	1.32	1.32	2.09	1.35	1.48	1.52	Relative P/E Ratio	1.60
--	--	--	--	--	--	--	--	--	--	--		Avg Ann'l Div'd Yield	Nil
--	24.5	50.1	97.5	140.4	197.5	345.9	590.8	803.5	1183.4	1843.4	2600	Sales ($mill) A	5000
--	21.2%	21.3%	29.9%	31.6%	33.7%	38.9%	34.4%	33.2%	37.1%	39.4%	40.0%	Operating Margin	38.0%
--	--	--	3.5	5.8	7.6	16.0	24.2	16.3	36.1	75.8	75.0	Depreciation ($mill)	130
--	3.5	6.5	15.9	24.1	39.3	78.1	123.9	170.5	279.2	462.7	675	Net Profit ($mill)	1235
--	37.3%	41.4%	43.3%	43.7%	40.5%	42.4%	32.6%	32.0%	32.0%	31.0%	32.0%	Income Tax Rate	32.0%
--	14.3%	12.9%	16.3%	17.2%	19.9%	22.6%	21.0%	21.2%	23.6%	25.1%	26.0%	Net Profit Margin	24.7%
--	--	--	21.5	41.5	118.5	166.4	227.8	310.1	533.1	735.1	1425	Working Cap'l ($mill)	4340
--	--	--	.4	--	1.9	2.0	--	1.9	--	--	Nil	Long-Term Debt ($mill)	Nil
--	8.3	14.6	30.7	54.4	139.3	239.1	375.5	561.8	918.6	1350.8	2140	Net Worth ($mill)	5335
--	42.3%	44.3%	51.0%	44.3%	27.8%	32.4%	33.0%	30.3%	30.4%	44.3%	31.5%	% Earned Total Cap'l	23.0%
--	42.3%	44.3%	51.7%	44.3%	28.2%	32.6%	33.0%	30.3%	30.4%	44.3%	31.5%	% Earned Net Worth	23.0%
--	42.3%	44.3%	51.7%	44.3%	28.2%	32.6%	33.0%	30.3%	30.4%	44.3%	31.5%	% Retained to Comm Eq	23.0%
--	--	--	--	--	--	--	--	--	--	--	Nil	% All Div'ds to Net Prof	Nil

BUSINESS: Microsoft Corp. is one of the three largest independent makers of personal computer software. Systems software & languages (36% of 1991 sales) include *MS-DOS* and *OS/2* (by far the most widely used operating systems for IBM PCs and compatibles), *Windows, XENIX,* and *LAN Manager.* Applications software (51%) includes word processing, spreadsheet and other business programs. *Microsoft Mouse,* other hardware and books (13%). R&D: 13% of sales. Foreign sales were 47% of sales and 46% of pre-tax profits in 1991. Has 8,225 empls. & 12,115 stkhldrs. Insiders own 54.1% of stock. Chrmn. and C.E.O.: William H. Gates. Pres. and C.O.O.: Michael R. Hallman. Inc.: DE. Add.: One Microsoft Way, Redmond, WA 98052-6399. Tel.: 206-882-8080.

Microsoft stock has soared to a new high. Since our report three months ago, the equity has advanced over 20%, fueled by the company's new product offerings and strong profit growth (see below). And the issue is top-ranked for year-ahead relative performance. However, this volatile equity's lofty price-earnings multiple leaves it vulnerable to any bad news, such as an adverse ruling in the Apple lawsuit contending that *Windows* infringes on Apple's copyrights, or earnings that fall short of expectations. Too, the current price discounts the earnings gains we expect by mid-decade; 3- to 5-year appreciation potential is below average.

Share net likely will hit a new high in fiscal '92 (the year ends June 30th). Microsoft's *Windows* user interface and its upgraded operating system, *MS-DOS 5.0,* are both selling extremely well. An upgrade for *Windows,* new spreadsheet and word processing applications for Apple's *Macintosh,* a multimedia version of *Works,* and a macro translator, which will make it easy for *1-2-3* users to switch to Microsoft's *Excel* spreadsheet, all scheduled for release in fiscal '92, should trigger further

sales. We also expect to see Microsoft's long-awaited database product before yearend. True, higher sales, marketing, and R&D costs, as well as increased competition, will pressure margins, as will a tax rate one percentage point higher than we had expected. Still, given the good product cycle, we have increased our share-earnings estimate for the full fiscal year by 25¢.

Microsoft appears set to maintain its momentum through the mid-Nineties. The company's strong grip on personal computer operating systems is being challenged by an alliance between Apple and IBM, but Microsoft likely will maintain its preeminent position. Microsoft has already shipped an early version of its followon operating system, code named New Technology, to test sites, and will probably release the system in late '92. We also expect the company to benefit from its efforts in the local area network and electronic mail fields. Too, Microsoft's resources should allow it to continue to turn out leading edge application software at a fast pace. In all, share net may well hit $6.00 by 1994-96.

George A. Niemond   *December 13, 1991*

(A) Fiscal year ends June 30th. (B) Primary earnings. Excludes nonrecurring loss: '87, 10¢. Next earnings report due mid-Jan. (C) In millions, adjusted for stock splits and dividends.

Company's Financial Strength	A+
Stock's Price Stability	25
Price Growth Persistence	90
Earnings Predictability	95

Figure 8-7 Page discussing Microsoft from *Value Line Investment Survey,* December 1991. (*Source:* Value Line, 711 Third Avenue, New York, N.Y. 10017.)

Many companies in the Computer Software and Services industry offer services or products that help businesses trim their costs, so their sales hold up well, even during periods of sluggish economic growth. Thus, many of these companies are able to post earnings gains, unlike their counterparts in other industries.

These relatively rosy prospects haven't gone unnoticed by investors, and shares of these companies have generally outpaced the market averages over the last three months. Too, the majority of software issues are ranked to outleg the year-ahead market. Conservative accounts should exercise care, though, since many of these equities are very volatile.

Recession? What Recession?

The end of the recession, which was officially reported to have occurred in this year's second quarter, does not appear to have been a boon for a number of businesses, judging from anemic third-quarter earnings reports and the many cuts in analysts' fourth-quarter earnings estimates. However, many software providers seem to be sailing thorough the tough times with little dislocation.

There are a number of reasons for software companies' relative immunity to economic ills. In many cases, they offer products or services that can cut a client's cost of doing business. For instance, it may be less expensive to buy an application to do a job, such as *System Software's* business packages, rather than hiring programmers to write a custom application. Too, some service providers can take over work that otherwise would be done in house, and do it cheaper because of economies of scale, as *Automatic Data Processing* does with its payroll processing services. In an increasing number of cases, companies farm out entire data processing operations, doing away with their investments in equipment and personnel. This trend should continue to fuel the growth of *General Motor's* Electronic Data Systems subsidiary. Finally, some of these firms can look to product cycles to drive continued growth. For instance, *Microsoft's* Windows user interface, which makes computers easier to use, thus cutting down on the need for training, has been selling very well, and its strength is boosting sales of applications that have been designed to run under Windows.

That's not to say that this industry is immune to

economic cycles. Customers most certainly can put off big projects that require large capital outlays. However, given the cost savings that many of these companies can generate, and the good product cycles that a number of the businesses are enjoying, we think that most software and service providers will see growth slow, at worst, and not shift into reverse.

Investment Considerations

Shares of companies in this industry, as a group, easily outperformed the broad market averages during the last three months, rising nearly 10%, while the broadly-based Value Line Composite declined almost 5%. The advance was led by companies with strong product cycles, such as *Borland* and *Microsoft*, as well as businesses whose fortunes are brightening after staggering, such as *System Software*. Investors looking for further near-term gains have many choices. Approximately half of the equities reviewed in the following pages are ranked to outleg the year-ahead market. A number of these equities also have above-average price appreciation potential for the 3 to 5 years ahead, as well.

Software stocks most certainly aren't for everyone, though. Just as they may run away from the market averages, so too are they subject to heart-stopping plunges. That's because these equities tend to be bid up to lofty multiples, on expectations that earnings will continue their meteoric ascents, or that a flow of new products will drive sales rapidly higher. Then, if those expectations aren't fully satisfied, holders unload the shares, driving prices sharply lower.

For investors seeking commitments in this industry, but who want to avoid some of the volatility, we suggest considering the shares of companies that have large recurring revenue streams, which not only insulate the businesses somewhat from tough economic times, but also tend to mitigate against earnings surprises. Note, though, that an accounting change, which will require many companies in this industry to revise their method of accounting for revenues, may cause some earnings shortfalls, and could spook unwary investors, lending extra volatility to software and service providers' shares.

George A. Niemond

Composite Statistics: COMPUTER SOFTWARE & SERV. IND.							
1987	1988	1989	1990	1991	1992		94-96E
10226	12221	14897	17259	19500	23000	Revenues ($mill)	38000
20.6%	21.3%	20.2%	21.3%	20.5%	21.0%	Operating Margin	21.0%
660.1	844.2	965.3	1108.9	1125	1275	Depreciation ($mill)	1750
943.2	1205.3	1386.5	1694.4	1900	2375	Net Profit ($mill)	4175
39.6%	35.1%	33.9%	35.0%	35.0%	35.0%	Income Tax Rate	35.0%
9.2%	9.9%	9.3%	9.8%	9.7%	10.3%	Net Profit Margin	11.0%
2318.8	2285.7	2636.2	3340.4	3875	4850	Working Cap'l ($mill)	11600
1221.7	1332.1	1309.8	998.6	950	900	Long-Term Debt ($mill)	900
4324.8	5461.0	6755.6	8387.6	10250	12575	Net Worth ($mill)	22675
17.5%	18.2%	17.8%	18.7%	17.5%	18.0%	% Earned Total Cap'l	18.0%
21.8%	22.1%	20.5%	20.2%	18.5%	19.0%	% Earned Net Worth	18.5%
19.1%	19.4%	17.2%	17.3%	16.0%	16.5%	% Retained to Comm Eq	17.0%
13%	13%	17%	15%	13%	13%	% All Div'ds to Net Prof	9%
18.9	16.7	16.3	16.8	*Bold figures are*		Avg Ann'l P/E Ratio	15.0
1.26	1.39	1.23	1.25	*Value Line*		Relative P/E Ratio	1.25
.7%	.7%	1.0%	.9%	*estimates*		Avg Ann'l Div'd Yield	.9%

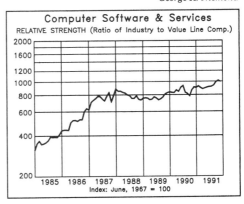

Computer Software & Services
RELATIVE STRENGTH (Ratio of Industry to Value Line Comp.)
Index: June, 1967 = 100

Figure 8-8 Sample analysis of computer software industry from *Value Line Investment Survey*, December 1991. (*Source:* Value Line, 711 Third Avenue, New York, N.Y. 10017.)

8-5 The Issuers of Securities

Issuers themselves are one of the best sources of investment information. The filing, registration, and other statements required by the NYSE, the SEC, the government agencies in charge of regulating various industries (such as the Civil Aeronautics Board, Interstate Commerce Commission, Federal Trade Commission, and Federal Communications Commission), and other institutions provide detailed information that is usually not published in corporations' annual and quarterly reports. Details about expenses, maintenance, interest, receivables, inventories, depreciation, sources and application of funds, employment costs, wasting assets, and treatment of nonrecurring special items must be reported to the SEC. Much of this information is available to the public.

Federal law prohibits the issuers of securities from making unjustified claims or forecasts or disseminating ungrounded opinions about the firm's prospects. As a result, some of the investment information provided by the issuers is more reliable than the information that comes out of research departments of brokerage houses because research departments are permitted to publish subjective forecasts and opinions. Furthermore, since brokerage houses' income is derived from commissions on clients' trading, the brokerage houses have a motive for giving investment advice that conflicts with customers' best interests. This problem is so serious that, as explained in Chapter 6, federal laws prohibit brokers from churning their clients' accounts.

Forms 8-K, 9-K, and 10-Q and Registration Statements

SEC regulations requiring that issuers of publicly traded securities provide "complete disclosure" of relevant investment information stipulate that those firms must file four reports: reports on registration, periodic reporting, insider trading, and proxy solicitations. The 8-K form is a report that firms required to register with the SEC must file each month in which any action occurs affecting the debt, equity, amount of capital assets, voting rights, or other aspects of the firm. The 9-K form is an unaudited report that is required every 6 months and that must contain revenues, expenses, gross sales, and special items. The 10-Q form is an unaudited quarterly report.

The information in the 8-K, 9-K, and 10-Q forms is only a portion of the information that firms required to register with the SEC must file when they plan to issue securities. As explained in Chapters 4 and 6, when preparing a primary issue of securities, the issuing firm is required by the Securities Act of 1933 to make a full disclosure of all the information listed in Box 4-2. This information is then made available to the public for the cost of photocopying and mailing.

Annual Reports and Executive Interviews

Investors may obtain information about a firm by reading its annual report or interviewing its executives. However, both sources are likely to be biased. Only events that have a favorable impact on the firm's prospects are usually discussed, because management is reluctant to publicize its errors.

Various financial organizations and publishing companies publish periodicals containing articles relevant to financial investing. We discuss some of the more prominent journals briefly here.

- *Financial Analysts Journal:* The *Financial Analysts Journal* (*FAJ*) is a bimonthly publication of the Association for Investment Management and Research, an affiliation of financial analysts. Subscriptions are $48 per year and may be obtained by writing to Association for Investment Management and Research, P.O. Box 7947, Charlottesville, Va. 22906.

- *Financial Management: Financial Management* is published quarterly by the Financial Management Association. The journal contains some investments articles. Subscriptions are $40 per year for individuals and may be obtained from Financial Management Association, Executive Director, College of Business Administration, University of South Florida, 4202 Fowler Ave., Tampa, Fla. 33620.

- *Institutional Investor: Institutional Investor* is a monthly publication aimed at professional investors and portfolio managers with emphasis on what is happening to the investment industry. Subscriptions are $295 per year and may be obtained from Institutional Investor, Inc., 488 Madison Ave., New York, N.Y. 10022.

- *Journal of Portfolio Management:* The *Journal of Portfolio Management* is a quarterly publication with the avowed intent of being a forum for academic research that is useful to the practicing portfolio manager. Subscriptions are $175 per year and may be obtained from *Journal of Portfolio Management,* Subscription Department, 488 Madison Ave., 14th floor, New York, N.Y. 10022.

- *Journal of Futures Markets:* This quarterly journal contains articles that investigate commodity markets, futures contracts, options, options on futures, hedging, arbitrage, and price movements in various speculative markets. Mathematics is used. Subscriptions cost $120 per year and may be obtained from *Journal of Futures Markets,* Subscription Department, John Wiley & Sons, Inc., 605 Third Ave., New York, N.Y. 10158.

- *Journal of Finance:* The *Journal of Finance* is published five times a year by the American Finance Association, an organization composed primarily of finance professors. Mathematics is used. An annual membership fee of $59 for institutions and $43 for students entitles members to a 1-year subscription. To obtain a subscription write to Professor Michael Keenan, Executive Secretary and Treasurer, Stern School of Business, New York University, 100 Trinity Place, New York, N.Y. 10006.

- *Journal of Financial and Quantitative Analysis:* The *Journal of Financial and Quantitative Analysis* is a quarterly academic finance journal that also publishes a few applied mathematics papers. Subscriptions cost $75 per year for firms and $35 per year for individuals. They may be obtained from the *Journal of Financial* and Quantitative Analysis, Graduate School of Business Administration, Mackenzie Hall, University of Washington, Seattle, Wash. 98195.

- *Journal of Financial Economics:* The *Journal of Financial Economics* (*JFE*) is a quarterly academic journal that typically contains articles that usually employ mathematics and/or statistics. Several investments articles are published in each issue. Student subscriptions cost $30 per year; individuals pay $95. Subscribers should contact Elsevier Sequoia S.A., P.O. Box 564, CH-1001, Lausanne 1, Switzerland.

- *Journal of Business:* The *Journal of Business* (*JOB*) is a quarterly academic journal published by the University of Chicago. Articles usually use mathematics. Subscriptions cost $22 per year and may be obtained from *Journal of Business,* The University of Chicago Press, Journals Division, P.O. Box 37005, Chicago, Ill. 60637.

- *Review of Quantitative Finance and Accounting:* This quarterly academic journal publishes articles that use mathematics and statistics. Institutional subscriptions are $147, and individual subscriptions are $60 per year. Write to Kluwer Academic Publishers Group, P.O. Box 322, 3300 AH Dordrecht, The Netherlands.

- *Financial Review: Financial Review* is a quarterly academic journal; most articles use mathematics or statistics. Each issue contains a few investments articles. Institutional subscriptions are $50, and individual subscriptions are $15 per year. Write to Office of Publication, College of Commerce and Business, University of Illinois, 1206 South Sixth St., Champaign, Ill. 61820.

- *The Review of Financial Studies:* This quarterly academic journal publishes articles that typically employ mathematics and/or statistics. Institutional subscriptions are $110, and individual subscriptions are $55 per year. Write to Journals Customer Service, Oxford University Press, 2001 Evans Road, New York, N.Y. 10016.

- *Journal of Financial Research:* The *Journal of Financial Research* is a quarterly academic research journal; most articles use quantitative analysis. Institutional subscriptions are $60.00, and individual subscriptions are $25.00 per year. Write to Journal of Financial Research, Department of Finance, College of Business, Arizona State University, Tempe, Ariz. 85287.

- *International Review of Financial Analysis:* The three annual issues of the *International Review of Financial Analysis* contain academic, quantitative financial research. Institutional subscriptions are $100 and individuals are $50 per year. Write to: *International Review of Financial Analysis,* JAI Press, 55 Old Post Road #2, P.O. Box 1678, Greenwich, Conn., 06836.

- *Mathematical Finance: Mathematical Finance* is a quarterly academic journal that publishes theoretical articles using advanced mathematics and statistical techniques. Institutional subscriptions are $120, and individual subscriptions are $60 per year. Write to Journals Marketing Manager, Basil Blackwell, Three Cambridge Center, Cambridge, Mass. 02142.

8-7 Tracking Professionally Managed Portfolios

217

*Chapter 8
Investment
Information
Sources*

Information about mutual funds (also known as *open-end investment companies*) and closed-end investment companies is published by the investment companies themselves.[9] Mutual funds are typically eager to send out free copies of prospectuses to potential investors. Some financial service firms also provide information about investment companies. The more prominent information providers are Morningstar, Arthur Wiesenberger Services, *Business Week* magazine, and *Donoghue's Moneyletter.*

Morningstar

The Morningstar Corporation produces books and pamphlets and floppy disks for personal computers that contain years of data for hundreds of common stock and bond mutual funds. These materials are sold primarily to mutual fund salespeople and individual investors.[10] Facts about each fund's investment objective, price data, performance data and an evaluation of that data, the fund's address and phone number, a graph of its historical performance, and facts about the composition of the fund's holdings are available to Morningstar subscribers.

Arthur Wiesenberger Services

Arthur Wiesenberger Services sells information about open-end and closed-end investment companies. The firm annually publishes a large book entitled **Investment Companies.** Several early chapters of *Investment Companies* are devoted to explaining the differences between open-end and closed-end investment companies, regulations pertaining to investment companies, pertinent tax laws, and other background facts. The greater part of the book is a description of the management, holdings, and history of large investment companies. One page for each company is devoted to presenting statistics. The Wiesenberger Service publications are sold primarily to sales representatives for investment companies. More information may be obtained by writing the company.[11]

Donoghue's *Moneyletter*

Diversified portfolios that invest only in debt securities maturing in less than 1 year (that is, money market securities) are called *money market funds.* William E. Donoghue's firm in Holliston, Massachusetts, compiles and tabulates investment data on the dozens of money market mutual funds operating in the United States.

---

[9] Open-end and closed-end investment companies were introduced in Chapters 3 and 6; Chapter 28 analyzes the performance of mutual funds.

[10] Subscription material may be obtained from Mutual Fund Values, Morningstar, 53 West Jackson Blvd., Chicago, Ill. 60604.

[11] Arthur Wiesenberger Services, Warren, Gorham and Lamont, Inc., 870 Seventh Ave., New York, N.Y. 10017.

Donoghue's *Moneyletter* is published 24 times a year and gives current information about money market fund investing. Donoghue's *Money Fund Report* is a similar periodical for larger investors.[12]

Business Week Magazine's Mutual Fund Scoreboard

Business Week, a weekly magazine, publishes facts and performance rankings on over 1000 mutual funds in special annual issues. More detailed mutual fund information can be obtained for use in a personal computer. *Business Week*'s Mutual Fund Scoreboard is a floppy diskette containing comprehensive facts and data on hundreds of mutual funds and programs to screen them in search of funds with desired characteristics; it is continually updated for subscribers.[13]

8-8   Historical Data Files for Computers

As computers have evolved, cost per computation has dropped. At the same time, equipment and programs have advanced and become easier to use. As a result, financial analysis in various forms is now being done by computer. Some firms compile and sell historical financial information in a form that may be read directly into a computer as raw input data.

The CRSP Tapes

The Center for Research in Security Prices (CRSP) has prepared magnetic tape files that provide raw input data about stock and U.S. government bond prices. The *monthly CRSP stock tape* contains monthly prices and quarterly dividends, both adjusted and unadjusted for stock dividends and splits, for over 5700 stocks listed on the NYSE since 1926 and the AMEX since 1962. Monthly data on over 9000 over-the-counter (or NASDAQ) stocks are available too. In addition, there is a daily **CRSP stock tape** that has the daily high, low, and closing prices and volume of shares traded for over 5000 NYSE and AMEX stocks since 1962 and over 9000 NASDAQ stocks since 1972. The CRSP also has a Government Bond File that contains monthly T-bill, T-note, and T-bond prices from 1925 to the present. The tapes may be purchased from the Center for Research on Security Prices, University of Chicago, 1101 East 58 St., Chicago, Ill. 60607.

Compustat

The **Compustat Services** division of Standard & Poor's Corporation sells a financial data base available on floppy disks and compact disks with read-only memory (called *CD-ROM*) for personal computers, and also on magnetic tapes for mainframe

---

[12] For more information write to Donoghue's *Moneyletter*, P&S Publications, Inc., P.O. Box 411, Holliston, Mass. 01746.

[13] *Business Week* magazine's Mutual Fund Scoreboard in diskette form is available free of charge to readers of this book if their instructor requests it. See end-of-book Appendix A.

computers. The Compustat system includes 20 years of annual data for about 6600 international corporations, 7000 active U.S. corporations, and 6000 inactive (for example, bankrupt or merged) U.S. corporations; quarterly data on 3900 U.S. corporations; and various U.S. industry (or product line) data. Compustat sells its massive data base in various prepackaged segments at reduced prices to colleges. Data bases may be updated several times a year for an additional charge over the annual subscription fee. Compustat information may be obtained by writing to Standard & Poor's Compustat Services, 1221 Avenue of the Americas, New York, NY 10020. Alternatively, write to 7400 South Alton Court, Englewood, Col. 80112-9970.

Value Line Data Base

The *Value Line Data Base* is available on both magnetic tape for mainframe computers and floppy disks for personal computers. Selected data from the income statements and balance sheets and quarterly stock price data on 1700 corporations are available going back to 1954. In addition, Value Line provides earnings estimates and investment desirability rankings for each of the 1700 firms. For details write to Value Line, 711 Third Ave., New York, N.Y. 10017.

The Berkeley Options Data Base

The University of California at Berkeley obtains market data from the Chicago Board of Options Exchange and compiles it for sale. Daily bid and asked prices and trading volume data on hundreds of put and call options are available from August 1976 to the present. Write the Berkeley Options Data Base, Institute of Business and Economic Research, University of California at Berkeley, 156 Barrows Hall, Berkeley, Cal., 94720.

The Chicago Board of Trade Commodity Data

The Chicago Board of Trade (CBT) has been compiling commodity price information in machine-readable form since 1981. These data are available on a transaction-to-transaction basis or on a daily basis. The CBT data may be purchased on magnetic tapes or in booklet form through the CBT. For more information write to Public Information Office, Chicago Board of Trade, LaSalle at Jackson, Chicago, Ill. 60604.

Disclosure Data

Legally required financial data filings with the Securities and Exchange Commission (SEC) are available on both magnetic tapes for mainframe computers and floppy disks for personal computers through the Disclosure Corporation. Complete financial statements, security prices, the names of corporate officers and auditors, data about foreign operations, names of subsidiaries, information about both inside and institutional investors, and employee information are available from the most recent filings back through 5 years of historical data. For more information contact Disclosure, 5161 River Rd., Bethesda, Md. 20816.

MUNIBASE is a machine-readable data base that contains the CUSIP number,[14] bond description, S&P or Moody's quality rating, call dates (if any), and details about each issue's protective provisions for thousands of municipal bond issues. Kenny Information Systems maintains MUNIBASE and allows investors to use it for a fee. For more information, contact Kenny Information Systems, 55 Broad St., New York, NY 10004.

[14] CUSIP numbers are identification numbers assigned to every security by a centralized registry in New York City that is managed by Standard and Poor's Corporation.

Table 8-1
Information Sources Provided by Dow Jones News Retrieval

A. Business and world news wires	
1. Dow Jones Business Newswires; searches the following leading news wire simultaneously:	Current news is held for 90 days.
a. Dow Jones News	Stories from Dow Jones News Service, *The Wall Street Journal,* and *Barron's.*
b. Dow Jones International News	News from Dow Jones's international news wires as well as *The Wall Street Journal, The Wall Street Journal Europe,* and *The Asian Wall Street Journal.*
c. Professional Investor Report	Unusual intraday trading activity on more than 5000 stocks traded on the NYSE and AMEX and the OTC National Market System.
d. Dow Jones Capital Markets Report	Comprehensive coverage of worldwide fixed income and financial-future markets.
e. Federal Filings	Coverage of merger and acquisition filings on 18,000 companies of high-yield and/or investment grade debt issuers and large cap companies.
f. Business Wire and PR Newswire	Press releases on corporations, government agencies, industry associations, labor unions, and stock exchanges.
2. Business and Finance Report	Top business and financial news culled from Dow Jones News Service, other news wires, and *The Wall Street Journal* is continuously updated.
3. News/Retrieval World Report	Top national and international news from the Associated Press, Dow Jones News Service, and other broadcast media is updated continuously.
4. Japan Economic Daily	Same-day coverage of Japanese economic, political, and financial market news from the Kyodo News Service.
B. Dow Jones Text Library	
1. Text-Search Services searches the following:	Total of 550 sources in either a menu-driven or a command version.
a. The Wall Street Journal	Full text of all news articles published or scheduled to appear since January 1984.
b. The Wall Street Journal Europe	Full text of most articles since January 1991.

c. The Asian Wall Street Journal	Full text of most articles from June 1991 to present.
d. Dow Jones News	Selected articles from *The Wall Street Journal, Barron's,* and Dow Jones News Service since June 1979.
e. Barron's	Full text of all articles back to January 1987.
f. The Washington Post	Full text of selected articles back to January 1984.
g. Business Week	Full text of all articles back to January 1985.
h. Business Library	Full text of selected articles from *Time, The Economist, Forbes, Fortune, American Demographics,* and more than 200 other business, industry, and general-interest publications.
i. Business Dateline	Full text of selected articles from 200 regional business publications.
j. McGraw-Hill Library	Full text of all articles published in McGraw-Hill's industry publications including *Aviation Week, BYTE, Platt's Oilgram Price Report,* and *ENR* since January 1985.
k. Press Release Wires	Full text of Business Wire and PR Newswire press releases since July 1989.
l. DataTimes	Full text of articles from 100 regional, national, and industry publications including *USA Today, San Francisco Chronicle,* and *The Dallas Morning News.*
2. DowQuest	Uses plain English to find articles on topics and trends from 350 publications; relevant articles or paragraphs may be used to refine the search.

C. Company and industry information

1. Corporate Canada Online	News and detailed financial information on 2300 public, private, and government-owned Canadian companies.
2. Dun's Financial Records	Financial reports and business information from Dun & Bradstreet on 1.5 million private and public companies.
3. Disclosure Database	10K extracts, company profiles, and other detailed data on over 12,000 publicly held companies from reports filed with the SEC and other sources.
4. Zacks Corporate Earnings Estimator	Consensus earnings per share estimates and P/E ratio forecasts given for 3500 companies and 100 industries.
5. Investext	Full text of 20,000 research reports covering 5000 American and international companies and 53 industries. New text-searching capability available.
6. Media General Financial Services	Financial and statistical information on 6200 companies and 180 industries. Makes possible comparisons of company to industry, two companies, or two industries.
7. Dow Jones Quick Search	One command gathers information from eight data bases: the latest news, current stock quotes, financial overview, income statements, company vs. industry performance, and more.
8. Standard & Poor's Online	4700 company profiles containing current and historical earnings and estimates, dividend and market figures.
9. Corporate Ownership Watch	Insider trading activity on more than 8000 publicly held companies and 80,000 individuals (officers, directors, or owners of over 10% of a class of company stock).
10. Worldscope	Reports on 45,000 corporations in 25 countries. Includes corporate profiles, operating summaries, balance sheets, income statements, financial ratios, stock data, and more.

D. Quotes, statistics, and commentary

1. Dow Jones — Quotes on common and preferred stocks, corporate and foreign bonds, mutual funds, U.S. Treasury issues, and options.

2. Dow Jones Real-Time — Up-to-the-minute stock price quotations.

3. Dow Jones Historical Quotes — Historical quotes for common and preferred stocks including daily quote history for 1 year, monthly summaries back to 1979, quarterly summaries back to 1978.

4. Tradeline — Up to 15 years of historical information on stocks, bonds, mutual funds exchange rates, and other international issue information. Option history back to 1 year.

5. Dow Jones Futures & Index Quotes — Current and historical quotes for over 80 contracts from major exchanges. Includes Dow Jones Industry Group & Equity Market Indexes.

6. Mutual Funds Performance Reports — Historical performance, assets, and background information on 1500 mutual funds. Search for funds meeting your investment requirements.

7. Historical Dow Jones Averages — Daily high, low, close, and volume for industrials, transportation, utilities, and 65-stock composite from May 1982.

8. Innovest Technical Analysis Reports — Based on price and volume analysis of more than 4500 stocks trading on NY and American exchanges and OTC.

9. MMS Weekly Market Analysis — U.S. money market and foreign exchange trends. Median forecasts indicators, equities, and debt market commentary.

10. Wall Street Week Online — Transcripts of the PBS program *Wall Street Week.*

E. General services

1. Magill Book Reviews — Reviews of recent fiction, nonfiction, and classics.

2. The National Business Employment Weekly — Career management advice.

3. Academic American Encyclopedia — 32,000 articles covering thousands of subjects.

4. Fidelity Investors EXPRESS — Electronic brokerage service. Places trades on-line for listed securities; monitors your portfolio.

5. MCI Mail — Mail service for sending printed and electronic communications next door or worldwide.

6. Cineman Movies Reviews — Reviews of the latest releases as well as thousands of movies back to 1926.

7. OAG Electronic Edition Travel Service — Airline schedules and fares, hotel and motel information, vacation packages, etc. On-line booking is available.

8. Peterson's College Selection Service — Guide to American and Canadian colleges and universities.

9. News/Retrieval Sports Report — Continuously updated scores, stats, standings, schedules, and stories.

10. Comp-U-Store OnLine — Electronic shopping for over 250,000 discounted brand name products.

11. News/Retrieval Weather Report — Accu-Weather forecasts for 100 cities worldwide.

F. Customized information

1. Dow Jones Clipping Service — Clips news automatically from seven top sources. Combines news codes, symbols, and words for a targeted search. Continuously scans incoming news and alerts you when news has been added to your folder.

2. Dow Jones Tracking Service — Creates five portfolios to monitor up to 125 companies. Automatically tracks news and quotes. Includes 30-day historical news feature.

8-9 Remote Computing

223

*Chapter 8
Investment
Information
Sources*

The historical financial data bases are good for financial research that might require massive *historical* data to evaluate some investment strategy. Those who make trading decisions, however, need *current* market information—and they need it quickly. Several firms sell up-to-the-minute security price quotations in a form that can be obtained via either personal or mainframe computers. Some firms that sell security price quotations and related investments information in machine-readable form are listed below:

- Dow Jones News Retrieval (800-832-1234)
- Compuserve (800-848-8199)
- Lotus One Source (800-554-5501)

Dow Jones News Retrieval (DJNR) is a popular source of information for investors. Table 8-1 itemizes the DJNR's comprehensive information sources. DJNR subscribers can instantly obtain the information they want as they sit in their home or office. DJNR subscribers with a personal computer, a modem, a telephone, and a printer can contact the DJNR mainframe computer, access the desired information sources, preview the material on their screen, and have the information printed out immediately on their own printer. Access fees are usually half price when the service is used nights and weekends. Subscribers can also submit buy and sell orders to brokers from their personal computers.

Summary

Investors can get current news that affects business easily by subscribing to *Investor's Business Daily, The New York Times,* and *The Wall Street Journal.* News about the American economy can also be obtained easily from the periodic newsletters sent out free by major banks and from U. S. government publications, such as the *Survey of Current Business.*

Information on selected industries and individual firms can be obtained by subscribing to an information service, such as Value Line, Standard & Poor's, or Moody's. The major brokerage houses disseminate free publications giving their investment opinions. Audited financial statements can also be obtained from the SEC.

Investors who wish to have their funds managed for them can obtain detailed information about the various mutual funds by buying reports published by Morningstar, Arthur Wiesenberger Services, *Business Week* magazine, and Donoghue's *Moneyletter.* Donoghue's *Moneyletter* focuses on money market mutual funds. Morningstar and Wiesenberger provide more information on a much broader array of investment companies. *Business Week* magazine's Mutual Fund Scoreboard provides massive data on a floppy diskette for personal computers.

Financial analysts who want to analyze masses of data may buy the raw data in machine-readable form from data base vendors. Computer software can be purchased to help complete the analysis.

Further
Reading

Meyers, Thomas A., *The Dow Jones–Irwin Guide to On-Line Investing,* (Homewood, Ill.: Dow Jones–Irwin, 1985).

Wasserman, Paul, ed. *Encyclopedia of Business Information Services,* 3d ed. (Detroit: Gale Research, 1976).

Questions and
Problem

Essay Questions

8-1 Select a publicly traded security and compare the reports on it found in Standard & Poor's *Stock Market Encyclopedia,* in *Moody's Handbook of Common Stocks,* and in the *Value Line Survey.* Be sure that all three reports cover the same time period in order to make them more suitable for comparison. What are the significant differences among these three sources? *Hint:* Review Figures 8-6 and 8-7.

8-2 Where could an investor interested in buying shares in a mutual fund find information about mutual funds and get data that would be helpful in choosing a fund? Do the sources of mutual fund information provide as much information as you would like? If not, explain.

8-3 If you had to prepare a graph of AAA-grade corporate bond (or any other high-grade bond) yields showing the path of the interest rate continuously for the last 10 years, where could you find the raw data quickly, easily, and inexpensively? Could you find the graph done for you in any publications?

8-4 Charles Brady wants to invest in a highly diversified high-yield corporate bond (also called a *junk bond*) mutual fund. Where can Charles get information to help him make an informed investment decision?

8-5 Name two sources where you can obtain numerical data about the U.S. gross national product (GNP) and the national income components that add up to the GNP every year for the past 5 years. How frequently are the numerical data available (quarterly, annually, etc.)? Are graphs of these data included in these publications? Why would a common stock or bond investor be interested in such macroeconomic data?

8-6 What is the name of the office within a large publicly traded corporation where you should write to request specific investment information about the firm? How can you find the name and address of these offices for corporations listed on the NYSE and the AMEX?

8-7 Why is a U.S. government economic publication like the *Survey of Current Business* full of details about business cycles and information about stock market indexes like the Standard & Poor's 500 Stocks Index? *Hint:* See Figure 17-5.

8-8 What is a 10-Q form? What information can be found on a 10-Q form? How does the 10-Q form differ from the 8-K and 9-K forms? How can an investor obtain these forms? *Hint:* See both this chapter and Chapter 6.

8-9 How could you get the current prices of every NYSE-listed stock delivered to your home or office every day at a reasonable price? Explain.

Problem

225

*Chapter 8
Investment
Information
Sources*

8-10   Thaddeus Smith is a 31-year-old assistant vice president at the First State Bank of Omaha (FSBO) in Omaha, Nebraska. Smith received his bachelor's degree in business finance from the University of Nebraska 9 years ago and after working for a large Minneapolis bank's trust department for 2 years, returned to his hometown of Omaha to take a position at the FSBO as a junior officer. Smith works at FSBO and takes night school courses toward an MBA in finance. He was promoted to assistant vice president 4 years ago. Since then, the young executive has impressed the FSBO's senior management so much that this middle-sized bank has offered to promote him to vice president and put him in charge of starting a trust department at FSBO.

The FSBO's executive committee has offered Smith the promotion and the trust department assignment with certain guidelines. A few days after Smith was offered this opportunity at FSBO by his boss, Fred Hannah, executive vice president in charge of business loans, he was summoned to the bank's executive conference room. At that time various members of the bank's executive committee cordially explained to Smith that even though usually only large banks started trust departments, they had nevertheless decided to offer Smith the chance to start one in their medium-sized bank. The FSBO had total deposits of $916 million and net income of $81 million last year. The bank has six branches in and around Omaha, and while it is a major bank in Omaha, it has no significant impact outside the Omaha area. In spite of the moderate size of the FSBO, its executive committee had decided that it was desirable for the bank to start a trust department to hold and attract depositors in the Omaha area. No other bank in or around Omaha had a trust department, and top management felt that FSBO would be able to attract substantial depositors by offering them the unique local service of a bank trust department to manage their investment portfolios. The executive committee told Smith that the trust department should charge 1 percent per year of the value of the assets managed and that the new department could spend all fees it collected. That is, the bank expected no profits from the trust department's fees. The majority of the members of FSBO's executive committee believed that the new trust department's customers would sooner or later bring their personal and business checking accounts to FSBO and that the bank would grow and profit therefrom. Thus, the trust department was visualized as a public relations and marketing service to attract deposits from among the wealthy people in the area. The members of the executive committee explained that for the first few years, at least, they did not envision the new trust department as consisting of more than the following personnel:

1. One full-time vice president—tentatively, Thaddeus Smith.
2. One full-time secretary-receptionist who would do work for both Smith and another vice president.
3. Assistance as needed from the FSBO's bookkeeping department to account for the clients' funds and send out periodic statements for the trust service.
4. Assistance from the FSBO's legal counsel, Larry Miller, in drawing up the legal fiduciary agreements specifying how the clients want their trusts administered.

Smith feels confident that with the contacts the other bank officers at FSBO can give him he can surely bring new trust business into the bank. He already knows of two different multimillion dollar corporate pension funds he can solicit, and the FSBO's corporate loan customers can be approached, too. Furthermore, one of the FSBO's senior vice presidents, Tom Hensley, is also membership committee chairman at an Omaha country club. Hensley has offered to share confidentially all the country club's membership applications with Smith and thus help Smith find wealthy local people who may be in need of the services of a trust department. Although the recruitment of clients will require much personal sales initiative, Smith is willing to tackle the new assignment.

The rank of vice president and the opportunity to have a private office greatly appeal to Smith. The promotion would also entail a pay raise. But Smith has some reservations about the new job; he has never managed an investment portfolio by himself (other than his family's small portfolio of $21,000). He is uncertain how to apply the investment management principles he learned in college to the management of millions of dollars of other people's money. Smith is trying to deal with his fears by writing down specific questions that concern him. He reasons that if he can find answers to these anticipated problems, then he will feel more able to tackle the new responsibilities. Can you offer suggestions to help Smith deal with his new trust management position? Smith's questions are listed below.

(*a*) Where could I get quality ratings to enable me to make safe bond and stock investment decisions? Would such quality ratings cost more than the fee FSBO will charge to manage the funds? Would these quality ratings be in a form such that I could show them to my clients, to senior management at the bank, and to bank examiners as a way to verify the judiciousness of my investment decisions?

(*b*) Where will I get economic forecasts about booms and recessions, the level of interest rates, and the profitability of various sectors of the economy? How much would such forecasts cost? Are good opinions on which to base my decisions available?

(*c*) Should I count on my close friend Bob Daley, who is an experienced stockbroker, to help me select investments? If I give Bob the brokerage commissions, he should be willing to help me manage the clients' accounts.

(*d*) Where can I get accurate financial analyses of every corporation in which I may consider investing? Can I get these analyses quickly when I need them? Will they be too expensive for the bank?

(*e*) If I get a $20 million or $30 million pension fund client, how will I invest all that money quickly? Is there a professional money management service I can use that is not too expensive? Will it reflect unfavorably on me if I use such a service? That is, how could I justify the use of such a service except by admitting personal incompetence?

Matching Questions

8-11 Match the following list of economic publications and government bodies on the left with the appropriate descriptions on the right.

A	1. Board of Governors of Federal Reserve System	A. Source of the monthly *Federal Reserve Bulletin*
E	2. Federal Reserve Bank of St. Louis, Research Department	B. Daily U.S. financial newspaper
B	3. *The Wall Street Journal*	C. Sources of forecasts and economic data
D	4. *Survey of Current Business*	D. Monthly U.S. government pamphlet full of economic data and attractive graphs
C	5. Newsletters from large New York City commercial banks	E. Source of good monetary economics analysis, graphs, and data

8-12 Match the following sources of financial information on the left with the most appropriate descriptions on the right.

C	1. *Moody's Handbook of Common Stocks*	A. Moody's periodicals about corporate and municipal debt
D	2. Value Line Rating	B. Thick volumes of data on hundreds of corporations

A 3. *Bond Outlook* and *Bond Survey*

B 4. *Moody's Manuals*

C. Financial booklet, similar to *S&P Stock Market Encyclopedia*

D. A numerical indicator of a stock's price appreciation potential

8-13 Match the following financial words and phrases on the left with the appropriate definitions on the right.

B 1. Form 9-K

A 2. Form 10-Q

D 3. Brokerage house research reports

C 4. Corporate annual reports

A. An unaudited quarterly financial report submitted to SEC

B. Semiannual financial report required by SEC-registered firms

C. Biased report of the good news affecting a firm

D. Free financial analysis provided to help brokers churn their clients for commissions

8-14 Match the following words and phrases about computers and finance on the left with the most appropriate definitions on the right.

C 1. CRSP tape

A 2. Dow Jones News Retrieval

B 3. Mutual Fund Scoreboard

A. A firm that rents out time, data, and software on its large computer

B. *Business Weekly* magazine's mutual fund data on diskettes

C. Center for Research in Security Prices file, a magnetic tape of common stock data

Multiple Choice Questions

8-15 Moody's Aa bond rating is economically equivalent to which of the following Standard & Poor's bond ratings? (*Hint:* See Chapter 10.)

(a) AA
(b) A
(c) BBB

(d) BB
(e) B

A

8-16 A report that firms are required to file for each month in which any action occurs affecting the debt, equity, amount of capital assets, voting rights, or other aspects of the firm. (*Hint:* See this chapter and Chapter 6.)

(a) The SEC's Form 8-K
(b) The SEC's Form 9-K
(c) The SEC's Form 10-Q
(d) Prospectus
(e) An SEC registration statement

A

8-17 Table 10-1 explains that when a bankruptcy court takes action to reorganize a corporation, Standard & Poor's assigns which of the following quality ratings to the common stock of the troubled corporation?

(a) C
(b) D

(c) F
(d) R

B

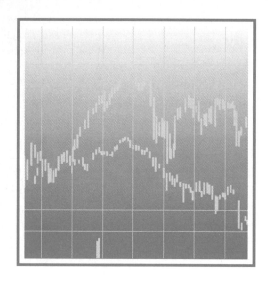

CHAPTER 9

ANALYSIS OF FINANCIAL STATEMENTS

Every potential investment should be researched. This research should delve into the overall condition of the nation's economy to determine the current level of business activity. The issuing firm's competitive position within its own industry should be ascertained. And, of course, the firm itself should be analyzed. The best single source of information about the firm is usually its own financial statements. This chapter reviews the principal financial statements that are used to report the progress of every business firm—the balance sheet and the income and expense statement. The remainder of the chapter is devoted to presenting financial ratios and interpreting their numerical values in order to assess the firm's financial health.

228

9-1   The Financial Statements

229

*Chapter 9
Analysis of
Financial
Statements*

Large corporations publish quarterly financial statements, while smaller firms may issue only annual statements. These financial statements can be a source of historical and current information about the firm's operations.

Financial statements are studied by bankers when a firm applies for a loan, by suppliers of raw materials when a firm purchases on credit, by stock and bond investors considering a firm's securities as an investment, by acquisition-oriented firms considering a merger, and by other lenders and investors. Each of these analysts might view the same firm's financial ratios from a slightly different perspective.

Financial statement analysis may be defined as the study of a firm's financial statements from various viewpoints. Different perspectives are used to help gain insights about the firm's relative strengths and weaknesses. The firm's own past performance, represented by its historical financial statements, can provide one perspective. Furthermore, past performance—good or bad—provides the foundation from which to forecast a firm's future.

The two main financial statements are the balance sheet and the income and expense statement. These two statements provide most of the data that financial analysts use to calculate financial ratios. The sections that follow will present financial statements from a hypothetical corporation. Statements for two consecutive years are provided in order to demonstrate how the preceding year furnishes a standard of comparison for the year that follows.

The Balance Sheet

A company's **balance sheet** represents an accounting picture of all the firm's sources of external funds (called *liabilities and stockholders' equity*) and uses of funds (that is, the assets) on one particular day. As Equation (9-1) shows (see Box 9-1), these amounts must balance. **Stockholders' equity** is also called the *net worth* or, simply, the *equity section* of the balance sheet. It measures the book value of the owners' investment.

Most firm's close their books annually at the end of a fiscal year, or accounting year, that ends on December 31. Thus, the balance sheet is simply a list of the assets, liabilities, and owner's equity that exists on December 31 (or whenever the firm's accounting year ends). Table 9-1 shows sample balance sheets for the General Resources (GR) Corporation for two consecutive years. The size of GR's investment in plant and equipment suggests that it is a manufacturing company instead of a service firm.

Box 9-1

DEFINITION: The Balance Sheet Equation

The equation that defines the balance sheet is shown below:

Total assets = liabilities + total stockholders' equity   (9-1)

$$A = L + SE$$

Table 9-1
Balance Sheet of General Resources (GR)
Corporation on December 31, 1991, and 1992

Acct. no.		1992	1991
	Assets (uses of funds)		
1	Cash	$ 12,571	$ 11,009
2	Marketable securities	7,519	5,977
3	Accounts receivable	31,053	33,581
4	Inventories	56,521	59,443
5	Other current assets	9,470	7,210
	Total current assets	$117,134	$117,220
6	Investments	29,818	28,122
7	Property, plant, and equipment	523,283	511,486
8	Total assets (TA)	$670,235	$656,828
	Liabilities and equity (sources of funds)		
9	Accounts payable	$ 44,343	$ 40,600
10	Other current liabilities:		
	Accrued expenses	19,006	17,800
	Notes payable	19,610	20,090
	Income taxes payable	1,200	1,101
	Total current liabilities	84,159	79,591
11	Long-term debt	$212,717	$234,090
12	Deferred tax	46,840	39,119
	Total long-term liabilities	259,557	$273,209
13	Shareholders' equity (EQ)	$326,519	$304,028
	Total liabilities and equity	$670,235	$656,828

The Income and Expense Statement

While balance sheets report **stocks** of assets and liabilities that exist at one particular date, income statements report **flows** of funds that have occurred over the accounting period. In the past, the **income and expense statement** was called the *profit and loss statement* because the *bottom line* of the statement revealed either the profits or losses from the firm's operations over the accounting period.

The so-called profit and loss statement also contained a lot of other information —such as the firm's income sources and itemized expenses. For these reasons the accounting profession has more accurately renamed the report the *income and expense statement,* usually calling it the *income statement.* Many financial officers, however, still use the profit and loss statement label. Box 9-2 shows the definition of the income and expense statement in its fundamental form.

Table 9-2 shows GR Corporation's income statements for the years 1991 and 1992. The line items in the table are numbered to follow in sequence the items in GR's balance sheet, shown in Table 9-1.

Box 9-2

DEFINITION: Income and Expense Statement

Sales − expenses = income or loss   (9-2)

9-2 Common-Sized Financial Statements

Firms' financial statements can be reformulated, or standardized, by stating all values as a percentage of a common base value. These are called *common-sized statements*. Stating all values as a percentage of a common base value may give financial

Table 9-2
Income and Expense Statements for
General Resources (GR) Corporation for the Years Ending
December 31, 1991, and 1992

Acct. no.		1992	1991
14	Sales	$1,130,439	$1,056,922
15	*Plus:* Other income	1,484	433
	Equals: Total revenue	$1,131,923	$1,057,355
16	Cost of goods sold	728,861	694,329
17	Excise taxes	207,452	196,335
18	Marketing and administrative expenses	110,641	100,385
	Less: Total operating expenses	$1,046,954	$ 991,049
	*Earnings before interest and taxes**	$ 84,969	$ 66,306
19	Interest expense	14,526	17,443
20	Other expenses	9,528	334
	Less: Total expenses	$1,071,008	$1,008,826
21	*Equals:* Earnings before tax (EBT)	$ 60,915	$ 48,529
22	*Less:* Corporate income taxes	30,019	21,980
23	*Equals:* Net income (NI) after taxes	$ 30,896	$ 26,549
24	*Less:* Cash dividend payments	15,448	13,270
25	*Equals:* Addition to retained earnings	$ 15,448	$ 13,279

	Per share data for common stock	1992	1991
26	Number of shares (NS) outstanding	19,310	19,310
27	Market price (P) per share of stock	$19.00	$15.50
28	Earnings per share (EPS) after tax	$ 1.60	$ 1.3748
29	Cash dividends per share (CDPS)	$ 0.80	$ 0.687
30	Price-earnings (P/E) ratio	11.875 times	11.27 times

* Earnings before interest and taxes (EBIT), between lines 18 and 19, is sometimes also referred to as the firm's **operating income**.

Table 9-3
Common-Sized Balance Sheet for General
Resources (GR) Corporation on December 31,
1991, and 1992, Percent of Total Assets

Acct. no.		*Percentage of total assets*	
		1992	*1991*
	Assets		
C1	Cash	1.9%	1.7%
C2	Marketable securities	1.1	.9
C3	Accounts receivables	4.6	5.1
C4	Inventories	8.4	9.0
C5	Other current assets	1.4	1.1
	Total current assets	17.4	17.8
C6	Investments and assets	4.5	4.3
C7	Property, plant, and equipment	78.1	77.9
C8	Total assets	100.0	100.0
	Liabilities and equity		
C9	Accounts payable	6.6%	6.2%
C10	Other current liabilities	6.0	5.9
	Total current liabilities	12.6	12.1
C11	Long-term debt	31.7	35.6
C12	Deferred taxes	7.0	6.0
	Total long-term liabilities	38.7	41.6
C13	Shareholders' equity	48.7	46.3
	Total liabilities and equity	100.0	100.0

analysts insights not readily apparent in dollar-denominated reports. Common-sized financial statements are also useful for comparing the statements of competing firms or the statements for one firm from different years.

Common-Sized Balance Sheet

Table 9-3 illustrates what is called a **common-sized balance sheet** for GR Corporation. Every value on such a statement has been standardized by stating it as a percentage of one number—the firm's total assets. Table 9-3 restates all assets, liabilities, and equity of GR Corporation relative to the firm's total assets, using raw data from GR's balance sheet, Table 9-1.

Common-Sized Income and Expense Statement

Just as a common-sized balance sheet expresses all items as a percent of a common base value, so does a **common-sized income and expense statement.** Table 9-4

Table 9-4
Common-Sized Income Statement for General
Resources (GR) Corporation 1991 and 1992
Operations, Percent of Sales

		Percentage of total revenues	
Acct. no.	Income and expense items	1992	1991
C14	Sales		
C15	*Plus:* Other income		
	Total revenue	100.0%	100.0 %
C16	Cost of goods sold	64.4	65.7
C17	Excise taxes	18.3	18.6
C18	Marketing, administrative, and general expenses	9.8	9.5
C19	Interest expense	1.3	1.6
C20	Other expense	.8	.03
	Total expense	94.6%	95.4 %
C21	Earnings before taxes	5.4%	4.6%
C22	*Less:* Income taxes	2.7	2.1
C23	*Equals:* Net income	2.7	2.5
C24	*Less:* Cash dividend payments	1.4	1.3
C25	*Equals:* Retained earnings	1.3%	1.2 %

presents a common-sized income and expense statement for GR in which every value has been standardized by dividing it by the firm's total revenue. The raw data used to compute the common-sized values in Table 9-4 came from Table 9-2.

9-3 Financial Ratios: Meaningful and Relevant Values

The item values in the financial statements of Tables 9-1 and 9-2 all convey important information of some kind. A **financial ratio** uses two meaningfully related values to produce new information that has additional value. The phrase "meaningfully related values" is important: The ratio of two unrelated values is a meaningless random number. Summarizing and quantifying financial relationships requires meaningful ratios.

Tables 9-3 and 9-4 are both tables of ratios, since percentages are simply one particular kind of ratio. These ratios provide insights because they involve meaningfully related values. For instance, the sum of the current and long-term liabilities in GR's common-sized balance sheet, Table 9-3, reveals that creditors of one form or another financed 51.3 percent of GR's assets in 1992. In contrast, it would be irrelevant to calculate GR's total liabilities as a percentage of, say, the number of elevators in the firm. The ratio of liabilities to elevators is meaningless because no real economic relationship exists between the two values. The remainder of this chapter discusses relevant financial ratios between meaningfully related economic variables.

9-4 Computing Financial Ratios

The main categories of useful financial ratios are:

- *Solvency ratios,* or *liquidity ratios,* which measure the extent to which a firm can meet its short-term obligations

- *Turnover ratios,* which measure the rate of use or the activity of various items within the firm

- *Coverage ratios,* which measure the extent to which the firm's earnings are able to pay (or cover) the interest expense and principal repayments on its debts

- *Leverage ratios,* which measure the extent to which the firm has been financed by creditors, provide a measure of the firm's financial risk. The Chrysler case (page 243) is a vivid illustration of how leverage ratios indicate risk.

- *Profitability ratios,* which measure the productivity of moneys invested in the firm

- *Common stock share data,* which measure per share quantities that affect the market price per share

- *Growth ratios,* which measure the contributions of various items to the firm's expansion

- *Risk analysis ratios,* which measure the dispersion of the firm's results around its expected outcome

As the list makes clear, most financial ratios have descriptive names that give the user clues about how to calculate the ratio and/or how to interpret its numerical value. The steps below show more precisely how the ratios are calculated. The numbers in parentheses in the equations refer to the individual item numbers from GR's financial statements in Tables 9-1 and 9-2. Brief comments about the interpretation of the ratio's value accompany some of the definitions. Additional information about how to assess the ratios is provided later in this chapter.

Solvency Ratios

One of the most widely used measures of a firm's solvency is the **current ratio:**

$$\text{Current ratio} = \frac{\text{current assets}}{\text{current liabilities}} = \frac{(1) + (2) + (3) + (4) + (5)}{(9) + (10)} \qquad (9\text{-}3)$$

$$= \frac{\$117,134}{\$84,159} = 1.39 = 139\% \text{ in 1992}$$

$$= \frac{\$117,220}{\$79,591} = 1.47 = 147\% \text{ in } 1991$$

The integer numbers in the parentheses above indicate that current assets, for instance, are a combination of line items (1) through (5) from GR's balance sheet (Table 9-1). The current ratio for GR Corporation indicates the firm had $1.39 of current assets for every dollar of bills coming due in 1992. This seems to indicate that the firm had plenty of current assets to pay its bills and was thus solvent. A more discerning look at liquidity can be obtained by also considering the "quick ratio."

The **quick ratio** is similar to the current ratio in two respects—both measure the firm's liquidity, and both have the same denominator. The numerators differ, however. The numerator in the quick ratio includes only those most liquid assets that can be *quickly* turned into cash. The **quick assets** include all current assets except inventory:

$$\text{Quick ratio} = \frac{\text{current assets } - \text{ inventory}}{\text{current liabilities}} = \frac{\text{quick assets}}{\text{current liabilities}} \qquad (9\text{-}4)$$

$$= \frac{(1) + (2) + (3) + (5)}{(9) + (10)}$$

$$= \frac{\$60,613}{\$84,159} = .7202 = 72.02\% \text{ in } 1992$$

$$= \frac{\$57,777}{\$79,591} = .7259 = 72.59\% \text{ in } 1991$$

Computing the quick ratio indicates that in 1992 GR Corporation had 72 cents of quick assets for every dollar of liabilities coming due that year. The quick ratio of .72 suggests that if the firm's inventory became worthless due to fashion obsolescence, water damage, mice in the warehouse, uninsured thievery, or any one of many other possible reasons, the GR Corporation could suffer a financial embarrassment called "insolvency."

Insolvency occurs when the firm has insufficient cash to pay its bills on time. Insolvency is the first step on the path to bankruptcy. A potential GR investor could conclude that the corporation is solvent, but that it doesn't have much of a margin for error if any of its current assets shrink in value for some reason.

Turnover Ratios

Turnover ratios measure different kinds of business activity within the firm. The general idea underlying all turnover ratios is that unused or inactive assets are nonearning assets. Once these inactive assets are pinpointed, actions can be taken to utilize the assets more effectively or to eliminate them. Turnover ratios are sometimes called **efficiency ratios** or **activity ratios.**

The **receivables turnover ratio** is used to scrutinize the liquidity of one of the primary current asset items, accounts receivable. If the credit customers are all paying their bills on time, then the accounts receivable should be turning over fairly frequently. The receivables turnover ratio is defined below. Here again, the numerals in parentheses refer to line items from GR Corporation's financial statements, shown in Tables 9-1 and 9-2.

$$\text{Receivables turnover} = \frac{\text{annual sales}}{\text{accounts receivable}} = \frac{(14)}{(3)} \qquad (9\text{-}5)$$

$$= \frac{\$1,130,439}{\$31,053} = 36.4 \text{ times in 1992}$$

$$= \frac{\$1,056,922}{\$33,581} = 31.47 \text{ times in 1991}$$

The calculations show that GR's accounts receivable turned over 36.4 times in 1992. If a firm's accounts receivables turned over every week, they would turn over 52 times a year. So, GR's receivables turned over less than once per week. Whether or not a receivables turnover of 36.4 times per year is too fast or too slow cannot be determined without knowing the company's credit conditions and the payment customs within its industry.

Another way to assess the liquidity of accounts receivable is to compute the number of days in a firm's **collection period.** This ratio, shown below, determines the speed at which bills are collected.

$$\text{Collection period} = \frac{\text{accounts receivable}}{\text{average day's sales}} \qquad (9\text{-}6)$$

$$= \frac{\text{accounts receivable}}{\text{annual sales/365 days}}$$

$$= \frac{(3)}{(14)/365 \text{ days}}$$

$$= \frac{\$31,053}{\$1,130,439/365 \text{ days}} = \frac{\$31,053}{\$3,097.09} =$$

$$= \frac{\$31,053}{\$3,097.09} = 10.03 \text{ days in 1992}$$

GR's average collection period was a little over 10 days during 1992. Applying the collection period calculation to GR's 1991 data indicates that the firm did a slightly better job of collecting its bills in 1992 than it did in 1991.

$$\text{Collection period} = \frac{\$33,581}{\$1,056,922/365 \text{ days}} = \frac{\$33,581}{\$2,895.68} = 11.59 \text{ days}$$

Another type of turnover measure is the **inventory turnover ratio,** a gauge of how efficiently the firm is employing the investment in its inventory. Calculations for this ratio are given below. Note that it is usually preferable to measure the firm's sales at the cost of goods sold value (that is, the wholesale cost, not the inventory's retail) in computing this ratio because inventories are carried on the books at their cost (instead of retail value) in most industries. If retail sales were divided by the inventory valued at cost, the resulting ratio would be significantly inflated.

Box 9-3

237

Chapter 9
Analysis of
Financial
Statements

PRINCIPLES: Financial Ratio Guidelines

GR's 1992 collection period of 10.03 days would be considered too rapid if GR were a manufacturing company that had credit terms of 2/15, net 60.* If this were the case, it would appear that GR had an accounts receivable collection officer so pushy that the customers might become irritated and find another source of supply. But if GR is in the business of selling fresh vegetables at the retail level, then 10 days might seem too long to let customers' bills go unpaid. Retail buyers of a perishable good like fresh vegetables should pay cash for their purchases, so the accounts receivable would be zero. The *appropriate* or *optimal* value for accounts receivable turnover or the length for the average collection period depends on the product being sold and competitors' credit terms.

* Terms of 2/15, net 60 mean that customers purchasing goods on credit are invited by the supplier to take a 2 percent cash discount if (and only if) they pay for the goods within 15 days after delivery. If the 2 percent cash discount is not taken, the supplier expects full payment within 60 days.

$$\text{Inventory turnover ratio} = \frac{\text{annual sales (valued at cost, not retail)}}{\text{average inventory (valued at cost)}} \quad (9\text{-}7)$$

$$= \frac{\text{cost of goods sold}}{\text{average inventory}} = \frac{(16)}{(4)}$$

$$= \frac{\$728,861}{\$56,521} = 12.89 \text{ times in 1992}$$

$$= \frac{\$694,329}{\$59,443} = 11.68 \text{ times in 1991}$$

In 1992 the GR Corporation turned its inventory over 12.89 times per year, or a little more than once per month. This is slightly faster than the inventory turned over in 1991. We must have more information, though, before we can say whether or not GR's turnover is too fast or too slow.

The **asset turnover ratio** measures how productive the firm's total assets (TA) are at producing final sales.

Box 9-4

PRINCIPLES: Inventory Turnover Guidelines

If GR manufactures aged whiskeys and has an inventory turnover of 11 or 12 times per year, the company must be producing their product so hastily that it isn't fit to drink. In contrast, if the firm is in the fresh vegetable business, inventory that is a month old is garbage. An industry-average inventory turnover figure would make an appropriate yardstick with which to compare GR's inventory turnover.

$$\text{Asset turnover ratio} = \frac{\text{annual sales}}{\text{total assets}} = \frac{(14)}{(8)} \tag{9-8}$$

$$= \frac{\$1,130,439}{\$670,235} = 1.69 \text{ times per year in 1992}$$

$$= \frac{\$1,056,992}{\$656,828} = 1.61 \text{ times in 1991}$$

The turnover of total assets per year varies from a low value like once per year for heavy manufacturing industries (steel mills and other smokestack industries) to over a dozen times a year for advertising agencies that own no tangible assets.

The **equity turnover ratio** measures the relationship between the dollar values of a firm's sales and its equity (EQ).

$$\text{Equity turnover ratio} = \frac{\text{sales}}{\text{equity}} = \frac{(14)}{(13)} \tag{9-9}$$

$$= \frac{\$1,130,439}{\$326,519} = 3.46 \text{ times in 1992}$$

$$= \frac{\$1,056,922}{\$304,028} = 3.48 \text{ times in 1991}$$

The computations show that GR Corporation has sales that were 3.46 times larger than its equity (or net worth) in 1992. The 1991 value was almost identical, so it appears that GR's equity turns over about 3.46 times per year fairly consistently. The firm's equity turns over faster than its assets because the firm uses financial leverage obtained from debt financing.

The components of GR's 1992 equity turnover ratio is algebraically decomposed into meaningful components below, and GR's 1992 data are analyzed.

$$\begin{array}{c} \text{Equity} \\ \text{turnover} \\ \text{ratio} \end{array} = \frac{\text{sales}}{\text{equity}} = \tag{9-9}$$

$$\text{Equity turnover ratio} = \frac{\text{sales}}{\text{total assets}} \times \frac{\text{total assets}}{\text{equity}} \tag{9-10}$$

$$= \begin{array}{c} \text{total} \\ \text{asset} \\ \text{turnover} \end{array} \times \begin{array}{c} \text{financial} \\ \text{leverage} \\ \text{ratio} \end{array}$$

$$3.46 \text{ times} = 1.69 \text{ times} \times 2.05 \text{ times, in 1992}$$

$$3.48 \text{ times} = 1.61 \text{ times} \times 2.16 \text{ times, in 1991}$$

The financial leverage ratio values (of 2.05 and 2.16) are derived and explained in more detail below; we will then reconsider the equity turnover ratio.

Coverage Ratios

239

*Chapter 9
Analysis of
Financial
Statements*

Coverage ratios measure how many times the firm's annual earnings cover its debt-service charges (like interest, sinking fund, and lease charges). The **times-interest-earned ratio** is probably the most widely used coverage ratio; it measures the firm's operating income as a percentage of interest payments.

As its name suggests, a firm's *operating income* is earnings from its ordinary operations. Extraordinary income is not included and nonoperating costs such as interest expenses and taxes are not deducted. Therefore, a firm's operating income is sometimes called its **earnings before interest and taxes,** or **EBIT.** In terms of the line item numbers in GR's income and expense statement, Table 9-2, GR's operating income equals (14) minus [(16) + (17) + (18)], as shown in the numerator below.

$$
\begin{aligned}
\text{Times-interest-} & = \frac{\text{annual operating income}}{\text{annual interest payments}} & (9\text{-}11) \\[2mm]
\text{earned ratio} & \\[4mm]
& = \frac{(14) - [(16) + (17) + (18)]}{(19)} \\[4mm]
& = \frac{\$1,130,439 - \$1,046,954}{\$14,526} = 5.75 \text{ times in 1992} \\[4mm]
& = \frac{\$1,056,922 - \$991,049}{\$17,443} = 3.77 \text{ times in 1991}
\end{aligned}
$$

Interpretation and Use The 1992 value of 5.75 for GR's times-interest-earned ratio suggests that the corporation's operating earnings could drop off 82.6 percent before paying the firm's annual interest payments of $14,526 (the denominator in 1992) becomes a problem, as shown below.

$$
\frac{\text{Operating income} - \text{Interest expense}}{\text{Operating income}} = \frac{\$83,485 - \$14,526}{\$83,485} = .826 = 82.6\%
$$

Thus, we see that the firm's operating income of $83,485 covers its debt servicing expenses 5.75 times in 1992.

Bond quality rating agencies like Moody's and the Standard & Poor's Corporation look closely at the times-interest-earned ratio when deciding what quality rating to assign to a bond issue. A firm with a times-interest-earned ratio of only 1.1 times, for instance, would have very little between it and insolvency if its earnings decreased. Such a firm would probably have its bonds assigned a *junk bond rating.*

Different Definitions for the Ratios Most financial analysts have their own favorite variations of each ratio. This is true for almost every financial ratio; the definitions of most ratios are not sacrosanct. The times-interest-earned ratio, for example, is defined by various bond analysts in different ways. Some use the firm's operating income while others prefer to use the firm's *pretax fixed-charge coverage* in the numerator.

The **pretax fixed-charge coverage ratio** is an income measure defined as the firm's net income plus income taxes plus gross interest charges. Some define the debt-service charges in the denominator to include only interest specified contractually in bond indentures, whereas others use gross interest expenses to measure the debt-service charges. The pretax fixed-charge coverage ratio is

$$\text{Pretax fixed-charge coverage ratio} = \frac{\text{pretax income} + \text{gross interest expense}}{\text{gross interest expense}} \quad (9\text{-}12)$$

Sometimes several different variations of the same ratio may be useful for different purposes. The important point is that *only consistently defined ratios should be compared.*

A Cashflow Ratio

Statements of cashflow are another type of financial statement prepared periodically by accountants. A firm's **cashflow** is defined as the sum of the following three quantities from its income and expense statement.

1. *Adjusted income:* This is the firm's normal operating income before taxes. Using the item numbers in Table 9-2, this is item (14) less the sum of items (16), (17), and (18). For 1992 it is $1,130,439 − $1,046,954 = $83,485 for GR Corporation.

2. *Interest expense on long-term debt:* This amount is added back into the firm's income after interest expense (because the income before interest expense is, obviously, a cashflow that may be used to pay interest expense). For GR this is item (19) in Table 9-2, and it equals $14,526 for 1992.

3. *Depreciation:* This noncash expense item is deducted from the firm's revenue to allow for the repair of plant and equipment that declines in value because of fair wear and tear. These repairs need not actually be made simply because the bookkeeping entry deducting depreciation expense is recorded. Depreciation is financially useful because it reduces the tax bill. Through its income tax deduction and resulting decreased tax bill, depreciation indirectly generates a cashflow that can be used for interest expense or to repair physical assets, or to pay for whatever else is needed. Stated differently, depreciation is an allocation of the cost of the asset over its useful productive life, not a deduction for actual repairs. GR's depreciation is hidden in its cost of goods sold, but we assume it is $65,000 for 1992.

Once a firm's cashflow has been calculated, the **cashflow to long-term debt ratio** can be determined. This ratio is

$$\text{Cashflow to long-term debt ratio} = \frac{\text{total annual cashflow}}{\text{long-term debt}} \quad (9\text{-}13)$$

GR's 1992 cashflow is its adjusted income of $83,485, plus $14,526 of interest expense, plus $65,000 depreciation, totaling $163,011. Long-term debt is debt that need not be repaid for more than 1 year; it is $212,717 for GR in 1992.

$$\text{Cashflow-to-long-term-debt ratio} = \frac{\$163,011}{\$212,717} = .76632 = 76.6\% \text{ for } 1992$$

If the firm's cashflow-to-long-term-debt ratio is less than the interest rate paid on total long-term debt, the firm might become insolvent, default on its interest payments, and wind up in bankruptcy court. A high cashflow-to-long-term-debt ratio, of 50 percent or more, suggests that the firm could probably experience a substantial decrease in cashflow without defaulting on its interest payments.[1] The calculations indicate that the GR Corporation has ample cashflows to cover its interest expense. (Box 10-2 shows how Standard & Poor's uses this ratio in assigning bond-quality ratings.)

Leverage Ratios

Leverage ratios gauge the extent to which a firm finances its operations with borrowed money rather than the owners' equity. The **total debt to total asset ratio** indicates what percent of a firm's assets are financed by creditors.

$$\text{Debt to assets ratio} = \frac{\text{total debt}}{\text{total assets}} = \frac{(9) + (10) + (11) + (12)}{(8)} \qquad (9\text{-}14)$$

$$= \frac{\$343,716}{\$670,235} = .5128 = 51.28\% \text{ in } 1992$$

$$= \frac{\$352,800}{\$656,828} = .5371 = 53.71\% \text{ in } 1991$$

Slightly over 51 cents out of every dollar's worth of assets that GR owned in 1992 was financed with borrowed money.

The **total debt to equity** ratio is defined in the following equation. The numerator is the same as the numerator in Equation (9-14) that defined the total debt to assets ratio.

$$\text{Debt to equity ratio} = \frac{\text{total debt}}{\text{equity}} = \frac{(9) + (10) + (11) + (12)}{(13)} \qquad (9\text{-}15)$$

$$= \frac{\$343,716}{\$326,519} = 1.0526 = 105.26\% \text{ in } 1992$$

$$= \frac{\$352,800}{\$304,028} = 1.16041 = 116.04\% \text{ in } 1991$$

The total debt to equity computations indicate that in 1992 creditors put up 105.26 percent as much money as the owners of the GR Corporation had invested in the

---

[1] For more information about analyzing cashflows see chapters 13 and 17 of Leopold A. Bernstein, *Financial Statement Analysis: Theory, Application, and Interpretation,* 4th ed. (Homewood, Ill.: Irwin, 1989).

firm. That seems like a substantial use of borrowed money. However, much of the borrowed money may be interest-free trade credit and accounts payable. The next ratio throws light on the proportions of long-term and short-term debt.

The **long-term debt to equity ratio** is calculated to ascertain the extent to which the firm has employed long-term borrowings (which are usually more rigidly fixed than short-term borrowings).

$$
\begin{array}{l}
\text{Long-term} \\
\text{debt to equity} \\
\text{ratio}
\end{array}
= \frac{\text{long-term debt}}{\text{equity}} = \frac{(11) + (12)}{(13)}
\tag{9-16}
$$

$$
= \frac{\$259,557}{\$326,519} = .7949 = 79.5\% \text{ in 1992}
$$

$$
= \frac{\$273,209}{\$304,028} = .89863 = 89.86\% \text{ in 1991}
$$

Since the long-term debt to equity ratio has significantly smaller values than the total debt to equity ratio for both 1992 and 1991 (79.49 percent versus 105 percent and 89.86 percent versus 116 percent), it appears that much of GR's debt is short-term. (If GR is to maximize its income, it would be best if these short-term debts are not interest-bearing.) Nevertheless, long-term lenders provided the GR Corporation with 79.5 percent as much funding as did its owners in 1992.

As our discussion of the pretax rate of return on long-term capital ratio will show, *capitalization* refers to a firm's permanently committed capital funds. A firm's capitalization is the sum of its permanently maintained current liabilities, long-term debt, preferred stock, and stockholders' equity.

The **long-term debt to capitalization ratio** for GR, calculated below, is similar to the long-term debt to equity ratio. It is used to determine what fraction of the firm's permanent capital is from debt.

$$
\begin{array}{l}
\text{Long-term debt} \\
\text{to capitalization} \\
\text{ratio}
\end{array}
= \frac{\text{long-term debt}}{\text{capitalization}} = \frac{(11) + (12)}{(11) + (12) + (13)}
\tag{9-17}
$$

$$
= \frac{\$259,557}{\$586,076} = .44287 = 44.287\% \text{ in 1992}
$$

$$
= \frac{\$273,209}{\$577,237} = .47330 = 47.33\% \text{ in 1991}
$$

It is impossible to tell from GR's balance sheet how much of the corporation's current liabilities are not currently coming due. Assuming that all of GR's current liabilities continue to roll over in 1992, then GR's long-term debt of $259,557, combined with its $326,519 of equity, adds up to $586,076 of **permanent capital.** Dividing this amount of permanent capital into $259,557 of long-term debt results in a ratio of 44.287 percent for 1992.

Another ratio that is used to evaluate a firm's degree of indebtedness is the **total asset to equity** (or **net-worth) ratio:**

CASE

Chrysler Almost Lost It in 1980

Chrysler was experiencing bad sales each year during the late 1970s. The automotive giant started losing money in 1978 and continued losing every year up to and including 1981. The firm had to lay people off and borrow just to meet its payrolls. The debts reached a peak in 1980, and Chrysler almost went bankrupt. Luckily for thousands of Chrysler's re-maining employees, new management and a $1.5 billion loan from the U.S. federal government turned the company around. Seven years of leverage ratios below document Chrysler's close brush with bank-ruptcy in 1980 and its recovery in the early 1980s. (See the Chrysler case in Chapter 10 for Chrysler's security prices and additional financial details.)

Chrysler's leverage ratios

Year	Sales, millions	Total debt / Total assets Eq. (9-14)	Total debt / Equity Eq. (9-15)	Long-term debt to Capitalization Eq. (9-17)
1978	$13,618	52.8%	136%	28.4%
1979	12,002	63.5	264%	33.8
1980	9,225	83.3	Negative equity	82.4 (Near
1981	10,822	71.4	Negative equity	70.8 bankruptcy)
1982	10,045	68.7	Negative equity	68.3
1983	13,240	67.3	399%	44.7
1984	19,573	53.8	147%	18.6

$$\text{Total assets to equity ratio} = \frac{\text{total assets}}{\text{equity}} = \frac{(8)}{(13)} \qquad (9\text{-}18)$$

$$= \frac{\$670,235}{\$326,519} = 2.052 = 205.2\% \text{ in } 1992$$

$$= \frac{\$656,828}{\$304,028} = 2.160 = 216.0\% \text{ in } 1991$$

The ratio shows that in 1992 GR had acquired 2.052 times as much in assets as it had in net worth (or equity). Total assets of 2.052 times more than stockholders' equity implies a significant amount of indebtedness. The fixed interest expenses that arise from such substantial long-term debt increases the risk that GR Corporation could default if its profitability slipped enough that it could not pay its fixed interest expenses.

Profitability Ratios

Profitability ratios compare a firm's earnings with various factors that generate earnings. The resulting ratios can throw light on the aspects of the business that are particularly profitable or unprofitable.

The **net profit margin** is a popular profitability ratio. It measures the contribution to net income that each sales dollar generates. The ratio is evaluated for GR below:

$$\text{Net profit margin} = \frac{\text{net income}}{\text{sales}} = \frac{(23)}{(14)} \qquad (9\text{-}19)$$

$$= \frac{\$30,896}{\$1,130,439} = .02733 = 2.73\% \text{ in 1992}$$

$$= \frac{\$26,549}{\$1,056,922} = .02511 = 2.51\% \text{ in 1991}$$

GR's net after-tax profit margin was about 2.7 and 2.5 percent of each sales dollar in 1992 and 1991, respectively.

The **rate of return on assets** is another profitability ratio. As the name suggests, this ratio measures net income after taxes as a percentage of the company's total asset investment. Calculations for GR Corporation are shown below:

$$\text{Return on assets} = \frac{\text{net income}}{\text{total assets}} = \frac{(23)}{(8)} \qquad (9\text{-}20)$$

$$= \frac{\$30,896}{\$670,235} = .046097 = 4.60\% \text{ in 1992}$$

$$= \frac{\$26,549}{\$656,828} = .040420 = 4.04\% \text{ in 1991}$$

GR's rate of return on total assets in 1992 means that the firm's average dollar's worth of assets yielded about 4.6 cents of after-tax earnings in 1992. Asset-intensive businesses like steel mills usually have low rates of return on huge investments in assets, while service companies that own virtually no assets are able to operate profitably and have high rates of return on tiny asset investments.

The **rate of return on equity (ROE)** is a profitability ratio that measures the rate of earnings on the owners' equity (EQ).

Box 9-5

PRINCIPLES: Net Profit Margin Guidelines

A net profit margin of 2.7 percent would be very low for, say, a full-service retail jewelry store, where the markups are usually very high. It is common for retail jewelers to sell their goods for twice the wholesale price; this results in net profit margins of 10 to 20 percent of sales after overhead expenses are deducted. On the other hand, large retail supermarkets operate on low markups and thin margins that would sometimes be even lower than GR's net profit margin. Thus, an appropriate standard of comparison is needed to obtain a more meaningful interpretation of the ratio's numerical value.

$$\text{Return on equity (ROE)} = \frac{\text{net income}}{\text{equity}} = \frac{(23)}{(13)} \tag{9-21}$$

$$= \frac{\$30,896}{\$326,519} = .094622 = 9.46\% \text{ in 1992}$$

$$= \frac{\$26,549}{\$304,028} = .087324 = 8.73\% \text{ in 1991}$$

The difference between rate of return on assets and rate of return on equity, the two preceding ratios, is attributable to the firm's use of borrowed money—or, synonymously, financial leverage. If a firm had no debts, these two ratios would yield identical values. Comparing GR's 1992 return on assets of 4.6 percent with its 1992 return on equity of 9.4 percent indicates that the company employed borrowed money advantageously to leverage its rate of return to its stockholders up above the positive rate of return it earned on its assets.[2]

A profitability ratio that is popular with bond quality rating agencies is the **pretax rate of return on long-term capital ratio.**

$$\begin{array}{c}\text{Pretax rate of return} \\ \text{on long-term capital} \\ \text{ratio}\end{array} = \frac{\text{interest} + \text{earnings before taxes}}{\text{long-term capital}} \tag{9-22}$$

The sum of earnings before taxes and interest expense is the total amount of income a firm has available to make its interest payments. **Long-term capital** is a firm's permanently committed capital funds; it is the sum of that portion of short-term debt that the firm permanently maintains to finance assets, long-term debt, preferred stock and common stock (or, synonymously, net worth or stockholders' equity). Sometimes a firm's long-term capital is also called its *permanent capital,* or simply its **capitalization.**

Figure 9-1 illustrates a firm's capital in terms of its balance sheet. **Net working**

---

[2] Financial leverage is counterproductive when a firm is suffering losses. Financial leverage magnifies both positive and negative rates of return on assets.

Figure 9-1 An illustration contrasting a company's balance sheet with its total capitalization.

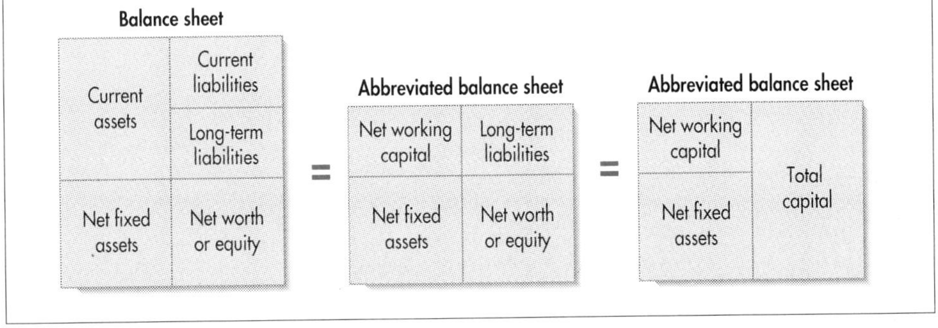

capital is defined as the excess of current assets over current liabilities. The only difference between the complete and the abbreviated balance sheets is that in the abbreviated statement some of the current assets have been used to pay all the current liabilities. Stated differently, a firm's total capital includes all its liabilities and net worth except its current liabilities.

The ratio for pretax rate of return (ROR) on long-term capital is computed for GR Corporation below:

$$\text{Pretax ROR on long-term capital ratio} = \frac{(21) + (19)}{(11) + (13)}$$

$$= \frac{\$60{,}915 + \$14{,}526}{\$212{,}717 + \$326{,}519}$$

$$= \frac{\$75{,}441}{\$539{,}236} = .13990 = 13.99\% \text{ in 1992}$$

GR's pretax ROR on long-term capital was less in 1991.

$$\text{Pretax ROR on long-term capital ratio} = \frac{\$48{,}529 + \$17{,}443}{\$234{,}090 + \$304{,}028} = 12.26\% \text{ in 1991}$$

The pretax rate of return on long-term capital ratio states the firm's income as a percent of its permanent capitalization. It is useful for comparison with current market interest rates. If the ratio does not exceed current interest rates, the company is not earning enough to pay its interest expense. This will result in low bond quality ratings and eventually lead to default if the situation does not improve.

Common Stock per Share Data

Common stock investors are particularly concerned about a few values that have a strong effect on the market price of their shares. The **earnings per share (EPS)** after income taxes is one of the most important determinants of a common stock's value, because it measures the earning power underlying the stock.

$$\text{Earnings per share} = \frac{\text{net income to common stockholders}}{\text{number of common shares outstanding}} = \frac{(23)}{(26)} \qquad (9\text{-}23)$$

$$= \frac{\$30{,}896}{19{,}310 \text{ shares}} = \$1.60 \text{ per share in 1992}$$

$$= \frac{\$26{,}549}{19{,}310 \text{ shares}} = \$1.3748 \text{ per share in 1991}$$

The earnings per share computations above indicate that GR Corporation earned $1.60 per share after taxes in 1992.

GR's income and expense statement reveals that the board of directors decided to pay out half the corporation's $30,896 of net income in the form of a cash dividend to the common stockholders in 1992. GR's **cash dividend per share** was 80 cents in 1992, calculated by dividing the corporation's total outlay for cash dividends by the number of shares of common stock outstanding.

$$\text{Cash dividend per share (CDPS)} = \frac{\text{total corporate cash dividend}}{\text{number of shares outstanding}} = \frac{(24)}{(26)} \qquad (9\text{-}24)$$

$$= \frac{\$15,448}{19,310 \text{ shares}} = \$0.80 \text{ per share in 1992}$$

$$= \frac{\$13,270}{19,310 \text{ shares}} = \$0.687 \text{ per share in 1991}$$

The calculations below show that GR's cash dividend of 80 cents per share in 1992 resulted in a **payout ratio** of 50 percent.

$$\text{Payout ratio} = \frac{\text{cash dividends per share}}{\text{earnings per share}} = \frac{(29)}{(28)} \qquad (9\text{-}25)$$

$$= \frac{\$0.80 \text{ per share}}{\$1.60 \text{ per share}} = .5 = 50 \text{ percent in 1992}$$

$$= \frac{\$0.687 \text{ per share}}{\$1.3748 \text{ per share}} = .4999 = 49.99 \text{ percent in 1991}$$

Another useful calculation is the retention rate (RR), which measures the fraction of a corporation's total after-tax earnings (or net income, denoted NI) that are retained within the firm to finance expansion. The **retention rate (RR)** is defined in terms of the corporation's annual retained earnings (RE) (item 25 in Table 9-2) stated as a fraction of the corporation's net income, as shown below:

$$\text{RR} = \frac{\text{net income} - \text{total cash dividends}}{\text{net income}} = \frac{\text{retained earnings}}{\text{net income}} = \frac{(25)}{(23)} \qquad (9\text{-}26)$$

$$= \frac{\$15,448}{\$30,896} = .5 = 50\% \text{ in 1992}$$

$$= \frac{\$13,279}{\$26,549} = .5001 = 50.01\% \text{ in 1991}$$

The equation below defines the retention ratio (RR) on a per share basis.

$$\text{RR} = \frac{\text{EPS} - \text{CDPS}}{\text{earnings per share}} = \frac{\text{retained earnings per share}}{\text{EPS}} \qquad (9\text{-}27)$$

$$= \frac{(28) - (29)}{(28)} = \frac{\$0.80}{\$1.60} = .5 = 50\% \text{ in 1992}$$

$$= \frac{\$0.687}{\$1.3748} = .5001 = 50.01\% \text{ in 1991}$$

Equations (9-26) and (9-27) appear to define the retention ratio differently, but they are equivalent. One uses corporate totals; the other uses per share data. Regardless of whether it is measured on an aggregate basis or on a per share basis, the retention ratio equals 1.0 less the payout ratio, as shown below.

Retention ratio = 1.0 − payout ratio

Common stock investors are also interested in their stock's **price-earnings ratio (P/E).**

$$\text{Price-earnings ratio} = \frac{\text{market price per share}}{\text{earnings per share}} = \frac{(27)}{(28)} \qquad (9\text{-}28)$$

$$= \frac{\$19.00}{\$1.60} = 11.875 \text{ times in } 1992$$

$$= \frac{\$15.50}{\$1.3748} = 11.27 \text{ times in } 1991$$

The price-earnings ratio is sometimes called the *earnings multiplier*. The calculations above show that in 1992 GR Corporation's stock was selling at 11.875 times its earnings per share. This is an average value for a price-earnings ratio. Most corporations' stock sells for 6 to 16 times their earnings. (Price-earnings ratios are discussed more fully in Chapter 13.)

9-5 Analyzing and Interpreting Ratios

Analysis of some financial ratios can yield more information than the ratio may appear to convey.

The DuPont Analytical Framework

Investors are always concerned about their corporation's growth because growth usually translates into stock price appreciation. The rate of return on equity (ROE) contributes to the firm's growth.

Analysis of ROE Breaking down the rate of return on equity into its financial components reveals some of the sources of a firm's growth. The rate of return on equity definition is shown again below so this formula can be analyzed further:

$$\text{Return on equity (ROE)} = \frac{\text{net income}}{\text{equity}} = \frac{\text{NI}}{\text{EQ}} = \frac{(23)}{(13)} \qquad (9\text{-}21)$$

$$= \frac{\$30,896}{\$326,519} = .09462 = 9.46\% \text{ in } 1992$$

$$= \frac{\$26,549}{\$304,028} = .08732 = 8.73\% \text{ in } 1991$$

(ROE = income / equity)

(ROA = income / assets)

Dividing both the numerator and the denominator of the ROE ratio by the firm's sales results in the mathematically equivalent way of stating the ROE ratio shown below:

$$\text{ROE} = \frac{\text{NI}}{\text{EQ}} = \frac{\text{sales}}{\text{EQ}} \times \frac{\text{NI}}{\text{sales}} \qquad (9\text{-}29)$$

$$= \text{equity turnover [Eq. (9-9)]} \times \text{net profit margin [Eq. (9-19)]}$$

$$= 3.46 \text{ times} \times 2.73\% = 9.46\% \text{ in 1992}$$

$$= 3.48 \text{ times} \times 2.51\% = 8.73\% \text{ in 1991}$$

There are different ways to restate the ROE formula algebraically that yield identical numerical results. The original ROE formula, Equation (9-21), is reformulated as Equation (9-29) to allow a deeper financial analysis because it breaks down a company's ROE into two other financially meaningful ratios. The ROE formula of Equation (9-29) can be further decomposed by using the equity turnover ratio, Equation (9-10), introduced earlier in this chapter.

$$\text{Equity turnover} = \frac{\text{sales}}{\text{EQ}} = \frac{\text{sales}}{\text{total assets}} \times \frac{\text{total assets}}{\text{EQ}} \qquad (9\text{-}10)$$

$$= \text{total asset turnover} \times \text{financial leverage ratio}$$

Substituting the equity turnover ratio into ROE Equation (9-29) allows the ROE formula to be broken down into the three components shown below:

$$\text{ROE} = \frac{\text{NI}}{\text{EQ}} = \frac{\text{sales}}{\text{EQ}} \times \frac{\text{NI}}{\text{sales}} \qquad (9\text{-}29)$$

$$= \frac{\text{equity}}{\text{turnover}} \times \frac{\text{net}}{\text{profit}}_{\text{margin}}$$

$$= \frac{\text{sales}}{\text{TA}} \times \frac{\text{TA}}{\text{EQ}} \times \frac{\text{NI}}{\text{sales}} \qquad (9\text{-}30)$$

$$= \frac{\text{total}}{\text{asset}}_{\text{turnover}} \times \frac{\text{financial}}{\text{leverage}}_{\text{ratio}} \times \frac{\text{net}}{\text{profit}}_{\text{margin}}$$

$$= \frac{1.69}{\text{times}} \times \frac{2.05}{\text{times}} \times 2.73\% = 9.46\% \text{ in 1992}$$

$$= \frac{1.61}{\text{times}} \times \frac{2.16}{\text{times}} \times 2.51\% = 8.73\% \text{ in 1991}$$

Breaking down the ROE formula into three components shows that a company's ROE can be increased in three different ways: (1) by more efficient asset usage (as measured by faster total asset turnover), (2) by increased use of debt (as measured by the financial leverage ratio), or (3) by increasing the profit margins (as measured by the net profit margin ratio). These three ROE components can contribute to the firm's growth if the earnings are reinvested in the firm.

Analysis of Growth   The *growth* of a corporation's common stock value depends on several factors. First, growth depends on the amount of earnings retained and reinvested in the firm. The rate of retained earnings is measured by the retention ratio (RR) that was defined in Equation (9-27).

Second, a corporation's growth rate depends on the rate of return on equity (ROE) earned on funds that are invested in the firm. Defining the growth rate in earnings as shown below shows how the ROE and the retention rate (RR) determine the retained earnings–induced growth rate.[3]

$$\text{Growth rate} = \text{RR} \times \text{ROE} \tag{9-31}$$

Substituting Equation (9-30)'s decomposed version of the ROE ratio into growth rate Equation (9-31) results in the more enlightening growth rate model shown below as Equation (9-32):

$$\text{Growth rate} = \text{RR} \times \frac{\text{sales}}{\text{TA}} \times \frac{\text{TA}}{\text{EQ}} \times \frac{\text{NI}}{\text{sales}} \tag{9-32}$$

Substituting RR = RE/NI [Equation (9-26)] into growth rate Equation (9-32) and rearranging the terms algebraically yields the equivalent formula for the growth rate:

$$\text{Growth rate} = \frac{\text{RE}}{\text{NI}} \times \frac{\text{NI}}{\text{sales}} \times \frac{\text{sales}}{\text{TA}} \times \frac{\text{TA}}{\text{EQ}} = \frac{\text{RE}}{\text{EQ}} \tag{9-33}$$

The various equivalent ways that the ROE and growth rate ratios can be restated highlight the manner in which different financial variables can add to or detract from the growth of a common stock's value. This approach to ratio analysis is called the DuPont analysis because it was popularized by the DuPont Corporation decades ago.[4]

Risk Analysis

Growing corporations are usually riskier than companies that are not growing. Regardless of whether a company is risky because of growth, management errors, tough competition, or other factors, risk is another aspect of an investment that should be analyzed. **Risk analysis** can be approached from several perspectives.

[3] This earnings growth rate analysis ignores expansion financed with funds from external financing sources.

[4] For additional discussion of the different factors that contribute to a firm's ROE and riskiness see Robert C. Higgins, *Analysis for Financial Management*, 2d ed. (Homewood, Ill.: Irwin, 1989), chaps. 1, 2, 3, and 4.

The Riskiness of Dollar-Denominated Quantities Various aspects of risk can be

251

*Chapter 9
Analysis of
Financial
Statements*

analyzed with a statistic called the **coefficient of variation (CV).** The CV of some variable is defined as the standard deviation divided by the average value, as shown below:

$$\text{CV of } x = \frac{\text{standard deviation of } x}{\text{average value of } x} = \frac{\sqrt{\sum\limits_{i=1}^{N} \frac{(x_i - \bar{x})^2}{N}}}{\sum\limits_{i=1}^{N} \frac{x_i}{N}} \tag{9-34}$$

where x_i = one value of x in the range of values

$\bar{x}$ = average of all the values

N = the number of values

The coefficient of variation formula is well known to statisticians, and many financial analysts use it too. The main advantage of using the CV is that it is a *normalized* (or standardized) statistic; that is, the standard deviation is normalized by dividing it by the average value so that the CVs of large firms are directly comparable with the CVs of small firms. This facilitates comparing the riskiness of dollar-denominated quantities of differing amounts.

The CV is a pure index number that measures variability around the average. The CV is a dimensionless statistic; it cannot be stated in terms of dollars, percentages, pounds, or inches. Comparisons of different kinds of variability are facilitated by this index-number quality of the CV.

Business risk: A firm's **business risk** is determined by volatility in its operating income. The CV of a series of annual operating income figures can be used to evaluate business risk. In order to calculate the CV of the firm's operating earnings, we let different time periods' operating income be the x values in the CV formula.[5] Looking into what makes a firm's operating income fluctuate reveals that business risk arises from both sales fluctuations and production cost fluctuations. Fluctuations that arise from changes in the way the firm finances its operations are not included in the CV of its operating income because financing costs are not considered in calculating operating income.

Other risk measurements: The **financial risks** a firm undertakes are measured with the coverage ratios and the leverage ratios explained earlier. In addition, **sales volatility** can be evaluated separately by calculating the CV of year-to-year sales. Riskiness from sales fluctuations can be measured by letting the firm's year-to-year sales figures furnish the values of x in the CV formula. Then the firm's financial ratios and its CVs can be compared with meaningful benchmarks in order to place the firm's values in perspective.

---

[5] Operating income is also called the firm's *earnings before interest and taxes (EBIT).* As shown in Table 9-2, *operating income* is usually defined to be equal to the firm's sales less its operating expenses (cost of goods sold plus marketing expenses plus administrative expenses plus general expenses plus excise taxes).

Rate-of-Return-Denominated Risk Analysis   In Chapter 1 the variance and standard deviation of an asset's one-period rates of return were defined in Box 1-9. These two rate-of-return-oriented risk measures need not be normalized by dividing them by their average value because the rate of return is not affected by the dollar size of the transaction. The rate of return is a percentage change.

The risk rankings of a group of corporations as measured by the standard deviations of their rates of return will be similar to (but not identical with) their risk ranking when risk is measured by the CV of some dollar-denominated income or sales measure. The risk rankings are similar because financial statement risk transfers through investors to become market risk.[6]

Interpreting Ratios with Standards of Comparison

Financial ratios and common-sized financial statements are valuable sources of information by themselves. They may be even more informative when they are compared with other relevant financial ratios. Financial analysts often do two comparisons—cross-sectional and time-series—in order to discern unusual levels in a ratio and to detect any trend.

Cross-Sectional Standards   A firm's financial ratios can be compared with other firms' ratios. Several categories of such **cross-sectional comparisons** may reveal strengths and/or weaknesses relative to the other firms. Several categories of cross-sectional comparisons can be helpful standards.[7]

Industry-average ratios are derived by averaging over the financial ratios of competing firms. Although the individual firms in any given industry typically have substantially different financial ratios, their average ratios provide good indications of the normal *level* of the financial ratios of similar firms. Industry-average financial ratios for dozens of different industries are published by companies like Moody's and Standard & Poor's.

By comparing the financial ratios of the firm being analyzed with the ratios of individual competing firms that are poorly or well-managed, a financial analyst may be able to detect differences that explain problems or successes, respectively.

Time-Series Standards   A firm's own ratios from other years can be surveyed. Such **time-series comparisons** are useful to highlight trends or changes that have occurred within the firm and to provide a context in which to place current trends. The financial ratios shown in the Chrysler case (earlier in this chapter) provide an example of a time series of several different financial ratios for a single firm that can give the financial analyst helpful clues.

---

[6] See W. Beaver, P. Kettler, and M. Scholes, "The Association between Market-Determined and Accounting-Determined Risk Measures," *Accounting Review,* October 1970, pp. 654–682. Also see D. J. Thompson, II, "Sources of Systematic Risk in Common Stocks," *Journal of Business,* vol. 49, no. 2, 1976, pp. 173–188.

[7] George Foster, *Financial Statement Analysis,* 2d ed. (Englewood Cliffs, N.J.: Prentice-Hall, 1986), chap. 6, discusses cross-sectional analysis of financial statements in more detail.

When the financial statements from adjoining years for the same firm are compared, there are so many pieces of information that it may not be easy to spot meaningful changes. However, if the analyst calculates the firm's financial ratios for adjoining years, significant changes may become more noticeable. By comparing data for several years, an analyst can assess if financial changes indicate a one-time-only change, a trend, or a cyclical fluctuation.

Trends may occur slowly from month to month and may go unnoticed by even close observers. However, when a time series of values for a particular ratio is observed annually over several years, the trend becomes apparent. Trends toward new ways of operating are worth considering to see if they have any implications for the investment's future value.

Potential Problems with Financial Analysis

Although financial analysis is a worthwhile way to gain information, it is not without its pitfalls. We'll look here at just three: inflationary distortion, vague definitions, and the effects of mergers.

Inflationary Distortions   Inflation can distort financial statements and the ratios calculated from accounting statements. For example, if several consecutive years of financial statements from a single corporation are compared, the comparison will be clouded by changes introduced by inflating prices. This is a particular problem with the balance sheet items because some fixed assets are carried on the balance sheet at historical costs that become increasingly irrelevant as inflation continues. Furthermore, some fixed assets are depreciated by accountants while their market values are actually appreciating. Thus, an astute financial analyst may find it necessary to adjust a firm's financial statements for inflation in order to calculate meaningful ratios.

The Vague Definition of Accounting Income   The generally accepted accounting principles used to define a firm's income are not so exact as they appear at first glance. Whether the firm's accountants use straight-line or accelerated depreciation, or various inventory valuation techniques (such as LIFO and FIFO), and whether sales are recognized as occurring when the order is signed by the customer or when the customer finally pays for the purchase are all important accounting decisions that modify a company's financial statements and its taxable income. These and other issues will be examined further in Chapter 14 and some guidelines for dealing with them suggested.

Mergers and Consolidated Financial Statements   The purchase of another company by a firm creates problems when the financial statements of acquirer and acquired are consolidated. Intangible items like "goodwill" often appear on the *consolidated balance sheet* after an acquisition. Financial analysts should be prepared to study these items and make adjustments in the firm's published financial statements to align them more closely with the economic realities of the situation. This can be a demanding task; the accounting departments at many colleges of business teach an entire course entitled "Consolidations" that deals with accounting for mergers and acquisitions.

Summary

The balance sheet and the income and expense statement are the two basic financial statements from which meaningful financial ratios can be calculated. Good financial analysis involves using ratios to distill voluminous data and make it easier to comprehend and convey. Relevant variables with cause-and-effect relationships are used to form meaningful ratios.

Investors can utilize many different categories of financial ratios, including common-sized financial statements, solvency ratios, coverage ratios, turnover ratios, profitability ratios, cashflow ratios, leverage ratios, growth ratios, ratios for analyzing per share data, and risk analysis statistics. The various ratios must be interpreted appropriately. Using ratios from firms doing the same type of business is one good approach to assessing them. Cross-section comparisons and time-series comparisons can provide benchmarks to aid the financial analysis.

Some caveats are in order. The financial ratios discussed above are not an exhaustive list of ratios, and some financial analysts prefer to use these ratios restated in a slightly different manner. Furthermore, when analyzing firms in some industries (such as the banks, for instance), analysts employ special ratios peculiar to that industry. Inflation, the differences between differing types of inventory accounting, and mergers can create headaches for financial analysts. If you are interested in the more esoteric aspects of financial analysis, you may wish to take an entire one-semester course devoted to the subject.

Further Reading

Bernstein, Leopold A., *Financial Statement Analysis: Theory, Application, and Interpretation,* 4th ed. (Homewood, Ill.: Irwin, 1989).
   An easy-to-read, accounting-oriented book that discusses traditional financial statement analysis in detail.

Briloff, Abraham J., *Unaccountable Accounting,* (New York: Harper & Row, 1972).
   This easy-to-read accounting book is full of actual names, dates, and examples of accounting gimmicks that major corporations have used to misrepresent the true economic events.

Foster, George, *Financial Statement Analysis,* 2d ed. (Englewood Cliffs, N.J.: Prentice-Hall, 1986).
   A statistical analysis–oriented book that presents new approaches to financial statement analysis that are often grounded in economic theory.

Questions and Problems

Essay Questions

9-1   Go to the library and gather financial data on two large corporations. First, consider Exxon Corporation, the largest petroleum company in the United States. Exxon drills oil wells, refines gas and oil, and retails petroleum products through an extensive chain of filling stations. Second, consider London-based Saatchi & Saatchi, the world's largest advertising agency. What differences might you expect in the following ratios for these two companies: (*a*) turnover ratios, (*b*) profit margins, (*c*) rate of return on equity, (*d*) leverage ratios? Why would you expect any differences?

9-2   What is the purpose of the coverage ratios? What information are these ratios supposed to convey? Who is most interested in coverage ratios?

9-3 Would you expect airline companies like Delta, American, or United to have the same business risk as a big public utility like American Telephone and Telegraph? Explain why or why not.

9-4 In recent years GR Corporation has earned about 10 percent rate of return on equity (ROE). Does this mean that the corporation is growing in value at about 10 percent per year? Explain why or why not.

9-5 In 1979 the IBM Corporation declared a 4-for-1 stock split that gave every stockholder three new shares of common stock in addition to every share owned before the split. Thus, there were 4 times as many shares of IBM stock outstanding after the split as there were before the split. One of the objectives of the split was to reduce the level of IBM's stock price from $300 per share to $75 per share. The price reduction was accomplished. But what did the 4-for-1 stock split do to IBM's earnings per share and cash dividends per share? Explain.

9-6 It is sometimes said that the balance sheet is like a *still photo* and, in contrast, the income statement is like a *moving picture*. What is meant by this analogy? Do you think it is true?

9-7 Consider three categories of people who use ratios to analyze corporations' financial statements: (*a*) potential investors, (*b*) the managers who run a corporation, and (*c*) suppliers of raw materials who are asked to extend credit to a corporation. Do these three categories of financial analysts have different interests? If so, on which ratios might each category of analyst tend to focus?

9-8 Is it possible that a company would have a high current ratio and still be unable to pay its bills? If so, explain how.

9-9 The values of the various financial ratios tend to vary from firm to firm. Nevertheless, the competing firms within each industry tend to have values for their financial ratios that cluster around unique industry-average values. What accounts for the differences in these industry-average values? Give a specific example to illustrate your answer.

Problems

9-10 Show whether each of the funds flows listed below increases, decreases, or has a negligible effect on the following balance sheet items of the affected firm's (*a*) net working capital, (*b*) net investment in plant after depreciation, (*c*) long-term debt, and (*d*) stockholder's equity. *Hint:* You may need to consult an introductory accounting textbook.

Funds flow into the firm from	*Stock-holders' equity*	*Net working capital*	*Net depreciated plant*	*Long-term debt*	
Long-term debt payoff	Negligible	Increase	Negligible	Decrease	(Sample answer)
Positive earnings					
Depreciation					
Sale of plant at price exceeding its positive book value					
Buy plant					
Cash dividends					

9-11 The current assets and liabilities of the Ultima Beauty Shop Supply Corporation are listed below, and some explanation of the way the firm operates is provided.

Current assets:		Current liabilities:	
Cash	$ 10,000	Accounts payable	$40,000
Accounts receivable	72,000	Accrued expenses	30,000
Inventories	80,000	Total	$70,000
Total	$162,000		

Ultima's inventory of beauty aid supplies is used to fill telephone orders from beauty salons; the orders are delivered within 1 working day after they are phoned in. Ultima has annual sales of $600,000, and the cost of the goods sold is $320,000. It is the custom in the beauty salon products industry for the beauty salons to pay cash on delivery for the goods. Ultima's chief executive officer and primary stockholder pays all his bills soon enough to enable him to take any cash discounts that are available. Ultima's accounts payable and accrued expenses include rent, employees' wages, utility bills, and taxes that are currently due. Calculate Ultima's (*a*) current ratio, (*b*) quick ratio, (*c*) inventory turnover ratio, (*d*) age of inventory, (*e*) accounts receivable turnover (assume that 10 percent of Ultima's sales are made on credit), and (*f*) age of accounts receivable. Do you think Ultima's current assets and liabilities are well managed? Explain.

9-12 Compare the following 1991 and 1992 income statements from the Mohawk Manufacturing Corporation:

	1992	1991
Sales	$960,000	$870,000
Less: Cost of goods sold	600,000	500,000
Equals: Gross profit	$360,000	$370,000
Less: Operating expenses	320,000	300,000
Equals: Earnings before interest and taxes	$ 40,000	$ 70,000

(*a*) Calculate Mohawk's income statement using common-sized percentages. (*b*) Calculate the percentage change from year to year for every item in Mohawk's income statement. (*c*) Why do you think Mohawk's 1992 earnings before interest and taxes are down from their 1991 level?

9-13 The Mohawk Manufacturing Corporation (from the preceding problem) has a 1992 balance sheet as shown below:

Mohawk Manufacturing Corporation, Balance Sheet, 1992

Current assets	$200,000
Fixed assets	500,000
Total assets	700,000
Current liabilities	$100,000
Long-term liabilities (at 9% interest)	300,000
Net worth	$300,000
Total liabilities and net worth	$700,000

Assume that Mohawk pays $27,000 per year interest expense, is in the 30 percent income tax bracket, and pays out 40 percent of its after-tax earnings as cash dividends. Calculate Mohawk's (*a*) common-sized balance sheet, (*b*) total asset turnover ratio, (*c*) after-tax profit margin on sales (assume Mohawk pays 30 percent of its income for taxes), (*d*) leverage as measured by the ratio of total assets divided by equity, and (*e*) rate of return on equity. (*f*) After considering all the information, at what rate do you think Mohawk's earnings will grow if the firm does not raise any more capital externally?

Multiple Choice Questions

9-14 The Acme Supermarket Company (ASC) and Baker's Jewelry Store (BJS) are located in the same block, and both these retail stores earn rates of return on equity that are about equal to each other every year. How might you expect the other financial ratios of these two establishments to compare?

    (*a*) ASC probably has higher profit margins and lower turnover ratios than BJS.
    (*b*) ASC probably has lower profit margins and higher turnover ratios than BJS.
    (*c*) ASC is less risky than BJS, but the supermarket uses more financial leverage than its neighbor.
    (*d*) ASC is more risky than BJS, but the supermarket uses less financial leverage than its neighbor.
    (*e*) Both (*a*) and (*d*) are true.

B

9-15 Financial analysts should not use the unaltered financial statements of many firms because of which of the following problems with financial statements?

    (*a*) Inflation undermines the validity of the depreciated purchase-price values used by accountants.
    (*b*) As accountants switch from LIFO to FIFO inventory valuation techniques, the reported results can be unrealistic.
    (*c*) Mergers result in consolidated financial statements that can contain "goodwill" and other confusing items that are of significant dollar value.
    (*d*) An accounting switch from the straight-line to an accelerated method of depreciation can result in unrealistic reported income for the firm.
    (*e*) All the above are true.

E

9-16 Coverage ratios are described by which of the following?

    (*a*) They are ratios that measure a firm's ability to pay its bills on time by gauging its net working capital position.
    (*b*) The times-interest-earned ratio is an example of a coverage ratio.
    (*c*) The current ratio is an example of a coverage ratio.
    (*d*) They are ratios that measure how well a firm should be able to meet its debt-servicing obligations.
    (*e*) Both (*b*) and (*d*) are true.

E

9-17 Which of the following ratios will increase as a firm uses more financial leverage?

    (*a*) The times-interest-earned ratio
    (*b*) The debt-to-equity ratio
    (*c*) The inventory turnover
    (*d*) Both (*a*) and (*b*)
    (*e*) Both (*a*) and (*c*)

B

9-18 Which of the following quantities may be observed on a firm's income and expense statement?

(a) Gross margin
(b) Net working capital
(c) Cost of goods sold
(d) Both (a) and (c)
(e) All the above

9-19 Which of the following factors would tend to increase the growth rate of a corporation?

(a) External borrowing
(b) The corporation's retention rate
(c) The corporation's rate of return on equity
(d) Both (a) and (b)
(e) All the above

9-20 How can a corporation's riskiness be gauged without using any financial ratios?

(a) The variability of return in the one-period rates of return from a corporation's common stock is a market-determined risk measure.
(b) The coefficient of variation in a corporation's income from year to year is a dimensionless index number that measures its riskiness.
(c) The coefficient of variation in a corporation's annual sales is a measure of its riskiness.
(d) Both (b) and (c) are true.
(e) All the above are true.

9-21 The phrase "common-sized financial statement" refers to which of the following?

(a) A collection of ratios calculated on one company at some particular point in time
(b) A reformulation of the balance sheet
(c) A standardized (or normalized) income and expense statement
(d) Both (b) and (c) are true
(e) All of the above

9-22 Cash, accounts receivable, inventory, and marketable securities are best described by which of the following statements?

(a) The productivity of these earning assets can be measured with various turnover ratios.
(b) The liquidity of the firm can be assessed with ratios that employ these liquid assets.
(c) Both (a) and (b) are true.
(d) The profitability of the firm is substantially determined by these earning assets.
(e) All the above are true.

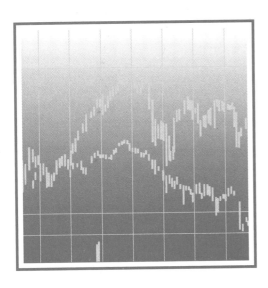

CHAPTER 10

THE DEFAULT-RISK FACTOR

An investment's total variability of return is a measure of its total risk. The sources of total risk include default risk, interest rate risk, management risk, and other factors. In this chapter, we explore default risk. The chapters that follow delve into other risk factors.[1]

---

[1] Chapter 26 is entitled Arbitrage Pricing Theory (APT). Chapters 10 and 11 lay the foundation for APT by defining risk factors, which are the building blocks of APT, and discussing each risk factor's diversifiable and undiversifiable parts.

> **DEFINITION: Default Risk**
>
> **Default risk** is that portion of an investment's total risk (or total variability of return) that results from changes in the financial strength of the investment. Default risk can also be called *financial risk* or *bankruptcy risk*.

10-1 Defining Default Risk

When a company that issues securities moves either farther away from or closer to bankruptcy, these changes in the firm's financial strength are reflected in the market prices of its securities. The variability of return that investors experience as a result of changes in the financial strength of an issuing firm is a measure of that investment's default risk.

Sources of Default Losses

Those who invest in corporate and municipal securities always face the possibility that the issuer can weaken financially, become insolvent, default on some payments, and, in the worst possible case, wind up bankrupt. But the actual bankruptcy is not the cause of catastrophic loss. Deteriorating financial ratios, falling quality ratings, and default on debt payments flash public signals for months or years before a bankruptcy is actually declared. Occasionally an act of God, such as a flood or earthquake, destroys a company's assets. If the firm has no insurance to cover the losses, a sudden and unforeseeable bankruptcy could result. But inadequate insurance is a *management risk*, not a financial risk (management risk is discussed in Chapter 19).

Most of the losses suffered by investors are caused by falling security prices, as the solvent firm that issued the securities grows weaker over a period of time. By the time actual bankruptcy occurs, the market prices of the firm's securities will have already declined to near zero, so actual bankruptcy losses are only a small part of the total losses resulting from the financial decline and default.

It is the possibility of default, rather than the actual bankruptcy, that causes most investor losses. Chrysler Corporation, the large automobile manufacturer, is a good example. It nearly went bankrupt in 1980, then was reborn with the help of massive loans. This interesting and well-documented case is reviewed here and referred to again in later chapters.

Warning Signs

As is the case in most defaults, Chrysler displayed some obvious warning signs before it hit bottom in late 1980. The case table shows that the firm's earnings, bond quality ratings, and security prices deteriorated precipitously from 1979 to 1980. Chrysler's board of directors voted to discontinue its already slashed common stock cash dividend in mid-1979. Preferred stock cash dividends were also canceled. Its bonds

CASE

Chrysler on the Precipice

Between 1979 and 1985, Chrysler slid rapidly toward bankruptcy, and then bounced back. It was able to avoid hitting bottom only because of a $1.5 billion federal loan authorized by Congress in 1980. This very unusual loan was made for two reasons: (1) Chrysler was a major U.S. defense contractor; the company had a subsidiary that manufactured tanks (later sold to raise cash). (2) The firm provided employment for thousands of U.S. citizens. On the strength of this highly publicized loan, the company was able to raise another $2 billion from private sources and so survive.

The accompanying table documents Chrysler's financial deterioration and the ensuing losses to investors. It lists quarterly bond ratings, bond prices, stock prices, quarterly earnings (or losses) per share, and cash dividend data for the years 1979 to 1985.

Historical Financial Data Documenting Chrysler Corporation's Near Bankruptcy and Recovery, 1979–1985

Date	Bond rating	Bond price	Bonds' yield-to-maturity	Common stock price	Quarterly earnings (loss) per share	Quarterly cash dividend
March 1979	BBB	$75⅛	12.50%	$10¼	$(0.95)	$0.10
June	BB	69½	13.62	9⅛	(3.31)	0.10
September	B	63½	15.00	8⅜	(7.15)	0
December	B	51½	18.49	6¾	(5.77)	0
March 1980	B	50⅛	19.03	6⅛	(6.84)	0
June	B	45½	20.91	6¾	(8.13)	0
September	B	49⅝	19.33	9⅛	(7.42)	0
December	B	43	22.18	4⅞	(3.61)	0
March 1981	CCC	41½	23	6¾	(4.56)	0
June	CCC	45⅞	21.04	6⅝	.06	0
September	CCC	44⅛	21.89	4⅝	(2.14)	0
December	CCC	40⅞	23.58	3⅜	(0.54)	0
March 1982	CCC	39⅜	24.50	4⅞	(1.31)	0
June	CCC	45	21.77	6⅞	1.30	0
September	CCC	55⅜	17.85	8¾	(.23)	0
December	CCC	58¾	16.98	17¾	(1.04)	0
March 1983	CCC	74	13.26	17	1.03	0
June	B	76	12.89	32	1.28	0
September	B	72⅝	13.66	29½	0.34	0
December	B	75	13.20	27⅝	1.64	0
March 1984	B	74½	13.36	25⅜	3.08	0.15
June	BB	69½	14.57	25	3.62	0.15
September	BB	72¼	13.99	30½	0.97	0.20
December	BBB	78	12.78	32	4.08	0.25
March 1985	BBB	80½	12.31	33⅜	4.10	0.25

were downgraded from BBB to BB in May 1979 and then further downgraded to B in August of the same year. The company's losses took on alarming proportions in 1979 to 1980, and its name was in the newspaper headlines around the world.[2]

The way that Chrysler's stock and bond prices collapsed month by month is instructive. The common stocks' price decline from over $20 per share in 1977 to less than $4 in 1981 indicates investors were aware of the firm's weakening condition for some time before it arrived at the brink of financial disaster. The continued excess of sellers over buyers caused the steadily declining security prices. The 3 years of falling stock and bond prices that preceded the financial low point when Chrysler obtained the $1.5 billion federal loan are an example of how *most losses from default risk precede a bankruptcy*. Only the most naive investors could have been surprised by Chrysler's need for drastic financial aid in 1980.

Upside and Downside

Of possible outcomes, the **downside risk** is the worst possible outcome—that everything is lost, and the rate of return is −100 percent. The **upside** refers to the best possible outcome. The stock price data for the Chrysler Corporation in the case table suggest that the upside for the Chrysler investors was that stock bought in December 1981 for $3.375 per share could be sold for $32 per share in June 1983. The $28.625 price increase equals a whopping 848 percent upside rate of return over that 17-month period.

10-2   Federal Bankruptcy Law

Since losses due to default risk occur as a firm's financial condition deteriorates in a way that increases the likelihood of bankruptcy, federal bankruptcy laws play a role in the scope of investor losses.

If a corporation fails to make a scheduled payment of interest or principal on a debt, the firm is said to be in **default** on that obligation. If payment is not made within a relatively short period, a lawsuit follows almost inevitably.

A corporation unable to meet its obligatory debt payments is said to be technically **insolvent**. If the value of a firm's assets falls below its liabilities, it is said to be insolvent in the bankruptcy sense. While details differ from case to case, the typical bankruptcy situation begins with a default on one or more legally required payments. If agreements with creditors cannot be obtained, the next step may be a filing of bankruptcy by the insolvent corporation itself. In some cases, creditors file a bankruptcy suit against the defaulting firm. Once proceedings are begun, a court decides the fate of the troubled firm.

---

[2] Steven Katz, Steven Lillien, and Bert Nelson, "Stock Market Behavior around Bankruptcy Model Distress and Recovery Predictions," *Financial Analysts Journal*, January–February 1985, pp. 70–74.

A question that arises in most bankruptcy hearings is whether the firm's assets should be liquidated at a public auction and the proceeds divided among the creditors. A **liquidation** occurs if the bankruptcy court feels the proceeds from a bankruptcy auction will exceed the amount investors will receive should the firm continue operations.

If the firm's assets are liquidated, the proceeds of the bankruptcy auction are paid out to creditors according to the following list of established **legal priorities of claimants.**

1. The attorney's fees and court costs associated with the bankruptcy proceeding are paid first.

2. If proceeds remain, back wages due to workers are paid next, up to a maximum of $2000 per worker.

3. Any remaining proceeds are used to pay back taxes owed to any federal, state, and local governments.

4. If any auction proceeds are left (and sometimes none are at this stage), creditors holding secured loans are paid. Mortgage lenders and the holders of collateralized loans made to the company would be paid.[3]

5. If any funds remain, the company's *general* (or unsecured) *creditors* are paid. Debenture bondholders and raw materials suppliers that sold to the firm on credit are in this category. It is common for general creditors to receive about 10 cents on every dollar owed them, but even this sum will not be paid unless all higher-priority claims have been paid in full.

6. Preferred stockholders are paid if any proceeds from the auction are left. Two cents on each dollar paid for preferred stock is an average liquidation receipt.

7. Common stockholders are paid last; they usually receive nothing. The law ensures that equity owners suffer the largest losses from a bankruptcy. This is fair because stockholders have a larger voice in corporate management than any other category of investor.

Reorganization

If the bankruptcy judge thinks that the value of the firm's assets employed as part of a "going concern" exceeds their liquidation value, the court may order a **reorganization** of the firm and its liabilities. At least two-thirds of the firm's creditors must

---

[3] This class of creditors typically receives only about 30 percent of the money owed to them by the bankrupt firm. The existence of collateral assets increases the likelihood of, but does not guarantee, repayment because even assets in excellent condition may bring depressed prices at auction. Or, collateral assets may be in varying stages of disrepair—they could be worn out junk, for example.

concur with the proposed reorganization. If substantial numbers of bonds are held by the public, the SEC must also approve.

Typically, creditors are given new claims on the reorganized firm, intended to be at least equal in value to the amounts that would have been received in liquidation. Holders of debentures might receive preferred stock; holders of subordinated debentures might be paid off with common stock; common stockholders might be left without any interest in the firm (that is, they lose their entire investment).

Among the goals of reorganization are fair treatment of various classes of securities and the elimination of debt obligations the troubled firm cannot possibly meet. Presumably, a plan that the troubled firm's debt and equity investors might agree upon among themselves would be considered equitable by the bankruptcy court.

Arrangements

Still another procedure is available to distressed corporations. Chapter XI of the Federal Bankruptcy Act authorizes certain corporations voluntarily to seek **arrangement** in which debts may be extended to longer maturities and/or reduced. For example, the court may order all creditors to wait 3 months for their payments. Or, the creditors might be ordered to accept 50 cents on the dollar for their claims. While Chapter XI proceedings are going on, the corporation is protected from creditor lawsuits. The troubled firm may continue to operate, but it must develop a plan for handling its debts within a few months or the creditors become eligible to propose a plan of their own. If a majority of creditors approve of a plan, the changes can be made and the firm returned to a solvent status to see if it can survive.

10-3 Quality Ratings

Quality ratings for stocks and bonds are risk measures. For example, the second column of the preceding case table lists the quality ratings of Chrysler's bonds. (Chrysler common stock's quality ratings are not included to save space, but they were highly positively correlated with the bond ratings.) Comparing the quality ratings with the other financial information about Chrysler shown in the table suggests that quality ratings gauge the likelihood that the issuer will fall into bankruptcy. Chrysler's bond ratings, for instance, dropped steadily from BBB in 1979 into the junk bond category of CCC by 1982 as the firm neared bankruptcy.

Financial services such as Standard & Poor's, Moody's, and Fitch's regularly analyze the financial situations of thousands of different corporations and assign and revise the quality ratings for their securities. The different rating agencies seldom give different ratings for the same security. If two financial services do give the same security different ratings, it is called a **split rating;** the few differences that do occur are rarely more than one rating grade level apart. Table 10-1 explains the meanings of the quality ratings that financial services like Moody's and Standard & Poor's assign to bond issues.

To assess the correlation between bond-quality ratings and actual defaults, financial analysts studied hundreds of different bond issues over several decades and

Table 10-1
Moody's and Standard & Poor's Bond Quality Ratings

Moody's	Standard & Poor's	Definition
Investment grade bonds		
Aaa	AAA	The AAA rating is the highest rating assigned to a debt instrument. It indicates extremely strong capacity to pay principal and interest. Bonds in this category are often referred to as *blue chips.*
Aa	AA	These are high-quality bonds by all standards. They are rated lower primarily because the margins of protection are not quite so strong as those of Aaa and AAA.
A	A	These bonds possess many favorable investment attributes, but there may be a susceptibility to impairment if adverse economic changes occur.
Baa	BBB	Bonds regarded as having adequate capacity to pay principal and interest are rated BBB if the bond issue lacks certain protective elements so that adverse economic conditions could lead to a weakened capacity for payment.
Speculative grade (or junk bonds)		
Ba	BB	These are bonds regarded as having minimum protection for principal and interest payments during both good and bad times. Bonds in this or any lower category are called *junk bonds* or *high-yield bonds.**
B	B	These bonds lack characteristics of other more desirable investments. Assurance of interest and principal payments over any long period of time may be very weak.
Caa	CCC	These are poor-quality issues that may be in default or in danger of default.
Ca	CC	These are highly speculative issues, often in default or possessing other marked shortcomings.
C		This is the lowest-rated class of bonds. These issues can be regarded as extremely poor in investment quality; they might go bankrupt, in Moody's opinion.
	C	Income bonds on which no interest is being paid are rated C by Standard & Poor's.
	D	A bond issue rated D by Standard & Poor's is in default, with principal and/or interest payments in arrears.

* See Box 4-3 in Chapter 4 for details about the junk bond market.

computed the percentage of firms in each quality-rating category that defaulted. Table 10-2 summarizes some of their findings; it shows that in each sample period a larger percentage of firms with low quality ratings defaulted. This strongly suggests that the quality ratings that financial services sell to subscribers do help in assessing the financial risks that can lead to default, reorganization, and bankruptcy.

Table 10-2 gives the percent of bonds with a given quality rating that defaulted each year. This single-year horizon does not reveal enough information to make long-run investment decisions. Table 10-3 shows the *default rates cumulated over a number of years* for bonds that started with a given quality rating. As the years passed, some bond issuers were downgraded (or upgraded) as their financial condition deteriorated (or improved). Some of the bond issues that were downgraded

Table 10-2

Single-Year Default Rates in Relation to the Issuers' Bond Quality Ratings, 1970–1990

	1970	1971	1972	1973	1974	1975	1976	1977	1978	1979	1980	1981	1982	1983	1984	1985	1986	1987	1988	1989	1990	Avg.
Aaa	0.0%	0.0	0.0%	0.0%	0.0%	0.0%	0.0%	0.0%	0.0%	0.0%	0.0%	0.0%	0.0%	0.0%	0.0%	0.0%	0.0%	0.0%	0.0%	0.0%	0.00%	0.00%
Aa	0.0	0.0	0.0	0.0	0.0	0.0	0.0	0.0	0.0	0.0	0.0	0.0	0.0	0.0	0.0	0.0	0.0	0.0	0.0	0.3	0.00	0.04
A	0.0	0.0	0.0	0.0	0.0	0.0	0.0	0.0	0.0	0.0	0.0	0.0	0.2	0.0	0.0	0.0	0.0	0.0	0.0	0.0	0.00	0.01
Baa	0.3	0.0	0.0	0.5	0.0	0.0	0.0	0.3	0.0	0.0	0.0	0.3	0.3	0.0	0.6	0.0	1.1	0.0	0.0	0.0	0.00	0.17
Ba	8.4	1.5	0.5	0.5	0.0	1.6	1.1	0.6	1.1	0.5	0.0	0.0	2.6	1.0	0.5	2.0	1.9	2.6	1.5	2.7	3.34	1.80
B	21.6	0.0	11.8	3.4	6.9	3.0	0.0	8.8	5.3	0.0	4.4	4.1	2.2	6.0	7.3	8.7	11.6	5.3	5.7	8.6	12.93	8.08
Overall average for investment grade bonds:	0.1	0.0	0.0	0.2	0.0	0.0	0.0	0.1	0.0	0.0	0.0	0.2	0.0	0.0	0.2	0.0	0.3	0.0	0.0	0.2	0.0	0.0
Overall average for speculative grade bonds:	10.9	1.6	3.7	1.4	1.4	2.3	1.4	1.9	1.8	0.4	1.5	0.7	3.4	3.4	3.5	4.4	5.7	4.0	3.4	5.8	5.8	4.18

Source: Jerome S. Fons and Andrew E. Kimball, "Corporate Bond Defaults and Default Rates," *The Journal of Fixed Income,* vol. 1, no. 1, June 1991, table 3, p. 44.

Table 10-3

Cumulative Default Rates for Issuers with Various Bond Quality Ratings, 1970–1990

	___ Year ___																			
	1	2	3	4	5	6	7	8	9	10	11	12	13	14	15	16	17	18	19	20
Aaa	0.0%	0.0	0.0%	0.1%	0.2%	0.3%	0.5%	0.6%	0.8%	1.0%	1.3%	1.6%	1.9%	2.3%	2.8%	3.4%	3.8%	4.2%	4.2%	4.2%
Aa	0.0	0.1	0.2	0.4	0.6	0.9	1.1	1.2	1.4	1.4	1.5	1.6	1.7	2.0	2.0	2.0	2.2	2.5	2.9	3.6
A	0.0	0.1	0.3	0.5	0.6	0.8	1.0	1.3	1.5	1.8	2.2	2.5	2.9	3.1	3.3	3.5	3.8	4.1	4.3	4.3
Baa	0.2	0.5	1.0	1.4	1.8	2.3	2.8	3.4	3.9	4.4	4.9	5.5	5.9	6.5	7.2	7.9	8.6	9.3	9.9	10.6
Ba	1.8	4.2	6.3	8.3	10.2	11.7	12.8	13.9	15.1	16.1	17.0	17.9	18.8	19.5	20.1	20.7	21.4	21.7	21.8	22.0
B	8.1	13.7	18.3	21.7	24.3	26.8	28.7	30.5	31.2	31.6	32.1	32.5	33.2	33.4	33.7	34.0	34.0	34.0	34.0	34.0
Overall average for investment grade bonds:	0.1	0.2	0.5	0.7	1.0	1.3	1.6	1.9	2.3	2.6	3.0	3.4	3.8	4.2	4.6	5.1	5.5	6.0	6.5	6.8
Overall average for speculative grade bonds:	4.2	7.7	10.6	12.9	15.0	16.8	18.1	19.2	20.3	21.2	22.0	22.8	23.7	24.2	24.8	25.3	25.8	26.0	26.1	26.3

Source: Jerome S. Fons and Andrew E. Kimball, "Corporate Bond Defaults and Default Rates," *The Journal of Fixed Income,* vol. 1, no. 1, June 1991, table 5, p. 44.

defaulted. About half the companies whose bond issues defaulted were able to avert bankruptcy and return to profitable operations, or were acquired by a "white knight" corporation that financed their recovery. Table 10-3 shows the cumulative default rates that resulted for investments ranging from 1 to 20 years. The lower long-term cumulative default rates for bonds that started with high quality ratings is evidence that few of these bonds deteriorated badly. However, the difference between the 1-year default rates in Table 10-2 and the cumulative default rates in Table 10-3 provides powerful evidence that investors' work is not finished when they select an investment—it is essential to reexamine investments continuously.

10-4 The Determinants of Ratings

The default-risk assessment and quality rating assigned to an issue are primarily determined by three factors.

- The issuer's ability to pay
- The strength of the security owner's claim
- The economic significance and size of the issuer

Ratio Analysis of Ability to Pay

Financial analysts use ratio analysis to analyze the present and forecasted earning power of the issuing corporation. As we saw in Chapter 9, ratio analysis of the issuer's financial statements yields insights about the strengths and weaknesses of the firm.

Ratio Analysis and Bond Ratings Bond rating agencies have written guidelines about what values each ratio should have within a particular quality rating. Box 10-2 shows some of the numerical guidelines that Standard & Poor's uses in rating bonds.

Different ratios are favored by individual bond analysts and rating agencies, and for any given set of ratios, different values are appropriate for each industry. Also, don't forget that the values of every firm's ratios vary in a cyclical fashion through the ups and downs of the business cycle.

Financial Analysis and Common Stock Ratings For common stocks, the usual measure of funds available to pay investors is earnings per share. The amount of funds "required" for common stock is the amount of cash dividends generally expected by investors. When a company has paid a certain level of cash dividends per share in the past, that amount influences the expected amount. If the trend has been upward, the usual expectation is that it will continue upward. Security analysts often extrapolate historical earnings per share to determine the expected amount. Dividends per share are usually forecasted to be some percentage of earnings per share, and these estimated amounts are considered the amounts required to fulfill common stock

Box 10-2

┌───┐

FINANCIAL: Average Financial Ratios for Each Bond Quality Rating

In explaining how it rates industrial bonds, Standard & Poor's (S&P) makes the following statement:

> Of all the financial ratios and measures that have been discussed, the ones that usually carry the most weight in rating determinations are pretax fixed-charge coverage, cash flow to long-term debt, pretax return on total capital invested, and long-term debt to capitalization. The accompanying table provides 5-year average values of those financial measures for a representative sample of industrial companies with long-term debt ratings in each of the rating categories . . .*

* *Standard & Poor's Rating Guide* (New York: McGraw-Hill, 1979), p. 42.

Average Relationships Between Ratios and Bond Ratings

Rating category	Pretax fixed-charge coverage, Eq. (9-12)	Cashflow to long-term debt, Eq. (9-13)	Pretax return on long-term capital, Eq. (9-22)	Long-term debt to capitalization, Eq. (9-17)
AAA	7.48 times	309.0%	25.6%	8.9%
AA	4.43	118.4	22.0	18.9
A	2.93	75.4	18.0	24.5
BBB	2.30	45.7	12.1	31.5
BB	2.04	27.0	13.8	45.5
B	1.51	18.9	12.0	52.0
CCC	0.75	15.1	2.7	69.3

Note: Equation numbers refer to financial ratios in Chapter 9.

Source: Standard & Poor's, *Debt Rating Criteria,* 1986, Standard & Poor's, New York; p. 51.

└───┘

investors' expectations. The greater the confidence of the analyst that these estimates will be realized in the future, the lower the risk level of the stock. (Common stock analysis is covered more fully in Chapters 13 and 14.)

The Strength of the Requirement to Pay

The laws requiring debtors to pay their bills can be modified by bond indenture contracts.

Indenture Provisions The bond owners' rights are spelled out in the legal instrument called the **indenture,** as explained in Chapters 2 and 6. The provisions spelled out in the indenture can raise an issue's quality rating as much as one or two grades if a strong issuer grants liberal protective provisions. In spite of the importance of these provisions, however, they are less significant than earning power. All the liberal protective provisions in the world won't get a high quality rating for a firm that faces a future of continuing losses.

The bond issuer commonly provides the following types of *protective provisions* to ensure the safety of the bondholder's investment:

- The issuer pledges specific assets as collateral.

- The issuer subordinates other legal claims on its assets or income.

- The issuer provides for a sinking fund with which to pay off the bonds even if the issuer goes bankrupt.

- The issuing firm's management promises to operate the firm in ways that protect the bondholders.

These four provisions are considered in more detail below.

Collateral: A paragraph in a bond indenture which specifies that certain assets of the issuing company become the property of the bond investors if the issuer defaults on the interest or principal payments of the bond issue is called a **collateral provision.** Many bond issues have no collateral provision, but those that do are rated somewhat higher (all other factors being equal).

Debentures are bonds that have no assets pledged as collateral. If the issuer goes bankrupt, debenture owners will find themselves placed in the undesirable category of *general creditors* by the bankruptcy court. If they want a collateral provision, investors can buy mortgage bonds. In bankruptcy, mortgage bonds have a priority claim on the specific asset pledged as collateral (for example, a new factory that the proceeds of the bond issue financed).

Bondholders don't get a collateral provision for nothing. If the issuer is not financially strong, a collateral provision increases the price per bond and lowers the interest rate. By buying collateralized bonds, the investor gives up some return in order to get a safer investment—this is a risk-return tradeoff.

The marketability and the market value of the collateral affect how much a collateral provision will raise the bond issue's quality rating. A fleet of old, broken-down trucks that has no significant market value will not impress the bond raters, for example.

Subordination: In order to make safety-conscious investors more willing to buy bonds, issuers can include clauses in the indenture that subordinate certain claims or assets. A **subordination clause** places specified bond issues or creditors in an inferior or secondary legal position with respect to the assets if the issuer defaults on the interest or principal payments.

The **after-acquired property clause** is an example. Such a clause states that if an issuer acquires additional assets after a first mortgage bond (or other type of collateralized bond) is outstanding, these new assets will automatically become part of this first mortgage bond's collateral. In effect, this clause subordinates the claim of any later mortgage bond buyers to the first mortgage bondholders' claim: first mortgage bondholders can claim their old assets and all the newer assets as collateral.

Another fairly common subordination is called the **dividend test clause.** This clause limits the claim of the common stockholders (who essentially run the corporation through their voting power at annual stockholders' meetings) on corporate profits. Profits may be used to pay cash dividends to stockholders or to pay interest to bondholders. The dividend test clause specifies that the issuer cannot pay annual cash dividends in excess of annual earnings. It helps ensure that if the firm suffers losses, its borrowing power and liquid assets will be retained to pay bondholders rather than used to pay cash dividends to common stockholders. Several other similar clauses subordinate maximization of common stockholders' profit to bondholders' safety.

Sinking funds: A **sinking fund provision** also subordinates the common stockholders' interest in maximizing corporate profits to the bondholders' desire for safety. As explained in Chapter 2, a sinking fund is a pool of money into which the bond issuer is required to make annual payments. The *indenture* stipulates that these deposits be held by a third party and be used solely to repurchase the bonds at some future date. Sinking funds are often collected at a bank that holds them in an escrow account, which is an account legally earmarked for a specific use. The sinking fund guarantees that the money needed to repay the bondholders' loan is being safely accumulated. This accumulation of funds does not maximize the issuer's profit, however. As a result, common stockholders who want their profits maximized typically object to granting sinking fund provisions.

A sinking fund clearly provides increased safety for bondholders. After a number of years' annual payments have been accumulated in the sinking fund, the rating agencies may acknowledge the protection provided by raising the issue's quality rating. An improved quality rating will increase the bond's market price and benefit the bondholders. Furthermore, well-funded sinking funds may provide *price supports* for their bonds. If the sinking fund has a policy of repurchasing bonds in the market when market prices fall sufficiently, this price support keeps prices from falling below that level. Sinking funds can also work to the detriment of bondholders, however, in two significant respects. First, some sinking fund provisions specify that bonds may be redeemed at stipulated dates before the issue matures. An investor may have gone to the trouble of evaluating a bond issue and purchasing a bond at what is considered to be an attractive yield-to-maturity, only to lose the investment to a sinking fund prematurity-date purchase. Such purchases are most likely to occur when interest rates are low and the investor has no good reinvestment alternative. Second, issues with sinking funds pay lower yields because they offer bondholders greater safety, another example of the risk-return tradeoff.

Other protective provisions: Some indenture contracts forbid the issuer to sell off some of its assets and then lease them back. Cash-hungry managements sometimes enter such **sale-and-leaseback** agreements to free capital invested in plant and equipment so that it can be spent for other purposes. Meanwhile, the use of the asset is assured because the corporation that sold the asset contracts to lease it back as part of the sales agreement. Bondholders want provisions against sale-and-leasebacks because they deplete the issuer's collateral assets—a leased asset provides no collateral.

Debt test clauses are common in issues of junk (or high-yield, or speculative-grade) bonds. Such provisions limit the issuer's ability to create additional debt and thereby protect bondholders in two ways. First, they limit the issuer's ability to undertake rapid expansion, which is usually risky. Second, if the issuer should go bankrupt, such clauses limit the number of creditors that must quarrel over the remaining assets.

Negative pledge clauses limit the issuer's ability to pledge assets as collateral in any future borrowings. This protects existing bondholders from later issues of collateralized bonds that might have prior claims in bankruptcy.

Prohibitions against the sale of subsidiary corporations are common. Such provisions allow the issuer to sell major subsidiaries only if it immediately repays the previously outstanding debt. This protects bondholders from losing important sources of income or collateral assets that the issuer owns through its subsidiaries.

There are an almost unlimited number of provisions that can be inserted in an indenture. Investment bankers eager to collect fees for floating a bond issue may encumber an issuing corporation almost to the point of paralysis with indenture provisions designed to make the bonds easier to sell. Potential investors should remember that every protective provision also probably reduces the rate of return they can expect to earn—this is the risk-return tradeoff again.

The Requirement to Pay Cash Dividends   A bond issuer is required by law to have an indenture contract that specifies specific payments on particular dates. In contrast, common stockholders enjoy no legal promise that they will receive cash dividends, and the consequences to the company of nonpayment of dividends are much less severe.

The strength of the requirement to pay cash dividends is determined by an unwritten understanding between the issuing corporation and its investors. If a corporation has paid cash dividends in the past because it had no highly profitable growth opportunities that it wanted to finance with retained earnings (most public utilities are this way, for example), it will attract a **clientele** of investors that want and expect regular cash dividend payments but little in the way of capital appreciation. Failure to pay this clientele the cash dividends they expect will be met with loud investor protests, an increase in investors selling the stock, and lowered stock prices. In contrast, growth firms attract a clientele of more aggressive investors that are willing to do without cash dividends, but that expect large capital gains.

The Economic Significance and Size of the Issuer

Bond raters and other financial analysts must consider more than a company's financial ratios and the provisions in its indenture. The competition, the firm's size, its importance in its industry, and many related factors must also be evaluated before assigning a quality rating or making an investment. This evaluation should start with the firm's industry.

The Issuer's Industry   To discern important facts about the industry within which a bond issuer operates, Standard & Poor's bond analysts study the seven points below:

1. *Position in the economy:* Is the firm in the capital-goods sector (such as machinery production), the consumer-durables sector (such as automobile production), or the consumer-nondurables sector (such as food processing)?

2. *Life cycle of the industry:* Is the industry in a growth, stable, or declining phase? (See Figure 13-3 for more information about industry life cycles.)

3. *Competitive nature:* What is the nature and intensity of the competition in the industry? Is the competition on a regional, national, or international basis? Is it based on price, quality of product, distribution capabilities, image, or some other factor? Is the industry regulated (as in broadcasting), which provides some competitive protection?

4. *Labor situation:* Is the industry unionized? If so, are labor contracts negotiated on an industrywide basis, and what is the recent negotiating history?

5. *Supply factors:* Does the industry generally have good control of key raw materials, or is there a dependence on questionable foreign sources?

6. *Volatility:* Is there an involvement with rapidly developing or changing technologies (such as computer software)? Is there a dependence on a relatively small number of major contracts (as is sometimes the case in the defense industry)?

7. *Major vulnerabilities:* Is the industry likely to be a prime target for some form of political pressure? Are substantial environmental expenditures likely to be mandated? Are near-term energy shortages possible? What is the ease of entry into the industry?

Answers to these questions inform the bond analyst about the industry's growth potential, problems that may plague the industry, and the stability of the industry's sales. The analysis can then move on to a closer consideration of the issuer's competitive situation within its industry.

Competitors   The key questions bond raters at S&P consider when evaluating the competition are listed below. The cost of the research can be limited by inquiring only into how the competition affects the bond issuer.

1. *Market share:* Does any company have a large enough portion of the market share (regional, national, or international) to influence industry dynamics significantly? Does the company have the opportunity to exercise price leadership? Does the company offer a full range of products or have proprietary products or a special niche in the market?

2. *Technological leadership:* Is the company usually among the first with new developments, or is it typically a follower? How do research and development expenditures compare with the industry average?

3. *Production efficiency:* Is the company a relatively low-cost producer? Are its facilities newer or more advanced than the average? Is it more or less vertically integrated than the average? If there are mandated expenditures (such as pollution control), has the company already complied to a greater or lesser extent than its competitors? Does the company face a more onerous labor situation than its competitors?

4. *Financial structure:* How does a company's use of leverage and various types of financing vehicles compare with that of others in the industry?

After the bond raters have answered these questions to their satisfaction, they are ready to make a decision. Corporations with strong competitive power in the marketplace experience less risk of default. Their securities should therefore enjoy quality ratings superior to those of weaker competitors, if all other factors are equal.

10-5 Default Risk and the Required Rate of Return

It would seem that investors should require issuers of high-risk securities to pay higher rates of return than issuers of low-risk securities; otherwise, why should investors assume the greater risk of default or even bankruptcy?

Table 10-4 shows average bond yields during the periods 1955 to 1967, 1968 to 1979, and 1980 to 1990. Risk avoidance is apparent. The statistics show that market yields increase with the level of default risk. Low-quality bonds must pay higher yields in the marketplace every day in order to attract risk-averse investors. Here again, the *risk-return relationship* seems to be determining yields—and therefore prices.

Figure 10-1 shows the relationship between risk and corporate bond yields at different times. Corporate bonds yield progressively higher interest rates as their quality ratings deteriorate. These market yields represent the **required rate of return** investors demand at each level of risk.

As we will see in Chapter 11, bond prices vary inversely with interest rates mathematically. As a result, a bond's quality rating directly affects its price, because the rating affects the bond's risk-adjusted interest rates. Federal Reserve Board policy, fiscal policy, the supply of and demand for lendable funds, and other factors that change continuously cause the relationship between discount rate and bond ratings to shift minute by minute every day. But investors always require higher rates of return to induce them to buy higher-risk bonds.

The tradeoff between the default risk that investors undertake and the rate of return they require is not limited to bonds. Stock investors are also risk-averse. As a

Table 10-4
Average Yields-to-Maturity for Different
Categories of Bonds over Various Sample Periods

Bond index	1955–1967 yield	1968–1979 yield	1980–1990 yield	March 1992 yield
Long-term Treasury bonds	3.88%	7.01%	10.41%	8.01%
AAA corporate bonds	4.25	7.88	10.87	8.30
AA corporate bonds	4.36	8.12	11.23	8.52
A corporate bonds	4.52	8.34	11.56	8.86
BBB corporate bonds	4.97	8.90	12.26	9.20

Source: Author's averages of data from *Standard & Poor's Trade and Securities Statistics,* 1992, Standard & Poor's, New York, N.Y.

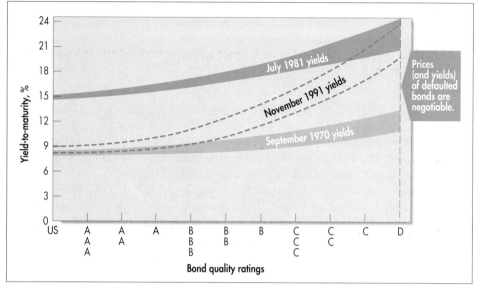

Figure 10-1   The risk structure of bond yields on September 1970, July 1981, and November 1991.

result, common stocks must, on average, pay higher rates of return than bonds because in a bankruptcy, common stockholders have only a residual claim against whatever assets (if any) the business has left over after all higher-priority debts (namely, bonds) are paid.

10-6   Undiversifiable and Diversifiable Default Risk

Although default risk is always present, the probability of default is increased under certain conditions. For instance, when the Federal Reserve tightens credit conditions and pushes up the level of market interest rates, this increases the likelihood that financially weak firms cannot borrow money. As a result, such firms may become insolvent and default. When a recession slows the flow of purchases, firms that are already on the brink of insolvency may fall into default. Tight credit conditions and a business recession are examples of forces that affect most firms simultaneously and systematically push them toward default. These systematic influences increase **undiversifiable default risk.**

In order to distinguish between undiversifiable and **diversifiable default risk,** consider a hypothetical situation. Suppose that a multimillionaire named Alicia Starwood borrowed heavily to build a luxurious hotel and gambling casino that she named Starwood Palace. If Starwood Palace went bankrupt because it could not pay off its excessively high debts during a period of time when all the other gambling casinos in the area were prospering, this would be an example of diversifiable default risk. It is unique to the company and not correlated with systematic economic forces. As a result, common stock in Starwood Palace could be placed in a highly diversified portfolio of stocks, and its unsystematic risk would be almost entirely averaged away to zero because it was idiosyncratic (or uncorrelated).

The

Wise investors choose assets that have both diversifiable and undiversifiable default-risk components only if they are paid an average rate of return enough above the return from a default-free investment (such as a T-bill) to compensate for exposure to the risk. The amount by which a risky interest rate exceeds the riskless T-bill rate is called the **risk premium.**

Summary

In investing, price and risk are related: the greater the risk, the lower the price and the greater the return. An investment's total risk has several sources, among which is default risk, the portion of total risk that results from changes in the financial strength of the investment. Most investment losses from default risk come long before bankruptcy, which is like the last act of the opera: market prices of its securities will go down steadily as the firm declines and be at the bottom when bankruptcy actually occurs. When a troubled firm defaults on one or more of its claims, investors worry that the firm will eventually go bankrupt, and the mere prospect is often enough to drive down market prices of securities.

U.S. bankruptcy laws encourage risk-averse behavior by stipulating a priority of claims that usually results in common stockholders losing everything if the firm in which they are invested goes bankrupt.

One gauge of default risk is the quality rating given a firm's stocks and bonds by financial service companies like Standard & Poor's and Moody's, which analyze thousands of different corporations on a regular basis and assign quality ratings to their securities. Changes in these quality ratings can be a signal of financial trouble, and a series of changes can document a firm's rise or fall. Quality ratings are determined primarily by three factors: (1) the issuer's ability to pay, (2) the strength of the security owner's claim, (3) the economic significance and size of the issuer.

Although every investment carries default risk, some of this risk is systematic—outside the firm's control—and some is idiosyncratic to that firm. When they choose assets with both diversifiable and undiversifiable default risk, wise investors demand a risk premium—an average rate of return above the risk-free or default-free rate.

Financial assets with high quality ratings usually pay fairly steady, positive rates of return. These low-risk assets tend to have low average rates of return because risk-averse investors are willing to accept low returns to avoid the higher default risks associated with securities that have low quality ratings.

But be forewarned: the default-risk and return tradeoff does not mean that buying financially risky investments automatically results in higher returns. Prudent investors should assess their ability to absorb losses before investing, and a thorough investigation should precede every investment. A risky investment should be made only if the security shows reasonable promise of paying a high enough rate of return to compensate the investor for the inherent dangers.

Further Reading

Altman, Edward I., *Corporate Financial Distress* (New York: Wiley, 1983).
This book explores the causes, effects, and results of bankruptcy. Mathematical statistics are used.

Cottle, Sidney, Roger F. Murray, and Frank E. Block, _Security Analysis,_ 5th ed. (New York: McGraw-Hill, 1988).

> _This classic book presents a nonmathematical approach that applies economic theory and intuition to realistic security analysis situations._

Foster, George, _Financial Statement Analysis,_ 2d ed. (Englewood Cliffs, N.J.: Prentice-Hall, 1986).

> _This book uses mathematical statistics and accounting statements to show how to analyze firms' default risk._

Ibbotson Associates, _Stocks, Bonds, Bills and Inflation: 1989 Yearbook,_ (Chicago: Capital Market Research Center, 1989).

> _This empirical study of the returns from investing in stocks and bonds uses only simple statistical tools to measure default-risk premiums and other risk premiums._

Standard & Poor's Rating Guide (New York: McGraw-Hill, 1979).

> _Written by Standard & Poor's employees, this nonmathematical book is rich with examples and guidelines from experienced financial analysts._

Questions and Problems

Essay Questions

10-1   Define "default risk." Does default risk occur before, when, or after a corporation is declared bankrupt? Explain.

10-2   Compare and contrast an insolvent firm, a defaulted firm, and a bankrupt firm. How does the default of securities relate to bankruptcy? Do any of the categories of firms have any chance for recovery?

10-3   What are the differences between the implications for the investor of bankruptcy and reorganization? If a firm in which you own securities goes into bankruptcy court, would your losses likely be affected if the firm were to be reorganized by the bankruptcy court?

10-4   Are there some instances when it would be impossible for anyone to foresee that a corporation is going to go bankrupt? How? If advance warnings exist, explain what they are and how they can be detected.

10-5   If bond rating agencies raise the rating of a bond issue from Baa or BBB to A, what effect will this probably have on the stock and bond prices of the firm? Explain.

10-6   Suppose you learn that a medical research group at a university is about to publish a research report concluding that cigarette smoking is definitely a cause of lung cancer and heart disease. The researchers are highly reputable, and their findings are well supported by clinical studies. As an investor how would you react if you knew this study were forthcoming? Why?

10-7   Is the variability of return that results from changes in security _investors' expectations_ about an issuer's financial abilities the same kind of risk as that caused by the _actual public announcements_ of changes in the issuer's financial abilities? Explain.

Problems

10-8   Reconsider the case of the Chrysler common stock investor's upside and downside risks. Use the raw data from the table and the same December 1981 buying and June 1983 selling dates cited at the end of section 10-1. Prepare your subjective estimate of the probability distribution that the Chrysler investor faced over the 17-month holding period. Let the expected rate of return be $E(r) = 374$ percent and let it have a probability of 8/20. The worst possible rate of return is -100 percent; let it have a probability of 1/20. The best possible return is 848 percent; let it occur with a 1/20 probability. Select two other rates of return that each have a probability of 5/20 and are equally far above and below the expected rate of return (so the probability distribution is symmetrical). Calculate the expected rate of return and the standard deviation of returns from these five rates of return. Sketch an illustration of what your risk and return statistics suggest that the probability distribution looks like. (*Hint*: Consult Chapter 1.)

10-9 Consider the financial data in the accompanying table, documenting the 1975 bankruptcy of a major retailer named the W. T. Grant Corporation. Use the financial ratio information from Chapter 9 to calculate a profitability ratio, a turnover ratio, a liquidity ratio, and a financial-leverage ratio every year for the years 1972, 1973, 1974, and 1975. (As explained in Chapter 8, the financial data for these ratios can be found in old S&P, Moody's, and other manuals at a business library.) From the 4 years of historical financial ratios you calculated, how far in advance can you tell that W. T. Grant was going bankrupt? Explain what signs give you advance warning.

The W. T. Grant Bankruptcy

Date	Standard & Poor's bond rating	Bonds' price per $100 of face value	Bonds' yield-to-maturity	Common stock price	Quarterly earnings per share	Quarterly cash dividend
1973:						
January	BBB	$80.125	6.88%	$39.00		
February	BBB	79.00	7.15	31.50	$ 2.70	$0.375
March	BBB	78.15	7.27	27.375		
April	BBB	76.875	7.44	22.375		
May	BBB	77.75	7.37	17.25	2.40	0.375
June	BBB	78.00	7.34	17.375		
July	BBB	69.875	8.57	19.00		
August	BBB	65.125	9.39	18.75	2.41	0.375
September	BBB	70.00	8.58	21.25		
October	BBB	74.125	7.95	18.75		
November	BBB	75.375	7.78	12.50	1.90	0.375
December	BB	65.00	9.49	10.875		
1974:						
January	BB	65.00	9.51	11.375		
February	BB	64.00	9.70	9.00	0.59	0.15
March	BB	61.00	10.31	7.625		
April	BB	61.125	10.32	7.25		
May	BB	51.00	12.62	6.625	0.50	0.15
June	BB	51.00	12.65	5.25		
July	B	50.875	12.72	4.625		
August	B	30.00	20.57	3.25	0.08	0
September	B	28.125	21.48	3.00		
October	B	31.125	20.07	2.625		
November	B	28.25	21.77	2.50	(0.47)*	0
December	CCC	23.00	25.67	1.875		

* Parentheses signify losses.

Date	Standard & Poor's bond rating	Bonds' price per $100 of face value	Bonds' yield-to-maturity	Common stock price	Quarterly earnings per share	Quarterly cash dividend
1975:						
January	CCC	28.00	22.07	2.375		
February	CCC	27.125	22.71	3.375	(0.47)*	0
March	CCC	32.50	19.67	5.00		
April	CCC	31.50	20.26	4.875		
May	CCC	35.00	18.61	4.125	(15.71)*	0
June	CCC	41.00	16.23	4.125		
July	CCC	39.00	17.05	4.00		
August	CCC	36.00	18.36	3.50	(19.06)*	0
September	CC	25.00	24.50	2.89		
October	C	15.00	Bankruptcy declared			

* Parentheses signify losses.

Source: Standard & Poor's *Bond Guide,* published monthly 1973–1975; *ISL Daily Stock Price Manuals.*

10-10 Some large organizations that either passed into bankruptcy or nearly became bankrupt in recent years are Penn Central Transportation in 1970, New York City in 1976, the Chrysler Corporation in 1980, International Harvester in 1984, LTV in 1986, and Pan Am Airways in 1991.

Select one of these organizations and gather financial data on it for the 4 years preceding the time of its financial difficulty. How far in advance can you foresee the financial difficulty? What signs suggest that the organization was in trouble? Did most of the losses to investors from these financially risky investments occur before, during, or after the bankruptcy declaration? Consult S&P and Moody's manuals for raw financial data and ratios.

10-11 The (hypothetical) Apex Tobacco Corporation has produced and sold snuff and chewing tobacco for over 100 years. Both products have fallen in popularity, and declines in sales and rising production costs resulted in a large deficit at the end of 19X8. Apex's balance sheet tells the story.

Apex Tobacco
Balance Sheet, December 31, 19X8
(in thousands of dollars)

Current assets	$375	Current liabilities	$450
Fixed assets	375	Long-term debt (unsecured)	225
		Capital stock	150
		Retained earnings (deficit)	(75)
Total assets	$750	Total claims	$750

**Selected Financial Data:
19X5–19X8**

Year	Sales	Net profit after tax before fixed charges
19X5	$2625	$ 262.5
19X6	2400	225.0
19X7	1425	(75.0)
19X8	1350	(112.5)

External appraisers suggested that the company would have a liquidation value of about $600,000. Management concluded that, as an alternative, a reorganization was possible with an additional investment of $300,000. Management was confident that the firm could undertake the manufacture of new smoking products, such as long, slim cigars for women, cigarette papers of varying colors for the growing roll-your-own market, Turkish water pipes, and stylish small pipes for customers who wish to smoke less than the normal full bowl. Outside consultants concluded that this broadened product line could be produced and marketed readily through Apex's existing marketing channels and concurred that a new investment of $300,000 was needed. However, these consultants also forecast that the additional investment would restore earnings to $125,000 a year after taxes and before fixed charges. Apex's common stock sells at about 8 times its earnings per share. Management is negotiating with a local investment group to obtain the additional investment of $300,000. If the funds are obtained, the holders of the long-term debt would be given half the common stock in the reorganized firm in place of their present claims.

Should the creditors agree to the reorganization, or should they force liquidation of the firm?

Multiple Choice Questions

10-12   When do the losses from default risk occur?

(*a*) Before the default
(*b*) Concurrently with the default
(*c*) After the default
(*d*) Both (*a*) and (*b*)
(*e*) All the above

E

10-13   How do the market prices of corporations that are involved in bankruptcy proceedings behave?

(*a*) The price of the firm's stock typically collapses and loses most of its market value if and only if the bankruptcy court declares the firm bankrupt and orders a liquidating auction.
(*b*) The price of the firm's stock typically collapses and loses most of its value before the default that led to the action in the bankruptcy court because stock prices tend to anticipate future events.
(*c*) The price of the firm's stock typically will not collapse until after an unsuccessful liquidation sale is completed and it becomes obvious that the proceeds from the liquidation auction are insufficient to repay the common stockholders for their investments.
(*d*) There is no typical pattern to the way that the price of the stock of a firm involved in a bankruptcy proceeding will behave.

B

10-14   Should a business firm be declared bankrupt and have all its assets liquidated whenever its liquidation value exceeds its value as a going concern?

(*a*) Yes; that would maximize the amount of funds that the stockholders and debtors could recover from the troubled firm.

(*b*) No; the stockholders have a moral and ethical duty to place the welfare of the employees above their profit motives. Therefore, they should continue to operate the firm for as long as the firm can meet its payroll.

(*c*) Usually, but not always. Some troubled firms may have a valuable patent application pending, be on the verge of obtaining a lucrative new customer, be on the verge of announcing an advantageous merger agreement, or have other unannounced assets about which the investing public is unaware. These firms might have their operating assets liquidated, pay one huge cash dividend, and then be allowed to continue as a holding company even through the firm can no longer operate profitably.

(*d*) No, troubled firms should be given the opportunity to lobby in Congress and/or their state legislature for public aid.

10-15   According to the bankruptcy law, which of the following classes of creditors has the most junior (that is, last) claim on the cash proceeds from a corporation's liquidation auction?

(*a*) Preferred stockholders

(*b*) Bond investors

(*c*) Employees with unpaid wages

(*d*) Debenture owners

(*e*) Utility companies with unpaid bills

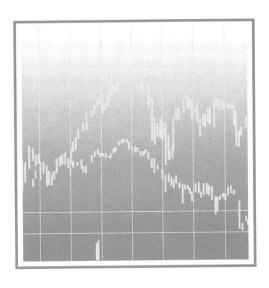

CHAPTER 11

THE INTEREST RATE
RISK FACTOR

Interest is the rent on borrowed money. The interest that borrowers pay lenders causes money to have a future value that differs from its present value. You could say that money has time value.

The present value of money fluctuates inversely with market interest rates. These fluctuations cause interest rate risk.

We begin this chapter by analyzing various aspects of the time value of money. Default risk is ignored initially so that we can focus on the time value of money. After

281

Box 11-1

> **DEFINITION: Interest Rate Risk**
>
> **Interest rate risk** is the variability of present value, or variability of the single-period rates of return, that results from fluctuations in market interest rates. Annuities, bonds, stocks, and other assets experience interest rate risk.

differentiating between the present value and the future value, the analysis turns to interest rate risk. The present and future values of securities that might default are considered at the end of this chapter.

11-1   The Time Value of Money

If the people who lent money did not charge interest, the future value and the present value would be the same. But, alas, most lenders charge interest.

The Future Value of Present Dollars

Money has time value because a dollar can be invested today and grow to be worth more than a dollar in the future. Table 11-1 shows the difference in value between a current dollar and an invested dollar received 1 year in the future. Table 11-1 was constructed with the one-period future-value-of-money equation:

$$\text{Future value} = (\text{present value})(1 + \text{interest rate}) \tag{11-1}$$

When you put a dollar in a 5 percent interest savings account at a bank for 1 year, this beginning deposit (or investment) of $1 grows to have a **future value** of $1.05.

$$\begin{aligned}\text{Future value} &= \$1(1.0 + 5\%) \\ &= \$1(1.0 + .05) = \$1(1.05) = \$1.05\end{aligned} \tag{11-1a}$$

$FV = PV(1+r_i)^t$

with t if compounded

Table 11-1
The Future Value of $1
in 1 Year

Present value	Annual interest rate	Interest on $1	Future value
$1.00	1%	$0.01	$1.01
1.00	5	0.05	1.05
1.00	10	0.10	1.10
1.00	15	0.15	1.15

If deposited money accumulates interest (or compounds) for more than one time period, a time-period exponent is added to Equation (10-1) to create Equation (10-2).

Future value = (present value)(1 + interest rate)^t (11-2)

The exponent t in Equation (11-2) gives the number of time periods the deposited money accumulates interest. For example, if you put a dollar in a 5 percent interest savings account at a bank for 2 years, this $1 deposit grows to have a future value of $1.1025, or $1.10 after rounding, after 2 years (or $t = 2$ years).

$$\text{Future value} = \$1(1.0 + 5\%)^t$$

$$= \$1(1.0 + .05)^2 = \$1(1.1025) \qquad (11\text{-}2a)$$

$$= \$1.1025$$

Figure 11-1 illustrates compounded future values of $1 over a span of years for several different interest rates.

The Present Value of Future Dollars

The time-value-of-money equation can also be used to find the **present value** of future dollar receipts. Dividing both sides of the single-period time-value-of-money equation by the quantity (1 + interest rate) results in the single-period present value model.

$$\text{Present value} = \frac{\text{future value}}{1 + \text{interest rate}} \qquad (11\text{-}3)$$

Figure 11-1   The inevitable march of compound interest.

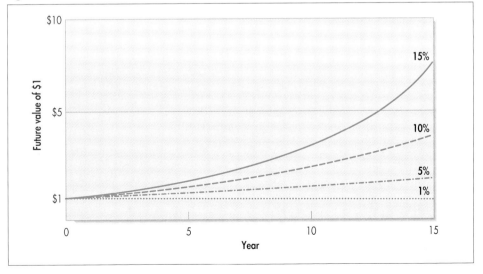

Table 11-2
Present Value of $1 Received in 1 Year

Future value in 1 year	Annual interest rate	Present value
$1.00	10%	$0.91
1.00	8	0.93
1.00	6	0.94
1.00	4	0.96

Table 11-2 was prepared using the single-period present value model, Equation (11-3). Table 11-2 shows that the present value of $1 to be received 1 year in the future is 91 cents if an interest rate or *discount rate* of 10 percent per year is used. The **discount rate** is the interest rate the investor views as being a *required rate of return* that is appropriate for the investment's riskiness. The present value of 91 cents was calculated as follows:

$$\text{Present value} = \frac{\text{future value}}{1 + \text{interest rate}}$$

$$= \frac{\$1.00}{1 + .10} = \frac{\$1.00}{1.1} = \$0.91 \tag{11-3a}$$

The multiple-period present value equation differs only slightly from the single-period present value equation, as shown below.

$$\text{Present value} = \frac{\text{future value}}{(1 + \text{interest rate})^t} \tag{11-4}$$

Table 11-3
Present Value of $1 Received
in Future Years

Number of years, t	Interest rate			
	1%	5%	10%	15%
1	$0.990	$0.952	$0.909	$0.870
2	0.980	0.907	0.826	0.756
3	0.971	0.864	0.751	0.658
4	0.961	0.823	0.683	0.572
5	0.951	0.784	0.621	0.497
8	0.923	0.677	0.467	0.327
10	0.905	0.614	0.386	0.247
15	0.861	0.481	0.239	0.123
20	0.820	0.377	0.149	0.061
25	0.780	0.295	0.092	0.030
30	0.742	0.231	0.057	0.015

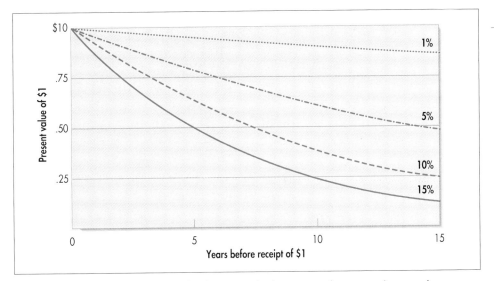

Figure 11-2 The present value of $1 decreases the longer you have to wait to get it.

As you can see, the single-period and the multiple-period present value equations differ only to the extent that the multiple-period equation has an exponent, the symbol *t*, in its denominator to account for the number of years in the future when the cashflow is to be received. For a time horizon of only 1 year (that is, when $t = 1$), the single-period and the multiple-period present value equations are identical. Table 11-3 lists the present values of a dollar that is received in different future years at various interest rates. These values are plotted in Figure 11-2. The values were calculated using the multiple-period present value model, Equation (11-4).

The present and future value computations above were all of the simplest possible type—they had only one cash inflow and one cash outflow. As explained in Chapter 2, most bonds pay a series of cashflows called *coupon interest payments.* Similarly, most pension funds pay fixed payments monthly. Next we will consider how to value these cashflow streams.

11-2   Present Value Applied to Annuity Payments

A common way to provide retirement income for yourself is to buy an annuity. An **annuity** is a contract to pay a beneficiary stipulated equal periodic amounts for a specified number of years. Most annuities are sold by life insurance companies or by large banks. A contract that promises to pay $1 per year at the end of each of the next 3 years is called a *3-year $1 annuity.* Table 11-4 shows that the present value of such an annuity would be about $2.72, assuming a 5 percent interest rate. Stated differently, in order to be able to receive a $1 per year annuity payment at the end of each of the next 3 years from a savings account paying a 5 percent rate of interest, you must put in

Table 11-4
Present Value of an Annuity of $1 per Year

Number of years, t	Interest rate			
	1%	*5%*	*10%*	*15%*
1	$ 0.990	$ 0.952	$0.909	$0.870
2	1.970	1.859	1.736	1.626
3	2.941	2.723	2.487	2.853
4	3.902	3.546	3.170	2.855
5	4.853	4.329	3.791	3.357
8	7.652	6.463	5.335	4.487
10	9.471	7.722	6.145	5.019
15	13.865	10.380	7.606	5.847
20	18.046	12.462	8.514	6.259
25	22.023	14.094	9.077	6.464
30	25.808	15.372	9.427	6.566

$2.72 to start. If a 10 percent interest rate were assumed, the annuity's present value would drop to about $2.49.[1]

To see how the present values in Table 11-4 were calculated, compare the values in each column of Table 11-4 with the sums of the values shown in the corresponding columns of Table 11-3. For example, Table 11-3 shows that the present values of $1 received 1, 2, and 3 years in the future at the 5 percent interest rate are 95.2 cents, 90.7 cents, and 86.4 cents, respectively. These three present values sum to $2.723; this is the amount shown in the 5% interest column of Table 11-4 for a 3-year annuity.

$$\text{Present value} = \frac{\$1.00}{(1.05)^1} + \frac{\$1.00}{(1.05)^2} + \frac{\$1.00}{(1.05)^3}$$

$$= \$0.952 + \$0.907 + \$0.864 = \$2.723$$

(11-5)

Present value tables like Tables 11-3 and 11-4 have been expanded to cover a larger number of interest rates and years and are published in many finance textbooks. In addition, several hand calculators and computers have built-in routines to calculate present values of annuity streams.

The Effect of Interest Rates on Present Values

As Table 11-4 makes clear, there is an *inverse relationship* between present values and interest rates. Suppose the interest rate rises from 5 percent to 10 percent. This change

---

[1] Most annuities pay nothing until the initial present value has been on deposit long enough to earn some interest income. An *annuity due* is a slightly different annuity. An annuity due makes its first payment on the same day you buy it, instead of waiting for some interest income to be earned. If everything else is equal, an annuity due is worth more (that is, has a larger present value) than an ordinary annuity because you get the cash sooner from the annuity due.

Box 11-2   287

> **PRINCIPLE: The First Present Value Principle**
>
> The present value of a cashflow varies inversely with the interest rate used as a discount rate.

would affect the present value of the 3-year annuity paying $1 per year, as shown in the following calculations:

$$\text{Present value} = \frac{\$1.00}{(1.10)^1} + \frac{\$1.00}{(1.10)^2} + \frac{\$1.00}{(1.10)^3} \qquad (11\text{-}6)$$

$$= \$0.9090 + \$0.8264 + \$0.7513 = \$2.487$$

$$PV = \frac{FV}{(1+i)}$$

This drop (of $2.723 - $2.486 = $0.237, or about 23⅔ cents) suggests that interest rates vary *inversely* with present values.

Now consider what happens when the interest rate decreases. Suppose the interest rate were to drop from 5 percent to 1 percent. The calculations below show how to compute the present value of a 3-year $1 annuity when the interest rate is 1 percent.

$$\text{Present value} = \frac{\$1.00}{(1.01)^1} + \frac{\$1.00}{(1.01)^2} + \frac{\$1.00}{(1.01)^3} \qquad (11\text{-}7)$$

$$= \$0.9901 + \$0.9803 + \$0.9706 = \$2.941$$

This present value of $2.941 is $0.218 (or about 22 cents) more than the present value calculated with the higher interest rate of 5 percent that was used before. Again, interest rates and present values are inversely related. The lower the interest rate, the higher the present value, and vice versa. This relationship gives rise to the first present value principle.

Table 11-3 provides a detailed comparison between present values and interest rates. The first present value principle can also be seen by comparing the four different curves in Figure 11-2. Select any given number of years and compare the different present values that result from using different interest rates with which to discount.

The Effect of Futurity on Present Value

The first present value principle provides the foundation for analyzing interest rate risk: it stipulates unequivocally that interest rates affect value. Additional insights into the nature of interest rate risk can be gained by noting the effect of a cashflow's time until payment, or **futurity**, on its present value. To see the effect of the futurity on an investment's cashflows, think about extending each of the three $1 annuity payments 1 year *further* into the future without changing the amount of the three annual cashflows. An example of this delayed annuity follows.

The present value of the delayed annuity paying $1 per year at the end of the second, third, and fourth years is calculated below for an interest rate of 10 percent.

$$\text{Present value} = \frac{\$0}{(1.10)^1} + \frac{\$1.00}{(1.10)^2} + \frac{\$1.00}{(1.10)^3} + \frac{\$1.00}{(1.10)^4}$$

(11-8)

$$= \$0 + \$0.8264 + \$0.7513 + \$0.6830 = \$2.261$$

If an interest rate of 5 percent is used, this delayed annuity's present value is found to be $2.594:

$$\text{Present value} = \frac{\$0}{(1.05)^1} + \frac{\$1.00}{(1.05)^2} + \frac{\$1.00}{(1.05)^3} + \frac{\$1.00}{(1.05)^4}$$

(11-9)

$$= \$0 + \$0.9070 + \$0.8638 + \$0.8227 = \$2.594$$

Finally, the delayed annuity has a discounted present value of $2.912 if an interest rate of 1 percent is used.

$$\text{Present value} = \frac{\$0}{(1.01)^1} + \frac{\$1.00}{(1.01)^2} + \frac{\$1.00}{(1.01)^3} + \frac{\$1.00}{(1.01)^4}$$

(11-10)

$$= \$0 + \$0.9803 + \$0.9706 + \$0.9610 = \$2.912$$

The 3-year $1 annuity delayed until the end of years 2, 3, and 4 pays a total cashflow of $3.00, just like the 3-year $1 annuity paid at the end of years 1, 2, and 3. Thus, the same cashflow total of $3.00 and the same interest rates are involved in both the 3-year and the delayed 3-year examples, but delaying the three $1 cashflows 1 year further into the future increased the interest rate risk of this investment in an annuity. To see how the interest rate risk increased with the futurity of the cashflows, compare the present values calculated over the 4-year span with the 1 percent and 10 percent interest rates. The difference between these present values is $2.912 − $2.261, or $0.651, for the 4-year time span. The difference between the highest and lowest present values over the shorter 3-year time span is only $2.941 − $2.487, or $0.454. The larger variability in present values that resulted from pushing the three cashflows ahead 1 year reveals how interest rate risk increases with the futurity of the investment—this principle is summarized in Box 11-3.

The information in Table 11-3 illustrates the second present value principle. It is clear that the difference between the present values of $1 received after 30 years and

Box 11-3

PRINCIPLE: The Second Present Value Principle

The interest rate risk of an investment increases with the futurity of the investment's cashflows. Stated differently, the present value of a series of cashflows varies inversely with interest rate fluctuations over a wider range as the futurity of the cashflows is increased.

discounted at 1 percent and discounted at 15 percent varies over a wider range than the present values of the dollar received at any earlier time. Figure 11-2 illustrates the same principle. The fact that the curves grow farther apart at the longer time periods in Figure 11-2 illustrates how interest rate risk increases with the futurity of the investment. Futurity is equivalent to a measure called *duration*. We will learn how to measure *duration* in Chapter 12.

The two present value principles presented above apply to stock and bond prices in the same way that they apply to the behavior of annuity contracts. The remainder of this chapter considers the interest rate risk in these other types of investments.

11-3   The Present Value of a Bond

As we noted in Chapter 2, a **bond** is a contract that requires the borrower to pay the lender (that is, the investor) interest income. Most bonds make fixed coupon payments every year until the bond matures. Bond coupons are like annuity payments. At maturity, the bond issuer must also repay the principal amount (or face value) of the bond. The market price of a bond equals its present value (Box 11-4).

Box 11-4

DEFINITION: The Present Value of a Bond

A bond's present value is

$$\frac{\text{Present}}{\text{value}} = \frac{\text{coupon}_1}{(1 + \text{YTM})^1} + \frac{\text{coupon}_2}{(1 + \text{YTM})^2} + \cdots + \frac{\text{coupon}_T + \text{face value}}{(1 + \text{YTM})^T} \qquad (11\text{-}11)$$

The three terms that appear on the right-hand side of the present value model, Equation (11-11), are explained below:

YTM: The yield-to-maturity is a market interest rate that changes constantly. Every bond has a different YTM. Many bonds' YTMs are published in daily newspapers or other market reports.*

Face value: The bond's face value (or principal) and the time when it is due to be repaid (its maturity date) are printed on the bond and cannot change throughout the bond's life.

Coupon: The coupon is the amount of interest paid each year. It is calculated by multiplying the coupon interest rate by the bond's face value.

* The YTM is the discount rate that equates the present value of all the bond's future expected cashflows with the current market price of the bond. The YTM is the compounded rate of return that will be earned if the bond is held to maturity and all cashflows are paid on time. The YTM is investigated further in Chapter 12.

A Bond with Annual Coupon Payments

Substituting the values assumed in the preceding paragraphs into the present value model, Equation (11-11), allows us to compute the value of a bond. For a hypothetical bond, assume a yield-to-maturity of YTM = 10 percent = .10, a $1000 face value that is to be repaid in 2 years (that is, $T = 2$), and a coupon rate of 6 percent. Thus the bond pays $60 (that is, $1000 \times .06$) of coupon interest at the end of each year of its life.

$$
\begin{aligned}
\frac{\text{Present}}{\text{value}} &= \frac{\text{coupon}_1}{(1 + \text{YTM})^1} + \frac{\text{coupon}_2 + \frac{\text{face}}{\text{value}}}{(1 + \text{YTM})^2} \\
&= \frac{\$60}{(1 + .10)^1} + \frac{\$60 + \$1000}{(1 + .10)^2} \\
&= \$54.545 + \$49.586 + \$826.446 = \$930.578
\end{aligned}
\tag{11-11a}
$$

The present value calculation above suggests that the bond is worth $930.58 (after rounding) if it pays coupons annually.

A Bond That Pays Semiannual Coupons

Most bonds pay their coupons every 6 months instead of only once per year. If the 6 percent coupon, $1000 bond above paid its annual coupon of $60 per year as $30 semiannually, the bond's present value would be calculated a little differently.

First, some cashflow adjustments are required. Bonds with semiannual coupons pay twice as many coupons over the life of the bond, but each coupon is only half as large as it would have been if they had been paid annually. In our example, $30 is paid semiannually instead of annual payments of $60.

The second change is that the number of time periods is counted differently. The exponents used in semiannual compounding occur at half-year intervals, and there are twice as many half-years as whole years. For example, the present value computations below in Equation (11-12) are appropriate for the 2-year bond that pays a 6 percent coupon rate, as in Equation (11-11a), if it pays its coupons semiannually instead of annually.

The third change is in the interest rate—the YTM. Since we have twice as many half-years as we do years, we must chop the interest rate in half to double the number of time periods. In our example, 10 percent per year is restated as 5 percent per 6-month time period.

$$
\begin{aligned}
\frac{\text{Present}}{\text{value}} &= \frac{\text{coupon}_1}{(1 + \text{YTM}/2)^1} + \frac{\text{coupon}_2}{(1 + \text{YTM}/2)^2} + \frac{\text{coupon}_3}{(1 + \text{YTM}/2)^3} + \frac{\text{coupon}_4 + \text{face value}}{(1 + \text{YTM}/2)^4} \\
&= \frac{\$30}{(1 + .05)^1} + \frac{\$30}{(1 + .05)^2} + \frac{\$30}{(1 + .05)^3} + \frac{\$30 + \$1000}{(1 + .05)^4} \\
&= \$30/1.05 + \$30/1.1025 + \$30/1.1576 + (\$30 + \$1000)/1.2155 \\
&= \$28.5142 + \$27.21088 + \$25.91513 + \$847.3835 \\
&= \$929.0809
\end{aligned}
\tag{11-12}
$$

One of the convenient aspects of bond valuation is that everyone in the world uses the same present value formula. Thus, everyone would agree that a 2-year bond paying a 6 percent semiannual coupon is worth $929.0809 when it is discounted at an annual interest rate of 10 percent interest.

Note that the present value of the 2-year bond paying a 6 percent coupon rate is slightly less when the coupons are discounted semiannually than when they were discounted annually. The present value is slightly less with semiannual coupon payments because the discount factors are compounded more times.[2]

The information needed to use the present value formula to value a bond is easy to obtain. The bond's principal amount, its coupon interest payments, and the dates of these cashflows are all printed on the bond, and they never change.

11-4 Default-Free U.S. Treasury Bonds

As explained in Chapter 2, U.S. Treasury bonds are default-free. However, even though they cannot go bankrupt, U.S. T-bonds nevertheless experience interest rate risk. In fact, interest rate risk is the main risk to which Treasury bonds are subject—and it can be substantial. In the past decade, for example, long-term U.S. Treasury bonds have fluctuated in price from as low as 80 percent to as high as 120 percent of their face values. This is called *price fluctuation risk*. In addition, there is *coupon-rate fluctuation risk*.

Price Fluctuation Risk

Treasury bonds are sometimes sold in denominations of $1000, but always in $5000, $10,000, $50,000, $100,000, and larger denominations. The market prices of these bonds fluctuate above and below their face values minute by minute. Their prices rarely equal their face values, except at maturity, when the principal must be repaid to the investor.

The factor that makes a $1000 Treasury bond with decades to maturity vary in price from $800 to $1200 is the changing interest rates in the bond market. The market price of a bond can be calculated to the penny by observing the current market interest rate (or yield-to-maturity) and using it to find the present value of the bond's cashflows. The **cashflows** are all known in advance. For example, a $1000 Treasury bond with a 10 percent coupon rate will pay $100 at prespecified dates each year until it matures and then repay the $1000 principal. The various present values this default-free bond may assume as its time to maturity varies from 0 to infinity are illustrated in Figure 11-3 for yields-to-maturity of 9, 10, and 11 percent. The market price of a bond will always exactly equal its present value, so these calculated values are informative.

Figure 11-3 illustrates the first present value principle. The present value of the bond is higher along the curve calculated with the 9 percent interest rate than it is

---

[2] For an enlightening discussion of this point see James T. Lindley, Billy P. Helms, and Mahmoud Haddad, "A Measurement of the Errors in Intra-period Compounding and Bond Valuation," *Financial Review*, Vol. 22, no. 1, February 1987, pp. 33–51.

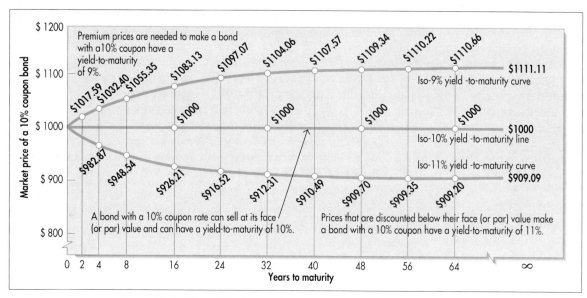

Figure 11-3 How differing market interest rates affect the market prices for a 10 percent coupon bond at various times to maturity.

along any curve that represents the same bond's present values calculated with a higher interest rate. Generally speaking, for any given time to maturity a bond's present value moves inversely with the interest rate that is used to discount the bond's cashflows.

Present value principle 2 is also relevant to Figure 11-3. The 10% Treasury bond's present values fluctuate over a much wider range at the longer maturities than at the shorter maturities. In other words, the bond has more interest rate risk as its futurity increases.

The price fluctuation risk caused by varying market interest rates is much less when the bond has only a few years to maturity. Note, for example, how the 9 percent and the 11 percent curves in Figure 11-3 come together at the bond's maturity date, when its present value and face value become the same. Figure 11-3 illustrates how buying shorter-term bonds reduces price fluctuation risk.

Coupon-Rate Risk

As we have seen, a bond investor seeking to avoid the interest rate risk arising from price fluctuations may do so by investing in short-term bonds (say, bonds with 1 year to maturity) rather than in bonds with more futurity. Then, however, another kind of interest rate risk is encountered–**coupon-rate risk.** Coupon-rate risk is also called **reinvestment rate risk.**

If an investor keeps funds invested over a number of years by buying a new 1-year bond every time another 1-year bond matures, each of these successive 1-year bonds will bear a different coupon interest rate. Bonds' coupon interest rates vary over just as wide a range as their market interest rates. Figure 11-4 indicates how

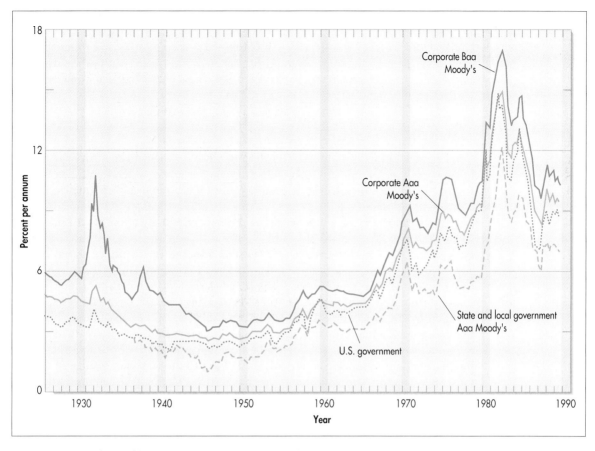

Figure 11-4 Market yields-to-maturity vary continuously.

market interest rates can vary over the years. Thus, an investor who buys only short-term bonds must buy a succession of bonds with coupon rates that vary with the market interest rates.

Coupon interest rates that fluctuate year to year (which are the source of the only cashflows from a bond before it matures) create coupon-rate risk. This risk can have hard consequences. Retired investors who depend on coupon income for household expenditures each month can suffer if this income decreases substantially. On the positive side, short-term bonds that have a lot of coupon-rate (or reinvestment rate) risk have less price fluctuations risk than bonds with longer periods to maturity.

Each investor must decide which type of interest rate risk is easier to bear—the risk arising from price fluctuations or coupon-rate risk. If bond investments can be held for years until they mature (this is how pension funds and life insurance companies invest much of their funds, for instance), then price fluctuations are not a problem. But if bond investments might have to be liquidated when market prices are low, then the risk from price fluctuations is unbearable and short-term bonds would be a more appropriate investment.

11-5   Bond Ratings and Default Risk

Unlike U.S. Treasury bonds, the bonds issued by corporations and municipalities sometimes default, and some even go bankrupt. Bond quality ratings are useful in assessing the risk of default and bankruptcy associated with particular bond issues, as we learned in Chapter 10.

Interest Rate Determinants

Bond ratings can determine a bond's discount rate (or yield-to-maturity, or market interest rate); see Figure 10-1. Regardless of whether market interest rates are high or low, all bonds are discounted at progressively higher rates as their quality ratings deteriorate (or their default risk increases). Since bond prices are determined by these discount rates, the ratings have an indirect but powerful effect on bond prices.

The nature of the relationship between the appropriate discount rate and bond ratings changes a little bit every day. Federal Reserve Board policy, fiscal policy, supply and demand for lendable funds, the rate of inflation, and other factors cause this relation to shift continuously. Figure 11-4 shows the extent to which market yields on bonds in different default-risk classes have varied in recent years. These changing credit conditions can turn bond markets into speculative markets, because the two present value principles apply to corporate and municipal bonds in exactly the same way they apply to the default-free Treasury bonds. Thus, corporate and municipal bonds that pay coupons are also subject to the same two sources of interest rate risk—coupon-rate risk and price change risk. The only difference is that the more risky corporate bonds must pay higher rates of interest than Treasuries in order to induce investors to assume their default risk. Since all interest rates tend to rise and fall together, the corporate bonds' interest rates merely fluctuate at a higher level than do the Treasury bonds (as shown in Figure 11-4).

Tax-Exempt Municipals

As explained in Chapters 2 and 7, the income tax exemption of municipal bonds greatly increases the desirability of this form of investing. As a result of this valuable tax exemption, municipal bonds' interest rates are low. Figure 11-4 shows that municipal bonds tend to have the lowest yields of all types of bonds.

Present value principles 1 and 2 also apply to municipal bonds; their tax exemption changes nothing. Municipals experience the same two sources of interest rate risk that affect all other bonds—price change risk and coupon-rate risk.

11-6   Stocks' Cash Dividend Yields

Most issues of preferred and common stocks pay cash dividends. The **dividend yield** from a share of preferred or common stock is defined as

$$\text{Dividend yield} = \frac{\text{annual cash dividend per share}}{\text{market price per share}} \tag{11-13}$$

The **coupon yield,** or **current yield,** from a bond is:

$$\text{Coupon yield} = \frac{\text{coupon interest per year}}{\text{market price per bond}} \qquad (11\text{-}14)$$

The dividend yield from a share of stock and the coupon yield from a bond are both rates of periodic cashflow that make up part of the investors' total rate of return. These two cash yield measures are somewhat different because of bankruptcy considerations. Nevertheless, most preferred and common stocks experience some interest rate risk, and it can be seen in terms of their cash yields.

A bond's coupon interest payment is a contractual payment that cannot vary in amount or timing, or the issuing company will be sued in bankruptcy court. Cumulative cash dividends on preferred stocks must also be paid if the issuing firm does not want trouble from its shareholders. But most preferred stock issues have noncumulative cash dividends, which may be skipped if the issuing corporation experiences hard times. Common stockholders' cash dividends are even less certain; they are paid only if the issuing firm's board of directors sees fit. This uncertainty makes the common stockholders' cash dividend yield more risky than bondholders' coupon yield.

In spite of the differences between stocks and bonds, the present value model is still relevant in determining the prices of both types of securities. It is through the present value mechanism that interest rate risk affects the prices of preferred and common stocks. Figure 11-5 illustrates how the average dividend yields of preferred

Figure 11-5 Stocks' cash dividend yields and bonds' coupon yields fluctuate with common interest rate risk factor.

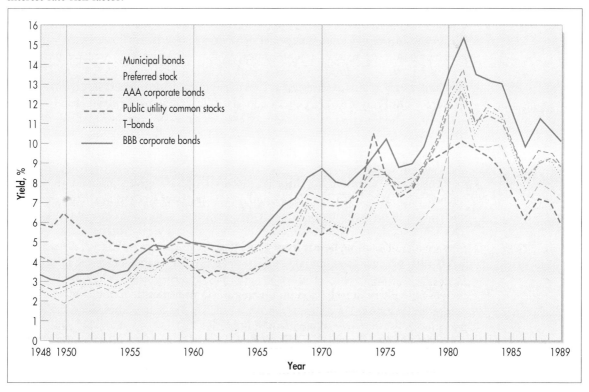

and common stocks and the average market interest rates of bonds fluctuated together over a period of years. They all tend to rise and fall together. The commonality illustrated in Figure 11-5 is the result of the different securities' common interest rate risk factor.

Common stocks and preferred stocks have interest rate risk because their values are estimated by computing the *discounted present values* of all future cash dividends. Thus, when the prevailing level of interest rates (also known as *discount rates*) changes, the discounted present values of all these securities change too. Preferred and common stock prices do not change exactly together with bond prices because stocks are more affected by default risk and management risk than are bonds. Also, common stocks have less interest rate risk than do preferred stocks because common stock dividends are affected so much by the firm's financial prospects. Interest rate risk is more evident in bonds because bond coupon payments are contractually specified and thus known in advance. As a result, interest rate risk is the dominant type of risk in bonds—especially in high-quality and default-free bonds.

11-7   Diversifiable and Undiversifiable Interest Rate Risk

Another look at Figures 11-4 and 11-5 shows that when the averages of different interest rates are plotted together through time, they all tend to rise and fall together. These systematic interest rate movements represent **undiversifiable interest rate risk.** Different interest rates are positively correlated because the same forces drive them.

To see why all interest rates tend to move together systematically, consider an example. Suppose that at some point in time the supply of AAA-grade bonds exceeds the demand from investors that prefer AAA-grade bonds. If all the other factors are held constant, the market interest rates of AAA-grade bonds will be bid up by borrowers' excess demand for capital funds. The resulting rise in AAA-grade interest rates will cause some investors who previously preferred to invest in other bonds to be lured into buying AAA-grade bonds. This flow of lendable funds to the AAA-grade bonds from other grades of bonds causes shortages of lendable funds in the markets for the other grades, and this causes the interest rates to be bid up in those markets too. *Systematic investor actions cause all market interest rates to tend to rise and fall together.*

There are exceptions to the rule, however. At any given moment the market interest rates of a few individual bond issues are uncorrelated with the prevailing movements in market interest rates for reasons peculiar to the issuers of those bonds. The Chrysler Corporation, for example, experienced a rise in the market interest rates on its outstanding bonds from 17.68 percent in January 1980 to 25.02 percent in April 1980 because the company was moving toward financial disaster at that time. Investors demanded higher interest rates because they perceived Chrysler to be increasingly likely to go bankrupt. During the same 4-month period, almost all other market interest rates were falling sharply as the United States entered a recession that curtailed most borrowers' demand for credit. The unsystematic behavior of the Chrysler Corporation's market interest rates during the first quarter of 1980 is an example of **diversifiable interest rate risk.**

Chrysler's bonds could have been purchased and included in a highly diversified portfolio of other bonds that were behaving in a more systematic fashion during early 1980. The average interest rates from this *highly diversified portfolio* would have been positively correlated with the market's prevailing interest rate movements. Chrysler's unsystematic movements would have been diversified away to obscurity in a large portfolio—that is why such unsystematic gyrations are diversifiable.

The interest rate risk in stocks, bonds, and all financial securities can thus be partitioned into two parts—diversifiable and undiversifiable. The systematic movements in market interest rates that affect the prices of all securities simultaneously constitute undiversifiable interest rate risk. Diversifiable interest rate risk is idiosyncratic to each security issue.

Summary

Interest rate risk is that portion of a security's total price variability caused by changes in the level of market interest rates. Interest rates affect security values in different ways, depending on the security. Market interest rates are used as the discount rates in calculating the present value of annuities, bonds, stocks, and other assets' cashflows. U.S. Treasury bonds, which are not affected by default risk and management risk, as are corporate securities, are totally susceptible to interest rate risk.

Present value principle 1 states that the interest (or discount) rate moves inversely with the present value. Present value principle 2 extends and refines principle 1: it states that the prices of long-term bonds fluctuate more than the prices of short-term bonds. The present value principles apply equally to annuities, U.S. government bonds, municipal bonds, corporate bonds, stocks, and other assets.

The interest rates and cash yields from different securities all tend to rise and fall together systematically because of common forces that create undiversifiable interest rate risk. Total interest rate risk is the sum of its diversifiable interest rate risk and undiversifiable interest rate risk. Diversifiable interest rate risk is caused by unsystematic movements.

Further Reading

Fabozzi, Frank J., and Irving M. Pollack, *The Handbook of Fixed Income Securities*, 2d ed. (Homewood, Ill.: Dow Jones–Irwin, 1987).
  This volume of edited readings has each chapter written by a different expert on that particular subject. Math beyond algebra is not used. A wide variety of topics dealing with interest rate risk, bonds, and preferred stock are discussed.

Homer, Sidney, and Martin L. Liebowitz, *Inside the Yield Book* (Englewood Cliffs, N.J.: Prentice-Hall, 1972).
  This book is devoted entirely to the topic of interest rate risk. Realistic numerical examples are used instead of abstract mathematics. Sophisticated bond trading strategies are explained.

Essay Questions

Questions and Problems

11-1 What tradeoffs are available to a bond investor when choosing between reinvestment rate (or coupon-rate) risk and price fluctuation risk?

11-2 Would a bond selling at a market price that is deeply discounted from its face value be more likely to have a long or short time until it matured? Explain why.

11-3 Look up information about the U.S. Treasury bond maturing in 2021 that pays an 8⅛ percent coupon rate. You could check a financial publication and/or call a securities broker. What is the dollar amount and the frequency of this bond's coupon interest payments for a bond with a $10,000 denomination?

11-4 Why do the market prices for default-free U.S. Treasury bonds decline as market interest rates rise, and vice versa? Why do these inverse movements occur between prices and market interest rates? Are there ever any times when a bond's price does not move inversely to its market interest rate?

11-5 Does the first present value principle tell us anything about the determination of the market prices of common stocks, which pay cash dividends instead of coupon interest? What about municipal bonds, which pay coupon interest that is exempt from federal income taxes?

11-6 Here are two instances of interest rate risk that need handling: (*a*) Assume that you and your twin each have $100,000 in cash. You are both very conservative, and you don't want to lose any of that money. Assume that you both invest your funds in U.S. Treasury notes due in 2 years at a price that yields 4 percent. Your twin then becomes concerned that a general increase in the level of interest rates will reduce the present value of the bond portfolio. What will you say to allay your twin's fears? (*b*) Assume you manage an investment counseling firm. One of your clients has read something about interest rate risk and is worried that if market interest rates decline, her coupon interest income will likewise decline. Her bond investments have maturities ranging from 15 to 30 years ahead. What can you tell this client to allay her fears?

Problems

11-7 If an investor puts $1000 in a savings account for 10 years and earns 6 percent annual rate of interest, what will be the value of this savings account at the end of 10 years? *Hint:* Use Equation (11-2).

11-8 If the discount rate is 10 percent, find the present value of the following opportunities: (*a*) Receive $100 at the end of 2 years. (*b*) Receive $100 at the end of each of the next 2 years. *Hint:* Use Equations (11-3) and (11-4).

11-9 If you make investments earning 10 percent, find your terminal wealth (or future value) if you (*a*) save $100 and leave it earning interest for 10 years; (*b*) invest $100 now and another $100 a year from now and withdraw the proceeds 2 years from now.

11-10 An employee is promised a retirement benefit of $100,000 at the end of 25 years of service. If the current interest rate is 10 percent, what is the present value of that benefit?

11-11 Mr. Smith can legally delay paying income tax on $5000 for 4 years without any penalties. Without the delaying tactic Smith must pay the tax immediately. Mr. Smith can earn 10 percent interest on his investments. How much does Mr. Smith gain at the end of the 4 years by delaying the $5000 tax?

11-12 Define interest rate risk. Use a graph of the different present values that can be generated for a bond that has a 3 percent coupon rate by varying the number of years to maturity and yield-to-maturity. Use yields-to-maturity of 2, 3, and 4 percent to illustrate your definition of interest rate risk. *Hint:* See Figure 11-3 for clues about how to construct the required illustration.

Multiple Choice Questions

11-13 How is the present value of a particular stream of cashflows affected by the timing of the receipt of the cashflows if everything else affecting the cash flows is held constant?

(a) The present value of the cashflows increases directly with the length of time in the future until the cashflows are received.
(b) The present value of the cashflows varies inversely with the length of time in the future until the cashflows are received.
(c) The present value of the cashflows is not affected by the length of time in the future until the cashflows are received.
(d) None of the above is true.

B

11-14 Look in the financial section of a newspaper and find the U.S. Treasury bond maturing in May of 2020 and determine the annual dollar amount of the coupon interest payments for one of these bonds that has a face value of $10,000.

(a) $72.50   (c) $437.25
(b) $300.00   (d) $1,206.00

C

11-15 If you want your initial deposit in a riskless account to double in value in 4 years, what annually compounded rate of return must you earn? *Hint:* Solve $(1 + x)^4 = 2$.

(a) 7%   (c) 15%
(b) 11%   (d) 19%

D

11-16 If you invest $100 in an FDIC-insured savings account at 8 percent interest for 10 years, how much will you be able to withdraw at the end of the decade?

(a) $100   (c) $186.01
(b) $130.86   (d) $215.90

D

11-17 Interest rate risk is defined by which of the following statements?

(a) Fluctuations in the coupon interest rates that occur from one bond issue to the next
(b) Systematic fluctuations in the market prices of bonds as their prices move inversely to the prevailing market interest rates
(c) The variability of return that investors experience as a result of fluctuations in market interest rates
(d) Both (a) and (b)
(e) All the above

E

11-18 Assume an interest rate of 5 percent and calculate the present value of a promise to receive $100 at the end of each of the next 2 years.

(a) $200.00   (c) $177.00
(b) $185.94   (d) $152.06

B

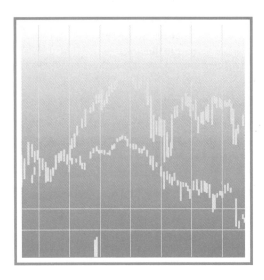

CHAPTER 12

BOND
SELECTION

After analyzing default risk and interest rate risk, we are now able to look beyond the individual bond issues and investigate how investment strategies can be used for different investment goals.

Financial newspapers list thousands of bonds issued by corporations, municipalities, and the federal government. In determining which bonds are appropriate for their needs, investors should consider a number of factors, including risk, expected rate of return, and the feasibility of purchasing a short-term or a long-term bond. Tax implications should also be considered.

12-1 Selecting Bonds

Selecting a bond is a two-step process:

1. The investor delineates a category, or several categories, of bonds that have an appropriate level of risk, the right tax status, acceptable callability, and other desirable characteristics.

2. Within whatever category or categories chosen, the investor chooses the specific bonds that offer the best terms available.

In selecting a category of bonds, the individual investor must decide how much risk to undertake. Institutional investors often have this decision made for them. In most states banks and life insurance companies are forbidden by state law to invest in anything riskier than BBB-grade bonds. Some states have **legal lists** of securities in which the financial institutions in that state are allowed to invest. These laws were enacted to keep banks and life insurance companies from buying bonds that are likely to default and undermine the institution's portfolio. They make it very clear what investment risks the state's banks and life insurance companies are allowed to undertake. Determining how much risk an individual investor should bear is more difficult: Individuals are not restricted by laws, but along with this latitude comes a greater margin for error (see Figure 1-4).

One way an individual can find out how much risk to bear is to read a bond rating agency's definitions of their quality ratings. Table 10-1, which defines the characteristics of Moody's and Standard & Poor's ratings, can be studied in light of the investor's emotional makeup and financial obligations to determine the most appropriate categories in which to invest. If an investor cannot tolerate any possibility that a bond issuer will go bankrupt, for instance, only default-free U.S. Treasury bonds would be appropriate. But even if the investment is limited to U.S. Treasury securities, the investor still must select specific bonds from among the hundreds of different issues.

The *second step* of the bond selection process is to choose the most desirable issues from the acceptable category. The attractiveness of a given issue depends on many characteristics. Determining how fast a bond can be expected to increase the investor's wealth is one of the more important considerations. Well-known formulas measure several different kinds of bond yields.

12-2 Bond Yield Measures

Most bonds have four different kinds of yields, or investment rate-of-return measures.

- A coupon interest rate is printed on the bonds. It never changes and states what fraction of the bond's face (or par) value is paid out annually as interest.

The other three measures are calculated after the amount of the annual coupon payment is known. They are:

- One-period rate of return

- Current yield

- Expected yield-to-maturity (YTM)

The One-Period Rate of Return

If a bond is purchased and then sold a few months later, its rate of return over this single holding period is as defined in Equation (12-1).

$$\text{Rate of return} = \frac{\text{price gain or loss during holding period} + \text{coupon interest, if any}}{\text{purchase price at beginning of holding period}} \qquad (12\text{-}1)$$

The **one-period rate of return** is sometimes called the **holding period return.** This continually fluctuating return measure can be calculated for any holding period—daily, monthly, or annually. It can assume negative values if the bond's price falls by an amount that exceeds the coupon payment.

The Current Yield

The **current yield** measures the annual rate (or percent) of cashflow the bond will pay if it is purchased at its current market price and the coupon interest is collected.

$$\text{Current yield} = \frac{\text{annual coupon payment}}{\text{current market price}} \qquad (12\text{-}2)$$

This measure is useful for investors who require a certain rate of cashflow from their investments every year. Investors should distinguish between the coupon rate and the current yield. If a bond is selling at its face value (a rare event that usually occurs only on the day the bond was issued and the day it matures), then and only then does the bond's coupon rate *equal* its current yield. Whenever a bond's market price differs from its face value, which is usually every day, the current yield will differ from the coupon interest rate.

Expected Yield-to-Maturity

An investor who buys a bond and holds it until it matures can hope to earn a rate of return we will call the expected **yield-to-maturity,** or **YTM.** That is, the owner of a bond with an YTM of, say, 10 percent will earn 10 percent compounded annually until the bond matures *if everything proceeds as expected.*

Box 12-1   303

Chapter 12
Bond
Selection

> **DEFINITION: The Approximate YTM (AYTM)**
>
> A bond's **approximate YTM,** or **AYTM,** can be calculated as follows.
>
> $$\text{AYTM} = \frac{I + \text{PD}/\text{years to maturity}}{(C + F)/2} \qquad (12\text{-}3)$$
>
> where I = annual coupon interest, \$
>
> $\quad$ PD = premium over or discount below par, \$
>
> $\quad$ C = current asked price, \$
>
> $\quad$ F = face value, \$

Earning the Expected YTM   *A bond investor will actually earn the YTM if and only if certain conditions are met.* The first condition is that the bond does not default. Any default will result in less than the expected yield-to-maturity. Second, the bond cannot be sold before it reaches maturity and repays its face value in full. Third, any and all coupon interest payments must be reinvested immediately upon payment at the YTM for the remainder of the bond's life. If any of the coupons from a bond are invested to earn a return less than the bond's YTM, the total return from the original bond investment will be pulled down accordingly.

Since the chance of all three conditions being met is not great, many bonds do not earn their expected yield-to-maturity. The word "expected" is included in the definition as a reminder that the YTM is not a *guaranteed* rate of return. The YTM is a particularly useful measure of the speed at which the investor's wealth is expected to increase. Since it measures the investor's rate of return, it facilitates comparing different bonds. For example, the YTM for a bond with a \$100 face value and 5 years to maturity can be compared with the YTM from a 10-year bond with a \$1000 par to determine which can be expected to earn higher returns.

Box 12-1 gives the formula for the approximate yield-to-maturity (AYTM); Box 12-2 shows how to calculate it. The advantages of using the AYTM formula are (1) it is informative and (2) you can compute it quickly and easily if you have a financial calculator.

Calculating Exact Yield-to-Maturity   The formula used to calculate the present value of a bond is also used to find the exact (rather than the approximate) expected yield-to-maturity (YTM). (For details, see Equation (11-11) for annual coupon bonds and Equation (11-12) for semiannual bonds.)

$$\text{Present value} = \frac{\text{coupon}_1}{(1 + \text{YTM})^1} + \frac{\text{coupon}_2 + \text{face value}}{(1 + \text{YTM})^2} \qquad (12\text{-}4)$$

The five terms in the present value model are the unknown market interest rate, or yield-to-maturity (YTM); the bond's \$10,000 face value; the number of years in the future when the bond matures, denoted $T = 2$; the $850 annual coupon; and the bond's present value or $9850 price. Four of these five terms have known values. The bond's price is printed in the daily financial news, and everything else except the YTM is printed on the bond. Thus, the present value formula for a bond with T time periods left until it matures can be solved for the only unknown value—the YTM.

The approximate yield-to-maturity (AYTM) of 9.32 percent in Box 12-2 differs from the exact YTM of 9.36 calculated in Box 12-3 by about four **basis points**—that is, $9.36 - 9.32$ is .04, or 4/100 of 1 percent. The AYTM differs from the exact YTM because the approximation did not employ precise compounding. Nevertheless, for small transactions the approximation is satisfactory and easy to compute.

Box 12-2

COMPUTATION: Calculating a Bond's AYTM

Consider a hypothetical Treasury bond that pays a coupon interest rate of 8½, or 8.5 percent, of its face value and matures in 2 years. If buyers are bidding 98.8 for this bond, potential investors are willing to pay 98⁸⁄₃₂, or 98.25 percent, of its face value. If sellers are asking 98.16 for the bond, they require 98¹⁶⁄₃₂, or 98.5 percent, of the face value. If purchased at the current asked (or offer) price of 98¹⁶⁄₃₂, the bond will yield approximately 9.32 percent per year if it is held to maturity; that is, the bond investor's AYTM from the 8½ coupon Treasury bond maturing in 2 years is 9.32 percent. Here are the calculations.

The Average Amount Invested

The denominator in Equation (12-3) is the average amount of money that remains invested in the bond over the remainder of its life. The average amount invested in our hypothetical T-bond is $9925 for a bond with a $10,000 face value:

$$\text{Average amount invested} = \frac{\text{asked price} + \text{face value}}{2}$$

$$= \frac{(\$9,850 + \$10,000)}{2} = \$9,925$$

The AYTM formula, Equation (12-3), is restated below in terms of the common denominator, the average amount invested:

$$\text{AYTM} = \frac{\text{annual coupon interest}}{\text{average investment}} + \frac{\text{average annual price change}}{\text{average investment}}$$

$$= \text{AYTM's coupon component} + \text{AYTM's price change component}$$

The coupon and price change components of the AYTM are calculated separately below.

$$Pv = \frac{P \cdot D + I}{YTM}$$
$$\frac{P + B}{2}$$

The Coupon Component

The coupon interest payment from our $10,000 T-bond's income is $850 per year (8.5% coupon rate times $10,000). Stated as a percentage of the average amount invested in the T-bond, the coupon component of the total AYTM equals 8.564 percent, as shown below:

$$\text{Coupon component} = \frac{\text{annual coupon}}{\text{average investment}} = \frac{\$850}{\$9925} = .08564 = 8.564\%$$

The Price Change Component

The asked price of our T-bond is 98.5 percent, which means the bond is selling at a discount of $150 ($10,000 − $9,850) from its $10,000 face value. When a bond's price is discounted below its face value, the price must rise up to its maturity (or face) value during the 2 years before the bond matures. Dividing the 2 years into the $150 total price gain shows that the average price increase is $75 per year [$150/(2 years)]. Dividing this $75 average annual price gain by the average amount invested gives the capital gain component of the total AYTM of almost 76/100 of 1 percent.

$$\text{Price change component} = \frac{\text{average capital gain}}{\text{average investment}} = \frac{\$75}{\$9925} = .0075566$$

The Total AYTM

The cash yield from the coupon component plus the price change component add up to an AYTM of 9.32 percent, as shown below:

Total AYTM = cash coupon component + price change component

$$= .08564 + .00756 = .0932 = 9.32\%$$

Using the AYTM formula

$$\text{AYTM} = \frac{\$850 + (\$150/2 \text{ years})}{(\$9,850 + \$10,000)/2} = \frac{\$850 + \$75}{\$9,925} = .0932 = 9.32\% \qquad (12\text{-}3a)$$

The bond's approximate expected yield-to-maturity is .0932, or 9.32 percent per year.

Box 12-3

COMPUTATION: Determining an Annual Coupon Bond's YTM

Solve the equation below to find the value of the YTM (or discount rate), that equates the present value of all the cashflows to the $9,850 cost of the bond.

$$\$9,850 = \frac{\$850}{(1 + \text{YTM})^1} + \frac{\$850 + \$10,000}{(1 + \text{YTM})^2}$$

$$= \frac{\$850}{(1 + .093568)^1} + \frac{\$850 + \$10,000}{(1 + .093568)^2}$$ (12-4a)

$$= \frac{\$850}{1.093568} + \frac{\$850 + \$10,000}{1.19589}$$

$$= \$777.272 + \$9,072.728$$

With annual compounding, the YTM is .093568 = 9.3568 percent per year. The solution can be calculated by hand using the laborious trial and error method, or a hand-held calculator can be used (see end-of-book Appendix B.)

Box 12-4

COMPUTATION: Determining a Semiannual Coupon Bond's YTM

Solve Equation (11-12) from page 290 using the values below to find the value of the **semiannual yield-to-maturity.**

$$\$9,850 = \frac{\$425}{(1 + \text{YTM}/2)^1} + \frac{\$425}{(1 + \text{YTM}/2)^2} + \cdots + \frac{\$425 + \$10,000}{(1 + \text{YTM}/2)^{2T}}$$

$$= \frac{\$425}{(1 + .046697)^1} + \frac{\$425}{(1 + .046697)^2} + \cdots + \frac{\$425 + \$10,000}{(1 + .046697)^{2 \times T}}$$

$$= \frac{\$425}{1.046697} + \frac{\$425}{1.095576} + \cdots + \frac{\$425 + \$10,000}{1.20028}$$

$$= \$406.04 + \$387.92 + \$370.62 + \$8685.42$$

If the bond pays $425 coupons every 6 months, its semiannual YTM is 4.6697 percent per 6 months, or 4.6697% × 2 = 9.34% at an annual rate. The annualized YTM is slightly smaller than the annual YTM because the semiannual coupons are compounded twice as often and, as a result, earn more income from interest on the interest. The solution can be calculated by hand using the laborious trial and error method, or a hand-held calculator can be used (see end-of-book Appendix B.)

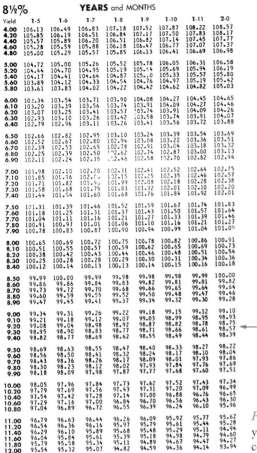

Figure 12-1 A page from a bond yield book for bonds with coupons of 8½ percent.

Using Bond Yield Tables Books of bond yield tables provide another way to find YTMs when the market prices of bonds are known. Figure 12-1 shows a page from a book of bond yield tables.

Each page in a **bond yield book** is appropriate for only one coupon rate. The page shown in Figure 12-1, for example, is only for bonds with coupon rates of 8.5 percent (shown at the upper-left-hand corner of the page). For example, reconsider the bond with 2 years 0 months to maturity whose asked price is 98.5. This bond is selling at 98.5 percent of its face value. Look down the column headed "2-0," which means 2 years and 0 months till maturity, until you find the number closest to the price of 98.5. In this case, the closest value is 98.57, which represents 98.57 percent of the bond's face value. If the number 98.5 could be found in the column headed "2-0," it would lie between the rows with values of 98.57 and 98.39. These two rows correspond to the YTMs in the left-hand corner of 9.3 and 9.4 percent, respectively. The bond's YTM may be estimated by interpolating between the 9.3 and 9.4 YTM rows; it appears that the bond's YTM is 9.3568 percent.

The table in Figure 12-1 can also be used to find a bond's price (or present value) if its YTM is known. Consider again the bond with an 8.5 percent coupon rate that matures in 2 years. If this bond pays annual coupons and its YTM is 9.356 percent, its present value is 98.50 percent of its face value. Thus, a bond with a $10,000 face value would be worth $9,850, as shown in Box 12-3. Box 12-4 shows that if a bond that is identical in every way, except that it pays its coupons *semiannually instead of annually* and its YTM is slightly less, 9.34 percent, it also has a present value of $9,850.

Up to now, we have focused on return measures that are useful to bond investors. The next section explains how changes in market interest rates determine bond price movements.

12-3   Bond Price Movements

If a bond does not default, its yield-to-maturity determines its market price—and vice versa. As a result of this mathematical interdependence, computing a bond's yield-to-maturity will tell us a lot about how its price will fluctuate in response to changes in market interest rates. Box 12-5 summarizes the relevant principles. The first four principles are illustrated in Figure 11-3 on page 292.

In the next section we turn away from the rate-of-return measures and how their changes affect bond prices and focus instead on another facet of a bond investment— the *time structure* of a bond.

Box 12-5

PRINCIPLES: Bond Price Movements

1. A bond's price moves inversely with its yield-to-maturity. (This is simply our old friend, the first present value principle from Box 11-2.)

2. For a given difference between the coupon rate and the yield-to-maturity, the accompanying price change will be greater the longer the term to maturity. That is, *interest rate risk* is greater for bonds with longer maturities. (This is the second present value principle from Box 11-3.)

3. The percentage price changes described in principle 2 increase at a diminishing rate as the bond's time left to maturity increases. Stated differently, interest rate risk increases at a diminishing rate with the bond's futurity. (See Figure 11-3 on page 292.)

4. For any given maturity, a decrease in a bond's yield causes a price increase that is larger than the price loss resulting from an equal increase in the bond's yield. That is, for equal-sized increases and decreases in the yield-to-maturity, price movements are not symmetrical.

5. The higher the coupon rate on a bond, the smaller the percentage price change for any given change in the bond's yield-to-maturity.

There are two similar but different approaches to studying the *time structure* of a bond investment. The most common way is to look at how many years will elapse until the bond matures and pays back its principal—this is called the asset's *time-to-maturity*, or its *years-to-maturity*. A second way to measure the futurity of an investment is to measure its average time until all interest coupons and the principal are recovered—or **Macaulay's duration,** as it is more commonly called.[1]

[1] The concept of duration was developed chronologically in the following pieces of published research: F. R. Macaulay, *Some Theoretical Problems Suggested by the Movement of Interest Rates, Bond Yields and Stock Prices in the United States Since 1856,* National Bureau of Economic Research (New York: Columbia, 1938). See also J. R. Hicks, *Value and Capital,* 2d ed. (New York: Oxford, 1965), p. 186; M. H. Hopewell and G. G. Kaufman, "Bond Price Volatility and Term to Maturity: A Generalized Respecification," *American Economic Review,* September 1973, pp. 749–753; and, R. A. Haugen and D. W. Wichern, "The Elasticity of Financial Assets," *Journal of Finance,* September 1974, pp. 1229–1240.

Box 12-6

DEFINITION: Macaulay's Duration (MD)

An investment's **duration** may be defined as the weighted average number of years until the cashflows occur, with the relative present values of each cash payment being used as the weights. The formula used to calculate Macaulay's duration (MD) for a bond is shown below:

$$MD = \frac{\text{maturities (or time}}{\text{periods) of payments}} \times \frac{\text{proportion of bond's value}}{\text{accounted for by the payment}}$$

$$MD = \frac{\sum\limits_{t=1}^{T} t[c_t/(1 + YTM)^t] + T\dfrac{\text{face value}}{(1 + YTM)^t}}{\sum\limits_{t=1}^{T} c_t/(1 + YTM)^t + \dfrac{\text{face value}}{(1 + YTM)^T}} \qquad (12\text{-}5)$$

where   MD = some number of years that measures the bond's duration

   c_t = the coupon interest payment the bond is scheduled to make in time period t

   t = an index number that counts the number of time periods

   T = the number of time periods until the terminal time period, when the last payments are made

   YTM = the bond's expected yield-to-maturity

Note that the denominator of Macaulay's duration formula is simply the present value formula.

Comparing the Duration of Two Bonds Numerically

Some numerical examples should clarify the duration computations. Consider two bonds that each have face values of $1000, expected yields-to-maturity of 6 percent (YTM = 6%), 3 years to maturity ($T = 3$), but different coupon rates. (See Boxes 12-7 and 12-8.) The durations of the two bonds in Boxes 12-7 and 12-8 are smaller than their 3 years-to-maturity.

Contrasting Duration with Years-to-Maturity

For bonds with periodic coupon interest payments (which most bonds have), Macaulay's duration for the bond will always be less than the number of years until the bond's maturity. In Box 12-7, for instance, the annual coupons of $70 caused the 3-year bond to have an average time until the bond repaid its invested funds, or duration, of 2.8107 years. Earlier and/or larger cashflows always shorten the duration of a bond investment. Consider the differences in the time structure of the two almost identical bonds in Boxes 12-7 and 12-8.

Box 12-7

COMPUTATION: The Duration of a 3-Year 7 Percent Coupon Bond

The present value of a 3-year bond with a 6 percent yield-to-maturity and a 7 percent coupon rate is $1026.73, as shown below:

Year, t (1)	Cashflow, c_t (2)	×	$1/(1 + YTM)^t$ (3)	=	$c_t/(1 + YTM)^t$ (4)
1	$ 70		$1/(1.06)^1 = .9434$		$ 66.04
2	70		$1/(1.06)^2 = .8900$		62.30
3	1,070*		$1/(1.06)^3 = .8396$		898.39
				Present value (p_0):	$1,026.73

* Includes principal.

Macaulay's duration for the 7 percent coupon bond is calculated by using the numerical values from the present value calculations above in the MD formula. The 3-year bond's duration is 2.8107 years, as computed below:

Year, t	Present value of cashflow, from (4) above	Cashflow's present value as proportion of total present value, (4)/p_0	$t \times (4)/p_0$
1	$ 66.04	.0643	.0643
2	62.30	.0607	.1214
3	898.39	.8750	2.6250
		1.0	MD = 2.8107 years

Box 12-8

311

Chapter 12
Bond
Selection

COMPUTATION: The Duration of a 3-Year 4 Percent Coupon Bond

The present value of a 3-year bond with a 4 percent coupon rate is $946.54 if YTM = 6.0 percent, as shown below:

Year, t (1)	Cashflow, c_t (2)	×	$1/(1 + YTM)^t$ (3)	=	$c_t/(1 + YTM)^t$ (4)
1	$ 40		$1/(1.06)^1 = .9434$		$ 37.74
2	40		$1/(1.06)^2 = .8899$		35.60
3	1,040*		$1/(1.06)^3 = .8396$		873.20
			Present value (p_0):		$946.54

* Includes principal.

The duration of this 4 percent coupon bond is 2.88 years, as calculated below:

Year, t	Present value of cashflow, from (4) above	Cashflow's present value as proportion of total present value, (4)/p_0	$t \times (4)/p_0$
1	$ 37.74	.0399	.0399
2	35.60	.0376	.0752
3	873.20	.9244	2.7732
		1.0	MD = 2.888 years

	First bond (Box 12-7)	Second bond (Box 12-8)
Face value	$1000	$1000
Coupon rate	7 percent	4 percent
Years-to-maturity	3.0	3.0
Macaulay's duration	2.811 years	2.888 years

The key to the difference between the two durations is that the bond with the larger coupon payments returns more of the invested funds to the investor sooner than the bond that pays smaller coupons. The bond with the smaller coupons therefore has a longer duration.

Table 12-1 shows the number of years' duration for several different bonds that have yields-to-maturity of 6.0 percent if held to maturity. Figure 12-2 illustrates the relationship between Macaulay's duration and the number of years-to-maturity for various bonds.

The duration of a zero coupon bond is simpler than that of a coupon-paying bond. A zero coupon bond has only one balloon payment to repay the principal and all interest on the date of maturity. So *a zero coupon bond's term to maturity is identical to its duration.*

Table 12-1
Bond Duration in Years for Bond Yielding 6 Percent under
Different Terms

Years to maturity	Various coupon rates			
	.02	.04	.06	.08
1	0.995	0.990	0.985	0.981
5	4.756	4.558	4.393	4.254
10	8.891	8.169	7.662	7.286
20	14.981	12.980	11.904	11.232
50	19.452	17.129	16.273	15.829
100	17.567	17.232	17.120	17.064
∞	17.667	17.667	17.667	17.667

Source: L. Fisher and R. L. Weil, "Coping with the Risk of Interest Rate Fluctuations: Returns to Bondholders from Naive and Optimal Strategies," *Journal of Business,* October 1971, p. 418.

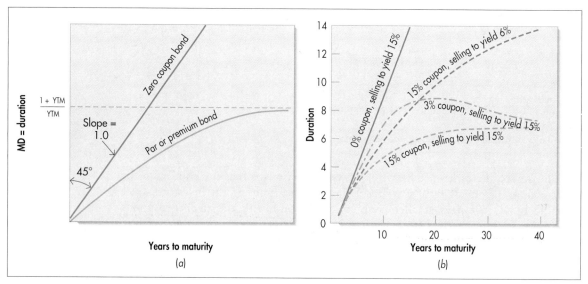

Figure 12-2 Relationships between duration and years-to-maturity for differing bonds. (*a*) Duration and term to maturity for premium, par, and zero coupon bonds. (*b*) Duration versus term to maturity for various bonds. (Reprinted by permission from The Revolution in Techniques for Managing Bond Portfolios, The Institute of Chartered Financial Analysts, 1983, p. 42. All rights reserved.)

Box 12-9

313

Chapter 12
Bond
Selection

> PRINCIPLES: Managing Interest Rate Risk
>
> 1. The interest rate risk of an investment increases directly with the duration of the investment's cashflows.
>
> 2. The duration and interest rate risk of an investment *usually* vary directly with the number of years left until the investment matures.
>
> 3. Bonds that pay zero coupons have durations equal to the number of years until the bond matures.
>
> 4. Coupon-paying bonds will always have durations that are less than the number of years until they mature.

In some respects a bond's years of duration are considered to be a better measure of the *time structure* of an investment's cashflows than its years-to-maturity because the duration reflects *the amount and timing of every cashflow* rather than just the length of time to the final payment. It might be said that duration is the best possible measure of a bond's futurity. Furthermore, a bond's duration is a measure of the bond's *interest rate risk*.

Box 12-9 summarizes some of the important points touched on so far in this chapter. (Some of these principles have their roots in Chapter 11.) The remainder of this chapter considers both the return and the duration of investments.

12-5   Bond Investing

The YTM and the duration are two dimensions of a bond that provide information useful for either of two buying strategies—investing or speculating. **Speculators** are aggressive traders who buy and sell frequently in an effort to profit from short-run price changes (see section 12-6). In contrast to speculators, **bond investors** buy a bond and hold it in their portfolio for years in order to obtain a long-term return. Investors do not trade so frequently as speculators.

Maximizing Return

Look again at the two-step investment strategy introduced earlier. The two steps boil down to this: select the bond with the highest YTM of all the bonds available in whatever quality rating (or other category) is appropriate. Unless the bond defaults, such an investment will ensure a relatively high rate of return in a suitable risk class. However, this plan ignores maturity date.

The investor may have financial obligations that will require future use of the funds invested in the bond market, before the maturity date. In this case, it would be appropriate to follow a three-step investment process.

- *Step 1:* Make a list of bonds that have a level of risk appropriate for the investor's particular situation.

• *Step 2:* Eliminate all bonds with maturity dates that come after the date on which the funds invested in the bond are needed for other purposes. (It would be ideal if several zero coupon bonds could be found with maturity dates that corresponded exactly with the date when the funds would be needed.)

• *Step 3:* Select the bond or bonds with the highest YTM that matures near the time when the funds are needed. (See the Bradley case below.)

Immunizing against Interest Rate Risk

While the three-step procedure outlined above has the advantage of being simple, it involves some interest rate risk. However, by *immunizing* a bond position, it may be possible to eliminate interest rate risk and lock in a high rate of return when one is available.

Macaulay's duration, Equation (12-5), considers the amount and timing of every cashflow and is also a good measure of the *time structure* of a bond's cashflows. Duration is also useful for immunizing bond investments against interest rate risk.

As we noted in Chapter 11, a bond's interest rate risk can come from two sources—coupon rate risk and price change risk—that arise when market interest rates change. Fortunately, *these two risks can offset each other.* For instance, when market interest rates rise, bond prices fall. Simultaneously, other new bond issues have higher coupon rates and offer richer reinvestment opportunities that tend to

---

CASE

Charles Bradley's Mutual Fund

Charles Bradley is a 52-year-old engineer who is planning his retirement. He wants to invest $50 to $100 per week where it can earn income and accumulate until he retires at age 65. Bradley has never taken an investments course and knows he will need some assistance.

Step 1—selecting a risk class: Bradley decided that speculative assets (like high-yield, or junk, bonds) involve too much default risk for him. However, he can live with the risks associated with assets that have moderately fluctuating market values. Essentially, Bradley decides that he can live with average risks, but that he will not gamble or speculate with his retirement funds.

After reading a book about mutual funds, Bradley has become convinced that this type of investment offers him (1) the full-time investment-management assistance he wants, (2) some risk-reducing diversification, (3) affordable management fees, of about 1 percent of the value of the assets managed per year, and (4) the ability to add increments as small as $100 to his retirement fund at frequent intervals.

Step 2—Time constraints: Bradley plans to retire in 13 years, so he has time to invest in short-term or long-term assets. His desire to earn high returns need not be constrained by time limitations on the investments he considers.

Step 3—Finding the highest YTM: Bradley has studied the historical average rates of return over the past years for each of several mutual funds. He has learned that some of the well-managed mutual funds that invest only in corporate bonds are expected to earn above-average rates of return. Furthermore, he believes that the leveraged buyout craze of the 1980s is over and that the bond market will be a safer place to invest in the 1990s. So, Charles Bradley decides to accumulate his retirement funds in the corporate bond fund with the highest YTM.

Ms. Smyth's Duration Matching Strategy*

Ms. W. W. Smyth has a $5000 bill that comes due in 12 months. This bill is a liability with both a time-to-maturity and a duration of 12 months. Smyth has the money to pay the bill now, but she doesn't want to pay early and lose the interest income that $5000 can earn in 1 year. So she invests about $4545 of her funds in coupon-paying bonds that have a yield-to-maturity of 10 percent, 13 months until maturity, and 12 months of duration. This bond investment is an asset with 12 months of duration. By equating the two $5000 terminal amounts and the 12-month durations of her liability and her asset, Ms. Smyth has immunized her portfolio against interest rate risk.

Immunization is like a hedge against interest rate risk. In 12 months Ms. Smyth's $4545 worth of bonds and the interest they have accumulated will have a total market value equal to the $5000 she needs to pay her $5000 liability, and she will have earned 10 percent rate of return from her bond investment. This will all occur regardless of whether the market interest rates rise or fall because Smyth is perfectly hedged with opposite and offsetting assets and liabilities. Thus, W. W. Smyth's immunization eliminated her interest rate risk exposure and *locked in* a guaranteed 10 percent rate of return until her funds were needed.†

* Technically speaking, duration matching will fully immunize a portfolio only if all interest rate changes can be represented by parallel shifts in the yield curve. If nonparallel shifts in the yield curve occur, duration matching will provide near total, but not complete, immunization.
† If Ms. Smyth wants to avoid default risk too, she can restrict her investments to default-free U.S. Treasury bonds.

offset the losses from the price declines. **Immunization** occurs when the coupon risk is balanced off against the price change risk so that total interest rate risk is minimized.

Duration can be redefined in terms of an immunization strategy. *Duration* is the length of time at which the coupon reinvestment risk and the price change risk of a bond portfolio are of equal and offsetting magnitudes. A specific example of how immunization can be achieved by matching the durations of an asset and an offsetting liability will clarify this new definition of duration.[2] See the Smyth case.

It might seem to have been simpler for Smyth to use a **maturity matching strategy,** by buying a $5,000 face value bond that matured in 12 months, instead of the more sophisticated **duration matching strategy** involving a bond that matured in 13 months but had a duration of 12 months. Although simpler, the maturity matching strategy would not have produced exactly the $5000 amount needed at the end of the 12 months because maturity matching ignores interest income. Further-

[2] For a more detailed discussion of immunizing to reduce interest rate risk see Lawrence Fisher and Roman L. Weil, "Coping with the Risk of Market Interest Rate Fluctuations: Returns to Bondholders from Naive and Optimal Strategies," *Journal of Business,* October 1971, pp. 408–431. See also G. O. Bierwag and George G. Kaufman, "Coping with Interest Rate Fluctuations: A Note," *Journal of Business,* vol. 50, no. 3, July 1977, p. 365.

more, a bond with the precise maturity date required for maturity matching frequently will not exist.

Immunizing a portfolio's interest rate risk using duration is an exacting process. Computer programs are available to do the mathematics for a large portfolio that might contain millions of dollars invested in dozens of different bond issues.[3]

Duration Rebalancing

If duration matching is going to immunize a portfolio against interest rate risk completely, the duration of the assets and the liabilities must be equal at every point in time. Keeping durations equal through time is not easy, because of **duration wandering:** durations do not change in a one-to-one correspondence with the passage of time, as was shown in Figure 12-2. Two particular problems arise with duration wandering: (1) a bond's duration decreases more slowly than its term to maturity, and (2) durations change whenever the market interest rates change (because they are the reinvestment rates). To overcome duration wandering it is necessary to "rebalance" a portfolio continuously until it matures.

Duration rebalancing involves buying and selling assets and/or liabilities in a portfolio in order to maintain the equality of the durations that is essential for complete immunization. The bond portfolio manager must continuously recalculate durations and modify the contents of the immunized portfolio to correct for the effects of duration wandering.

For bond investors who are willing to accept the risks that accompany a more aggressive strategy, a riskier and more complicated set of trading rules can be used to speculate on bond price changes. Investors who speculate and lose will wish they had immunized to avert risks. But if the investor speculates profitably, the gains may more than compensate for the work, risk, and worry involved.

12-6 Aggressive Trading

Speculators are different from investors because they actively buy and sell whereas investors buy and hold. Speculative trading incurs the additional costs of the security broker's commissions for the trades, the additional analysis and planning work, and the added risk of making a disastrous decision. Some shrewd strategies are needed to make trading more profitable than buy and hold investing.

---

[3] For more details and additional numerical examples of duration and immunization see Frank J. Fabozzi, T. Dessa Fabozzi, and Irving M. Pollack, eds. *The Handbook of Fixed Income Securities* (Homewood, Ill.: Dow Jones–Irwin, 1991). In particular, see chaps. 42 and 43. A program to immunize a bond portfolio that is written in BASIC language can be found in Richard Bookstaber, *The Complete Investment Book* (Glenview, Ill.: Scott, Foresman, 1985), chapter 8. Also, see Appendix A at the end of this book about similar computer software that accompanies this book.

Speculative strategies are frequently discussed in terms of the bonds' YTMs and the first present value principle that was discussed in Chapter 11. The first present value principle says that when market interest rates change, bond prices move inversely. Figure 11-3 illustrates this inverse relationship. An aggressive bond trader who can forecast the rise and fall of market interest rates can profit handsomely by buying when market interest rates are high, which means bond prices are low, and selling when market interest rates are low, which means bond prices are high. The rest of this chapter describes various tools that aid in forecasting market interest rates. The second present value principle can be adapted to suggest a profitable refinement in the buy low and sell high strategy. This principle tells us that the prices of long-term bonds will fluctuate more than the prices of similar short-term bonds if everything else is the same.

There is one big problem with all aggressive buy low and sell high bond trading strategies: *Forecasting market interest rates correctly is difficult work.* Stock and bond prices adjust quickly and efficiently to reflect the latest information. As a result, new information affects security prices around the world within seconds after it becomes public. Changes in the Federal Reserve's monetary policy or the U.S. Treasury's fiscal policy, the outbreak of war somewhere, OPEC oil price changes, changes in the level of corporate profits, surprising numbers in the American government's weekly announcements of business statistics, as well as many other factors keep the prices of bonds and stocks moving in a way that make millions of dollars in profits for investors who can process information quickly. Those who process information slowly or make wrong decisions can lose millions too. In view of the stakes, it is worthwhile to examine more closely the forces that move market interest rates.

The Rate of Inflation   One of the primary forces that move market interest rates is the rate of inflation. When the inflation rate rises to a high level, interest rates tend to rise to high levels too. A falling inflation rate tends to pull down all interest rates. (The relationship between the inflation rate and the level of market interest rates and the way inflation influences investment decisions are discussed in more detail in Chapters 17 and 18.)

There tends to be approximately a one-to-one relationship between the rate of inflation and the level of all market interest rates. For example, if the inflation rate increases, or decreases, three percentage points, market interest rates also tend to rise, or decrease, about three percentage points, respectively. As a result of this direct relationship, forecasting the inflation rate is an essential part of forecasting market interest rates. And forecasting market interest rates is an efficient way to forecast the price moves of thousands of different bonds. Let us consider some determinants of inflation and interest rates.

The Level of Business Activity   Inflation and interest rates tend to rise and fall with business activity. A speedup in business activity will have many effects. Most factories operate closer to full capacity, and the national economy moves toward a peak in the business cycle. Busier production schedules require overtime and higher overtime wages. Bottlenecks caused by late deliveries and machine breakdowns are more likely. Labor unions are more willing to go on strike and demand large wage increases because there is usually a labor shortage. These factors result in higher costs, and corporations usually raise their prices in an effort to maintain their profit margins. In such a situation, there is a tendency for inflation to speed up and for market interest rates to rise.

A slowdown in business activity reverses the process: declining market interest rates result. Bond price speculators should bear in mind this tendency of inflation rates and interest rates to vary with business activity. However, factors other than the phase of the business cycle can also put pressure on the inflation rate and interest rates.

Financing Federal Deficits   The U.S. Congress determines what the government will spend and what it will collect in federal income taxes. The U.S. Treasury then performs the checkwriting and tax-collecting tasks. The fiscal policy decision left to the Treasury Department is to decide what to do when income does not equal expenditures.

Congress occasionally legislates lower spending than is provided by income tax revenues, and the difference is called a **federal budget surplus.** In those rare years when a surplus occurs, the Treasury uses it to pay off part of the U.S. federal debt (that is, to buy back some outstanding U.S. Treasury bonds). But almost every year Congress legislates *more* spending than taxes will pay for, so in most years the Treasury must spend more than it takes in. This is called a *budget deficit,* and it results in **deficit spending.** The U.S. Treasury has difficulties making fiscal policy because deficit spending occurs year after year, and financing the deficit creates problems for the financial markets. Bond price speculators need to be political observers in order to forecast whether any surplus- or deficit-induced bond price changes lie ahead.

If the **federal deficit** is financed by debt that is purchased with new money created by the Federal Reserve System specifically to pay for the government's deficit spending, the increased money supply is inflationary. Increasing the nation's money supply this way provides more credit along with (after a few months of lagged response) higher inflation rates and higher interest rates. If the U.S. Treasury sells new bonds to finance a deficit, private borrowers can be crowded out of the debt markets by the high Treasury bond interest rates that are needed to sell the new T-bonds. But the "crowding out" approach is not an inflation accelerator, like increasing the money supply. Crowding out leads to tight credit conditions that can slow business borrowing and expansion.

In addition to watching the business cycle and congressional spending in order to forecast the major trends in interest rates and bond prices, bond traders should also be cognizant of some basic relationships among different interest rates.

Yield Spreads

Table 12-2 shows some yield spread statistics. For example, over the 1955 to 1964 period, AAA-grade corporate bonds paid an average risk premium of .40 percent, or 40 basis points, over similar-term (that is, intermediate-term) U.S. Treasury bonds (.40 = 4.13 − 3.73). Statistics on the inflation rate, the unemployment rate, and the average percentage of utilized U.S. plant capacity are shown at the bottom of the table.

Box 12-10

319

Chapter 12
Bond
Selection

> **DEFINITION: Risk Premiums**
>
> A **yield spread** is the difference between the yields-to-maturity (YTMs) on any pair of bonds—usually U.S. Treasury bonds and other, more risky bonds.
>
> Yield spread = yield on a risky bond − yield on a U.S. Treasury bond
>
> Yield spreads may also be called **risk premiums** because they measure the additional YTM that risky bonds pay to induce investors to buy the risky bonds rather than riskless bonds.

The statistics in Table 12-2 suggest how the business cycle affects yield spreads. The data show that yield spreads were larger on average in the 1965 to 1975 period than they were in the 1955 to 1964 period. The data also demonstrate how the levels of interest rates and the yield spreads have varied. Table 12-3 presents yield spreads at key points in the business cycle. The last column of Table 12-3 shows how one

Table 12-2
Average Yields and Related Economic Statistics

	1955–1964 average	1965–1974 average	1975–1984 average	1985–1990 average
Yields-to-maturity*:				
AAA corporate bonds	4.13%	7.06%	10.74%	9.56%
AA corporate bonds	4.25	7.29	11.06	9.98
A corporate bonds	4.42	7.51	11.32	10.26
BBB corporate bonds	4.93	8.06	12.04	10.84
Long-term Treasury bonds	3.76	5.82	10.20	9.03
Intermediate-term T-bonds	3.73	6.30	10.13	8.72
Short-term Treasury bonds	3.51	6.18	8.85	8.13
Monetary sector:				
Inflation rate†	2.02	5.48	6.55	4.07
Real sector:				
Unemployment rate‡	5.47	5.02	7.57	5.89
Capacity utilization rate§	81.87	86.41	79.87	82.03

* Standard & Poor's, *Standard & Poor's Trade and Securities Statistics,* New York, 1976.

† U.S. Department of Commerce, *Survey of Current Business,* (U. S. Government Printing Office, Washington D.C., monthly); GNP implicit deflator.

‡ Board of Governors of the Federal Reserve System, *Federal Reserve Bulletin,* Washington D.C., published monthly.

§ U.S. Department of Commerce, *Survey of Current Business,* (U. S. Government Printing Office, Washington D.C., monthly); manufacturing sector data.

Table 12-3
Yields at Peaks and Troughs in Business Activity

Month, year (economy)	AAA	AA	A	BBB	I-T*	BBB less I-T*
August 1957 (peak)	4.13%	4.27%	4.39%	5.11%	3.84%	1.27%
April 1958 (trough)	3.63	3.82	4.03	4.82	2.58	2.24
April 1960 (peak)	4.44	4.56	4.75	5.34	4.13	1.21
February 1961 (trough)	4.28	4.40	4.66	5.22	3.74	1.48
December 1969 (peak)	7.65	7.83	8.10	8.67	7.47	1.20
November 1970 (trough)	7.79	8.31	8.69	9.38	6.52	2.86
November 1973 (peak)	7.76	7.95	8.17	8.67	6.83	1.84
March 1975 (trough)	8.63	8.86	9.08	9.66	6.92	2.74
January 1980 (peak)	10.98	11.36	11.59	12.12	10.70	1.42
July 1980 (trough)	10.63	10.96	11.25	12.10	9.72	2.38
July 1981 (peak)	14.11	14.54	14.79	15.74	14.11	1.63
November 1982 (trough)	10.95	11.33	11.88	13.19	10.09	3.10
July 1990 (peak)	9.25	9.57	9.94	10.21	8.46	1.75

* I-T stands for an average yield of intermediate-term U.S. Treasury bonds.
Source: Official National Bureau of Economics Research (NBER) peak and trough dates.

yield spread varies with the business cycle and that it tends to be larger at economic *troughs* than at *peaks* of business activity.

Risk premiums are higher at economic troughs for two main reasons. First, unemployment, fear of job loss, and risk aversion are greater during recessions. Therefore, most investors demand larger risk premiums to buy risky bonds. Second, the corporations that issue bonds typically experience reduced sales and profits. Since issuers are more subject to bankruptcy during recessions, investors again require larger risk premiums. These changes in risk premiums occur in a fairly consistent and predictable fashion as the business cycle progresses from recession to boom to recession. Bond traders who buy and sell may be able to increase their profits by finding an unusual yield spread and then investing to profit from bond price changes that should occur in order to restore normal yield spreads. Other strategies that may profit bond investors involve studying the term structure of interest rates.

12-7   The Term Structure of Interest Rates

As we have seen, different bond issues have unequal terms to maturity and various YTMs. For a given issuer, the relationship between the YTMs of bonds and their years-to-maturity (assuming that the bonds differ in only these two respects) is called the **term structure of interest rates** or the **yield curve.** Figure 12-3 shows how a yield curve, which is a graph of the term structure of interest rates, is constructed. The information in this figure is derived from a source like Figure 2-1.

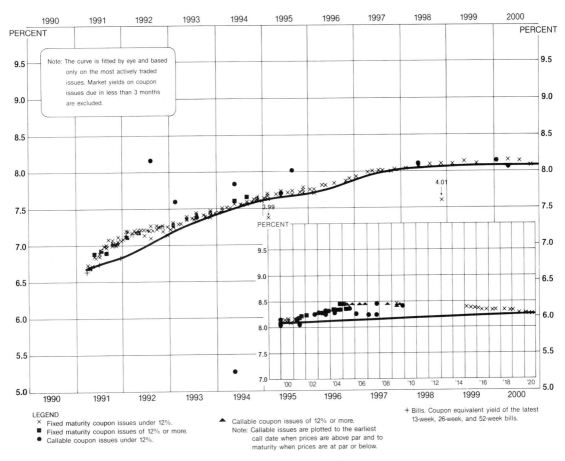

YIELDS OF TREASURY SECURITIES, DEC. 31, 1990
Based on closing bid quotations

LEGEND
× Fixed maturity coupon issues under 12%.
■ Fixed maturity coupon issues of 12% or more.
● Callable coupon issues under 12%.

▲ Callable coupon issues of 12% or more.
Note: Callable issues are plotted to the earliest
call date when prices are above par and to
maturity when prices are at par or below.

+ Bills. Coupon equivalent yield of the latest
13-week, 26-week, and 52-week bills.

Figure 12-3 The Treasury yield curve of June 30, 1988. The yield curve is a
line-of-best-fit through the Treasury bonds' YTMs that exist on a particular date. (Office
of the Secretary, U.S. Department of the Treasury, Washington, D.C., *Treasury Bulletin*,
September 1988, p. 51.)

There are different yield curves for the bonds in each risk class, or quality-rating
category, and these curves change a little every day. The yield curve for AAA-rated
corporate bonds, for example, is different from the yield curve for U.S. Treasury
bonds on any given day. The yield curves for bonds in different risk classes are
separated by risk premiums (or yield spreads). This difference is illustrated in Figure
12-4.

By eliminating all variables that do not affect the yield curve (such as default
risks), we can simplify our discussion. This simplification limits us to U.S. Treasury
securities, which are free of default risk. *The **Treasury yield curve** may be defined as
the relationship between yields and maturities for all the bonds issued by the U.S.
Treasury.* This yield curve can assume many different shapes, as shown in Figure
12-5.

321

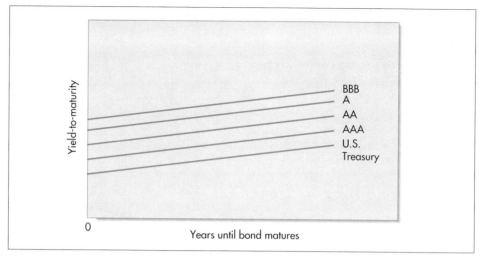

Figure 12-4 Different yield curves for bonds in different default risk categories, all observed on the same day.

Yield Curve Hypotheses

The rate of inflation is the main determinant of the *level* of all interest rates. In addition, three hypotheses have been suggested to explain why the yield curve has the *shape* it has at any given moment: (1) the expectations hypothesis, (2) the liquidity premium hypothesis, and (3) the segmentation hypothesis.

The Expectations Hypothesis Bond investors and traders who expect market interest rates to rise substantially will avoid buying long-term bonds because, if the interest rates actually do rise, the prices of long-term bonds will fall (as stated in the first present value principle). Short-term bonds will be preferable because their prices will fall less than the prices of long-term bonds (as stated in the second present value principle). If declining market interest rates are expected, investors will prefer to buy long-term bonds because the capital gains will exceed those from short-term bonds. Furthermore, a long-term investment at high yields will yield high coupon interest payments for years. Thus, differing investor expectations will be reflected in yield differences for bonds of different maturities, as illustrated in Figures 12-6 and 12-7.

Investors' expectations of future interest rates are revealed by the shape of the yield curve because, the **expectations hypothesis** asserts, the long-term rates are the average of the short-term rates expected to prevail between the current period and the maturity date of the bonds. The calculations in Box 12-11 show how bond investors' expectations about future interest rates determine the consensus yields-to-maturity that make up yield curves.

The Liquidity Premium Hypothesis "Liquidity premiums" also help shape yield curves. The **liquidity premium hypothesis** asserts that long-term yields should average more than short-term yields. This theory maintains that investors pay a price premium (resulting in lower yields) for short maturities to avoid the interest rate risk

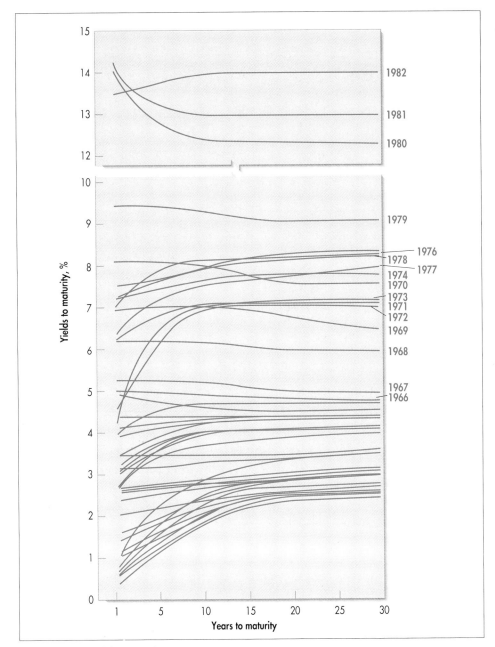

Figure 12-5 Yield curves from 1930 to 1982.

that is more prevalent in the long maturities. Essentially, the liquidity premium hypothesis asserts that an upward sloping yield curve is considered normal.

As the second present value principle taught us, long-term bonds have more interest rate risk than short-term bonds. As a result, the prices of long-term bonds fluctuate more than the prices of shorter-term bonds (even though long-term rates

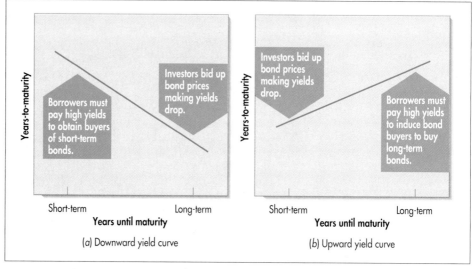

Figure 12-6 Investor expectations determine the shape of yield curves. (*a*) An expected decline in interest rates causes the yield curve to slope downward. (*b*) An expected increase in interest rates causes the yield curve to slope upward.

Box 12-11

COMPUTATION: Expected Future Rates Shape the Yield Curve

Using the simple arithmetic average, if 1-year rates are now 10 percent and the interest rates on 1-year bonds are expected to rise to 11 percent next year, then rates on current 2-year bonds will be approximately 10.5 percent.

$$\text{Two-year average} = \frac{10\% + 11\%}{2 \text{ years}} = 10.5\%$$

If the consensus of bond investors expects the future interest rates in 3 years to be 15 percent, then the current (or spot) rate on a 3-year loan is the average of the next 3 consecutive 1-year future rates, or approximately 12 percent, as shown below.*

$$\text{Three-year average} = \frac{10\% + 11\% + 15\%}{3 \text{ years}} = 12\%$$

* Technically, the expectations theory should be formulated in terms of the *geometric mean return* instead of the arithmetic average return. For a more detailed explanation of the theory see Jack Clark Francis, *Investments: Analysis and Management*, 5th ed. (New York: McGraw-Hill, 1991), chap. 12, pp. 344–349. To be precise, the 3-year geometric mean is $\sqrt[3]{(1.1)(1.11)(1.15)} - 1.0 = .1197 = 11.97\%$.

fluctuate less than short-term rates). The larger price fluctuation in the longer-term bonds is the basis for the liquidity premium hypothesis.

The Segmentation Hypothesis   Segmented markets for bonds with different maturities also help shape yield curves. The **segmentation hypothesis** asserts that lenders and borrowers confine themselves to certain segments of the yield curve for the following reasons:

1. Legal regulations, such as *legal lists,* which limit the investments that certain institutional investors are allowed to make.

2. The high cost of gathering information, which causes investors to specialize in one market segment.

3. The fact that various bond investors tend to have a fixed maturity structure of liabilities (for example, life insurance companies and pension funds tend to have long-term liabilities that can be accurately forecast by an actuary). The fixed (or almost fixed) maturity dates of the liabilities cause these investors to hedge their interest rate risk with assets of equivalent maturity. For this reason, the segmentation theory is also referred to as the **hedging theory.**

As a result of these factors, the rates on different maturities tend to be determined independently by the supply and demand conditions in the various market segments.

Forecasting Interest Rates with the Yield Curve

The yield curve can be plotted in 5 minutes using Treasury bond–yield data from a newspaper, and then market interest rates can be forecast by studying the shape of the yield curve. Since bond investors' expectations about interest rates determine the shape of the yield curve, we could say that the shape of the yield curve must reveal bond investors' expectations about interest rates. The yield curves in Figure 12-7 are interpreted in the legend; the comments there suggest how to find the consensus of bond investors' expectations about interest rates by observing the shape of a yield curve.

Yield curves' implicit forecasts are valuable because they reflect the consensus of the expectations of bond investors who vote with dollars. Larger investors have more impact on the yield curve than small investors. Since bond prices move inversely with market interest rates, interest rate forecasts obtained from yield curves can be valuable to both investors and speculators. Forecasts from yield curves are like other forecasts in that they can change at any time and sometimes turn out to be wrong. However, forecasts derived from yield curves are especially valuable because they reflect the expectations of professional investors more than they reflect the expectations of amateurs.

Riding the Yield Curve

When the yield curve is upward sloping (that is, when long-term rates are higher than short-term rates), some bond portfolio managers attempt to increase their yields by using a strategy called **riding the yield curve.** The bond investor purchases an

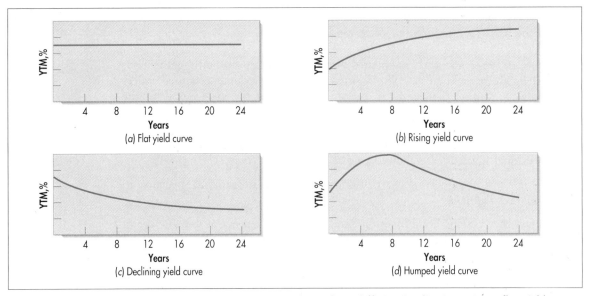

Figure 12-7 Different yield curve shapes have differing implications. (*a*) A flat yield curve results from the investors' consensus that interest rates will remain unchanged. (*b*) A rising yield curve means the consensus expects interest rates to rise continuously in the years ahead. (*c*) A declining yield curve means, the consensus of investors expects interest rates to fall in the future. (*d*) The humped yield curve reflects a consensus that interest rates will rise for a few years and then decline in the years after that.

intermediate-term or long-term bond to hold. The investment in a longer-term bond is maintained to obtain the capital gains that occur as the bond moves closer to its maturity date and thus "rides down the yield curve" to the lower interest rates that will be appropriate when it becomes a shorter-term bond. As a result, in addition to the coupon interest, the bond investor earns capital gains that result from the lower yields near its maturity date.

The danger inherent in trying to ride the yield curve is that the level of interest rates may rise or the short-term end of the yield curve may swing upward. Either development would cause capital losses. To avoid these dangers the bond investor must continuously monitor the shape of the yield curve and be alert to disadvantageous shifts in market interest rates.

Speculating on Quality-Ratings Changes

The profit and loss opportunities arising from interest rate changes cause professional bond investors to work at forecasting the yield curve. However, forecasting other types of bond changes can also be profitable. Figure 12-4 shows a series of parallel yield curves, each one representing bonds with a different quality rating. The difference in yields between any two yield curves is the *yield spread*, or *risk premium*, between the two quality ratings on a particular date. When a bond's quality rating is

Table 12-4
Revision Statistics for Corporate Bond Ratings

Rating at time of issue	Rating at time of maturity					
	AAA	AA	A	BBB	BB–C	Unrated
AAA (or Aaa)	57%	21%	7%	6%	9%	0%
AA (or Aa)	9	56	13	7	13	2
A	2	12	45	18	21	2
BBB (or Baa)	1	2	15	43	35	4
BB to C (or Ba to C)	1	1	3	14	75	6

Source: W. Braddock Hickman, *Corporate Bond Quality and Investor Experience* (New York: National Bureau of Economic Research, 1958), p. 158. Ratings are a composite of the ratings of various agencies.

revised, it moves from one yield curve to another, and the price of the bond moves accordingly. Such moves will always adhere to the first present value principle.

If the quality rating of a bond issue is raised, the bond is then in a safer default-risk class. As a result, bond investors bid up the issue's market price, and its YTM moves inversely. Such changes can be unrelated to the economic conditions in the bond market. A financial analyst who can anticipate bond quality rating changes can reap handsome trading profits. The techniques for analyzing the default risk of bonds discussed in Chapter 10 are the key to anticipating bond quality rating changes. In order to see if it is worthwhile to perform the needed bond analysis, let's consider some actual cases.

The case in Chapter 10 covering Chrysler's brush with bankruptcy suggested how the price of Chrysler bonds plummeted from $78 in February of 1979 to $34.50 just 23 months later. During the same period, the company's bond rating fell from BBB to CCC. Bond analysts who could see this decline coming could sell Chrysler bonds at advantageous prices. Figure 10-1 illustrates the relationship between quality ratings and bond yields in a more general context. The market data show that quality-rating changes vary directly with changes in the prices of the bonds.

Table 12-4 shows how often bond quality ratings change. It indicates that 57 percent of the bonds rated AAA by Standard & Poor's (or Aaa by Moody's) when they were newly issued remained unchanged. It also shows that 1 percent of the BBB (or Baa) bonds were upgraded all the way to AAA (or Aaa). The capital gains from this upgrading were spectacular. Clearly, a trading strategy based on correct rating-change forecasts can be lucrative. Of course, if the forecasts are wrong, the losses can also be spectacular.

Summary

Bond yield measures and present value principles 1 and 2 can be used in formulating bond investment and trading plans. Investors who buy and hold follow a step-by-step process: they select the bonds that have the highest rate of return in the appropriate risk class and that mature at the time the invested funds are needed. Investors can also use Macaulay's duration to gauge the time structure and interest rate risk of a bond. Duration can also be used to immunize bond investments against interest rate risk.

Other trading strategies are useful for more aggressive bond buyers. Risk premiums are the yield spreads between different bonds. Some bond speculators look for unusual yield spreads to suggest bonds that may be over- or underpriced.

The yield curve is the relationship between the number of years until a group of similar bonds matures and those bonds' YTMs. The expectations theory explains the shape of the yield curve and also provides implicit interest rate forecasts. Thoughtful bond traders can obtain forecasts of interest rate movements by studying the various shapes the yield curve assumes.

Since bond prices always move inversely with market interest rates, forecasting interest rates provides a way to forecast bond price swings. For the financial analyst, a bond trading strategy based on quality-rating changes can also be effective. There are ample opportunities in the bond markets to earn handsome rewards by correctly forecasting either interest rate changes or changes in bond quality ratings.

Further Reading

Bierwag, G. O., George G. Kaufman, and Alden Toevs, "Duration: Its Development and Use in Bond Portfolio Management," *Financial Analysts Journal,* July-August 1983, pp. 15–35.
   An easy-to-read survey of the research that led to duration as a useful tool for bond portfolio managers. A little elementary algebra is used.

Homer, Sidney, and Martin L. Leibowitz, *Inside the Yield Book: New Tools for Bond Market Strategy* (Englewood Cliffs, N.J.: Prentice-Hall; New York: New York Institute of Finance, 1972).
   This book describes various bond trading strategies, using easy-to-read examples that employ no mathematics at a level higher than basic arithmetic.

Questions and Problems

Essay Questions

12-1   Compare and contrast changes in bond prices caused by varying levels of interest rates with changes caused by reshaping the yield curve. Draw a graph with all parts labeled to illustrate your points.

12-2   If you managed a portfolio of bonds, what would you do if you were convinced that a period of temporarily tight credit conditions was beginning that would drive market interest rates up substantially? Explain your plan.

12-3   Define the phrase "yield curve." What financial variables that affect interest rates are held constant when constructing the yield curve? Why are these variables held constant?

12-4   Why should an investment manager care about the yield curve? Provide a hypothetical example.

12-5   Define the term "yield spread." What does the yield spread measure? Does a given yield spread ever change? Explain.

12-6   Compare and contrast bond investing and bond trading.

12-7 "Bonds are a good hedge against inflation because their market prices tend to rise with inflation." Is this assertion true, false, or uncertain? Explain.

12-8 Consider the three hypotheses about what determines the shape of the yield curve—the expectations hypothesis, the liquidity premium hypothesis, and the segmentation hypothesis. Are these three mutually exclusive, or are they compatible? Explain.

12-9 What does the phrase "duration wandering" mean? What problems are created by duration wandering?

Problems

12-10 A $1000-face-value bond pays a 7 percent coupon rate annually, matures in 3 years, and has a yield-to-maturity of 6 percent. (*a*) What is its present value? (*b*) What is its duration? Show your computations.

12-11 Calculate three different rates of return for a bond that pays an 8 percent coupon rate annually on its $1000 face value, matures in 4 years, and is selling for $967.59. Calculate the (*a*) current yield, (*b*) approximate yield-to-maturity (AYTM), and (*c*) exact YTM. Show your calculations and label your work.

12-12 Calculate the duration of a bond that pays an 8 percent coupon annually, matures in 4 years, is selling for $967.59, and has a yield-to-maturity of 9 percent per annum. Show your calculations and label your work. *Hint:* Your calculations from Problem 12-11 will be helpful with this problem.

12-13 Mr. John Marcus has an $8000 debt coming due for payment in 2 years. He currently has $8000 cash with which to pay the debt off. He wants to invest the cash so it can earn interest until the debt payment date arrives. Mr. Marcus wants an investment that is free from default risk or interest rate risk that he will not have to worry about. What do you suggest? *Hint:* Consider duration.

12-14 Get a copy of a newspaper that lists this week's Treasury bond prices (as in Figure 2-1). Plot a yield curve; that is, prepare a graph of the Treasury bonds' YTMs against their term to maturity. Why do some of the bonds plot away from any smooth yield curve you draw? (*Hint:* Consider the difference between ordinary income taxes and capital gains taxes that was explained in Chapter 7.) As you graph the yield curve, consider the following helpful pointers: (1) Prices are stated as percentages of the bonds' face value. The numbers after the decimal point are in thirty-seconds. For example, 98.22 is $98^{22}/_{32}$ percent. (2) On callable issues, market convention treats the yields to the earliest call date as more significant when an issue is selling above par and the yields-to-maturity as more significant when it is selling at par or below.

Multiple Choice Questions

12-15 If the present value of $220 paid at the end of 1 year is $180, what is the 1-year discount factor used to find the present value? More concisely, what is the value of $1/(1 + k)$?

(*a*) .22   (*c*) 1.22

(*b*) .82   (*d*) .88   B

12-16 For a particular interest rate, the associated yearly discount factors $1/(1 + k)$ do which of the following?

      (*a*) Rise in early years and then begin to taper off

C   (*b*) Decline toward zero as the quality rating rises

      (*c*) Vary inversely with the interest rate

      (*d*) None of the above

12-17 A bond's duration equals the number of years until the bond matures under which one of the following conditions?

      (*a*) The bond's coupon rate equals the market interest rate when the bond is issued.

D   (*b*) The bond's quality rating does not change.

      (*c*) Market interest rates do not fluctuate.

      (*d*) The bond pays no coupon interest.

12-18 A bond will not earn its expected yield-to-maturity without satisfying which of the following conditions?

      (*a*) The issuer will not default.

D   (*b*) All cashflows are immediately reinvested at the yield-to-maturity.

      (*c*) The bond will not be sold before it matures.

      (*d*) All the above are necessary conditions.

12-19 A bond's current yield is which of the following?

      (*a*) The after-tax income from the bond's coupon interest

D   (*b*) The bond's capital gain or loss plus its coupon interest during some period all divided by the bond's purchase price

      (*c*) The bond's inflation adjusted rate of return for the current year

      (*d*) The bond's annual coupon interest divided by its current market price

12-20 A bond's duration is defined as which of the following?

      (*a*) The length of time until the bond defaults

B   (*b*) The weighted average number of years until the bond's cashflows occur using the present value of each cashflow for weights

      (*c*) The number of years the issuer must make payments into the issue's sinking fund

      (*d*) The weighted average number of years until the bond matures using the probabilities of the issue's being assigned to each different quality rating for weights

12-21 If a U.S. Treasury bond is held until it matures, the interest rate on reinvestment opportunities affects the investor's realized rate of return because of which one of the following?

      (*a*) Interest on the interest.

A   (*b*) The bond's price fluctuates inversely with market interest rates every day of its life.

      (*c*) The coupon interest payments can only be consumed.

      (*d*) The coupon rate fluctuates along with the current market interest rates.

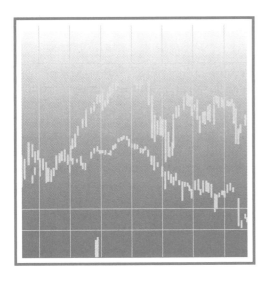

CHAPTER 13

COMMON
STOCK
ANALYSIS

This chapter and the one following focus on the information investors need to make informed common and preferred stock selections. Both kinds of stock are valued the same way. The objective of these chapters is to suggest how to identify underpriced and overpriced stocks. The value of a share of common or preferred stock depends primarily on its earnings per share, but other factors are also important.

The present value model introduced in Chapters 11 and 12 is used to find the discounted present value of all future cashflows that a shareholder may expect to receive. Financial analysts call this present value the **intrinsic value** of a share of stock. We also discuss something called a stock's *price-earnings ratio*, which is a popular shortcut method of assessing a stock's intrinsic value per share.

13-1   Estimating Intrinsic Value

When buying a share of common stock, the cash dividends per share are the only cashflows the investor can hope to receive. The discounted present value of these cash dividends determines how much the share is worth. If the corporation is acquired in a merger, the shareholder will receive cash or new securities. We can calculate the present value of any of these outcomes the same way we calculate the present value of cash dividends from the premerger shares. If the corporation develops new products as its old products become obsolete and has an effective management-development program, it should exist for a long time—perhaps forever. A corporation's cash dividends may increase (have a positive growth rate, $g > 0$) or decrease (experience a negative growth rate, $g < 0$). Either way, the present value, denoted P_0, of all the future cash dividends a shareholder expects to receive can be calculated as shown below.[1]

$$P_0 = \frac{D_1}{(1+k)^1} + \frac{D_2}{(1+k)^2} + \frac{D_3}{(1+k)^3} + \cdots \qquad (13\text{-}1)$$

$$= \frac{D_0(1+g)^1}{(1+k)^1} + \frac{D_0(1+g)^2}{(1+k)^2} + \frac{D_0(1+g)^3}{(1+k)^3} + \cdots \qquad (13\text{-}1a)$$

$$= \sum_{t=1}^{\infty} \frac{D_0(1+g)^t}{(1+k)^t} \qquad (13\text{-}1b)$$

$$= \frac{D_1}{k-g} \qquad (13\text{-}1c)$$

where P_0 = present value

D = cash dividend

k = discount rate

g = growth rate (assumed constant)

t = time period being considered

Equation (13-1c) is a simple valuation model; let us consider how to use it. The numerator of Equation (13-1c), D_1, should be your best estimate of a stock's cash dividend per share next year. Cash dividends are assumed to grow at a *constant rate* denoted g, as shown in Equation (13-2)—g represents the average yearly growth rate in the firm's cash dividends per share (for instance, $g = .02 = 2.0\%$).

$$D_t = D_0(1+g)^t \qquad (13\text{-}2)$$

Figure 11-1, page 283, illustrates how something like cash dividends per share might grow at different constant growth rates.[2]

---

[1] The constant perpetual growth present value model for stock valuation is derived mathematically in Jack Clark Francis, *Investments: Analysis and Management*, 5th ed. (New York: McGraw-Hill, 1991), chap. 15.

[2] Figure 11-1 was prepared in terms of an interest rate denoted i. By substituting the growth rate g in place of the interest rate i, the figure can be used to illustrate different rates of growth.

Box 13-1

333

Chapter 13
Common
Stock
Analysis

COMPUTATION: The present value of a share of stock

Consider a share of stock that has an annual cash dividend of $5 per share for next year and an average growth rate of 2 percent per year in its cash dividends. Assume that this stock is in a risk class requiring a 10 percent per year rate of return to attract investors. Using the present value of constantly growing dividends model, Equation (13-1c), we can compute this share's present value of $62.50, as shown below:

$$P_0 = \frac{D_1}{k - g}$$

$$= \frac{\$5}{.10 - .02} = \frac{\$5}{.08} = \$62.50 \text{ per share}$$

(13-3)

The discount rate k in Equation (13-1) is a **risk-adjusted discount rate** that can be estimated from a risk-return relationship like those in Figure 10-1. The risk-adjusted discount rate is the discount (or interest) rate the investor chooses to compute the present value. It is said to be *risk-adjusted* because it is the **required rate of return,** what investors consider sufficient to induce them to accept the investment's risk. If an investment's required rate of return equals its *expected rate of return*, the asset is in equilibrium and its price equals its present value. But, if the investment's required rate of return exceeds its expected rate of return, then the asset is overpriced; it is underpriced if the required rate of return is less than the expected rate of return.

Now we will see how the present value of constantly growing dividends model can be used in some hypothetical, but nevertheless realistic, investment situations.

If the Business Gets Riskier

Suppose a firm becomes riskier. Perhaps a tough new competitor appears or the Environmental Protection Agency sues the firm for not cleaning up its waste. Such events would probably reduce sales or raise operating expenses. As a result, profits and the cash available for dividends would be reduced, and these changes would make the firm's stock riskier. Investors would require that the stock earn a higher rate of return to compensate for the additional risk. These changes may be represented in the model by raising the risk-adjusted discount rate k.

The discount rate used to find the present value of cash dividends is a risk-adjusted rate of return. If we are valuing shares of common stock in a blue-chip corporation (say, Coca-Cola), then a discount rate of 10 percent is appropriate. If the risk is increased (for example, the federal government removes some import restrictions on foreign soft drinks, so that Coca-Cola faces tougher foreign competition), the appropriate risk-adjusted discount rate rises slightly. Investors would recognize that increased foreign competition could hurt sales, profits, and cash dividends. A higher rate of return will compensate them for the additional risk. Table 13-1 offers some guidelines that may be helpful in selecting an appropriate discount rate.

Table 13-1
Risk-Adjusted Discount Rates Observed for Selected Common Stocks in Normal Times*

Risk level	Type of firm	Appropriate discount rate
Very low	Large, top-grade, bluest of the blue chips (Coca-Cola, ARCO, Pfizer, Carter-Wallace, Kellog, Anheuser-Busch, and Hershey are graded A+).	8%
Low	Large, established blue chips (IBM, Borden, Woolworth, Procter & Gamble, Boeing, Gillette are grade-A).	10
Low-medium	Established top-50 firms (Zurn, AT&T, Chubb, NYNEX, Walt Disney, and Exxon are A−).	12
Medium	Established top-100 firms (Kodak, Xerox, Whirlpool, Dow Chemical, Polaroid, CBS, Chevron, Atlantic Richfield, Apple, and Mobil are graded B+).	14
High-medium	Established Fortune 500 firms (GM, Black & Decker, Champion International, Alcoa, and Lockheed are B).	16
High	Risky Fortune 1000 firms (Caterpillar, Chase-Manhattan, Avon are B−).	18
Very high	Very risky (Data General, Tidewater, Bally, Beverly Enterprises, Teladyne, and Unisys are C-grade).	20
Speculative	Defaulted firms are grade-D. Firms do not remain in this status for long.	25
Very speculative	Small new firms (Joe's Bar & Grill, if Joe has never drunk).	33
Gamble	Small, risky firms (Joe's Bar & Grill, if Joe is a reformed alcoholic).	50
Bad gamble	Small, failing firms (Joe's Bar & Grill, if Joe is drinking).	66

* The common stock quality ratings were assigned by Standard & Poor's and were current in 1991, but may change at any time.

Source: Standard & Poors, *Stock Market Encyclopedia,* August 1991.

Box 13-2

> ## COMPUTATION: The Present Value with a Higher Risk-Adjusted Discount Rate
>
> Consider a share of stock that is expected to pay an annual cash dividend of $5 per share next year, $D_1 = \$5$, and has an average growth rate of $g = 2\%$ per year in its cash dividends. Assume that this stock was in a risk class requiring a $k = 10\%$ per year rate of return to attract investors. When an increase in the firm's risk increases the appropriate discount rate from $k = 10\%$ to $k = 12\%$, the present value of the stock falls from $P_0 = \$62.50$ per share to $P_0 = \$50.00$, as shown below. This drop in value makes sense—a riskier stock should be worth less. Compare this result with Box 13-1.
>
> $$P_0 = \frac{D_1}{k - g}$$
>
> $$= \frac{\$5}{.12 - .02} = \frac{\$5}{.1} = \$50$$
>
> (13-4)

334

Box 13-3

335

*Chapter 13
Common
Stock
Analysis*

COMPUTATION: The Present Value with a Higher Growth Rate

The present value per share P_0 for a corporation that had a risk-adjusted discount rate of $k = 10\%$ and a $D_1 = \$5$ per share cash dividend would skyrocket from $P_0 = \$62.50$ with a $g = 2\%$ growth rate to $P_0 = \$250.00$ with a new growth rate of 8%. (See Box 13-1 for comparison.)

$$P_0 = \frac{D_1}{k - g}$$

$$= \frac{\$5}{.10 - .08} = \frac{\$5}{.02} = \$250$$

(13-5)

This result is realistic. When a firm's growth rate is expected to accelerate, the value of the firm's common stock can quickly double, triple, or even quadruple just because its future dividends are expected to grow faster.

If Growth Prospects Heat Up

Suppose the rate of growth in a firm's cash dividends increases. More specifically, assume the stock becomes a "hot" growth stock with a higher expected growth rate. Such growth might result from a new discovery the firm was able to patent or the bankruptcy of a tough competitor.

The price of Chrysler's common stock furnishes a well-known case study of the effects of rapidly improved growth prospects. As the case table on page 261 of Chapter 10 shows, Chrysler's stock went from less than $5 per share in the first quarter of 1982 to over $30 in the summer of 1983 because in 1983 investors perceived that the firm's prospects had improved. Note that during this time Chrysler purchased no major assets, hired back only a fraction of its laid-off workers, and experienced a shrinkage in its capitalization. Chrysler's stock price did not skyrocket because of physical growth in the firm. The 600 percent price rise can be attributed mostly to changes in investors' *expectations* about the firm's growth prospects.

If There Is a Cut in Cash Dividend per Share

Finally, let us consider how a change in the cash dividend affects the value of a stock. Suppose, for instance, that the $5 cash dividend in Box 13-1 were halved to $D_1 = \$2.50$ because the corporation's earning power had diminished. This might happen if the firm lost its biggest customer to a competitor. Box 13-4 presents a numerical example.

Preferred stock is sometimes called a *fixed income security* because it is supposed to pay a stipulated cash dividend every year. In contrast, every quarter many corporate boards of directors meet to consider whether to increase or decrease their common stock's cash dividends that quarter. As a result, cash dividend changes are more likely to affect common stock values than preferred.

Box 13-4

> **COMPUTATION: The Present Value with the Cash Dividend Halved**
>
> The present value per share P_0 for a corporation that had a risk-adjusted discount rate of $k = 10\%$, a growth rate of $g = 2\%$, and a $D_1 = \$5$ per share cash dividend would collapse if the cash dividend were halved.
>
> $$P_0 = \frac{D_1}{k - g}$$
>
> $$= \frac{\$2.50}{.10 - .02} = \frac{\$2.50}{.08} = \$31.25$$
>
> (13-6)
>
> The present value of $P_0 = \$62.50$ per share falls to $P_0 = \$31.25$ when the cash dividend is cut from $D_1 = \$5$ to $D_1 = \$2.50$ per share.

[handwritten margin note: PV Div & price should be riskier less?]

If You Sell in a Few Years

The stock valuation model used so far in this chapter, Equation (13-1c), assumes the investor holds the stock forever. Instead, if the stock is sold after a few years, two types of income can be earned—cash dividends and the change in the stock's price. Equation (13-7) and Box 13-5 show how to value a share of stock that is held for $T = 2$ years (where $P_2 =$ its price when sold).

$$P_0 = \frac{D_1}{(1 + k)^1} + \frac{D_2}{(1 + k)^2} + \frac{P_2}{(1 + k)^2}$$

(13-7)

Box 13-5

> **COMPUTATION: Amjet's Present Value over a 3-Year Holding Period**
>
> An investor in the Amjet Corporation's common stock expects it to pay annual cash dividends of $2.00 and $2.30 per share during the next 2 years. This investor plans to sell the stock for $33 at the end of the second year, after collecting the two dividends. Amjet stock's required rate of return is 10 percent. Using the present value over a finite holding period model, Equation (13-7), we can compute this share's present value of $30.99, as shown below:
>
> $$P_0 = \frac{\$2.00}{(1 + .1)^1} + \frac{\$2.30}{(1 + .1)^2} + \frac{\$33}{(1 + .1)^2}$$
>
> $$= \frac{\$2.00}{1.1} + \frac{\$2.30}{1.21} + \frac{\$33}{1.21}$$
>
> (13-7a)
>
> $$= \$1.82 + \$1.90 + \$27.27 = \$30.99$$
>
> $\underbrace{\$1.82 + \$1.90}_{\text{Present value of dividends}}$ $\underbrace{\$27.27}_{\text{Present value of price}}$

Box 13-6

337

Chapter 13
Common
Stock
Analysis

DEFINITION: Intrinsic Value per Share

$$\text{Intrinsic value per share} = \text{normalized EPS} \times \text{expected P/E ratio} \qquad (13\text{-}8)$$

Note that simply multiplying P/E times E to obtain the price would be mathematical tautology if the actual P/E ratio were employed. However, when the unobservable, but *expected* (or forecast), price-earnings ratio, denoted E(P/E), is used instead of the actual P/E ratio, multiplying E(P/E) by E becomes a logical basis for forecasting the intrinsic value per share.

A *model* is a simplified version of reality. We cannot expect simplified valuation models to explain every movement in the price of every stock. To create a model that is more useful, the earnings of the firm (the source of cash dividends) and other factors must also be considered. For this, we use a technique called *fundamental analysis*.

13-2   Fundamental Analysis

Different security analysts use various techniques to estimate the value of a stock. The most popular method is fundamental analysis. Analysts who use this method are called *fundamental analysts*. Fundamental analysts study basic financial and economic facts about a security issuer in order to prepare an estimate of the security's value. They examine the level and trend of the firm's sales and earnings, the quality of the firm's products, the firm's competitive position in the markets where its products are sold, its labor relations, sources of raw materials, the government rules that apply to the firm, and many other factors that may affect the value of the firm's common stock. The goal of all this research is to estimate two key numbers: the *normalized earnings per share (EPS)* and the *price-earnings ratio (P/E)*. As explained in Equation (9-23), the EPS is the firm's net income after taxes divided by the number of shares outstanding. The EPS is *normalized* by disregarding temporary fluctuations in its value (see Chapter 14). The P/E ratio is the price per share of a firm's stock divided by EPS. To estimate the *intrinsic value per share*, fundamental analysts multiply EPS by the expected P/E ratio (see Box 13-6).

The E(P/E) Ratio

Fundamental analysis requires investors to calculate forecasts of the stock's **expected price-earnings ratio,** denoted **E(P/E).** The E(P/E) value is formed by dividing the present value per share by the *expected* normalized earnings per share, denoted E(EPS), as shown below:

$$E(P/E) = \frac{\text{present value per share}}{E(EPS)} \qquad (13\text{-}9)$$

To increase the usefulness of Equation (13-9) the security analyst should substitute the stock's present value of dividends formula, Equation (13-1c), into the numerator of Equation (13-9). Rearranging the terms results in a model that explains the theory underlying the E(P/E), Equation (13-9a).

$$E(P/E) = \frac{\text{cash dividend}/E(EPS)}{\text{discount rate} - \text{growth rate}} = \frac{D/E(EPS)}{k - g} \tag{13-9a}$$

Coincidentally, the numerator of Equation (13-9a) is called the expected cash dividend **payout ratio.** (It was introduced in Equation (9-25) and is discussed further in a later section of this chapter.)

$$\text{Payout ratio} = \text{cash dividend per share}/EPS = D/E \tag{9-25}$$

Equations (13-9a) and (13-25) show that in order to estimate the price-earnings ratio, the fundamental analyst must forecast (1) the stock's risk-adjusted discount rate, (2) its growth rate, (3) its cash dividend per share, (4) its earnings per share (EPS), and (5) its payout ratio (*D/E*).

Comparing Expected and Actual P/E Ratios

Fundamental analysts compare their E(P/E) with the actual P/E ratio that is based on the stock's current market price. The current, or **actual, P/E ratio** is defined below.

$$\text{Actual P/E ratio} = \frac{\text{current market price per share}}{\text{current earnings per share}} \tag{13-10}$$

The results of this comparison are used to reach one of three conclusions:

 1. If the current P/E ratio is larger than the E(P/E) ratio, the stock is overpriced; it should be sold before its price falls.

2. If the current P/E ratio is smaller than the E(P/E) ratio, the stock is underpriced; it could be purchased with a reasonable expectation that its price will rise.

3. If the current P/E ratio equals the E(P/E) ratio, the stock is correctly priced; no significant price changes are likely to occur.

The fundamental analysis process is summarized in Figure 13-1. This procedure is a widely used method of making decisions about buying and selling common stock. Thousands of professional security analysts who manage billions of dollars use this procedure. The result is that overpriced shares have their prices and P/E ratios driven down to appropriate levels by selling pressure, underpriced stocks have their prices and P/E ratios bid up, and correctly priced stocks experience no consistent buying or selling pressures to cause their prices to change. Market pressures tend to keep stock prices near the intrinsic values reached by the fundamental analysts' consensus.[3]

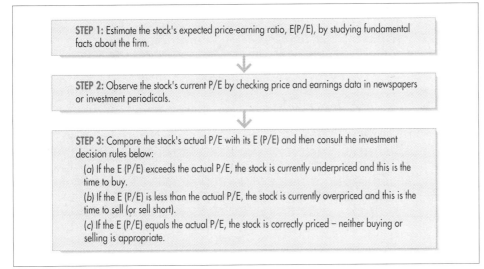

STEP 1: Estimate the stock's expected price-earning ratio, E(P/E), by studying fundamental facts about the firm.

STEP 2: Observe the stock's current P/E by checking price and earnings data in newspapers or investment periodicals.

STEP 3: Compare the stock's actual P/E with its E (P/E) and then consult the investment decision rules below:

(a) If the E (P/E) exceeds the actual P/E, the stock is currently underpriced and this is the time to buy.

(b) If the E (P/E) is less than the actual P/E, the stock is currently overpriced and this is the time to sell (or sell short).

(c) If the E (P/E) equals the actual P/E, the stock is correctly priced – neither buying or selling is appropriate.

Figure 13-1   Fundamental analysis flowchart.

Earnings Multipliers

P/E ratios are sometimes called **earnings multipliers** because the E(P/E) ratio is multiplied by the EPS to obtain an estimate of the intrinsic value per share. Table 13-2 shows partially calculated E(P/E) ratios, which are ready for comparison with actual P/E ratios. The (D/E) symbols in Table 13-2 represent the payout ratio. Note that the payout ratio is in the numerator of Equation (13-9a), the model that explains the expected price-earnings ratio, E(P/E). Thus, when the payout ratio for a given stock is determined, it can be multiplied by the associated number in Table 13-2 to obtain the E(P/E) ratio. The expected price-earnings ratio is then multiplied by the stock's EPS to get an estimate of the intrinsic value per share. For instance, consider the value of a stock with a $k = 12\%$ discount rate, a $g = 2\%$ per year growth rate, and a payout ratio of $D/E = .60 = 60$ percent. Table 13-2 indicates that the appropriate P/E ratio [that is, the E(P/E) ratio] for this stock is 6 (or $10 \times .6$).

The Payout Ratio

About 60 percent of the average NYSE-listed corporation's earnings are typically paid out in the form of cash dividends to shareholders. The remaining 40 percent becomes retained earnings. A corporation's cash dividend payout is determined at

---

[3] For an important empirical investigation of P/E ratios see Sanjay Basu, "The Information Content of Price Earnings Ratios," *Financial Management,* vol. 4, no. 2, 1975, pp. 53–64. Also see S. Basu, "The Relationship between Earnings' Yield, Market Value and Return for NYSE Common Stocks: Further Evidence," *Journal of Financial Economics,* vol. 12, no. 1, 1983, pp. 129–156, and S. Basu, "The Investment Performance of Common Stocks in Relation to Their Price-Earnings Ratios: A Test of the Efficient Market Hypothesis," *Journal of Finance,* vol. 32, no. 3, 1977, pp. 663–682.

Table 13-2
Expected P/E Ratios Appropriate for
Different Discount Rates and Growth Rates*

Risk-adjusted discount rate, k	Growth rate, g				
	0%	2%	4%	6%	8%
8%	12.5(D/E)	16.66(D/E)	25(D/E)	50(D/E)	Undefined
10	10(D/E)	12.5(D/E)	16.66(D/E)	25(D/E)	50(D/E)
12	8.33(D/E)	10(D/E)	12.5(D/E)	16.66(D/E)	25(D/E)
14	7.14(D/E)	8.33(D/E)	10(D/E)	12.5(D/E)	16.66(D/E)
16	6.25(D/E)	7.14(D/E)	8.33(D/E)	10(D/E)	12.5(D/E)
18	5.55(D/E)	6.25(D/E)	7.14(D/E)	8.33(D/E)	10(D/E)
20	5(D/E)	5.55(D/E)	6.25(D/E)	7.14(D/E)	8.33(D/E)
25	4(D/E)	4.34(D/E)	4.76(D/E)	5.26(D/E)	5.88(D/E)
33	3(D/E)	3.22(D/E)	3.44(D/E)	3.70(D/E)	4.0(D/E)
50	2(D/E)	2.08(D/E)	2.17(D/E)	2.17(D/E)	2.38(D/E)

* The values in the table were calculated with the following model:

$$E(P/E) = \frac{\text{cash dividend}/E(EPS)}{\text{discount rate} - \text{growth rate}}$$

$$= \frac{D/E}{\text{discount rate} - \text{growth rate}}$$

$$= \left(\frac{1}{\text{discount rate} - \text{growth rate}}\right)(D/E)$$

quarterly meetings of the board of directors. If a corporation pays cash dividends, the payout ratio is an important variable in estimating its intrinsic value. The relationship between a corporation's cash dividend payout and its intrinsic value per share is explained here with respect to the dividend payout policies of growth firms, declining firms, and normal firms.

Cash Dividends for Growth Firms Firms that earn a return on funds invested within the firm that is higher than their cost of capital are **growth firms.** Growth firms maximize their value by retaining earnings for internal investment. For example, environmental protection firms and corporations that manufacture high-tech medical products have been growth stocks recently because of technological breakthroughs that gave them superior products. These firms could raise capital (for example, by selling bonds and paying interest) at some cost of capital and then reinvest these funds internally to earn a rate of return that exceeds their cost of capital. Firms with such profitable internal investment opportunities usually reinvest most of their earnings inside the firm to finance profitable growth. *Paying cash dividends tends to decrease a growth firm's value per share.*

Cash Dividends for Declining Firms Firms that do not have profitable opportunities to invest are **declining firms.** Typically, a firm declines because its products become obsolete, its sales decline, and further investment within the firm is not profitable. Declining firms can be found in the industry that manufactures film for still photo cameras, for example. Electronic camcorders have stolen market share away from the traditional still camera. As a result, manufacturers of film for still cameras have so few profitable investment opportunities in the film business that their rate of return on internal investment remains below their cost of capital. Declining firms can maximize share value by paying out whatever they earn in cash dividends.

In many cases the optimal action for a declining firm is to liquidate all the firm's assets and pay one big, final cash dividend. The shareowners who receive these dividends will either spend them or look for better investments. Either way, the capital will be used more productively outside the declining firm. Usually, *there is no reason to continue investing in a declining firm;* its profits get smaller each year and eventually turn into losses as the firm moves toward bankruptcy.[4]

Cash Dividends for Normal Firms   The vast majority of firms have only a few modest growth opportunities. These firms are in economic equilibrium; the rate of return from their internal investments *equals* their cost of capital. For these firms, *dividend policy has no effect on value;* that is, no matter what percentage of earnings such firms pay out in dividends, the value of their common stock is unchanged.

Figure 11-1 contrasts the way cash dividends might grow for corporations that had very fast growth of 15 percent per year, swift growth of 10 percent, above average growth of 5 percent, and a slow 1 percent rate. This discussion suggests an intricate relationship between the variables that determine P/E ratios and share values. You may wonder whether there isn't a simpler way to determine the value of common stock. Let's see.

Book Value, Appraised Value, and Intrinsic Value

After considering the logic behind using P/E ratios to value common stocks, you might think that it would be simpler and more appropriate to base common stock values on a stock's book value, or on the value of the firm's physical assets. However, a profitable corporation is more than a collection of physical assets; a profitable corporation produces some item or service of value and earns income. If the corporation's assets cannot produce income, they have no economic value. As a result, *the market values of physical assets are usually irrelevant.*

The liquidation value of assets can be estimated by consulting an appraiser. The asset value of a security can be assessed by estimating the liquidation value of the firm, deducting the claims of creditors, and allocating the value of the remaining assets to the outstanding securities.

Usually asset values are important in determining the market value of a company

---

[4] This discussion ignores strategic corporate moves like doing research and development to develop new products, acquiring firms with growth products, and other forms of diversification. Or, if the declining firm owns some valuable assets (such as patents, real estate, and/or natural resources), it might be worthwhile to continue operating while these assets are sold off in an orderly manner.

Box 13-7

FINANCIAL EXAMPLE: More and Less Meaningful per Share Data

Table 13-3 shows financial data for the International Business Machine (IBM) Corporation that might be used in estimating the intrinsic value of the firm's common stock. The lack of relationship between the book value of equity and the market value of the firm's stock is apparent in these data. Note, for instance, how IBM's lowest stock price per share is always more than $18 above the book value per share. Furthermore, IBM's book value per share rises while the peak market prices for the stock fell in 1980, 1981, and 1984. This suggests that asset values and accounting book values can be ignored when valuing common stock. Generally speaking, the book value and the liquidation value give very small clues to what the common stock of a profitable corporation is actually worth.

Table 13-3
Selected Financial Data for IBM Common Stock
on a per Share Basis

Year	Per share book value	Range of market price	Per share earnings	Average price-earnings ratio	Per share cash dividend	Cash dividend payout ratio
1991	$64.69	$ 83–139	$(4.95)	UND	$4.84	UND
1990	75.01	96–123	10.51	10	4.84	46%
1989	67.00	93–130	6.47	17	4.73	73
1988	62.87	104–129	9.80	13	4.40	45
1987	64.09	102–176	8.72	16	4.40	50
1986	56.73	119–161	7.81	18	4.40	56
1985	51.98	117–158	10.67	13	4.40	41
1984	43.23	99–128	10.77	10	4.10	38
1983	38.02	92–134	9.04	12	3.71	41
1982	33.13	55–98	7.39	11	3.44	46
1981	30.66	48–71	5.63	11	3.44	61
1980	28.18	50–72	6.10	10	3.44	56
1979	25.64	61–80	5.16	13	3.44	66

Note: UND means undefined.

only if it may (1) go bankrupt or (2) be acquired for its physical assets. In that case the firm's income and dividends will not continue and will therefore have little value; the firm's value will depend on the value of its physical assets. For prosperous firms, however, the intrinsic value typically far exceeds the value of the firm's physical assets.

13-3   Some Practical Considerations

343

*Chapter 13
Common
Stock
Analysis*

Much of the fundamental analyst's work centers on determining the appropriate earnings multiplier, E(P/E), to use in valuing securities. Several interrelated factors determine earnings multipliers, including the issuer's level of risk, growth rate, and payout ratio. Table 13-2 indicates the general nature of the relationship between risk-adjusted discount rates, multipliers, and the growth rate. The table shows that if all other factors are held constant:

- Price-earnings ratios vary inversely with the risk-adjusted discount rate.

- Increased growth prospects imply higher price-earnings ratios.

The values given by the models must be adjusted to account for various other factors.

Business Cycles

The discussion of the E(P/E) ratios so far considers earnings multipliers under normal market conditions, which occur when security prices are experiencing slow, steady growth and the average P/E ratios prevail. The left side of Figure 13-2 illustrates how the risk-adjusted interest rates (or capitalization rates) used in present value calculations rise and fall as market conditions change from bearish to bullish, respectively. On the right-hand side of Figure 13-2 we can see how earnings multipliers move inversely with discount rates as the condition of the market changes. (Figure 13-5, introduced later, shows cyclical fluctuations in the stock market.)

Figure 13-2 Capitalization rates and multipliers are affected by risk and economic conditions. *Left,* discount rates are affected by the risk of the stock and the condition of the market. *Right,* earnings multipliers vary inversely with discount rates.

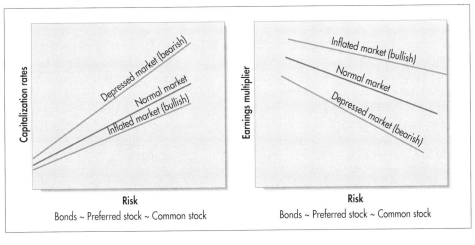

The discount (or capitalization) rates presented in Table 13-2 are for normal markets. If the analysis is being performed in an inflated (or bullish) market, the capitalization rates should be adjusted downward to increase the earnings multipliers in line with prevailing conditions. The reverse is true if pessimism prevails and market prices are depressed.

The Margin for Error

Errors may creep into estimates of a share of stock's normalized earnings, dividend payout ratio, capitalization rate, and dividend growth rate. It is possible that an error of plus or minus 20 percent of the true intrinsic value could occur, even in a carefully prepared analysis, so it is wise to consider the intrinsic value to be within 20 percent of the estimated value. For example, a $20 estimate for the intrinsic value of a share of stock should be understood to mean that the value is within the range of $16 to $24. Analysts should always be explicit about this margin for error so that inexperienced investors will not depend too much on the accuracy of the estimate. To continue the example: if the stock were selling at $15, it would seem to be underpriced and therefore a good buy. But if it were selling at $18.50 or $21.75, it would be priced appropriately after allowing for a 20 percent error from the $20 intrinsic value estimate.

The Payout Ratio and the Earnings Multiplier

The effects of the dividend payout ratio are fairly direct and easy to see. All other things being equal, reducing a corporation's dividend payout tends to cut its earnings multiplier and thus its intrinsic value. However, measuring the payout ratio can be problem. Since dividends per share are a different percentage of corporations' earnings per share practically every quarter, what is the best estimate of its payout ratio? A glance at the right-hand column of Table 13-3, for example, shows that IBM's payout ratio fluctuated from 73 to 38 percent from 1979 to 1990. Most corporations' payout ratios fluctuate more than this because they try to maintain the same level of cash dividends with varying earnings. When a corporation incurs a loss (that is, has negative earnings per share), its payout ratio is simply undefined for that period. This happened to IBM in 1991, for example.

Estimating the payout ratio of a fairly stable firm like IBM is not too difficult. As Table 13-3 shows, the payout ratio usually fluctuated above and below 50 percent. For a more risky company, which experiences more volatile earnings fluctuations, it is necessary to estimate *normalized earnings per share*. Although we will postpone our investigation of earnings and the procedures for finding normalized earnings until the next chapter, we can state here that a firm's earnings should be averaged over a complete business cycle to smooth out temporary fluctuations. The resulting normalized earnings per share can be used to find a normalized payout ratio for use in determining an earnings multiplier, as shown below.

$$\frac{\text{Normalized}}{\text{payout ratio}} = \frac{\text{regular cash dividend per share}}{\text{normalized earnings per share}} \qquad (13\text{-}11)$$

There are, however, a few cases where this straightforward procedure is inappropriate. Some corporations seeking rapid growth reinvest all earnings to maximize internally financed growth—that is, no cash dividends are paid. As explained above, this is logical for a growing firm.

There are other unusual cases in which the present value of constantly growing dividends model will not work. Consider a corporation that pays cash dividends that bear no relation to its earnings. While experiencing losses in 1978 and 1979, Chrysler continued to pay cash dividends with borrowed money. In such cases, the analyst might be able to use past earnings multipliers as a starting point. Historical earnings multipliers might then be adjusted to obtain the best possible estimate of a share's current intrinsic value.

13-4 The Product Life Cycle

Figure 13-3 presents a product (or industry) life cycle model that may be useful in forecasting the profitability of a corporation.[5] The life cycle depicted in Figure 13-3 shows the four stages of a product's life: introduction, expansion, maturity, and decline.

[5] The industry life cycle theory is discussed in *Techniques of Profitability Analysis* by Sam R. Goodman, John Wiley & Sons, 1970; in particular, see chapter four. Also see *Modern Economic Growth,* Yale University Press, New Haven, Conn., 1966, by Simon S. Kuznets.

Figure 13-3 Product life cycle curves.

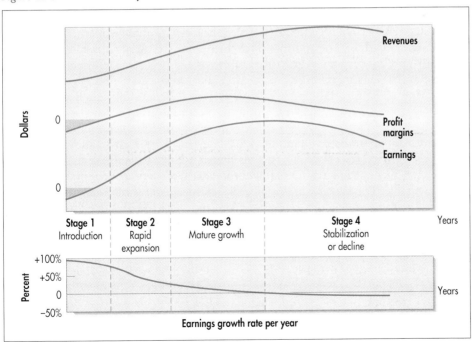

Stage 1: Introduction   In this phase, the product starts with zero sales and may operate with initial losses. If the product survives, its manufacturer may be recognized by the more perceptive security analysts. A share in a corporation that is growing successfully by the time it arrives at the end of stage one is called an **emerging growth stock.** Emerging growth stocks can be lucrative investments if they survive.

Stage 2: Rapid Expansion   Sales grow rapidly and consistent annual profits usually begin to emerge during the second stage of a product's life. Firms in this second stage must reinvest earnings and borrow heavily to finance the new plant, new equipment, increased inventory, and larger accounts receivable needed to sustain rapid growth. Solvency is difficult to maintain under these conditions, and many rapidly developing firms with good products go bankrupt during stage two simply because they cannot finance their expansion.

Stage 3: Mature Growth   After years of rapid growth during which the products and firms in an industry tend to acquire stable market shares come the years of slower growth that comprise stage three. Mature growth companies may begin to pay consistent cash dividends, and they usually repay any excessive debt acquired during the years of rapid expansion. Profit margins stated as a percent of sales typically start to shrink because of price competition, but annual dollar profits continue to grow—although at a slower rate.

Stage 4: Stability or Decline   When a product reaches stage four of its life cycle, unit sales stabilize for the individual firms and for the entire industry. Unit sales can decline if the product becomes obsolete, but dollar sales and dollar profits may continue to grow slowly at a rate about equal to the rate of inflation. Firms in this fourth stage are usually very liquid, but they have few profitable internal investment opportunities within the industry. Such firms must typically diversify into new fields to sustain corporate growth. During the 1990s, for example, computer companies (IBM, Wang, Unisys, Burroughs), tobacco companies (American Brands, Philip Morris, Liggett Group, Lorillard, RJR Nabisco), and auto manufacturers (Ford, GM, and Chrysler) may pass from the third into the fourth stage.

The product life cycle theory is better at explaining the behavior of industries than at explaining the behavior of individual firms, because many small firms fall into bankruptcy during stages one and two. And even in those cases where it is applicable, the life cycle theory can be difficult to interpret because there are no set time limits on a product's life. For instance, cameras that develop pictures internally (such as the Polaroid) and most fad goods reach stage four of their life cycles in a fraction of the number of years it took for the automobile and the printing industries to mature and stabilize.

In spite of these difficulties, however, the theory can still yield valuable insights. The theory can be particularly valuable to the analyst who is trying to estimate growth rates in sales, earnings, and/or dividends. If a corporation's products can be categorized into one of the four stages, the life cycle theory suggests growth estimates for the industry and whether these growth rates should be increasing or decreasing.

In estimating a stock's intrinsic economic value, many factors can be evaluated only subjectively. The firm's management, its research and development program, accounting inconsistencies, and industry factors are some of the more important subjective considerations that can affect value.

Management   In forecasting the risk and earnings of a given corporation, the fundamental security analyst ought to appraise the quality of the firm's management. The depth and experience of management; managers' age, education, and health; individuals who constitute bottlenecks; and ability to react to change all affect the firm's risk and its future income. Management evaluation is not simple, for capable managers do not fit easily recognizable stereotypes. Chapter 19 delves into management assessment in more detail.

Research and Development (R&D)   Research and development (R&D) programs can have an important impact on the value of the firm. For example, if a company has made new discoveries or possesses advanced technology that will give it a competitive advantage in the future, the potential benefits tend to have a favorable effect on the intrinsic value of its securities. But assessing the value of ongoing research is difficult, since seemingly minor technological developments can sometimes be extremely profitable. Making such evaluations involves as much skill as science.

Accounting Inconsistencies   As we noted in Chapter 9, accounting statements and financial ratios are useful tools for assessing a firm. Financial analysts should be wary of certain accounting statement inconsistencies. Three of the more drastic accounting changes that should be watched for are (1) changes in the way sales are reported each year, (2) changes in the way inventories are valued, and (3) changes in the way asset values are depreciated.

1. *Changes in the way sales are reported each year:* A firm could change from recognizing sales as occurring as early as when the customer signs a sales agreement, before a single penny is paid, to recognizing sales as occurring as late as when the last payment is received (which might be years later). This accounting inconsistency will alter sales in the first year of the change, and the difference can be huge. Suppose, for example, the sale is of a new skyscraper.

2. *Changes in the way inventories are valued:* Switching from what accountants call first-in-first-out (FIFO) to last-in-first-out (LIFO) inventory valuation will tend to change the firm's reported profits in the year after the change. Some firms that carry large inventories have been able to change losses into profits by switching from LIFO to FIFO. When these one-time changes are used to conceal poor earnings, the practice is called *cooking the books*.

3. *Changes in the way asset values are depreciated:* A switch from what is called *straight-line depreciation accounting* to an accelerated form of depreciation accounting (such as the accelerated cost recovery system) changes the firm's reported profits. Essentially, switching from straight line to any kind of accelerated depreciation technique decreases the firm's accounting earnings in the first few years after the change and increases later years' earnings.

Investors can detect accounting inconsistencies and other gimmicks by analyzing the firm's financial statements and reading the footnotes to the statements. Investors can also examine consistently defined financial statements and ratios by consulting such investor services as Standard & Poor's, Value Line, and Moody's.

Industry Factors   Many industry factors should be considered when analyzing a corporation's securities, including legislation that subsidizes or curtails the industry, environmental problems that are unique to the industry, the stage in the product life cycle in which the industry finds itself (see Figure 13-3), the aggressiveness of foreign competition, and new technology that may make the industry's product more or less competitive.

13-6   Playing the Market: Stock Market Timing

Some long-term investors try to buy stocks whose market prices are at or below their estimated intrinsic value and then hold them for long-run price appreciation and cash dividends. Those who follow this buy and hold strategy make no attempt to buy low and sell high or otherwise outguess the market. Life insurance companies, pension funds, and bank trust departments are examples of institutional investors that typically follow a *buy and hold strategy.* In contrast, some investors are **active traders,** who work aggressively to forecast the rises and falls in the market and time their trades so that they buy at cyclically low prices and sell at cyclically high prices. Like the bond speculators of Chapter 12, stock traders hope their aggressive trading will earn them higher profits.

Virtually all free markets for securities and commodities periodically fall precipitously, offering traders who can anticipate these turns ample opportunity to profit from timely security trading. Figure 17-1 shows recent bull and bear market periods in the U.S. stock market. As it illustrates, a trader who buys at market low points and sells at high points can avoid capital losses and earn larger trading profits than someone following a buy-and-hold strategy. However, buying low and selling high is more easily said than done.

It is difficult to outguess the market because there are thousands of investors watching it, and some of these investors are knowledgeable in finance and economics. Furthermore, some of these knowledgeable investors also have high levels of intelligence and energy, and they study the market every day. Many of these sophisticated investors are amateurs, but a few thousand are professional money managers. The combined efforts of these bright, energetic, and well-trained investors keep the prices of most securities close to their intrinsic (or present) values. Even though new information arrives continuously and in a random fashion, securities prices fluctuate in close pursuit of their underlying values. As a result of this **efficient markets** mechanism, it is not easy to find underpriced securities.

In this section we will discuss the tools an active trader can use to try to forecast the rises and falls in security markets. A fundamental analyst can begin to predict the timing of security price movements by studying economic forecasts and leading economic indicators for the entire economy.

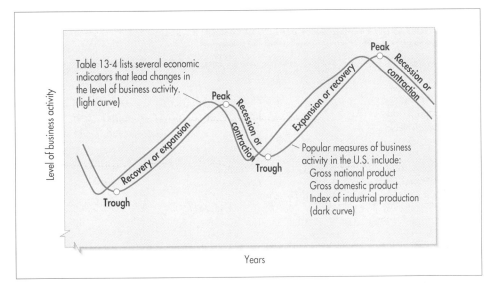

Figure 13-4 Stages of business cycles.

Leading Economic Indicators

No two business cycles are precisely the same, but typically business activity increases for several years until the *economic expansion* peaks, and then a *recession* starts (see Figure 13-4). It usually takes a year or two for a recession to reach its trough so that the next period of expansion can begin. All economic activity does not rise and fall together simultaneously. Corporate profits and cash dividend payments are called a **lagging indicator** of economic activity because they rise and fall with the level of business activity, but their peaks and troughs follow several months behind those in the level of general business activity.

Millions of investors follow the economic news. Many work out forecasts of when the next economic peak or trough will occur. Some of the largest investors have detailed forecasts that extend for over a year into the future. It is because of this economic forecasting that stock prices are a **leading indicator** of economic activity. Stock market indexes (like the S&P 500) crash months in advance of recessions because the investors with economic forecasts see the recessions coming and start selling their stocks months before corporate profits and cash dividends collapse.

Economic forecasts can help investors forecast the market's turns and help them to buy low and sell high. Four leading economic indicators that frequently anticipate changes in the nation's gross domestic product (GDP) are discussed below.

- *Private housing starts:* The number of new residential homes started into production each year is a leading indicator because sales of construction material, furniture, carpeting, and drapery follow housing starts. Home construction and home furnishings make up a large sector of the American economy.

- *New durable goods orders:* Automobiles, appliances, machinery, and other durable goods on order from manufacturers are a leading indicator because at the

Table 13-4
Lead Times for Leading Economic Indicators

Indicator	Months of lead time ahead of GDP
Private housing starts	2–37
New durable goods orders	1–30
Average workweek	0–20
S&P 500 stocks index	2–11

Sources: See Jesse Levin, "Prophetic Leaders," *Financial Analysts Journal,* July–August 1970, p. 89; Geoffrey H. Moore, *Business Cycles, Inflation, and Forecasting,* National Bureau of Economic Research Study No. 24 (Cambridge, Mass.: Ballinger, 1980), chap. 9, entitled Security Markets and Business Cycles; R. D. Arnott and W. A. Copeland, "The Business Cycle and Security Selection," *Financial Analysts Journal,* March-April 1985, pp. 26–32; B. G. Malkiel and J. G. Cragg, "Expectations and the Structure of Share Prices," *American Economic Review,* September 1970, pp. 615–616; and Raymond Piccini, "Stock Market Behavior around Business Cycle Peaks," *Financial Analysts Journal,* July-August 1980, pp. 55–57.

end of a recession, for example, people who are reemployed and businesses that are starting to enjoy sales increases may need to spend some of their increasing incomes to replace the durable goods that deteriorated when they were surviving on accumulated capital during the recession.

- *Average workweek:* The number of hours worked per week averaged over thousands of workers is a leading indicator, because fatter paychecks turn into increased consumer spending. This spending, in turn, causes businesses to increase production, employment, and investments in inventories and new machinery.

- *Stock price indexes:* The average price of common stocks, as reflected in the S&P 500 index, for example, is a leading indicator because investors who foresee an economic downturn sell their stocks and thus cause bear markets months before a recession starts.

Table 13-4 suggests the lead times for each of these economic indicators.

Forecasting

Some investors do not bother to forecast the entire U.S. economy. Instead, they simply follow some economic indicators that tend to lead stock prices. Since bull and bear markets have preceded every recession in the United States by almost a year, a forecast should extend more than 1 year into the future to be useful in anticipating

Box 13-8

351

*Chapter 13
Common
Stock
Analysis*

> **PRINCIPLES: Buy Low, Sell High**
>
> After a strong bull market has pushed the prices of most stocks to high levels, the market's optimism will be reflected in certain financial ratios. The market average price-earnings ratio will be notably high, and the average stock's cash dividend yield will be remarkably low. The converse of these statements would be true after the market has been bearish for a long period—the market average price-earnings ratio will be low and the cash dividend yield high. The tendencies of these market average ratios can be used as guidelines for selling out or buying into the market. Figure 13-5 presents graphs of historical statistics for the Standard & Poor's 500 Stocks Composite Index (S&P 500).
>
> Figure 13-5*a* shows that the S&P 500 average's price-earnings ratio seldom gets as high as 19 or as low as 8; these extremes may therefore be interpreted as sell and buy signals, respectively. Figure 13-5*d* shows that the cash dividend yield for the S&P 500 rarely rises above 5 percent or falls below 3 percent; so these values can also be used as buy and sell signals.
>
> Comparing the buy and sell signals from (*a*) and (*d*) with the S&P 500 index shown in (*b*) and (*c*) reveals that the signals were not optimal. They were useful, however, in providing perspective and in making worthwhile trading suggestions. In particular, note that both (*a*) and (*d*) gave almost simultaneous signals to sell several months before the October 1987 crash. Likewise, both indicators gave strong buy signals in 1974 that would have been profitable to follow.

turns in the stock market. The forecast ideally would include the timing of changes and provide some detail about inflation and other matters that are useful in making investment decisions. Economic forecasts may be purchased from consultants or obtained from newspapers and magazines.

Ultimately, the ability of an economic forecast to predict dollar quantities is not so important as its ability to foretell the *timing* and *direction* of changes in the various rates of economic growth. Indications of shifts in the direction of the economy are most useful in anticipating similar changes in the stock market. This type of information allows an investor to assume a defensive position when bear markets are anticipated and to be aggressive when bullish conditions are expected.

When forecasting that a particular security's price will rise or fall, the fundamental analyst must estimate the earnings multipliers for each quarter.

Forecasting Earnings Multipliers   As Table 13-4 indicated, security prices anticipate the economy by 2 to 11 months in the United States. These data imply that an economic forecast for 1 year into the future can be expected to lead changes in the level of security prices by 1 to 10 months. Because of the variable time lag between the anticipatory stock prices and the underlying economic activity, however, even the best forecasts cannot be expected to pinpoint the turn in the securities markets within much less than several months.

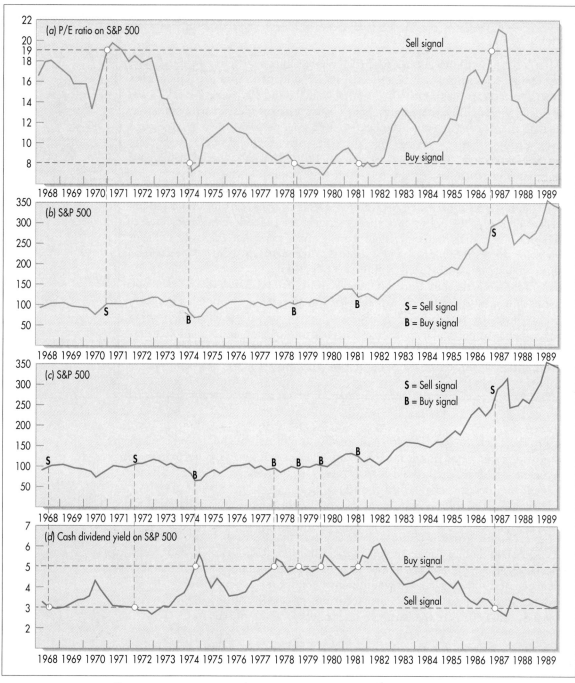

Figure 13-5 S&P 500 market statistics, 1968–1990, for (*a*) P/E ratio, (*b*) S&P 500 market index, (*c*) S&P 500 market index (with different buy-sell signals), (*d*) cash dividend yield. (*Trendline, 25 Broadway, New York, NY 10004.*)

Price-earnings ratios fluctuate continuously, as Table 13-5 shows. A significant portion of this fluctuation is systematic market-related movement. As a result, it can be useful to forecast stock market levels in terms of the P/E ratio for some stock market index. Studying past P/E ratios for a highly diversified stock market indicator (such as the Standard & Poor's 500) and studying the associated economic conditions

Table 13-5
Price-Earnings Ratios for Selected Firms, 1981–1990*

Industry and firm	1981	1982	1983	1984	1985	1986	1987	1988	1989	1990
Airlines:										
Delta	8	67	NM	8	7	38	8	7	7	11.5
Automobiles:										
Chrysler	NM	NM	10	2.5	2.5	4	5.5	5	17	49
Ford	NM	NM	3.5	2.5	3.5	4	4.5	4	6	28
General Motors	43	16	6	5	6	9	7	5	7	NM
Honda	4	11	8	9	9.5	7	13	12	19	28
Banks:										
Bankers Trust	4.5	4.5	5	5	6	7	NM	4.5	NM	5
Chase Manhattan	4.5	6	5	5	5	6	NM	2.5	NM	NM
Citicorp	6	5.5	6	5	6	8	NM	5	26	35
BankAmerica	8	8	10	10.5	NM	NM	NM	4.5	7	7
Photography:										
Eastman Kodak	8	11	23	12	32	35	16	10	28	18
Polaroid	27	31	19	36	29	17	15	NM	22	15
Raw materials:										
Exxon	5	6	6	6	8	9	12	10	19	12
Weyerhaeuser	19	34	27	19	22	19	14	10	19	12
Dow Chemical	10	13	21	10	NM	13	13	7	7	11
Rubber:										
Goodyear	5	8	11	14	10	42	6.5	9.5	15	NM
Goodrich	5	NM	54	12	NM	NM	15	12	8.5	9
Beverages:										
Coca-Cola	9	11	17	12	14.5	15	17	14	18.5	20
Anheuser-Busch	7	9	10	8	12	14	16.5	13	14	13
Computers:										
COMPAQ	NA	NM	90	19	9	11	13.5	9.5	11	NA
Digital Equipment	15	11	19	16	15	18	17	11.5	NM	12
Texas Instrument	21	18	NM	10	NM	NM	19	12	12	NA
IBM	10		12	10	13	18	16	12	17	11
Mining:										
Homestake	31	36	28	49	51	54	12	24	NM	NM
Advertising:										
Saatchi	NA	NA	19	17	15	16	11	8	NM	NA
Market index:										
S&P 500 Index	8.5	9.1	12	10	12.2	16.3	18.5	13.1	13.6	15.1

* The price-earnings ratios are the averages of the high and low values for each year.

Source: Standard & Poor's Corporation, *Stock Market Encyclopedia*, August 1991.

Note: NM means not meaningful because of negative earnings; NA means not available.

Box 13-9

COMPUTATION: Estimating IBM's Intrinsic Value per Share

A securities analyst was considering buying a share of IBM common stock early in 1991 and selling it late in 1994. The analyst's 1991 estimates of the earnings per share, cash dividend payout ratio, cash dividends per share, appropriate risk-adjusted discount rate*, and present value of all cashflows are shown below. These computations provide an example of how to use Equation (13-7) to estimate the intrinsic value per share.

Part A: The present value (PV) of 4 years of cash dividends per share is $17.94.

Year	Estimated earnings per share (5% annual growth)	×	Estimated cash dividend payout	=	Estimated cash dividend per share	×	12% PV factor	=	PV of estimated cash dividend
1990	$10.51		.46		$4.84		NA		Actual
1991	11.04		.5		5.52		.893		$ 4.93[a]
1992	11.59		.5		5.80		.797		4.62[a]
1993	12.17		.5		6.08		.712		4.33[a]
1994	12.77		.5		6.39		.636		4.06[a]

1991 present value of forecast cash dividends: $17.94

[a] Forecast values.

Part B: The present value of the estimated 1994 selling price is $81.22 for the share.

Year	Estimated earnings per share	×	Price-earnings ratio	=	Estimated value per share	×	12% PV factor	=	E(PV per share)
1994	$12.77		10 times		$127.70		.636		$81.22

Part C: The 1991 estimate of the intrinsic value per share for IBM stock is $81.22.

$17.94 (from part A) + $81.22 (from part B) = $99.16 = E(PV per share)

These computations suggest that the value of IBM was $99.16 per share in 1991. IBM's market price actually fluctuated as high as $139 in 1991 but ended the year at $83.

* Determining the appropriate risk-adjusted discount rate to use when finding the present value of an asset is the subject of Chapters 10 and 12 (see Figures 10-1 and 12-4) and some later chapters.

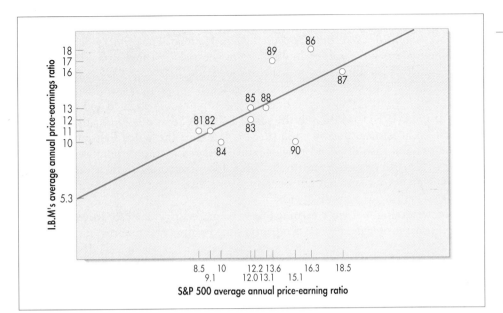

Figure 13-6 IBM's price-earnings ratio regressed on the S&P 500 average price-earnings ratio.

can help the fundamental analyst in converting economic forecasts into forecasts of the market's average earnings multiplier. The bottom row of Table 13-5 shows how earnings multipliers from the Standard & Poor's 500 stocks index varied over several years. Table 13-5 shows that most P/E ratios tend to rise and fall together with bull and bear markets, unless something idiosyncratic to the issuer causes the P/E to change unsystematically.

After forecasting the earnings multiplier for some market indicator, the analyst can use a scatter diagram such as the one shown in Figure 13-6 to convert the market forecast into earnings multipliers for individual securities. The price-earnings ratio may be viewed as an index of investor confidence. Since investor confidence in all securities tends to rise and fall with the level of the market, useful relationships between the market's average earnings multiplier and individual securities' earnings multipliers are common. Figure 13-6, for instance, shows that the S&P 500's P/E ratio can be used to help explain IBM's P/E. Box 13-9 shows how an analyst would estimate IBM's intrinsic value per share.

Summary

A stock is worth the present value of all future cashflows an investor can expect to receive from it. If something makes those cashflows riskier, a higher discount rate should be used to find their present value. The increased riskiness and higher discount rate will tend to lower the present value. If the rate at which the cashflows from an asset are expected to grow increases, their present value increases accordingly.

Fundamental analysts value stock by using price-earnings ratios. These earnings multipliers can be derived from the present value formula. The primary determinants of a common stock's earnings multiplier are the risk-adjusted discount rate, the growth rate for cash dividends, and the payout ratio.

Comparing estimates of a common stock's appropriate price-earnings ratio, E(P/E), with its actual P/E ratio is one way to pinpoint undervalued and overvalued stocks. If the E(P/E) ratio exceeds the actual P/E ratio, that is a sign that the stock is undervalued; it is overvalued if the E(P/E) is less than the actual P/E ratio.

The optimal cash dividend payout ratio is related to the corporation's growth prospects. Growth firms can maximize their value by retaining all their earnings; the cash dividend payout ratio has no effect on normal firms; and declining firms should pay out everything as cash dividends.

In determining a stock's earnings multiplier, security analysts may encounter some practical problems. Forecasts must be stated with a margin for error. Furthermore, assessments of a corporation's management, its research and development, industry factors, and any accounting inconsistencies are subjective processes, but nevertheless important in determining the appropriate earnings multiplier.

The timing of trades is important to price speculators who hope to profit from short-run price changes. Economic forecasts and leading economic indicators can be useful in refining the forecast of a common stock's earnings per share and its earnings multiplier.

Further Reading

Financial Analysts Journal, November-December 1985, was devoted to various articles about valuing common stocks with discounted present value of cash dividend models: J. L. Farrell, Jr., "The Dividend Discount Model: A Primer," pp. 16–25; P. W. Estep, "A New Method for Valuing Common Stocks," pp. 26–34; B. D. Fielitz and F. L. Muller, "A Simplified Approach to Common Stock Valuation," pp. 35–41; Daniel Rie, "How Trustworthy Is Your Valuation Model?" pp. 42–47; R. O. Michaud, "A Scenario-Dependent Dividend Discount Model: Bridging the Gap between Top-Down Investment Information and Bottom-Up Forecasts," pp. 49–59; and E. H. Sorenson and D. A. Williamson, "Some Evidence on the Value of Dividend Discount Models," pp. 60–64.

Francis, Jack Clark, "Analysis of Equity Returns: A Survey with Extensions," *Journal of Economics and Business,* Spring-Summer 1977. Reprinted in J. C. Francis, C. F. Lee, and Donald E. Farrar, eds., *Readings in Investments* (New York: McGraw-Hill, 1980).
  Econometric analysis of earnings per share, price-earnings multipliers, and stock price changes reveals insights.

Graham, B., D. Dodd, and S. Cottle, *Security Analysis,* 4th ed. (New York: McGraw-Hill, 1962).
  This nonmathematical book is used by most fundamental analysts; it should be read by anyone who aspires to be one.

Malkiel, B. G., "The Valuation of Public Utility Equities," *The Bell Journal of Economics and Management Science,* 1970.
  A statistical test of the present value of the constantly growing dividends model.

Whitbeck, V., and M. Kisor, "A New Tool in Investment Decision Making," *Financial Analysts Journal,* May-June 1963.
  An easy-to-read empirical study of earnings per share and multipliers.

Essay Questions

13-1 "A fundamental analyst's estimate of intrinsic value is different from the present value of all income." Is this statement true, false, or questionable? Explain.

13-2 Does an increase in a firm's cash dividend growth rate always mean an increase in its intrinsic value? Explain why or why not.

13-3 Can factors external to the firm, such as national economic conditions, affect the intrinsic value of a share of stock? Explain.

13-4 "An increase in a firm's liquidity ratios means the firm is well managed and safe, and this will always increase its price-earnings multipliers." Is the preceding statement true, false, or questionable? Explain.

13-5 An experienced fundamental security analyst claims that the procedures for estimating intrinsic value used by professional analysts lead to realistic estimates of true value that are based on "all the facts" and on realistic assumptions. Comment on this claim.

13-6 "The price-earnings multiplier is an index of investor optimism. Stocks that the public likes have high P/E ratios, and stocks that have fallen from favor have low P/E ratios." Is the preceding statement true, false, or questionable? Explain.

13-7 Answer the following question that is taken from the June 1981 Chartered Financial Analysts (CFA) exam.

The value of an asset is the present value of the expected returns from the asset during the holding period. An investment will provide a stream of returns during this period and it is necessary to discount this stream of returns at an appropriate rate to determine the asset's present value. A dividend valuation such as the following is frequently used.

$$\text{Present value} = \frac{\text{cash dividend per share}}{\text{discount rate} - \text{growth rate}}$$

A. Identify the three factors that must be estimated for any valuation model and explain why these estimates are more difficult to derive for common stocks than for bonds. (9 minutes)

B. Explain the principal problems involved in using a dividend valuation model to value the following: (i) Companies whose operations are closely correlated with economic cycles. (ii) Companies that are of giant size and are maturing. (iii) Companies that are small size and are growing rapidly (assume all companies pay dividends). (6 minutes)

Problems

13-8 The Ajax Manufacturing Corporation has been reporting slowly declining sales and annual losses every year for the last 5 years. Ajax's annual losses are small, but the losses keep getting a little larger each year. Rumors that Ajax will soon file for bankruptcy have driven the price per share of its common stock down to $11 per share—the lowest level in over 20 years. Analyzing Ajax's audited financial statements reveals that the corporation has no debts and holds a surprisingly large amount of cash and marketable securities; these liquid assets alone are worth $7.50 per share. In addition, Ajax has another $9 per share worth of real estate and old plant and equipment that is almost fully depreciated on its books. The Ajax plant has been well kept and is in a highly desirable industrial area. Should you ignore the fact that Ajax has financial and physical assets with a value of $7.50 + $9.00 = $16.50 per share? Why is Ajax stock selling for only $11 per share? What would you be willing to pay for a share of Ajax?

13-9   The Blume Company is a small, growing manufacturer of lawn care equipment planning to go public. Mr. Blume, the president of the firm, has hired you as a financial consultant to estimate the price per share at which the stock should be issued. The Westerfield Corporation and the Pettit Corporation are also young lawn equipment manufacturers that provide insightful comparisons; they have recently gone public and have similar product lines. Data on the three corporations are shown below.

Earnings per share	*Westerfield*	*Pettit*	*Blume's totals*
Earnings per share	$5	$11	$1,000,000
Average earnings per share	$5	$8	$780,000
Median market price	$29	$145	
Average price	$27	$110	
Dividends per share	$3	$7.20	$500,000
Average dividends	$2.80	$6.50	$390,000
Book value per share	$81.23	$112.10	$131,500
Growth in earnings per share	0%	5%	6%
Debt-equity ratio	9%	42%	45%
Current ratio	3.1	1.9	2.0
Employees	180	90	80
Sales	$170,000,000	$9,800,000	$8,800,000

The sales, earnings, and stock prices of all lawn equipment manufacturers have paralleled changes in GNP in the past few years. Historical data show that for the two public firms, 10 percent is an appropriate discount rate (or cost of equity capital). The future for the lawn equipment industry is bright because of an increase in the suburban population and rising affluence. The economic outlook is for steady growth, and securities markets are normal. If Blume issues 1 million shares, what price per share will you recommend? Explain how you arrived at your estimated value per share.

13-10   Ten percent is an appropriate discount rate to use in valuing the common stock issued by the Archer Corporation. Archer's normalized earnings of $2 per share are all paid out in cash dividends. Per share cash dividends have been growing at 3 percent per year for some time, and the current market price of $28.60 reflects this growth. However, because of a technological breakthrough, Archer's earnings are expected to grow at a rate of 6 percent per year in the foreseeable future. What effect do you think this technological innovation will have on Archer's market price per share when the news of Archer's innovation becomes public? Explain.

13-11   Consider the following two investment opportunities: (*a*) A U.S. Treasury bond that matures in 25 years and has a face value of $1000, a coupon rate of 3.5 percent, a current market price of $770, and a yield-to-maturity of 5.15 percent; (*b*) A share of common stock in an automobile corporation that pays $1.75 annual cash dividend and that can be purchased at $38.50 per share. If you had $770 to invest, would you rather buy the Treasury bond or 20 shares of the common stock? What are the advantages and disadvantages of each investment?

Multiple Choice Questions

359

Chapter 13
Common
Stock
Analysis

13-12 The value of a share of stock is primarily determined by which of the following?

(*a*) Risk-adjusted discount rate
(*b*) Income per share
(*c*) Expected growth rate
(*d*) All the above
(*e*) The value of the firm's assets

D

13-13 Fundamental analysts deal with which of the following quantities when they estimate a common stock's value?

(*a*) Earnings per share
(*b*) The asset's appraised values
(*c*) Price-earnings ratios
(*d*) Both (*a*) and (*c*)
(*e*) All the above

D

13-14 Changes in the gross domestic product (GDP) are anticipated fairly consistently by which of the following economic indicators?

(*a*) The unemployment rate
(*b*) Market interest rates
(*c*) Private housing starts
(*d*) The rate of inflation

C

13-15 A common stock's payout ratio:

(*a*) Is directly related to the issuing firm's growth rate in most cases
(*b*) Can be zero for a profitable growth stock and yet the stock can still be a wise investment
(*c*) Measures the share's rate of cashflow as a percentage of its market price
(*d*) Measures the percent of future years in which cash dividends are expected to be paid
(*e*) All the above

B

13-16 Which one of the following statements is true?

(*a*) If the market value of a corporation's physical assets is below the value of the firm's total common stock outstanding, the stock is overvalued.
(*b*) If a stock's P/E ratio exceeds the industry average P/E ratio, the stock is overvalued.
(*c*) Stocks issued by rapidly growing corporations usually have higher than average P/E ratios.
(*d*) If a stock's price exceeds its value, it is a good investment.

C

13-17 Which of the following is irrelevant when estimating a stock's intrinsic value?

D

(*a*) Earnings per share   (*c*) Cash dividend payout ratio
(*b*) Growth rate   (*d*) Par value per share

13-18 Corporations that pay no cash dividends are probably in which of the following categories?

(*a*) Nearly insolvent and/or bankrupt
(*b*) Growth firms
(*c*) Subsidiaries of large parent firms
(*d*) Either (*a*) or (*b*)
(*e*) All the above

D

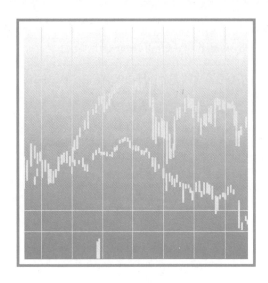

CHAPTER 14

ANALYZING EARNINGS

This chapter extends the common stock analysis discussion begun in Chapter 13 to earnings analysis. As we saw in Chapter 13, the intrinsic value of a share of common stock can be estimated by multiplying the stock's *normalized earnings per share*, or *EPS*, by the appropriate *earnings multiplier*, the E(P/E) ratio. We will repeat from Chapter 13 the fundamental analysts' model to estimate the intrinsic value of a share of common stock:

Intrinsic value per share = EPS × E(P/E) ratio

In our examination of fundamental analysis, we focused on the earnings multiplier and did not delve deeply into the EPS. This chapter focuses on EPS as a key component in share valuation. As the formula makes clear, the value of a stock's EPS must be determined in order to estimate its intrinsic value. The stock analyst must scrutinize the accountants' EPS figure and sometimes "normalize" it by making adjustments. For example, suppose a consistently profitable corporation is struck by its labor union and has its factories closed for 3 months. One quarter's earnings are then reported as zero by the firm's accountants. But an analyst would not use zero as an EPS value when estimating the intrinsic value of the corporation's stock; the stock is certainly not worthless because it earned nothing during one quarter. Instead, the analyst should estimate what the EPS will be when the strike is over and *normal* operations resume. The analyst should adjust for unusual or temporary situations and use this *normalized earnings* figure to estimate the stock's intrinsic value.

The remainder of this chapter explains the adjustments to EPS reported by a firm's accountants that are sometimes needed to obtain realistic estimates of the firm's true income. Two different income concepts are discussed: *economic earnings* and *accounting earnings.* Each may be calculated differently, and each has different implications for the fundamental analyst.

14-1 Economic Earnings and Accounting Earnings

The definition of economic earnings given in Box 14-1 is stated in terms of **consumption opportunities,** actual chances to use up real economic goods. Examples include food that can be eaten and clothing that can be worn. If someone gives you $1000 cash and tells you that you can do what you want with this money, you would truly have $1000 worth of consumption opportunities. If accountants report earnings of $1000, this does not usually entitle the recipient to $1000 worth of consumption opportunities. **Accounting earnings**—earnings reported by accountants—may be biased by misleading conventions and temporary devices. These biases may make the firm's financial statements appear to be better or worse than they actually are. Financial analysts should use the definition of economic earnings as a standard of comparison in order to determine if accounting earnings require adjustment.

Part of a corporation's accounting earnings are not paid out to owners; on the firm's income and expense statement this portion is called **retained earnings.** The shareholders may never be able to get this money and spend it. As a result, investors should not think that their firm's accounting earnings will always translate into consumption opportunities for them.

Economic earnings are defined in terms of consumption opportunities for three reasons: (1) because earnings that cannot be consumed are not really earnings, (2) because we want to avoid using the phrase "retained earnings" (which are not always

Box 14-1

> DEFINITION: The Economic Earnings of a Firm
>
> The **economic earnings of a company** during a given period are the maximum amount that can be *consumed* by the owners of the firm during that period without decreasing the future consumption opportunities they can get from their investment in the firm.

earnings that can be consumed), and (3) because we need to compare dollars of earnings received in different years that may not have directly comparable purchasing power (because of inflation).

Economic earnings can be measured over a period of any length. However, since most firms normally produce new financial statements at quarterly and annual intervals, economic earnings are usually estimated at quarterly and annual intervals too.

Economic earnings do not include the sale of all or any part of a firm needed to *maintain the firm's future earning power* at the same level as present earnings. If a firm is sold in its entirety, for instance, the sales proceeds should not be counted as economic earnings, because nothing would be left to produce earnings with which to pay for future consumption. However, if a firm were to make a discovery that allowed it to increase its profits for 1 year, that new discovery and the additional earnings it generates could be sold and counted as economic earnings. So long as enough of the firm is left to continue future earnings undiminished, then discoveries, inventions, unused patents, and unrelated subsidiaries and/or other pieces of the firm can be sold and these sale proceeds counted as economic earnings.

To gain more understanding of what is included in a firm's economic earnings, let us look at specific examples. Deriving a firm's economic earnings from its income and expense statement is also useful for learning how to detect accounting inconsistencies and biases.

Generally Accepted Accounting Procedures

Someone who is unfamiliar with the complex array of accounting procedures can get the impression that accounting earnings are a narrowly defined quantity. The neat financial statements in annual reports seem to imply that the figures are not open to dispute or interpretation. Look back at the income and expense statement introduced in Chapter 9. Table 9-2 outlines the essentials of the statement. Despite its seeming simplicity, many questions arise concerning the definition and measurement of the items that determine accounting earnings. For answers to these questions, the accounting profession can turn to several sources.

In most cases, accountants use the **GAAP** (**generally accepted accounting procedures**). These are procedures that have been established by a number of different authorities and that continue to evolve. The American Institute of Certified Public Accountants (AICPA) hands down opinions as to which practices are acceptable and which are not. Often these opinions eliminate the less desirable alternatives while still allowing several choices. The result is a narrowing of practices but not the creation of uniform accounting: The same economic event can often legitimately be reported in several different ways by certified public accountants (CPAs).

The existing body of accounting practice has also been shaped by professional organizations, government agencies, and legislation. The most important institutions are the AICPA, the American Accounting Association, and two federal government agencies—the Securities and Exchange Commission (SEC) and the Internal Revenue Service (IRS).

The IRS, for instance, limits the range of permissible accounting. If a given accounting procedure is used by a firm for tax purposes, it also must be used in the published financial statements of that firm. Such rulings increase the consistency of the accounting statements given to shareholders and the IRS in any given year. The IRS also may contest the propriety of certain generally accepted accounting procedures when these tend to help the firm evade income taxes. But such policies do not necessarily tend to align a firm's reported (or accounting) earnings with its economic earnings. In the final analysis, the responsibility for ferreting out a firm's economic earnings lies with the fundamental securities analyst.

The latitude accountants are permitted does not necessarily mean that a firm's accounting earnings will differ significantly from its economic earnings. Accountants truly need some leeway to be sure the accounting procedure used most clearly reports the true economic consequence of a given transaction. Accountants who produce income and expense statements that fundamental analysts find necessary to alter have usually:

1. Used a procedure that is inappropriate for the transaction

2. Been pressured by management to minimize the firm's accounting earnings (and thus also the firm's income taxes)

3. Been pressured by management to make the firm's accounting earnings as large as possible in order to impress investors

Comparing Income and Expense Statements

Many firms prepare two different income statements. Each statement is rational and legal, and the two are compatible. One income statement minimizing taxable income may be prepared for the IRS, and a second income statement may be kept confidential and used by management as a basis for decision making. Presumably, this second statement better reflects the firm's true economic earnings.

Table 14-1 shows two income and expense statements for the same company in the same year that are identical in every way except for the accounting procedures used to derive them. Statement A was prepared to minimize taxable income; statement B gives the true economic earnings for the firm. The differences in the accounting procedures followed in developing statements A and B are legal, commonplace, and generally accepted by practicing accountants. Only statement B is correct in the sense of providing a true picture of the economic results of the firm's operations.

The differences in the five pairs of items connected by numbered arrows in Table 14-1 are explained below; they are a representative, but not exhaustive, set of instances in which confusion and deception can enter into measurement of a firm's earning power.

⟨1⟩ *Sales* Statement B includes in its sales item both cash sales and all current installment sales. The firm sells (or factors) its accounts receivables to collection agents as soon as they arise and thus realizes the cash proceeds from installment contract sales, after an estimated allowance for bad debts has been deducted, almost immediately. However, statement A does not recognize these sales until the customer's final cash payment is actually received and the factoring company has no

Table 14-1
Comparison of Income and Expense Statements

	Statement A (in thousands)	Statement B (in thousands)
Sales	$9,200 ◄——⟨1⟩——►$11,000	
Less: Returns and allowances	−1,000	−1,000
Net sales	$8,200	$10,000
Beginning inventory	$2,000 $2,000	
Purchases and freight in	6,000 6,000	
Net purchases	$8,000 $8,000	
Less: Ending inventory	−2,000◄——⟨2⟩——► −3,000	
Less: Cost of goods sold	−6,000	−5,000
Gross margin	$2,200	$5,000
Less: Operating expenses		
Selling costs	−$1,500 −$1,500	
Depreciation	−500◄——⟨3⟩——► −300	
Pension	−100◄——⟨4⟩——► −20	
Other costs	−200◄——⟨5⟩——► −50	
Salaries	−200 −200	
Bonuses	−100 −100	
Total operating expenses	−2,600	−2,170
Net operating income (loss)	$ (400)	$2,830
Less: Interest expense	−100	−100
Taxable earnings (loss)	$ (500)	$2,730
Less: Federal taxes of 50% (or refunds)	+250	−1,365
Net earnings (loss)	$ (250)	$1,365

Note: The bracketed numbers are explained in text.

potential bad-debt claims. Both practices are acceptable. However, many of the installment contracts are never paid off in full, so the procedure used in statement B is a truer reflection of the actual transaction and should be used to estimate the firm's economic earnings.

Sales can be realized as early as the date the sales order is signed, or as late as the day delivery of the completed product is made, which may be years after the contract is signed (for example, construction of a large building). Between these extremes are many points in time when the accountant may choose to recognize sales revenue in the financial statement.

⟨2⟩ *Inventory*   Statement B uses the **first-in-first-out (FIFO)** method of inventory valuation, while statement A uses the **last-in-first-out (LIFO)** method. During periods of inflation the FIFO method tends to result in higher reported profits.

Perhaps the easiest way to understand LIFO and FIFO is by an example. Imagine that 1-ton steel ingots are the inventory items and that one ingot is always carried in inventory. Assume that early in the accounting year represented in Table 14-2 the cost of ingots rose from $2000 to $3000. The inventory is valued at cost, and the beginning inventory value of the one-ingot inventory is assumed to be $2000,

Table 14-2
Inventory Valuation during 50% Inflation

365

Chapter 14
Analyzing
Earnings

A. *LIFO valuation*

Beginning inventory (1 ingot at $2,000)	$2,000
Plus: Purchases (2 ingots at $3,000 each)	6,000
Cost of goods available for sale	$8,000
Less: Ending inventory (1 ingot at $2,000)	−2,000 (undervalued)
Cost of goods sold	$6,000 (overvalued)

B. *FIFO valuation*

Beginning inventory (1 ingot at $2,000)	$2,000
Plus: Purchases (2 ingots at $3,000 each)	6,000
Cost of goods available for sale	$8,000
Less: Ending inventory (1 ingot at $3,000)	−3,000 (market value)
Cost of goods sold	$5,000

whether FIFO or LIFO is used. This value is shown for "Beginning inventory" in Tables 14-1 and 14-2.

If the newest ingots are assumed to be used in production first, then the LIFO method is appropriate for valuing the inventory. Thus, during the inflationary accounting period when ingot prices rose 50 percent and only one ingot was carried in stock, the value of the inventory was constant; that is, the value of the ingot in ending inventory is assumed to be unchanged. So, relative to the year's ending market price of $3000 per ingot, LIFO undervalues ending inventory, overestimates the cost of goods sold, and underestimates profits during inflation. As shown in part B of Table 14-2, if the FIFO method had been used, the ending inventory (of one ingot purchased for $3000) would have been valued at $3000 and the cost of goods sold would have been $5000.

FIFO incorporates inventory capital gains or losses into regular income, whereas LIFO does not. Thus, the FIFO method often causes profits to be more volatile. FIFO is the more realistic (although less advantageous for tax purposes) method of inventory valuation in this case for two reasons. First, the firm represented in statements A and B does indeed use its oldest inventory first. Second, profits and losses on the inventory are reflected in reported income as they occur.

Not only do LIFO and FIFO have different effects on income, but switching from one of these inventory valuation techniques to the other can result in the year the switch is made in changes to a firm's reported accounting earnings that are unrelated to the true economic facts.

⟨3⟩ *Depreciation*   The manner in which a firm depreciates its assets for accounting purposes can also result in changes in accounting earnings that are unrelated to the economic facts. There are various depreciation techniques, including the straight-line method, the double-declining balance method, the sum-of-the-years'-digits method, and the accelerated cost recovery system (ACRS). The last three methods are called **accelerated depreciation** techniques. Figure 14-1 contrasts different depreciated values over the life of an asset.

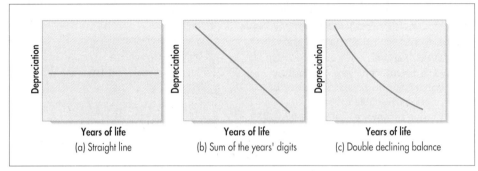

Figure 14-1 Different amounts of annual depreciation over the life of a given asset.

Assuming that no new technology or unusually heavy use is likely to depreciate the value of the assets used by the firm before they are worn out, the **straight-line depreciation** used in statement B is more honest (but less desirable for tax purposes) than the accelerated **sum-of-the-years'-digits depreciation** procedure employed in statement A.

Accelerated depreciation increases depreciation costs in the early years of a new asset's life, and decreases accounting earnings and income tax on these earnings when the asset is new. Essentially, accelerated depreciation postpones income taxes on earnings. *Postponing taxes is like obtaining an interest-free loan from the federal government. The total depreciation expense is unchanged; only the timing is altered.* As

Box 14-2

COMPUTATION: Straight-Line versus Accelerated Depreciation

Imagine an asset that costs $1000 and has an expected life of 3 years. By use of the straight-line method, depreciation is $1000/3 years = $333.33 for each of the 3 years. By use of the sum-of-the-years'-digits method, the annual depreciation starts large and diminishes each year because the fraction that is multiplied by the cost of the asset to determine each year's depreciation decreases. The numerator of this fraction, which represents the number of years left in the life of the asset, decreases by 1 each year, as shown in the table below. The denominator of the fraction remains stable; it is a sum related to the total number of years in the life of the asset. For example, if the life expectancy of an asset were 3 years, the denominator would be 6 (that is, 1 + 2 + 3).

Year	*Depreciation as fraction of cost*	*Sum-of-the-years'-digits depreciation*
1	³⁄₆	$ 500.00
2	²⁄₆	333.33
3	¹⁄₆	166.67
Total	1	$1000.00

Table 14-1 shows, however, these bookkeeping procedures can affect a particular year's reported accounting earnings significantly.

Businesses are allowed to decide whether they want to use straight line or one of the accelerated depreciation techniques in their annual reports, but they are allowed no alternatives when they compute their federal income taxes. The Internal Revenue Service (IRS) requires all firms to use the *accelerated cost recovery system (ACRS)* for tax purposes. It depreciates assets more rapidly than they can realistically wear out from fair wear and tear and faster than any of the traditional accelerated techniques.

⟨4⟩ *Pension*   If a firm has a pension plan for its employees, accounting for pension costs also affects accounting earnings. Statement A in Table 14-1 reflects the maximum allowable pension cost and statement B the minimum. The maximum pension cost is the normal cost for current employee services, plus 10 percent of any unpaid past employee service costs and/or 10 percent of any change in prior service costs. The maximum allowable cost is based on the notion that pension payments are due to individual employees. The minimum is the normal pension cost plus the equivalent of an interest payment on any unfunded prior employee service costs. The minimum cost is based on the idea the payments are put into a pension fund from which all present and all future employees can draw payment. The maximum recognizes prior-services expense during the life span of individuals (a short time span), whereas the minimum spreads the cost over the life of the pension plan (perhaps to 90 years). On the assumption that the firm has a youthful labor force with few employees near retirement age, statement B's treatment of pension costs is the more forthright approach (although it furnishes less of an income tax shelter).

There are several methods of determining pension costs. For pension funds that provide for setting aside the anticipated cash needs in advance of the actual payment of employee benefits, these costs must be estimated. Usually a statistical analyst called an *actuary* evaluates a company's contractual pension liabilities by forecasting its labor turnover, the age pattern of its employees, the rate of return that can be earned on the funds invested, and the mortality rates of the pensioners. On the basis of these forecasts, the actuary estimates the pension's future costs to the firm. The reported pension costs deducted in any given year thus depend on both the accounting procedure used and the actuary's forecasts.

In a footnote to the financial statements, companies are required to disclose the pension accounting and funding policy, the pension charge for the year, the unfunded vested liability of the company, the amount of unfunded past-service obligations (such obligations can exceed the net worth of a company in extreme cases), and the rate of return (or discount rate) the actuary assumes when finding the present value of the pension's liability. These crucial values can be disclosed so vaguely that they are misleading. If so, what appears to be the accounting earnings can differ from the true (but concealed) economic earnings.

⟨5⟩ *Other Costs*   There are many business expenses that accountants may decide to write off as current business expenses, or capitalize and then amortize over a period of years. For example, motion picture production costs, oil well exploration costs, advertising campaign costs, and many other items are not clearly either a current expense or an asset that should go on the balance sheet and be amortized over a number of years. Reporting these is a matter of managerial discretion—and items the fundamental analyst should scrutinize.

Statements A and B differ because some outlays expensed on statement A were capitalized and amortized on statement B. The analyst should consider this difference in comparing the two income statements. An analyst who believes the outlays should be expensed should adjust statement B accordingly.

Conclusions As the income statements in Table 14-1 clearly show, key differences in accounting procedures can affect a firm's reported accounting earnings. Statement A indicates that the firm need not pay any income taxes; instead, it receives a $250,000 federal income tax refund that partially offsets its losses. In contrast, statement B shows the firm must pay $1,365,000 in federal income taxes. It is hard to believe that statements A and B represent the same firm in the same year. Both taxpayers and investors who use statement A would be misled by the accounting earnings reported in that statement. However, the firm would have little difficulty in getting a certified public accountant to make a written certification that either statement conforms to *generally accepted accounting procedures.*

Some financial executives and accountants take advantage of this leeway in accounting procedures and manipulate the firm's accounting earnings to suit their purposes. Since many amateur investors do not have the time or the training to detect problems and make the proper adjustments, accountants should be required to make liberal use of footnotes to explain areas where they used discretion.

When evaluating a firm's income statements, the analyst should bear two points in mind. First, the true economic earnings of a firm may be greater or smaller than its reported accounting earnings. Second, it is difficult for outsiders to detect unethical practices and deliberate misrepresentation in any given set of accounting statements. Executives can manage the flow of information to accountants in such a way as to have a major impact on the firm's reported earnings.[1]

Even after the analyst has resolved the various ambiguities that may creep into a firm's income and expense statement, the earnings analysis is not finished. The firm's reported earnings per share must also be examined closely.

14-2 Reported Earnings per Share

Investors should be concerned with EPS when they are estimating the value of a share of stock: EPS is the dollar amount that a share of common stock earned during the reporting period. If a company has convertible securities, warrants, stock options, or other contracts that permit the number of shares of common stock outstanding to be increased in future periods, more than one measure of EPS should be reported. Moreover, income or losses caused by extraordinary events should also lead to the reporting of other measures of EPS.

---

[1] For a classic book that documents many cases where large, well-known corporations used unethical and misleading accounting practices, see Abraham J. Briloff, *Unaccountable Accounting* (New York: Harper & Row, 1972).

Box 14-3   369

Chapter 14
Analyzing
Earnings

DEFINITION: Accounting Earnings per Share

A common stock's **earnings per share** is the net income after taxes less preferred stock dividend payments divided by the weighted average number of shares of common stock outstanding during the accounting period. In computing the weighted average number of shares outstanding, the weights are determined by the length of time the shares are outstanding during the reporting period.

For example, if there were 1.2 million shares outstanding for the first 8 months of the reporting year and 1.5 million shares for the last 4 months, then the weighted average number of shares is 1.3 million, determined as follows:

Shares outstanding	Weight	Product
1.2 million shares	$\frac{8}{12}$	.8 million shares
1.5 million shares	$\frac{4}{12}$	.5 million shares
Total	1.0	1.3 million shares

Dilution of Earnings per Share

The total earnings of a company may increase over time, but any increase in the number of shares of common stock outstanding tends to dilute the corporation's future EPS. An increase in the outstanding common stock can occur when management elects to sell more shares or when contracts exist that permit investors to purchase additional common stock from the company. Among such contracts are warrants, convertible bonds, convertible preferred stock, and executive options to purchase common stock.

Professional accountants have adopted a generally accepted accounting procedure for reporting dilution from increases in the number of shares outstanding. If the potential dilution due to the existence of convertible security contracts cannot result in a decline of more than 3 percent in EPS, it need not be reported; only a single presentation of EPS need be made. For companies with contracts that allow a total potential EPS dilution in excess of 3 percent, EPS will be presented in two ways. First, dilution that considers only common stock equivalents is used to determine EPS. **Common stock equivalents** are options or warrants to purchase common stock and certain convertible securities.[2] This first measure is called **primary earnings per share.** Second, the maximum potential dilution of EPS must be reported. This measure is **fully diluted earnings per share.**

[2] For a convertible security to be considered a common stock equivalent, the cash yield of the security at the time of issue has to be less than two-thirds of the prime rate of interest when the security was issued.

Extraordinary Gains and Losses

Security analysts attempt to estimate a corporation's normalized economic earnings. However, extraordinary events may distort normal earnings—an example is loss due to a major casualty, such as a flood. Events that accountants do not consider to be extraordinary are the write-down of inventory, gains or losses due to foreign exchange fluctuations, and gains or losses from the disposition of a segment of the business. How should extraordinary items be reported in the firm's income statement?

Accountants have long debated this point. Some take the view that extraordinary items should be reported on the income statement for the current period. Others believe that these items distort the firm's reported accounting earnings and hence should not appear on the income statement. This second group has argued that such items should simply be charged or credited directly to retained earnings on the firm's balance sheet.

For a transaction to be considered "extraordinary," accountants require that the item be both unusual in nature and unlikely to recur in the foreseeable future.[3] The SEC requires "extraordinary" items to be reported as separate sources of income and to make clear that these sources of income will probably not recur in the normal course of business.

Inflation

A major criticism of published financial statements is that they do not require any analysis of the impact of inflation. Accountants' financial statements can be seriously biased because of inflation. For example, in 1982 American Telephone and Telegraph (AT&T) reported conventional earnings of $7 billion and inflation-adjusted earnings of only $1.4 billion. In that same year Exxon's conventional earnings were reported as $4.2 billion, but these turned into losses after being adjusted to reflect price level changes. Since the accounting profession has never required inflation-adjusted reports, AT&T and Exxon understandably eliminated their inflation-adjusted financial statements in the years that followed.

When the purchasing power of accounting earnings is eroded by inflation, the ability of a firm to maintain its operating capacity is reduced, for two reasons. First, the earnings retained in the corporation will have less purchasing power with which to buy new plant and equipment. Second, fewer dollars will probably be retained, since cash dividends and taxes are based on inflated accounting earnings rather than on inflation-adjusted earnings.[4] Chapter 18 suggests methods investments analysts should use to deal with the purchasing power risk that results from inflation.

---

[3] APB Opinion No. 30, "Reporting the Results of Operations" (New York: AICPA, 1973).

[4] Not all accountants agree with the inflation findings reported in this text. For example, see William H. Beaver and Stephen G. Ryan, "How Well Do Statement No. 33 Earnings Explain Stock Returns?" *Financial Analysts Journal*, September-October 1985, pp. 66–71. This study suggests that earnings which are not inflation-adjusted are just as highly correlated with corporations' stock prices as are inflation-adjusted earnings.

Two approaches have been suggested for taking into account the impact of inflation: *constant dollar accounting* and *current cost accounting*. Constant dollar accounting deals with changes in the general price level, while current cost accounting adjusts for changes in individual items. These two approaches should be viewed as complementary.

Unfortunately, neither approach has become popular, and as a result, financial statements continue to be based on *historical costs* and *nominal dollars*. Assets like plant and equipment, which might have been purchased decades ago, are carried on the books at their low historical cost. The result is book values that significantly underestimate the assets' market values. Furthermore, reporting each year's business transactions in that year's unique nominal dollar values makes it difficult to compare financial statements from the same firm if they are more than a few years apart.[5]

14-3 Adjusting Earnings

Since accounting earnings can differ from economic earnings, security analysts may find it necessary to adjust or normalize the reported accounting earnings figure to a more realistic value that is defined consistently from year to year. Because there are few precisely defined terms in accounting, realistic definitions must be developed. This is where the economists' definition of earnings in Box 14-4 becomes useful.

The definition in Box 14-4 means that a stock share's economic income equals any price change (which can be negative or positive) plus any cash dividends earned during the holding period, after these amounts are adjusted to reflect any changes in the cost of living.

When analyzing a share's earnings, the analyst should try to discern any trends because this will affect the per share earnings. Typically, this is done by gathering financial statements for the past several years. Then, through reference to the footnotes, the statements can be adjusted so the items in all years are defined consistently. Once these adjustments are made, year-by-year comparisons of economic earnings are more useful for detecting real changes and trends.

[5] Inflation-adjusted financial statements were seriously considered during the 1970s when double-digit inflation became a problem in the United States. At this writing the inflation rate is a much lower 4 percent, and there seems to be little interest in inflation-adjusted accounting.

Box 14-4

DEFINITION: Economic Earnings per Share for a Common Stock

The **economic earnings per share** from a stock during a given period equals the maximum amount of real, physical consumption opportunities that can be withdrawn from the share during that period without diminishing the consumption opportunities that can be obtained from the share in the future.

When adjusting accounting data, some key aspects of the definition of an equity share's economic earnings are worthy of further discussion.

- *Inflation:* The reference to "real, physical consumption opportunities" is to inflation-adjusted dollars rather than nominal dollar values that can be distorted by inflation.

- *Withdrawals:* An equity share's economic earnings do not actually have to be withdrawn and consumed, but the consumption *opportunity* must exist or else the earnings are not real. For example, if a firm must retain some accounting earnings to survive, those retained earnings are not true economic earnings that the share owner can consume without diminishing the share's future earning power.

- *Depreciation:* The economic earnings must be the earnings left after an allowance for fair wear and tear of assets is deducted. This depreciation or depletion allowance, which must be reinvested in the assets to maintain their future productivity, is not consumable and cannot be considered economic earnings.

- *Market values:* A share's current economic earnings include its gain or loss in market value, regardless of whether the share is sold and the gain or loss is actually realized. Any increase (decrease) in a security's price constitutes economic earnings because the price change increases (decreases) the investor's consumption opportunities.

14-4   Forecasting Earnings per Share

After accounting earnings have been normalized to yield a consistently defined series of estimates of the firm's economic earnings, future earnings can be forecast. (Remember that it is necessary to estimate a stock's future earnings because the value of the share is the present value of its *future* cashflows.)

Obtaining Earnings per Share Forecasts

Short-term forecasts (that is, projections of up to 1 year) of a firm's EPS are useful to speculators who want to buy and sell quickly in hopes of profiting from a short-run price change. Short-run forecasts may be prepared from discussions with the management of the firm and/or competitors. Professional forecasts may also be purchased from financial services.

The Lynch, Jones and Ryan financial services corporation in New York City provides Institutional Brokers Estimate System (IBES) forecasts of EPS of about 3600 U.S., Canadian, and foreign corporations. These forecasts are obtained by surveying hundreds of professional investment analysts and then publishing summary statistics. The forecasts of each stock's earnings are averaged, and these averages are then published by IBES.

A useful feature of the IBES forecasts is that, for each firm and for each industry, they include the average of the earnings forecasts for each stock, the range of forecast statistics for each stock, and the dates the forecasts were made. The range statistics allow a subscriber to evaluate how much agreement there is among the analysts. IBES is available on a subscription basis.[6]

Preparing Earnings per Share Forecasts

Many corporations' earnings tend to grow at some constant rate—either positive or negative. For those firms whose earnings are in a trend, Equation (14-1) can be used to obtain earnings projections.

$$EPS_t(1.0 + g)^T = EPS_{t+T} \quad \Leftarrow forecasting\ future\ EPS \qquad (14\text{-}1)$$

Starting at time period *t*, this equation assumes that earnings per share grow at the fixed rate of *g* to attain a level of EPS_{t+T} after *T* time periods. A formula like Equation (14-1) was used to calculate Figure 11-1, on page 283, which illustrates how $1 grows at various growth rates.

Practically speaking, however, forecasting a corporation's future EPS is usually not a simple task. Growth rates change continuously, varying with the intensity of competitive pressures and the stages of the business cycle. In addition, products have life cycles. [Chapter 13 investigates the product (or industry) life cycle for additional factors that affect companies' growth rates.] Since the growth rate is also an important factor in determining the earnings multiplier (see Table 13-2), this rate must be estimated carefully.

If the managers of the issuing corporation are aggressive and want to ensure continued growth, they will phase out products that are becoming obsolete and introduce new products generated through an ongoing research and development program. However, if top management becomes emotionally tied to traditional products, the company may falter as products that provided growth in the past become obsolete. Growth rates can also drop suddenly when patents expire, competition becomes more aggressive, or economically turbulent periods occur. One of the purposes of fundamental analysis is to anticipate these events in order to make a sound estimate of the issuing firm's future.

To stay abreast of all the new information about a product, many professional fundamental analysts specialize in one industry. They attend trade conventions for that industry, get to know each firm's products, meet with industry executives, follow legislation affecting the industry's product, and take other steps to ensure that they have up-to-date information.

14-5 Cashflow-Oriented Financial Analysis

Earlier sections of this chapter described ambiguities in the way accounting earnings are derived and suggested guidelines to derive more meaningful income measurements. Cashflow analysis is one acceptable way to avoid these pitfalls.

---

[6] The Lynch, Jones and Ryan Corporation, 345 Hudson St., New York, NY 10014, phone 212-243-3137, graciously makes the valuable IBES data available free to college professors and their students who sign a statement promising the data will be used only for academic research.

Measuring a firm's cashflows is a good way to estimate its economic income. **Cashflow from operations** is a well-known income measure found in most accounting textbooks. It can be computed simply by listing the elements of revenue that generate cash and the operating expenses that use cash. Cashflow from operations ignores extraordinary cash inflows (such as when a manufacturing firm sells some old machinery) and nonrecurring outflows (for instance, if a lawsuit is lost and damages must be paid).[7]

Recognizing the inadequacy of information provided by accountants' income and expense statements and the value of additional information provided by cashflow analysis, in 1987 the Financial Accounting Standards Board (FASB) issued FASB Statement No. 95. It requires all firms to include cashflow statements in publicly disclosed financial statements after 1988. Various cashflow measures have been developed to meet this requirement.

Free cash flow, or **FCF,** is a comprehensive measure that includes cashflows from operations and depreciation (since depreciation is not a cash expense); deducts any purchases of Treasury stock; considers changes in relevant balance sheet items; considers items from the sources and uses statement; and considers some footnote items such as changes in the firm's pension surplus, reserves, and accruals. To ferret out the firm's FCF, the analyst must find and unravel any gimmicks accountants might have used to smooth the firm's accounting profit from year to year and/or conceal "corporate fat" in reserve accounts, surpluses, and/or accruals.

Cash dividends provide only a crude estimate of the average amount of FCF for many corporations. FCF numbers reveal more current information because they vary every year with the firm's activities, while cash dividends are usually changed only every few years. Different financial analysts might develop different estimates of the FCF for a given firm in a particular year. These differences can be attributed to differences in the analysts' approach and the level of detail in the analysis. Equation (14-2) defines FCF formally.[8]

$$\text{Free cashflow} = \text{revenue} - \text{operating costs} - \text{investments to sustain earnings} \tag{14-2}$$

A corporation's FCFs are an excellent measure of its economic income. The present value of the FCF on a per share basis, Equation (14-3), is as logical and

---

[7] See Leopold A. Bernstein, *Financial Statement Analysis,* 4th ed. (Homewood, Ill.: Irwin, 1989), chap. 13 and its appendixes, especially app. A. Also see L. A. Bernstein and M. M. Makay, "Again Now: How Do We Measure Cashflows from Operations?" *Financial Analysts Journal,* vol. 41, no. 4, pp. 74–77. Alternatively, see George Foster, *Financial Statement Analysis,* 2d ed. (Englewood Cliffs, N.J.: Prentice-Hall, 1986), table 3.4 on p. 63. See also A. C. Sondhi, G. H. Sorter, and G. I. White, "Transactional Analysis," *Financial Analysts Journal,* September–October 1987, pp. 57–64.

[8] Equation (14-2)'s definition of FCF is written by two Nobel Prize-winning economists; see M. H. Miller and F. Modigliani, "Dividend Policy, Growth and the Valuation of Shares," *Journal of Business,* October 1961, pp. 411–433. For a more in-depth discussion of cashflow analysis see J. C. Francis, *Investments: Analysis and Management,* 5th ed. (New York, McGraw-Hill), 1991, chap. 16.

acceptable a measure of the share's value as is the venerable present value of cash dividends model explained in Chapter 13.

$$\text{Present value per share} = \sum_{t=1}^{\infty} \frac{\text{FCF per share}_t}{(1 + k)^t} \qquad (14\text{-}3)$$

where k is a risk-adjusted discount rate. Focusing on a single share of stock instead of the entire corporation allows us to formulate another definition of a firm's present value on a FCF per share basis.

Summary

Another part of common stock analysis is earnings analysis. Economic earnings per share are the maximum amount of consumption opportunity an equity share can yield. Economic earnings do not always coincide with accountants' reported earnings. When they differ significantly, accounting earnings have to be adjusted to obtain consistently defined economic earnings. Long-range forecasts should be made on the basis of normalized economic earnings that are comparable through time. Good earnings forecasts are important because, as the fundamental analysts' intrinsic value per share estimating methods of Chapter 13 revealed, earnings per share is a key part of stock price prediction.

In 1988 the accounting profession began requiring corporations to provide investors a cashflow statement. Cashflows cannot be manipulated by switching inventory valuation techniques or depreciation guidelines, and they provide a readily discernible measure of a firm's economic income on either the aggregate level or a per share basis. The present value of an equity share's FCF provides a good estimate of its intrinsic value.

Further
Reading

Bernstein, Leopold A., *Financial Statement Analysis*, 4th ed. (Homewood, Ill.: Irwin, 1989).
  This accounting-oriented textbook explains traditional financial statement analysis in detail and provides interesting examples.

Briloff, Abraham J., *Unaccountable Accounting* (New York: Harper & Row, 1972).
  This easy-to-read book presents names, dates, and other explicit details in its review of actual cases of accounting misrepresentation.

Foster, George, *Financial Statement Analysis*, 2d ed. (Englewood Cliffs, N.J.: Prentice-Hall, 1986).
  This textbook uses economic theory and statistics to analyze financial statement data. Financial forecasting techniques are explained.

Essay Questions

14-1   Consider the definitions of economic earnings (*a*) for a firm and (*b*) for a share of common stock. What are the common elements in these two concepts of income?

14-2   In your opinion, when should an automobile manufacturer recognize the $20,000 income from selling a new car: (*a*) when the car is shipped to the dealer from the manufacturing plant, (*b*) weeks later when the new car's buyer signs the purchase order in the showroom of the auto dealer, or (*c*) 2 to 5 years later when the car buyer makes the last monthly installment payment to pay off the car completely? How would each of these three alternatives affect the auto manufacturer's annual income if all the corporation's car sales were consistently reported this way?

14-3 Describe three ways in which a company could manipulate its earnings within the framework of generally accepted accounting procedures (GAAP).

14-4 In Chapter 6 we learned that the Securities and Exchange Commission requires corporations to report their "extraordinary income" on a Form 8-K. (*a*) What is the difference between an extraordinary income item and a firm's normal earnings? (*b*) Why should the SEC require that extraordinary income be specially reported?

14-5 Compare and contrast these three income measures: cash dividends per share, accounting earnings per share, and economic earnings per share? Which has the greatest impact on common stock values and prices? What are the advantages and disadvantages inherent in the use of each measure?

14-6 In a 1984 U.S. Supreme Court decision Chief Justice Burger stated: "By certifying the public reports that collectively depict a corporation's financial status, the independent auditor assumes a *public* responsibility transcending any employment relationship with the client." (For further discussion see Lee Burton, "Investors Call CPAs to Account," *The Wall Street Journal*, Jan. 28, 1985. Also see the Financial Accounting Standards Board discussion memorandum dated July 31, 1979, entitled "An Analysis of Issues Related to Reporting Earnings.") If you make an investment based on audited financial statement information that misrepresents the facts, and as a result of this misconception, you incur losses, what do you think the Chief Justice would suggest you do to obtain justice?

14-7 Answer following questions about financial analysis, taken from the CFA exam, level I, June 1982:

There are certain accounting signals that might be viewed as tipoffs to deteriorating earnings capacity and financial position. While these signals are not prima facie evidence of trouble, they are an indication that further financial analysis is in order. For each of the following, discuss why deterioration might be implied.

    (*a*) Increase in receivables
    (*b*) Changes in accounting policies
    (*c*) Intangible assets increase
    (*d*) Increase in non-recurring income
    (*e*) Reserve manipulations

14-8 Answer the following three-part question about the reporting of corporate income, taken from the level I, 1980 CFA exam:

    (*a*) Generally accepted accounting procedures require the presentation of corporate earnings per share data on the face of the income statement. (1) Explain the meaning of "primary earnings per share." (2) Explain how "fully diluted earnings per share" differs from "primary earnings per share."
    (*b*) Comment on the probable reason(s) why an individual company might choose to use straight-line depreciation for financial reporting purposes while using accelerated depreciation for tax purposes.
    (*c*) Briefly discuss the impact of the accounting recognition of deferred income taxes on a company's cashflows.

14-9 (*a*) Explain the difference between a company's after-tax income and its cashflows. (*b*) Why are financial analysts sometimes more interested in a company's cashflows than in its after-tax income?

Problems

14-10 The Hypothetical Corporation earns $200 taxable income every year and is in the 50 percent federal income tax bracket. The corporation bought a $100 computer program in 19X1. What will the after-tax income of the Hypothetical Corporation be in the years 19X1 through 19X5 inclusive if it (*a*) writes off the $100 outlay as a 19X1 expense, or (*b*) calls the computer program an asset and depreciates it over 5 years using straight-line depreciation? Both (*a*) and (*b*) are generally accepted accounting procedures. (*c*) Explain which method you would rather see the corporation use if you were a potential investor in its stock.

14-11 The Meadows Corporation earned a net income of $12,672,000, as shown below:

Sales revenue	$51,108,000
Less: Depreciation on machinery	3,200,000
Less: Labor	11,003,000
Less: Raw materials	16,705,000
Less: Accrued expenses	1,000,000
Taxable income	$19,200,000
Less: Corporate income taxes (34%)	6,528,000
Net income	$12,672,000
Less: Retained earnings	2,672,000
Cash dividends	$10,000,000

The Meadows Corporation has 5,000,000 shares of common stock outstanding. Calculate Meadows's (*a*) cash dividends per share, (*b*) earnings per share, and (*c*) cashflow per share. (*d*) Which of these three per share income measures is the most useful and insightful to a potential investor?

Multiple Choice Questions

14-12 Economic income is a more logical concept than is accounting income because economic income provides needed allowances for which of the following?

(*a*) Replacement of assets worn out from fair wear and tear and obsolescence
(*b*) Inflation or deflation
(*c*) The market values of assets
(*d*) Both (*b*) and (*c*)
(*e*) All the above

14-13 Generally accepted accounting procedures (GAAP) are:

(*a*) Determined by fundamental security analysts' consensus
(*b*) Affected by rulings of the Internal Revenue Service
(*c*) Not affected by the Securities and Exchange Commission
(*d*) Modified by the common law developed by court rulings
(*e*) Described by all the above

14-14 Accountants may define a firm's sales vaguely because of which of the following:

(*a*) Cash sales and credit sales may be recognized at different times or at the same time.
(*b*) Reserves for anticipated bad-debt losses may or may not be deducted from credit sales.

(c) Reserves for sales returns may or may not be deducted from sales.
(d) All the above are true.

14-15   The LIFO inventory valuation technique has which of the following characteristics?

(a) It underestimates the firm's cost of goods sold during inflationary periods.
(b) It tends to minimize the firm's income taxes during inflation.
(c) In an inflationary environment it presents a better reflection of the firm's true economic earnings.
(d) Switching to another inventory valuation procedure distorts the firm's reported sales figures.
(e) All the above are true.

14-16   Accelerated depreciation accounting is characterized by which of the following?

(a) The units-of-production method of depreciation accelerates the least.
(b) The sum-of-the-years'-digits method is the most accelerated depreciation schedule.
(c) It helps companies reduce the total amount of income taxes they pay during the life of a depreciable asset.
(d) The accelerated cost recovery system (ACRS) is the most accelerated depreciation schedule.

14-17   According to generally accepted accounting procedures, a legal and ethical way for a firm to deduct its $1,000,000 cost for an advertising campaign from its taxable income is described by which of the following statements?

(a) Put the $1,000,000 outlay on the balance sheet as an intangible asset and depreciate (or amortize) it over future years.
(b) Advertising is not a legally deductible expense because of its intangible nature.
(c) Deduct the entire $1,000,000 outlay as a current expense in the year of the advertising campaign.
(d) Either (a) or (c).

14-18   Which of the following items might result in a dilution of a corporation's earnings per share?

(a) Convertible bonds
(b) Stock options given as incentives to top executives
(c) Warrants
(d) All the above

14-19   The accounting profession has suggested which of the following ways for producing inflation-adjusted financial statements?

(a) Base year costing restates all financial data for the latest 3 years in terms equivalent to the current year's value of the wholesale price index.
(b) Current value accounting uses price level adjustments for individual items.
(c) General price level accounting provides equal adjustments for all items.
(d) Both (b) and (c).

14-20   The definition of an investment's economic earnings includes which of the following concepts?

(a) Cash dividends plus retained earnings
(b) Implicit inflation allowances
(c) Withdrawable consumption opportunities
(d) Both (b) and (c)
(e) All the above

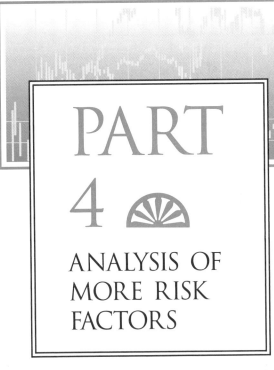

PART 4

ANALYSIS OF MORE RISK FACTORS

SECURITY PRICES fluctuate during short spans of time—from day to day or from week to week. Chapters 15 and 16 open Part 4 by examining the course of security prices. Do security prices tend to move in repetitive patterns that can be useful to price forecasters? Are securities market prices equal to their intrinsic (or present) values? If so, why should security analysts bother to estimate securities values? Finding the answers to these questions provides essential investment information.

Looking at security price fluctuations over a period of ten years or more reveals that the market indexes tend to rise to peaks and fall to troughs that delineate, respectively, bull markets and bear markets. Bull and bear market fluctuations are powerful economic influences that create what is called *market risk*. Chapter 17 compares the ways that security prices behave during bull markets and bear markets, and pinpoints some meaningful differences.

Inflation causes the prices of most, but not all, goods to rise. The prices of food, clothing, housing, medical care, and other living costs increase during inflationary periods and, in so doing, diminish the purchasing power that our money and our savings accounts will have in the years ahead. Chapter 18 shows ways to deal with this *purchasing-power risk*.

Business people are mortals. No matter how long their corporate limousine may be or how high their annual income, an executive is still capable of making bad decisions. Chapter 19 investigates the kinds of errors top executives make, suggesting how to spot trouble and providing ways to assess *management risk*.

Chapter 20 defines long positions, short positions, hedges, and arbitrage. The chapter also shows how to use these positions to create different strategies to protect yourself from investment losses that can result from the risks that investors must face.

379

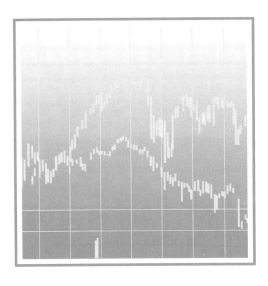

CHAPTER 15

TECHNICAL ANALYSIS

A technical analyst is a security analyst who uses an approach completely different from that of the fundamental analyst. A **technical analyst,** or *technician,* believes it is not productive to sift through all the fundamental facts about an issuing corporation —company earnings, its products, forthcoming legislation that might affect the firm, and so forth. Instead, technical analysts believe that the fundamentals are all summarized in the market prices of a security. Technical analysts therefore focus on charts of security market prices and summary statistics about security transactions. As a result, they are sometimes called **chartists.** Although most technical analysts prepare and study charts of various financial variables in order to make forecasts about security prices, some use quantitative rather than graphic tools.[1] In this chapter we explore some of the more prominent techniques used by technical analysts to measure supply and demand and to forecast securities prices: the Dow theory, bar charts, odd-lot theory, breadth-of-market indicators, relative-strength analysis, volume of shares traded, and moving-average analysis. Then we'll compare and evaluate methods of analysis. But first we will briefly review the philosophy behind technical analysis.

15-1 The Theory of Technical Analysis

Technical analysis is based on the widely accepted premise that security prices are determined by the supply of and the demand for securities. The tools of technical analysis are therefore designed to measure supply and demand indicators. Typically, technical analysts record historical financial data on charts, study these charts in search of meaningful patterns, and endeavor to use the patterns to predict the future.

[1] Dr. Richard Bookstaber has proposed a modern, computer-based quantitative approach to technical analysis; see Richard Bookstaber, *The Complete Investment Book* (Glenview, Ill.: Scott, Foresman, 1985), chaps. 14–20.

Box 15-1

PRINCIPLES: The Basis of Technical Analysis

A classic book by Edwards and Magee* articulates the basic assumptions underlying technical analysis:

- Market value is determined by the interaction of supply and demand.

- Supply and demand are governed by numerous factors, both rational and irrational.

- Despite minor fluctuations in the market, security prices tend to move in trends that persist for an appreciable length of time.

- Changes in a trend are caused by shifts in supply and demand.

- Shifts in supply and demand, no matter why they occur, can be detected sooner or later in charts of market transactions.

- Some chart patterns tend to repeat themselves.

In essence, technical analysts believe that past patterns will recur in the future and can therefore be used for predictions.

* R. D. Edwards and John Magee, Jr., *Technical Analysis of Stock Trends,* 4th ed. (Springfield, Mass: John Magee Inc., 1958), p. 86.

Most charts are used to forecast the price of a single security or the value of a market index. Some technicians use the same charting techniques to forecast market indexes, stock prices, bond prices, commodity prices, foreign exchange rates, and interest rates.

Chapters 13 and 14 explained how fundamental analysts estimate the *value of* shares of stock. Technical analysts form *price estimates* instead. They tend to ignore fundamental valuation facts, such as risk and earnings growth, in favor of various barometers of supply and demand they have devised. As a classic technical analysis book lyrically asserts:

> It is futile to assign an intrinsic value to a stock certificate. One share of United States Steel, for example, was worth $261 in the early fall of 1929, but you could buy it for only $22 in June 1932. By March 1937, it was selling for $126 and just one year later for $38. . . . This sort of thing, this wide divergence between presumed value and actual value, is not the exception; it is the rule; it is going on all the time. The fact is that the real value of a share of U.S. Steel common is determined at any given time solely, definitely and inexorably by supply and demand, which are accurately reflected in the transactions consummated on the floor of the . . . Exchange.
>
> Of course, the statistics which the fundamentalists study play a part in the supply and demand equation—that is freely admitted. But there are many other factors affecting it. The market price reflects not only the differing value opinions of many orthodox security appraisers but also the hopes and fears and guesses and moods, rational and irrational, of hundreds of potential buyers and sellers, as well as their needs and their resources—in total, factors which defy analysis and for which no statistics are obtainable, but which are nevertheless all synthesized, weighted and finally expressed in one precise figure at which a buyer and seller get together and make a deal (through their agents, their respective brokers). This is the only figure that counts. . . .
>
> In brief, the going price as established by the market itself comprehends all the fundamental information which the statistical analyst can hope to learn (plus some which is perhaps secret to him, known only to a few insiders) and much else besides of equal or even greater importance.[2]

In discussing their practices, most technical analysts do not accuse fundamental analysts of being illogical. In fact, some security analysts use both fundamental and technical analysis tools. However, technical purists assert the superiority of their methods by pointing out that technical analysis is easier, faster, and can be applied simultaneously to more stocks than can fundamental analysis. While these claims are true, if the results do not predict security prices very well, the fact that technical analysis is easier to learn or simpler to use is irrelevant.

Many technical analysts would say that fundamental analysis is not worthless, just too much trouble. First, even if fundamental analysts do find what they believe to be an underpriced security, they must wait and hope that the rest of the market agrees with their assessment and bids the price up. Second, fundamental analysis is hard

[2] Robert D. Edwards and John Magee, *Technical Analysis of Stock Trends,* rev. 5th ed. (Boston, Mass.: John Magee, 1966), pp. 5–6.

384

Part 4
Analysis of
More Risk
Factors

Box 15-2

> DEFINITION: The Dow Theory
>
> The market is always considered as having three movements, all going at the same time. The first is the narrow movement from day to day. The second is the short swing, running from 2 weeks to a month or more; the third is the main movement, covering at least 4 years in duration.*
>
> *The Wall Street Journal, Dec. 19, 1900.

work. Third, technical analysts cite problems with accountants' income statements, which form the basis for much fundamental analysis. Finally, technical analysts point out the subjective aspects of the earnings multipliers used by fundamental analysts.

15-2   The Dow Theory

The **Dow theory** is one of the oldest and most famous technical tools; it was originated by Charles Dow, a founder of the Dow Jones Company and editor of *The Wall Street Journal* at the turn of the century. Dow died in 1902, and the Dow theory was developed further and given its name by staff members at *The Wall Street Journal.* Today, the theory is the basis for much of the work done by technical analysts; it is used to delineate trends in the market as a whole or in individual securities.

Dow theory practitioners refer to the three components outlined by Charles Dow as:

- **Primary trends,** which are long-term movements, commonly called *bear* or *bull markets.* Delineating the beginnings and endings of the primary trends is the main goal of Dow theorists.

- **Secondary movements,** which last only a few months. Secondary movements are sometimes called **corrections.**

- **Tertiary moves,** which are simply the daily fluctuations. The Dow theory asserts that daily fluctuations are essentially meaningless random wiggles. Nonetheless, the chartist should plot an asset's price or the market average each day in order to trace the primary and secondary trends.

Figure 15-1 is a line chart that a Dow theorist might develop. **Line charts** are constructed by plotting each day's closing (or opening, or high, or low) prices and then drawing a line through these points. Figure 15-1 shows a primary uptrend existing from period t to the peak price that occurred just before day $t+j$. On trading day $t+j$, an abortive recovery takes place, signaling a change in the direction of the market's primary movement. An **abortive recovery is said to occur** when a secondary movement fails to rise above the preceding top. Before day $t+j$, all the tops

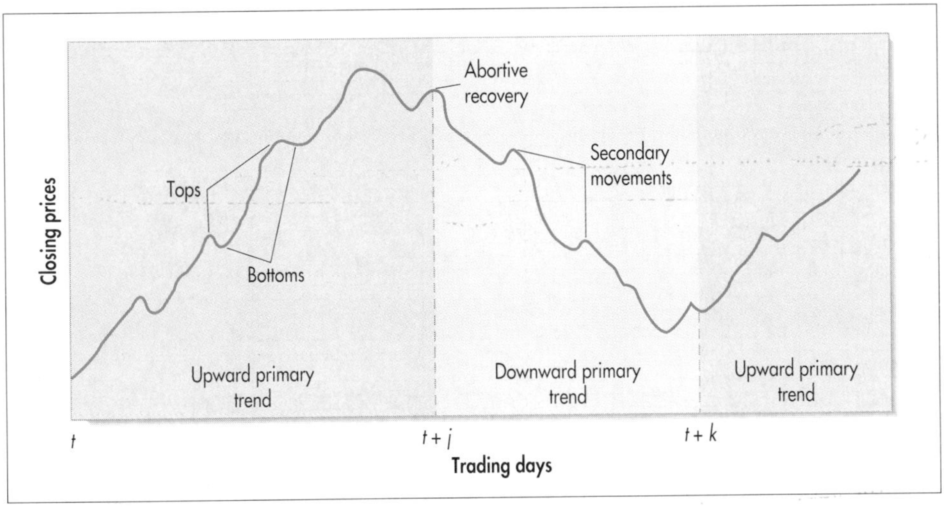

Figure 15-1 A line chart of daily prices annotated with Dow theory signals.

are ascending; after the abortive recovery, the tops descend until just before day $t+k$. At $t+k$, a secondary movement fails to reach a new bottom, signaling the start of a bull market. Most Dow theorists do not believe a new primary trend has emerged until they see confirmation. **Confirmation** occurs when the pattern of ascending or descending tops also occurs in both the industrial and the railroad averages.[3]

Statistically speaking, the Dow theory is based on trends that can be measured by serial correlation (or autocorrelation) coefficients that are significantly different from zero. In 1988 Fama and French reported statistically significant trends in security prices measured over 3- to 5-year time periods. The longer-term serial correlations they reported measure the types of trends on which the Dow theory and some other technical analysis theories are based.[4]

15-3 Bar Charts

The line chart in Figure 15-1 is one type of chart; the bar chart is another. Figure 15-2 illustrates price movements over an 11-month period. Bar charts can be prepared for a market index or for an individual asset. **Bar charts** have one vertical bar representing each day's price movement. Each bar spans the distance from the day's highest price to the day's lowest price, and a small cross on each bar marks that day's closing price.

[3] A supportive empirical test of the Dow theory is reported by David A. Glickstein and Rolf E. Wubbels, "Dow Theory Is Alive and Well," *Journal of Portfolio Management,* April 1983, pp. 28–31.

[4] See E. F. Fama and K. R. French, "Permanent and Temporary Components of Stock Prices," *Journal of Political Economy,* April 1988, vol. 96, no. 2, pp. 246–273.

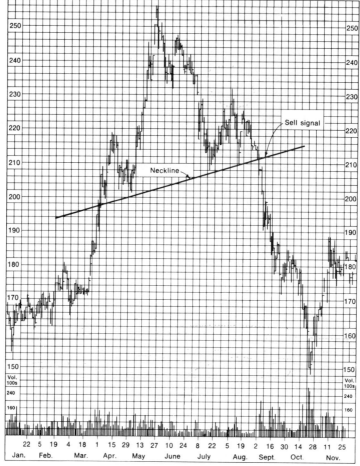

Figure 15-2 A bar chart of a head and shoulders top formation.

Line charts and bar charts usually have secondary graphs along the bottom showing the volume of shares traded at each date. Figure 15-2 shows such volume data. Many technicians believe that trading volume is the second most important statistic they follow, after prices. As an example of how technical analysts try to relate stock price moves and the volume of shares traded, consider a pattern called the *head and shoulders formation.*

A Head and Shoulders Top

A **head and shoulders top** formation is supposed to signal that the security's price has reached a top and will decline in the future. As its name suggests, the head and shoulders top pattern has a left shoulder, a head, and a right shoulder. The market action that forms a head and shoulders top can be broken down into four phases, as illustrated in Figure 15-2.

1. *Left shoulder:* A period of heavy buying followed by a lull in trading pushes the price up to a new peak before the price begins to slide down.

2. *Head:* A spurt of heavy buying raises prices to a new high and then allows the price to fall back below the top of the left shoulder.

3. *Right shoulder:* A moderate rally lifts the price somewhat but fails to push prices as high as the top of the head before a decline begins.

4. *Breakout:* Prices fall below the *neckline,* that is, the line drawn tangent to the left and right shoulders. This breakout presumably precedes a price drop and is a signal to sell.

Chart Patterns

Technical analysts have described numerous patterns in both line and bar charts that they believe indicate the direction of future price movements. Triangles, pennants, flags, channels, rectangles, double tops, triple tops, wedge formations, and diamonds are only some of the patterns for which chartists search. A minority of chartists employ even more complex techniques, some of which have names like point-and-figure charting and the Elliot wave theory. There is no consensus among technical analysts about which charting technique or which chart patterns are the best for the job.

15-4   Odd-Lot Theory

Theories of contrary opinion advocate doing the opposite of what some particular group of investors is doing. The **odd-lot theory,** for instance, assumes that small investors are usually wrong and it is therefore advantageous to pursue strategies that are the opposite of what they are doing.

Round lots are transactions involving multiples of 100 shares; *odd lots* are transactions of less than 100 shares. Since the sales commissions on odd lots are higher than the commissions on round lots, professional investors rarely trade odd lots; most odd-lot purchases are made by amateur investors with limited resources.

Odd-lot trading volume is reported in the financial section of many large newspapers. Odd-lot statistics are broken down into number of shares purchased, sold, and sold short. Most odd-lot theorists chart the ratio of odd-lot sales to odd-lot purchases week by week. The odd-lot purchases/sales index is typically plotted concurrently with some market index. It is used by some chartists as a leading indicator of market prices. High odd-lot purchases/sales ratios are presumed to forecast falls in market prices, and low purchases/sales ratios are presumed to occur toward the end of bear markets.

Figure 15-3 charts the odd-lot purchases/sales ratio along with S&P 500 Stocks Composite Index and the Dow Jones Industrial Average. The October 1987 stock

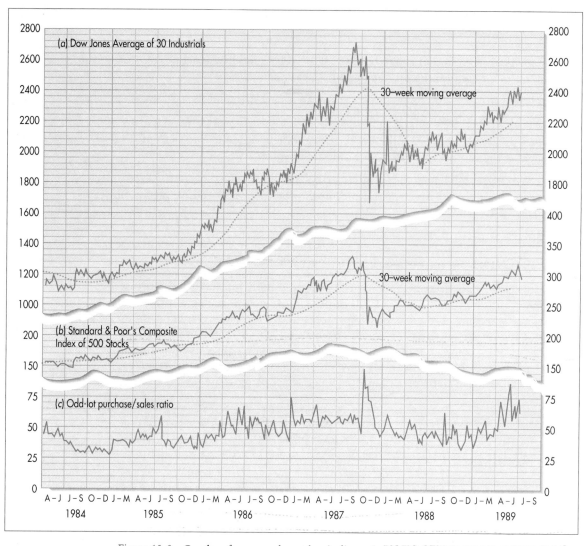

Figure 15-3 Graphs of two stock market indicators and the Odd-Lotters purchases/sales ratio. (*Source: Daily Action Stock Charts,* July 1989, published by Trendline, a division of Standard & Poor's, 25 Broadway, New York, N.Y., 10004.)

market crash is a noteworthy event: stock prices around the world collapsed, and there is no consensus explanation about what caused it. Let us focus on what the technical indicators suggested before that event. During the weeks prior to the crash, in opposition to the odd-lot theory, odd-lotters were selling more shares than they bought as the market rose precipitously. After the crash, odd-lotters sensibly became big buyers when stock prices were near their lows. These rational trading patterns by odd-lotters defy the contrary opinion theory about them.[5]

[5] For a different view see T. J. Kewley and R. A. Stevenson, "The Odd-Lot Theory for Individual Stocks," *Financial Analysts Journal,* January-February 1969.

MARKET DIARY

	Tues	Mon	Fri	Thur	Wed	Tues
Issues traded	1,531	1,532	1,562	1,597	1,582	1,616
Advances	582	669	255	468	994	745
Declines	657	589	1,118	914	391	634
Unchanged	292	274	189	215	197	237
New highs.	3	4	1	9	14	8
New lows	49	41	42	31	24	38

Figure 15-4 Data about the volume of shares traded on the NYSE.

To avoid being hurt by technical analysis theories that do not perform as they should, chartists typically search for *confirmation* from other indicators. As more technical indicators simultaneously issue the same signal to buy or sell, the technical analyst grows more confident that it is time to consummate a trade.

15-5   Breadth-of-Market Indicators

Breadth-of-market indicators are used to measure the underlying strength of market advances or declines. For example, it is possible that the Dow Jones Industrial Average, which takes into account only 30 blue-chip stocks, would still be rising for some time after the market for the majority of lesser-known stocks had already turned down. This occurred for several weeks before the October 1987 international stock market crash, for example. If one is to gauge the real underlying strength of the market, tools are needed to measure the breadth of the market's moves.

Calculating Advance-Decline Statistics

One of the easiest methods for measuring the breadth of the market is to subtract the number of issues that declined in price from the number that advanced in price in some particular market, such as the NYSE. Daily computations will yield the daily **net advances or declines.** Data on advances and declines are published each day in most financial and national newspapers; Figure 15-4 shows a sample newspaper excerpt.

The breadth-of-market statistic is obtained by cumulating the net advances and declines, so it is also called the **advance-decline line.** This advance-decline statistic may become negative during a bear market, as it did in the example in Table 15-1.

Table 15-1
Daily Advance-Decline Calculations

Day	Advances	minus	Declines	equals	Daily net advances and declines	Breadth
Tuesday	745		634		+111	111
Wednesday	994		391		+603	714
Thursday	468		914		−446	268
Friday	255		1,118		−863	−595
Monday	669		589		+80	−515
Tuesday	582		657		−75	−590

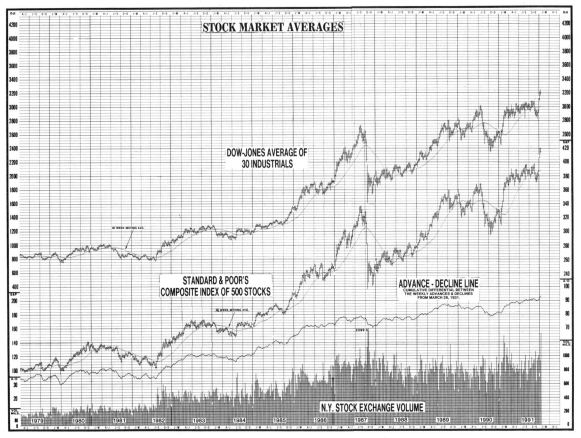

Figure 15-5 Chart of two stock market indicators and their moving averages, advance-decline line, and trading volume, 1986–1989, page 533. (*Source: Daily Action Stock Charts,* June 16, 1989, cover page, published by Trendline, a division of Standard & Poor's, 25 Broadway, New York, NY 10004.)

This is no cause for alarm, however, since the *level* of the cumulative advances and declines is entirely arbitrary. Only the *direction* of the advance-decline statistic is relevant.

Interpreting Breadth Data

Figure 15-5 shows breadth-of-market data for the NYSE. As the figure shows, the advance-decline line and the market indicators usually move in tandem. Technical analysts watch for the trend in the advance-decline line to diverge from the trend in the market.

Before the October 1987 international stock market crash, the advance-decline line had been declining for almost 6 weeks. This downturn indicated that many small stocks were falling in price. Such an indicator of weakening market demand gave technical analysts warning of the market collapse to come.

Another indicator that technical analysis relies on is the relative strength exhibited by some securities. The **relative-strength** approach suggests that the prices of some securities rise relatively faster in a bull market and decline relatively slowly in a bear market compared with other securities. Technicians who use this approach invest in securities that have demonstrated relative strength in the recent past, because relative strength sometimes continues undiminished for a considerable period. As a result,

Box 15-3

FINANCIAL: Measuring Relative Strength: Analysis of Anonymous Corporation

Consider the data for Anonymous Corporation (denoted A), a hypothetical growth firm in the electronics industry (EI). Table 15-2 presents some relative-strength data for this corporation.

Table 15-2
Relative-Strength Data for Anonymous Corporation

Quarter	Price of A	Average price of EI	Average price of MI	P_A/P_{EIA}	P_A/P_{MIA}	P_{EIA}/P_{MIA}
1	$30	$17	$210	30/17 = 1.78	30/210 = .144	17/210 = .081
2	36	18	250	36/18 = 2	36/250 = .144	18/250 = .072
3	72	20	285	72/20 = 3.6	72/285 = .253	20/285 = .070

Note: P_A is the average price of Anonymous Corporation for the quarter; P_{EIA} is the S&P electronics industry average for the quarter; P_{MIA} represents S&P 500 market index average for the quarter.

From the first quarter to the second Anonymous did slightly better than most of the firms in the electronics industry. The price of Anonymous rose relatively more than the electronics industry average; the ratio P_A/P_{EIA} advanced from 1.78 to 2. Moreover, from quarter 1 to 2 the electronics industry showed weakness relative to all industrial stocks: the ratio P_{EIA}/P_{MIA} declined from .081 to .072. From quarter 1 to 2 Anonymous showed no increased relative strength compared with the index average: the ratio P_A/P_{MIA} was invariant at .144. But from quarter 2 to 3 Anonymous showed considerable strength relative both to its industry and to the market, while the rest of the electronics industry performed weakly.

why can you extrapolate?

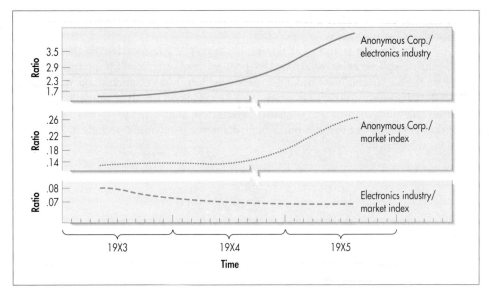

Figure 15-6 Relative-strength data for Anonymous Corporation and the electronics industry.

these investors expect to earn higher returns.[6] The relative-strength concept may be applied to individual securities or to whole industries.

To interpret relative-strength data, a technician typically plots the ratios of the security relative to its industry and to the market. A chart like the one shown in Figure 15-6 might result for Anonymous Corporation.[7] Figure 15-6 shows that although the electronics industry is failing to keep pace with the market, Anonymous Corporation is developing relative strength both in its industry and in the market. After preparing charts like this for firms from different industries over a period of time, the technician selects industries and firms that demonstrated relative strength as promising investment opportunities.

[6] For empirical evidence that supports relative strength see J. Brush, "Eight Relative Strength Models Compared," *Journal of Portfolio Management,* Fall 1986, pp. 21–28. Also see M. Greene and B. Fielitz, "Long-Term Dependence of Common Stock Returns," *Journal of Financial Economics,* May 1977, pp. 339–349; J. Bohan, "Relative Strength: Further Positive Evidence," *Journal of Portfolio Management,* Fall 1981, pp. 36–39; and J. Brush and K. Boles, "The Predictive Power in Relative Strength and CAPM," *Journal of Portfolio Management,* Summer 1983, pp. 20–23.

[7] For a discussion of measuring relative strength by computer see chap. 18 of Richard Bookstaber, *The Complete Investment Book* (Glenview, Ill.: Scott, Foresman, 1985). For further discussion of relative-strength computations see sec. 6 of J. W. Wilder, *New Concepts in Technical Trading Systems* (Greensboro, N.C.: Trend Research, 1978).

A chartist can calculate a few different relative strength ratios daily for each of dozens of different stocks. When all these ratios are graphed, they enable the technician to easily pick out those securities that have relative strength—they are the current "hot investments." Or, if the technical analyst is willing to spend some money, it is also possible to purchase graphs on hundreds of stocks and have them delivered at frequent intervals.

15-7 Volume of Shares Traded

Many technical analysts believe they can get a better idea of whether a market is bullish or bearish by studying the **volume of shares traded,** because volume is thought to measure the intensity of investors' aggregate desires. Most financial newspapers publish the previous day's total volume of shares traded in various security markets. Some financial newspapers also publish the number of shares traded in selected individual issues. Figure 15-4 presents a typical newspaper excerpt.

There is a Wall Street adage that "it takes volume to move a stock," either up or down in price. Indeed, a large amount of trading volume is often associated with large price changes, so it is reasonable for chartists to study volume data in an effort to discern the causes of specific stock price movements. But the cause-and-effect relationship between the volume of shares traded and the price change in the traded security is vague and hard to unravel. Security transactions are sometimes grouped into two categories: *information trading* and *liquidity trading.* Sometimes a large volume of liquidity trading can take place without causing any price change.[8]

Technicians watch volume most closely on days when supply and demand appear to be moving to a new equilibrium. If high volume occurs on days when prices move up, the market is considered to be bullish. High volume on days when prices are falling is a bearish sign. If the same price changes occurred with low trading volume, they would be considered less significant. There is one occasion when falling prices and high volume are considered bullish. When technicians feel the end of a bear market is near, they watch for a high volume of selling as the last of the bearish investors liquidate their holdings in what is called a **selling climax.** A selling climax is supposed to eliminate the last of the bears who drive prices down and clear the way for the market to turn up.

Some technicians also look for a **speculative blowoff** to mark the end of a bull market. A speculative blowoff is a high volume of buying that pushes prices up to a

---

[8] Research into the implications of the volume of shares traded includes Prem C. Jain and Gun-Ho Joh, "The Dependence between Hourly Prices and Trading Volume," *Journal of Financial and Quantitative Analysis,* vol. 23, no. 3, September 1988, pp. 269–284. Also see J. M. Karpoff, "The Relation between Price Changes and Trading Volume: A Survey," *Journal of Financial and Quantitative Analysis,* vol. 22, no. 1, March 1987, pp. 109–126; and G. E. Tauchen and M. Pitts, "The Price Variability-Volume Relationship on Speculative Markets," *Econometrica,* vol. 51, March 1983, pp. 485–505.

peak; it is supposed to exhaust the enthusiasm of speculators and make way for a bear market. Technicians who hold this belief say that "bulls must die with a bang, not a whimper."

Figure 15-5 shows the daily volume on the NYSE plotted alongside bar charts of the DJIA and Standard & Poor's 500 Stocks Composite Index. October 1987 provides a case when high trading volume was clearly associated with a substantial move in market prices.

15-8   Moving-Average Analysis

A *moving-average stock price* is used to provide a smoothed reference value against which daily fluctuations can be compared. As a result, technical analysis done with moving averages is also called *rate-of-change analysis*.

Constructing a Moving-Average Chart

The *moving-average price* changes each day as the most recent day's stock price is added and the oldest day's price is dropped from the average. The span of time over which the moving average is calculated affects the volatility of the moving average. Some technicians use a 200-day moving average of closing prices. Here is the formula for calculating a 200-day moving average (MA_t) of the DJIA on day t.

$$MA_t = \frac{1}{200} \sum_{j=1}^{200} DJIA_{t-j}$$

$$= \frac{1}{200} (DJIA_{t-1} + DJIA_{t-2} + \cdots + DJIA_{t-200})$$

where t = a day counter
   j = the number of days back from day t for each
        of the 200 DJIA values in the sum

Figure 15-5 shows the 30-week moving average of the DJIA and the S&P 500 Stocks Composite Index as dotted lines. Technicians obtain their information from the relationship between the market prices and the moving average. Moving-average analysis is used for individual securities and market indexes.

Interpreting Moving-Average Charts

When daily prices penetrate the moving-average line, technicians interpret this *penetration* as a signal to buy or sell. When the daily prices move downward through the moving average, they frequently fail to rise again for many months. Thus, a downward penetration of a flattened moving average suggests selling. When actual prices are above the moving average but the difference is narrowing, this is a signal that a bull market may be ending.

1. The moving average flattens out and the stock's price rises through the moving average.

2. The price of a stock falls below a moving-average line that is rising.

3. A price that is above the moving-average line falls but turns around and begins to rise again without yet reaching the moving-average line.

Moving-average chartists recommend selling a stock when:

1. The moving-average line flattens out and the stock's price drops downward through the moving-average line.

2. A stock's price rises above a declining moving-average line.

3. A price falls downward through the moving-average line and turns around to rise but then falls again before getting above the moving-average line.

The buy and sell signals initiated by a moving-average trading system vary with the length of time over which the average is calculated. Moving averages calculated over short time spans tend to touch off many unfruitful trades, but adherence to the moving-average trading rules over many months and many different stocks shows that sometimes profitable trades are also signaled. Most technical analysts therefore use more than one tool and compare the various buy and sell signals before they actually trade.

bad for short term

15-9 Evaluating Technical Analysis

Let us summarize the technical analysis philosophy and sampling of tools presented in this chapter and reach some conclusions.

Fundamental analysts analyze a firm's financial statements, its competitors, the condition of the economy, governmental actions that may affect the firm, and other fundamental facts that may affect the future value of the firm's common stock. Fundamental analysts largely ignore the unpredictable short-run swings that constantly alter the stock's current price. They work to find new information before other investors so they can get into a position to profit from anticipated price changes.

Technical analysts, in sharp contrast, largely ignore the facts that determine the intrinsic value of a corporation's common stock. Technical analysts do not concern themselves with trying to estimate a stock's value. They study graphs of historical stock prices, market averages, and other indications of market trends in search of patterns that may have predictive value.

All technical analysis tools try to measure some aspect of supply and demand. Shifts in supply and demand are presumed to be gradual rather than instantaneous. When shifts in prices are detected, they are presumed to be the result of *gradual shifts* in supply and demand rather than a series of *independent shifts* that all happened to be in the same direction. Since these shifts are assumed to continue as prices *react gradually to new information,* they are used to predict further price changes.

Many economists believe that technical analysis cannot measure supply and demand or predict prices. They suggest that security markets are highly efficient (as illustrated in Figure 16-2*a*) and that security prices reflect new information instantly so that price changes are therefore random and unpredictable. When a security's price moves in the same direction for several days, efficient markets theorists interpret these movements as a series of independent changes in supply or demand, all of which happen to move the price in the same direction by coincidence. They assert that technical analysts are wrong in believing that supply and demand adjust gradually, causing trends that may be used for predicting future prices. Evidence supporting the efficient markets hypothesis will be examined in Chapter 16.

Summary

Security analysts who prepare charts of security prices and study them in order to find patterns that may be useful in predicting future prices are called *technical analysts,* or *chartists.* Most technical analysts say they use charts to detect the shifts in supply and demand that determine market prices. Technical analysts chart data on individual securities, on market averages, and on various technical indicators such as odd-lot trading and moving averages. Most chartists use two different types of charts: line charts and bar charts.

The Dow theory is one of the oldest and most well known instruments in the chartists' toolbox. The Dow theory focuses on trying to detect and ride along with the prevailing bull or bear market trends.

Theories of contrary opinion advocate doing the opposite of what is being done by a certain group of investors. The odd-lot theory, for example, advocates buying when investors who trade in odd lots of stocks are selling, and vice versa.

Breadth-of-market statistics can be useful in determining how widespread a trend is in some market index. Breadth of market is measured by counting the number of stocks in a market that are having advances and declines and cumulating the net total of advances less declines each trading day.

Relative-strength ratios are plotted over time to see which securities have strength relative to other securities in the same industry and relative to the market averages. Chartists follow the volume of shares traded because volume is believed to be a key to interpreting the importance of price moves. Moving-average analysis is used to smooth over short-term price fluctuations in order to see long-run trends more clearly.

Further Reading

Bookstaber, Richard, *The Complete Investment Book* (Glenview, Ill.: Scott, Foresman, 1985).
> *Chapters 14 through 20 explain various technical analysis tools. Computer programs to do technical analysis that are written in BASIC language are printed at the end of each chapter.*

Edwards, R. D., and John Magee, Jr., *Technical Analysis of Stock Trends,* rev. 5th ed. (Springfield, Mass.: John Magee Inc., 1966).
> *This classic book has been used for years by technical analysts. It is easy to read and explains many different techniques.*

Jiler, William L., *How Charts Can Help You in the Stock Market* (New York: Trendline, 1962).
   This book on charting explains many techniques and provides good illustrative examples.

Pring, Martin J., *Technical Analysis Explained*, 2d ed. (New York: McGraw-Hill, 1985).
   This comprehensive book presents a large number of technical analysis techniques that are used with individual stocks, bonds, commodities, and market averages. Helpful illustrations are provided.

Tully, Shawn, "Princeton's Rich Commodity Scholars," *Fortune*, Feb. 9, 1981, pp. 94–98.
   This article provides an admiring report about the profitability of one group's use of technical analysis in commodity trading.

Trendline, a division of Standard & Poor's, 25 Broadway, New York, NY 10004.
   Trendline purveys books of stock price charts showing the details of short-run price moves and, also, books illustrating long-term price histories.

Wilder, J. Welles, *New Concepts in Technical Trading Systems* (Greensboro, N.C.: Trend Research, 1978).
   This book explains precisely how to execute different technical analysis trading rules. Computer programs written by author Welles may also be purchased.

Essay Questions

15-1 According to the Dow theory, what is the significance of an abortive recovery following a series of ascending tops?

15-2 How is the moving average used in analyzing stock prices? Can it be meaningfully calculated in different ways? Explain.

15-3 Which of the technical indicators discussed in this chapter do you think provided the clearest and most unambiguous forewarning of the October 1987 international stock market crash? Explain.

15-4 What significance do technical analysts attribute to the volume of odd-lot trading? Explain.

15-5 (*a*) How are data on the number of shares that advance and decline on a given trading day used by technical analysts? (*b*) Does knowing the number of advances and declines for only 1 day convey meaningful information? Explain.

15-6 Compare and contrast the concepts of relative strength and undiversifiable systematic risk. If a stock has high relative strength, what is the implication for that stock's rates of return?

15-7 Define the phrases "speculative blowoff" and "selling climax." What do these concepts have in common?

15-8 Are the technical analysis tools presented in this chapter useful for analyzing individual securities, market indexes, or both? Explain.

15-9 "Experienced technical analysts usually have one favorite tool that they follow closely." Is the statement true, false, or questionable? Explain.

Problems

15-10 Consider the following 14 days of data for the Hemmel Corporation's common stock. On which day do you think the market received important new information affecting the value of Hemmel's stock?

Day	Closing price	Volume of shares traded	Day	Closing price	Volume of shares traded
1	$29.25	1,000	8	31.50	14,000
2	31.125	11,000	9	31.75	2,000
3	32.50	3,000	10	33.125	500
4	33.125	2,000	11	34.50	2,000
5	33.75	500	12	34.00	3,000
6	32.875	2,000	13	33.75	2,000
7	32.125	1,000	14	32.625	500

15-11 (*a*) Calculate a 5-day moving average from the Hemmel Corporation's closing price data from Problem 15-10. *Note:* You will be able to calculate only 10 moving-average prices, since it is impossible to calculate the average for the first 4 days. (*b*) Over what range does Hemmel's price vary? (*c*) Over what range do the moving-average values of Hemmel's prices vary?

15-12 Daily stock price and volume data for the Flexible Flyer Sled Corporation are listed below. Draw a bar graph of these stock prices and chart the volume data along the bottom of your illustration.

Trading day	High price	Low price	Closing price	Number of shares traded
1	48	47¼	48	37,100
2	48	47	48	38,200
3	48	47⅜	47⅜	28,600
4	48⅛	47⅜	48⅛	36,500
5	49	48¼	48½	59,700
6	48¾	48¼	48⅝	29,500
7	49	48	48¼	44,200
8	48⅞	48¼	48½	29,500
9	49¾	48½	49¾	75,700
10	49⅞	49½	49⅝	48,200
11	49¾	49¼	49⅝	31,800
12	49¾	49¼	49¾	29,200
13	49¾	49⅜	49⅝	21,500
14	50	49⅜	50	55,200
15	50⅜	50	50⅜	45,700
16	50¾	50¼	50⅜	41,100
17	50⅞	50⅜	50¾	37,100
18	51	50⅝	50¾	40,100
19	51	50⅝	51	35,300
20	50⅞	50⅜	50⅜	26,400
21	50⅛	49¾	50⅛	39,300

Trading day	Closing price	Sledding industry index	Standard & Poor's 500 Index
1	48	28	270
2	48	27	268
3	47⅜	27	269
4	48⅛	27	270
5	48½	28	270
6	48⅝	29	269
7	48¼	28	271
8	48½	29	272
9	49¾	29	271
10	49⅝	30	273
11	49⅝	29	274
12	49¾	30	276
13	49⅝	31	278
14	50	29	276
15	50⅜	31	279
16	50⅜	31	280
17	50¾	30	279
18	50¾	31	281
19	51	32	282
20	50⅜	32	283
21	50⅛	31	282

15-13 Daily closing stock price data for the Flexible Flyer Sled Corporation (FFSC) are listed above beside the closing values for an index of sledding industry stock prices and the S&P 500 Stocks Composite Index. Calculate relative-strength statistics for FFSC relative to the industry and relative to the market. Do your findings suggest that FFSC has relative strength, relative weakness, or what? What does this imply about the kinds of returns an investor might expect from FFSC?

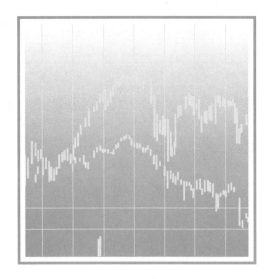

CHAPTER 16

THE EFFICIENT MARKETS HYPOTHESIS

In 1900 a French mathematician named Louis Bachelier wrote a scientific paper suggesting that the day-to-day security price fluctuations were random.[1] His idea became known as the **random-walk theory**.[2] However, as we saw in Chapter 15, technical analysts do not think security price fluctuations are random. Technicians claim to see meaningful patterns in their price charts. Who is right? Are security prices determined by chance or do they move in an orderly fashion? Furthermore, what about the intrinsic values we studied in Chapters 13 and 14? If stock prices fluctuate randomly or move in well-defined patterns, intrinsic values seem to have little meaning. What should we conclude from these conflicting notions? This chapter introduces the efficient markets theory to clear up the contradictions and explain the process that determines security prices.

16-1   Price Is Determined by Value

Security price fluctuations may appear to be meaningless gyrations, but upon closer examination it appears that prices move in pursuit of their ever-changing values.

Cootner's Model: Liquidity Traders and Information Traders

In 1962 an economist named Paul Cootner suggested that security prices can be viewed as a series of constrained random fluctuations around their intrinsic value.[3] Cootner's constraints resulted from the actions of two groups of investors. The first group is made up of those who find themselves with excess cash they want to invest or who need to liquidate some of their investments to pay for a sudden expense. These **liquidity traders** base investment decisions on the arrival of an income tax refund, an inheritance, lottery winnings, or other random good fortune. They might sell their investments when they need to pay a medical bill, buy a new furnace for the house, or pay for a wedding. These are unsophisticated investors who recognize few divergences from intrinsic values. Essentially, liquidity traders buy and sell at random times, and they do not investigate before they invest.

The second group is made up of **information traders**, those who have the

---

[1] Louis Bachelier, "Theory of Speculation," *Ann. Sci. Ecole Norm. Sup. (3),* no. 1018, Gauthier-Villars, Paris, 1900.

[2] The mathematical random-walk theory is a very negative statement. It says that absolutely no patterns exist in price changes, that technical analysis techniques are entirely worthless, and that the daily changes in the Dow Jones Industrial Average (DJIA) are totally random. It is quite easy to find counterexamples to these rigid assertions. These counterexamples do not deny what we might call a "rational investor's random-walk model," however. A *rational investor's random-walk model* says that short-run price fluctuations are so hard to predict that on an after-commissions, risk-adjusted basis it is nearly impossible to outperform a naive buy-and-hold strategy.

[3] See P. H. Cootner, "Stock Prices: Random versus Systematic Changes," *Industrial Management Review,* vol. 3, no. 2 (Spring) 1962, pp. 24–45.

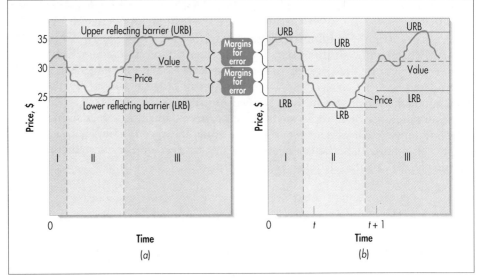

Figure 16-1 Random stock price fluctuations within reflecting barriers. (*a*) No change in intrinsic value; (*b*) intrinsic value changes at times *t* and *t*+1.

resources to discover new information and develop estimates of securities' values. Information traders recognize significant deviations from intrinsic value and initiate trading that tends to align market price with intrinsic value.

An Intrinsic Value Random-Walk Market

Figure 16-1 illustrates how security prices might fluctuate in Cootner's model. The dashed lines represent the professional investors' consensus value estimate. Note that the intrinsic value of the security in Figure 16-1*b* changes at times *t* and *t*+1, while the value remains unchanged at $30 in Figure 16-1*a*. Since liquidity trading is not necessarily based on correct analysis of the latest news, these traders may buy securities whose market prices are above their intrinsic values. This buying is illustrated in Figure 16-1*a* and 16-1*b* by the price fluctuating above the value in phase I. After this initial overoptimistic buying, liquidity traders may sell the stock when its price is below its value, as shown in phase II. Unprofitable liquidity-motivated trades are largely responsible for the aimless price fluctuations that can cause prices to diverge from values.

When a security's price does differ significantly from its true intrinsic value, information traders find it profitable to correct the disequilibrium. Small deviations are not worth correcting, because the profits will not be enough to pay for the brokerage commissions. But when prices are significantly out of line, information traders will bid up low prices or push down prices of overpriced securities by selling them. In effect, information traders erect "reflecting barriers" around the intrinsic value. These barriers are represented by the solid lines above and below the intrinsic value lines in Figure 16-1. The *upper reflecting barrier* is denoted "URB" and the *lower reflecting barrier* is "LRB." Prices will fluctuate freely between the barriers. When prices reach the barriers, the actions of information traders will cause prices to move toward their intrinsic value. Professor Eugene Fama called Cootner's model an **intrinsic value random-walk market.**[4]

A Market with Varying Degrees of Efficiency

Figure 16-2 illustrates three different scenarios about how the price of a security might vary around its value. Figure 16-2*a* portrays the price fluctuating closely around its value in what we will call a *strongly efficient market.* Figure 16-2*b* depicts more significant departures in a *semistrongly efficient market.* Figure 16-2*c* represents a *weakly efficient market* in which price and value diverge substantially. Varying degrees of market efficiency can be expected to exist in different securities markets.

[4] See Eugene Fama, "The Behavior of Stock Market Prices," *Journal of Business,* January 1955, p. 36.

Figure 16-2 Varying degrees of pricing efficiency.

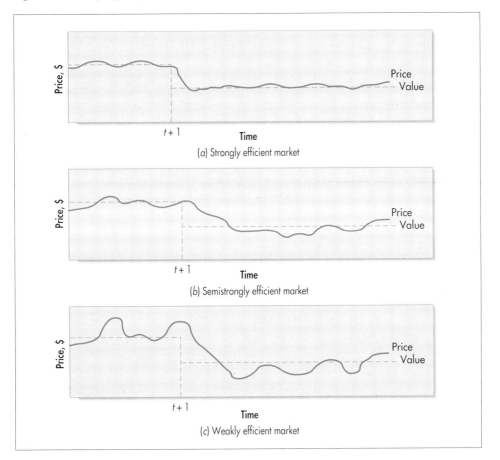

(a) Strongly efficient market

(b) Semistrongly efficient market

(c) Weakly efficient market

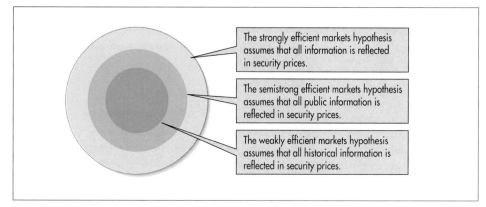

Figure 16-3 A Venn diagram of the three levels of information that might be reflected in stock prices.

The prices of over-the-counter (OTC) stocks might be expected to fluctuate around their values less efficiently than the prices of NYSE-listed stocks because there is typically less investor interest and a lower level of trading in most OTC stocks. The prices in foreign security markets may be less efficient than NYSE prices, too, because overseas security laws do not require corporations to disclose as much information. As a result, there is more uncertainty surrounding the values of these securities.[5]

The levels of information dispersal required by the three hypotheses about market efficiency are compared graphically in Figure 16-3. *These three hypotheses are not mutually exclusive;* they differ only in the degree of information required. The information dissemination needed for the weaker hypothesis to be true, plus some additional knowledge, is necessary for the stronger hypothesis to be true.

But before we evaluate evidence about how efficient the security markets are, let us consider why market efficiency is an important topic. Investors should form an opinion about the degree of efficiency they think exists in security markets because that belief will determine whether they manage their investments passively or aggressively.

16-2 Aggressive versus Passive Investment Management

Although considerable evidence suggests that security markets in the United States are highly efficient, few people would seriously argue that they have actually attained perfect efficiency so that the price of every security always equals its value. Scientific evidence shows that market inefficiencies create opportunities for security analysts to

[5] See Gabriel A. Hawawini, *European Equity Markets: Price Behavior and Efficiency,* Monograph 1984–4/5, Salomon Brothers Center for the Study of Financial Institutions, Graduate School of Business, New York University, New York City.

profit from undervalued and overvalued securities.[6] The existence of these lucrative opportunities motivates some investors to become **aggressive investment managers** who buy and sell securities in order to maximize their trading profits.

Aggressive Management

Active security analysis is at the core of aggressive investment management. The analyst must accurately estimate the intrinsic value of a security so that this estimate can be compared with its market price in order to make buy-sell decisions. Aggressive securities analysts usually trade actively, because every time they discover a mispriced asset, they either buy or sell—whichever appears to be profitable.

There are a few thousand professional security analysts who work full time in the United States, aggressively analyzing publicly traded securities and trading actively on their findings. As a result of their activities, it is difficult to find securities that are substantially mispriced. Empirical evidence that securities markets in the United States are highly efficient is presented later in this chapter. This evidence means, essentially, that the prices of most securities are usually close to their values.

Passive Management

Because a large amount of evidence[7] has been published showing that the prices of securities are highly efficient, **passive investment management** became popular during the 1970s. Passive investors reasoned that if many investors are well-informed and some consensus exists about intrinsic values, security analysis and aggressive trading are too much trouble and too risky. As a result, passive investors chose to invest in special portfolios called *index funds.*

Index funds are diversified portfolios that buy and hold the same securities that are used in some securities market index. Emulating the Standard & Poor's 500 Stocks Composite Index is the objective of several index funds. These portfolio managers buy the same 500 stocks that make up the S&P 500 index and maintain them in their portfolios in exactly the same proportions they are held in the index. Several index funds manage billions of dollars for thousands of passive investors. In

[6] See Sanjay Basu, "The Investment Performance of Common Stocks Relative to Their Price-Earnings Ratios: A Test of the Efficient Markets," *Journal of Finance*, vol. 32, no. 3, June 1977, pp. 663–682. See also, Robert J. Shiller, "Do Stock Prices Move Too Much to Be Justified by Subsequent Changes in Dividends?" *American Economic Review*, vol. 71, June 1981, pp. 421–436, and Bruce I. Jacobs and Kenneth N. Levy, "Disentangling Equity Return Regularities: New Insights and Investment Opportunities," *Financial Analysts Journal*, May-June 1988, pp. 18–43. For a review of dozens of anomalies in the efficient markets theory see chap. 18, "Behavior of Stock Market Prices," in J. C. Francis, *Investments: Analysis and Management*, 5th ed. (New York: McGraw-Hill, 1991).

[7] Eugene F. Fama, "Efficient Capital Markets: A Review of Theory and Empirical Work," *Journal of Finance*, May 1970, pp. 383–417, and Eugene F. Fama, "The Behavior of Stock Market Prices," *Journal of Business*, January 1965.

Box 16-1

DEFINITION: Weakly Efficient Markets

Weakly efficient markets are markets in which historical prices provide no information about future prices that would allow a short-term trader to earn a return above what could be attained with a naive buy-and-hold strategy.

---

particular, Wells Fargo Investment Advisors, a subsidiary of Wells Fargo Bank in San Francisco; Batterymarch Financial Management Corporation in Boston; and the trust department of the American National Bank and Trust Company in Chicago manage large index funds. Efficient markets research has made such passive management practices a respectable alternative to estimating values, comparing them with prices, and trading aggressively.[8] Passive investment management offers the benefits of being inexpensive and providing performance that will match some designated market index.

Let us consider empirical evidence that will allow you to decide whether you should be a passive investor who indexes your funds, or an aggressive investor who searches for good buys.

16-3   The Weakly Efficient Markets Hypothesis

First we examine the hypothesis that markets are weakly efficient, as illustrated in Figures 16-2c and 16-3. Since the weakly efficient markets hypothesis maintains that past performance is irrelevant to future strategies, it implicitly suggests that technical analysis is worthless. Stock market data provide support for the weakly efficient markets hypothesis.

The weakly efficient markets definition does not suggest that short-term traders, speculators, and technical analysts will never earn a positive rate of return. It means that, on average, short-term speculators will not outperform a blindfolded investor picking securities with a dart. Of course, some lucky traders do better than investors using a naive buy-and-hold strategy, and unlucky traders do worse, but on average the buy-and-hold strategy cannot be beaten by chartists or liquid traders. Let us look at some scientific evidence to back this assertion.

Filter Rules

A **filter rule** is a mechanical trading rule that operates as described in Box 16-2 and illustrated in Figure 16-4. Filter rules typically place the trader in short positions periodically. A *short position* involves selling an asset the short seller does not own in

---

[8] See Peter C. Aldrich, "Active versus Passive: A New Look," *Journal of Portfolio Management,* vol. 14, no. 1, 1987, pp. 9–11.

Box 16-2

407

Chapter 16
The Efficient
Markets
Hypothesis

> **DEFINITION: An *X* Percent Filter Rule**
>
> If the price of a security rises at least *x* percent, buy and hold the security until its price drops at least *x* percent from a subsequent high. When the price decreases from a peak level by *x* percent, liquidate the holding and assume a short position as the price falls and hold the short position until the price reaches a low point and then rises *x* percent.

hopes of buying the asset later at a lower price in order to profit from a price decline. (Short sales are analyzed further in Chapter 20.)

A computer program can be written to trade a filter rule mechanically, and one can test different filter rules by varying the value of *x*. If stock price changes are random, filter rules should not perform better than a naive buy-and-hold strategy. Filter rules should earn significant profits, however, if they can discern the bull and bear market trends on which the Dow theory is based.

Figure 16-4 illustrates how a 10 percent filter rule would operate as the price of a hypothetical stock fluctuates between $18 and $40 over a period of a few years. Note that the stock price rises from a $20 purchase price to a $36 sale price, for a $16 per share profit during a bullish trend of about 18 months' duration.

Studies have been published using different stocks and different filters. Filters as small as one-half of 1 percent (*x* = 0.5) and as large as 50 percent (*x* = 50.0) have been tested. The tests were performed with stock price data gathered at various intervals. One test used daily stock prices over several years. Occasionally, a filter rule earned a return above what would have been earned with a naive buy-and-hold strategy, if the

Figure 16-4   Using a 10 percent filter rule to trade as the price fluctuates.

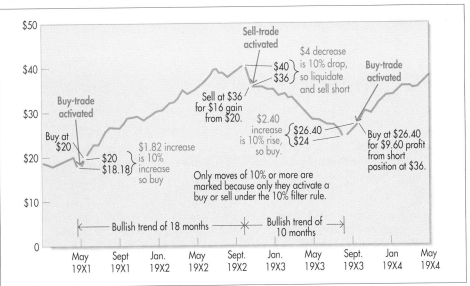

commissions incurred in buying and selling were ignored. However, *after commissions were deducted, the filter rules do not outperform a naive buy-and-hold strategy.* In fact, some filter rules resulted in considerable net losses after commission expenses were deducted. If there are price patterns that can be used as bases for a profitable trading strategy, filter rules do not seem able to detect them. This evidence supports the weakly efficient markets hypothesis; it suggests that charting stock prices may be a waste of time.[9]

Serial Correlations

While technical analysts maintain that security prices seem to have *momentum* (this means they sometimes move in trends), scientific investigation suggests they do not; that is, consecutive short-term changes in a particular direction (up or down) are not necessarily followed by further changes in the same direction. Filter rules should detect such patterns if they did exist. Security prices may also follow a pattern of **reversals** in which price changes in one direction tend to be followed by changes in the opposite direction. While filter rules might not detect a pattern of erratic reversals, serial correlation tests should.

Serial correlation (or autocorrelation) measures the correlation coefficient in a series of numbers (stock prices in this case) with lagging values in the same time series (that is, in past prices of the same stock). (Appendix 5A at the end of Chapter 5 defines the correlation coefficient.) Both trends and reversals can be detected. We can measure the correlation between security price changes in one time period and price changes in the same security in later periods. Of course, there is a long-term upward trend in security prices; so if "one time period" covers a number of years, a positive serial correlation would be observed. But long-term trends are of no interest here, since they are already known to exist. The question is the existence of patterns in short-term (daily or weekly) price changes that can be used to earn larger profits after commissions than a naive buy-and-hold strategy.

Figure 16-5 depicts some of the patterns serial-correlation tests would detect. Many serial-correlation studies of security prices have been published, and they have failed to detect any significant correlations.[10] Most serial-correlation coefficients are not significantly different from zero; this finding suggests prices fluctuate randomly. This is another piece of evidence in support of the weakly efficient markets hypothesis.

[9] See E. F. Fama and M. E. Blume, "Filter Rules and Stock Market Trading," *Journal of Business,* January 1966, pp. 226–241. For more refined results see Richard J. Sweeney, "Some New Filter Rule Tests: Methods and Results," *Journal of Financial and Quantitative Analysis,* vol. 23, no. 3, September 1988, pp. 285–300.

[10] See Eugene F. Fama, "The Behavior of Stock Market Prices," *Journal of Business,* January 1955, vol. 38, no. 1, pp. 34–105. Also see Sidney Alexander, "Price Movements in Speculative Markets: Trends or Random Walks," *Industrial Management Review,* May 1961, pp. 7–26. And, see M. G. Kendall, "The Analysis of Economic Time Series, Part I," *Journal of the Royal Statistical Society,* 96, 1953, pp. 11–25.

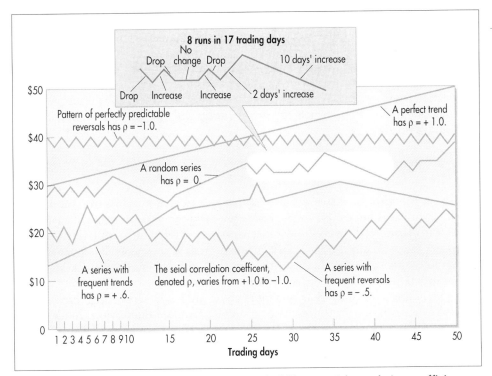

Figure 16-5 Price fluctuations for five stocks with different serial-correlation coefficients.

Runs Tests

It is possible that security prices might change randomly most of the time but *occasionally* follow trends that filter rules and serial correlations cannot detect. Runs tests can be used to determine if there are irregular trends in price changes.

Statisticians are able to determine how many positive, negative, or zero runs may be expected to occur in a series of truly random numbers of any size. This number of runs is then used as a standard against which actual price changes are compared. A

Box 16-3

> **DEFINITION: Statistical Runs**
>
> A **run** is something that happens in a series of numbers whenever the *changes* between consecutive numbers switch direction. For example, in a bear market, a security price that declines for 10 consecutive trading days will generate nine negative daily price changes but only one negative run. A zero run occurs when prices remain flat for a period of any duration. The highlighted panel of Figure 16-5 illustrates eight runs (four negative runs, one zero run, and three positive runs) that occurred during the 17 trading days from day 25 to day 42.

series of price changes for a security containing either too many or too few runs (relative to what would be expected in a series of random numbers) is evidence of some kind of nonrandomness. Published runs tests suggest that the runs in price changes of stocks are not significantly different from the runs in a series of random numbers. This evidence, along with the conclusions from filter rules and serial-correlation tests, suggests that short-run traders looking for various types of nonrandom trends from which to earn a profit will not be able to beat a naive buy-and-hold strategy.

Indirect Tests

The problem with the statistical tests is that the securities' values are not actually used, because it is impossible to determine precisely the intrinsic value of a common stock. Furthermore, different fundamental analysts develop different estimates of the intrinsic value of any given security. Since there is no generally accepted and observable intrinsic value estimate to compare with the security's market price, *technical analysis must be subjected to indirect tests.*

The indirect statistical tests presented above are based on the idea that intrinsic values of securities ought to fluctuate randomly. Random fluctuations result from a market mechanism in which the intrinsic value of a share of stock changes whenever more recent news about the security reaches the public. This is a reasonable assumption, but the semistrongly efficient markets hypothesis we examine next uses more direct techniques.

16-4   The Semistrongly Efficient Markets Hypothesis

The weakly efficient markets hypothesis asserts only that security prices do not tend to follow patterns; the *semistrongly efficient markets hypothesis* requires more evidence of market efficiency.

If the semistrongly efficient markets hypothesis is true, then only a few insiders trading on short-run price changes can earn a profit larger than what could be earned by using a naive buy-and-hold strategy. Evidence points to the conclusion that U.S. securities markets are semistrongly efficient.

In the free and competitive market, prices adjust so that they balance supply and demand. When supply and demand are in equilibrium, a market price emerges that represents a consensus of opinion. For common stocks, this equilibrium price is

Box 16-4

DEFINITION: Semistrongly Efficient Markets

Semistrongly efficient markets are those in which all relevant publicly available information is fully reflected in security prices. As a result, nothing that will lead to profitable trades can be gained from public sources in a semistrongly efficient market.

---

called the *intrinsic value.* When a new piece of information reaches the market, supply and/or demand will react. The faster the fresh news is assimilated and the new equilibrium price emerges, the more efficient the market. In the United States prices adjust rapidly enough to support the semistrong hypothesis.

Absence of Learning Lags

In order for markets to be semistrongly efficient, there can be no learning lags; prompt dissemination and assimilation of news are essential if prices are to reflect all relevant information immediately.

Think of what would happen if there were learning lags. Suppose the financial news released in New York did not spread beyond that state's boundaries on the day it was released. If the news favorably affected a corporation's stock, the price would probably move up slightly as New Yorkers acted upon it. The second day after the announcement, if the news traveled as far west as the Mississippi River, the rest of the eastern investors would bid the price up a bit farther. By the third day the news would have traveled as far west as the Rocky Mountains and midwestern investors would then bid prices up farther as they got the information. On the fourth day, the news would reach the Pacific coast. The price would then be bid up again.

As a result of the learning lag, two events would occur. First, there would be a 4-day trend in a security's price, rather than one immediate effect. Second, for over 3 days the corporation's stock price would not fully reflect all available information. The studies in the section on the weakly efficient market hypothesis revealed practically no evidence of such trends, which indicates that in the United States, financial news is assimilated into security prices quickly. As a result, prices tend to reflect all publicly available information. Charting stock prices in search of trends will not be worthwhile.

Effects of the Fed's Discount Rate Changes

Interest rates affect security prices because they determine the appropriate discount rate to use in determining present values (see Chapters 11, 12, and 13). Therefore, when the Board of Governors of the Federal Reserve System announces changes in its Federal Reserve discount rate, that event could be expected to change securities' prices. This is particularly true because announcements of changes in the Fed's discount rate are publicized by the press immediately. The **Federal Reserve discount rate** is the interest rate charged at the discount windows of the 12 Federal Reserve Banks when they lend money to banks. The discount rate is important because it affects the interest rates banks pay to get deposits and charge for lent funds. The Federal Reserve does not change its discount rate frequently, and the changes always make the headlines and the TV news.

Research on discount rate changes has shown that the average security's price changes a tiny but significant amount (never exceeding one-half of 1 percent) on the first trading day following the public announcement of a change in the discount rate.[11] This change can be viewed as an **announcement effect;** it is not large enough

---

[11] R. N. Waud, "Public Interpretation of Discount Rate Changes: Evidence on the Announcement Effect," *Econometrica,* vol. 38, March 1970, pp. 231–250.

to yield a trading profit after paying the trading commissions. In fact, most of the price change associated with the announcements occurs *before* the announcement. Traders watch the Federal Reserve Board closely and are usually able to anticipate changes in its discount rate. The semistrongly efficient markets hypothesis is again supported.

Stock Splits and Stock Dividends

Stock splits and stock dividends, which were introduced in Chapter 3, are occasionally used by corporations that want to broaden the market for their shares. For example, if a firm's shares are selling for $100 each, a 2-for-1 split (or 100 percent stock dividend) will reduce the cost of a round lot from 100 shares × $100 = $10,000 to half that much. Splitting shares may enlarge the potential shareholder group to include investors who do not have large amounts to invest.

Box 16-5

COMPUTATION: How Stock Splits or Stock Dividends Affect Investor Returns

Table 16-1 shows how a share of stock selling for $100 per share falls to $50 per share owing to a 2-for-1 split or 100 percent stock dividend without changing the owner's 5 percent rate of return. The hypothetical change in the unit of account occurs between periods 2 and 3. The investor owns twice as many shares after the change, but since each share has half the previous market price, the market value of the investor's total investment is unchanged. The investor's income in this example is $5 of cash dividends per period per $100 of investment, both before and after the change in the unit of account. As a result, investors earn an invariant 5 percent per period rate of return.

Table 16-1
The Effects of a 2-for-1 Stock Split or a 100 Percent Stock Dividend*

	Time period			
	t=1	*t=2*	*t=3*	*t=4*
Market price per share	$100	$100	$50	$50
Cash dividend per share	$ 5	$ 5	$ 2.50	$ 2.50
Earnings per share	$ 10	$ 10	$ 5	$ 5
Number of shares held per $100 of original investment	1	1	2	2
Percentage price change per $100 invested	0	0	0	0
One-period rate of return with Equation (1-4)	5%	5%	5%	5%

* The 100% stock dividend or 2-for-1 stock split occurs between periods 2 and 3.

IBM Reduces Its Stock Price from $315 to $72

In June 1979, when its stock was selling for $315 per share, IBM declared a 300 percent common stock dividend (which is financially equivalent to a 4-for-1 split). Next month IBM's stock was selling at $73 dollars a share. Four times $73 is $292 per pre-stock dividend share. The correct way to interpret this price decline from $315 to $73 in a few weeks is that IBM's change in its unit of account had no effect on the aggregate market value or rate of return from the corporation's common stock. A June 1979 investment of $315 in IBM's stock would have fallen to a $292 market value a month later regardless of whether or not IBM's 300 percent stock dividend had been declared. The decline in price from $315 for one share to $292 for four shares can be attributed to fundamental conditions within the corporation and/or market conditions that are external to the corporation, but not to the 300 percent stock dividend.

Studies of stock dividends and splits have reviewed hundreds of disparate cases from hundreds of different corporations and dissimilar sample periods to make allowances for unusually good gains or bad results (such as IBM experienced in 1979) that cloud the changes which can be attributed purely to the change in the unit of account.

Several studies have analyzed whether stock splits or stock dividends had any influence on the aggregate market value of the common stock.[12] All the common stock shares were adjusted for the stock splits and stock dividends before their one-period rates of return were calculated using Equation (1-4). This adjustment ensured that only real changes in investors' wealth would be measured, rather than erroneously assigning significance to the price changes resulting purely from changes in the unit of account.

Studies of hundreds of different stock dividends and splits support the hypothesis that markets are semistrongly efficient. *Stock dividends and stock splits usually have no discernible effects on aggregate investment values or investor returns.* This evidence is impressive in view of the popular folklore about the importance of stock dividends and stock splits. Unusual price changes near the time of splits generally result from rational investor reactions to changes in the corporation's earning power rather than from the split or stock dividend. The IBM experience is a case in point.

New Exchange Listings

If a corporation that is traded over the counter grows large enough to meet the listing requirements for an organized exchange, it may apply to be listed on the AMEX or NYSE to attain increased prestige, a more liquid market, and/or a higher stock price. Advocates of the semistrongly efficient markets hypothesis point out that, since an

---

[12] See E. Fama, L. Fisher, M. Jensen, and R. Roll, "The Adjustment of Stock Prices to New Information," *International Economic Review,* February 1969, pp. 1–21. Also see Sasson Bar-Yosef and Lawrence D. Brown, "A Reexamination of Stock Splits Using Moving Betas," *Journal of Finance,* September 1977, pp. 1069–1080.

exchange listing involves no fundamental changes in the firm, its value should not change as a result of the listing. Although researchers differ slightly about the details, the fairly consistent conclusion about new listings is that the value of the corporation's stock is not increased by listing it on an exchange. The price of the stock tends to rise a little for several weeks before the listing and then to diminish to about where it was before the corporation applied for the listing.[13] These findings support the semistrong hypothesis.

16-5 The Strongly Efficient Markets Hypothesis

Economists sometimes refer to the strongly efficient markets illustrated in Figures 16-2a and 16-3 as *perfectly efficient markets*.

The strongly efficient markets hypothesis can be refuted because evidence shows that *insiders* have been able to profit without violating the laws against using their privileged information. Jaffee and Seyhun studied SEC filings by insiders reporting their trading in their own corporation's common stock and these insiders' subsequent rates of return from their inside trading.[14] The insiders did not profit from their trading in every instance. But, averaged over many cases, the insiders earned a few percentage points more than a naive buy-and-hold strategy. These findings (and others we will not take the time to review here) lead to the rejection of the strongly efficient market hypothesis.

This rejection does not mean that the hypothesis is totally inaccurate, however. Financial analysts studying the risk-adjusted rates of return from hundreds of mutual

[13] See Richard W. Furst, "Does Listing Increase the Market Price of Common Stocks?" *Journal of Business,* vol. 43, no. 2, 1970, pp. 174–180. Also see Waldemar M. Goulet, "Price Changes, Managerial Actions and Insider Trading at the Time of Listing," *Financial Management,* vol. 3, no. 1, 1974, pp. 30–36; Frank J. Fabozzi, "Does Listing on the AMEX Increase the Value of Equity?" *Financial Management,* vol. 10, no. 1, 1981, pp. 43–50; David A. Dubofsky and John C. Groth, "Exchange Listing and Stock Liquidity," *Journal of Financial Research,* vol. 7, no. 4, 1984, pp. 291–302; Theoharry Grammatikos and George J. Papaioannou, "The Informational Value of Listing on the New York Stock Exchange," *Financial Review,* vol. 21, no. 4, 1986, pp. 485–499; and Theoharry Grammatikos and George Papaioannou, "Market Reaction to NYSE Listings: Tests of the Marketability Gains Hypothesis," *Journal of Financial Research,* vol. 9, no. 3, 1986, pp. 215–228.

[14] Jeffrey Jaffee, "Special Information and Insider Trading," *Journal of Business,* vol. 47, no. 3, July 1974, pp. 410–428. In addition, see H. N. Seyhun, "Insiders Profits, Costs of Trading, and Market Efficiency," *Journal of Financial Economics,* vol. 16, 1986, pp. 189–212.

Box 16-6

DEFINITION: Strongly Efficient Markets

In **strongly efficient markets** all information (not just publicly available information) is reflected in security prices.

funds over decades usually find that these professionally managed portfolios cannot outperform a naive buy-and-hold strategy. For instance, after researching 115 mutual funds over a decade, Jensen concluded that:

> Although these tests certainly do not imply that the strong form of the [efficient markets] hypothesis holds for all investors and for all time they provide strong evidence in support of that hypothesis. One must realize that these [mutual fund] analysts are extremely well endowed. Moreover they operate in the securities markets every day and have wide-ranging contacts and associations in both the business and financial communities. Thus, the fact that they are apparently unable to forecast returns accurately enough to recover their research and transactions costs is a striking piece of evidence in favor of the strong form of the [efficient markets] hypothesis.[15]

The strongly efficient markets hypothesis is partially supported by the evidence. If you accept all the efficient markets hypotheses, some of the implications of the theory can be difficult to swallow. One implication of the semistrong hypothesis, for example, is that information published by *The Wall Street Journal,* Standard & Poor's, and other financial news services is not worth reading. This conclusion follows because, if the security markets are semistrongly efficient, then by the time information is published and disseminated, it should have no value to investors. The next section presents some anomalies which suggest that the efficient markets theory and its implications should not be taken too literally.

16-6   Anomalies in the Efficient Markets Theory

We have presented empirical evidence supporting varying degrees of market efficiency, but the theory is nevertheless flawed. Empirically observable return regularities undercut the models of totally random price movements and perfectly efficient prices. **Return regularities** are predictable patterns of security price behavior that fly in the face of the efficient markets theory.

Anomalies in the Weakly Efficient Markets Hypothesis

Some of the evidence above suggested that studying charts of historical stock prices will not reveal any patterns that are useful for making price forecasts. Nevertheless, some patterns have been reported.

The Weekend Effect   There is a small but significant **weekend effect** in stock price movements.[16] Stock prices tend to rise all week long to a peak on Fridays. The stocks

---

[15] M. Jensen, "Risk, the Pricing of Capital Assets, and the Evaluation of Investment Portfolios," *Journal of Business,* April 1969, p. 170. Words in brackets added. Mutual fund performance is the topic of chap. 28.

[16] See Frank Cross, "The Behavior of Stock Prices on Fridays and Mondays," *Financial Analysts Journal,* November-December 1973, pp. 67–69. More recently, see R. A. Connolly, "An Examination of the Robustness of the Weekend Effect," *Journal of Financial and Quantitative Analysis,* June 1989, pp. 133–169. Connolly's findings suggest that the weekend effect ended about 1975, for reasons that are not known.

then tend to trade on Mondays at reduced prices, before they begin the next week's price rise. This tendency is so small, however, that if a trader bought stocks on Mondays and sold them on Fridays, the profits would be too little to pay the brokerage commissions. Furthermore, stock prices do not follow this pattern every week. The weekend effect is a small but significant deviation from perfectly random price movements that violates the weakly efficient markets hypothesis. As with most of the anomalies, researchers have been unable to prove what causes it.

The January Effect   Another anomalous pattern in stock price movements is the **January effect.** Researchers have reported a tendency for stock prices, especially the prices of stocks in small firms, to fall slightly late in December and then rise during the first 3 weeks of January.[17] It has been suggested that the January effect might result from last-minute selling by investors who have accumulated losses on stocks and want to realize some of these losses to reduce their income taxes for the year. Other investigators have suggested that it may simply be an irrational behavior pattern. The cause of this second anomaly remains as much a mystery as the cause of most other anomalies.

The weekend and January effects make it impossible to conclude that stock prices align perfectly with the weakly efficient markets hypothesis. They are not the basis for any profitable trading strategies, however, and so they appear to have limited economic significance.

Anomalies in the Semistrongly Efficient Markets Hypothesis

Several anomalies in the semistrongly efficient markets hypothesis have been reported. These anomalies cause significant return regularities that can be replicated using publicly available information.

The Size Effect   Studies indicate that common stock investments in small-sized firms tend to earn significantly higher rates of return than comparable investments in large corporations. In one early study, Rolf Banz showed that NYSE-listed firms with the smallest 20 percent of the market values of total common stock outstanding earned 19.8 percent per year more than the largest 20 percent of the firms in a sample that included hundreds of corporations.[18] While there were periods when firms in the quintile containing the largest corporations' stocks outperformed the quintile of small stocks, the rates of return from common stock investments in the smallest quintile outperformed those in the larger quintiles by a significant amount over longer periods. Since the total market value of all of a corporation's outstanding

[17] See E. Dyl, "Capital Gains Taxation and Year End Stock Market Behavior," *Journal of Finance,* March 1977, pp. 165–175. Also see W. DeBondt and R. Thaler, "Further Evidence of Investor Overreaction and Stock Market Seasonality," *Journal of Finance,* July 1987, pp. 557–581.

[18] See Rolf Banz, "The Relationship between Return and Market Value of Common Stocks," *Journal of Financial Economics,* vol. 9, Mar. 3–18, 1981. Also see *Stocks, Bonds, Bills and Inflation: Yearbook* (Chicago: Ibbotson Assoc., published annually).

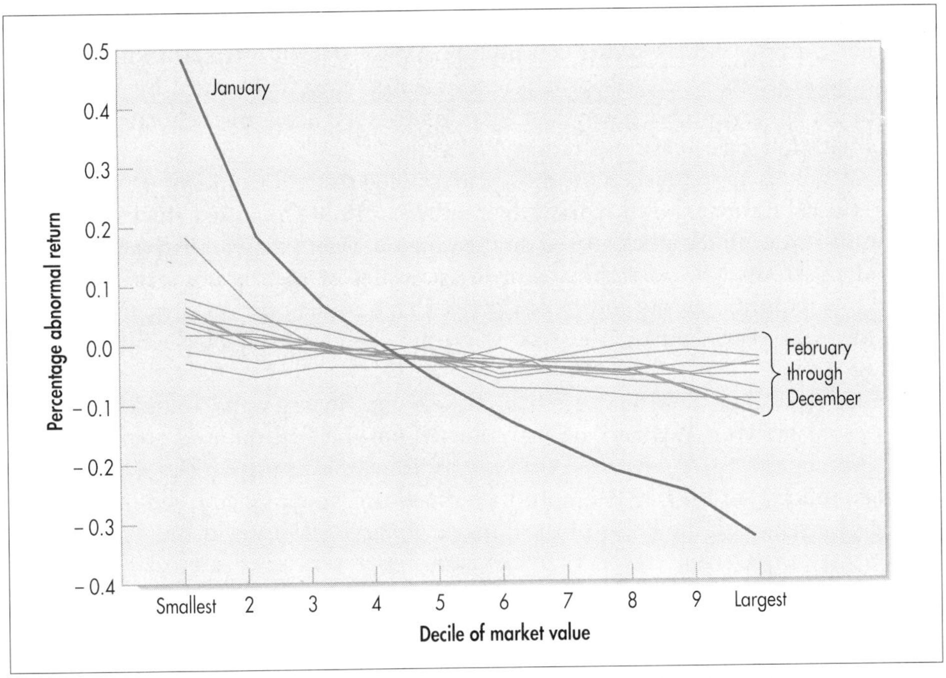

Figure 16-6   The size effect and the January effect are interrelated for the period 1963 to 1979. (*Source:* Donald B. Keim, "Size-Related Anomalies and Stock Return Seasonality: Further Empirical Evidence," *Journal of Financial Economics,* vol. 12, no. 1, June 1983, p. 21.)

common stock is a matter of public record, the **size effect** findings weigh against the semistrongly and weakly efficient markets hypotheses.

The cumulative impact of the size effect over several decades is illustrated in Figure 1-5; here the index for the quintile of small firms is compared with the S&P 500 Stocks Composite Index. If the quintile of the smallest firms were compared with the quintile of the largest firms, the difference would be even more dramatic.

Several different economic variables may ultimately be shown to cause the size effect, although at present there is no clear-cut theory.[19] What is known, however, is that the size effect and the January effect interact in a predictable manner. Figure 16-6 shows how size deciles of stocks perform in each month, averaged over a 17-year sample period.[20] The figure shows that the small stocks are the source of most of the January effect.

[19] The small firms may have low price-earnings ratios or freedom from agency costs that explain what appears at first to be a size effect. Further research may show that it is merely a statistical measurement error or some other economic variable that was difficult to discern in the initial research. For empirical work, see S. Basu, "The Relationship between Earnings Yield, Market Value, and the Return for NYSE Common Stocks: Further Evidence," *Journal of Financial Economics,* vol. 12, no. 1, 1983.

[20] See Donald B. Keim, "Size-Related Anomalies and Stock Return Seasonality: Further Empirical Evidence," *Journal of Financial Economics,* vol. 12, no. 1, June 1983, pp. 13–32.

The Low P/E Ratio Effect   Chapter 13 explained how fundamental security analysts use price-earnings ratios (or earnings multipliers) to estimate intrinsic value per share for common stock. One well-known investment strategy, advocated by Value Line Investment Survey, other money managers, and several economic scholars, is to buy stocks with low price-earnings ratios (P/E's).[21]

Sanjay Basu has published the most widely cited study documenting the **low P/E ratio effect**.[22] Basu analyzed market data on over 750 NYSE-listed stocks. His first step was to array all the stocks based on the values of their year-end P/E's. Second, he formed five 150-stock portfolios from the quintiles of each year's array of P/E's. Third, the monthly rates of return of the five P/E quintile portfolios were calculated over the next year. Fourth, the risk was estimated for each of the five quintile portfolios.

Basu replicated these four steps each year for 14 years and found an inverse relationship between P/E and average return from the P/E quintile portfolios. He took precautions to remove any risk effects from the returns by preparing risk-adjusted returns for the five P/E quintile portfolios. These risk-adjusted returns also varied inversely with the P/E's of the quintile portfolios. This evidence supports the notion that, on average, low P/E stocks earn better raw returns and risk-adjusted returns than stocks with higher P/E ratios.

But the resounding success of simply buying stocks with low P/E's gave Basu some pause; it appeared to be too easy to "beat the market." He therefore deducted the brokerage commissions his strategy would have incurred, a modest research fee of one-quarter of 1 percent each year, and federal income taxes appropriate for an investor in the 50 percent federal income tax bracket. After these costs were deducted from the returns for the quintile portfolio with the lowest P/E ratios, that portfolio earned from half of 1.0 percent to 2.5 percent per annum more than a randomly selected portfolio (that is, one formed without regard to the stocks' P/E's) in the same risk class. Since there is no logical reason why stocks with low P/E ratios should outperform stocks with high P/E's, and since P/E ratios are published daily in newspapers, Basu's findings point to another flaw in the semistrongly efficient markets hypothesis.

Effect of Quarterly Earnings Announcements   Stock prices react to corporations' quarterly earnings per share announcements in a manner that allows traders to earn

---

[21] See Fischer Black, "Yes, Virginia, There Is Hope: Tests of the Value Line Ranking System," *Financial Analysts Journal*, September-October 1973. Also see T. E. Copeland and D. Mayers, "The Value Line Enigma, 1965–1978: A Case Study of Performance Evaluation Issues," *Journal of Financial Economics*, vol. 10, 1982, pp. 289–321, and Volkert S. Whitbeck and Manown Kisor, Jr., "A New Tool in Investment Decision-Making," *Financial Analysts Journal*, May-June 1973, pp. 55–62.

[22] See Sanjay Basu, "The Investment Performance of Common Stocks in Relation to Their Price-Earnings Ratios: A Test of the Efficient Markets Hypothesis," *Journal of Finance*, vol. 32, no. 3, June 1977, pp. 663–682. More recently, assertions that the P/E ratio subsumes the size effect are made in S. Basu, "The Relationship between Earnings Yield, Market Value, and the Return for NYSE Common Stocks: Further Evidence," *Journal of Financial Economics*, vol. 12, no. 1, 1983.

profits, but not in a way that supports the semistrongly efficient markets hypothesis. There is both good news and bad news in this finding for the efficient markets advocates. The good news is that stock prices tend to anticipate quarterly earnings announcements by several months. The bad news is that stock prices also continue to react to these announcements for several months *afterward.* An investor can read newspaper announcements of quarterly earnings and buy (or sell) stocks that reported surprisingly good (or bad) earnings and, averaged over many such trades, outperform a naive buy-and-hold strategy.[23]

The Managerial Ownership Effect Agency theory, explained in more detail in Chapter 19, suggests that corporate executives, in their roles as agents for the stockholders, may not always intend to make decisions that maximize the value of the firm for its owners. In fact, empirical evidence suggests that *agency costs* tend to cause the average rate of return from common stocks to vary directly with the percentage of the corporations' stock owned by the managers of the corporation.[24] This finding implies that corporations managed by executives who are also owners will tend to be better investments than firms managed by executives who are merely employees. Since ownership data are public knowledge for publicly traded stocks, this return regularity presents another loophole in the semistrongly efficient markets theory from which investments analysts can hope to profit.

16-7 Some Conclusions

This chapter has probably raised as many questions as it has answered. Can we expect technical analysis to be highly profitable? Does the anomalous evidence overwhelm the efficient markets hypotheses? Let's review the three hypotheses.

Weakly Efficient Markets

Empirical tests of the weakly efficient markets hypothesis (namely, filter rules, serial correlations, and runs) support the hypothesis. There have been a few minor anomalies, such as the weekend and January effects, but they are not capable of

[23] See Victor Niederhoffer and Patrick Reagan, "Earnings Changes, Analysts Forecasts, and Stock Prices," *Financial Analysts Journal,* vol. 28, no. 3, May-June 1972, pp. 66–68. Also see Henry A. Latane and C. Jones, "Standardized Unexpected Earnings—1971–77," *Journal of Finance,* vol. 34, June 1979, pp. 717–724. For a more definitive study see George Foster, Chris Olsen, and Terry Shevlin, "Earnings Releases, Anomalies and the Behavior of Security Returns," *Accounting Review,* vol. 59, no. 4, October 1984, pp. 574–603.

[24] The first to suggest this hypothesis were Wi Saeng Kim, Jae Won Lee, and Jack Clark Francis, "Investment Performance of Common Stocks in Relation to Inside Ownership," *Financial Review,* vol. 23, no. 1, February 1988, pp. 53–64. For a contrary view see G. Tsetsekos and R. DeFusco, "Portfolio Performance, Managerial Ownership, and the Size Effect," *Journal of Portfolio Management,* vol. 16, no. 3 (Spring), 1990, pp. 33–39. For strong supporting evidence see C. D. Hudson, John Jahara, and W. P. Lloyd, "Further Evidence on the Relationship between Ownership and Performance," *Financial Review,* vol. 27, no. 2, May 1992, pp. 227–239.

generating large trading profits after commission costs are paid. No scientific studies have overturned the weakly efficient markets hypothesis. Those who earn a living by selling charting services assert that short-run security price changes are not random and offer unscientific claims to back these assertions, but objective people would have little trouble accepting the weakly efficient markets hypothesis as realistic.

Belief in the weakly efficient markets hypothesis has two implications for investors. The first is that it is a waste of time to chart stock prices. The second implication is that it is worthwhile for fundamental analysts to estimate intrinsic values, because prices tend to pursue their fluctuating values.

Semistrongly Efficient Markets

Moody's manuals, Standard & Poor's reports, and audited financial information filed with the SEC are readily available to the investing public. Financial newspapers and the news services compete to deliver news as quickly as possible, at an affordable cost. And libraries are free. This publicly available information provides prospective investors what they need to evaluate investment opportunities. On average, investors tend to interpret the news correctly. When news affects the value of a security, it will cause reevaluations and trading. Such trading begins whenever fresh news is announced; market prices immediately start adjusting toward their new intrinsic value. Studies show that security prices not only react immediately and rationally to news, but sometimes even *anticipate* it. Thus, we may conclude that security prices reflect most publicly available relevant information, as suggested by the semistrongly efficient markets hypothesis.

Some anomalies to the semistrongly efficient markets hypothesis have been reported. The effects of low P/E ratios, firm size, delayed reactions to quarterly earnings announcements, and managerial ownership create return regularities that are inefficient. However, these effects may really be only proxies for some rational but more subtle economic effect that remains to be discovered. In any event, the anomalies are not capable of helping anyone get rich quick, because of the modest size of the effects.

Strongly Efficient Markets

There is little doubt that stock prices in the United States tend to pursue their intrinsic values. For example, none of the hundreds of mutual funds that provide professional investment management services seem to be able consistently to outperform a naive buy-and-hold strategy. But, some opposing evidence exists. Federal law allows insiders to trade on their valuable knowledge if they follow certain guidelines and keep the SEC notified of every trade. These law-abiding insiders are able to outperform a naive buy-and-hold strategy by a modest amount. As a result, virtually no one advocates that the security markets anywhere in the world are perfectly efficient.

Although the weakly efficient and semistrongly efficient markets hypotheses are fairly well supported by the facts, some anomalous evidence prevents us from accepting these hypotheses without reservation. And significant evidence suggests that the strongly efficient market hypothesis is not appropriate. Nevertheless, for practical purposes, security markets in the United States are markets in which prices tend to fluctuate randomly in pursuit of constantly changing intrinsic values. Such markets may be best described as intrinsic value random-walk markets.

The question of whether technical analysis or fundamental analysis is more rewarding reduces to questions of whether stock prices exhibit patterns (as technical analysts claim) or whether prices fluctuate randomly around intrinsic values (as fundamental analysts claim). We concluded here that securities markets are intrinsic value random-walk markets. In such a market, fundamental analysis can be a valuable aid in detecting the occasional mispriced securities, whereas technical analysis is of dubious value.

Summary

The efficient markets theory focuses on the question of whether stock prices fluctuate randomly or move in well-defined patterns. It appears that prices move in close pursuit of their ever-changing values. This idea is supported by Cootner's model of liquidity traders and information traders—what others have called the *intrinsic value random-walk market*—which shows the results of the activities of liquidity and information traders.

Three different scenarios illustrate how the price of a security can vary around its value: the weakly efficient markets hypothesis, the semistrongly efficient markets hypothesis, and the strongly efficient markets hypothesis. These are not mutually exclusive; they vary only in the level of information required. Having some opinion about market efficiency is important for investors because it determines whether they will manage their investments actively or passively.

The weakly efficient markets hypothesis maintains that past performance is irrelevant to future strategies and implies that technical analysis is worthless. Support for this idea comes from filter rules, serial correlations, runs tests, and some indirect tests. The semistrongly efficient markets hypothesis asserts that all relevant publicly available information is fully reflected in security prices, and therefore the only traders who can do better than a naive buy-and-hold strategy are insiders. Support for this hypothesis comes from the absence of learning lags, the effects of discount rate changes by the Fed, the lack of effects from stock splits and dividends, and the effect of a new exchange listing. The strongly efficient markets hypothesis, which holds that markets are perfectly efficient, can easily be refuted. But it is not altogether wrong: the hypothesis is partially supported by the evidence.

Flaws in the efficient markets theory are illustrated by anomalies such as the weekend and January effects in the weakly efficient hypothesis. The size effect, Basu's low P/E ratio effect, the effect of quarterly earnings announcements, and the managerial ownership effect are flaws in the semistrong hypothesis. The strongly efficient markets hypothesis suffers from more than flaws, it is simply untrue.

Brealey, Richard A., "How to Combine Active Management with Index Funds," *Journal of Portfolio Management*, vol. 12, no. 2, 1986, pp. 4–10.
  The article considers active (or aggressive) management, passive management, and a combination of both as methods for portfolio management.

Fama, Eugene F., "Efficient Capital Markets: A Review of Theory and Empirical Work," *Journal of Finance,* May 1970, pp. 383–417.

> *This article develops the distinction between the weakly efficient, semistrongly efficient, and strongly efficient markets hypotheses and reviews some empirical studies. Mathematical statistics are used.*

Good, Walter R., Robert Ferguson, and Jack Treynor, "A Guide to the Index Fund Controversy," *Financial Analysts Journal,* vol. 32, no. 6, 1976, pp. 27–38.

> *This article defines terms and concepts used by index funds.*

Stevenson, Richard A., and Robert M. Bear, "Commodity Futures: Trends or Random Walks?" *Journal of Finance,* March 1970, pp. 65–81.

> *Those interested in commodities trading may read about the application of filter rules and other tests explained in this chapter to commodity prices. Some weak trends are found in commodity prices.*

Questions and Problems

Essay Questions

16-1   Define the following phrases: (*a*) weakly efficient market, (*b*) semistrongly efficient market, and (*c*) strongly efficient market. (*d*) What do these three concepts have in common?

16-2   Should the value of a security remain stable in equilibrium? What might change the value of a security? How often might such changes occur?

16-3   For what purpose are (*a*) runs tests, (*b*) serial correlations, and (*c*) filter rules used in testing the efficient markets theory? (*d*) What investment information was obtained from these tests?

16-4   "Stock prices are random numbers." Is this statement true, false, or questionable? Explain.

16-5   Suppose the chairman of the board of General Motors Corporation appears on the late-night news of every U.S. television station and announces that GM has discovered an oil well on every parking lot it owns around the world. Assuming the executive would not distort the truth, how do you think the market would react to such a public announcement? Would the price of GM move upward in a trend as more and more investors learned of the GM discovery each day and then bid the stock's price up as they reached their decisions to buy the stock?

16-6   Assume your next-door neighbor is a business executive who is also an amateur astronomer. Suppose your neighbor has noticed on several occasions that the spots on the sun's surface are more active during bull markets. Should you begin to study sunspot activity as a way to beat the stock market? Why or why not?

16-7   What are the arguments in favor of using technical analysis instead of fundamental analysis? Are these valid arguments? Why or why not?

16-8   What theories of technical analysis are tested by the filter rules? Explain.

16-9   There are millions of part-time amateur investors in the United States. However, there are only a few thousand chartered financial analysts (CFAs), experienced portfolio managers, and other professional investments analysts who actually manage other people's money full time. (The chartered financial analyst is somewhat like the certified public accountant (CPA) among public accountants. Both must be recommended by professionals in the field, serve a 3-year apprenticeship, and pass a series of professional exams on the subject.) Given that there are millions of amateur investors and only thousands of professional investors, which group do you think has the dominate role in determining stock market prices? Explain your view.

16-10   If you were managing a billion-dollar pension fund portfolio, do you think it would be wiser for you to pursue (*a*) a passive investment policy of indexing the billion dollars so that you could earn 10 percent per annum over the long run or (*b*) an aggressive investment management program that required you to spend many thousands of dollars annually on security analysis and brokerage commissions in order to earn a 12 percent per year rate of return over the long run? Explain your decision.

16-11   Ruby Young bought a book entitled *Get Rich Using Technical Analysis* and studied it. With the assistance of her securities broker, Ima Rorschach, Ms. Young has used the knowledge she gained from the book to chart stock market prices. She recently traced out the left shoulder and the head of a head and shoulders top (HST) price chart formation (consult Figure 15-2). Her charting book and her broker both say that this is a sell signal. Ms. Young has invested a major part of her life savings in stocks and is therefore very concerned about this liquidation signal. What advice can you offer Ms. Young?

Problems

16-12   Panels (*a*) and (*b*) below illustrate two different ways a stock's price might react to new information. Suppose that unequivocal new information suggesting that the value of Zair Corporation's common stock fell from $80 to $40 per share reaches the market at time *t+k*. Zair's price reacts instantly in panel (*a*). In contrast, in panel (*b*) Zair's stock price reacts to the arrival of the same new information at the same time with a lag that lasts from time *t+k* until time *t+k*+Lag. If you were a technical analyst, would you rather work in a market like the one in panel (*a*) or (*b*)? Why? Which panel's price reaction more closely resembles the way prices react on the New York Stock Exchange? Explain. What market mechanisms might explain the difference in the two price reactions illustrated in the figure?

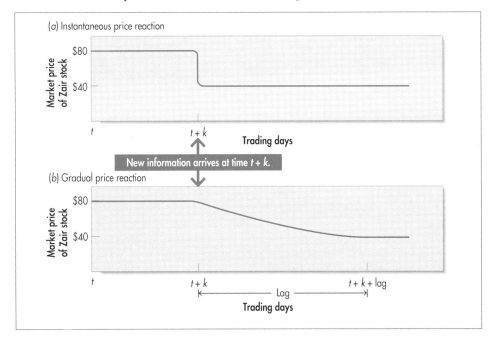

16-13 Reconsider the 14 days of stock price data on the Hemmel Corporation's stock that is listed with Question 15-10. Analyze these data using an x percent filter rule. On what days would you buy and sell Hemmel's stock if you used (a) and x = 4 percent filter rule? (b) An x = 8 percent filter rule?

Multiple Choice Questions

16-14 Statistically measuring a security's serial correlation should detect which of the following patterns in security prices? *Hint:* Consult Figure 16-5.

    (a) Head and shoulders pattern (See Figure 15-2.)
    (b) Trends
    (c) Reversal patterns
    (d) Both (b) and (c)

16-15 If securities prices are semistrongly efficient, which of the following activities would not be profitable to perform?

    (a) Charting prices
    (b) Buying common stocks before a stock dividend or split is announced
    (c) Studying Moody's or Standard & Poor's to get hot tips
    (d) All the above

16-16 If security markets in the United States were all strongly (or perfectly) efficient, which of the following would be true?

    (a) It would be easy for unethical traders to manipulate security prices.
    (b) The markets must also be weakly and semistrongly efficient.
    (c) Playing the market could be both fun and profitable for many.
    (d) Some profitable patterns could be detected in graphs of stock price movements.

16-17 Anomalous evidence that flaws the semistrongly efficient markets hypothesis includes which of the following?

    (a) The low price-earnings effect
    (b) The quarterly effect
    (c) The size effect
    (d) Both (a) and (c)

16-18 Stock splits can be best described by which of the following statements?

    (a) A paper shuffling activity that does not change the price or value of anything
    (b) A good way to reduce the price of a high-priced stock so that more small investors can afford to purchase it, and thus increase its price after the split
    (c) The economic equivalent of a stock dividend
    (d) Both (a) and (c)

16-19 The erratic price changes that marketable securities experience are caused by which of the following?

    (a) The supply and demand conditions for new issues in the primary market
    (b) The continuous arrival of new information
    (c) Purchases and sales of large blocks of securities that may occur even without new information, in order for the seller to obtain needed cash
    (d) Clerical errors and other "backroom problems" that sometimes occur on Wall Street

16-20 This chapter presented a model of a security price determination that is best described by which one of the following statements?

    (*a*) Prices and values both fluctuate.
    (*b*) Prices fluctuate around their value.
    (*c*) Prices fluctuate within upper and lower reflecting barriers.
    (*d*) All the above are true.

D

16-21 The theories about random-walk prices and efficient markets are best characterized by which one of the following statements?

    (*a*) New public information affecting a company's prospects is disseminated slowly.
    (*b*) The price of a stock represents the consensus of varying value assessments from different investors.
    (*c*) Stock prices follow several different discernible patterns that repeat themselves from time to time and can be forecast.
    (*d*) The more efficient a stock's price is, the less it fluctuates.

B

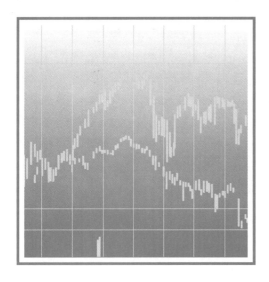

CHAPTER 17

THE MARKET
RISK FACTOR

Analysis of individual bonds and stocks was the topic of Chapters 11 through 14; Chapters 15 and 16 focused on technical analysis and the efficient markets theory. Now we move on to the topic of market risk. This chapter is directed both to those who invest in diversified portfolios and to those who speculate in the price moves of individual securities. The chapter delves into the bull and bear markets introduced in Box 5-1. First we will look at the **market risk factor** that arises from bull and bear market conditions and then estimate the parameters of these alternating forces. The remainder of the chapter investigates the causes of the bear markets that can make investors lose money, have insomnia, default on their financial obligations, go

Box 17-1

427

Chapter 17
The Market
Risk Factor

> DEFINITION: Market Risk
>
> **Market risk** is that portion of total variability of return caused by the alternating forces of bull and bear markets.

bankrupt, and in some extreme cases, even commit suicide. One of the main points of this chapter is that *even a well-diversified portfolio will not be able to withstand the depressing effects of a bear market.*[1]

17-1   Analyzing the Market Risk Factor

In Chapter 1, Definition Box 1-9 defined an asset's *total risk* as its total variability of returns, and showed how to assess total risk statistically. Market risk is one of the risk factors that make up total risk.

Using Security Market Indicators

As we saw in Chapter 5, security market indicators can be used to gauge the ups and downs of a market. In this chapter, stock market indexes from Standard & Poor's and stock price data from the Center for Research on Security Prices (CRSP) are used to analyze bull and bear markets. The CRSP file includes all NYSE-listed stocks plus some stocks that are traded at the American Stock Exchange (AMEX) and over-the-counter (OTC). The AMEX stocks entered the monthly CRSP file in 1962. Data on the OTC stocks begins in 1972.

It's Bull and Then Bear and Then Bull and Then . . .

When a security index rises from a market low point called a **trough** and moves haltingly upward for a significant period of time, this trend is called a **bull market.** A bull market ends when the market index climbs to a **peak** and starts down. The period of time during which the market declines from a peak to the next trough is called a **bear market.**

The alternating bull and bear markets are illustrated in Figure 17-1. Each bear

---

[1] Empirical research into the arbitrage pricing theory (APT) indicates that the market risk factor is the most statistically significant portion of total risk. For example, see Nai-Fu Chen, Richard Roll, and Stephen A. Ross, "Economic Forces and the Stock Market: Testing the APT and Alternative Asset Pricing Theories," *Journal of Business,* July 1986. The APT model that brings this and the risk factors introduced in the other chapters together under one unifying theory is the topic of Chapter 26.

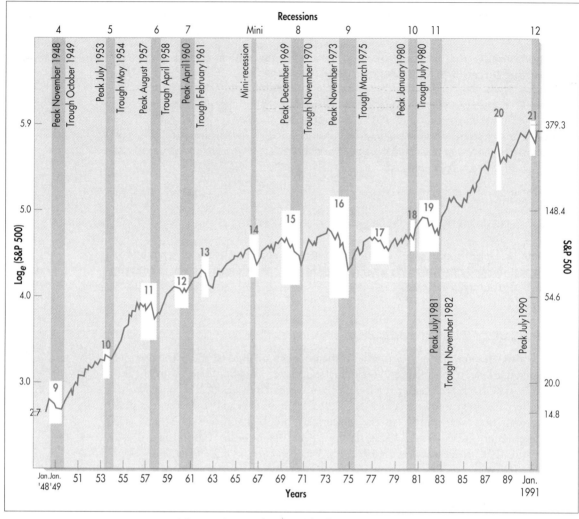

Figure 17-1 Time-series graph of Standard & Poor's 500 Stocks Composite Index, 1948–1991.

market in the figure is delineated by a rectangle with its left side at the peak of the bull market that preceded the downturn.

Recessions are represented by shaded vertical bands in Figure 17-1. These economic downturns will be examined more closely later. Table 17-1 provides some summary statistics about the bear markets. The bear market rectangles in Figure 17-1 are numbered to correspond to the lines in Table 17-1.

Figure 17-1 and Table 17-1 indicate that in recent decades bear markets have lasted for periods ranging from 3 months to almost 3 years, with an average duration of a little over 13 months. The values at the bottom of the table give the average bear market's duration and average percentage change. During these bear market periods the S&P 500 market index fell between 8 percent and 82 percent, with an average

Box 17-2

429

Chapter 17
The Market
Risk Factor

> **DEFINITION: Recession**
>
> A **recession** is a period during which a nation's *real gross national product* (GNP) decreases for at least two consecutive quarters. Recessions always depress aggregate personal income, corporate earnings, and corporate cash dividend payments. The significant 1966 turndown in business activity lasted a little less than 6 months and cannot be classified as a recession; it is called a **minirecession.**

decline of about 25 percent. Of course, these statistics depend on the delineation of the bear markets. Any market decline that exceeded 10 percent or lasted at least 3 months was classified as a bear market in compiling the statistics reported in this chapter. This definition is not sacrosanct; in particular, some of the smallest bear markets might be contested.

Table 17-1
Bear Market Summary Statistics, 1929–1991

Bear market	Bear market dates, peak–trough	Length, in months	S&P index, peak–trough	Change in S&P, %
1	10/29–6/32	33	25.14–4.43	−82.38%
2	10/32–3/33	6	6.96–5.66	−18.68
3	3/34–3/35	13	10.75–8.47	−21.21
4	3/37–4/38	15	18.09–8.50	−53.01
5	12/38–4/39	5	13.21–10.92	−17.34
6	11/39–6/40	8	12.49–9.27	−25.78
7	8/41–4/42	9	10.30–7.66	−25.63
8	6/46–11/46	6	18.43–14.67	−20.40
9	7/48–6/49	12	16.54–14.16	−14.39
10	2/53–9/53	8	25.90–23.32	−9.96
11	8/56–12/57	17	47.91–39.99	−16.53
12	7/59–10/60	16	60.51–53.39	−11.77
13	1/62–6/62	6	69.96–54.75	−21.74
14	12/65–10/66	11	92.88–76.56	−17.57
15	12/68–6/70	19	103.86–72.72	−29.98
16	1/73–10/74	22	116.03–63.54	−45.24
17	10/76–3/78	18	107.46–87.04	−19.00
18	3/80–5/80	3	111.24–102.09	−8.83
19	12/80–7/82	19	136.00–107.09	−21.26
20	9/87–11/87	3	321.83–230.30	−28.44
21	6/90–10/90	5	361.55–297.81	−17.62
Average		12.1 months		−25.08

Source: CRSP Monthly File.

What Percent Go Up and What Percent Go Down? A glance at Figure 17-1 shows that every bear market includes one or more brief upturns in the market. Furthermore, if we were to study graphs of the prices of individual stocks, we would see that they can also rise when the market indexes are falling. That is, a given stock can move in the opposite direction from the market averages, at least temporarily. These observations allow us to say that a bear market is a period of time during which pessimism prevails and security prices show a *tendency* to decline.

You might wonder whether some unusual stocks have had higher prices at the end of a bear market than they had at its start. This is an important question because the profitability of investing during a bear market depends on the proportion of stocks that experience rising prices. To answer this question, the market prices of every NYSE stock plus all the AMEX and OTC stocks on the CRSP file were tabulated by computer for each bear market covered in Table 17-1.

The computer program examined only those stocks that were listed throughout each bear market. Corporations that went bankrupt or were merged and so lost their identity were not considered. The program checked the market prices of every continuously listed stock at the start and end of each bear market to see whether its price had advanced or declined overall. Table 17-2 presents the results.

The figures at the bottom of the table indicate that, on average, about 82 percent

Table 17-2
Advance-Decline Data for Bear Markets, 1929–1987

Bear Market	Listed stocks	Stocks rising	Percent rising	Stocks same	Percent same	Stocks down	Percent down
1	656	25	3.81%	0	0%	631	96.19%
2	710	155	21.83	0	0	555	78.17
3	700	147	21.00	0	0	553	79.00
4	749	9	1.20	0	0	740	98.75
5	777	59	7.59	2	.3	716	92.15
6	776	71	9.15	2	.3	705	90.85
7	798	52	6.52	2	.3	746	93.48
8	879	18	2.05	2	.2	861	97.95
9	960	148	15.42	2	.2	812	84.58
10	1034	112	10.83	2	.2	922	89.17
11	1024	193	18.85	2	.2	831	81.15
12	1057	282	26.68	2	.2	775	73.32
13	1133	23	2.03	2	.2	1110	97.97
14	1218	206	16.91	2	.2	1012	83.09
15	1189	51	4.29	2	.2	1138	95.71
16	1439	120	8.34	2	.1	1319	91.66
17	1494	921	61.65	2	.1	573	38.35
18	1524	1340	87.93	11	.7	175	11.48
19	1424	524	36.80	11	.7	900	63.20
20	1588	36	2.22	13	.8	1550	97.61
21	1510	223	14.76	0	0	1287	85.23
Average			17.94		.2		81.86

Source: CRSP Monthly File.

of NYSE stocks finished the bear market with a price lower than the price at which they started the downturn. The analysis also revealed that almost every stock rose in price for at least 1 month during every bear market period. Nevertheless, the prices of the vast majority of stocks moved downward in most months.

Are Some Segments of the Market Able to Rise during a Bear Market? The Standard & Poor's 500 Stocks Composite Index is composed of four smaller, more homogeneous, stock indexes that S&P publishes. The S&P 500 is the aggregate of the S&P 400 Industrial Stocks Index, S&P 40 Public Utility Stocks Index, S&P 20 Transportation Stocks Index, and S&P 40 Financial Stocks Index. Some of these 500 stocks are from large corporations, and some are from small ones. Some of the corporations issuing the stocks are highly profitable, and some are teetering on the verge of bankruptcy. Most are listed on the New York and American stock exchanges, but some are traded over the counter. To illustrate more about the way the stock market behaves during bear markets, Figure 17-2 compares three of the smaller, mutually exclusive, S&P stock indexes with the composite index.

Figure 17-2 Standard & Poor's utility, industrial, rails, and composite price indexes, 1926–1990.

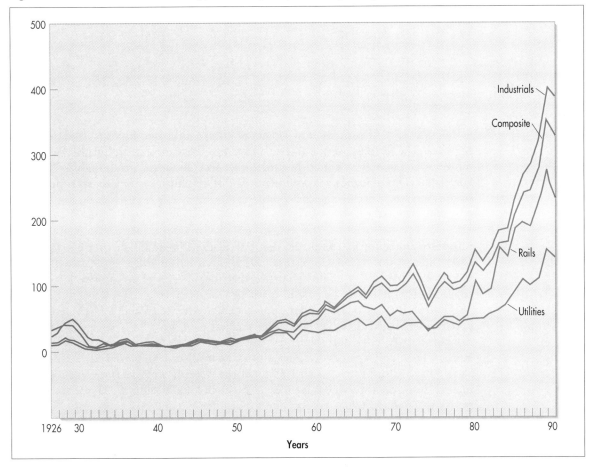

Table 17-3
Bull Market Summary Statistics, 1929–1987

Bull market	Bull market dates, trough–peak	Length of period, months	S&P index, trough–peak	Change in S&P, %
1	7/32–9/32	14	6.10–8.39	37.54%
2	4/33–2/34	10	8.32–11.17	34.25
3	4/35–1/37	10	9.28–17.83	92.13
4	5/38–11/38	6	9.27–13.17	42.07
5	5/39–10/39	5	10.86–13.02	19.89
6	7/40–7/41	10	9.31–11.08	19.01
7	5/42–5/46	48	8.15–19.18	135.34
8	12/46–6/48	18	14.00–16.74	19.57
9	7/49–1/53	42	15.04–26.57	76.66
10	10/53–7/56	33	24.54–49.39	101.26
11	1/58–6/59	17	40.84–58.68	43.68
12	11/60–12/61	13	55.54–71.55	28.83
13	7/62–11/65	17	56.27–92.42	64.24
14	11/66–11/68	24	80.33–108.37	34.91
15	7/70–12/72	30	78.05–118.05	51.25
16	11/74–9/76	22	68.56–105.24	53.50
17	4/78–2/80	22	93.15–114.16	22.56
18	6/80–11/80	6	114.24–140.52	23.00
19	8/82–8/87	61	119.51–329.80	175.96
20	12/87–5/90	30	241.86–352.19	45.61
Average		21.9 months		56.06

Source: CRSP Monthly File.

Figure 17-2 illustrates how some of S&P's different indexes tend to move together. The indexes do not all rise and fall to the same extent, but they generally move in the same direction at the same time. S&P's indexes are all highly positively correlated. This evidence suggests that it is difficult for investors not to suffer losses in the stock market during a bearish period.

Bull Market Parameters   The overall upward trend in the stock market index illustrated in Figure 17-1 indicates that bull markets predominate over bear markets. Over the past few decades investors have enjoyed bull markets about two-thirds of the time. Table 17-3 contains statistics that measure just how profitable common stock investing tends to be in bull markets.

The S&P stock market index appreciated an average of about 56 percent in the bull markets listed in Table 17-3. The smallest gain was 19.01 percent, in the bull market of 1940–1941, and the largest was 175.96 percent during the 1982–1987 bull market. This 175.96 percent gain means that an investor who picked stocks at random should have reaped gains worth 1.75 times the value of their initial investment. (The income from cash dividends would have equaled an additional 33 percent of the portfolio's value.) While results like these point up what is called the "thrill of investing," don't forget that even during the five bullish years from 1982 to 1987 a few bad stock selections could have bankrupted an unlucky investor. There is no guarantee that every investor will do as well as the averages during a bull market—some investors will do worse, some will do better.

Table 17-3 shows that the bull markets varied in length from 5 to 61 months, with an average life of almost 22 months. Note that the average life span of bear markets, just over 13 months, is substantially briefer than that of bull markets.

Investors may fantasize about the market's long-term upward trend and project those bullish times when the market more than doubled (for example, in the 1942–1946, 1953–1956, or 1982–1987 bull markets) into their own future. However, the thought of losing more than 80 cents out of every dollar invested in common stocks in less than 3 years (as was the case in the 1929–1932 bear market) brings a person's feet back down to the ground with a discomforting thud. The compelling question is: What causes the stock market indexes to rise and fall like a roller coaster?

17-2 The Business Cycle and Market Timing

Some aggressive investors endeavor to take advantage of the highs and lows of the business cycle by trying to anticipate bull and bear markets and execute stock purchases and sales at advantageous times. Their objective is to buy low and sell high. Those investors who have the good luck to buy low and sell high across many trades are said to have **good market timing.**

The main element that causes the stock market to rise bullishly and then fall bearishly over and over again is the fact that the nation's economy follows a repetitive business cycle of recessions and expansions.[2] Recessions are described by the statistics in Table 17-4.

---

[2] For an expert discussion, see Geoffrey H. Moore, *Business Cycles, Inflation and Forecasting,* National Bureau of Economic Research Studies in Business Cycle No. 24 (Cambridge, Mass.: Ballinger, 1980), chap. 9.

Box 17-3

DEFINITION: Business Cycle

A **business cycle** can be defined as a type of fluctuation found in the aggregate economic activity of nations that organize their work mainly in business enterprises. A cycle consists of expansions occurring at about the same time in many economic activities, followed by similarly general recessions, contractions, and revivals that merge into the expansion phase of the next cycle. This sequence of changes is recurrent but not periodic; in duration, business cycles may last from more than 1 year to 10 or 12 years. They are not divisible into shorter cycles of similar character with amplitudes approximating their own.[*]

[*] W. C. Mitchell and A. F. Burns, *Measuring Business Cycles* (New York: National Bureau of Economic Research, 1946).

Table 17-4
Official National Bureau of Economic Research (NBER)
Recession Statistics

Recession number	Peak month	Trough month	Duration, in months
1	August 1929	March 1933	43
2	May 1937	June 1938	13
3	February 1945	October 1945	8
4	November 1948	October 1949	11
5	July 1953	May 1954	10
6	August 1957	April 1958	8
7	April 1960	February 1961	10
8*	December 1969	November 1970	11
9	November 1973	March 1975	16
10	January 1980	July 1980	6
11	July 1981	November 1982	18
12	July 1990	April 1991**	9
Average			14 months

* There was a minirecession in 1966.

** April is the estimated trough month.

Bear Markets

Figure 17-1 and the data in Tables 17-1 and 17-4 reveal that the stock market tends to fall into a bear market before and during the first part of most recessions. The bear market that started in January 1973, for instance, preceded by 10 months the recession that started in November 1973. Occasionally, the stock market falls into bearish periods when no recession is at hand. For example, the bear markets in 1946, 1962, 1966, 1977, 1987, and some earlier years were not associated with recessions. However, the majority of the 21 bear markets shown in Table 17-1 and Figure 17-1 were associated with recessions. And almost all the recession-related bear markets *anticipated* recessions that were correctly forecast by security analysts. As a result, many investors study recessions so that they can attempt to forecast them (the next section looks at this matter more closely). If investors can correctly forecast a recession far enough in advance, they might be able to protect their wealth by withdrawing investments before the onset of the bear market that usually precedes the recession.[3]

[3] Valuable information about business cycle indicators can be gained from the following references: U.S. Department of Commerce, *Survey of Current Business* (Washington, D.C.: U.S. Government Printing Office, published monthly). Studies of security price movements that each explain different viewpoints include William Poole, "The Relationship of Monetary Decelerations to Business Cycle Peaks; Another Look at the Evidence," *Journal of Finance*, June 30, 1975, pp. 697–711, and J. J. Shiller, "Do Stock Prices Move Too Much to Be Justified by Subsequent Changes in Dividends?" *American Economic Review*, vol. 71, June 1981, pp. 421–436.

Economist Raymond Piccini has studied over a dozen recessions in an effort to determine the length of time that normally elapses between a stock market peak (which is the start of a bear market) and the onset of a recession.[4] Although the durations of bear markets and recessions differ, Piccini was able to detect some notable tendencies. His first observation was that, on average, a good time for an investor to sell all common stocks is 1 to 3 months before a recession starts. Piccini reached this conclusion because the stock market typically peaks 1 to 3 months before the peak month in economic activity. Piccini's second observation was that if an investor waits until 6 months after a recession starts (that is, after the peak of business activity), the market index will be down, on average, 11 percent from where it was when the recession started. This low is a good time to start thinking about buying common stocks in order to benefit from the next bull market.

The common thread that ties these investment hints together is the *anticipation* of future events, rather than the reaction to past events. In the next section we examine business cycles and recessions in more detail, in order to understand how they work.

17-3   Analyzing Recessions

During a recession, business activity slows. As a result, factories run at less than full capacity, and both employment and business profits fall. Recessions always depress a nation's aggregate personal income, corporate earnings, and corporate cash dividend payments. Forecasts of a recession cause common stock investors to sell and drive down the stock price indexes. Since either real or erroneously forecast recessions seem to cause bear markets, the obvious question for investors to ask is: How do you foretell a recession? The answer: study past recessions and the economic signs that pointed to them and see if you can learn to forecast.

The Real Sector of the Nation's Economy

Figure 17-3 illustrates how aspects of the physical goods sector of the nation's economy behave during recessions. Economists call this physical goods sector of the economy the **real sector.** Figure 17-3 shows recessions as shaded vertical strips that start at a peak (denoted "P") in economic activity (for instance, January 1980 is a peak month) and end at a trough (denoted "T," such as July 1980).

Figure 17-3 has four panels. The top panel charts the number of people employed in nonagricultural (or manufacturing, service, and other industrial) jobs. It shows that layoffs outnumber hirings during recessions; the reverse is true during expansionary periods. The second panel shows how aggregate personal income (from salaries, wages, commissions, and other sources) in the United States tends to decline during recessions and climb during boom periods. These total personal income

[4] R. Piccini, "Stock Market Behavior around Business Cycle Peaks," *Financial Analysts Journal,* July–August 1980, pp. 55–57.

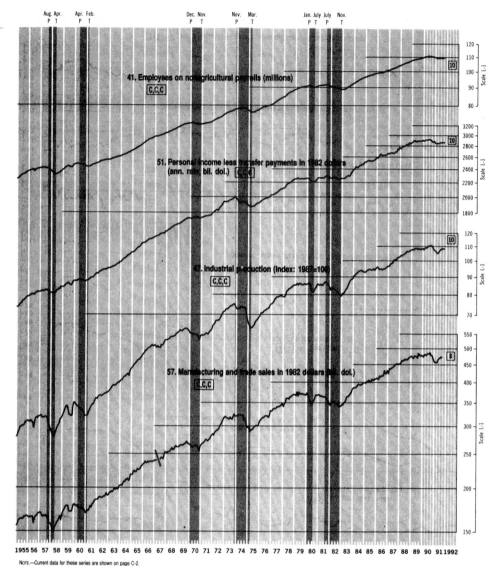

Figure 17-3 Business cycle indicators for the real sector of the U.S. economy. (*Source:* U.S. Department of Commerce.)

figures have been adjusted to 1982 price levels to eliminate any upward bias from inflation. The third panel tracks the index of industrial production (IIP), a measure of tangible business activity (like production output and the length of the average workweek). Note that the IIP falls during every recession. This fall can be seen as confirming the existence of a recession that was signaled by a decrease in the real GNP.

The bottom panel is a graph of manufacturing and trade (or nonagricultural) sales in 1982 dollars. Sharp sales declines are evident during every recession. If each year's current prices had been used instead of inflation-adjusted prices, the sales decreases caused by recessions would have been deeper, because many businesses cut prices in an effort to spur slumping sales.

The statistics in Figure 17-3 are published by the U.S. government for both government and public use. They are utilized by knowledgeable security analysts and business economists. The recessionary patterns seen in the figure repeat themselves because falling business revenues and reduced levels of business activity cause profit levels to decline and, as a result, businesses are forced to lay off workers. Layoffs cause the level of aggregate personal income to fall. This business cycle pattern is important in valuing common stocks, because security values are determined primarily by the income they yield (as explained in Chapters 13 and 14). Thus, recession-induced periods of decreased corporate earnings cause stock market values to shrink.

As we saw above, the stock market typically starts declining a few months before a recession begins. Professional financial analysts foresee the recession and the reduced corporate earnings that will be available to pay cash dividends on most common stock issues. Investors react to forecasts of a recession by selling stocks in any portfolios they manage, and this selling pressure pushes prices down. Later, when the recession actually begins and employee layoffs start, the nation's level of aggregate personal income declines. Lower incomes cause investors to stop investing in securities in order to save money for necessary expenses. Stock prices thus continue to fall after the recession gets started.

The Monetary Sector of the Nation's Economy

In contrast with the physical elements in the real sector, the **monetary sector** of a nation's economy consists of abstract variables such as the money supply, inflation rates, and interest rates. Recessions cause important changes in this sector of the nation's economy. Let us begin our discussion of the monetary sector by explaining how to calculate the rate of inflation.

The CPI and INF The rate of inflation can be measured by using one of several different price level indexes. The popular **consumer price index (CPI)** is tabulated by the U.S. government's Bureau of Labor Statistics every month. It measures the cost of a representative market basket of 300 different consumer goods. The percentage change in the CPI measures the **rate of inflation (INF)**. The rate of inflation between January and February, for instance, is represented by Equation (17-1).

$$\text{INF} = \frac{\text{February CPI} - \text{January CPI}}{\text{January CPI}} \tag{17-1}$$

If the cost of the market basket goes from \$121.1 to \$121.6 between January and February, the rate of inflation would be 41/100 of 1 percent in that month.

$$\text{INF} = \frac{\$121.6 - \$121.1}{\$121.1} = \frac{\$0.5}{\$121.1} = .0041 = \frac{41}{100} \text{ of } 1.0\%$$

Table 17-5
1990 Inflation Rates Calculated from CPI Data

Month	CPI's Value (1967=100)	Month's percent change, INF
January	127.4	1.03
February	128.0	0.47
March	128.7	0.55
April	128.9	0.16
May	129.2	0.23
June	129.9	0.54
July	130.4	0.38
August	131.6	0.92
September	132.7	0.84
October	133.5	0.60
November	133.8	0.22
December	133.8	0.00

Source: U.S. Department of Commerce.

Essentially, if the CPI increases a certain percent in a month, this monthly rate is multiplied by 12 to get the **annualized** rate of inflation. An inflation rate of 41/100 of 1 percent per month is equivalent to an annual rate of .0041 × 12 months = .0495 = 4.95 percent.[5] It is common to annualize inflation rates and interest rates to facilitate comparisons.

Table 17-5 contains month-by-month data for the CPI and the rate of inflation. Column 3 contains the monthly rates of inflation (INF) that are calculated with Equation (17-1).

INF and Nominal Interest Rates   The effect of recessions on the rate of inflation and market interest rates can be seen in Figure 17-4. The figure shows that the rate of inflation, represented by the vertical bars, tends to be lowered by recessions. Recessions reduce the inflation rate because many businesses and consumers have reduced incomes, and therefore they buy less. This reduced demand for goods and services makes labor unions and businesses afraid to raise wages and prices.

The time path of the market interest rate on U.S. Treasury bonds is illustrated in Figure 17-4. Variations in the rate of inflation over the business cycle causes corresponding increases and decreases in the level of market interest rates. In fact, the yields-to-maturity of all bonds and the interest rates on bank loans are similarly affected. The next section will explore reasons for this relationship between market interest rates and the rate of inflation.

---

[5] To be precise, the monthly rate of inflation or interest, denoted *mr*, should have 1 added to it and then be raised to the twelfth power to get 1 plus the annual rate, ar.

$$(1.0 + mr)^{12} = (1.0 + ar)$$

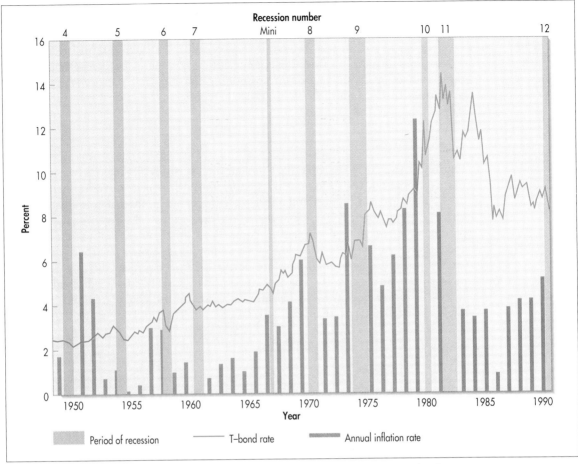

Figure 17-4 Market interest rates on Treasury bonds rise and fall with the rate of inflation. (*Source:* U.S. Department of Commerce.)

17-4 Changing Market Interest Rates

Chapter 11 analyzed the impact interest rates have on the present values of marketable assets. This section shows that the fluctuations in market interest rates are primarily determined by two varying factors: (1) risk premiums and (2) the rate of inflation. The manner in which these factors combine to influence **market interest rates,** or **nominal interest rates,** is summarized as follows:

$$\begin{matrix} \text{Market} \\ \text{interest rate} \end{matrix} = \begin{matrix} \text{riskless rate} \\ \text{of interest} \end{matrix} + \begin{matrix} \text{risk} \\ \text{premium} \end{matrix} + \begin{matrix} \text{rate of} \\ \text{inflation} \end{matrix} \qquad (17\text{-}2)$$

Equation (17-2) is sometimes called the **Fisher equation,** after Irving Fisher, a famous economist who first explained the effect of inflation on market interest rates.[6] We will look at the components of Equation (17-2) below.

[6] Another interest rate, called the *real rate of return,* is discussed further in Chapter 18 when purchasing-power risk is analyzed.

The Riskless Rate of Interest

The **riskless rate of interest** is a low interest rate that is called "riskless" because it involves zero variability of return; it is also called the **pure rate of interest.** The riskless rate includes no risk premiums or inflation allowances. It represents what a saver or investor should be paid for postponing consumption in order to invest funds in an asset that has no risks of any kind. It represents the reward for waiting.

Risk Premiums

One of the two basic variables that fluctuate and cause market interest rates to vary is the risk premium (or yield spread). Lenders always require an additional amount, called a **risk premium,** over and above the riskless rate of interest to induce them to invest (or lend) their funds when the risk of loss exists. The determination of risk premiums for bonds is illustrated in Figure 11-4. It shows that as interest rates rise and fall over the business cycle, U.S. government bonds always pay the lowest rate of interest—because Treasury bonds are default-free. In contrast, the average interest rates on the BBB-grade (or Baa-grade) corporate junk bonds are the highest rates shown in Figure 11-4. This is because the lowest-grade corporate bonds are more likely to go bankrupt than the other bonds in the illustration, and they must

Box 17-4

COMPUTATION: How Market Interest Rates Influence Loan Rates

Suppose someone lends $100 for a year at 5 percent interest. The lender will be repaid $105. If a 10 percent inflation rate exists, this $105 will have the purchasing power of only $95.45 when it is repaid a year later:

$$\text{Future purchasing power} = \frac{\text{future dollars}}{1.0 + \text{inflation rate}} = \frac{\$105}{1.10} = \$95.45$$

In this inflationary environment professional lenders will charge 15 percent interest per year to allow a real interest rate of 5 percent plus a 10 percent inflation allowance. In this case, the lender will be repaid $115. After the 10 percent inflation, the $115 has a real purchasing power of $104.54.

$$\text{Future purchasing power} = \frac{\text{future dollars}}{1.0 + \text{inflation rate}} = \frac{\$115}{1.10} = \$104.54$$

The lender thus gained only $4.54, or 4.54 percent, in purchasing power by lending money at 15 percent interest during a year in which inflation was 10 percent. *Lenders should raise their nominal interest rates by at least the rate of inflation in order to maintain the real purchasing power of their wealth.*

therefore offer investors a *risk premium* of a few extra percentage points of interest to induce them to assume this default risk. Figure 10-1 presents an alternative view of the determinants of risk premiums.

Market Interest Rates and the Inflation Rate

The rate of inflation (INF) is an important and highly variable determinant of interest rate levels. All market interest rates must allow for price level changes so that lenders' wealth will not be dissipated by inflation.

As shown by the vertical bars in Figure 17-4, the inflation rate has fluctuated from a low of about 1 percent per year around 1955 to over 10 percent by the end of the 1970s. Note how market interest rates have tended to rise with the inflation rate. The Fisher equation, Equation (17-2), formalizes this relationship between interest rates and the rate of inflation. In actuality, though, market interest rates do not always rise and fall in unison with the inflation rate exactly as the Fisher equation suggests.[7] Market interest rates usually adjust more slowly and less precisely. Nevertheless, the Fisher equation is a useful indicator for investors and financial analysts.

Changing Interest Rates and Bond Prices

Just as common stock prices have fallen and risen dramatically in recent years, so have the prices of default-free U.S. Treasury bonds. Bonds have experienced gyrations from as low as $800 to as high as $1200 for a bond with a $1000 face value. These bond price fluctuations are largely attributable to changes in the level of market interest rates.

The mathematical formulas used to value bonds and stocks cause their market prices to vary inversely with market interest rates because the market rates are the discount rates in the present value formulas. This inverse relation is more prevalent for bonds than for stocks because interest rates are more important in the formula used to value bonds. This is because coupon interest rates printed on bonds cannot vary after the bonds are issued, but market interest rates fluctuate continuously. Box 17-5 presents an example of this relationship. A 20-year Treasury bond with a face value of $1000 principal and an 8 percent coupon rate is repaid in 20 years. However, during the bond's life, market interest rates may fluctuate above and below the bond's fixed coupon rate.

[7] The received theory of interest rates and inflation is presented in this book. The theory is attributed to Irving Fisher, *The Theory of Interest* (New York: Macmillan, 1930). Fisher's theory has been supported empirically over selected sample periods by, among others, W. E. Gibson, "Interest Rates and Inflationary Expectations: New Evidence," *American Economic Review,* December 1972, pp. 854–865. The received theory about risk premiums is supported by, among others, Lawrence Fisher, "Determinants of Risk Premiums on Corporate Bonds," *Journal of Political Economy,* June 1959, pp. 217–237. For a critique of the received theory about the determinants of market interest rate levels and some empirical data to substantiate that critique, see Steven C. Leuthold, "Interest Rates, Inflation and Deflation," *Financial Analysts Journal,* January-February 1981, pp. 28–41.

442

Part 4
Analysis of
More Risk
Factors

Box 17-5

COMPUTATION: Pricing an 8 Percent Coupon Bond When the Market Rate Is Not 8 Percent

Case 1: 8 percent coupon rate is *less* than the market rate of interest. If the market interest rate rises above the bond's coupon rate for a default-free 8 percent coupon rate, the only way an investor wanting to sell the bond can make it yield a competitive market interest rate (above 8 percent) is to offer to sell the bond at a **discount** below its $1000 face value. The bond must be sold for a large enough price *discount* below its face value to provide capital gains that make up the difference between the bond's fixed 8 percent coupon rate and the higher market interest rate. Stated differently, the discount below the bond's face value is a capital gain the investor who buys the bond will get if he or she holds the bond until it matures and gets back the $1000 principal. As a result of these bond pricing realities, bond prices must always be at a discount when the market interest rate is above the bond's coupon rate.

Case 2: 8 percent coupon rate is *greater* than the market rate of interest. If market interest rates fall *below* the bond's 8 percent coupon rate, the bond will have to be sold at a **premium** above its face value. In this case, investors who buy at the premium price and hold the bond until they get its $1000 face value at maturity will suffer capital losses sufficient to offset the bond's above-market-rate fixed coupon rate. Thus, this 8 percent coupon bond will have a yield-to-maturity that equals competitive market interest rates. This explains why a bond's market price is always at a premium above its face value when market interest rates are below the bond's coupon rate.

As we learned in Box 11-2, bond market prices always vary inversely with market interest rates. If a bond pays no coupon interest and sells at a discount from its face value (even when it is newly issued) in order to yield its investor income in the form of price appreciation, its market price must still vary inversely with market interest rates. Thus the prices of zero coupon bonds like U.S. Treasury bills vary inversely with market interest rates even though such bonds are always traded at discount prices.

Figures 11-3, 11-4, and 17-4 highlight the effect of market risk on bond prices. Swings in market interest rates cause bond market prices to move in bullish and bearish trends as they fluctuate inversely with the level of market interest rates.

17-5 Undiversifiable and Diversifiable Market Risk

A combination of systematic forces called the **undiversifiable market risk factor** causes the majority of securities to rise or fall together during bull or bear markets. Table 17-2, for instance, shows that over 80 percent of the NYSE-listed stocks fall in price during bear markets. Most of these systematic forces can ultimately be traced to the consensus business cycle forecast. Regardless of whether it turns out to be correct or incorrect, a widespread view that a recession is coming causes investors to begin selling, and that precipitates a bear market. However, even when an expected recession actually occurs and the market prices of most securities are being drawn down by bearish forces, the data in Table 17-2 show that some stocks will nevertheless rise. These unsystematic movements make up **diversifiable market risk.**

An individual security might experience market price movements that are uncorrelated with the prevailing market trend (and are therefore diversifiable) for any one of several different reasons. The prices of a few securities might rise during a bear market, for example, because the issuing corporations were recently granted valuable new patents, just obtained control of a lucrative additional share of the market for their product, or will benefit from the bankruptcy of a tough competitor. Such unsystematic price fluctuations are diversifiable because they can be combined into a diversified portfolio and the unsystematic fluctuations tend to cancel each other out.

Table 17-6
Economic Statistics That Make Up the Leading, Coincident,
and Lagging Economic Indicators

Leading index components

(1)	Average weekly hours worked in manufacturing
(5)	Average weekly initial claims for unemployment insurance (inverted)
(8)	New orders for consumer goods and materials, in 1982 dollars*
(19)	Standard & Poor's 500 Stocks Composite Index
(20)	Contracts and orders for plant and equipment, in 1982 dollars*
(29)	Building permits for new private housing units
(32)	Vendor performance, slower deliveries diffusion index
(83)	Index of consumer expectations
(92)	Change in unfilled orders for durable goods, in 1982 dollars*
(99)	Change in sensitive materials prices, smoothed
(106)	M2 money supply, in 1982 dollars*

Coincident index components

(41)	Employees on nonagricultural payrolls
(47)	Industrial production
(51)	Personal income less transfer payments, in 1982 dollars*
(57)	Manufacturing and trade sales, in 1982 dollars*

Lagging index components

(62)	Change in labor cost per unit of output in manufacturing
(77)	Ratio of manufacturing and trade inventories to sales, in 1982 dollars*
(91)	Average duration of unemployment
(95)	Ratio of consumer installment credit to personal income
(101)	Commercial and industrial loans made by banks, in 1982 dollars*
(109)	Average prime interest rate
(120)	Change in consumer price index for services, smoothed

* Inflation-adjusted 1982 dollar equivalents.

Note: The numbers preceding each indicator are U.S. Department of Commerce economic series numbers.

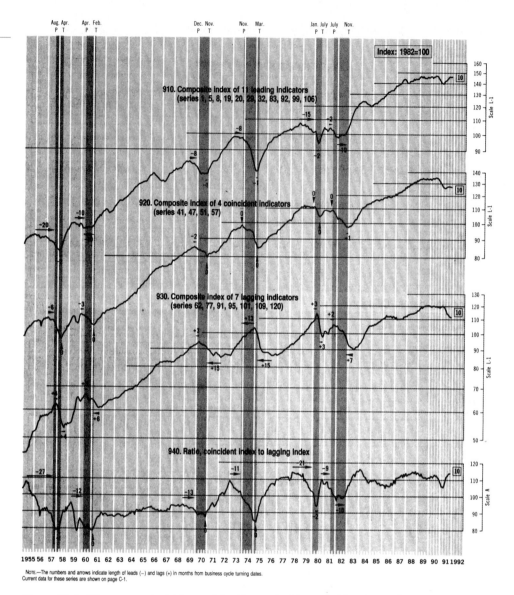

NOTE.—The numbers and arrows indicate length of leads (−) and lags (+) in months from business cycle turning dates.
Current data for these series are shown on page C-1.

Figure 17-5   The composite indexes of leading, coincident, and lagging indicators during recessions. (*Source:* U.S. Department of Commerce, *Survey of Current Business.*)

17-6   Leading and Lagging Indicators

Professional investors usually develop their own economic forecasts that they use to try to forecast bear markets. Those who have fewer resources can use a shortcut to forecasting that involves leading and lagging indicators. A **leading economic indicator** is an economic time series that usually moves up or down *before* the general level of business activity and can therefore be used to obtain forecasts of booms and recessions. Stock market indexes like the S&P 500 Composite Index or the Dow Jones

Industrial Average are leading economic indicators. A **lagging economic indicator** follows the level of business activity. The prime rate is an example of a lagging indicator.

The U.S. Department of Commerce monthly publication called the *Survey of Current Business* contains numerical tables and graphs of dozens of economic time series. Table 17-6 lists the numbers and names of the Commerce Department's economic time series that are added together to form the federal government's indexes of leading, coincident, and lagging economic indicators. Figure 17-5 shows how these indexes have varied over several business cycles.

Recessions are indicated by shaded vertical bands in Figure 17-5. This figure shows that, as its name suggests, the **index of leading economic indicators** declines months before each recession. The **index of coincident economic indicators** declines simultaneously with each recession. The **index of lagging economic indicators** declines months after each recession has started. These three indexes of economic activity are helpful in trying to forecast the business cycle. However, *since the stock market indexes are leading indicators, investors must use leading indicators that have longer lead times over business activity than the stock market indexes to help them forecast the stock markets.*

Forecasting the twists and turns of stock market indexes is a hard and risky business. Many try, and many suffer losses as the forecasts turn out to be wrong. As explained in Section 16-2, investors can take two different points of view about trying to buy low and sell high. The *aggressive investors* work hard at forecasting and use their projections as a basis for trading frequently. In contrast, investors who believe that security prices are efficient estimates of their present values become *passive investors* and follow a buy-and-hold strategy or invest in one or more *index funds*.

Summary

Both stocks and bonds are affected by alternating bull and bear markets, during which market prices rise and fall. Stock and bond prices can move in divergent directions or in similar directions and, as a result, are uncorrelated. Investors can sometimes reduce the market risk of a portfolio by diversifying their investments across stocks and bonds. Such a portfolio can be expected to be less risky than a portfolio consisting of similar securities from one market. In contrast, a homogeneous portfolio of NYSE stocks will be highly subject to the systematic market variations that make up undiversifiable stock market risk.

Economic forecasting can be helpful in anticipating and reacting to changes in the stock and bond markets. Bearish stock markets precede most recessions. Bearish bond markets result from high market interest rates, which are usually pushed up by high rates of inflation. If an investor can make forecasts of recessions and the inflation rate, or at least react quickly to unforeseen turns in these variables, investment decisions can be executed to avoid serious losses. But economic forecasting is hard work, and very few forecasters are able to make accurate forecasts consistently.

Further Reading

Moore, Geoffrey H., *Business Cycles, Inflation, and Forecasting*, National Bureau of Economic Research Studies in Business Cycles No. 24 (Cambridge, Mass.: Ballinger, 1980).

Chapter 9 explicitly discusses the determinants of bull and bear markets. The book contains tables of supporting economic data and graphs that are easy to understand.

Siegel, Jeremy J., "Does It Pay Stock Investors to Forecast Business Cycles?," *Journal of Portfolio Management*, Fall 1991, pp. 27–34.

> *This empirical study analyzes the length of time by which the stock market leads general business activity.*

Stocks, Bonds, Bills and Inflation: Yearbook (Chicago: R. G. Ibbotson).

> *This empirical study compares the returns from common stocks, corporate bonds, Treasury bills and T-bonds with the consumer price index. The easy-to-read book contains many tables of informative data from 1925 to the present.*

U.S. Department of Commerce, Bureau of Economic Analysis, *Survey of Current Business* (Washington, D.C.: U.S. Government Printing Office, published monthly).

> *This U.S. government publication may be subscribed to for $29 per year; it contains numerous time series of economic data and attractive charts of the data that are useful in analyzing the business cycle.*

Questions and Problems

Essay Questions

17-1 Define the terms (*a*) bull market, (*b*) bear market, (*c*) market risk, and (*d*) business cycle. How do these four concepts interrelate?

17-2 Clyde Cuming was overheard to say: "The average bear market lasts 14 months. Since we are now in the fourteenth month of the current bear market, it must be about over. Therefore, I am going to quickly invest all the money I can borrow before the next bull market starts." What do you think of Mr. Cuming's investment plan? Explain.

17-3 Abigail Scott observed that some common stocks experienced good price rises during the last bear market. Therefore, she plans to continue to be a consistently active investor in the future regardless of whether the stock market is experiencing a bullish trend or a bearish trend. Scott says that she has studied past bear market stock prices and "found several good price-gaining stocks during every month of the last two bear markets." Comment on Ms. Scott's investment plans for the future.

17-4 Sally Stanton heard two different economists predict that the current economic boom would peak and turn downward into a recession. Both economists predicted that this forthcoming recession was expected to start 5 months ahead. On the basis of the two economists' forecasts, Stanton has decided to invest in a widely diversified portfolio of common stocks and then to liquidate 4 months from now, 1 month before the forecasted recession starts. Stanton reasons that this strategy will allow her to take advantage of the last few months of bullish price rises before the bear market starts. How do you evaluate Stanton's strategy?

17-5 On Friday, November 22, 1963, President John F. Kennedy was assassinated as he rode in a car in a parade in Dallas, Texas. The news services wired the news of the killing around the world instantly. When the news reached the NYSE, hysterical selling began that caused officials to close the exchange early. In the 27 minutes between the arrival of the news of the assassination on the NYSE floor and the closing, many stock prices dropped by as much as $5 or $10 per share. The DJIA fell 24.5 points in those 27 minutes. However, when the exchange reopened on the following trading day (that is, on Monday, November 25), the shares opened at about the same prices they had been before the tragic news. On the first trading day following the funeral, the DJIA leaped 32 points. In your opinion, did the market temporarily collapse because of default risk, management risk, interest rate risk, bull and bear market risk, or what? Explain.

17-6   Explain how you would expect bond prices to react to a substantial change in the rate of inflation. Your explanation should include mention of the Fisher equation, Equation (17-2) and the first principle of present value from Box 11-2.

17-7   Consider Chrysler's common stock prices shown in the case cited in Chapter 10 and the stock market index data illustrated in Figure 17-1. Did Chrysler's price experience any unsystematic movements during those periods of time included in the case study and in Figure 17-1? At what dates did Chrysler's stock move unsystematically? Why did these countercyclical price moves occur? Did these countercyclical price variations reflect diversifiable or undiversifiable risk?

17-8   Compare Figure 17-3, showing the real economic variables, with Figure 17-4, showing the monetary sector variables. Also consider the leading, coincident, and lagging economic indicators shown in Figure 17-5. In view of this information, would you classify market interest rates as a (*a*) leading, (*b*) concurrent, or (*c*) lagging indicator of business activity in the real sector of the economy? Explain.

17-9   Consider the accompanying graph of the Dow Jones Industrial Average illustrating the 1929–1932 Great Crash. Do you think fundamental factors such as the nation's income and aggregate corporate profits declined by an amount to be sufficient to be justify this market collapse? Or do you think the Great Crash involved some irrational overreaction? Explain. *Hint:* Consult an economic history book.

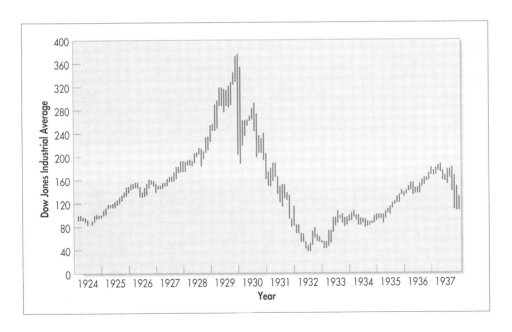

17-10   Compare Figure 15-5 with the bear market dates delineated in Figure 17-1 of this chapter. For the years in which the two overlap, do you agree with this chapter's definition of bear markets? Or, would you delineate different periods as being the bear markets? Explain.

17-11 This chapter explained that the stock market declines bearishly before recessions. In fact, the stock market anticipates recessions so well that it typically declines significantly for at least a few months, and sometimes nearly a whole year, before a recession starts. This chapter went on to explain how an accurate economic forecast of recessions would be helpful in predicting bear markets. (*a*) Explain how a perfectly accurate economic forecast can be useful in forecasting bear markets if the stock market declines *before* every recession. (*b*) Do you think it would be easy to find a perfectly accurate economic forecast? Explain.

Problems

17-12 Sometimes the value of a security market price index might move upward and downward in a narrow range for weeks or months without having either bull or bear market trends. If so, this market movement is called a *sideways market* or a *directionless market.* Draw a probability distribution (like the three in Figure 1-2) of the rates of change in the S&P 500 Stocks Composite Index over a sample period that includes at least one complete business cycle. Then delineate and label parts of that distribution as (*a*) bull market returns, (*b*) sideways market returns, and (*c*) bear market returns.

Matching Question

17-13 Match the words and phrases listed below with the most appropriate definitions or descriptions.

C 1. Trough

A. Systematic price movements that sweep most stocks along in alternating bull and bear market price swings

E 2. Business cycle

B. A period of prevailing optimism that carries the prices of most securities to higher levels

D 3. Real sector

C. The lowest point in a cyclical movement

A 4. Undiversifiable market risk

D. Those activities in a country's economy that involve tangible production work

B 5. Bull market

E. Alternating periods of expansion and recession that punctuate a country's economic activity

Multiple Choice Questions

17-14 Which of the following statements accurately characterizes the phrase "business cycle"?

E
    (*a*) A cycle that recurs but is not generally predictable with any great degree of accuracy.
    (*b*) Patterns of business activity that are similar in timing and amplitude.
    (*c*) A cycle of business activity that ranges from 1 to 2 years.
    (*d*) Ups and downs in the business cycle lead the bull and bear markets, respectively, by 6 to 12 months.
    (*e*) Both (*a*) and (*b*) are true.

17-15 Why should an investor need a 1-year forecast of business activity in order to achieve good investment timing?

B
    (*a*) There is a one-to-one correspondence between the timing of the stock price indexes and the level of business activity; so, a 1-year forecast of business activity converts into a 1-year stock market forecast.

(*b*) Because a bear stock market precedes every recession by 1 year or less. Thus, a 1-year business activity forecast has immediate stock market implications.

(*c*) Because market interest rates tend to rise with the level of business activity, causing bond prices to rise bullishly.

(*d*) Because the stock market is a leading indicator of business activity that has a 6- to 12-month lead.

(*e*) Both (*b*) and (*d*) are true.

17-16   Market risk can be accurately described by which of the following statements?

(*a*) It is an unimportant source of investors' total variability of return.

(*b*) It causes the type of stock price fluctuations that can be diversified away by forming a portfolio of many different stocks.

(*c*) It includes major bear markets, which occur before recessions and at other times too.

(*d*) It is the result of the alternating sociological forces of optimism and pessimism.

C

17-17   The real sector of the U.S. economy is best described by which of the following statements?

(*a*) Gross national product (GNP), employment, and other physical measures of business activity are components of the real sector.

(*b*) Credit, the money supply, interest rates, and the rate of inflation are all components of the real sector.

(*c*) Turns in the stock market are an economic indicator that leads turns in the real sector by as much as a year sometimes.

(*d*) Both (*a*) and (*c*) are true.

C

17-18   Bull markets are best described by which of the following statements?

(*a*) Bull and bear markets may be viewed as alternating periods of time during which financial optimism and pessimism prevail.

(*b*) On average, bull markets last about 50 percent longer than bear markets.

(*c*) About 95 percent of the stocks listed on the NYSE increased in price, on average, during bull markets.

(*d*) Both (*a*) and (*b*) are true.

(*e*) All the above are true.

D

17-19   A bull market is correctly defined by which of the following phrases?

(*a*) An upward move in a market index

(*b*) An upward trend that is punctuated with some small, temporary declines

(*c*) A period during which the volume of shares purchased is larger than the volume of shares sold

(*d*) A period during which market pessimism prevails

(*e*) All the above

B

CHAPTER 18

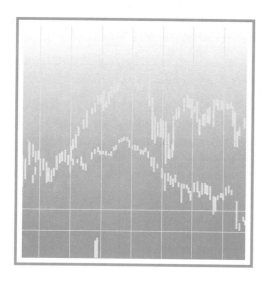

PURCHASING-POWER RISK AND OTHER RISK FACTORS

An investment can be risky for a number of reasons. The risk of default increases when the financial health of an issuer of securities deteriorates. Fluctuating credit market conditions cause interest rate risk. Alternating bull and bear forces generate market risk, and the value of securities can diminish. Another force that erodes the value of money is inflation. In this chapter, we first explore purchasing power risk, in both the domestic and the international contexts. Then we turn to other risk factors: liquidity risk, political risk, call risk, and convertibility risk.

Assets that can be sold quickly only by marking down their price significantly or by paying a large sales commission are not highly liquid assets. The *liquidity risk factor* reduces the marketability of some investments.

Box 18-1

451

*Chapter 18
Purchasing-
Power Risk
and Other
Risk Factors*

> **DEFINITION: Purchasing-Power Risk**
>
> **Purchasing-power risk** is that portion of an asset's total variability in real (or inflation-adjusted) returns that is caused by changes in the general level of prices. Inflation is the primary cause of purchasing-power risk; it reduces the purchasing power of monetary assets (like cash and bonds) that are denominated in fixed dollar amounts.

Investors face two sources of political risk: Tax assessments imposed by federal, state, or local governments are the primary source of *domestic political risk.* Investors who buy securities issued by companies and governments located outside the United States must deal with *international political risks.*

Securities that are either callable or convertible should pay higher rates of return than securities that are not callable or convertible to compensate investors for enduring their respective *call risk* or *conversion risk.*

18-1   The Purchasing-Power Risk Factor

When the general price level is rising, the movement is called **inflation.** The inflation rate was defined in Equation (17-1). If the price level declines, Equation (17-1) will also measure the rate of **deflation.** Chapter 17 analyzed the impact of inflation on interest rates. This chapter considers the effects of inflation on certain investments; the impact on other assets is discussed in later chapters. If deflation occurs, the purchasing power of your dollars will increase: *deflation appears infrequently.*

The Money Illusion

Purchasing-power risk is different from interest rate risk and market risk, because *an investment can lose its purchasing power even though its price is rising.* Investors who do not understand how this can happen—how they are actually poorer when on paper they appear to be richer—suffer what economists call *money illusion.*

Those who have **money illusion** mistakenly believe that if they have more money they must be richer. This belief ignores the effects of inflation. For example, if the amount of wealth you have doubles during a period of time when the general price level quadruples, you are *poorer.* Even though you may have twice as many dollars to spend, you have only half as much purchasing power if the cost of living quadruples.

Inflation has seriously eroded the purchasing power of dollars in the United States in recent decades. An average national inflation rate of 3.5 percent per year for the 40 years from 1950 to 1990 means that a 1990 dollar will buy only 25 cents worth of 1950 goods and services.

Real versus Nominal Returns

Inflation also reduces the purchasing power of investment returns. In order for investors to see through the deceptive veil of money and discern the actual purchasing power of investment returns, inflation should be measured and compared with investment returns. When you read a newspaper ad saying that a savings account pays a certain rate of return, for example, that advertised rate is the **nominal rate of return.** Nominal rates of return are **money rates of return;** they are not adjusted for the effects of inflation. A key question is: Are your investments' nominal rates of return higher than the rate of inflation?

Calculating Real Returns

An asset with a present value of $100 earning a nominal rate of $r = .06 = 6.0\%$ for one period has a nominal future value of

$$\text{Nominal future value} = (\text{present value})(1.0 + r)$$
$$= \$100(1.06) = \$106 \tag{18-1}$$

Once the nominal future value is calculated, an asset's real (or inflation-adjusted) future value can be calculated as shown in the following equation:

$$\text{Real future value} = \frac{\text{nominal future value}}{1.0 + \text{inflation rate}} \tag{18-2}$$

Box 18-2 presents an example of how inflation can cause real future value to be less than nominal future value.

The real purchasing power earned by an investment, its **real rate of return** during some time period, is calculated by dividing 1 plus the asset's nominal rate of return $(1.0 + r)$ by 1 plus the rate of inflation $(1 + INF)$. The resulting real rate of return is denoted rr.

$$1.0 + rr = \frac{1.0 + r}{1.0 + INF} \tag{18-3}$$

Equation (18-3) can be manipulated algebraically and restated equivalently as

$$rr = \frac{1.0 + r}{1.0 + INF} - 1.0 \tag{18-3a}$$

For example, if a common stock earns a 10 percent nominal rate of return, $r = .1 = 10\%$, for a year when the inflation rate is 8 percent, $INF = .08 = 8\%$, the stock's real rate of return is less than 2 percent in that year.

$$rr = \frac{1.10}{1.08} - 1.0 = .0185 = 1.85\%$$

Box 18-2

453

COMPUTATION: Inflation Erodes Purchasing Power

Assume that a savings deposit earns a nominal interest rate (or nominal rate of return) of $r = .06 = 6\%$ during some 1-year period so that if $100 were deposited, it would grow to $106 in that year.

Nominal future value $= \$100(1.0 + r) = \$100(1.06) = \$106$

If we also assume that the rate of inflation during that year is INF $= .06 = 6\%$, then the real value (that is, dollars of purchasing power) of the $100 savings at the end of the year is still only $100, as shown below.

$$\text{Real future value} = \frac{(\$100)(1.0 + r)}{(1.0 + \text{INF})}$$

$$= \frac{\$100(1.06)}{1.06} = \$100$$

In this example the nominal rate of return is eroded by an inflation rate of equal size, so that the savings account's purchasing power did not increase even though there were 6 percent more dollars in the account.

This investment in common stock resulted in a 1.85 percent increase in purchasing power. The only portion of an investment's nominal rate of return that results in increased consumption opportunities for an investor is the *real* portion of the return; the rest is lost to inflation. Investors who suffer from the money illusion fail to realize this and believe erroneously that the investment in this example yields more than a 1.85 percent real gain. It is also possible for an investment earning a positive *nominal* rate of return to earn a negative *real* return.[1]

---

[1] To avoid doing decimal-point-accurate division, an approximate formula can be derived from Equation (18-3).

$$1.0 + \text{rr} = \frac{1.0 + r}{1.0 + \text{INF}} \tag{18-3}$$

$$1.0 + r = (1.0 + \text{rr})(1.0 + \text{INF})$$

$$r = \text{rr} + \text{INF} + (\text{INF})(\text{rr})$$

If the product of INF times rr is a tiny number, it can be ignored to obtain the following approximation:

$$r \cong \text{rr} + \text{INF}$$

Box 18-3

COMPUTATION: A Negative Real Rate of Return

Consider a savings account that pays 6 percent interest in a year when inflation is 8 percent. This savings account has a negative real rate of return, as shown below.

$$rr = \frac{1.0 + r}{1.0 + INF} - 1 = \frac{1.06}{1.08} - 1 = .9815 - 1 = -.0185 = -1.85\%$$

Investors who have the money illusion think that the savings account increased their wealth by 6 percent when, in fact, their purchasing power actually shrank by 1.85 percent.

If an investment has a negative real rate of return, that does not necessarily mean the investor would have been better off without it. After all, if money had been held in cash (earning zero rate of return) instead of being invested in the 6 percent savings account in the boxed example, the investor would have suffered an 7.4 percent loss in purchasing power.

$$rr = \frac{1.0 + r}{1.0 + INF} - 1 = \frac{1.0}{1.08} - 1 = .926 - 1 = -.0740 = -7.4\%$$

Thus, even when the inflation rate exceeds an investment's nominal rate, loss of purchasing power will be greater if a nonearning asset like cash is held. To maximize their purchasing power, investors should try to ensure that their nominal rates of return are greater than the inflation rate, and focus on the real return from investments.[2]

18-2 Inflation Rates in Foreign Countries

This section compares the nominal returns investors earn from different investments with the concurrent rates of inflation. The purpose of making this comparison is to discover which investments yield the best real returns.

Table 18-1 shows rates of inflation and the associated consumer price index (CPI)

---

[2] Some detailed studies on the effect of inflation on stock prices include Rene M. Stulz, "Asset Pricing and Expected Inflation," *Journal of Finance*, vol. 41, no. 1, 1986, pp. 209–224; Eric C. Chang and J. Michael Pinegar, "Risk and Inflation," *Journal of Financial and Quantitative Analysis*, vol. 22, no. 1, 1987, pp. 89–100; John Huizinga and Frederic S. Mishkin, "Inflation and Real Interest Rates on Assets with Different Risk Characteristics," *Journal of Finance*, vol. 39, no. 3, 1984, pp. 699–712; Steven C. Leuthold, "Interest Rates, Inflation and Deflation," *Financial Analysts Journal*, vol. 37, no. 1, 1981, pp. 28–41; Douglas K. Pearce and V. Vance Roley, "Firm Characteristics, Unanticipated Inflation, and Stock Returns," *Journal of Finance*, vol. 43, no. 4, 1988, pp. 965–981; and G. William Schwert, "The Adjustment of Stock Prices to Information about Inflation," *Journal of Finance*, vol. 36, no. 1, 1981, pp. 15–29.

Table 18-1
Foreign Countries' Consumer Price Indexes, 1926–1989

455

Chapter 18
Purchasing-
Power Risk
and Other
Risk Factors

	Canada		France		Germany	
Decade	Rate of change	Index	Rate of change	Index	Rate of change	Index
1926–29	0.18%	1.01	8.52%	1.39	0.33%	1.01
1930–39	−1.80	0.84	3.08	1.88	−1.96	0.83
1940–49	4.52	1.31	31.48	29.02	5.23	1.38
1950–59	2.36	1.65	6.40	53.97	1.05	1.53
1960–69	2.59	2.13	3.78	78.17	2.47	1.96
1970–79	7.54	4.41	9.09	186.66	5.02	3.20
1980–89	6.45	12.80	8.34	727.32	2.88	5.33

	Italy		Japan		Sweden	
Decade	Rate of change	Index	Rate of change	Index	Rate of change	Index
1926–29	−2.82%	0.89	−4.46%	0.83	−0.98%	0.96
1930–39	0.24	0.91	2.11	1.03	0.10	0.97
1940–49	47.72	45.19	66.80	171.17	4.10	1.45
1950–59	2.65	58.69	2.42	217.50	4.39	2.23
1960–69	3.66	84.09	5.51	371.97	3.52	3.15
1970–79	12.88	282.43	8.94	876.08	8.72	7.27
1980–89	11.05	1832.27	2.50	1364.15	7.89	26.83

	Switzerland		United Kingdom		United States	
Decade	Rate of change	Index	Rate of change	Index	Rate of change	Index
1926–29	−1.05%	0.96	−1.68%	0.93	−1.09%	0.96
1930–39	−1.53	0.82	−0.41	0.90	−2.05	0.78
1940–49	4.76	1.31	5.69	1.56	5.41	1.32
1950–59	1.08	1.46	4.36	2.39	1.02	1.64
1960–69	3.20	1.99	3.68	3.44	2.52	2.10
1970–79	4.99	3.25	13.04	11.71	7.37	4.28
1980–89	3.26	5.72	7.35	39.51	5.49	10.41

Notes: Rates of change equal the annual compound rates of change in percent, for the decade or subperiod indicated. The indexes are the cumulative price indexes initialized at 1.00 on Dec. 31, 1925.

Sources: Starting 1960, International Financial Statistics (various issues), published by the International Monetary Fund, Washington, D.C., and prior to 1960, reproduced from R. G. Ibbotson and Gary P. Brinson, Investment Markets (Englewood Cliffs, N.J.: Prentice-Hall, 1987), p. 174.

for different countries during a 64-year sample period. This table shows, for example, that deflation occurred in the United States during the late 1920s and early 1930s. From 1926 to 1929, the cost of a representative market basket of consumer goods dropped 1.9 percent per year, on average. That is, INF $= -.0109 = -1.09\%$. This deflation resulted from the Great Depression, a period of great economic suffering when the unemployment rate reached 25 percent and thousands of U.S. banks went bankrupt.

Table 18-1 also shows that since the Depression ended, the United States has endured 4 decades with average rates of inflation that ranged from 1.02 percent during the 1950s to 7.37 percent during the 1970s. Cumulated over the entire 64-year period, the U.S. consumer price index (CPI) rose from a base value of 1.0 on December 31, 1925, to a value of 10.41 on December 31, 1989.

$$(1 + INF_{1926})(1 + INF_{1927}) \dots (1 + INF_{1989}) = 10.41 = CPI_{1989} = 10.41$$

This means that the average American who purchased a market basket of consumer goods had to pay 10.41 times as much on December 31, 1989, as he or she would have had to pay on December 31, 1925.

Table 18-1 also shows that over the 64 years Germany, one of the most stable economies in the world, experienced only about half ($[5.33/10.41] = .512$) as much inflation as the United States. In contrast, Italy had over 176 times ($[1832.27/10.41] = 176.01$) more. These inflation rates mean that, ignoring how the countries' securities prices might have appreciated or depreciated, an international investor would certainly rather have money invested in German deutsche marks than in Italian lire. Stated differently, if Italian common stocks enjoyed a price rise that was twice as large as the German stocks, an investor's purchasing power would still have increased more in the German stocks because the German deutsche mark holds its purchasing power more than 343 times better ($[1832.27/5.33] = 343.76$) than the Italian lira. Comparisons like this make it clear why international investors should be wary of purchasing-power risk. Germany and Switzerland had lower rates of inflation over the 64-year sample period than the United States. Relatively low inflation is why Germany, Switzerland, and the United States are generally viewed as being among the most desirable places in the world to invest.

Investors should beware of investments in countries that have unstable political systems. Table 18-2 shows 3 decades of inflation statistics for three countries that have high and accelerating rates of inflation. Brazil, for instance, has had average price rises of 230 percent per year during the 1980s. *Hyperinflation* like this not only discourages investors, it also makes accounting for a business's profits from year to year nearly impossible (see also Chapter 14).

18-3   Real Rates of Return from U.S. Investments

To simulate the average investor's experience with different types of assets and analyze the merits of each, financial analysts have prepared hypothetical portfolios. In this section we will examine representative samples of common stocks (including stocks from small corporations), corporate bonds, U.S. Treasury bills, and U.S.

457

*Chapter 18
Purchasing-
Power Risk
and Other
Risk Factors*

Table 18-2
Three Countries with High and Accelerating Rates of Inflation

	Brazil		Israel		Mexico	
Period	*Rate of change*	*Index*	*Rate of change*	*Index*	*Rate of change*	*Index*
1960–69	44.20%	38.88	5.22%	1.66	2.53%	1.29
1970–79	29.95	533.79	31.01	24.78	14.45	4.97
1980–89	230.00	60,918,426.00	99.20*	70,000.00*	65.04	1,912.72

* Author's estimate, because data was unavailable for 1980.

Notes: Rates of change equal the annual compound rates of change in percent, for the decade or subperiod indicated. The indexes are the cumulative price indexes initialized at 1.00 on Dec. 31, 1959.

Sources: International Financial Statistics (various issues), published by the International Monetary Fund, Washington, D.C., and R. G. Ibbotson and Gary P. Brinson, *Investment Markets* (Englewood Cliffs, N.J.: Prentice-Hall, 1987), p. 187.

Treasury bonds that were used to form hypothetical portfolios in the United States. The portfolios were constructed without any attempt to pick the best or the worst securities in each category; they were intended to represent the *average* investors' experience. The investment indexes (or portfolio values) are interesting by themselves —for comparison with each other, and for comparison with the rate of inflation.

Figure 1-5 shows how $1 would have grown if it had been invested in different types of investment portfolios on Dec. 31, 1925, and then kept invested that way for the next 6 decades. The consumer price index (CPI), also illustrated in Figure 1-5, provides a standard of comparison against which the different investment portfolios can be prepared.

Table 18-3 lists the annual nominal and real rates of return for each category of assets. Figures 1-4 and 1-5 and Table 18-1 all refer to the same underlying data. As you study Figures 1-4 and 1-5 and Table 18-3, look for answers to the following questions:

1. Which category of assets enriched investors the most in nominal terms? The least?

2. Which category of assets experienced the most variability in nominal terms? The least?

3. Which categories of assets earned positive real rates of return over the decades? Negative real returns?

4. Which categories of assets earned positive real rates of return during every one of the years?

The summary statistics in Figure 1-4 suggest that T-bills had a small positive nominal rate of return, but their real rate of return was practically zero. As might be expected, the low-return T-bills also had the least variability of return of any

Table 18-3
Annual Rates of Return for Different Categories of Assets in Nominal and Real Terms, 1926–1988

Year	Nominal							Inflation-adjusted					
	Common stocks	Small-company stocks	Long-term corporate bonds	Long-term government bonds	Intermediate-term government bonds	U.S. Treasury bills	Consumer price index	Common stocks	Small-company stocks	Long-term corporate bonds	Long-term government bonds	Intermediate-term government bonds	U.S. Treasury bills
1926	0.1162	0.0028	0.0737	0.0777	0.0538	0.0327	-0.0149	0.1331	0.0179	0.0900	0.0940	0.0697	0.0483
1927	0.3749	0.2210	0.0744	0.0893	0.0452	0.0312	-0.0208	0.4041	0.2469	0.0973	0.1124	0.0674	0.0531
1928	0.4361	0.3969	0.0284	0.0010	0.0092	0.0356	-0.0097	0.4501	0.4106	0.0384	0.0108	0.0190	0.0457
1929	-0.0842	-0.5136	0.0327	0.0342	0.0601	0.0475	0.0019	-0.0859	-0.5145	0.0307	0.0322	0.0581	0.0454
1930	-0.2490	-0.3815	0.0798	0.0466	0.0671	0.0241	-0.0603	-0.2008	-0.3418	0.1491	0.1137	0.1356	0.0898
1931	-0.4334	-0.4975	-0.0185	-0.0531	-0.0232	0.0107	-0.0952	-0.3737	-0.4446	0.0848	0.0465	0.0796	0.1171
1932	-0.0819	-0.0539	0.1082	0.1684	0.0881	0.0096	-0.1030	0.0235	0.0547	0.2354	0.3025	0.2130	0.1255
1933	0.5399	1.4287	0.1038	-0.0008	0.0182	0.0030	0.0051	0.5321	1.4163	0.0982	-0.0058	0.0131	-0.0021
1934	-0.0144	0.2422	0.1384	0.1002	0.0900	0.0016	0.0203	-0.0340	0.2175	0.1158	0.0784	0.0683	-0.0183
1935	0.4767	0.4019	0.0961	0.0498	0.0701	0.0017	0.0299	0.4339	0.3613	0.0644	0.0194	0.0390	-0.0273
1936	0.3392	0.6480	0.0674	0.0751	0.0306	0.0018	0.0121	0.3232	0.6283	0.0547	0.0623	0.0183	-0.0102
1937	-0.3503	-0.5801	0.0275	0.0023	0.0156	0.0031	0.0310	-0.3698	-0.5927	-0.0035	-0.0279	-0.0150	-0.0271
1938	0.3112	0.3280	0.0613	0.0553	0.0623	-0.0002	-0.0278	0.3487	0.3659	0.0917	0.0855	0.0926	0.0284
1939	-0.0041	0.0035	0.0397	0.0594	0.0452	-0.0002	-0.0048	0.0007	0.0083	0.0446	0.0645	0.0502	0.0050
1940	-0.0978	-0.0516	0.0339	0.0609	0.0296	0.0000	0.0096	-0.1064	-0.0605	0.0241	0.0508	0.0198	-0.0094
1941	-0.1159	-0.0900	0.0273	0.0093	0.0049	0.0006	0.0972	-0.1942	-0.1706	-0.0637	-0.0801	-0.0841	-0.0880
1942	0.2034	0.4451	0.0260	0.0322	0.0194	0.0027	0.0929	0.1011	0.3223	-0.0612	-0.0555	-0.0673	-0.0825
1943	0.2590	0.8837	0.0283	0.0208	0.0281	0.0035	0.0316	0.2204	0.8260	-0.0032	-0.0105	-0.0034	-0.0273
1944	0.1975	0.5372	0.0473	0.0281	0.0180	0.0033	0.0211	0.1728	0.5055	0.0257	0.0069	-0.0031	-0.0174
1945	0.3644	0.7361	0.0408	0.1073	0.0222	0.0033	0.0225	0.3343	0.6979	0.0178	0.0830	-0.0003	-0.0188
1946	-0.0807	-0.1163	0.0172	-0.0010	0.0100	0.0035	0.1817	-0.2220	-0.2521	-0.1391	-0.1546	-0.1452	-0.1507
1947	0.0571	0.0092	-0.0234	-0.0263	0.0091	0.0050	0.0901	-0.0303	-0.0742	-0.1041	-0.1067	-0.0743	-0.0780
1948	0.0550	-0.0211	0.0414	0.0340	0.0185	0.0081	0.0271	0.0272	-0.0469	0.0139	0.0067	-0.0084	-0.0185
1949	0.1879	0.1975	0.0331	0.0645	0.0232	0.0110	-0.0180	0.2097	0.2195	0.0521	0.0840	0.0420	0.0296
1950	0.3171	0.3875	0.0212	0.0006	0.0070	0.0120	0.0579	0.2450	0.3115	-0.0347	-0.0542	-0.0481	-0.0434
1951	0.2402	0.0780	-0.0269	-0.0394	0.0036	0.0149	0.0587	0.1714	0.0182	-0.0809	-0.0927	-0.0521	-0.0414
1952	0.1837	0.0303	0.0352	0.0116	0.0163	0.0166	0.0088	0.1733	0.0213	0.0262	0.0027	0.0074	0.0077
1953	-0.0099	-0.0649	0.0341	0.0363	0.0323	0.0182	0.0063	-0.0160	-0.0707	0.0277	0.0299	0.0259	0.0119
1954	0.5262	0.6058	0.0539	0.0719	0.0268	0.0086	-0.0050	0.5339	0.6138	0.0591	0.0772	0.0319	0.0137
1955	0.3156	0.2044	0.0048	-0.0130	-0.0065	0.0157	0.0037	0.3107	0.1999	0.0010	-0.0166	-0.0102	0.0119
1956	0.0656	0.0428	-0.0681	-0.0559	-0.0042	0.0246	0.0286	0.0359	0.0138	-0.0941	-0.0821	-0.0319	-0.0039
1957	-0.1078	-0.1457	0.0871	0.0745	0.0784	0.0314	0.0302	-0.1340	-0.1708	0.0552	0.0430	0.0467	0.0011
1958	0.4336	0.6489	-0.0222	-0.0610	-0.0129	0.0154	0.0176	0.4088	0.6203	-0.0391	-0.0772	-0.0300	-0.0022
1959	0.1196	0.1640	-0.0097	-0.0226	-0.0039	0.0295	0.0150	0.1030	0.1468	-0.0243	-0.0370	-0.0187	0.0143

	Nominal							Inflation-adjusted					
Year	Common stocks	Small-company stocks	Long-term corporate bonds	Long-term government bonds	Intermediate-term government bonds	U.S. Treasury bills	Consumer price index	Common stocks	Small-company stocks	Long-term corporate bonds	Long-term government bonds	Intermediate-term government bonds	U.S. Treasury bills
1960	0.0047	−0.0329	0.0907	0.1378	0.1175	0.0266	0.0148	−0.0099	−0.0470	0.0748	0.1212	0.1013	0.0117
1961	0.2689	0.3209	0.0482	0.0097	0.0185	0.0213	0.0067	0.2604	0.3121	0.0412	0.0030	0.0117	0.0144
1962	−0.0873	−0.1190	0.0795	0.0689	0.0556	0.0273	0.0122	−0.0983	−0.1297	0.0664	0.0559	0.0429	0.0149
1963	0.2280	0.2357	0.0219	0.0121	0.0164	0.0312	0.0165	0.2081	0.2156	0.0054	−0.0043	−0.0001	0.0144
1964	0.1648	0.2352	0.0477	0.0351	0.0404	0.0354	0.0119	0.1511	0.2207	0.0354	0.0229	0.0282	0.0232
1965	0.1245	0.4175	−0.0046	0.0071	0.0102	0.0393	0.0192	0.1033	0.3908	−0.0234	−0.0119	−0.0089	0.0197
1966	−0.1006	−0.0701	0.0020	0.0365	0.0468	0.0476	0.0335	−0.1298	−0.1003	−0.0306	0.0029	0.0129	0.0136
1967	0.2398	0.8357	−0.0495	−0.0919	0.0101	0.0421	0.0304	0.2031	0.7815	−0.0776	−0.1187	−0.0198	0.0113
1968	0.1106	0.3597	0.0257	−0.0026	0.0453	0.0521	0.0472	0.0605	0.2984	−0.0205	−0.0476	−0.0018	0.0046
1969	−0.0850	−0.2505	−0.0809	−0.0508	−0.0074	0.0658	0.0611	−0.1377	−0.2937	−0.1338	−0.1054	−0.0645	0.0045
1970	0.0401	−0.1743	0.1837	0.1210	0.1686	0.0653	0.0549	−0.0141	−0.2173	0.1221	0.0627	0.1078	0.0098
1971	0.1431	0.1650	0.1101	0.1323	0.0872	0.0439	0.0336	0.1060	0.1271	0.0741	0.0955	0.0519	0.0099
1972	0.1898	0.0443	0.0726	0.0568	0.0516	0.0384	0.0341	0.1505	0.0099	0.0372	0.0220	0.0169	0.0041
1973	−0.1466	−0.3090	0.0114	−0.0111	0.0460	0.0693	0.0880	−0.2156	−0.3649	−0.0704	−0.0911	−0.0385	−0.0172
1974	−0.2647	−0.1995	−0.0306	0.0435	0.0569	0.0800	0.1220	−0.3446	−0.2865	−0.1360	−0.0700	−0.0581	−0.0374
1975	0.3720	0.5282	0.1464	0.0919	0.0783	0.0580	0.0701	0.2821	0.4280	0.0713	0.0204	0.0076	−0.0113
1976	0.2384	0.5738	0.1865	0.1675	0.1287	0.0508	0.0481	0.1816	0.5015	0.1320	0.1140	0.0769	0.0026
1977	−0.0718	0.2538	0.0171	−0.0067	0.0140	0.0512	0.0677	−0.1307	0.1743	−0.0474	−0.0697	−0.0503	−0.0155
1978	0.0656	0.2346	−0.0007	−0.0116	0.0348	0.0718	0.0903	−0.0226	0.1324	−0.0834	−0.0934	−0.0508	−0.0169
1979	0.1844	0.4346	−0.0418	−0.0122	0.0409	0.1038	0.1331	0.0453	0.2662	−0.1543	−0.1282	−0.0813	−0.0259
1980	0.3242	0.3988	−0.0262	−0.0395	0.0391	0.1124	0.1240	0.1781	0.2445	−0.1336	−0.1455	−0.0756	−0.0103
1981	−0.0491	0.1388	−0.0096	0.0185	0.0945	0.1471	0.0894	−0.1271	0.0453	−0.0909	−0.0651	0.0047	0.0530
1982	0.2141	0.2801	0.4379	0.4035	0.2910	0.1054	0.0387	0.1688	0.2323	0.3843	0.3512	0.2428	0.0642
1983	0.2251	0.3967	0.0470	0.0068	0.0741	0.0880	0.0380	0.1803	0.3456	0.0087	−0.0300	0.0348	0.0482
1984	0.0627	−0.0667	0.1639	0.1543	0.1402	0.0985	0.0395	0.0222	−0.1022	0.1196	0.1104	0.0968	0.0567
1985	0.3216	0.2466	0.3090	0.3097	0.2033	0.0772	0.0377	0.2736	0.2013	0.2615	0.2621	0.1596	0.0381
1986	0.1847	0.0685	0.1985	0.2444	0.1514	0.0616	0.0113	0.1715	0.0566	0.1851	0.2305	0.1385	0.0498
1987	0.0523	−0.0930	−0.0027	−0.0269	0.0290	0.0547	0.0441	0.0079	−0.1313	−0.0448	−0.0680	−0.0144	0.0101
1988	0.1681	0.2287	0.1070	0.0967	0.0610	0.0635	0.0442	0.1187	0.1767	0.0602	0.0503	0.0161	0.0185

Source: Stocks, Bonds, Bills and Inflation: 1989 Yearbook (Chicago: R. G. Ibbotson Assoc.) Ibbotson compounded monthly returns to get both the real and the nominal annual data above. As a result, the real and nominal annual returns do not differ precisely by the amount that would be obtained by either dividing or subtracting out the annual rate of inflation.

Table 18-4
Average Rate of Return and Risk Statistics in Real Terms
for Different Categories of Securities, 1926–1988

Series	Geometric mean	Arithmetic mean	Standard deviation
Inflation-adjusted common stocks	6.7%	8.8%	21.1%
Inflation-adjusted small stocks	8.9	14.3	34.9
Inflation-adjusted long-term corporate bonds	1.9	2.4	10.0
Inflation-adjusted long-term government bonds	1.2	1.7	10.1
Inflation-adjusted intermediate-term government bonds	1.7	1.9	7.0
Inflation-adjusted U.S. Treasury bills (real interest rates)	0.5	0.5	4.4

Source: Stocks, Bonds, Bills and Inflation: The Past and the Future, 1989 Yearbook (Chicago: R. G. Ibbotson Assoc.), exh. 27, p. 84.

category of investments. At the other extreme, the common stocks of small corporations had the highest risk along with the highest average rate of return. The stocks of small firms earned high average rates of return, in both the nominal and the real sense.

Table 18-4 provides some summary statistics about the average *real rates of return* and risks of the different categories of investment securities described above. The real return statistics in Table 18-4 should be compared with the nominal return statistics for the same asset categories shown in Figure 1-4. Note that although the real returns are less than the nominal returns for every category of asset, the *real risk statistics are larger* than the nominal risk statistics for every category except the small stocks.

Dealing with purchasing-power risk is more complicated than we have indicated so far. We also need to consider whether the variations in an investment's real rates of return are diversifiable or undiversifiable.

18-4 Diversifiable and Undiversifiable Purchasing-Power Risk

An investment may experience purchasing-power risk even though its market price never fluctuates. As we have seen, purchasing-power risk results from fluctuations in the purchasing power of the asset's real, or inflation-adjusted, price, not just from fluctuations in its nominal, or market, price. Investment assets can be categorized into two groups based on whether their purchasing-power risk is likely to be undiversifiable or diversifiable. Those assets that have undiversifiable purchasing-power risk are typically *monetary assets.* Investment assets with diversifiable purchasing-power risk are often **real assets,** physical assets like diamonds, real estate, gold, and silver. During periods of time when the rate of inflation is positive, the prices of the real assets usually rise along with the general price level so that the real asset investments do not lose purchasing power. This is why the real assets have **diversifiable purchasing-power risk.**

Including real assets in a portfolio of monetary assets is a good way to help reduce the portfolio's loss of purchasing power. Because their market prices tend to be positively correlated with the inflation rate, real assets are called *good inflation hedges.* (Chapter 23 explores real asset investing in detail.) In contrast, monetary assets tend to be bad inflation hedges.

Monetary assets are denominated in fixed dollar amounts. Cash, bonds, and savings account deposits are examples. During inflationary periods the prices of monetary assets cannot change, because they are dollar-denominated. As a result, the monetary assets lose purchasing power whenever inflation is positive. Thus, the real returns from monetary assets are negatively correlated with the rate of inflation. Monetary assets have **undiversifiable purchasing-power risk** because they lose purchasing power when the general price level rises. Even a highly diversified portfolio that contained only monetary assets would lose purchasing power during inflationary periods, because the portfolio would contain a large amount of undiversifiable purchasing-power risk.

461

*Chapter 18
Purchasing-
Power Risk
and Other
Risk Factors*

18-5 The Liquidity Risk Factor

Next, let us consider the risk that an investment may be difficult to sell. Perfectly liquid assets can be sold without suffering any price reductions. U.S. dollars are a perfectly liquid medium of exchange because a $5 bill can easily be exchanged for five $1 bills without paying anyone a commission. U.S. Treasury securities and blue-chip common stocks are other examples of highly liquid assets. But municipal bonds and the common stocks of small, unknown corporations are usually not very liquid.

Stated negatively, **illiquid assets** are not readily marketable. Most homes are examples of illiquid assets. Significant price discounts must be given or significant sales commissions must be paid, or both, in order to find a new investor for an illiquid asset. The more illiquid an asset is, the larger the price discounts and/or commissions that must be given up by the seller in order to effect a quick sale.

The **bid–asked spread** is a transaction cost for exchanging an asset. The bid price is the highest price bid by potential buyers. It is always below the asked price, as shown in Figure 3-2b. The asked price is the lowest price at which potential sellers offer to sell.

The bid–asked spread can be thought of as being the amount the seller has to give up to sell the asset quickly. This seller's loss equals the broker's commission for

Box 18-4

DEFINITION: Liquidity Risk

Liquidity risk is that portion of an asset's total variability of return which results from price discounts, sales commissions paid by the seller, and any other concessions that must be given in order to liquidate an asset hastily.

---

handling the transaction plus the dealer's inducement to carry the asset in inventory until a new buyer can be found. A highly liquid common stock like IBM or General Motors will have a bid–asked spread of about 12.5 to 25 cents per share. A less liquid stock might have a larger bid–asked spread. Liquidity (or marketability) risk is an important factor to consider when selecting investments.[3]

18-6   Political Risk Factors

In any country in the world, various groups endeavor to improve their relative positions by competing in the political arena. The goods or privileges allocated via political processes have direct dollar costs (for example, tax laws) or can have dollar costs imputed to them (the costs of environmental damage, for instance). Whether the changes are sought by political, social, or economic interests, the resulting variability of return is called *political risk* if it is accomplished through political manipulation of the legislative, judicial, or administrative branches of the government.

The International Political Risk Factor

International investors face political risk in the form of expropriation of nonresidents' assets, foreign exchange controls that do not let investors change their foreign funds into dollars, disadvantageous tax and tariff treatments, requirements that nonresident investors give partial ownership to local residents, unreimbursed destruction of foreign-owned assets by hostile residents of the foreign country, and other costly actions. Foreign investors make allowances for **international political risk** by requiring higher expected rates of return from foreign than from domestic investments, by obtaining written guarantees from high-level government officials, and by using nonrecourse financing provided by the foreign country to finance their foreign investments.

Not all political risk is international; domestic political risk can also affect investment decisions.

[3] For a statistical analysis of the determinants of the bid–asked spread see Seha Tinic, "The Economics of Liquidity Services," *Quarterly Journal of Economics,* February 1972. For an easy-to-read discussion that goes into more detail than this chapter see Jack Clark Francis, *Investments: Analysis and Management,* 5th ed. (New York: McGraw-Hill, 1991), pp. 84–86.

Box 18-5

> DEFINITION: Political Risk
>
> **Political risk** is the variability in incomes and asset values that arises from actions by federal, state, or local governments or governmental bodies.

The Domestic Political Risk Factor

Domestic political risk takes the form of environmental regulations, zoning requirements, fees, licenses, and, most frequently, taxes of one form or another. The taxes may be property taxes, sales taxes, income taxes, or employment taxes. Such taxes are levied on a readily identifiable group, such as owners of real estate, buyers of luxury or "sinful" goods (such as the consumers of liquor), high-income earners, or

463

employers. The passage of new tax laws or the modification of previously existing taxes can be significant and difficult to forecast; so, investors must cope with political uncertainty.

Political Risk and Value

The effects of political risk on investment values can be analyzed using the discounted present value of cash dividends valuation model from Chapter 13. This model states that the present value of a share of stock equals the discounted present value of all cash dividends the share is expected to pay to its owners from now (that is, time period $t = 0$) to infinity:

$$P_0 = \frac{D_1}{(1 + k)^1} + \frac{D_2}{(1 + k)^2} + \frac{D_3}{(1 + k)^3} + \cdots$$

where D_t is the cash dividend per share paid in time period t, k is the risk-adjusted discount rate (from Figure 10-1, for example), and P_0 is the stock's present value.

Political risk can change the value of the share of common stock in the present value model above in two different ways. First, if a new corporate income tax is imposed or an existing income tax is raised, the firm would not be able to pay investors cash dividends as large as those expected before the tax increase. This politically legislated tax would therefore reduce the investment's value.

The second way political risk can cause variability in common stock value is through risk changes, as shown in Box 13-2. Care must be taken to avoid "double counting" when risk adjustments are made, however. If cash dividends were correctly adjusted in the numerator of the present value of cash dividends model, only pure risk changes justify a further adjustment to the discount rate in the denominator.[4]

18-7 The Call Risk Factor

As we saw in Chapters 2 and 3, some issues of bonds and preferred stock are accompanied by a provision allowing the issuer to call, or repurchase, the securities before they mature. Issuers like the call provisions because it allows them to replace outstanding fixed-payment securities with a newer issue if market interest rates drop below the level being paid on the older issue. Whatever the issuing

---

[4] For further discussion see Tamir Agmon and M. Chapman Findlay, "Domestic Political Risk and Stock Valuation," *Financial Analysts Journal*, November–December, 1982, pp. 3–6.

Box 18-6

> DEFINITION: Call Risk
>
> That portion of a security's total variability of return derived from the possibility that the issue may be called by its issuer is the **call risk factor.**

465

*Chapter 18
Purchasing-
Power Risk
and Other
Risk Factors*

company gains by calling in an issue is at the expense of the investors who had their securities called. Investors should view the call provision as a threat that may deprive them of a good investment at a time when they can reinvest their funds only at a lower yield.

Call risk commands a risk premium in the form of a slightly higher expected rate of return. This additional return should increase as the probability that the issue will be called rises. The categories below show how the call risk increases as more terms are attached to the call provision.

1. Securities that are noncallable at any time during their life have zero call risk.

2. An issue that is noncallable for refunding (or rolling over with a new issue), but that can be redeemed with funds from sources other than a refunding (such as retained earnings) is the category second-best protected from call risk.

3. The third category is the largest and most difficult to define because it involves one or both of two different kinds of call protection. One kind of protection is a stipulation that the issue may not be called for a certain number of years, but is callable on short notice after that period ends. The other kind of call protection is a call premium that allows the issuer to call the securities at any time, but only at a premium (10 percent, for example) over the face value of the callable securities. The risk protection from these provisions increases with the number of years before the call may be allowed and/or with the size of the call premium.

4. Callability risk is greatest with issues that are callable at any time on short notice. These securities may pay risk premiums as much as seven- or eight-tenths of a percentage point more yield than an equivalent issue that is not callable under any conditions.[5]

18-8 The Convertibility Risk Factor

Call risk and convertibility risk are similar. First, both provisions are contractual stipulations that are included in the terms of the original security issue. Second, both provisions alter the variability of return (that is, the risk) of the security.

---

[5] For more information about callable securities see Edwin Elton and Martin Gruber, "The Economic Value of the Call Option," *Journal of Finance,* September 1972. Also see Gordon Pye, "The Value of a Call Option on a Bond," *Journal of Political Economy,* April 1966, and Gordon Pye, "The Value of Call Deferment on a Bond: Some Empirical Results," *Journal of Finance,* December 1967.

Box 18-7

DEFINITION: Convertibility Risk

Convertibility risk is that portion of the total variability of return that a convertible bond or preferred stock investor experiences because of the contractual possibility that the investment may be converted into the issuer's common stock under terms that modify the value of the investment.

Sometimes bonds and preferred stocks are issued with the stipulation that they may be converted into the issuing corporation's common stock if the investor wishes to do so (as explained in Chapters 2 and 3). The convertibility right attached to these bonds and/or preferred stocks gives investors the implicit (or embedded) option to buy shares of the corporation's common stock at some future date for some stipulated price by using the face value of the bond or preferred stock to pay for the purchase. The value of the conversion right of a security can be assessed by comparing the price of a similar nonconvertible security with the price of the convertible.[6]

Summary

An investment is a multifaceted opportunity to earn a profitable return or suffer losses.

A wise investor should compare the current inflation rate with the nominal rates of return from different potential investments to see if the investments' real rates of return are positive or negative. Investors should focus on the real returns to select the opportunities that will maximize their purchasing power.

An analysis of sample portfolios of different investments reveals that common stocks issued by small corporations have the highest long-run real returns of any of the securities considered, while Treasury bills display the weakest inflation-adjusted performance. The summary statistics presented in this chapter show that although the monetary assets listed in Figure 1-4 and Table 18-3 lost some purchasing power to the rising price level, there are *varying degrees* of undiversifiable purchasing-power risk. If basic economic conditions change, these historical-average relationships are likely to change too. However, it is reasonable to generalize and say that monetary assets will usually be poorer inflation hedges than real assets because real assets usually maintain their purchasing power during inflationary periods.

Liquidity risk is that portion of an asset's total variability of return that results from price discounts, sales commissions paid by the seller, and any other concessions the seller must grant to liquidate an asset *hastily*. Political risk is the variability of return that results from actions stemming from or revolving around federal, state, or local governments or governmental bodies. That portion of a security's total variability of return that is derived from the possibility that the issue may be called by its issuer before its maturity date is the call risk. Convertibility risk is that portion of the total variability of return a convertible security investor experiences because of the contractual possibility that the investment may be converted into the issuer's common stock under terms that modify its value.

Each of the non-purchasing-power risk factors may or may not be present in any given security. U.S. Treasury bills, for instance, suffer no liquidity, callability, convertibility, default, or management (the topic of Chapter 19) risk. Common stock, in contrast, can suffer from default, management, interest rate, political, and market

[6] Convertible securities are discussed by Michael J. Brennan and Eduardo S. Schwartz, "Analyzing Convertible Bonds," *Journal of Financial and Quantitative Analysis,* vol. 15, no. 4, 1980, pp. 907–929. In addition, see Milton Harris and Artur Raviv, "A Sequential Signaling Model of Convertible Debt Call Policy," *Journal of Finance,* vol. 40, no. 5, 1985, pp. 1263–1281.

risk. In addition, securities that are traded infrequently (like municipal bonds) can suffer from liquidity risk. Each different investment opportunity must be evaluated in order to determine the risk factors it involves and the compensation for bearing them.

Stocks, Bonds, Bills and Inflation: Yearbook (Chicago: R. G. Ibbotson Assoc.).
This empirical study compares the returns from common stocks, corporate bonds, Treasury bills and T-bonds with the consumer price index. The easy-to-read book contains many tables of informative data from 1925 to the latest yearbook.

U.S. Department of Commerce, Bureau of Economic Analysis, *Survey of Current Business* (Washington, D.C.: U.S. Government Printing Office).
This monthly U.S. government publication may be subscribed to for $29 a year; it contains numerous time series of economic data and attractive charts of the data that are useful in analyzing the business cycle.

Essay Questions

18-1   Define the following terms, and explain how they are related: (*a*) nominal rate of interest, (*b*) rate of inflation, (*c*) real rate of interest, and (*d*) risk premium. *Hint:* Check the Fisher equation, Equation (17-2), and the associated discussion.

18-2   Explain how the market price of a U.S. Treasury bond that has 10 years until it matures would probably be affected by an increase in the rate of inflation from 5 percent to 10 percent per annum.

18-3   Does purchasing-power risk pose more of a threat to working people who are starting their career or to older people who have already retired? Explain.

18-4   (*a*) Define the phrase "inflation hedge." (*b*) Which of the following two categories of investment assets is the better hedge against inflation—real assets (such as real estate, homes, diamonds, gold, silver, and rental property) or monetary assets (such as savings account deposits, cash, and/or bond investments)? Why is one a better inflation hedge? (*c*) What factors unrelated to purchasing-power risk should also be considered in selecting between these two categories of investment assets?

18-5   Consider how inflation might affect people who borrow money and people who lend money. Does inflation help or hinder debtors and creditors in any way? Explain.

18-6   Why do convertible bonds from a given firm sell at a lower yield-to-maturity than nonconvertible bonds issued by the same firm that are identical in every respect except the convertibility feature?

18-7   Assume a well-to-do relative died and willed you $900,000. Inheritance and estate taxes took one-third of it, leaving you a net inheritance of $600,000. When you receive the $600,000, it is invested in a diversified portfolio of common stocks. This portfolio earns $20,000 per year in cash dividends for you. It also earns about $30,000 per year, on average, in capital gains. The bank trust officer who managed this portfolio for your deceased benefactor gives you the following recommendations: (*a*) Leave the portfolio with the bank's trust department to be managed, since they are professional money managers. (*b*) You can safely consume the $20,000 per year in cash dividends from the portfolio. (*c*) Do not sell off any of the stocks in order to consume part of the $600,000 principal. This would reduce your dividend-earning principal and thus decrease your future years' income. (*d*) If you follow this advice, you will be able to consume $400 per week (that is, the $20,000 per year in cash dividends) for the rest of your life. This plan assures you that you will have absolutely no worry about decreasing your principal. What do you think of the bank trust officer's advice? Does the advice ignore inflationary effects? Can you think of better guidelines than those offered by the banker? Explain.

Problems

18-8 Suppose that a representative basket of consumer goods cost $200 on January 1, 19X6, and that the same basket cost $242 on January 1, 19X8. What was the rate of inflation per year for 19X6 and 19X8? Show your calculations. *Hint:* See Equation (17-1).

18-9 Suppose you purchased IBM common stock at $130 per share and sold it 6 months later for $150 per share. During these 6 months the stock paid a $6 cash dividend per share. (*a*) What was your annualized nominal rate of return? Further suppose that the CPI rose from 110 to 115.5 during the same 6-month period. (*b*) What was the annualized rate of inflation? (*c*) What was the real rate of return from your 6-month investment in IBM? *Hint:* See Equations (17-1) and (18-3).

18-10 If your money earns a nominal rate of interest of 12 percent per year while inflation is 6 percent, (*a*) how long will it take your invested dollars to double? (*b*) How much will the purchasing power of your dollars increase while your number of dollars doubles in this inflationary investment environment?

18-11 Suppose a woman who is in the 34 percent income tax bracket has all her money invested in a savings account that pays a guaranteed interest rate of 10 percent. If the rate of inflation is 5 percent, (*a*) what is this woman's real rate of return before taxes? *Hint:* Use Equation (18-3). (*b*) What is her real rate of return after taxes? *Hint:* Equation (18-3) must be extended to include the appropriate income tax deductions.

18-12 Answer the following question from the level I, 1983 CFA exam:
The following regression equation describes the relationship between the annual percentage change in the stock of money (M1) and the annual percentage change in retail sales of automobile units.

Percent change
 in retail auto = −.295 + 4.4(percent change in M1)
 sales in units

Based on the regression and the following table of expected M1 growth under three economic scenarios, calculate the expected percent change in automobile units sold during the next 12 months. Show your calculations.

Economic scenario	Percent change in M1	Probability
1	6%	.3
2	8%	.5
3	10%	.2

469

*Chapter 18
Purchasing-
Power Risk
and Other
Risk Factors*

18-13   Maria has almost finished the table below that shows the different investment returns required to yield a 2 percent real rate of return after taxes under various assumptions about the rate of inflation. Can you fill in the blanks?

Marginal income tax rate	Rate of inflation (INF)				
	4.0%	5.0%	6.0%	7.0%	8.0%
25%	8.0%	9.3%	10.7%	12.0%	13.3%
30	8.6				14.3
35	9.3				15.4
40	10.0	11.7	13.4	15.0	16.7

18-14   Bob Meyers retired in 19X1 at the age of 65 as a salesman at a department store. Mr. Meyers and his family were thrifty people who worked hard and saved their money; they had accumulated $60,000, which was all invested in a conservatively managed mutual fund. In addition to their own residence, the Meyers family owns two small homes that it rents to responsible tenants. Over the years the family has completely paid off the three mortgages on the homes and owes no debts to anyone. Mr. and Mrs. Meyers enjoy good health in their retirement. Mr. Meyers works as a part-time salesclerk during busy seasons and when vacations create temporary openings at the store where he had been personnel director. The Meyers' retirement income is listed below, along with the CPI.

Year	Social Security	Rental income*	Hourly wages	Mutual fund†	Total income	CPI
19X2	$4000	$2000	$2300	$2500	$11,800	171.5
19X3	4200	3100	2000	2700	12,000	188.1
19X4	4400	3100	2500	2600	12,600	202.0
19X5	4400	3400	1900	2800	12,500	229.9
19X6	4600	3400	1100	3000	12,100	258.4
19X7	4600	3500	1600	3100	12,800	281.0

* Net after property taxes, insurance, maintenance, and other expenses.

† The mutual fund income includes only cash dividends.

(*a*) What has the family income been, in constant (that is, inflation-adjusted) 19X2 dollars since Mr. Meyers' retirement? (*b*) Which sources of income involve the most (and the least) purchasing-power risk? (*c*) Do you anticipate any future problems for the Meyers family? Explain.

Matching Questions

18-15   Match the following risk factors with their correct definitions.

Risk factor	Definition
C 1. Purchasing-power risk	A. The portion of an asset's total risk which is caused by discounts and selling commissions which must be given up to sell it
G 2. Bull and bear market risk	B. Variability of return caused by the fact that a security may legally be called by its issuer for an early redemption

Risk factor	Definition
A 3. Liquidity risk	C. Variability of return caused by changes in the price level
F 4. Political risk	D. Variability of return caused by the fact that a debt security may be converted into a common stock
B 5. Callability risk	E. The aggregate variability of return an asset derives from all its risk factors
D 6. Convertibility risk	F. The portion of an asset's total variability of return caused by changes in the political environment that affects the asset's price
E 7. Total risk	G. Variability of return caused by simultaneous fluctuations in the prices of most securities in a market

Multiple Choice Questions

18-16 The real rate of return may be accurately described by which of the following?

D

(*a*) It is an inflation-adjusted interest rate.
(*b*) It is the rate at which an investor's purchasing power changes.
(*c*) The market value of the investor's portfolio is rising steadily.
(*d*) Both (*a*) and (*b*) are true.
(*e*) All the above are true.

18-17 Which of the following investment situations will always enhance an investor's economic welfare?

C

(*a*) The nominal rate of return is positive.
(*b*) The rate of inflation is zero.
(*c*) The real rate of return is positive.
(*d*) The market price of the investor's portfolio is rising.

18-18 When the rate of inflation accelerates from 3 percent to 6 percent, the market (or nominal) interest rates tend to do which of the following? *Hint:* See Equation (17-2).

C

(*a*) Decline
(*b*) Be less than real interest rates
(*c*) Increase by about 300 basis points
(*d*) Rise and fall with the unemployment rate

18-19 Which of the following statements accurately describes nominal interest rates?

A

(*a*) They are identical with market interest rates.
(*b*) They are less than real interest rates.
(*c*) They don't fluctuate much.
(*d*) They tend to rise and fall with the unemployment rate.
(*e*) Both (*a*) and (*c*) are true.

18-20 Which of the following will help minimize the purchasing-power risk in investing?

C

(*a*) Seek out bond investments whose interest rates do not vary much.
(*b*) Seek assets with high positive nominal rates of return.

(c) Seek assets with high positive real rates of return.
(d) Do not invest during inflationary periods.
(e) Follow both (b) and (d).

471

*Chapter 18
Purchasing-
Power Risk
and Other
Risk Factors*

18-21   If money is saved at a 7 percent rate of interest for a year in which the inflation rate is 8 percent, which of the following is the saver's real rate of return?

(a) Negative one percent
(b) Zero
(c) Positive one percent
(d) Seven percent

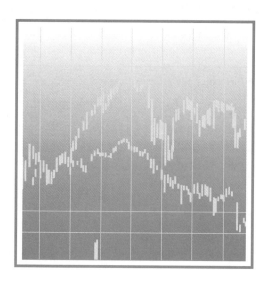

CHAPTER 19

MANAGEMENT RISK AND OTHER RISK FACTORS

This chapter analyzes management risk from three perspectives. First, some management errors are examined to provide examples of how incompetent managers can diminish the investors' wealth. Second, agency theory is used to explain more subtle sources of management risk. The chapter ends by drawing a distinction between diversifiable and undiversifiable management risk.

Box 19-1

> DEFINITION: Management Risk
>
> **Management risk** is that portion of the total variability of return experienced by an investor that can be attributed to decisions made by the agents (or people) the investor employs to manage the investments.

19-1 Who Is Responsible for Management Risk?

473

Chapter 19
Management
Risk and
Other Risk
Factors

Management errors are one cause of management risk. But sometimes the responsibility is hard to assign. Let us begin by considering some specific problems.

Acts of God

Some high-level executives earn princely salaries, occupy luxurious offices, and wield enormous power within their organizations. But these status symbols should not make us forget that even the very highest executive is merely mortal and capable of making a poor decision. Management risk can arise, for example, from the way an executive deals with so-called acts of God. An extraordinary interruption of events by a natural cause is called an **act of God.** Hurricanes, earthquakes, and bolts of lightning are examples. These extraordinary occurrences usually entail great costs to those involved, and they cannot be foreseen or prevented.

Agricultural Losses   Those who invest in agricultural goods and agricultural futures contracts traded at commodity exchanges suffer continual risk exposure from acts of God such as floods; droughts; hordes of insects; and epidemics of fungus, blight, or disease that affects plants and animals. A month-long summer drought in the midwestern part of the United States will harm the corn, wheat, soybean, and other crops grown there. The diminished grain harvest expectations that result from the drought cause the prices of the grain commodities and the futures contracts on the grains to skyrocket. Well-managed farms will insure against drought losses by planting a diversified assortment of crops and/or by installing an irrigation system. Investors in commodity futures contracts and wise farmers will also use hedges set up at commodity futures exchanges to protect the value of their positions from such catastrophes.

Destruction of Corporate Assets   The same acts of God that regularly affect the prices of commodities and commodity futures contracts can also affect the value of a corporation's securities. Conscientious business managers can reduce the risk of great financial loss by insuring their plant, equipment, and key personnel, and taking other steps to prepare for catastrophes. When an act of God wreaks disaster upon a business firm, the costs of the misfortune typically fall on the firm's insurance company (if the firm has insurance), on any employees who may be harmed, and ultimately, on the firm's investors. Consider the eruption of Mount St. Helens in Washington State in May 1980 (Box 19-2).

Shortsighted executives have caused many companies to suffer financial losses from acts of God. Myopic management plans that fail to include insurance or other provisions for protection against acts of God reduce the value of the securities of these firms in the financial markets.

Product Obsolescence

Theoretically, a corporation can live forever if it is well managed. When share owners sell out or employees change jobs, die, or retire, new people take their places. This transfer of roles enables businesses to survive for generations.

Box 19-2

FINANCIAL: The Mount St. Helens Eruption in 1980

Geologists estimate that Mount St. Helens spewed out about 1.5 cubic miles of debris. This stupendous explosion of trapped gases generated about 500 times the force of the atomic bomb dropped on Hiroshima in 1945. People were killed and millions of dollars worth of losses occurred. For example, the eruption destroyed 150 square miles of timber worth about $200 million (in 1980 dollars). Many of these losses would have been reduced if prudent business managers had built their facilities farther away from the volcano or purchased insurance against losses due to volcanic eruptions. Investors suffered financially when their investments were buried in volcanic ash.

Products, too, must sometimes be replaced if they grow old, go out of style, suffer decreasing usefulness, or otherwise become obsolete. It is up to management to overcome the problem of obsolescence by developing and maintaining active *research and development* (R&D) programs. A generous annual expenditure for R&D is a sign of a farsighted top management. For example, if the buggy manufacturers of 1900 had reinvested some of their profits in R&D, they might have survived in the 1930s as horseless carriage manufacturers. The steam engine manufacturers of the 1940s either learned to manufacture diesel locomotives to compete in the 1960s or had their customers pulled away by competitors who did. Manufacturers of black-and-white television sets in the 1950s had to develop color sets to compete in the markets of the 1960s. Today, Detroit's automotive giants must produce smaller, more fuel-efficient cars that have higher quality and lower price tags if they are to survive foreign-car competition in the 1990s. The product life cycle curve in Figure 13-3 shows in abstract form how management must work to avoid product obsolescence.

The road to corporate success is littered with bankrupt corporations that did not develop new products to replace obsolete ones. In many cases, blame can be directly attributed to management error: Not enough profits were spent to develop new products. Instead, nearsighted top managers tried to make bigger short-run profits by cutting R&D budgets. The short-run cost savings resulted in permanent losses for the firms' investors.

Maintaining Sales

A product usually becomes obsolete gradually over a period of years. In contrast, it is common for a business to lose customers abruptly because of competition. A firm that suddenly loses a sufficiently *large* customer can just as suddenly go bankrupt.

It is a management error to let a company become dependent on one customer or a few customers whose loss could financially embarrass the firm or even force it into bankruptcy. Every firm's top management should strive to develop a diversified customer base.

It is easy to obtain a diversified customer group in some industries. Retail department stores, supermarkets, dry cleaning stores, filling stations, airlines, and theaters, for example, usually do not depend on any one customer to maintain a profitable level of sales. However, some businesses are extremely dependent on one or a few customers. Any small firm that supplies only one product (say, rearview mirrors, floor carpets, or radio antennas) to an automobile manufacturer (like GM or Ford) or a large retail chain (like Sears Roebuck or J. C. Penney) is likely to be highly dependent on its giant customer. Small firms often lack the diversified sales force and manufacturing technology needed to get new customers and may exist solely to supply one customer. Investors should be wary of firms like these.

Manufacturers of defense equipment are another category of firms prone to have a poorly diversified list of customers. Top management may be composed of engineers who concentrate their efforts on developing a weapons system for the government of one country, for example. These managers may ignore the necessity of diversification into nondefense products until it is too late. Should the government that is their main customer impose a budget cut or reduce defense spending, the company will be left without any buyers.

475

*Chapter 19
Management
Risk and
Other Risk
Factors*

Box 19-3

FINANCIAL: Dynamic Leadership Governs Sears Expansion

In the mid-1920s America's farmers were starting to buy Model T cars and drive into town to shop. So Sears opened retail stores to expand its marketing channels beyond the original mail-order business. Then Sears centralized the buying and promotion for all its stores at its home office in Chicago to achieve economies of scale and specialization within these two separate administrative activities. At the same time, the stores were decentralized by allowing the individual store managers to arrange the stores to fit local conditions. In the 1930s Sears diversified by starting its own insurance company. Today, Allstate Insurance is a profitable part of Sears' total operation. In the mid-1950s Sears drastically changed its character, from a hardware-oriented store to a full-line department store. Then it diversified into the financial services industry in the early 1980s with the acquisition of the Dean Witter securities brokerage and investment banking firm, and the Coldwell Banker real estate business. As a result, Sears became a financial supermarket. In 1990 it announced it would start carrying brand name goods at prices that were below the manufacturers' list prices to make Sears stores more like discount stores. These strategies have made Sears a retailing giant. Its history furnishes a good example of how dynamic and flexible top management decision making helps a firm grow in an ever-changing world.*

* See J. McDonald, "Sears Makes It Look Easy," *Fortune*, May 1964. See also S. Furst and M. Sherman, eds., *Business Decisions That Changed Our Lives* (New York: Random House, 1964) and Eric N. Berg, "Sears Says It Will Cut 21,000 Jobs," *The New York Times*, Jan. 4, 1991, p. D1.

The Nixon administration's cutback in spending for the Vietnamese war in 1968 and 1969 is an example of how lack of diversified customers can hurt a large manufacturer. In 1969, sales to the U.S. government accounted for 89 percent of the total sales of Lockheed Aircraft. The firm manufactured missiles, cargo transport planes, antisubmarine aircraft, rocket motors, radar systems, and ground vehicles used in Vietnam. When the U.S. Department of Defense cut its outlays on these programs, Lockheed suffered greatly, as did thousands of its employees. Net sales decreased about 10 percent in 1968. In 1969 sales went down another 10 percent. These two 10 percent sales drops would have been larger were it not for the hasty addition of some less profitable new customers. Lockheed suffered multimillion-dollar losses in 1969 and 1970. In 1970 the firm nearly went bankrupt.

Although the company eventually survived, the effect of these losses on its common stock investors was horrendous. Lockheed's common stock price fell from a high of $73 per share in 1967 to a low of $7 per share in 1970; investors lost over 90 cents of every dollar they had invested in 1967. Undoubtedly, by 1970 these investors felt that the firm's management should have taken steps to diversify when things were rosy in 1967. In fact, after the near bankruptcy, the firm's top management included some new faces. The Sears Roebuck experience shows what can happen when top management is alert (Box 19-3).

Management Errors—An Infinite Variety

Not all management errors are so obvious as failure to insure against natural disasters, failure to invest in R&D, or dependence on one customer. Investors must also be wary of managers who make less glaring errors.

Executives can make so many different kinds of errors that we cannot cover all of them. However, we will review a few cases in order to get a feeling for what management risks investors should try to avoid. The situations described here are unlikely to recur precisely the same way again—they are unique. They are provided to broaden your appreciation of how wide a range of problem areas must be considered. Watching for management errors requires vigilance and sensitivity.

First, consider Detroit's initial attempt to market the economy-sized Corvair, discussed in Box 19-4.

It is not clear how GM should have handled the Nader affair. It is clear, however, that management error crippled sales of an automotive product that was years ahead of its time. The ill-fated Corvair was similar to the small economy cars so popular in the 1980s and 1990s. If GM's management had dealt more openly and honestly with Nader's charges, they might have ultimately been able to keep the Corvair as a profitable and increasingly popular product.

Another sort of management problem was experienced by National Cash Register (NCR). Although recently NCR has become an example of a well-managed firm, an inflexible management caused problems for the company in the 1970s, as seen in Box 19-5.

The NCR case documents two facts. First, good management can make a big difference in the performance of an investment. Second, bad management can be replaced by better managers.

Box 19-4

477

*Chapter 19
Management
Risk and
Other Risk
Factors*

FINANCIAL: Ralph Nader versus General Motors

In 1965 an unknown attorney, Ralph Nader, published a book entitled *Unsafe at Any Speed* that severely criticized a compact car manufactured by General Motors called the Corvair. The book documented how passengers in this small economy car were not so safe as passengers in larger, heavier cars that cost more money to purchase and operate. The book gave names and dates to document passenger injuries in Corvairs. Nader published statistics showing that the death rate from accidents in the Corvair was significantly higher than the death rate in full-sized cars. In more recent times, when higher gasoline prices have made small cars very popular, a book like Nader's would probably be dismissed. But when it was published in 1965, small cars were not very popular. As a result, the book was widely read and quoted, and GM experienced declining Corvair sales. The first Corvair had been sold in 1959. Sales peaked at 304,000 cars in 1962 and were down to only 15,000 in 1968, 3 years after *Unsafe at Any Speed* was published. In an effort to destroy Nader's credibility and dissuade him from making negative comments about its Corvair, GM harassed him.

Nader sued GM in 1966 for invasion of privacy. In his suit, Nader complained that GM had hired a private detective firm run by Vincent Gillen to tail him, make threatening and obnoxious phone calls to him at all hours, interrogate his acquaintances, tap his telephone, and cast aspersions on his integrity. After stalling Nader's case via a series of legal technicalities for 3½ years, GM settled out of court in 1970 for $425,000.

GM's out-of-pocket payoff to Nader does not represent an admission of guilt. However, it is suggestive. Furthermore, Mr. Gillen was quoted as saying he had been hired to shadow Nader, and James Roche, then president of GM, told a Senate subcommittee that the inquiry into Nader's affairs had been "most unworthy of American business." But more costly to GM than the $425,000 settlement was the fact that the corporation was forced to close down its entire Corvair operation in 1970 because of lack of demand. As a result of this shutdown, GM wrote off millions of dollars of losses on Corvair manufacturing equipment. GM management's handling of Ralph Nader not only embarrassed the firm, but also cost GM's investors dearly.*

* The New York Times, Jan. 9, 1970, p. 22, col. 1; The New York Times, Aug. 14, 1970, p. 1.

19-2 Agency Theory

This section investigates a category of management problems that is more subtle than those of the previous section. An economic theory called *agency theory* can help. Agency theory was developed in 1932 by Professors A. A. Berle and Gardiner Means.[1]

---

[1] A. A. Berle and Gardiner C. Means, *The Modern Corporation and Private Property* (New York: Macmillan, 1932).

Box 19-5

FINANCIAL: NCR Enters the Electronic Age

Until 1970, Dayton, Ohio–based NCR dominated the business machine field. NCR was a glamorous growth stock selling at $21 per share for a price-earnings multiple of 63 times its 1970 earnings per share. The firm manufactured cash registers, adding machines, calculators, and accounting and bookkeeping machines and was attempting to enter the computer field.

J.C. Penney, Kroger Food, Sears, and other large retailing customers asked NCR to modernize its mechanical cash registers. The big retailers wanted computerized point-of-sale information-entry systems that would update inventory records every time a sale was rung up. At that time, the Singer Corporation happened to be interested in diversifying its operations and thus was eager to develop the desired point-of-sale electronic cash register systems. NCR's top management resisted and continued to make mechanical cash registers.

> Puzzled critics attributed NCR's inertia to a "Dayton" mentality. With a long record of corporate success to look back on, the company's top managers often tended to look backward instead of forward. To visitors' eyes, the NCR complex in Dayton seemed old-fashioned in appearance, customs, and style. "We had a living retirement program going on here," one vice president recalls.
>
> NCR spun such a tight cocoon around its Dayton operations that employees in other cities were called "outsiders." The computer division in California seemed to bear little relation to the electromechanical cash registers and accounting machines manufactured in Dayton. No one seemed able to muster the vision to connect the two.*

In mid-1970, NCR sales and profits started to decline. The common stock suffered as the stock's price fell from $21 a share to $8 and sold for only four times that year's earnings per share. Finally, things started to change in Dayton.

NCR's board of directors selected a new president and gave him full authority to make major changes. The Dayton work force was reduced from 15,700 to 2000 by 1976. Some top executives took early retirement; others found new jobs elsewhere. Seven senior managers were demoted. The new, leaner management ushered NCR into the electronic age. But the firm had gotten a late start. In the United States, both Singer and Pitney-Bowes had larger annual sales of electronic cash registers than NCR by the mid-1970s. NCR led the pack only in sales of mechanical cash registers, and this was not the big growth segment of the cash register industry.†

During the 1980s NCR perfected its electronic cash registers and was able to reassert the firm's dominance in the business machine field. NCR slipped by IBM in 1990 to become the world leader in the automated teller machine (ATM) business that was revolutionizing retail banking. Not everything was rosy for NCR, however. During the 1980s, personal computers had become very popular, and NCR joined the competition in that new arena. But it came up with a nonstandard personal computer (PC) that was not supported with much

479

*Chapter 19
Management
Risk and
Other Risk
Factors*

software. As a result, IBM, Apple, Compaq, Sun, Hewlett-Packard, DEC, and other computer manufacturers enjoyed growth rates in the PC market that were denied to NCR. Then, in 1990 NCR's CEO Charles Exley forced the company to move aggressively to the technology forefront by developing a fast, new desktop computer to work with Intel's 80486 chip.‡ NCR also lined up some software companies to provide the software needed to spur the sales of their new computer. American Telegraph and Telephone (AT&T) was so impressed by NCR's new computer technology and management skills that it acquired NCR in a $7 billion hostile takeover in 1990 to 1991.§ NCR had transformed itself from a tired old cash register company whose stock was selling for $8 per share in 1975 into an attractive, diversified, high-tech, $110 per share ATT takeover candidate in 1991.

* "What Happened at NCR after the Boss Declared Martial Law," *Fortune*, September 1975, p. 102.
† "The Coming Battle at the Supermarket Counter," *Fortune*, September 1975, p. 105; "Point of Sale Cash Registers Are Becoming a Growth Industry," *The New York Times*, July 7, 1964.
‡ "NCR Is Revamping Its Computer Lines in Wrenching Change," *The Wall Street Journal*, June 20, 1990, p. 1.
§ See "AT&T Seeks NCR Ousters," *The New York Times*, Jan. 3, 1991, p. D17. Also see Peter Coy, "Can AT&T Keep NCR's Clients On-Line?" *Business Week*, Jan. 14, 1991, p. 38.

Agency theory suggests that a corporation run by hired managers who own no stock would be worth less than a company run by owner-managers because the hired managers would not be motivated to work as hard to maximize the value of the owners' shares. Furthermore, the hired managers might consume more perquisites (such as chauffeur-driven company cars) than owner-managers. Over the years, a significant body of evidence in support of agency theory has accumulated.[2]

Table 19-1 summarizes some agency costs involved in principal-agent relationships that are of interest to investors. The first problem in Table 19-1, churning, is the only one that was previously discussed (see page 149) and the only one that is illegal.

[2] See W. J. Baumol, *Business Behavior, Value and Growth* (New York: Macmillan, 1959). Also see Robin Marris, *The Economic Theory of "Managerial" Capitalism* (London: Macmillan, 1964); Oliver E. Williamson, "Managerial Discretion and Business Behavior," *American Economic Review*, vol. 53, December 1963, pp. 1032–1057; and Robert J. Larner, *Management Control and the Large Corporation* (New York: Dunellen, 1970). More recently, see Michael C. Jensen and William H. Meckling, "Theory of the Firm: Managerial Behavior, Agency Costs and Ownership Structure," *Journal of Financial Economics*, vol. 3, 1976, 305–360, and Michael C. Jensen and William H. Meckling, "Rights and Production Functions: An Application to Labor-Managed Firms and Codetermination," *Journal of Business*, vol. 52, 1979, 469–506.

Box 19-6

> **DEFINITION: Agency Theory**
>
> **Agency theory** analyzes **principal-agency relationships.** The theory defines the stockholders of a corporation as the **principals** and the executives hired to manage the business as the share owners' **agents.** Within this corporate context, **agency costs** are the difference between what a corporation is worth if it is managed by its owners (or principals) versus the (presumably smaller) amount it would be worth if it were managed by hired executives acting as the absentee owners' agents.

Performance Shares for Top Executives

Some large corporations pay their top executives astronomically high salaries, give these executives free rein to work as hard or as little as they wish, place chauffeured limousines and corporate airplanes at their disposal, and provide luxurious offices and personal assistants. Granting such perquisites can become a problem because

Table 19-1
Principal-Agent Relationships Involve Agency Costs

Principal	Agent	Agency costs	Legal
Investor	Securities broker	Churning depletes the client's account.	No
Stockholders	Hired executives who own no stock	Perquisites, such as a chauffeur, huge salary, private plane, and "assistants."	Yes
Stockholders	Hired executives who own no stock	Costs of going private, namely, a reduced stock price to facilitate management's takeover.	Yes
Stockholders	Hired executives who own no stock	Greenmail paid to keep away potential buyers so incompetent managers can keep their jobs.	Yes
Stockholders	Hired executives who own no stock	Poison pills and golden parachutes to protect entrenched, inept top managers, paid with stockholders' money.	Yes
Stockholders	Executives who own voting stock	Classified common stock can be used to let entrenched managers reelect themselves even when incompetent.	Yes

corporations let the top managers award perquisites to themselves almost without control. As a result, some unscrupulous executives are overpaid and underworked, and live luxuriously at the expense of shareholders (or principals). How can shareholders who are absentee owners control the executives who are supposed to be working to maximize the value of their shares?

481

*Chapter 19
Management
Risk and
Other Risk
Factors*

There are laws against stealing, embezzlement, and other white-collar crimes. There are also proxy votes to allow shareholders to select someone other than themselves (who is presumably better informed) to vote their shares. There are management malpractice laws designed to protect the shareholders of a corporation from those who might gain control of the firm and manage it badly. But these laws are difficult to enforce. One way for shareholders to defend themselves against abuses by hired executives is to *establish a system of managerial incentives.*

In recent years financial research has uncovered an impressive amount of evidence documenting the *agency costs* inherent in the principal-agent relationship that exists between shareholders and their hired executives. As a result, more corporations are establishing **performance plans** to unify the interests of owners and hired managers. Some corporations give executives financial incentives to maximize profits. These firms supplement executive salaries by giving them stock in the corporation, called **performance shares,** for achieving high and growing earnings per share, rates of return in excess of the corporation's targeted level, or other criteria that tend to benefit shareholders. Managers who receive performance shares experience an increase in wealth whether or not the market price of the stock happens to rise, so this incentive cannot be ruined by temporary market downturns in the stock's price. Most corporations that give their executives performance shares stipulate that these shares do not vest (that is, ownership does not become permanent) until several years after the bonus is granted. The delayed vesting provision is designed to increase executive loyalty (or reduce management turnover).

Some shareholders view granting of performance shares to their corporation's executives as an extravagance. However, studies show that corporations who grant these incentives are more profitable than those that do not.

Taking a Corporation Private

From their privileged positions at the helm of a corporation, top management can sometimes see opportunities that are not visible to the absentee owners. When this happens, the top-level managers may take a corporation private: they get together to buy the corporation from the absentee owners. **Management buyouts,** or MBOs, often involve massive amounts of borrowing by the new owners that place the privately owned firm in danger of bankruptcy if the plan goes astray. Some people believe that gains for the executives who take over the corporation are gains that should have gone to the corporation's previous absentee owners (or the previous principals). To make matters even worse, it is in the interest of the acquisition-minded managers to try to drive down the market price of the shares of the corporation that employs them before they announce the MBO so they can later acquire those shares at a lower cost.

MBOs are actually a special kind of **leveraged buyout (LBO).** In 1988 a top management team at the Hospital Corporation of America borrowed $4.91 billion and purchased control of that corporation; the top managers of Montgomery Ward acquired control of that firm with $3.8 billion of borrowed funds in 1988; the top executives of the Fort Howard Paper Company purchased a controlling interest in that business by raising $3.58 billion in outside funds to finance their MBO in 1988; and in 1987 Morgan-Stanley helped finance the top managers of Burlington Industries when they acquired control from that firm's shareholders for $2.63 billion.

MBOs are legal. Unfortunately, some shareholders that sell to management in an MBO are being exploited by deceitful agents they hired to act as top executives. Some of these shareholders are voting to place more outside directors on the corporation's board, instead of the corporation's own top executives, to help them control top management.

Hostile Takeover Attempts and Greenmail

If a corporation has a good product, valuable natural resources, and/or widespread customer recognition, it may have an *intrinsic value* that exceeds its market price. Such underpriced firms make attractive targets for **corporate raiders.** In addition, if such a corporation is poorly managed, its earnings and market price per share may be depressed and the gap between its market price and its intrinsic value may be even larger. These underpriced and poorly managed firms are especially good candidates for a hostile takeover.

A **hostile takeover** occurs when an aggressive outside investor sets out to acquire enough stock of a **target corporation** to gain control of it and the management of the target corporation opposes the takeover. These takeover attempts are called *hostile* because it is typically the intention of the acquirer to change the management of the acquired firm. The acquirers often replace top managers with more aggressive executives. A typical takeover plan is to increase the profitability of the acquired firm and then resell it at a higher price a few years later.

Hostile takeovers involving large sums of money make headlines in the news media. T. Boone Pickens' (chairman of Mesa Petroleum) 1983 purchases of Gulf Oil stock, Carl Icahn's takeover of Trans World Airlines (TWA) in 1986, Ronald Perlman's takeover of Revlon in 1986, Sir James Goldsmith's acquisition of Crown-Zellerbach in 1985, and AT&T's takeover of NCR in 1990–91 are examples of widely publicized hostile takeovers.

Some hostile takeovers have consequences that are harmful to stockholders and/or the general population. For example, in order to prevent the hostile takeover of their firm in 1984, Texaco's management (acting as the agents of the corporation's shareholders) bought 13 million shares of Texaco stock from the Bass organization at $50 per share while the stock was selling on the NYSE at less than $40. The $130 million premium ($10 per share difference times 13 million shares) that management paid for Texaco stock represents an outlay of stockholders' cash that was paid as **greenmail** to the Bass organization, presumably so Texaco's executives would not lose their jobs in the threatened takeover. If Texaco's shareholders had been allowed to make this decision, they would probably have voted to let Bass take over. The price of their stock would have already been bid up, and in addition, the stockholders would still have had the $130 million of greenmail management paid Bass to protect their jobs. Greenmail is a form of blackmail that can grow out of the principal-agent relationship that exists between a corporation's shareholders and its executives—it is an agency cost. Greenmail payments are legal, although people argue that they should not be.

483

*Chapter 19
Management
Risk and
Other Risk
Factors*

Some people who do not understand corporate takeovers naively assume that all hostile takeovers are bad.[3] In truth, many hostile takeovers will benefit both stockholders and society at large. Each case must be evaluated on its individual merits.

Most hostile takeovers are beneficial for the stockholders—especially the owners of the acquired firm. For example, NCR's stock price was bid up from $70 to an all-time high of $110 per share in 1991 as AT&T acquired NCR. This aligned NCR's market price with its market value and enriched the owners of NCR stock by billions of dollars. Regardless of whether or not the takeover is beneficial for society at large, however, there are always some fired executives, laid-off blue-collar workers, disgruntled labor union leaders, or other complainers who claim that the corporate raiders are evil villains who are out to exploit the innocent.

Golden Parachutes and Poison Pills

There are many ways that top managers can legally extract millions of dollars from the pockets of the absentee owners of the corporation that employs them.

Golden Parachutes   Multimillion-dollar severance pay plans for each executive are sometimes arranged by those who fear they will lose their jobs in a hostile takeover. The executives who arrange these **golden parachutes** for themselves sometimes defend them on the grounds that, because the parachutes will financially cripple the corporation that employs them, they will discourage hostile takeovers. Of course, a better defense would be for top management to work hard to maximize the value of investors' shares so the takeover would be too expensive to tempt corporate raiders.

Poison Pills   Self-destructive measures that corporate top managers arrange to make their corporation unattractive to suitors are called **poison pills.** Examples include Disney's decision to sell large blocks of its stock to "friendly" investors at lower-than-market prices in the event of a hostile takeover attempt. The Carleton Corporation provided huge retirement bonuses to its executives in case they were deposed in a takeover. The payments were so large they constituted a major portion of the corporation's assets and made the firm too costly to be a desirable acquisition. Some corporate managers have written debt contract provisions so that millions of

---

[3] In an effort to attract new businesses, the state of Pennsylvania enacted laws to make it more difficult for corporate raiders to carry out hostile takeovers in that state. But, responsible executives at several Pennsylvania corporations asked to be exempted from these protective laws because they realized that the laws reduced the demand for their stock and thus tended to lower the share prices. For information, see Jonathan M. Karpoff and Paul H. Malatesta, "Evidence on State Antitakeover Laws," *Financial Analysts Journal*, July-August 1990, pp. 8–13. For more details see Jonathan M. Karpoff and Paul H. Malatesta, "The Wealth Effects of Second-Generation State Takeover Legislation," *Journal of Financial Economics*, vol. 25, no. 2, December 1989, pp. 291–322.

dollars of debt come due for payment whenever a hostile takeover is completed, effectively bringing the firm close to bankruptcy. The cost of such schemes is an agency cost that shareholders unwillingly but unknowingly pay to support managers who should be replaced.

Classified Common Stock

For years U.S. government officials went into communist and socialist countries around the world and extolled the virtues of their competitive business system—they called it **democratic capitalism.** They explained that democratic capitalism allowed even the poorest citizen to buy a share in the biggest corporation and thereby have some voice in its management. As we saw in Chapter 3, however, classified common stock eliminates the "one share, one vote" principle that underlies democratic capitalism.

Classified common stock typically means a corporation has Class A common stock as nonvoting, dividend-paying stock that is sold to the public. Class B common stock is voting stock held by management, which therefore controls the firm. Class B pays no dividends, but the owners can benefit from capital appreciation.[4]

Issuing classified common stock is one way for the management of a corporation to stop corporate raiders from tendering hostile takeover offers that threaten their job security. Executives simply use their Class B common stock, which has voting power, to vote down any unwanted offers. In 1924 the New York Stock Exchange stopped listing issues of nonvoting, classified stock. When the General Motors (GM) Corporation came out with its class E stock with the acquisition of the Electronics Data Systems (EDS) Corporation in 1984, however, the prospect of not being able to trade GM shares denied the NYSE so much brokerage commission income that the exchange changed its long-standing policy of delisting corporations that issued classified stock. A few years later the NYSE forbade *new listings* (which typically trade in low volume) from having classified stock, while permitting the large, old firms like GM to continue with their classified stock. Some top-level SEC administrators made public statements in favor of the "one share, one vote" principle, but so far no national policy has been mandated to resolve the matter.

The principal-agent problems discussed in this section involve agency costs that investors should seek to avoid because the money comes out of their pockets. A written ethics code for top management should be installed, incentive pay systems should be initiated, classified common stock should be eliminated, luxurious perquisites should be denied, poison pills and golden parachutes should be disallowed, greenmail should not be paid, and very few members of the board of directors should be employees of the corporation. Absentee shareholders should strive to control the agents they hire to manage their business.

---

[4] Important investigations into classified common stock have been published by H. DeAngelo and L. DeAngelo, "Managerial Ownership of Voting Rights: A Study of Public Corporations with Dual Classes of Common Stock," *Journal of Financial Economics,* vol. 14, 1985, pp. 33–69. Also see M. Partch, "The Creation of a Class of Limited Voting Common Stock and Shareholders' Wealth," *Journal of Financial Economics,* vol. 18, no. 2, June 1987, pp. 313–340.

19-3 Diversifiable and Undiversifiable Management Risk

485

*Chapter 19
Management
Risk and
Other Risk
Factors*

In normal times some unfortunate executive decisions do occur and cause losses, because executives make human errors under even the best of circumstances. Normal management errors result in what is called **diversifiable management risks;** they occur unsystematically (or at random). Investors can guard against unsystematic losses by diversifying their holdings across securities from different companies—that is why these risks are called *diversifiable management risks.*

But suppose that when extenuating circumstances occur (such as the emergence of tough foreign competition, new pollution-control regulations, a recession, or higher petroleum prices) the rate of management errors *quadruples* in those firms that are affected. In this oversimplified scenario, rational investors would be reluctant to invest in the common stocks of corporations they believed had weak managements that were subject to systematic pressures of any kind. Equation (19-1) illustrates how, under extenuating circumstances, the market price would drop and the expected return would rise for one of the corporations perceived to have weak management.

$$\uparrow E(r) = \frac{\text{capital gains or losses } + \text{ cash dividends, if any}}{\downarrow \text{ purchase price}} \qquad (19\text{-}1)$$

If all corporations with weak managements reacted this way, it would cause a systematic market price movement. Under such conditions investors could not protect themselves from the associated losses by simply diversifying their holdings. That is why this is called **undiversifiable management risk.** Securities perceived by investors to involve undiversifiable management risks would have to pay higher rates of return (or risk premiums) to get investors to buy them.[5]

Assessing the management risk factor is more subjective than evaluating many other risk factors (for example, default risk, where explicit financial ratios can be calculated and compared). An infinite number of potential problems must be considered.

Acts of God are beyond the control of any business executive. However, good managers will have contingency plans and insurance coverage to sustain the firm. Product obsolescence, in contrast, may be foreseen, and R&D can be undertaken to avoid it. Unfortunately, some executives may fail to notice that demand for their product is declining. The loss of an important customer is traumatic to any firm, so a well-managed firm will endeavor to maintain a diversified list of customers. All customers are free to change suppliers, and most customers do so periodically; this is why management should always avoid dependence on one or a few customers.

---

[5] See W. S. Kim, J. C. Francis, and J. W. Lee, "Investment Performance of Common Stocks in Relation to Inside Ownership," *The Financial Review*, vol. 23, no. 1, February 1988, pp. 53–64. For supporting evidence see C. D. Hudson, J. S. Jehara, Jr., and W. P. Lloyd, "Further Evidence on the Relationship between Ownership and Performance," *Financial Review,* vol. 27, no. 2, May 1992, pp. 227–239.

The list of possible management errors is very long. Also, each problem with which management must deal is unique. A corporation's managers are under continuous pressure to handle whatever problems arise so that investors in the firm will not suffer. Thus, investors need to scrutinize the management of a firm before investing in it.

Agency theory offers insights for discerning some subtle management problems. Executives who lavish costly perquisites on themselves, use MBOs to take over and exploit their former employer, insert poison pills into the corporation that employs them to protect their jobs by preventing takeovers, and issue classified common stock to enable them to maintain control of the corporation that employs them are the adversaries of the principals (or absentee owners) that employ them.

Further Reading

Hampton, David R., *Management*, 3d ed. (New York: McGraw-Hill, 1986).

Harlow, J. Heneman, "The Financial Analyst and Management," *Readings in Financial Analysis*, 2d ed. (Homewood, Ill.: Irwin, 1970).

Henderson, Richard, *Performance Appraisal* (Reston, VA.: Reston, 1980).

Questions and Problems

Essay Questions

19-1   Suppose that a medical research group has broken away from a reputable university and then publicly announces the development of a new kind of cigarette that absolutely does not increase the smokers' risks of contracting lung cancer and heart disease. The researchers are highly reputable medical doctors and technicians, and their findings are well supported by clinical studies. Furthermore, these researchers have incorporated and are preparing to mass-produce their revolutionary new smoking product under the brand name of SafeSigarets. As an investor, how would you react to the opportunity to invest in this emerging corporation and its new smoking technology? Explain your approach to this investment opportunity.

19-2   What are the advantages and the disadvantages of corporate research and development expenditures from the investors' point of view?

19-3   Compare and contrast a centralized top management structure with a decentralized top management structure. Which is better? Why? [Hint: For outside reading see Chapter 9 of David R. Hampton, *Management*, 3d ed. (New York: McGraw-Hill, 1986).]

19-4   Does a corporation's board of directors serve the common stockholders' interests in any way? Explain why, or why not.

19-5   Think about the investor as being the principal and the securities broker as being the investor's agent. Are there any potential agency problems inherent in the usual client-broker relationships?

19-6   Shaw Stores is a retail chain that was one of the first companies in the United States to offer both its blue-collar and white-collar employees a generous retirement plan if they stayed with the firm for over 10 years. Under this plan the retirement benefits increased directly with the length of time the employee stayed with Shaw Stores. Someone who had worked as a janitor in Shaw Stores for 30 or more years, for example, could retire with an income equal to 70

487

*Chapter 19
Management
Risk and
Other Risk
Factors*

percent of his or her working wages—an unusually high percentage for a blue-collar employee. Some of Shaw's stockholders have complained that the corporation should cut back on the employees' retirement benefits and use the money saved to pay higher cash dividends to Shaw's common stockholders. What do you think of Shaw's management policy about employee retirement benefits? Explain the implications of your thinking for potential investors in Shaw's common stock.

19-7   Dr. C. F. Lee is the 86-year-old chairman of the board and chief executive officer of the Lee Corporation. Although Dr. Lee founded the corporation years ago, he and his family controlled only about 30 percent of the outstanding shares of stock in the corporation in 1990. Dr. Lee gave up the majority of the voting stock in what he calls "his company" years ago when he issued common stock on several occasions to finance the growth of the firm. In nominating people to be on the Lee Corporation's board of directors, Dr. Lee prefers to nominate only senior executives from the Lee Corporation because he says their years of experience with the firm make them expert in its management. Do you agree with Dr. Lee, or do you think the firm should have a majority of outside directors? Explain.

19-8   In recent years the IBM Corporation has spent almost 10 cents out of every dollar's sales on research, development, and engineering. Each year when the firm budgets these billions of dollars, it is not certain whether or not any profitable developments will be forthcoming from the various think tanks, laboratories, and other research facilities that are supported. And even if something profitable is developed, years may pass from the time when the research was undertaken until a profitable product is actually ready to go on sale. How can IBM's top management justify these large outlays in view of the uncertainty and lengthy delays involved?

19-9   Do you think the United States needs legislation outlawing the agency problems outlined in Table 19-1? Explain why or why not.

19-10   In addition to its original $1.666 par value per share common stock, the General Motors Corporation (GM) also has class E and class H classified common stocks. Do you think GM's top management established the classified common stocks to protect itself from hostile takeovers? Explain why or why not. [*Hint:* Check an annual report from GM (or Moody's or Standard & Poor's) to find out the purpose of its classes E and H.]

Matching Questions

19-11   Match the management words and phrases listed below with the most appropriate definitions or descriptions.

Word or phrase	*Definition or description*
1. Undiversifiable management risk	A. Difference in expenses at owner-managed and employee-managed firms
2. Compensation incentives	B. Some combination of salary and bonuses that links an executive's income to the shareholders' wealth
3. Outside director	C. A member of the board who is not an employee of the corporation
4. Agency cost	D. Costly management errors that occur systematically at the worst times

19-12 Match the management evaluation words and phrases listed below with the most appropriate information-gathering technique for the potential investor to employ.

Aspect of management being evaluated	*Appropriate inquiry*
1. Board of directors	A. Look for telecommunications, inflation-adjusted financial statements in annual report, and compliance with federal pollution and hiring guidelines.
2. Long-range growth and profit plans	B. Look for bonuses, stock options, and other executive incentive plans designed to minimize agency costs.
3. Management of profits	C. Check annual report for outside directors and, at least, quarterly meetings.
4. Modern management techniques	D. Check annual report for R&D expenditures and diversified sales.
5. Incentive compensation plan	E. Check for profit and, at least, sales data broken out by product line and/or subsidiary, and compare rates of return with competitors.

Multiple Choice Questions

19-13 The Chevrolet Corvair is best described by which one of the following statements?

(*a*) A small economy car that was the subject of Ralph Nader's book *Unsafe at Any Speed.*

(*b*) Detroit's first entry into the American compact car market that foreign cars came to dominate in the decades that followed.

(*c*) An example of how mismanagement of a public information problem can cost a corporation a profitable product that was probably destined for decades of future profits.

(*d*) An unfortunate case in which a well-intentioned Ralph Nader did more to hurt the United States than help it. After all, the subcompact foreign cars that are popular in the United States today are probably no safer than the U.S.-built Corvair of the 1960s, and at least the Corvair would have provided jobs for Americans.

(*e*) All the above are true.

19-14 The consumption by top-level corporate executives of excessive amounts of nonpecuniary benefits such as expensive chauffeur-driven autos, private plane services, luxurious meetings scheduled at glamour spots, and special residences can be explained best by which of the following statements?

(*a*) The high-consumption-oriented top executives are simply enjoying pleasures to which they are entitled because they were denied such luxuries as junior executives when they were working their way up the "corporate ladder."

(*b*) High consumption of nonpecuniary benefits by top executives is an agency cost that is inherent in the principal-agent relationship between employed managers and stockholders who are the absentee owners that employ the managers.

(*c*) High consumption of expense account benefits by executives is evidence of bad management, because the firm needs more expense account spending guidelines.

(*d*) Both (*a*) and (*c*) are true.

19-15 What is the difference between what a company would be worth if it were managed by its owners and what that same company would be worth if it were managed by hired executives?

489

Chapter 19
Management
Risk and
Other Risk
Factors

(a) The bid–asked spread
(b) An agency cost
(c) The difference between wholesale and retail
(d) A surplus bestowed on the firm by professional managers
(e) A fair profit for the founders

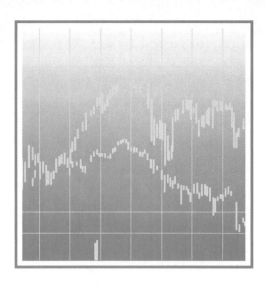

CHAPTER 20

MAKING BUY-SELL DECISIONS

This chapter begins by distinguishing between a security's market price and its present value and explaining how buying underpriced and selling overpriced securities helps align prices with values. Long and short positions are introduced as ways to buy and sell securities, and to create hedges. Imperfect hedges are analyzed and revealed to be the foundation for arbitrage. But first, let us review the way that security prices fluctuate.

There is no readily discernible pattern in price movements on most trading days. On one day a stock's price might move upward continuously throughout the day. In the next few days, the price may move "sideways"—that is, it may fluctuate without any trend. Then for the next 2 days the price might tend to move down. Sometimes a price moves in continuous trends and sometimes it fluctuates aimlessly, as Figures 15-2, 15-3, and 15-5 illustrate. What causes security prices to fluctuate the way they do? To answer this question, let's consider the basic economic process that determines security prices.

20-1 The Venerable Present Value Model

A security's price is determined by its value. To see how this happens, we review the present value model introduced in the first half of Chapter 11. Although the process used to find the value of securities varies with the type of security, the one outlined in Box 20-1 is the basic economic model for valuing most assets.

The model shown in Box 20-1 illustrates how a security's present value (or economic value or intrinsic value) is calculated. Assume, for instance, you are thinking of purchasing a share of stock that you require to earn a $k = .10 = 10$ percent rate of return to induce you to undertake the risks you perceive in the investment.[1] If you expect to sell the stock for $45 after you collect cash dividends of $3 per share at the end of each of the next 2 years, the following equation suggests you should be willing to pay as much as $42.40 for this investment:

$$\text{Present value} = \frac{D_1}{(1 + k)^1} + \frac{D_2 + S}{(1 + k)^2}$$

$$= \frac{\$3}{(1.10)^1} + \frac{\$3 + \$45}{(1.10)^2} = \$42.40$$

where D_1, D_2 = first and second cash dividends, respectively

S = sale price or liquidation value

k = required rate of return

[1]Figure 10-1 showed how to determine the risk-adjusted discount rate (or the required rate of return) needed to calculate the present value of a bond. Chapter 26 explains how to determine the risk-adjusted discount rate using a more comprehensive (arbitrage pricing theory) model that considers all relevant risks.

Box 20-1

DEFINITION: The Present Value Model

The present value of an asset is the sum of all discounted incomes an investor may expect to receive from it.

$$\frac{\text{Present}}{\text{value}} = \frac{\text{income}_1}{(1 + k)^1} + \frac{\text{income}_2}{(1 + k)^2} + \frac{\text{income}_3}{(1 + k)^3} + \cdots \qquad (20\text{-}1)$$

Equation 20-1 defines the present value of an income stream expected to start at time period $t = 1$. The dollars of income (or cashflows) are discounted at the investor's required (or risk-adjusted) rate of return k.

Stated differently, you estimate the stock's *value* to be $42.40. If its *market price* happens to be less than the estimated value, you would say the stock is a good investment because it is underpriced.

After the security's present value is determined, a buy-sell investment decision can be made by comparing market price and present value. For example, if the present value of a security is $42.40 at a time when its market price is $60, that security is overpriced and should be sold. Box 20-2 outlines the investment decision-making process.

20-2 Value versus Price

Unfortunately for them, not all the 30 million people in the United States who own securities know that value determines price. These unfortunate investors are the ones most likely to misunderstand why security prices change erratically. Professional investors follow the more scientific procedure of forming estimates of a security's value before they make a buy or sell decision. To see how these value estimates determine security prices, examine the buy-sell decision rules summarized in Box 20-2.

The price-value, buy-sell rules in Box 20-2 are easy to understand, but they are difficult to implement because it is difficult to obtain good estimates of an asset's present value. Hundreds of security analysts earn annual salaries in excess of $100,000 per year just for providing value estimates for a few securities. An expert automotive analyst, for example, might be responsible for, say, Ford, Chrysler, General Motors, Volvo, Nissan, and Honda. If this analyst can correctly predict the direction of the prices of these six stocks, that analyst will develop a track record and attract a following of investors. A stock brokerage can pay this analyst a six-figure annual salary because the expert's following will generate high trading commissions for the brokerage firm.

The way the buy-sell rules in Box 20-2 determine security prices is straightforward. *Underpriced securities get purchased, and this bids their prices upward. Overpriced securities get sold, and this drives their prices down. As a result of these pressures, securities' prices tend to be aligned with their values.*

20-3 The Valuation and Investment Procedure

The valuation process is actually more complex than suggested in Boxes 20-1 and 20-2. One problem involves the amount of confidence to place in a security analyst's estimate. The estimate is rarely a single price; instead, it is given as a price with a **margin for error.** For example, an expert might estimate that XYZ stock is worth $30 per share plus or minus a $6 per share margin for error. The equity share's value is thus estimated to be within the $24 to $36 range. The buy-sell rules in Box 20-2 are oversimplified because they are based on one specific value estimate.

Another practical problem results from the fact that a security's risk and return, and thus also its value, usually change with time. Selling a security puts downward pressure on its market price (if market supply exceeds market demand at the moment

Box 20-2

493

*Chapter 20
Making
Buy-Sell
Decisions*

PRINCIPLES: The Buy-Sell Decision Rules

The buy rule: If a security's price is below its value, it is *underpriced* and should be bought and held for future gain. At a point in time denoted t, if the market price of a security is p_t and its intrinsic (or present) value is v_t, and if v_t exceeds p_t, then that security appears to be a profitable investment.

$$\text{If } (p_t < v_t) \rightarrow \text{buy}$$

Stated differently but equivalently, if an asset's expected return $E(r)$ exceeds the required (or risk-adjusted) rate of return k that the investor considers appropriate for the asset's riskiness, buy it.

$$\text{If } [E(r) > k] \rightarrow \text{buy}$$

The don't trade rule: If an asset's market price equals its value, then the price is in equilibrium and the asset is not expected to experience unusual gains or losses. The asset is correctly priced, and there is no abnormal profit to be made from buying or selling it.

$$\text{If } (p_t = v_t) \rightarrow \text{don't trade}$$

Equivalently, if an asset's expected return equals the investor's risk-adjusted rate of return, that asset is expected to earn no more than its expected return and is not profitable to trade.

$$\text{If } [E(r) = k] \rightarrow \text{don't trade}$$

The sell rule: If a security's price is above its estimated value, then the security is *overpriced* and should be sold to avoid losses when the price falls toward its actual value.

$$\text{If } (p_t > v_t) \rightarrow \text{sell (or sell short)}$$

If the asset's expected return is below the investor's required rate of return, the asset should be sold.

$$\text{If } [E(r) < k] \rightarrow \text{sell (or sell short)}$$

Selling short is a sophisticated way to sell a security that is explained later in this chapter.

Note: The rate-of-return buy-sell rules will become clearer after you have completed Chapters 25 and 26.

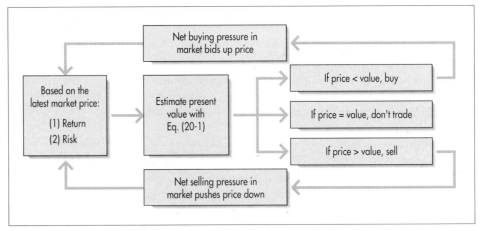

Figure 20-1 The continuous valuation process.

of the sale), and buying a security may bid up its price (if the market's supply for sale of the security does not increase simultaneously). As a result of any change in price level, the security's expected future capital gains or losses must be revised, which in turn affects estimated future income. The security's risk may change as well.

The continuous valuation process security analysts use is more realistically represented by the flowchart in Figure 20-1. The dynamic valuation process is a never-ending loop of reconsidering value, comparing price and value, and then reconsidering the buy-sell decision on the basis of the latest estimates. Every time a new piece of information about a security appears, that security's value may change. *Since new information arrives continuously, the value estimates fluctuate continuously too.* And the buying and selling pressures keep market prices in continuous motion as they react to continuously changing values.

The buy-sell decision rules in Box 20-2 suggest when to buy and when to sell. The next section analyzes the buying and selling transactions and introduces another way to sell securities.

20-4 Long and Short Positions

Investors may assume either or both of two basic positions in a market asset. Most investors are only aware of the **long position,** which involves simply buying and holding the asset until it is sold. The short position is more complex.

Selling Short

Although it may sound strange, short selling is a common investment activity. The **short seller** sells a second party, called the *buyer,* securities that the short seller does not own. The short seller expects, *at some later date,* to be able to purchase securities to cover the short position at a lower price and return them to a third party who lent them. People who sell short can usually borrow the securities from their broker with ease. Brokerage houses are able to lend securities because they usually hold their clients' securities in safe-deposit boxes at the brokerage's office as a free customer service.[2]

Minutes, days, weeks, or months after the short position is established, the short seller purchases securities in the market to repay the third party who lent them (usually the short seller's broker). If the securities purchased to replace the borrowed securities have a lower price than the price at which they were sold short, the short seller profits from the price decline. But if the price of the security rises before the short seller replaces the borrowed securities, the short seller loses because the borrowed securities must be purchased at a price higher than their earlier selling price.

Short sellers usually sell an asset short because they expect its price to fall and they want to profit from that price drop—they are bearish. The bearish short seller sells an asset to a buyer who takes a long position. The buyer typically expects the price to rise. Thus, a short sale requires a short seller who is bearish and a long buyer who is bullish about the same asset at the same time; it is a case of opposites being attracted in search of profit. If the price of the asset that was sold short does fall (or rise), the short seller profits (or loses) by the difference between the price paid for the asset to give to the third party and the price at which the asset was previously sold short to the long buyer, less any commission costs. Aside from the commission costs taken by the broker, the short seller's profit equals the long buyer's loss—or vice versa, if the asset's price rises after the short sale.

Another reason to sell short is to create a new position that is negatively correlated with an existing long position in order to reduce aggregate risk. That is, a short position can establish a risk-reducing, two-position portfolio comprising a long position and a short position. This strategy, discussed later in this chapter, is called *hedging*.

Some Complications

Short sales are complicated for several reasons. First, short sales of NYSE common stocks can be made only on an ''uptick''—that is, after a trade in which the stock's price was bid up. This NYSE rule is designed to keep short sellers from adding to a downturn in the price of a stock. A second possible complication involves cash dividends. If a common stock that is sold short pays a cash dividend while on loan to the short seller, the short seller must pay that dividend out of his or her own pocket to the third-party owner who lent the shares. A third potential entanglement is that the short seller may be required to put up margin money equaling as much as 100

---

[2]All brokerage houses require every short selling client to sign a legal form called a *short seller's agreement* that gives the broker the limited power of attorney to buy shares at the client's expense (by liquidating assets in the client's account) to cover the client's short positions without obtaining the client's prior permission. Brokerage firms require each potential short seller to sign these agreements because these documents permit the brokerage to limit its losses if the short seller fails to cover the short position.

percent of the value of the borrowed shares as collateral to protect the third party lender. Yet a fourth problem is that the short seller can be involuntarily "forced out" of the short position at any time if the third party lender demands the shares back immediately (see the accompanying case).

Some Gain-Loss Illustrations

Figure 20-2 shows the long and the short positions in a fashion that should help clarify them. The vertical axes in these gain-loss graphs show the dollars of profit above the origin and the dollars of loss below the origin. The horizontal axes show

Figure 20-2 Gain-loss illustrations. (*a*) Long position; (*b*) short position.

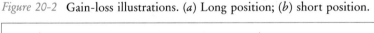

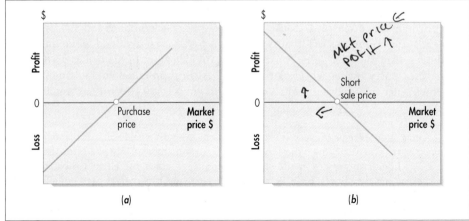

496

the potential market prices of the asset held in either the long or the short position. (The market price rises along the axis toward the right.)

The gain-loss graph for the long position (Figure 20-2a) has a slope of positive unity, indicating that the person holding the long position makes a dollar of profit (or loss) for each dollar the market price rises (or falls). In contrast, the gain-loss graph for the short position (Figure 20-2b) has a slope of negative unity, indicating a dollar of loss (or profit) for the short seller for each dollar the market price rises (or falls).

Short sales have been conducted on the floor of the New York Stock Exchange (amid what is predominantly long buying) for decades. The volume of short sales is reported daily in financial newspapers under the heading "short interest." The **short interest** is the total number of shares that brokers have listed in their accounts as being sold short; it is usually below 5 percent of the total volume of shares traded (and the NYSE specialists do most of it).

20-5 Hedged Positions

A person may take a short position for different reasons. First, and most obvious, is the desire to make a speculative gain from an expected price drop. Second, a risk-averse investor may sell short to hedge against possible losses. Hedging is an important investment strategy. Security investors, commodity processors, futures contract traders, put and call option traders, foreign exchange traders, and others hedge to limit their risk exposure.

Hedging occurs when someone simultaneously buys and sells the same or similar assets. There are different types of hedges: Some hedges are set up with the expectation of reaping profits. The easiest hedge of all to explain is discussed first. It is the **perfect hedge,** from which no profits or losses can be earned. Figure 20-3 is a series of graphs illustrating the perfect hedge.

The Perfect Hedge

Figure 20-3a is a gain-loss graph that combines the long position from Figure 20-2a and the short position from Figure 20-2b at the same purchase and sale prices, respectively. The hedger is thus perfectly protected: the profits and losses from the two positions sum to zero at any value the market price may attain. This situation might result, for instance, if an investor purchased a long position of 100 shares of the Acme Corporation's common stock at $64 per share. At the same time, the investor

Box 20-3

> DEFINITION: Hedging
>
> **Hedging** is the establishment of offsetting long and short positions to diminish the loss that could result from an adverse price movement.

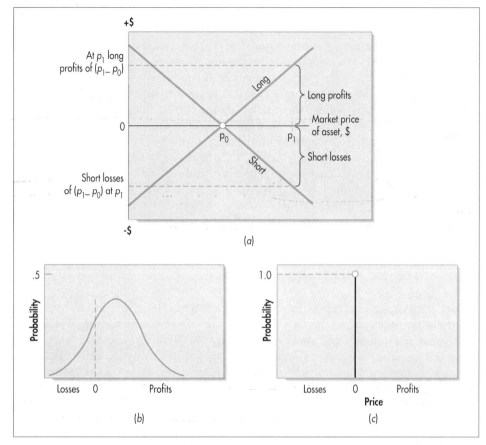

Figure 20-3 A perfect hedge. (*a*) Gain-loss illustration; (*b*) probability distribution from unhedged position; (*c*) probability distribution for a perfectly hedged position.

sells short 100 shares of Acme's stock at $64 per share. Figure 20-3*a* shows that if the market price of the hedged asset rises above p_0, which is the initial price for both the long and the short positions, to, say, p_1 dollars, then the profit on the long position will be exactly offset by the loss on the short position. The hedger can have neither profits nor losses, because the hedge is perfect.

Figure 20-3*b* shows a probability distribution for the various possible outcomes from an unhedged long or short position. Figure 20-3*c* illustrates the probability distribution of outcomes for a perfect hedge. Perfect hedges are typically created by risk averters who are seeking to decrease their exposure to risk and are willing to give up any opportunity to earn gains in order to limit possible losses.

For a hedge to be perfect, it is essential that (1) equal dollar amounts must be held in both the long and the short positions and (2) the purchase price for the long position be identical with the sales price for the short sale. Technically, the long and short positions do not have to be of equal dollar magnitude to create a perfect hedge. For instance, an investment that involved only half as many dollars in an offsetting short position that had twice the price elasticity could result in a perfect hedge if the two positions were perfectly inversely correlated. Options and financial futures, introduced in Chapters 21 and 22, can be used to create these sophisticated trading positions.

Imperfect Hedges

Not all hedges are perfect. In fact, most hedges are imperfect—and this is sometimes desirable. Imperfect hedges arise for either of two reasons: if the dollar commitments to the long and the short positions are not equal, or if the short sale price is not equal to the purchase price for the long position. This second imperfection often results from opening the long and the short positions at different times. In hedging parlance, the long position is called one *leg* of the hedge and the short position is the other leg; the second imperfection is sometimes described as "legging into the hedge" at different prices.

Figure 20-4 illustrates two imperfect hedges. Since the size of the dollar commitments to the long and the short positions cannot be illustrated in Figure 20-4, let us assume that they are equal. The hedges are imperfect because the short sales prices p_s differ from the purchase prices for the long positions p_p.

The hedge in Figure 20-4a shows a purchase price for the long position that is *above* the sales price for the short position, $p_p > p_s$. The resulting hedge will yield an *invariant loss* at whatever value the market price may assume, and this loss will equal the excess of the purchase price over the short sale price $(p_p - p_s)$.

The hedge in Figure 20-4b is imperfect because its short sales price is *above* the purchase price for its long position. As a result, the hedge will yield an *invariant profit* equal to the excess of the short sale price over the purchase price. It is impossible for the imperfect hedge in Figure 20-4b to do anything except yield a profit of $(p_s - p_p)$ regardless of what value the market price of the hedged asset assumes.

Figure 20-4 Gain-loss illustrations of imperfect hedges. (*a*) Invariant losses; (*b*) invariant profits.

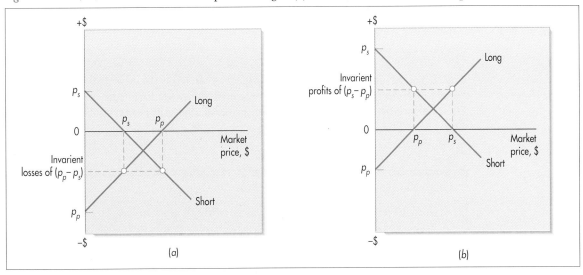

Box 20-4

> **DEFINITION: Arbitrage**
>
> **Arbitrage** can be defined as simultaneously buying long and selling short the same (or similar) assets in an effort to earn riskless profits from unrealistic price differentials.

20-6 Arbitrage

An investor might enter into a hedged short position to carry on arbitrage. Arbitraging is somewhat like hedging because both the hedger and the arbitrageur buy and sell similar items, but unlike hedging, which seeks zero gains and losses, arbitrageurs are seeking gains. Arbitrage may take place in the same or in different markets. For an example of arbitrage between different markets consider international arbitrage in IBM common stock.

International Stock Price Arbitrage

If IBM stock is sold in the United States and also in a European market at different prices, arbitrage can be profitable. Profit-seeking arbitrageurs facilitate enforcement of the **law of one price** by buying the stock in the market where its price is lowest and selling in the market where its price is highest. Arbitrageurs will go on buying at the low price and selling at the high price until the price of IBM stock is the same in all free markets around the world. Technically, the price may never be exactly identical in all markets because of transactions costs. However, with the exception of these costs (a few cents per share), IBM stock should cost the same no matter where in the world it is traded. The law of one price should never be broken, or profit seekers will exploit the opportunity until a single prevailing price is restored. Box 20-6 shows how this works.

Risky and Riskless Arbitrage

The arbitrage procedure can yield *riskless* profits for the arbitrageur because the arbitrageur can remain hedged while repeating the procedure again and again. Figure 20-4*b* illustrates the imperfect but profitable hedge arbitrageurs strive to establish.

Box 20-5

> **DEFINITION: The Law of One Price**
>
> At any given moment, identical goods should sell at identical prices everywhere in the world. If the same item sells at different prices, arbitrage will work to bring the disparate prices together.

Box 20-6

501

Chapter 20
Making
Buy-Sell
Decisions

PRINCIPLES: Rules for Profitable Arbitraging

1. Sell short in the market where the item is offered at the higher price. For example, sell IBM stock short for $100 per share in London if the price of IBM is higher in London than elsewhere. This selling tends to drive down the London price.

2. Buy a long position in the same quantity of the same item in the market where it is offered at the lowest price. Simultaneously buy IBM stock for $99 at the New York Stock Exchange (or anywhere else it sells for less than the short sale price). This tends to bid up the low price.

3. Deliver the item purchased at the low price for the long position at a higher selling price to fulfill the delivery requirements of the short sale. Buy IBM for $99 at the NYSE, sell it short for $100 in London, deliver the shares purchased on the NYSE for $99, and make $1 per share profit for each share delivered under these terms.

4. Continue to profit from buying for the long position where the price is lower and selling short where the price is higher. Repeat this procedure until the lower price is bid up by the market force of the demand, the high price is driven down by the supply, and the same price prevails in all markets.

As the short sale price and the long purchase price are driven together, the arbitrage pays off regardless of any other price fluctuations. The general level of the prices could double or fall to zero, for instance, and the arbitrage will still be profitable so long as the differing prices come together.[3]

20-7 Selling Short against the Box

As we have seen, short sales are used to accomplish different objectives. They are used by bearish speculators in search of profits from a price decline. They are also used by risk-averse hedgers. Furthermore, some hedgers can be seeking more than simply risk

[3]For a discussion of a gold and other arbitrage positions see chap. 3 in Richard Bookstaber, *The Complete Investment Book* (Glenview, Ill.: Scott, Foresman, 1985.)

Box 20-7

DEFINITION: Selling Short against the Box

When an investor has a long position in securities held in a safe-deposit box (or some safe place) and simultaneously borrows equivalent securities to sell short, that is called **selling short against the box.**

aversion. They use a technique called *selling short against the box.* The accompanying cases provide some examples.

Investors sometimes sell short against the box in order to carry a short-term capital gain for sufficient time for it to turn into a long-term capital gain and thereby decrease their income taxes. It can also be used as a sophisticated way to delay income tax payments. Furthermore, an investor who sells short against the box can carry a taxable gain from a high-income year into a low-income year and thus decrease income taxes.

As the cases make clear, short sales are not always undertaken for profit. They may be used like insurance to hedge away risks, to maintain control, to distribute income tax burdens to later years, or to arbitrage differential prices into equilibrium. Speculators, risk averters, and arbitrageurs use short sales for different purposes.

The present value model provides the intrinsic value estimates that should be used as the basis for rational, well-informed, wealth-maximizing investment decisions. Once an estimate of a security's intrinsic value is obtained, the buy-sell investment decision rules presented in Box 20-2 are simple to use. The intrinsic value estimates and the buy-sell decisions will probably be used more than once for each security, however. Every time a piece of new information arrives, it may change the intrinsic value estimates for one or more securities. As a result, a never-ending series of investment decisions keeps securities analysts busy.

The market prices of securities fluctuate in an unpredictable fashion because they are pursuing ever-changing intrinsic values. Securities' intrinsic values change continuously because every time a piece of new information becomes available, it may cause analysts to change their assessment of the intrinsic value of one or more securities. These changes in the intrinsic value motivate investors either to buy and bid up, or to sell and push down, the ever-changing securities prices. Some investors pursue this aggressive investment management style eagerly.

Buying and holding an asset in a long position to profit from some cashflows and/or price appreciation is the simplest and most popular position assumed by investors. Selling short in order to profit from price declines is a more sophisticated but less common practice. Short sales are complicated by certain requirements—that the position be taken only on an uptick in price, that any cash dividends be paid by the short seller to the third party who lent the shares, by delays until the short seller enjoys any liquidity the position may generate, and by the risk that the borrowed shares may be unexpectedly recalled.

Long and short positions in similar assets can be combined to create a hedged position. Perfect hedges are rare positions sought by risk averters. Most hedges are imperfect, which can be highly desirable if the imperfect hedge has a profit built into it. Imperfect hedges with built-in riskless profits are desirable arbitrage situations. Arbitrage involves the simultaneous purchase and short sale of the same or similar assets in an effort to profit from unrealistic price differentials. Arbitrage becomes profitable to perform any time the law of one price is violated.

Fabozzi, Frank J., and Gregory M. Kipnis, eds., *Stock Index Futures,* (Homewood, Ill.: Dow Jones–Irwin, 1984).
> *Chapters 10 and 16 deal with arbitrage, Chapter 12 with hedging. The book is easy to read. Elementary algebra is used sparingly. Many numerical examples enrich the discussion in this book.*

Figlewski, Stephen, *Hedging with Financial Futures for Institutional Investors* (Cambridge, Mass.: Ballinger, 1986).
> *A mathematical book about hedging that has numerical examples.*

Kaufman, Perry J., *Handbook of Futures Markets* (New York: Wiley-Interscience, 1984).
> *Chapters 9 and 10 introduce hedging and arbitrage with a minimum of mathematical notation so that it is easy to read. Only very elementary algebra is used.*

Welles, Chris, "Inside the Arbitrage Game," *Institutional Investor*, August 1981, pp. 41–44. This easy-to-read magazine article discusses **risk arbitrage**, which is a form of speculating on corporate reorganizations instead of true arbitrage.

Questions and Problems

Essay Questions

20-1 Why must a security analyst have estimates of a security's risk and return before preparing estimates of the security's value? Explain your answer in terms of the present value formula.

20-2 When the present value of all future cashflows model is used to value a share of common stock, the model discounts all future cash dividends that the share of stock can be expected to earn (see Box 20-1). What is the economic theory for finding the discounted present value of a share's future cash dividends when a corporation's board of directors can decrease the cash dividend payout to zero at any time they choose to do so?

20-3 Are short sellers primarily risk-taking speculators or risk-averse hedgers? Explain.

20-4 Mr. John Malone was bearish about the stock issued by American Telegraph and Telephone (AT&T). He expected the price of AT&T to fall significantly within the next 3 months, so he sold 100 shares short. Mr. Malone's stockbroker arranged to lend Mr. Malone's account the 100 shares to deliver with the understanding that these shares would be replaced with other AT&T shares later. A month after Mr. Malone opened his short position, AT&T announced a cash dividend of $3.50 per share. How will this cash dividend affect Mr. Malone while he is selling AT&T stock short?

20-5 Risk averters can create riskless hedges quickly and easily by assuming a long and a short position in similar securities. Is the preceding statement true, false, or questionable? Explain.

20-6 Consider two positively correlated common stocks—say, Ford and General Motors. Assume the correlation coefficient between the rates of return from these two automotive stocks is +0.6. If you take a long position in GM and a short position in Ford of exactly equal dollar values, will you be perfectly hedged? Explain why, or why not.

20-7 Are there any conditions under which someone who thought that the price of IBM stock would *rise* would want to become involved in a short position in the stock? Explain.

20-8 Suppose that a small company named the Crocket Cereal Company (CCC) has just obtained the largest order it has ever had in its history. A large national supermarket chain has signed a sales contract to buy several boxcar loads of Crocket's Shredded Wheat periodically during the next year for a price that works out to $4.00 per bushel. It costs $1.00 per bushel to manufacture the cereal, and the raw material (namely, the wheat) currently sells for $2.80 per bushel in the cash market. Thus, CCC hopes to earn $4.00 − $1.00 − $2.80 = $0.20 per bushel profit from the order. But the president of CCC is worried that the price of wheat may rise from the current cash price of $2.80 to above $3.00 per bushel in the year ahead and turn CCC's potential profits to losses. What can CCC do to protect the biggest profit opportunity the firm has ever had?

Problems

505

*Chapter 20
Making
Buy-Sell
Decisions*

20-9   After comparing their prices and values, decide whether buying, no action, or selling is appropriate for the following common stocks? Explain each investment decision.

Corporation's name	Market price of stock	Estimated value per share	Buy, sell or no action?
Acme Corp.	$87.75	$90	
Baker Inc.	11.125	13	
Crown Corp.	31.75	40	
Delta Inc.	19.50	25	
Evans Corp.	44.25	30	

20-10   Read the narrative below and then fill in the appropriate dollar amounts in the blanks that follow the narrative.

Jane Trader has bought a long position in General Motors (GM) common stock at a purchase price of $60 per share. If the price of GM stock goes up to $80 per share, Figure 20-5a shows that Jane has a profit of (a) per share before commissions and taxes. But if Jane was bullish when she should have been bearish and the stock's price falls to $45 per share, she has a loss of (b) per share.

If Ms. Trader were bearish about GM's stock rise, she could sell the stock short at $60 per share, as shown in Figure 20-5b. If the price then fell to $45 per share, she would have a profit before commissions and taxes of (c) per share from her short position. But if Jane judged the stock incorrectly and its price appreciated to $80 per share, she would suffer a loss of (d) per share from the short sale. Note the symmetry of the long and short positions. Figure 20-5a is the mirror image of 20-5b.

Finally, consider Ms. Trader's position if she had taken both a long and a short position. Figure 20-5c is a gain-loss graph, which combines Jane Trader's long position from Figure

Figure 20-5   Position graph for Jane Trader's perfect hedge at $60.

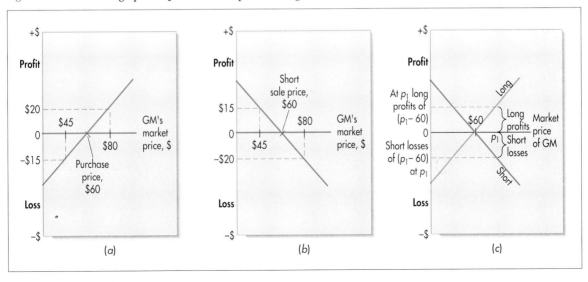

20-5*a* with her short position from Figure 20-5*b*, with both positions being taken simultaneously at the same $60 per share price. Figure 20-5*c* illustrates what happens if Jane Trader hedged herself perfectly. If she purchased a long position of 100 shares of GM's common stock at $60 per share and simultaneously sold 100 shares of GM's stock short at $60 per share, she would be perfectly hedged. Figure 20-5*c* shows that if the market price of the hedged asset rises above the $60 purchase price to the higher price of $80 dollars, then the (*e*) per share profit on the long position will be offset by a (*f*) per share loss on the short position, for a net profit of (*g*). In contrast, if the market price of GM fell from $60 to $45, the loss of (*h*) per share on Ms. Trader's long position would have been offset by a gain of (*i*) per share on her short position for a net profit of (*j*).

Fill in the dollar amounts that should go in the 10 blanks embedded in Jane Trader's case.

(*a*) Profit of _____
(*b*) Loss of _____ per share
(*c*) Profit before commissions and taxes of _____
(*d*) Loss of _____ per share
(*e*) _____ per share profit
(*f*) _____ per share loss
(*g*) Net profit of _____
(*h*) Loss of _____
(*i*) Gain of _____ per share
(*j*) Net profit of _____

20-11 Write out the formulas for the one-period rates of return for an investor who (*a*) buys a share of the Ace Corporation's common stock for $40, holds the stock in a long position for 6 months while collecting a $2 cash dividend, and sells it for $42; and (*b*) sells a share of Ace common stock short at $40 per share, holds the short position open for 6 months while Ace pays a $2 cash dividend, and covers the short position at $42 per share.

Matching Questions

20-12 Match the following terms on the left with their definitions on the right.

1. Price per share	A. A quantity estimated by an informed analyst
2. Passive investment management	B. A quantity determined by market processes that can sometimes be irrational
3. Intrinsic value per share	C. A buy and hold without trading strategy
4. Buy a security	D. The appropriate decision when an underpriced security is discovered

Multiple Choice Questions

20-13 Which of the following is a true statement concerning the value of an investment security?

(*a*) Value and price are synonyms as they pertain to securities.
(*b*) Value equals the discounted present value of the security's future income.
(*c*) A security's value depends on the assessed value of the firm's physical assets.
(*d*) A security's equilibrium value never fluctuates.

20-14 The value of a security depends on which of the following factors?

(*a*) Whether the security is over- or underpriced in the market
(*b*) The risk-adjusted discount rate

(c) The size of the security's trading volume

(d) The efficiency of the market in which the security is traded

20-15   The economic law of one price is correctly described by which of the following statements?

(a) Identical goods must sell at identical prices.

(b) Arbitrageurs enforce the law of one price.

(c) The same goods can sell at different prices if the differences are limited to transportation costs between the markets where the goods are sold.

(d) All the above are true.

(e) Only (a) and (b) are true.

20-16   Selling short against the box is illegal under which of the following conditions?

(a) If it is used as an income tax evasion tactic.

(b) If it is used by an insider.

(c) If a wash sale occurs.

(d) All the above are true.

(e) Only (b) and (c) are true.

20-17   According to the investor's buy-sell decision rules, which one of the following statements is wise and rational?

(a) If price > value, then buy.

(b) If price < value, then don't trade.

(c) If price = value, then buy.

(d) If price < value, then buy.

20-18   In assessing the value of a manufacturing corporation's common stock, which of the following rules makes sense?

(a) You cannot really know the value of the firm until an appraiser estimates the value of the plant and equipment.

(b) Professional investors who manage multimillion-dollar investment portfolios create support areas that keep the prices of stock from ever falling to as low as $2 or $3 per share.

(c) Most common stocks are worth their normal earnings per share.

(d) The value of a share of stock is equal to the present value of all future income from the stock.

20-19   What characteristics do the long and short positions have in common?

(a) The potential profits from a long position and the potential losses from a short position are both infinite if the price of the underlying security rises to infinity.

(b) There is a one-to-one correspondence between movements in the price of the underlying security and the profits of the investor with both the positions.

(c) Both (a) and (b) are true.

(d) The investor loses money if the price of an asset held in either position declines.

(e) All the above are true.

20-20   Under which of the following conditions would someone who thought that the price of a stock was going to rise want to become involved in a short position in that stock?

(a) If the short sale were part of a larger plan to sell short against the box in order to maintain voting control through the shares.

(b) If the short sale were part of an imperfect hedge that was expected to yield arbitrage profits.

(c) Both (a) and (b) are true.

(d) If the short sale were part of a perfect hedge the investor was setting up in order to reap large profits.

(e) All the above are true.

20-21 Short selling is complicated by which of the following problems?

(a) Short sales can take place only on an uptick in some security exchanges.

(b) The law forbids insiders from profiting on short sales.

(c) If a stock in a short position pays a cash dividend, short sellers must pay for this cash dividend out of their own pockets.

(d) Only (b) and (c) are true.

(e) All the above are true.

20-22 A short seller's profits are best described by which of the following statements?

(a) The per share profit from short selling is limited to an amount equal to the price at which the shares were sold short.

(b) The short seller earns $1 profit for every $1 fall in price of the security.

(c) Short sellers must pay for any cash dividends the stock might declare while they are borrowing it, and this decreases the profits from selling short.

(d) Short selling can help arbitrageurs earn profits.

(e) All the above are true.

20-23 For a hedge to be perfect, which of the following conditions must be met?

(a) The short sale must be initiated at the same price that was paid for the long position.

(b) The dollar values of the long and the short positions should be identical.

(c) If the dollar values of the long and the offsetting short positions differ, some arrangements must be made so that the two positions' price elasticities are exactly offsetting.

(d) All the above are true.

(e) The long and the short positions must be initiated simultaneously.

20-24 Selling short against the box involves which of the following conditions?

(a) The owner of the securities can continue to own them and, thus, exercise whatever voting power they convey.

(b) A short position of equal dollar value, and in the identical security that is held in the long position, must be established if a perfect hedge is desired.

(c) If the dollar values of the long and the short positions differ, an imperfect hedge can be established that leaves the party who is selling short against the box partially exposed to risk.

(d) Both (a) and (b) are true.

(e) All the above are true.

20-25 Selling securities short is useful in which of the following activities?

(a) Speculating

(b) Hedging

(c) Selling short against the box

(d) Arbitrage

(e) All the above

20-26 Profitable arbitrage is best described by which of the following statements?

    (*a*) If the long and short positions exactly offset each other, then profitable arbitrage is impossible.

    (*b*) An imperfect hedge is a necessary ingredient if an arbitrage position is to be profitable.

    (*c*) It involves only small risks.

    (*d*) Only (*a*) and (*b*) are true.

    (*e*) All the above are true.

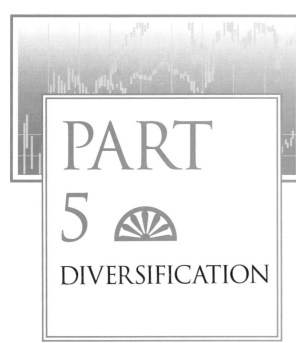

PART 5
DIVERSIFICATION

PART 5 begins by suggesting some additional vehicles with which to diversify. Chapter 21 delves into put and call options, warrants on stock, and fixed income securities that can be converted into common stock. Futures contracts are the topic of Chapter 22. The chapter defines agricultural and financial futures, but is primarily focused on financial futures. The Appendix to Chapter 22 investigates options on futures contracts. Investing in real assets like real estate, precious stones, gold, silver, and paintings is reviewed in Chapter 23. After Chapters 21, 22, and 23 expand our menu of investment assets, Chapters 24 through 28 analyze the concept of diversification.

Chapters 24 through 28 share some common threads: these chapters are theoretical and they involve some financial engineering. *Financial engineering* is a new phrase that refers to plugging financial numbers into formulas to solve problems and make investment decisions; it is similar to the way engineers work. These chapters on theory were combined at the end of the book to focus your analysis and evaluation of the investment possibilities presented in Chapters 1 through 24.

Chapter 24, entitled "Portfolio Analysis," compares and contrasts random diversification, diversifying across securities in different industries, and Markowitz's portfolio theory. (As you might imagine, the Nobel-prize-winning portfolio theory is shown to offer benefits that the simpler approaches to diversification cannot provide.)

The focus on Markowitz's portfolio theory in Chapter 24 provides the foundation for the capital market theory presented in Chapter 25. Capital market theory provides some rather profound risk-return models that are so intuitively pleasing they are easy to learn. Essentially, the chapter shows how to use quantitative risk surrogates (like the standard deviation and the beta coefficient) to help investors find under- and over-priced assets. Professors

Tobin and Sharpe won Nobel prizes for their contibutions to capital market theory; this is glamorous and exciting material.

Professor Steve Ross will probably win a Nobel prize someday for creating arbitrage pricing theory—called simply APT. Ross's APT is the topic of Chapter 26. APT shows how to extend the concepts of hedging and arbitrage (introduced in Chapter 20) to develop asset pricing models. These APT models are somewhat analogous to the capital market theory models in Chapter 25. However, Chapter 26 extends the capital market theory to include more different risk factors. It sounds contradictory, but it is nevertheless true that the APT is both simpler and more complex than the capital market theory.

International investment opportunities are explored in Chapter 27. The chapter analyzes the benefits and problems of multinational diversification in terms of the economic theories discussed in Chapters 24 through 26.

"Investment Performance Evaluation" is the title of Chapter 28. It seems appropriate for this subject to close the book because this final chapter analyzes real world investment results to see which approaches to investment management work best.

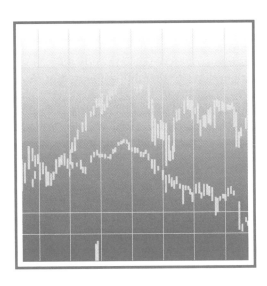

CHAPTER 21

OPTIONS, WARRANTS, AND CONVERTIBLES

The array of instruments investors may use to maximize return and manage risks contains many more exotic possibilities than the simple buy and hold strategy. Put options, call options, warrants, and index options are specialized financial instruments that can be used for speculating or hedging. Each instrument can be used for a

Box 21-1

> **DEFINITION: Call Option**
>
> A **call** option gives its owner the right, but not the obligation, to buy an asset. Most calls are negotiable contracts giving the call buyer the option to buy a stated number of shares of a specific security within a fixed period of time at a predetermined price. Calls can also be purchased to "call in" cash settlements based on the value of a market index or other economic quantity.

different purpose: for the immediate excitement of a quick gamble, for the short-run thrill of a price change speculation, for the long-run rewards associated with investing successfully, or as a basis for a risk-averting hedge. Whether the financial position turns out to be a short-run speculation, a long-run investment, or a hedge depends in each case on how long and why that position is kept open.

21-1   Calls and Puts

In addition to taking long and/or short positions in order to speculate or hedge, investors can also buy and sell options. **Options** are marketable **financial instruments** that give their owners the right but not the obligation to buy or sell a stated number of shares (usually 100) of a particular security at a fixed price within a predetermined time period. The buyers of options are also referred to as the "holders" or "owners." As its name implies, the *exercise price* is the predetermined price at which an option is to be exercised. There are two basic types of options—the put option and the call option.

The Characteristics of Options

New puts and calls on common stocks that have maturities of as long as 18 months into the future are originated at intervals of 3 months. As a result of these continuously originating new options, several different options on the same security (with different maturity dates) may be traded simultaneously. In the 1990s exchange-

Box 21-2

> **DEFINITION: Put Option**
>
> A **put** option gives its owner the right, but not the obligation, to sell (or put) an asset to someone else. Most puts are negotiable contracts giving the put owner the option to sell a stated number of shares of a specified security within a fixed period of time at a predetermined price. Puts can also be purchased that allow their owner to collect cash settlements that are based on the value of a market index and other economic quantity.

listed put and call options with maturities as long as 24 months began trading on selected common stocks and on the S&P 100 Stock Index. These options are called *long-term equity appreciation securities,* or *LEAPS.*

Options can be written on a variety of securities, as well as on other goods. In addition to common stocks, options are actively traded on bonds, stock market indexes, foreign currencies, commodity futures contracts (see the appendix to Chapter 22) and even economic indexes (index options will be explained later in this chapter). Although the goods to be delivered may differ, the basic structure of puts and calls remains the same.

On any trading day before the expiration date, the owner of a put or call may choose to do any one of the following three things:

1. Do nothing and hold the option longer

2. Sell the option at its current market price, thereby ending the position

3. Exercise the option

Different people and prices are involved in all three choices.

515

*Chapter 21
Options,
Warrants,
and
Convertibles*

The People, the Prices, and the Markets

Option Parties   There are three parties to every option:

1. The **option seller** receives a price (or premium) for granting someone else the option. The seller is also called the **option writer.**

2. The **option buyer** pays a price to the option seller in order to induce the seller to write (or grant) the option.

3. The securities broker finds option buyers and option sellers and acts as their agent in order to consummate transactions. Brokers receive commission fees, which come out of the option's premium, to induce them to arrange the transactions.

Option Prices   Every option has three prices associated with it:

1. *The price of the optioned asset:* This is the fluctuating market price of the optioned security, asset, or other economic quantity.

2. *The option's premium, or purchase price:* The **premium** is the price the option buyer pays to the option writer when the option is originated. Later, the option may be resold at a different premium because premiums fluctuate to reflect market conditions.

3. *The exercise price:* The **striking price,** or **contract price,** or **exercise price** is the price at which the option writer can be legally required to execute the option. This price does not change during the life of the option.

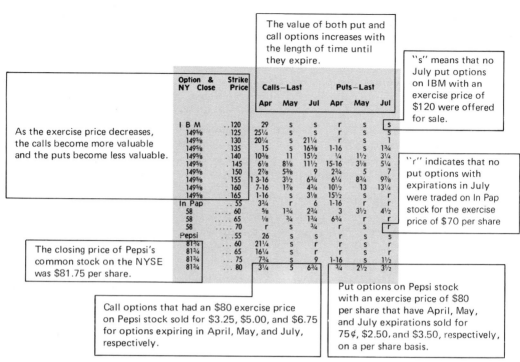

The value of both put and call options increases with the length of time until they expire.

"s" means that no July put options on IBM with an exercise price of $120 were offered for sale.

As the exercise price decreases, the calls become more valuable and the puts become less valuable.

"r" indicates that no put options with expirations in July were traded on In Pap stock for the exercise price of $70 per share

The closing price of Pepsi's common stock on the NYSE was $81.75 per share.

Call options that had an $80 exercise price on Pepsi stock sold for $3.25, $5.00, and $6.75 for options expiring in April, May, and July, respectively.

Put options on Pepsi stock with an exercise price of $80 per share that have April, May, and July expirations sold for 75¢, $2.50, and $3.50, respectively, on a per share basis.

Option & NY Close	Strike Price	Calls—Last			Puts—Last		
		Apr	May	Jul	Apr	May	Jul
I B M	..120	29	s	s	r	s	s
149⅝	.125	25¼	s	s	r	s	s
149⅝	.130	20¼	s	21¼	r	s	1
149⅝	.135	15	s	16⅜	1-16	s	1¾
149⅝	.140	10⅜	11	15½	¼	1½	3¼
149⅝	.145	6⅛	8⅛	11½	15-16	3⅛	5¼
149⅝	.150	2⅞	5⅜	9	2¾	5	7
149⅝	.155	1 3-16	3½	6¾	6¼	8¾	9⅞
149⅝	.160	7-16	1⅞	4¾	10½	13	13¼
149⅝	.165	1-16	s	3⅛	15½	s	r
In Pap	..55	3¾	r	6	1-16	r	r
58	60	⅝	1¾	2¾	3	3½	4½
58	65	⅛	¾	1¾	6¾	r	r
58	70	r	s	¾	r	s	r
Pepsi	...55	26	s	s	r	s	s
81¾	...60	21¼	s	r	r	s	r
81¾	...65	16¼	s	r	r	s	r
81¾	...75	7¾	s	9	1-16	s	1½
81¾	...80	3¼	5	6¾	¾	2½	3½

Figure 21-1 Newspaper excerpt showing 1 day's market data for call and put options.

Markets for Options In 1973 a new options market called the *Chicago Board Options Exchange (CBOE)* began operations. The CBOE is America's first and largest options exchange and organized secondary market for options. It began by trading call options on about two dozen stocks. Trading flourished, and by 1990 the CBOE had expanded to over 3600 options on over 130 stocks. (The CBOE was originally started by the largest, oldest commodity futures exchange in the United States, the Chicago Board of Trade. However, the CBOE is now independent.) Option trading thrived elsewhere too. Today the well-known American Stock Exchange (AMEX) is also the second-largest options exchange in the United States. The venerable Philadelphia Stock Exchange (PHLX) lists options on over a half-dozen foreign currencies and dozens of common stocks, in addition to conducting its traditional common stock trading activities. The Pacific Stock Exchange (PSE) and the New York Stock Exchange (NYSE) also have options markets to supplement their stock exchanges.

Buying an Option To buy an option, an investor should learn the current option prices published daily in many newspapers. A phone call to a stockbroker is all that is needed to carry out a purchase. Figure 21-1 presents a newspaper excerpt listing 1 day's option prices and explains their meaning. The prices shown are of various put and call options traded on the CBOE.

The Options Clearing Corporation The CBOE, AMEX, PHLX, PSE, and NYSE clear their option transactions through the Options Clearing Corporation (OCC). The OCC is headquartered in Chicago, with operations in the four cities where the

517

*Chapter 21
Options,
Warrants,
and
Convertibles*

option exchanges it services are located. It is owned by the five exchanges it services. The OCC and the markets for options are regulated by the Securities and Exchange Commission (SEC).

The OCC issues the options traded at the options exchanges. However, it does not write options; it acts as an intermediary or clearinghouse for the purchase and sale of options. In so doing, the OCC substitutes its ability to deliver for the option writer's ability to deliver.

The OCC's role as intermediary in every option transaction facilitates trading. Owners of options can choose to close out their positions at any time before the option expires by simply selling the option back to the OCC at the current market price. The OCC then simply resells the position to another option buyer at the same current market price. Having a strong clearinghouse like the OCC is fundamental to the maintenance of a smoothly functioning secondary market where options can be traded actively.

The CBOE, AMEX, PHLX, PSE, and NYSE keep track of their trades with computers operated by the OCC and through brokerage firms that are clearing members of the OCC. Since the OCC inserts its own name into every option contract, it essentially becomes the seller in every purchase and the buyer in every sale—thus removing the need for contact between the buyers and the sellers of OCC options. The OCC's role also expedites the clearing process because the computers need bring together only the final buyer and seller, with the OCC as intermediary in order to close out each option contract. All intermediate buyers and sellers who may have owned the option at any time before its expiration are erased from the computer's memory when they sell to the next option buyer.

In addition to clearing functions, the OCC also performs a *guarantee function.* The OCC stands behind and guarantees every option it issues on the CBOE, AMEX, PHLX, PSE, and NYSE. If an option seller defaults on an option obligation, the OCC steps in and delivers on the contract at its own expense. As a result, the options issued at the options exchanges are highly marketable securities. Buyers need not check the credit of the party writing an option before buying it, because the OCC stands behind every option.

Gain-Loss Illustrations for Calls

An investor who thinks a security's price is likely to move upward may want to buy a call. If the security's price falls, only the premium is lost. But if the security's price rises, the buyer of the call can reap capital gains from purchasing the security at the exercise price stated in the call option contract and then selling the security at the higher current market price.

The gain-loss positions of an option buyer and an option writer can be depicted graphically, as shown in Figure 21-2. These graphs are like the gain-loss graphs for the long and short positions in Figure 20-2. Profit or loss is graphed on the vertical axis, and the market price of the optioned security is on the horizontal axis. The **intrinsic value** of each position on the date *when the call expires* is shown by the dashed line in Figure 21-2. The solid curve indicates the expected market price (or premium) of the position *1 month before the call expires.* The distance between the dashed line and the dotted curve measures the call's time value. **Time value** is equal to the premium, or market price, minus the intrinsic value. Note that the time value is

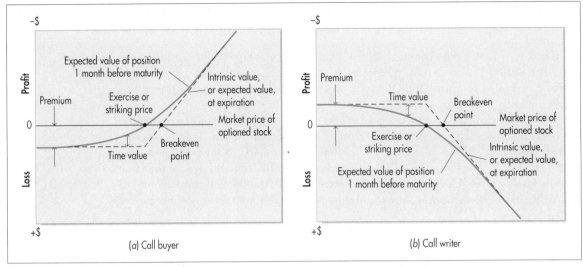

Figure 21-2 Gain-loss graph for the parties to a call option. (*a*) Call buyer; (*b*) call writer.

greatest when the price of the optioned asset equals the exercise price. An option's time value diminishes gradually down to zero on the day it expires.

The Call Buyer's Position The graph of the call option buyer's position, Figure 21-2*a*, shows a loss equal to the premium up to the point where the market price rises above the call contract's exercise price. Where the market price exceeds the exercise price by just enough to cover the premium, the buyer's profit is zero if the buyer exercises the option. The buyer might actually exercise the option at the zero-profit (or break-even) point if he or she thought the price of the security would not rise any higher and simply wanted to recoup an amount equal to the premium. If the market price rises above the break-even point, the buyer can reap a profit (over and above the initial outlay for the premium) by requiring the call writer to sell the optioned security at the exercise price, whereupon the buyer can immediately resell it at the higher market price.[1]

The Call Writer's Position Figure 21-2*b* shows that if the price of the optioned stock stays near zero, it will not be profitable for the call buyer to exercise the option and, as a result, the call writer gets to keep all the premium income. But if the price of the optioned stock rises above the exercise price, the call buyer will find it profitable to exercise the option and the option buyer's profits will equal the option writer's losses.

Before turning from the call option, let's consider what determines the amount of the premium a call writer gets paid to grant a call option. The same factors that determine the amount of a call's price also determine the put premium. Therefore, the principles in Box 21-3 will be equally relevant to puts and to calls.

---

[1] For a discussion of how options are taxed, see Don M. Chance, *Options and Futures* (Orlando, FL: Dryden Press, 1989), pp. 58–61.

James Byer purchases a call option on American Express (AXP) common stock from option writer Carla Rider. Byer pays Rider a premium of $4.50 per share (or $450 for the call option on 100 shares) for a 6-month call with a $50 exercise price. If the market price of AXP's stock rises to $63, Byer can call the stock from Rider at $50 to earn a profit of $13 per share (less the $4.50 premium Byer has already paid) by turning around and immediately selling the stock at $63. Since one party's gains are the other party's losses, this outcome would cost Rider $13 per share (less the $4.50 per share premium she received for writing the option). If Byer exercised his call, Rider would have to buy AXP at $63 and immediately deliver it to Byer at the contract price of $50 and, in so doing, lose $13 per share. Figure 21-3 outlines the gains and losses for Byer and Rider, respectively.

Rider's call-writing position would be justified should the price of AXP stock decline to $40 per share. Then, Byer would lose money if he called the stock from Rider at $50 per share, because he could sell it for only $40. Byer presumably would not exercise his call and would lose the premium of $4.50 per share paid for the option. In this case, Rider would keep the $450 total premium Byer paid her for doing nothing.

21-2   Call Premium Determinants

The six factors listed in Principles Box 21-3 have a readily observable impact on option prices. Some of these factors interact differently in determining call and put premiums. Here we consider how they interact to determine call premiums; put premiums will be analyzed later in the chapter.

Figure 21-3   Gain-loss illustrations for a call on American Express Stock (AXP). (*a*) James Byer; (*b*) Carla Rider.

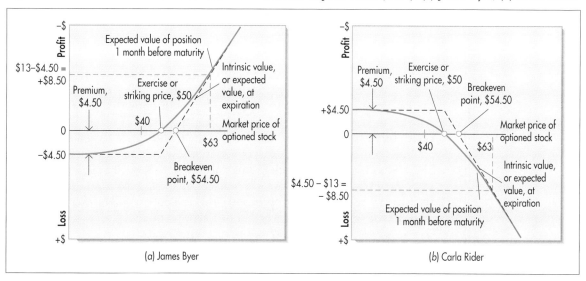

PRINCIPLES: Determining Put and Call Premiums

Six factors determine the price, or premium, that the put or call buyer must pay for an option:

1. *The market price of the optioned security:* It takes a larger premium to induce the option writer to assume the risks associated with 100 shares of high-priced stock because the potential losses are larger than for 100 shares of a low-priced stock. If market prices change 10 percent, the change in value of 100 shares of a $20 stock is only $200, whereas a 10 percent change in value of 100 shares of a $150 stock is $1500, for example.

2. *The length of time remaining in the option's life:* When an option is purchased, the buyer is told the length of time during which the option may be exercised. Writers of longer-term options charge larger premiums than writers of shorter-term options on the same security. The charge is higher simply because the probability that the option will be exercised and that the writer will lose money rises with the length of time the option remains exercisable.

3. *The riskiness of the underlying asset:* The riskiness (or variability of return) of the optioned security matters because a sizable price change can make it profitable for the option owner to exercise the option. The most important factor affecting a security's risk is the asset's price volatility. Option writers assess the riskiness of the underlying asset and require higher premiums to write options on riskier assets because the options on high-risk securities are more likely to be exercised and cause the option writer to take a loss.

   Figure 21-4 shows why the call premium should be higher for an option on a stock like XYZ than on a stock like ABC that is identical in every way, except that ABC is less risky. The best possible outcomes in the right-hand tail of the probability distributions are higher for the riskier XYZ stock, and as a result, the call on XYZ has more profit potential.

4. *The exercise price:* The exercise price of an option is usually approximately equal to the market price of the security on the day the option was originally written. Sometimes the exercise price of a put or call is "points away" from the market price (that is, the exercise price is above or below the market price by several dollars). Say, a 9-month option is originally sold with an exercise price of $50, which is near the optioned security's market price at that time. Three months later, if the market price has fallen to $40 and the option is resold to a new buyer, it is now a six-month option with a $50 exercise price on a stock selling for $40 per share. When the exercise price is several dollars above the current market price of the optioned security, there is a different probability that the option will be exercised. As a result, the option will be worth a different premium.

5. *The riskless rate of interest:* The level of market interest rates on default-free securities like U.S. Treasury bills affects option prices through the relation-

ship between the exercise price and the security's market price explained in item (4). The present value of the exercise price varies inversely with market interest rates; this, in turn, affects the option's premium. Call premiums respond directly, and put prices are inversely related, to the current level of the riskless interest rate.

6. *Cash dividends:* On the first trading day after a common stock makes a cash dividend payment (the ex-dividend date), the market price of the stock drops off by approximately the amount of the cash dividend per share that was paid (since the value of the corporation was depleted by the unrecoverable cash dividend payment). This lower price on the optioned security changes the value of any options on the security [as explained in item (1)].

521

Chapter 21
Options,
Warrants,
and
Convertibles

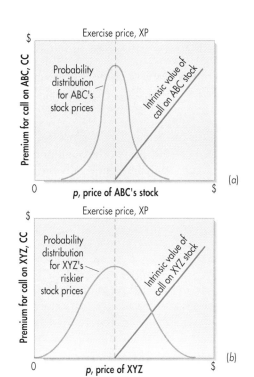

Figure 21-4 Call premiums are affected by risk. (*a*) Call model and probability distribution for ABC's stock prices; (*b*) call model and probability distribution for XYZ's stock prices; (*c*) determining the premiums for calls on ABC and XYZ.

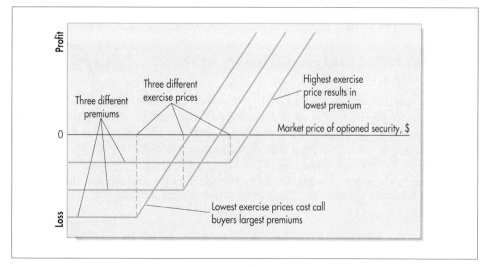

Figure 21-5 Gain-loss graph showing the relationships between call premiums and exercise prices.

How Exercise Price Affects Call Premiums

Figure 21-5 illustrates the relationship between exercise prices, the premium, and the potential gains and losses from a call. The figure compares three calls on the same stock that differ only with respect to their exercise prices. Lower exercise prices result in higher call premiums because the call writer will have to pay larger amounts if the call buyer finds it profitable to exercise.

How Call Premium Determinants Interact

The interaction of the various factors that determine a call premium is illustrated in Figure 21-6. The dashed curves represent the prices for calls that differ only in the number of months until they expire. The figure shows that the premium on a call rises as the market price of the optioned security rises, and also demonstrates that premiums on long-lived calls exceed premiums on short-lived options.

The Maximum Value Line Figure 21-6 contains a line emanating from the origin of the graph that represents an upper price limit for calls; it is labeled **maximum value line** and contains all the points at which the call's price equals the price of the optioned stock, since the call is never more valuable than the price of the optioned stock.

The Minimum Value Line Figure 21-6 also contains a line projecting from the exercise price labeled the **minimum value line,** which represents all the costs of calls (or premiums), denoted CC, larger than or equal to the amount by which the price of the optioned stock P exceeds the exercise price XP. The minimum value line can be represented symbolically as

$$CC > (P - XP) \tag{21-1}$$

523

Chapter 21
Options,
Warrants,
and
Convertibles

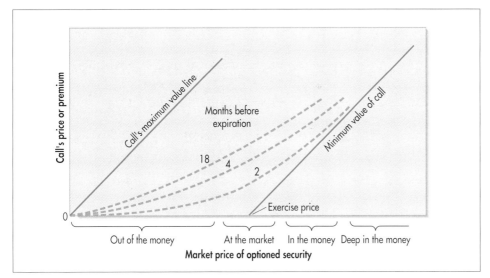

Figure 21-6   The determination of call premiums.

No investor should ever let a call's premium fall below $P - XP$. If this happens, the call can be bought at the ridiculously low price CC and exercised at price XP. Thus, by spending only CC + XP dollars, an investor could acquire the optioned stock at less than its market price of P dollars. The optioned stock could then be sold at its higher market price for an easy profit of $P - (CC + XP)$ dollars per share.

Limited Liability   After a call buyer pays for a call, the option can never create a debt for its owner. Call prices can never attain negative values (become liabilities). As a result of this *limited liability*, call prices are always larger than or equal to zero (that is, CC ≥ 0). This means that call prices never fall below the horizontal axis of Figure 21-6.

The maximum and minimum value lines in Figure 21-6 delineate the area within which call prices may fluctuate. Within these boundaries, call prices tend to lie along one of the dashed curves. The economic factors that determine the shapes of the dashed curves are discussed in Principles Box 21-3.

Note the labels on the horizontal stock price axis in Figure 21-6. These phrases describe the value of a call and are defined as follows:

- A call that is **out of the money** is usually not worth much because the market price of the optioned security is less than the exercise price.

- A call option that is **at the market** has a market price for the optioned security approximately equal to the call's exercise price.

- A call that is **in the money** has a market price for its optioned securities above the call's exercise price.

- A call that is **deep in the money** is highly valued because the market price of the optioned security is far above the exercise price.

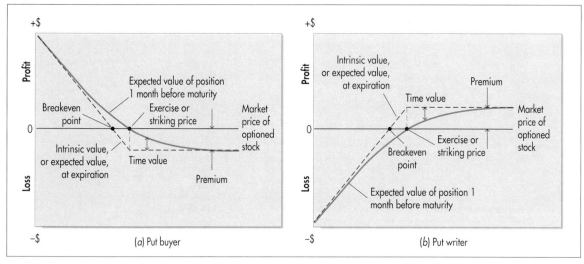

Figure 21-7 Gain-loss graphs for the parties to a put. (*a*) Put buyer; (*b*) put writer.

The call option is an interesting investment for a bullish price speculator. A bearish speculator might wish to sell a call option, but wouldn't want to buy one. A bear might buy a put option in order to profit from a security price decline.

21-3 Put Options

A put option offers profit possibilities similar in some respects to those derived from a short position, but offers other benefits a bearish price speculator cannot obtain with a short sale. The buyer of a put option profits if the market price of the optioned security falls, just as a short seller would. But unlike the short seller, the put buyer has *limited liability,* because only the premium can be lost if the optioned security experiences a price rise.

Gain-Loss Illustrations

Position graphs for the writer and the buyer of a put are shown in Figure 21-7. The buyer receives the maximum gain if the market price of the optioned security falls to zero; that is, if the issuer of the optioned security goes bankrupt and the security becomes worthless, the put buyer's profits are maximized. In this case the bearish put buyer could buy the optioned stock for nothing and then put it to the option writer (that is, legally force the put's writer to buy the stock) at the exercise price. The gains for the put buyer (Figure 21-7*a*) are losses for the put's (Figure 21-7*b*) writer.

Figure 21-7*b* shows that if the price of the security rises, the writer gains the put premium (denoted PP) but no more. Options writers' gains are always limited to the amount of the premiums they receive. But the put writer's losses are also limited. Figure 21-7*b* shows that the put writer's maximum loss equals the option's exercise price less the put premium received per share, or XP − PP dollars.

525

Chapter 21
Options,
Warrants,
and
Convertibles

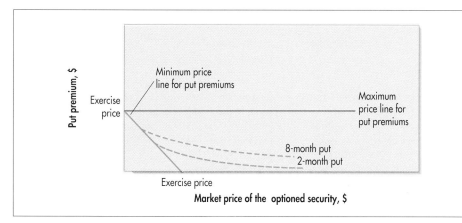

Figure 21-8 Determinants of put premiums.

Put Premiums

The market price of a put option is determined by the factors discussed in Box 21-3. Some of these factors interact differently to determine call prices. Figure 21-8 illustrates how put prices are determined by the price of the optioned security and the length of time the option remains open.

The dashed curves in Figure 21-8 show how put prices move inversely with the price of the optioned security. The two dashed curves also indicate that a longer-lived put is worth more than one with a shorter life. The solid lines trace the maximum and minimum prices for put premiums, denoted PP. The accompanying case (page 526) looks at factors to consider in deciding whether to buy an option, sell short, or buy a stock directly.

Table 21-1 compares and contrasts the rights and obligations of the parties that buy and sell securities and options.

Table 21-1
**Rights and Obligations of Buyers and Sellers
of Options and Securities**

	Buyer	*Seller*
Call	*Right* to buy on or before the expiration date at the exercise price	*Obligation* to sell at the exercise price on or before the expiration date
Put	*Right* to sell on or before the expiration date at the exercise price	*Obligation* to buy at exercise price on or before the expiration date
Short	Not applicable	*Obligation* to deliver securities and accept the current market price
Long	*Right* to buy at the current market price	*Right* to sell at the current market price

CASE

Two Investors Face Decisions

Ms. Bullish and Mr. Bear are faced with decisions over whether to buy an option or take a direct position in a security. Their situations are as follows.

Ms. Bullish believes the price of the ABC stock is going to rise sharply in the very near future. She cannot decide whether she should take a long position directly in ABC stock or buy a call option on ABC stock. She can tell that either of the two positions will be profitable if the price rises enough to cover the brokerage commissions paid to obtain the position. But which one is the more desirable?

Mr. Bear thinks the price of XYZ Corporation's stock will decline sharply in the near future. He cannot decide whether to sell XYZ short or buy a put option on XYZ stock. His calculations have shown that both positions will be profitable if the price of XYZ drops enough to cover the brokerage commissions incurred to establish them. But which position is the more profitable?

Factors Favoring Options

An investor who wants to speculate that the price of some security will change must choose between buying an option and taking a position directly in the underlying security. Purchasing the option can be more desirable for two reasons.

1. *Financial leverage:* The investment in an option is limited to the premium paid for it. In contrast, taking a position directly in the underlying security requires a larger sum of money (even after allowing for the use of margins). The option position offers more financial leverage than the long or short position. Stated differently, each dollar invested in a option premium can generate more dollars of profit than a dollar invested directly in the underlying security. Figure 21-9 illustrates this concept, in the steeper lines for the options positions.

2. *Limited liability:* The holder of an option can lose no more than the premium if the price of the optioned security moves adversely. In contrast, the losses associated with a direct position in the underlying security will almost always be larger if the price of the optioned asset declines significantly. Figure 21-9*b* shows that the potential losses extend downward without limit for the short sale.

Be careful not to misinterpret Figure 21-9*a*. Although the figure shows the potential loss is 100 percent of the invested funds for both the call and the long position, do not forget that many more dollars must be invested to establish the long position (even with margins) than to buy a call on the same security.

Financial leverage and limited liability are the two main reasons to prefer options over taking a position directly in the asset. Other factors also favor buying put options.

3. *No interest lost:* A third advantage to buying a put over selling short is that short sellers lose the use of the proceeds from their short sale without being paid any interest for the funds. Typically, the short seller's brokerage takes the cash proceeds from the short sale and uses these funds without paying any interest on them. In contrast, there is no problem with lost interest on untouchable proceeds to hinder the put buyer.

4. *No cash dividends to pay:* The put buyer does not have to pay cash dividends to a third party; a short seller must make up any cash dividends the issuing corporation paid to the owner of the borrowed shares.

5. *No constraint:* Short sales can be made only on an uptick in some markets—that is, after the price has risen in the preceding trade—while a put can be purchased at any time.

6. *No involuntarily endings:* Short sellers may be involuntarily closed out of the position if the third party who lent the shares demands them back. **American puts** can be exercised any time during their life. (**European options** can be exercised only on the day they expire.)

One Big Advantage of the Direct Positions

The advantages of financial leverage and the limited liability associated with the option tend to be somewhat offset by one advantage of trading in the underlying security directly: expiration. *Options expire and become worthless if the price of the underlying security does not move far enough within*

526

the period of time covered by the option's life. In contrast, the long and short positions can be held open indefinitely without incurring any additional costs. (This last factor can pale in significance if the investor is confident that the price of a stock is poised for a profitable, sharp, short-term move. The length of the option's life is a consideration that should be reflected in the price of the option.)

In the final analysis, there is no single correct solution for the decisions facing Ms. Bullish and Mr. Bear. Each investment situation is unique and must be judged on its own merits.

21-4 Index and Other Options

Index options are puts and calls whose premiums are based on the value of a market index. Index options are traded in the United States at the exchanges listed in Table 21-2. Some market indexes are based on a highly diversified list of stocks—such the Standard & Poor's 500 Stocks Composite Index. Others are based on a small number of homogeneous securities called *subindexes* or *industry indexes.* The options on the subindexes are usually called **subindex options.**

Index options are all cash settlement options. **Cash settlement** means that the bundle of securities underlying the index is not delivered to the owner of the option when it is exercised. Instead, if the option is "in the money," upon either exercise or maturity the owner of the option receives an amount of cash based on the difference between the value of the index and the index option's exercise price.

The same factors that determine the prices of options on individual securities (see the Principles Box 21-3) also determine the premiums on index options. The intrinsic value of a call option on an index equals the amount by which the underlying index exceeds the call's exercise price. For example, if the value of the S&P 500 Index is 380, a call with an exercise price of 375 will have an intrinsic value of 5. The *time value* of a

Figure 21-9 Rate-of-return diagrams. (*a*) Buying a call versus buying the underlying security; (*b*) buying a put versus selling the underlying security short.

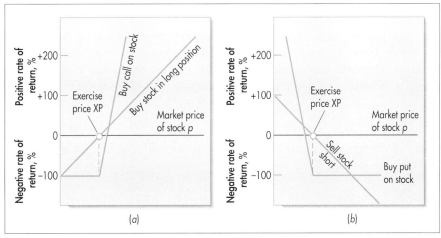

(*a*)

(*b*)

Table 21-2
Index Options and Their Exchanges

Name of index option	Exchange
AMEX Computer Technology Index	AMEX
AMEX Institutional	AMEX
AMEX Major Market Index	AMEX
AMEX Oil & Gas Index	AMEX
AMEX Transportation Index	AMEX
CRB Commodities Index	NYFE
Financial News Composite Index	PSE
Japan Index	AMEX
NYSE Composite Index	NYSE
PSE Gold-Silver	PSE
PSE Over-the-Counter	PSE
PSE Utility	PSE
PSE Technology Index	PSE
S&P 500 Index (SPX)*	CBOE
S&P 500 Index LEAPS†	CBOE
Value Line Arithmetic	PSE
Value Line Index	KCBT

* This is the most popular (highest-volume) option in the world.

† "LEAPS" stands for "long-term equity appreciation securities." This option has denominations one-tenth as large as the similar option, and maturities as long as 24 months.

call will make its premium exceed its intrinsic value. The S&P 500 call might have a *premium* of 8.5, for example, which implies that its time value is 8.5 − 5.0 = 3.5. The market value of that index option will be $100 × 8.5 = $850 because most index options are priced at $100 times their premium. The prices of the index options fluctuate continuously as dictated by the fluctuating value of the underlying index, the exercise price of the index option, the length of time until the option matures, the perceived riskiness of the index, and market interest rates.

Figure 21-10 shows some stock index options price (or premium) quotations. To interpret these listings, consider as an example the CBOE's May call on the S&P 100 that has an exercise (or striking) price of 215. This call has an intrinsic value of 218.46 − 215 = 3.46. The call's premium of 8⅞ (or 8.875) therefore contains a time value of 8.875 − 3.46 = 5.415. The price of the contract will be 8.875 × $100 = $887.50.

Uses of Index Options

Consider two categories of investment risk that we will call diversifiable, stock-specific risk and undiversifiable market risk.

Diversifiable, Stock-Specific Risk   Stock-specific risk stems from the idiosyncratic price fluctuations of each stock. An investor can try to manage stock-specific risk by processing information about a stock rapidly in an effort to buy and sell advanta-

529

*Chapter 21
Options,
Warrants,
and
Convertibles*

Index Options

Chicago

S. & P 100

Option & NY Close	Strike Price	Calls-Last Apr	May	Jun	Puts-Last Apr	May	Jun
SP100 185		r	r	s	r	⅛	s
218.46 ..190		29	28½	s	1-16	⅛	s
218.46 ..195		24¼	24¼	s	1-16	3-16	s
218.46 ..200		r	19¼	20½	1-16	½	1¼
218.46 ..205		14¼	16¼	17¾	⅛	1⅛	2⅛
218.46 ..210		9⅜	12	14¼	7-16	2	3⅜
218.46 ..215		5¾	8⅞	11½	1½	3¾	5¼
218.46 ..220		2¾	6⅛	8¼	3½	6¼	7½
218.46 ..225		1¼	4⅛	6¼	7⅛	4	10¼
218.46 ..230		7-16	2⅝	4½	11½	12½	15
218.46 ..235		3-16	1 9-16	3¼	16½	17½	18
218.46 ..240		1-16	⅞	2¼	22	23	r

Total call vol. 343,460 Call open int. 798,191
Total put vol. 246,817 Put open int. 592,655

American

Major Market Index

Option & NY Close	Strike Price	Calls-Last Apr	May	Jun	Puts-Last Apr	May	Jun
MMIdx 290		30½	r	s	1-16	7-16	s
321.21 ..295		27½	r	s	⅛	1 1-16	s
321.21 ..300		19½	22	s	3-16	1¾	s
321.21 ..305		16½	20¾	s	⅜	2½	s
321.21 ..310		14	17	r	1 1-16	4	6½
321.21 ..315		9	14¼	17¾	2⅜	6½	9
321.21 ..320		6⅞	12¼	17	4¾	8⅜	12
321.21 ..325		4¼	9¼	12¼	7¼	10¾	14¾
321.21 ..330		2⅝	7⅛	r	10½	13	r
321.21 ..335		1½	5½	9⅜	13⅞	17	r
321.21 ..340		1	4¼	6⅜	17¾	r	r
321.21 ..345		⅝	2⅞	5⅛	27	r	r
321.21 ..350		⅜	2½	4⅝	29	29	31⅝
321.21 ..355		3-16	1¾	4	r	r	31
321.21 ..360		1-16	1 5-16	2⅜	r	r	38⅛

Total call vol. 64,168 Call open int. 136,220
Total put vol. 30,719 Put open int. 78,195

Computer Technology Index

Option & NY Close	Strike Price	Calls-Last Apr	May	Jun	Puts-Last Apr	May	Jun
CTIdx 110		r	r	r	½	r	r
115.22 ..115		1 9-16	r	r	2¼	r	r
115.22 ..120		⅜	r	r	r	r	r

Total call vol. 20 Call open int. 896
Total put vol. 21 Put open int. 655

Figure 21-10 Newspaper excerpt showing price quotations for some stock index options.

geously. But since the market prices are efficient, that is not easy. Stock-specific risk can be reduced to zero via simple diversification (as illustrated in Figure 24-1); as a result, it is nonexistent in diversified portfolios and market indexes.

Undiversifiable Market Risk   In contrast, market risk is a systematic risk that simple diversification will not reduce. As Chapter 17 explained, *market risk* affects all assets simultaneously. Since market risk is undiversifiable, it is equal to the total risk in highly diversified portfolios and market indexes.

Three different strategies may be useful in managing the effects of undiversifiable market risk: sophisticated diversification techniques (discussed in Chapter 24), superior market timing (which is extremely difficult), and use of index options to hedge (or insure). Index options provide a convenient way to hedge and thus reduce a portfolio's exposure to undiversifiable market risk.

Box 21-4

COMPUTATION: Betting on the Market with an Index Option

Mary Gherkil wants to bet that the S&P 100 stock market index will rise above its current level of 216. So, she decides to buy a call option. That way, if she is wrong and the market declines, she loses only the cost of the unexercised call. Before leaving for lunch, Mary calls her broker and selects from among the list of calls that are being traded a May call on the OEX with an exercise price of 215. This call has a premium of $7 and a $700 purchase price ($100 × $7). While Mary is having lunch, the S&P 100 Index advances to 218, causing her OEX call's premium to rise to $12. She immediately goes to the phone and tells her broker to sell the option for $1200 ($100 × $12). Mary gambled on the market and had a gross gain of $500.

Sales price for OEX of $100 times $12 equals:	$1,200
Less: Purchase price of $100 times $7 equals:	700
Gross profit	$ 500

Mary's broker charges her a $50 commission to buy and sell the OEX option. So, during lunch she makes a net taxable gain of ($500 gross gain less $50 commission) $450.

Index options are not only useful for reducing market risk, they also provide a way of betting on the direction the market will take (Box 21-4).

The Options on the S&P Indexes

The options on the S&P 100 and 500 stocks indexes are the most popular options of all; trading volume frequently exceeds 50 percent of the total volume of options traded at the CBOE. And the CBOE is the biggest option exchange in the United States—it makes markets in over 3600 options on various stocks and indexes. At any given moment there are between 200 and 400 floor traders and market makers in the S&P index options trading pit at the CBOE actively trading this phenomenal financial instrument. These particular index options are so popular because investors understand the S&P indexes and use the options on them to hedge market risk. Many others simply like to bet on the market.[2]

Other Options

Interest rate options are like equity options that apply to interest rate–sensitive debt securities. The CBOE trades puts and calls on short-term and long-term debt securities. These options give their owners the right to sell or buy debt at a certain

---

[2] The CBOE and AMEX started offering capped stock index options in 1991. These put and call options have limits on their profitability and, as a result, are cheaper than the traditional options.

531

*Chapter 21
Options,
Warrants,
and
Convertibles*

price before a specified date. These interest rate options should be called *debt options* because they apply to dollar-denominated debt securities instead of interest rate–denominated debt securities. However, a cash settlement call or put on a debt security behaves like a cash settlement put or call, respectively, on the debt security's interest rate because a bond's price and yield move inversely. This close inverse relationship is probably why options on debt securities are also called *interest rate options.*

Trading in the interest rate options has never become very active. But, options on debt futures contracts are actively traded on T-bills, T-notes, T-bonds, Eurodollar bonds, municipal bonds, and other debt securities at Chicago's futures exchanges (see Chapter 22).

Options on foreign currencies with various maturities are traded at the Philadelphia Stock Exchange on Australian dollars, Canadian dollars, British pounds, German marks, Japanese yen, and Swiss francs. Importers, exporters, and international investors use these options to hedge their foreign exchange risks.

Embedded options are puts and calls that are implicit in a contract. Home buyers with mortgages have an embedded option that allows them to pay the mortgage off before it matures. Mortgage borrowers have the option to *put* their mortgage back to their lender. This ability to get out of a mortgage contract is valuable because it gives the homeowner the ability to sell the home and move. We will examine other kinds of securities that have embedded options, such as warrants and convertible securities, in the remainder of this chapter.

21-5 Warrants

Warrants are options to buy shares of common stock. They are like calls to the extent that they are options to buy a fixed number of shares at a predetermined price during some specified period of time. But warrants are also different: A warrant is written by the corporation that issues the optioned stock rather than by an independent option writer. Warrants are usually given away by the issuing corporation as attachments to a new issue of bonds or preferred stock to "sweeten" the new issue—to raise the sales price per share and to make the issue easier to sell. Financially troubled corporations that anticipate problems in selling a new issue of preferred stock to raise needed capital are typical warrant writers.

Like call options, warrants may expire at a certain date. They may also be perpetual warrants, which never expire. Most warrants are detachable from the bond or preferred stock to which they were attached at issue. After they are detached, warrants can be traded as independent securities, like call options.

Warrant Prices

The *exercise price* of a warrant is what the owner must pay to purchase the stated number of optioned shares. The *intrinsic value* of a warrant is the market price P per share of stock, less the exercise price of XP dollars per share, multiplied by the number of shares of common stock N obtained with one warrant, or zero, whichever amount is more:

Box 21-5

COMPUTATION: The Intrinsic Value of a Warrant

A warrant that entitles its owner to buy two shares of stock ($N = 2$) at an exercise price of $50 per share (XP = $50) while the market price is $60 per share ($P = $60) has an intrinsic value of $20 per warrant [2($60 − $50)].

$$\text{Intrinsic value} = N(P - \text{XP}) \qquad (21\text{-}2)$$

or zero, whichever is more.

Figure 21-11 illustrates some of the factors that determine the market value of a warrant. Note that when the market price of the optioned security is below the exercise price ($P <$ XP), the warrant may still have a positive intrinsic value. A warrant (or any other option) cannot have a negative value, because no one can force the warrant owner to take a harmful action. When the market price of the optioned security is above the warrant's exercise price, the warrant has a positive intrinsic value that increases directly with the price of the optioned security.

The actual market price of the warrant follows the dashed curves in Figure 21-11. These curves show that a warrant (like all other call options) has a market price (or premium) lying above its intrinsic value. The amount by which a warrant's price exceeds its intrinsic value (the option's time value) is determined by expectations about future stock prices in the same way that other option premiums are determined (see Principles Box 21-3). In fact, a comparison of Figure 21-6, which illustrates the determinants of a call option's premium, with Figure 21-11 reveals that the two figures are essentially identical. Call options and warrants differ significantly only in their writers and in the warrants' dilution effects (because exercising a warrant causes new shares to be issued).

Figure 21-11 The determinants of a warrant's price.

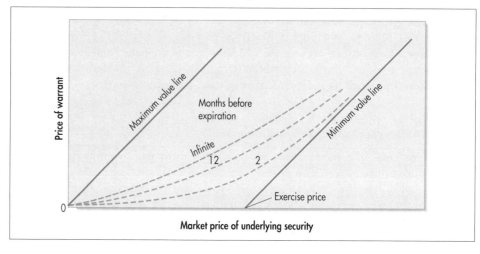

The Warrant Agreement

533

*Chapter 21
Options,
Warrants,
and
Convertibles*

The terms of a warrant are specified in a legal contract called the **warrant agreement.** This agreement stipulates when the warrant may be exercised, among other important details. Most warrants are like long-term call options—that is, they may be exercised at any time within 5 to 10 years. A few warrants have perpetual lives, while others may be exercised only at specific times.

Most warrants are protected against stock splits and stock dividends. If the security to which the warrant applies undergoes a 2-for-1 split, for instance, the warrant is adjusted so that it entitles its owner to two of the new split shares for every one of the old shares (since the new shares are worth half of what the old shares would have been worth if they had not been split). However, most warrants are not protected against the eroding effect of cash dividends on the price of the optioned security. When a common stock starts to trade on the first day after it pays a cash dividend (called *trading ex-dividend*), its market price drops off by an amount equal to the cash dividend just paid. This drop in price simultaneously decreases the value of the warrant, as illustrated in Figure 21-11 by movement to the left along one of the dashed curves.

Some warrants are *nondetachable*, which means that they cannot be separated from their associated securities, but most are *detachable* and may be traded as independent securities. The warrant agreement outlines all such rights and provisions.

21-6   Convertible Securities

As explained in Chapter 3, most convertible preferred stocks and convertible bonds grant their owners the right to convert into another security, usually the common stock of the corporation that issued the convertibles. Occasionally a convertible bond can be converted into the issuer's preferred stock. The conversion is not a taxable exchange.

Analysis of the Embedded Options

Convertible securities can be viewed as a combination of a nonconvertible security and an embedded call option on the issuer's stock. As a result, the price of a convertible security equals the sum of the two components:

$$P_C = P_E + P_{CO}$$

where P_C = price of convertible security   (21-3)

P_E = price of equivalent nonconvertible security

P_{CO} = price for call option on the issuer's stock

Since call options have positive values, convertible securities typically sell at prices that are slightly above (and yields that are slightly below) nonconvertible securities that are equivalent in every other way. The embedded call options are nondetachable and cannot be traded independently. When a conversion occurs, the call option must be turned in with the associated bond or preferred stock so the convertible security can be used to pay for the new stock.

Most convertible securities are callable. The buyer of a **callable convertible** has essentially purchased a nonconvertible security, purchased a call option on the issuer's stock, and sold the issuer a call option on the nonconvertible security—all at once. These three components are reflected in the price of a convertible that is callable.[3]

$$P_{CC} = P_{ENC} + P_{CO} - P_{CON}$$

where P_{CC} = price of callable convertible security (21-4)

P_{ENC} = price of equivalent nonconvertible and noncallable security

P_{CO} = price for a call option on the issuer's stock

P_{CON} = price for a call option on the nonconvertible security

Traditional Analysis of Convertibles

Every issue of convertible securities stipulates a par conversion price, a conversion ratio, or both. If only a conversion price is given, the conversion ratio may be determined

$$\text{Conversion ratio} = \frac{\text{face value of the convertible security}}{\text{par conversion price of the issuer's stock}}$$

(21-5)

The **conversion ratio** gives the number of shares of stock received for each convertible security. If only the conversion ratio is given, the **par conversion price** can be obtained by dividing the conversion ratio into the face (or par) value of the convertible security. For example, a conversion ratio of 4 combined with a convertible preferred stock that had a face value of $100 per share, as is the case in Table 21-3 and Figure 21-12, implies a par conversion price of $25 per share for the stock. This means that it will be increasingly profitable to convert the security as the underlying stock's market price rises above $25 per share.

[3] The options that are embedded in a convertible security can be evaluated by using the Black-Scholes formula to value the call option and the put-call parity formula to value the put option. These formulas are in the appendixes to this chapter.

535

*Chapter 21
Options,
Warrants,
and
Convertibles*

Table 21-3
Data for Two Convertible Securities

	ABC's convertible preferred stock	*XYZ's convertible bond*
Known data:		
Market price of convertible	$110	$1100
Par conversion price of the underlying common stock	$25	$250
Conversion ratio, Eq. (21-5)	4	4
Calculated data:		
Estimated value of equivalent nonconvertible security	$90	$900
Conversion value, Eq. (21-7)	$100	$1000
Downside risk percentage, Eq. (21-6)	22.2%	22.2%
Convertible security's percentage conversion premium, Eq. (21-9)	10%	10%

Estimating Comparable Market Price   An integral part of the analysis of a convertible bond or preferred stock is to estimate the market price of an equivalent nonconvertible security that can be used as a standard for comparison. Assessing what the convertible security would be selling for if it did not have the embedded call option on the issuer's stock is easy if the issuer has a similar issue of nonconvertible (or straight, or pure) securities outstanding. If the issuer does not have a similar nonconvertible issue outstanding, the price of an equivalent nonconvertible security must be estimated by surveying other firms' nonconvertible securities that have the

Figure 21-12   The price of a convertible security relative to the price of the underlying stock.

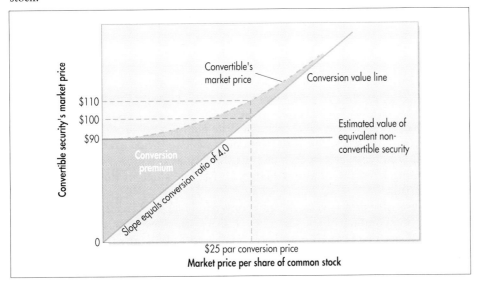

same quality rating and approximately the same time until maturity, coupon rate, and other characteristics. The data in Table 21-3 assume that equivalent nonconvertible preferred stocks and nonconvertible bonds are selling for $90 and $900, respectively.

The market price of an equivalent nonconvertible security provides a floor below which the price of the convertible security's price cannot fall. As explained in Chapter 11, bond prices and market interest rates move inversely. So, this floor moves inversely with market interest rates.

Calculating Downside Risk   After the market price of an equivalent nonconvertible security has been determined, the convertible security's downside risk percentage can be calculated.

$$D = \frac{P_C - P_{NC}}{P_{NC}} \tag{21-6}$$

where D = percentage of downside risk

P_C = market price of convertible

P_{NC} = price of an equivalent nonconvertible security

This figure measures the percentage price decline convertible investors would suffer if the option to convert into the issuer's stock became worthless. It also measures the convertible's **price premium** over the price of an equivalent nonconvertible security.

If a convertible preferred stock or bond were selling for 110 percent of its face value of $100 or $1000, respectively, while a nonconvertible equivalent security was selling for 90 percent of the convertible's face value, for example, the downside risk would be 22.2 percent:

$$\frac{\$110 - \$90}{\$90} = \frac{\$1100 - \$900}{\$900} = 22.2\%$$

Determining Conversion Value   To make advantageous conversion decisions, the investor should also determine the **conversion value** of a convertible security.

$$\begin{matrix} \text{conversion} \\ \text{value} \end{matrix} = \begin{matrix} \text{conversion} \\ \text{ratio} \end{matrix} \times \begin{matrix} \text{market price per share} \\ \text{for the issuer's stock} \end{matrix} \tag{21-7}$$

The conversion (or parity) value represents the market value of the convertible if it were converted into stock; this is the minimum value of the convertible based on the current price of the issuer's stock. The conversion value is represented by the straight line emanating from the origin in Figure 21-12. The slope of this line equals the conversion ratio.

If a convertible preferred stock had a conversion ratio of 4 and the market price of the underlying common stock was $25 per share, the conversion value would be 4 shares × $25 per share = $100 per share. A convertible bond with a conversion ratio of 4 and a stock price of $250, like the one in Table 21-3, implies a conversion value of $1000 per bond.

Determining the Conversion Premium   As Figure 21-12 shows, the market price of a

537

*Chapter 21
Options,
Warrants,
and
Convertibles*

convertible usually exceeds its conversion value by the amount of the conversion premium. An investor can determine the **conversion premium** included in the price of a convertible security using the following formula:

$$\text{Conversion premium in dollars} = \text{convertible's market price} - \text{convertible's conversion value} \qquad (21\text{-}8)$$

The conversion premium is represented by the shaded area in Figure 21-12. The premium is stated as a percentage of the convertible security's conversion value, as shown below, to facilitate comparisons with different convertible securities.

$$CP = \frac{P_C - CV}{CV} \qquad (21\text{-}9)$$

where CP = conversion premium as a percentage

      P_C = market price of convertible

      CV = conversion value of convertible

A convertible preferred stock that was selling for $110 while its conversion value was $100, for example, would be selling with a 10 percent conversion premium.

$$\frac{\$110 - \$100}{\$100} = 10\%$$

Similarly, a convertible bond that had a conversion value of $1000 and was selling at $1100 would contain a 10 percent conversion premium.

Figure 21-12 shows that the conversion premium diminishes toward zero as the price of the underlying stock appreciates. Figure 21-13 shows how the percentage conversion premium and the percentage price premium (or the percentage of

Figure 21-13 Response curves for a convertible security's price premiums as the price of the underlying stock varies.

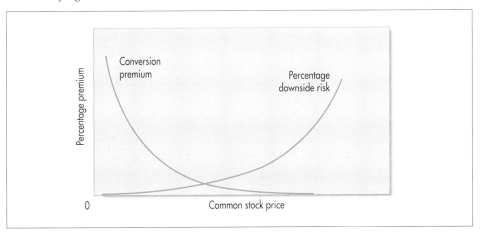

downside risk) over an equivalent nonconvertible security vary inversely as the underlying stock's price fluctuates.

Comparing Cash Yield Comparing the cash yield of the convertible security with the cash yields from investment alternatives provides another perspective on the analysis of convertibles.

$$\text{Cash yield} = \frac{\text{annual cash dividend or coupon}}{\text{market price of security}} \tag{21-10}$$

The convertible bond's coupon yield is typically about twice as high as the common stock's cash dividend yield. The convertible preferred stock's cash dividend yield also usually exceeds the yield from the underlying common stock. Convertible investors typically enjoy these high rates of cash yield until such time as the common stock's price rises significantly. Then, if the issuing corporation flourishes, the investor can convert to stock. The ability of investors to enjoy the senior position and the high cash yields from owning a fixed income security while maintaining the option of converting their security and participating in stockholders' price gains makes convertible securities attractive.

Summary

The assortment of investment positions from which an investor may choose is exceedingly diverse. In the simplest case, an investor can profit from price increases or decreases by assuming a long or a short position. Investors who are risk-averse can create hedges by combining long and short positions.

On a more sophisticated level, investors can profit from price increases or decreases by purchasing calls or puts, respectively. When a price rise is expected, buying a call option may have advantages over buying the security long. And buying a put may be more desirable than selling short when a price drop is expected. Buying options may be more profitable than taking long or short positions for two reasons: Options offer financial leverage and limited liability, both of which are unavailable in the analogous long and short positions.

Another option possibility exists through warrants, which are offered by corporations as "sweeteners" for new issues of bonds, preferred stock, or common stock that are difficult to sell. Warrants have value and work like call options.

Convertible preferred stock and convertible bonds combine the benefits of fixed income investing (namely, coupon income and a high-priority claim on corporate assets in the event of a bankruptcy) with the option of sharing in the price appreciation benefits normally reserved for the common stockholders.

Further Reading

Bookstaber, Richard, *The Complete Investment Book* (Glenview, Ill.: Scott, Foresman, 1985).
Chapters 21 through 27 discuss various aspects of option analysis. Most chapters list computer programs written in BASIC language that are ready to run.

McMillan, Lawrence G., *Options as a Strategic Investment*, 2d ed. (New York: New York Institute of Finance, 1986).
This nonmathematical book provides numerous numerical examples. Options and option strategies are explained in an easy-to-understand manner.

Mesler, Donald T., *Stock Index Options* (Chicago: Probus, 1985).

This totally nonmathematical book explains the institutions and financial instruments in an easy-to-read manner.

Essay Questions

21-1 "Risk averters do not sell short; short selling is done by speculators." Is the quotation true, false, or questionable? Explain.

21-2 Who are the parties to the sale of put and call options, and what functions are performed by each party?

21-3 (*a*) What are the main factors determining put and call premiums? Write one sentence explaining how each determinant affects option premiums. (*b*) What are the main factors determining the market price of a warrant?

21-4 Explain how to create the economic equivalent of a short position (called a *synthetic short position*) by combining two different options. Illustrate your solution with graphs. *Hint:* Consider how to create Figure 20-2*b* from Figures 21-2*b* and 21-7*a*.

21-5 Does the CBOE ever trade more than one option (which, e.g., has the same expiration date but different exercise prices) on the same underlying security? Why or why not?

21-6 Compare the following two investments in the Sportee Kayak Boat Company (SKBC): (*a*) Buy 10 shares of SKBC common stock at $100 per share; this is a total investment of $1000. (*b*) Buy a call option on 100 shares of SKBC stock that has a $100 exercise price for a call premium of $10 per share. This 100-share call option's total cost is $1000 ($10 per share premium × 100 shares) before commissions. Figure 21-14 illustrates these investment

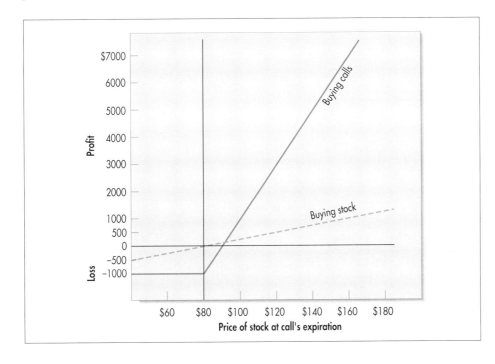

Figure 21-14
Positions in Sportee Kayak Boat stock.

alternatives. Which investment do you prefer? Why? Under what conditions would you prefer the other investment?

21-7 What are the differences between a warrant and a call option on the same corporation's stock?

21-8 When you buy a call option on a stock market index (like the SPX option), are you speculating on diversifiable risk, undiversifiable risk, or total (that is, both diversifiable and undiversifiable) risk? Explain.

21-9 Is there any difference between exercising a call option on an individual stock and exercising a call option on a stock market index? Explain.

21-10 Assume that as you look ahead 3 months into the future you are very bullish about the nation's economy and the stock market and, as a result, you are fairly certain that the S&P 500 will rise. (*a*) If you expect the market to rise, would you be better off buying shares in a mutual fund that is indexed to the S&P 500 Index, buying call options on the S&P 500 Index, or, writing (or selling) put options on the S&P 500 Index? What if you, instead, are bearish and expect the S&P 500 to go down? (*b*) If you expect the market to fall, would you be better off selling short a portfolio of shares that is indexed to the S&P 500 Index, writing call options on the S&P 500 index, or buying put options on the S&P 500 index? In both scenarios, rank the desirability of the three alternatives and explain your ranking.

Problems

21-11 Before 1986, when capital gains on investments held for over 6 months were taxed at a lower income tax rate than ordinary income, Ms. Bullish bought 100 shares of GM stock at $40 per share on February 1, 19X1. She held the shares for price appreciation, which she expected to occur over the next 6 months. Five months after purchasing the shares, on July 4, 19X1, to be exact, the price of GM reached $80 per share. Then, Ms. Bullish turned bearish about GM and wanted to sell the stock. Her accountant informed her at that time that if she held the 100 shares until August of 19X1, she would have held it for over 6 months, so her $4000 total gain [($80 − $40) × 100 shares] would be taxed at her long-term capital gains tax rate of 20 percent rather than at the 40 percent ordinary income tax rate that she would have to pay if she held the investment less than 6 months. Ms. Bullish wanted to pay the lower capital gains tax rate, but she was convinced that GM's stock price peaked at $80 per share on July 4, 19X1, and was destined to fall drastically before August. (*a*) Would you recommend that she sell the stock in July or wait until August? (*b*) How could she have kept her $40 per share gain and still have it taxed at the more desirable long-term capital gains tax rate? (See Chapter 7 for more details about capital gains taxes. The long-term capital gains tax was reinstated in 1990 at a more modest tax savings.)

21-12 On July 6, 1973, the only call on the common stock of Texas Instruments (TI) that was being traded on the CBOE was a July call with a $90 exercise price. The optioned stock's price had just fallen to $83 per share, so the TI call was out of the money. It was selling for only 1⅜, or $1.375, per optioned share of stock. Assume you had purchased this July call on July 6, 1973, for 1⅜ (or $1.375). On July 27, in the short time before the option expired, the price of TI stock shot up to $108.75. (*a*) What do you estimate the July call of TI's stock was worth when the optioned stock price hit $108.75? (*b*) What is the percentage gain in the price of the call from 1⅜ to the July 27 price (or premium) that you estimated? (*Note:* This remarkable case is true.)

541

*Chapter 21
Options,
Warrants,
and
Convertibles*

21-13 The cash market price of gold bullion advanced rapidly from $345 per ounce on July 7, 1986, to $387 on August 14, 1986. As a result, the prices of options on gold bullion changed, too, as the following prices for options expiring in October 1986 indicate. For instance, one October call with an exercise price of $340 per ounce on 100 ounces of gold at Comex Commodity Exchange in New York City cost $1250 on July 7, 1986, and it could be sold for $5010 on August 14, 1986.

Date	Oct. 340 call	Oct. 350 call	Oct. 360 call	Oct. 340 put	Oct. 350 put	Oct. 360 put
7-7-86	$1,250	$ 650	$ 350	$ 430	$ 770	$ 1,450
8-14-86	5,010	4,040	3,090	40	60	120
Gain (loss)	$3,260	$3,390	$2,740	$(390)	$(710)	$(1,330)
Commission	−50	−50	−50	−50	−50	−50
Net gain	$3,210	$3,340	$21,690	$(440)	$(760)	$(1,380)

Which one of the six options above would have been the best one to buy on July 7, 1986, if you had known what the price of gold was going to be on August 14, 1986? Show your calculations and explain how you selected the best one.

21-14 The Carleton Corporation's convertible bonds are selling for $1100. The bond has a conversion ratio of 50 shares of common stock per bond. Carleton's common stock is currently selling for $25 per share. Equivalent nonconvertible bonds are selling for $1150. What do you recommend?

21-15 The following question is from the 1987 level I Chartered Financial Analyst (CFA) exam.

In examining a company's straight debentures and subordinated convertible debentures, both issued at the same time with the same maturity and at par, you note that the coupon and yield for the subordinated convertible debenture is lower than for the straight debenture. Discuss the return potential for the convertible bond in an environment of stable interest rates and rising stock prices that would explain its lower coupon and yield. (5 minutes)

Multiple Choice Questions

21-16 Which one of the following statements is true?
   (*a*) The premium of the call option is inversely related to the stock price.
   (*b*) The premium of the call option does not depend on the volatility of the underlying stock.
   (*c*) Option prices are not affected by market interest rates.
   (*d*) The striking price is inversely related to the premium of a call option.
   (*e*) All of the above are true.

21-17 A call option is correctly defined by which of the following?
   (*a*) It is an option to collect any cash dividends paid by the optioned stock.
   (*b*) It is an option to buy securities at a prearranged contract price.
   (*c*) It expires after a prearranged time, unless it is exercised first.
   (*d*) Both (*b*) and (*c*) are correct.
   (*e*) All of the above are true.

21-18   Which of the following correctly describes the position of a put writer?

(*a*) The put writer has paid for the option of writing a certified letter to someone which contains securities the recipient of the letter must purchase at a preset price.

(*b*) The put writer has granted the put buyer the right to require the writer to purchase 100 shares of a stock at a preset price, if the put buyer desires to do so.

(*c*) The put writer usually wants to sell the optioned securities.

(*d*) The put writer is paid a premium by the option exchange.

21-19   Put buying has which of the following advantages over short selling?

(*a*) The short seller is not affected by cash dividend payments.

(*b*) The put buyer gets financial leverage.

(*c*) The put buyer is exposed to only limited liability.

(*d*) Both (*b*) and (*c*) are advantages.

(*e*) All of the above are true.

21-20   Warrants differ from call options in which of the following ways?

(*a*) Warrants increase the number of shares outstanding when they are exercised.

(*b*) Warrants all have perpetual lives.

(*c*) Warrants are written by the option exchange.

(*d*) Warrants offer no financial leverage.

21-21   The call option premium curve has the steepest slope when which one of the following conditions occurs?

(*a*) The call is at the market.

(*b*) The call is out of the money.

(*c*) The call is far out of the money.

(*d*) The call is deep in the money.

21-22   An increase in the volatility of the underlying stock might result in which one of the following?

(*a*) A simultaneous increase in the premiums of both the calls and the puts on the stock

(*b*) An increase in the put premium and a decrease in the call premium

(*c*) An increase in the premiums of call options and a decrease in the premiums of put options

(*d*) An increase in the premiums of call options and no effect on premiums of put options

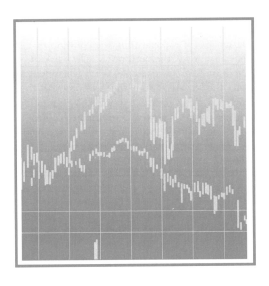

APPENDIX 21A

THE BLACK-SCHOLES CALL OPTION PRICING FORMULA

Fischer Black and Myron Scholes derived a widely accepted mathematical model that gives the values of put and call option premiums.[1] The Black-Scholes call option formula is shown in Definition Box 21A-1. The call prices suggested by the model are represented by the dashed curves in Figure 21-6.

[1] F. Black and M. Scholes, "The Pricing of Options and Corporate Liabilities," *Journal of Political Economy,* May-June 1973, pp. 637–654. See also Robert C. Merton, "The Theory of Rational Option Pricing," *The Bell Journal of Economics and Management Science* (Spring), 1973, pp. 161–183.

Box 21A-1

> **DEFINITION: The Black-Scholes Call Option Pricing Formula**
>
> A call option's premium CC is determined by the formula
>
> $$CC = N(z)P - \frac{N(y)XP}{\exp(Rd)} \qquad (21A\text{-}1)$$
>
> where the symbol "exp" means take the antilogarithm to the base e of the value in the parentheses and $e = 2.718$. The exercise price is XP, and z, y and $N(y)$ are defined below.
>
> $$z = \frac{\ln (P/XP) + \{R + .5[\mathrm{VAR}(r)]\}d}{\sqrt{\mathrm{VAR}(r)}\ \sqrt{d}} \qquad (21A\text{-}2)$$
>
> $$y = z - \sqrt{\mathrm{VAR}(r)}\ \sqrt{d} \qquad (21A\text{-}3)$$

The market price of the optioned security is represented by P; XP stands for the exercise price; ln denotes the natural (or naperian, or base e) logarithm; the convention VAR(r) denotes the variance of the rates of price change for the optioned stock, a risk measure; and the term R denotes the riskless rate of interest (for example, the market interest rate on Treasury bills). The symbol d denotes the length of time until expiration of the call, stated as a fraction of 1 year (for example, $d = \frac{1}{12}$ means 1 month). $N(y)$ represents a cumulative normal-density function of the argument y. $N(y)$ gives the probability that a value of less than y will occur in a normal probability distribution that has a mean of 0 and a standard deviation equal to 1. $N(-\infty) = 0$, $N(0) = .5$, and $N(+\infty) = 1.0$. [See Table 21A-1 for values of $N(y)$ and Table 21A-2 for natural logarithms.]

Table 21A-1
Values of $N(x)$ for Given Values of x for a
Cumulative Normal Probability Distribution Function
with Zero Mean and Unit Variance

x	$N(x)$	x	$N(x)$	x	$N(x)$	x	$N(x)$	x	$N(x)$	x	$N(x)$
		−2.00	.0228	−1.00	.1587	.00	.5000	1.00	.8413	2.00	.9773
−2.95	.0016	−1.95	.0256	−.95	.1711	.05	.5199	1.05	.8531	2.05	.9798
−2.90	.0019	−1.90	.0287	−.90	.1841	.10	.5398	1.10	.8643	2.10	.9821
−2.85	.0022	−1.85	.0322	−.85	.1977	.15	.5596	1.15	.8749	2.15	.9842
−2.80	.0026	−1.80	.0359	−.80	.2119	.20	.5793	1.20	.8849	2.20	.9861
−2.75	.0030	−1.75	.0401	−.75	.2266	.25	.5987	1.25	.8944	2.25	.9878
−2.70	.0035	−1.70	.0446	−.70	.2420	.30	.6179	1.30	.9032	2.30	.9893
−2.65	.0040	−1.65	.0495	−.65	.2578	.35	.6368	1.35	.9115	2.35	.9906
−2.60	.0047	−1.60	.0548	−.60	.2743	.40	.6554	1.40	.9192	2.40	.9918
−2.55	.0054	−1.55	.0606	−.55	.2912	.45	.6736	1.45	.9265	2.45	.9929
−2.50	.0062	−1.50	.0668	−.50	.3085	.50	.6915	1.50	.9332	2.50	.9938
−2.45	.0071	−1.45	.0735	−.45	.3264	.55	.7088	1.55	.9394	2.55	.9946
−2.40	.0082	−1.40	.0808	−.40	.3446	.60	.7257	1.60	.9452	2.60	.9953
−2.35	.0094	−1.35	.0885	−.35	.3632	.65	.7422	1.65	.9505	2.65	.9960
−2.30	.0107	−1.30	.0968	−.30	.3821	.70	.7580	1.70	.9554	2.70	.9965
−2.25	.0122	−1.25	.1057	−.25	.4013	.75	.7734	1.75	.9599	2.75	.9970
−2.20	.0139	−1.20	.1151	−.20	.4207	.80	.7881	1.80	.9641	2.80	.9974
−2.15	.0158	−1.15	.1251	−.15	.4404	.85	.8023	1.85	.9678	2.85	.9978
−2.10	.0179	−1.10	.1357	−.10	.4602	.90	.8159	1.90	.9713	2.90	.9981
−2.05	.0202	−1.05	.1469	−.05	.4801	.95	.8289	1.95	.9744	2.95	.9984

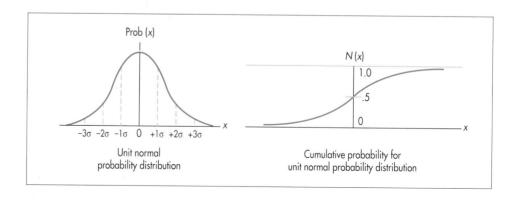

Prob (x)

−3σ −2σ −1σ 0 +1σ +2σ +3σ   x

Unit normal
probability distribution

N (x)

1.0

.5

0   x

Cumulative probability for
unit normal probability distribution

545

Chapter 21
Options,
Warrants,
and
Convertibles

Table 21A-2
Natural Logarithms

$\frac{\ln y}{x}$	$\frac{y}{e^x}$	$\frac{\ln y}{x}$	$\frac{y}{e^x}$
0.00	1.0000	0.25	0.2840
0.01	1.0101	0.26	1.2969
0.02	1.0202	0.27	1.3100
0.03	1.0305	0.28	1.3231
0.04	1.0408	0.29	1.3364
0.05	1.0513	0.30	1.3499
0.06	1.0618	0.31	1.3634
0.07	1.0725	0.32	1.3771
0.08	1.0833	0.33	1.3910
0.09	1.0942	0.34	1.4049
0.10	1.1052	0.35	1.4191
0.11	1.1163	0.36	1.4333
0.12	1.1275	0.37	1.4477
0.13	1.1388	0.38	1.4623
0.14	1.1503	0.39	1.4770
0.15	1.1618	0.40	1.4918
0.16	1.1735	0.41	1.5068
0.17	1.1853	0.42	1.5220
0.18	1.1972	0.43	1.5373
0.19	1.2092	0.44	1.5527
0.20	1.2214	0.45	1.5683
0.21	1.2337	0.46	1.5841
0.22	1.2461	0.47	1.6000
0.23	1.2586	0.48	1.6161
0.24	1.2712	0.49	1.6323

Pricing a Call with the Black-Scholes Model

All that is needed to use the Black-Scholes model are a table of natural logarithms and a table of cumulative normal distribution probabilities for computing $N(z)$ and $N(y)$. The values for $N(z)$ and $N(y)$ can be looked up in Table 21A-1. Table 21A-2 contains natural logarithms and antilogarithms or use a hand-held calculator.

In the following example of how to apply the Black-Scholes model, $P = \$60$, $XP = \$50$, $d = .333$ (which represents 120 days out of a 360-day year), $R = .07$ (which represents 7 percent per annum), and $\sqrt{VAR(r)} = \sqrt{.144} = .379$. The quantity z is given by

$$z = \frac{\ln(P/XP) + \{R + .5[VAR(r)]\}d}{\sqrt{VAR(r)}\,\sqrt{d}}$$

$$= \frac{\ln(\$60/\$50) + [.07 + .5(.144)](.333)}{\sqrt{.144}\,\sqrt{.333}}$$

$$= \frac{.182 + .142(.333)}{.379(.577)} = \frac{.2296}{.2191} = 1.048$$

The quantity y is

$$y = z - \sqrt{VAR(r)} \sqrt{d}$$

$$= z - (\sqrt{.144} \sqrt{.333}) = 1.048 - .2191 = .829$$

Substituting the values for z and y into the formula for CC yields

$$CC = N(1.048)(\$60) - \frac{[N(.829)](\$50)}{\exp[(.07)(.333)]}$$

Looking up the values of the antilogarithm in Table 21A-2 and the cumulative normal distribution in Table 21A-1 and doing some interpolating yields

$$CC = N(z)P - \frac{N(y)XP}{\exp(Rd)}$$

$$= (.851)(\$60) - \frac{(.800)(\$50)}{1.0236}$$

$$= \$51.060 - \$39.076 = \$11.98$$

The calculations indicate the call option's value to be \$11.98. Slight differences in the way various people interpolate between the values in Table 21A-1 may result in slightly different answers.

Two Call Pricing Problems

Use the Black-Scholes call option pricing formula to find the value of call options on the following optioned stocks. (*Hint:* The call option on XYZ is worth about 3 times as much as the call on ABC.)

Name of the optioned stock	ABC	XYZ
Time to maturity	4 months	88 days
Standard deviation, $\sqrt{VAR(r)}$	.30	.40
Exercise price, XP	\$40	\$60
Price of optioned stock, P	\$40	\$68
Riskless interest rate, R	.12	.06

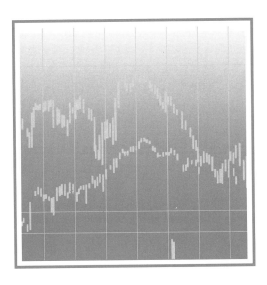

THE PUT-CALL
PARITY FORMULA

The put-call parity formula presented in this appendix can be used for two purposes: (1) to calculate put option premiums after the call option premium is obtained and (2) to detect mispriced puts and/or calls. The put-call parity formula specifies a fair-value relationship between a put and a call written on the same underlying security.

Pricing Puts with the Put-Call Parity Formula

The put-call parity formula below specifies that the premium on a put option should be

$$PP = CC + \frac{XP}{(1 + R)^d} - P \tag{21B-1}$$

where PP = premium on put

CC = premium on call

XP = exercise price

R = riskless interest rate

d = fraction of 1 year until option expires (e.g., d = ½ for 6 months)

P = price of the security

The same values from the computation in Appendix 21A that showed how to apply the Black-Scholes call valuation formula can be used to determine the value of a put option on the same stock.

The following data describe the optioned security: P = \$60, XP = \$50, d = .333 (which represents 120 days out of a 360-day year), R = .07 (which represents 7 percent per annum), and VAR(r) = .144. In Appendix 21A, the Black-Scholes model placed a value on this 4-month call of \$11.98. The value of the put is calculated below by substituting these values into the put-call parity formula.

$$PP = CC + \frac{XP}{(1 + R)^d} - P$$

$$= \$11.98 + \frac{\$50.00}{(1.0 + .07)^{.333}} - \$60.00$$

$$= \$11.98 + \frac{\$50.00}{1.0227} - \$60.00$$

$$= \$11.98 + \$48.89 - \$60.00$$

$$= \$60.87 - \$60.00 = \$0.87$$

Two Put Pricing Problems

Refer back to the table at the end of Appendix 21A containing pricing information for options on ABC and XYZ stock. Use that information to compute the put option premiums on ABC and XYZ.

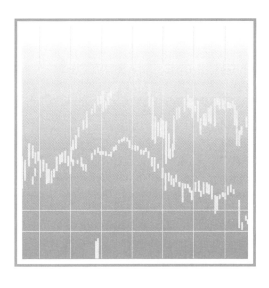

CHAPTER 22

COMMODITY FUTURES

Farmers and merchants started using "forward contracts" many centuries ago in an effort to reduce business risks. In a **forward contract,** a buyer promises to pay a seller some fixed price for a specified quantity of a particular good when it is delivered at some future (or forward) date. But if one party does not perform as agreed, the injured party must pursue the defaulting party for damages.

Forward contracts are still widely used today. While they are better than making no arrangement for future uncertainties, they still leave both parties exposed to the risk that one party will not perform as promised. Shoddy goods can be delivered. The delivery can be made at an unanticipated location. The amount can be wrong. As a result of these problems, an improved version of the forward contract called the *futures contract* came into existence at European trade fairs around the twelfth century. These original futures contracts have been improved, and as will be explained later in this chapter, today's futures contracts guarantee the buyer and the seller that their contracts will be fully executed as promised.

22-1   Futures Contracts

A **futures contract** is a legal agreement between a potential buyer and a potential seller of a commodity. It stipulates that the future seller will deliver to a designated location a specified quantity of well-defined goods that are to be sold to the buyer at a prearranged price on some preset future date. For example, seller ABC agrees to deliver to buyer XYZ at a bank in New York five U.S. Treasury bonds that each have $100,000 face values and at least 15 years to maturity in December of next year, and buyer XYZ agrees to pay cash on delivery for these bonds. Such contracts are called *December T-bond futures.*

Futures Trading

Futures contracts are negotiable financial instruments that are bought and sold freely, but only through members of a commodity exchange. If you wish to buy or sell a commodity futures contract, you must pay a commodities broker a commission to conduct the transaction for you on the floor of a commodity exchange. Orders to buy or sell a futures contract are initiated by calling a commodities broker, opening an account, and then phoning in your buy and/or sell orders.

Commodity futures contracts are called simply *futures.* When an investor buys a futures contract, the investor is said to be *long futures,* or in a *long position.* If an investor initiates trading by selling futures, that trader is said to be in a *short position,* or *short futures.*

When a commodity trader with a long position sells an identical futures contract, or when a trader who is short futures buys such a contract, the transaction is called a **reversing trade.** Reversing trades are used to eliminate (or "reverse out of") previously established positions. Such transactions offset the initial position and leave the trader with no position (or a neutral position, or holding cash).

Futures contracts can be sold at prices that differ with each transaction. The owner of a contract experiences a profit or loss depending on whether the sales price was above or below the price in the previous transaction.

Figure 22-1 shows a newspaper excerpt that lists the futures prices of some exchange-listed commodities. Many daily newspapers publish these prices as well as *open interest* statistics for every commodity contract. The **open interest** is the number of futures contracts currently outstanding and is one of the more widely watched commodity futures statistics.

When trading begins in a new futures contract, the open interest advances from 0 to 1 when the first contract is sold. During the early part of a contract's trading life (1 year for most commodities) many contracts are opened, and the open interest soars to thousands of contracts within a few months. Later, as the delivery dates near, more

Futures

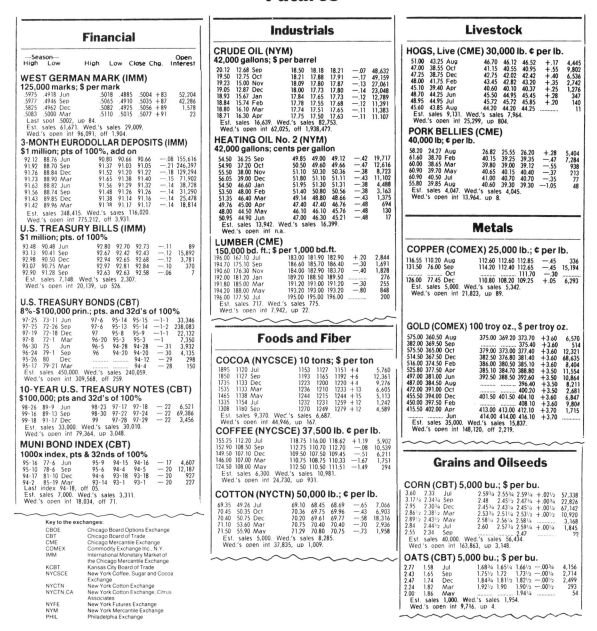

Financial

—Season—						Open
High	Low	High	Low	Close	Chg.	Interest

WEST GERMAN MARK (IMM)
125,000 marks; $ per mark
.5975	.4918	Jun	.5018	.4885	.5004	+83	52,204
.5977	.4946	Sep	.5065	.4910	.5035	+87	42,286
.5825	.4962	Dec	.5082	.4925	.5056	+89	1,578
.5083	.5000	Mar		.5110	.5015	.5077	+91	23
Last spot .5002, up 84.
Est. sales 61,671. Wed.'s sales 29,009.
Wed.'s open int 96,091, off 1,904.

3-MONTH EURODOLLAR DEPOSITS (IMM)
$1 million; pts of 100%, add on
92.12	88.76	Jun	90.80	90.66	90.66	—.08	155,616
91.92	88.70	Sep	91.37	91.03	91.05	—.21	246,397
91.76	88.84	Dec	91.52	91.20	91.22	—.18	129,294
91.73	88.90	Mar	91.65	91.38	91.40	—.15	71,902
91.63	88.82	Jun	91.56	91.29	91.32	—.14	38,728
91.56	88.74	Sep	91.48	91.26	91.28	—.14	31,290
91.43	89.85	Dec	91.38	91.14	91.16	—.14	25,478
91.42	89.96	Mar	91.39	91.17	91.17	—.14	18,814
Est. sales 348,415. Wed.'s sales 116,020.
Wed.'s open int 775,212, off 3,931.

U.S. TREASURY BILLS (IMM)
$1 million; pts. of 100%
93.48	90.48	Jun	92.80	92.70	92.73	—.11	89
93.13	90.41	Sep	92.67	92.42	92.43	—.12	15,892
92.98	90.50	Dec	92.94	92.65	92.68	—.12	3,781
93.07	90.75	Mar	92.97	92.81	92.84	—.10	370
92.90	91.28	Sep	92.63	92.63	92.58	—.06	7
Est. sales 7,148. Wed.'s sales 2,307.
Wed.'s open int 20,139, up 526.

U.S. TREASURY BONDS (CBT)
8%-$100,000 prin.; pts. and 32d's of 100%
97-25	73-11	Jun	97-6	95-15	95-15	—1	33,346
97-25	72-26	Sep	97-6	95-13	95-14	—1-2	238,083
97-19	72-18	Dec	97	95-8	95-9	—1	22,132
97-8	72-1	Mar	96-20	95-3	95-3	—1	7,350
96-30	75	Jun	96-5	94-28	94-28	—31	3,932
96-24	79-1	Sep	96	94-20	94-20	—30	4,135
95-26	80	Dec			94-12	—29	298
95-17	79-21	Mar			94-4	—28	150
Est. sales 450,000. Wed.'s sales 240,059.
Wed.'s open int 309,568, off 259.

10-YEAR U.S. TREASURY NOTES (CBT)
$100,000; pts and 32d's of 100%
98-26	89-9	Jun	98-23	97-17	97-18	—22	6,521
99-16	89-13	Sep	98-30	97-22	97-24	—22	69,386
99-18	91-17	Dec	99	97-28	97-29	—22	3,456
Est. sales 33,000. Wed.'s sales 30,010.
Wed.'s open int 79,364, up 3,048.

MUNI BOND INDEX (CBT)
1000x index, pts & 32nds of 100%
95-16	77-6	Jun	95-9	94-9	94-16	—17	4,607
95-10	78-6	Sep	95-6	94-4	94-5	—20	12,187
94-17	81-10	Dec	94-6	93-18	93-18	—20	927
94-2	85-19	Mar	93-14	93-1	93-1	—20	227
Last index 94-18, off 05.
Est. sales 7,000. Wed.'s sales 3,311.
Wed.'s open int 18,034, off 71.

Key to the exchanges:
CBOE	Chicago Board Options Exchange
CBT	Chicago Board of Trade
CME	Chicago Mercantile Exchange
COMEX	Commodity Exchange Inc., N.Y.
IMM	International Monetary Market of the Chicago Mercantile Exchange
KCBT	Kansas City Board of Trade
NYCSCE	New York Coffee, Sugar and Cocoa Exchange
NYCTN	New York Cotton Exchange
NYCTN,CA	New York Cotton Exchange, Citrus Associates
NYFE	New York Futures Exchange
NYM	New York Mercantile Exchange
PHIL	Philadelphia Exchange

Industrials

CRUDE OIL (NYM)
42,000 gallons; $ per barrel
20.12	12.68	Sep	18.50	18.18	18.21	—.07	48,632
19.50	12.75	Oct	18.21	17.88	17.91	—.17	49,159
19.23	15.00	Nov	18.09	17.80	17.87	—.13	27,061
19.05	12.87	Dec	18.00	17.73	17.80	—.14	23,048
18.93	15.67	Jan	17.84	17.65	17.73	—.12	12,789
18.84	15.74	Feb	17.78	17.55	17.68	—.12	11,391
18.80	16.10	Mar	17.74	17.51	17.65	—.11	11,383
18.71	16.30	Apr	17.75	17.50	17.63	—.11	11.107
Est. sales 16,639. Wed.'s sales 82,753.
Wed.'s open int 62,025, off 1,938,472.

HEATING OIL No. 2 (NYM)
42,000 gallons; cents per gallon
54.50	36.25	Sep	49.85	49.00	49.12	—.42	19,717
54.90	37.20	Oct	50.50	49.60	49.66	—.47	12,616
55.50	38.00	Nov	51.10	50.30	50.36	—.38	8,723
56.05	39.00	Dec	51.80	51.10	51.11	—.43	11,102
54.50	46.60	Jan	51.95	51.30	51.31	—.38	4,488
53.50	48.00	Feb	51.40	50.80	50.56	—.38	3,163
51.35	46.40	Mar	49.14	48.80	48.66	—.43	1,375
49.76	45.00	Apr	47.40	47.40	46.76	—.48	694
48.40	44.50	May	46.10	46.10	45.76	—.48	130
50.95	44.90	Jun	47.00	46.30	45.21	—.48	17
Est. sales 13,942. Wed.'s sales 16,399.
Wed.'s open int n.a.

LUMBER (CME)
150,000 bd. ft.; $ per 1,000 bd.ft.
196.00	167.10	Jul	183.00	181.90	182.90	+.20	2,844
194.70	175.10	Sep	186.60	185.70	186.40	—.30	1,691
190.60	176.30	Nov	184.00	182.90	183.70	—.40	1,828
192.00	181.20	Jan	189.20	188.50	189.50		276
191.80	185.00	Mar	191.20	191.00	191.20	—.30	255
194.20	188.00	May	193.20	193.00	193.20	—.80	848
196.00	177.50	Jul	195.00	195.00	196.00		200
Est. sales 717. Wed.'s sales 775.
Wed.'s open int 7,942, up 22.

Foods and Fiber

COCOA (NYCSCE) 10 tons; $ per ton
1895	1120	Jul	1153	1127	1151	+4	5,760
1850	1127	Sep	1193	1165	1192	+6	12,361
1735	1133	Dec	1223	1200	1220	+4	9,276
1535	1133	Mar	1236	1210	1233	+13	6,605
1465	1138	May	1244	1215	1244	+15	5,113
1335	1154	Jul	1232	1231	1259	+12	1,242
1308	1180	Sep	1270	1249	1279	+12	4,589
Est. sales 9,370. Wed.'s sales 6,687.
Wed.'s open int 44,946, up 167.

COFFEE (NYCSCE) 37,500 lb. ¢ per lb.
155.25	112.20	Jul	118.75	116.00	118.62	+1.19	5,902
152.90	108.50	Sep	112.75	110.70	112.74	—.08	10,539
149.50	107.10	Dec	109.50	107.50	109.45	—.51	6,211
146.00	107.00	Mar	110.75	108.75	110.51	—1.67	1,751
124.50	108.00	May	112.50	110.50	111.51	—1.49	294
Est. sales 6,300. Wed.'s sales 10,981.
Wed.'s open int 24,730, up 931.

COTTON (NYCTN) 50,000 lb.; ¢ per lb.
69.35	49.26	Jul	69.10	68.45	68.69	—.65	7,066
70.45	50.35	Oct	70.36	69.75	69.96	—.43	6,903
70.40	50.75	Dec	70.20	69.61	69.77	—.58	18,316
71.10	53.60	Mar	70.75	70.40	70.40	—.70	2,936
71.50	55.90	May	71.29	70.80	70.75	—.73	1,958
Est. sales 5,000. Wed.'s sales 8,285.
Wed.'s open int 37,835, up 1,009.

Livestock

HOGS, Live (CME) 30,000 lb. ¢ per lb.
51.00	43.25	Aug	46.70	46.12	46.52	+.17	4,445
47.00	38.55	Oct	41.15	40.55	40.95	+.55	9,802
47.25	38.75	Dec	42.75	42.02	42.42	+.40	6,536
48.00	41.75	Feb	43.45	42.82	43.20	+.35	2,742
45.10	39.40	Apr	40.60	40.10	40.37	+.25	1,276
48.70	44.25	Jun	45.50	44.95	45.45	+.28	347
48.95	44.95	Jul	45.72	45.72	45.85	+.20	140
45.60	43.85	Aug	44.20	44.20	44.25		11
Est. sales 9,131. Wed.'s sales 7,964.
Wed.'s open int 25,299, up 804.

PORK BELLIES (CME)
40,000 lb; ¢ per lb.
58.20	24.27	Aug	26.82	25.55	26.20	+.28	5,404
61.60	38.70	Feb	40.15	39.25	39.35	—.47	7,284
60.00	38.65	Mar	39.80	39.00	39.12	—.55	938
60.90	39.70	May	40.65	40.15	40.40	—.37	213
60.90	40.50	Jul	41.00	40.70	40.70	—.35	77
55.80	39.85	Aug	40.60	39.30	39.30	—1.05	48
Est. sales 4,047. Wed.'s sales 4,045.
Wed.'s open int 13,964, up 8.

Metals

COPPER (COMEX) 25,000 lb.; ¢ per lb.
116.55	110.20	Aug	112.60	112.60	112.85	—.45	336
131.50	76.00	Sep	114.20	112.40	112.65	—.45	15,194
		Oct			111.70	—.30	
126.00	77.45	Dec	110.80	108.20	109.25	+.05	6,293
Est. sales 5,000. Wed.'s sales 5,342.
Wed.'s open int 21,823, up 89.

GOLD (COMEX) 100 troy oz., $ per troy oz.
575.00	360.50	Aug	375.00	369.20	373.70	+3.60	6,570
382.00	369.50	Sep			375.40	+3.60	514
575.50	365.00	Oct	379.00	373.00	377.40	+3.60	12,321
514.50	367.50	Dec	382.50	376.80	381.40	+3.60	68,635
516.00	374.50	Feb	386.00	380.50	385.10	+3.60	8,404
525.80	377.50	Apr	385.10	384.70	388.80	+3.50	11,554
497.00	381.00	Jun	392.50	388.50	392.60	+3.50	10,864
487.00	384.50	Aug			396.40	+3.50	8,211
472.00	391.00	Oct			400.20	+3.50	2,681
455.50	394.00	Dec	401.50	401.50	404.10	+3.60	6,847
450.00	397.50	Feb			408.10	+3.60	9,804
415.50	402.00	Apr	413.00	413.00	412.10	+3.70	1,715
		Jun	414.00	414.00	416.10	+3.70	
Est. sales 35,000. Wed.'s sales 15,837.
Wed.'s open int 148,120, off 2,219.

Grains and Oilseeds

CORN (CBT) 5,000 bu.; $ per bu.
3.60	2.33	Jul	2.59¾	2.55¾	2.59¼	+.02½	57,338
3.17¼	2.34¾	Sep	2.48	2.45½	2.47¼	+.03¾	22,826
2.95	2.30¾	Dec	2.45¾	2.43¼	2.45¼	+.00¼	67,142
2.86½	2.38½	Mar	2.53¾	2.51¼	2.53½	+.00½	10,920
2.89½	2.43½	May	2.58¼	2.56¼	2.58¼		3,168
2.84	2.44½	Jul	2.60	2.57¾	2.59¼	+.00¼	1,845
2.55	2.34	Sep			2.47		72
Est. sales 40,000. Wed.'s sales 56,434.
Wed.'s open int 163,863, up 3,148.

OATS (CBT) 5,000 bu.; $ per bu.
2.77	1.58	Jul	1.68¾	1.65¼	1.66½	—.00¾	4,156
2.43	1.65	Sep	1.75½	1.72	1.73½	—.00¼	2,714
2.47	1.74	Dec	1.84¾	1.81½	1.82½	—.00½	2,499
2.24	1.82	Mar	1.92½	1.90	1.90½	—.00½	293
2.00	1.86	May			1.94¼		54
Est. sales 1,000. Wed.'s sales 1,954.
Wed.'s open int 9,716, up 4.

Figure 22-1 A newspaper excerpt showing commodity futures price quotations.

positions are closed out through reversing trades, and the open interest declines back to 0 on the contract's delivery date. Only about 1 percent of all the futures contracts opened are ever actually delivered; the rest disappear when reversing trades wipe them out.

551

Only those futures contracts that are scheduled for delivery more than 1 month in the future are referred to as futures contracts. Futures contracts that are due to be delivered within the current month are called **spot contracts.** Futures contracts become spot contracts in the month before they expire. Both spot and futures contracts are traded at commodity exchanges.

Financial Futures

Before 1972 the only commodities on which futures were traded included agricultural goods (like grains or meats), imported foodstuffs (such as coffee and sugar), and industrial commodities (like silver and copper). In 1972 the Chicago Mercantile Exchange (or CME, or the "Merc") pioneered trading in financial futures: contracts on T-bills, T-notes, T-bonds, Eurodollar CDs, a municipal bond index, several stock market indexes, and other monetary commodities. Other commodity exchanges soon followed. Trading in financial futures flourished, and today the aggregate dollar value of trading in financial futures exceeds the value of trading in the traditional commodities.

22-2   Commodity Markets

People are usually surprised to learn that real, physical commodities are not traded at commodity exchanges.

Cash Markets and Futures Markets

Physical commodities are traded in what are called *cash markets:* futures contracts are traded at *futures exchanges.* Grain elevators and stockyards, where farmers deliver and sell their products, and stock exchanges are examples of **cash markets,** even though some of the trades are paid for with credit instead of cash. Cash markets are also called **physicals markets.**

Futures exchanges are also called *commodity exchanges.* But the name "commodity exchange" is misleading because no commodities are traded at most of these exchanges. **Commodity exchanges** are centralized locations where buyers' and sellers' agents meet to trade futures on whichever commodities that particular exchange lists for trading. Trading is conducted via open outcry in designated areas called **trading pits.**

The Chicago Board of Trade (CBT) is the largest, oldest commodities exchange in the United States. The CBT has trading pits for corn, oats, soybeans, soybean oil, soybean meal, wheat, gold, silver, Treasury bonds, Treasury notes, and a stock market index called the *Major Markets Index.* The Chicago Mercantile Exchange is the second-largest exchange in the United States. It trades contracts on pork bellies, live cattle, live hogs, feeder cattle, and the Standard & Poor's stock market index. The International Monetary Market, a division of the Chicago Merc, trades futures on the British pound, the Canadian dollar, the Japanese yen, the Swiss franc, the German mark, the Australian dollar, gold, Treasury bills, and Eurodollars. There are four futures exchanges in Chicago and four in New York City. Kansas City, Philadelphia, and Minneapolis also have commodity exchanges.

Trading   There are usually several **trading rooms** at a large commodity exchange, which only the exchange members and their employees may enter. Trading itself occurs in **trading rings** or pits in the trading room. Exchange members who want to buy or sell futures in some commodity go to the appropriate trading room, step into the trading pit, and indicate their intentions by making hand signals and/or shouting. When buyer and seller settle on terms, clerks immediately send news of the latest price out via telecommunications.

Floor brokers are self-employed members of the exchange; they do most of the trading. For a commission, they buy and sell futures for their customers. Orders to buy and sell come to the floor brokers by phone. They then step into the appropriate trading pit, execute the trades, and notify customers of the results via return call.

The structure of events in and around a commodity exchange is complex, as Figure 22-2 illustrates.

Determining Prices   The prices of futures contracts are directly related to the prices of their underlying commodities. Commodity prices are determined by supply and demand. The supply of agricultural commodities is affected by such natural events as flood, disease, insects, and drought, as well as by governmental acts such as the imposition of import-export quotas, subsidies, and foreign exchange rate changes. In contrast to the uncertain supply, the demand for most agricultural commodities is fairly steady. Farm products are traded in what economists call **perfect markets**— markets where there are many sellers and many buyers, none of whom is large enough to control prices. As a result, price fluctuations are largely determined by changes in supply, since demand changes gradually from year to year. Figure 22-3, which shows a stable demand curve for corn and a supply curve that changes from season to season, models the economic process that determines the market price of corn.

22-3   The Activities in a Commodities Exchange

Commodity futures exchanges are usually nonprofit corporations that collect just enough in fees from each transaction to pay their operating costs—salaries for a president, several vice presidents, and a staff of administrative workers, as well as the upkeep of a building where futures are traded.

The Commodity Board

For any given commodity, several delivery months may be specified in the futures contract. The price of the futures in any given commodity varies with the month in which the commodity is to be delivered. Thus, March #2 winter wheat deliverable at Chicago has a different price per bushel from the price of the same type of wheat deliverable at the same place in May. These prices are listed on a commodity board in the trading rooms. Futures traders watch the board continuously as they trade.

Table 22-1 contains an example of a hypothetical commodity board found on the wall of a commodity exchange's wheat trading room. The top line of the **commodity board** gives the highest and lowest prices at which the commodity has been traded

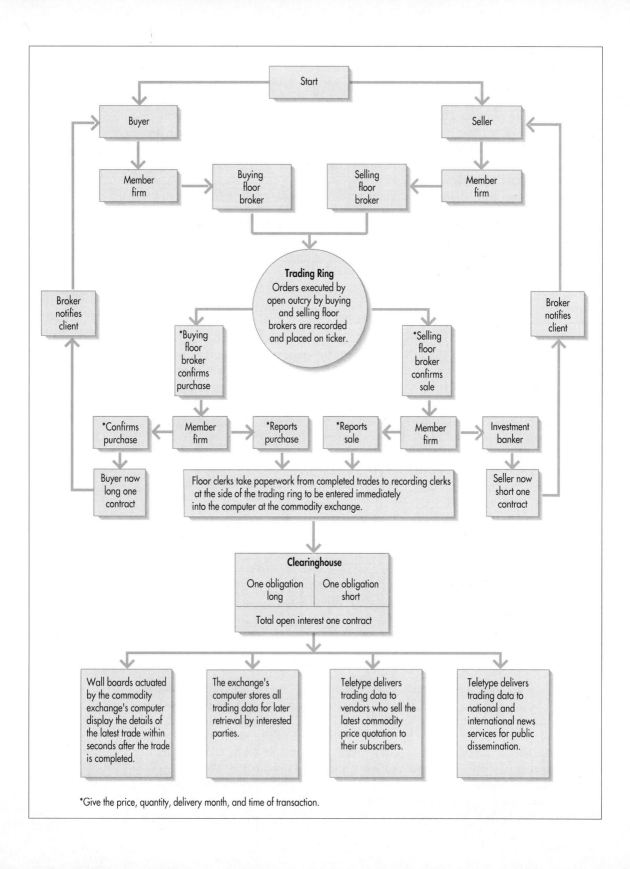

Figure 22-2 The structure of events associated with the origination and execution of a commodity futures contract (shown opposite page).

555

Chapter 22
Commodity
Futures

since contracts with that particular delivery month started trading. (All prices are in cents per bushel for wheat.) The second line of the board lists the **delivery months.** Table 22-1 shows that Chicago wheat futures, like most futures, are not available for delivery in every month. The delivery months for futures are determined by the commodity exchange. The third line of the board gives the closing price of the commodity on the previous trading day. The closing price is also called the **settlement price;** this is the price on which all margin requirement calculations are based.[1] The bottom four lines give the opening, highest, and lowest prices for the day, along with the current ("ticker") price for the commodity. The board is updated constantly by clerks, and current prices are wired to other commodities exchanges and commodities brokerages around the world.

Price Fluctuation Limits

Commodity futures prices have both minimum and maximum price fluctuation limits imposed on them by the exchange in which they are traded. Bid and asked prices must be changed from the price of the last transaction by at least the amount of

---

[1] Several orders may arrive at the trading floor simultaneously as the bell rings to signal the close of trading for the day. These orders sometimes have different prices. Each exchange has a method of dealing with the question of which should be considered the day's closing price. Most exchanges use the median price from the orders that were submitted simultaneously at the closing bell. Determining the settlement price is not an insignificant question, because every trader's margin requirements are recomputed and settled daily based on that day's settlement price.

Figure 22-3 A stable demand curve and shifting supply curve determine corn prices.

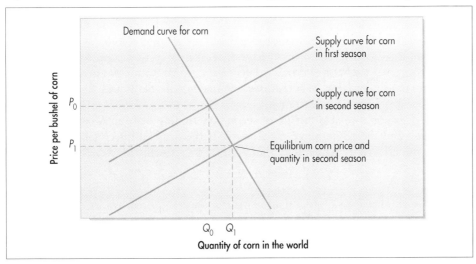

Table 22-1
Commodity Board for Chicago Wheat

High and low	390–351	399–370	391–366	379–359	384–360
Trading months	December	March	May	July	September
Previous close	370	377⅛	379	355	363⅜
Opening today	371½	377	378⅞	353	362
Today's high	371	379	379	353	362
Today's low	368⅝	377¼	377	350½	361
Ticker	369	379	378	350	361⅛

the **minimum daily price fluctuation limit,** which is called a **tick.** Otherwise, the exchange will not accept the new bid or asked price. The minimum price limit fluctuations are designed to prevent haggling over insignificant price changes. Offers to buy or sell at the old price are always accepted, but they may not result in trades if the bid prices are too low to attract sellers or the selling prices asked are too high to interest buyers.[2]

Maximum daily price fluctuation limits are set by each commodity exchange to prevent wild trading, which might result from successive large price changes. If a commodity's price rises or falls by the day's limit, trading in that commodity cannot exceed that **limit move** for the remainder of the day. All trading is stopped, unless the price starts to move in the opposite direction. The next day, trading resumes at the price that stopped the previous day's trading. These maximum price fluctuation limits cause trading in any given commodity to be halted only a few days each year.

The Clearinghouse

The **clearinghouse** is an organization within every commodity exchange which guarantees that every futures contract will be fulfilled. By acting as an intermediary in every transaction, the clearinghouse frees futures contracts from performance uncertainties. The clearinghouse makes delivery to all buyers and is the buyer that accepts all scheduled deliveries and pays for them. For a small fee charged on each contract, the clearinghouse also agrees to act as buyer if the buyer defaults or as seller if the seller defaults. The clearinghouse acts like an insurance company: It saves part of the fees it collects in an insurance fund. If one party to a contract defaults, the clearinghouse pays whatever costs are necessary to carry out the contract from its insurance fund, ensuring that futures contracts will be liquid and completely interchangeable financial instruments.

The clearinghouse also facilitates secondary trading of futures contracts before they expire and the commodity is delivered. If the original buyer sells the contract and the second buyer then resells the contract to a third, the clearinghouse keeps

---

[2] For a theoretical analysis of price limit moves, see Michael J. Brennan, "A Theory of Price Limits in Futures Markets," *Journal of Financial Economics,* vol. 16, no. 2, June 1986, pp. 213–234.

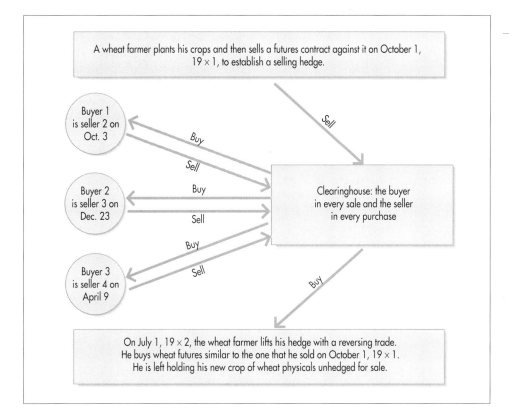

Figure 22-4   A series of futures contract trades.

track of the current owner. When the time comes to deliver on the contract, the clearinghouse arranges for delivery to be made to the last buyer. In practice, the clearinghouse actually rewrites every futures contract as two separate contracts and inserts its name in both. The various buyers and sellers never know one another's names; the clearinghouse keeps track of these details and deals directly with each buyer and seller separately, as shown in Figure 22-4. (The various futures trading transactions in the figure will be explained later in this chapter.)

Trading

Commodity traders who are not members of an exchange must trade through brokers. Brokers are employees of brokerage firms with seats on a commodity exchange. Agents trade futures contracts for the brokerages' clients so that commodity investors do not need to know much about the physical characteristics of the commodities they trade. In fact, they need not ever see the commodities.

Commodity futures contracts are traded only in standard **units.** The size of the unit depends on the commodity. For example, on the Chicago Board of Trade 100 tons is one unit, or one contract, of soybean meal; a wheat contract is for 5000 bushels; and a unit of lard is 40,000 pounds. The unit for the T-bond contract is one

Treasury bond with a face value of $100,000. To sell a futures contract, the trader notifies the broker. The broker finds out whether the customer wants to buy or sell. Clients may sell their own futures contract or take a short position by selling a contract they do not own. Or clients may buy futures to establish a long position or buy to cover (or reverse out of) a previously arranged short position. The broker also works with the client to determine the price, margin requirements, units, total cost, and delivery month.

Every futures contract specifies the **deliverable grade** of commodity. For agricultural commodities, the deliverable grade sets a minimum quality standard. For financial futures, the deliverable grade specifies a standard acceptable security. For the Treasury note contract traded on the Chicago Board of Trade, for example, only T-notes with a denomination of $100,000 and between 6.5 and 10 years to maturity will be accepted for delivery. If the physical commodity presented for delivery is unacceptable, the delivering party defaults on the contract. In that case the clearinghouse fulfills the contract instantly (and sues the defaulting party later). Some contracts allow the party delivering below-grade goods to accept a price lower than the price stipulated in the futures contract according to a prespecified schedule of penalties.

The broker takes the client's order and transmits it to the commodity exchange. At that time the customer is required to pay the 2 to 10 percent *initial margin*. Both buyers and sellers are required to post initial margin money, to help ensure performance. When it is time to deliver on a contract, the seller can do any one of the following: (1) deliver the actual commodity (if the seller owns any), (2) buy back (reverse out of) the contract in the spot market, (3) buy the physical commodity in the cash market and deliver it to fulfill the futures contract.

22-4   Trading Futures for Profit or Protection

As is the case with any investment, futures traders can reap profits or incur losses. For example, if a trader buys a silver futures contract for 5000 ounces (one unit of silver) at a price of 822 cents per ounce and sells it before its delivery date at a price of 852 cents per ounce, a gain of 30 cents per ounce (or $1500 profit) is earned before commissions. However, if the same trader has the misfortune to sell the silver at 802 cents per ounce after buying it at 822 cents per ounce, a loss of 20 cents an ounce (or $1000, plus the commission cost) would be incurred. Traders deal with the riskiness of futures trading in two ways—some become hedgers and some are speculators—depending on their degree of risk aversion.

Speculating

Speculators earn their living by continually buying and selling futures contracts in order to profit from the price changes. While speculators trade futures contracts frequently, they do not actually want to receive delivery on any contract. Their willingness to buy and sell frequently makes futures markets more liquid. Speculators can increase their profits (or losses) by using margins.

Buying on Margin   When speculators buy and sell futures, they usually make only small down payments called **margins** to bind their transactions. Using margins rather than paying cash for the entire amount of the contract increases the *financial leverage* and the risk exposure the trader incurs. Commodity brokerages define a client's margin as the equity in the client's account. The equity equals the sum of the following amounts: cash, cashlike securities (U.S. Treasury bills), net paper profits (which may be positive or negative), and equity in any positions owned.

Exchange officials may curtail overly aggressive speculation by raising the margin requirements if they fear that speculators may not have the money to cover their commitments. Margin requirements are thus set by the commodity exchanges to control pyramiding of debt that might collapse and then initiate or accentuate a market downturn.

Initial and Maintenance Margin Requirements   Commodity exchanges require purchasers of futures (or short sellers) to put up margin money to guarantee they will perform as contracted. Initial margin requirements of 2 to 10 percent are common.

Box 22-1

EXAMPLE: Bearish Sheila Sells the Market Short

Sheila started feeling bearish about the stock market on Monday, November 11, 1991. Even though the market kept creeping upward all week long, she continued to feel bearish. Then, on Friday the 15th, Sheila got out of a late morning meeting and discovered that the market had started down.* Quickly, before she went to lunch, she called her broker and sold one futures contract on the Standard & Poor's 500 Stocks Composite Index at 390. The S&P 500 futures contract is valued at $500 times the value of the S&P 500 index, so Sheila made a $390 \times \$500 = \$195,000$ short sale. This short sale required an initial margin of 3 percent of the contract's total market value, or $\$195,000 \times 3.0\% = \$5850$. After lunch Sheila called her broker and found out that the S&P 500 had fallen to 386. She reversed out of her short position by buying one S&P 500 contract at 386. Sheila's transaction is summarized below.

Transaction	*Contract price*	*3% initial margin*
1. Sell one contract at 390 × $500	$195,000	$ 5,850
2. Buy one contract at 386 × $500	193,000	
Profit	$ 2,000	

Sheila speculated by putting an initial margin of $5850 down on one S&P 500 contract and borrowing $189,150 from her brokerage. After lunch she was $2000 richer for her effort.

---

*The stock market indexes usually fluctuate less than 1 percent per day. November 15, 1991, was an unusual day; the markets all dropped more than 4 percent.

(Note that commodity futures margins are much lower than the common stock margin requirement of about 50 percent.) The **initial margin** is usually a sufficient guarantee, unless the margined commodity's price falls a significant amount on a long position (or rises a significant amount on a short position). Then the trader receives a *margin call* to put up more margin money as evidence of continued financial solvency.

Maintenance margins, or **variation margins,** as they are also called, are additional amounts of guarantee money that traders may be required to pay their brokerage to ensure performance if the commodity price fluctuates adversely. For example, if a speculator buys a futures contract on 5 percent initial margin and the commodity's price then falls 5 percent, the speculator's original margin is wiped out. There will be zero equity (that is, none of the investor's own money) left in the margined account. In such a case the broker will ask the speculator to put up maintenance margin money. If the speculator does not do so, the broker will liquidate the futures contract being held as collateral for the loan to buy the contract. Thus, a margin call forces speculators to put up the maintenance margin, or **mark to the market,** as it is called, to avoid having their accounts liquidated.[3]

Hedging

Hedgers are usually business people who need to buy or sell a physical commodity in order to conduct their business. They use futures to guard against disadvantageous price changes. This risk-averse strategy is used, for example, by silverware manufacturers who buy silver bullion in the silver futures market, by breakfast cereal manufacturers who buy grain futures, by farmers who want to be sure of selling their crops at a profit, and by investors who want to buy or sell securities at a favorable price. These buyers and sellers want to receive income from their normal business rather than from price fluctuations. Hedgers use futures contracts to pass price risks on to speculators. As we saw in Chapter 20, hedging is not an activity designed to make profits; it is usually done to protect a position. In fact, *perfect hedges* result in zero profits and zero losses.

A perfectly hedged futures trader, just like a perfectly hedged securities trader, owns identical long and short positions. A perfectly hedged trader has simultaneously contracted to buy and to sell the same goods at the same price. Since the purchase price equals the sales price, the hedger will earn no profit and suffer no loss because price movements of the two positions exactly offset each other. A perfect hedge can be formed with cash positions, spot contracts, or futures contracts.

---

[3] For a numerical example showing how traders are required to mark to the market daily, see Daniel R. Siegel and Diane Siegel, *Futures Markets* (Orlando, Fla.: Dryden, 1990), pp. 16–22. For a discussion of marking to the market that also explains the tax aspects of the transactions, see Perry J. Kaufman, *Handbook of Futures Markets* (New York: Wiley-Interscience, 1984), pp. 10–20 of chap. 6.

Between most risk-averse hedged sellers and most risk-averse hedged buyers is a risk-taking speculator. While the speculator also dislikes risk, the professional takes many risks in both buying and selling because these risks tend to cancel each other out over many trades.

A speculator will buy a futures contract that a seller who is establishing a hedge wants to sell. The speculator does not ever want to receive delivery of the physical commodity from this futures contract, but hopes to profit from a price change in the futures contract and then eliminate the position with a reversing trade. When the speculator does make the reversing trade and sells the futures contract to some other party, this second buyer may be another hedger who wants to buy a futures contract to establish a hedge. Speculators thus create a series of diversified trades for their portfolios and, in the process, help make futures markets more liquid.

Hedging buyers and hedging sellers pass the risks they seek to avoid on to speculators. Speculators who can forecast prices correctly should earn a profit while they provide opportunities for hedgers. However, if the number of hedging buyers does not exactly equal the number of hedging sellers (and it rarely does), the speculator is left holding some long and short futures contracts that are not hedged.

Box 22-2

EXAMPLE: A Risk-Averse Silver Manufacturing Corporation

The Chippendale Silverware Corporation has a written corporate policy from its board of directors stating that its executives should try to earn profits by manufacturing silverware and, at the same time, avoid taking risks arising from changes in the fluctuating market prices of silver bullion. In January Chippendale's contracted to deliver 10,000 ounces of finished silver products to Alexander's Department Stores in June at a price of $6.66 per ounce plus a fixed fee of $20,000 for silversmith work. When the sales contract with Alexander's was signed in January, Chippendale's purchased a July silver futures contract on 10,000 ounces (one contract) at $6.66 per ounce to eliminate the risks associated with silver price fluctuations. This long position in July silver would be delivered after Alexander's June delivery date; the contract was purchased to establish a hedge against price fluctuations in the silver bullion.

Chippendale's obtains the silver bullion needed to start manufacturing by *lifting its physicals-futures hedge.* In April Chippendale's simultaneously (1) buys 10,000 ounces of silver bullion in the cash market to produce the silverware for Alexander's order, and (2) buys back (reverses out of) its July silver futures contract. If the price level of silver changes between January and April, the profits on Chippendale's futures position will be exactly offset by the losses on its contract to deliver to Alexander's, or vice versa, so the silverware manufacturer can neither benefit nor lose from silver price fluctuations. Figure 22-5 illustrates the silversmith's hedge.

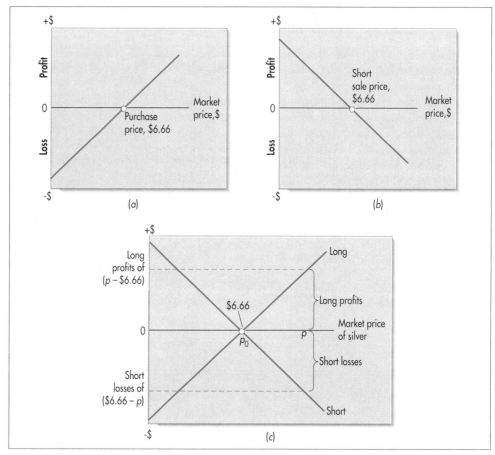

Figure 22-5   Profit graphs for (*a*) the silversmith's long futures position, (*b*) the silversmith's short position in physical silver, (*c*) the silversmith's perfect hedge.

In such situations, speculators hope that the price forecasts on which they based their decisions are correct. The fact that commodity exchanges have been growing for over a century suggests that the parties to these arrangements usually benefit from them.

22-5   Spot and Futures Prices

The prices of spot and futures contracts on a given commodity usually rise and fall together—but not always.

The Basis

The market price of a futures contract is called a **futures price,** and the price of a spot contract is called the **spot price.** For any given commodity futures contract on any given day, the futures price normally exceeds the spot price. The excess of the futures price over the spot price is called the **basis**:

$$\text{Basis} = \text{futures price} - \text{spot price} \qquad (22\text{-}1)$$

When the basis is a positive amount, it is said that futures are selling at a **premium** over spot prices.

In **normal market** conditions, the premium is just sufficient to cover the commodity's carrying cost. The carrying cost for grain commodities, for example, is about 4 cents per bushel per month. The carrying cost for agricultural commodities includes interest expense, charges for storage, quality inspection, insurance, and other expenses incurred while holding a physical commodity in inventory for future delivery. The carrying cost for financial futures equals the current short-term interest rate. The premium is necessary to compensate speculators for buying physical commodities when cash prices are low (for example, at harvest time) and carrying them in inventory until prices rise.

In an **inverted market** the futures price is less than the spot price. This excess of spot over future prices is called a **discount**. Futures can sell at discount to spot, for example, when the current supply of a commodity is short, keeping cash and spot prices high, and the future is expected to yield a large harvest, ensuring plentiful supplies and low future prices.

Delivery Date Convergence

The cash (or physicals) price and the future price for any particular commodity converge as they approach the future contract's delivery date because when delivery is made on the expiring futures contract, it is transformed into the physical commodity. This price **convergence** may not be perfect because a few transactions costs differentiate the physical commodity from the warehouse receipt that is handed over at the contract's delivery. But the futures price will converge on the cash price fairly closely as the delivery date draws near. More generally, cash prices, spot prices, and futures prices for a given commodity tend to be highly positively correlated as their basis diminishes and they converge, as shown in Figure 22-6.

22-6   Sources of Information

To a large extent, spot and futures prices are determined by consensus expectations about supply and demand. Periodicals dedicated to discussing the factors that determine supply and demand are excellent references for the investor. Sources for the information that determine the prices of financial assets are presented in Chapter 8. Sources of information for agricultural goods are listed below.

Government reports: The U.S. Department of Agriculture (USDA) issues periodic crop reports and news bulletins on farm commodities. These reports are released to the public and are usually the most accurate information available. The USDA also gathers and publishes information from U.S. embassies abroad

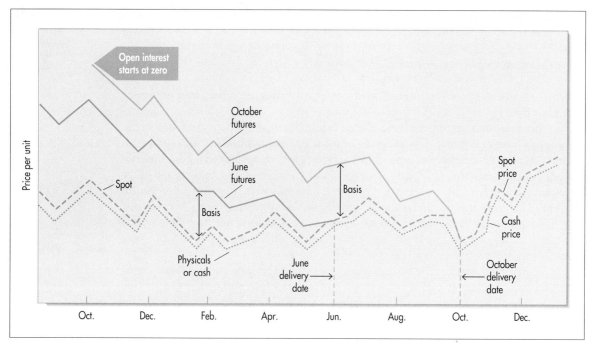

Figure 22-6 The prices of spot and futures converge at the contract delivery date, while the cash and futures prices for storable commodities do not quite converge.

about the commodity situation in foreign lands. The USDA bulletins are typically more accurate than official commodity reports issued by the foreign governments themselves.

Situation reports: The major price-making influences in specific commodities are discussed in various situation reports, two of which are *The Poultry and Egg Situation* and the *Wheat Situation.* Situation reports are available for every major commodity; they discuss all the issues that might affect prices. Since there are so many factors to consider in commodity speculating, most speculators specialize in only a few commodities.

Commodity research organizations: Some research companies publish newsletters, charts of commodity prices, supply and demand statistics, analyses of current news, and even buy and sell recommendations. The Commodity Research Bureau in New York City is the largest of these services, but there are many others.

Newspapers: The New York Times has a section devoted to commodities futures; *The Wall Street Journal* publishes commodity news, too. The *Journal of Commerce* is primarily devoted to commodity news.

Brokerage houses: Commodities brokerages usually have research departments that issue free newsletters to prospective and actual customers.

Successful speculation is based on fast and accurate information processing because prices are determined by buyers' and sellers' expectations. Commodity futures trading is fast and exciting. Those who process information quickly and anticipate price changes correctly profit handsomely. Trading can be a risky business, however, especially when futures contracts are purchased with small margins as down payments.

Summary

Futures contracts on agricultural commodities were used over a century ago; futures on financial assets did not begin trading until the 1970s. Futures on Treasury securities are called *interest rate futures*. The contracts on securities markets indexes might be called *futures on anticipated profits*. The popularity of financial futures has soared since their inception in the 1970s.

Business people use futures contracts to protect themselves against the risk of adverse price fluctuations. Futures are bought and sold at commodity exchanges in trading rings, where buyers and sellers who are members of the exchange come together. The bid prices of potential buyers and the asked prices of potential sellers are determined by their expectations concerning supply and demand.

Speculators sell futures short, expecting to gain by selling at a higher price than the price for which they later cover their short position. Speculators do not usually intend to take delivery on their contracts; they buy futures contracts hoping a price increase will enable them to sell at a profit. Hedgers use futures contracts to reduce their risk exposure rather than as a way to earn speculative profits. Speculators and hedgers sell and buy futures contracts to and from each other as they pursue their speculative profits and risk-averting hedges.

Further
Reading

Chance, Donald M., *An Introduction to Options and Futures,* 2d ed. (Orlando, Fla.: Dryden, 1991.)
> *This readable textbook uses algebra; it provides an up-to-date explanation of the theories and research about what determines the market prices of options and futures.*

Hull, John, *Introduction to Futures and Options Markets* (Englewood Cliffs, N.J.: Prentice-Hall, 1991).
> *Algebra and statistics are used in this comprehensive introduction to the workings of the markets for options and futures.*

Kaufman, Perry J., *Handbook of Futures Markets* (New York: Wiley-Interscience, 1984).
> *This is a comprehensive volume full of details about commodities, commodity markets, commodity regulations, trading strategies, and related economic topics.*

Kolb, Robert W., *Understanding Futures Markets,* 3d ed. (Miami, Fla.: Kolb, 1991).
> *This nonmathematical book uses graphs and tables of numerical data to supplement its detailed discussion of many aspects of futures trading.*

Leuthold, Raymond M., Joan Junkus, and Jean E. Cordier, *The Theory and Practice of Futures Markets* (Lexington, Mass.: Lexington Books, 1989).
> *This book uses mathematics, statistics, and economic theory to analyze futures prices and futures markets.*

Petzel, Todd E., *Financial Futures and Options* (Westport, Conn.: Quorum Books, 1989).
> *This book is rich with facts and theories. The author's experiences as both a professor and a vice president at the Chicago Mercantile Exchange enrich this readable book.*

Powers, Mark J., *Getting Started in Commodity Futures* (Cedar Falls, Iowa: Investor Publications, 1983).
> *This easy-to-read paperback defines many of the essential words and concepts used by commodity traders.*

Tucker, Alan L., *Financial Futures, Options, and Swaps* (St. Paul, Minn.: West, 1991).
> *Over half the chapters in this textbook deal with futures markets. In addition, the book addresses statistical concepts, utility theory, and portfolio theories and shows how they help determine market prices.*

Questions and Problems

Essay Questions

22-1   What functions are performed by a commodity exchange's clearinghouse? (*a*) What can a clearinghouse do to make the commodity exchange function more smoothly? (*b*) What can a clearinghouse do to improve the commodity futures contracts it administers?

22-2   What is an inverted market? Give an example of how and why an inverted market might occur.

22-3   "The futures price is determined after a commodity's spot prices is known. Carrying costs are added to the spot prices to determine futures prices." (*a*) Is this statement true, false, or questionable? Explain. (*b*) Are spot and futures prices for a given commodity ever equal?

22-4   "Speculation is a pastime for wealthy dilettantes. It destabilizes prices, misallocates resources, and should be made illegal." Is this statement true, false, or questionable? Explain.

22-5   (*a*) Why do you suppose there are no futures markets for raisins and salt? (*b*) Do you think that the absence of such markets means that no speculation in these commodities occurs? (*Note:* The answer is not in this book; this is a think question.)

22-6   If wheat futures were selling at $3 per bushel at noon one day and some occurrence instantly changed the equilibrium price to $3.50 per bushel, what would this do to trading in wheat futures? Explain what would happen and why such results will always occur.

22-7   The premise that makes hedging possible is that cash (or physical) prices, spot prices, and futures prices behave in a certain manner. Explain how and why the cash, spot, and futures prices of a given commodity interact the way they do.

22-8   Describe the principal differences between futures contracts and forward contracts.

22-9   Write two short, but different, one-sentence definitions of hedging that are both correct.

22-10   Is the graph of wheat prices that follows normal or abnormal? Is it possible that the price of physical (or cash) wheat will coincide with the September wheat futures price? What economic process does the graph represent?

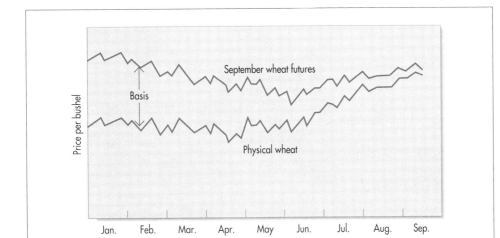

Problems

22-11 Assume that the following data are the commodity prices of wheat futures:

July	$2.39 per bushel
December	2.60
March	2.71
May	2.81
July	2.70
September	2.78

From the data, (*a*) estimate the cost of carrying a bushel of wheat in storage for 1 month. (*b*) Judging from the data, in which month do you think the wheat is harvested? Explain how you obtain your answers.

22-12 Joe Speculator is bearish on the stock market. (*a*) What will Joe make if the S&P 500 index is currently at 130 and Joe sells 10 S&P 500 futures contracts short? Assume that 6 months from now the S&P 500 has fallen to 100. (*b*) Calculate Joe's rate of return in part (a) if he had invested 10 percent margin. (*c*) How much would Joe earn if the S&P 500 index increased to 150 over 6 months?

22-13 It is June 1 and you expect the price of wheat to increase over the next 3 months. Initial margin requirements call for a minimum of 10 percent down, and the current price of wheat is $3 per bushel. (*a*) If you have $10,000 to invest, what should you do? Assume a $40 commission per contract. (*b*) Assume you purchased six wheat contracts on June 1 and the price of wheat then goes to $3.50 per bushel over the next 3 months. How much will you earn or lose, net of commission costs? (*c*) How much will you earn or lose, net of commission costs, if you take the long position on June 1 and the price of wheat goes to $2.25 per bushel over the next 3 months?

22-14 In March you are bearish on the price of gold over the next 6 months. If you sell 10 gold futures contracts short at the price of $450 per troy ounce, what will you earn if the price of gold goes to $400 per troy ounce over this time period? Assume a $1500 margin and a $35 commission per contract.

22-15   Assume you were managing a $7.5 million portfolio of common stock and were bearish about the next 6 months. (*a*) If 6-month futures contracts are available on the S&P 500 and the S&P 500 index is currently at 150, how can you advantageously use your bearish expectations to hedge your long position in the stock market? (*b*) What will happen to the overall value of the portfolio if it has been fully hedged and the common stock portfolio declines in value by $1.5 million to a total value of $6 million and the S&P 500 index simultaneously falls to 120?

Matching Question

22-16   Match the commodity words and phrases listed below with the most appropriate definitions or descriptions.

Word or phrase	Definition or description
1. Carrying charges	A. The maximum daily price change allowed for a commodity by an exchange
2. Deliverable grades	B. The official closing price
3. Inverted market	C. Storage rent + interest expense + insurance cost for a grain commodity
4. Open interest	D. Quality levels acceptable for delivery on a futures contract
5. Limit move	E. When the spot price exceeds the futures price
6. Settlement price	F. Total number of contracts in a given commodity that are for sale or are on order

Multiple Choice Questions

22-17   A farmer who anticipates making a cash sale at harvest could hedge his crop by performing which of the following?

(*a*) Buying futures contracts before the crop is harvested
(*b*) Selling futures contracts before the crop is harvested
(*c*) Both of the above
(*d*) Neither of the above

22-18   The clearinghouse at a commodity exchange is best described by which of the following?

(*a*) It is the seller to every buyer.
(*b*) It is the buyer from every seller.
(*c*) It delivers on defaulted contracts.
(*d*) It is all of the above.
(*e*) It is insured by the FDIC.

22-19   An inverted market is best described by which of the following?

(*a*) Prices decline bearishly as pessimism predominates.
(*b*) Futures prices are at a discount to spot prices.
(*c*) The supply for sale exceeds buyer's demands.
(*d*) Both (*a*) and (*b*).

22-20   Hedges can be best described by which of the following statements?

(a) One speculator and one risk averter typically form one hedged position.
(b) Profits can be made or lost from speculating.
(c) Hedges are used by risk avoiders to reduce their risk exposure.
(d) All the above.

22-21   The "open interest" is best defined by which of the following statements?

(a) The number of unhedged futures contracts in force.
(b) The number of futures contracts currently in force.
(c) The number of buyers (but not sellers) of futures contracts.
(d) It expands as a futures contract becomes a spot contract.

22-22   Which one of the following would serve as a good source for commodity news?

(a) *The Journal of Commerce*
(b) USDA
(c) Foreign embassies
(d) Both (a) and (b)

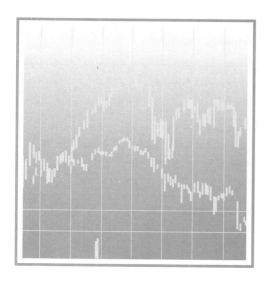

CHAPTER 23

INVESTING IN REAL ASSETS

Real assets are physical assets like diamonds, oil paintings, a stamp collection, real estate, or other investments in physical things. Investing in real assets is different from investing in securities for several reasons. This chapter focuses on these differences and then examines the various types of real asset investments and their advantages and disadvantages.

23-1   Analysis of Real Assets

Real assets differ significantly from securities in three respects: One is the type of income derived from investments in real assets, a second is the way real assets must be analyzed, and the third is the way inflation affects real assets.

570

Like securities investors, most real asset investors hope for financial gain. In addition, many also expect to derive *psychic income.* Consider, for example, the pleasure many homeowners obtain from their residences. Similarly, many people take great pride in owning and wearing fine jewelry. Such pleasures provide a nonfinancial income called **psychic income** that cannot be measured in dollars.

The existence of a significant but unmeasurable quantity like psychic income makes it difficult to analyze the risk and income characteristics of investments in real assets. However, real assets are a large and growing part of many investment portfolios; this category of assets should not be ignored, even if emotions tend to obscure the analysis.

Psychic income is not usually a problem for institutional investors like banks and insurance companies; they typically own a large and highly diversified portfolio containing pieces of real estate, diamonds, gold, or perhaps other types of real assets. Funds controlled by institutional investors are managed by committees of investment professionals who get no psychic income from the assets in which their institution invests. Nevertheless, there are unavoidable problems in analyzing real assets that even institutional investors must confront.

Every Real Asset Is Unique

Investors must work harder to analyze real assets because of their inherent uniqueness. No two homes are completely alike, for instance. Even if two houses were identically designed and constructed, their locations must differ. Two diamonds of the same size and cut will have different degrees of clarity, different colors, different flaws. In contrast, most securities are homogeneous. One share of IBM common stock is just like every other share of IBM common stock. Analyzing real assets is more difficult than analyzing securities because investors must evaluate every asset individually. Real assets do have some compensatory advantages, however.

Real Assets versus Monetary Assets

Monetary assets and real assets can be viewed as two different investment categories. **Monetary assets** are legal claims on financial instruments that are denominated in dollars. Cash, bank account deposits, cash-value life insurance, promissory notes, and bonds are examples. Real assets are physical goods, such as real estate (land, houses, buildings), precious metals (gold, silver), precious stones (diamonds, rubies), art objects (paintings, sculpture), and other collectibles (rare stamps, antiques). *Real assets are not denominated in dollars*—an important fact that differentiates them from monetary assets.

Inflation Hedges   Research has shown that real assets tend to be good inflation hedges. As we saw in Chapters 5 and 18, assets that are good **inflation hedges** typically appreciate more rapidly than the rate of inflation. Table 5-5 and Figure 5-1 compare the average annual rates of return for various types of investment assets with the rate of inflation (measured by the consumer price index).

Monetary assets are not usually good inflation hedges because they do not inflate in price when the inflation rate rises. For example, if you had put $100 in a savings account at 5 percent interest during 1973 or 1979, years of double-digit inflation, your savings dollars would have lost purchasing power. If you had taken your $100 principal plus $5 of interest income from your 1-year deposit, this $105 would *not* have as much purchasing power as the original $100 deposit had a year earlier. And since the income from most monetary assets is subject to income taxes in the period in which it is earned, your purchasing power from a monetary asset investment would be further reduced. In contrast, the income from most real assets is not taxable until the asset is sold and the gain is realized. If, instead, you had invested your money in real assets, the real assets would probably have increased in value at a rate at least equal to the inflation rate. Stated differently, the purchasing power of your investment would not have suffered. This does not mean investing in real assets is riskless, however.

Lack of Guarantees   There is no guarantee that the value of any real asset will appreciate as fast or faster than the rate of inflation. The prices of many homes declined (in both the nominal and the real sense) during the recession of 1981 to 1982 and before, during, and after the 1990 to 1991 recession. The prices of investment grade diamonds fell about one-third from March 1980 to February 1981, and the price of silver fell by 75 percent in the first half of 1980. These examples serve as reminders that although real assets tend to be good inflation hedges, they do not always yield high returns and they are far from being riskless.

Table 23-1 presents rate-of-return data for various types of real and monetary assets. Note how the rate-of-return rankings change over different holding periods.

23-2   Real Estate

For many people the purchase of a residence is the biggest and the best investment they make in their entire lives. Potential investors should also consider the many other forms of real estate ownership available. Figure 5-1 shows that, on average, various categories of real estate have risen in value about as fast as or faster than most corporate and government securities. Table 5-5 contains risk and return statistics that break down the performance of these investments into the subcategories of business, residential, and farm. The statistics show that farm investments have dominated the NYSE average—that is, farms yielded slightly higher returns than did stocks on the NYSE, while experiencing less variability of return during some periods. Residential housing has experienced less return and less risk than the average NYSE stock investment.

Two additional factors should be considered when evaluating the data in Figure 5-1 and Table 5-5. First, when the psychic income that most homeowners and farmers derive from their investments is considered, these forms of real estate compare even more favorably with alternative investment vehicles. And second, just as the data in Figure 5-1 and Table 5-5 are representative of economic conditions in the 1960 to 1984 sample period, different sample periods can be expected to yield statistics that

Table 23-1

573

Chapter 23
Investing in
Real Assets

Annualized Rates of Return for Real Assets and Monetary Assets[a]

Asset category	20-yr Return	Rank	10-yr Return	Rank	5-yr Return	Rank	1-yr Return	Rank
Old masters[b]	12.3%	1	15.8%	2	23.44%	1	6.5%	5
U.S. common stocks[c]	11.7	2	16.0	1	13.3	3	11.8	3
Chinese ceramics[d]	11.6	3	8.1	5	15.1	2	3.6	8
Gold	11.5	4	−2.9	12	1.0	12	−0.7	12
Diamonds[e]	10.5	5	6.4	5	10.2	4	0.0	11
Stamps[f]	10.0	6	−0.7	10	−2.43	13	−7.67	13
Bonds[g]	9.4	7	15.2	3	9.7	5	13.2	2
Oil[h]	8.9	8	−5.9	13	8.5	6	20.7	1
T-bills, 3-month	8.6	9	8.8	4	7.0	7	7.1	4
Housing[i]	7.3	10	4.4	7	4.6	9	4.7	7
Inflation[j]	6.3	11	4.3	8	4.5	10	5.0	6
U. S. farmland	6.3	12	−1.8	11	1.3	11	2.1	9
Silver	5.0	13	−9.3	14	−4.8	14	−18.9	14
Foreign exchange[k]	4.5	14	3.6	9	5.4	8	0.2	10

[a] Salomon Brothers, New York, NY 10004. All returns are for the period ending June 1, 1991, and are based on the latest data available. Reprinted with permission of R. S. Salomon, Jr.

[b] Data on old masters oil paintings are from Sotheby's in New York City.

[c] Stock returns assume quarterly reinvestment of cash dividends.

[d] Data on Chinese ceramics from Sotheby's in New York City.

[e] Diamond data from the Diamond Registry.

[f] Stamp data from Scott Incorporated.

[g] Bond returns assume quarterly reinvestment of coupons.

[h] U.S. Department of Energy data.

[i] Housing data from National Association of Realtors.

[j] The inflation rate is the percentage change in the consumer price index (CPI).

[k] The rate of return from a diversified portfolio of different currencies.

reflect different economic conditions. Compare the statistics from alternative investments shown in Table 23-2 for the periods 1947 to 1959, 1960 to 1972, and 1973 to 1984. All forms of real estate investing (especially farmland) were more lucrative during the 1973 to 1984 period than during the other sample periods. One of the conclusions from all these data is that if you are thinking of investing in farmland, you should ask yourself if the economic environment that existed during the years 1973 to 1984 can be expected to exist in the future. Some other factors real estate investors should consider are addressed below.

Table 23-2
Investment Statistics from Real Estate and Other Categories of Assets
Measured over Three Different Sample Periods

Investment	1947–1959		1960–1972		1973–1984	
	Average rate of return, %	Standard deviation	Average rate of return, %	Standard deviation	Average rate of return, %	Standard deviation
Residential real estate	5.42%	2.73%	6.58%	2.31%	10.53%	4.44%
Farmland	9.94	6.01	9.93	3.56	14.03	11.06
Business real estate	NA	NA	6.38	3.94	10.78	2.77
Common stocks	18.34	18.06	9.55	12.94	9.62	19.71
Corporate bonds	1.23	4.15	4.21	6.92	7.51	13.92
Small stocks	16.44	24.65	15.13	29.73	21.96	28.11

Note: NA means not available.

Source: James R. Webb and Jack H. Rubens, "How Much in Real Estate? A Surprising Answer," *Journal of Portfolio Management,* vol. 13 (Spring), no. 3, 1987, pp. 10–14.

Forms of Ownership

A real estate investor can choose to own an asset directly or indirectly. If you buy a piece of real estate *directly,* the title is in your name. The advantage of direct ownership is that you have complete control over the asset. However, you are also solely responsible for any damage to the property, or for personal injuries that may occur on the property. Indirect ownership is more complicated.

A real estate investor who does not want direct ownership can choose among several alternatives. First, the investor can make a mortgage loan to someone else, with real estate as collateral for the loan. Second, the investor can buy a mortgage-backed security issued by Fannie Mae or Ginnie Mae (see Chapter 3). A third approach would be to form a real estate syndicate with partners. Some partners could be limited partners who merely invest money and take a share of any profits; some partners could be managers who also draw salaries. Still another approach is the real estate investment trust (REIT), an interesting form of indirect ownership.

Syndicates A **syndicate** is usually formed by a real estate manager, who raises capital from individual investors. A syndicate offers the inexperienced investor an opportunity to participate in a large real estate venture. Syndicates offer an investor very specific advantages and disadvantages. They are frequently organized as **limited partnerships.** The risks of limited partners are limited to their investment, and there is no double taxation (at the corporate level and then again at the investor level) on real estate limited partnerships: income is taxed only when the investor receives it. Furthermore, accounting losses may offset income from other sources. However, limited-partnership interests are not readily marketable. Investors in a real estate syndicate may have to wait an undetermined number of years until the syndicate manager decides to liquidate the assets and distribute the invested funds. The three main investment objectives of real estate limited partnerships are to offer tax shelter, to provide tax-free cash flow, and to convert ordinary income into long-term capital gains that receive more favorable tax treatment.

Real Estate Investment Trusts   A **real estate investment trust,** or **REIT,** is a closed-end investment company that invests only in real estate. REITs are exempt from federal income tax if they do not violate any of the following conditions:

1. Keep 75 percent or more of their assets invested in real estate, mortgages, cash, or government securities

2. Derive 75 percent of their gross income from real estate

3. Distribute at least 90 percent of their income to shareholders (officially called *beneficiaries*)

4. Have at least 100 shareholders, no 5 of whom can control more than half the shares

REITs were granted tax exemption in order to eliminate double taxation (at both the corporate and the investor levels) and to encourage publicly held institutions to divert funds into real estate investing. Shares of REITs are generally marketable, especially those listed on national or regional stock exchanges. Share prices are determined in the open market and may be above or below the actual value of the real estate holdings. There are many types of REITs: some emphasize owning real estate, some concentrate on mortgage investing, and others make construction loans.[1]

After selecting a form of real estate ownership, the investor must still decide what type of real estate to buy.

Types of Real Estate

All real estate investments are different, but they can nevertheless be classified into several broad categories:

- *Raw land:* Undeveloped land may be purchased by an investor who hopes that its market price will rise in the years ahead. If the investor is energetic and the location desirable, the land can be developed by subdividing it and installing roads and sewers and other amenities. Then parcels of the developed land can be sold.

- *Rental residences:* Investors may purchase residential space to generate rental income. The owner or hired manager must collect rents, maintain the premises, and keep the premises rented.

---

[1] For more information about REITs contact the National Association of Real Estate Investment Trusts, Inc., in Washington, D.C., for their annual *REIT Fact Book* or monthly and quarterly periodicals that the organization publishes. Also see John S. Howe and James D. Shilling, "Capital Structure Theory and REIT Security Offerings," *Journal of Finance,* vol. 43, no. 4, 1988, pp. 983–993.

• *Office buildings:* Rental income from a commercial office building can be tax-sheltered. Keeping the building well maintained and rented to compatible tenants usually requires professional management.

• *Warehouses:* A building that is to be leased as storage space does not require much active management with a responsible tenant that will sign a long-term lease.

• *Neighborhood shopping centers:* A profitable shopping center can be a wonderful "money pump" so long as the neighborhood remains attractive and competing shopping centers are scarce. Developing a new center is costly, however; and the process can take several years from acquiring of land to opening day.

• *Travel accommodations:* A hotel or motel located near a heavily traveled route can be profitable, but such an asset generally requires professional management.

• *Private residences:* The single-family residence remains the most popular investment in the United States. In fact, the psychic income associated with home ownership clouds the rational economic thinking of many prospective buyers. The usual financial considerations involved in the purchase of an owner-occupied home are reviewed in Box 23-1.

Advantages of Real Estate Investing

Besides psychic income and the inflation hedge, investors can benefit from other advantages to real estate ownership.

Financial Leverage   Financial leverage can be defined as the use of borrowed money to buy an investment with a larger value than what the buyer could have afforded without any borrowed money. When an individual can invest borrowed money and

Box 23-1

COMPUTATION: Buying a Residence

Consider the purchase of a $150,000 home. The real estate agent who sells the home typically informs the potential home buyer where to apply for a mortgage loan. If a husband and wife are buying the house and both are gainfully employed, a mortgage loan for 80 percent of the home's value can usually be obtained. However, the home buyers must be able to make a 20 percent down payment. In other words, $30,000 (20 percent of $150,000) of cash equity is required to obtain the mortgage. If the home buyers are gainfully employed, have good credit records, and can make the required down payment, the bank will probably grant a $120,000 mortgage loan to be paid off over the next 30 years at 10 percent interest, in equal monthly installments of $1053. Table 23-3 shows a budget for this home purchase.*

* Fixed-rate mortgages with lives of 15 to 30 years are common. Variable-rate mortgages are also popular.

Table 23-3
Budget for Purchase of a $150,000 Home
with a $30,000 Down Payment

Monthly payments:*

Mortgage†	$1,053
Real estate taxes	180
Heat, lights, and water	160
Home insurance	40
Repairs and upkeep	120
Total monthly payments	$1,553

Monthly savings:*

Income tax reduction‡	$ 354
Price appreciation§	250
Equity accumulation¶	53
Total monthly savings	$ 657

Excess of monthly payments
over savings ($1,553 − $657) $ 896 per month

* To the nearest dollar.

† A $120,000 mortgage at a fixed rate of 10% for 30 years.

‡ $1000 of the $1053 monthly mortgage payment is interest expense. This $1000 interest and the $180 real estate tax are both tax-deductible. If you are in the 30% income tax bracket, you save 30% of $1,000 + $180, or $354 per month in income taxes.

§ Assume 2 percent per year price appreciation, or $3000 appreciation in the first year (or $250 per month).

¶ $636 of the $120,000 loan will be paid off in the first year, which represents $53 per month of equity accumulation (apart from the appreciation).

Table 23-3 indicates that if the price of the new home rises 2 percent per year, the home purchase will *decrease* its owner's wealth by $896 per month in the first year. Moreover, the home buyer should not forget that the capital gain of $3000 per year cannot be spent while the buyer continues to own the home. This accumulating capital will not be available until the home is sold, and the same is true of the equity accumulation.

The price appreciation and the equity accumulation associated with the home purchase are like savings programs from which no withdrawals are allowed. The $354 income tax savings is the only reduction in cash outflows that results from the home purchase. Therefore, the home buyers must be prepared to make cash payments of $1199 (that is, $1553 − $354) per month from their income. Considering the income and expense figures above, and the illiquidity of a home investment (6% sales commission to buy and 6% to sell), buying a home should be considered a long-term investment that restricts the investor's flexibility.

earn a rate of return higher than the rate of interest payable on the loan, the financial leverage is profitable. Traditionally, real estate investors borrow from 60 to 80 percent of the value of the properties they acquire, which is a much higher leverage ratio (of loan to asset value) than is available on most other forms of investment.

When the interest rate on borrowed money is less than the rate at which the real estate's market value goes up (which was not the case in Table 23-3), increased use of financial leverage increases the rate at which the owner's equity grows. For an income-producing property, this growth often means a higher dollar cashflow per dollar of equity investment. A high leverage ratio also tends to increase the tax deductions for property taxes, interest expense, and depreciation (because leverage facilitates a larger investment), which can shelter more of the cashflow from income taxes.

A high leverage ratio also involves some disadvantages for the investor. It increases the risk undertaken by the borrower. If an income-producing property becomes distressed and its ability to generate cashflows shrinks to the point that the property cannot pay for itself, and there is no income from the property against which to write off the tax-deductible expenses (of interest, depreciation, and property taxes), investors must use their own cash to pay off the debt. This can lead to bankruptcy if the debt exceeds the investor's liquid assets. Thus, financial leverage offers both great potential benefits and great potential risks.

Tax Shelter   Real estate investors benefit from tax laws that encourage real estate ownership. Rental property can be depreciated, and this depreciation is a tax-deductible expense that will reduce taxes on the rental income. When a piece of real estate is held longer than 1 year and sold for more than it cost, this long-term capital gain is taxed at a lower tax rate than ordinary (such as rental) income. (See Chapter 7 about capital gains tax law.) Furthermore, both the interest expense on a mortgage loan and the real estate property taxes can be deducted from taxable income by either landlords or owner-occupants (see Table 23-3). The resulting tax savings are essentially government subsidies for real estate investors.

Control   Real estate owners can control all physical aspects of their properties—the color their house is painted, how often the grass is cut, how soon leaking plumbing is repaired, and other factors, all of which may give them psychic income.

Disadvantages of Real Estate Investing

Although real estate investments offer substantial benefits to investors, they can also involve problems. Real estate investors should weigh the advantages against the disadvantages carefully before undertaking an investment. Here are some of the problems that can arise.

Structural Flaws   A home or building can have termites, sinking or shifting foundations, a leaky basement or roof, or other flaws. Furthermore, such flaws may be extremely difficult to detect and may involve difficult and costly repairs.

Change in Neighborhood Quality   Location has a tremendous impact on the value of a piece of real estate. If a famous actor moves into a home next door to a piece of real estate you own, the value of your property might increase substantially overnight. If the municipality in which your real estate is located buys the lot next to yours and uses it as a garbage dump, the value of your investment would plummet. Such changes in value are generally beyond the investor's control.

Liquidity   Liquidity is gauged by the ease with which an asset can be converted to cash. An asset is considered to have high liquidity when it can be sold quickly without lowering the price. Real estate is an example of an asset that typically has low liquidity. If you were forced to sell your house in a hurry because you had to move to keep your job, for instance, you might have to sell it for only half what you paid for it if credit conditions are tight or the economy is depressed. Lack of liquidity can be a costly flaw in an investment.

Financial Risk   Most real estate investors obtain mortgage loans to finance their purchases. Some mortgages have floating, or variable, interest rates. If market interest rates rise or fall, the interest on such a **variable-rate mortgage,** or **VRM,** rises or falls correspondingly. Since most of each monthly mortgage payment is interest expense, rising interest rates on a VRM can spell financial disaster for an investor.

The Landlord's Duties   Managing rental property is hard work. A landlord must keep the property rented, execute legally enforceable rental contracts, collect rent and deal with delinquent payments, stop violations of leases, keep peace between the tenants, and maintain the property in good condition.

Brokers' Fees   Real estate agents typically receive 6 percent of the value of the transaction when a property is purchased. They collect the same commission rate again when the property is sold. These brokerage fees can easily consume several years of after-tax income. Note that the typical real estate brokers' fees of 6 percent are much higher than, for example, the commissions of 1 percent (or less) that most securities brokers receive. This difference implies that securities are typically more liquid investments than real estate.

23-3   Precious Stones

Diamonds, rubies, emeralds, and sapphires are **precious stones.** Diamonds have been regarded as investments for a longer time, are traded in more active markets, and are worth more per carat than other gemstones. Occasionally, a very large green emerald of very high quality will bring a price that exceeds that of a diamond of comparable size and quality. Table 23-4 shows the price history of diamonds.

Diamonds

The largest and most expensive precious stones (among all other valuable collectibles) are bought and sold regularly at two New York City auction houses—Christie's and Sotheby Parke Bernet. A few blocks away, on 47th Street, is a teeming diamond market composed of dozens of independent wholesale and retail dealers. And, of

Table 23-4
Wholesale Cost per Carat of Various Gemstones, 1976–1990
(in thousands of dollars)

Year	1976	1978	1980	1982	1984	1986	1988	1990
Diamond (1-carat, D-flawless*)	$6.7	$18	$64	$40	$10	$8	$17	$18
Diamond (1-carat, F-flawless*)	4.6	9	28	11	5.5	4	9.2	11

* Grades D, E, and F are all in the colorless category on the color rating scale for diamonds; the scale runs from a top grade of D (for perfectly white) to a bottom grade of Z for yellowish diamonds.

Source: Author's estimates. The prices of all gemstones are negotiable.

course, almost every city in the world has retail jewelry stores where precious stones are sold.

Most of the diamonds in the world come from one firm, DeBeers Consolidated Mines Limited, an old South African company. DeBeers owns about one-third of the diamond mines in the world and has contracts to purchase the output of many other diamond mines. The firm therefore controls most of the supply of new diamonds each year. This control, combined with billions of dollars in working capital, allows the firm to exert some control over the price of diamonds. DeBeers also mines and buys new diamonds itself. Whenever diamond prices do not rise, DeBeers curtails its selling and buys diamonds in an effort to keep prices up. The price drop that began in 1981 was the first decline in diamond prices in decades (see Table 23-4).

The quality of a diamond is appraised in terms of the **four C's**—carat weight, cut, clarity, and color. The quality of a diamond has a major impact on its price. A perfect diamond weighing 1 carat (that is, 1/142 of 1 ounce) might sell for as much as $20,000 wholesale, while another diamond of the same size and shape that looks the same to the untrained observer may bring only $4000. To help investors assess the quality of any diamond, the Gemological Institute of America (GIA) inspects diamonds. For $80 per stone, the GIA will issue a certificate describing the diamond in terms of the four C's and register any flaws. It is more difficult for an investor to obtain assessments of the quality of the other precious stones.

Colored Stones

Rubies, sapphires, and emeralds are called **colored stones.** A high-quality ruby is "pigeon-blood red" and clear. Sapphires must be clear and pure blue in color; traces of green, gray, or violet and lack of clarity greatly reduce the quality (and the price) of a sapphire. Emeralds should be a deep, translucent green; however, Colombian emeralds from the Muzo mine can have a firelike yellowish-green color that is considered attractive.

Colored stones are all much scarcer than diamonds. Nevertheless, diamonds have traditionally brought a higher price per carat than the colored stones for several possible reasons: there are so many more diamonds and they are traded more actively than the colored stones; jewelry lovers simply prefer clear stones to colored stones; industrially manufactured small colored stones cannot be differentiated from genuine stones, thus keeping their value suppressed; and, the DeBeers Company supports diamond prices, which helps maintain their price supremacy. We may never know why diamond prices are highest, but potential investors should not ignore the fact that diamonds are a more liquid asset than colored stones.

There are no tax advantages associated with investments in gemstones. The prices of many precious stones fell by about 50 percent during the Depression of the early 1930s. If another depression were to occur or a major new mine for diamonds or colored stones were to be discovered, it is safe to assume that prices would decline significantly, at least temporarily. Thus, there are risks in investing in gemstones.

The prices of the various types of precious stones do tend to be somewhat independent of each other. The drop in diamond prices in the early 1980s did not pull down the prices of the colored stones as much. In fact, prices for some colored stones did not decline at all. These price movements suggest that diversifying among the different types of precious stones could be an effective way to reduce risk.

The difference between the purchase price and the sales price of any stone on any given day (that is, the wholesaler's commission) can easily be 10 to 50 percent. And the retail jeweler's markup is often as much as 100 percent over the wholesale price. Such high trading costs considerably reduce the liquidity of an investment in gemstones.

23-4   Precious Metals

In contrast with investments in precious stones, investments in precious metals are more liquid and involve lower commissions. Gold and silver are the **precious metals** that are most popular for investing. Other expensive metals include copper, magnesium, manganese, molybdenum, nickel, platinum, titanium, and zinc. Members of this latter group are primarily industrial materials, and thus lack certain investment properties. Like precious stones, gold and silver are priced as aesthetically attractive substances. Precious metals and precious stones are also valued because they have what is called **moneyness.** A substance possesses moneyness when it is (1) a store of value, (2) durable, (3) easy to own anonymously, (4) easy to subdivide into small pieces that are also valuable, (5) easy to authenticate, and (6) interchangeable (that is, homogeneous, or fungible). Gold and silver and other objects that possess the six characteristics listed above have been used as money at one time or another. This quality of moneyness gives gold and silver a special value apart from their value in industry and as jewelry.

The History of Silver and Gold

As moneylike assets, gold and silver have been at the core of domestic and international monetary systems for centuries. They are excellent inflation hedges; furthermore, their values tend to rise during crises such as hyperinflation, political upheaval, and war.

Some U.S. Silver History   The Coinage Act of 1965 ended the use of silver to make dimes and quarters, which was the first step in ending the use of silver as a form of money in the United States. In 1967 the U.S. Treasury stopped supporting the price of silver at $1.29 per ounce; the price jumped to $1.87 per ounce and began to fluctuate. In 1968 the secretary of the treasury declared that dollar bills called *silver certificates* were no longer redeemable in silver—silver was demonetized. By the mid-1970s silver prices had gradually fluctuated up to $5 per ounce. Some investors made millions when silver briefly soared to $50 per ounce in 1980, as the wealthy Hunt family of Texas sought to manipulate the price. But, then many silver investors (including the Hunts) lost millions as prices collapsed. Since 1983, silver prices have fluctuated between $5 and $10 per ounce.

Some U.S. Gold History   In 1933 President Roosevelt devalued the dollar against gold and made it more difficult for citizens to buy and sell gold. In August 1971 the United States stopped its gold dealings with foreign dollar holders, which snapped the link between the dollar and gold. On December 31, 1974, the U.S. government ended a 41-year ban on American citizens' ownership of gold; a week later, on January 6, 1975, the government started auctioning a portion of its gold stock on the open market. The auction meant that the U.S. government had removed the gold backing for the dollar and was handling gold as though it were just another commodity. Gold prices have fluctuated between $300 and $500 per ounce in recent years.

Empirical Data   Table 23-5 shows some risk and return statistics contrasting gold and silver with investments in monetary assets. Market indexes were used to get the stock and bond returns. Monthly rates of return were calculated by assuming that at the end of every month each asset is sold and immediately repurchased. After 17 years of monthly buying and selling, summary statistics were tabulated. They indicate that gold and silver are the riskiest—they have the largest standard deviations. Investing in common stocks issued by small corporations dominated silver and gold investing; the small stocks offered higher average returns with less risk. Furthermore, commissions on securities are typically much lower than commissions on real assets.

Investing in Silver and Gold

Although silver and gold possess some moneyness, they should be viewed as commodities whose prices fluctuate freely. Investments in silver and gold can take two basic forms—physical and nonphysical. The physical forms include bars of bullion, coins, and jewelry. Nonphysical gold investments include warehouse receipts

Table 23-5
Monthly Average Rates of Return and Risk Statistics from Investments in Alternative Asset Categories, 1971–1987

Investment category	Average return	Standard deviation	Maximum return	Minimum return
Gold	1.56%	7.88	28.66%	−22.29%
Silver	1.51	11.58	57.46	−59.52
Inflation*	0.54	0.37	1.81	−0.46
Treasury bills	0.64	0.24	1.35	0.25
Treasury bonds	0.75	3.43	15.24	−8.46
Long-term corporate bonds	0.76	3.27	14.19	−8.90
Small stocks	1.57	6.53	22.67	−24.27
Common stocks	1.06	4.51	16.57	−11.70

* Percentage change in the consumer price index (CPI), or inflation rates in the U.S.

Source: Jeffrey F. Jaffe, "Gold and Gold Stocks as Investments for Institutional Portfolios," *Financial Analysts Journal,* March-April 1989, table 1, p. 54.

documenting possession of stored gold or silver, futures contracts on gold or silver, and shares of stock in companies that mine precious metals.

Bullion or Ingots Private holdings of silver or gold bars, called **bullion,** or *ingots,* are handled by a few banks and by dealers. There is a wide range of bar sizes from which to choose, but there are important disadvantages to holding silver or gold in this form. For one thing, no current income can be realized. For another, small bars are usually purchased at a premium price and sold at a discount price. The wholesaler's profit is the spread between the premium and discount prices. As a percentage of the total cost, the wholesaler's profit (or the investor's commission costs) are usually largest on the smallest quantities. So the investor should purchase the biggest bar possible. Once you have your bar, you can store it or you can arrange to have a financial institution store it for a fee. You should also provide for insurance on your holdings. The carrying costs alone can be 2 to 3 percent of the value of the bullion per year, or more if you are not a careful shopper.

The loss of current income, the commissions and sales taxes on transactions, and the costs incurred while owning silver or gold mean that the price must rise substantially for the investor to break even. Assay (or appraisal) fees may be required upon sale if an investor decides to accept physical delivery of bullion. In addition, unless the investor deals with bullion dealers of the highest reputation, there is the possibility of fraud.

Coins Coins may or may not have numismatic (or collectors) value. We will concentrate on those gold coins, such as the South African Krugerrand, that are held for investment purposes because of their gold content. The Krugerrand contains 1 ounce of gold and sells at a premium of from 5 to 8 percent above its value as bullion. Millions of these coins have been sold in the United States, giving the market for Krugerrands some liquidity. However, even with a reasonably good secondary market, investors should buy only from reputable sources. Late in 1979 the Canadian government started selling its 1-ounce gold maple leaf coin to compete with the Krugerrand. These Canadian coins are sold at the prevailing gold price plus 3 percent to cover minting and other costs. The U.S. government issued American eagle gold coins and silver coins in sizes from 1/10 to 1 ounce. The American eagle coins are sold at fluctuating prices through banks, brokers, and precious metals dealers.

Jewelry Jewelry containing silver or gold provides psychic income while also working as an investment. However, the quality of jewelry varies widely. Low-quality gold jewelry is of 14-karat gold; pure gold is 24-karat. The highest-quality silver jewelry is 100 percent fine silver—that is, the silver is not diluted with a cheaper metal. A disadvantage of jewelry investments is that aesthetic value, and thus investment value, varies with the taste of the beholder.

Warehouse Certificates Warehouse certificates for gold or silver are nontransferable statements of ownership for bullion stored in banks or warehouses usually located in places that do not levy sales taxes. The minimum acceptable investment is normally several thousand dollars. In addition, commissions average 3 percent on the purchase and 1 percent on the sale. The major drawback of investing in warehouse certificates is lack of liquidity.

Futures Contracts The contract unit is 10,000 ounces for silver and 100 ounces for gold. The purchase of these futures can be highly leveraged; that is, investors can buy with small down payments (or margins). As with other commodities, investors buying gold or silver futures on margin tend to realize substantial gains when the price advances, but they also stand to lose a large portion of their initial investment if the price declines.

Shares of Stock Buying shares of common stock in a corporation that mines silver or gold is another indirect way of investing in precious metals. Such stock is a highly leveraged investment because a small movement in the price of gold or silver can result in a great change in the earnings of a mine and the price of its stock. Many mining stocks are issued by South African companies. The major American gold and silver producers include Sunshine Mining Company and Homestake Mining. Campbell Resources is a big Canadian mining company. Several gold mutual funds offer an alternative to investing in gold or in gold stocks. Some have combination portfolios of bullion and stocks; others hold only stocks.

Problems with Silver and Gold Investing

Although gold and silver have been popular investment assets for centuries, they are not a riskless path to profits.

Disadvantages   First, as with most investments, the value of silver and gold at any given time depends on factors over which the investor has no control. Second, although gold and silver generally appreciate in price, they earn no interest; furthermore, prices sometimes depreciate dramatically. A third factor is the carrying costs of storage, interest, and insurance. Fourth, there are commissions (although they are not high compared with, say, those charged on precious stones). Finally, the possibility of fraud arises when dealing in physical gold or silver, and only costly assaying can prevent it.

Price Determinants   Silver and gold prices are determined by supply and demand interactions in worldwide markets. Supplies come from mines and from carefully hoarded inventories. Both precious metals are demanded by jewelry makers. Both gold and silver have moneyness, but differences between the two affect the gold-to-silver price ratio and the management of investments.

A fundamental change has taken place since the days when silver and gold were used only for luxury goods and coin. Today, silver has important industrial uses: It is a basic component of such manufactured items as photographic and radiology film, electronic conductors, and dental supplies, as well as of such traditional crafted goods as mirrors, tableware, and jewelry. About 55 percent of American silver consumption is for use in photography and electronics; less than 25 percent is accounted for by silverware, jewelry, works of art, and commemorative objects. In contrast, jewelry still comprises the single largest use for gold.

23-5   Art Objects

A dictionary defines **art** as the "production of aesthetic objects through skill, taste, and creative imagination." This broad definition encompasses paintings, sculpture, decorative furniture, etchings, jewelry, and many other items. Since it determines the prices of art objects, let's stop to consider what makes up the **art market:**

• Creative artists

• Private investors and collectors

• Agents, auctioneers, and dealers

• Museums and other institutions

If you wish to invest in an art object and you have no inside connections, you are well advised to buy at auction rather than from an art dealer. After all, you are better off when you are competing with a dealer attempting to buy at a wholesale price than when you are buying the same objects at the dealer's retail price. Before you buy any art, however, you need to know what determines the value of this type of investment.

The value of art objects varies according to rarity, artistic quality, authenticity, condition, historic appeal, fashion, and origin. Before buying anything, an investor should consult an expert. This is not the place to look for bargains or buy on impulse. Go to the exhibitions that precede art auctions and find out about the objects that appeal to you and that are also sound investments.

Table 23-6
Real Annual Rates of Return from Two Studies
of Investments in Famous Paintings

Financial analysts	*Sample period*	*Number of buy-sell transactions*	*Inflation-adjusted returns*		
			Average	*Minimum*	*Maximum*
Baumol	1652–1961	640	0.6%	−19%	+27%
Frey and Pommerehne	1635–1987	1198	1.5	−19	+26

Sources: B. S. Frey and W. W. Pommerehne, "Art Investment: An Empirical Inquiry," *Southern Economic Journal,* vol. 56, no. 2, October 1989, table IV, p. 405. W. J. Baumol, "Unnatural Value or Art Investment as a Floating Crap Game," *American Economic Review, Papers and Proceedings,* May 1986, pp. 10–16.

The supply of most art objects and of all genuine antiques is fixed because most of the artists are dead. However, the demand has increased in recent years for a number of reasons. First, growth in the number of museums means less art is available to private buyers. Second, income tax laws encourage wealthy collectors to donate art objects to museums rather than to sell them. Third, the number of corporate purchasers of art and antiques is growing. Finally, the general public has developed an increasing interest in art objects. It seems, then, that we have an almost perfect investment situation: limited supply and increasing demand. One study of investments in paintings pointed out that:

> In April 1987 van Gogh's "Sunflowers" was sold at Christie's London for $39.9 million, only to be surpassed in November 1987 by van Gogh's "Irises," sold by Sotheby's New York for $53.9 million (including the auction house's 10 percent commission). . . . These enormous prices that are paid today for some masterpieces create a widespread belief that the rate of return from such investments is in general and on average very high.[2]

Unfortunately, the empirical statistics in Table 23-6 burst the euphoric art investment bubble. Two studies are summarized in the table; these data are representative of those reported by a number of different studies. Table 23-6 presents the inflation-adjusted (or real) rates of return from numerous long-term investments in paintings done by world-famous artists over the last 3 centuries.

One of the studies summarized in Table 23-6 concludes:

> There are reasons to assume that the low rate of return on investment in paintings may even be biased upward, not only because of the already mentioned cost of maintenance, restoration and insurance (here left out of account), but also because of the *inherent selection bias:* in general only successful art is repeatedly auctioned.[3]

[2] Bruno S. Frey and Werner W. Pommerehne, "Art Investment: An Empirical Inquiry," *Southern Economic Journal,* vol. 56, no. 2, October 1989, p. 396.

[3] Ibid., p. 406.

An investor should be prepared to hold an art object for decades. This can be difficult, because art objects do not produce income and are usually illiquid. The statistics in Table 23-6 conceal the fads that can send the price of an art object currently in vogue skyrocketing. Some lucky speculators have captured some very high short-term rates of return by purchasing a piece of art by an unknown artist, riding up on a speculative bubble, and then selling before the bubble bursts. Art investors view such price volatility as an undesirable speculative risk-taking.

23-6   Collectibles

Like art objects, collectibles are enjoying increasing interest, which tends to raise prices. **Collectibles** include such items as dolls, antique toys, slot machines, jukeboxes, political buttons, stamps, and coins. Collecting can be risky because the interest in some items may change considerably. After the interest peak passes, the market value of the items can diminish substantially. Since coins and stamps are among the oldest and most popular collectibles, let us confine our attention to them.

Coins

Every coin has three different values—face value, intrinsic value, and numismatic value:

- **Face value** is the amount of standardized monetary value stamped on the coin. For example, the U.S. $20 liberty gold coin has a face value of $20.

- **Intrinsic value** (or ''bullion value'') is the current market value of the metal of which the coin is composed. The U.S. $20 liberty gold coin contains .9675 ounces of fine gold, which places its intrinsic value at about $350 per coin.

- **Numismatic value** is determined by the rarity of the coin (that is, how many such coins there are in existence) and the condition of the coin in relation to its initial, mint state. The coin industry has systems for evaluating rarity and condition that are accepted by all reputable dealers. The U.S. $20 liberty gold coin may have a numismatic value of anywhere between $100 and $150,000.

Table 23-7 shows the face value, intrinsic value, and numismatic value of several different coins, most of which are rare and one of which is a common penny. You can see that coins of low face value tend to have lower intrinsic values, because they contain little valuable metal. The numismatic value, in contrast, has no particular relation to either face or intrinsic value.

The condition of a coin has a very important bearing on its numismatic value. Condition can be classified into three categories.

- **Proof coins** are made especially for collectors from highly polished dies and are struck to bring out the coin's design.

- **Uncirculated coins** are made for circulation but are preserved in near-perfect form.

- **Circulated coins** (or worn coins) have been used and show signs of wear.

Table 23-7
The Values of Various Coins

Date	Metal	Condition	Face value	Intrinsic value*	Numismatic value	Rarity
1857	Copper	Proof	$0.005	$0.02	$3,000	Rare
1959	Copper	Uncirculated	0.01	0.01	0.03	Common
1815	Silver	Uncirculated	0.25	3	5,000	Rare
1841	Gold	Proof	2.50	50	100,000	Rare
1926	Gold	Uncirculated	10	200	2,000	Rare

* Subject to change as the market fluctuates.
Source: Max Liebler, "Mining the Mints," in Arthur Levitt, Jr., ed., *How to Make Your Money Make Money* (Homewood, Ill.: Dow Jones–Irwin, 1981), table 10-1, p. 167.

Proof coins are worth more than uncirculated coins, and both are worth more than worn coins. An uncirculated coin might sell for 80 percent as much as an otherwise identical proof coin, for instance. A circulated coin might sell for only a third as much as the corresponding proof coin.

Coin investors should usually seek the aid of a *coin agent,* who can provide guidance in assessing and predicting numismatic trends and help the investor design a profit-maximizing collecting strategy. The leading journal of numismatics, *Coin World,* contains advertisements by many coin agents. Most numismatic firms offer genuine coins for sale, accurate grading of coins, fair prices, and helpful advice.

Stamps

The condition of a stamp is a very important factor in determining its value. Poor-quality stamps sell at deep discounts from the prices for identical stamps in good condition. The type of paper on which the stamp is printed, the watermarks, the type of color separation used, and the printing technique are also important in valuing a stamp. In addition, if a stamp has a historical background that makes it unique, that history can add to its value.

Rare stamps should be stored in dry places with stable temperatures. Stamps should not be handled. They should be held for years. Dealers normally charge commission of 20 to 30 percent for buying or selling, and these high transactions costs reduce the liquidity of the asset.

People with limited funds to invest can begin investing in stamps. By purchasing one stamp from every new U.S. Post Office stamp issue, you can accumulate a valuable collection over the years at a modest cost.

The best and cheapest way to learn about stamps is by reading the *Scott Stamp Catalog,* a five-volume set that lists every stamp ever issued in the world.[4] The catalog

[4] For the *Scott Stamp Catalog,* write to *Coin World,* Subscription Department, P.O. Box 150, Sidney, Ohio 45365, phone 513-498-0800. The five volumes cost $26 each.

Table 23-8
Performance of a Portfolio of Selected U.S. Stamps

Scott Catalog number	Stamp's description	1925	1980*	Increase
1–2	1847 first issues (set)	$ 180.00	$ 18,000.00	10,000%
230–245	1893 Columbian Expo (set)	45.33	11,169.00	24,050
285–293	1898 Trans. Miss. (set)	23.83	4,827.00	20,000
323–327	1904 La. Purchase (set)	2.13	442.00	22,000
C3a	1918 24c Biplane (invert)	750.00	115,000.00	14,800
	Total	$1,001.29	$149,438.00	14,800
	Gold price (London)†	$20.67	$512.00	2,300
	DJIA†	159.40	838.74	425
	Cost of living (CPI)‡	52.50	230.00	338

* *Scott Specialized Catalog* prices, 1980. Prices are for average-condition mint stamps. The premium for superb U.S. nineteenth-century stamps can be at about 200 to 600 percent of the catalog price.

† As of December 31, 1979. Cash dividends are not included in the Dow Jones Industrial Average of stock prices.

‡ The base year is 1967, when the consumer price index was set at 100.

Source: Max Liebler, "Mining the Mints," in Arthur Levitt, Jr., ed., *How to Make Your Money Make Money* (Homewood, Ill.: Dow Jones–Irwin, 1981), p. 180.

also lists prices for both new and used stamps. It can keep an inexperienced investor from being exploited.

Table 23-8 presents some summary statistics showing how a diversified investment portfolio of five selected U.S. stamps appreciated over a 55-year holding period. The bottom of the table also provides comparative statistics for investments in gold, the Dow Jones Industrial Average (DJIA), and the consumer price index (CPI) over the same period. All five stamps selected for the portfolio outperformed gold and the stock market by a wide margin. This impressive portfolio was constructed to demonstrate the profit potential in stamp collecting. Do not be misled by these impressive results, however. Many stamps are lost or damaged; many stamps never appreciate in value; and commissions and taxes would take a large chunk out of the profits of the stamps in Table 23-8. Like other forms of investing, stamp portfolios can be very risky.

Real assets can bring both psychic income and valuable diversification to an investor's holdings. Furthermore, real assets tend to be better hedges against inflation than monetary assets.

Real estate is the most common real asset investment. Over the years an investment in property has usually yielded good returns. However, real estate returns

Summary

were bad from 1988 through the early 1990s. Real estate ownership offers several tax advantages. Commercial and rental residential real estate can be profitable, but the investor should be prepared for extensive management responsibilities.

Other forms of real asset investing involve difficulties too. The time necessary to obtain a good return from real assets tends to be longer than the time for securities because the spread between the purchase price and the resale price (that is, the intermediary's commission) is usually much larger for real assets. Furthermore, most real assets produce no income (such as interest or dividends), and, so, precious stones, precious metals, art objects, antiques, and collectibles do not usually appreciate as rapidly as financial assets (like common stocks), on average.

The market for a real asset is not highly liquid. As a result, a real asset may have to be sold at a substantial discount. Even if a liquid market is available, expert advice may be needed to transact business profitably. Each real asset is unique, and each requires time-consuming study before investment.

Further Reading

Blume, Marshall E., and Jack P. Freidman, eds., *Encyclopedia of Investments* (Boston: Warren, Gorham and Lamont, 1982).
> *This large volume contains 62 chapters about investing in every real asset from rugs to real estate, plus some financial assets. A few chapters introduce some investment theories. Mathematics is not used in the book.*

Coin World, 911 Vandermark Rd., P.O. Box 4315, Sidney, Ohio 45365-9944.
> Coin World *is a weekly newspaper for coin collectors. Subscriptions are $26 per year and can be obtained from* Coin World; *call 513-498-0800.*

Khoury, Sarkis J., *The Valuation and Investment Merits of Diamonds* (Westport, Conn.: Quorum Books, 1990).
> *This little book contains informative background material, empirical data, and some theory about the determinants of diamond prices.*

Levitt, Arthur, Jr., Ed., *How to Make Your Money Make Money* (Homewood, Ill.: Dow Jones–Irwin, 1981).
> *This is a collection of 20 essays written by experts in 20 fields of real asset investing. No math is used.*

Solnik, Bruno, *International Investments* (Reading, Mass.: Addison-Wesley, 1988).
> *Chapter 11, entitled Gold and Gold-Linked Investments, discusses precious metal investing.*

Questions and Problems

Essay Questions

23-1 In what significant respects does a home investment differ from an investment in other real assets? Can a real estate investment be used to reduce the investor's taxes? Explain.

23-2 (*a*) What are REITs and what forms do they take? (*b*) What are the advantages and disadvantages of investing in a REIT compared with investing directly in a piece of real estate?

23-3 Which type of precious stone makes the most desirable investment? Why? Could the desirability of the different kinds of precious stones as investments change in future years? Explain your thinking.

23-4   Would you invest in any precious metals? Which seems to be the best investment vehicle—physical or nonphysical holdings? Explain your investment decision.

23-5   How are the returns of real assets correlated with the returns of financial assets? Why? What are the implications of these correlations? (Hint: See Table 5-4.)

23-6   In what different types of real estate might a person invest? Which of these would be the most difficult for an individual investor to manage? Why?

23-7   What are the differences between purchasing common stock investments on margin and buying real estate with the aid of mortgage debt? Explain. (*Hint:* If you wish to review some tax laws, see Chapter 7.)

23-8   Compare the real rates of return from the investment categories shown in Figure 5-1 and Tables 5-5, 18-3, and 18-4 with the real rates of return from real (physical, not financial) assets that can be computed from the data shown in Tables 23-1 and 23-5. What category of assets seems to yield the highest real rate of return? The lowest real rates of return?

23-9   What is the difference between the assessed value of a real asset, as assessed by a reputable assessor, and the liquidation value (or market price) of a real asset? To what do you attribute this difference? (*Hint:* This question requires outside research.)

23-10   Rank the following categories of investment assets with respect to liquidity: (*a*) common stocks, (*b*) real estate, (*c*) U.S. Treasury bonds, (*d*) gold, and (*e*) diamonds. Should investors give more weight to the rate of return, the risk, or the liquidity when shopping for an investment?

23-11   The following question is from the level III, 1985 CFA exam:

You are considering the addition of real estate investments to the equity portion of the portfolios you manage. Identify and explain three characteristics which make real estate equity investments attractive relative to common stock investments.

Research Projects

Outside research is especially appropriate for this chapter because only a few pages are devoted to topics on which volumes have been written.

23-12   What are the advantages and disadvantages of investing in real estate, compared with investing in financial assets. [*Hint:* For more information see W. Burns and D. Epley, "The Performance of REITs and Common Stocks," *Journal of Portfolio Management* (Spring), 1982, pp. 37–42; R. H. Zerbst and B. R. Cambon, "Real Estate: Historical Returns and Risk," *Journal of Portfolio Management* (Spring), 1984, pp. 5–20; H. R. Fogler, "20% in Real Estate: Can Theory Justify It?" *Journal of Portfolio Management* (Winter), 1984, pp. 6–13; H. M. Kaplan, "Farmland as a Portfolio Investment," *Journal of Portfolio Management* (Winter), 1985, pp. 73–79; C. Froland, R. Gorlow, and R. Sampson, "The Market Risk of Real Estate," *Journal of Portfolio Management* (Spring), 1986, pp. 12–19; G. Wilson and G. Sullivan, "Farmland Price Behavior: A Study in Diversity," published by the Federal Reserve Bank of Atlanta, April 1985; and, in the book *Real Estate Investing*, edited by T. S. Sale (Homewood, Ill.: Dow Jones–Irwin, 1985), see, by S. E. Roulac, "Games the Stock Market Did Not Teach You," and also, by J. S. Lillard, "The Myths and Realities of Investing in Real Estate."]

23-13 Should someone who is interested in precious metal investing select gold or silver or some other metal? (*Hint:* For more information see G. A. Brauer and R. Ravichandran, "How Sweet Is Silver?" *Journal of Portfolio Management* (Summer), 1986, pp. 33–42; E. J. Sherman, "A Gold Pricing Model," *Journal of Portfolio Management* (Spring), 1983, pp. 68–70; and S. Lee, "Gold: The Ultimate Burglar Alarm," *Forbes*, Sept. 23, 1985, pp. 130–131.)

23-14 Can stamp collectors expect to earn high enough returns to make their hobby rewarding economically as well as psychologically? (*Hint:* For more information see W. M. Taylor, "The Estimation of Quality-Adjusted Rates of Return in Stamp Auctions," *Journal of Finance*, vol. 38, no. 4, September 1983, pp. 1095–1110; J. Boland, "Postage Due," *Barron's*, Jan. 28, 1980; and, "How to Sell a Stamp Collection," *Changing Times*, May 1985.)

Multiple Choice Questions

23-15 Analyzing the investment merits of real assets is more difficult than analyzing financial assets because of which of the following complications?

    (*a*) Unlike the stocks or bonds from a given issuer, every real asset is unique and requires a separate appraisal.

    (*b*) Real assets (such as a home or a hobbyist's stamp collection) yield psychic income that is difficult to assess objectively.

    (*c*) The prices of real assets are more volatile than the prices of financial assets.

    (*d*) Both (*a*) and (*b*) are true.

23-16 A good inflation hedge is best described by which of the following statements?

    (*a*) The price of an investment asset normally increases proportionately as much as or more than the consumer price index.

    (*b*) Corporate bonds are normally a good inflation hedge.

    (*c*) Real assets tend to be better inflation hedges than monetary assets.

    (*d*) Both (*a*) and (*c*) are true.

23-17 Which of the following are advantages that favor real estate investing over investing in common stocks?

    (*a*) Real estate tax shelters and tax subsidies are built into the U.S. tax laws.

    (*b*) Real estate brokers charge lower commission rates than do securities brokers.

    (*c*) Real estate down payments are relatively smaller than margins required to buy common stocks, so more financial leverage is available in real estate.

    (*d*) Both (*a*) and (*c*) are true.

23-18 Precious stones include which of the following?

    (*a*) Emeralds   (*c*) Rubies

    (*b*) Sapphires   (*d*) All the above

23-19 The quality of an investment grade diamond depends on which of the following factors?

    (*a*) Cut   (*d*) All the above

    (*b*) Carat weight   (*e*) Both (*a*) and (*b*)

    (*c*) Coarseness

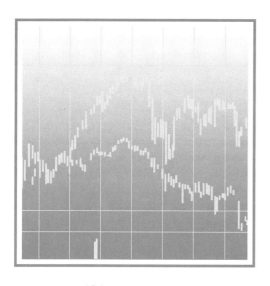

CHAPTER 24

PORTFOLIO
ANALYSIS

An investment **portfolio** is the group of assets that one investor owns. As we have
seen throughout this text, the risk-reducing benefits of diversification make it wiser
to invest in a diversified portfolio than in a single asset. Sinking all of an investor's
funds in a single security is not an investment, it is a *speculation* on the future of one
risky asset. A diversified portfolio might contain common stocks, bonds, options,
future contracts, real estate, diamonds, cash, gold, savings accounts, and other assets.

This chapter shows how a portfolio manager can analyze stocks, bonds, and
other assets to develop diversified portfolios having the maximum rate of return that
can be expected at each level of risk. (The discussion of risk and return in Chapter 1
provides the necessary background for the discussion in this chapter.) Knowledge of
the rates of return from individual assets is necessary for portfolio analysis. This
chapter analyzes various approaches to portfolio analysis to help you select assets on

593

the basis of rates of return, variances of returns, and correlations with the returns from other securities. The statistics needed to perform portfolio analysis are like the expected rate of return and risk information shown in Table 5-5 and the correlation coefficients between these asset categories shown in Table 5-4.

24-1   Dominant Assets and Efficient Portfolios

Portfolio analysis begins when a portfolio manager has the expected rate of return and risk statistics for the various bonds, stocks, and other potential investments. A simple way to select assets worthy of investment is to use the dominance principle (introduced in Box 1-10). We will review this principle below.

The Dominance Principle

The **dominance principle** states that among all investments with a given expected rate of return, the one with the least risk is the most desirable. Conversely, among all investments in a given risk class, the one with the highest expected rate of return is the most desirable. Now reconsider the investment opportunities listed in Table 1-3.

The GM bond listed in Table 1-3 is "dominated" by American Telegraph & Telephone (ATT) stock because the telephone stock has a higher expected rate of return than GM's bond, although both are in the same risk group (of 13.4 percent). Figure 1-3 illustrates the dominance principle. Points that are higher in Figure 1-3 have higher expected rates of return. Points farther to the right are riskier. Thus, Figure 1-3 indicates that the GM bond can be eliminated from consideration because it is a dominated investment. GM's stock, on the other hand, dominates Borden's (BN) stock; their expected rates of return are the same, but GM presents less risk. So BN should be ignored because it too is dominated.

The dominance principle suggests that the GM bond and Borden's stock are inferior investments. The nondominated investments are the common stocks issued by ATT, GM, and Firestone (FIR). The dominance principle has thus narrowed the choices from five assets to three. There is a positive risk-return tradeoff available to investors selecting from the nondominated assets—the riskier dominant assets tend to have the higher returns. It is too soon to make final selections, however, because we have not yet considered diversification. To learn more about diversification, let us consider efficient portfolios.

Efficient Portfolios

Although GM's stock is a nondominated asset, an examination of Figure 1-3 shows that its risk-and-return position does not seem so appealing as those of ATT and Firestone because of certain portfolio effects. Suppose ATT and FIR were combined to form a two-asset portfolio. A two-asset portfolio's expected rate of return is simply the weighted average of the expected rates of return of the two assets in the portfolio. For example, the two-asset portfolio with five-sixths of its funds invested in ATT and the other one-sixth invested in FIR has the same 10 percent expected rate of return as GM's stock, as shown below:

Box 24-1

595

*Chapter 24
Portfolio
Analysis*

> **DEFINITION: Efficient Portfolios**
>
> An **efficient portfolio** is any asset, or combination of assets, that has the maximum expected rate of return in its risk class or, conversely, the minimum risk at its level of expected rate of return.

$$E(r_{GM}) = (5/6)E(r_{ATT}) + (1/6)E(r_{FIR})$$

$$= (5/6)(8\%) + (1/6)(20\%) = 10\%$$

$$E(R_P) = (\% \, Ass_1)(E(r_{Ass_1}) + (\% \, Ass_2)(E(r)Ass_2)$$

The straight line from ATT to FIR in Figure 1-3 represents the risk and return of all the portfolios that can be formed from various proportions of ATT and FIR. (Note, though, that this line ignores some risk-reducing effects of diversification that will be introduced later in this chapter.) GM's stock is a dominated asset if portfolios are considered as possible assets, because the line from ATT to FIR dominates GM's stock.

The objective of portfolio management is to delineate efficient portfolios. As Figure 1-3 shows, there are an infinite number of efficient portfolios lying along the straight line. This group is called the *efficient set* of portfolios. The efficient set in turn defines the *efficient frontier* in risk-return space. As first suggested in Box 1-11, the **efficient frontier** is the locus of points in risk-return space having the maximum return at each level of risk. The efficient frontier dominates all other investment opportunities.

Let's see how diversification can be used to reduce risk and help the investor attain the efficient frontier.

24-2 Simple Diversification

Even the simplest kind of diversification usually reduces portfolio risk substantially. As the number of different assets added to a randomly diversified portfolio increases, the portfolio's total risk tends to decrease. Diversifying across common stocks randomly will usually decrease the unsystematic portion of total risk toward zero until approximately 15 stocks are added to the portfolio. Additional risk reduction cannot usually be gained by diversifying across more than about 15 stocks. Simple diversification (see Box 24-2) will not usually reduce the undiversifiable risk component at all.

Box 24-2

> **DEFINITION: Simple Diversification**
>
> **Simple diversification** involves selecting different securities randomly in order to reduce portfolio risk; it does not involve any effort to diversify across securities from different industries or any analytical procedure—it is the most naive kind of diversification.

We have examined the causes of undiversifiable and diversifiable risk from various factors in earlier chapters. Several studies have shown that the total risk of most securities, as measured by variance in rates of return over time, can be divided into two parts. The exact proportions of systematic and unsystematic risk vary from security to security; but for a large number of NYSE-listed common stocks, systematic risk has been shown to make up about one-quarter of the total risk, on average.

With simple random diversification, the average portfolio's total risk will decline because unsystematic price fluctuations are uncorrelated with the market's systematic fluctuations. That is, the unsystematic variability in different firms' rates of return averages out to zero when added together to form a portfolio.

Figure 24-1 shows how simple diversification over randomly selected common stocks reduces the total risk in portfolios of various sizes. The figure was prepared using empirical data on 470 common stocks from the NYSE during a 10-year period. The average standard deviation of returns for all 470 stocks was .21. Different portfolios of each size were constructed randomly, that is, 470 one-security portfolios, 235 two-security portfolios, 156 three-security portfolios, and so on up to 11 mutually exclusive forty-security portfolios. The portfolios were constructed so that each randomly selected security was allocated an equal weight in every portfolio. Then the average standard deviation of returns was calculated for all the portfolios of each size. Figure 24-1 shows these average standard deviations for each size of portfolio. We can see that, on average, randomly combining about 15 NYSE-listed stocks will reduce portfolio risk to the systematic level of variation found in the market average. Spreading the assets over 30 or 40 (or even 500 or 1,000) randomly selected stocks cannot be expected to reduce the portfolio's total risk below the level of the undiversifiable systematic risk.

Figure 24-1 Simple diversification over 10 to 20 randomly selected common stocks eliminates unsystematic risk. (*Source:* J. Evans and S. H. Archer, "Diversification and the Reduction of Dispersion: An Empirical Analysis," *Journal of Finance*, December 1968, pp. 761–767.)

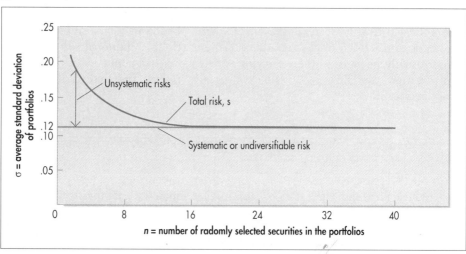

Unsystematic risk is so easily reduced to zero by simply selecting different stocks randomly that *investors require no risk premium (or no additional required rate of return) for assuming diversifiable risks.* Stated differently, risk-averse investors who diversify are not afraid of the unsystematic components of the different risk factors, because they will average away to nothing in portfolios composed of as few as 15 randomly selected stocks. As a result, none of the unsystematic risk components has any effect on the assets' expected returns.

24-3   Diversifying across Industries

Some investment counselors advocate selecting securities from unrelated industries to achieve better diversification. It is certainly better to follow this advice than to choose all the securities from one industry. But **diversifying across industries** is not much more effective than simply selecting securities randomly; analysis reveals that both procedures have equal risk-reduction powers.

The easiest way to see how meager are the benefits of diversifying across industries is to examine the movement of different stock market indexes. Studies of the rates of return of securities have shown that many industries are highly correlated with one another. Figure 17-2 shows how stock market indexes from mutually exclusive industries tend to move together month after month. This systematic variability of return cannot be reduced merely by selecting securities from different industries.

One study tested the effectiveness of diversifying across industries and increasing the number of different assets in the portfolio. Portfolios containing 8, 16, 32, and 128 NYSE-listed common stocks were formed using two approaches. The first was random selection; the second involved selecting each stock from different industries. Numerous portfolios of each size were constructed using both methods, and all the portfolios' risk statistics were calculated. Table 24-1 summarizes the results of the study. In particular, note the average portfolio risk statistics in the right-hand column.

Table 24-1
A Comparison of Simple Diversification
versus Diversification across Industries

Number of stocks	Type of diversification	Min. return	Max. return	Avg. return	Average portfolio's standard deviation
8	Simple	−47%	164%	13%	.22
	Across industries	−47	158	13	.22
16	Simple	−37	121	13	.21
	Across industries	−35	121	13	.21
32	Simple	−31	98	13	.20
	Across industries	−29	93	13	.20
128	Simple	−29	76	13	.19

Source: L. Fisher and J. Lorie, "Some Studies of Variability of Returns on Investments in Common Stocks," *Journal of Business,* April 1970, table 5, p. 112.

The two main conclusions to be drawn from Table 24-1 are that diversifying across industries is no better than simple diversification and that increasing the number of different assets held in the portfolio beyond about 15 does not usually reduce the portfolio's risk much further.

24-4   Superfluous Diversification

Simple diversification will ordinarily reduce risk to the systematic level in the market. However, portfolio managers should not spread their funds over too many assets. The studies summarized in Figure 24-1 and Table 24-1 suggests that if 15 different assets have been selected for a portfolio, the maximum benefit from simple diversification has probably been attained. Further spreading of the portfolio's assets is *superfluous diversification* and will usually result in the following investment-management problems:

- *Purchase of lackluster performers:* Selecting numerous different assets will lead to acquiring some investments that will not yield an adequate return.

- *Information problems:* If a portfolio contains too many different securities, it is practically impossible for a manager to keep informed about all of them simultaneously.

- *High research costs:* The larger the number of assets to be selected for the portfolio, the more expensive it is to search for them and maintain current information about each one.

- *High transaction costs:* Frequent purchases of small quantities of shares will result in larger brokerage commissions than will less frequent purchases of larger blocks of securities.

More time and money must be spent to manage a superfluously diversified portfolio, and there will most likely be no real improvement in performance. In fact, superfluous diversification may actually lower the portfolio owner's net return.

In spite of the negative side effects from superfluous diversification, most large institutional portfolios contain hundreds of different securities. This is usually because professional managers do not want to invest the millions of dollars they manage in a few stocks, since they would wind up with a controlling interest in some of the corporations in which they invest. Portfolio managers do not want to be corporation managers too, so they make smaller investments in more corporations. (The performance of professional portfolio managers is evaluated in Chapter 28.)

The next section presents the optimal diversification method, which considers how the correlations among assets affect the portfolio risk.

24-5   Markowitz Diversification

Markowitz diversification (Box 24-3) is named after Harry Markowitz, who originated the analysis in his classic article "Portfolio Selection," *Journal of Finance,* March 1952, and who won a Nobel Prize for the work in 1991. It is a more scientific

Box 24-3

599

Chapter 24
Portfolio
Analysis

> DEFINITION: Markowitz Diversification
>
> **Markowitz diversification** is an analytical procedure that involves combining assets that are less than perfectly positively correlated in order to form efficient portfolios.

process than simple diversification, since it considers the assets' correlation coefficients. (Chapter 5 Appendix discusses correlation coefficients.) Consider what happens when two stocks, Summer Resorts, Inc. (SR) and Universal Umbrella Corp. (UU), which have perfectly negatively (that is, inversely) correlated rates of return, are combined into a portfolio. Table 24-2 shows the results from combining the stock in SR, which booms in the sunshine and suffers when it rains, with the stock in umbrella manufacturer UU, which enjoys a booming business only in rainy weather.

The portfolio spread 50-50 across the SR and UU common stocks has zero variability of return over the 4 years analyzed in Table 24-2. This elimination of risk is due to the perfect negative correlation of the rates of return of assets UU and SR; the gains on one exactly offset the losses on the other. Figure 24-2 depicts graphically how three different portfolios composed of equal parts of SR and UU stocks behave differently if the correlation coefficient between the two stocks assumes different values.

A more general discussion of Markowitz diversification considers the risk and return of a two-asset portfolio as the correlation coefficient between the two assets varies. Computational Box 24-4 presents financial data about the U.S. Telephone (UST) and Dynamics International (DI) corporations. Only the summary statistics in Table 24-6 are needed to perform portfolio analysis; the information about the companies is provided to show how the statistics needed for portfolio analysis are calculated. In the box, Table 24-3, the joint probability distribution of returns, shows how stocks in UST and DI vary over a complete business cycle. (It is assumed that the probability distributions for both the UST and the DI stocks are symmetrical. In fact,

Table 24-2
Markowitz Diversification with
Perfectly Negatively Correlated Rates of Return

	Year 1, heavy rain	Year 2, rain	Year 3, rain and shine	Year 4, heavy rain	Variance of 4 years' returns*
Stock in SR	5%	10%	15%	5%	.0017
Stock in UU	25	20	15	25	.0017
Portfolio of half SR and half UU	15	15	15	15	0

* See Box 1-9 for a discussion of calculating the variance statistics.

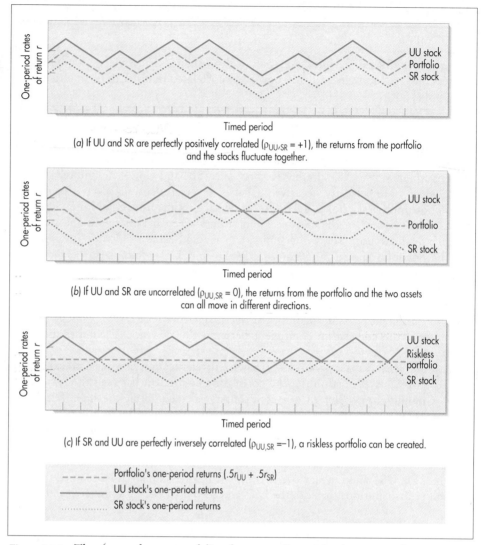

Figure 24-2 The returns from a portfolio of two equally weighted assets are determined by the returns from the component assets.

the probability distribution for DI is symmetrical, but the distribution for UST is slightly skewed to the left.[1] This skewness is assumed to be insignificant and can be ignored. Markowitz's mean-variance portfolio analysis is appropriate under these circumstances.) The box then shows how the two stocks' annual rates of return fluctuate over a 10-year period and how their expected return and risk statistics are calculated.

[1] *Skewness* refers to the lopsidedness of a probability distribution. Symmetrical distributions have zero skewness. Most stocks and bonds have probability distributions that are approximately symmetrical.

Box 24-4

601

Chapter 24
Portfolio
Analysis

COMPUTATION: Markowitz Diversification with U. S. Telephone (UST) and Dynamics International (DI) Stocks

Table 24-3
Joint Probability Distribution of Rates of Return for
U.S. Telephone (UST) and Dynamics International (DI) Common Stocks

State of nature (stage of the business cycle)	Occurrence per decade	Probability	UST Return	DI Return	State of nature counter
Very fast advance	1 year	.1 = 10%	.3 = 30%	.9 = 90%	s = 1
Fast advance	2 years	.2 = 20	.2 = 20	.5 = 50	s = 2
Slow advance	4 years	.4 = 40	.1 = 10	.2 = 20	s = 3
Mild recession	2 years	.2 = 20	−.1 = −10	−.1 = −10	s = 4
Deep recession*	1 year	.1 = 10	−.2 = −20	−.5 = −50	s = 5*
Total		1.0 = 100			

* There is a one-to-one correspondence between the states of nature in this table and the annual outcomes seen in Tables 24-4 and 24-5. For instance, note that this example's deep recession occurring once in 10 years occurs in the third year in Tables 24-4 and 24-5.

The expected-rate-of-return formula for probabilistic rates of return are shown below, where $P(s)$ denotes the probability that state s occurs, and $S = 5$ economic states of nature are assumed to exist.

$$E(r) = \sum_{s=1}^{S=5} P(s)(r_s) = P(1)(r_1) + P(s)(r_2) + \cdots + P(s)(r_5)$$

Table 24-4
U.S. Telephone (UST) Common Stock's
Annual Rate of Return and Risk Statistics over 10 Years

Year	UST return r	$P(t)$ equals $1/T$	Product, $P(s) \times r$	Deviation, $r - E(r)$	Probability times squared deviation $P(s) \times [r - E(r)]^2$
1	.1 = 10%	.1	(.1)(.1) = .01	.1 − .07 = .03	(.1)(.03)² = .00009
2	.2 = 20	.1	(.1)(.2) = .02	.2 − .07 = .13	(.1)(.13)² = .00169
3	−.2 = −20	.1	(.1)(.2) = .02	−.2 − .07 = −.27	(.1)(−.27)² = .00729
4	−.1 = −10	.1	(.1)(−.1) = −.01	−.1 − .07 = −.17	(.1)(−.17)² = .00289
5	.3 = 30	.1	(.1)(.3) = .03	.3 − .07 = .23	(.1)(.23)² = .00529
6	.1 = 10	.1	(.1)(.1) = .01	.1 − .07 = .03	(.1)(.03)² = .00009
7	.1 = 10	.1	(.1)(.1) = .01	.1 − .07 = .03	(.1)(.03)² = .00009
8	.1 = 10	.1	(.1)(.1) = .01	.1 − .07 = .03	(.1)(.03)² = .00009
9	−.1 = −10	.1	(.1)(−.1) = −.01	−.1 − .07 = −.17	(.1)(−.17)² = .00289
10	.2 = 20	.1	(.1)(.2) = .02	.2 − .07 = .13	(.1)(.13)² = .00169
Totals:		1.0	$E(r_{UST})$ = .07		$VAR(r_{UST})$ = .0221

The variance-of-returns formula for probabilistic rates of return is

$$\text{VAR}(r) = \sum_{s=1}^{S=5} P(s)[r_s - E(r)]^2$$

$$= P(1)[r_1 - E(r)]^2 + P(2)[r_2 - E(r)]^2 + \cdots + P(5)[r_5 - E(r)]^2$$

The expected-rate-of-return formula for T equally likely annual rates of return occurring with the probability $\frac{1}{10} = .10$ is as follows:

$$E(r) = \frac{1}{T} \sum_{t=1}^{T} r_t = \frac{1}{T}(r_1 + r_2 + r_3 + \cdots + r_T)$$

The variance-of-returns formula for T equally likely annual rates of return is

$$\text{VAR}(r) = \frac{1}{T} \sum_{t=1}^{T} [r_t - E(r)]^2 = \frac{1}{T}[r_1 - E(r)]^2 + \frac{1}{T}[r_2 - E(r)]^2 + \cdots + \frac{1}{T}[r_T - E(r)]^2$$

The standard deviation for UST is the square root of the formula above.

$$\sigma_{\text{UST}} = \sqrt{\text{VAR}(r_{\text{UST}})} = \sqrt{.0221} = .14866$$

Table 24-5
Dynamics International (DI) Common Stock's Annual Rate of Return and Risk Statistics over 10 Years

Year	DI return r	$P(t)$ equals $\frac{1}{T}$	Product, $P(s) \times r$	Derivation, $r - E(r)$	Probability times squared deviation, $P(s) \times [r - E(r)]^2$
1	$.2 = 20\%$	.1	$(.1)(.2) = .02$	$.2 - .2 = 0$	$(.1)(0)^2 = 0$
2	$.5 = 50$	.1	$(.1)(.5) = .05$	$.5 - .2 = .3$	$(.1)(.3)^2 = .009$
3	$-.5 = -50$	.1	$(.1)(-.5) = -.05$	$-.5 - .2 = -.7$	$(.1)(-.7)^2 = .049$
4	$-.1 = -10$	.1	$(.1)(-.1) = .01$	$-.1 - .2 = -.3$	$(.1)(-.3)^2 = .009$
5	$.9 = 90$	.1	$(.1)(.9) = .09$	$.9 - .2 = .7$	$(.1)(.7)^2 = .049$
6	$.2 = 20$	.1	$(.1)(.2) = .02$	$.2 - .2 = 0$	$(.1)(0)^2 = 0$
7	$-.1 = -10$	.1	$(.1)(-.1) = -.01$	$-.1 - .2 = -.3$	$(.1)(-.3)^2 = .009$
8	$.2 = 20$	.1	$(.1)(.2) = .02$	$.2 - .2 = 0$	$(.1)(0)^2 = 0$
9	$.2 = 20$	.1	$(.1)(.2) = .02$	$.2 - .2 = 0$	$(.1)(0)^2 = 0$
10	$.5 = 50$	.1	$(.1)(.5) = .05$	$.5 - .2 = .3$	$(.1)(.3)^2 = .009$
	Totals:	1.0	$E(r_{\text{DI}}) = .2$		$\text{VAR}(r_{\text{DI}}) = .134$

The expected-rate-of-return and variance formulas above can also be used for DI.

The standard deviation for DI is

$$\sigma_{\text{DI}} = \sqrt{\text{VAR}(r_{\text{DI}})} = \sqrt{.134} = .36606$$

Table 24-6
Risk and Return Summary Statistics
for U.S. Telephone (UST)
and Dynamics International (DI) Common Stocks

	Expected rate of return	*Variance of returns*	*Standard deviation of returns, σ*
U.S. Telephone	.07 = 7.0%	.0221	.14866
Dynamics International	.2 = 20.0	.134	.366

A Two-Asset Portfolio's Expected Rate of Return

The **expected rate of return for a portfolio** $E(r_P)$, made up of two assets, is the weighted average of the returns from the two assets in the portfolio. Its value is given by the formula

$$E(r_P) = x_1 E(r_1) + x_2 E(r_2) \tag{24-1}$$

where $E(r_P)$ = portfolio's expected rate of return
x_1, x_2 = fraction of portfolio made up of assets 1 and 2, respectively
$E(r_1), E(r_2)$ = expected rate of return for assets 1 and 2, respectively

Box 24-5 gives an example of computing the expected rate of return for a two-asset portfolio.

The fraction of funds invested in an asset is sometimes referred to as the **weight** or the **participation level** invested in that asset. In Box 24-5 these weights are denoted x_{UST} and x_{DI}. These can more generally be shown as x_1 and x_2. Note that the fraction of the portfolio invested in asset 1 plus the fraction in asset 2 must sum to 1, as indicated below, or the formulas defining the portfolio are meaningless.

Box 24-5

COMPUTATION: A Portfolio's Expected Rate of Return

If 71.1 percent of a two-asset portfolio's funds are invested in U.S. Telephone (UST) stock, and the remaining 28.9 percent are invested in Dynamic International (DI) stock, the resulting portfolio's expected rate of return is 10.75 percent, as shown below:

$$E(r_P) = x_{UST} E(r_{UST}) + x_{DI} E(r_{DI})$$
$$= (.711)(7\%) + (.289)(20\%) \tag{24-1a}$$
$$= 4.97\% + 5.78\% = 10.75\%$$

Although all the invested funds must be accounted for, this does not mean that all the funds must be invested in risky assets. For example, cash or a riskless asset may be one of the investments.

The risk and return statistics for assets UST and DI from Table 24-6 are illustrated in the risk-return space in Figure 24-3. Risk, as measured by the standard

Figure 24-3 Portfolio analysis of two assets in risk-return space. (*a*) The portfolios that can be constructed from DI and UST when they are perfectly positively correlated lie along a straight line. (*b*) When DI and UST are uncorrelated, the portfolio possibilities lie along a curve. (*c*) If UST and DI are perfectly negatively correlated, the portfolios that can be created include the riskless portfolio Z. (*d*) The correlation between the assets determines which efficient frontier is possible.

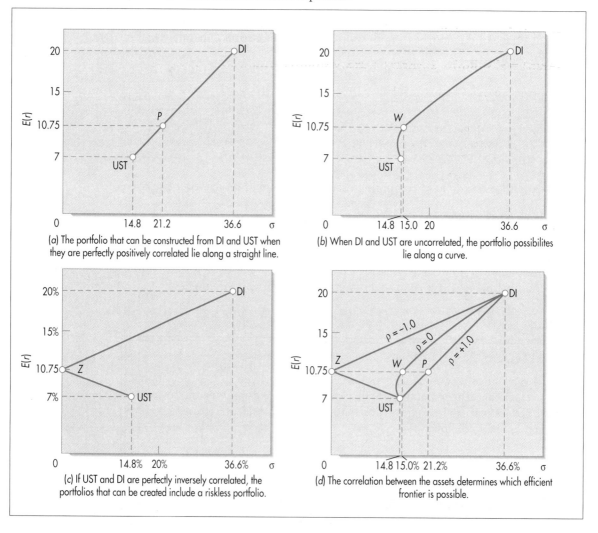

(a) The portfolio that can be constructed from DI and UST when they are perfectly positively correlated lie along a straight line.

(b) When DI and UST are uncorrelated, the portfolio possibilites lie along a curve.

(c) If UST and DI are perfectly inversely correlated, the portfolios that can be created include a riskless portfolio.

(d) The correlation between the assets determines which efficient frontier is possible.

deviation of the rates of return, is on the horizontal axis. The expected return $E(r)$ is on the vertical axis. Figure 24-3 illustrates Markowitz portfolio in a risk-return graph.

Consider the three portfolios at points P, W, and Z in Figure 24-3*a*, *b*, and *c*, respectively. All three portfolios have 71.1 percent of their funds invested in asset UST and the remaining 28.9 percent invested in DI stock. Since the weights in assets UST and DI are identical in the three portfolios, they all have the same weighted average rate of return of 10.75 percent. In all parts of Figure 24-3, portfolios P, W, and Z lie at 10.75 percent on the vertical axis. Notice, however, that the riskiness of the portfolios varies considerably in spite of the fact that all contain the same assets in the same proportions. Figure 24-3*d* combines Figure 24-3*a*, *b*, and *c* to facilitate comparisons.

A Two-Asset Portfolio's Risk

In order to understand the relationship between the risk statistics of individual assets and the risk of a portfolio created from those assets, it is necessary to consider the risk formula for a portfolio.

$$\text{VAR}(r_P) = x_1^2 \text{VAR}(r_1) + x_2^2 \text{VAR}(r_2) + 2x_1x_2\sqrt{\text{VAR}(r_1)}\sqrt{\text{VAR}(r_2)}\,\rho_{1,2} \qquad (24\text{-}3)$$

The risk formula above says that the variance of returns from a two-asset portfolio, denoted $\text{VAR}(r_P)$, equals the squared weight (or proportion) of the funds invested in asset 1, denoted x_1^2, multiplied by asset 1's variance of returns, $\text{VAR}(r_1)$; plus the square of the weight invested in asset 2, x_2^2, multiplied by the variance of asset 2, $\text{VAR}(r_2)$; plus two times the product of the weights of assets 1 and 2, their two standard deviations, represented by $\sqrt{\text{VAR}(r)}$, and the correlation between them, $\rho_{1,2}$.

The risk of the two-asset portfolio graphed in the panels of Figure 24-3 varies as the correlation coefficient between the returns from assets DI and UST is set to three different values.[2] The investigation will focus on three specific values of the correlation coefficient.

---

[2] Statisticians define the large product term in the portfolio risk formula as the **covariance** of returns between assets 1 and 2. The covariance is defined mathematically as follows.

$$\text{COV}(r_1, r_2) = \sqrt{\text{VAR}(r_1)}\sqrt{\text{VAR}(r_2)}\,\rho_{1,2}$$

where $\rho_{1,2}$ denotes the correlation between assets 1 and 2.

The covariance can also be calculated from T annual rates of return as follows.

$$\text{COV}(r_1, r_2) = \frac{1}{T}\sum_{t=1}^{T}[r_{1t} - E(r_1)][r_{2t} - E(r_2)]$$

where the subscript t counts the time periods and $E(r)$ denotes the expected or average rate of return. The probability of each outcome is treated as being equally likely, so that the probabilities would be $1/T = 1/10 = .1$ if data from 10 time periods ($T = 10$) were analyzed. Tables 25-2 and 25-3 show numerical examples of how to calculate the covariance.

Box 24-6

> ## COMPUTATION: Perfectly Positively Correlated Assets
>
> The risk of a two-asset portfolio with 71.1 percent of its funds invested in UST and 28.9 percent of its funds invested in DI is calculated as follows:
>
> $$\sigma_P = \sqrt{x^2_{\text{UST}}\text{VAR}(r_{\text{UST}}) + x^2_{\text{DI}}\text{VAR}(r_{\text{DI}}) + 2x_{\text{UST}}x_{\text{DI}}\sqrt{\text{VAR}(r_{\text{UST}})}\sqrt{\text{VAR}(r_{\text{DI}})}\,\rho_{\text{UST,DI}}}$$
>
> $$= \sqrt{(.711)^2(.022) + (.289)^2(.134) + 2(.711)(.289)(.148)(.366)(+1.0)}$$
>
> $$= \sqrt{.011 + .011 + (.022)(+1.0)} = \sqrt{.044}$$
>
> $$= .212 = 21.2\% = \text{standard deviation of portfolio P in Figure 24-3}a$$

Perfect Positive Correlation   The correlation coefficient is a statistic that has an upper limit of +1.0. When the correlation coefficient between the rates of return of assets UST and DI is +1.0, the linear risk-return relationship shown in Figure 24-3a results.

Zero Correlation   When the correlation is zero, that is, $\rho_{\text{UST, DI}} = 0$, the returns are statistically unrelated; they are independent and uncorrelated. When the correlation coefficient between the rates of return of assets UST and DI is zero, substantial risk reduction can be obtained by diversifying between the two. This risk reduction is illustrated in Figure 24-3b. At zero correlation, the assets' rates of return occasionally move in opposite directions (and, thus, sometimes offset each other's changes). This interaction reduces portfolio variability.

   Note how portfolio W in Figure 24-3b has less risk than portfolio P in Figure 24-3a. Both portfolios have identical weighted average rates of return of 10.75 percent, but portfolio W is less risky than portfolio P because the value of the correlation coefficient between assets UST and DI used to create portfolio W is less than the correlation that underlies portfolio P.

Perfect Negative Correlation   The lowest possible value any correlation coefficient can attain is −1.0. When the correlation coefficient between assets UST and DI

Box 24-7

> ## COMPUTATION: Portfolio Analysis of Uncorrelated Assets
>
> The risk of the same portfolio with 71.1 percent of its assets invested in UST and 28.98 percent in DI is calculated below:
>
> $$\sigma_W = \sqrt{x^2_{\text{UST}}\text{VAR}(r_{\text{UST}}) + x^2_{\text{DI}}\text{VAR}(r_{\text{DI}}) + 2x_{\text{UST}}x_{\text{DI}}\sqrt{\text{VAR}(r_{\text{UST}})}\sqrt{\text{VAR}(r_{\text{DI}})}\,\rho_{\text{UST,DI}}}$$
>
> $$= \sqrt{(.711)^2(.022) + (.289)^2(.134) + 2(.711)(.289)(.148)(.366)(0)}$$
>
> $$= \sqrt{.011 + .011 + 2(.011)(0)} = \sqrt{.0225}$$
>
> $$= .150 = 15.0\% = \text{standard deviation for portfolio W in Figure 24-3}b$$

Box 24-8

607

*Chapter 24
Portfolio
Analysis*

> **COMPUTATION: Perfectly Negatively Correlated Assets**
>
> The calculations below confirm the riskless nature of portfolio Z in Figure 24-3c.
>
> $$\sigma_Z = \sqrt{x^2_{UST}VAR(r_{UST}) + x^2_{DI}VAR(r_{DI}) + 2x_{UST}x_{DI}\sqrt{VAR(r_{UST})}\sqrt{VAR(r_{DI})}\,\rho_{UST,DI}}$$
>
> $$= \sqrt{(.711)^2(.0221) + (.289)^2(.134) + 2(.711)(.289)(.148)(.366)(-1.0)}$$
>
> $$\sqrt{(.011) + (.011) + 2(.011)(-1.0)} = \sqrt{0}$$
>
> $$= 0 = \text{standard deviation for portfolio Z in Figure 24-3c.}$$

equals its minimum value of -1.0, then regardless of what values the assets' weights assume, portfolio risk will be at a minimum. In fact, for one particular mix of assets UST and DI, the portfolio's risk can be reduced to zero. In particular, Figure 24-3c shows that when 71.1 percent of the funds are invested in asset UST and 28.9 percent in asset DI and the correlation is perfectly inverse (or perfectly negative) the resulting portfolio at point Z is riskless: $VAR(r_Z) = 0$.

If it seems impossible that two *risky* assets like UST and DI could be combined to form a *riskless portfolio* like the one at point Z in Figure 24-3c, look again at Table 24-2.

Some Conclusions about Markowitz Diversification

As Figure 24-3 shows, when 71.1 percent of a portfolio's funds are invested in asset UST and the other 28.9 percent in asset DI and the correlation between UST and DI is $+1.0$, the portfolio's standard deviation is 21.2 percent—see portfolio P in Figure 24-3a. If the correlation is zero, the portfolio's risk is 15 percent—see portfolio W in Figure 24-3b. When the correlation is -1.0, the portfolio has zero risk—see portfolio Z in Figure 24-3c. Thus, Markowitz diversification can lower risk below the systematic level if the securities in the portfolio have low enough correlations. Unfortunately, there are very few securities with negative correlations, so investors must usually diversify between securities that have low positive correlations.

Markowitz diversification applied on a large scale to multiple assets is called **Markowitz portfolio analysis.** (Such analysis is usually done by computer.) Markowitz portfolio analysis requires that many equations be solved simultaneously, using a mathematical technique called **quadratic programming,** which delineates the asset weights that minimize the portfolio's risk at each level of return. It can evaluate the risk and return of dozens, hundreds, or thousands of different securities simultaneously (the number is limited only by the size of the computer and the number of securities for which the analyst has risk and return statistics). Such mathematical analysis is a more powerful method of analyzing a portfolio than using some executive's brain or selecting investments by committee.

A diversified portfolio derived by Markowitz portfolio analysis will usually be spread across industries. However, it will not usually contain a large number of different securities. Some of the securities included will surprise you, but they are added to the portfolio primarily to obtain risk reduction due to their low correlations with other assets. Not all assets in a dominant portfolio will have either high rates of return or low standard deviations—some may have low correlations instead.

24-6 The Efficient Frontier

The risk and return of all individual assets plotted in risk-return space would be dominated by efficient portfolios. Figure 24-4 represents the total set of investment opportunities in the securities markets. The set contains individual assets (issues of stock and bonds, for example) represented by dots, while the efficient frontier is represented by the heavy curve from E to F. Only portfolios will lie on the efficient frontier; that is, portfolios will always dominate individual assets because they enjoy the risk-reducing benefits of diversification.

Portfolio Analysis Markowitz diversification applied to all marketable assets would generate the efficient set of portfolios that forms an efficient frontier. The curve of the efficient frontier will always bulge toward the vertical (expected rate of return) axis, because almost all assets have correlation coefficients between zero and +1.0. As Figure 24-3*a* shows, only perfectly positively correlated assets can generate an efficient frontier that is a straight line. Because negatively correlated assets are so rare, only occasionally will an efficient frontier touch the vertical axis (see Figure 24-3*c*).
Not all portfolios will lie on the efficient frontier; some will dominate others.

Figure 24-4 Investment opportunities.

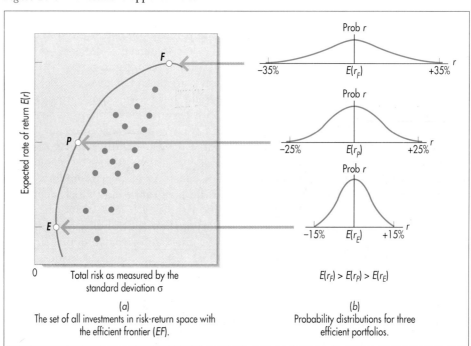

(a)
The set of all investments in risk-return space with the efficient frontier (*EF*).

(b)
Probability distributions for three efficient portfolios.

$E(r_F) > E(r_P) > E(r_E)$

Markowitz diversification, for example, will generate portfolios that dominate simply diversified portfolios.

Portfolio Selection Each investor has different preferences. An aggressive investor might select portfolio F in Figure 24-4. A timid investor might maximize the happiness he or she derives from investing by selecting portfolio E. Both the aggressive investor and the timid investor are risk-averse; their preferences differ because the timid investor is more risk-averse than the aggressive investor.

24-7 Asset Allocation

Asset allocation is the process of choosing the optimal proportions of investments from different asset categories. Portfolio managers usually focus on the stock-bond mix; the controversy often boils down to the best long-run stock/bond distribution —30/70, 60/40, 50/50, 40/60, 70/30.[3]

Individual securities are not analyzed in asset allocation problems; instead, the risk and return statistics supposed to be representative of different *asset categories* are analyzed. Table 24-7 shows statistics representing two categories of assets that might be considered—common stocks and bonds.

[3] To gain insight, see K. P. Ambachtsheer, ''Pension Fund Asset Allocation: In Defense Of A 60/40 Equity/Debt Asset Mix,'' *Financial Analysts Journal*, September–October 1987. For a varied selection of readings on this topic, see Robert D. Arnott and Frank J. Fabozzi, *Asset Allocation*, Probus Publishing Company, Chicago, Ill., 1988.

Table 24-7
Return, Risk, and Correlation Statistics for Two Categories of Assets

	(a) Expected rates of return	
Common stocks, s	12.0%	
Treasury bonds, b	4.6%	
	(b) Variance-covariance matrix	
	Common Stocks, s	*Treasury bonds, b*
Common stocks, s	$\sigma_s = 21.1\% = \sqrt{445.21}$	$COV(s,b) = 19.7\%$
L-T Treasury bonds, b		$\sigma_b = 8.5\% = \sqrt{72.25}$
	(c) Correlation matrix	
	Common stocks, s	*Treasury bonds, b*
Common stocks, s	1.0	.11
Treasury bonds, b		1.0

Source: Stocks, Bonds, Bills and Inflation (SBBI): 1982 Edition, by R. G. Ibbotson and Rex A. Sinquefield, updated in *SBBI 1988 Yearbook*, Exhibits 8 and 32, Ibbotson Associates Inc., 8 South Michigan Avenue, Suite 707, Chicago, Ill. (See Figure 1–4 and its discussion for an explanation of these statistics.)

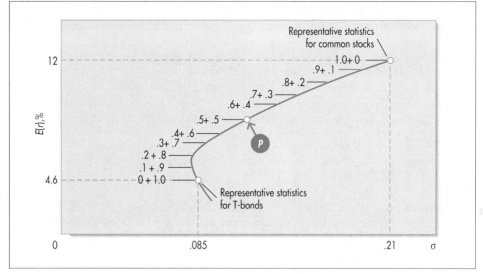

Figure 24-5 The efficient frontier derived from two asset categories.

The Menu of Optimal Asset Allocations

Some portfolio managers choose to use equally weighted categories of assets. Others use judgment and intuition to select the asset mix for their portfolios. The more scientific managers will use Markowitz portfolio analysis to define the set of optimal asset mixes from which they can select. Table 24-8 lists the menu of alternatives delineated using the Markowitz method; Figure 24-5 illustrates these alternatives.

Some portfolio managers prefer to make allocation decisions before selecting individual securities to buy. These managers believe selecting the optimal asset mix is more important to performance than security selection and/or active asset management.[4] They think it is wise to spend considerable effort preparing estimates of risk-return statistics for the categories of assets they are considering. They believe the analysis of individual securities should wait until after the optimal allocation decision has been made.

Selecting an Optimal Asset Allocation

Table 24-8 and Figure 24-5 display alternative allocations of stocks and bonds obtained by using the Markowitz portfolio analysis tools introduced in Figure 24-3. All these allocations are dominant strategies that will minimize the investor's risk at

---

[4] See G. P. Brinson, J. J. Diermeier, and G. G. Schlarbaum, "A Composite Portfolio Benchmark for Pension Plans," *Financial Analysts Journal,* March–April 1986, pages 271–280. Also see Richard O. Michaud, "Pension Policy and Benchmark Optimization," *Industrial Management Review,* March–April 1989, pages 25–30, and Richard O. Michaud, "The Markowitz Optimization Enigma: Is 'Optimized' Optimal?" *Financial Analysts Journal,* January–February 1989, pages 31–42.

Table 24-8
The Efficient Frontier of Optimal Asset Mixes

Portfolio's expected return	Portfolio's standard deviation	Weight in common stock	Weight in T-bill
12.0%	21.1%	100%	0
11.3	19.1	90	10
10.5	17.1	80	20
9.8	15.3	70	30
9.0	13.5	60	40
8.3	11.8	50	50
7.6	10.3	40	60
6.8	9.1	30	70
6.1	8.4	20	80
5.3	8.2	10	90
4.6	8.5	0	100

whatever level of return is selected. Different investors will select different allocations from the efficient frontier of possibilities because each person has different risk-return preferences. A very aggressive investor might find a stock/bond allocation of 90/10 optimal, while a highly risk-averse investor might be happiest with a 10/90 allocation. Someone with less extreme preferences might select the 50/50 stock/bond mix at point *P* in Figure 24-5.

Summary

Diversification is essential to the investor seeking the minimum risk at a given level of return. The dominance principle can be used to select desirable assets and to define an approximate efficient frontier, but Markowitz portfolio analysis is required to delineate the true efficient frontier. Portfolio selection is a personal choice about how much risk an investor is willing to assume in order to obtain higher returns. Rational, wealth-seeking investors should always select an efficient portfolio.

Diversification reduces risk, and Markowitz diversification is the most effective way to diversify. Unlike simple diversification, diversifying across industries, and superfluous diversification, Markowitz diversification is scientific. It focuses on the correlation coefficients between the returns from all possible investment candidates. Low correlations are essential for reducing the risk in a portfolio.

Further Reading

Francis, Jack Clark, *Investments: Analysis and Management*, 5th ed. (New York: McGraw-Hill, 1991).
   Chapters 9 through 11 inclusive use algebra to delve into the mathematical aspects of diversification, portfolio analysis, and investment performance evaluation. Calculus is used only in a few appendixes. The discussion is augmented by numerical examples and graphs.

Francis, Jack Clark, and Gordon Alexander, *Portfolio Analysis,* 3d ed. (Englewood Cliffs, N.J.: Prentice-Hall, 1986).

> *This monograph uses algebra, calculus, advanced calculus, and matrix algebra liberally in order to explore the frontiers of knowledge about modern portfolio theory. The discussion uses numerical examples in most places.*

Markowitz, Harry, *Portfolio Selection: Efficient Diversification of Investments* (New York: Wiley, 1959).

> *This monograph contains the first complete presentation of Markowitz's portfolio analysis theory. Elementary algebra supplemented with graphs and numerical examples is used, so this scholarly book is engaging and not difficult to read.*

Questions and Problems

Essay Questions

24-1   (*a*) After you have estimates of each individual security's expected rate of return, how do you calculate a portfolio's weighted average rate of return? (*b*) What is assumed about the weights (or proportions) of the individual assets in a portfolio?

24-2   How can you relate the risk statistics from the assets that are investment candidates to the portfolio possibilities that might be generated from these candidate assets? Be as explicit and mathematical as possible.

24-3   (*a*) What is simple diversification? (*b*) Will it reduce total risk? (*c*) Will it reduce unsystematic risk? (*d*) Will it reduce systematic risk? Explain your response to each question.

24-4   (*a*) What is superfluous diversification? (*b*) What problems frequently exist when a portfolio is diversified superfluously?

24-5   (*a*) Define Markowitz diversification. (*b*) What statistic is key to obtaining the risk-reducing benefits of Markowitz diversification? (*c*) Do Markowitz-diversified portfolios suffer lower returns in order to achieve risk-reductions?

24-6   What does it mean when two variables have (*a*) perfect positive correlation, (*b*) zero correlation, (*c*) perfect negative correlation? (*d*) Draw three graphs illustrating examples of each of the three correlations. (*Hint:* See the appendix to Chapter 5 and Figure 24-3.)

24-7   Explain why the curve representing the efficient frontier in Figure 24-4 *must* bulge toward the vertical axis (or, the expected return axis) rather than away from it.

24-8   "A portfolio of many different assets from many different industries will be a well-diversified portfolio." Is this statement true, false, or questionable? Explain.

24-9   "Apart from negatively correlated stocks, all the gains from diversification come from averaging over the independent components of the returns and risks of individual stocks. Among positively correlated stocks, there would be no gains from diversification if independent variations (that is, unsystematic risk) were absent." Interpret the preceding statement.

24-10   What is the objective of portfolio analysis? That is, what should a portfolio manager seek to obtain from Markowitz diversification?

24-11 Compute the expected rate of return and standard deviation for the UST common stock shown in Table 24-3 over the five states of nature. Show your calculations. Compare the statistics you calculated with the statistics calculated in Table 24-4 for the UST stock over the 10 annual rates of return shown there. Do the statistics you calculated from the data in Table 24-3 differ from the statistics for the same stock shown in Table 24-4? If so, explain the difference.

24-12 (*a*) Fill in the appropriate boxes below with formulas for the risk and expected rate of return for a two-asset portfolio. (*b*) Calculate the risk and expected rate of return statistics for two-asset portfolios made up of the common stocks issued by the Crown (C) and the Southwest (S) Corporations.

Asset	Expected rate of return, E(r)	Standard deviation of returns, σ
Crown (C)	.14 = 14%	.06 = 6%
Southwest (S)	.08 = 8	.03 = 3

(*c*) Calculate the portfolio risk and return statistics for three different assumptions about the correlation between assets C and S: $\rho_{C,S} = +1.0$; $\rho_{C,S} = 0$; and $\rho_{C,S} = -1.0$.

	Three correlations	Assumed weights for C				First, fill in the essential formulas below.
		1.0	.4	.2	Zero	
x_S	$\rho = +1$					$x_S =$
	$\rho = 0$					
	$\rho = -1$					
$E(r_P)$	$\rho = +1$					$E(r_P) =$
	$\rho = 0$					
	$\rho = -1$					
Portfolio standard deviation	$\rho = +1$					$SD(r_P) =$
	$\rho = 0$					
	$\rho = -1$					

(*d*) Draw a graph in risk-return space to illustrate the two-asset portfolio possibilities you calculated.

24-13 Which of the two accompanying graphs is incorrect? Why is it incorrect?

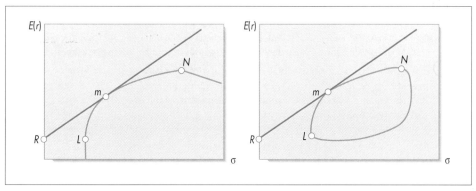

24-14 Consider the different two-asset portfolios you can construct from assets A and B if the correlation coefficient between them varies over the three values: +1.0, 0, and −1.0.

	Asset A	*Asset B*
Expected return	9.0%	21.0%
Standard deviation	11.0%	22.0%

Fill in the blank statistics (rounded to the nearest tenth) in the following table:

			Portfolio's standard deviation		
Percent in A	*Percent in B*	*Portfolio's E(r)*	*+1.0 correlation*	*Zero correlation*	*−1.0 correlation*
100%	0%	9.0%	11.0%	11.0%	11.0%
—	10	10.2	12.1	10.1	7.7
80	20	11.4	13.2	9.8	4.4
70	—	12.6	14.3	10.1	1.1
60	40	13.8	15.4	11.0	2.2
50	50	—	16.5	12.3	5.5
40	60	16.2	17.6	13.9	8.8
30	70	17.4	18.7	—	12.1
20	80	18.6	19.8	17.7	15.4
10	90	19.8	20.9	19.8	—
0	100	21.0	22.0	22.0	22.0

Multiple Choice Questions

24-15 Under what conditions may risky assets be combined to form a riskless portfolio?

(*a*) The assets should be perfectly inversely correlated.
(*b*) The assets must be combined precisely in proportions of 50-50.
(*c*) The risky assets can contain no undiversifiable risk.
(*d*) Combining risky assets into a portfolio always results in a risky portfolio that is more risky than any of the individual securities in the portfolio.

24-16 Dominant assets have which of the following characteristics?

(*a*) The highest rate of return
(*b*) The lowest risk
(*c*) The highest return in their risk class
(*d*) Both (*a*) and (*b*)

24-17 Simple diversification is best described by which of the following statements?

(*a*) It is as effective as diversifying across industries as a way to reduce risk.
(*b*) It is almost completely futile as a means of reducing risk.
(*c*) It is the most effective risk-reduction technique available.
(*d*) It is rarely employed to reduce risk.

24-18 Efficient assets are best described by which of the following statements?

(*a*) Dominant assets
(*b*) Diversified portfolios

(c) The minimum risk
(d) Both *(a)* and *(b)*

24-19 Superfluous diversification is best described by which of the following statements?

(a) It will reduce risk in the same way as simple diversification, but it has accompanying disadvantages.
(b) The administrative costs of tracking a large number of investments can be substantial.
(c) It will minimize total risk.
(d) Both *(a)* and *(b)* are correct.

24-20 Markowitz diversification is best described by which of the following statements?

(a) It maximizes the portfolio's return.
(b) It selects the minimum risk assets with which to build portfolios.
(c) It establishes that the correlation coefficient (or the covariance) between the assets is the key in delineating efficient portfolios.
(d) All the above are true.

24-21 The objective of Markowitz portfolio analysis is which of the following?

(a) To delineate those portfolios that have the maximum rate of return at each risk class
(b) To delineate the minimum risk portfolios at each risk class
(c) To constrain the sum of the positive weights in each portfolio to equal the sum of the negative weights in the portfolio
(d) Both *(b)* and *(c)*

24-22 Markowitz portfolio analysis computes which of the following?

(a) The risk statistics of each individual asset.
(b) The correlation coefficients between each investment candidate.
(c) The weights of the assets in the efficient portfolios.
(d) The expected rate of return for each individual asset.

24-23 Which of the following statements correctly describes the use of the correlation coefficient?

(a) It is an index number ranging in value from zero to one.
(b) It is a measure of unsystematic risk.
(c) Assets with low correlations are good for reducing risk in a portfolio.
(d) It can be used to measure the unsystematic risk of assets.

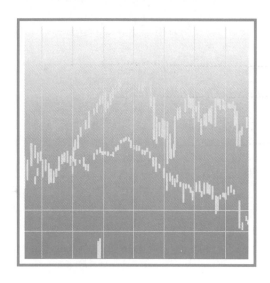

CHAPTER 25

CAPITAL
MARKET
THEORY

Capital market theory (CMT) is an extension of Markowitz portfolio analysis, which was introduced in Chapter 24. CMT is an asset valuation model similar in many respects to the arbitrage pricing theory (APT) presented in Chapter 26.

　　Both CMT and APT consider all investments—stocks, bonds, options, commodities, diamonds, gold, art objects and other assets—at the same time. Both theories explain how to determine the market prices of all assets. Some concepts important to the study of both APT and CMT have already been introduced, including total risk, systematic (or undiversifiable) risk, unsystematic (or diversifiable) risk, and the efficient frontier.[1] This chapter draws these, and some other new

Note: Chapter 25 presumes a familiarity with the material in Chapters 1 and 24.

[1] CMT was developed by W. F. Sharpe, "Capital Asset Prices: A Theory of Market Equilibrium under Conditions of Risk," *Journal of Finance,* September 1964, pp. 425–552. APT did not emerge until later (see S. A. Ross, "The Arbitrage Pricing Theory of Capital Asset Pricing," *Journal of Economic Theory,* December 1976, pp. 344–360). Even though APT is a newer theory, CMT has nevertheless been shown to be a special case of APT.

ideas, together and shows how they interact. Both the APT and CMT conclude that the undiversifiable (or systematic) portion of an asset's total risk is the main cause of risk-averse investors demanding higher rates of return. Diversifiable (or unsystematic) risk has no impact on the required rate of return, k.

As we saw in Chapter 24, the risk and return statistics for all individual assets graphed in risk-return space are dominated by efficient portfolios. Figure 24-4a shows the set of investment opportunities. The individual assets are represented by dots and the efficient frontier, by the heavy curve between points E and F. The figure shows, essentially, that if opportunities to borrow and lend at a fixed interest rate are ignored, the efficient frontier curve bulges toward the vertical axis in risk-return space. Only Markowitz-diversified portfolios can attain the efficient frontier.

25-1 The Capital Market Line (CML)

If the opportunity to borrow and lend at a fixed interest rate is introduced into the analysis, a more desirable set of investment opportunities emerges, represented by a *straight line* called the **capital market line (CML)**.

Point R in Figures 25-1 and 25-2 represents a **riskless asset;** it is riskless because it has no variability of return, that is, $\text{VAR}(R) = 0$. A U.S. Treasury bill held to maturity is one example of a riskless asset. By combining one riskless asset and one risky asset, portfolios can be created that extend the possibilities illustrated in Figure 24-3 to the more comprehensive situation depicted in Figure 25-1. The weighted average rate of return of a two-asset portfolio composed of risky asset m and riskless asset R would lie on the CML shown in Figure 25-1.

The investment opportunities along the CML dominate all other opportunities, even the portfolios along curve EF. The CML is the new efficient frontier that emerges when borrowing and lending at a riskless rate of interest are permitted.

Box 25-1

> DEFINITION: The Capital Market Line (CML)
>
> The CML is a risk-return relationship for *efficient portfolios.* The CML states that the required rates of return for portfolios are a positive linear function of the portfolios' standard deviations (or total risk). The formula for the CML is
>
> $$E(r_P) = R + \frac{E(r_m) - R}{\sigma_m} \sigma_P \qquad (25\text{-}1)$$
>
> where $E(r_P)$ = portfolio's expected rate of return
>
> R = return on a riskless asset
>
> $E(r_m)$ = expected return on asset m
>
> σ_m = standard deviation of asset m
>
> σ_P = standard deviation of the portfolio
>
> Figure 25-1 illustrates the CML relative to the efficient frontier without borrowing and lending opportunities; Figure 25-2 shows the CML alone.

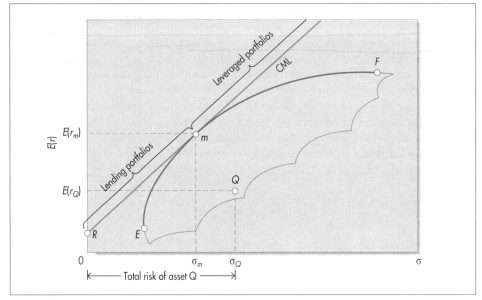

Figure 25-1   The capital market line (CML) is tangent to the efficient frontier.

Lending Portfolios

In Figure 25-1 the portfolio represented by point *m* is the only portfolio on the curved efficient frontier that is also on the CML. Portfolio *m* does not utilize the opportunity to borrow or lend. The portfolios along the CML between points *R* and *m* are **lending portfolios:** these portfolios include some money lent out at the riskless

Figure 25-2   A numerical example of the capital market line.

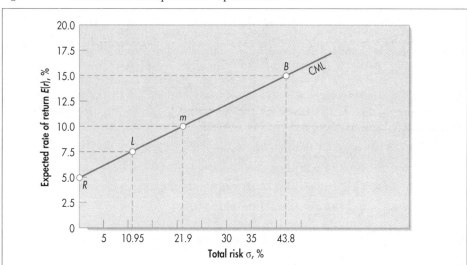

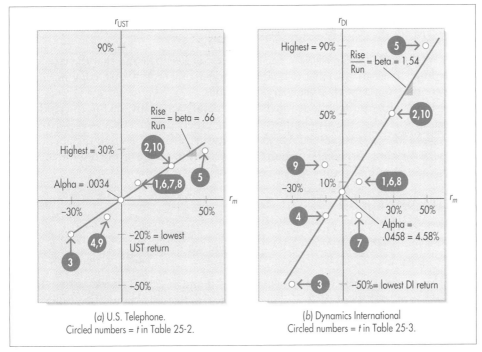

Figure 25-3 Characteristic regression lines for (*a*) U.S. Telephone (UST) and (*b*) Dynamics International (DI). The circled numbers correspond to the times *t* given for UST and DI, respectively, in Tables 25-2 and 25-3.

rate of interest *R*. This is like depositing money in a bank and earning a fixed rate of interest from an FDIC-insured savings account. The rest of the investor's funds are invested in the risky efficient portfolio *m*.

Borrowing (or Leveraged) Portfolios

Capital market theory can be extended and made more realistic by including investments financed with borrowed money, such as margin accounts. The portfolios above point *m* along the CML are all leveraged (or margined)—that is, they are **borrowing portfolios.** These portfolios were constructed by borrowing at the riskless interest rate *R* and investing the borrowed funds in the risky portfolio *m*. This money could be borrowed by any investor who was able, for example, to issue bonds that promised to pay an invariant (or riskless) rate of return, denoted *R*. Borrowing more money leverages the portfolio farther out on the CML and increases the investor's risk exposure.

Table 25-1 presents statistics for points on the CML. These statistics can be used to describe the CML in the formula below:

$$E(r_P) = R + \frac{E(r_m) - R}{\sigma_m} \sigma_P = 5\% + \frac{10\% - 5\%}{21.9\%} \sigma_P \qquad (25\text{-}1a)$$

Box 25-2

COMPUTATION: A Lending Portfolio

Let us assume that the riskless rate of interest is $R = 5\%$ and that the efficient portfolio m earns an expected rate of return of $E(r_m) = 10\%$. Figure 25-2 illustrates a CML with these market statistics.

If a lending portfolio, denoted L, has half its assets invested in the riskless asset, $x_R = .5$, then the weight invested in the other asset in a two-asset portfolio must be $(1.0 - x_R) = (1.0 - .5) = .5$. Substituting these values into the portfolio expected-return formula, Equation (24-1), results in a lending portfolio that has an expected rate of return of 7.5 percent, as shown below:

$$E(r_L) = x_R R + (1.0 - x_R)E(r_m) \tag{25-2}$$
$$= (.5)(5\%) + (1.0 - .5)(10\%)$$
$$= 2.5\% + 5\% = 7.5\%$$

Since R does not fluctuate, $\text{VAR}(R) = 0$ and $\rho_{R,m} = 0$. If we assume that portfolio m has risk of $\sigma_m = 21.9\%$, then the risk formula [a modified Equation (24-3)] for a two-asset lending portfolio L is

$$\text{VAR}(r_L) = x_R^2\text{VAR}(R) + (1 - x_R)^2\text{VAR}(r_m) + 2x_R(1 - x_R)\sqrt{\text{VAR}(R)}\sqrt{\text{VAR}(r_m)}\,\rho_{R,m}$$
$$= (.5)^2 (0)^2 + (.5)^2 (21.9\%)^2 + 2(.5)(.5)\sqrt{\text{VAR}(R)}\sqrt{\text{VAR}(r_m)}\,(0) \tag{25-3}$$
$$= 0 + (.25)(.04796) + 0 = .01199$$

Taking the square root of the variance of this lending portfolio to get the standard deviation yields $\sigma_L = .1095 = 10.95\%$. This risk and the expected rate of return of $E(r_L) = 7.5\%$ for the lending portfolio are plotted at point L on the CML in Figure 25-2.

Table 25-1
Statistics for R and m and Other Points on CML

Assets R and m	Expected return	Total risk, σ	Weight in R	Weight in m
Riskless asset, R	$R = 5\%$	0	1.0	0
Market portfolio, m	$E(r_m) = 10$	$\sigma_m = 21.9$	0	1.0

Portfolios created from assets R and m	Weighted average return	Portfolio's total risk, σ	Weight in R	Weight in m
Lending portfolio, L	$E(r_L) = 7.5\%$	10.95%	.5	.5
Borrowing portfolio, B	$E(r_B) = 15$	43.8	−1.0	2.0

Box 25-3 621

*Chapter 25
Capital
Market
Theory*

COMPUTATION: A Borrowing Portfolio

Borrowing at the riskless weight is represented mathematically by negative weights for the riskless asset—symbolically, $x_R < 0$. Assume that an amount of money equal to the investor's original equity was borrowed at the riskless interest rate R. This borrowing is represented by $x_R = -100\% = -1.0$. The borrowed money plus the investor's original equity ($100\% = 1.0$) has a weight of 2 times the investor's original equity, as calculated in Equation (25-4) below, using Equation (24-2).

$$[1.0 - x_R] = 1.0 - (-1.0) = 1.0 + 1.0 = 2.0 \qquad (25\text{-}4)$$

These funds were then invested in the market portfolio m to create the borrowing portfolio at point B in Figure 25-2. The expected rate of return of 15 percent for this borrowing portfolio is calculated in Equation (25-5) below, using Equation (24-1).

$$\begin{aligned} E(r_B) &= x_R R + (1.0 - x_R)\, E(r_m) \\ &= (-1.0)(5\%) + [1.0 - (-1.0)](10\%) \qquad (25\text{-}5) \\ &= -5\% + [2.0](10\%) = -5\% + 20\% = 15\% \end{aligned}$$

The risk of the borrowing portfolio, denoted σ_B, is calculated with Equation (25-6) below—using Equation (24-3).

$$\begin{aligned} \mathrm{VAR}(r_B) &= x_R^2 \mathrm{VAR}(R) + (1 - x_R)^2 \mathrm{VAR}(r_m) + 2x_R(1 - x_R)\sqrt{\mathrm{VAR}(R)}\sqrt{\mathrm{VAR}(r_m)}\rho_{R,m} \\ &= (-1.0)^2(0)^2 + (2.0)^2(21.9\%)^2 + 2(-1.0)(2.0)\sqrt{\mathrm{VAR}(R)}\sqrt{\mathrm{VAR}(r_m)}(0) \\ &= 0 + (4)(.04796) + 0 = .19184 \qquad (25\text{-}6) \end{aligned}$$

Taking the square root of the borrowing portfolio's variance yields a standard deviation of $\sqrt{\mathrm{VAR}(r_B)} = \sigma_B = .438 = 43.8\%$. This borrowing portfolio is plotted as point B on the CML illustrated in Figure 25-2.

Box 25-4

DEFINITION: The Market Portfolio, m

Portfolio m is called the **market portfolio.** The market portfolio is the most desirable portfolio in the world because it is the only asset that allows investors to create the dominant opportunities along the CML. Since every portfolio on the CML is some combination of the riskless asset R and the risky market portfolio m, it follows that the market portfolio must be a unique portfolio that contains all assets in the world in the proportion in which they exist. Value-weighted market indexes like the Standard & Poor's 500 Stocks Composite Index are real-world estimates of the theoretical market portfolio.

Undiversifiable Risk

When assets lie on a straight line in risk-return space, they must be perfectly positively correlated, as shown in Figure 24-3a. This means that the returns from portfolios along the CML have had their unsystematic risk diversified down to zero; perfectly positively correlated systematic fluctuations are the only risk present along the CML.

An individual asset, represented by point Q in Figure 25-1, is not efficient, because total risk includes both undiversifiable and diversifiable risk; individual assets cannot have their total risk reduced by diversification. As a result, individual assets can never lie on the CML.

25-2   The Characteristic Regression Line (CRL)

Changes in the economic, political, and sociological environment that affect securities markets are sources of systematic risk. Figure 17-2 and Figure 27-1 (note the October 1987 crash, for instance) show how mutually exclusive stock market

Box 25-5

DEFINITION: The Characteristic Regression Line

The **characteristic regression line,** or **CRL,** is a simple linear regression model estimated for one asset to statistically measure its diversifiable and undiversifiable risks.* For the ith asset the CRL model is

$$r_{i,t} = a_i + b_i r_{m,t} + e_{i,t} \tag{25-7}$$

where t is a counter for $1, 2, \ldots, T$ consecutive time periods' returns. The alpha a_i and beta b_i statistics are the intercept and slope of a straight line, respectively. The symbol $e_{i,t}$ is the unexplained residual return around the ith asset's regression line that occurs in time period t. The independent (or causal) variables in the CRL are the rates of change for some estimate of the market portfolio, represented by $r_{m,t}$. The dependent (or explained) regression variables are the one-period rates of return from the ith asset, denoted $r_{i,t}$.

Figure 25-3 illustrates the characteristic regression line for two different common stocks. The beta slope coefficient is a measure of undiversifiable risk. The unexplained residual variance around the regression line, VAR(e), is a measure of diversifiable risk.

* The first printed discussion of the CRL was by Harry Markowitz, *Portfolio Selection* (New York: Wiley, 1959), pp. 97–101; Markowitz called it an *index model.* The next printed record of the model appeared in W. F. Sharpe's doctoral dissertation. Sharpe referred to the model as the *single-index model* in an article summarizing his dissertation entitled ''A Simplified Model for Portfolio Analysis,'' *Management Science,* vol. 9, no. 2, January 1963, pp. 277–293. Working independently of Markowitz and Sharpe, Jack L. Treynor published an article entitled ''How to Rate Management of Investment Funds,'' *Harvard Business Review,* vol. 43, no. 1, January–February 1965, pp. 63–75, in which he referred to the model as the *characteristic line.*

indexes tend to vary together systematically. The resulting undiversifiable risk can be measured statistically with a tool to be introduced in this section.

A Time-Series Regression Line

Undiversifiable risk can be measured statistically with a simple linear regression called the *characteristic regression line (CRL)*. A characteristic regression line may be statistically estimated for a stock, a bond, a futures contract, a piece of real estate, or any marketable asset.

The Independent Variable

The action of market forces is measured along the horizontal axis of Figure 25-3 in terms of rates of change in the market at different time periods, $r_{m,t}$. We will calculate these rates of change using Standard & Poor's (S&P) market index; other market indexes could also have been used just as satisfactorily. And, the cash dividends from the stocks in the index, denoted "S&P-Div$_t$," could have been eliminated without significantly changing the resulting statistics (since dividends fluctuate very little).

$$r_{m,t} = \frac{S\&P_{t+1} - S\&P_t + S\&P\text{-Div}_t}{S\&P_t} \tag{25-8}$$

In Equation (25-8), $S\&P_{t+1}$ and $S\&P_{t+1}$ represent the value of the S&P index at the beginning and end of time period t, respectively. Essentially, $r_{m,t}$ measures the percentage changes in a market index.[2]

The Dependent Variable

Rates of return that the characteristic regression line seeks to explain can be calculated with the one-period rate of return formula for a share of common stock. Equation (1-4) is repeated below.

$$r_{i,t} = \frac{p_{i,t+1} - p_{i,t} + d_{i,t}}{p_{i,t}} = \frac{\overset{\text{price}}{\text{change}} + \overset{\text{cash}}{\text{dividend (if any)}}}{\text{purchase price}} \tag{1-4}$$

The symbols $p_{i,t}$ and p_{t+1} denote the market price of a share of stock i at the beginning and end, respectively, of time period t; $d_{i,t}$ stands for the cash dividends per share (if

---

[2] Various empirical estimates of the returns from the market portfolio exist. See R. G. Ibbotson and Carol L. Fall, "The US Wealth Portfolio: Components of Capital Market Values and Returns," *Journal of Portfolio Management* (Fall), 1979, pp. 82–92; R. G. Ibbotson, R. C. Carr and A. W. Robinson, "International Equity and Bond Returns," *Financial Analysts Journal,* July–August 1982, fig. C, p. 66; R. C. Ibbotson and R. A. Sinquefield, *Stocks, Bonds, Bills and Inflation: The Past and the Future* (Charlottesville, Va.: Financial Analysts Research Foundation, 1982); and Roger G. Ibbotson, Laurence Siegel, and Kathryn S. Love, "World Wealth: Market Values and Returns," *Journal of Portfolio Management* (Fall), 1985, pp. 4–23. (See Chapter 5 for more information.)

any) that the stock paid in period t. The rates of return from a bond, real estate investment, diamond, or any other asset could also be used as a dependent variable in the CRL.

The rates of return from the ith asset are the dependent variable on the vertical axis of Figure 25-3. If asset i has any systematic risk, part of its variation in rates of return is determined by the simultaneous market returns—the independent variable. The CRL measures the statistical relationship between the ith asset and the market portfolio m. Each characteristic regression line is thus a **market model** for one particular asset.

Box 25-6 presents market rates of return for U.S. Telephone (UST) and Dynamics International (DI) common stocks. Tables 25-2 and 25-3 in the box list the

Box 25-6

COMPUTATION: Rates of Return and Statistics for U.S. Telephone (UST) and Dynamics International (DI) Common Stocks

Table 25-2
Rates of Return and Statistics for U.S. Telephone (UST)
Common Stock's Characteristic Regression Line

$$\text{COV}(r_{\text{UST}}, r_m) = \frac{1}{T}\sum_{t=1}^{T} [r_{\text{UST},t} - E(r_{\text{UST}})][r_{m,t} - E(r_m)] \tag{25-9}$$

Time period	UST Return, r_{UST}	UST Deviation, $r_{\text{UST}} - E(r)$	Market portfolio, m Return, r_m	Market portfolio, m Deviation, $r_m - E(r)$	Probability $(1/T)$	Probability times deviations, $P[r_{\text{UST}} - E(r)][r_m - E(r)]$
1	$.1 = 10\%$	.03	$.1 = 10\%$	0	.1	$(.1)(.03)(0) = 0$
2	$.2 = 20$	.13	$.3 = 30\%$	.2	.1	$(.1)(.13)(.2) = .0026$
3	$-.2 = -20$	$-.27$	$-.3 = -30\%$	$-.4$	.1	$(.1)(-.27)(-.4) = .0108$
4	$-.1 = -10$	$-.17$	$-.1 = -10\%$	$-.2$	.1	$(.1)(-.17)(-.2) = .0034$
5	$.3 = 30$	.23	$.5 = 50\%$	.4	.1	$(.1)(.23)(.4) = .0092$
6	$.1 = 10$	.03	$.1 = 10\%$	0	.1	$(.1)(.03)(0) = 0$
7	$.1 = 10$	.03	$.1 = 10\%$	0	.1	$(.1)(.03)(0) = 0$
8	$.1 = 10$	.03	$.1 = 10\%$	0	.1	$(.1)(.03)(0) = 0$
9	$-.1 = -10$	$-.17$	$-.1 = -10\%$	$-.2$	.1	$(.1)(-.17)(-.2) = .0034$
10	$.2 = 20$	.13	$.3 = 30\%$	.2	.1	$(.1)(.13)(.2) = .0026$
					1.0	$\text{COV}(r_{\text{UST}}, r_m) = .032$

Note: The probabilistic rates of return for UST over the complete business cycle were listed in Box 24-4 in Table 24-3. UST's annual rates of return were listed in Table 24-4 and assigned the equally likely probabilities of $(1/T) = (1/10) = .1$. UST's expected rate of return, $E(r) = .07 = 7\%$, and standard deviation, $\sigma = .148$, were calculated in Box 24-4.

$$\text{Beta} = \frac{\text{COV}(r_{\text{UST}}, r_m)}{\text{VAR}(r_m)} = \frac{.032}{.048} = .666 \tag{25-10}$$

$$\text{Alpha} = a_{\text{UST}} = E(r_{\text{UST}}) - b_{\text{UST}}E(r_m) = .07 - (.666)(.10) = .07 - .0666 = .0034 \tag{25-11}$$

$$\text{Correlation} = \frac{\text{COV}(r_{\text{UST}}, r_m)}{\sigma_m \sigma_{\text{UST}}} = \frac{.032}{(.219)(.148)} = \frac{.032}{.0325} = .9833 = \rho_{\text{UST},m} \qquad (25\text{-}12)$$

Table 25-3
Rates of Return and Statistics for Dynamics International (DI)
Common Stock's Characteristic Regression Line (CRL)

$$\text{COV}(r_{\text{DI}}, r_m) = \frac{1}{T}\sum_{t=1}^{T}[r_{\text{DI},t} - E(r_{\text{DI}})][r_{m,t} - E(r_m)] \qquad (25\text{-}13)$$

Time period	DI Return, r_{DI}	DI Deviation $r_{\text{DI}} - E(r)$	Market portfolio, m Return, r_m	Market portfolio, m Deviation $r_m - E(r)$	Probability $(1/T)$	Probability times deviations, $P[r_{\text{DI}} - E(r)][r_m - E(r)]$
1	.2 = 20%	0	.1 = 10%	0	.1	(.1)(0)(0) = 0
2	.5 = 50	.3	.3 = 30	.2	.1	(.1)(.3)(.2) = .006
3	−.5 = −50	−.7	−.3 = −30	−.4	.1	(.1)(−.7)(−.4) = .028
4	−.1 = −10	−.3	−.1 = −10	−.2	.1	(.1)(−.3)(−.2) = .006
5	.9 = 90	.7	.5 = 50	.4	.1	(.1)(.7)(.4) = .028
6	.2 = 20	0	.1 = 10	0	.1	(.1)(0)(0) = 0
7	−.1 = −10	−.3	.1 = 10	0	.1	(.1)(−.3)(0) = 0
8	.2 = 20	0	.1 = 10	0	.1	(.1)(0)(0) = 0
9	.2 = 20	0	−.1 = 10	−.2	.1	(.1)(0)(−.2) = 0
10	.5 = 50	.3	.3 = 30	.2	.1	(.1)(.3)(.2) = .006
					1.0	$\text{COV}(r_{\text{DI}}, r_m)$ = .074

Note: The probabilistic rates of return for DI over the complete business cycle were listed in Box 24-4 in Table 24-3. DI's annual rates of return were listed in Table 24-5 and assigned the equally likely probabilities of $(1/T) = (1/10) = .1$. DI's expected rate of return, $E(r) = .2 = 20\%$, and standard deviation, $\sigma = .366$, were also calculated in Box 24-4.

$$\text{Beta for DI} = \frac{\text{COV}(r_{\text{DI}}, r_m)}{\text{VAR}(r_m)} = \frac{.074}{.048} = 1.54 \qquad (25\text{-}14)$$

$$\text{Alpha} = a_{\text{DI}} = E(r_{\text{DI}}) - b_{\text{DI}}E(r_m) = .20 - (1.54)(.10) = .20 - .154 = .0458. \qquad (25\text{-}15)$$

$$\text{Correlation} = \frac{\text{COV}(r_{\text{DI}}, r_m)}{\sigma_{\text{DI}}\sigma_m} = \frac{.074}{(.366)(.219)} = \frac{.074}{.080} = .923 = \rho_{\text{DI},m} \qquad (25\text{-}16)$$

Table 25-4
Summary Statistics for the Characteristic Regression Lines (CRL)

Statistic	UST	DI
Expected return, $E(r)$	.07 = 7%	.2 = 20%
Variance of returns, VAR(r)	.0221	.134
Standard deviation of returns, σ	.148 = 14.8%	.366 = 36.6%
Covariance with m, COV($r_p r_m$)	.032	.074
Alpha intercept, a	.0034 = .34%	.0458 = 4.58%
Beta slope, b	.666	1.54
Correlation coefficient, ρ	.983	.923
Coefficient of determination, ρ^2	.967	.852

market rates of return for the two stocks and the market index over a 10-year sample period. The tables also show how the CRL statistics are calculated. Table 25-4, at the end of the box, provides summary statistics for UST's and DI's characteristic regression lines.

Partitioning an Asset's Total Risk

As we saw in Chapter 24, an asset's total risk is measured by its variance of returns, denoted VAR(r). This measure of total risk may be partitioned into systematic and unsystematic components by computing the variance of the CRL, as shown here. By substituting $a_i + b_i r_{m,t} + e_{i,t}$ for $r_{i,t}$,

$$VAR(r_{i,t}) = VAR(a_i + b_i r_{m,t} + e_{i,t})$$
$$= VAR(a_i) + VAR(b_i r_{m,t}) + VAR(e_{i,t})$$

Since VAR(a_i) = 0, we can simplify as follows:

$$VAR(r_{i,t}) = 0 + VAR(b_i r_{m,t}) + VAR(e_{i,t})$$
$$= b_i^2 VAR(r_{m,t}) + VAR(e_{i,t}) \tag{25-17}$$
$$= \text{systematic risk} + \text{unsystematic risk}$$

The unsystematic risk measure, VAR($e_{i,t}$), is called the **residual variance** by statisticians; financial analysts call it *diversifiable risk.* The systematic risk, VAR($b_i r_{m,t}$) = b_i^2VAR($r_{m,t}$), is the undiversifiable part of the ith asset's total risk. The squared correlation coefficient is a measure of the percentage of the ith asset's total risk that is undiversifiable; it is called the **coefficient of determination.**[3]

$$\frac{\text{Undiversifiable risk}}{\text{Total risk}} = \frac{b_i^2 VAR(r_m)}{VAR(r_i)} = \rho^2 \tag{25-18}$$

Studies of the characteristic lines of hundreds of stocks indicate that the average correlation coefficient for a characteristic regression line is about ρ = .5. This means that about ρ^2 = (.5)^2 = 25% of the total variability of return in the average common stock is explained by the market. These market-induced movements are systematic fluctuations that are undiversifiable. Investment assets with high coefficients of determination ρ^2 have small potential for risk-reducing diversification because a large portion of their total risk is undiversifiable.

[3] Appendix A to Chapter 5 discusses correlation. For empirical statistics see J. C. Francis, "Statistical Analysis of Risk Surrogates for NYSE Stocks," *Journal of Financial and Quantitative Analysis,* December 1979, pp. 981–997.

Financial Interpretation of the CRL

The unexplained residual returns from every CRL sum up to zero when summed over all the time periods observed. Symbolically,

$$\sum_{t=1}^{T} e_{i,t} = e_{i,1} + e_{i,2} + \cdots + e_{i,T} = 0$$

Since its expected value is zero, the symbol e need not appear in every statement of an asset's CRL, as shown in Equation (25-19).

$$r_i = a_i + b_i r_m \tag{25-19}$$

The time subscripts in the CRL formula above have also been omitted to show that the CRL can be used to represent a span of multiple time periods instead of only one period.

In the CRL the **alpha** coefficient a_i for security i is the intercept point where the characteristic line intercepts the vertical axis in Figure 25-3. Alpha is an estimate of the ith asset's rate of return when the market is stationary, $r_{m,t} = 0$. The **beta** coefficient b_i measures the slope of the CRL.

$$\text{Beta} = \frac{\text{units of rise}}{\text{units of run}} = \text{slope of characteristic regression line}$$

The average stock has a beta equal to 1.0. Beta coefficients are measures of systematic risk and, so, may be used for ranking the undiversifiable risk of different assets. If the beta is larger than 1.0, $b > 1.0$, then the asset is more volatile than the market and is called an **aggressive asset.** If the beta is less than 1.0, $b < 1.0$, the asset is a **defensive asset;** it is less volatile than the market. Most assets' beta coefficients are in the range from .5 to 1.5.

U.S. Telephone (UST)   The statistics from Tables 25-2 and 25-4 that are illustrated in Figure 25-3*a* indicate that UST is a defensive investment, since its beta has a below-average value of .666. Stated differently, UST's returns tend to rise .666 as much as the market during a bull market. UST's correlation of .983 is a remarkably high goodness-of-fit statistic indicating that this stock's characteristic regression line explains $\rho^2 = (.983)^2 = .967 = 96.7\%$ of the variation in the stock's returns by using the market's returns. UST has a small amount of total risk, $\text{VAR}(r_{\text{UST}}) = .0221$. Since 96.7 percent of this modest total risk is undiversifiable, UST's diversifiable risk is very small. Only $1.0 - \rho^2 = 1.0 - .967 = .033 = 3.3\%$ of UST's small total variance can be attributed to unsystematic movements. UST's tiny alpha of .0034 means that when the market is neither bullish nor bearish, that is, $r_m = 0$, UST's stock may be expected to earn a return of 34/100 of 1 percent (almost nothing), unless some idiosyncratic event imparts a significant value to the residual term e at that time.

Dynamics International   Figure 25-3*b* shows that DI is an aggressive stock with a high degree of systematic risk. DI's beta of 1.54 indicates that when the market falls, DI's return tends to fall 154 percent of the decrease in the market. The characteristic line for DI has an above-average value for its correlation coefficient, $\rho_{DI} = .923$, indicating that the returns on this security follow its particular characteristic line more closely than the average stock. DI's alpha of 4.58 percent can be interpreted to mean that when the market is neither advancing nor retreating, that is, $r_m = 0$, DI's stock may be expected to earn a return of 4.58 percent, unless some event that is idiosyncratic to DI occurs to give some negative or positive value to the residual term e.

The characteristic regression line allows us to measure an asset's undiversifiable risk statistically. Furthermore, the amount of systematic beta risk in an asset's returns has implications for the asset's price, as we see in the next section.

25-3   The Capital Asset Pricing Model (CAPM)

As we saw in Figure 24-1, diversifiable risk can easily be eliminated by the simplest kind of diversification. As a result, investors should focus on an asset's undiversifiable systematic risk when they search for dominant (or efficient) assets. Investors will, therefore, bid up the prices of assets with low systematic risk—or low beta coefficients. In contrast, assets with high beta coefficients will experience low demand and will sell at relatively low market prices. Because of this risk-averse behavior, investors require that assets with high levels of systematic risk yield high rates of return. Figure 25-4 presents the capital asset pricing model (CAPM), or the **security market line (SML)**, as it is also called, which graphically depicts the results of price adjustments from the risk-averse trading described above.

Interpreting the CAPM

Any vertical line drawn on Figure 25-4 is a **risk class** for that particular amount of systematic risk. The CAPM relates a required rate of return to each beta risk class—or level of systematic risk. The CAPM rates of return are the returns that

Figure 25-4   The capital asset pricing model (CAPM).

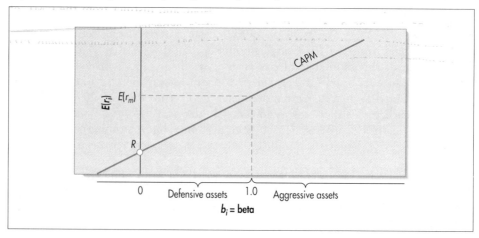

Box 25-7

629

Chapter 25
Capital
Market
Theory

DEFINITION: The Capital Asset Pricing Model (CAPM)

The **capital asset pricing model** is a linear relationship in which the required rate of return k from an asset is determined by that asset's undiversifiable (or systematic, or beta) risk. The CAPM is represented mathematically by

$$k_i = R + [E(r_m) - R]b_i \qquad (25\text{-}20)$$

where b_i is the independent variable representing the systematic risk of the ith asset, and the asset's dependent variable k measures its required rate of return. The CAPM intersects the vertical axis at the riskless rate R; the quantity $E(r_m) - R$ is the slope of the CAPM (since $b_m = 1.0$).

---

investors require to induce them to accept each different amount of undiversifiable risk along the CAPM.

The CAPM suggests a required rate of return that is made up of two separate components:

- The CAPM's intercept R represents the **price of time**. This component of the ith asset's required rate of return compensates the investor for delaying consumption in order to invest.
- The slope of the CAPM, $E(r_m) - R$, the second component, is the **market price of risk.**

The market price of risk is multiplied by the ith asset's beta risk coefficient. The product of this multiplication determines the appropriate **risk premium** (or additional return) that should be added to the riskless rate to find the asset's required rate of return. This risk premium is what induces investors to take on risk.

The linear set of required returns illustrated in Figure 25-4 is the CAPM. The CAPM is a risk-return relationship that is separate and distinct from the CML of Figures 25-1 and 25-2. An *individual* security's expected return and beta risk statistics should lie on the CAPM, but *below* the CML. Only efficient *portfolios'* $E(r)$ and standard deviations will lie *on* the CML. In contrast, the $E(r)$ and beta statistics of all portfolios (even the inefficient ones) should plot on the CAPM. The CML will never include all points if efficient portfolios, inefficient portfolios, and individual securities are plotted together on one graph. The individual assets and the inefficient portfolios should plot as points *below* the CML because their total risk includes diversifiable risk.

Undiversifiable risk is the main factor that risk-averse investors should consider in deciding whether a security yields enough rate of return to induce them to buy it. Other factors, such as the "glamour" of the stock and the company's financial ratios, are important only to the extent that they affect the security's systematic risk and return. *Diversifiable risk is not considered in the CAPM or in the CML.*

The CAPM's Asset Pricing Implications

The CAPM has asset pricing implications because it tells what risk-adjusted discount rate (or required rate of return) should be used to find the present value of an asset with any particular beta. After an asset's expected rate of return and beta have been estimated, they may be plotted in reference to the CAPM. In equilibrium, every asset's expected return and beta systematic risk coefficient should plot as one point on the CAPM. If an asset's expected rate of return differs from its required rate of return, that asset is over- or underpriced. To see why this is true, consider Figure 25-5, which shows two assets denoted H and L.

The CAPM tells us that asset L is priced too low because its average rate of return is inappropriately high for the level of systematic risk it bears. Asset H is priced too high because its expected rate of return is below the rate of return that investors require to induce them to accept its undiversifiable risk. These two assets should move toward their equilibrium-required return positions on the CAPM, as shown by the arrows in Figure 25-5.

To see why assets H and L are incorrectly priced, reconsider Equation (1-4), which defines the one-period rate of return for a common stock. The expected return is:

$$E(r) = \frac{\text{expected capital gain or loss} + \text{expected cash dividends}}{\text{purchase price}}$$

To reach their required-rate-of-return positions on the CAPM, assets H and L must go through a temporary price readjustment. Assuming their systematic risk remains unchanged, the expected return of L must fall to $E(L)$ and the expected return of H must rise to $E(H)$. To accomplish this move to an equilibrium rate of return, the denominator of the asset's expected return formula above must rise for asset L and fall for asset H. Asset H or L or any marketable capital asset will be in disequilibrium unless its risk and return lie on the CAPM. Such disequilibriums from the CAPM

Figure 25-5 The asset pricing implications of the capital asset pricing model (CAPM).

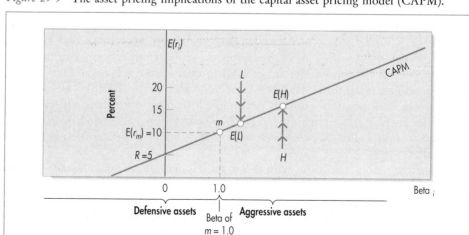

will be corrected as supply and demand set to work as outlined above. Box 20-2 on page 493 delineates the buy-sell decision rules.

The CRL and CAPM models are useful only if the beta coefficients are stable through time. Research indicates that the majority of market assets have betas that do not change significantly from one 5-year sample to the next mutually exclusive 5-year period. However, the betas of a significant minority of assets do change with the passage of time as the nature of the asset's underlying earning power changes.[4] Finding assets with disequilibrium prices is the task of the security analysts. It will be profitable to buy under-priced assets and sell short the assets that are over-priced.

Summary

The total risk of an asset can be assessed by measuring its total variability of returns. Total risk can be partitioned into two parts—systematic risk and unsystematic risk. Both these risks can be assessed with the CRL, which explains an asset's systematic variability in terms of a market index. The sources of the market's systematic changes are fluctuations that affect all assets simultaneously.

Unsystematic risk is the portion of total risk that is not explained by an asset's characteristic regression line. This diversifiable variability of returns is unique to each asset and is caused by idiosyncratic price fluctuations.

Figure 24-1 illustrates how unsystematic risk can be diversified away to zero by simply spreading the funds to be invested across about 15 randomly selected stocks. Systematic risk, on the other hand, is more difficult to diversify because, in varying degrees, it is common to almost every asset in the market. Therefore, assets with high degrees of systematic risk must be priced to yield high rates of return in order to induce investors to accept high degrees of undiversifiable risk. The CAPM illustrates the positive relation between assets' systematic risks and their required rates of return.

Further
Reading

Francis, Jack Clark, *Investments: Analysis and Management,* 5th ed. (New York: McGraw-Hill, 1991).
  Chapters 9 through 11, 20, and 21 inclusive use algebra to delve into the mathematical aspects of diversification, portfolio analysis, and investment performance evaluation. Calculus is used only in a few appendixes. The discussion is augmented by numerical examples and graphs.

Francis, Jack Clark, and Gordon Alexander, *Portfolio Analysis,* 3d ed. (Englewood Cliffs, N.J.: Prentice-Hall, 1986).
  This monograph uses algebra, calculus, advanced calculus, and matrix algebra liberally in order to explore the frontiers of knowledge about modern portfolio theory. The discussion uses some numerical examples. Chapters 5 through 10 delve into the capital market theory using rigorous mathematics and statistics.

[4] For empirical research into the stability of betas see Jack Clark Francis, "Statistical Analysis of Risk Coefficients for NYSE Stocks," *Journal of Financial and Quantitative Analysis,* vol. 14, no. 5, December 1979, pp. 981–997, or see Appendix 10A, entitled Stability of Risk Statistics, in Jack Clark Francis, *Investments: Analysis and Management,* 5th ed. (New York: McGraw-Hill, 1991), pp. 289–294.

Sharpe, William F., "Capital Asset Prices: A Theory of Market Equilibrium under Conditions of Risk," _Journal of Finance,_ September 1964, pp. 425–552.

> _This classic article written by a Nobel Prize winner presents a simple but complete statement of the early capital market theory._

Questions and Problems

Essay Questions

25-1 Define, compare, and contrast each of the following risk concepts: (_a_) total risk, (_b_) systematic risk, (_c_) unsystematic risk, (_d_) diversifiable risk, and (_e_) undiversifiable risk.

25-2 Considering the capital market theory, how might you expect the total risk of a share in a mutual fund to be divided between systematic and unsystematic risk? Explain.

25-3 As a security analyst, could you expect to find any worthwhile information by studying the residual errors from an investment's characteristic line regression? Explain why or why not.

25-4 Define the market portfolio. Suggest a realistic way to create an empirically observable prototype of the theoretical market portfolio.

25-5 "Since the assumptions underlying the capital market theory are unrealistic, the theory is not a valid description of reality." True, false, or questionable? Explain.

25-6 "The best (or most desirable) portfolio will never be the one on the Markowitz efficient frontier with the lowest attainable risk or the highest attainable expected rate of return." Is the preceding sentence true, false, or questionable? Explain.

25-7 Compare and contrast the price behavior of aggressive and defensive common stocks in a bear market.

25-8 Given the assumptions underlying capital market theory, rationalize the following _separability theorem:_ The investment decision of which asset to buy is a separate and independent decision from the financing decision of whether to borrow or lend.

25-9 What does it mean to assume that all investors have "homogeneous expectations" or that "idealized uncertainty" exists? Why is this assumption necessary to capital market theory?

25-10 Compare and contrast the CML and the CAPM. What assets lie on both lines in equilibrium? What assets should never lie on the CML? Why?

Problems

25-11 Suppose that a highly cyclical automobile manufacturer merges with a countercyclical red ink manufacturer of about equal size and equal profitability. How do you think this merger will affect the value of the auto firm's stock? Construct a diagram of the CAPM to illustrate the asset pricing implications of this merger.

25-12 Reconsider the risk and expected-rate-of-return statistics that were introduced in Problem 24-12 for the two-asset portfolios made up of the common stocks issued by the Crown (C) and the Southwest (S) corporations. Use the portfolio risk and return statistics you calculated for three different assumptions about the correlation between assets C and S: (a) $\rho_{C,S}$ = +1.0, (b) $\rho_{C,S}$ = 0, and (c) $\rho_{C,S}$ = −1.0. These data can be used to analyze the effects of *selling short* one of the securities to obtain funds to buy a leveraged position in the other security. Short selling is represented by a negative weight. For example, $x_C = -.2$ represents a short sale of Crown stock equal in dollar value to 20 percent of the portfolio owner's equity (or initial cash) investment. The cash proceeds from the short sale are used to purchase an amount of Southwest stock that exceeds the portfolio's initial cash investment, that is, $x_s = 1.2 = 120\%$. Such short sales are legal and economically logical so long as the weights always sum to 1, $x_c + x_s = 1.0$.

	Three correlations	Assumed weights for C			First, fill in the three essential formulas below:
		1.3	1.0	−.2	
x_S	$\rho = +1$				$x_S =$
	$\rho = 0$				
	$\rho = -1$				
$E(r_P)$	$\rho = +1$				$E(r_P) =$
	$\rho = 0$				
	$\rho = -1$				
Portfolio standard deviation	$\rho = +1$				$\sqrt{\text{VAR}(r_P)} =$
	$\rho = 0$				
	$\rho = -1$				

Extend the graph you drew when you answered Problem 24-12 to include the short selling results you obtained here.

25-13 (a) Gather quarterly data for the 10 years from 1979-1Q to 1988-1Q inclusive for IBM common stock and prepare a characteristic regression line like those in Figure 25-3. The needed stock market index data will have to be obtained from the library. (See Chapter 8, Investment Information Sources.) Use S&P500 Index data. (b) Calculate rates of return for the asset, and estimate the characteristic regression line for the asset. Is it a defensive or an aggressive asset? (*Hint:* Use a computer or calculator to expedite these computations; see end-of-book Appendixes A and B.) (c) Does the characteristic line for IBM have much predictive power? How can you tell? (d) Does IBM appear to be a good candidate for risk-reducing diversification purposes within a well-diversified portfolio of other common stocks? Explain. (e) Did the 4-for-1 stock split in 1979 tend to increase the adjusted price of the stock after the split? Did the 4-for-1 split have any statistically measurable effect? *Note:* This is a large problem; it could make a term project.

Multiple Choice Questions

25-14 Which of the following statements most accurately describes undiversifiable risk? Systematic

(a) It is caused by changes in the political, economic, or sociological environment that affect all assets at the same time.

(b) It leads to default and frequently even bankruptcy.

(c) It can be reduced to zero by diversifying an investment portfolio across enough different assets.

(d) It is caused by the factors that affect only low-quality market assets.

25-15 Undiversifiable risk can be correctly characterized by which of the following descriptions?

(*a*) Systematic variability of return.

(*b*) It includes bankruptcy risk unique to each firm.

(*c*) It encompasses price fluctuations associated with quality rating changes.

(*d*) Unsystematic risk.

25-16 The capital market line (CML) is best described by which of the following statements?

(*a*) It is an asset pricing model for stocks and bonds.

(*b*) It is a time-series regression model for a single asset's rates of return.

(*c*) It is a portfolio pricing model.

(*d*) It distinguishes between the securities issued by small corporations and large corporations.

25-17 The market portfolio is best described by which of the following statements?

(*a*) It is the most desirable risky asset.

(*b*) It is perfectly positively correlated with the riskless interest rate.

(*c*) It contains all assets in the world in proportion to their market values relative to the aggregate market value.

(*d*) Both (*a*) and (*c*) are true.

25-18 The capital market line (CML):

(*a*) Includes only portfolios that have perfectly positively correlated rates of return

(*b*) Is a portfolio made up only of real assets

(*c*) Is a portfolio pricing model that roughly approximates the risk and return statistics of blue-chip stocks

(*d*) Is a credit rating model

CHAPTER 26

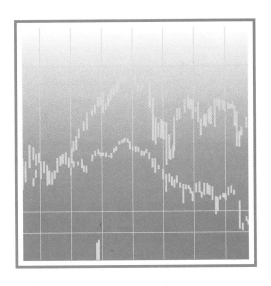

ARBITRAGE PRICING
THEORY

Among the tools at the disposal of investors and investment managers is an economic model called **arbitrage pricing theory (APT).** The APT model is a risk-return relationship that uses the weighted average of default risk from Chapter 10, interest rate risk of Chapter 11, market risk of Chapter 17, purchasing-power risk of Chapter 18, management risk of Chapter 19, and whatever other risk factors might be relevant for valuing a particular asset. APT shows how the relevant risk factors determine the required rate of return (or risk-adjusted discount rate) that is appropriate for finding an asset's present value.

APT is a portfolio theory that is simpler and more general than the older capital market theory of Chapter 25. APT requires fewer and simpler assumptions than

635

capital market theory, but is nevertheless able to contain the capital asset pricing model (CAPM) as a special case of APT. This chapter requires an understanding of Chapters 1, 20, 24, and 25.

26-1 APT's Underlying Assumptions

All **models** are simplified versions of reality. Economic models are abstract models that are constructed by making some basic assumptions and then working out their implications.

The first simplifying assumption of the APT model is that most people prefer more wealth to less wealth. Second, APT assumes that people are risk-averse. Third, APT assumes that investors can assess any asset's risk factor (or factors) numerically. These three underlying assumptions are realistic, yielding an intuitively logical theory. Today a number of major financial research firms use the APT theory.[1]

As its name makes clear, APT involves arbitrage. Therefore, we will start our introduction to the theory with a brief review of how arbitrage works. **Arbitrage** (Box 20-4) is the simultaneous purchase and sale of the same or equivalent assets to create an **imperfect hedge** that is profitable. The **law of one price (Box 20-5) says** that at any given time the same good should always sell at the same price. The law of one price should never be broken or else profit seekers will execute the profitable arbitrage procedure until a single price prevails. Arbitrageurs' eagerness to profit by correcting deviations from the law of one price provides the engine that powers arbitrage pricing theory.

26-2 One-Factor APT

The simplest APT model assumes there is only one source of risk. This single-factor model can be presented as a formula or a graph of the formula.

The Arbitrage Pricing Line

The three basic assumptions of arbitrage pricing theory result in the **arbitrage pricing line.** Figure 26-1 illustrates this risk-return relationship.

---

[1] Professor Steve Ross at Yale University, the creator of APT, and Professor Richard Roll of UCLA, Ross's fellow researcher, use arbitrage pricing management to manage $7 billion of other peoples' money. For details about the money management firm named Roll and Ross Asset Management, see Stephen E. Clark, "Practicing What They Teach," *Institutional Investor,* November 1991, pp. 92-99. In addition, some of the oldest, largest investments consulting firms have switched from single-factor models (like the capital asset pricing model) to models that employ multiple risk factors. For example, BARRA Associates, headquartered in Berkeley, California, and Frank Russell and Company, headquartered in Tacoma, Washington, both have offices around the world, manage billions of dollars, employ many Ph.D.s (some of whom used to be finance professors), and use multifactor models. See H. Russell Fogler, "Common Stock Management in the 1990s," *Journal of Portfolio Management* (Winter), 1990, pp. 26–35.

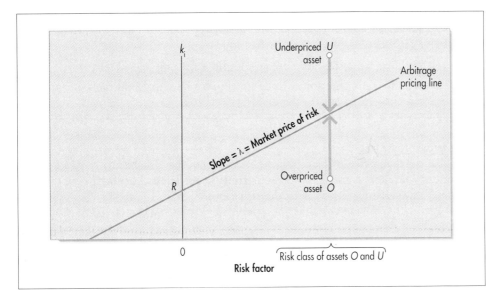

Figure 26-1   The APT model for one risk factor.

Risk is measured along the horizontal axis of Figure 26-1. The APT considers all assets (such as assets O and U in Figure 26-1) that are in the same risk class to be perfect substitutes that should yield the same rate of return. An asset's required rate of return, denoted k_i for the ith asset,[2] is measured along the vertical axis of the figure. These **required rates of return** are the minimum rates of return investors require to induce them to bear the associated level of risk.

The arbitrage pricing line intersects the vertical axis at point R, which represents the **riskless rate of interest.** The riskless rate of interest is like the fixed interest rate that a federally insured bank pays on its savings deposits; it is the lowest interest rate that exists in the model. Investments that involve zero risk can pay the low riskless rate of interest and still be appealing to highly risk-averse investors.[3]

Equation (26-1) below defines the one-factor APT model shown in Figure 26-1.

$$k_i = R + \lambda\, b_i \tag{26-1}$$

where k_i represents the required rate of return for asset i; R stands for the riskless rate of interest; λ (lambda) stands for the slope of the arbitrage pricing line—sometimes

[2] Any particular asset is referred to as simply the ith asset. If n different assets are being considered, think of the assets as being numbered $i = 1, 2, 3, \ldots , n$. Using these mathematical subscripts keeps the discussion concise and keeps us from diverting our attention to whether we "like" or "dislike" particular features of the individual assets.

[3] The arbitrage pricing line is identical to the *capital asset pricing model* (CAPM) when the only risk factor is the *market portfolio*. In fact, the CAPM is one special case of the more general APT.

Box 26-1

DEFINITION: Law of One Price Restated
At any given moment identical goods should have identical expected rates of return everywhere in the world. If identical items have different rates of return, arbitrage will work to equate the disparate returns.

λ

called the **market price of risk** because it measures the risk-return tradeoff in the investments markets—and b_i is a **sensitivity coefficient,** or **factor beta,** that measures how sensitive asset i is to the risk factor.[4]

Overpriced and Underpriced Assets

It is possible to illustrate mispriced assets graphically by restating the law of one price from Box 20-5 in an equivalent but slightly different form (see Box 26-1).

Consider two assets in the same risk class, like the two assets at points U and O in Figure 26-1. Assets U and O violate the restated law of one price because they are both in the same risk class (and therefore have equal risks) but do not have the same expected rate of return. The restated law of one price suggests that these two assets should be located together on the arbitrage pricing line. In fact, according to APT, the forces of supply and demand should drive all assets to lie on the arbitrage pricing line as arbitrageurs profit from assets that violate the restated law of one price.

Even though they are *equally risky,* asset O in Figure 26-1 offers a lower rate of return than asset U. Risk-averse investors will sell asset O because it is a less desirable investment. The resulting excess of supply over demand for asset O will drive down its market price. As the price of asset O is driven down, the one-period expected rate of return for asset O will rise; this price-adjustment process is indicated by the arrows in Equation (26-2).

$$\uparrow E(r_i) = \frac{[E(p_{t+1}) - p_t] + d_t}{\downarrow p_t} \tag{26-2}$$

In this single-period expected-rate-of-return equation, $E(r_i)$ denotes the expected rate of return from asset i (which might be shares of a common stock like O or U).

---

[4] Those who prefer decimal-point statistical accuracy may estimate the sensitivity coefficients, the b_i coefficients, empirically using time-series regressions. The sensitivity coefficients (or factor betas) can be estimated with one first-pass regression for each asset using time-series data. Then the Greek letter lambda λ can be estimated as the slope coefficient from a cross-sectional regression. In estimating λ, a second-pass regression is determined using the sensitivity coefficients b_i and the required (or average) rates of return k_i for each asset as raw data. For a more detailed explanation, see J. C. Francis, *Investments: Analysis and Management,* 5th ed., New York: McGraw-Hill, Inc., chap. 11, entitled Arbitrage Pricing Theory.

This *i*th stock has an expected price at the end of one investment period of $E(p_{t+1})$, a cash dividend of d_t per share, and a purchase price (or a beginning-of-the-period price) of p_t. Equation (26-2) is restated below as Equation (26-2a).

$$\begin{array}{c}\text{Expected} \\ \uparrow \text{ rate of} \\ \text{return}\end{array} = \dfrac{\begin{array}{c}\text{expected capital} \\ \text{gain or loss}\end{array} + \begin{array}{c}\text{cash dividend,} \\ \text{if any}\end{array}}{\downarrow \text{purchase price}} \tag{26-2a}$$

Risk-averse investors will continue to sell asset O until its price is driven down and its expected rate of return rises to the arbitrage pricing line in Figure 26-1. The upward pointing arrow in the figure traces the path that asset O's expected rate of return should follow until it reaches its equilibrium point on the arbitrage pricing line.

The most aggressive investors will not only sell asset O if they own any of it, they will also want to sell asset O short to profit from its anticipated price drop. Assuming the short seller gets to keep the cash proceeds from the short sale, this investor can use these funds to buy a long position in asset U. Here we encounter a *fourth assumption* that underlies APT. This assumption remained unstated in Section 26-1 because it was premature and confusing to bring up at that point. The fourth assumption is that investors can obtain all the cash proceeds when they sell a security short. Short sellers will take their cash proceeds and buy asset U in order to enjoy its expected rate of return—which lies above the arbitrage pricing line in Figure 26-1. As these profit seekers buy asset U in order to obtain its high return, they will bid up its price. But, as the price of asset U is bid higher, its expected rate of return will come down. The way the economic pressures work on asset U can be traced by reversing the direction of the arrows in Equations (26-2) and (26-2a).

The assumption that most people prefer more wealth to less wealth will ensure that asset U experiences more buyers than sellers until its purchase price is bid so high that its expected rate of return is moved down onto the arbitrage pricing line in Figure 26-1. The asset's price will then be in equilibrium.

This price-adjustment process will work for all assets in all risk classes. *Every asset that plots above the arbitrage pricing line in Figure 26-1 is underpriced* (like asset U), and its price will adjust upward. *Every asset that plots below the arbitrage pricing line is overpriced* (like asset O), and its price will fall.

Establishing an Arbitrage Portfolio

To maximize profits, the most aggressive investors will sell an overpriced asset short and *simultaneously* buy a long position of equal dollar value in an underpriced asset. These investors will create an **arbitrage portfolio.** To do this they will not need to invest any of their own funds, because they can take the cash proceeds from the short sale of asset O and use them to buy a long position of equal value in asset U. They will not be exposed to any risk because their arbitrage portfolio is fully hedged with long and short positions that offset each other's gains and losses. Furthermore, the arbitrage portfolio will earn a riskless return of $E(r_U) - E(r_O)$ by raising funds from the short sale on which the arbitrageur must pay a rate of return of $E(r_O)$ and simultaneously investing these funds in the long position at a higher rate of return of $E(r_U)$. Figure 20-4b provides another illustration of a two-asset arbitrage portfolio.

In summary, an *arbitrage portfolio* will:

1. Have zero money invested

2. Be a riskless investment

3. Earn a predetermined positive profit

26-3 APT with Two Risk Factors

Consider what APT is like if two risk factors are relevant, as is the case with a U.S. Treasury bond. Like all other bonds, Treasury bonds have interest rate risk and purchasing-power risk.

The Two-Factor APT Model: Two Types of Undiversifiable Risk

Equation (26-3) is a two-factor APT model for our hypothetical T-bond.

$$k_{TB} = R + \lambda_1 b_{TB,1} + \lambda_2 b_{TB,2} \tag{26-3}$$

where k_{TB} = required rate of return for a T-bond

   R = riskless rate of interest

   λ_1 = market price of risk for the first risk factor,
      which we will assume to be interest rate risk

   $b_{TB,1}$ = sensitivity of the Treasury bond (TB) to the interest rate risk factor

   λ_2 = market price of risk for the second risk factor,
      which we assumed was purchasing-power risk

   $b_{TB,2}$ = sensitivity of the ith T-bond to the purchasing-power risk factor

The sensitivity coefficients in APT can be viewed as indexes of various kinds of **undiversifiable** (or **systematic**) **risk.** The average value of the sensitivity coefficients for all assets and for all risk factors is +1.0. When b_{ij} = 1.0, the rates of return from the ith asset tend to fluctuate in a one-to-one correspondence with the jth risk factor. If b_{ij} = 1.5, the ith asset's returns tend to rise and fall 50 percent more than average. If b_{ij} = .5, asset i is only half as volatile as the average in its response to the jth risk factor. An asset that had a sensitivity coefficient of zero for the jth risk factor would have none of that particular kind of undiversifiable risk. Boxes 26-2 and 26-3 present some examples.

The Arbitrage Pricing Plane

The two-factor APT model is illustrated in Figure 26-2 as a three-dimensional surface called the **arbitrage pricing plane.** The arbitrage pricing plane in Figure 26-2 is an extension of the arbitrage pricing line of Figure 26-1. As in Figure 26-1, assets' required rates of return are measured along the vertical axis. The interest rate risk and

Box 26-2

641

*Chapter 26
Arbitrage Pricing
Theory*

COMPUTATION: A Riskless Asset Seen through the Two-Factor APT Model

If asset c has none of the two risk factors to which an asset of its type falls victim (that is, $b_{c1} = 0$ and $b_{c2} = 0$), then the two-factor APT model simplifies as shown below.

$$k_c = R + \lambda_1 b_{c1} + \lambda_2 b_{c2}$$

$$= R + \lambda_1(0) + \lambda_2(0) \qquad \text{if asset } c \text{ is a riskless asset} \qquad (26\text{-}4)$$

$$= R$$

The appropriate required rate of return for an asset that was free from undiversifiable risk would equal the riskless rate R.

the purchasing-power risk factors are measured along the depth and width axes, respectively, of Figure 26-2.

Consider the economic reasons that certain assets will assume certain positions on the arbitrage pricing plane. One day before the maturity date, a Treasury bond has essentially zero interest rate risk and zero purchasing-power risk left. At this point in time the maturing T-bond is practically a *totally riskless* asset that should pay a rate of return equal to the riskless rate of interest. Speaking graphically, maturing Treasury bills should plot on the arbitrage pricing plane of Figure 26-2 very near point R.

Box 26-3

COMPUTATION: The Expected Return for a Risky Asset with Positive Amounts of Risk Factors 1 and 2

Suppose an investor estimated the riskless rate of return to be $R = 4\%$ and the market price of risk to be $\lambda_1 = 1.1$ for interest rate risk and $\lambda_2 = .9$ for purchasing-power risk. Further, suppose that asset g has 40 percent more than the average amount of the interest rate risk factor (that is, $b_{g1} = 1.4$) combined with an average amount of purchasing-power risk, $b_{g2} = 1.0$. The required rate of return for asset g would be 6.44 percent, as shown below.

$$k_g = R + \lambda_1 b_{g1} + \lambda_2 b_{g2} \qquad (26\text{-}5)$$

$$= 4\% + 1.1(1.4) + .9(1.0) = 4\% + 1.54\% + .9\% = 6.44\%$$

An investor who used APT would not buy asset g unless it earned at least the required rate of return of 6.44 percent. Or, if the investor wanted to compute the present value of asset g, $k = 6.44\%$ would be used as the risk-adjusted discount rate.

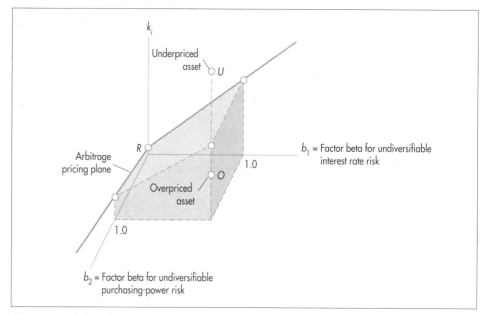

Figure 26-2 The arbitrage pricing plane for two risk factors.

Treasury bonds that have several years left to maturity will entail larger amounts of interest rate risk and purchasing-power risk. These longer-term T-bonds should therefore plot on the arbitrage pricing plane somewhere sufficiently above point *R* to compensate investors for assuming these increased levels of risk.

Consider T-bonds of all maturities, or any other asset that has its required rate of return determined solely by interest rate risk and purchasing-power risk. *All such assets that plot above the surface of the arbitrage pricing plane are underpriced,* as asset *U* was shown to be in Figure 26-1. The actions of arbitrageurs should continue to bid up the prices of all these underpriced assets until their expected rates are driven down onto the arbitrage pricing plane in Figure 26-2. Similarly, *all assets that plot below the arbitrage pricing plane are overpriced and should experience price declines until their expected rate of return rises to the arbitrage pricing plane,* as asset *O* was shown to do in Figures 26-1 and 26-2.

Investors who wish to use APT start their security analysis work by preparing estimates of the b_{ij} risk factor sensitivity coefficients for the assets and the market prices of risk λ. Then, to use the APT model to find over- and underpriced assets, financial analysts compare where each asset lies in relation to the arbitrage pricing line or arbitrage pricing plane they have estimated.

26-4 APT with *f* Risk Factors

Earlier chapters in this text introduced a variety of risk factors. Investors might also consider some other risk factors. For example, during the Persian Gulf crisis of 1990 to 1991, oil prices became a risk factor that temporarily explained much about

Box 26-4

643

Chapter 26
Arbitrage Pricing
Theory

COMPUTATION: A Risk Premium Is the Product of a Sensitivity Coefficient and a λ

The sensitivity coefficients (or factor betas) are indexes of undiversifiable risk with respect to some risk factor. Sensitivity coefficients estimating the eleventh asset's reaction to the second risk factor with high (1.6), medium (1.0), and low (.5) values are explained below.

$b_{11,2} = 1.6$ Means that the eleventh asset has 160 percent as much undiversifiable risk from the second risk factor as the average asset.

$b_{11,2} = 1.0$ Means that the eleventh asset has just as much undiversifiable risk from the second risk factor as the average asset in the market.

$b_{11,2} = .5$ Means that the eleventh asset has half as much undiversifiable risk from the second risk factor as the average asset.

The λ measures the slope of the arbitrage pricing line (or of the arbitrage pricing plane).

$\lambda_2 = .08$ Means that the risk-return tradeoff in the market for the second risk factor equals 8 percent (or .08) of required rate of return k for each unit of undiversifiable risk from the second risk factor.

Risk premiums are the products of the appropriate lambdas λ and the betas b.

$(\lambda_2)(b_{11,2}) = (.08)(.5) = .04$ Means that asset 11 has a risk premium of 4 percent (or .04) of expected return added to the riskless interest rate and any other risk premiums that may be appropriate for asset 11 to compensate for undiversifiable risk from the second risk factor.

security price movements. Multifactor APT models may have old risk factors deleted and/or have new risk factors added when risk factors change. These multifactor APT models are called *f-factor models,* where f can be any positive integer. The integer f counts the number of different risk factors that have a statistically significant impact on security prices.

The f-Factor APT Model

Equation (26-6) represents the f-factor APT model that considers f different risk factors in determining the ith asset's expected rate of return.

$$k_i = R + \lambda_1 b_{i1} + \lambda_2 b_{i2} + \ldots + \lambda_f b_{if} \qquad (26\text{-}6)$$

Note that there are two subscripts on each risk factor's beta in Equation (26-6). The subscript i is a counter that refers to the ith investment asset's arbitrarily assigned identification number. For instance, asset $i = 23$ might be GM's common stock, asset $i = 24$ might be a GM bond issue, and asset $i = 25$ might be IBM's common stock. The other subscript is a counter for the risk factors. There are $j = 1, 2, \ldots, f$ risk factors considered in this APT model. Let us refer to any unspecified risk factor as the jth risk factor—note that the subscript j itself does not appear in Equation (26-6). The jth risk factor refers to one particular risk factor, where j might be risk factor $j = 1$, or risk factor $j = 2$, or any other integer value of j up to and including $j = f$.

The integer f is the last (or total number of) risk factors. The value of f is left unspecified for the sake of generality. The Greek lambda with subscript j, λ_j, measures the *market price of risk* for the jth risk factor. Graphically speaking, λ_j measures the slope of the APT pricing plane from the starting point R out along the axis that measures the jth risk factor.

If λ_j equals zero, that particular risk factor receives zero weight in the determination of the expected rate of return. Economically speaking, if the market price of risk factor j is zero, this means that it is irrelevant (or, it is not priced) in the market.

APT gives financial researchers no clues about which risk factors may affect the pricing of any given asset. Analysts must be detectives and use clues from economic theory to identify the relevant sensitivity coefficients b_{ij}. The top half of Table 26-1 (in Section 26-5) lists some of the systematic risk factors likely to be found in an f-factor APT model. The numerical values of the sensitivity coefficients usually lie between 0 and +2, with an average value of 1, that is, $0 < b_{ij} < 2$. If asset i has a sensitivity coefficient with respect to the jth risk factor that is greater than 1, the ith asset is more sensitive to the jth risk factor than the average, and conversely, if the coefficient is less than 1, the asset is less sensitive. Each sensitivity coefficient b_{ij} is an index indicating the amount of the jth undiversifiable risk factor present in asset i.

The f-Dimensional Hyperplane

It is impossible to draw graphs that have more than three dimensions. Since the required-rate-of-return variable k on the vertical axis uses one dimension, the f-factor APT model cannot be represented graphically if more than two risk factors are considered, because then more than a total of three variables (or graphic dimensions) are involved. The f-factor APT model is what mathematicians call an **f-dimensional hyperplane.** Any asset that has a required rate of return lying above this f-dimensional hyperplane is underpriced, and its price should seek an economic equilibrium at a higher level. Any asset with an expected rate of return below the f-dimensional hyperplane is overpriced, and its price should seek an economic equilibrium at a lower value. Box 26-5 shows computation for a 5-factor APT model.

26-5 The Components of Total Risk in the APT Model

One of the few shreds of information that APT gives investors about which risk factors to include in the APT model is that only undiversifiable risk should be considered. Table 26-1 lists various risk factors that were introduced and defined as

Box 26-5

645

*Chapter 26
Arbitrage Pricing
Theory*

> ## COMPUTATION: Using a Five-Factor APT Model to Estimate the Risk-Adjusted Discount Rate for a Common Stock
>
> Suppose investment analysts estimated the riskless rate of return for an asset to be $R = 5\%$ and the relevant market prices of risk as listed below:
>
> $\lambda_1 = 1.1$ for interest rate risk
>
> $\lambda_2 = .9$ for purchasing-power risk
>
> $\lambda_3 = 1.0$ for management risk
>
> $\lambda_4 = .8$ for market risk
>
> $\lambda_5 = 1.2$ for default risk
>
> If a particular common stock, denoted *d*, had average amounts of all five risk factors, then for all five of that asset's indexes of undiversifiable risk, the coefficient will equal positive unity.
>
> $$b_{d1} = b_{d2} = b_{d3} = b_{d4} = b_{d5} = 1.0$$
>
> The required rate of return for common stock *d* is calculated with Equation (26-7) below:
>
> $$k_d = R + \lambda_1 b_{d1} + \lambda_2 b_{d2} + \lambda_3 b_{d3} + \lambda_4 b_{d4} + \lambda_5 b_{d5} \qquad (26\text{-}7)$$
>
> $$k_d = 5\% + 1.1(1.0) + .9(1.0) + 1.0(1.0) + .8(1.0) + 1.2(1.0)$$
>
> $$= 5\% + 1.1\% + .9\% + 1.0\% + .8\% + 1.2\% = 10\%$$
>
> Ten percent would be the required rate of return (or appropriate risk-adjusted discount rate) for an asset with the undiversifiable risk factors indicated above.

possible components of an asset's total risk in earlier chapters. It categorizes these risk factors under headings indicating how each component of total risk contributes to the asset's diversifiable and undiversifiable risk.

Only the systematic risk factors are used in APT, because they are the undiversifiable risks that cannot be eliminated. The unsystematic risk factors can easily be diversified away to zero and therefore play no role in APT. Stated differently, APT ignores unsystematic risk because it assumes that investors are rational risk averters who diversify.

26-6 Simple Diversification

Simple diversification can be described as "not putting all your eggs in one basket." Simple diversification can usually be expected to reduce substantially the unsystematic (or diversifiable) risk of a portfolio. But as we saw in Chapters 10, 11, 17, 18 and 19,

Table 26-1
Diversifiable and Undiversifiable Risk Factors an Asset Might Have

1. Possible sources of undiversifiable risk:
   Systematic interest rate risk, b_1
   Systematic purchasing-power risk, b_2
   Systematic market risk, b_3
   Systematic management risk, b_4
   Systematic default risk, b_5
   Systematic liquidity risk, b_6
   Systematic callability risk, b_7
   Systematic convertibility risk, b_8
   The first additional systematic risk, b_9
   Other additional systematic risk factors, b_{10}

2. Possible sources of diversifiable risk:*
   Unsystematic interest rate risk
   Unsystematic purchasing-power risk
   Unsystematic market risk
   Unsystematic management risk
   Unsystematic default risk
   Unsystematic liquidity risk
   Unsystematic callability risk
   Unsystematic convertibility risk
   The first additional unsystematic risk
   Other additional unsystematic risk factors

Note: The sum of all the items in (1) and (2) equals the total risk of the investment.

* Diversifiable risk plays no role in the APT models.

covering specific investment risks, simple diversification cannot be expected to reduce undiversifiable risk.

Figure 24-1 summarizes graphically the risk-reducing powers of simple diversification. Simple diversification will usually cause the diversifiable portion of a portfolio's total risk to decrease, until approximately 15 securities have been included in the portfolio. This happens because the unsystematic portions of the assets' rates of return vary independently of each other—they are zero correlated. These uncorrelated unsystematic variations tend to add to zero when different securities are combined to form a portfolio because the diversifiable components of each asset's return average to zero when they are combined. Adding more than about 15 randomly selected securities to a portfolio cannot be expected to reduce its unsystematic risk further, however, because all the diversifiable risk will have already been eliminated.

While simple diversification is an effective way to reduce a portfolio's unsystematic risk to zero, it does nothing to reduce the systematic (or undiversifiable) risk. Therefore, it is this undiversifiable risk that determines assets' required rates of return.

The discussion has focused, thus far, on using APT to determine the required rate of return k. This risk-adjusted rate of return can be used to find the present values of actively traded securities or of assets that are not traded in active markets (such as privately owned companies, manufacturing machines, art objects, and real estate).[5] The buy-sell rules we examined in Box 20-2 can then be used to make decisions.

In addition to being useful for calculating present values, an asset's required rate

---

[5] Stephen A. Ross, "A Simple Approach to the Valuation of Risky Streams," *Journal of Business,* vol. 51, no. 3, July 1978, pp. 453–475.

CASE

Evaluating IBM's Common Stock with a Five-Factor APT Model

Marie Esposito began to do some common stock analysis by preparing the estimates of the riskless rate of return and lambdas (or market prices of risk, or Marie's personal weighting system) listed below.

$R = 5\%$

$\lambda_1 = .9$ for interest rate risk

$\lambda_2 = .8$ for purchasing-power risk

$\lambda_3 = 1.6$ for management risk

$\lambda_4 = 1.75$ for market risk

$\lambda_5 = 1.6583$ for default risk

After doing some additional research, Ms. Esposito assigned IBM's common stock the following five factor betas (or sensitivity coefficients):

$b_1 = .9$ for interest rate risk

$b_2 = .9$ for purchasing-power risk

$b_3 = 1.3$ for management risk

$b_4 = .8$ for market risk

$b_5 = 1.2$ for default risk

Then Marie used the riskless rate, lambdas, and betas to estimate the required rate of return (or appropriate risk-adjusted discount rate) for IBM's common stock. Marie used the five-factor APT model below and found IBM's required rate of return to be $k_1 = 12\%$.

$$k_1 = R + \lambda_1\,b_{11} + \lambda_2\,b_{12} + \lambda_3\,b_{13} \quad (26\text{-}8)$$
$$+ \lambda_4\,b_{14} + \lambda_5 b_{15}$$

$$= 5\% + .9(.9) + .8(.9) +$$
$$1.6(1.3) + 1.75(.8) + 1.6583(1.2)$$

$$= 5\% + .81\% + .72\% + 2.08\% +$$
$$1.4\% + 1.99\% = 12.0\%$$

Next, Ms. Esposito prepared a probability distribution of IBM's returns and estimated its expected rate of return to be $E(r_1) = 10\%$, as shown below in Equation (26-9).

$$E(r_1) = (P_1)(r_1) + (P_2)(r_2) + (P_3)(r_3) + \quad (26\text{-}9)$$
$$(P_4)(r_4) + (P_5)(r_5)$$

$$= (.1)(40\%) + (.2)(30\%) + (.4)(10\%) +$$
$$(.2)(-10\%) + (.1)(-20)$$

$$= .04 + .06 + .04 - .02 -$$
$$.02 = .1 = 10\%$$

Finally, Marie compared IBM's required rate of return of 12 percent with its expected return of 10 percent and concluded that IBM's common stock was not a good investment at that time, $10\% = E(r_1) < k_1 = 12\%$.

of return k can be compared with its expected return, $E(r)$. Box 1-7 showed how to compute an investment's expected return.

Assets whose present values exceed their market prices are good investments, because they will also have expected returns that exceed their required rates of return. Speaking graphically, these underpriced assets lie above the arbitrage pricing line in Figure 26-1, or above the arbitrage pricing plane in Figure 26-2.

Some number crunching is required to use the APT models, as the accompanying case box shows. To implement APT you must first estimate sensitivity coefficients (that is, the factor betas b_{ij}) for every relevant risk factor associated with each potential investment. You must then multiply every sensitivity coefficient by the associated market prices of risk (namely, the slope coefficients λ) and then add up these products to obtain each asset's expected rate of return. Even if you wish to avoid these computations, however, the APT models can be useful.

APT can help your thinking. The APT model directs you to assess all risk factors, attach weights to your risk assessments (you can think of the λ's as being the weights), and try to discriminate between over- and underpriced investments. Even if you do not perform all the computations, it is wiser to make investment decisions by following these guidelines than aimlessly to chase "hot tips."

Summary

When they find deviations from the law of one price, arbitrageurs earn riskless profits by entering different imperfect hedges and, in so doing, creating arbitrage portfolios of overpriced and underpriced assets. In the process of maximizing their profits arbitrageurs eliminate deviations from the law of one price. Arbitrageurs' eagerness to repeat this profitable procedure over and over causes the risk-adjusted discount rates k from all assets to increase with whatever risk factors characterize each asset, as illustrated in Figures 26-1 and 26-2.

APT is based on the assumption that most investors prefer more wealth to less wealth, and are risk-averse. This realistic assumption means that a positive risk-return tradeoff must exist to induce risk-averse investors to buy risky assets. In the simplest cases this risk-return tradeoff may take the form of an arbitrage pricing line or an arbitrage pricing plane, but when analyzing common stocks and other assets that have several different risk factors, it is necessary to use the f-factor APT model. From the simplest to the most complex APT model, however, one characteristic that all APT models have in common is their use of only the undiversifiable portion of the relevant risk factors. Unsystematic risks are so easy to diversify away to zero that they play no role in APT or in the determination of the required rates of return.

APT can be useful in assessing asset value. The arbitrage pricing line, arbitrage pricing plane, and the f-factor arbitrage pricing hyperplane can be used to pinpoint over- and underpriced assets, as illustrated with assets O and U in Figures 26-1 and 26-2. APT can also be used to suggest the appropriate risk-adjusted discount rate with which to find the present value of a potential investment.

Further Reading

Alexander, Gordon J., and Jack Clark Francis, *Portfolio Analysis*, 3d ed. (Englewood Cliffs, N.J.: Prentice-Hall, 1986).

Chapter 14 contains a mathematical introduction to the arbitrage pricing theory.

Francis, Jack Clark, *Investments: Analysis and Management*, 5th ed. (New York: McGraw-Hill, 1991).

> Chapters 1, 8, 11, and 20 use elementary algebra and statistics to discuss various theoretical and empirical aspects of the APT.

Roll, Richard, and S. Ross, "An Empirical Investigation of the Arbitrage Pricing Theory," *Journal of Finance*, vol. 35, December 1980, 1073–1103.

> This article reviews the APT model and presents initial empirical tests. It is difficult to read, however, because matrix algebra is used.

Roll, R., and S. Ross, "The Arbitrage Pricing Theory Approach to Strategic Portfolio Planning," *Financial Analysts Journal*, May–June 1984, pp. 14–26.

> Roll and Ross suggest that their empirical research has identified four factors: (1) unanticipated changes in inflation, (2) unanticipated changes in industrial production, (3) unanticipated changes in risk premiums (as measured by the yield spread between low-grade and high-grade bonds), and (4) unanticipated changes in the slope of the yield curve.

Ross, S. A., "The Arbitrage Pricing Theory of Capital Asset Pricing," *Journal of Economic Theory*, December 1976, pp. 344–360.

> The development of arbitrage pricing theory can be attributed to Prof. Stephen Ross; it has been suggested that someday he will earn a Nobel Prize for this theory.

Essay Questions

26-1   How do arbitrageurs profit by correcting deviations from the law of one price? Explain your answer using a graph of a one-factor APT model. Label all parts of the graph.

26-2   "It is possible to own a portfolio of different common stock positions without investing any money and/or without taking any investment risks." Is the preceding statement true, false, or questionable? Explain. (*Hint:* Consider the fourth APT assumption.)

26-3   What does APT tell investors about the risk factors that determine the returns from assets? Be specific about what the theory does and does not specify.

26-4   Consider the various risk factors that were introduced in Chapters 10, 11, 17, 18, and 19 of this text. What risk factors might be relevant in the APT? Explain.

26-5   List the four assumptions that underlie the APT. Which of the four assumptions is the least plausible to you? Explain what you do not like about whichever assumption you find least plausible.

26-6   "All components of an asset's total risk should be considered by APT in determining the asset's expected rate of return." Is the preceding statement true, false, or questionable? Explain.

26-7   "APT cannot be used to assess the value of physical assets (for instance, machines) that cannot be sold short and that are usually evaluated by finding the present value of their cashflows over a number of future years." Is the preceding statement true, false, or questionable? Explain.

26-8 "If an asset's expected rate of return lies below the arbitrage pricing line (or plane, or hyperplane), the asset is underpriced." Is this statement true, false, or questionable? Explain.

Problems

26-9 Consider a situation in which the riskless rate of interest is $R = 5\%$ and the market prices of certain risk factors are as follows:

$\lambda_1 = 1.1$ for interest rate risk

$\lambda_2 = 1.5$ for purchasing-power risk

$\lambda_3 = .8$ for default risk

Asset h has the following beta sensitivity indexes of undiversifiable risk:

$b_{h1} = 1.5$

$b_{h2} = .8$

$b_{h3} = -.6$

(a) What expected rate of return does APT suggest is appropriate for asset h? (b) Assume that asset h will be sold after 1 year and yield $110 at that time, and that is the only cashflow that the asset is expected to produce. What is asset h worth? Show your computations and label all variables in the formulas.

26-10 If the total risk of asset z is diversifiable, unsystematic risk, what does APT suggest that its rate of return should be? Explain your answer.

26-11 Assume you are using APT to evaluate two different U.S. Treasury bills that you plan to hold until they mature. One T-bill matures in 1 month and the other in 2 months. Assume money market interest rates range between 5 and 7 percent per annum. Since market interest rates are not high and the T-bills' maturities are so short, purchasing-power risk is the only nonzero risk factor for these two default-free bonds. A financial consultant estimates the market price of purchasing-power risk (PPR) to be $\lambda_{PPR} = .1$ and the sensitivity to changes in the price level to be $b_1 = .1$ for the T-bill with 1 month to maturity and $b_2 = .2$ for the 2-month T-bill. Both the 1-month and the 2-month T-bills are priced to yield 7 percent if held to maturity. The riskless interest rate is $R = 5\%$. (a) What is the appropriate APT model with which to evaluate these two T-bills? (b) What are the required rates of return for these two money market securities? (c) Are the two T-bills priced correctly? (d) Draw a graph to illustrate your answer.

Multiple Choice Questions

26-12 APT is a model which suggests that investors consider all risk factors affecting an asset and then calculate a weighted average of every asset's nonzero factor beta (or sensitivity coefficient) using which one of the following for the weights?
 (a) Equal weights
 (b) The market price of risk, the λ_i coefficients for each different risk factor that is not zero
 (c) The dollar value of each asset stated as a fraction of the aggregate value of all assets in the market
 (d) The actual rate of return that each asset is priced to yield

26-13 Investors who do not have access to expert estimates of the market prices of risk λ for every relevant risk factor and all the beta sensitivity coefficients for every asset should view APT in which of the following ways?

(*a*) Use the theory intuitively when making investment decisions by simply trying to be cognizant of the various undiversifiable risks that affect every potential investment.

(*b*) Discard the teachings of the theory if all the statistical inputs needed to implement it are not available.

(*c*) The theory is a sterile, academic exercise that has no practical applications; the beta and lambda statistics cannot realistically be estimated.

(*d*) An amateur investor working alone should be able to prepare estimates of all the lambdas λ_j and betas b_{ij} within 2-decimal-point accuracy in order to implement APT.

26-14 The beta sensitivity coefficient for a certain common stock with respect to the interest rate risk factor is best described by which of the following statements?

(*a*) The beta can be viewed as an elasticity measure that gauges the percentage change in the price of the stock that should occur in response to any given percentage change in the level of market interest rates.

(*b*) The beta coefficient is an index of the undiversifiable risk impact that a change in market interest rates will have on the price of the stock.

(*c*) The beta should be multiplied by the lambda that measures the market price of risk for the interest rate risk factor to determine the interest rate risk premium that is appropriate in the expected rate of return for the stock.

(*d*) All the above are true.

26-15 The lambda coefficients are best described by which of the following statements?

(*a*) If the lambda coefficient for a particular risk factor is zero, then that risk factor has no effect on the rate of return that should be expected from any asset in the market.

(*b*) If all the lambdas in an APT model equal 1, the market is in equilibrium.

(*c*) Lambdas are empirically estimated using a cross-sectional multiple regression across many different assets to calculate the weights that investors implicitly attach to the assets' different risk sensitivities.

(*d*) Both (*a*) and (*c*) above are true.

26-16 Which of the following statements best describes the assumption made about short selling with the APT?

(*a*) The APT assumes that short selling is not possible.

(*b*) The APT assumes that some investors can keep all the cash proceeds they get when they sell an asset that they do not own.

(*c*) The APT assumes that any investor who desires to do so can borrow at the riskless rate of interest to finance a short position.

(*d*) The APT assumes that investors can only sell short the riskless asset to obtain funds needed to establish a self-financing position.

26-17 An arbitrage portfolio is best described by which of the following statements?

(*a*) It is a self-financing position that requires the investor to invest zero money.

(*b*) It is a riskless position because the portfolio is perfectly hedged against losses from all relevant risk factors.

(*c*) The arbitrage portfolio yields a profit, with certainty.

(*d*) All the above are true.

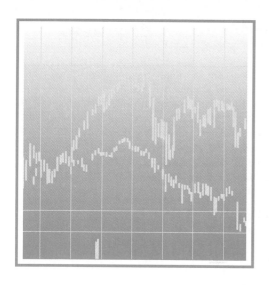

CHAPTER 27

INTERNATIONAL INVESTING

The 23 stock exchanges around the world listed in Table 4-5, page 113, can be viewed as components of one global stock market. Telecommunication networks that disseminate news instantly enable the participants in this worldwide stock market to enjoy equal access to all public information. Figure 27-1 illustrates the stock market crash of October 1987; the simultaneity of the crash in each of these foreign markets provides evidence that the world's disparate stock markets are all part of one global market.

Stock around the Clock   Most security exchanges around the world close at night. This does not mean that the global market is closed; it is always daytime in some part of the world. Since the most actively traded securities (for instance, IBM, Nestlé, Sony, and Exxon) are traded in markets around the world, the market for these securities is open around the world and around the clock.

New York, Tokyo, and London have the three largest financial markets in the world. Indexes of these markets, along with other international financial markets, are

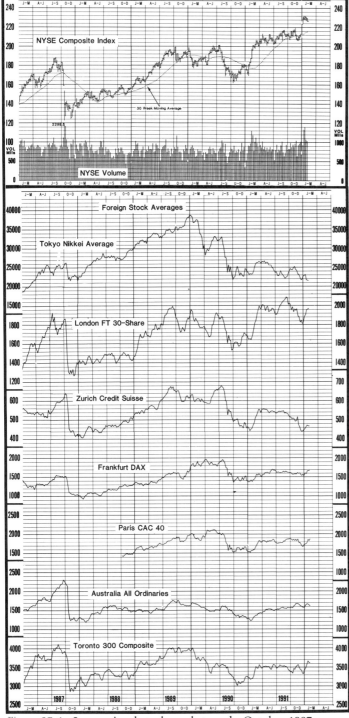

Figure 27-1 International stock market crash, October 1987.
(*Source:* Daily Action Stock Charts, June 16, 1989, published by
Trendline, a division of Standard & Poor's Corporation.)

Stock Market Indexes

EXCHANGE	3/26/92 CLOSE	NET CHG	PCT CHG
Tokyo Nikkei Average	19885.49 −	341.29	− 1.69
Tokyo Topix Index	1446.76 −	2.02	− 0.14
London FT 30-share	1938.3 +	8.4	+ 0.44
London 100-share	2472.2 +	7.3	+ 0.30
London Gold Mines	1938.3 +	8.4	+ 0.44
Frankfurt DAX	1719.02 +	2.76	+ 0.16
Zurich Credit Suisse	479.6 −	0.1	− 0.02
Paris CAC 40	1934.75 +	6.47	+ 0.34
Milan Stock Index	978 −	4	− 0.41
Amsterdam ANP-CBS General	205.0 +	0.2	+ 0.10
Stockholm Affarsvarlden	1004.10 −	5.2	− 0.52
Brussels Bel-20 Index	1190.63 −	2.74	− 0.23
Australia All Ordinaries	1571.2 −	10.8	− 0.68
Hong Kong Hang Seng	5037.71 −	14.52	− 0.30
Singapore Straits Times	1439.72 −	9.94	− 0.69
Johannesburg J'burg Gold	1124 −	16	− 1.40
Madrid General Index	255.57 +	1.52	+ 0.60
Mexico I.P.C.	1907.29 +	6.67	+ 0.35
Toronto 300 Composite	3448.51 −	3.79	− 0.11
Euro, Aust, Far East MSCI-p	768.0 +	0.4	+ 0.05

p-Preliminary
na-Not available

	Mar 25	Mar 24	% This Year
U.S.	381.8	382.9	− 2.2
Britain	732.4	731.3	− 0.6
Canada	389.0	387.5	− 1.7
Japan	836.0	833.2	− 15.5
France	547.5	538.4	+ 9.4
Germany	264.8	263.6	+ 8.8
Hong Kong	3686.9	3702.5	+ 19.1
Switzerland	224.3	223.7	+ 9.4
Australia	338.7	339.2	− 3.6
World index	493.0	492.0	− 7.9

Figure 27-2 Newspaper excerpt showing daily values of stock market indexes from around the world. (*a*) Foreign stock market indexes; (*b*) Morgan-Stanley indexes.

published regularly in the financial press.[1] Figure 27-2 presents one such newspaper listing. Market indicators like these help keep geographically segregated markets linked economically. Nevertheless, the cultures and institutions of the countries of the world differ sufficiently to create some interesting disparities among their markets.

International Investment Risks Multinational investors face the same risks that domestic investors face plus some additional ones—international marketability risk, international political risk, foreign exchange risk, international legal risks, and inferior information risk.

Most foreign markets are not so efficient and liquid as the securities markets in the United States. Furthermore, there are added legal risks in some foreign countries—for example, security price manipulation that is illegal in the United States is permitted in some foreign markets.

International political risk and foreign exchange risk are usually interrelated. Many of the foreign exchange rates in the world are fixed by the governments of the countries that issue the currencies, rather than being freely floating exchange rates determined by supply and demand. However, foreign investors can use currency options and foreign exchange futures contracts to reduce their foreign exchange risk via hedging.

---

[1] For empirical estimates of the value of a worldwide market portfolio and the rates of return it yields, see R. G. Ibbotson, L. B. Siegel, and K. S. Love, "World Wealth: Market Values and Returns," *Journal of Portfolio Management*, vol. 12 (Fall), no. 1, 1985, pp. 1–11. Also, see R. G. Ibbotson, R. C. Carr, and A. W. Robinson, "International Equity and Bond Returns," *Financial Analysts Journal*, vol. 38, no. 4, July-August 1982, pp. 61–83. Some of this material is in chap. 5 of this book. For empirical bond return data see M. Adler, "Global Fixed-Income Management," *Financial Analysts Journal*, vol. 39, no. 5, September-October 1983, pp. 44–50.

The risk of being forced to compete against foreign investors who probably have faster access to public information about their country, who may have inside information, and who may even be able to manipulate security prices in their country places the outside investor at a disadvantage. Some large international banks (like Morgan-Guaranty, Citibank, and Bank of America) and other institutional investors have foreign offices that manage investments in the host country and are partly staffed by nationals of the foreign country. Such foreign nationals not only make low-cost employees, they may also be able to gather valuable information for their employers.

Although the dissimilarities between the securities markets of the world create risks, they also provide opportunities to benefit from diversification.

27-1 Multinational Investing and Efficient Portfolios

The portfolio analysis tools of Chapter 24 are useful for evaluating the possibilities available through multinational investing.

International Portfolio Analysis

A portfolio of marketable securities diversified between two countries would have an expected return that is determined by the expected returns in each country and the proportion of assets invested in each country, as specified in the equation below:

$$E(r_p) = xE(r_1) + (1 - x)E(r_2) \qquad (27\text{-}1)$$

where $E(r_p)$ = expected return from an international portfolio of securities from
   countries 1 and 2

   $E(r_i)$ = expected return from country i (in this case, i = 1 or 2)

   x = proportion of the international portfolio's assets
   invested in country 1, $1.0 > x > 0$

   $1 - x$ = proportion of assets invested in country 2

The variance of this two-country portfolio $\text{VAR}(r_p)$ would be determined by the variances of returns from each country, the proportion of assets invested in each country, and the correlation between both countries' returns, as shown below.

$$\text{VAR}(r_p) = x^2\text{VAR}(r_1) + (1 - x)^2\text{VAR}(r_2) + 2(x)(1 - x)\,\sigma_1\sigma_2\rho_{1,2} \qquad (27\text{-}2)$$

where $\text{VAR}(r_1) = \sigma_1^2$ = variance of returns for an investor in country 1

   $\text{VAR}(r_2) = \sigma_1^2$ = variance of returns in country 2 for an investor in country 1
   includes no foreign exchange risk because the exchange rates
   are presumed to be pegged

   $\rho_{1,2}$ = correlation coefficient between the two countries' investment returns

Computation Box 27-1 illustrates the risk reduction benefits available to the international investor as the correlation between the two countries' rates of return is

Box 27-1

COMPUTATION: The Impact of Intercountry Return Correlations on the Variance from an International Portfolio

$E(r_1) = E(r_2) = 10\% =$ expected returns in the two countries

$\sigma_1^2 = \sigma_1^2 = 16\% =$ variance of returns in both countries

$x = (1 - x) = .50 =$ proportion of assets invested in each country

$E(r_p) = xE(r_1) + (1 - x)E(r_2)$

(27-1)

$E(r_p) = (.5)(.1) + (1.0 - .5)(.1) = .1 = 10.0\%$ (27-1a)

$VAR(r_p) = x_1^2 \, VAR(r_1) + (1 - x)^2 \, VAR(r_2) +$
$\qquad + 2(x)(1 - x)\sigma_1\sigma_2\rho_{1,2}$

(27-2)

$VAR(r_p) = (.5)^2(.16) + (1.0 - .5)^2(.16) +$
$\qquad + 2(.5)(1.0 - .5) \sqrt{(.16)}\sqrt{(.16)}\rho_{1,2}$

(27-2a)

$VAR(r_p) = .08 + .08(\rho_{1,2})$ (27-2b)

The following table illustrates the variance reduction:

If the correlation is:	+1.0	+.50	0.0	−.50	−1.0
the VAR(r_p) will be:	.16	.12	.08	.04	0

varied. The intercountry correlation is important in multinational diversification. Table 27-1 presents empirical estimates of the correlations between common stock portfolios in the United States and various foreign countries that can be used to estimate the potential for risk reduction. Table 5-4 shows the intercountry correlations between various categories of foreign investment. Investors can insert the correlations from Tables 27-1 and 5-4 into the analytical format suggested in Computation Box 27-1 to analyze international portfolios.

Table 27-1 shows that estimates of the correlation between the U.S. stock market and foreign stock markets have ranged from as high as .8598 with the Canadian market to as low as −.26 with the Japanese market. (The correlation coefficients in Table 27-1 contain sampling error, as do all statistics. For example, the correlations between the United States and Belgium range from .1080 to 0.83, and the correlations between the United States and Japan from −.26 to 0.5279.) Applying the correlations from Table 27-1 in the risk analysis model shown in Box 27-1 shows that equal investments in Canada and the United States, for example, would produce a portfolio variance of only 14.88 percent (assuming $\rho = .8598$) versus 16.0 percent for an investment that was limited to the United States. Equal investments in the United

Table 27-1
Summary of Correlations between
U.S. and Foreign Markets

	Sources of data*					
	(1)	(2)	(3)	(4)	(5)	(6)
Canada	.7025		.8598	.4895		.263
U.K.	.2414	.578	.5836	.6420	.26	.225
West Germany	.3008	.335	.4062	.4337	.43	.141
France	.1938	.542	.4139	.1820	.34	.196
Italy	.1465				.09	
Belgium	.1080	.621			.83	
Netherlands	.2107	.583			.53	.189
Japan	.1149		.1796	.5279	−.26	.107
Australia	.0584		.4311	.6626		.225
South Africa	−.1620				.08	
Switzerland		.68				.201
Spain			.0098	.3230		
Venezuela					−.17	
Austria					.26	
Denmark					.19	
Mexico					.02	
New Zealand					.08	

* The data given in the numbered columns were taken from the following correspondingly numbered sources:

	Author	Sampled period	Publication
(1)	H. Grubel	1959–1966, annual	1968 Am. Econ. Rev.
(2)	B. Jacquillat and B. Solnik	1974–1976, monthly	1978 J. of Portfolio Management
(3)	A. M. Rugman	1951–1975, annual	1977 J. of Econ. and Bus.
(4)	A. M. Rugman	1970–1975, monthly	1977 J. of Econ. and Bus.
(5)	H. Levy and M. Sarnat	1951–1967, annual	1970 Am. Econ. Rev.
(6)	Cho, Eun, and Senbet	1973–1983, monthly	1986 J. of Finance

States and Japan could have lowered the portfolio's variance to only 5.92 percent (assuming $\rho = -.26$). These results suggest that international diversification could have benefited U.S. investors—and, foreign investors as well.[2]

[2] Monthly rates of return from foreign investments in common stocks can be calculated with the equation below after the prices are processed to reflect changes in foreign exchange rates:

$$\text{Effective monthly} \atop \text{rate of return} = \left[\frac{(\text{annual cash dividend} \div 12) + p_t}{p_{t-1}} \right]^{12} - 1.0$$

where p_t is the market price of the foreign security (or foreign stock market index) existing at the end of time period t.

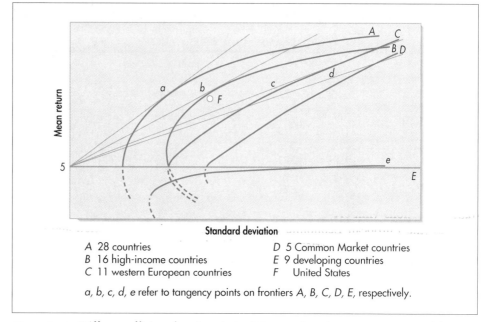

A 28 countries
B 16 high-income countries
C 11 western European countries

D 5 Common Market countries
E 9 developing countries
F United States

a, b, c, d, e refer to tangency points on frontiers *A, B, C, D, E*, respectively.

Figure 27-3 Different efficient frontiers derived from various investment opportunities. (*Source:* H. Levy and M. Sarnat, "International Diversification of Investment Portfolios," *American Economic Review,* September 1970, pp. 668–675.)

The International Investor's Efficient Frontier

It is possible to analyze the effect of multinational diversification in terms of the efficient frontier (from Chapter 24). As might be expected, as the number of countries in which investments are made increases, more desirable efficient frontiers become attainable.

Point *F* in Figure 27-3 indicates the risk level and rate of return for the U.S. stock market alone. Efficient frontier E shows the risk and return combinations available from investing only in developing countries; as the figure shows, this option is dominated by all the other investment alternatives. Even though point *F* in the figure represents a portfolio that is fully diversified within the United States, this portfolio is not efficient in an international context. Efficient frontier D indicates the efficient frontier if investments are limited to the five countries that were members of the European Economic Community (EEC) in 1970. If the investment universe is expanded beyond the EEC to include all western European countries, efficient frontier C becomes attainable. When all high-income countries are considered, the possibilities expand to efficient frontier B. Finally, when all countries, including the developing countries, are allowed into the solution, efficient frontier A is reached. **Multinational efficient frontier** A dominates all other investment opportunities in Figure 27-3.

This analysis suggests that the dominant portfolio in every risk class tends to be composed of investments from many different countries.[3] However, barriers to capital flows may make this theoretically optimal portfolio impossible to obtain.

Reasons for Low Intercountry Market Correlations

The key factor that improves investment opportunities in the international capital market is the low correlations among various countries' securities markets. Intercountry correlations are low because different countries and their economic prospects are not tied closely together. Countries have different political systems (capitalism versus socialism), different currencies (French francs and Japanese yen), different foreign exchange regulations (fixed versus floating exchange rates), different trade restrictions (import and export limitations and tariffs), different political alliances (the European Economic Community and the United States), and other distinctions that serve as barriers to international trade.

Furthermore, at any given time different countries may find themselves at different phases in their business cycle (for example, the United States might be starting a recession just as another country is ending one); interest rates, monetary policies, and/or fiscal policies differ (for instance, one country may have an inflationary federal budget deficit as another country has a budget surplus and deflation); military postures can diverge (such as peace versus active aggression); or foreign exchange rates can change (because of differing intercountry inflation rates or governmental decrees). As a result of these dissimilar situations, different countries' security markets are seldom highly synchronized (or highly positively correlated) with one another.[4]

27-2 Multinational Diversification

Barriers to international investment can actually enhance the benefits typically obtained from multinational diversification. These "beneficial" barriers may include restrictions on currency flows, lack of English translations of foreign financial statements, lack of familiarity with local accounting conventions, social and cultural

---

[3] For readings about international investing see Carl Beidleman, ed., *Handbook of International Investing* (Chicago: Probus, 1987); in particular, see Raj Aggarwal, "Alternatives for International Portfolio Diversification," pp. 57–96. For a multiperiod study of the benefits of international diversification see Robert R. Grauer and Nils H. Hakansson, "Gains from International Diversification: 1968–85 Returns on Portfolios of Stocks and Bonds," *Journal of Finance,* vol. 42, no. 3, July 1987, pp. 721–739.

[4] For empirical risk and return statistics from various investments in foreign countries see Yasushi Hamao, "Japanese Stocks, Bonds, Bills and Inflation, 1973–1987," *Journal of Portfolio Management* (Winter), 1989, pp. 20–26. Also see Daniel Wydler, "Swiss Stocks, Bonds and Inflation, 1926–1987," *Journal of Portfolio Management* (Winter), 1989, pp. 27–32.

Box 27-2

DEFINITION: Homogeneous Markets

Homogeneous markets have identical business practices, economic conditions, laws, languages, and social customs. Multinational diversification will not offer any beneficial risk-reducing opportunities over domestic diversification if the multinational markets are perfectly homogeneous.

differences, government restrictions on foreign ownership, markets where significant insider trading is allowed to affect security prices, and markets that are thin with respect to volume of trading or number of traders.[5] When such barriers exist, they cause **international market segmentation.** If such barriers to international diversification did not exist, we would have homogeneous markets.

Heterogeneous markets have barriers to entry that create international market segmentation and international investment risks. However, these troublesome barriers to entry make international diversification superior to domestic diversification.

Of course, the diversification possibilities are bounded because investors have limited funds. Consequently, it is worthwhile to have guidelines for diversifying in foreign countries. One such set of guidelines was prepared by Bruno Solnik. Using weekly returns from eight different countries over 5 consecutive years, Solnik calculated the proportion of variance that could be eliminated from portfolios by increasing the number of assets in the portfolio. For each country, portfolios of various sizes were constructed from randomly selected stocks, and the variance of these portfolios was calculated. These variances were averaged for each portfolio size.[6]

In each country, average portfolio variance declined rapidly until portfolios of approximately 15 randomly selected securities were attained; after that, little additional reduction in the average portfolio's variance was achieved by adding more securities. (Similar results were reported for simple diversification across domestic U.S. securities, as shown in Figure 24-1.) Panels (*a*) through (*c*) of Figure 27-4 illustrate some risk reduction possibilities suggested by Solnik's study.

To determine how best to diversify, Solnik examined three strategies of selecting different numbers of randomly selected common stocks. Stocks were selected (1) across countries, (2) across industries, and (3) across both countries and industries. Figure 27-4*a*, *b*, and *c* shows that selection across countries and across both countries and industries are superior to selecting only across industries. These experiments

[5] For more details about international investment risks see Bruno Solnik, *International Investments*, 2d ed. (Reading, Mass.: Addison-Wesley, 1991). Also see Gunter Dufey and Ian Giddy, *The International Money Market* (Englewood Cliffs, N.J.: Prentice-Hall, 1978), and Vihang Errunza and Etienne Losq, "International Asset Pricing under Mild Segmentation: Theory and Text," *Journal of Finance*, March 1985, pp. 105–124.

[6] Solnik was essentially extending the methodology developed by John L. Evans and Stephen H. Archer in "Diversification and the Reduction of Dispersion: Empirical Analysis," *Journal of Finance*, December 1968, pp. 761–767. The Evans-Archer results were presented in Figure 24-1.

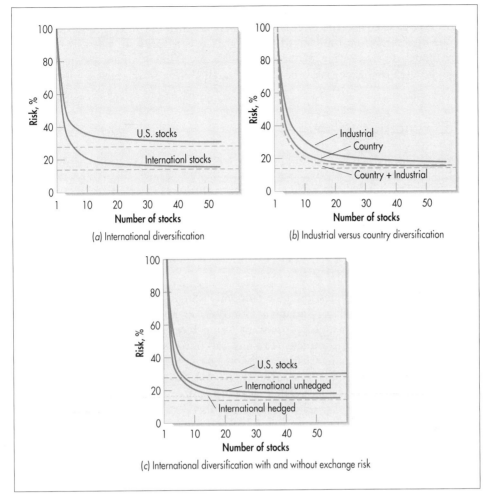

Figure 27-4 Illustrated results of different diversification strategies. (*Source:* Bruno H. Solnik, "Why Not Diversify Internationally?" *Financial Analysts Journal,* July-August 1974, pp. 48–54.)

with simple diversification suggest that portfolios of about 15 common stocks diversified randomly across countries will reduce total risk down to the undiversifiable, systematic level. (One simple way to diversify internationally without bumping into problems with foreign languages and foreign accounting conventions is to buy shares in one large corporation that is active multinationally. Ford Motor Company has over 30 percent of its sales outside the United States, for instance. Sony is a Japanese corporation that has 35 percent of its sales in the United States. Unfortunately, research suggests that this approach is not a powerful way to reduce risk.[7])

An important consideration for investors in foreign securities is foreign exchange risk. Figure 27-4c indicates that a substantial portion of the value of multinational

[7] See Bertrand Jacquillat and Bruno Solnik, "Multinationals Are Poor Tools for Diversification," *Journal of Portfolio Management,* vol. 4 (Winter), no. 2, 1978, pp. 8–11.

diversification is not affected by foreign exchange losses. The portfolio hedged against foreign exchange losses does have lower risk than the unhedged portfolio, but the rate of return from the hedged portfolio is also reduced. In short, the value of international diversification exists either with or without a concurrent currency hedge. Foreign exchange risk is considered more closely in the next section.

27-3   Foreign Exchange Risk

Fluctuating foreign exchange rates can have a significant effect on investors' returns. If a domestic investor and a foreign investor put the same amount in the same security at the same time, they will nevertheless earn different rates of return over identical holding periods if the foreign exchange rate fluctuates. The case considers the fortunes of two such investors.

Hedging Foreign Exchange Risk

Many foreign exchange rates fluctuate randomly.[8] Steps can be taken to diminish or even eliminate the resulting foreign exchange risk. Some multinational investors hedge their foreign exchange positions by using foreign exchange options and/or foreign exchange futures contracts. (Put and call options were discussed in Chapter 21, and futures contracts in Chapter 22.)

In 1983 the Philadelphia Stock Exchange (PHLX) started trading listed options on the major foreign currencies. The PHLX lists put and call options on Australian dollars, British pounds, Canadian dollars, German deutsche marks (DM), Japanese yen, Swiss francs, and the European Currency Unit (ECU).[9] More recently, the Chicago Board of Options Exchange (CBOE) also began listing currency options.[10]

For decades before currency options were listed at exchanges, banks wishing to hedge their foreign exchange risks bought forward contracts in an informal interbank market. This informal forward market in large, tailor-made foreign exchange contracts still exists, but only large banks and selected clients have access to it. In 1972 currency hedgers were presented with an alternative to the illiquid forward contracts; the International Monetary Market (IMM) in Chicago started trading futures contracts at a commodity exchange. The IMM trades futures on British pounds, Canadian dollars, German deutsche marks, Japanese yen, and Swiss francs.

---

[8] Gunter Dufey and Ian Giddy, "The Random Behavior of Flexible Exchange Rates: Implications for Forecasting," *Journal of International Business Studies,* vol. 6 (Spring), no. 1, 1975, pp. 1–32.

[9] The ECU is a weighted average composite of the currencies of the European countries that are members of the European Monetary Cooperation Fund.

[10] A pamphlet about the PHLX may be obtained free by writing to the Federal Reserve Bank of Philadelphia, Research Dept., Ten Independence Mall, Philadelphia, PA 19106, and asking for "New Markets in Foreign Currency Options," by Brian Gendreau, *Business Review,* July-August 1984, pp. 3–12. Alternatively, contact the PHLX and/or the CBOE directly for free information.

Fluctuating Exchange Rates Cause Different Returns

◁▷

The Domestic Investor's Return Let r_d denote the single-period rate of return that a domestic investor earns after paying for a domestic security with the local currency. The familiar single-period rate of return [based on Equations (1-2) and (1-3)] is restated as Equation (27-3) to define formally a **domestic investor's return.**

$$r_d = \frac{p_t - p_{t-1} + c_t}{p_{t-1}} \qquad (27\text{-}3)$$

where p_t = market price of a security at the end of time period t

p_{t-1} = price at the end of the preceding period (or, equivalently, at the beginning of period t)

c_t = cash flow, if any, from cash dividends or coupon interest received during time period t.

If a German invests 50 deutsche marks (DM) in Volkswagen common stock that pays no cash dividends and then sells it one period later for DM55, the German earns r_d = (DM55 − DM50 + 0)/DM50 = 10%. However, if an American made the same investment, it would be a different story.

The Foreign Investor's Return An American investing U.S. dollars in Volkswagen stock would be a foreign investor. A **foreign investor's return** is measured by

$$r_f = \frac{x_t p_t - x_{t-1} p_{t-1} + x_t c_t}{x_{t-1} p_{t-1}} \qquad (27\text{-}4)$$

where x_t stands for the DM-to-dollars exchange rate at time period t, and the price and cash flow variables are defined as they were above, in Equation (27-3). If the foreign exchange rate equals x = DM2/\$1 at time $t-1$, then an American investor must pay 50 cents for

1 DM. This translates into a purchase price of $(x_{t-1})(p_{t-1})$ = (.50)(DM50) = \$25 per share of Volkswagen stock. If the exchange rate is invariant, the American will earn the same 10 percent rate of return from the German security that the German investor earned.

But suppose that between time $t-1$ and time t the dollar depreciates relative to the DM so that when the American investor sells the Volkswagen stock the exchange rate is x_t = .55. The American will then make a 10 percent gain on the investment in the German currency, as shown below.

$$r_c = \frac{x_t - x_{t-1}}{x_{t-1}} = \frac{.55 - .50}{.50} = 10\% \qquad (27\text{-}5)$$

where x_t stands for the DM-to-dollars exchange rate at time period t, and r_c denotes the one-period rate of return from the American's investment in the DM currency. Under these more favorable circumstances, the American investor can sell the German security for $(x_t)(p_t)$ = (.55)(DM55) = \$30.25. Equation (27-4) shows that in this case the American investor's total rate of return is 21 percent = [(.55)(DM55) − (.50)(DM50) + 0]/[(.50)(DM50)], before commissions, fees, and taxes.

The Components of Total Return Manipulating Equations (27-3), (27-4), and (27-5) algebraically results in Equation (27-6), a statement of total return from foreign investment r_f.

$$r_f = r_d + r_c + r_d r_c \qquad (27\text{-}6)$$

Equation (27-6) allows us to decompose the American investor's 21 percent total return from the foreign investment into a pure gain on the Volkswagen stock of r_d = 10% plus a gain of the investment in the DM currency of r_c = 10% plus a cross product of $(r_d)(r_c)$ = (.1)(.1) = 1%.

The MidAmerica Commodity Exchange in Chicago lists futures contracts on some of the same currencies, but the units are smaller.[11]

27-4 American Depository Receipts

Trading in multinational securities can be complicated, and the brokerage commissions can be expensive. To transact international security trades, some brokerage houses charge double the commission rate for executing domestic orders. Other brokers simply refuse to execute multinational transactions. While investors may choose to use a full-service brokerage house—which charges full-service commission rates—they may opt instead to purchase international securities another way. Major banks with large international departments and with a network of foreign banking offices (like Citibank and Morgan-Guaranty) issue **American depository receipts,** or **ADRs,** at commission rates that compare favorably with the rates charged for ordinary domestic transactions.

Banks issue ADRs by purchasing securities in a foreign corporation for domestic U.S. clients. The bank keeps these securities in the vault of its foreign branch, registered in the bank's name, and the client is issued a marketable ADR stating that the bank is holding securities for whoever buys the ADR. For example, you might purchase an ADR showing that Morgan-Guaranty Bank is holding 100 shares of Sony common stock in its vault at the bank's Tokyo branch. The bank collects cash dividends or coupon interest for whoever owns the ADR and either reinvests the money or converts it into U.S. dollars and pays it to the current ADR investor— whichever is requested. ADRs are available for a modest fee of a penny or two out of each security's cash payment, and they are as liquid as the underlying security.

Although most of the corporations for which banks issue ADRs are large and reputable, these security issuers enjoy a kind of diplomatic immunity from most of the regulations of the U.S. Securities and Exchange Commission. However, the immunity has not hurt the marketability of their securities. Every day hundreds of thousands of foreign shares represented by ADRs are traded in the organized security exchanges and over the counter in the United States. In fact, sometimes more shares of a popular stock (like Sony) are traded using ADRs in the United States than are traded in the issuer's home country.[12]

---

[11] For more details about currency futures and options, see one of the following textbooks: Don M. Chance, *Options and Futures,* 2d ed. (Orlando, Fla.: Dryden, 1991), chap. 13; David A. Dubofsky, *Options and Financial Futures* (New York: McGraw-Hill 1992), chap. 18 and 19; Franklin R. Edwards and Cindy Ma, *Futures and Options* (New York: McGraw-Hill 1992), chap. 14; R. W. Kolb, *Understanding Futures Markets,* 3d ed. (Miami, Fla.: Kolb, 1991), chap. 11; John F. Marshall, *Futures and Options Contracting* (Cincinnati, Ohio: South-Western Publishing, 1989), chap. 11; and Todd E. Petzel, *Financial Futures and Options* (Westport, Conn.: Quorum, 1989), chap. 6.

[12] For more details about ADRs, see D. T. Officer and J. R. Hoffmeister, "ADRs: A Substitute for the Real Thing?" *Journal of Portfolio Management,* vol. 13 (Winter), no. 2, 1987, pp. 61–67. Also see Leonard Rosenthal et al., "An Empirical Test of the Efficiency of the ADR Market," *Journal of Banking and Finance,* vol. 7, no. 1, March 1983, pp. 17–29.

ADR holders receive all the benefits of direct ownership, but without the costs of additional brokerage commissions, without losing any marketability, and without the bother of collecting cash dividends in a foreign currency.

665

Chapter 27
International
Investing

ADR holders receive all the benefits of direct ownership, but without the costs of additional brokerage commissions, without losing any marketability, and without the bother of collecting cash dividends in a foreign currency.

27-5 Global Investment Companies

Four main approaches can be taken to investing multinationally. As we have seen, investing in foreign stocks, investing in multinational corporations, and investing in ADRs each offer unique benefits. These three were discussed above. The fourth approach to international investing is using global investment companies. (Alternatives to international common stock investing are international bonds, real estate, and gold.)[13]

Global investment company shares are like mutual fund shares. However, the shares of foreign investment companies require additional analysis to take foreign exchange risks into account. Research indicates that, like the American mutual funds, the global investment companies do not seem to outperform buying a randomly selected portfolio like the Standard & Poor's 500 Stocks Composite Index.[14]

The investment objectives of global investment companies tend to fall into three categories—investing only in stocks, investing only in bonds, or investing only in securities from specific countries. The Korea Fund and the Taiwan Fund, for instance, are closed-end common stock investment companies that invest only in Korean and Taiwanese enterprises, respectively. There are many **country funds,** and their popularity is growing. International investors can construct portfolios of different country fund shares to achieve whatever goals they seek.

Summary

Telecommunications networks have given investors around the world equal access to the information that determines security prices, and also provided investors the opportunity to trade securities listed in foreign lands. As a result, we have a global securities market.

In spite of their links, the securities exchanges around the world are still heterogeneous in many respects. Foreign exchange risk, different social and business customs, and many other significant disparities create barriers to entry for foreign investors. These barriers reduce the correlations between the security returns from

[13] See H. Levy and Zvi Lerman, "The Benefits of International Diversification in Bonds," *Financial Analysts Journal,* September-October 1988, pp. 56–64; J. R. Webb and J. H. Rubens, "Portfolio Considerations in the Valuation of Real Estate," *AREUEA Journal* (Fall), 1986, and R. Aggarwal and Luc A. Soenen, "The Nature and Efficiency of the Gold Market," *Journal of Portfolio Management,* vol. 14, 1988, pp. 18–21.

[14] See Ramesh P. Rao and Raj Aggarwal, "Performance of U.S.-Based International Mutual Funds," *Akron Business and Economic Review* (Winter), 1987, pp. 98–107. Also see R. E. Cumby and J. D. Glen, "Evaluating the Performance of International Mutual Funds," *Journal of Finance,* vol. 45, no. 2, June 1990, pp. 497–521.

different countries and make international diversification desirable. The risk-reducing benefits from international diversification usually more than offset the disadvantageous risks that international investors face. Multinational investing opportunities offer a more dominant efficient frontier from which to choose than is available through domestic diversification.

A foreign investor can get a highly diversified portfolio of foreign securities without doing security analysis by buying shares in a mutual fund that invests only in foreign securities. More aggressive international investors can buy country funds, pay U.S. dollars for ADRs on stocks issued by foreign corporations, or buy foreign exchange and invest directly in foreign securities. The more aggressive approaches are riskier than simply paying dollars for shares in an internationally diversified mutual fund.

Further Reading

Fabozzi, Frank J., and Irving M. Pollack, *The Handbook of Fixed Income Securities*, 2d ed. (Homewood, Ill.: Dow Jones–Irwin, 1987).
> *Chapters 49 through 52, inclusive, present insightful information about managing different types of international bond portfolios.*

Grabbe, J. Orlin, *International Financial Markets* (Amsterdam, Neth.: Elsevier, 1986).
> *This MBA-level textbook explores foreign currencies, currency futures, currency options, currency markets, interest rate and currency swaps, and the Eurobond and other international bond markets using no math beyond algebra.*

Institute of Chartered Financial Analysts, *International Bonds and Currencies* (Homewood, Ill.: Dow Jones–Irwin, 1986).
> *This book is useful to someone studying for the Chartered Financial Analysts (CFA) exam.*

Roll, Richard, "The International Crash of 1987," *Financial Analysts Journal*, September-October 1988, pp. 19–35.
> *This statistical study of the way the October 1987 stock market crash affected 23 different stock markets around the world provides insights into the workings of each of these markets.*

Solnik, Bruno, *International Investments*, 2d ed. (Reading, Mass.: Addison-Wesley, 1991).
> *This 12-chapter textbook about international investing introduces the relevant topics and provides good references as to where additional detailed studies can be found. Elementary algebra and statistics are used.*

Questions and Problems

Essay Questions

27-1 How might a multinational investor based in the United States use foreign exchange futures to hedge against the risk that the foreign exchange rate might change? (*Hint:* Some material about financial futures is in Chapter 22, but outside research will be beneficial.)

27-2 Which risks are specific to international investing? Stated differently, which factors, in addition to the usual domestic investment risks, should be of particular concern to the multinational investor?

27-3 What induces investors to invest internationally even though they face additional risks that are specific to multinational investing?

27-4   Does every international investment opportunity provide the investor with new investment opportunities that dominate the old opportunities in a risk-return analysis? Explain.

27-5   What factors explain why the intercountry correlations between securities markets are low? (*Hint:* You may benefit from consulting an international economics or an international finance textbook.)

27-6   Clifford Davis just bought a Nissan 300Z Turbo and is so impressed by the car that he wants to invest in the Nissan Corporation's stock. However, Nissan is a Japanese company, and Clifford does not want to get involved in foreign exchange and the other administrative problems that might arise from a foreign investment. How can Clifford buy shares in Nissan without getting involved in international complications?

27-7   Victoria Jones is interested in multinational diversification but does not have the time or expertise to select individual foreign assets in which to invest. Is there some way she can diversify internationally?

27-8   Since the intercountry correlation between securities markets plays such an important role in international diversification, consider the trend in the multinational correlation statistics. Do you think that, in general, these correlations should increase, stay the same, or decrease with the passage of time? Explain why.

Problems

27-9   Françoise LeClerq is a fashion designer in New York City who offers investment advice to her twin brother François, an automotive engineer in Paris. Françoise and François both simultaneously bought stock in Michelin Tire at the price of 180 French francs (FF) per share. At the time of the purchase the exchange ratio was $x_0 = \$1/FF6 = \$.1666$ per franc. (*a*) How many dollars per share did Françoise pay for her stock? How many FF per share did François pay for his?

The expert advice of Françoise enabled them to sell their Michelin stock for FF200 2 months later; they received no cash dividends. At the time of the sale the dollar had depreciated relative to the FF; the exchange ratio was $x_1 = \$1/FF5 = \$0.20$ per franc. (*b*) What rates of return did François and his sister earn over the 2 months they owned Michelin? (*c*) How did the change in the exchange rate affect Françoise?

27-10   Assume the expected rate of return and standard deviation of returns from investing British pounds in Barclays Bank, which is headquartered in England, is 10 percent and .2, respectively. The pound has been appreciating relative to the dollar at a rate of 5 percent per year with a standard deviation of .1. Also assume that the correlation coefficient between the returns from Barclays stock and the British pound is .5. How much return and total risk should a U.S. investor that pays British pounds for stock in Barclays Bank expect? [*Hint:* Use Equations (27-1), (27-2), (27-4), and (27-5).]

27-11   While working as a chemist at a laboratory in New York, Rolf Kierulf won $100,000 in the state lottery and decided he wanted to invest in the common stock of his previous employer, Hoffman LaRoche, a large pharmaceutical corporation headquartered in Switzerland. Rolf bought Swiss francs (SF) in the United States at the rate of $x_0 = \$1/SF1.5 = \$0.666$ per franc. He purchased Hoffman LaRoche stock at a price of SF150,000 per share. (*a*) How many dollars per share did Rolf pay for one share of the stock?

Rolf sold the stock for SF160,000 three months later without receiving any cash dividends. He converted the proceeds of the sale to dollars at a rate of $x_1 = \$1/1.6 = \$.625$ per

SF. (*b*) What rate of return did Rolf earn over the 3-month holding period? (*c*) How did the dollar-to-SF exchange rate affect Rolf's return?

27-12 The stock in King's Public Limited Corporation (PLC) is currently selling for 30 pounds per share on the London Stock Exchange. A year earlier the stock sold for 25 pounds. During the past year the stock paid no dividend. The current exchange rate between the pound and the dollar is $1.25 per pound. However, a year earlier, it was $1.15 per pound. Determine the rate of return from King's during the past year for (*a*) a U.S. investor and (*b*) a British investor.

27-13 Currently, the Japanese yen is trading at $0.0076923 per yen. A year ago the yen was trading at $0.0083333 per yen. If the return on Japanese stocks had been 25 percent last year, what would be the net return to a U.S. investor?

The following international security market returns are to be used with Problems 27-14 through 27-18:

Year	U.K.	Japan	Canada	Australia	U.S.
1981	47.99%	46.55%	14.13%	−1.54%	18.16%
1982	3.93	126.56	33.12	21.06	17.71
1983	−23.44	−20.13	−3.11	−12.06	−18.68
1984	−50.33	−15.65	−26.52	−32.97	−27.77
1985	115.06	19.84	15.07	50.71	37.49
1986	−12.55	25.8	9.71	−10.00	26.68
1987	56.49	15.7	−1.37	11.25	−3.03
1988	14.63	53.33	20.55	22.24	8.53
1989	22.2	−11.69	52.52	43.44	24.18
1990	38.8	29.7	22.00	52.20	33.22

27-14 (*a*) Determine the correlation of returns for the United States, the United Kingdom, and Japan over the 10-year period. (*b*) Determine the standard deviation of returns for the three countries over the same period of time. (*Hint:* You might want to use a computer or calculator to calculate the statistics; see end-of-book appendixes A and B.)

27-15 (*a*) Determine the correlation between the returns from Australia and Canada over the 10-year period. (*b*) Also determine the standard deviation of returns over the same time period.

27-16 With the information generated in Problem 27-14, determine the expected return and risk (as measured by the standard deviation) for a portfolio of 25 percent U.K., 25 percent Japanese, and 50 percent U.S. stocks. Assume the historical means, standard deviations, and correlation coefficients are the expected values. *Note:* Outside research will be required to find the risk formula for a 3-asset portfolio.

27-17 Using the information generated in Problem 27-15, determine the expected return and standard deviation of return for a portfolio of 40 percent Australian and 60 percent Canadian stocks. Again, assume that the historical statistics are the expected values.

27-18 Using the information generated in Problems 27-14 and 27-15, determine the standard deviation of returns for a portfolio of 50 percent U.S. and 50 percent Canadian stocks.

27-19   The following question is from the 1987, level I Chartered Financial Analyst (CFA) exam. This question lets you preview questions that have been on the CFA exam.

Unique risks are associated with international investing. Briefly describe *three* such risks. (5 minutes)

27-20   Exam question 12 from the 1987, level I Chartered Financial Analyst (CFA) exam follows. The question will require some additional reading to supplement the information in this textbook, but you should be able to figure out the answer to this question.

An investor in foreign currency bonds should view the prospects for return both in an absolute sense and relative to returns expected in the investor's domestic market. **Briefly discuss** *three* key issues that should be considered when analyzing the prospects for return on foreign currency bonds relative to returns expected on bonds in the investor's domestic market. (10 minutes)

Multiple Choice Questions

27-21   Differences between intercountry rate-of-return correlations result from which of the following?
   (*a*) Different currencies and foreign exchange regulations
   (*b*) Different languages, accounting systems, and trade restrictions
   (*c*) Different political systems and, in the same vein, different political and military alliances
   (*d*) Both (*b*) and (*c*)
   (*e*) All the above

27-22   Bruno Solnik's empirical study of international diversification suggests which of the following conclusions?
   (*a*) Simple diversification within the borders of a single country does not appear to result in substantial risk reduction.
   (*b*) Every country in the world appears to have some level of systematic (or undiversifiable) risk, below which simple diversification cannot reduce the total risk of a portfolio.
   (*c*) Multinational investing reduced risk below domestic diversification for every country studied by Solnik.
   (*d*) Both (*b*) and (*c*).
   (*e*) All the above.

27-23   Suppose a U.S. investor converts dollars into French francs and then invests those francs in a French security that earns zero rate of return in terms of the French francs. Which of the following statements best describes this investor's dollar rate of return after liquidating the French investment and converting the francs back to dollars?
   (*a*) The U.S. investor earned zero rate of return on the dollars invested if the dollar-to-franc foreign exchange rate was invariant.
   (*b*) The U.S. investor earned a positive rate of return on the dollars invested if the French franc appreciated in value relative to the dollar during the investment period.
   (*c*) The U.S. investor earned a negative rate of return on the dollars invested if the dollar appreciated in value relative to the French franc during the life of the investment.
   (*d*) None of the above is correct.

27-24 Someone who invests in an ADR will receive which of the following?

(a) If the foreign investment happens to go bankrupt the international investor receives a legal claim on the bankrupt corporation's assets that is prior to the claim of the corporation's common stockholders who bought ordinary shares instead of ADRs.

(b) Coupon interest, as the foreign corporation pays it.

(c) Safe storage for the investor's securities.

(d) Both (b) and (c).

(e) Both (a) and (c).

27-25 Comparing common stock price indexes from different countries over a number of years reveals which of the following conclusions? (*Hint:* See Figure 27-1.)

(a) Most stock markets in the world reach their peaks in the same year, and most stock markets in the world reach their troughs in the same year.

(b) Because of lags in responding to different stimuli, the stock markets in a few countries will be at their peaks while other countries' stock markets will be between their peaks and troughs. Furthermore, sometimes the stock markets in a few countries will be at their troughs while other countries' stock markets will be between their peaks and troughs. But, the lags between countries is not so large that we commonly find some countries having peaks while others are having stock market troughs; some internationally systematic price movements are evident.

(c) In any given year approximately one-third of the countries' stock markets are peaking, about one-third are at their troughs, and about one-third are between their peaks and troughs. Furthermore, the large oil-producing nations always tend to lead the other nations through the turns of the business cycle.

(d) There is no discernible pattern to the way that different countries' stock markets behave.

27-26 Homogeneous security markets:

(a) Have all their securities denominated in the same currency even though the markets are located in different countries

(b) List almost all the same securities

(c) Provide no opportunities for international diversification that exceed those that can be attained with domestic diversification

(d) Are described by both (a) and (c)

(e) Are described by all the above

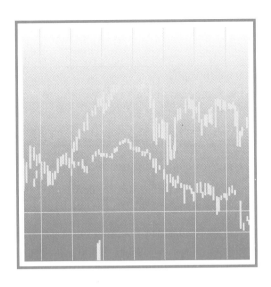

CHAPTER 28

INVESTMENT
PERFORMANCE
EVALUATION

Much of this text has focused on tools investors can use to manage their own
investments. In reality, most investors rely on hundreds of professional money
management firms known as **institutional investors** that manage hundreds of
billions of dollars of marketable securities. Some examples of institutional investors
are listed below.[1]

Chapter 28 presumes a knowledge of Chapters 1, 24, and 25.

[1] Details about the 300 largest institutional money managers are published annually in the July
issue of *Institutional Investor*, 488 Madison Ave., New York, NY 10022. See *Institutional
Investor,* July 1991, pp. 73–110, for instance.

671

- Investment advisory services:

  For average investors: Value Line sells investment advice via subscription and manages money through its mutual funds.

  For large investors: Frank Russell & Company in Tacoma, Washington, oversees more than $10 billion of pension funds.

- The trust departments of large commercial banks: Morgan-Guaranty Bank and Bankers Trust, both of New York City, each manage over $100 billion of money, primarily from wealthy "widows and orphans" and pensions.

- The investment-management departments of life insurance companies: Prudential Insurance Company of Newark, New Jersey, manages over $150 billion of "other people's money."

- Investment companies, which include:

  Mutual funds: T. Rowe Price Associates of Baltimore, Maryland, and Fidelity Funds of Boston each manage mutual fund empires with assets of over $30 billion.

  Closed-end investment companies:

  Domestic: Duff & Phelps Selected Utilities is a large closed-end fund with assets of about $1.7 billion.

  Country funds: Korea Fund, Mexico Fund, Japan Fund, Brazil Fund, and others. These funds typically have assets of $50 to $100 million.

The investment-management services listed above are provided by professional money managers that receive the funds they manage from clients and investors such as those listed below:

- Pension funds (by far, the largest pool of funds):[2]

  Corporate: AT&T and General Motors each have over $40 billion pension funds.

  Governmental units: California Public Employees Retirement System (CALPERS) has over $60 billion in its pension fund.

- College endowments: Old, private universities like Harvard and Yale have large endowments.

- Charitable foundations: The Ford and Rockefeller Foundations have billions in assets and give millions to charities annually.

- Individual investors:

  Average: Most of their funds are invested in pensions and homes.

  Wealthy: Professional money managers are usually retained.

---

[2] Details about the pension funds of hundreds of corporations and governmental units are published in each year's January issue of *Institutional Investor*. See pp. 103–184 of the January 1992 issue, for instance.

Although the clients maintain ownership and legal control of their funds, they delegate investment decisions to portfolio managers. Before delegating the investment-management function to a money manager, however, the investor must select one.

For Average Investors   Value Line offers worthwhile investment advice about which stocks to buy and sell for subscription fees of a few hundred dollars per year.[3] Value Line also manages several mutual funds that involve no **sales commissions** (that is, load fees, redemption fees, exit fees, or 12b-1 fees, as they are variously called). There are over 2000 mutual funds investing primarily in equities and over 1000 fixed income funds from which to select in the United States. The Fidelity Group in Boston, for example, manages about 80 different mutual funds, and a few are popular (namely, the Magellan Fund). Unfortunately for investors, in addition to the annual **management fee** of about 1 percent per year of the market value of the assets managed, which all money managers charge, Fidelity charges sales commissions that reduce the net returns to investors. Many money managers include selling fees or sales commissions of some kind in their fee structures, but these fees provide nothing of any value to the investors.

For Large Investors   Some money management firms will not manage modest amounts of money. The trust departments at Morgan-Guaranty Bank and Bankers Trust, for instance, refuse to open accounts of less than $5 million. Management fees vary with the money manager and the size of the account, but usually amount to about 1 percent per year of the value of the assets managed. Large and small accounts both require about the same amount of work, but the management fees from the large account are many times larger.

This chapter shows how to differentiate between the money management services that are good and those that are not so good. To evaluate the performance of a portfolio manager requires rate-of-return data. Unfortunately, not all money management services make adequate data about their performance available to the public. The *investment company industry,* however, is a category of professional money managers that federal law requires to disclose their dealings. There are over 3000 mutual funds operating in the U.S.—too many to discuss in one chapter. Therefore, we will analyze only a small random sampling of the funds to demonstrate the analysis. Nevertheless, the selection principles are the same whether you are investing thousands, millions, or billions of dollars with a money manager.

---

[3] See Fisher Black, "Yes, Virginia, There Is Hope: Tests of the Value Line Ranking System," *Financial Analysts Journal,* September–October 1973. Also see L. D. Brown and M. S. Rozoff, "The Superiority of Analyst Forecasts as a Measure of Expectations: Evidence from Earnings," *Journal of Finance,* vol. 33, no. 1, March 1978, pp. 1–16. For a study that employed Value Line's approach for selecting stocks see S. Basu, "The Investment Performance of Common Stocks in Relation to Their Price-Earning Ratios," *Journal of Finance,* vol. 32, no. 3, June 1977, pp. 663–682. Also see T. E. Copeland and D. Mayers, "The Value Line Enigma (1965–1978): A Case Study of Performance Evaluation Issues," *Journal of Financial Economics,* November 1982, pp. 289–321. These studies suggest that Value Line's recommendations earn returns that beat the returns from a naive buy-and-hold strategy (Definition Box 5-5).

28-1 Investment Companies

The **Investment Company Act of 1940** created three kinds of investment companies:

1. Unit investment trusts
2. Closed-end investment companies
3. Open-end investment companies

We will begin our discussion with open-end investment companies, or mutual funds, because they are the most popular.

Mutual Funds

As explained in Chapters 3 and 6, mutual funds commingle money invested by different clients. These funds are called **open-end companies** because they can keep selling new shares and growing so long as anyone will invest. The funds are invested in a diversified portfolio of securities selected by professional money managers. The owners of mutual fund shares may invest more money or withdraw all or part of their money at any time. When an investor withdraws funds, it is called a **redemption.** The total assets invested in a mutual fund shrink when old shares are redeemed and grow when new shares are purchased by an investor.

The Investment Company Act of 1940 requires that mutual funds fully disclose details of their operations. (Investment companies are also governed by the Securities Act of 1933, the Securities Exchange Act of 1934, and the Investment Advisers Act of 1940. These laws are discussed in Chapter 6.) Provisions of the act also restrict mutual funds' ability to use leverage (that is, to borrow money), to buy on margin, to take more than 9 percent of the proceeds from the sale of new shares for sales commissions, to sell the funds' shares on margin, and to sell shares without making full, written disclosures of their operations to investors before they invest. These limitations ensure a certain amount of similarity among mutual funds.

Federal law also requires each mutual fund to give every current and prospective investor a written statement describing its investment objective. Table 28-1 lists these goals and the number of funds in each category.

Mutual funds are typically tax-exempt. The Internal Revenue Service (IRS) does not tax mutual fund income and then tax that same income again as personal income when it is paid out to the investors—that would be **double taxation.** Therefore, a mutual fund's income is tax-exempt unless the IRS judges that the fund is being used in a tax evasion scheme. To be tax-exempt, a mutual fund must pay out almost all income to its investors in the same year the income is earned. This income is then taxed as the investor's personal income. (If investors desire to do so, their after-tax income may be immediately reinvested in additional shares of the same mutual fund.)

A Mutual Fund's One-Period Rate of Return

Federal law requires that mutual funds sell and redeem their shares at the current **net asset value per share (NAVS).** An investment company's NAVS is computed by dividing the total market value of all the mutual fund's holdings (less any liabilities)

Table 28-1
Census of Mutual Funds Categorized
by Published Investment Objectives

	Number of funds	Percent of aggregate funds' assets
Types of common stock funds:		
Aggressive growth	213	6.7%
Growth	352	11.9
Growth and income	271	16.5
Global	48	2.5
Types of income funds:		
Income from equities	73	4.2
Income from bonds	102	2.4
Income from mixed sources	75	2.8
Income from options	13	0.7
Types of balanced (stock and bond) funds:		
Balanced, not highly flexible	59	2.4
Balanced and flexible	45	0.8
Types of bond funds:		
U.S. government bond income	205	14.7
GNMA	57	5.1
Corporate bonds	58	2.1
Money market and short-term municipals	664	
Global	29	0.6
High-yield (or junk)	104	5.1
Municipal bond funds:		
One-state, long-term municipals	258	7.4
Multistate, long-term municipals	180	11.6
Other categories of funds:		
Precious metals	36	0.7
International	75	1.8
Total:	2918	100.0

Sources: Author's information and the 1990 *Mutual Fund Fact Book*, Investment Company Institute, Washington, D.C., pp. 29 and 82.

by the number of the fund's outstanding shares. Mutual funds' NAVS are published in newspapers each business day. After the NAVS is known, the fund's one-period rate of return is calculated, as shown below:

$$\text{Rate of return} = \frac{\text{income from change in NAVS} + \text{interest or cash dividend disbursements} + \text{capital gains disbursements}}{\text{NAVS at beginning of period}} \tag{28-1}$$

The numerator of the mutual fund's rate of return formula above shows three types of income: (1) income from changes in NAVS, which includes unrealized capital gains or losses ("paper" profits and losses) and realized but undistributed capital gains, dividends, and interest income. Investors can realize their "paper gains or losses" at any time by redeeming the mutual fund shares at their NAVS. (2) Coupon interest from bonds and/or cash dividends from common stocks in the portfolio that are disbursed to the investors. (3) Capital gains disbursements, which are funds paid to the shareholders from realized price appreciation. Each investor's share of the income is divided by the beginning-of-period NAVS—this is what the share would have cost if it had been purchased at the start of that time period. The rate of return should be calculated using per share (rather than aggregate) data so that changes in the size of a fund resulting from its sales and redemption of shares will not be erroneously counted as investors' gains and losses.

Other Kinds of Investment Companies

As mentioned above, the Investment Company Act of 1940 established two other kinds of investment companies: closed-end investment companies and unit investment trusts. Because neither is a very popular vehicle, and one of them—the unit investment trust—is not actively managed, we will examine them only briefly here. We will concentrate instead on the mutual funds, which are very popular.

CASE

Muriel's Mutual Fund Return

Muriel paid the NAVS of $20.64 for shares in the Janus Twenty Fund on October 1, 1991. On December 31, 1991, the fund's NAVS was $24.19, and Muriel received a disbursement of cash dividends the fund had received of 3 cents per share and income from realized capital gains of 37 cents per share. Thus, over the 3 months that she owned the shares, Muriel's income per share was:

Change in NAVS ($24.19 − $20.64)	$3.55
Cash dividends disbursement	0.03
Disbursement of realized capital gains	0.37
Total income	$3.95

Over the last 3 months of 1991 Muriel's rate of return was 19.14 percent, as shown below in Equation (28-1a):

One-period rate of return (28-1a)

$$= \frac{\begin{array}{c}\text{income} \\ \text{from change} \\ \text{in NAVS}\end{array} + \begin{array}{c}\text{cash} \\ \text{dividends}\end{array} + \begin{array}{c}\text{capital gains} \\ \text{disbursements}\end{array}}{\text{beginning NAVS (or purchase price)}}$$

$$= \frac{\$3.55 + \$0.03 + \$0.37}{\$20.64}$$

$$= \frac{\$3.95}{\$20.64} = .1914 = 19.14\%$$

Since there are four 3-month periods in a year, Muriel's annualized rate of return was 101.46 percent!

$$(1 + r)^4 - 1 = (1.1914)^4 - 1 = 2.0146 - 1$$
$$= 1.0146 = 101.46\%$$

Closed-End Investment Companies   Unlike the open-end mutual funds, which may continually offer new shares to investors, **closed-end investment companies** are forbidden by law to sell additional shares after their initial public offering. They differ from open-end companies in another important way: Closed-end funds do not stand ready to redeem their shares when a shareholder wants to sell. The shares in closed-end funds are bought and sold in the secondary stock market (like the NYSE or the OTC market) at prices that rarely equal their NAVS. Sometimes closed-end funds' shares trade at a **premium** above their NAVS, and sometimes they trade at a **discount** below their NAVS.[4] This disconcerting price behavior detracts from the popularity of investing in closed-end funds.

There are only about 100 closed-end funds in the United States, and they attract certain investors. Seven dual-purpose funds were started in 1967. **Dual-purpose funds** are unusual because they have two classes of shares: income shares and capital shares. Owners of the *income shares* receive all the portfolio's cash dividend income. *Capital shares* participate in the changes in the entire portfolio's market value. Country funds are a newer variety of closed-end funds. A **country fund** invests in only the securities from a specific country: the Korea Fund, the Italy Fund, and the Taiwan Fund are examples.

Unit Investment Trusts   A **unit investment trust** owns the same fixed assets throughout the company's life. (Note that what Americans would call a *mutual fund* is called a *unit investment trust* in England.) In America a unit investment trust might buy $20,000,000 worth of bonds, for instance, and sell shares in the trust to finance the bond purchase. The bonds are held by a third party in trust, and when they mature, their principal amount is used to pay off shares in the unit investment trust. If shareholders request it, some unit investment trusts will sell some of the trust assets and use the proceeds to buy back the investor's shares at their net asset before they reach their contractual expiration date.

28-2   Evaluating the Skills of Mutual Fund Managers

Mutual funds (and, by implication, their managers) can be evaluated by analyzing their rates of return and riskiness. The tools presented in this chapter are also useful to evaluate and rank the desirability of closed-end funds, unit investment trusts, individual stocks, individual bonds, oil paintings, and many other investments.

---

[4] See Greggory A. Brauer, "Closed-End Fund Shares' Abnormal Returns and the Information Content of Discounts and Premiums," *Journal of Finance,* vol. 43, no. 1, 1988, pp. 113–127; R. Malcolm Richards, Donald R. Fraser, and John C. Groth, "The Attractions of Closed-End Bond Funds," *Journal of Portfolio Management,* vol. 8, no. 2, 1982, pp. 56–61; and Rex Thompson, "The Information Content of Discounts and Premiums on Closed-End Fund Shares," *Journal of Financial Economics,* vol. 6, no. 2–3, 1978, pp. 151–186.

One way to assess performance is to rank rates of return averaged over a complete business cycle. [See Equation (28-1) for a mutual fund's one-period rate of return formula.] Table 28-2 shows rate-of-return rankings for 20 randomly selected mutual funds' annual returns over a decade. The sampled statistics cover a decade in order to average out the bull and bear market conditions that would bias results from just a few years.

Column 1 of Table 28-2 shows the arithmetic average rate of return that each mutual fund earned over the decade of the 1980s. This return is what would have been earned if a tax-exempt investor had purchased shares on January 1, 1980, held them throughout the decade while reinvesting all cash disbursements, and then sold the shares at the end of the 10 years.[5] Only 3 of the 20 mutual funds in Table 28-2

[5] Since different readers are in different income tax brackets, it is impossible to know which tax rate is most appropriate to report. Therefore, tax-exempt returns are reported. Furthermore, the largest investors in the United States, pension funds, are tax-exempt.

Table 28-2
Annual Rate-of-Return Rankings for 20 Mutual Funds, January 1980 through December 1989

Name of fund	Average return per year*	Return rank									
		1980	1981	1982	1983	1984	1985	1986	1987	1988	1989
Magellan Fund	0.2695	1	20	1	1	10	1	4	7	1	3
IDS Growth	0.2231	2	3	2	7	20	2	1	2	5	2
Sigma Trust Shares	0.2096	14	11	12	10	5	10	14	14	6	1
S&P 500 Index†	0.1770										
Sequoia	0.1757	17	1	6	5	1	8	15	9	16	7
Mutual Shares	0.1754	11	2	19	2	4	9	7	5	2	17
Putnam Investors	0.1665	3	19	3	18	14	4	10	10	18	4
IDS Stock (investors' stock)	0.1528	8	19	8	13	12	13	2	1	14	6
Vanguard Index	0.1521	12	16	13	17	8	3	8	4	7	5
American Balanced	0.1519	16	6	5	12	6	5	9	8	9	9
Wellington	0.1510	9	8	9	11	3	6	6	13	15	16
Kemper Total Return	0.1472	5	13	10	6	16	7	5	20	19	11
Franklin Funds, Income Series	0.1455	10	10	4	15	2	20	3	11	17	13
Dreyfus	0.1412	7	5	16	9	11	12	11	3	20	14
Oppenheimer Special	0.1369	4	17	11	3	19	19	13	19	3	10
Pioneer	0.1318	6	14	17	4	17	11	20	6	4	8
Wellesley Income	0.1059	19	7	14	8	7	16	18	17	12	15
Keystone Income K-1	0.1040	15	9	20	20	13	14	16	15	11	12
Riskless rate‡	0.1034										
IDS Mutual, (Investors' Mutual)	0.1003	13	15	15	16	15	18	12	16	13	18
Composite Bond and Stock	0.0995	18	12	18	14	18	15	17	12	8	19
Oppenheimer High Yield	0.0871	20	4	7	19	9	17	19	18	10	20

* Annualized average rate of return.

† S&P 500 represents a naive buy-and-hold strategy.

‡ The average of 30-day Treasury bill yields over the decade.

were able to earn an average rate of return above the 17.7 percent earned by the S&P 500 Index. The rate of return on the S&P 500 is what an investor could have expected to earn by picking stocks randomly, or by using some other naive buy-and-hold strategy. (Box 5-6 defines the naive buy-and-hold strategy.)

The data in Table 28-2 indicate that most mutual funds do not do better than the S&P 500's naive buy and hold strategy. Other studies of mutual funds over different sample periods yield the same discouraging results. However, the high rates of return earned by Fidelity's Magellan Fund, IDS Growth Fund, and Sigma Trust Shares appear to represent superior investment management skills. Of the 20 funds in Table 28-2, Fidelity's Magellan Fund earned the highest average rate of return. Its 26.95 percent average annual return exceeded the average return from the S&P 500 index by 9.25 percentage points. This superficially impressive result needs closer examination, however.

Columns 2 through 11 of Table 28-2 show the ranking of the 20 funds' yearly rates of return. The most striking feature of these annual return rankings is their lack of consistency. No fund was in the top half of the rankings in all 10 years. *Moreover, none of the 20 mutual funds was able to outperform the S&P 500 index, a naive buy-and-hold strategy, in every one of the 10 years.*

Considering Risk and Return Together

Are the majority of mutual funds really as poor at managing investments as the data in Table 28-2 seem to suggest? We should consider the possibility that some funds maximize their returns at a low level of risk, where high returns are not available. If so, it could be that the funds are dominant assets along the bottom portion of the efficient frontier. Figure 28-1 illustrates the performance of 23 mutual funds relative

Figure 28-1 The performance of 23 mutual funds graphed in risk-return space. (*Source:* Donald E. Farrar, *The Investment Decision under Uncertainty*, Englewood Cliffs, N.J.: Prentice-Hall, 1962, p. 73.)

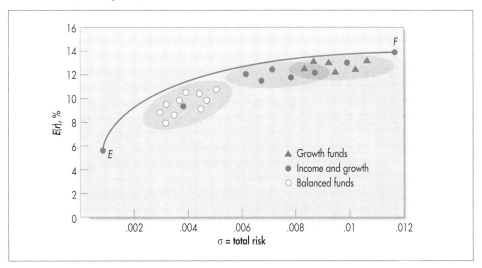

to the efficient frontier (curve *EF*). As the figure makes clear, none of the 23 funds was an efficient asset; only a few had an average rate of return within one percentage point of the efficient frontier. This suggests that mutual funds' average rates of return cannot be attributed to management's seeking a position on the low-risk end of the efficient frontiers. Instead, it appears that perhaps the professionals who managed the 23 funds were simply not as good as their advertisements suggested.

Even though no individual mutual funds are sufficiently well-managed to attain the efficient frontier, they can still be useful when forming a **portfolio of portfolios** that dominates the individual mutual funds. Selecting among the mutual funds is an **asset allocation** problem; it can be done scientifically by using Markowitz diversification, as illustrated in Figures 24-4 and 24-5. A portfolio analysis problem can be formulated to treat each mutual fund as a separate asset and solved to find the efficient frontier made from various mutual funds: each point on this efficient frontier represents the combination of mutual funds in that particular dominant portfolio of portfolios. Many asset allocators use less scientific methods; they simply select a few mutual funds or other categories of assets and divide the money among them using intuition.[6]

Statements of Investment Objectives

The Investment Company Act of 1940 requires mutual funds to publish a **statement of investment objectives,** which can be changed only if a majority of the shareholders consent. On the basis of the published statements of the 23 common stock mutual funds illustrated in Figure 28-1, their investment objectives were grouped into three categories:

1. **Growth funds** seek high rates of return from capital gains and undertake significant risks in order to earn these gains. Emerging growth stocks are sought.

2. **Growth and income funds** seek both cash dividend income and capital gains and, as a result, are less risky than growth funds. Blue-chip common stocks and preferred stock are typical investments.

3. **Balanced funds** claim to be in pursuit of income, growth, and stability. However, conservation of principal is placed above earning high returns. Public utility common stocks, high-quality preferred stocks, and high-grade corporate and government bonds are typical investments.

Note that the funds in Figure 28-1 tend to cluster into three groups. Those whose stated objective was to seek growth and that were willing to assume risk form a cluster that lies above the funds with less aggressive objectives. This finding suggests that fund managers are able to pinpoint the risk and return characteristics of their investments and stay in a preferred risk class fairly consistently. But, although they tended to stay in the same groupings fairly consistently over time, the groupings did

---

[6] For a collection of papers discussing different asset allocation tactics and strategies, see Robert D. Arnott and Frank Fabozzi, *Asset Allocation* (Chicago: Probus, 1988).

not always correspond with the particular fund's stated objective. In a few cases quantitative risk measures (such as the standard deviation of returns) give a clearer picture of mutual funds' investment objectives than does fund managements' published objective statements.

Do Not Ignore Risk!

As the rankings in Table 28-2 suggest, portfolios' rates of return vary widely over time as the market alternates between bullish and bearish periods. As a result, rates of return alone are not enough to rank investment performance. An investment's average rate of return should be evaluated along with its risk because risk and return are directly related.

28-3 Sharpe's Performance Index (SPI)

Sharpe's performance index, or **SPI,** yields a single value that can be used for investment performance rankings.[7] The SPI assigns the highest values to assets that have the best **risk-adjusted average rate of return.** The difference between an investment's expected rate of return and the riskless rate, $E(r) - R$, is called the **risk premium.** This risk premium is divided by the asset's standard deviation to compute the SPI.

Risk Premium
$$\overline{\sigma}$$

Computing SPI

The risk and average-rate-of-return statistics for the three most desirable mutual funds in Table 28-3 are plotted as points in risk-return space in Figure 28-2. Graphically, each investment's SPI value equals the slopes of lines drawn in Figure

[7] The SPI was developed by William F. Sharpe, "Mutual Fund Performances," *Journal of Business,* Suppl., January 1966, p. 125.

Box 28-1

DEFINITION: Sharpe's Performance Index (SPI)

The **risk premium per unit of standard deviation,** or SPI, is simply the formula for calculating the slope of a line in risk-return space that starts at point R.

$$\text{SPI} = \frac{\begin{array}{c}\text{asset's average} \quad \text{riskless rate} \\ \text{rate of return} \; - \; \text{of return } R\end{array}}{\begin{array}{c}\text{asset's standard deviation} \\ \text{of rates of return } \sigma\end{array}} = \frac{\text{risk premium}}{\text{standard deviation}} \qquad (28\text{-}2)$$

SPI can logically be used to rank the desirability of portfolios, but not individual assets (which still contain their diversifiable risk).

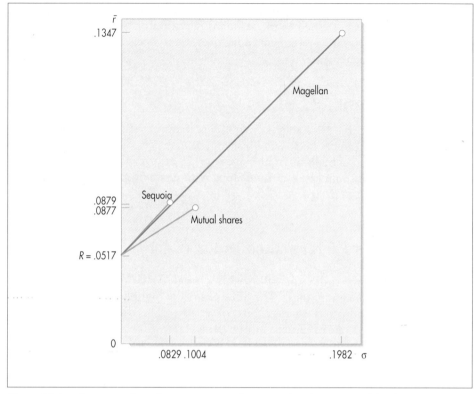

Figure 28-2 The SPI index of investment performance for three mutual funds.

28-2. A line is drawn from each of the three points to point *R*, representing a riskless investment of 5.17 percent per period. Each of these lines represents the infinite number of two-asset portfolios that could be constructed from various combinations of a risky investment in the mutual fund and a riskless investment in *R* = 5.17 percent.

After the straight lines from point *R* to each risky asset are determined, the selection of the best investment is straightforward: The asset on which the dominant investment possibilities line is based is the best investment. Figure 28-2 shows that the Sequoia Fund is the most desirable of the three dominant mutual funds when risk and return are considered simultaneously; Sequoia dominates all others.

Interpreting the SPI's Risk-Adjusted Returns

Note that the Sequoia Fund, which dominates the rankings in Table 28-3 and Figure 28-2, *did not have the highest average rate of return* in Table 28-2; the Magellan Fund did. But, The Magellan Fund's managers took such great risks to earn the high returns that its risk-adjusted return was not the most desirable.

Calculating Sequoia's Index   Assuming the riskless interest rate is *R* = 5.17% per 6-month period, the calculation of the Sequoia Fund's SPI index is shown below.

Table 28-3
Semiannual Risk and Return Statistics for 20 Mutual Funds
Arrayed on Their SPI Values

Name of mutual fund	Average semiannual return	Standard deviation of semiannual returns	SPI performance measure	Fund's investment objective
Sequoia*	0.0879	0.0829	0.4363	Growth
Fidelity's Magellan Fund*	0.1347	0.1982	0.4190	Growth
Mutual Shares*	0.0877	0.1004	0.3586	Growth-income
American Balanced	0.0760	0.0842	0.2881	Balanced
Sigma Trust Shares	0.1048	0.1948	0.2726	Balanced
IDS Growth	0.1115	0.2211	0.2706	Growth
Franklin Funds: Income Series	0.0728	0.0811	0.2600	Income
Wellington	0.0755	0.0928	0.2566	Balanced
IDS Stock (Investors' Stock)	0.0764	0.1204	0.2049	Growth-income
Dreyfus	0.0706	0.0945	0.1998	Growth-income
Putnam Investors	0.0833	0.1606	0.1965	Growth
Vanguard Index	0.0760	0.1251	0.1945	Growth-income
Kemper Total Return	0.0736	0.1321	0.1659	Balanced
Oppenheimer Special	0.0684	0.1265	0.1323	Growth
Pioneer	0.0659	0.1299	0.1092	Growth-income
Wellesley Income	0.0529	0.0670	0.0184	Income
Keystone Income K-1	0.0520	0.0714	0.0041	Income
IDS Mutual (Investors' Mutual)	0.0501	0.0721	−0.0216	Balanced
Composite Bond and Stock	0.0497	0.0832	−0.0236	Balanced
Oppenheimer High Yield	0.0435	0.0762	−0.1071	Income

* The three most desirable mutual funds are illustrated in Figure 28-2.

The semiannual data from Table 28-3 were used in the SPI computations to obtain 20 returns from 10 years of data.

$$\text{SPI for Sequoia Fund} = \frac{8.79\% - 5.17\%}{8.29\%} = \frac{3.62\%}{8.29\%} = .4363$$

Sales Commissions Another factor to take into consideration in assessing the desirability of investments is the sales commissions. Mutual fund sales commissions paid at the time of purchase are called **load fees** and range from zero to as much as 9 percent. In addition, some mutual funds charge redemption (or exit) fees, 12b-1 (promotional) fees, and other fees. Money that mutual fund managers spend on sales promotion does not aid the investor. If the promotions increase investments in the portfolio, the fund managers can collect their percentage-of-assets-per-year management fee on more assets.

Investing in mutual funds that charge no sales commissions allows investors to avoid paying sales promotion fees that only enrich the portfolio's managers. There is, for example, a 3 percent load fee on Fidelity's Magellan Fund, but Sequoia is a no-load fund. When these load fees are considered, Sequoia is even more desirable than Magellan.

28-4 Treynor's Performance Index (TPI)

Jack Treynor conceived an index of portfolio performance that is based on systematic risk, as measured by portfolios' beta coefficients, rather than on total risk (as measured by the standard deviations).[8] To use Treynor's measure, the mutual fund's characteristic regression line below must first be calculated to find the beta.

$$r_{p,t} = a_p + b_p r_{m,t} + e_{p,t} \qquad\qquad t = 1, 2, \ldots, T \qquad\qquad (28\text{-}3)$$

where $r_{p,t}$ = rate of return on portfolio p in time period t

$r_{m,t}$ = return on market index in period t

$e_{p,t}$ = unexplained residual return for portfolio p in period t

a_p = regression line's intercept term for portfolio p

b_p = beta coefficient for portfolio p, a measure of the portfolio's undiversifiable systematic risk

Figure 28-3 shows the characteristic lines for two portfolios with different beta slope coefficients.

Chapter 25 introduced characteristic regression lines and the beta coefficient as an index of undiversifiable risk. As with individual assets, the beta coefficient from a portfolio's characteristic line is an index of undiversifiable systematic risk. Using

[8] J. Treynor, "How to Rate Management of Investment Funds," *Harvard Business Review,* January-February 1965, pp. 63–75.

Figure 28-3   Characteristic regression lines for two mutual funds.

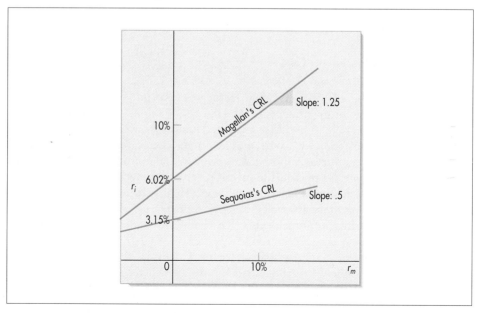

Box 28-2

685

Chapter 28
Investment
Performance
Evaluation

DEFINITION: Treynor's Performance Index (TPI)

Treynor's single-parameter investment performance index number for ranking purposes is defined by

$$TPI_p = \frac{\text{portfolio's average rate of return} - \text{riskless rate of interest } R}{\text{beta coefficient for portfolio } p} \qquad (28\text{-}4)$$

TPI can be used to rank the desirability of portfolios and individual assets together, since diversifiable risk is ignored.

only simple diversification, the unsystematic variability of returns of the individual assets in a portfolio typically average out to zero, and the portfolio is left with only systematic risk. Therefore, Treynor suggests measuring a portfolio's return relative to its systematic risk rather than relative to its total risk (which the SPI assesses).

Calculations with the TPI Formula

Graphically, **Treynor's performance index** for portfolio p, TPI_p, is a measure of the slope of the line from R to the portfolio, as shown in Figure 28-4. As this figure illustrates, Sequoia is a more desirable portfolio than Magellan because Sequoia earned more risk premium per unit of systematic risk; that is, $TPI_{\text{Sequoia}} = .0725 > .0665 = TPI_{\text{Magellan}}$.

Figure 28-4 Comparison of Treynor's performance index (TPI) for two assets.

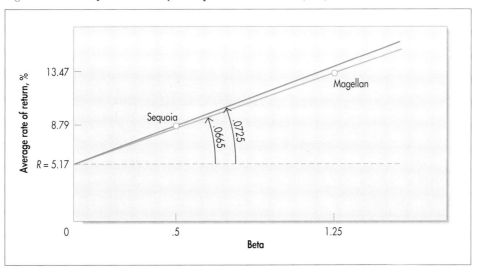

Table 28-4
Semiannual Risk and Return Statistics for 20 Mutual Funds
Arrayed on Their TPI Values

	Average semiannual return	*Beta*	*Risk premium, $r - R$*	*Treynor's performance index (TPI)*
Sequoia	0.0879	0.4990	0.0362	0.0725
Fidelity Magellan Fund	0.1347	1.2493	0.0830	0.0665
Sigma Trust Shares	0.1048	0.8560	0.0531	0.0621
Mutual Shares	0.0877	0.6614	0.0360	0.0544
Franklin Income Fund	0.0728	0.4340	0.0211	0.0486
IDS Growth	0.1115	1.5004	0.0598	0.0399
American Balanced	0.0760	0.6105	0.0243	0.0397
Wellington	0.0755	0.6286	0.0238	0.0379
Dreyfus	0.0706	0.6780	0.0189	0.0279
IDS Investors' Stock	0.0764	0.8894	0.0247	0.0278
Putnam Investors	0.0833	1.1606	0.0316	0.0272
Vanguard Index	0.0760	0.9587	0.0243	0.0254
Kemper Total Return	0.0736	0.9249	0.0219	0.0237
Oppenheimer Special	0.0684	0.8498	0.0167	0.0197
Pioneer	0.0659	0.9393	0.0142	0.0151
Wellesley Income	0.0529	0.4644	0.0012	0.0026
Keystone Income K-1	0.0520	0.5213	0.0003	0.0006
IDS Investors' Mutual	0.0501	0.5210	−0.0016	−0.0030
Composite Bond and Stock	0.0497	0.5720	−0.0020	−0.0034
Oppenheimer High Yield	0.0435	0.4141	−0.0082	−0.0197

Table 28-4 lists risk and return data for the same 20 mutual funds listed in Table 28-3. The two tables differ because Table 28-3 is arrayed on the mutual funds' SPI statistics while Table 28-4 is arrayed on their TPI statistics.

Comparing the SPI and TPI Measures

Treynor's portfolio performance index TPI_p is similar to Sharpe's index SPI_p; both divide an asset's risk premium by a quantitative measure of risk. But the two differ because they do not use the same risk measures. Sharpe's measure ranks assets' dominance in the CML's standard-deviation-and-return space, and Treynor's measures dominance in the CAPM's beta-and-return space. Both measures implicitly assume that money may be freely borrowed or lent at R. This assumption is required to generate the linear investment opportunities that emerge out of R and allow funds in different risk classes to be contrasted. Compare the mutual fund rankings in Tables 28-3 and 28-4 and you will note that in spite of the different risk measures they employ, both performance measures tend to yield similar rankings.

The data in Tables 28-3 and 28-4 are similar in another respect: only 5 of the 20 mutual funds in Table 28-4 had higher TPI scores than the S&P 500 Stock Index.

Other scientific studies that used larger samples of different portfolios from different sample periods reached similar conclusions. It seems that most mutual fund managers' salaries and other professional management expenses do not contribute to shareholder returns, because these outlays do not generate offsetting increases in the mutual funds' rates of return.

28-5 Advantages of Investing in Mutual Funds

Portfolio performance analysis of mutual funds suggests that investors could expect higher rates of return and less risk if they invested their own funds by selecting securities randomly. Realization of this is what made indexed mutual funds the most rapidly growing type of fund during the 1980s. **Index funds** have the stated objective of investing in the same stocks and in the same proportions that are used to compute some broad stock market index; they do this so they can earn the same return as the market average. The S&P 500 Index is the market index to which several index funds are indexed.

Not all mutual funds perform worse than a naive buy-and-hold strategy. Furthermore, mutual funds can perform valuable services for many investors, as Box 28-3 shows.

The risk-reducing diversification available from investing in a mutual fund is significant and should not be overlooked. Most mutual funds are usually able to reduce their risk to the systematic level of the market's fluctuations. In addition, most mutual funds' long-run average rates of return exceed the rates paid on FDIC-insured savings accounts. Investors receive some added return for assuming risk—unless they are forced to liquidate their holdings during a period of depressed prices. Mutual funds can also help an investor remain in a preferred risk class.

Box 28-3

COMPUTATION: John Smith's Mutual Fund Decision

Consider an investor named John Smith, who has $9000 to invest. If we suppose that Smith will purchase stocks only in round lots (to avoid paying the higher odd-lot commissions) and that the stocks have an average market price of $30 per share, Smith would probably be well advised to invest in a good mutual fund. An investor such as Smith, acting alone, would be able to buy round lots in only three securities, as shown below:

$$\text{Cost of 100-share round lot} = \$30 \text{ per share} \times 100 \text{ shares} = \$3000$$

$$\text{Number of round lots} = \frac{\$9000 \text{ for investment}}{\$3000 \text{ per round lot}} = 3 \text{ round lots}$$

Since three is too few securities to diversify adequately, Smith should look for a mutual fund in which to invest. He can achieve better diversification that way.

Summary

This chapter introduced two scientific investment performance evaluation tools that can be used to appraise the desirability of a stream of investment returns: The SPI and TPI measures were used to assess the performance of 20 mutual funds. From the results, certain conclusions can be drawn regarding mutual funds and the skill of their portfolio managers.

Ranking portfolios' yearly rates of return reveals whether any of them are consistently able to outperform competitors. However, such rankings may make efficient, low-risk portfolios that earn low returns appear to be doing poorly when they are actually doing quite well. To evaluate a portfolio adequately, the level of risk assumed must be considered *simultaneously with* the rate of return. The SPI and TPI measures consider the risk premium per unit of risk borne by individual portfolios. These two measures yield a single index number for each asset that can be used to rank the performances of a group of completely different investments.

Further Reading

Admati, Anat R., Sudipto Bhattacharya, Paul Pfleiderer, and Stephen A. Ross, "On Timing and Selectivity," *Journal of Finance*, vol. 41, no. 3, 1986, pp. 715–729.
> *Advanced mathematics is used to analyze how an investor might be able to determine if a portfolio manager has good market timing skills (that is, the ability to buy at the market lows and sell at the highs), good security selection skills, or both.*

Business Week, a weekly business magazine that is sold worldwide, publishes two special issues in February of each year that contain substantial information on mutual funds and investment results. The first issue in February is devoted to about 700 common stock mutual funds; the next one is devoted to hundreds of bond mutual funds. The articles contain investment advice that is based on the risk-adjusted rate-of-return performance measurements introduced in this chapter, although that analysis is not published. Only simple summary facts are presented.

Cumby, R. E., and J. D. Glen, "Evaluating the Performance of International Mutual Funds," *Journal of Finance*, vol. 45, no. 2, June 1990, pp. 497–521.
> *This article is an empirical investigation of 15 funds that uses 1982–1988 data with the Jensen and the Treynor-Mazuy performance measures. It reports that, like the domestic funds, the international mutual funds do not outperform the S&P 500 on a risk-adjusted basis.*

Sharpe, William F., "Mutual Fund Performance," *Journal of Business*, Supplement on Security Prices, January 1966, pp. 119–138.
> *This risk-return analysis of mutual fund performance uses correlation, regression, and statistical inference to develop Sharpe's SPI.*

Questions and Problems

Essay Questions

28-1 (*a*) Define the *net asset value per share (NAVS)* for a mutual fund. (*b*) "Open-end investment companies redeem their shares at the current net asset value per share (NAVS)." Is this statement true, false, or debatable? Explain.

28-2 "Sharpe's SPI will rank the performances of a group of investments about the same way they would be ranked if they were ranked purely in terms of their average rates of return; this is because the average rate of return is given more weight than risk in Sharpe's index." Is this statement true, false, or debatable? Explain.

28-3 Compare and contrast open-end investment companies with closed-end investment companies.

28-4 (*a*) Define the one-period rate of return for a mutual fund. (*b*) Define each of the income components that an open-end investment company investor receives (that is, each element in the numerator of the one-period rate of return).

28-5 "Rankings of portfolios' average rates of returns show that although the average mutual fund does not outperform the market, a few truly superior funds consistently beat the market." Is this statement true, false, or debatable? Explain.

28-6 Explain why ranking mutual funds by rate of return is a poor way to evaluate performance.

28-7 How well does the mutual fund industry perform relative to a naive buy-and-hold strategy? Explain. (*Hint:* See Box 5-5.)

28-8 Assume you have been put in charge of a mutual fund with a large staff of fundamental analysts and millions of dollars of assets spread over more than 150 different common stocks. The fund's gross return is about average for the industry, but its management expenses are high, so its net yield to its investors is slightly below-average. The previous management did not try to specialize as a growth or income fund, but ran the firm as a general-purpose fund. What do you plan to do with your fund? Explain why.

28-9 What federal laws govern the administration of mutual fund income? (*Hint:* Some outside research into the tax law and the Investment Company Act will be essential.)

28-10 Compare and contrast the way the Sharpe and Treynor portfolio performance ranking tools would rank the performance of the same set of mutual funds over identical sample periods.

28-11 Why is it necessary for both the Sharpe and the Treynor investment performance models to unrealistically assume that money can be borrowed and lent at some riskless rate of interest?

Problems

28-12 Consider the following summary statistics about five investment portfolios and the riskless rate of interest.

Portfolio	Average return	Standard deviation	Beta
Alpha	7%	3	.4
Beta	10	8	1.0
Gamma	13	6	1.1
Delta	15	13	1.2
Epsilon	18	15	1.4
R	3	0	0

(a) Which of the five portfolios performed the best according to Sharpe's measure? (b) Which performed the worst? (c) Draw a graph analogous to the CML illustrating the five portfolios' individual opportunity lines. (d) Which of the five portfolios performed the best according to Treynor's measure? (e) Which performed the worst? (f) Draw a graph analogous to the CAPM illustrating the five portfolios' individual opportunity lines. Show all calculations and label the graphs clearly.

28-13 Reconsider the five investment portfolios listed in Problem 28-12. However, now assume that the riskless rate of interest was 6 percent, instead of 3 percent. (a) Which portfolio ranks first according to Sharpe's measure under this new assumption? (b) Draw a graph analogous to the CML illustrating the five portfolios' individual opportunity lines at both $R = 3\%$ and $R = 6\%$. (Note: This merely extends the graph you were asked to draw in Problem 28-12c.) (c) Which portfolio performed best according to Treynor's measure? (d) Draw a graph analogous to the CAPM illustrating the five portfolios' individual opportunity lines at both $R = 3\%$ and $R = 6\%$. (Note: This merely extends the graph from Problem 28-12f.) Show all calculations and label all variables in your graphs.

Multiple Choice Questions

28-14 A mutual fund's net asset value per share (NAVS) is defined by which one of the following?

(a) (Purchase price of the fund's total assets − total liabilities)/number of shares outstanding = NAVS

(b) (Current market value of the fund's total investments − any current liabilities)/number of shares outstanding = NAVS

(c) (Current market value of the fund's total investments − any current liabilities)/number of authorized shares = NAVS

(d) (Purchase price of the fund's total investments − total liabilities)/number of authorized shares = NAVS

28-15 Dr. Donald Farrar's study of 23 mutual funds' investment efficiency, illustrated in Figure 28-1, indicated which of the following conclusions?

(a) The growth funds tended to have the highest risk and returns, and the balanced funds tended to have the lowest risk and returns.

(b) A few of the mutual funds didn't perform in the risk class the fund had stated in its legally required statement of investment objective.

(c) None of the 23 mutual funds attained the efficient frontier.

(d) All the above are correct.

28-16 Investing in mutual fund shares provides which one of the following advantages?

(a) Expert professional management guarantees consistently high rates of return.

(b) Small investors with only a few hundred or a few thousand dollars to invest can obtain a diversified portfolio without paying odd-lot commissions and incurring high administrative expenses if they buy a no-load fund.

(c) The majority of mutual funds consistently seek to attain the same investment objective that the law requires them to publish.

(d) Both (b) and (c) are true.

28-17 Money market mutual funds invest in which of the following categories of assets? (*Hint:* Consult Chapter 2 about money market securities.)

(*a*) Foreign exchange
(*b*) U.S. Treasury bonds
(*c*) Securities that have less than 1 year until their maturity
(*d*) Treasury bills
(*e*) Both (*b*) and (*d*)

28-18 Ranking the annual rates of return earned by mutual funds year by year reveals which of the following conclusions?

(*a*) No mutual funds consistently earn the lowest rates of return.
(*b*) The same mutual funds consistently earn the highest rates of return.
(*c*) No mutual funds consistently earn the highest rates of return.
(*d*) The same mutual funds consistently earn the lowest rates of return.
(*e*) Both (*a*) and (*c*) are true.

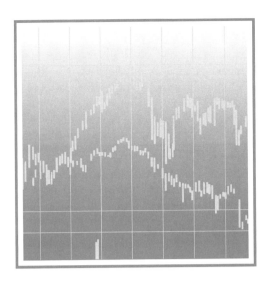

APPENDIX A

COMPUTER
SOFTWARE
AND DATA

The third edition of *Management of Investments* was written to be used without computers, as most instructors wished. However, some instructors have requested computer software and investments data to accompany the book. This appendix describes several 5.25-inch floppy diskettes for an IBM-PC or compatible.

The package of investments analysis data and software to accompany the third edition is large and comprehensive, and has been prepared by professionals. If a piece of software fails to work, it is probably because of system-level differences between your personal computer and the standard IBM-PC. Such incompatibilities are typically easy to circumvent.

The disks will produce color displays if the user's computer has color capabilities. None of the software is copy-protected, so everyone in the class can have a personal copy to take home. All the disks have menu-driven programs that require no previous computer experience. The diskettes can be read directly into an IBM-PC or compatible personal computer, or uploaded to a mainframe computer for use there.

The software is designed to do a variety of investment analyses, including:

1. Mutual fund data and programs
2. BASIC language programs
3. Lotus 1-2-3 templates
4. McCann's QP program

Mutual Fund Data and Investment Analysis Programs

This diskette contains data on hundreds of different mutual funds and a computer program to supply answers to questions mutual fund investors frequently ask.

Business Week Mutual Fund Scoreboard

Business Week magazine prepares the mutual fund disk, which it calls its Mutual Fund Scoreboard, and sells thousands of copies for subscriptions of $299 per year. Two different subscriptions are available: one covers the mutual funds that invest only in common stocks, and the other covers funds that invest in fixed income securities. For subscription information please write to: Business Week Mutual Fund Diskettes, P.O. Box 1597, Fort Lee, New Jersey 07024; Fax: (201) 461-9808.

The free diskette provided by McGraw-Hill is the Mutual Fund Scoreboard for common stocks. The sample of portfolios on the diskette includes hundreds of common stock mutual funds in the United States. Most of the facts on the diskette (such as load fee and total assets) are from a recent year. In addition, some historical data about each fund (such as average rates of return) are on the disk, too. Up-to-date disks are prepared monthly by *Business Week* for subscribers to the service. Updates cannot be obtained free.

Data

The mutual fund diskette has several monitor screens full of data on each of its mutual funds. Management fee, load fee, redemption fee, total assets, year-to-year change in total assets, address, phone number, principal holdings, performance ranking, investment recommendation, and other facts are available for every fund. Average rates of return over different periods for both the fund and the S&P 500 stock market average are presented for direct comparison. Beta systematic risk statistics, the portfolio's turnover rate, average rates of return from over various years, and other data are also available.

Screening

The mutual fund diskette contains a screening program that can be used to sort and select either one individual fund or all the funds that meet selected criteria. Any funds meeting the desired screening criteria will instantly be listed on the screen.

Ease of Use

The user merely needs to type a few letters (printed on the diskette), and the diskette's internal program starts itself. The diskette is menu-driven, so the user need select only the mutual fund or category of mutual funds of interest. The program then automatically presents the user with another menu from which to select a computation program to do the type of analysis desired. Most of the computations a mutual fund investor might want are stored on the diskette. The screening programs can be used to sort through the hundreds of mutual funds on the diskette for the characteristics that interest the analyst.

Data on the disk can be transferred (or exported or downloaded) to Lotus 1-2-3 or other computer programs for further analysis. Menu-driven programs are provided on the diskette to download the mutual fund data. The mutual fund diskette supplements Chapter 28 of this edition of *Management of Investments.*

BASIC Language Programs for Investments Analysis

This diskette contains BASIC language programs to do a number of financial computations. It is entirely menu-driven and requires no computer programming skills in order for the user to perform the analysis.

Program 1: Generates a page out of a bond table (or bond price book) for any combination of coupon rate and years-to-maturity the user requests. Different tables for annual and semiannual compounding can be tabulated.

Programs 2–6: Analyzes an individual bond and includes the following computations: present value (program 2), yield-to-maturity (3), duration (4), realized compound yields (5), and bond price volatility analysis (6).

Program 7: Calculates an interest rate risk immunization portfolio. A linear programming computer program that simultaneously analyzes the durations of different potential bond investments and determines exactly which bonds should be included in a portfolio, and in what proportions, to immunize the portfolio against interest rate risk.

Program 8: Performs stock analysis, including calculation of the present value of future dividends.

Program 9: Performs common stock analysis: the program reads in the market prices of one or more securities and simultaneous observations on some market index and calculates statistics such as period-by-period rates of return, beta coefficients, average rates of return, standard deviations, and correlations with the market.

Program 10: Performs put and call computations based on the Black-Scholes option pricing model and includes call premiums (or prices) and put premiums (or prices).

Program 11: Performs Markowitz portfolio analysis; calculates and displays the risk, return, and weights of the assets in efficient portfolios. This is a quadratic programming program.

Lotus 1-2-3 Templates

You need not know how to use Lotus 1-2-3 to use these templates; they are all menu-driven so that you need select only what you want to do from a menu and then interactively supply the needed values when asked for them. Each diskette contains templates to do the following kinds of investments analysis:

Template 1: BONDTAB generates a page out of a bond table (or bond price book) for any combination of coupon rate and years-to-maturity that the user requests. Different tables for annual and semiannual compounding are available.

Template 2: BOND1 analyzes an individual bond to include the following computations for either annual or semi-annual compounding: (*a*) present value, (*b*) yield-to-maturity, and (*c*) duration. Special consideration is given to convertible bonds and after-tax results.

Template 3: BOND2 analyzes an individual bond with semiannual compounding to include the following computations: (*a*) present value, (*b*) yield-to-maturity, and (*c*) duration. BOND2 is a simplified version of BOND1.

Template 4: STKVAL analyzes common stock that has a constant perpetual growth rate and includes the calculation of (*a*) the present value of future dividends, (*b*) the required rate of return (or discount rate) implicit in a given stock price, and (*c*) the growth rate implicit in any given stock price.

Template 5: 2STAGE analyzes a common stock that has two different stages of growth and includes the calculation of (*a*) the present value of future dividends, (*b*) the required rate of return (or discount rate) implicit in a given stock price, and (*c*) the growth rate implicit in any given stock price.

Template 6: 3PHASE analyzes common stock that has three different stages of growth and includes the calculation of (*a*) the present value of future dividends, (*b*) the required rate of return (or discount rate) implicit in a given stock price, and (*c*) the growth rate implicit in any given stock price.[1]

Template 7: OPTION1 performs simple put and call computations based on the Black-Scholes option pricing model and includes: (*a*) call premiums (or prices) and (*b*) put premiums (or prices).

Template 8: OPTION2 performs detailed put and call computations based on the Black-Scholes option pricing model and includes: (*a*) call premiums (or prices) and (*b*) put premiums (or prices). Specific expiration times and cash dividend payments may also be analyzed. OPTION2 is a sophisticated version of OPTION1.

Template 9: MARKPRT performs Markowitz portfolio analysis of a two-asset portfolio. The risk, return, and weights of the assets in portfolios are calculated, and the resulting efficient frontier can be displayed graphically. Either efficient or inefficient portfolios can be analyzed.

Template 10: PEMODEL calculates price-earnings ratios for any risk-adjusted discount rate (k), growth rate (g), and number of years (n) of growth desired.

Various Lotus 1-2-3 templates contain investments problems that may be solved with the Lotus 1-2-3 templates above. These problem templates have names like PROBMRK for problems to do with Markowitz portfolio analysis, PROBOND for bond problems, PRO-BOPS for put and call option problems, and PROBSTK for common stock problems.

Each Lotus 1-2-3 template generates either monochrome or color displays, has a one- or two-page introduction, includes problems for students to work and answers, and generates graphs to illustrate the analysis if desired. The print screen (PrtSc) key can be used to print out the introduction, the problems, and/or the solutions to the problems, if desired.

A Sophisticated Quadratic Program

Professor Douglas McCann has written a sophisticated quadratic programming (QP) computer program in the highly efficient C language, and he has graciously made demonstration copies available to us for free. The demonstration copy is compiled and has been constrained so that it will analyze only a maximum of 10 assets. McCann's QP handles the full-covariance matrix and, unlike simpler QP codes, allows constraints on each variable. Professor McCann sells this QP for $2500 without the constraint that limits it to only 10 assets.

How to Obtain Disks

At the request of an adopting instructor, the local McGraw-Hill representative will provide information about the floppy disks.

---

[1] This three-phase algorithm is not discussed in the text. It was included here for comparison purposes and to please Moldovsky aficionados.

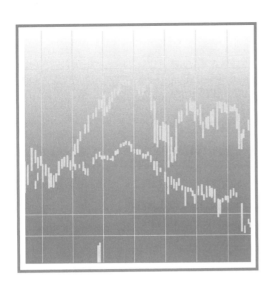

APPENDIX B

INVESTMENTS ANALYSIS WITH HAND-HELD CALCULATORS

Hand-held financial calculators are widely used in financial analysis. This appendix explains some fundamental applications using two of the more popular calculators:

- The Texas Instruments Student Business Analyst, the BA 35 hereafter, has a list price of $28.

- The Hewlett-Packard Advanced Financial Programmable calculator, the HP 12C, has a list price of $95.

Hand-held financial calculators have built-in financial functions. These financial functions are addressed with five keys on both the BA 35 and HP 12C, defined below.

1. n or N is the number of periods

2. i or %i is the rate of return (entered as a percent)

3. PMT is payment (a cashflow, like a bond's coupon)

4. PV is present value

5. FV is future value

Both the BA 35 and HP 12C have continuous memories. Values stay in the memory of the calculator even when it is turned off (if the battery is charged). The continuous memory feature is helpful, but it can also cause problems if irrelevant values from previous calculations are not cleared out of the memory. The memories are called *registers*. To clear the HP 12C

Note: This appendix draws heavily on the expertise of Professor Richard Taylor, Ph.D., CFA, Arkansas State University.

registers, you must use the gold-colored f key. The f key permits you to use the gold-lettered functions. For example, when you press f clear REG , you will clear the registers of the HP 12C. In a similar manner, the blue-colored g key allows you to use the blue-lettered functions. With the BA 35, pressing the 2nd key allows you to execute the functions appearing above the keys. For example, pressing 2nd FIN puts you in the finance mode and clears the financial registers.

You may want to control the number of decimal places displayed on your calculator. With the BA 35 you have two choices—two decimal places or a variable number. Push in sequence 2nd STO to set the level at two. Note that "Dec 2" will appear in the face of the calculator when two decimal places are being used. By pushing 2nd STO again, the setting is reversed and you return to the variable decimal mode. With the HP 12C, push f followed by the desired number of decimal places; for example, f 3 sets the level to three.

The following pages explain several financial applications for both calculators—time value of money, a bond's yield to maturity, stock analysis, geometric mean, arithmetic mean, and standard deviation. The HP 12C has additional features available, including simple regression.

The Time Value of Money

To begin with, consider four time-value-of-money applications: the present and future values of single sums, and the present and future values of annuities. Some combination of the five financial keys listed above can be used to do any of these calculations. With both calculators, if you know three of the four variables in question, the calculator will solve for the unknown fourth variable. You simply key in the values of the three variables you know and then push the button or series of buttons to solve for the value you do not know. Let's look at some examples.

Future Value

If you place $100,000 in a savings account that earns 12 percent for 15 years, how much will you have in the account at the end of 15 years? The solution is:

BA 35	HP 12C
1. ON/C 2nd STO	1. ON f 2
2. 2nd FIN (clears memory)	2. f clear FIN
3. 100,000 PV	3. 100,000 CHS PV
4. 15 N	4. 15 n
5. 12 %i	5. 12 i
6. CPT FV	6. FV
Answer: $547,356.57.	*Answer:* $547,356.58.

The CHS means "change sign" and is used on the HP 12C to distinguish between cash inflows and outflows.

Present Value

What is the present value of $200,000 to be received in 12 years at an interest rate of 9 percent?

BA 35	HP 12C
1. 200,000 FV	1. 200,000 CHS FV
2. 12 N	2. 12 n
3. 9 %i	3. 9 i
4. CPT PV	4. PV

Answer: $71,106.95.   *Answer:* $71,106.95.

Note that since we are already in the finance mode and have the number of decimal places set to two, it is not necessary to repeat these settings. Also, since the same four keys are being used, it is not necessary to clear the calculator.

Future Value of an Annuity

If at the end of each year you place $2000 in a savings account for 20 years for retirement purposes, how much will have accumulated at the end of 20 years if the return is assumed to be 10 percent per year?

BA 35	HP 12C
1. 2nd FIN (clears memory)	1. f clear FIN
2. 2000 +/− PMT	2. 2000 CHS PMT
3. 20 N	3. 20 n
4. 10 %i	4. 10 i
5. CPT FV	5. FV

Answer: $114,550.   *Answer:* $114,550.

Present Value of an Annuity

Mr. Jay expects to receive $10,000 at the end of each year for the next 10 years. What is the present value of these cash flows if the appropriate rate of return is 14 percent?

BA 35	HP 12C
1. 2nd FIN (clears memory)	1. f clear FIN
2. 10,000 PMT	2. 10,000 CHS PMT
3. 14 %i	3. 14 i
4. 10 N	4. 10 n
5. CPT PV	5. PV

Answer: $52,161.16.   *Answer:* $52,161.16.

Bond Analysis

Calculating a bond's yield-to-maturity will be explained after learning how to find the present value of a bond.

Bond Valuation

Determine the present value (or price) of bonds issued by the Mack Corporation that have 15 years until maturity. The bonds have a coupon rate of 12 percent (semiannual interest) and a maturity value of $1000. If the yield-to-maturity for bonds of this type is 14 percent, what is the price of the bond issue?

	BA 35	
1.	2nd	FIN
2.	1000	FV
3.	60	PMT
4.	30	N
5.	7	%i
6.	CPT	PV

Answer: 875.91.

	HP 12C	
1.	f clear	FIN
2.	1000	FV
3.	60	PMT
4.	30	n
5.	7	i
6.	PV	

Answer: 875.91.

Yield-to-Maturity

Find the yield-to-maturity of the Mack Corporation bonds described above if the current price is $1100.

	BA 35	
1.	2nd	FIN
2.	1000	FV
3.	60	PMT
4.	30	N
5.	1100	PV
6.	CPT	%i

Answer: 5.33 × 2 =10.65% annual rate.

	HP 12C		
1.	f clear	FIN	
2.	1000	CHS	FV
3.	60	CHS	PMT
4.	30	n	
5.	1100	PV	
6.	i		

Answer: 5.33 × 2 = 10.65%.

Since the same five keys are being used, it is not necessary to clear the calculator to solve the next problem. For example, if you wanted to compute the yield-to-maturity that is implied by a different bond price while all other factors remained unchanged, all you would have to do is enter a new value for PV (the price) and compute i . The longer approach was used to show

how to compute a yield-to-maturity from the beginning. Also note that for the HP 12C the
signs of the cash flows in steps 2, 3, and 5 could all be reversed.

B-5

*Appendix B
Investments
Analysis with
Hand-Held
Calculators*

Stock Analysis

The BA 35 and the HP 12C calculators can be used to value stocks and find the investor's rate
of return from a stock investment.

Stock Value

Suppose an investor expects to receive the following stream of cash flows if he purchases a share
of XYZ Corporation stock: $2.00, $2.50, and $3.00 in total dividends at the end of years 1, 2,
and 3, respectively. The investor also expects to sell the stock for $30 per share at the end of
year 3. If the investor requires a return of 15 percent, what price should he pay for the stock?

BA 35	HP 12C
1. ON/C 2nd FIN	1. f clear REG
2. 0 STO	2. f 2
3. 2nd STO	3. 15 i
4. 15 %i	4. 0 g CF$_o$
5. 2 FV	5. 2 g CF$_j$
6. 1 N CPT PV SUM	6. 2.5 g CF$_j$
7. 2.5 FV	7. 33 g CF$_j$
8. 2 N CPT PV SUM	8. f NPV
9. 33 FV	
10. 3 N CPT PV SUM	*Answer:* $25.33 per share.
11. RCL	

Answer: $25.33 per share.

The HP 12C uses its built-in net present value routine that is designated NPV .

A Stock's Return

If the investor pays $24 per share for the XYZ stock, what return will be earned? The BA 35
has no built-in internal rate of return (IRR) function, so the procedure is like that given in the
bond valuation problem, except that you should select a return, calculate the present value of
the expected cash flows, and compare the calculated present value with the stock price.
Essentially, you find the IRR by trial and error. When you find a discount rate that makes the

present value of the expected cash flows equal to the price, you have found the IRR. The HP 12C solution is much easier.

With the HP 12C, the built-in IRR routine is used as follows:

HP 12C
_____

1. f clear REG

2. 24 CHS g CF$_o$

3. 2 g CF$_j$

4. 2.5 g CF$_j$

5. 33 g CF$_j$

6. f IRR

Answer: 17.24%.

Means and Standard Deviations

Financial calculators can also be used to calculate common statistics.

Geometric Mean

The geometric mean, arithmetic mean, and standard deviation can easily be calculated with the BA 35 and HP 12C. Suppose ABC Corporation had the following equally likely annual returns:

Year	Return, %
1	−5
2	10
3	15

To calculate the geometric mean return, denoted GMR, the following formula should be used:

$$GMR = \{[(1 + r_1)(1 + r_2) \cdots (1 + r_N)]^{1/N} - 1.0\} \times 100$$

The formula should be applied to the example in the following manner:

$$GMR = [(.95 \times 1.1 \times 1.15)^{1/3} - 1.0] \times 100$$

The two calculators can be used to obtain the solution as follows:

BA 35	HP 12C

1. ON/C ON/C

2. .95 x

1. ON f 4

2. .95 ENTER

BA 35	HP 12C
3. 1.1 [x]	3. 1.1 [x]
4. 1.15 [x]	4. 1.15 [x]
5. [yˣ]	5. 3
6. 3	6. [1/X]
7. [1/X]	7. [yˣ]
8. [=]	8. 1
9. [−] 1	9. [−]
10. [=]	10. 100
11. [x] 100	11. [x]
12. [=]	*Answer: 6.3175%.*

Answer: 6.32%.

Standard Deviation

Calculate the standard deviation and arithmetic mean as follows:

BA 35	HP 12C
1. [ON/C] [ON/C]	1. [f] 4
2. [2nd] [STAT]	2. [f] [clear] [Σ]
3. 5 [+/−] [Σ+]	3. 5 [CHS] [Σ+]
4. 10 [Σ+]	4. 10 [Σ+]
5. 15 [Σ+]	5. 15 [Σ+]
6. [x̄] (mean)	6. [g] [x̄] (mean)
Answer: 6.67%.	*Answer: 6.6667%.*
7. [σn − 1] (sample standard deviation)	7. [g] [s] (Sample standard deviation)
Answer: 10.41%.	*Answer: 10.4083%.*
8. [σn] (Population standard deviation)	

Answer: 8.50%.

To calculate the population standard deviation with the HP 12C, push the following keys in sequence: [g] [x̄] [Σ+] [g] [s]. The answer is 8.4984%. This sequence should be executed after the sample standard deviation has been determined.

The BA 35 can also be used to calculate the mean, standard deviation, and variance of a discrete probability distribution. For example, consider the following discrete probability distribution:

Probability	Rate of return, %
.2	10
.3	20
.3	25
.2	30
1.0	

The mean, standard deviation, and variance are calculated as follows. Note that the returns are entered first and then the probabilities are entered as integers.

1. ON/C ON/C

2. 2nd STAT

3. 10 FRQ 20 Σ+

4. 20 FRQ 30 Σ+

5. 25 FRQ 30 Σ+

6. 30 FRQ 20 Σ+

7. X (mean)

Answer: 21.5.

8. σ_n (standard deviation)

Answer: 6.73.

9. 2nd x² (variance)

Answer: 45.25.

Linear Regression

Simple linear regression can be performed with the HP 12C. One dependent variable (usually called y) and one independent variable (or explanatory variable, usually called x) are used. An example will illustrate. Suppose you want to calculate the beta coefficient for the returns of the QRT Corporation with the following data:

Year	QRT Stock Returns, % (y)	Market Returns, % (x)
1	15	17
2	−5	−7
3	9	11
4	12	14

The procedure on the HP 12C is as follows:

1. f clear Σ   Clears statistical registers
2. 15 ENTER   1st y value
3. 17 Σ+   1st x value
4. 5 CHS ENTER   2d y value
5. 7 CHS Σ+   2d x value
6. 9 ENTER   3d y value
7. 11 Σ+   3d x value
8. 12 ENTER   4th y value
9. 14 Σ+   4th x value
10. 0 g ŷ, r   Calculates a intercept

Answer: .5806.

11. STO 0

12. 0 g x̂, r

13. CHS

14. RCL 0 X ⪌ Y ÷   Slope, or beta value

Answer: .8194.

Therefore, the characteristic line is in the form

$$y = a + bx$$

$$r_i = .5806 + .8194 r_m$$

After the regression equation is derived, the correlation can also be easily calculated. To calculate the correlation coefficient, press g ŷ, r X ⪌ Y or g x̂, r X ⪌ Y. In the regression above, the correlation coefficient is .9987.

Analyzing Bonds between Interest Payment Dates

One of the most useful built-in finance functions on the HP 12C is the bond function. A present value and yield-to-maturity can be calculated for a bond between interest payment dates. To show how this can be done, we will solve the following two problems:

   1. You are considering purchasing a 9 percent Jones Corporation bond today (March 30, 1990). If the bond matures on June 4, 2004, what price should you pay for the bond? Assume the appropriate YTM is 12 percent. The sequence of steps to follow on the HP 12C is as follows:

B-10

*Appendix B
Investments
Analysis with
Hand-Held
Calculators*

1.	[f] 4	Sets decimal to 4
2.	[f] clear [REG]	Clears registers
3.	12 [i]	Enters yield-to-maturity
4.	9 [PMT]	Enters coupon rate
5.	[g] [M.DY]	Sets month-day-year format
6.	3.301990 [ENTER]	Purchase date
7.	6.042004	Maturity date
8.	[f] [PRICE]	Calculates bond's price as a percent of par—that is, $797.58

Answer: 79.7581.

9.	[+]	Bond's price plus accrued interest (in dollars, $826.26).

Answer: 82.6262.

2. Suppose in the previous problem that you know the price (as a percent of par) but do not know the yield-to-maturity. What is the yield-to-maturity of the Jones Corporation bond if its price is 110 percent of par?

1. [f] clear [REG]

2. 110 [PV]

3. 9 [PMT]

4. 3.301990 [ENTER]

5. 6.042004

6. [f] [YTM]

Answer: 7.8184%.

These calculations are for semi-annual bond coupons and a 365-day year.[1]

---

[1] For some additional HP 12C programming examples, see Richard Taylor, "Option Valuation for Alternative Instruments with Black-Scholes Model: A Pedagogical Note," *Journal of Financial Education* (Fall), 1987, pp. 73–77 and Richard Taylor, "Bond Duration Analysis: A Pedagogical Note," *Financial Analysts Journal*, July-August 1987, pp. 71–72. See also W. Scott Bauman, Jaroslaw Komarynsky, and John C. Siska Goytre, *Investment Securities Program Guide Using the HP-12C* (New York: McGraw-Hill, 1987). For a briefer, but still good, guide, see the 79-page, double-spaced typewritten manuscript "Quick Acquaint Course for the Hewlett-Packard HP 12C Electronic Calculator," by Profs. Stephen D. Messner and Mark H. Goldman, Finance Department, School of Business, University of Connecticut, Storrs, Conn.

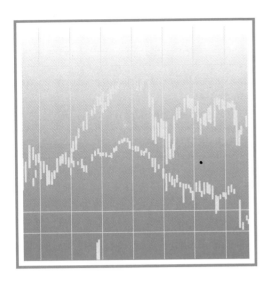

APPENDIX C

ANSWERS TO PROBLEMS
AND QUESTIONS

Chapter 1

1-8 20%; 50%; −50%; −10%; 90%; 20%; −10%; 20%; 20%; 50%

1-9 $E(r) = 20\%$; $VAR(r) = .134$; $SD = 36.606\%$.

1-10 (a) $E(r) = 20\%$. (b) Weighted average equals $E(r)$. (c) Unweighted return is 20%. (d) Arithmetic mean could be either (b) or (c).

1-11 $E(r) = 20\%$; $VAR(r) = .143$; $SD = .378 = 37.8\%$.

1-12 (a) $E(r) = 13\%$; (b) $VAR(r) = .09953$; (c) $SD = 31.548\%$; (d) distribution skewed right.

1-13 Federal Sys. Co.: $E(r) = .10$, $VAR(r) = .0840$; Turtle Express: $E(r) = .08$, $VAR(r) = .02560$; Standard Pacific: $E(r) = .20$, $VAR(r) = .0840$; National Distributors: $E(r) = .08$, $VAR(r) = .01004$ (a) Federal Systems Co. dominated by Standard Pacific. Turtle is dominated by National Distributors. (b) Choose between Standard Pacific and National Distributors or a portfolio of the two or speculate on Standard Pacific.

1-14 b	1-17 a
1-15 d	1-18 e
1-16 b	1-19 c

Chapter 2

2-8 (a) Several hundred Treasury issues are outstanding. (b) Difference between zero and 350 basis points. (c) Maturities from a few days to 30 years. (d) T-bills have no coupons. (e) Savings bonds nonmarketable.

2-9 Zero's has 1-year return: 12.5%.

2-10 (a) T-bill worth $9500. (b) 5.6% 1-period return.

2-11 T-bill buyer earns 4.17% for 65 days. Bond equivalent yield is 23.077% per annum for a 360-day year.

2-12 13.3745% over 10 years.

2-13 For the municipal bond the before-tax and after-tax returns are equal; the corporate after-tax return of 8% (that is 12% − 4%) is better.

2-14 XYZ's 1-year return is 15.38%.

2-15 The buyer earns 4.17% over 65 days; the bond equivalent yield for a 360-day year is 23.077%; for a 365-day year, 25.76%.

2-16 The 30-day gain is 1.04%; the bond equivalent yield is 12.48% for a 360-day year, or 13.44% for a 365-day year.

2-17 1-A; 2-B; 3-C.		2-23 d	
2-18 1-D; 2-C; 3-B; 4-A.		2-24 d	
2-19 b		2-25 d	
2-20 d		2-26 d	
2-21 d		2-27 d	
2-22 d			

Chapter 3

3-7 The GGG conversion value is $20 \times \$40 = \$800$.

3-8 The GGG conversion premium is $\$950 - \$800 = \$150$.

3-9 (a) Before-tax return is 40%. (b) $(40\%)(1.0 - .33) = 26.66\%$ after-tax return. (c) After the commission and taxes, her income was 1.66%.

3-10 Frame owes preferred shareholders $100,000 from last year, plus $100,000 for this year; this exhausts Frame's $200,000 profit. Common stockholders will be displeased.

3-11 (a) After the initial offering:

Par value, $1 per share, 100,000 shares	$ 100,000
Additional paid-in capital, $9 per share	900,000
Total net worth (or equity)	$1,000,000

(b) After 1-year of manufacturing:

Par value, $1 per share, 100,000 shares	$ 100,000
Additional paid-in capital, $9 per share	900,000
Retained earnings	50,000
Total net worth	$1,050,000

3-12 (a) Conversion premium = $5 per share, or 25%. (b) $1000/$25 = 40 shares; ($30 per share)(40 shares) = $1200

$$\text{Return on convertible} = \frac{\text{price change, \$200 + coupon interest, \$80}}{\text{purchase price, \$1000}} = 28\%$$

$1000 into common equals 50 shares = $1000/20.

$$\text{Return on common} = \frac{(\$30 - \$20)(50 \text{ shares}) + (\$0.60)(50)}{\$1000} = 53\%$$

Thus, the investor in common stock would receive the higher return.
     (c) Converted bond equals $21 \times 40 = \$840$.

$$\text{Return on convertible} = \frac{(\$1000 - \$1000) + \$80}{\$1000} = 8\%$$

$$\text{Return on common} = \frac{(\$21 - \$20)(50) + (\$.60)(50)}{\$1000} = \frac{\$80}{\$1000} = 8\%$$

(d) The bond's converted value is $18 \times 40 = \$720$. The return on the convertible is the same as (c).

$$\text{Return on common} = \frac{[(\$18 - \$20) + (\$0.60)](50 \text{ shares})}{\$1000} = -7\%$$

Thus, the investor in the convertible would receive the higher return.

3-13 (a) NG&E's preferred is cumulative, so the 19X1 dividend must have been made up in 19X2, since common dividends were paid. The return over 3 years is $80 + 0 + ($80 \times 2) = $240. The 13% preferred is noncumulative; the dividend is not made up. The investor over 3 years receives $130 + 0 + $130 = $260. The investor could buy $1000/$40 = 25 shares of common and over 3 years would receive ($0.80 \times 25) + 0 + ($1 \times 25) = $45. (b) Noncumulative received more income than cumulative because its higher return covered the missed dividend.

3-14 Intercorporate cash dividends are 85% tax-exempt. (a) After-tax bond yield: $(1.0 - .25)(10\%) = 7.5\%$. (b) $.15 \times .25 = 3.75\%$ of the dividend for taxes leaves 96.25% of preferred's 8% cash, or 7.7% after taxes. Preferred's after-tax yield is higher.

3-15 (a) Biddle return for year 2 is -38%; for year 3, 55%. (b) The 2-for-1 split means per share values must be halved:

Year	Adjusted ending prices	Dividend
$t + 1$	$25	$1.00
$t + 2$	15	.50
$t + 3$	22.50	.75

Thus, the return for year 2 is -38%; for year 3, 55%; the returns are unchanged.

3-16	e		3-20	c
3-17	d		3-21	d
3-18	d		3-22	c
3-19	e		3-23	c

Chapter 4

4-11 $500 \times \$40 \times .6 = \$12,000$.

4-12 500 shares $\times \$40 \times .75 = \$15,000$.

4-13 100 shares $\times \$50 \times .65 = \$3250$.

4-14 See Equation (4-2); margin transformed a 100% price rise into a 173.6% gain, ignoring commissions.

4-15 300 shares $\times \$50 \times .65 = \$9750$ margin and $5250 debt from ESIC initially. Maintenance margin is

300 shares × $50 × (.35) = $5250. Solved price: $26.92. Thus, there would be a decline of $50 − $26.92 = $23.08 before call.

4-16 (300 shares)($50/share)(1 − .35) = $9750. Jones has debt of $5250. The maintenance margin requirement is also $5250. If the price falls to $15, $2325 additional cash is required.

4-17 ($25.00 − $2.10)/$32.50 = 70.46%

4-18 Nonmargined return: [($75 − $50) + 0]/$50 = 50%

4-19 (1) Thin and shallow; (2) thin and deep; (3) broad and shallow; (4) broad and deep.

4-20 (a) and (b)

Acct.	Mkt. value	Equity	Margin requirement 50%	75%
Able	$0	$ 8,000	$16,000	$10,666
Baker	8,000	4,000	Zero	Mrg. call
Jones	20,000	16,000	$12,000	$1,333
Smith	30,000	10,000	Mrg. call	Mrg. call

(c) Brokers lend clients money to maximize commission income.

4-21

Mvmt.	Change in cash account	Change in margin account
100% gain	$r_c = +100\%$	$r_m = +182\%$
50% decline	$r_c = -50\%$	$r_m = -91\%$

4-22 1-D; 2-C; 3-E; 4-F; 5-B; 6-A.

4-23 d

4-24 b

4-25 a

4-26 d

4-27 b

4-28 e

4-29 c

4-30 d

4-31 d

Chapter 5

5-8

Stock	Price change
Mite	+250%
Middie	+ 50
Maxum	+ 33

Index	Value of the index
(a) Value-weighted	42.68 %
(b) Price-weighted	75.0
(c) Equally weighted	110.999

(d) The value-weighted index suggested the smallest rate of price appreciation, 42.68%, because value weighting assigns largest weight to the largest issuer, Maxum, which in this case had the smallest percent gain. The equally weighted index registered the largest percent price gain because it gave equal weights to the large 250% gain of the Mite stock and the more modest gains from the two larger issuers. The price-weighted index yielded an intermediate value of 75%.

5-9 Case's 10% change had a small impact on the average because it is a price-weighted average and Case has a low price. When Ace rose 10%, this had a larger effect on the average because Ace has a high price. Price-weighting is inappropriate in many applications and can result in misleading values (like the DJIA).

5-10 (a) Gurlz Cloz arithmetic mean is 11.5%; (b) SD = 13.154847%; (c) GMR = 10.72%.

5-11 (a) IBM's mean return is 8.045%, and standard deviation is 10.5925%; (b) GMR is 7.549%.

5-12 e

5-13 c

5-14 e

5-15 d

5-16 b

5-17 c

5-18 e

5-19 d

5-20 b

Chapter 6

6-9 1-H; 2-I; 3-J; 4-K; 5-L; 6-A; 7-B; 8-C; 9-D; 10-E; 11-F; 12-G.

6-10 1-C; 2-E; 3-F; 4-D; 5-G; 6-A; 7-B.

6-11 c

6-12 c

6-13 a

6-14 d

6-15 e

6-16 d

6-17 b

6-18 c

6-19 d

Chapter 7

7-10

Taylors' ordinary income	$20,000
Net capital loss ($5,000 less $6,000)	(1,000)
	$19,000
Less: 2 exemptions (2 × $2,150)	4,300
	$14,700
Less: Standard deduction	5,700
	$ 9,000
Less: Tax on $10,000 (Table 7-1)	1,350
After-tax income	$ 7,650

7-11 $(1.0 - .33) \times 8\% = 5.3\% < 6.0\%$; therefore, the municipal bond is the better investment for Lind.

7-12

Gross estate of Mary Jones	$1,800,000
Less: Unlimited marital deduction	1,800,000
Adjusted gross estate	$ 0
Plus: Lifetime gifts	
(½ × $500,000 less $10,000	
annual exclusion)	240,000
Taxable estate	$ 240,000
Tax on $240,000	$ 28,000
Less: Unified credit	
available in 1988	192,800
Tax due on estate of Mary Jones	$ 0
Gross estate of John Jones	$2,000,000
Less: Unlimited marital deduction	0
Adjusted gross estate	$2,000,000
Plus: Lifetime gifts	
(½ × $500,000 less $10,000	
annual exclusion)	240,000
Taxable estate	$2,240,000
Tax on $2,240,000	$ 898,400
Less: Unified credit	
available in 1988	192,800
Tax due on estate of John Jones	$ 705,600

7-13 (*a*) For a 28% tax rate on both capital gains and ordinary income, the taxable return is 14.4%. (*b*) If the capital gains tax is half [(.5)(28%) = 14%] the tax rate on ordinary income, the after-tax return is 16.64%.

7-14 The coupon income is tax-exempt, but Rose owes 25% taxes (or $100) on the $400 short-term gain.

7-15 Sontab's average tax rate is $10,000/$60,000 = 16.6%, with a 25% marginal tax rate.

7-16 Chambers should not take the bank loan to buy the bond.

7-17 *b*		**7-19** *c*	
7-18 *b*		**7-20** *c*	

Chapter 8

8-11 1-A; 2-E; 3-B; 4-D; 5-C.

8-12 1-C; 2-D; 3-A; 4-B.

8-13 1-B; 2-A; 3-D; 4-C.

8-14 1-C; 2-A; 3-B.

8-15 *a*

8-16 *a*

8-17 *b*

Chapter 9

9-10

From	Equity	N.W.C.	Net L-T plant	L-T debt
L-T debt pay.	Negligible	+	Negligible	−
Pos. earn.	+	+	Negligible	Negligible
Deprec.	Negligible	+	−	Negligible
Sale above book	+	+	−	Negligible
Buy plant	Negligible	−	+	Negligible or +
Cash div.	−	−	Negligible	Negligible

9-11 (*a*) Ultima's current ratio of 2.31 is too high; (*b*) its quick ratio of 1.17 times is a little too high; (*c*) its inventory turnover of 4 times per year seems slow; (*d*) its average age of inventory of 91 days is too high; (*e*) even if 10% of Ultima's annual sales are on credit, the firm's accounts receivable turnover would be only .86 times per year—too slow for a company that carries no inventory of finished goods. Credit terms are too lenient. (*f*) The accounts receivable turnover of only .86 times per year is too slow; this implies that the average age of accounts receivable is 424.4 days old. The firm is highly profitable, but the owner-manager is ignoring its inventory and accounts receivable.

(a)

	1991		1992	
Sales	$870,000	100%	$960,000	100%
−$ Goods sold	500,000	57	600,000	63
Gross profit	$370,000	43	$360,000	37
− Oper. exp.	300,000	35	320,000	33
EBIT*	$ 70,000	8	$ 40,000	4

*EBIT stands for "earnings before interest and taxes," or operating income.

(b)

	1991	1992	Percentage change
Sales	$870,000	$960,000	10%
−$ Goods sold	500,000	600,000	20
Gross profit	$370,000	$360,000	(3)
− Oper. exp.	300,000	320,000	7
EBIT	$ 70,000	$ 40,000	(43)

(c) The percentage change calculations indicate Mohawk suffered a 43% decline in its earnings before interest and taxes even though its sales are up 10%. This profit erosion is attributable to a 20% increase in Mohawk's cost of goods sold. The decrease in profits would have been even worse if operating expenses had not shrunk from 35% of sales to 33%.

9-13 (a) 1992 common-sized balance sheet; total assets 100%:

Curr. assets	$200,000	Curr. liabilities		$100,000
	28.6%			14.2%
		L-T liabilities		$300,000
		(at 9% int.)		42.9%
Fixed assets	$500,000	Net worth		$300,000
	71.4%			42.9%

(b) Total asset turnover was $960k/$700k = 1.37 times. (c) After-tax income is:

EBIT	$40,000
Less: Interest expense (9% × $300,000)	27,000
Taxable income	$13,000
Less: 30% taxes (30% of $13,000)	3,900
After-tax income	$ 9,100

After-tax profit margin on sales is $9,100/$960,000 = 95/100 of 1%. (d) Total assets to equity ratio is 2.333 times.

(e)
$$\frac{\text{Net income}}{\text{Equity}} = \frac{\text{sales}}{\text{T.A.}} \times \frac{\text{T.A.}}{\text{equity}} \times \frac{\text{income}}{\text{sales}} = \text{ROE}$$

$$\frac{\$9,100}{\$300,000} = \frac{\$960,000}{\$700,000} \times \frac{\$700,000}{\$300,000} \times \frac{\$9,100}{\$960,000} = 3.03\%$$

(f) Growth rate = percent of net income retained × ROE = (100% − 40% payout rate = 60%) × 3.0% = 1.8%. Growth rate can be decomposed:

$$\text{Growth rate} = \frac{\text{RE}}{\text{NI}} \times \frac{\text{NI}}{\text{sales}} \times \frac{\text{sales}}{\text{TA}} \times \frac{\text{TA}}{\text{EQ}} = \frac{\text{RE}}{\text{EQ}}$$

1.8% = .018 = .6 × .0095 × 1.37 times × 2.33 times

Growth rate of 1.8% could be doubled if Mohawk could cut its cost of goods sold enough to regain past profitability.

9-14	b	9-19	e
9-15	e	9-20	e
9-16	e	9-21	e
9-17	b	9-22	b
9-18	d		

Chapter 10

10-8 One plausible answer is suggested below:

Rate of return	Probability	
−100% = −1.0	1/20 = .05	Worst
+298% = 2.98	5/20 = .25	Arbitrarily
+374% = 3.74	8/20 = .40	(E)r
+450% = 4.50	5/20 = .25	Arbitrarily
+848% = 8.48	1/20 = .05	Best
	1.0 = 1.0	

$E(r) = 3.74 = 374\%$; $VAR(r) = 46.0904$; and SD = 6.7889. The probability distribution of returns should be symmetric, with the lower end at −100%, the upper end at 848%, and the mean, or $E(r)$, at 374%.

10-9 Grant started experiencing declining profits in 1966. These declines turned into losses in 1974 and 1975, and the firm had to borrow money to stay solvent. Grant's financial leverage ratios had been rising for years and reached dangerously high levels in 1974 and 1975 as losses grew rapidly. Obvious external warning signals were the cash dividend cut in 1974, declining bond quality ratings, and falling prices of Grant's bonds and stock.

10-10 The preceding answer about the W. T. Grant bankruptcy suggests ideas.

10-11 Apex's lengthy solution is in the instructor's manual.

10-12 *e*

10-14 *c*

10-13 *b*

10-15 *a*

Chapter 11

11-7 $1,000 (1 + 6\%)^{10 \text{ years}} = \$17,908$

11-8 (*a*) $\$100/(1 + 10\%)^2 = \$82.64$

(*b*) $\$100/(1 + 10\%) + \$100/(1 + 10\%)^2 = \$173.55$

11-9 (*a*) $\$100(1 + 10\%)^{10 \text{ years}} = \$259.37$

(*b*) $\$100(1 + 10\%)^2 + \$100(1 + 10\%)^1 = \$231$

11-10 $\$100,000/(1 + 10)^{25} = \$9,229.60$

11-11 $\$5000 (1 + 10\%)^4 - \$5000 = \$5000 (1.4641) - \$5000 = \$2320.50$ gain

11-12 Figure 11-3 should be recreated for a 3% coupon bond.

11-13 *b*

11-16 *d*

11-14 *c*

11-17 *e*

11-15 *d*

11-18 *b*

Chapter 12

12-10 (*a*) Equation (12-4) indicates that the present value of a 3-year bond with $1000 face value and a 7% coupon is $1026.73. (*b*) Equation (12-5) indicates that the 3-year bond's Macaulay's duration is 2.8107 years.

12-11 See Equations (12-2), (12-3), and (12-4) in the textbook for an 8.0% coupon, $1000 bond. (*a*) Current yield is $80/\$967.59 = 8.26\%$; (*b*) AYTM is 8.955%; (*c*) the bond's exact YTM is 9.0004%.

12-12 The 4-year bond's Macaulay's duration is 3.56946 years.

12-13 Invest $8000 in T-bonds to earn interest income without default risk. To omit interest rate risk use either of two strategies: (1) maturity matching: buy a bond that matures in 2 years with an $8000 maturity value or (2) duration matching: buy a bond with a Macaulay's duration of 2 years that can accumulate a total value of $8000 in 2 years.

12-14 Create a graph like Figure 12-3.

12-15 *b*

12-19 *d*

12-16 *c*

12-20 *b*

12-17 *d*

12-21 *a*

12-18 *d*

Chapter 13

13-8 Liquidation value becomes more relevant, since Ajax is teetering on the edge of bankruptcy. Analysis suggests Ajax stock may be worth its asset value of $16 per share, or more. If the assets have been maintained, the plant and equipment probably have a liquidation value substantially above depreciated book value. Thus, Ajax may be a good buy at its market price of $11 per share, or even at its per share asset liquidation value. The assets could conceivably bring in enough cash to make the stock worth $18 or $20 per share.

13-9 Lengthy answer is in instructor's manual.

13-10 Technological innovation should cause Archer stock to appreciate to $50 per share, since $d_1/(k - g) = \$2(1.06)/(.10 - .06) = \$2.12/.04 = \$53$. A price increase of approximately $24.40 (i.e., $53 − $28.60) per share should occur. This gain results from an increase in Archer's earnings multiplier from $(D/EPS)/(k - g) = 1/(10\% - 3\%) = 14.29$ times up to $1/(10\% - 6\%) = 25$ times, presuming the cash dividend payout ratio remains at $D/EPS = 1.0 = 100\%$. This increase results from an expected increase in the growth rate from 3% to 6%.

13-11 Both assets have present values of approximately $770, their current market price. Therefore, other factors are relevant. The T-bond is appropriate for a highly risk-averse investor, while a more aggressive investor would prefer the stock.

Salient characteristics	T-bond	Auto stock
Cashflow	$35	$35
Rate of app.	1.65%	6%
Default risk	Zero	Significant
Int. rate risk	Large	Negligible
Mgt. voice	Zero	Stockholders' meeting
Life	25 years	Indefinite, perhaps infinity

13-12 *d*

13-14 *c*

13-13 *d*

13-15 *b*

Chapter 14

14-9 (*a*) Cashflow = after-tax income + noncash expenses (like depreciation). (*b*) Unlike accounting income, cashflow is not distorted by the inventory valuation convention used or changes in the depreciation guidelines.

14-10

	(*a*) Expensed in 19X1			
	19X1	19X2	through	19X5
Gross income	$200	$200		$200
Less: Program's cost	100	0		0
Taxable income	$100	$200		$200
Times: Tax rate	.5	.5		.5
Income tax	$ 50	$100	. . . . . .	$100
After-tax income	$ 50	$100	. . . . . .	$100

	(*b*) Depreciated		
	19X1	through	19X5
Gross income	$200		$200
Less: Program's cost	20		20
Taxable income	$180		$180
Times: Tax rate	.5		.5
Income tax	$ 90	. . . . . .	$ 90
After-tax income	$ 90	. . . . . .	$ 90

(*c*) Expensing the program off in 1 year provides a truer reflection of the facts, which some investors appreciate. But, depreciating the software delays paying the income taxes; the investors would benefit from that interest-free loan.

14-11 (*a*) With 5,000,000 shares of stock Meadows' cash dividends per share are $2.00, and (*b*) earnings per share are $2.53. (*c*) Total cash flow = net income + noncash expenses (depreciation) + accrued expenses = $12,672,000 + $3,200,000 + $1,000,000 = $16,872,000, or $3.37 per share cashflow. (*d*) Cashflow analysis reveals that Meadows is more profitable than its cash dividends or net income suggests. If depreciation is straight-line, it is a substantial future cashflow.

14-12 *e*   14-17 *d*

14-13 *b*   14-18 *d*

Chapter 15

15-10 The larger-than-average price change on day 1 coupled with a large volume of shares traded on day 2 suggests that the market probably received new information about Hemmel's and some *information traders* bought the stock. The large volume of shares traded on day 8 is probably just a big *liquidity trade* not associated with new information. The larger-than-average price move on day 10 is also probably just another meaningless price move, because so few shares were traded.

15-11 (*a*) $31.95, $32.675, $32.875, $32.675, $32.40, $32.275, $32.60, $32.975, $33.425, $33.60; (*b*) price range of $5.25; (*c*) moving averages range of $1.65.

15-12 A graph is required.

15-13 FFSC demonstrates slight weakness relative to the sled industry and relative to the S&P 500; therefore, it should have slightly below-average returns.

Chapter 16

16-12 (*a*) The gradual price decline in Figure 16-7(*b*) would be more conducive to technical analysis than an instantaneous reaction would. Gradual reaction causes price trends (positive serial correlation). (*b*) NYSE prices react instantaneously, as in Figure 16-7(*a*), because the NYSE-listed stocks are closely observed by many information traders. (*c*) The gradual reaction in Figure 16-7(*b*) could result from learning lags. However, competition between Associated Press International (API) and United Press International (UPI) should get the news around the world instantly, so the learning lags illustrated in Figure 16-7(*b*) do not occur.

16-13 Hemmel's stock would generate four buys and zero sells with a 4% filter, and no trades with the 8% filter.

16-14 *d*   16-18 *c*

16-15 *d*   16-19 *b*

16-16 *b*   16-20 *d*

16-17 *d*   16-21 *b*

Chapter 17

17-12 Bull market returns should fill the right-hand tail of a probability distribution of returns, returns near zero should fill the middle of the probability distribution, and bear market returns should fill up most of the left-hand (or negative) tail of a stock's distribution.

17-13 1-C; 2-E; 3-D; 4-A; 5-B.

17-14 *e*		**17-17** *c*
17-15 *b*		**17-18** *d*
17-16 *c*		**17-19** *b*

Chapter 18

18-8 $(1.0 + 10\% \text{ annual inflation})^2 - (1.10)^2 = 1.21$

18-9 (*a*) ($150 + $6)/$130 = 1.2 = 1.0 + 20% per 6 months, or $(1.2)^2 = 1.44 = 1.0 + 44\%$ per year. (*b*) 115.5/110 = 1.05 = 1.0 + 5% per 6 months inflation, or $(1.05)^2 = 1.1025 = 1.0 + 10.25\%$ annualized inflation rate. (*c*) 1.2/1.05 = 1.14286 = 1.0 + 14.286% real return over 6 months, or $(1.14286)^2 = 1.30612 = 1.0 + 30.612\%$ annual real return.

18-10 (*a*) If $(1.12)^T = 2.0$, then $T = 6.11625$ years causes doubling. (*b*) In $T = 6.11625$ years the cost of living will increase: $(1.06)^{6.11625} = 1.42816 = 1.0 + 42.816\%$. The purchasing power of twice as many dollars will be 40% more: 2/1.42816 = 1.40 = 1.0 + 40.0% increase in real purchasing power.

18-11 (*a*) (1 + 10%)/(1 + 5%) = 1.1/1.05 = 1.0476 = 1.0 + 4.76% annual increase in pretax purchasing power. (*b*) Nominal after-tax return: 10%(1.0 − .34) = 6.6% per annum. After 5% inflation, the real after-tax rate of return is 1.066/1.05 = 1.0152 = 1.0 + 1.52% after-tax real rate per year.

18-12 CFA solution to question: A 33.6975% increase in unit sales is expected in auto sales.

Scenario	Forecasts	×	Probability	=	Product
1	−.295 + 4.4(6%) = 26.105%	×	.3	=	7.8316%
2	−.295 + 4.4(8%) = 34.25%	×	.5	=	17.125%
3	−.295 + 4.4(10%) = 43.705%	×	.2	=	8.741%
Expected percentage increase					33.6975%

Marginal income tax rate	Rate of inflation (INF)				
	4.0%	5.0%	6.0%	7.0%	8.0%
25%	8.0%	9.3%	10.7%	12.0%	13.3%
30	8.6	10.0	11.5	12.9	14.3
35	9.3	10.8	12.3	13.9	15.4
40	10.0	11.7	13.4	15.0	16.7

18-14 To get inflation-adjusted (or constant 19X2 purchasing-power) dollars for the Meyers family, inflation must be divided out of each year's income. The cost of living is expected to rise 63.84% during the next 5 years, so retirement income in constant 19X2 dollars is:

Year	S.S.	Rent	Wages	Cash Div.	Tot. Inc.
19X2	$4,000	$12,000	$2,300	$2,500	$20,800
19X3	3,830	11,945	1,823	2,462	20,060
19X4	3,736	11,122	2,123	2,207	19,188
19X5	3,282	9,996	1,417	2,089	16,784
19X6	3,053	8,894	730	1,991	14,668
19X7	2,807	8,240	977	1,892	13,916

(*a*) Mr. Meyers' real income from all sources other than rent decreased from 19X2 to 19X7, so the Meyers' total real income decreased 33% from 19X2 to 19X7. (*b*) Mr. Meyers' wages have shrunk the most, and dividends the least, constant dollars and also nominal dollars. (*c*) The Meyers family faces continued erosion of the purchasing power of their income.

18-15 1-C; 2-G; 3-A; 4-F; 5-B; 6-D; 7-E.

18-16 *d*		**18-19** *a*
18-17 *c*		**18-20** *c*
18-18 *c*		**18-21** *a*

19-11   1-D; 2-B; 3-C; 4-A.

19-12   1-C; 2-D; 3-E; 4-A; 5-B.

19-13   *e*   19-15   *b*

19-14   *b*

Chapter 20

20-9

Corporate name	Price of stock	Est. value per share	Buy, sell, or no action?
Acme Corp.	$87.75	$90	No action
Baker Inc.	11.125	13	No action
Crown Corp.	31.75	40	Buy
Delta Inc.	19.50	25	Buy
Evans Corp.	44.25	30	Sell

20-10   (*a*) $20; (*b*) $15; (*c*) $15; (*d*) $20; (*e*) $20; (*f*) $20; (*g*) zero; (*h*) $15; (*i*) $15; (*j*) zero.

20-11   (*a*) Long position returns 10% over 6 months; (*b*) short position returns −10% (loss) over 6 months.

20-12   1-B; 2-C; 3-A; 4-D.

20-13   *b*   20-20   *c*

20-14   *b*   20-21   *e*

20-15   *d*   20-22   *e*

20-16   *d*   20-23   *d*

20-17   *d*   20-24   *e*

20-18   *d*   20-25   *e*

20-19   *c*   20-26   *d*

Chapter 21

21-11   (*a*) Bullish should hedge her position by either selling 100 shares of GM short at $80 per share or buying a put option on GM with an $80 striking price. (*b*) Bullish could carry her $40 per share gain into the future and have it taxed at the lower long-term capital gains tax rate by holding either the perfect hedge (obtainable with the offsetting short position) or the imperfect hedge (that requires purchasing a put).

21-12   (*a*) The intrinsic value per share of TI call was $108.75 − $90 = $18.75. (*b*) The estimated gain was Selling price/purchase price = $18.75/$1.375 = 13.636 = 1363.6%.

21-13   The puts all lost money. The October call with an exercise price of $350 was the most profitable in dollar terms, but not the most desirable.

	Call option		
	Oct. 340	Oct. 350	Oct. 360
Gains	$\dfrac{\$3260}{\$1250} = 2.608$	$\dfrac{\$3390}{\$\,650} = 5.215$	$\dfrac{\$2740}{\$\,350} = 7.828$
Prem.			

The October call with an exercise price of $360 had the highest precommission rate of return, 782.8%, over the 5 weeks.

21-14   Carleton's convertible $1100 bonds can be converted into 50 shares of stock at a cost of $1100/50 = $22 per share. Since the market price of Carleton's stock is $25 per share, the conversion would result in a profit of $25 − $22 = $3 per share. So Carleton's convertibles are underpriced. If the stock's price is at $25 per share, the bond's $1250 conversion value exceeds the convertible bond's market price of $1100, so arbitrage will be profitable until the price of the convertible bond is bid up to $1250.

21-15   Lengthy CFA answer in instructor's manual.

21-16   *d*   21-20   *a*

21-17   *d*   21-21   *d*

21-18   *b*   21-22   *a*

21-19   *d*

Chapter 22

22-11   (*a*) The average price rise in the noninverted months is about 4 cents per bushel per month. (*b*) The drop in the futures price to (an inverted level of) $270 per bushel in July probably results from anticipations that a large new crop will be harvested.

22-12   (*a*) If Joe sells short 10 S&P 500 contracts, his gain is 130 − 100 = 30 points per contract, for a total gain of $30(10 \text{ contracts})(\$500) = \$150,000$. Joe's equity would be his 100% initial margin of $10(130 \text{ per contract})(\$500) = \$650,000$; the return would be $\$150,000/\$650,000 = 23.07\%$ over 6 months. (b) This is 231% on 10% margin. (c) If Joe perversely sells short 10 S&P 500 contracts, he loses $130 - 150 = 20$ points per contract, for a total loss of $\$20(10 \text{ contracts})(\$500) = -\$100,000$. Joe's equity would be his initial payment of $(10)(130 \text{ per contract})(\$500) = \$650,000$; his rate of loss would be $-\$100,000/\$650,000 = -15.38\%$ over 6 months. Initial margin investment would be only $10(130)(\$500)(.10) = \$65,000$, so Joe's rate of loss would be $-\$100,000/\$65,000 = 153.8\%$ over the 6 months.

22-13 (a) Each wheat contract has a market value of $\$3(5000 \text{ bushels}) = \$15,000$. Assuming an initial margin of 10%, the cash outlay is $1500 per contract. Six contracts cost $6 \times \$1500 = \$9000$ plus $6 \times \$40 = \$240$ commissions, so $760 is left. (b) You earn 50 cents per bushel gain, or $\$0.50(6)(5000) = \$15,000$ gain, less $240 in commissions for a net gain of $14,760. Your holding period rate of return is (total net price gain)/(total investment) = $\$14,760/\$9,000 = 1.64$, or 64% over 3 months. (c) If the price of wheat falls to $2.25, you lose 75 cents a bushel, for a total loss of $\$0.75(6)(5000) = \$22,500$, plus $240 in commissions.

22-14 Your investment is $15,000 plus $350 of commissions. Your gain from the price decline is $50 per contract, for a total gain of $50(10 \text{ contracts})(100 \text{ ounces per contract}) = \$50,000$, minus $350 of commissions, for a net gain of $47,650.

22-15 (a) To hedge the position fully, sell short $\$7,500,000/(150 \times \$500) = 100$ S&P 500 futures contracts. (b) The total gross gain on the short futures contract is $150 - 120 = 30$ points on the S&P 500 Index, for a total gain of $\$30(100 \text{ contracts})(\$500) = \$1,500,000$, if we ignore commission costs.

22-16 1-C; 2-D; 3-E; 4-F; 5-A; 6-B.

22-17 *b*   **22-20** *d*

22-18 *d*   **22-21** *b*

22-19 *b*   **22-22** *d*

Chapter 23

23-12 There are several advantages of investing in real estate relative to investing in financial assets: (1) leverage, (2) tax shields, (3) more control. Relative to investing in financial assets, there are several disadvantages to invest-

ing in real estate: (1) structural flaws, (2) neighborhood risk, (3) lack of liquidity.

23-13 Gold is more liquid, a better inflation edge, and a better store of value than silver or other (industrial) metals. The precious metals other than gold do not possess the qualities of "moneyness" as gold does.

23-14 Most stamps appreciate slowly, if at all. Furthermore, most stamp collecting activities can be financially rewarding only if the stamp collector-investor assigns no cost to the time spent working on (buying, tending, displaying, and selling) the stamps. Also, stamps are illiquid investments.

23-15 *d*

23-16 *d*

23-17 *d*

23-18 *d*

23-19 *e*

Chapter 24

24-11 The risk and return statistics should be identical whether they are calculated with the ex ante data from Table 24-3 or the ex post data shown in Table 24-4. The difference is that Table 24-3 is an expected future joint probability distribution, whereas Table 24-4 is a historical record of the same returns shown in Table 24-3. $E(r_{\text{UST}}) = .07 = 7\%$ and $\text{VAR}(r_{\text{UST}}) = .0221$.

24-13 Figure 24-3 illustrates that the portfolio possibilities cannot be convex away from the $E(r)$ axis. So the graph on the right is wrong.

24-14

| | | | Port. std. dev. | | |
Percent in A	Percent in B	Portfolio's E(r)	+1.0 Corr.	Zero Corr.	−1.0 Corr.
90	10	10.2	12.1	10.1	7.7
70	30	12.6	14.3	10.1	1.1
50	50	15.0	16.5	12.3	5.5
30	70	17.4	18.7	15.7	12.1
10	90	19.8	20.9	19.8	18.7

24-15 *a*   **24-20** *c*

24-16 *c*   **24-21** *a*

24-17 *a*   **24-22** *c*

24-18 *d*   **24-23** *c*

24-19 *d*

| | Three correlations | Assumed weights for C | | | | Fill in the three essential formulas below. |
		1.0	.4	.2	Zero	
x_S	$\rho = +1$	0	.5	.8	1.0	$x_S = 1.0 - x_C$
	$\rho = 0$	0	.5	.8	1.0	
	$\rho = -1$	0	.5	.8	1.0	
$E(r_P)$	$\rho = +1$	8.0%	10.4%	9.2%	14.0%	$E(r_P) = x_C E(r_C) + x_S E(r_S)$
	$\rho = 0$	8.0%	10.4%	9.2%	14.0%	
	$\rho = -1$	8.0%	10.4%	9.2%	14.0%	
Portfolio	$\rho = +1$	3.0%	4.2%	3.6%	6.0%	
standard	$\rho = 0$	3.0%	3.0%	2.7%	6.0%	$SD(r_P) = x_C \sigma_C + x_S \sigma_S + \sqrt{2x_C x_S \sigma_C \sigma_S}$
deviation	$\rho = -1$	3.0%	.6%	1.2%	6.0%	

(d) A graph is required.

Chapter 25

25-11 Cyclical auto manufacturer A has a beta coefficient of $b_A = 1.5$. Red ink manufacturer I has returns that covary inversely with the market because red ink sells better in recessions, when accountants make entries in red ink; the beta coefficient is $b_1 = -.5$ before the merger. Assume that firms A and I are of equal value and are merged into one firm denoted "F" with a weighted average beta of 1.0: $b_F = .5b_A + .5b_1 = 1.0 = (.5)(1.5) + (.5)(-.5)$. Since required rates of return are a function of systematic risk, the two firms' required returns array as follows: $k_A > k_F = R > k_1$.

25-13 (a) The Standard & Poor's 500 Stocks Composite Index data and the IBM stock data are in the

25-12 (a), (b), and (c)

instructor's manual. (b) IBM's beta = 1.021; alpha = -0.998; VAR(r) = 5001.340; and coefficient of determination = 0.56176. IBM's beta is that of a slightly aggressive stock. (c) IBM's coefficient of determination explains over 56% of IBM's total variance. (d) IBM's high beta and high coefficient of determination suggest that it is a little worse than average as a candidate for risk-reducing diversification. (e) IBM's stock price fell more than the 4-for-1 split in 1979 suggested it should; the CRL had negative residual returns for a few months after its stock split.

25-14 a	25-17 d
25-15 a	25-18 a
25-16 c	

| | Three correl- -ations | Assumed weights for C | | | First, fill in the three essential formulas below: |
		1.3	1.0	−.2	
x_S	$\rho = +1$	−.3	0	1.2	$x_S = 1.0 - x_C$
	$\rho = 0$	−.3	0	1.2	
	$\rho = -1$	−.3	0	1.2	
$E(r_P)$	$\rho = +1$	15.8%	8.0%	6.8%	$E(r_P) = x_C E(r_C) + x_S E(r_S)$
	$\rho = 0$	15.8%	8.0%	6.8%	
	$\rho = -1$	15.8%	8.0%	6.8%	
Portfolio	$\rho = +1$	6.9%	3.0%	2.4%	
standard	$\rho = 0$	7.8%	3.0%	3.8%	$\sqrt{VAR(r_P)} = x^2_C \sigma^2_C + x^2_S \sigma^2_S + 2x_C x_S \sigma_C \sigma_S$
deviation	$\rho = -1$	8.6%	3.0%	4.8%	

(d) A graph is required.

Chapter 26

26-9 (*a*) APT suggests that the $E(r)$ for asset h should be:

$$E(r_h) = R + \lambda_1 b_{h1} + \lambda_2 b_{h2} + \lambda_3 b_{h3}$$

$$= 5\% + 1.1(1.5) + 1.5(.8) + .8(-.6) = 7.37\%$$

(*b*) $E(r) = 7.37\%$ for asset h is the discount rate to find the present value. The present value of a $110 cashflow expected in 1 year is $p = \$110/[1.0 + E(r)] = \$110/1.0737 = \$102.45$

26-10 Consider the following hypothetical three-factor APT model:

$$k_z = R + \lambda_1 b_{z1} + \lambda_2 b_{z2} + \lambda_3 b_{z3}$$

If the total risk of asset z is unsystematic risk, then all its beta sensitivity coefficients are zero, b_{z1}, b_{z2}, and $b_{z3} = 0$. Thus, the APT model above reduces to the simple model: $E(r_z) = R$

26-11 (*a*) The appropriate single-factor APT model is:

$$E(r_i) = R + .1b_i = .05 + .1b_i$$

(*b*) The 1-month T-bill has $E(r_1) = .05 + .1b_i = .05 + .01 = .06 = 6.0\%$. The 2-month T-bill has $E(r_i) = .05 + .1b_i = .05 + .02 = .07 = 7.0\%$. (*c*) The $E(r_2) = 7\%$ yield is above the $E(r_1) = 6\%$ yield for the 1-month T-bill; therefore, it is underpriced. The 7% yield equals the $E(r_2) = 7\%$ for the 2-month T-bill; therefore, the 2-month T-bill is priced correctly. (*d*) A graph would illustrate that the actual yield of 7% on the 1-month T-bill is above $E(r_1) = 6\%$, while the 2-month T-bill is correctly priced to yield 7%.

26-12 *b*		**26-15** *d*	
26-13 *a*		**26-16** *b*	
26-14 *d*		**26-17** *d*	

Chapter 27

27-9 (*a*) François paid FF180 per share for Michelin. At an exchange rate of $1/FF6 = $0.1666 Françoise paid FF180(.1666) = $30 per share, since she is a foreign investor. (*b*) François earned a rate of return of (FF200 − FF180)/FF180 = 11.1% over his 2-month holding period. Françoise earned {[FF200(.20) = $40] − [FF180(.1666) = $30]}/[FF180(.1666) = $30] = 33.3%.

(*c*) François made a 20% gain in the foreign exchange market because the dollar depreciated to $x_1 = \$1/FF5 = \$0.20$ per franc in time for her to convert FF200 back into $40; she would have gotten only FF200(.1666) = $33.32 if the dollar had not fallen relative to the FF.

27-10 An American would be a foreign investor in Barclays. Equation (27-6) suggests the investor earns 15.5%:

$$r_f = r_d + r_c + r_d r_c = 10\% + 5\% + 10\%(5\%) = 15.5\%$$

Total risk would be a combination of the stock's risk and the currency risk and their covariance:

$$VAR(r_f)$$
$$= VAR(r_c) + VAR(r_d) + \sqrt{VAR(r_c)}\sqrt{VAR(r_d)}\,\rho_{cd}$$

$$= (.2)^2 + (.1)^2 + 2(.2)(.1)(.5) = .04 + .01 + .02 = .07$$

27-11 (*a*) Kierulf paid $100,000, or SF150,000, for one share of H-LR stock. (*b*) His 3-month rate of return is zero. (*c*) He made a SF160,000/SF150,000 = 1.066666667 = 6.66% price gain on H-LR. However, he suffered a loss on the SF foreign exchange ($0.625/$0.66666 = .9375) of 6.25% that wiped out his gain from price appreciation on H-LR:

$$(1.0 + \text{H-LR return})(1.0 + \text{currency return}) =$$
$$1.0666666(.9375) = 1.0 = 1.0 + \text{zero return}$$

27-12 (*a*) The 25 pounds converted to dollars is $21.73913, and 30 pounds converted to dollars is $24.00. The return is $24/$21.73913 = 1.104, or 10.4% return. Foreign exchange risk hurt the American investor. (*b*) British investor: 30 pounds/25 pounds = 1.2, or 20% return.

27-13 Last year, at time $t − 1$, $1 American would purchase 1/.0083333 = 120 yen. But the dollar appreciated 10%, so that at time t $1 would buy 1/.007575757 = 130 yen. The currency gain is 10%, and the total gain is 37.5%, that is, (1 + market return)(1 + currency percent change) = 1.25(1.10) = 1.375, or 37.5% gain.

27-14

	Correlation matrix			Standard
	U.S.	U.K.	Japan	deviation
U.S.	1.00			21.843%
U.K.	.659	1.00		46.754
Japan	.389	.152	1.00	43.092

27-15 (*a*) The correlation between Australia and Canada is .747. (*b*) The standard deviations of Australia and Canada are 28.867% and 21.407%, respectively.

27-16 $E(r_p)$ from the 25-25-50 portfolio is 17.895%, and the standard deviation is 25.88%.

27-17   The 60-40 portfolio's $E(r)$ = 13.92%, and the standard deviation is 22.80361%. See Equation (27-2).

27-18   Standard deviation of the 50-50 portfolio is 20.08931%.

27-19   The lengthy CFA solution is in the instructor's manual.

27-20   The lengthy CFA solution is in the instructor's manual.

27-21	e		27-24	c
27-22	d		27-25	b
27-23	a		27-26	c

Chapter 28

28-12 and 28-13

Portfolio	S_i for R = 3%	S_i for R = 6%
Alpha	1.333	.333 (worst)
Beta	.875 (worst)	.5
Gamma	1.666 (best)	1.1666 (best)
Delta	.9230	.6923
Epsilon	1.0	.80

Portfolio	T_i for R = 3%	T_i for R = 6%
Alpha	.10	.025 (worst)
Beta	.07 (worst)	.04
Gamma	.0909	.0636
Delta	.10	.075
Epsilon	.107 (best)	.0857 (best)

The required graph is in the instructor's manual.

28-14	b		28-17	c
28-15	d		28-18	e
28-16	d			

GLOSSARY

Accelerated depreciation Writing off larger amounts of depreciation in the early years of an asset's life than in the asset's later years. Sum-of-the-years'-digits and double-declining balance are two examples of accelerated depreciation.

Accounting earnings The net income on the income and expense statement prepared by an accountant who uses generally accepted accounting procedures.

Accounting inconsistencies Changes in the generally accepted accounting procedure used by a firm to account for some event that changes the firm's *accounting* earnings per share even though *true* economic earnings are unchanged.

Active traders Investors that buy and sell securities frequently and aggressively in hopes of earning additional returns. The opposite of passive, or inactive, traders.

Agency cost The difference between what an enterprise is worth if it is managed by its owners compared with the presumably smaller amount it is worth if it is managed by the owners' agents. (See also **agency-principal relationship**.)

Agency-principal relationship The arrangement between one party (called the *principal*) who pays another party (called the *agent*) to manage the principal's assets and make decisions on behalf of the principal. If assets are not managed in the principal's best interests, *agency costs* result.

Aggressive asset An asset with a beta coefficient greater than 1. (See also **defensive asset**.)

Alpha The regression intercept term in the **characteristic regression line (CRL)**.

American depository receipt (ADR) Documents issued by large international banks evidencing a bank's ownership of shares of foreign securities, which it holds in its safe while the ADRs are traded. The bank passes any interest or cash dividends through to the holder of the ADR.

Annuity A financial contract that provides its owner with equal annual cash receipts for a specified number of years into the future.

Arbitrage Buying an asset at a low price and simultaneously selling it or a similar asset at a higher price in order to profit from a perceived pricing discrepancy that violates the **law of one price.**

Arbitrage pricing theory (APT) A risk-return asset pricing model that can be based on one or more undiversifiable risk factors. [See also **capital asset pricing model (CAPM)**.]

Arrangement Provision of Chapter XI of the Bankruptcy Act. If a company is not judged bankrupt or is not weak enough to require reorganization, an officer of the court meets with creditors and arranges to postpone debt repayments or reduce them to save the firm from bankruptcy.

Arrears Cash dividend payments that are due to cumulative preferred stock investors but that have not yet been paid.

G-1

Art market The artists, the investors, the collectors, the agents, the auctioneers, the dealers, and the museums that create and purvey art.

Asked price See **bid–asked prices.**

Asset-backed securities Marketable debt securities collateralized by illiquid financial assets like mortgages, accounts receivable, leases, and installment loan contracts, used to finance the assets of a closed-end investment pool. Most issues are liquid because the investment banking firm that securitized the assets enhances their credit rating and maintains an active secondary market in them. (See also **securitization**.)

Average tax rate A taxpayer's total taxes stated as a percentage of the taxpayer's total taxable income. The average tax rate is always less than the **marginal tax rate** in a **progressive tax** system.

Balance sheet A financial statement that lists all the sources (namely, the liabilities and net worth) and uses (or assets) a firm has at the close of its accounting period.

Banker's acceptance A document ordering a bank to pay money to another party. When the bank signs (or accepts) a banker's acceptance on behalf of its customer in order to help the customer pay a bill, the acceptance becomes a money market security the bank can sell to another investor. It is payable within less than 270 days.

Banking Act of 1933 See **Glass-Steagall Act of 1933.**

Bankruptcy The condition that exists when a company or a person is unable to meet financial obligations and is ordered by a bankruptcy court to auction off any remaining assets to pay debts. (Compare with **reorganization** and **arrangement**.)

Bar chart In a financial context, a graph of a security's price created by drawing tiny vertical lines (or bars) from the highest to the lowest prices on each trading day.

Basis The difference between the spot price and the futures price for a given commodity; equals the commodity's carrying cost in normal market conditions.

Basis point A hundredth of a percentage point.

Bear market A market condition in which the market indexes and the prices of most securities decline and pessimism prevails. The volume of shares traded is typically low.

Beta The regression slope coefficient from the characteristic regression line (CRL) that measures the systematic (or undiversifiable) risk of an asset. **Factor betas** are multiple beta coefficients in the arbitrage pricing theory (APT), one for each different risk factor.

Bid–asked prices The bid price is the highest price a potential buyer is willing to pay; the asked (or offering) price is the lowest price potential sellers are willing to take. The bid price is always below the asked price. The *bid–asked spread* varies inversely with the liquidity of the asset.

Block trader A broker or dealer who specializes in trades involving blocks of stock—that is, 10,000 or more shares per transaction.

Blue sky laws A nickname for state laws regulating securities transactions.

Bond A debt security issued by a governmental unit or a firm that promises interest income of one form or another to its investors.

Bond issue An initial public offering (IPO) of bonds that are sold at the same time by the same issuer.

Bond quality ratings See **quality ratings.**

Bond trading Actively buying and selling bonds in an effort to profit from short-run changes in prices, rather than simply buying bonds and holding them as long-run investments.

Bond yield tables (or book) A book full of tables of numbers that associate a yield-to-maturity with a coupon rate, term to maturity, and market price for bonds purchased and held to maturity without suffering any default.

Book value per share An accounting term obtained by subtracting total liabilities and preferred stock from total assets (to get a firm's net worth, or *total* book value) and then dividing this amount by the number of shares outstanding.

Breadth of market A tool of technical analysis based on the number of advancing and declining issues of stock; used to predict the direction of the market.

Broker A security sales representative who assists investors in selling their securities to new investors for a commission. Unlike dealers, brokers never take title to the securities.

Bull market A market condition, lasting months or years, during which the market indexes and the prices of most securities in a given market rise in value, and optimism prevails.

Business cycle A period lasting from 1 to 12 years during which general business activity first expands, then contracts, and finally revives to start the expansion phase of the next cycle; marked by peaks and troughs of activity.

Call option A marketable contract whereby a buyer pays an option writer an option premium (or price) for the right (but not the obligation) to call (or buy) a specified security at a predetermined price within some stated time period.

Call provision A legal right incorporated in the terms of an issue of bonds or preferred stock that gives the issuer the opportunity to redeem the issue before it matures. The issuer must pay an additional amount over the face value (the *call premium*) to exercise this option.

Capital asset pricing model (CAPM) A risk-return asset pricing theory based on the beta coefficient. The CAPM is a linear formula, or a graph of the formula, that uses the beta index of undiversifiable (or systematic) risk as an independent variable.

Capitalization Long-term funds that are committed to a firm. All equity or net worth, preferred stock, and long-term liabilities are part of a firm's capitalization.

Capitalizing expenses An accounting procedure that places current business expenses (such as advertising) on the firm's balance sheet to be depreciated or amortized.

Capital market line (CML) A portfolio possibility line emanating out of the riskless rate R and passing through the market portfolio, denoted m. The CML is the efficient frontier when borrowing and lending are considered.

Cash dividend dropoff The decrease in the market price of a common stock on the first day it trades after paying a cash dividend (that is, trades **ex-dividend date**).

Cash dividends Cash payments to stockholders, usually paid quarterly. Many corporations pay about half their earnings out in cash dividends.

Cash markets Markets where physical commodities are bought and sold for cash. (Compare with **futures exchange**.)

Cash settlement Termination with *cash* rather than physical delivery of some real good for futures contracts on abstract things like market indexes that cannot actually be delivered when the contract matures.

CATS An acronym for "certificates of accrual on Treasury securities," zero coupon bonds Salomon Brothers created by stripping coupons from T-bonds and selling them separately.

Characteristic regression line (CRL) The simple linear time-series regression $r_{i,t} = a_i + b_i r_{m,t} + e_{i,t}$ for an individual asset that has the beta measure of undiversifiable risk as a slope coefficient.

Chartist See **technical analyst**.

Churning An illegal but nevertheless common practice in which unethical salespeople get clients to buy and sell securities fruitlessly in order to turn the account over (that is, churn it) and thus generate commission income for the broker.

Classified common stock See **Common stock.**

Clearinghouse An organization within a commodity exchange that guarantees the execution of every futures contract by inserting itself between each buyer and seller, thus making it the buyer in every sale and the seller in every purchase.

Closed-end investment company A type of investment company that (1) owns a diversified portfolio of investment securities, (2) is not allowed by law to sell more shares, and (3) has a net asset value per share that usually differs from its market price per share. (See also **Investment Company Act of 1940**, and **mutual fund**.)

Collateral Assets pledged to ensure repayment of a debt.

Collectibles Real assets such as dolls, antiques, toys, stamps, coins, and other unique physical objects that some people collect for hobbies, investment, or both.

Colored stones Rubies, sapphires, and emeralds, but not diamonds.

Commercial mortgage A combined loan and claim against business buildings, land, or both to guarantee that if the loan is not paid off, the lender can sell the real estate to recover the lent funds.

Commercial paper Promissory note maturing in 270 days or less sold by a major corporation to obtain a short-term loan.

Commodities Homogeneous, fungible market goods that are generally divided into categories such as agricultural commodities, financial commodities, metallic commodities.

Commodity board An electronic board on the wall of the trading room in a commodity exchange that displays up-to-the-second market prices and other statistics about the commodity being traded there.

Commodity Futures Trading Commission (CFTC) The federal regulatory agency that oversees and governs commodity exchanges and the trading of futures contracts.

Common stock The owners' equity shares in a corporation. Common stock has a residual claim on the corporation's assets and income, and may be issued with different voting rights and dividend provisions as *classified* common stock.

Compounded rate of return See **geometric mean rate of return.**

Confirmation According to technical analysts, the point at which two or more technical indicators generate the same trading signal at the same time, thus corroborating each other.

Consumer price index (CPI) A general cost-of-living price level index prepared monthly by the U.S. government's Bureau of Labor Statistics and based on the cost of a representative market basket of goods that the average American family buys.

Contract price See **exercise price.**

Conversion ratio The number of shares of common stock obtainable from one convertible security.

Conversion value The price a convertible security would have if it were converted to common stock; equals the conversion ratio times the price per share of common stock.

Convertibility risk That portion of a security's total variability of return caused by the possibility that investors exercise their options to convert securities into shares of stock.

Convertible security A senior security (that is, a bond or preferred stock) which gives the investor the option of converting it into a prespecified number of shares of that issuer's common stock.

Cornering the market An illegal price manipulating scheme in which one buyer obtains all the supply offered for sale and then raises the price in order to sell at a profit.

Corporation An artificial entity created by governmental authority, which has whatever powers, privileges, and limitations the government confers on it. Like a person, corporations can sue or be sued, own property, make legal contracts, have a name, and hire employees. Corporations are owned by shareholders who share profits but have limited liability.

Correlation coefficient An index number between +1.0 and −1.0 that measures how two variables tend to covary together.

Coupon rate The fixed interest rate printed on a coupon-paying bond; it is stated as a fraction of the bond's face value.

Coupon yield A bond's coupon payment per year stated as a percentage of the bond's current market price. (See also **current yield**.)

Coupons Prespecified interest payments that are usually payable annually or semiannually to the owner of a coupon-paying bond until it matures.

Covariance A statistical measure of the way two random variables covary. Mathematically, the covariance between random variables i and m is COV $(i,m) = \rho_{i,m}\sigma_i\sigma_m$, where $\rho_{i,m}$ denotes the correlation between i and m, and σ_i and σ_m are the standard deviations of i and m, respectively.

Coverage ratios Financial ratios measuring how well a company's earnings cover the fixed charges associated with a bond issue.

Credit enhancement A guarantee, insurance policy, overcollateralization, surety bond, or other valuable promise attached to a pool of financial assets to assure investors that the asset-backed securities issued to finance the pool will pay off as promised and are therefore worthy of a high quality rating.

Cumulative preferred stock An issue of preferred stock that promises to cumulate any missed preferred stock cash dividends and pay them in the future before any common stock dividends are paid. (Compare with **noncumulative preferred stock**.)

Current ratio A financial ratio designed to measure a firm's liquidity and solvency, calculated by dividing total current assets by total current liabilities.

Current yield A stock's or bond's cashflow to investors in the form of cash dividends or interest stated as a percentage (or equivalent fraction) of the security's current market price.

Day trade Purchase and sale of a security in 1 day.

Dealer A securities vendor who buys securities and holds them in inventory for resale in the hope of earning a profit from the purchase and resale price difference. (See also **market maker**.)

Debenture A promissory note (a bond) issued by a company that is backed by the firm's general credit but has no collateral pledged.

Debt securities Certificates evidencing a creditor claim that are transferable and can be traded. Bonds, debentures, zeros, T-notes, and money market securities are examples of debt securities.

Default Failure to pay a legal debt in full, on time, or both.

Default risk That portion of an asset's total variability of return caused by changes in the chance that the issuer of the securities might default. Also called *financial risk* or *bankruptcy risk*.

Defensive asset An asset with a beta coefficient of less than 1. (Compare with **aggressive asset**.)

Deficit spending The excess of federal spending over tax collections, which occurs whenever Congress votes such spending. The deficit is financed by increasing the national debt.

Depreciation Allowance for fair wear and tear, obsolescence, and decreasing value, which accountants deduct from an asset's book value regardless of whether or not the asset actually depreciates. (See **accelerated depreciation** and **straight-line depreciation**.)

Depression The economic collapse in the United States starting in 1929, during which 5000 banks went bankrupt and the unemployment rate reached a high of 25 percent in 1933.

Depth That aspect of market liquidity which refers to the existence of buy and sell orders both above and below the price at which a security is trading. A market that lacks depth is said to be *shallow*.

Dilution A reduction in the actual or potential value of a common stock that may result from issuing more shares of the security without a proportionate increase in the issuer's total assets and total earnings.

Discount Pricing a security so that it sells below its face value. T-bills and zeros are always sold at discount prices, for example.

Discount broker A securities brokerage firm that provides only essential brokerage services for its clients and charges minimal commission rates.

Discount rate The interest rate used in finding a present (or discounted present) value. Alternatively, the interest rate at which the Federal Reserve makes loans to commercial banks.

Discounted bond price The market price of a bond when it is selling below the bond's face value.

Discounted futures price The price of a futures contract when it is below the spot price for that commodity. The futures price is said to be at a discount to the spot price; this occurs when the market is *inverted*.

Diversifiable risk Variability of return caused by sources that are unique to one or a few assets. Creating even a simply diversified portfolio from as few as 15 securities averages such variability out to zero and thus eliminates the diversifiable risk from the total risk of the portfolio. It is also called *unsystematic variability of return*. (Compare with **undiversifiable risk**.)

Dominance principle A guideline which asserts that *dominant assets* have the highest expected rate of return in their risk class or, conversely, the minimum risk at any selected level of return. (See also **efficient frontier**.)

Double taxation Taxation of the same income twice; for example, the General Motors Corporation pays corporate income taxes on its earnings, and then the GM investors pay personal income taxes on the cash dividends from their GM stock.

Dow theory A theory originated by Charles Dow (a founder of the Dow Jones Company) about charting patterns in security prices in order to ascertain whether it is a bull or bear market (that is, the direction of the primary trend).

Dropoff See **Cash dividend dropoff.**

Duration A measure of the time structure of a bond and the bond's interest rate risk; the weighted average time that funds remain invested in a bond using the present value of each dollar of cashflow to weight the time period in which the cashflow is received. Also called **Macaulay's duration,** it equals time to maturity for zero coupon bonds. Macaulay's duration is less than the time to maturity for all coupon-paying bonds.

Earnings multiplier See **price-earnings ratio.**

Earnings per share A corporation's total earnings divided by the number of shares of common stock outstanding; an accountant's estimate of the earning power behind a share of stock.

Economic earnings of a common stock The maximum amount of real, physical consumption opportunities that can be withdrawn from the share without diminishing the consumption opportunities available in future periods.

Efficient frontier The set of assets that have (1) the maximum expected rate of return at each risk class and (2) the minimum risk at each level of return; the set of all dominant assets.

Efficient portfolio A portfolio with the greatest expected return at a given level of risk.

Efficient prices Market prices that do not fluctuate very far from the value of the underlying security, even though the value itself may fluctuate continuously; prices that furnish good, unbiased estimates of securities value.

Embedded options Options that are implicit or explicit within securities, such as the option of a mortgage borrower to repay the mortgage fully at any time.

Employees Retirement Income Security Act of 1974 (ERISA) A federal law requiring that pension funds be managed in a prudent manner to protect the retiring workers' interests.

Equally weighted index A securities price index that gives equal weighting to the return from every asset used to compute the index. (See also **naive buy and hold strategy.**)

Estate tax A progressive tax on the assets left by deceased parties. (See also **gift tax.**)

Eurodollar bonds U.S. dollar–denominated bonds traded primarily in foreign markets.

Ex-dividend date A stock that is trading during the 4 days after a cash dividend was just paid.

Exemptions Legally specified amounts of tax-exempt income allowed for each dependent a taxpayer supports.

Exercise price The price at which a security covered by a put or call option (or warrant) can be sold or purchased, respectively. Also called the *strike price* or **contract price.**

Expectations theory about the yield curve A theory which asserts that long-term interest rates are the average of all the short-term interest rates expected to exist during the life of the long-term bond.

Expected rate of return The weighted average rate of return using probability of each return for the weights: $E(r) = \Sigma \, [\text{Prob}(r_i)][r_i].$

Extraordinary gain (or loss) An unusual gain (or loss) that may occur, for example, when a manufacturing firm sells a plant at a gain (or loss); a nonrecurring source of income (or loss).

Face value The nominal amount printed on a security that represents its presumed value when it reaches maturity.

Factor betas The *sensitivity coefficients* that are indexes of undiversifiable risk with respect to some risk factor in arbitrage pricing theory (APT).

Federal agency bonds Bonds issued by an agency of the U.S. government such as the Federal Home Loan Bank, Federal Home Loan Mortgage Corporation (Freddie Mac), or Federal National Mortgage Association (Fannie Mae).

Federal funds rate The interest rate on excess reserves that one bank lends to another bank overnight in the U.S. money market.

Federal income tax The fraction of taxable income that American income earners are required by law to pay to the Internal Revenue Service (IRS), a branch of the U.S. Treasury.

Federal Reserve The monetary authority in the United States that oversees the banking system, money supply, interest rates, inflation rates, and balance of payments.

FIFO An acronym for the "first-in-first-out" inventory accounting rule.

Filter rule A mechanical trading rule used to generate buy-sell orders in the hope of earning profits without doing any intellectual work.

Financial futures Futures contracts on stock market indexes, Treasury bonds, U.S. government agency bonds, and other monetary quantities.

Financial instruments Securities like put and call options and futures contracts that differ somewhat from the traditional securities (that is, stocks and bonds).

Financial ratios Ratios of values from a firm's financial statements studied because they are indicators of the firm's liquidity, profitability, or indebtedness.

Fiscal policy The operating procedures adopted by the U.S. Treasury Department in matters of federal spending, federal tax collections, financing of federal deficits, and management of the national debt.

Fixed income securities Securities such as bonds and preferred stock, which have fixed cashflows scheduled to occur periodically.

Fixed minimum commission The NYSE's price-fixing agreement (or requirement) that all members charge fixed minimum commissions on all common stock trades, a requirement outlawed on May 1, 1975.

Floating-rate bonds Bonds on which the coupon interest rate is periodically reset to reflect current credit market interest rates, instead of remaining fixed like most bond coupon rates.

Floor broker A freelance NYSE member who executes orders for commission brokers with more orders than they can handle.

Fourth market A communications network that works between block traders, where commission rates are minimal.

Fraud Deliberate deception in order to obtain unfair or illegal gain. Insider trading, wash sales, price manipulation, and churning are examples of fraudulent activities in the securities business.

Free cashflow A comprehensive income measure that includes cashflows from operations and depreciation (since depreciation is not a cash expense); deducts any purchases of Treasury stock; considers changes in relevant balance sheet items; considers items from the sources and uses statement; and considers some footnote items such as changes in the firm's pension surplus, reserves, and accruals.

Full service brokerage A securities brokerage firm that charges clients high commission rates and provides services that include margin credit, free investment research, and free safekeeping of securities. (Compare with **discount broker**.)

Fully diluted earnings per share A common stock share's earnings after the maximum possible allowance is made for future diluting affects. (Compare with **primary earnings per share**.)

Fundamental security analysis Research into the basic facts that determine a security's value: the issuing firm's industry and the company's sales, assets, earnings, products, and market penetration; the firm's management; and its competitors. The security's intrinsic value is estimated by multiplying normalized earnings per share by the appropriate price-earnings ratio.

Future value The inverse of present value: future value = (present value)(1.0 + interest rate).

Futures exchange Also called a *commodity futures market*. A securities market in which contracts to deliver agricultural and financial commodities at a specified future date are actively traded. (Compare with **cash markets**.)

Futures price The amount that must be paid on some future date when the contracted delivery of goods is made.

General creditor A creditor who has no collateral pledged to guarantee repayment.

General obligation (GO) bond A municipal bond backed by the full faith and credit of a municipality rather than the revenues of one specific project.

Generally accepted accounting principles (GAAP) Accounting procedures that have been established gradually by a number of different authorities and that continue to evolve. The American Institute of Certified Public Accountants (AICPA) and the IRS, for instance, hand down opinions on which accounting practices are acceptable and which are unacceptable.

Geometric mean rate of return A compounded average rate of return over a number of time periods equal to or less than the arithmetic average rate of return over the same time periods.

Gift tax A progressive tax on goods given to parties that are not tax-deductible charities. Gift taxes are figured along with the **estate tax** of the deceased donor using the **unified transfer tax** schedule.

Glass-Steagall Act of 1933 Also called the **Banking Act of 1933**. A federal law which (1) required that commercial banking activities and investment banking activities be separated into different and independent companies, (2) forbade commercial banks to pay interest on checking accounts, and (3) established the FDIC.

Golden parachute Agreement that provides huge severance payments for high-level executives; sometimes arranged by top executives who fear they will lose their jobs in a hostile takeover.

Good-till-canceled (GTC) order Also called an *open order*. A broker's instruction to buy or sell that remains in effect until it is either executed or canceled.

Gross income Income from wages, salaries, and rent before income tax deductions are subtracted.

Growth firm A firm that can acquire funds at a lower cost of capital than the rate it earns on internally invested funds so that additional investments increase the firm's value.

Growth fund A so-called go-go mutual fund; it invests only in common stocks offering large capital gain possibilities, even if substantial risks are involved.

Growth rate The percentage per year by which an economic quantity changes. The growth rates in earnings and stock prices, for example, usually lie in the range between minus 20% to plus 30% per year.

Head and shoulders A pattern discernible in graphs of security prices that technical analysts believe has implications about the direction of a security's price in the future.

Hedging The strategy of taking offsetting long and short positions in the same asset at the same time to minimize possible losses from adverse price fluctuations.

High-yield bonds See **junk bonds**.

Holding period The planning or investment horizon, measured in months and years, over which the investor anticipates holding an investment before selling it.

Homogeneous markets Markets so similar that they would be highly positively correlated. International diversification would not offer any better benefits than domestic diversification if the markets were homogeneous.

Hostile takeover An attempt by a so-called corporate raider to obtain control of a corporation in which the executives of the target corporation resist the acquisition.

Immunization A bond management strategy to eliminate interest rate risk: the construction of a portfolio of different bonds so that the coupon reinvestment risk exactly offsets the price change risk to create a portfolio with a value on some future date that can be predetermined even if market interest rates change.

Imperfect hedge A hedge that involves invariant profits or invariant losses. Imperfect hedges that involve invariant profits are called *arbitrage positions.*

Indenture A legal contract detailing the interest rate, maturity date, protective provisions, and other terms governing a bond issue.

Index A pure indicator number devoid of any dollar or other dimensions. (See also **security market index.**)

Index fund A mutual fund or other portfolio designed to mimic the market actions of a specified market index (such as the S&P 500 Index).

Index options Put and call options on market indexes (such as the Standard & Poor's 500 Stocks Composite Index).

Industry life cycle See **product life cycle.**

Inflation An increase in the general price level. Thus, even though a few prices may fall, the overall cost of living and cost of doing business rise because most prices increase.

Inflation hedge An asset which has a market price which rises as fast as or faster than the rate of inflation so that the owner of the asset suffers no loss of purchasing power from investing in the asset.

Inflation rate The percentage change (usually at an annualized rate) in some price level index, such as the consumer price index.

Inheritance tax A steeply progressive death tax, which takes a large percentage of estates in excess of $600,000. (See also the **unified transfer tax.**)

Initial margin The percentage down payment required for an initial purchase of securities. Initial margins are about 50 percent for stocks and about 3 percent for futures contracts, for example.

Initial public offering An offering of new securities for sale to the public, in which a dealer registers the issue with the SEC and disseminates prospectuses to all potential investors.

Insiders The directors, officers, other executives, secretaries, and technicians (such as outside consultants and auditors) who have access to material, nonpublic information about a company and are therefore legally restricted in their investment activities in the securities of that company.

Insolvent The financial status of a debtor who has no liquid assets with which to pay just bills. Insolvency leads to default and perhaps even bankruptcy if the situation cannot be corrected.

Institutional investors Pension funds, trust departments of banks, life insurance companies, mutual funds, and other large, commercially managed investment portfolios.

Insured home mortgage A loan to purchase a home in which the mortgaged home is the collateral and some third party (such as FHA, FNMA, or GNMA) insures that the loan will be repaid. The insurance removes default risk and makes the mortgage a readily marketable security.

Intercorporate cash dividend A cash dividend paid by one corporation to another corporation that owns some of its common stock and is therefore subject to a preferential income tax rate on that dividend.

Interest rate risk Variability of return to investors caused by changes in market (or nominal) rates of interest.

Intrinsic value The true economic worth of a share of stock, calculated, for example, by finding the discounted present value of all the share's future income. Fundamental common stock analysts estimate a stock's intrinsic value in order to see if its market price is too high or too low.

Inverted market A relationship between the futures prices for a given commodity such that the spot price exceeds the futures price.

Investment banker A securities broker and dealer firm that underwrites primary issues.

Investment Company Act of 1940 The federal law governing the management practices of mutual funds, closed-end investment companies, and unit investment trusts.

Investment performance index A number derived from simultaneously weighing an asset's expected (or average) rate of return and the asset's risk through a formula which yields an index number suitable to use in ranking the desirability of different investments. [See also **Sharpe's performance index (SPI)** and **Treynor's performance index (TPI).**]

Investment timing See **timing.**

January effect The tendency for stock market prices to decrease during the last few days of December and then appreciate relatively rapidly during the first 3 weeks of January.

Junk bonds Any corporate bond that is rated below Standard & Poor's BBB or, equivalently, below Moody's Baa; also called **high-yield bonds.**

Keogh plan A tax-sheltered retirement plan for self-employed people, which allows them to save certain amounts of their annual income for retirement and deduct these savings from their taxable income.

Lagging economic indicators See **leading and lagging indicators.**

Law of one price   An economic law stating that the same good cannot sell simultaneously at prices that differ by more than the transportation costs to ship the good from the market where its price is lowest to the market where its price is the highest.

Leading and lagging indicators   Economic variables (such as the stock market indexes) that tend to anticipate, and therefore *lead,* changes in the general level of business activity, and economic variables (such as market interest rates) that tend to follow, or *lag* behind, changes in the general level of business activity.

Leverage ratios   A group of financial ratios designed to measure a firm's use of borrowed money.

Lien   A legal claim on the property of someone else to ensure that the person pays off a just debt.

Life cycle of an industry   Also called the *life cycle of a product;* the general tendency for a new product's high initial profitability to diminish as the product matures and competition intensifies over the years.

LIFO   An acronym for the "last-in-first-out" inventory accounting rule.

Limit order   Also called a *limited price order.* A customer's order instructing a brokerage to buy or sell a specific quantity of a given security at a fixed price, or at a better price if a better price is available after the order reaches the trading floor.

Limited liability   U.S. law freeing common stock owners from responsibility for the debts of the corporation in which they invest.

Limited obligation bonds   See **revenue bond.**

Liquid asset fund   A mutual fund that invests only in money market securities.

Liquidity   The ease with which an asset can be converted to cash without suffering a decrease in price in order to effect a hasty sale.

Listing requirements   The requirements that an organized securities exchange demands of an issuer of securities before it will make a market in (that is, list) those securities.

Load fee   Sales commissions charged by some mutual funds.

Long position   Buying and holding an asset in the hope of profiting from its cash dividends, interest, price increases, or other benefits.

Long-term capital gains   Investment income from price appreciation that, in past years, has been taxed at a lower preferential income tax rate if the assets were held for over 1 year.

Macaulay's duration   See **duration.**

Maintenance margin   The minimum amount of equity that must be maintained after a margin position is established in order to avoid a margin call. Maintenance margins are smaller than the initial margins, and are maintained by **marking to the market.**

Maloney Act of 1936   An amendment to the Securities and Exchange Act of 1934 governing the over-the-counter market that requires the registration of national securities associations and establishes standards for such associations.

Management buyout (MBO)   A transaction in which the top managers of a corporation borrow the money to acquire control of the corporation that employs them.

Management risk   Variability in investors' rates of return caused by management deficiencies.

Margin   The equity portion of a security's purchase price an investor pays when using money borrowed from a brokerage to buy the securities.

Marginal tax rate   The percentage of income taxes that must be paid on the next additional increment of income. (Compare with **average tax rate.**)

Market maker   A securities dealer who invests in an inventory of a security and earns the bid–ask spread for facilitating trading in that security.

Market order   An order from an investor to a brokerage to buy or sell a security at the best price available at the time the order reaches the trading floor.

Market portfolio   The unique most desirable portfolio of risky assets in existence in the capital market theory; it must contain all assets in the world in the proportions in which they exist in equilibrium.

Market risk   The variability of return to investors caused by the alternating forces of bull and bear markets.

Market value weighting   A weighting system used in the construction of market indexes that assigns weights to the component securities that are proportional to their market value in the relevant securities market.

Marking to the market   The procedure in which margin traders must pay additional maintenance margin money or withdraw cash proceeds at the end of every trading day when the market price of their asset moves either adversely or favorably, respectively.

Markowitz diversification   Combining assets that are less than perfectly positively correlated in order to reduce risk in the portfolio without sacrificing any expected return.

Model   A simplified version of reality.

Monetary assets   Assets that are denominated in dollars —such as cash, bonds, and savings accounts—and thus tend to make poor inflation hedges.

Monetary policy   The operating procedures selected by the board of governors of the Federal Reserve System to be used in managing the American money supply, inflation rate, interest rates, banking system, and credit regulations.

Monetary sector of the economy   The private commercial banks and loan companies that handle loan applications, the nation's central bank, which regulates credit conditions, and the interaction of these money managers to determine the level of inflation and interest rates. (Compare with **real sector of the economy**.)

Money illusion   The widely held, but nonetheless naive, belief that merely owning more dollars makes a person wealthier. This belief is naive because it ignores inflation: a person whose dollar wealth doubled would be poorer if the price level quadrupled at the same time.

Money market securities High-grade promissory notes that mature in less than 270 days and are marketable securities; examples are commercial paper and bankers' acceptances.

Mortgage A loan collateralized with a home (for a *home mortgage*) or with a piece of land or a building (for a **commercial mortgage**).

Mortgage-backed securities Bonds that have a pool of insured home mortgages as collateral. (See also **asset-backed securities.**)

Mortgage bond A bond issued under an indenture that grants a lien on real estate as collateral for the bond issue.

Mutual fund See **open-end investment company** and **net asset value per share (NAVS).**

Naive buy and hold strategy A simple strategy of randomly selecting one or more securities without regard to their investment qualities, buying them, and holding this random selection regardless of what additional information becomes available. This is how some security market indexes are constructed; it provides a standard of comparison useful in evaluating the performance of portfolio managers. The Standard & Poor's 500 Stocks Composite Index is a well-known example.

NASDAQ Acronym for "National Association of Securities Dealers Automated Quotations," a nationwide computerized securities market.

National Association of Securities Dealers (NASD) A trade association for securities dealers and brokers in the over-the-counter market that enforces rules and ethics.

Negotiated commissions Stock brokerage commissions arrived at by bargaining between client and broker; usually significantly lower than the fixed minimum commission rates the NYSE required before May 1, 1975.

Net asset value per share (NAVS) The value at which mutual fund shares can always be redeemed; equals the total value of the portfolio's assets, less any liabilities, divided by the number of outstanding shares.

Net working capital The amount by which a firm's current assets exceed its current liabilities.

Nominal interest rates The money interest rates advertised in the newspapers that have a built-in hidden inflation allowance.

Nominal rate of return See **nominal interest rates.**

Noncumulative preferred stock Preferred stock which involves no promise from the issuer that cash dividends that are omitted will be made up later. (Compare with **cumulative preferred stock.**)

Nonmarketable bonds U.S. Treasury promissory notes that can be redeemed only at a federal office and are not traded in any secondary market—U.S. savings bonds are a well-known example.

Normal firm A typical firm, in which the value of its stock is not affected by its cash dividend payout ratio. Cash dividend payout policy is irrelevant because the firm's cost of capital equals its internal rate of return, and the present value cost of new financing equals the present value of the new investment, so that value per share is not affected by changes in dividend policies.

Normal market A price structure in commodity futures markets in which the futures price exceeds the spot price by an amount equal to the commodity's carrying charge.

Normalized earnings per share A share of common stock's true economic earnings per share, which is derived by adjusting accounting earnings per share to remove temporary fluctuations or deviations introduced by misleading accounting procedures, acts of God, or other unusual events.

Numismatic value The value of a coin that is based on its rarity and its condition.

Odd lots Transaction sizes involving less than 100 shares of a given stock. (Compare with **round lots.**)

Offering price A synonym for **asked price.** (See also **bid–asked prices.**)

Open-end investment company Also called a **mutual fund.** A publicly owned company that (1) owns diversified portfolios of securities, (2) can keep selling more shares and growing indefinitely, and (3) has shares that can always be redeemed at their **net asset value per share (NAVS).**

Open interest The aggregate number of uncovered futures contracts outstanding at a given moment.

Option pool An illegal association between two or more parties formed with the intention of acquiring stock at advantageous prices through options granted by a friendly management and reselling at a profitable higher price that is achieved through manipulation.

Option premium The price that a put or a call option buyer must pay to purchase the option; also called the option's *price.*

Organized exchange A formal organization that conducts orderly markets for the securities in which it chooses to make a market, such as The New York Stock Exchange.

Options Speculative securities called *puts* and *calls.*

Option writer A party that sells a put or a call.

Over-the-counter (OTC) market A market in securities that are not traded solely on organized securities exchanges; it is composed of securities dealers in all 50 states and some foreign countries.

Overcollateralized assets Assets backed by collateral exceeding their face value—for example, a pool of mortgages that has an aggregate face value 125 percent of the face value of the mortgage-backed securities issued to finance that pool.

Overhanging issue An issue of convertible securities the owners cannot be forced to convert to common stock, because the stock price is not high enough to make the conversion profitable.

Par value   An arbitrary value typically ranging from $0 to $10 that is assigned to a share of common stock when it is issued. For bonds and preferred stock, par value is synonymous with **face value.**

Participating bond   A bond that pays its investors cash dividends when the issuer earns large profits.

Participating preferred stock   Preferred stock that is entitled to special cash dividends in excess of the regular dividend if the corporation is highly profitable.

Payout ratio   Cash dividends stated as a fraction (or equivalent percentage) of a common stock's earnings. (Compare with **retention ratio.**)

Perfectly efficient price   A price that is continuously equal to the security's value as they vibrate together randomly; also called *strongly efficient price* fluctuation and *continuous equilibrium.*

Pit   See **trading ring.**

Political risk   Variability of return caused as politically strong groups exploit politically weak groups.

Portfolio   A list or collection of different investments.

Portfolio turnover   A measure of security trading within a portfolio during some time period.

Preemptive right   Stockholders' right to subscribe to any new issue of stock so as to maintain the fraction of the total number of shares outstanding they owned before the new offering.

Preferred stock   Ownership shares in a corporation that have a junior claim on assets compared with bondholders, but a senior claim relative to stockholders, if the corporation goes bankrupt. Fixed cash dividends are usually paid.

Premium over a bond's face value   When the yield-to-maturity for a bond is below the bond's coupon rate, its market price will be above its face value and the bond is said to sell at a premium over its face value.

Present value   The discounted value of future dollar quantities: present value = future value ÷ (1.0 + interest rate).

Present value model   A well-known formula for finding the discounted value of future receipts. (See also **value.**)

Price   The dollar amount that equates the demand for a security with the supply offered for sale; the amount reported in market quotations. (Compare with **value.**)

Price-earnings ratio   A stock's price per share divided by its earnings per share; also called the **earnings multiplier.**

Primary earnings per share   A common stock's measure of earnings per share which considers the conversion of common stock equivalents which may dilute future earnings per share. (Compare with **fully diluted earnings per share.**)

Primary issue   The sale by an underwriter (or investment banker) of an initial public offering (IPO) of securities.

Primary market   The market for primary (or new) issues of securities. (Compare with **secondary market.**) Investment bankers create a primary market, and the issuer gets the sale proceeds.

Primary trends   The bull and bear market trends that the Dow theory seeks to discern.

Principal   See **agency-principal relationship.**

Private placement   The sale of an entire issue to one large investor.

Probability   A number between 0 and 1 that indicates the relative likelihood of an uncertain event's occurring.

Probability distribution   A graph or table that associates a probability with every possible outcome of an experiment involving chance.

Product life cycle   Also called **industry life cycle.** A theoretical passage of a product through four phases: (1) introductory, (2) rapid expansion, (3) mature growth, and (4) stabilization or decline.

Product obsolescence   A decrease in demand in an old product because of technologically superior competitors, shifts in consumer taste, or both.

Profitability ratios   Ratios designed to measure a firm's profitability—for instance, the rate-of-return-on-total-assets ratio.

Progressive tax   A graduated tax that takes a larger percentage of taxes from taxpayers with larger incomes. (See also **marginal tax rate.**)

Prospectus   A pamphlet of information about a primary issue of securities that must be given to every potential investor according to federal law.

Protective provisions   Guarantees or assurances specified in a bond issue's indenture to protect the bond investors.

Proxy   A written authorization that a shareholder can sign to give his or her voting rights to another party.

Psychic income   Nonpecuniary income: happiness or pride derived from a possession.

Purchasing-power risk   Variability of investors' returns caused by changes in the rate of inflation.

Put bond   A bond that has its market price supported by a legal option in the bond issue's indenture allowing investors to sell (or put) the bond back to the issuer at some specified price; also called *extendible* or *retractable bond.*

Put option   A marketable contract in which the put's buyer pays an option premium (or price) to the put's writer for the right (but not the obligation) of putting (selling) a specific security to the put's writer for a predetermined price anytime within a stated time period.

Quality ratings   The letter grades that Standard & Poor's and Moody's use to measure the probability that a security issue will default.

Random walk theory   A theory about security price movements which says that new information affecting security values arrives randomly, causing values and prices to fluctuate randomly; sometimes called the *efficient markets theory.*

Rate of return   A percentage (or equivalent fraction) which measures the rate of gain or loss of an investment over a holding period. Gains or losses of wealth are measured by positive or negative rates of return, respectively.

Real assets   Physical assets like real estate, gold, and jewelry that are not denominated in dollars and typically make good inflation hedges.

Real rate of return   The amount or return left over after the inflation rate is subtracted from the nominal rate of interest. It measures the rate at which real physical purchasing power is changing; also called the *real rate of interest.* (Compare with **nominal interest rates** and **inflation rate.**)

Real sector of the economy   A sector of the economy that produces real physical goods (such as houses and cars) and services (such as dining and entertainment). (Compare with **monetary sector of the economy.**)

Recession   A period of time during which general business activity contracts for several months or a few years.

Registration   Filing of a prospectus and other information with the SEC as required by the Securities Act of 1933 in order to give investors full information they need to make investment decisions.

REIT   A real estate investment trust; a closed-end investment company formed to invest in real estate.

Reorganization   A legal process in Chapter X of the Bankruptcy Act in which a bankruptcy court, deeming a business able to survive if reorganized and relieved of some of its debts, cancels some junior obligations (such as common stockholders claims) and downgrades senior claims (for instance, by converting bonds to common stock). (Compare with **arrangement.**)

Required rate of return   The minimum acceptable risk-adjusted discount rate (or rate of return) investors want when they buy an investment.

Requirement to pay   Obligation to pay bondholders' claims. The strength of the obligation affects the issue's quality rating. Collateralized bonds have stronger (or more senior, or prior) requirements to pay than debenture bonds do, for example.

Residual claim   The lowest-priority (or last) claim. For instance, common stockholders have a residual claim on their corporation's income and assets.

Retained earnings   The part of a company's net income reinvested within the firm rather than made available to the owners for their consumption purposes.

Retention ratio   The percentage of a corporation's earnings retained for internal investment; the complement of the stock's **payout ratio.**

Return   The investor's income; the reward for undertaking an investment. (See also **rate of return.**)

Revenue bond   A municipal bond that is supported by revenues from the asset it was used to finance. (For instance, a toll bridge bond issue is paid off with the tolls.)

Risk   Variability of return or dispersion of outcome. Total risk equals diversifiable risk plus undiversifiable risk. (See also **standard deviation.**)

Risk-adjusted discount rate   Also called the *appropriate discount rate.* The rate of interest on default-free securities (namely, the U.S. Treasury bill rate) plus a risk premium sufficient to compensate the investor for assuming the risks associated with the particular assets. (See also **required rate of return.**)

Risk aversion   Investors' natural fear and dislike of risk.

Risk premium portion of an interest rate   That portion of an interest rate which exceeds the interest rate on a default-free security (U.S. Treasury bill, for example) to induce investors to place their money at risk. (See also **yield spread.**)

Risk-return relationship   See **risk-return tradeoff.**

Risk-return space   Also called *risk-return graph.* Points representing assets plotted on a two-dimensional graph with total risk on the horizontal axis and expected rate of return on the vertical axis.

Risk-return tradeoff   The generally observed economic phenomenon in which risk aversion is evidenced as investors require higher rates of return to induce them to buy riskier investments.

Riskless interest rate   The interest rate that has zero variability of return within the holding period—the interest rate on a government-insured savings account, for example.

Round lots   Transaction sizes involving shares in multiples of 100. (Compare with **odd lots.**)

Runs   Series of changes that all have the same positive, zero, or negative sign. Runs tests are used to test statistically whether security prices fluctuate randomly.

SEC forms   The 8-K, 10-K, 10-Q, 13-D, and other forms some corporations are required to file with the SEC to disclose required information.

SEC Rule 19C-3   A Securities and Exchange Commission requirement which went into effect April 26, 1979, and which endeavors to weaken the New York Stock Exchange's (NYSE) market-making monopoly on certain stocks. The rule allows NYSE members to trade NYSE-listed securities in the over-the-counter market.

Secondary distribution   The sale to different investors of a block of securities that has already been outstanding.

Secondary market   Markets such as the New York Stock Exchange or the over-the-counter market where previously issued securities are traded. The issuer of the security receives no cashflow from secondary market trades between investors. (Compare with **primary market.**)

Securities and Exchange Commission (SEC)   An agency of the U.S. government established by the Securities Exchange Act of 1934 to ensure full disclosure of financial information of interest to investors and to promote honest trading.

Securities Investors Protection Corporation (SIPC) A nonprofit corporation which has securities brokerages for members; each member brokerage pays dues to SIPC to ensure clients' accounts in case the brokerage goes bankrupt.

Securitization A process in which **asset-backed securities** are issued to raise the money to finance a pool of illiquid financial assets like mortgages, accounts receivable, leases, and installment loan contracts.

Security A document that provides evidence of either creditorship or ownership, depending on whether it is a bond or a stock, respectively.

Security market index An indicator of the activity (namely, the price level) in a securities market. A dimensionless ratio that indicates changes (usually in the aggregate dollar value) in a security market. Indexes are more sophisticated measures than averages.

Segmentation theory The hypothesis that each maturity segment of the yield curve is determined by supply and demand factors that are unique to that maturity range; also called the *hedging theory*.

Segmented international market structure The condition that exists when international trading impediments like foreign exchange restrictions, accounting conventions that differ from country to country, thin foreign markets, and lack of information about foreign investments make multinational diversification advantageous. Synonymous with *heterogeneous international market structure*. *Homogeneous* international markets exist when no barriers impede international trading.

Semistrongly efficient market A market in which the securities prices reflect all *public* knowledge.

Sensitivity coefficient See **factor betas.**

Serial bond A bond in an issue that matures part by part over a series of years.

Sharpe's performance index (SPI) A risk-adjusted rate-of-return measure calculated by dividing an asset's risk premium, $E(r) - R$, by its standard deviation of return; used to rank the investment performance of different assets.

Short position Selling an asset the seller does not possess at the time of the sale in the hope of purchasing the asset profitably at a lower price in the future to make the promised delivery; synonym for *short sale.*

Simple diversification "Not putting all one's eggs in one basket," or spreading the risks across different assets—an easy way to reduce the diversifiable (or unsystematic) risk in a portfolio.

Sinking fund An amount of money set aside periodically by the issuer and accumulated to buy back outstanding bonds or preferred stock.

Sinking fund bond A bond in an issue for which the indenture requires the issuer to set money aside in a sinking fund in order to repurchase the bonds.

Size effect The statistical finding that small firms earn

higher rates of return than large firms, on average, if everything else is equal.

Specialist A member of an organized securities exchange who makes an orderly market in one or a few stocks by standing ready to buy or sell any of the assigned securities offered for sale at the current price.

Speculation Purchase of an asset to be held for weeks or months in the hope of reselling it at a higher price.

Speculators Active traders who purchase (or sell short) securities, futures contracts, or any other asset with the expectation that they will be able to profit from a short-term price movement.

Spot contract A futures contract that is in the final month of its life and is thus about to be executed by delivering the specified commodity.

Spot price The market price of a spot futures contract. (See also **spot contract.**)

Standard deviation A statistical measure of the dispersion of outcomes around their expected (or mean) value. It is used to measure total risk and is the square root of the variance. (See also **risk.**)

Stock dividend A prorated distribution to stockholders of additional common stock shares. Except for a few bookkeeping entries, it is like a stock split.

Stock split A procedure in which all common stockholders receive a certain percentage increase in the number of shares they hold. This dilutes each share's value proportionally and leaves the total value of all shares unchanged.

Straight-line depreciation A fictitious expense allowance for wear, tear, and obsolescence that accountants write off against an asset in equal annual amounts regardless of whether the asset actually appreciates or depreciates. (Compare with **accelerated depreciation.**)

Stripped bonds Zero coupon bonds created by stripping (or separating) the coupons from (the corpus of) coupon-paying bonds and then selling the coupons and the corpus of the bond separately.

Strongly efficient market A market in which security prices reflect all information—both public and inside information. Also called a *perfectly efficient market* and a *market in continuous equilibrium.*

Subordination provisions Paragraphs in a bond's indenture that place a bond issue in a legal position that is inferior to other issues.

Superfluous diversification The spreading of investment assets across so many different assets that the portfolio becomes large and difficult to manage without enjoying an associated reduction in risk.

Systematic variability of return See **undiversifiable risk.**

Taxable income Gross income less (1) any essential business expenses, (2) legal deductions (such as charitable contributions and local taxes), and (3) legal exemptions for dependents.

Tax-exempt bonds Bonds issued by municipalities (such as cities, states, and towns) which have interest payments exempt from federal income taxes.

Tax-sheltered retirement savings Individual retirement accounts (IRAs), Keogh plans, tax-sheltered annuities, appropriately administered company pension plans, profit-sharing plans, etc.

Technical analyst A market analyst or security analyst who typically charts indexes, prices, or other market statistics in search of patterns that may have predictive value about the future. A technical analyst is also called **a chartist.**

Term structure of interest rates See **yield curve.**

Third market An over-the-counter market in exchange-listed stocks.

Time value of money The value of money attributable to the fact that a dollar can grow to a dollar plus interest income in the future.

Timing Also called *market timing.* The ability to select the times when security prices are low to make purchases and the times when security prices are near their peaks to sell in order to maximize profits from aggressive trading.

Total risk Total variability of the investor's holding period rate of return; equals diversifiable plus undiversifiable risk and can be measured by the standard deviation or the variance.

Trading pool An illegal stock price manipulation between two or more parties that hope to profit by destabilizing prices through massive trading.

Trading ring Also called the *trading pit.* Where buyers and sellers meet on the floor of a commodity exchange to trade futures contracts.

Trading volume The number of shares of a security (or of all securities in a market) traded during a specified time period; also called the *volume of trading.*

Tranches The categories of bonds issued to finance a pool of collateralized mortgage obligations (CMOs); each tranche has a different claim on the cashflows from the pool.

Transfer agent A third party, usually a bank, that keeps the names, addresses, and number of shares owned for each shareholder in a corporation and sees that stock certificates are transferred to new owners.

Treasury bills Also simply called T-bills. Money market securities issued by the U.S. Treasury sold at a discount rather than paying coupon interest, and maturing within 1 year or less from the date of issue; an example of a default-free security.

Treasury bonds Coupon bonds issued by the U.S. Treasury that have original maturities in excess of 10 years but less than 30 years.

Treasury notes Coupon bonds issued by the U.S. Treasury that have original maturities in excess of 1 year but less than 10 years.

Treynor's performance index (TPI) An index used to rank the investment performance of different assets. It is a risk-adjusted rate-of-return measure calculated by dividing an asset's risk premium, $E(r) - R,$ by its beta coefficient.

Trustee A third party, usually a bank, that acts as liaison between a bond issuer and the bond buyers in administering the indenture contract.

Turnover rate A measure of the frequency with which assets in a portfolio are being traded during a given time period; it is useful in detecting **churning.**

Uncorrelated Moving independently of another factor; having a correlation coefficient of zero.

Underwriting syndicate A group of securities brokers and dealers who cooperate in underwriting a new issue and selling the securities to the public.

Undiversifiable risk Also called *systematic risk.* Variability of the investors' rates of return caused by economic factors (for example, recessions), political factors (for example, election of a new administration), or sociological factors (for example, the mass hysteria on the NYSE following President Kennedy's assassination) which affect all assets systematically in some way.

Unified transfer tax A steeply progressive tax on the gifts and inheritances left by a deceased benefactor.

Unit Also called *contract unit.* The standardized size, or minimum quantity, that is delivered under the terms of a futures contract.

Unsystematic variability of return See **diversifiable risk.**

Value The economic worth, intrinsic value, present value, estimated worth, or dollar appraisal, which may be greater or less than the item's market price.

Value-earnings ratio The appropriate or theoretically correct value that a stock's price-earnings ratio should reach in equilibrium.

Variability of return Investment risk.

Variable-rate bond A type of bond that has a coupon rate which varies with current market interest rates according to some formula.

Variance The standard deviation squared; a quantitative risk surrogate.

Warrant A call option written by the corporation that issued an optioned security giving the warrant investor the opportunity (or option), but not the obligation, to purchase the security at a prespecified price.

Wash sale A phony, illegal transaction in which the buyer and seller of a security are the same party. It is done to create the illusion that trading is occurring.

Weakly efficient market A market in which securities prices reflect all *historical* information. (Compare with **semistrongly** and **strongly efficient markets.**)

Weekend effect The empirically observed tendency for stock prices to rise slightly from a low on Mondays to a high on Fridays.

Yield curve Also called the **term structure of interest rates.** The relationship between the number of years to maturity and the yield-to-maturity for a group of bonds in the same default risk class. The yield curve is usually studied for U.S. Treasury securities.

Yield spread The amount by which some market interest rate exceeds the market rate of interest on a default-free security (such as U.S. Treasury bills); measured in nominal terms. Also called a *risk premium,* this difference represents the investor's reward for undertaking a risky investment. (See also **risk premium portion of an interest rate.**)

Yield-to-maturity A bond's compound average rate of return over its remaining life; a market-determined interest rate that fluctuates inversely with the bond's market price; the discount rate that equates the present value of a bond's expected cashflows to its current market price.

Zero coupon bonds Bonds that pay no coupon interest but are instead issued at a discount from their face (or maturity) value to yield income from capital appreciation.

NAME INDEX

I-1

SUBJECT INDEX

Present Value of $1

Period	1%	2%	3%	4%	5%	6%	7%	8%	9%	10%
2	0.980	0.961	0.943	0.925	0.907	0.890	0.873	0.857	0.842	0.826
4	0.961	0.924	0.888	0.855	0.823	0.792	0.763	0.735	0.708	0.683
6	0.942	0.888	0.837	0.790	0.746	0.705	0.666	0.630	0.596	0.564
8	0.923	0.853	0.789	0.731	0.677	0.627	0.582	0.540	0.502	0.467
10	0.905	0.820	0.744	0.676	0.614	0.558	0.508	0.463	0.422	0.386
12	0.887	0.788	0.701	0.625	0.557	0.497	0.444	0.397	0.356	0.319
14	0.870	0.758	0.661	0.577	0.505	0.442	0.388	0.340	0.299	0.263
16	0.853	0.728	0.623	0.534	0.458	0.394	0.339	0.292	0.252	0.218
18	0.836	0.700	0.587	0.494	0.416	0.350	0.296	0.250	0.212	0.180
20	0.820	0.673	0.554	0.456	0.377	0.312	0.258	0.215	0.178	0.149
22	0.803	0.647	0.522	0.422	0.342	0.278	0.226	0.184	0.150	0.123
24	0.788	0.622	0.492	0.390	0.310	0.247	0.197	0.158	0.126	0.102
26	0.772	0.598	0.464	0.361	0.281	0.220	0.172	0.135	0.106	0.084
28	0.757	0.574	0.437	0.333	0.255	0.196	0.150	0.116	0.090	0.069
30	0.742	0.552	0.412	0.308	0.231	0.174	0.131	0.099	0.075	0.057
40	0.672	0.453	0.307	0.208	0.142	0.097	0.067	0.046	0.032	0.022
50	0.608	0.372	0.228	0.141	0.087	0.054	0.034	0.021	0.013	0.009

Period	12%	14%	16%	18%	20%	22%	24%	26%	28%	30%
2	0.797	0.769	0.743	0.718	0.694	0.672	0.650	0.630	0.610	0.592
4	0.636	0.592	0.552	0.516	0.482	0.451	0.423	0.397	0.373	0.350
6	0.507	0.456	0.410	0.370	0.335	0.303	0.275	0.250	0.227	0.207
8	0.404	0.351	0.305	0.266	0.233	0.204	0.179	0.157	0.139	0.123
10	0.322	0.270	0.227	0.191	0.162	0.137	0.116	0.099	0.085	0.073
12	0.257	0.208	0.168	0.137	0.112	0.092	0.076	0.062	0.052	0.043
14	0.205	0.160	0.125	0.099	0.078	0.062	0.049	0.039	0.032	0.025
16	0.163	0.123	0.093	0.071	0.054	0.042	0.032	0.025	0.019	0.015
18	0.130	0.095	0.069	0.051	0.038	0.028	0.021	0.016	0.012	0.009
20	0.104	0.073	0.051	0.037	0.026	0.019	0.014	0.010	0.007	0.005
22	0.083	0.056	0.038	0.026	0.018	0.013	0.009	0.006	0.004	0.003
24	0.066	0.043	0.028	0.019	0.013	0.008	0.006	0.004	0.003	0.002
26	0.053	0.033	0.021	0.014	0.009	0.006	0.004	0.002	0.002	0.001
28	0.042	0.026	0.016	0.010	0.006	0.004	0.002	0.002	0.001	0.001
30	0.033	0.020	0.012	0.007	0.004	0.003	0.002	0.001	0.001	0.000
40	0.11	0.005	0.003	0.001	0.001	0.000	0.000	0.000	0.000	0.000
50	0.003	0.001	0.001	0.000	0.000	0.000	0.000	0.000	0.000	0.000